MADACEEV

D0012737

# Thailand
## a Lonely Planet travel survival kit

### Joe Cummings

**Thailand**

**7th edition**

**Published by**
**Lonely Planet Publications**
Head Office:   PO Box 617, Hawthorn, Vic 3122, Australia
Branches:      155 Filbert St, Suite 251, Oakland, CA 94607, USA
               10 Barley Mow Passage, Chiswick, London W4 4PH, UK
               71 bis rue du Cardinal Lemoine, 75005 Paris, France

**Printed by**
SNP Printing Pte Ltd, Singapore

**Photographs by**

| | |
|---|---|
| Glenn Beanland | Richard I'Anson |
| Paul Beinssen | Mark Kirby |
| Michael Clark | Bernard Napthine |
| Sara Jane Cleland | Richard Nebesky |
| Joe Cummings | Tourism Authority of Thailand (TAT) |
| John Demodena | Dale Wahren |

Front cover: Royal guards, Bangkok (Mark Kirby)

**First Published**
February 1982

**This Edition**
March 1997

**Although the authors and publisher have tried to make the information as accurate as possible, they accept no responsibility for any loss, injury or inconvenience sustained by any person using this book.**

National Library of Australia Cataloguing in Publication Data

Cummings, Joe.
    Thailand.

    7th ed.
    Includes index.
    ISBN 0 86442 411 6.

    1. Thailand – Guidebooks. I. Title
    (Series: Lonely Planet travel survival kit).

915.930444

text & maps © Lonely Planet 1997
photos © photographers as indicated 1997
climate charts compiled from information supplied by Patrick J Tyson, © Patrick J Tyson, 1997

All rights reserved. No part of this publication may be reproduced, stored in a retrieval system or transmitted in any form by any means, electronic, mechanical, photocopying, recording or otherwise, except brief extracts for the purpose of review, without the written permission of the publisher and copyright owner.

**Joe Cummings**
Joe has travelled extensively in Thailand since 1977. Before travel writing became a full-time job, he was a Peace Corps volunteer in Thailand, an extra in the Indochina War film *The Deer Hunter*, a translator/interpreter of Thai, a graduate student of Thai language and Asian art history at the University of California at Berkeley, a columnist for *The Asia Record*, an East-West Center Scholar in Hawaii, a university lecturer in Malaysia and a bilingual studies consultant in the USA and Taiwan.

Able to speak, read and write Thai fluently, Joe has travelled through all 76 of the kingdom's provinces. Joe is also the author of Lonely Planet's *Thai* phrasebook and guides to *Bangkok*, *Laos* and *Myanmar*, and a contributor to LP guides to *South-East Asia, China, Malaysia/Singapore & Brunei* and *Indonesia*. He occasionally writes for *Geographical, World & I, Outside, Worldview, Earth Journal, BBC Holidays, The Independent, Bangkok Post, The Nation, Sawasdee, Ambassador, Asia Magazine* and other periodicals.

**From the Author**
Thanks to the following people in Thailand who assisted along the way: Nicole Altclass, Rachel Foord, Andrew Forbes, David Henley, Jill Fain, Charles Henn, Guy Gorias, Steve Rosse, Uthit Sawat, Krista Schumacher, Veronika Martin, Nanthirat Prasertzup, Nuansri Vongchanyakul, Max & Tick, Michael Wilson, Julian & Pao, Eileen Stuart, Phra Sujato, Jan Jacobs, Kristinn Sigfus Kristjan, Sue Hughes and Sharon London.

The Tourism Authority of Thailand and its employees throughout Thailand, as usual, were of considerable assistance, as were my research assistants/travel companions Jennifer Bartlett, Lynne Cummings, John Demodena and Sarah Lynch. Thank you Dan Heck for displaying grit in the face of insurgent armies, potentially rabid dogs, killer chillies and other routine hazards.

Thanks also to the hundreds of travellers who have taken time to write, especially letter-writers Andrew Coop, Jim Enright, Christopher Hilburn, Bernie Hodges, Tony Jurica, Mark Karaczun, Vermeulen Laurent, Carol O'Hare, Mark Ord and Jim Paulin.

I've tried to name everyone who was of direct help but know I've forgotten a few names along the way. Please forgive me if you're not listed and accept my heartfelt thanks.

**Author's Note to Readers**
When using the information contained in this guide to find your way around Thailand,

keep in mind the Buddhist concept of *anicca*, or 'impermanence'. All things in the world of travel especially are in a constant state of flux and Thailand is no exception. What you read here are conceptual snapshots of single moments in time, filtered through one person's perceptions. They represent the very best of my research efforts at the time of writing, but were bound to change the second I turned my attention away from research and began writing it all down, a necessary part of the process in getting this book to you. Don't expect to find things to be exactly as described in the text – stay flexible and you'll enjoy yourself more.

## From the Publisher
The 7th edition of *Thailand* was edited by Megan Fraser and designed by Glenn Beanland in LP's Melbourne office. Jane Rawson, Anne Mulvaney, Kristin Odijk and Greg Alford assisted with editing and proofing. Maps were drawn and coordinated by Paul Piaia and Chris Love, with help from Sally Gerdan, Chris Lee Ack, Indra Kilfoyle and Trudi Canavan. All the new illustrations were done by Trudi and the index was compiled by Sharon Wertheim. Dan Levin designed the special Thai fonts and made sure the script behaved properly. Simon Bracken created the front cover design and Adam McCrow looked after the back.

Thanks to all the travellers who took the time to write to us about their experiences. Their names appear at the back of the book.

## Warning & Request
Things change – prices go up, schedules change, good places go bad and bad places go bankrupt – nothing stays the same. So, if you find things better or worse, recently opened or long since closed, please tell us and help make the next edition even more accurate and useful.

We value all of the feedback we receive from travellers. Julie Young coordinates a small team who read and acknowledge every letter, postcard and email, and ensure that every morsel of information finds its way to the appropriate authors, editors and publishers.

Everyone who writes to us will find their name in the next edition of the appropriate guide and will also receive a free subscription to our quarterly newsletter, *Planet Talk*. The very best contributions will be rewarded with a free Lonely Planet guide.

Excerpts from your correspondence may appear in updates (which we add to the end pages of reprints); new editions of this guide; in our newsletter, *Planet Talk*; or in the Postcards section of our Web site – so please let us know if you don't want your letter published or your name acknowledged.

# Contents

# Map Legend

## BOUNDARIES

............... International Boundary
............... Regional Boundary

## ROUTES

............................................. Freeway
............................................. Highway
..................................... Major Road
............... Unsealed Road or Track
.................................... City Road
..................................... City Street
..................................... Railway
............... Underground Railway
..................................... Tram
............... Walking Track
..................................... Walking Tour
..................................... Ferry Route
............... Cable Car or Chairlift

## AREA FEATURES

............................................. Parks
..................... Built-Up Area
..................... Pedestrian Mall
..................... Market
............... Cemetery
............... Reef
..................... Beach or Desert
..................... Rocks

## HYDROGRAPHIC FEATURES

............... Coastline
..................... River, Creek
............... Intermittent River or Creek
..................... Rapids, Waterfalls
............... Lake, Intermittent Lake
............... Canal
..................... Swamp

## SYMBOLS

| | | |
|---|---|---|
| ✪ CAPITAL | ....................... National Capital | |
| ◉ Capital | ............................. Regional Capital | |
| 🌑 CITY | ............................. Major City | |
| ● City | ............................................. City | |
| ● Town | ..................................... Town | |
| ● Village | ..................................... Village | |

| | | |
|---|---|---|
| ■ ▼ | ...... Place to Stay, Place to Eat | |
| ☕ 🍺 | ..................... Cafe, Pub or Bar | |
| ✉ ☎ | ............... Post Office, Telephone | |
| ❶ ⬧ | ........... Tourist Information, Bank | |
| ◔ 🅿 | ............... Transport, Parking | |
| 🏛 ⌂ | ............... Museum, Youth Hostel | |
| ⚑ ⚲ | Caravan Park, Camping Ground | |
| ✚ ✚ | ............... Church, Cathedral | |
| ☪ ✡ | ............... Mosque, Synagogue | |
| ▲ ▣ | ............... Temple, Tomb | |
| ◆ ★ | ............... Hospital, Police Station | |

| | | |
|---|---|---|
| ⊘ � | ......... Embassy, Petrol Station | |
| ✈ ✝ | ......................... Airport, Airfield | |
| ▭ ✿ | ......... Swimming Pool, Gardens | |
| ❖ 🐘 | ......... Shopping Centre, Zoo | |
| ⚘ 🌲 | ... Winery or Vineyard, Picnic Site | |
| ← A25 | One Way Street, Route Number | |
| 🏛 ⚑ | ......... Stately Home, Monument | |
| ♜ ✗ | ..................... Castle, Battlefield | |
| ⌒ ⌂ | ............... Cave, Hut or Chalet | |
| ▲ ※ | ......... Mountain or Hill, Lookout | |
| 🕯 ⚓ | ......... Lighthouse, Shipwreck | |
| )( ◎ | ..................... Pass, Spring | |
| 🏄 ⛷ | ..................... Beach, Surf Beach | |
| ⛳ ⬒ | ......... Golf Course, Dive Site | |

............... Ancient or City Wall
............... Cliff or Escarpment, Tunnel
............... Railway Station

Note: not all symbols displayed above appear in this book

# Introduction

Thailand, or Siam as it was called until 1939, has never been colonised by a foreign power, while all of its South-East Asian neighbours have undergone European imperialism (or more recently, ideological domination by communism – which originated in Europe) at one time or another. True, it has suffered periodic invasions on the part of the Burmese and the Khmers and was briefly occupied by the Japanese in WWII, but the kingdom was never externally controlled long enough to dampen the Thais' serious individualism. Although the Thais are often depicted as fun-loving, happy-go-lucky folk (which they often are), they are also very strong-minded and have struggled for centuries to preserve their independence of spirit.

This is not to say that Thailand has not experienced any western influence. Like other Asian countries it has both suffered and benefited from contact with foreign cultures. But the ever-changing spirit of Thai culture has remained dominant, even in modern city life.

The end result is that Thailand has much to interest the traveller: historic culture, lively arts, exotic islands, nightlife, a tradition of friendliness and hospitality to strangers, and one of the world's most exciting cuisines.

Travel in this tropical country is fairly comfortable and down-to-earth. The rail, bus and air travel network is extensive and every place worth visiting is easily accessible. There are many places that warrant a stop, many sights to see, a multifaceted culture to experience and it is all very affordable by today's international travel standards.

Travellers will, from time to time, notice that the spelling of place names in this book is at variance with other sources. This is because Thai uses a totally different script from our own 'roman' script. Any Thai name has to be transliterated for those of us who don't read Thai, and transliteration is very often a matter of opinion. For more information on Thai spellings, see the Language section in the Facts about the Country chapter. ■

# Facts about the Country

## HISTORY

### Prehistory

The history of the geographical area now known as Thailand reaches far back into hoary antiquity. World-renowned scholar Paul Benedict (author of *Austro-Thai Language & Culture*) found that modern linguistic theory (which ties numerous key items in ancient Chinese culture to an early Thai linguistic group), together with recent archaeological finds in Thailand, enable us to establish South-East Asia as a 'focal area in the emergent cultural development of *Homo sapiens*. It now seems likely that the first true agriculturists anywhere, perhaps also the first true metalworkers, were Austro-Thai speakers'.

The Maekhong River valley and Khorat Plateau areas of what today encompasses significant parts of Laos, Cambodia and Thailand were inhabited as far back as 10,000 years ago. Currently the most reliable sources for archaeological evidence are the Ban Chiang and Ban Prasat areas of North-Eastern Thailand, where rice was cultivated as early as 4000 BC (China by contrast was growing and consuming millet at the time). The Ban Chiang culture had begun bronze metallurgy before 3000 BC; the Middle East's Bronze Age arrived around 2800 BC, China's a thousand years later.

### Thai Migration

The ancestors of today's Thais were scattered amidst a vast, nonunified zone of Austro-Thai influence that involved periodic migrations along several different geographic lines. The early Thais proliferated all over South-East Asia, including the islands of Indonesia, and some later settled in south and south-west China, later to 're-migrate' to north Thailand to establish the first Thai kingdom in the 13th century.

A linguistic map of south China, northeast India and South-East Asia clearly shows that the preferred zones of occupation by the Thai peoples have been river valleys, from the Red River (Hong River) in south China and Vietnam to the Brahmaputra River in Assam, India. At one time there were two terminals for movement into what is now Thailand – the 'north terminal' in the Yuan Jiang and other river areas in China's modern-day Yunnan and Guangxi provinces, and the 'south terminal' along central Thailand's Chao Phraya River. The populations remain quite concentrated in these areas today, while areas between the two were intermediate relay points and as such have always been far less populated.

The Maekhong River valley between Thailand and Laos was one such intermediate migrational zone, as were river valleys along the Nan, Ping, Kok, Yom and Wang rivers in Northern Thailand, plus various river areas in Laos and in the Shan State of Myanmar (Burma). The migrant Thais established local polities along traditional social schemata according to *meuang* (roughly 'principality' or 'district'), under the hereditary rule of chieftains or sovereigns called *jâo meuang* (meuang lord).

Each meuang was based in a river valley or section of a valley. Some meuang were loosely collected under one jâo meuang or an alliance of several. One of the largest collections of meuang – though not necessarily united – was in south China and was known as Nam Chao (Naam Jao), or Lord(s) of the River(s). Yunnan's present-day Xishuangbanna district (Sipsongpanna in Thai), a homeland for Northern Thai and Thai Lü groups, is often cited as the point of origin for all Thais, but in-depth histories place Thai groups everywhere along the Thai diaspora from Dien Bien Phu in Vietnam to Assam.

In the mid-13th century, the rise to power of the Mongols under Kublai Khan in Sung dynasty China caused a more dramatic southward migration of Thai peoples. Wherever Thais met indigenous populations of

Tibeto-Burmans and Mon-Khmers in the move south (into what is now Myanmar, Thailand, Laos and Cambodia), they were somehow able to displace, assimilate or coopt them without force. The most probable explanation for this relatively smooth assimilation is that there were already Thai peoples in the area. Such a supposition finds considerable support in current research on the development of Austro-Thai language and culture.

### Early Kingdoms

With no written records or chronologies it is difficult to say with certainty what kind of cultures existed among the meuangs of Thailand before the middle of the first millennium AD. However, by the 6th century an important network of agricultural communities was thriving as far south as modern-day Pattani and Yala, and as far north and northeast as Lamphun and Muang Fa Daet (near Khon Kaen). Theravada Buddhism was flourishing and may have entered the region during India's Ashoka period, in the 3rd or 2nd centuries BC, when Indian missionaries were said to have been sent to a land called Suvannabhumi (Land of Gold). Suvannabhumi most likely corresponds to a remarkably fertile area stretching from southern Myanmar, across central Thailand, to eastern Cambodia. Two different cities in Thailand's central river basin have long been called Suphanburi (City of Gold) and U Thong (Cradle of Gold).

**Dvaravati** This loose collection of city-states was given the Sanskrit name Dvaravati (literally, 'place having gates'), the city of Krishna in the Indian epic poem *Mahabharata*. The French art historian George Coedes discovered the name on some coins that were excavated in the Nakhon Pathom area, which seems to have been the centre of Dvaravati culture. The Dvaravati period lasted until the 11th or 12th century AD and produced many fine works of art, including distinctive Buddha images (showing Indian Gupta influence), stucco reliefs on temples and in caves, some architecture (little of which remains intact), some exquisite terracotta heads, votive tablets and other miscellaneous sculpture.

Dvaravati may have been a cultural relay point for the pre-Angkor cultures of ancient Cambodia and Champa to the east. The Chinese, through the travels of the famous pilgrim Xuan Zang, knew the area as Tuoluobodi, located between Sriksetra (northern Myanmar) and Tsanapura (Sambor Prei Kuk-Kambuja).

The ethnology of the Dvaravati peoples is a controversial subject, though the standard decree is that they were Mon or Mon-Khmer. The Mon themselves seem to have been descended from a group of Indian immigrants from Kalinga, an area overlapping the boundaries of the modern Indian states of Orissa and Andhra Pradesh. The Dvaravati Mon may have been an ethnic mix of these people and people indigenous to the region (the original Thais). In any event, the Dvaravati culture quickly declined in the 11th century under the political domination of the invading Khmers, who made their headquarters in Lopburi. The area around Lamphun, then called Hariphunchai, held out until the late 12th or early 13th century, as evidenced by the Dvaravati architecture of Wat Kukut in Lamphun.

**Khmer Influence** The concurrent Khmer conquests of the 7th to 11th centuries brought Khmer cultural influence in the form of art, language and religion. Some of the Sanskrit terms in Mon-Thai vocabulary entered the language during the Khmer or Lopburi period between the 11th and 13th centuries. Monuments from this period located in Kanchanaburi, Lopburi and many other North-Eastern towns were constructed in the Khmer style and compare favourably with architecture in Angkor. Elements of Brahmanism, Theravada Buddhism and Mahayana Buddhism were intermixed as Lopburi became a religious centre, and some of each religious Buddhist school – along with Brahmanism – remains to this day in Thai religious and court ceremonies.

Detail from a Thai mural painting – murals were often applied to temple interiors to decorate as well as to depict scenes from the Buddhist scriptures.

**Other Kingdoms** While all this was taking place, a distinctly Thai state called Nan Chao or Nam Chao (650-1250 AD) was flourishing in what later became Yunnan and Sichuan in China. Nam Chao maintained close relations with imperial China and the two neighbours enjoyed much cultural exchange. The Mongols, under Kublai Khan, conquered Nam Chao in 1253, but long before they came, the Thai peoples began migrating southward, homesteading in and around what is today Laos and Northern Thailand.

A number of Thais became mercenaries for the Khmer armies in the early 12th century, as depicted on the walls of Angkor Wat. The Khmers called the Thais 'Syam', possibly from the Sanskrit *shyama* meaning 'golden' or 'swarthy', because of their relatively deeper skin colour at the time. Another theory claims the word means 'free'. Whatever the meaning, this was how the Thai kingdom eventually came to be called Syam or Sayam. In north-western Thailand and Myanmar the pronunciation of Syam became 'Shan'. English trader James Lancaster penned the first known English transliteration of the name as 'Siam' in 1592.

Meanwhile southern Thailand – the upper Malay peninsula – was under the control of the Srivijaya empire, the headquarters of which may have been in Palembang, Sumatra, between the 8th and 13th centuries. The regional centre for Srivijaya was Chaiya, near the modern town of Surat Thani. Srivijaya art remains can still be seen in Chaiya and its environs.

**Sukhothai & Lan Na Thai Periods**
Several Thai principalities in the Maekhong River valley united in the 13th and 14th centuries, when Thai princes wrested the lower north from the Khmers – whose Angkor government was declining fast – to create Sukhothai (or 'Rising of Happiness'). They later took Hariphunchai from the Mon

to form Lan Na Thai (literally, 'million Thai rice fields').

The Sukhothai kingdom declared its independence in 1238 under King Si Intharathit and quickly expanded its sphere of influence, taking advantage not only of the declining Khmer power but the weakening Srivijaya domain in the south. Sukhothai is considered by the Thais to be the first true Thai kingdom. It was annexed by Ayuthaya in 1376, by which time a national identity of sorts had been forged. Many Thais today view the Sukhothai period with sentimental vision, seeing it as a 'golden age' of Thai politics, religion and culture – an egalitarian, noble period when everyone had enough to eat and the kingdom was unconquerable. A famous passage from Sukhothai's so-called Ramkhamhaeng inscription reads:

This land of Sukhothai is thriving. There is fish in the water and rice in the fields...**The King** has hung a bell in the opening of the gate over there; if any commoner has a grievance which sickens his belly and grips his heart, he goes and strikes the bell; **King Ram Khamhaeng** questions the man, examines the case and decides it justly for him.

Among other accomplishments, the third Sukhothai king, Ramkhamhaeng, sponsored a fledgling Thai writing system which became the basis for modern Thai; he also codified the Thai form of Theravada Buddhism, as borrowed from the Sinhalese. Under Ramkhamhaeng, the Sukhothai kingdom extended as far as Nakhon Si Thammarat in the south, to the upper Maekhong River valley in Laos, and to Bago (Pegu) in southern Myanmar. For a short time (1448-86) the Sukhothai capital was moved to Phitsanulok.

Ramkhamhaeng also supported Chao Mangrai (also spelt 'Mengrai') of Chiang Mai, and Chao Khun Ngam Meuang of Phayao, two northern Thai jâo meuang, in the 1296 founding of Lan Na Thai, nowadays often known simply as 'Lanna'. Lanna extended across northern Thailand to include the meuang of Wiang Chan along the middle reaches of the Maekhong River. In the 14th century, Wiang Chan was taken from Lanna by Chao Fa Ngum of Luang Prabang, who made it part of his Lan Xang (Million Elephants) kingdom. Wiang Chan later flourished as an independent kingdom for a short time during the mid-16th century and eventually became the capital of Laos in its royal, French (where it got its more popular international spelling, 'Vientiane') and now socialist incarnations. After a period of dynastic decline, Lanna fell to the Burmese in 1558.

## Ayuthaya Period

The Thai kings of Ayuthaya grew very powerful in the 14th and 15th centuries, taking over U Thong and Lopburi, former Khmer strongholds, and moving east in their conquests until Angkor was defeated in 1431. Even though the Khmers were their adversaries in battle, the Ayuthaya kings incorporated large portions of Khmer court customs and language. One result of this acculturation was that the Thai monarch gained more absolute authority during the Ayuthaya period and assumed the title *devaraja* (god-king; *thewarâat* in Thai) as opposed to the *dhammaraja* (dharma-king; *thammárâat* in Thai) title used in Sukhothai.

Ayuthaya was one of the greatest and wealthiest cities in Asia, a thriving seaport envied not only by the Burmese but by the Europeans who were in great awe of the city. It has been said that London, at the time, was a mere village in comparison. The kingdom sustained an unbroken monarchical succession through 34 reigns, from King U Thong (1350-69) to King Ekathat (1758-67), over a period of 400 years.

By the early 16th century Ayuthaya was receiving European visitors, and a Portuguese embassy was established in 1511. The Portuguese were followed by the Dutch in 1605, the English in 1612, the Danes in 1621 and the French in 1662. In the mid-16th century Ayuthaya and the independent kingdom of Lanna came under the control of the Burmese, but the Thais regained rule of both by the end of the century. In 1690 Londoner Engelbert Campfer proclaimed 'Among the Asian nations, the Kingdom of

Siam is the greatest. The magnificence of the Ayuthaya Court is incomparable'.

A rather exceptional episode unfolded in Ayuthaya when a Greek, Constantine Phaulkon, became a very high official in Siam under King Narai from 1675 to 1688. He kept out the Dutch and the English but allowed the French to station 600 soldiers in the kingdom. Eventually the Thais, fearing a takeover, forcibly expelled the French and executed Phaulkon. The word for a 'foreigner' (of European descent) in modern Thai is *faràng*, an abbreviated form of *faràngsèt*, meaning 'French'. Siam sealed itself from the west for 150 years following this experience with farangs.

The Burmese again invaded Ayuthaya in 1765 and the capital fell after two years of fierce battle. This time the Burmese destroyed everything sacred to the Thais, including manuscripts, temples and religious sculpture. The Burmese, despite their effectiveness in sacking Ayuthaya, could not maintain a foothold in the kingdom, and Phaya Taksin, a half-Chinese, half-Thai general, made himself king in 1769, ruling from the new capital of Thonburi on the banks of the Chao Phraya River, opposite Bangkok. The Thais regained control of their country and further united the disparate provinces to the north with central Siam.

Taksin eventually came to regard himself as the next Buddha; his ministers, who did not approve of his religious fantasies, deposed and then executed him in the custom reserved for royalty – by beating him to death in a velvet sack so that no royal blood touched the ground.

## Chakri Dynasty

Another general, Chao Phaya Chakri, came to power and was crowned in 1782 under the title Phutthayotfa Chulalok. He moved the royal capital across the river to Bangkok and ruled as the first king of the Chakri dynasty. In 1809 his son, Loet La, took the throne and reigned until 1824. Both monarchs assumed the task of restoring the culture so severely damaged by the Burmese decades earlier.

The third Chakri king, Phra Nang Klao (1824-51), went beyond reviving tradition and developed trade with China while increasing domestic agricultural production. He also established a new royal title system, posthumously conferring 'Rama I' and 'Rama II' upon his two predecessors and taking the title 'Rama III' for himself. During Nang Klao's reign, American missionary James Low brought the first printing press to Siam and produced the country's first printed document in Thai script. Missionary Dan Bradley published the first Thai newspaper, the monthly *Bangkok Recorder*, from 1844 to 1845.

Rama IV, commonly known as King Mongkut (Phra Chom Klao to the Thais), was one of the more colourful and innovative of the early Chakri kings. He originally missed out on the throne in deference to his half-brother, Rama III, and lived as a

## Chakri Dynasty

| Crown Title | Reign | Common Westernised Name | Thai Pronunciation |
|---|---|---|---|
| Rama I | 1782-1809 | Yot Fa | Phutthayotfa Chulalok |
| Rama II | 1809-24 | Loet La | Phutthaloetla Naphalai |
| Rama III | 1824-51 | Nang Klao | same |
| Rama IV | 1851-68 | Mongkut | Phra Chom Klao |
| Rama V | 1868-1910 | Chulalongkorn | Chula Chom Klao |
| Rama VI | 1910-25 | Vajiravudh | Mongkut Klao |
| Rama VII | 1925-35 | Prajadhipok | Pokklao |
| Rama VIII | 1935-46 | Ananda Mahidol | Anantha Mahidon |
| Rama IX | 1946-present | Bhumibol Adulyadej | Phumiphon Adunyadet |

Buddhist monk for 27 years. During his long monastic term he became adept in the Sanskrit, Pali, Latin and English languages, studied western sciences and adopted the strict discipline of local Mon monks. He kept an eye on the outside world and when he took the throne in 1851 immediately courted diplomatic relations with European nations, while avoiding colonialisation.

In addition, he attempted to align Buddhist cosmology with modern science, with the aim of demythologising the Thai religion (a process yet to be fully accomplished), and founded the Thammayut monastic sect, based on the strict discipline he had followed as a monk. (Today, the Thammayut remains a minority sect in relation to the Mahanikai, which comprises the largest number of Buddhist monks in Thailand.)

Thai trade restrictions were loosened by King Mongkut and many western powers signed trade agreements with the monarch. He also sponsored Siam's first printing press and instituted educational reforms, developing a school system along European lines. Although the king courted the west, he did so with caution and warned his subjects: 'Whatever they have invented or done which we should know of and do, we can imitate and learn from them, but do not wholeheartedly believe in them'. Mongkut was the first monarch to show Thai commoners his face in public; he died of malaria in 1868.

His son, King Chulalongkorn (known to the Thais as Chula Chom Klao or Rama V, 1868-1910), continued Mongkut's tradition of reform, especially in the legal and administrative realms. Educated by European tutors, Chula abolished prostration before the king as well as slavery and corvée (state labour). Siam further benefited from relations with European nations and the USA: railways were built, a civil service established and the legal code restructured. Though Siam still managed to avoid colonialisation, the king was compelled to concede territory to French Indochina (Laos in 1893, Cambodia in 1907) and British Burma (three Malayan states in 1909) during his reign.

Chula's son, King Vajiravudh (also known as Mongkut Klao or Rama VI, 1910-25), was educated in Britain and during his rather short reign introduced compulsory education and other educational reforms. He further 'westernised' the nation by making the Thai calendar conform to western models. His reign was somewhat clouded by a top-down push for Thai nationalism that resulted in strong anti-Chinese sentiment.

Before Rama VI's reign, Thai parents gave each of their children a single, original name, with no surname to identify family origins. In 1909 a royal decree required the adoption of Thai surnames for all Thai citizens – a move designed as much to parallel the European system of family surnames as to weed out Chinese names.

In 1912 a group of Thai military officers unsuccessfully attempted to overthrow the monarchy, the first in a series of 20th century coup attempts that has continued to the present day. As a show of support for the Allies in WWI, Rama VI sent 1300 Thai troops to France in 1918.

## Revolution

While Vajiravudh's brother, King Prajadhipok (Pokklao or Rama VII, 1925-35) ruled, a group of Thai students living in Paris became so enamoured of democratic ideology that they mounted a successful coup d'état in 1932 against absolute monarchy in Siam. This bloodless revolution led to the development of a constitutional monarchy along British lines, with a mixed military-civilian group in power.

A royalist revolt in 1933 sought to reinstate absolute monarchy, but it failed and left Prajadhipok isolated from both the royalist revolutionaries and the constitution-minded ministers. One of the king's last official acts was to outlaw polygamy in 1934, leaving behind the cultural underpinnings for consorts, concubines and minor wives that now support Thai prostitution.

In 1935 the king abdicated without naming a successor and retired to Britain. The cabinet promoted his nephew, 10 year old Ananda Mahidol, to the throne as Rama

VIII, though Ananda didn't return to Thailand from school in Switzerland until 1945. Phibun (Phibul) Songkhram, a key military leader in the 1932 coup, maintained an effective position of power from 1938 until the end of WWII.

Under the influence of Phibun's government, the country's name was officially changed from 'Siam' to 'Thailand' in 1939 – rendered in Thai as 'Prathêt Thai'. ('Prathêt' is derived from the Sanskrit *pradesha* or 'country'. 'Thai' is considered to have the connotation of 'free', though in actual usage it simply refers to the Thai, Tai or T'ai peoples, who are found as far east as Tonkin, as far west as Assam, as far north as south China, and as far south as north Malaysia.)

Ananda Mahidol ascended the throne in 1945 but was shot dead in his bedroom under mysterious circumstances in 1946. Although there was apparently no physical evidence to suggest assassination, three of Ananda's attendants were arrested two years after his death and executed in 1954. No public charges were ever filed, and the consensus among historians today is that the attendants were 'sacrificed' to settle a karmic debt for allowing the king to die during their watch. His brother, Bhumibol Adulyadej, succeeded him as Rama IX. Nowadays no-one ever speaks or writes publicly about Ananda's death. Even as recently as 1993 a chapter chronicling the known circumstances surrounding the event in David Wyatt's *A Short History of Thailand* had to be excised before the Thai publisher would print and distribute the title in Thailand.

## WWII & Postwar Periods

During their invasion of South-East Asia, the Japanese outflanked Allied troops in Malaya and Myanmar in 1941. The Phibun government complied with the Japanese in this action by allowing them into the Gulf of Thailand; consequently the Japanese troops occupied a portion of Thailand itself. Phibun declared war on the USA and Britain in 1942 but Seni Pramoj, the Thai ambassador in Washington, refused to deliver the declaration. Phibun resigned in 1944 under pressure from the Thai underground resistance (known as Thai Seri), and after V-J Day in 1945, Seni became premier.

In 1946 Seni and his brother Kukrit were unseated in a general election and a democratic civilian group took power under Pridi Phanomyong, a law professor who had been instrumental in the 1932 revolution. Pridi's civilian government, which changed the country's name back to 'Siam', ruled for a short time, only to be overthrown by Phibun, now field marshal, in 1947. Phibun suspended the constitution and reinstated 'Thailand' as the country's official name in 1949. Under Phibun the government took an extreme anti-communist stance, refused to recognise the People's Republic of China and became a loyal supporter of French and US foreign policy in South-East Asia.

In 1951 power was wrested from Phibun by General Sarit Thanarat, who continued the tradition of military dictatorship. However, Phibun somehow retained the actual title of premier until 1957 when Sarit finally had him exiled. Elections that same year forced Sarit to resign and go abroad for 'medical treatment'; he returned in 1958 to launch another coup. This time he abolished the constitution, dissolved the parliament and banned all political parties, maintaining effective power until he died of cirrhosis in 1963. From 1964 to 1973 the Thai nation was ruled by army officers Thanom Kittikachorn and Praphat Charusathien, during which time Thailand allowed the USA to establish several army bases within its borders in support of the US campaign in Vietnam.

Reacting to political repression, 10,000 Thai students publicly demanded a real constitution in June 1973. In October of the same year the military brutally suppressed a large demonstration at Thammasat University in Bangkok, but King Bhumibol and General Krit Sivara, who sympathised with the students, refused to support further bloodshed, forcing Thanom and Praphat to leave Thailand. Oxford-educated Kukrit Pramoj took charge of a 14 party coalition government and steered a leftist agenda past a conservative

PAUL BEINSSEN

RICHARD NEBESKY

Top: Street billboard for new Thai action blockbuster
Bottom: Colourful bow of the *kaw-lae* – the traditional fishing boat of the South

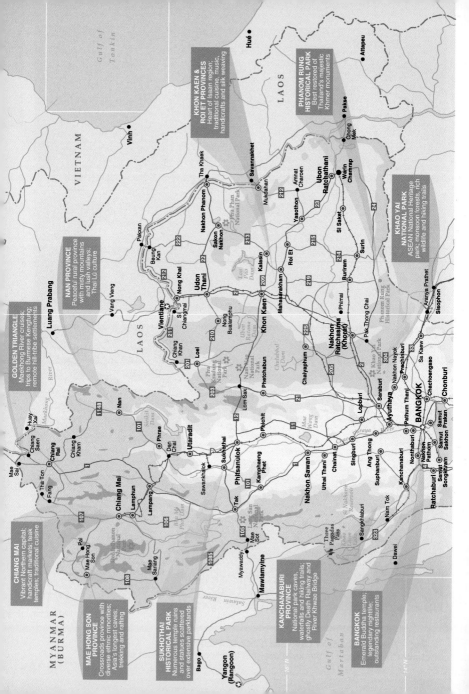

**GULF OF TONKIN**

**Gulf of Tonkin**

Hué •

Attapeu •

VIETNAM

Vinh •

**KHON KAEN & ROI ET PROVINCES**
Heart of Isaan region;
traditional culture, music,
handicrafts and silk weaving

**PHANOM RUNG HISTORICAL PARK**
Best-restored Khmer monuments

Pakse •

LAOS

Chong Mek

Tha Khaek

Savannakhet

Mun

Nakhon Phanom

Amnat Charoen

Ubon Ratchathani

Warin Chamrap

**212**

Sakon Nakhon

Yasothon

**23**

Si Saket

**24**

Phu Phan National Park

**213**

Kalasin

Roi Et

**215**

Pakxan

Beung Kan

**222**

Nong Khai

**22**

Udon Thani

**2**

Khon Kaen

**209**

Mahasarakham

**214**

Surin

Buriram

**219**

**KHAO YAI NATIONAL PARK**
ASEAN National Heritage
park; monsoon forests, rich
wildlife and hiking trails

Aranya Prathet

Sisophon

Vang Vieng

Vientiane

Si Chiangmai

**211**

Chiang Khan

Loei

**201**

Nong Bualamphu

Phu Kradung National Park

Ubon Ratmai National Park

Nam Nao National Park

Lom Pao Dam

**210**

Phetchabun

Chaiyaphum

**225**

Nakhon Ratchasima (Khorat)

Phimai

Pak Thong Chai

**205**

**2**

Phanom Rung Historical Park

Chalerm Dam

Khao Yai National Park

Sa Kaew

**33**

**GOLDEN TRIANGLE**
Maekhong River cruises;
trips to Burmese Kengtung;
remote hill-tribe settlements

Luang Prabang

**NAN PROVINCE**
Peaceful, rural province
with misty mountains
and lush valleys;
Thai Lu culture

Lom Sak

**12**

Saraburi

Lopburi

Nakhon Nayok

Prachinburi

**304**

Chachoengsao

Chonburi

Mekhong River

Huay Xai

Chiang Saen

Nan

**1148**

Mae Sai

Chiang Rai

**101**

Chiang Kham

Uthai Thani

Fang

Tha Ton

Phrae

Den Chai

Uttaradit

Phitsanulok

Sawankhalok

Sukhothai

Kamphaeng Phet

Nakhon Sawan

**1**

Chainat

Singburi

Ang Thong

Ayuthaya

Pathum Thani

Nonthaburi

**BANGKOK**

Samut Prakan

**CHIANG MAI**
Vibrant Northern capital;
handicraft markets; teak
temples; traditional cuisine

Chiang Mai

Lamphun

Lampang

**106**

**107**

Pai

Mae Hong Son

Mae Sariang

**108**

Bhumibol Dam

Tak

**101**

Mae Sot

**105**

Mae Wong Dam

Suphanburi

Nakhon Pathom

Samut Sakhon

Samut Songkhram

**MAE HONG SON PROVINCE**
Crossroads province with
diverse ethnic minorities;
Asia's longest caves;
trekking and rafting

**SUKHOTHAI HISTORICAL PARK**
Numerous temple ruins
and statues scattered
over extensive parklands

**KANCHANABURI PROVINCE**
National park caves,
waterfalls and hiking trails;
ghostly Death Railway and
River Kwae Bridge

**BANGKOK**
Emerald Buddha temple;
legendary nightlife;
outstanding restaurants

MYANMAR (BURMA)

Myawaddy

Mawlamyine

Salween River

Three Pagodas Pass

Sangkhlaburi

**323**

Nam Tok

Kanchanaburi

Ratchaburi

Phetchburi

Bago

Yangon (Rangoon)

Dawei

Gulf of Martaban

**16 N**

**12 N**

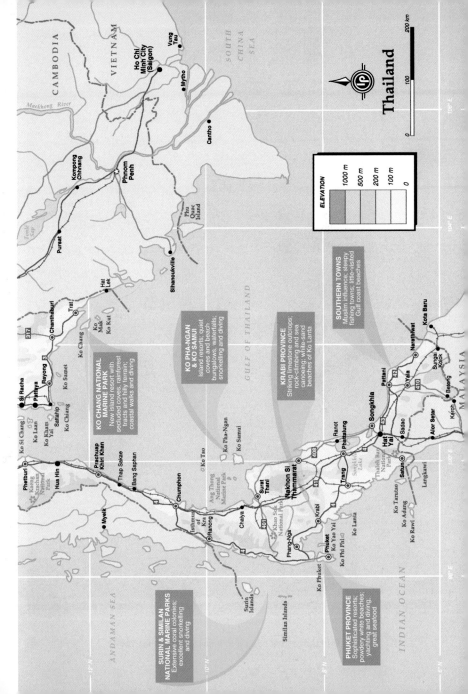

# Thailand

**ELEVATION**
1000 m
500 m
200 m
100 m
0

0   100   200 km

---

**SURIN & SIMILAN NATIONAL MARINE PARKS**
Extensive coral colonies; excellent snorkelling and diving

**KO CHANG NATIONAL MARINE PARK**
National land reserve with secluded coves and rainforest tracts and hilly terrain; coastal walks and diving

**KO PHA-NGAN & KO SAMUI**
Island resorts; quiet coves and beach bungalows; waterfalls; snorkelling and diving

**KRABI PROVINCE**
Striking limestone outcrops; rock-climbing and sea canoeing; white-sand beaches of Ko Lanta

**SOUTHERN TOWNS**
Muslim influence; sleepy fishing towns; little-visited Gulf coast beaches

**PHUKET PROVINCE**
Sophisticated resorts; powdery white beaches; yachting and diving; great seafood

---

CAMBODIA

VIETNAM

MALAYSIA

SOUTH CHINA SEA

GULF OF THAILAND

ANDAMAN SEA

INDIAN OCEAN

Maekhong River

Tonle Sap

Vung Tau
Ho Chi Minh City (Saigon)
Mytho
Cantho
Phnom Penh
Kompong Chhnang
Pursat
Phu Quoc Island
Sihanoukville

Hat Lek
Chanthaburi
Ko Mak
Ko Kut
Ko Chang
Trat
Ko Samet
Rayong
Pattaya
Si Racha
Ko Si Chang
Ko Laan
Ko Kham Yai
Ko Chang
Sattahip

Phetburi
Kaeng Krachan National Park
Hua Hin
Prachuap Khiri Khan
Thap Sakae
Bang Saphan
Myeik
Isthmus of Kra
Ranong
Chumphon
Chaiya
Surat Thani
Ang Thong National Marine Park
Ko Tao
Ko Pha-Ngan
Ko Samui

Khao Sok National Park
Phang-Nga
Ko Phi Phi
Ko Yao Yai
Phuket
Ko Phuket
Similan Islands
Surin Islands

Krabi
Ko Lanta
Nakhon Si Thammarat
Ranot
Phatthalung
Trang
Songkhla Lake
Thaleh Ban National Park
Songkhla
Hat Yai
Sadao
Satun
Ko Tarutao
Ko Adang
Ko Rawi
Langkawi
Alor Setar
Kroh
Betong
Yala
Pattani
Narathiwat
Sungai Kolok
Kota Baru

JOE CUMMINGS

Buddhist monk caught in festival traffic, Hat Yai

parliament. Among his lasting successes were a national minimum wage, the repeal of anti-communist laws and the ejection of US forces from Thailand.

**Polarisation & Stabilisation**

Kukrit's elected, constitutional government ruled until October 1976 when students demonstrated again, this time protesting Thanom's return to Thailand as a monk. Thammasat University again became a battlefield as border patrol police, along with right-wing, paramilitary civilian groups (Nawaphon, the Red Guards and the Village Scouts), assaulted a group of 2000 students holding a sit-in. Hundreds of students were killed and injured in the fracas; more than a thousand were arrested. Using public disorder as an excuse, the military stepped in and installed a new right-wing government with Thanin Kraivichien as premier.

This bloody incident disillusioned many Thai students and older intellectuals not directly involved with the demonstrations, the result being that numerous idealists 'dropped out' of Thai society and joined the People's Liberation Army of Thailand (PLAT) – armed communist insurgents based in the hills who had been active in Thailand since the 1930s.

In October 1977 the military replaced Thanin with the more moderate General Kriangsak Chomanand in an effort to conciliate anti-government factions. When this failed, the military-backed position changed hands again in 1980, leaving Prem Tinsulanonda at the helm. By this time the PLAT had reached a peak force numbering around 10,000.

Prem served as prime minister through 1988 and is credited with the political and economic stabilisation of Thailand in the post-Indochina War years (only one coup attempt in the 1980s!). The major accomplishment of the Prem years was a complete dismantling of the Communist Party of Thailand and PLAT through an effective combination of amnesty programmes (which brought the students back from the forests) and military action. His administra-

tion is also considered responsible for a gradual democratisation of Thailand which culminated in the 1988 election of his successor, Chatichai Choonhavan.

It may be difficult for new arrivals to Thailand to appreciate the political distance Thailand covered in the 1980s. Between 1976 and 1981, freedom of speech and the press were rather curtailed in Thailand and a strict curfew was enforced in Bangkok. Anyone caught in the streets past 1 am risked spending the night in one of Bangkok's mosquito-infested 'detention areas'. Under Prem, the curfew was lifted, and dissenting opinions began to be heard again in public.

Traditionally, every leading political figure in Thailand, including Prem, has needed the support of the Thai military, who are generally staunch reactionaries. Considering Thailand's geographic position, it's not difficult to understand, to some extent, the fears of this ultra-conservative group. But as the threat of communist takeover (either from within or from nearby Indochinese states) diminished, the military gradually began loosening its hold on national politics. Under Chatichai, Thailand enjoyed a brief period of unprecedented popular participation in government.

Approximately 60% of Chatichai's cabinet were former business executives rather than ex-military officers, as compared to 38% in the previous cabinet. Thailand seemed to be entering a new era in which the country's double-digit economic boom ran concurrently with democratisation. Critics praised the political maturation of Thailand, even if they grumbled that corruption seemed as rife as ever. By the end of the 1980s, however, certain high-ranking military officers had become increasingly disappointed with this *coup d'argent*, complaining that Thailand was being run by a plutocracy.

**February 1991 Coup**

On 23 February 1991, in a move that shocked Thailand observers around the world, the military overthrew the Chatichai administration in a bloodless coup (Thai: *pàtìwát*) and handed power to the newly formed National

Peace-Keeping Council (NPKC), led by General Suchinda Kraprayoon. Although it was Thailand's 19th coup attempt and one of 10 successful coups since 1932, it was only the second coup to overthrow a democratically elected civilian government. Chatichai lasted longer than any other elected prime minister in Thailand's history: two years and seven months. Charging Chatichai's civilian government with corruption and vote-buying, the NPKC abolished the 1978 constitution and dissolved the parliament. Rights of public assembly were curtailed but the press was closed down for only one day.

Whether or not Chatichai's government was guilty of vote-buying, one of Chatichai's major mistakes was the appointment of General Chaovalit Yongchaiyuth and former army commander Arthit Kamlang-ek as defence and deputy defence minister respectively. Both were adversaries of the generals who engineered the coup, ie Suchinda and his main ally General Sunthorn Kongsompong (both 'Class 5' officers – those who had graduated from the Chulachomklao Royal Military Academy in 1958 and who formed the backbone of the NPKC's support). Chatichai was also moving into areas of foreign policy traditionally reserved for the military, especially relations with Myanmar, Laos and Cambodia, and the generals may have feared that the prime minister would fire them. It was the same old story: a power struggle between military bureaucrats and capitalist politicians.

Following the coup, the NPKC appointed a hand-picked civilian prime minister, Anand Panyarachun, former ambassador to the USA, Germany, Canada and the UN, to dispel public fears that the junta was planning a return to 100% military rule. Anand claimed to be his own man, but like his predecessors – elected or not – he was allowed the freedom to make his own decisions only in so far as they didn't affect the military. In spite of obvious constraints, many observers felt Anand's temporary premiership and cabinet were the best Thailand had ever had.

In December 1991, Thailand's national assembly passed a new constitution that guaranteed a NPKC-biased parliament – 270 appointed senators in the upper house stacked against 360 elected representatives. Under this constitution, regardless of who was chosen as the next prime minister or which political parties filled the lower house, the government would remain largely in the hands of the military. The new charter includes a provisional clause allowing for a 'four year transitional period' to full democracy, a provision which sounds suspiciously close to the military subterfuge in neighbouring Myanmar.

## Elections & Demonstrations

A general election in March 1992 ushered in a five party coalition government with Narong Wongwan, whose Samakkhitham (Justice Unity) Party received the most votes, as premier. But amid allegations that Narong was involved in Thailand's drug trade, the military exercised its constitutional prerogative and immediately replaced Narong with (surprise, surprise) General Suchinda in April.

The NPKC promised to eradicate corruption and build democracy, a claim that was difficult to accept since they had previously done little on either score. In many ways, it was like letting the proverbial fox guard the henhouse, as the military is perhaps the most corrupt institution in the country – always claiming to be free of politics and yet forever meddling in it. Thailand's independent political pundits agreed there was more oppression under the NPKC than under any administration since pre-1981 days.

In May 1992, several huge demonstrations demanding Suchinda's resignation – led by charismatic Bangkok governor Chamlong Srimuang – rocked Bangkok and larger provincial capitals. Chamlong won the 1992 Magsaysay Award (a humanitarian service award issued by a foundation in the Philippines) for his role in galvanising the public to reject Suchinda. After street confrontations between the protesters and the military near Bangkok's Democracy Monument resulted in nearly 50 deaths and hundreds of injuries, Suchinda resigned after less than six weeks as premier. The military backed government also agreed to institute a constitutional amendment requiring that Thailand's prime minister come from the ranks of elected MPs. Anand Panyarachun was reinstated as interim premier, once again winning praise from several circles for his even-handed and efficient administration.

The September 1992 elections squeezed in veteran Democrats Party leader Chuan Leekpai with a five seat majority. Chuan led a coalition government consisting of the Democrats, New Aspiration, Palang Dharma and Solidarity parties. A food vendor's son and native of Trang Province, the new premier didn't fit the usual Thai prime minister mould since he was neither general nor tycoon nor academic. Though well regarded for his honesty and high morals, Chuan accomplished little in the areas of concern to the majority of Thais, most pointedly Bangkok traffic, national infrastructure and the undemocratic NPKC constitution. By the end of 1993 the opposition was calling for parliamentary dissolution and a royal command appointed a new cabinet for Chuan in December 1994.

Chuan never completed his four year term and a new general election ushered in a seven party coalition led by the Chart Thai (Thai Nationality) Party. At the helm was 63 year old billionaire Banharn Silapa-archa, whom the Thai press called a 'walking ATM (automatic teller machine)'. Two of the largest partners in the coalition, the Palang Dharma and New Aspiration parties, were former participants from the Chuan coalition. Banharn wasn't very popular with the Thai media, who immediately attacked his tendency to appoint from a pool of rural politicians known to be heavily involved in money politics. In September 1996 the Banharn government collapsed, amidst a spate of corruption scandals and a crisis of confidence. The November national election, marked by electoral violence and accusations of vote buying, saw former

deputy prime minister and army commander, Chavalit Yongchaiyudh of the New Aspiration Party, secure premiership with a dubious mix of coalition partners.

In most ways since the coup/counter-coup events of 1991 and 1992, Thailand has experienced 'business as usual'. Thai cynics will tell you that things *never* change – it depends on how closely you observe politics. The temporary military takeover undoubtedly hurt Thailand's international image, especially among those observers who had seen Thailand moving towards increased democratisation.

Optimists now see Suchinda's hasty resignation as a sign that the coup was only a minor detour on the country's road towards a more responsive and democratic national government. Others say the democratic Chatichai, Chuan, Banharn and Chavalit governments may merely be short-lived deviations from the norm of military rule. Hardened cynics might hold the view that Thailand's 20th century coups and counter-coups are a mere extension of the warlordism of early Thai jâo meuangs. Corruption remains a major problem; the Berlin-based watchdog Transparency International recently ranked Thailand third behind Indonesia and the Philippines in terms of corruptive tendencies. Without question, until the constitution is fully amended to remove objectionable provisions for parliamentary succession, Thailand's claims to democratic status and political stability will remain as shaky as ever.

## GEOGRAPHY

Thailand has an area of 517,000 sq km, making it slightly smaller than the state of Texas in the USA, or about the size of France. Its shape on the map has been compared to the head of an elephant, with its trunk extending down the Malay peninsula, looking as if someone has squeezed the lower part of the 'boot' of Italy, forcing the volume into the top portion while reducing the bottom. The centre of Thailand, Bangkok, is at about 14° north latitude, putting it on a level with Madras, Manila, Guatemala and Khartoum.

## Opium & the Golden Triangle

The opium poppy, *Papaver somniferum*, has been cultivated and its resins extracted for use as a narcotic at least since the time of the early Greek empire. The Chinese were introduced to opium by Arab traders during the time of Kublai Khan (1279-94). The drug was so highly valued for its medicinal properties that hill-tribe minorities in south China began cultivating the opium poppy in order to raise money to pay taxes to their Han Chinese rulers. Easy to grow, opium became a way for the nomadic hill tribes to raise what cash they needed in transactions (willing and unwilling) with the lowland world. Many of the hill tribes that migrated to Thailand and Laos in the post-WWII era in order to avoid persecution in Myanmar and China took with them their one cash crop, the poppy. The poppy is well suited to hillside cultivation as it flourishes on steep slopes and in nutrient-poor soils.

The opium trade became especially lucrative in South-East Asia during the 1960s and early 1970s when US armed forces were embroiled in Vietnam. Alfred McCoy's *The Politics of Heroin in Southeast Asia* recounts how contact with the GI market not only expanded the immediate Asian market, but provided outlets to world markets. Before this time the source of most of the world's heroin was the Middle East. Soon everybody wanted in and various parties alternately quarrelled over and cooperated in illegal opium commerce. Most notable were the Nationalist Chinese Army refugees living in northern Myanmar and Northern Thailand, and the anti-Yangon rebels, in particular the Burmese Communist Party (BCP), the Shan States Army and the Shan United Army (SUA).

The American CIA eventually became involved in a big way, using profits from heroin runs aboard US aircraft to Vietnam and farther afield to finance covert operations throughout Indochina. This of course led to an increase in the availability of heroin throughout the world, which in turn led to increased production in the remote northern areas of Thailand, Myanmar and Laos, where there was little government interference. This area came to be known as the 'Golden Triangle' because of local fortunes amassed by the 'opium warlords' – Burmese and Chinese military-businesspeople who controlled the movement of opium across three international borders.

As more opium became available, more was consumed and the demand increased along with the profits – so the cycle expanded. As a result, opium cultivation became a full-time job for some hill tribes within the Golden Triangle. Hill economies were destabilised to the point where opium production became a necessary means of survival for thousands of people, including the less nomadic Shan people.

One of the Golden Triangle's most colourful figures is Khun Sa (also known as Chang Chi-Fu, or Sao Mong Khawn), a half-Chinese, half-Shan opium warlord who got his start in the 1950s and 1960s working for the Kuomintang (KMT) – Chiang Kai-shek's Nationalist Chinese troops, some of whom had fled to Myanmar. The KMT were carrying out military operations against the Chinese communists along the Myanmar-China border, financed by the smuggling of opium (with CIA protection). They employed Khun Sa as one of their prime local supporters/advisors. Khun Sa broke with the KMT in the early 1960s after establishing his own opium-smuggling business with heroin refineries in Northern Thailand.

From that time on, the history of heroin smuggling in the Golden Triangle was intertwined with the exploits of Khun Sa. In 1966, the Burmese government deputised Khun Sa as head of 'village defence forces' against the BCP, which was at maximum strength at this time and fully involved in opium trade. Khun Sa cleverly used his government backing to consolidate power and build up his own militia by developing the SUA, an anti-government insurgent group heavily involved in opium throughout the Golden Triangle in competition with the BCP and KMT.

When the KMT attempted an 'embargo' on SUA opium trade by blocking caravan routes into Thailand and Laos, Khun Sa initiated what has come to be known as the Opium War of 1967 and thwarted the embargo. However, the KMT managed to chase Khun Sa, along with a contingent of SUA troops running an opium caravan routed for Thailand, into Laos, where Burmese officials arrested him and the Laotian government seized the opium. Khun Sa escaped Burmese custody by means of a carefully planned combination of extortion and bribery in 1975 and returned to take command of the SUA. About the same time, the Myanmar government broke KMT control of opium trafficking and Khun Sa stepped in to become the prime opium warlord in the Triangle, working from his headquarters in Ban Hin Taek, Chiang Rai Province, Thailand. Coincidentally, US forces pulled out of Indochina so there was no longer any competition from CIA conduits in Laos.

Since the late 1970s, Khun Sa and his ilk continued to buy opium from the Shan and hill-tribe cultivators in Myanmar, Laos and Thailand, transporting and selling the product to Yunnanese-operated heroin refineries in China, Laos and Thailand, who in turn sell to ethnic Chinese (usually Tae Jiu/Chao Zhou) syndicates which control access to world markets via Thailand and Yunnan.

A turning point in Khun Sa's fortunes occurred in 1982 and 1983 when the Thais launched a full-scale attack on his Ban Hin Taek stronghold, forcing him to flee over the mountains and across the border to Ho Mong, Myanmar, where he directed his independent empire from a fortified network of underground tunnels. This move led to the breaking up of opium and heroin production in the Mae Salong-Ban Hin Taek area.

The SUA merged with several other Shan armies to form the Muang (Mong) Tai Army (MTA), led by the Shan State Restoration Council. The MTA reached an estimated strength of 25,000 – the largest and best equipped ethnic army in Myanmar – before Khun Sa's surprise surrender to Yangon in 1996. His retreat to an island off the coast of Myanmar smacks of collusion with the Yangon-based military.

Meanwhile Khun Sa's former Northern Thailand stronghold has undergone heavy 'pacification' or Thai nationalisation. At great expense to the Thai government, tea, coffee, corn and Chinese herbs are now grown where opium once thrived. Whether this particular project is successful or not is another question, but the government's strategy seems to be one of isolating and then pushing pockets of the opium trade out of Thailand and into Myanmar and Laos, where it continues uninterrupted. During a bumper year, the entire Triangle output approaches 4000 tonnes, most of it from north-eastern Myanmar. In Thailand, the average yield is a high 2.2 kg of raw opium per *rai* (one rai is equal to 1600 sq m); an estimated two tonnes of heroin is smuggled out of the country each year.

North-western Laos is dotted with heroin refineries which process Burmese and Laotian opium. Smuggling routes for Laotian opium and heroin continue to intersect the Thai border at several points throughout the North and North-East, including the provinces of Chiang Mai (via Myanmar), Chiang Rai, Nan, Loei, Nong Khai and Nakhon Phanom.

By all estimates there has been a steady increase in Triangle production during the last 10 years; only around 2% of the opium crop is intercepted by national or international authorities each year. Whenever they receive a large financial contribution from the US Drug Enforcement Agency (DEA), Thai army rangers sweep Northern Thailand from Tak to Chiang Rai and Mae Hong Son, destroying poppy fields and heroin refineries but rarely making arrests. A typical sweep costs US$1 million and accomplishes the destruction of 25,000 or more rai of poppy fields in Thailand's nine poppy-growing provinces – Tak, Mae Hong Son, Chiang Mai, Chiang Rai, Nan, Phayao, Phitsanulok, Phetchabun and Loei. Hill-tribe and Shan cultivators, at the bottom of the profit scale, stand by helplessly while their primary means of livelihood is hacked or burned to the ground. A crop substitution programme, developed by the Thai royal family in 1959 (a year earlier, cultivation of the opium poppy for profit had been made illegal), has had mixed results. Success has only occurred in selected areas where crop substitution is accompanied by a concentrated effort to indoctrinate hill tribes into mainstream Thai culture.

Meanwhile, power shifts from warlord to warlord while the hill-tribe and Shan cultivators continue as unwilling pawns in the opium-heroin cycle. The planting of the poppy and the sale of its collected resins has never been a simple moral issue. Cultivators who have been farming poppies for centuries and heroin addicts who consume the end product have both been exploited by governments and crime syndicates who trade in opium for the advancement of their own interests. Because of the complexities involved, opium production in the Golden Triangle must be dealt with as a political, social, cultural and economic problem and not simply as a conventional law-enforcement matter.

So far, a one-sided approach has resulted only in the unthinking destruction of minority culture and economy in the Golden Triangle area, rather than an end to the opium and heroin problem. Although the Thai government outlawed the opium trade in 1839, any hill-tribe settlement may legally plant a limited crop of opium poppies for medical consumption. Small plots of land are thus sometimes 'leased' by opium merchants who have allowed production to decentralise in order for poppy resin collection to appear legal. Due to crackdowns on Burmese and Lao opiate imports – which resulted in doubling the average price per kilo – poppy cultivation in Thailand for personal/local consumption increased 60% in 1995-96. ■

The country's longest north-south distance is about 1860 km, but its shape makes distances in any other direction a thousand km or less. Because the north-south reach spans roughly 16 latitudinal degrees, Thailand has perhaps the most diverse climate in South-East Asia. The topography varies from high mountains in the North (the southernmost extreme of a series of ranges that extend across northern Myanmar and southwest China to the south-eastern edges of the Tibet Plateau) to limestone-encrusted tropical islands in the South that are part of the Malay Archipelago. The rivers and tributaries of Northern and Central Thailand drain into the Gulf of Thailand via the Chao Phraya Delta near Bangkok; those of the Mun River and other North-Eastern waterways exit into the South China Sea via the Maekhong River.

These broad geographic characteristics divide the country into four main zones: the fertile centre region, dominated by the Chao Phraya River; the north-east plateau, the kingdom's poorest region (thanks to 'thin' soil plus occasional droughts and floods), rising some 300m above the central plain; Northern Thailand, a region of mountains and fertile valleys; and the Southern peninsular region, which extends to the Malaysian frontier and is predominantly rainforest. The Southern region receives the most annual rainfall and the North-East the least, although the North is less humid.

Extending from the east coast of the Malay peninsula to Vietnam, the Sunda Shelf separates the Gulf of Thailand from the South China Sea. On the opposite side of the Thai-Malay peninsula, the Andaman Sea encompasses that part of the Indian Ocean found east of India's Andaman and Nicobar islands. Thailand's Andaman Sea and Gulf of Thailand coastlines form 2710 km of beaches, hard shores and wetlands. Hundreds of oceanic and continental islands are found offshore on both sides – those with tourist facilities constitute only a fraction of the total. Offshore depths in the Gulf range from 30 to 80m, while offshore Andaman depths reach over 100m.

## CLIMATE
### Rainfall
Thailand's climate is ruled by monsoons that produce three seasons in Northern, North-Eastern and Central Thailand, and two seasons in Southern Thailand. The three season zone, which extends roughly from Thailand's northernmost reaches to Phetburi Province on the Southern peninsula, experiences a 'dry and wet monsoon climate', with the south-west monsoon arriving between May and July and lasting into November. This is followed by a dry period from November to May, a period that begins with lower relative temperatures (because of the influences of the north-east monsoon, which bypasses this part of Thailand but results in cool breezes) till mid-February, followed by much higher relative temperatures from March to May.

It rains more and longer in the South, which is subject to the north-east monsoon from November to January, as well as the south-west monsoon. Hence most of Southern Thailand has only two seasons, a wet and a dry, with smaller temperature differences between the two.

Although the rains 'officially' begin in July (according to the Thai agricultural calendar), they actually depend on the monsoons in any given year. As a rule of thumb, the dry season is shorter the farther south you go. From Chiang Mai north the dry season may last six months (mid-November to May); in most of Central and North-Eastern Thailand five months (December to May); on the upper peninsula three months (February to May); and below Surat Thani only two months (March and April). Occasional rains in the dry season are known as 'mango showers' (as they arrive on the onset of the mango season).

In Central Thailand it rains most during August and September, though there may be floods in October since the ground has reached full saturation by then. If you are in Bangkok in early October don't be surprised if you find yourself in hip-deep water in certain parts of the city. It rains a little less in the North, August being the peak month. The

North-East gets less rain and periodically suffers droughts. In Phuket it rains most in May (an average of 21 out of 30 days) and in October (an average of 22 out of 30 days), as this area undergoes both monsoons. Travelling in the rainy season is generally not unpleasant, but unpaved roads may occasionally be impassable.

## Temperature

Most of Thailand – with the mountains in the North and the Khorat Plateau of the North-East notable exceptions – is very humid, with an overall average humidity of 66% to 82%, depending on the season and time of day. The hot part of the dry season reaches its hottest along the north-east plain, and temperatures easily soar to 39°C in the daytime, dropping only a few degrees at night. The temperature can drop to 13°C at night during the cool season in Chiang Mai and even lower in Mae Hong Son – if you're visiting the North during the cooler months, long-sleeved shirts and pullovers would be in order. Because temperatures are more even year-round in the South, when it is 35°C in Bangkok it may be only 32°C in Phuket.

## ECOLOGY & ENVIRONMENT
### Flora

Unique in South-East Asia because its north-south axis extends some 1800 km from mainland to peninsular South-East Asia, Thailand provides potential habitats for an astounding variety of flora and fauna. As in the rest of tropical Asia, most indigenous vegetation in Thailand is associated with two basic types of tropical forest: monsoon forest (with a distinctive dry season of three months or more) and rainforest (where rain falls more than nine months per year).

Monsoon forests amount to about a quarter of all remaining natural forest cover in the country; they are marked by deciduous tree varieties which shed their leaves during the dry season to conserve water. About half of all forest cover consists of rainforests, which are typically evergreen. Central, Northern, Eastern and North-Eastern Thailand mainly contain monsoon forests while

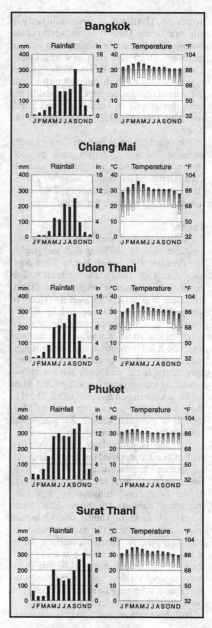

Southern Thailand is predominantly a rainforest zone. There is much overlap of the two – some forest zones support a mix of monsoon forest and rainforest vegetation. The remaining quarter of the country's forest cover consists of freshwater swamp forests in the delta regions, forested crags amidst the karst topography of both North and South and pine forests at higher altitudes in the North.

The country's most famous flora includes an incredible array of fruit trees, bamboo (more species than any country outside China), tropical hardwoods and over 27,000 flowering species, including Thailand's national floral symbol, the orchid.

## Fauna

As with plant life, variation in the animal kingdom closely affiliates with geographic and climatic differences. Hence the indigenous fauna of Thailand's northern half is mostly of Indochinese origin while that of the South is generally Sundaic (ie typical of Malaysia, Sumatra, Borneo and Java). The invisible dividing line between the two zoogeographical zones is across the Isthmus of Kra, about halfway down the Southern peninsula. The large overlap area between zoogeographical and vegetative zones – extending from around Prachuap Khiri Khan on the Southern peninsula to Uthai Thani in the lower north – means that much of Thailand is a potential habitat for plants and animals from both zones.

Thailand is particularly rich in birdlife, with over 1000 recorded resident and migrating species – approximately 10% of all world bird species. Coastal and inland waterways of the Southern peninsula are especially important habitats for South-East Asian waterfowl. Loss of habitat due to human intervention remains the greatest threat to bird survival in Thailand; shrimp farms along the coast are robbing waterfowl of their rich intertidal diets, while the over-harvesting of swiftlet nests in the South for bird's nest soup may threaten the continued survival of the nests' creators.

Indigenous mammals, mostly found in dwindling numbers within Thailand's national parks or wildlife sanctuaries, include tigers, leopards, elephants, Asiatic black bears, Malayan sun bears, gaur (Indian bison), banteng (wild cattle), serow (an Asiatic goat-antelope), sambar deer, barking deer, mouse deer, tapir, pangolin, gibbons, macaques, dolphins and dugongs (sea cows). Forty of Thailand's 300 mammal species, including clouded leopard, Malayan tapir, tiger, Irawaddy dolphin, goral, jungle cat, dusky langur and pileated gibbon, are on the International Union for Conservation of Nature (IUCN) list of endangered species.

Herpetofauna in Thailand numbers around 313 reptiles and 107 amphibians, and includes four sea-turtle species along with numerous snake varieties, of which six are venomous: the common cobra (six subspecies), king cobra (hamadryad), banded krait (three species), Malayan viper, green viper and Russell's pit viper. Although the relatively rare king cobra can reach up to six metres in length, the nation's largest snake is the reticulated python, which can reach a whopping 15m. The country's many lizard species include two commonly seen in homes and older hotels or guesthouses, the túk-kae (a large gecko) and the jing-jòk (a smaller house lizard), as well as larger species like the black jungle monitor.

Insects number some 6000 species, while the country's rich marine environment counts tens of thousands of other species.

## National Parks, Reserves & Wildlife Sanctuaries

Despite Thailand's rich diversity of flora and fauna, it has only been in recent years that most of the 79 national parks (only 50 of which receive an annual budget), 89 'non-hunting areas' and wildlife sanctuaries and 35 forest reserves have been established. Eighteen of the national parks are marine parks that protect coastal, insular and open-sea areas. Together these cover 13% of the country's land and sea area, one of the highest ratios of protected to unprotected areas of any nation in the world (compare

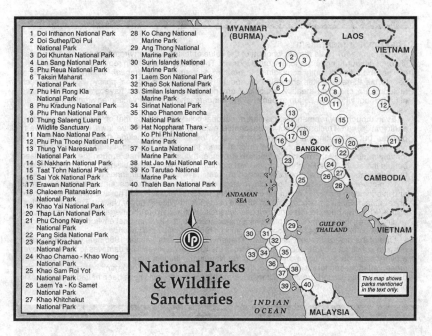

| | |
|---|---|
| 1 Doi Inthanon National Park | 28 Ko Chang National |
| 2 Doi Suthep/Doi Pui | Marine Park |
| National Park | 29 Ang Thong National |
| 3 Doi Khuntan National Park | Marine Park |
| 4 Lan Sang National Park | 30 Surin Islands National |
| 5 Phu Reua National Park | Marine Park |
| 6 Taksin Maharat | 31 Laem Son National Park |
| National Park | 32 Khao Sok National Park |
| 7 Phu Hin Rong Kla | 33 Similan Islands National |
| National Park | Marine Park |
| 8 Phu Kradung National Park | 34 Sirinat National Park |
| 9 Phu Phan National Park | 35 Khao Phanom Bencha |
| 10 Thung Salaeng Luang | National Park |
| Wildlife Sanctuary | 36 Hat Noppharat Thara - |
| 11 Nam Nao National Park | Ko Phi Phi National |
| 12 Phu Pha Thoep National Park | Marine Park |
| 13 Thung Yai Naresuan | 37 Ko Lanta National |
| National Park | Marine Park |
| 14 Si Nakharin National Park | 38 Hat Jao Mai National Park |
| 15 Taat Tohn National Park | 39 Ko Tarutao National |
| 16 Sai Yok National Park | Marine Park |
| 17 Erawan National Park | 40 Thaleh Ban National Park |
| 18 Chaloem Ratanakosin | |
| National Park | |
| 19 Khao Yai National Park | |
| 20 Thap Lan National Park | |
| 21 Phu Chong Nayoi | |
| National Park | |
| 22 Pang Sida National Park | |
| 23 Kaeng Krachan | |
| National Park | |
| 24 Khao Chamao - Khao Wong | |
| National Park | |
| 25 Khao Sam Roi Yot | |
| National Park | |
| 26 Laem Ya - Ko Samet | |
| National Park | |
| 27 Khao Khitchakut | |
| National Park | |

National Parks
& Wildlife
Sanctuaries

this figure with India at 4.2%, Japan 6.5%, France 8.8% and the USA 10.5%).

A system of wildlife sanctuaries was first provided for in the Wild Animals Reservation and Protection Act of 1960, followed by the National Parks Act of 1961 which established the kingdom's national park programme with the setting up of Khao Yai National Park. The majority of the parks, reserves and sanctuaries are well maintained by the Forestry Department, but a few have allowed rampant tourism to threaten the natural environment. Poaching, illegal logging and shifting cultivation have also taken their toll on protected lands, but since 1990 the government has been cracking down with some success.

Most of the national parks are easily accessible, yet only around 5% of the average annual number of visitors is non-Thai. Most parks charge a small fee to visit (typically 3 to 5B for Thais, 15 to 25B for foreigners) and there is usually somewhere to stay for a reasonable fee. For more information on staying in national parks, see Accommodation in the Facts for the Visitor chapter.

Recommended reading for those interested in a more in-depth description of Thailand's protected areas is the well researched *National Parks of Thailand* by Denis Gray, Colin Piprell & Mark Graham.

For a true appreciation of Thailand's geography and natural history, a visit to at least one national park is a must. In Bangkok the reservations office is at the national parks division of the Forestry Department (☎ (2) 579-4842/0529), Phahonyothin Rd, Bangkhen (north Bangkok). Bookings from Bangkok must be paid in advance.

### Environmental Policy
Like all countries with high population densities, Thailand has applied enormous pressure on the ecosystems within its borders. Fifty years ago the countryside was

## Thai Environmentalism

A large number of Thais remain ignorant of the value of taking a pro-environment stance in everyday life or of encouraging ecologically sound tourism. The director of a certain regional Tourism Authority of Thailand office recently complained to me that ecotourism was *lambàak* (inconvenient) for Thai people but there was little she could do about it because 'that's national policy'. Fortunately such attitudes are changing steadily, especially among younger Thais who have grown up in relative affluence but who have begun to perceive the dangers inherent in neglecting environmental conservation.

Even though environmentalism is part of national policy it's obvious that only with strong popular participation can Thailand effect a reasonable enforcement of protective laws which are already plentiful but often ignored. Current examples of 'people power' include the hundreds of forest monasteries that voluntarily protect chunks of forest throughout Thailand. When one such wat was forcibly removed by the military in Buriram Province, thousands of Thais around the country rallied behind the abbot, Phra Prachak, and the wat's protectorship was re-established. On the other side of the coin, wats with less ecologically minded trustees have sold off virgin lands to developers.

Non-governmental organisations play a large role in surveying and designating threatened areas and in educating the public about the environment. In 1983 Wildlife Fund Thailand (WFT) was created under Queen Sirikit's patronage as an affiliate of the World-Wide Fund for Nature. The main function of the WFT has been to raise public consciousness with regard to the illegal trade in endangered wildlife. Citing the country's free press as a major incentive, the international environmental watchdog organisation Greenpeace may soon be opening a regional office in Thailand.

One of the greatest recent victories by Thai environmentalists was the 1986 defeat of government plans to construct a hydroelectric facility across the Khwae Yai River. The dam was to be placed over a river section in the middle of the Thung Yai Naresuan National Park, one of the largest and best preserved monsoon forest areas in South-East Asia. It took four years of organised protest to halt the dam. Since this ground-breaking victory several other power projects have been halted through public protest. ■

around 70% forest; as of 1995 an estimated 25% of the natural forest cover remained. Logging and agriculture are mainly to blame for the decline, and the loss of forest cover has been accompanied by dwindling wildlife resources. Species notably extinct in Thailand include the kouprey (a type of wild cattle), Schomburgk's deer and the Javan rhino, but innumerable smaller species have also fallen by the wayside.

In response to environmental degradation, the Thai government has created a large number of protected parks, reserves and sanctuaries since the 1970s, and has enacted legislation to protect specific plant and animal species. The government hopes to raise total forest cover to 40% by the middle of next century. Thailand has also become a signatory to the UN Convention on International Trade in Endangered Species (CITES).

In 1989, logging was banned in Thailand following a 1988 disaster in which hundreds of tonnes of cut timber washed down deforested slopes in Surat Thani Province, killing more than 100 people and burying a number of villages. It is now illegal to sell timber felled in the country, and all imported timber is theoretically accounted for before going on the market. The illegal timber trade has further diminished with Cambodia's recent ban on all timber exports, along with the termination of all Thai contracts by the Burmese. Laos is now the number one source for imported timber in Thailand, both legal and illegal.

These days builders even need government permission to use timber salvaged from old houses. This has helped curb illegal logging operations in the interior (unfortunately Thai timber brokers are now turning their attention to Laos and Myanmar, neither of which are CITES signatories), but corruption remains a problem.

Corruption also impedes government attempts to shelter 'exotic' species from the illic global wildlife trade and to preserve Thailand's sensitive coastal areas. The Forestry Department is currently under pressure to take immediate action in those areas where preservation laws have gone unenforced, including coastal zones where illegal tourist accommodation has flourished. There has also been a crackdown on restaurants serving 'jungle food' (aahāan pàa), which consists of exotic and often endangered wildlife species like barking deer, bear, pangolin, civet and gaur.

The tiger is one of the most endangered of Thailand's large mammals. Although tiger hunting or trapping is illegal, poachers continue to kill the cats for the lucrative overseas Chinese pharmaceutical market; among the Chinese, the ingestion of tiger penis and bone are thought to have curative effects. Taipei, where at least two-thirds of the pharmacies deal in tiger parts (in spite of the fact that such trade is forbidden by Taiwanese law), is the world centre for Thai tiger consumption. Around 200 to 300 wild tigers are thought to be hanging on in the national parks of Khao Yai, Kaeng Krachan, Thap Lan, Mae Wong and Khao Sok.

Forestry Department efforts are limited by lack of personnel and funds. The average ranger is paid only 75B a day – some aren't paid at all but receive only food and lodging – to take on armed poachers backed by the rich and powerful godfathers who control illicit timber and wildlife businesses.

Marine resources are also threatened by a lack of long-range conservation goals. The upper portion of the Gulf of Thailand, between Rayong and Prachuap Khiri Khan, was once one of the most fertile marine areas in the world. Now it is virtually dead due to overfishing and the release of mainland pollutants.

Experts say it's not too late to rehabilitate the upper Gulf by reducing pollution and the number of trawlers, and by restricting commercial fishing to certain zones. An effective ban on the harvest of plaa tuu (mackerel) in the spawning stages has brought this fish back from the brink of total depletion. The Bangkok Metropolitan Administration (BMA) is currently developing a system of sewage treatment plants in the Chao Phraya Delta area with the intention of halting all large-scale dumping of sewage into Gulf waters, but similar action needs to be taken along the entire eastern seaboard, which is rapidly becoming Thailand's new industrial centre.

Overdevelopment on Ko Phuket and Ko Phi Phi is starving the surrounding coral reefs by blocking nutrient-rich run-off from the island's interior, as well as smothering the reefs with pollutants. Ko Samui and Ko Samet face a similar fate if action isn't taken soon to control growth and improve waste-disposal standards.

One encouraging move by the government has been the passing of the 1992 Environmental Act, which provides for environmental quality standards and the establishment of national authority to designate conservation and pollution control areas. Pattaya and Phuket immediately became the first locales to be decreed pollution control areas, thus making them eligible for government cleanup funds. With such assistance, officials in Pattaya now claim they'll be able to restore Pattaya Bay – exposed to improper waste disposal for at least the last 20 years – to its original purity by the end of this decade.

### Tourism & the Environment

In some instances tourism has had positive effects on environmental conservation in Thailand. Conscious that the country's natural beauty is a major tourist attraction for both residents and foreigners, and that tourism is one of Thailand's major revenue earners, the government has stepped up efforts to protect wilderness areas and to add more acreage to the park system. In Khao Yai National Park, for example, all hotel and golf-course facilities were removed in order to reduce human influences on the park environment. As a result of government and private sector pressure on the fishing industry, coral dynamiting has been all but eliminated in the Similan and Surin islands, to preserve the area for tourist visitation.

As described in *National Parks of Thailand*:

A growing number of conservationists, development experts and government officials believe that boundary markers and even guns do little to halt encroachment. The surrounding communities must somehow be allowed to share in whatever economic benefits a park can offer. Some sanctuaries, like Huay Kha Khaeng, recruit employees from local villages. In [Thaleh Noi Wildlife Preserve], local fishermen are hired to take visitors around the lake in their boats to view the rich bird life. Rangers at Laem Son National Park encourage local fishermen to take visitors to outlying islands rather than over-fish the sea. Phu Kradung National Park takes on several hundred locals as porters to carry hikers' gear up the mountain. Some have become so protective of their park that they report violations of regulations to the rangers.

However, tourism has also made negative contributions. Eager to make fistfuls of cash, hotel developers and tour operators have rushed to provide ecologically inappropriate services for visitors in sensitive areas. Concerns about this issue are causing the government to look more closely at Ko Phi Phi and Ko Samet – two national park islands notorious for overdevelopment. Part of the problem is that it's not always clear which lands are protected and which are privately owned.

Common problems in marine areas include the anchoring of tour boats on coral reefs and the dumping of rubbish into the sea. Coral and seashells are also illegally collected and sold in tourist shops. 'Jungle food' restaurants, with endangered species on the menu, flourish near inland national parks. Perhaps the most visible abuses occur in areas without basic garbage and sewage services, where there are piles of rotting garbage, mountains of plastic and open sewage run-off.

One of the saddest sights in Thailand is the piles of discarded plastic water bottles on popular beaches. Worse yet are those seen floating in the sea or in rivers, where they are sometimes ingested by marine or riparian wildlife with fatal results. Many of these bottles started out on a beach only to be washed into the sea during the monsoon season.

What can the average visitor to Thailand do to minimise the impact of tourism on the environment? Firstly, they can avoid all restaurants serving 'exotic' wildlife species; visitors should also consider taking down the names of such restaurants and filing a letter of complaint with the Tourism Authority of Thailand (TAT), the Wildlife Fund Thailand (WFT) and the Forestry Department (addresses below). The main patrons of this type of cuisine are the Thais themselves, along with visiting Chinese from Hong Kong and Taiwan. Municipal markets selling endangered species, such as Bangkok's Chatuchak Market, should also be duly noted – consider enclosing photographs to support your complaints. For a list of endangered species in Thailand, contact the WFT.

When using hired boats in the vicinity of coral reefs, insist that boat operators not lower anchors onto coral formations. This is becoming less of a problem with established boating outfits, some of whom mark off sensitive areas with blue-flagged buoys, but is common among small-time pilots. Likewise, volunteer to collect (and later dispose of) rubbish if it's obvious that the usual mode is to throw everything overboard.

Obviously, you should refrain from purchasing coral or items made from coral while in Thailand. Thai law forbids the collection of coral or seashells anywhere in the country – report any observed violations in tourist or marine park areas to the TAT and Forestry Department, or in other places to the WFT.

One of the difficulties in dealing with rubbish and sewage problems in tourist areas is that many Thais don't understand why tourists should expect different methods of disposal than are used elsewhere in the country. In urban areas or populated rural areas throughout Thailand, piles of rotting rubbish and open sewage lines are frequently the norm – after all, Thailand is still a 'developing' country. Thais sensitive to western paternalism are quick to point out that on a global scale the so-called 'developed' countries contribute far more environmental damage than does Thailand (eg per capita greenhouse emissions for Australia, Canada or the USA average over five tonnes each while ASEAN countries contribute less than 0.5 tonnes per capita).

Hence, in making complaints or suggestions to Thais employed in the tourist industry, it's important to emphasise that you want to work *with* them rather than against them in improving environmental standards.

Whether on land or at sea, refrain from purchasing or accepting drinking water offered in plastic bottles wherever possible. When there's a choice, request glass water bottles, which are recyclable in Thailand. The 4B deposit is refundable when you return the bottle to any vendor who sells drinking water in glass bottles. For those occasions where only plastic-bottled water is available, you might consider transferring the contents to your own reusable water container, if the vendor/source of the plastic bottle is a more suitable disposal point than your destination. If not, take the bottle with you and dispose of it at a dumpster or other legitimate collection site.

A few guesthouses now offer drinking water from large, reusable plastic water containers as an alternative to the disposable individual containers. This service is available in most areas of Thailand (even relatively remote areas like Ko Chang). Encourage hotel and guesthouse staff to switch from disposable plastic to either glass or reusable plastic.

In outdoor areas where rubbish has accumulated, consider organising an impromptu cleanup crew to collect plastic, styrofoam and other nonbiodegradables for delivery to a regular rubbish pickup point. If there isn't a pickup somewhere nearby, enquire about the location of the nearest collection point and deliver the refuse yourself.

By expressing your desire to use environmentally friendly materials – and by taking direct action to avoid the use and indiscriminate disposal of plastic – you can provide an example of environmental consciousness not only for the Thais but for other international visitors. A recent letter from a reader said:

[Your] guide suggested that travellers fill their own bottles from guesthouses. This is an excellent and highly practical idea; you simply carry your own water bottle and refill it where convenient. I used only about two bottles in a month doing this, and guesthouses as well as restaurants were always happy to refill for at most 2 or 3B, if not free. It educates them and saves waste – I think this idea should be given more prominence.

Write to the following organisations to offer your support for stricter environmental policies or to air specific complaints or suggestions:

Asian Society for Environmental Protection – c/o CDG-SEAPO, Asian Institute of Technology, GPO 2754, Bangkok 10501

Bird Conservation Society of Thailand – PO Box 13, Ratchathewi Post Office, Bangkok 10401

Community Ecological Development Programme – PO Box 140, Chiang Rai 57000

Friends of Nature – 670/437 Charansavatwong Rd, Bangkok 10700

Magic Eyes – Bangkok Bank Building, 15th floor, 333 Silom Rd, Bangkok 10400

Office of the National Environment Board – 60/1 Soi Prachasumphan 4, Rama IV Rd, Bangkok 10400

Project for Ecological Recovery – 77/3 Soi Nomjit, Naret Rd, Bangkok 10500

Raindrop Association – 105-107 Ban Pho Rd, Thapthiang, Trang 92000

Royal Forestry Department – 61 Phahonyothin Rd, Bangkhen, Bangkok 10900

Siam Environmental Club – Chulalongkorn University, Phayathai Rd, Bangkok 10330

The Siam Society – 131 Soi Asoke, Sukhumvit Rd, Bangkok 10110

Thailand Information Centre of Environmental Foundation – 58/1 Sakol Land, Chaeng Wattana Rd, Pak Kret, Nonthaburi

Tourism Authority of Thailand – 372 Bamrung Meuang Rd, Bangkok 10100

Wildlife Fund Thailand – 251/88-90 Phahonyothin Rd, Bangkhen, Bangkok 10220
255 Soi Asoke, Sukhumvit 21, Bangkok 10110

## GOVERNMENT & POLITICS
### The 1991 Constitution
Since 1932, the government of the Kingdom of Thailand has nominally been a constitutional

monarchy inspired by the bicameral British model but with myriad subtle differences. Thailand's 15th constitution, enacted on 9 December 1991 by the coup regime's now-defunct National Peace-Keeping Council (NPKC), replaced that promulgated in December 1978 and allows for limited public participation in the choosing of government officials. National polls elect the 360 member lower house (House of Representatives) and prime minister, but the 260 senators of the upper house (Senate) are appointed by the prime minister. In Thailand the Senate is not as powerful as the House of Representatives; the latter writes and approves legislation, while the Senate votes on constitutional changes.

Constitutional amendments proposed in February 1995 lower the voting age from 20 to 18, reduce the number of non-elected Senate seats, require senators to declare their assets upon taking office and establish an election commission to oversee public polls.

## Elected & Non-Elected Administrative Officials

Candidates for prime minister need not come from the national assembly, and there is no limit on the number of non-elected cabinet members in the prime minister's council of ministers, which numbers 13 in all. The upper and lower houses vote jointly on no-confidence motions, which means that a majority Senate would need only 46 MPs to oust the government and elect a new prime minister. The NPKC claimed that such a system was necessary to guard against the potential for vote-buying, especially in rural areas. However, neither they nor anyone else ever offered conclusive evidence to show that vote-buying was pervasive in previously elected administrations. Meanwhile the premier's position has become a revolving door with no elected prime minister lasting longer than two and a half years.

A portion of the government's annual budget is provided by over 60 state-owned enterprises – including major manufacturing and transport industries – administered by the prime minister's office and various government ministries.

## Administrative Divisions

For administrative purposes, Thailand is divided into 76 *jangwàat* or provinces. Each province is subdivided into *amphoe* or districts, which are further subdivided into *kìng-amphoe* (subdistricts), *tambon* (communes or village groups), *mùu-bâan* (villages), *sukhãaphibaan* (sanitation districts) and *thêtsàbaan* (municipalities). Urban areas with more than 50,000 inhabitants and a population density of over 3000 per sq km are designated *nákhon*; those with populations of 10,000 to 50,000 with not less than 3000 per sq km are *meuang* (usually spelt 'muang' on roman-script highway signs). The term 'meuang' is also used loosely to mean metropolitan area (as opposed to an area within strict municipal limits).

A provincial capital is an *amphoe meuang*. An amphoe meuang takes the same name as the province of which it is capital, eg amphoe meuang Chiang Mai (often abbreviated as 'meuang Chiang Mai') means the city of Chiang Mai, capital of Chiang Mai Province.

Except for Krungthep Mahanakhon (Metropolitan Bangkok), provincial governors *(phûu wâa râatchakaan)* are appointed to their four year terms by the Ministry of the Interior – a system that leaves much potential for corruption. Bangkok's governor and provincial assembly were elected for the first time in November 1985, when Chamlong Srimuang, a strict Buddhist and a former major general, won by a landslide. The mid-1996 elections saw independent Dr Pichit Ruttakul take over from Chamlong as Bangkok governor.

District officers *(nai amphoe)* are also appointed by the Ministry of the Interior but are responsible to their provincial governors. The cities are headed by elected mayors *(naiyók thêtsàmontrii)*, tambons by elected commune heads *(kamnan)* and villages by elected village chiefs *(phûu yài bâan)*.

## Armed Forces & Police

Thailand's armed services include the Royal Thai Army (280,000 troops), Royal Thai Air Force (44,000) and Royal Thai Navy (40,000) under the Ministry of Defence, as well as the National Police Department (120,000) under the Ministry of the Interior. The latter department is divided into provincial police, metropolitan police, border patrol police and the central investigation bureau. The central bureau includes railway, marine, highway and forestry police along with special branches concerned with transprovincial crime and national security issues. Police corruption is common; recruits earn just US$150 a month on salary, so many take 'tea money' whenever they can.

Ever since the 1932 revolution, and particularly following WWII, the Thai military has had a substantial influence on the nation's political affairs. Since the constitutional monarchy was established in 1932, generals have commanded the premiership for 46 out of 64 years. Anand Panyarachun, interim premier for two short terms in 1991 and 1992, was able to diminish the military's power considerably when he revoked a 14 year old ministerial order which gave the supreme commander powers as 'internal peace-keeping director'. At the same time he disbanded the Capital Security Command, an organ that was instrumental in the May 1992 bloodbath. This has effectively dissolved all legal and physical structures introduced after the infamous October 1976 coup, including the special command and task forces which had allowed the use of military forces for internal peace-keeping since that time.

Such task forces have not been the military's only source of political ascendancy. High-ranking officers have traditionally held key positions in the telecommunications, shipping and public transport industries as well, thus forming a powerful partnership with big business interests. Another of Anand's accomplishments was the ousting of military brass from executive posts at the Telephone Organization of Thailand and Thai Airways International.

Following the events of 1991-92, even the generals were admitting that the role of the military had to be reduced. In 1992 General Vimol Wongwanich of the State Railway of Thailand voluntarily resigned his board chairmanship to assume his new position as commander-in-chief – a move that would have been unheard-of 20 years ago. Vimol claims he will depoliticise the army and has declared the coup d'état 'obsolete'. One of his first acts was to reshuffle key postings in the Thai armed forces in order to break up the anti-democratic Class 5 clique. Current political conditions suggest that military coups are less likely to occur than before – if so, this shift represents a watershed in 20th century Thai politics.

## The Monarchy

His Majesty Bhumibol Adulyadej (pronounced 'Phumíphon Adunyádèt') is the ninth king of the Chakri dynasty (founded in 1782) and as of 1988 the longest reigning king in Thai history. Born in the USA in 1927 and schooled in Bangkok and Switzerland, King Bhumibol was a nephew of Rama VII (King Prajadhipok, 1925-35) as well as the younger brother of Rama VIII (King Ananda Mahidol). His full name – including royal title – is Phrabaatsomdet Boramintaramahaphumiphonadunyadet.

His Majesty ascended the throne in 1946 following the death of Rama VIII, who had reigned as king for only one year (Ananda served as regent for 10 years after his uncle's abdication in 1935 – see History earlier).

A jazz composer and saxophonist, King Bhumibol wrote the royal anthem, *Falling Rain*, which accompanies photos of the royal family shown before every film at cinemas throughout the country. His royal motorcade is occasionally seen passing along Ratchadamnoen (Royal Promenade) Rd in Bangkok's Banglamphu district; the king is usually seated in a yellow vintage Rolls Royce or a 1950s Cadillac.

The king has his own privy council comprised of up to 14 royal appointees who assist with the king's formal duties; the president

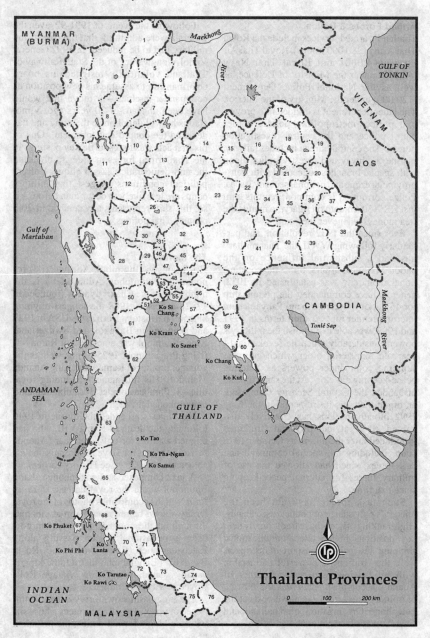

Thailand Provinces

| 1 | Chiang Rai | 27 | Uthai Thani | 53 | Nonthaburi |
|---|---|---|---|---|---|
| 2 | Mae Hong Son | 28 | Kanchanaburi | 54 | Bangkok |
| 3 | Chiang Mai | 29 | Suphanburi | 55 | Samut Prakan |
| 4 | Lampang | 30 | Chai Nat | 56 | Chachoengsao |
| 5 | Phayao | 31 | Singburi | 57 | Chonburi |
| 6 | Nan | 32 | Lopburi | 58 | Rayong |
| 7 | Phrae | 33 | Nakhon Ratchasima | 59 | Chanthaburi |
| 8 | Lamphun | 34 | Mahasarakham | 60 | Trat |
| 9 | Utaradit | 35 | Roi Et | 61 | Phetburi |
| 10 | Sukhothai | 36 | Yasothon | 62 | Prachuap Khiri |
| 11 | Tak | 37 | Amnat Charoen | | Khan |
| 12 | Kamphaeng Phet | 38 | Ubon Ratchathani | 63 | Chumphon |
| 13 | Phitsanulok | 39 | Si Saket | 64 | Ranong |
| 14 | Loei | 40 | Surin | 65 | Surat Thani |
| 15 | Nong Bualamphu | 41 | Buriram | 66 | Phang-Nga |
| 16 | Udon Thani | 42 | Sa Kaew | 67 | Phuket |
| 17 | Nong Khai | 43 | Prachinburi | 68 | Krabi |
| 18 | Sakon Nakhon | 44 | Nakhon Nayok | 69 | Nakhon Si |
| 19 | Nakhon Phanom | 45 | Saraburi | | Thammarat |
| 20 | Mukdahan | 46 | Ang Thong | 70 | Trang |
| 21 | Kalasin | 47 | Ayuthaya | 71 | Phattalung |
| 22 | Khon Kaen | 48 | Pathum Thani | 72 | Satun |
| 23 | Chaiyaphum | 49 | Nakhon Pathom | 73 | Songkhla |
| 24 | Phetchabun | 50 | Ratchaburi | 74 | Pattani |
| 25 | Phichit | 51 | Samut Songkhram | 75 | Yala |
| 26 | Nakhon Sawan | 52 | Samut Sakhon | 76 | Narathiwat |

of the privy council serves as interim regent until an heir is throned.

The king and his wife, Queen Sirikit, have four children: Princess Ubol Ratana (born 1951), Crown Prince Maha Vajiralongkorn (1952), Princess Mahachakri Sirindhorn (1955) and Princess Chulabhorn (1957). A royal decree issued by King Trailok (1448-88) to standardise succession in a polygamous dynasty makes the king's senior son or full brother his *uparaja* (Thai: *ùpàrâat)* or heir apparent. Thus Prince Maha Vajiralongkorn was officially designated as crown prince and heir when he reached 20 years of age in 1972; if he were to decline the crown or be unable to ascend the throne due to incurable illness or death, the senior princess (Ubol Ratana) would be next in line.

Princess Ubol Ratana married American Peter Jensen in 1972 against palace wishes, thus forfeiting her royal rank, but was reinstated a few years ago. The crown prince has married twice, most recently to an ex-actress. His son Prince Juthavachara is the eldest male of the next Chakri generation.

Though Thailand's political system is officially classified as a constitutional monarchy, the Thai constitution stipulates that the king be 'enthroned in a position of revered worship' and not be exposed 'to any sort of accusation or action'. With or without legal writ, the vast majority of Thai citizens regard King Bhumibol as a sort of demigod, partly in deference to tradition but also because of his impressive public works record.

Neither the constitution nor the monarchy's high status prevent Thai people from gossiping about the royal family in private, however. Gathered together, the various whisperings and speculations with regard to royal intrigue would make a fine medieval fable. Many Thais, for example, favour Princess Sirindhorn for succession to the Thai throne, though none would say this publicly, nor would this popular sentiment appear in the Thai media. Among the nation's soothsayers, it has long been prophesied that the Chakri dynasty will end with Rama IX; current political conditions, however, suggest the contrary.

It is often repeated that the Thai king has

no political power (by law his position is strictly titular and ceremonial) but in times of national political crisis, Thais have often looked to the king for leadership. Two attempted coups d'état in the 1980s may have failed because they received tacit royal disapproval. By implication, the successful military coup of February 1991 must have had palace approval, whether *post facto* or *a priori*.

The NPKC's 1991 draft constitution was widely condemned until just a few days before its final reading in the national assembly, when the king spoke out during his annual birthday address in favour of leaving the draft unchanged. Out of respect, the assembly passed the constitution in spite of a few anti-democratic clauses contained therein, even though it would have taken only a few extra days to revise the draft. This foot-dragging on the part of the government indirectly led to the violence six months later. The unamended constitution continues to be a major source of friction between Thailand's political parties, although in 1995 the national assembly finally began introducing amendments to reflect the popular sentiment so passionately expressed in 1992.

Along with nation and religion, the monarchy is very highly regarded in Thai society – negative comment about the king or any member of the royal family is a social as well as legal taboo. See the Society & Conduct section later in this chapter.

## ECONOMY

During the 1980s, Thailand maintained a steady GNP growth rate which by 1988 had reached 13% per annum. Thailand in the 1990s finds itself on the threshold of attaining the exclusive rank of NIC or 'newly industrialised country'. Soon, economic experts say, Thailand will be joining Asia's 'little dragons', also known as the Four Tigers – South Korea, Taiwan, Hong Kong and Singapore – in becoming a leader in the Pacific Rim economic boom.

Sixty percent of Thailand's exports are agricultural; the country ranks first in the world for rice (followed by the USA and

Vietnam), second in tapioca (after Brazil) and fifth in coconut (following Indonesia, the Philippines, India and Sri Lanka). Since 1991 Thailand has been the world's largest producer of natural rubber, although it still ranks behind Malaysia in total rubber exports. Other important agricultural exports include sugar, maize, pineapple, cotton, jute, green bean, soybean and palm oil. Processed food and beverages – especially canned shrimp, tuna and pineapple – also account for significant export earnings. Thailand's top export markets are the USA, Japan and Singapore.

About 60% of the Thai labour force is engaged in agriculture, 10% each in commerce and services and 20% in manufacturing. Manufactured goods have become an increasingly important source of foreign exchange revenue and now account for at least 30% of Thailand's exports. Textiles, cement and electronics lead the way, with car and truck manufacture coming up fast. Thailand now boasts the second largest pickup truck market in the world after the USA; several international truck manufacturers have established factories in the country – mostly along the eastern seaboard – including Ford, Mazda, Mitsubishi, GM, Toyota and Honda. The country also has substantial natural resources, including tin, petroleum and natural gas.

Since 1987, tourism has become a leading earner of foreign exchange, occasionally outdistancing even Thailand's largest single export, textiles, with receipts as high as US$5.7 billion per annum. The government's economic strategy remains focused, however, on export-led growth through the continued development of textiles and other light industries such as electronics, backed by rich reserves of natural resources and a large, inexpensive labour force. Observers predict that such a broad-based economy will make Thailand a major economic competitor in Asia in the long-term.

Raw average per capita income by 1996 was US$2680 per year; if measured using the purchasing power parity method (which takes into account price differences between countries), the Thais average US$6870 per capita annually. With an average net escalation of 11.2% per annum since 1985, Thailand has ranked highest in Asia in terms of real GDP growth per employee over the last decade. Regional inequities, however, mean that local averages range from US$400 in the North-East to US$3000 in Bangkok.

The minimum wage in Bangkok and surrounding provinces is 145B (US$5.80) per day; it can be as low as 95B a day in the outer provinces. Although it doesn't reach the world's top 50 list in terms of raw per capita GNP, on a worldwide scale Thailand's economy ranks approximately 20th if measured by the GDP purchasing power parity method. An estimated 20% of Thai citizens – most of them in Bangkok or Phuket – control 63% of the wealth.

The incidence of poverty in Thailand (defined by the World Bank in concert with the Ministry of Public Health as falling below the level of income a person needs to buy a basket of food that will satisfy their daily nutritional requirements, along with necessary non-food items) has steadily declined, from 30% in 1976 to 6.4% in 1995-96. Conversely the average income has increased to nearly 19 times what it was in 1962-63. Thais rank seventh worldwide, just ahead of the Japanese, for gross savings of GDP income at 37%.

The current inflation rate is a relatively low 7% per annum; travellers should keep this in mind when referring to prices in this edition. As in most other countries, prices continue to rise. Unemployment hovers at around 1.4%, tied with Taiwan for the lowest in Asia; 56.5% of the population – the highest percentage in Asia – participate in the general labour force.

## Regional Economies

Thailand's North-East has the lowest inflation rate and cost of living. This region is poorer than the rest of the country and doesn't get as much tourism; it therefore offers excellent value for the traveller and is in need of your travel dollar. Hand-woven textiles and farming remain the primary means of livelihood in this area, although Nakhon Ratchasima (Khorat) is an emerging centre for metals and the automotive industry.

In the South, fishing, tin mining and rubber production keep the local economy fairly stable, with tourism a seasonal runner-up.

Central Thailand grows fruit (especially pineapples), sugar cane and rice for export, and supports most of Thailand's ever-expanding industry (textiles, food processing and cement).

Northern Thailand produces mountain or dry rice (as opposed to water rice, the bulk of the crop produced in Thailand) for domestic use, maize, tea, various fruits and flowers, and is very dependent on tourism. Teak and other lumber were once major products of the North, but since 1989 all logging has been banned in Thailand in order to prevent further deforestation.

## Infrastructure & Growth

The 1990-92 recession was a blessing in disguise inasmuch as it allowed Thailand's overheated economy to cool down. Widespread flooding in November 1995 damaged agricultural output for that year, with negative carry-over well into the next. As of 1996 the growth rate had slowed to 8% and was not expected to increase over the following two years or so. Even at this rate, Thailand will remain one of the world's fastest growing economies.

Some say that Thailand has been growing faster than its infrastructure can handle. Although adequate for most domestic trade, the transport and telecommunications systems are in dire need of upgrading for purposes of international trade. Incoming ships have to wait as long as a week before they can get a berth at Bangkok's busy Khlong Toey Port. Access to Khlong Toey is limited to ships of less than 10,000 tonnes or 8.5m draft; larger vessels must off-load at the mouth of the Chao Phraya River or offshore near the country's second largest ports at Si Racha and Sattahip. Thirty smaller ports along the Gulf of Thailand and Andaman Sea

## Thailand's Relationship with Myanmar

Thailand shares its longest international border with Myanmar, all the way from Sop Ruak in the extreme north to Ranong in the middle of the Malay peninsula. Historically the two countries have warred long and frequently. Northern Thailand was conquered by invading Burman and Shan armies in the 11th and 16th centuries, and many Thai citizens will never forgive their largest neighbour for destroying their most magnificent royal capital, Ayuthaya, in 1757.

During WWII, Thailand suffered again when invading Japanese forces used Kanchanaburi as a base for building a railway link with eastern Myanmar (from 1886 to 1989 the English name for the country was 'Burma'), with the support of the Burmese underground.

In the latter part of this century, following Myanmar's independence from Great Britain, ties between the neighbouring countries have grown stronger but have never risen beyond cordial diplomacy. Official trade between the two is not very significant when compared with trade between Thailand and other South-East Asian neighbours, eg Malaysia, Laos, Indonesia or Singapore. Unofficially, black-market border trade has thrived for centuries.

Thailand and Myanmar have endured several border disputes since the British abandoned the Raj in the 1940s. The latest involves 32 sq km of territory in Mae Ai district, south-west of Mae Sai in Chiang Rai Province, an area vacated by Shan insurgent armies when it was seized by Yangon (Rangoon) troops. Another dispute involves the banks of the Moei River in Tak Province near Mae Sot, where the two governments had originally agreed to build a bridge; Yangon backed down on the bridge deal after construction began and now both sides claim the other is stealing land reclaimed from the riverbed.

The latest issue to demand diplomatic attention from Thailand has been the stand-off between Myanmar's totalitarian military regime and its main domestic opposition, the National League for Democracy (NLD), which won a democratic election in 1990 but so far hasn't been permitted to assume power. As a member of the Association of South-East Asian Nations (ASEAN), Thailand has supported the group's official stance toward Yangon – a policy of 'constructive engagement'.

The professed objective of this policy is to maintain normal diplomatic and business ties in order to foster stability and economic development in Myanmar. Whether this policy has borne fruit is debatable; cynics say it's just business as usual. South-East Asian diplomats argue that it has had limited success, while activists are clamouring for a policy of disengagement, believing that an internationally isolated Yangon would be forced to hand over power to the elected opposition. The Thai response to this is that 37 years of self-imposed isolation in Myanmar (from the time the Burmese military seized control of the economy in 1962 till it began loosening its grip in 1989) didn't bring democracy and neither will externally motivated isolation.

Nevertheless, of all the South-East Asian governments, Thailand has done the most to reach out to the NLD. In July 1995, when charismatic NLD spokesperson Aung San Suu Kyi was released from nearly six years of house arrest, the Thai ambassador to Myanmar, Poksak Hilubol, was the first South-East Asian representative to visit her. And in May 1996, when the NLD convened its first congress since the ill-fated 1990 election, a Yangon-based Thai diplomat was the only South-East Asian government representative to attend its opening.

The Yangon government has responded by crossing Thailand off its recent list of diplomatic stopovers for General Than Shwe, the leader of Myanmar's State Law & Order Restoration Council (SLORC), whose recent diplomatic travels have favoured China, Singapore, Indonesia, Laos and Vietnam. ■

serve fishing fleets and smaller import-export operations.

Engineers are working hard to meet the shipping demands – a new deep-water port in the Gulf has opened at Laem Chabang, near Si Racha, and is linked to an export-processing zone. Another industrial park and port is under development at Maptaphut, farther east along the Gulf, for the petrochemical and fertiliser industries. Plans are underway to enlarge ports along the west

coast – at Krabi and/or Satun – and to build a transpeninsular freeway to create a 'Southern Land Bridge' connecting the Andaman Sea with the Gulf of Thailand.

One of the biggest dilemmas facing the economic planners is whether to acquire a larger foreign debt in order to finance the development of an infrastructure which is capable of handling continued high growth, or whether to allow growth to slow while the infrastructure catches up. Continued rapid growth will probably result in a disproportionate development of the more industrialised Central and Southern regions, leaving the agricultural North and North-East behind.

Advocates of a slow-growth approach hope for better distribution of wealth around the country through a combination of agribusiness projects and welfare programmes that would bring a higher standard of living to poor rural areas. This makes good sense when one considers the relative differences between Thailand and the Four Tigers (in the proportion of rural to urban dwellers and the high fertility of the land).

### Indochina, ASEAN & Pacific Trade

Aside from its own export-oriented growth, Thailand stands to profit from increased international trade in Laos, Cambodia and Vietnam. At the moment Bangkok is the main launching base for foreign investments in Indochina, and the Thai baht is second only to the US dollar as the currency of choice for regional commerce. In Laos and Cambodia the only foreign banks are Thai; Vientiane and Phnom Penh have even started building up portions of their national reserves in baht, thus forming a 'baht bloc'. Thailand continues to profit from the overland transshipment of international goods to Vietnam via Laos, even with the 1994 lifting of the US-Vietnam trade embargo.

In 1994 the ASEAN countries (Thailand, Malaysia, Singapore, Brunei, the Philippines, Indonesia and Vietnam) established the ASEAN Free Trade Area (AFTA), which will gradually reduce import tariffs and nontariff barriers among ASEAN nations until total free trade is reached by 2008. This agreement should prove very advantageous for Thailand's economy since Thailand has a highly educated, inexpensive labour pool and a large manufacturing sector.

Thailand is also a member of the Asia-Pacific Economic Cooperation (APEC) bloc, which comprises the ASEAN countries plus the USA, Canada, Japan, Australia, New Zealand, South Korea, Hong Kong, Taiwan, China, Papua New Guinea, Mexico and Chile. APEC meets periodically to discuss trade issues of mutual interest, occasionally agreeing to lower or eliminate trade barriers on specific products.

The kingdom's latest efforts for regional economic influence include plans for a 'southern growth triangle' that would link trade growth in Thailand's five southernmost provinces with Malaysia and Indonesia, and the 'northern growth quadrangle' joining Northern Thailand, China's Yunnan Province, northern Laos and north-eastern Myanmar. For the latter plan, the Thai government is offering significant financial assistance for road development between the four countries, beginning with north-south highways connecting Yunnan and Northern Thailand via both Myanmar and Laos.

### Tourism

According to statistics put together by the Tourism Authority of Thailand (TAT), the country is currently averaging about seven million tourist arrivals per year, a 64 fold increase since 1960 when the government first began keeping statistics. Historically the country's largest increase in tourism occurred in 1963, a year that saw a 49% increase in visitation over the previous year, possibly encouraged by the arrival of foreign troops in Vietnam. Ten years later there was another sizeable increase (+28% in 1972 and +26% in 1973) as the 'overland trail' from Amsterdam to Australia hit its peak. The country's most recent boom occurred during 1986-90, when arrivals grew by 10% to 23% per annum.

In 1995 – the most recent year for which full statistics are available – 60% of all visitors (4.2 million total) came from East and South-East Asia, with Malaysians leading the way at 1.1 million, followed by Japanese (840,000), Taiwanese (475,000), Koreans (446,000) and Singaporeans (390,000). Europeans as a whole made up approximately 1.5 million of the total, with Germans at the top (350,200), followed by Britons (268,000), French (219,000) and Italians (130,000). US visitors accounted for 292,000 of the total, and Australians 198,000.

Other major markets include Hong Kong (310,000), China (257,000), India (108,000) and Switzerland (98,000). Thailand's fastest-growing tourist segments in 1995 were China (up 47%), United Arab Emirates (up 40%), South Korea (up 35.8%) and Argentina (up 32%).

The biggest growth in tourism since 1990 has been among the Thais themselves. Spurred by steady economic growth, an estimated 40 million Thais per year are now taking domestic leisure trips. Ten years ago western tourists often outnumbered Thais at some of the nation's most famous tourist attractions. Now the opposite is true; except at major international beach destinations like Phuket and Ko Samui, Thai tourists tend to outnumber foreign tourists in most places at a rate of more than five to one.

Tourist revenues amount to some US$5.7 billion a year. A recent study carried out by the Thailand Development Research Institute confirms that 'although the daily expenditure of typical guesthouse tourists may not be as high as that of hotel dwellers, they do, in fact, normally spend more because they usually stay in the country much longer. Income generated by these tourists is thought to penetrate more deeply and widely to the poorer segments of the industry'.

## POPULATION & PEOPLE

The population of Thailand is about 61 million and currently growing at a rate of 1.5% per annum (as opposed to 2.5% in 1979), thanks to Mechai Viravaidya's nationwide family-planning campaign (see the boxed aside on Aids in the following chapter).

Over a third of all Thais live in urban areas. Bangkok is by far the largest city in the kingdom, with a population of over six million (more than 10% of the total population) – too many for the scope of its public services and what little 'city planning' exists. Ranking the nation's other cities by population depends on whether you look at thetsabaan (municipal district) limits or at meuang (metropolitan district) limits. By the former measure, the four most populated cities in descending order (not counting the densely populated 'suburb' provinces of Samut Prakan and Nonthaburi, which would rank second and third if considered separately from Bangkok) are Nakhon Ratchasima (Khorat), Chiang Mai, Hat Yai and Khon Kaen. Using the rather misleading meuang measure, the ranking runs Udon Thani, Lop-buri, Nakhon Ratchasima (Khorat) and Khon Kaen. Most of the other towns in Thailand have populations of well below 100,000.

The average life expectancy in Thailand is 69, the highest in mainland South-East Asia. Yet only an estimated 59% of all Thais have access to local health services; in this the nation ranks 75th worldwide, behind even countries with lower national incomes such as Sudan and Guatemala. There is only one doctor per 4316 people, and infant mortality figures are 26 per 1000 births (figures for neighbouring countries vary from 110 per 1000 in Cambodia to 12 in Malaysia). Thailand as a whole has a relatively youthful population; only about 12% are older than 50.

### The Thai Majority

About 75% of citizens are ethnic Thais, who can be divided into the Central Thais or Siamese of the Chao Phraya Delta (the most densely populated region of the country); the Thai Lao of North-Eastern Thailand; the Thai Pak Tai of Southern Thailand; and the Northern Thais. Each group speaks their own Thai dialect and to a certain extent practises customs unique to their region. Politically and economically the Central Thais are the dominant group, although they barely outnumber the Thai Lao of the North-East.

Smaller groups with their own Thai dialects include the Shan (Mae Hong Son), the Thai Lü (Nan, Chiang Rai), the Lao Song (Phetburi and Ratchaburi), the Phuan (Chaiyaphum, Phetburi, Prachinburi), the Thai Khorat or Sawoei (Khorat), the Phu Thai (Mukdahan, Sakon Nakhon), the Yaw (Nakhon Phanom, Sakon Nakhon) and the Thai-Malay (Satun, Trang, Krabi).

## Thailand's Largest Cities

| Population | Thetsabaan (municipal district) | Meuang (metropolitan district) |
|---|---|---|
| Bangkok | not applicable | 6+ million (1569 sq km) |
| Chaiyaphum | 25,600 (2.8 sq km) | 157,700 (1169 sq km) |
| Chiang Rai | 36,542 (10.6 sq km) | 167,318 (1622 sq km) |
| Chiang Mai | 154,777 (40 sq km) | 164,490 (152 sq km) |
| Hat Yai | 139,400 (21 sq km) | 149,800 (1154 sq km) |
| Khon Kaen | 130,300 (46 sq km) | 197,400 (953 sq km) |
| Nakhon Ratchasima (Khorat) | 202,403 (37 sq km) | 208,800 (571 sq km) |
| Lampang | 43,369 (9 sq km) | 184,000 (1156 sq km) |
| Lopburi | 40,000 (6.8 sq km) | 211,400 (565 sq km) |
| Nakhon Pathom | 45,000 (5.3 sq km) | 181,700 (417 sq km) |
| Nakhon Si Thammarat | 71,500 (11.7 sq km) | 216,708 (765 sq km) |
| Nonthaburi | 46,400 (2.5 sq km) | 240,000 (77 sq km) |
| Sakon Nakhon | 24,800 (13 sq km) | 178,000 (1815 sq km) |
| Samut Prakan | 71,400 (7.3 sq km) | 266,000 (190 sq km) |
| Surin | 40,000 (11.4 sq km) | 237,000 (1279 sq km) |
| Udon Thani | 95,000 (3.7 sq km) | 277,000 (1094 sq km) |

## The Chinese

People of Chinese ancestry make up 11% of the population, most of whom are second or third generation Hokkien (Hakka), Tae Jiu (Chao Zhou/Chiu Chao) or Cantonese. In the North there is also a substantial number of Hui – Chinese Muslims who emigrated from Yunnan to Thailand in the late 19th century to avoid religious and ethnic persecution during the Ch'ing dynasty.

Ethnic Chinese probably enjoy better relations with the majority population here than in any other country in South-East Asia, due partly to historical reasons and partly to the traditional Thai tolerance of other cultures (although there was a brief spell of anti-Chinese sentiment during the reign of Rama VI). Rama V used Chinese businesspeople to infiltrate European trading houses, a manoeuvre that helped defeat European colonial designs on Siam. Wealthy Chinese also introduced their daughters to the royal court as consorts, developing royal connections and adding a Chinese bloodline that extends to the current king.

## Minorities

The second largest ethnic minority group living in Thailand are the Malays (3.5%), most of whom reside in the provinces of Songkhla, Yala, Pattani and Narathiwat. The remaining 10.5% of the population is divided among smaller non Thai-speaking groups like the Vietnamese, Khmer, Mon, Semang (Sakai), Moken (chao leh or 'sea gypsies'), Htin, Mabri, Khamu and a variety of hill tribes (described more fully in the Northern Thailand chapter).

A small number of Europeans and other non-Asians live in Bangkok and the provinces – their total numbers aren't recorded since very few have immigrant status.

## EDUCATION

The literacy rate in Thailand runs at 93.8%, one of the highest rates in mainland South-East Asia. In 1993 the government raised compulsory schooling from six to nine years. Although a high social value is placed on education as a way to achieve material success, the system itself favours rote learning over independent thinking at most levels.

Thailand's public school system is organised around six years at the *pràthõm* (primary) level beginning at age six, followed by three years of *máthãyom* (middle) and three years of *udom* (high) school. In reality less than nine years of formal education is the national norm. These statistics don't take into account the education provided by Buddhist wats in remote rural areas, where monastic schooling may be the only formal education available.

Private and international schools for the foreign and local elite are found in Bangkok and Chiang Mai, and to a lesser extent in other larger cities. The country has 12 public and five private universities, plus numerous trade schools and technical colleges. A teaching certificate may be obtained after attending a two year, post-máthãyom programme at one of the many teachers' colleges scattered throughout the country.

## SOCIETY & CONDUCT

When outsiders speak of 'Thai culture' they're referring to a complex of behavioural modes rooted in the history of Thai migration throughout South-East Asia, with many commonalities shared by the Lao of neighbouring Laos, the Shan of north-eastern Myanmar and the numerous tribal Thais found in isolated pockets from Dien Bien Phu, Vietnam, all the way to Assam, India. Nowhere are such norms more generalised than in Thailand, the largest of the Thai homelands.

Practically every ethnicity represented in Thailand, whether of Thai ancestry or not, has to a greater or lesser degree been assimilated into the Thai mainstream. Although Thailand is the most 'modernised' of the existing Thai (more precisely, Austro-Thai) societies, the cultural underpinnings are evident in virtually every facet of everyday life. Those aspects that might be deemed 'westernisation' – eg the wearing of trousers instead of *phâakhamãa* (wraparound), the presence of automobiles, cinemas and 7 Elevens – show how Thailand has adopted and adapted tools invented elsewhere.

Such adaptations do not necessarily represent cultural loss. Ekawit Na Talang, a scholar of Thai culture and head of the government's National Culture Commission, defines culture as 'the system of thought and behaviour of a particular society – something which is dynamic and never static'. Talang and other world culture experts agree that it's paradoxical to try and protect a culture from foreign influences, realising that cultures cannot exist in a vacuum. Culture evolves naturally as outside influences undergo processes of naturalisation. From this perspective, trying to maintain a 'pure' culture is like breeding pedigreed dogs: it eventually leads to a weakening of the species. As Talang has said, 'Anything obsolete, people will reject and anything that has a relevant role in life, people will adopt and make it part of their culture'.

Nevertheless there are certain aspects of Thai society that virtually everyone recognises as 'Thai' cultural markers. The Thais themselves don't really have a word that corresponds to the English term 'culture'. The nearest equivalent, *wátánátham*, emphasises fine arts and ceremonies over other aspects usually covered by the concept. So if you ask Thais to define their culture, they'll often talk about architecture, food, dance, festivals and the like. Religion – obviously a big influence on culture as defined in the western sense – is considered more or less separate from wátánátham.

### Sanùk

The Thai word *sanùk* means 'fun'. In Thailand anything worth doing – even work – should have an element of sanùk, otherwise it automatically becomes drudgery. This doesn't mean Thais don't want to work or strive, just that they tend to approach tasks with a sense of playfulness. Nothing condemns an activity more than the description *mâi sanùk*, 'not fun'. Sit down beside a rice field and watch workers planting, transplanting or harvesting rice some time while you're in Thailand. That it's back-breaking labour is obvious, but participants generally inject the activity with lots of sanùk – flirtation between the sexes, singing, trading insults and cracking jokes. The same goes in an office or a bank, or other white-collar work situations – at least when the office in question is predominantly Thai (businesses run by non-Thais don't necessarily exhibit sanùk). The famous Thai smile comes partially out of this desire to make sanùk.

## Face

Thais believe strongly in the concept of 'saving face', that is avoiding confrontation and endeavouring not to embarrass themselves or other people (except when it's sanùk to do so!). The ideal face-saver doesn't bring up negative topics in everyday conversation, and when they notice stress in another's life, they usually won't say anything unless that person complains or asks for help. Laughing at minor accidents – like when someone trips and falls down – may seem callous to outsiders but it's really just an attempt to save face on behalf of the person undergoing the mishap. This is another source of the Thai smile – it's the best possible face to put on in almost any situation.

### Phûu Yài-Phûu Náwy & Phii-Nawng

All relationships in traditional Thai society – and virtually all relationships in the modern Thai milieu as well – are governed by connections between *phûu yài* (literally, 'big person') and *phûu náwy* ('little person'). Phûu náwy are supposed to defer to phûu yài following simple lines of social rank defined by age, wealth, status and personal and political power. Examples of 'automatic' phûu yài status include adults (vs children), bosses (vs employees), elder classmates (vs younger classmates), elder siblings (vs younger siblings), teachers (vs pupils), military (vs civilian), Thai (vs non-Thai) and so on.

While this tendency toward social ranking is to some degree shared by many societies around the world, the Thai twist lies in the set of mutual obligations linking phûu yài to phûu náwy. Sociologists have referred to this phenomenon as the 'patron-client relationship'. Phûu náwy are supposed to show a degree of obedience and respect (together these concepts are covered by the single Thai term *'kreng jai'*) toward phûu yài, but in return phûu yài are obligated to care for or 'sponsor' the phûu náwy they have frequent contact with. In such relationships phûu náwy can, for example, ask phûu yài for favours involving money or job access. Phûu yài re-affirm their rank by granting such requests when possible; to refuse would be to risk loss of face and status.

Age is a large determinant where other factors are absent or weak. In such cases the terms *phîi* (elder sibling) and *náwng* (younger sibling) apply more than phûu yài/phûu náwy although the intertwined obligations remain the same. Even people unrelated by blood quickly establish who's phii and who's nawng; this is why one of the first questions Thais ask new acquaintances is 'How old are you?'.

When dining, touring or entertaining, the phûu yài always picks up the tab; if a group is involved, the person with most social rank pays the check for everyone, even if it empties his or her wallet. For a phûu náwy to try and pay would risk loss of face. Money plays a large role in defining phûu yài status in most situations. A person who turned out to be successful in his or her post-school career would never think of allowing an ex-classmate of lesser success – even if they were once on an equal social footing – to pay the bill. Likewise a young, successful executive will pay an older person's way in spite of the age difference.

The implication is that whatever wealth you come into is to be shared – at least partially – with those who have been less fortunate. This doesn't apply to strangers – the average Thai isn't big on charity – but always comes into play with friends and relatives.

Foreigners often feel offended when they encounter such phenomena as two tiered pricing for hotels or sightseeing attractions – one price for Thais, a higher price for foreigners. But this is simply another expression of the traditional patron-client relationship. On the one hand foreigners who can afford to travel to Thailand from abroad are seen to have more wealth than Thai citizens (on average this is self-evident), hence they're expected to help subsidise Thai enjoyment of these commodities; and at the same time, paradoxically, the Thais feel they are due certain special privileges as homelanders – what might be termed the 'home-town discount'. Another example: in a post office line, Thais get served first as part of their nature-given national privilege.

## Comportment

Personal power (baará-mii, sometimes mistranslated as 'charisma') also has a bearing on one's social status, and can be gained by cleaving as close as possible to the ideal 'Thai' behaviour. 'Thai-ness' is first and foremost defined, as might be expected, by the ability to speak Thai. It doesn't matter which dialect, although Southern Thai – with its Malay/Yawi influences – is slightly more suspect, mainly due to the South's association with the 'foreign' religion of Islam.

Other hallmarks of the Thai ideal – heavily influenced by Thai Buddhism – include discretion in behaviour toward the opposite sex, modest dress, a neat and clean appearance, and modes of expression and comportment that value the quiet, subtle and indirect rather than the loud, obvious and direct.

The degree to which Thais can conform to these ideals matches the degree of respect they receive from most of their associates. Although high rank – based on age or civil, military or clerical roles – will exempt certain individuals from chastisement by their social 'inferiors', it doesn't exempt them from the way they are perceived by other Thais. This goes for foreigners as well, even though most first-time visitors can hardly be expected to speak idiomatic Thai. But if you do learn some Thai, and you do make an effort to respect Thai social ideals, you'll come closer to enjoying some of the perks awarded for Thai-ness.

## Avoiding Offence

Monarchy and religion are the two sacred

cows in Thailand. Thais are tolerant of most kinds of behaviour as long as it doesn't insult either of these.

**King & Country** The monarchy is held in considerable respect in Thailand and visitors should be respectful too – avoid disparaging remarks about the king, queen or anyone in the royal family. One of Thailand's leading intellectuals, Sulak Sivaraksa, was arrested in the early 1980s for lese-majesty because of a passing reference to the king's fondness for yachting (Sulak referred to His Majesty as 'the skipper') and again in 1991 when he referred to the royal family as 'ordinary people'. Although on that occasion he received a royal pardon, later in 1991 Sulak had to flee the country to avoid prosecution again, for alleged remarks delivered at Thammasat University about the ruling military junta, with reference to the king (Sulak has since returned under a suspended sentence). The penalty for lese-majesty is seven years imprisonment.

While it's OK to criticise the Thai government and even Thai culture openly, it's considered a grave insult to Thai nationhood as well as to the monarchy not to stand when you hear the national or royal anthems. Radio and TV stations in Thailand broadcast the national anthem daily at 8 am and 6 pm; in towns and villages (even in some Bangkok neighbourhoods) this can be heard over public loudspeakers in the streets. The Thais stop whatever they're doing to stand during the anthem (except in Bangkok where nobody can hear anything above the street noise) and visitors are expected to do likewise. The royal anthem is played just before films are shown in public cinemas; again, the audience always stands until it's over.

**Religion** Correct behaviour in temples entails several considerations, the most important of which is to dress neatly and to take your shoes off when you enter any building that contains a Buddha image. Buddha images are sacred objects, so don't pose in front of them for pictures and definitely do not clamber upon them.

Shorts or sleeveless shirts are considered improper dress for both men and women when visiting temples. Thai citizens wearing either would be turned away by monastic authorities, but except for the most sacred temples in the country (eg Wat Phra Kaew in Bangkok and Wat Phra That Doi Suthep near Chiang Mai), Thais are often too polite to refuse entry to improperly clad foreigners. Some wats will offer trousers or long sarongs for rent so that tourists dressed in shorts may enter the compound.

Monks are not supposed to touch or be touched by women. If a woman wants to hand something to a monk, the object should be placed within reach of the monk, not handed directly to him.

When sitting in a religious edifice, keep your feet pointed away from any Buddha images. The usual way to do this is to sit in the 'mermaid' pose in which your legs are folded to the side, with the feet pointing backwards.

A few of the larger wats in Bangkok charge small entry fees. In other temples, offering a small donation before leaving the compound is appropriate but not mandatory. Usually there are donation boxes near the entry of the *bòt* (central sanctuary) or next to the central Buddha image at the rear. In rural wats, there may be no donation box available; in these places, it's OK to leave money on the floor next to the central image or even by the doorway, where temple attendants will collect it later.

**Social Gestures & Attitudes** Traditionally Thais greet each other not with a handshake but with a prayer-like palms-together gesture known as a *wâi*. If someone wais you, you should wai back (unless wai-ed by a child). Most urban Thais are familiar with the western-style handshake and will offer the same to a foreigner, although a wai is always appreciated.

Thais are often addressed by their first name with the honorific *khun* or other title preceding it. Other formal terms of address include *nai* (Mr) and *naang* (Miss or Mrs). Friends often use nicknames or kinship terms like *phîi* (elder sibling), *náwng*

(younger sibling), *mâe* (mother) or *lung* (uncle), depending on the age differential.

A smile and *sawàt-dii khráp/khâ* (the all-purpose Thai greeting) goes a long way toward calming the initial trepidation that locals may feel upon seeing a foreigner, whether in the city or the countryside.

When encounters take a turn for the worse, try to refrain from getting angry – it won't help matters, since losing one's temper means loss of face for everyone present. Remember that this is Asia, where keeping your cool is the paramount rule. Talking loudly is perceived as rude behaviour by cultured Thais, whatever the situation. See the previous sections on Face and Comportment regarding the rewards for 'Thai-ness' – the pushy foreigner often gets served last.

The feet are the lowest part of the body (spiritually as well as physically) so don't point your feet at people or point at things with your feet. In the same context, the head is regarded as the highest part of the body, so don't touch Thais on the head either.

Don't sit on pillows meant for sleeping, as this represents a variant of the taboo against head-touching. I recently watched a young woman on Ko Samet bring a bed pillow from her bungalow to sit on while watching TV; the Thai staff got very upset and she didn't understand why.

When handing things to other people you should use both hands or your right hand only, never the left hand (reserved for toilet ablutions). Books and other written material are given a special status over other secular objects. Hence you shouldn't slide books or documents across a table or counter-top, and never place them on the floor – use a chair instead if table space isn't available.

**Dress & Nudity** Shorts (except knee-length walking shorts), sleeveless shirts, tank tops (singlets) and other beach-style attire are not considered appropriate dress in Thailand for anything other than sporting events. Such dress is especially counterproductive if worn to government offices (eg when applying for a visa extension). The attitude of 'This is how I dress at home and no-one is going to stop me' gains nothing but contempt or disrespect from the Thais.

Sandals or slip-on shoes are OK for almost any but the most formal occasions. Short-sleeved shirts and blouses with capped sleeves likewise are quite acceptable.

Regardless of what the Thais may (or may not) have been accustomed to centuries ago, they are quite offended by public nudity today. Bathing nude at beaches in Thailand is illegal. If you are at a truly deserted beach and are sure no Thais may come along, there's nothing stopping you – however, at most beaches travellers should wear suitable attire. Likewise, topless bathing for females is frowned upon in most places except on heavily touristed islands like Phuket, Samui, Samet and Pha-Ngan. Many Thais say that nudity on the beaches is what bothers them most about foreign travellers. These Thais take nudity as a sign of disrespect for the locals, rather than as a libertarian symbol or modern custom. Thais are extremely modest in this respect (despite racy billboards in Bangkok) and it should not be the visitor's intention to 'reform' them.

**Upcountry** When travelling in minority villages, try to find out what the local customs and taboos are, either by asking someone or by taking the time to observe local behaviour. Here are several other guidelines for minimising the impact you can have on local communities.

- Many tribes fear photography, so you should always ask permission – through hand gestures if necessary – before pointing your camera at tribespeople and/or their dwellings.
- Show respect for religious symbols and rituals. Avoid touching spirit houses, household altars, village totems and other religious symbols, as this often 'pollutes' them spiritually and may force the villagers to perform purification rituals after you have moved on. Keep your distance from ceremonies being performed unless you're asked to participate.
- Do not enter a village house without the permission or invitation of its inhabitants.

- Practise restraint in giving things to tribespeople or bartering with them. Food and medicine are not necessarily appropriate gifts if they result in altering traditional dietary and healing practices. The same goes for clothing. If you want to give something to the people you encounter, the best thing is to make a donation to the village school or other community fund.

**Message from a Reader** As a final comment on avoiding offence, here is a plea from a reader who wrote to me following an extended visit she had in Thailand:

Please do whatever you can to impress on travellers the importance of treating the Thai people, who are so generous and unassuming, with the respect they deserve. If people sunbathe topless, take snapshots of the people like animals in a zoo, and demand western standards then they are both offending the Thai people and contributing to the opinion many of them have of us as being rich, demanding and promiscuous.

## RELIGION
### Buddhism
Approximately 95% of the Thai citizenry are Theravada Buddhists. The Thais themselves frequently call their religion Lankavamsa (Sinhalese lineage) Buddhism because Thailand originally received Buddhism from Sri Lanka during the Sukhothai period. Strictly speaking, Theravada refers only to the earliest forms of Buddhism practised during the Ashokan and immediate post-Ashokan periods in South Asia. The early Dvaravati and pre-Dvaravati forms of Buddhism – those which existed up until the 10th or 11th century – are not the same as that which developed in Thai territories after the 13th century.

Since the Sukhothai period (13th to 15th centuries), Thailand has maintained an unbroken canonical tradition and 'pure' ordination lineage, the only country among the Theravadin countries to have done so. Ironically, when the ordination lineage in Sri Lanka broke down during the 18th century under Dutch persecution, it was Thailand that restored the Sangha (Buddhist brotherhood) there. To this day the major sect in Sri Lanka is called Siamopalivamsa (Siam-Upali lineage, Upali being the name of the Siamese monk who led the expedition to Ceylon), or simply Siam Nikaya (the Siamese sect).

Basically, the Theravada school of Buddhism is an earlier and, according to its followers, less corrupted form of Buddhism than the Mahayana schools found in East Asia or in the Himalayan lands. The Theravada (literally, 'teaching of the elders') school is also called the 'southern' school since it took a southern route from India, its place of origin, through South-East Asia (Myanmar, Thailand, Laos and Cambodia in this case), while the 'northern' school proceeded north into Nepal, Tibet, China, Korea, Mongolia, Vietnam and Japan. Because the Theravada school tried to preserve or limit the Buddhist doctrines to only those canons codified in the early Buddhist era, the Mahayana school gave Theravada Buddhism the name Hinayana, or the 'lesser vehicle'. The Mahayana school was the 'great vehicle', because it built upon the earlier teachings, 'expanding' the doctrine in such a way as to respond more to the needs of lay people, or so it is claimed.

Theravada or Hinayana doctrine stresses the three principal aspects of existence: *dukkha* (stress, unsatisfactoriness, disease), *anicca* (impermanence, transience of all things) and *anatta* (non-substantiality or non-essentiality of reality – no permanent 'soul'). The truth of anicca reveals that no experience, no state of mind, no physical object lasts; trying to hold onto experience, states of mind and objects that are constantly changing creates dukkha; anatta is the understanding that there is no part of the changing world that we can point to and say 'This is me' or 'This is God' or 'This is the soul'. These three concepts, when 'discovered' by Siddhartha Gautama in the 6th century BC, were in direct contrast to the Hindu belief in an eternal, blissful self *(paramatman)*. Hence Buddhism was originally a 'heresy' against India's Brahmanic religion.

Gautama, an Indian prince-turned-ascetic, subjected himself to many years of severe austerity before he realised that this was not

the way to reach the end of suffering. He turned his attention to investigating the arising and passing away of the mind and body in the present moment. Seeing that even the most blissful and refined states of mind were subject to decay, he abandoned all desire for what he now saw as unreliable and unsatisfying. He then became known as Buddha, 'the enlightened' or 'the awakened'. Gautama Buddha spoke of four noble truths which had the power to liberate any human being who could realise them. These four noble truths are:

1. The truth of dukkha: 'All forms of existence are subject to dukkha (disease, unsatisfactoriness, stress, imperfection)'
2. The truth of the cause of dukkha: 'Dukkha is caused by *tanha* (desire)'
3. The truth of the cessation of dukkha: 'Eliminate the cause of dukkha (ie desire) and dukkha will cease to arise'
4. The truth of the path: 'The Eightfold Path is the way to eliminate desire/extinguish dukkha'

The Eightfold Path (Atthangika-Magga), which if followed will put an end to dukkha, consists of:

1. Right understanding
2. Right mindedness (right thought)
3. Right speech
4. Right bodily conduct
5. Right livelihood
6. Right effort
7. Right attentiveness
8. Right concentration

These eight limbs belong to three different 'pillars' of practice: wisdom or *pañña* (1 and 2), morality or *sila* (3 to 5) and concentration or *samadhi* (6 to 8). The path is also called the 'Middle Way', since ideally it avoids both extreme austerity and extreme sensuality. Some Buddhists believe it is to be taken in successive stages, while others say the pillars and/or limbs are interdependent. Another key point is that the word 'right' can also be translated as 'complete' or 'full'.

The ultimate end of Theravada Buddhism is *nibbana* (Sanskrit: *nirvana)*, which literally means the 'blowing out' or extinction of

## Spirit Houses

Every Thai house or building has to have a spirit house to go with it – a place for the spirits of the site, or *phra phum*, to live in. Without this vital structure you're likely to have the spirits living in the house with you, which can cause all sorts of trouble. A spirit house looks rather like a birdhouse-sized Thai temple mounted on a pedestal – at least your average spirit house does. A big hotel may have a shrine covering 100 sq m or more.

How do you ensure that the spirits take up residence in your spirit house rather than in the main house with you? Mainly by making the spirit house a more auspicious place to live in than the main building, through daily offerings of food, flowers, candles and incense. The spirit house should also have a prominent location and should not be shaded by the main house. Thus its position has to be planned from the very beginning and installed with due ceremony. If your own house is improved or enlarged then the spirit house should be as well. The local *phâw khru* or *mâe khruu* (father or mother teacher) usually presides over the initial installation as well as later improvements.

The interior of a spirit house is usually decorated with ceramic or plastic figurines representing the property's guardian spirits. The most important figurine, the *châo thîi* or 'place lord', embodies a phra phum who reigns over a specific part of the property (see the list of guardian spirits below). Larger or more elaborate spirit houses may also contain figurines that serve as family, retainers or servants for these resident spirits. Thai believers purchase these figurines – as well as the bowls, dishes and other accoutrements for making daily offerings – at rural temples or, in larger cities, at supermarkets and department stores.

An abandoned or damaged spirit house can't simply be tossed aside like a broken appliance, left to rot or dismantled for firewood. Instead, it should be deposited against the base of a sacred banyan tree or in the corner of a sympathetic wat where benevolent spirits will watch over it.

| *Guardian Spirit* | *Sphere of Influence* |
| --- | --- |
| Phra Chaimongkhon | houses |
| Phra Nakhonrat | gates, portals, ladders |
| Phra Khonthan | honeymoon homes |
| Phra Khan Thoraphon | corrals, cattle pens |
| Phra Chai Kassapa | granaries |
| Phra Thamahora | fields |
| Phra Than Thirat | gardens, orchards |
| Phra Chaimongkut | farmyards, compounds |
| Phra That Tara | temples, shrines, monasteries |

all desire and thus of all suffering (dukkha). Effectively, it is also an end to the cycle of rebirths (both moment to moment and life to life) that is existence. In reality, most Thai Buddhists aim for rebirth in a 'better' existence rather than the supramundane goal of nibbana, which is highly misunderstood by Asians as well as westerners.

Many Thais express the feeling that they are somehow unworthy of nibbana. By feeding monks, giving donations to temples and performing regular worship at the local *wát* (temple) they hope to improve their lot, acquiring enough merit (Pali: *puñña*; Thai: *bun*) to prevent or at least lessen the number of rebirths. The making of merit *(tham bun)* is an important social and religious activity in Thailand. The concept of reincarnation is almost universally accepted in Thailand, even by non-Buddhists, and the Buddhist theory of karma is well expressed in the Thai proverb *tham dii, dâi dii; tham chûa, dâi chûa* (do good and receive good; do evil and receive evil).

The Triratna, or Triple Gems, highly respected by Thai Buddhists, include the Buddha, the Dhamma (the teachings) and the Sangha (the Buddhist brotherhood). All are quite visible in Thailand. The Buddha, in his myriad and omnipresent sculptural forms, is found on a high shelf in the lowliest roadside restaurants as well as in the lounges of expensive Bangkok hotels. The Dhamma is chanted morning and evening in every wat and taught to every Thai citizen in primary school. The Sangha is seen everywhere in the presence of orange-robed monks, especially in the early morning hours when they perform their alms-rounds, in what has almost become a travel-guide cliché in motion.

Thai Buddhism has no particular 'Sabbath' or day of the week when Thais are supposed to make temple visits. Nor is there anything corresponding to a liturgy or mass over which a priest presides. Instead Thai Buddhists visit the wat whenever they feel like it, most often on *wan phrá* (literally, 'excellent days') which occur with every full and new moon, ie every 15 days. On such a visit typical activities include: the traditional offering of lotus buds, incense and candles at various altars and bone reliquaries around the wat compound; the offering of food to the temple Sangha (monks, nuns and lay residents – monks always eat first); meditating (individually or in groups); listening to monks chanting *suttas* or Buddhist discourse; and attending a *thêt* or Dhamma talk by the abbot or some other respected teacher. Visitors may also seek counsel from individual monks or nuns regarding new or ongoing life problems.

**Monks & Nuns** Socially, every Thai male is expected to become a monk for a short period in his life, optimally between the time he finishes school and the time he starts a career or marries. Men or boys under 20 years of age may enter the Sangha as novices – this is not unusual since a family earns great merit when one of its sons takes robe and bowl. Traditionally, the length of time spent in the wat is three months, during the Buddhist lent *(phansāa)* which begins in July and coincides with the rainy season. However, nowadays men may spend as little as a week or 15 days to accrue merit as monks. There are about 32,000 monasteries in Thailand and 200,000 monks; many of these monks ordain for a lifetime. Of these a large percentage become scholars and teachers, while some specialise in healing and/or folk magic.

The Sangha is divided into two sects: the Mahanikai and the Thammayut (from the Pali *dhammayutika* or 'dharma-adhering'). The latter is a minority sect (the ratio being one Thammayut to 35 Mahanikai) begun by King Mongkut and patterned after an early Mon form of monastic discipline which he had practised as a monk *(bhikkhu)*. Members of both sects must adhere to 227 monastic vows or precepts as laid out in the Vinaya Pitaka – Buddhist scriptures dealing with monastic discipline. Overall discipline for Thammayut monks, however, is generally stricter. For example, they eat only once a day – before noon – and must eat only what is in their alms bowl, whereas Mahanikais eat twice before noon and may accept side dishes. Thammayut monks are expected to attain proficiency in meditation as well as Buddhist scholarship or scripture study; the Mahanikai monks typically 'specialise' in one or the other. Other factors may supersede sectarian divisions when it comes to disciplinary disparities. Monks who live in the city, for example, usually emphasise study of the Buddhist scriptures while those living in the forest tend to emphasise meditation.

At one time the Theravada Buddhist world had a separate Buddhist monastic lineage for females, who called themselves *bhikkhuni* and observed more vows than monks did – 311 precepts as opposed to the 227 followed by monks. Started in Sri Lanka around two centuries after the Buddha's lifetime by the daughter of King Ashoka (a Buddhist king in India), the bhikkhuni tradition in Sri Lanka eventually died out and was unfortunately never restored.

In Thailand, the modern equivalent is the *mâe chii* (Thai for 'nun,' literally 'mother priest') – women who live the monastic life as *atthasila* or 'Eight-Precept' nuns. Thai nuns shave their heads, wear white robes and take vows in an ordination procedure similar to that undergone by monks. Generally speaking, nunhood in Thailand isn't considered as 'prestigious' as monkhood. The average Thai Buddhist makes a great show of offering new robes and household items to the monks at their local wat but pays much less attention to the nuns. This is mainly due to the fact that nuns generally don't perform ceremonies on behalf of laypeople, so there is often less incentive for self-interested laypeople to make offerings to them. Furthermore, many Thais equate the number of precepts observed with the total Buddhist merit achieved, hence nunhood is seen as less 'meritorious' than monkhood since mae chiis keep only eight precepts.

This difference in prestige represents social Buddhism, however, and is not how those with a serious interest in Buddhist practice regard the mae chii. Nuns engage in the same fundamental eremitic activities – meditation and Dhamma study – as monks do, activities which are the core of monastic life. The reality is that wats which draw sizeable contingents of mae chiis are highly respected, since women don't choose temples for reasons of clerical status. When more than a few nuns reside at one temple, it's usually a sign that the teachings there are particularly strong.

Recently a small movement to restore the bhikkhuni Sangha in Thailand has arisen. Some women now ordain in Taiwan, where the Mahayana tradition has maintained a bhikkhuni lineage, then return to Thailand to practice with full bhikkhuni status.

An increasing number of foreigners come to Thailand to ordain as Buddhist monks or nuns, especially to study with the famed meditation masters of the forest wats in North-Eastern Thailand.

**Further Information** If you wish to find out more about Buddhism you can contact the World Fellowship of Buddhists (☎ (2) 251-1188), 33 Sukhumvit Rd (between sois 1 and 3), Bangkok. Senior farang monks hold English-language Dhamma/meditation classes here on the first Sunday of each month from 2 to 6 pm; all are welcome.

A Buddhist bookshop across the street from the north entrance to Wat Bovornives (Bowonniwet) in Bangkok sells a variety of English-language books on Buddhism. Asia Books and DK Book House also stock Buddhist literature.

For more information on meditation study in Thailand, see the Courses section in the Facts for the Visitor chapter, and also the Meditation Study section in the Bangkok chapter.

Recommended books about Buddhism include:

*Buddhism Explained* – by Phra Khantipalo
*Buddhism, Imperialism, and War* – by Trevor Ling
*Buddhism in the Modern World* – edited by Heinrich Dumoulin
*Buddhism in Transition* – by Donald K Swearer
*Buddhist Dictionary* – by Mahathera Nyanatiloka
*The Buddhist World of Southeast Asia* – by Donald K Swearer
*The Central Conception of Buddhism* – by Th Stcherbatsky
*Heartwood of the Bodhi Tree* – by Buddhasa Bhikku
*In This Very Life: The Liberation Teachings of the Buddha* – by Sayadaw U Pandita
*Living Buddhist Masters* – by Jack Kornfield
*A Still Forest Pool: the Teaching of Ajaan Chaa at Wat Paa Pong* – compiled by Jack Kornfield & Paul Breiter
*The Mind and the Way* – by Ajaan Sumedho
*What the Buddha Never Taught* – by Timothy Ward
*What the Buddha Taught* – by Walpola Rahula
*World Conqueror and World Renouncer* – by Stanley Tambiah

## Other Religions

A small percentage of Thais and most of the Malays in the South, amounting to about 4% of the total population, are followers of Islam. Half a percent of the population – primarily missionised hill tribes and Vietnamese immigrants – profess Christian beliefs, while the remaining half percent are Confucianists, Taoists, Mahayana Buddhists and Hindus. Mosques (in the South) and Chinese temples are both common enough that you will probably come across some in your travels in Thailand. Before entering *any* temple, sanctuary or mosque you must remove your shoes, and in a mosque your head must be covered.

# Thai Arts & Architecture

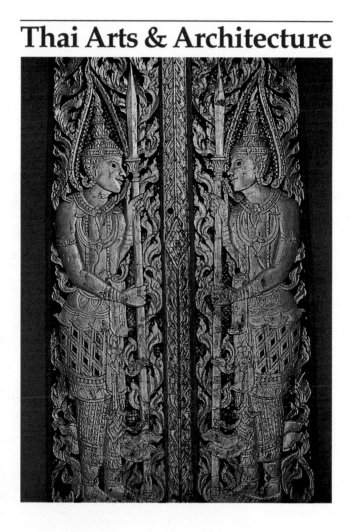

A s the centrepoint of Indianised South-East Asia – as distinct from Sinicised South-East Asia east of the Annamite Chain of mountains – Thailand's long-standing artistic traditions owe their greatest debt to the arts of India. As in India, traditional art in Thailand revolved around religious symbols borrowed from Hindu and Buddhist cosmology as well as literary epics such as the *Ramayana* and *Mahabharata*. The *shastras* of India *(sàat* in Thai) – semi-sacred texts which systematised the way in which these symbols were to be sculpted, painted and applied to architecture – became equally important in Thailand subsequent to their importation.

These symbols and texts arrived in Thailand by many avenues, including Indian traders, Mon immigrants, Sinhalese missionaries, Indonesian sailors and Khmer soldiers – each of which acted as cultural and artistic filters. When further modified by Thai artists and artisans, they attained their own native characteristics which resulted in distinctively Thai modes of artistic expression.

*Title Page: An elaborately carved door detail from Wat Klang, Trat Province (photo by Richard Nebesky).*

*Right: The decorative yaks (mythical giants) at Wat Phra Kaew, Bangkok.*

JOHN DEMODENA

# Architecture

Considered the highest art form in traditional Thai society, architecture creates and adapts structures within which the people eat, sleep, work and worship. In addition to native Siamese styles of building, within Thailand's borders you'll find splendid examples from historical Khmer, Mon, Lao and Northern Thai traditions. Early texts used by these builders trace the power of all architecture to the Hindu-Buddhist deity Vishvakarman, architect of the universe. Today the power transfers to modern practitioners of the art, who are among the most highly celebrated individuals in Thai society.

## Traditional Architecture

Traditional home and temple architecture followed relatively strict rules of design that dictated proportion, placement, materials and ornamentation. With the modernisation of Thailand in the 19th and 20th centuries, stylistic codification gave way first to European functionalism and then to stylistic innovation in more recent times.

JOE CUMMINGS

*Red and green roof tiles, Chinese porcelain dishes, gilded umbrellas and holy orange cloth decorate the main chedi at Wat Phra Mahathat, Nakhon Si Thammarat.*

JOE CUMMINGS

*Phanom Rung in Buriram Province is one of the most outstanding examples of Angkor-period architecture in Thailand. The temple complex was constructed between the 10th and 13th centuries, during the reign of King Suryjavarman II (1113-50), a period which represented the apex of Angkor-period architecture. Though smaller than Cambodia's Angkor Wat, the hill-top location of Phanom Rung adds to its grandeur.*

## What's a Wat

Technically speaking, a *wát* (a Thai word, from the Pali-Sanskrit *avasatha* or 'dwelling for pupils and ascetics') is a Buddhist compound where men or women can be ordained as monks or nuns. Virtually every village in Thailand has at least one wat, while in towns and cities they're quite numerous. Without an ordination area (designated by *sěma* or stone ordination markers), a monastic centre where monks or nuns reside is simply a *săm-nák sŏng* (Sangha residence). The latter are often established as meditation retreat facilities in forest areas, sometimes in conjunction with larger *wát pàa* (or forest monasteries).

The typical wat compound in Thailand will contain: an *uposatha (bòt* in Thai), a consecrated chapel where monastic ordinations are held; a *vihara (wihăan* in Thai), where important Buddha images are housed; a *sala (săalaa)* or open-sided shelter for community meetings and Dhamma (Buddhist teachings) lectures; a number of *kùti* or monastic quarters; a *hăw trai* or *tripitaka* library where Buddhist scriptures are stored; a *hăw klawng* or drum tower (sometimes with a *hăw rákhang* or bell tower); various *chedis* or stupas (the smaller squarish stupas are *thâat kràdùk* or bone reliquaries), where the ashes of worshippers are interred; plus various ancillary buildings – such as schools or clinics – that differ from wat to wat according to local community needs. Many wats also have a *hăw phĭi khun wát* or spirit house for the temple's reigning earth spirit.

In rural Thailand, the wat often serves as a combination religious centre, grammar school, health clinic, herbal sauna house, community centre, astrology house, transient guesthouse, funeral home and geriatric ward, with monks and nuns serving as staff for one or more of these functions.

The typical wat is also a focus for much festival activity and is thus an important social centre for Thais. Especially lively are the *ngaan wát* or temple fairs; these take place regularly on certain auspicious dates (eg the advent and end of the Rains Retreat; the anniversary of the Buddha's birth, enlightenment and death; the anniversary of the first Dhamma lecture etc) and usually feature music, feasting, outdoor cinema and occasional fireworks. Another common type of celebration is the *ngaan sòp* or funeral ceremony. A typical ngaan sòp includes a lively procession (with musical accompaniment) from the deceased's home to the wat. ■

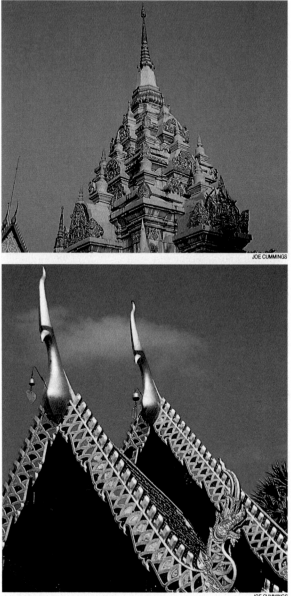

JOE CUMMINGS

*This chedi at Wat Phra Boromathat in Chaiya, built during the Srivijaya period, resembles the candis or Hindu-Buddhist stupas of central Java in its 'stacked' appearance.*

JOE CUMMINGS

*The hook-like gable fixtures found at the roofline corners of Thai temples are called jaofao or 'sky lords'. Their cryptic spiritual function is to protect the temple interior from any unsavoury spirits that might fall out of the sky. In earlier temple architecture these fixtures often represented naga heads (the dragon-serpent of Hindu-Buddhist mythology); in the later, more stylised versions they almost resemble exotic bird heads.*

JOE CUMMINGS

*During their periods of oc-
cupation, the Burmese and
Shan built many of the older
Northern Thai temples out
of wood, especially teak.*

The scheme presented at the end of this architecture section is the latest
one used by Thai art historians to categorise historical styles of Thai art,
principally sculpture and architecture (since very little painting prior to
the 19th century has survived).

A good way to acquaint yourself with these styles, if you are interested,
is to visit the National Museum in Bangkok, where works from each of
these periods are on display. Then, as you travel upcountry and view old
monuments and sculpture, you'll know what you're seeing, as well as
what to look for.

Since 1981, the Thai government has made the restoration of nine
key archaeological sites part of its national economic development plan.
As a result, the Fine Arts Department, under the Ministry of Education,
has developed nine historical parks *(ùthayaan pràwátisàat)*: Sukhothai
Historical Park and Si Satchanalai-Chaliang Historical Park in Sukhothai
Province; Ayuthaya Historical Park in Ayuthaya Province; Phanom Rung
Historical Park in Buriram Province; Si Thep Historical Park in
Phetchabun Province; Phra Nakhon Khiri Historical Park in Phetburi
Province; Prasat Hin Phimai Historical Park in Nakhon Ratchasima
Province; Muang Singh Historical Park in Kanchanaburi Province; and
Kamphaeng Phet Historical Park in Kamphaeng Phet Province.

*The construction and main-
tenance of spirit houses – to
pay respect to nature spirits
residing on any piece of
land chosen as a building
site – is a Thai custom that
predates Buddhism. The
interior of a spirit house is
usually decorated with
ceramic or plastic figurines
representing the property's
guardian spirits. The most
important of the figurines,
chaothii or 'place lord', embodies the spirit who reigns
over the property. Daily
offerings of rice, sacred
leaves and incense ensure
that the spirits are placated
and won't bring grief to the
human occupants.*

JOE CUMMINGS

## National Museums

Thailand's Fine Arts Department operates an excellent network of national museums in areas of the country known for historic art and archaeology. The museums typically offer a small exhibit of artefacts from around the country as well as more extensive displays featuring works of local provenance. At present visitors have a choice of 35 museums. Since 1996, most national museums have changed their opening schedules so that they are now open daily from 9 am to 5 pm; a few still follow the pre-1996 schedule, open 9 am to 5 pm from Wednesday to Sunday only. Those most worth visiting include the following listed below. Museums are in provincial capitals unless otherwise stated.

| Provincial Capital | Museum |
| --- | --- |
| Ayuthaya | Chao Sam Phraya National Museum |
| | Chan Kasem Palace |
| Bangkok | National Museum |
| | National Royal Barges Museum |
| | Wat Benchamabophit National Museum |
| Chiang Mai | Chiang Mai National Museum |
| Chiang Rai | Chiang Saen National Museum (Chiang Saen) |
| Kamphaeng Phet | Kamphaeng Phet National Museum |
| Kanchanaburi | Ban Kao Neolithic Museum (Ban Kao) |
| Khon Kaen | Khon Kaen National Museum |
| Lamphun | Lamphun National Museum |
| Lopburi | Lopburi National Museum |
| Nakhon Pathom | Phra Pathom Chedi National Museum |
| Nakhon Ratchasima | Mahawirawong National Museum |
| | Phimai National Museum (Phimai) |
| Nakhon Si Thammarat | Nakhon Si Thammarat National Museum |
| Nan | Nan National Museum |
| Phetburi | Phra Nakhon Khiri Historical Park |
| Phitsanulok | Phra Phuttha Chinnarat National Museum |
| | (at Wat Phra Si Ratana Mahathat) |
| Songkhla | Matchimawat National Museum |
| | Songkhla National Museum |
| Sukhothai | Ramkhamhaeng National Museum |
| | Sawanworanayok Museum |
| Suphanburi | U Thong National Museum |
| Surat Thani | Chaiya National Museum (Chaiya) |
| Ubon Ratchathani | Ubon National Museum |
| Udon Thani | Ban Chiang National Museum (Ban Chiang) |

JOE CUMMINGS

*In temples of the far north, doorways, windows and lintels are often decorated with colour glass mosaics, an ornamental technique of the Shan.*

JOE CUMMINGS

*The principle chedi at Wat Phra Mahathat in Nakhon Si Thammarat, displays Sinhalese influence in its simplistic hemispherical shape.*

JOE CUMMINGS

*These layered and stream-lined chedis at Wat Pho are 'Ratanakosin' or 'old Bangkok' monuments built to commemorate the first three kings of the Chakri royal dynasty.*

These parks are administered by the Fine Arts Department to guard against theft and vandalism, and to protect tourists from bandits at the more remote sites. The department even managed to get the famous Phra Narai lintel returned to Phanom Rung from the Art Institute of Chicago Museum in 1988. UNESCO has declared the ruins at Ayuthaya, Sukhothai, Si Satchanalai-Chaliang and Kamphaeng Phet as World Heritage Sites, which makes them eligible for UN funds and/or expertise in future restoration projects.

Additional areas of historical interest for art and architecture include Thonburi, Nakhon Pathom, Sawankhalok, Chiang Mai, Phitsanulok, Chiang Saen, Lamphun, Nan, Lopburi, Khorat, Surin, Buriram, Si Saket, Chaiya and Nakhon Si Thammarat. Some of the monuments at these sites have also been restored by the Fine Arts Department and/or by local interests. For more details on these historical parks and sites, see the relevant destination chapters in this book.

Recommended books on Thai art are AB Griswold's classic *Arts of Thailand* (Indiana University Press, 1960), the similarly titled *The Arts of Thailand* (Thames & Hudson, 1991) by Steve Van Beek and *A Concise History of Buddhist Art in Siam* (Tokyo, 1963) by Reginald Le May. Even the newest of these three books is out of date, since research in Thai art history has progressed rapidly in recent years, but they still serve as good introductions. There are several decent English-language books on various aspects of Thai art for sale at the national museums around Thailand (particularly at the Bangkok National Museum) and at the Ancient City (Muang Boran) office on Ratchadamnoen Klang Rd in Bangkok.

For information about the export of antiques or *objet d'art* from Thailand, see the Customs section in the Facts for the Visitor chapter.

## Modern Architecture

Modern Thai architects are among the most daring in South-East Asia, as even a short visit to Bangkok will confirm. Thais began mixing traditional Thai with European forms in the late 19th and early 20th centuries, as exemplified by Bangkok's Vimanmek Teak Mansion, the Author's Wing of the Oriental Hotel, the Chakri Mahaprasat next to Wat Phra Kaew, the Thai-Chinese Chamber of Commerce on Sathon Tai Rd and any number of older residences and shophouses in Bangkok or provincial capitals throughout Thailand. This style is usually referred to

*Bangkok's glossy World Trade Centre, a relatively new office and shopping complex containing the city's trendiest food centre.*

JOE CUMMINGS

RICHARD NEBESKY

as 'old Bangkok' or 'Ratanakosin'. The recently completed Old Siam Plaza shopping centre, adjacent to Bangkok's Chalermkrung Royal Theatre, is an attempt to revive the old Bangkok school.

In the 1920s and 1930s a simple Thai Deco style emerged, blending European Art Deco with functionalist restraint; surviving examples include the restored Chalermkrung Royal Theatre, the Royal Hotel, Ratchadamnoen Boxing Stadium, Hualamphong station, the GPO building and several buildings along Ratchadamnoen Klang Rd. According to world Deco expert Carol Rosenstein, Bangkok possesses the richest trove of Art Deco in South-East Asia, surpassing even former colonial capitals such as Jakarta, Kuala Lumpur, Singapore, Hanoi and Yangon (Rangoon).

Buildings of mixed heritage in the North and North-East exhibit French and English influences, while those in the South typically show Portuguese influence. Shophouses throughout the country, whether 100 years or 100 days old, share the basic Chinese shophouse *(hâwng tháew* in Thai) design in which the ground floor is reserved for trading purposes while the upper floors contain offices or residences.

During most of the post-WWII era, the trend in modern Thai architecture – inspired by the European Bauhaus movement – was towards a boring functionalism in which the average building looked like a giant egg carton turned on its side. The Thai aesthetic, so vibrant in prewar eras, almost entirely disappeared in this characterless style of architecture.

When Thai architects finally began experimenting again during the building boom of the mid-1980s, it was to provide high-tech designs like Sumet Jumsai's famous robot-shaped Bank of Asia on Sathon Tai Rd in Bangkok. Few people seemed to find the space-age look endearing, but at least it was different. Another trend affixed gaudy Roman and Greek-style columns to rectangular Art Deco boxes in what was almost a parody of western classical architecture. One of the outcomes of this fashion has been the widespread use of curvilinear banisters on the balconies of almost every new shophouse, apartment or condominium throughout Thailand, often with visually disturbing results.

More recently, a handful of rebellious architects have begun reincorporating traditional Thai motifs – mixed with updated western classics – in new buildings. Rangsan Torsuwan, a graduate of MIT (Massachusetts Institute of Technology), introduced the neoclassic (or neo-Thai) style, the best example of which is the new Grand Hyatt Erawan in Bangkok. Another architect using traditional Thai architecture in modern functions is Pinyo Suwankiri, who has designed a number of government buildings in Bangkok as well as the Cittaphawan Buddhist School in Chonburi.

A good book for those with a general interest in Thai residential design, interior or exterior, is William Warren's *Thai Style* (Asia Books), a coffee-table tome with excellent photography by Luca Invernizzi Tettoni.

*Detail from a typical 19th century Chinese shophouse in Southern Thailand, displaying elements of Portuguese design.*

JOE CUMMINGS

*Wat Doi Suthep's octagonal chedi in Chiang Mai is typical of the Lanna or Chiang Saen style (13th to 15th centuries).*

## Thai Art Styles

**Mon Art (formerly Dvaravati 6th to 11th C & Hariphunchai 11th to 13th C)**
Originating in Central, North and North-Eastern Thailand, Mon Art is an adaptation of Indian styles, principally Gupta.

**Lanna (formerly Chiang Saen) – 13th to 15th C**
Centred in Chiang Mai, Chiang Rai, Phayao, Lamphun and Lampang, Lanna is influenced by Shan/Burmese and Lao traditions and mixed with local styles.

*Mon (Dvaravati)*

*Lanna*

*Mon (Hariphunchai)*

**Sukhothai – 13th to 15th C**
Centred in Sukhothai, Si Satchanalai, Kamphaeng Phet and Phitsanulok, this style is unique to Thailand.

**Khmer Art – 7th to 13th C**
Centred in the Central and North-Eastern areas of Thailand, this style is characterised by post-classic Khmer styles accompanying the spread of Khmer empires.

**Peninsular Art (formerly Srivijaya period)**
Centred in Chaiya and Nakhon Si Thammarat, this style exhibits Indian influence 3rd to 5th C, Mon and local influence 5th to 13th C and Khmer influence 11th to 14th C.

*Sukhothai*

**Lopburi – 10th to 13th C**
This Central Thailand style is characterised by a mix of Khmer, Pala and local styles.

*Suphanburi-Sangkhlaburi*

**Ayuthaya A – 1350-1488**
Central Thailand style characterised by Khmer influences and gradually replaced by revived Sukhothai influences.

**Ayuthaya B – 1488-1630**
Central Thailand style with characteristic ornamentation distinctive of Ayuthaya style, eg crowns and jewels on Buddhas.

*Lopburi*

**Suphanburi-Sangkhlaburi (formerly U Thong) – 13th to 15th C**
A Central Thailand style combining Mon, Khmer and local styles. A prototype for the later Ayuthaya style.

**Ayuthaya C – 1630-1767**
Central Thailand style heralding baroque stage and then decline.

**Ratanakosin – 19th C to the present**
Bangkok style heralding a return to simpler designs and the beginning of European influences.

JOE CUMMINGS

*This graceful motif is found repeatedly in traditional Thai painting, sculpture and architecture. Its shape suggests an image of an unfurling lotus bud fused with that of a dying flame – symbolising the cooling effect of Buddhist Dhamma (teachings) upon the fires of passion.*

JOE CUMMINGS

*Red, green, orange and yellow are colours associated with Theravada Buddhist art and architecture in Thailand. The scales of this naga were created from plant materials for a float in Chiang Mai's annual flower festival.*

# Sculpture

On an international scale, Thailand has probably distinguished itself more in sculpture than in any other art form. Although the country hasn't produced any individually world-famous classical or modern sculptors, within the realm of Buddhist art Thai work is quite well known and well appreciated internationally.

Delicate clay and terracotta engravings found on cave walls and on votive tablets date as far back as the 6th century in Thailand, although if you count the bronze culture of Ban Chiang then sculptural endeavours began at least 4000 years ago. Historically the most commonly sculpted materials have consisted of wood, stone, ivory, clay and metal. Depending on the material, artisans use a variety of techniques – including carving, modelling, construction and casting – to achieve their designs.

Thailand's most famous sculptural output has been its bronze Buddha images, coveted the world over for their originality and grace. Nowadays historic bronzes have all but disappeared from the art market in Thailand. Most are zealously protected by temples, museums or private collectors.

*The 15m reclining Buddha at Bangkok's Wat Pho is one of the largest such images in the world. This posture represents the passing of Buddha from the human world into the realm of parinibbana – the ultimate release from the cycle of birth and death.*

JOE CUMMINGS

## Sculptural Symbolism

Buddha images throughout Thailand are for the most part sculpted according to strict iconographical rules found in Buddhist art texts dating to the 3rd century AD. The way the monastic robes drape over the body, the direction in which the hair curls, the proportions for each body part are all to some degree canonised by these texts. The tradition does leave room for innovation, however, allowing the various 'schools' of Buddhist art to distinguish themselves over the centuries.

One aspect of the tradition that almost never varies is the posture *(asana)* and hand position *(mudra)* of Buddha images. There are four basic postures and positions: standing, sitting, walking and reclining. The first three are associated with the daily activities of the Buddha, ie teaching, meditating and offering refuge to his disciples.

JOE CUMMINGS

*Phitsanulok's Chinnarat Buddha is one of Thailand's most revered and copied images. This famous bronze was cast in the late Sukhothai style, but its striking uniqueness comes from the flame-like halo around the head and torso; the halo turns up at the bottom to become naga heads to either side of the image. The head of this Buddha is a little wider than standard Sukhothai, giving the statue a very solid feel.*

**Bhumisparsa** In this classic mudra the right hand touches the ground while the left rests in the lap. This hand position symbolises the point in the Buddha's legendary life story when he sat in meditation beneath the banyan tree and vowed not to budge from the spot until he gained enlightenment. Mara, the Buddhist equivalent of Satan, tried to interrupt the Buddha's meditation by invoking a series of distractions (including tempests, floods, feasts and nubile young maidens); the Buddha's response was to touch the earth, thus calling on nature to witness his resolve. The bhumisparsa mudra is one of the most common mudras seen in Thai sculpture; it's also known as the *maravijaya* ('victory over Mara') mudra.

**Vitarka or Dhammachakka** When the thumb and forefinger of one hand (vitarka) or both hands (dhammachakka) form a circle with the other fingers curving outward the mudra evokes the first public discourse on Buddhist doctrine.

**Dhyana** Both hands rest palms up on the Buddha's lap, with the right hand on top, signifying meditation.

**Abhaya** One or both hands extend forward, palms out, fingers pointing upward, to symbolise the Buddha's offer of protection or freedom from fear to his followers. This mudra is most commonly seen in conjunction with standing or walking Buddhas.

**Calling for Rain** In Northern Thailand – especially in Chiang Rai, Nan and Phrae provinces – one occasionally sees a non-canonical mudra in which the arms of a standing image extend straight downward with the palms facing the thighs. Among Thai worshippers this pose symbolises a call for rain to nourish the rice fields.

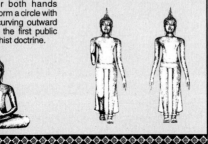

The Sukhothai style of Buddhist sculpture is considered by many art historians to be the most innovative and original of all. Often described as 'pneumatic' because of the slightly distended appearance of body and limbs, Sukhothai Buddhas are also noted for their elegance of proportion. The 'boneless' appearance of the finger, elbow, hand and leg joints symbolises the lack of physical tension achieved in nibbana.

JOE CUMMINGS

Naga Buddhas – images seated on a coiled, hooded and multi-headed serpent – were common in Thailand during the 8th-13th centuries. Such figures depict a climactic episode in the Buddha's life when he vowed not to budge from meditation until he had attained enlightenment. When heavy rains flooded the area around him, a huge cobra is said to have coiled itself beneath the Buddha to raise him above the floodwaters.

JOE CUMMINGS

JOE CUMMINGS

*Human-like from the waist up, ostrich-like from the waist down, the fabled kinnari (human-bird princess) represents celestial love and compassion. It's usually paired with its male counterpart, the kinnara.*

JOE CUMMINGS

*The wheel is a common motif in Buddhist iconography and can represent Buddhism's Eightfold Path (if it has eight sections or spokes), the cycle of dependent causation (12 spokes) or the lotus pedestal that grew beneath the Buddha as he meditated to attain enlightenment (more than 12 spokes).*

JOE CUMMINGS

*An astonishing variety of scenes from both secular and religious life embellish the inner walls of temples throughout Thailand. Windows and door panels were also decorated with motifs. This wall mural from Wat Phra Kaew displays the vivid colours and rich textural detail that characterise the paintings of the Ratanakosin or old Bangkok period.*

# Painting

As with sculpture, Thai painting traditions were mostly confined to religious art, in which the application of natural pigments to temple walls became the favoured medium. Always instructional in intent, such painted images ranged from depiction of the *jatakas* (life stories of the Buddha) and scenes from the Indian Hindu epic *Ramayana*, to elaborate scenes detailing daily life in Thailand. Lacking the durability of architecture and sculpture, pre-20th century religious painting is limited to very few surviving examples. However the study and application of mural painting techniques have been kept very much alive, and modern mural projects are undertaken practically every day of the year somewhere in the country. Influenced by international styles, a uniquely Thai movement in secular painting is also flourishing.

## Traditional Painting

Except for prehistoric and historic cave or rock-wall murals found throughout the country, not much formal painting predating the 18th century exists in Thailand. Presumably there were a great number of temple murals in Ayuthaya that were destroyed by the Burmese invasion of 1767. The earliest surviving temple examples are found at Ayuthaya's Wat Ratburana (1424), Wat Chong Nonsii in Bangkok (1657-1707) and Phetburi's Wat Yai Suwannaram (late 17th century).

Nineteenth century religious painting has fared better; Ratanakosin-style temple art is in fact more highly esteemed for painting than for sculpture or architecture. Typical temple murals feature rich colours and lively detail. Some of the finest are found in Wat Phra Kaew's Wihan Buddhaisawan (Phutthaisawan) Chapel in Bangkok and at Wat Suwannaram in Thonburi.

RICHARD NEBESKY

## Modern Painting

The beginnings of Thailand's modern art movement are usually attributed to Italian artist Corrado Feroci, who was first invited to Thailand by Rama VI in 1924. Feroci's design of Bangkok's Democracy Monument was inspired by Italy's fascist art movement of the 1930s – in Italy, he earned his reputation as a designer of war memorials under Mussolini. He also created the bronze statue of Rama I which stands at the entry to Memorial Bridge and several monuments around the city. Feroci founded the country's first fine arts institute in 1933, a school which eventually developed into Silpakorn University, Thailand's premier training ground for artists and art historians. In gratitude for his contributions, the Thai government gave Feroci the Thai name Silpa Bhirasri.

Today contemporary Thai painting is exhibited at a number of Bangkok and Chiang Mai venues. One of the most important modern movements in Thai art was an updating of Buddhist themes, begun in the 1970s by painters Pichai Nirand, Thawan Duchanee and Prateung Emjaroen. The movement has grown stronger since their early efforts combined modern western schemata with Thai motifs. One Bangkok gallery, the Visual Dhamma Art Gallery (off Soi Asoke), specialises in the display of modern Thai Buddhist art by a number of different artists.

Another important venue and source of support for modern art are Bangkok's luxury hotels. The largest collection of modern Thai painting anywhere in the world is found in the lobbies and public areas of the Grand Hyatt Erawan; the displays are changed regularly.

*Wat Phra Kaew in Bangkok features some of the finest examples of Thai temple mural painting from the 19th century.*

# Music

Throughout Thailand you'll find a wide variety of musical genres and styles, from the serene court music that accompanies classical dance-drama to the chest-thumping house music played at Bangkok's latest discos. Even in Thai monasteries – where music is proscribed by the *vinaya* or monastic discipline – the chanting of the monks exhibits musical qualities.

## Traditional Music

From a western perspective, traditional Thai music is some of the most bizarre on the planet, but to acquire a taste for it is well worth the effort. The classical Central Thai music is spicy, like Thai food, and features an

JOE CUMMINGS

*Chiang Mai has its own style of Northern folk music, played by small ensembles such as this.*

*A Northern Thai musician playing the phin, a banjo-like instrument plucked with a large plectrum.*

JOE CUMMINGS

incredible array of textures and subtleties, hair-raising tempos and pastoral melodies.

The classical orchestra is called the *pìi-phâat* and can include as few as five players or more than 20. Among the more common instruments is the *pìi*, a woodwind instrument which has a reed mouthpiece; it is heard prominently at Thai boxing matches. The pìi is a relative of a similar Indian instrument, while the *phin*, a stringed instrument whose name comes from the Indian *vina*, is considered native to Thailand. A bowed instrument similar to ones played in China and Japan is aptly called the *saw*. The *ranâat èk* is a bamboo-keyed percussion instrument resembling the western xylophone, while the *khlui* is a wooden flute.

One of the more amazing Thai instruments is the *khawng wong yài*, tuned gongs arranged in a semicircle. There are also several different kinds of drums, some played with the hands, some with sticks. The most important Thai percussion instrument is the *tà-phon* (or *thon*), a double-headed hand-drum which sets the tempo for the ensemble. Prior to a performance, the players make offerings of incense and flowers to the tà-phon, which is considered to be the 'conductor' of the music's spiritual content.

The pìi-phâat ensemble was originally developed to accompany classical dance-drama and shadow theatre but can be heard in straightforward performance these days, in temple fairs as well as concerts. One reason classical Thai music may sound strange to the western ear is that it does not use the tempered scale we have been accustomed to hearing since Bach's time. The standard Thai scale does feature an eight-note octave but it is arranged in seven full-tone intervals, with no semi-tones. Thai scales were first transcribed by Thai-German composer Peter Feit (Phra Chen Duriyanga), who also composed Thailand's national anthem in 1932.

In the North and North-East there are several popular reed instruments with multiple bamboo pipes, which function basically like a mouth-organ. Chief among these is the *khaen*, which originated in Laos; when played by an adept musician it sounds like a rhythmic, churning calliope. The funky *lûuk thûng* (or country; literally 'children of the fields') style, which originated in the North-East, has become a favourite throughout Thailand.

If you're interested in learning how to play traditional Thai instruments, contact the Bangkok YMCA (☎ (2) 286-1542/2580) to enquire about its weekly classes.

Recommended books include *The Traditional Music of Thailand* by David Morton, and *Thai Music* by Phra Chen Duriyanga (Peter Feit).

# Modern Music

Popular Thai music has borrowed much from western music, particularly its instruments, but still retains a distinct flavour of its own. Although Bangkok bar bands can play fair imitations of everything from Hank Williams to Madonna, there is a growing preference among Thais for a blend of Thai and international styles.

The best example of this is Thailand's famous rock group Carabao. Recording and performing for nearly 20 years now, Carabao is by far the most popular musical group in Thailand and has even scored hits in Malaysia, Singapore, Indonesia and the Philippines with songs like 'Made in Thailand' (the chorus is in English). This band and others have crafted an exciting fusion of Thai classical and lûuk thûng forms with heavy metal. These days almost every other Thai pop group sounds like a Carabao clone, and individual members of the original band are putting out their own albums using the now-classic Carabao sound.

Another major influence on Thai pop was a 1970s group called Caravan, which created a modern Thai folk style known as *phleng phêua chii-wít* or 'songs for life'. Songs of this nature have political and environmental topics rather than the usual moonstruck love themes; during the authoritarian dictatorships of the 1970s many of Caravan's songs were officially banned by the government. Though this band dissolved in the early 1980s, they re-form for the occasional live concert. The group's most gifted songwriter, Surachai, continues to record and release solo efforts.

Yet another inspiring movement in modern Thai music is the fusion of international jazz with Thai classical and folk motifs. The leading exponent of this newer genre is the composer and instrumentalist Tewan Sapsanyakorn (also known as Tong Tewan), whose performances mix western and Thai instruments. The melodies of his compositions are often Thai-based but the improvisations and rhythms are drawn from such heady sources as Sonny Rollins and Jean-Luc Ponty. Tewan himself plays soprano and alto sax, violin and khlui with equal virtuosity. When Tewan isn't touring internationally you may catch him and his extremely capable band Tewan Noveljazz at the Cool Tango and other Bangkok clubs.

Other notable groups fusing international jazz and indigenous Thai music include Kangsadarn and Boy Thai; the latter adds Brazilian *samba* to the mix. Thai instrumentation in world music settings are specialities of Todd Lavelle and Nupap Savantrachas, each of whom scored hits in Thailand during the late 1990s. Fong Nam, a Thai orchestra led by American composer Bruce Gaston, performs an inspiring blend of western and Thai classical motifs.

Cassette tapes of Thai music are readily available throughout the country in department stores, cassette shops and street vendors. The average price for a Thai music cassette is 55 to 75B. Western tapes are cheaper (about 30B each) if bootlegged, but the days of pirate tapes in Thailand are numbered now that the US music industry is enforcing international copyright laws. Licensed western music tapes cost 90 to 110B, still a good deal by the pricing standards of most western nations.

*A craftsman in Si Kaew, Roi Et Province, tests out a new khaen, the quintessential folk instrument in Isaan (North-Eastern Thailand).*

JOE CUMMINGS

# Theatre & Dance

Traditional Thai theatre consists of six dramatic forms: *khŏn*, formal masked dance-drama depicting scenes from the *Ramakian* (the Thai version of India's *Ramayana)* and originally performed only for the royal court; *lákhon*, a general term covering several types of dance-dramas (usually for non-royal occasions) as well as western theatre; *lí-khe* (likay), a partly improvised, often bawdy folk play featuring dancing, comedy, melodrama and music; *mánohra*, the Southern Thai equivalent of lí-khe, but based on a 2000 year old Indian story; *năng* or shadow plays, limited to Southern Thailand; and *lákhon lék* or *hùn lŭang* – puppet theatre.

## Khŏn

In all khŏn performances, four types of characters are represented – male humans, female humans, monkeys and demons. Monkey and demon figures are always masked with the elaborate head coverings often seen in tourist promo material. Behind the masks and make-up, all actors are male. Traditional khŏn is a very expensive production – Ravana's retinue alone (Ravana is the *Ramakian's* principal villain) consists of over a hundred demons, each with a distinctive mask. Perhaps because it was once limited to royal venues and hence never gained a popular following, the khŏn or *Ramakian* dance-drama tradition nearly died out in Thailand. Bangkok's National Theatre was once the only place where khŏn was regularly performed for the public; the

*Scenes from the Ramakian are played out in a khŏn performance at the Chalermkrung Royal Theatre in Bangkok.*

TAT

renovated Chalermkrung Royal Theatre now hosts weekly khŏn performances enhanced by laser graphics and high-tech audio.

Scenes performed in traditional khŏn (and lákhon performances) come from the *Ramayana*, the classic 'epic journey' tale with obvious archetypal parallels in the Greek epic the *Odyssey*, and the Greek myth of Jason and the Argonauts. The central story revolves around Prince Rama's search for his beloved Princess Sita, who has been abducted by the evil 10-headed demon Ravana and taken to the island of Lanka. Rama is assisted in his search and in the final battle against Ravana by a host of mythical half-animal, half-human characters including the monkey-god Hanuman. See the following Literature section for some details on the differences between the Indian *Ramayana* and the Thai *Ramakian*.

TAT

# Lákhon

The more formal *lákhon nai* (inner lákhon) was originally performed for lower nobility by all-female ensembles; today it's a dying art, even more so than royal khŏn. In addition to scenes from the *Ramakian*, lákhon nai performances may include traditional Thai folk tales; whatever the story, text is always sung.

*Lákhon nâwk* (outer lákhon) deals exclusively with folk tales and features a mix of sung and spoken text, sometimes with improvisation. Both male and female performers are permitted. Like khŏn and lákhon nai, performances are becoming increasingly rare. More common these days is the less refined *lákhon chatrii*, a fast-paced, costumed dance-drama usually performed at upcountry temple festivals or at shrines (commissioned by a shrine devotee whose wish was granted by the shrine deity). Chatrii stories have been influenced by the older *mánohra* theatre of southern Thailand (see the following Mánohra section).

*Lákhon phûut* (speaking lákhon) is the equivalent of western theatre based on the Greek model – all dialogue is spoken rather than sung. This is the most modern of Thailand's theatre traditions as well as the most popular in cities and larger towns.

*The costuming for Thai classical dancers – heavily embroidered silks, silver jewellery and the chadok or royal headdresses – can weigh up to several kilos. All dances are perfomed barefoot.*

# Lí-khe

In rural and small-town Thailand this is the most popular type of live theatre. Thought to have descended from drama-rituals brought to Southern Thailand by Arab and Malay traders, the first native public performance in Central Thailand came about when a group of Thai Muslims staged a lí-khe for Rama V (1868-1910) in Bangkok during the funeral commemoration of Queen Sunantha. Lí-khe grew very popular under Rama VI and has remained so ever since.

Most often performed at festivals by troupes of travelling performers, lí-khe presents a colourful mixture of folk and classical music, outrageous costumes, melodrama, slapstick comedy, sexual innuendo and up-to-date commentary on Thai politics and society. Farangs – even those who speak fluent Thai – are often left behind by the highly idiomatic, culture-specific language and gestures. Most lí-khe performances begin with the *àwk khàek*, a prelude in which an actor dressed in Malay costume takes the stage to pay homage to the troupe's teacher and to narrate a brief summary of the play to the audience. For true lí-khe aficionados, the coming of a renowned troupe is a bigger occasion than the release of a new James Bond sequel at the local cinema.

## Mánohra

Also known simply as *nora*, this is Southern Thailand's equivalent to
lí-khe and the oldest surviving Thai dance-drama. The basic story line
bears some similarities to the *Ramayana*. In this case the protagonist,
Prince Suthon (Sudhana in Pali), sets off to rescue the kidnapped
Mánohra, a *kinnari* or woman-bird princess. As in lí-khe, performers add
extemporaneous comic rhymed commentary – famed nora masters
sometimes compete at local festivals to determine who's the best rapper.

## Nãng

Shadow-puppet theatre – in which two-dimensional figures are manipu-
lated between a cloth screen and light source at night-time performances
– has been a South-East Asian tradition for perhaps five centuries.
Originally brought to the Malay peninsula by Middle Eastern traders, the
technique eventually spread to all parts of mainland and peninsular
South-East Asia; in Thailand it is mostly found only in the South. As in
Malaysia and Indonesia, shadow puppets in Thailand are carved from
dried buffalo or cow hides *(nãng* in Thai).

Two distinct shadow-play traditions survive in Thailand. The most
common, *nãng thálung*, is named after Phattalung Province, where it
developed based on Malay models. Like their Malay-Indonesian counterparts, the Thai shadow puppets represent an array of characters from
classical and folk drama, principally the *Ramakian* and *Phra Aphaimani*
in Thailand. A single puppet master manipulates the cutouts, which are
bound to the ends of buffalo-horn handles. Nãng thálung is still occasionally seen at temple fairs in the South, mostly in Songkhla and Nakhon

*The two-dimensional Thai
shadow puppets are deli-
cately carved from dried
bovine hide.*

TAT

JOE CUMMINGS

*Performers participating in a traditional dance at Bangkok's Erawan Shrine.*

Si Thammarat provinces. Performances are also held periodically for tour groups or visiting dignitaries from Bangkok.

The second tradition, *năng yài* (literally, 'big hide'), uses much larger cutouts, each bound to two wooden poles held by a puppet master; several masters (almost always male) may participate in a single performance. Năng yài is rarely performed nowadays because of the lack of trained năng masters and the expense of the shadow puppets. Most năng yài made today are sold to interior decorators or tourists – a well crafted hide puppet may cost as much as 5000B. In 1994, in order to celebrate the king's 50th year on the throne, the Fine Arts Department initiated a project to restore the original 180-year-old set of năng yài figures used by the Thai royal court. The project required the refurbishing of 352 puppets along with the creation of a hundred new ones to complete the royal set, known as Phra Nakhon Wai ('City-Shaking') – a tribute to the impact they had on audiences nearly two centuries ago. In addition to the occasional performance in Nakhon Si Thammarat or Bangkok, năng yài can be seen at Wat Khanon in Ratchaburi Province, where năng yài master Khru Chalat is passing the art along to younger men.

# Lákhon Lék

Like khŏn, lákhon lék or 'little theatre' (also known as hùn lŭang or 'royal puppets') was once reserved for court performances. Metre-high marionettes made of *koi* paper and wire, wearing elaborate costumes modelled on those of the khŏn, are used to convey similar themes, music and dance movements. Two Thai puppetmasters are required to manipulate each hùn lŭang – including arms, legs, hands, even fingers and eyes – by means of wires attached to long poles. Stories are drawn from Thai folk tales, particularly *Phra Aphaimani,* and occasionally from the *Ramakian.*

Hùn lŭang is no longer performed, as the performance techniques and puppet-making skills have been lost. The hùn lŭang puppets themselves are highly collectable; the Bangkok National Museum has only one example in its collection. Surviving examples of a smaller, 30 cm court version called *hùn lék* (little puppets) are occasionally used in live performances; only one puppeteer is required for each marionette in hùn lék.

Another Thai puppet theatre called *hùn kràbòk* (cylinder puppets) is based on popular Hainanese puppet shows. It uses 30 cm hand puppets that are carved from wood, and they are viewed from the waist up. Hùn kràbòk marionettes are still being crafted and used in performance.

# Literature

Of all classical Thai literature, the *Ramakian* is the most pervasive and influential in Thai culture. The Indian source – the *Ramayana* – came to Thailand with the Khmers 900 years ago, first appearing as stone reliefs on Prasat Hin Phimai and other Angkor temples in the North-East. Oral and written versions may also have been available; eventually, though, the Thais developed their own version of the epic, first written down during the reign of Rama I (1782-1809). This version contained 60,000 stanzas, about 25% longer than the Sanskrit original.

Although the main theme remains the same, the Thais embroidered the *Ramayana* by providing much more biographic detail on arch-villain Ravana (Dasakantha, called Thótsàkan or '10-necked' in the *Ramakian)* and his wife Montho. Hanuman the monkey-god differs substantially in the Thai version insofar as he is very flirtatious with females (in the Hindu version he follows a strict vow of chastity). One of the classic *Ramakian* reliefs at Bangkok's Wat Pho depicts Hanuman clasping a maiden's bared breast as if it were an apple.

Also passed on from Indian tradition are the many jatakas or life stories of the Buddha *(chaa-tòk* in Thai). Of the 547 jataka tales in the Pali tripitaka (Buddhist canon) – each one chronicling a different past life – most appear in Thailand almost word-for-word as they were first written down in Sri Lanka. A group of 50 'extra' stories, based on Thai folk tales of the time, were added by Pali scholars in Chiang Mai 300 to 400 years ago. The most popular jataka in Thailand is one of the Pali originals known as the Mahajati or Mahavessandara (Mahaa-Wetsandon in Thai), the story of the Buddha's penultimate life. Interior murals in the bòt or ordination chapel of Thai wats typically depict this jataka and nine others: Temiya, Mahaachanaka, Suwannasama, Nemiraja, Mahaasotha, Bhuritat, Chantakumara, Nartha and Vithura.

*The Ramakian provides the source for the most pervasive and potent classical literature in Thailand.*

The 30,000-line *Phra Aphaimani*, composed by poet Sunthorn Phu in the late 18th century, is Thailand's most famous classical literary work. Like many of its epic predecessors around the world, it tells the story of an exiled prince who must complete an odyssey of love and war before returning to his kingdom in victory.

## Poetry

During the Ayuthaya period, Thailand developed a classical poetic tradition based on five types of verse – *chan, kap, khlong, khlon* and *rai*. Each of these forms uses a complex set of strict rules to regulate metre, rhyming patterns and number of syllables. Although all of these poetic systems use the Thai language, chan and kap are derived from Sanskrit verse forms from India while khlong, khlon and rai are native forms. The Indian forms have all but disappeared from 20th century use. During the political upheavals of the 1970s, several Thai newspaper editors, most notably Kukrit Pramoj, composed lightly disguised political commentary in khlon verse. Modern Thai poets seldom use the classical forms, preferring to compose in blank verse or with song-style rhyming.

GLENN BEANLAND

## LANGUAGE

Learning some Thai is indispensable for travelling in the kingdom; naturally, the more language you pick up, the closer you get to Thailand's culture and people. Foreigners who speak Thai are so rare in Thailand that it doesn't take much to impress most Thais with a few words in their own language.

Your first attempts to speak the language will probably meet with mixed success, but keep trying. When learning new words or phrases, listen closely to the way the Thais themselves use the various tones – you'll catch on quickly. Don't let laughter at your linguistic forays discourage you; this amusement is an expression of their appreciation.

I would particularly urge travellers, young and old, to make the effort to meet Thai college and university students. Thai students are, by and large, eager to meet visitors from other countries. They will often know some English, so communication is not as difficult as it may be with shop owners, civil servants etc, plus they are generally willing to teach you useful Thai words and phrases.

For a complete selection of phrases, basic vocabulary and grammar for travel in Thailand, see the updated and expanded 3rd edition of Lonely Planet's *Thai phrasebook*.

Many people have reported modest success with *Robertson's Practical English-Thai Dictionary* (Charles E Tuttle Co, Tokyo), which has a phonetic guide to pronunciation with tones and is compact in size. It may be difficult to find, so write to the publisher at 2-6 Suido 1-chome, Bunkyo-ku, Tokyo, Japan.

More serious learners of the Thai language should get Mary Haas' *Thai-English Student's Dictionary* (Stanford University Press, Stanford, California) and George McFarland's *Thai-English Dictionary* (also Stanford University Press) – the cream of the crop. Both of these require that you know the Thai script. The US State Department's *Thai Reference Grammar* by RB Noss (Foreign Service Institute, Washington, DC, 1964) is good for an in-depth look at Thai syntax.

Other learning texts worth seeking out include:

*AUA Language Center Thai Course: Reading & Writing* (two volumes) – AUA Language Center (Bangkok), 1979

*AUA Language Center Thai Course* (three volumes) – AUA Language Center (Bangkok), 1969

*Foundations of Thai* (two volumes) – by EM Anthony, University of Michigan Press, 1973

*A Programmed Course in Reading Thai Syllables* – by EM Anthony, University of Hawaii, 1979

*Teaching Grammar of Thai* – by William Kuo, University of California at Berkeley, 1982

*Thai Basic Reader* – by Gething & Bilmes, University of Hawaii, 1977

*Thai Cultural Reader* (two volumes) – by RB Jones, Cornell University, 1969

*Thai Reader* – by Mary Haas, American Council of Learned Societies, Program in Oriental Languages, 1954

*The Thai System of Writing* – by Mary Haas, American Council of Learned Societies, Program in Oriental Languages, 1954

*A Workbook for Writing Thai* – by William Kuo, University of California at Berkeley, 1979

For information on language courses, see Thai Language Study under Courses in the Facts for the Visitor chapter.

### Dialects

Thailand's official language is Thai as spoken and written in Central Thailand. This dialect has successfully become the lingua franca of all Thai and non-Thai ethnic groups in the kingdom. Of course, native Thai is spoken with differing tonal accents and with slightly differing vocabularies as you move from one part of the country to the next, especially in a north to south direction. But it is the Central Thai dialect that is most widely understood.

All Thai dialects are members of the Thai half of the Thai-Kadai family of languages and are closely related to languages spoken in Laos (Lao, Northern Thai, Thai Lü), northern Myanmar (Shan, Northern Thai), north-western Vietnam (Nung, Tho), Assam (Ahom) and pockets of south China (Zhuang, Thai Lü).

Modern Thai linguists recognise four basic dialects within Thailand: Central Thai (spoken as a first dialect through Central Thailand and throughout the country as a second dialect); Northern Thai (spoken from

Tak Province north to the Myanmar border); North-Eastern Thai (north-eastern provinces towards the Lao and Cambodian borders); and Southern Thai (from Chumphon Province south to the Malaysian border). Each of these can be further divided into subdialects; North-Eastern Thai, for example, has nine regional variations easily distinguished by those who know Thai well. There are also a number of Thai minority dialects such as those spoken by the Phu Thai, Thai Dam, Thai Daeng, Phu Noi, Phuan and other tribal Thai groups, most of whom reside in the North and North-East.

## Vocabulary Differences

Like most languages, Thai makes distinctions between 'vulgar' and 'polite' vocabulary, so that *thaan*, for example, is a more polite everyday word for 'eat' than *kin*, and *sĭi-sà* for 'head' is more polite than *hŭa*. When given a choice, foreigners are better off learning and using the polite terms since these are less likely to lead to unconscious offence.

A special set of words, collectively called *kham râatchaasàp* (royal vocabulary), is set aside for use with Thai royalty within the semantic fields of kinship, body parts, physical and mental actions, clothing and housing. For example, in everyday language Thais use the word *kin* or *thaan* for 'eat', while with reference to the royal family they say *ráppràthaan*. For the most part these terms are used only when speaking to or referring to the king, queen and their children, hence as a foreigner you will have little need to learn them.

## Script

The Thai script, a fairly recent development in comparison with the spoken language, consists of 44 consonants (but only 21 separate sounds) and 48 vowel and diphthong possibilities (32 separate signs). Experts disagree as to the exact origins of the script, but it was apparently developed around 800 years ago using Mon and possibly Khmer models, both of which were in turn inspired by south Indian scripts. Like these languages, written Thai proceeds from left to right, though vowel signs may be written before, above, below, 'around' (before, above *and* after), *or* after consonants, depending on the sign.

Though learning the alphabet is not difficult, the writing system itself is fairly complex, so unless you are planning a lengthy stay in Thailand it should perhaps be foregone in favour of learning to actually speak the language. Where possible, place names occurring in headings in this book are given in Thai script as well as in roman script, so that you can at least 'read' the names of destinations at a pinch, or point to them if necessary.

## Tones & Pronunciation

In Thai the meaning of a single syllable may be altered by means of five different tones (in standard Central Thai): level or mid tone, low tone, falling tone, high tone and rising tone. Consequently, the syllable *mai*, for example, can mean, depending on the tone, 'new', 'burn', 'wood', 'not?' or 'not', eg *Mái mài mâi mâi măi* ('New wood doesn't burn, does it?'). This makes it rather tricky to learn at first, especially for those of us who come from non-tonal language traditions. Even when we 'know' what the correct tone in Thai should be, our tendency to denote emotion, verbal stress, the interrogative etc, through tone modulation often interferes with speaking the correct tone. Therefore the first rule in learning to speak Thai is to divorce emotions from your speech, at least until you have learned the Thai way to express them without changing essential tone value.

The following is a brief attempt to explain the tones. The only way to really understand the differences is by listening to a native or fluent non-native speaker. The range of all five tones is relative to each speaker's vocal range so there is no fixed 'pitch' intrinsic to the language.

1.  The level or mid tone is pronounced 'flat', at the relative middle of the speaker's vocal range. Eg: *dii* means good. (No tone mark used.)

2.  The low tone is 'flat' like the mid tone, but pronounced at the relative *bottom* of one's vocal range. It is low, level and with no inflection. Eg: *bàat* means baht (the Thai currency).
3.  The falling tone is pronounced as if you were emphasising a word, or calling someone's name from afar. Eg: *mâi* means 'no' or 'not'.
4.  The high tone is usually the most difficult for westerners. It is pronounced near the relative top of the vocal range, as level as possible. Eg: *níi* means 'this'.
5.  The rising tone sounds like the inflection generally given by English speakers to a question – 'Yes?' Eg: *sǎam* means 'three'.

If the tones were to be represented on a visual curve they might look like this:

| Mid | Low | Falling | High | Rising |

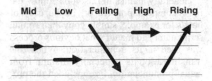

Words in Thai that appear to have more than one syllable are usually compounds made up of two or more word units, each with its own tone. They may be words taken directly from Sanskrit, Pali or English, in which case each syllable must still have its own tone. Sometimes the tone of the first syllable is not as important as that of the last, so for these I am omitting the tone mark.

Here is a guide to the phonetic system which has been used in the Language and special Thai Cuisine sections, as well as throughout the book when transcribing directly from Thai. It is based on the Royal Thai General System of transcription (RTGS), except that it distinguishes between: vowels of short and long duration (eg 'i' and 'ii'; 'a' and 'aa'; 'e' and 'eh'; 'o' and 'oh'); between 'o' and 'aw' (both would be 'o' in the RTGS); between 'u' and 'eu' (both 'u' in the RTGS); and between 'ch' and 'j' (both 'ch' in the RTGS).

### Consonants

**th**  as the 't' in 'tea'
**ph**  as the 'p' in 'put' (never as the 'ph' in 'phone')
**kh**  as the 'k' in 'kite'
**k**  as the 'k' in 'skin'; similar to 'g' in 'good', but unaspirated (no accompanying puff of air) and unvoiced
**t**  as the 't' in 'forty', unaspirated; similar to 'd' but unvoiced
**p**  as the 'p' in 'stopper', unvoiced and unaspirated (not like the 'p' in 'put')
**ng**  as the 'ng' in 'sing'; used as an initial consonant in Thai (practise by saying 'sing' without the 'si')
**r**  similar to the 'r' in 'run' but flapped (tongue touches palate); in everyday speech often pronounced like 'l'

All the remaining consonants correspond closely to their English counterparts.

### Vowels

**i**  as the 'i' in 'it'
**ii**  as the 'ee' in 'feet'
**ai**  as the 'i' in 'pipe'
**aa**  as the 'a' in 'father'
**a**  half as long as *aa*
**ae**  as the 'a' in 'bat' or 'tab' (for British English speakers, as in 'there')
**e**  as the 'e' in 'hen'
**eh**  as the 'a' in 'hate'
**oe**  as the 'u' in 'hut' but more closed
**u**  as the 'u' in 'flute'
**uu**  as the 'oo' in 'food', longer than *u*
**eu**  as the 'eu' in French 'deux', or the 'i' in 'sir'
**ao**  as the 'ow' in 'now'
**aw**  as the 'aw' in 'jaw' or 'prawn'
**o**  as the 'o' in 'bone'
**oh**  as the 'o' in 'toe'
**eua**  diphthong, or combination, of *eu* and *a*
**ia**  as 'ee-ya', or as the 'ie' in French *rien*
**ua**  as the 'ou' in 'tour'
**uay**  as the 'ewy' in 'Dewey'
**iu**  as the 'ew' in 'yew'
**iaw**  as the 'io' in 'Rio' or Italian *mio* or *dio*

On the following page are a few extra hints to help you with the alphabetic tangle.

- Remember that 'ph' is not meant to be pronounced like the 'ph' in phone but like the 'p' in 'pound' (the 'h' is added to distinguish this consonant sound from the Thai 'p' which is closer to the English 'b'). This can be seen written as 'p', 'ph', and even 'bh'.
- There is no 'v' sound in Thai; Sukhumvit is pronounced Sukhumwit and Vieng is really Wieng.
- 'L' or 'r' at the end of a word is always pronounced like an 'n'; hence, Satul is pronounced Satun, Wihar is really Wihan. The exception to this is when 'er' or 'ur' are used to indicate the sound 'oe', as in 'ampher' (amphoe). In the same way 'or' is sometimes used for the sound 'aw' as in 'Porn' (phawn).
- 'L' and 'r' are often used interchangeably in speech and this shows up in some transliterations. For example, naliga (clock) may appear as 'nariga' and râat nâa (a type of noodle dish) might be rendered 'laat naa' or 'lat na'.
- 'U' is often used to represent the short 'a' sound, as in tam or nam, which may appear as 'tum' and 'num'. It is also used to represent the 'eu' sound, as when beung (swamp) is spelt 'bung'.
- Phonetically all Thai words end in a vowel (a, e, i, o, u), semi-vowel (y, w), nasal (m, n or ng) or one of three stops: p, t and k. That's it. Words transcribed with 'ch', 'j', 's' or 'd' endings – like Panich, Raj, Chuanpis and Had – should be pronounced as if they end in 't', as in Panit, Rat, Chuanpit and Hat. Likewise 'g' becomes 'k' (Ralug is actually Raluk) and 'b' becomes 'p' (Thab becomes Thap).
- Finally, the 'r' in 'sri' is always silent, so that word should be pronounced 'sii' (extended 'i' sound, too).

## Transliteration

Writing Thai in roman script is a perennial problem – no truly satisfactory system has yet been devised to assure both consistency and readability. The Thai government uses the Royal Thai General System of transcription for official government documents in English and for most highway signs. However, local variations crop up on hotel signs, city street signs, menus, and so on in such a way that visitors often become confused. Add to this the fact that even the government system has its flaws. For example, 'o' is used for two very different sounds ('o' and the 'aw' in the Vowels section above), as is 'u' ('u' and 'eu' above). Likewise for 'ch', which is used to represent

two different consonant sounds ('ch' and 'j'). The government transcription system also does not distinguish between short and long vowel sounds, which affect the tonal value of every word.

To top it off, many Thai words (especially people and place names) have Sanskrit and Pali spellings but the actual pronunciation bears little relation to that spelling if romanised strictly according to the original Sanskrit/Pali. Thus Nakhon Si Thammarat, if transliterated literally, becomes 'Nagara Sri Dhammaraja'. If you tried to pronounce it using this Pali transcription, very few Thais would be able to understand you.

Generally, names in this book follow the most common practice or, in the case of hotels for example, simply copy their roman script name, no matter what devious process was used in its transliteration! When this transliteration is especially distant from actual pronunciation, I've included the pronunciation (following the system outlined in this section) in parentheses after the transliteration. Where no roman model was available, names were transliterated phonetically directly from Thai. Of course, this will only be helpful to readers who bother to acquaint themselves with the language – I'm constantly amazed at how many people manage to stay for great lengths of time in Thailand without learning a word of Thai.

Problems often arise when a name is transliterated differently, even at the same place. 'Thawi', for example, can be Tavi, Thawee, Thavi, Tavee or various other versions. Outside the International Phonetic Alphabet, there is no 'proper' way to transliterate Thai – only wrong ways. The Thais themselves are incredibly inconsistent in this matter, often using English letters that have no equivalent sound in Thai: Faisal for Phaisan, Bhumibol for Phumiphon, Vanich for Wanit, Vibhavadi for Wiphawadi. Sometimes they even mix literal Sanskrit transcription with Thai pronunciation, as in King Bhumibol (which is pronounced Phumiphon and if transliterated according to the Sanskrit would be Bhumibala).

Here are a few words that are commonly

spelt in a way that encourages mispronunciation among native English speakers:

| Common Spelling | Pronunciation | Meaning |
|---|---|---|
| bung | beung | pond or swamp |
| ko or koh | kàw | island |
| muang | meuang | city |
| nakhon or nakorn | nákhawn | large city |
| raja | usually râatchá if at the beginning of a word, râat at the end of a word | royal |

## Greetings & Civilities

When being polite, the speaker ends his or her sentence with *khráp* (for men) or *khâ* (for women). It is the gender of the *speaker* that is being expressed here; it is also the common way to answer 'yes' to a question or show agreement.

Greetings/Hello.
　*sawàt-dii (khráp/khâ)*　สวัสดี (ครับ/ค่ะ)
How are you?
　*pen yangai?*　เป็นยังไง?
I'm fine.
　*sabàay dii*　สบายดี
Thank you.
　*khàwp khun*　ขอบคุณ
Excuse me.
　*khăw thôht*　ขอโทษ

## Small Talk

you
　*khun* (for peers)　คุณ
　*thâan* (for elders, people in authority)　ท่าน
　*phŏm* (for men)　ผม (ผู้ชาย)
　*dii chăn* (for women)　ดีฉัน (ผู้หญิง)
What is your name?
　*khun chêu arai?*　คุณชื่ออะไร?
My name is ...
　*phŏm chêu ...* (men)　ผมชื่อ...
　*dii chăn chêu ...* (women)　ดีฉันชื่อ...
Do you have ...?
　*mii ... mǎi/... mii mǎi?*　มี...ไหม?
　　(..มีไหม?)

No
　*mâi châi*　ไม่ใช่
No?
　*mǎi/châi mǎi?*　ไหมฝ่?/ใช่ไหม?

go
　*pai*　ไป
come
　*maa*　มา
(I) like ...
　*châwp ...*　ชอบ...
(I) do not like ...
　*mâi châwp ...*　ไม่ชอบ...
(I) would like ... (+ verb)
　*yàak jà ...*　อยากจะ...
(I) would like ... (+ noun)
　*yàak dâi ...*　อยากได้...
when
　*mêu-arai*　เมื่อไร
It doesn't matter.
　*mâi pen rai*　ไม่เป็นไร
What is this?
　*níi arai?*　นี่อะไร?

## Language Difficulties

I understand.
　*khâo jai*　เข้าใจ
I don't understand.
　*mâi khâo jai*　ไม่เข้าใจ
Do you understand?
　*khâo jai mǎi?*　เข้าใจไหม?
a little
　*nít nàwy*　นิดหน่อย
What do you call this in Thai?
　*níi phaasǎa thai rîak wâa arai?*　นี่ภาษาไทยเรียกว่า
　　:ไร?

## Getting Around

I would like to go ...
　*yàak jà pai ...*　อยากจะไป...
Where is (the) ...?
　*... yùu thîi nǎi?*　...อยู่ที่ไหน?
airport
　*sanǎam bin*　สนามบิน
bus station
　*sathǎanii rót meh*　สถานีรถเมล์
bus stop
　*thîi jàwt rót pràjam*　ที่จอดรถประจำ

railway station
  *sathãanii rót fai*  สถานีรถไฟ
taxi stand
  *thîi jàwt rót tháek-sîi*  ที่จอดรถแท็กซี่
I would like a ticket.
  *yàak dâi tũa*  อยากได้ตั๋ว
What time will the train leave?
  *kìi mohng rót jà àwk?*  กี่โมงรถจะออกฯ
motorcycle
  *rót maw-toe-sai*  รถมอเตอร์ไซ
train
  *rót fai*  รถไฟ
bus
  *rót meh/rót bát*  รถเมล์/รถบัส
car
  *rót yon*  รถยนต์
straight ahead
  *trong pai*  ตรงไป
left
  *sáai*  ซ้าย
right
  *khwãa*  ขวา
far/not far
  *klai/mâi klai*  ไกล/ไม่ไกล

## Accommodation
hotel
  *rohng raem*  โรงแรม
guesthouse
  *bâan phák (kèt háo)*  บ้านพัก
    (เกสต์เฮาส์)

Do you have a room?
  *mii hâwng mãi?*  มีห้องไหมฯ
How much per night?
  *kheun-lá thâo rai?*  คืนละเท่าไรฯ
bathroom
  *hâwng náam*  ห้องน้ำ
toilet
  *hâwng sûam*  ห้องส้วม
room
  *hâwng*  ห้อง
hot
  *ráwn*  ร้อน
cold
  *não*  หนาว
bath/shower
  *àap náam*  อาบน้ำ

towel
  *phâa chét tua*  ผ้าเช็ดตัว

## Around Town
Can (I/we) change money here?
  *lâek ngoen thîi nîi dâi mái?*  แลกเงินที่นี่ได้ไหม
    มฯ
What time does it open/close?
  *raan poed muea rai/pit muea rai?*  ร้านเปิดเมื่อไร/ปิดเม
    ื่อไร
bank
  *thanaakhaan*  ธนาคาร
beach
  *hàat*  หาด
hospital
  *rohng phayaabaan*  โรงพยาบาล
market
  *talàat*  ตลาด
museum
  *phíphíth phan*  พิพิธภัณฑ์
post office
  *praisanii*  ไปรษณีย์
restaurant
  *ráan aahãan*  ร้านอาหาร
tourist office
  *sãmnák-ngaan thâwng thîaw*  สำนักงานท่อง
    เที่ยว

## Shopping
How much?
  *thâo raí?*  เท่าไรฯ
How much is this?
  *nîi thâo rai/kìi bàat?*  นี้เท่าไร (กี่บาท)
too expensive
  *phaeng pai*  แพงไป
cheap, inexpensive
  *thùuk*  ถูก

## Health & Emergencies
(I) need a doctor.
  *tâwng-kaan mãw*  ต้องการหมอ
chemist/pharmacy
  *ráan khãai yaa*  ร้านขายยา
Help!
  *chûay dûay*  ช่วยด้วย

Stop!
*yàt*  หยุด
Go away!
*bai sí*  ไปซิ
I'm lost.
*chãn lõng thaang*  ฉันหลงทาง

## Time
What's the time?
*kìi mohng láew?*  กี่โมงแล้วๆ
today
*wan níi*  วันนี้
tomorrow
*phrûng níi*  พรุ่งนี้
yesterday
*mêua waan*  เมื่อวาน

## Days of the Week
Sunday
*wan aathít*  วันอาทิตย์
Monday
*wan jan*  วันจันทร์
Tuesday
*wan angkhaan*  วันอังคาร
Wednesday
*wan phút*  วันพุธ
Thursday
*wan phréuhàt*  วันพฤหัส
Friday
*wan sùk*  วันศุกร์
Saturday
*wan são*  วันเสาร์

## Numbers
| | | |
|---|---|---|
| 0 | *sũun* | ศูนย์ |
| 1 | *nèung* | หนึ่ง |
| 2 | *sãwng* | สอง |
| 3 | *sãam* | สาม |
| 4 | *sìi* | สี่ |
| 5 | *hâa* | ห้า |
| 6 | *hòk* | หก |
| 7 | *jèt* | เจ็ด |
| 8 | *pàet* | แปด |
| 9 | *kâo* | เก้า |
| 10 | *sìp* | สิบ |
| 11 | *sìp-èt* | สิบเอ็ด |
| 12 | *sìp-sãwng* | สิบสอง |
| 13 | *sìp-sãam* | สิบสาม |
| 14 | *sìp-sìi* | สิบสี่ |
| 20 | *yîi-sìp* | ยี่สิบ |
| 21 | *yîi-sìp-èt* | ยี่สิบเอ็ด |
| 22 | *yîi-sìp-sãwng* | ยี่สิบสอง |
| 23 | *yîi-sìp-sãam* | ยี่สิบสาม |
| 30 | *sãam-sìp* | สามสิบ |
| 40 | *sìi-sìp* | สี่สิบ |
| 50 | *hâa-sìp* | ห้าสิบ |
| 100 | *ráwy* | ร้อย |
| 200 | *sãwng ráwy* | สองร้อย |
| 300 | *sãam ráwy* | สามร้อย |
| 1000 | *phan* | พัน |
| 10,0000 | *mèun* | หมื่น |
| 100,000 | *sãen* | แสน |
| 1,000,000 | *láan* | ล้าน |
| billion | *phan láan* | พันล้าน |

# Facts for the Visitor

## PLANNING
### When to Go
The best overall time for visiting most of Thailand vis-à-vis climate falls between November and March – during these months it rains least and is not so hot. Remember that temperatures are more even in the south, so the south makes a good refuge when the rest of Thailand is miserably hot (April to June). The north is best from mid-November to early December or in February when it begins warming up again. If you're spending time in Bangkok, be prepared to roast in April and do some wading in October – probably the two worst months, weather-wise, for the capital.

The peak months for tourist visitation are November, December, February, March and August, with secondary peak months in January and July. Consider travelling during the least crowded months of April, May, June, September and October if avoiding crowds of vacationers is your main objective and you want to take advantage of discounted rooms and other low-season rates. On the other hand it's not difficult to leave the crowds behind even during peak months if you simply avoid the most popular destinations (eg Chiang Mai, all islands and beaches).

### Maps
Lonely Planet publishes the 1:1,150,000 scale *Thailand travel atlas*, a 44 page country map booklet designed for maximum accuracy and portability. The atlas includes place names in both Thai and roman script, travel information in five languages (English, French, German, Spanish and Japanese), topographic shading and a complete geographic index. It has been spot-checked on the ground for accuracy and currency by this author. The atlas is readily available for around US$9 at many Bangkok bookshops as well as overseas.

Nelles Maps and Bartholomew Maps each publish decent 1:500,000 scale maps of Thailand with general topographic shading. The Bartholomew map tends to be more up-to-date and accurate than the Nelles.

A few years back Bartholomew, in conjunction with DK Book House, came out with the *Handy Map of Thailand*, an ingeniously folded 22 x 13 cm road atlas that can be opened like a book to any section without refolding the map – perfect for the backpacker. Although it's not 100% accurate, the convenience and durable coated paper make it a bargain at 90 to 100B – if you can find it. Other companies have issued similar – but much less readable and accurate – accordion maps.

Even better is the huge four-map set issued by Thailand's Highway Department (although also not 100% accurate). For less than 100B you get a very detailed, full-colour road map of the Central, Northern, North-Eastern and Southern regions. The 1:1,000,000 scale maps include information on 'roads not under control by the Highway Department' – many of the roads you may travel on in the north, for example. Bookshops sometimes sell this set for 200B, including a mailing tube, but the Highway Department on Si Ayuthaya Rd in Bangkok offers the set at the lower price. The mailing tube is not worth the extra 100B or more.

The Roads Association of Thailand publishes a large format, 48 page, bilingual road atlas called *Thailand Highway Map*. The atlas has cut the Highway Department maps to a more manageable size and includes dozens of city maps, driving distances and lots of travel and sightseeing information. It costs 100 to 120B depending on the vendor, but beware of inferior knock-offs.

The Lonely Planet atlas, or the maps from either the Highway Department or Bartholomew/DK Book House, are more than adequate for most people. Thai military maps, which focus on areas no larger than the *amphoe* (local district), come complete with elevations and contour lines. They are rarely offered for sale (DK Book House carries a few on occasion) but can sometimes be photocopied at university libraries.

**City Maps** *Bangkok Bus Map*, issued by Bangkok Guide Co, is the most accurate of the general Bangkok maps available. *Latest Tour's Guide to Bangkok & Thailand* has a bus map of Bangkok on one side and a fair map of Thailand on the other. Both maps are usually priced around 35B and are available at most Bangkok bookshops which carry English-language materials.

*Nancy Chandler's* city maps of Bangkok and Chiang Mai are also very useful. Revised annually, these colourful maps serve as up-to-date and informative guides, spotlighting local sights, noting local markets and their wares, outlining local transport and even recommending restaurants. Her maps are available at most English-language bookshops as well as some map stores abroad. (See Books later in this chapter as well as the Orientation section of the Bangkok chapter.)

**What to Bring**
Bring as little as possible – one medium-sized shoulder bag or backpack should do. Pack light, natural-fibre clothes, unless you're going to be in the North in the cool season, in which case you should have a pullover. Pick up a *phâakhamāa* (short Thai-style sarong for men) or a *phâasîn* (a longer sarong for women) to wear in your room, on the beach or when bathing outdoors. These can be bought at any local market (different patterns and colours can be found in different parts of the country) and the vendors will show you how to tie them.

The sarong is a very handy item; it can be used to sleep on or as a light bedspread, as a makeshift 'shopping bag', as a turban/scarf to keep off the sun and absorb perspiration, as a towel, as a small hammock and as a device with which to climb coconut palms – to name just a few of its many functions. It is not considered proper street attire, however.

Sunglasses are a must for most people and can be bought cheaply in Bangkok. Slip-on shoes or sandals are highly recommended – besides being cooler than lace-up shoes, they are easily removed before entering a Thai home or temple. A small torch (flashlight) is a good idea, as it makes it easier to find your way back to your bungalow at night if you are staying at the beach or at a remote guesthouse. A few other handy things include a compass, a plastic lighter for lighting candles and mosquito coils (lighters, candles and mossie coils are available in Thailand) and foam ear plugs for noisy nights.

Toothpaste, soap and most other toiletries can be purchased anywhere in Thailand. Sun block and mosquito repellent (except high-percentage DEET – see the Health section in this chapter) are available, although they can be expensive and the quality of both is generally substandard. If you plan to wash your own clothes, bring along a universal sink plug, a few plastic clothes pegs and three metres of plastic cord or plastic hangers for hanging wet clothes out to dry.

If you plan to spend a great deal of time in one or more of Thailand's beach areas, you might want to bring your own snorkel and mask (see Diving & Snorkelling under Activities in this chapter). This would save you having to rent such gear and would also assure a proper fit. Shoes designed for water sports, eg aquasocks, are great for wearing in the water whether you're diving or not. They protect your feet from coral cuts, which easily become infected.

If you plan on attempting computer modem communications in Thailand, see the Online Services section later in this chapter.

**SUGGESTED ITINERARIES**
See the special Thailand's Highlights section beginning on page 110 for a listing of the country's more outstanding attractions.

With the exception of the upper Southern peninsula from Phetburi to Surat Thani, Thailand's asymmetric shape doesn't lend itself to simple linear north-south or east-west routes. Depending on your interests and available time you might pick from the following circuits or combine parts of several to create your own travel route.

The standard Tourist Visa is valid for two months, though only a relatively small percentage of visitors stays that long. The 30 days granted to visitors from most countries who arrive without a visa usually suffices and can be extended by simply crossing the border into a neighbouring country and re-entering Thailand the same day.

The itineraries suggested below assume you want to see as much of the country as possible within a given interval. Another approach would be to spend more time in a few places rather than less time in many. Depending on your inclinations, you might decide to spend a full two weeks or even more just exploring the North. If you're into Isaan culture, a month spent in the towns and cities along the Maekhong River could be very rewarding. And of course some people choose to hole up on a beach or island for their entire stay.

Most visitors begin their journey in Bangkok. Depending on how much time you have available, you might want to save your Bangkok explorations until after you've seen other parts of the country. That way Bangkok won't seem quite so overwhelming as on first arrival. You'll also understand more about the Thai character after travelling around the country, and in Bangkok it pays to be a good judge of character – in order to separate the touts from the genuinely friendly.

## One Week
**Temples & Gulf Beaches** For a short Thailand sampler, start with a two day taste of Bangkok's heavily gilded temples and urban intensity, then flee toward the former royal capital of Ayuthaya to take in the 400 year old temple and palace ruins, right in the centre of the city. A day in Ayuthaya is enough for most people in a hurry. Transit back through Bangkok and head south-east to Ko Samet off the eastern Gulf of Thailand coast for two or three nights on this all-season island before saying farewell to Thailand. Substitute Jomtien Beach near Pattaya for Samet if your tastes run toward international-class hotels rather than simpler beach bungalows.

**Floating Markets, River Kwai & Lopburi** From Bangkok get an early morning start for one of the floating markets south-west of the city – Damnoen Saduak is the most well known but there are several others in the vicinity (see the Samut Sakhon & Songkhram provinces section in the Central Thailand chapter). Spend the night in Nakhon Pathom and take in the world's tallest Buddhist monument, Phra Pathom Chedi. Continue on to Kanchanaburi by bus or train to see the world-famous 'Bridge Over the River Kwai' and experience a fairly typical provincial Thai town. Return to Bangkok via Suphanburi and Lopburi, passing through the country's 'rice bowl' and stopping for a night in Lopburi to catch the Khmer and Thai temple ruins there.

## Two Weeks
**Northern Thailand** After completing one of the above circuits, take an overnight train (or fly) to Chiang Mai. Shop till you flop at the Chiang Mai Night Bazaar, sample the city's excellent Northern Thai cuisine, and decide whether to move north-west to Mae Hong Son or north-east to Nan. Both areas offer mountain trekking, national parks and hilltribe populations.

**North-Eastern Thailand** Start with one of the Central Thailand circuits, then take a train to Nakhon Ratchasima (Khorat) and visit the nearby Angkor-period ruins at Phimai. If you want to see more Khmer architectural splendour, make a short journey to the Phanom Rung Historical Park in Buriram Province.

Finish with a travel sector along the Maekhong River – from Chiang Khan to Si Chiangmai if you prefer small towns and villages, from Nakhon Phanom to Ubon Ratchathani if you like cities.

**Bangkok to the Malaysian Border** After you've had your fill of Bangkok – three or four days does the trick for most people who have two weeks to spend in the country – start your roll down the Malay peninsula with a two night, one day stopover in

Phetburi, a city of venerable late Ayuthaya-period temples and a hill-top royal palace.

After Phetburi, take your pick among the beaches at Cha-am, Hua Hin or in the vicinity of Prachuap Khiri Khan – all places where middle-class Thais like to vacation. And/or visit Khao Sam Roi Yot National Park, good for coastal and hillside hiking.

For some serious beach time, zero in on one or more of the three major islands off the coast of Chumphon and Surat Thani provinces – Ko Tao, Ko Pha-Ngan and Ko Samui – depending on your tastes (see Islands & Beaches in the special Thailand's Highlights section for descriptive summaries).

If you're ready for a little culture, sail back to the mainland and visit Chaiya (Srivijaya-era ruins and a world-famous meditation monastery) or Songkhla (Sino-Portuguese architecture and a national museum).

Follow with a night or two in Hat Yai to sample some of Thailand's best Chinese food outside Bangkok and to shop for Southern Thai or Malay textiles. For your entry into Malaysia, take the east coast route via Narathiwat for the best natural scenery, the west coast if you're in a rush to reach Penang or Kuala Lumpur.

## One Month

**Temples, Trekking & Beaches** In a month you can sample many of Thailand's major highlights. After a few days in Bangkok (or leave the city for the end), take a slow ride north with two night stopovers in Lopburi, Phitsanulok and Sukhothai to take in some of Thailand's most historic temple architecture, ancient as well as modern. From the latter head south-west to Mae Sot, amidst a zone of Karen and Burmese influence, and explore the less-than-beaten path – with waterfalls, trekking, rafting, working elephants – stretching from Um Phang to Mae Sariang. Continue north from Mae Sariang along the Mae Hong Son loop to Tha Ton on the Kok River, and either boat down the Kok to Chiang Rai or take a ride on a *sǎng tháew* (songthaew; pickup truck) through the mountains along the Myanmar border to the Yunnanese settlement of Mae Salong.

With roughly a week left in your itinerary, choose an island or beach along the upper Gulf of Thailand coast (Pattaya, Ko Samet, Ko Chang or Hua Hin) if you want to get there quickly via Bangkok, or pick from either the Andaman coast (Phuket, Khao Lak, Krabi, Trang) or lower Gulf coast (Ko Samui, Ko Pha-Ngan, Ko Tao) if you don't mind a longer trip by air, road or rail. If you like your beaches untrammelled it might be worth the extra effort to visit one of the national marine parks off the Andaman coast – Ko Tarutao, Ko Similan or Ko Surin.

If you have time while in the South, make a side trip to Khao Sok National Park, one of Thailand's most important refuges for tigers and rainforest.

**North by North-East** If beaches don't matter much to you, go for a major intake of culture and nature by starting with the Lopburi to Mae Salong route described above. From the latter continue eastward to Nan and Phrae, two of the North's less travelled provinces, then segue across to Loei Province for the Maekhong River loop from Chiang Khan to Ubon.

If there's time at the end of the latter, head into the interior to visit Prasat Hin Phimai and Phanom Rung. The more adventurous can substitute a whirl along the Cambodian border from Ubon to Aranya Prathet via Surin and Si Saket – provinces that are home to a number of smaller, lesser known Khmer temple sites. Or if temple-trekking has paled by this point, go hiking in Khao Yai National Park, one of Thailand's largest and oldest protected areas.

## Two Months

In two months you can combine two or three of the above itineraries to link Central, Northern, North-Eastern and Southern Thailand.

## TOURIST OFFICES

The Tourism Authority of Thailand (TAT) is a government-operated tourist information/promotion service attached to the prime minister's office, with several offices within the country and overseas. In 1991 TAT was granted regulatory powers for the monitoring of tourism-related businesses throughout Thailand, including hotels, tour operators, travel agencies and transport companies, in an effort to upgrade the quality of these services and to prosecute unscrupulous operators.

## Local TAT Offices

Ayuthaya – Si Sanphet Rd (temporary office), Ayuthaya 13000 (☎ (35) 246076/7; fax 246078)

Bangkok – 372 Bamrung Meuang Rd, Bangkok 10100 (☎ (2) 226-0060/72; fax 224-6221)

Cha-am – 500/51 Phetkasem Highway, Amphoe Cha-am, Phetburi 76 (☎ (32) 471005/8; fax 471502)

Chiang Mai – 105/1 Chiang Mai-Lamphun Rd, Chiang Mai 50000 (☎ (53) 248604/7; fax 248605)

Chiang Rai – Singkhlai Rd, Chiang Rai 57000 (☎ (53) 717433; fax 717434)

Hat Yai – 1/1 Soi 2, Niphat Uthit 3 Rd, Hat Yai, Songkhla 90110 (☎ (74) 243747; fax 245986)

Kanchanaburi – Saengchuto Rd, Kanchanaburi 71000 (☎ /fax (34) 511200)

Khon Kaen – 15/5 Prachasamoson Rd, Khon Kaen 40000 (☎ (43) 244498/9; fax 244497)

Lopburi – HM The Queen's Celebration Building (temporary office), Provincial Hall, Narai Maharat Rd, Lopburi 15000 (☎ (36) 422768; fax 422769)

Nakhon Nayok – Kh/1 084/23 Suwannason Rd, Nakhon Nayok 26000 (☎ (37) 312282; fax 312286)

Nakhon Phanom – 184/1 Sonthonvichit Rd, Nakhon Phanom 48000 (☎ (42) 513490/1; fax 513492)

Nakhon Ratchasima (Khorat) – 2102-2104 Mittaphap Rd, Nakhon Ratchasima 30000 (☎ (44) 213666; fax 213667)

Nakhon Si Thammarat – Sanam Na Meuang, Ratchadamnoen Klang Rd, Nakhon Si Thammarat 80000 (☎ (75) 346515/6; fax 346517)

Narathiwat (Sungai Kolok) – Asia Hwy 18 (temporary office), Sungai Kolok, Narathiwat 96120 (☎ (73) 612126; fax 615230)

Pattaya – 382/1 Chai Hat Rd, Pattaya Beach, South Pattaya 21000 (☎ (38) 427667; fax 429113)

Phitsanulok – 209/7-8 Surasi Trade Center, Borom Trailokanat Rd, Phitsanulok 85000 (☎ (55) 252742/3; fax 252742)

Phuket – 73-75 Phuket Rd, Phuket 83000 (☎ (76) 212213, 211036; fax 213582)

Rayong – 153/4 Sukhumvit Rd, Rayong 21000 (☎ /fax (38) 655420/1; fax 655422)

Surat Thani – 5 Talaat Mai Rd, Ban Don, Surat Thani 84000 (☎ (77) 288818/9; fax 282828)

Trat (Laem Ngop) – 100 Muu 1, Trat-Laem Ngop Rd, Laem Ngop, Trat 23120 (☎ /fax (38) 597255)

Ubon Ratchathani – 264/1 Kheuan Thani Rd, Ubon Ratchathani 34000 (☎ (45) 243770/1; fax 243771)

Udon Thani – Provincial Education Office (temporary office), Phosi Rd, Udon Thani 41000 (☎ /fax (42) 241968)

## Overseas TAT Offices

Australia – Level 2, National Australia Bank House, 255 George St, Sydney, NSW 2000 (☎ (02) 9247-7549; fax 9251-2465)

France – 90 Avenue des Champs Elysées, 75008 Paris (☎ 01 45 62 86 56; fax 01 45 63 78 88)

Germany – Bethmannstrasse 58, 60311 Frankfurt/Main (☎ (069) 295-704/804; fax 281-468)

Hong Kong – Room 401, Fairmont House, 8 Cotton Tree Drive, Central (☎ 2868-0732; fax 2868-4585)

Italy – Via Barberini 50, 00187 Rome (☎ (06) 487-3479; fax 487-3500)

Japan – 2nd floor, South Tower, Yurakucho Denki Bldg, 1-7-1 Yurakucho, Chiyoda-ku, Tokyo 100 (☎ (03) 3218-0337; fax 3218-0655)
5th floor, Hiranomachi Yachiyo Bldg, 1-18-13 Hiranomachi, Chuo-ku, Osaka 514 (☎ (06) 231-4434; fax 231-4337)

Korea – Room No 2003, 20th floor, Coryo Daeyungek Center Bldg 25-5, 1-ka, Chungmu-Ro, Chung-Ku, Seoul 100-706 (☎ (02) 779-5417; fax 779-5419)

Malaysia – c/o Royal Thai Embassy, 206 Jalan Ampang, Kuala Lumpur (☎ (03) 248-0958; fax 241-3002)

Singapore – c/o Royal Thai Embassy, 370 Orchard Rd, 238870 (☎ 235-7694; fax 733-5653)

Taiwan – 13th floor, Boss Tower, 109-111 Sung Chiang Rd, Taipei 104 (☎ (02) 502-1600; fax 502-1603)

UK – 49 Albemarle St, London W1X 3FE (☎ (0171) 499-7679; fax 629-5519)

USA – 5 World Trade Center, Suite 3443, New York, NY 10048 (☎ (212) 432-0433; fax 912-0920)
3440 Wilshire Blvd, Suite 1100, Los Angeles, CA 90010 (☎ (213) 382-2353/5; fax 389-7544)
303 East Wacker Drive, Suite 400, Chicago, IL 60601 (☎ (312) 819-3990/5; fax 565-0359)

## VISAS & DOCUMENTS
### Passports

Entry into Thailand requires a passport valid for at least three months from the time of entry. If you anticipate your passport expiring while you're in Thailand, you should obtain a new one before arrival or enquire from your government whether your embassy in Thailand (if one exists – see the list of foreign embassies further on) can issue a new one after arrival.

## Visa Categories

Whichever type of visa you have, be sure to check your passport immediately after stamping. Overworked officials sometimes stamp 15 or 30 days on arrival even when you hold a longer visa; if you point out the error before you've left the immigration area at your port of entry, officials will make the necessary corrections. If you don't notice this until you've left the port of entry, go to Bangkok and plead your case at the central immigration office.

Once a visa is issued, it must be used (ie you must enter Thailand) within 90 days.

**Transit & Tourist Visas** The Thai government allows 56 different nationalities to enter the country without a visa for 30 days at no charge. Shining exceptions are visitors with New Zealand, Swedish or South Korean passports, who may enter Thailand for up to 90 days without a visa!

Seventy-six other nationalities – those from smaller European countries like Andorra or Liechtenstein or from West Africa, South Asia or Latin America – can obtain 15 day Transit Visas on arrival upon payment of a 300B fee.

A few nationalities, eg Hungarians, must obtain a visa in advance of arrival or they'll be turned back. Check with a Thai embassy or consulate in advance to be sure if you plan arriving without a visa.

Without proof of an onward ticket and sufficient funds for one's projected stay any visitor can be denied entry, but in practice your ticket and funds are rarely checked if you're dressed neatly for the immigration check. See Exchange Control in the Money section in this chapter for the amount of funds required per visa type.

Next in length of validity is the Tourist Visa, which is good for 60 days and costs US$15. Three passport photos must accompany all applications.

**Non-Immigrant Visas** The Non-Immigrant Visa is good for 90 days, must be applied for in your home country, costs US$20 and is not difficult to obtain if you can offer a good reason for your visit. Business, study, retirement and extended family visits are among the purposes considered valid. If you want to stay longer than six months, this is the one to get.

## Visa Extensions

Sixty day Tourist Visas may be extended up to 30 days at the discretion of Thai immigration authorities. The Bangkok office (☎ (2) 287-3101) is on Soi Suan Phlu, Sathon Tai Rd, but you can apply at any immigration office in the country – every province that borders a neighbouring country has at least one. The usual fee for extension of a Tourist Visa is 500B. Bring along one photo and one copy each of the photo and visa pages of your passport. Normally only one 30 day extension is granted.

The 30 day, no-visa stay can be extended for seven to 10 days (depending on the immigration office) for 500B. You can also leave the country and return immediately to obtain another 30 day stay. There is no limit on the number of times you can do this, nor is there a minimum interval you must spend outside the country.

Extension of the 15 day, on-arrival Transit Visa is only allowed if you hold a passport from a country that has no Thai embassy.

If you overstay your visa, the usual penalty is a fine of 100B each extra day, with a 20,000B limit; fines can be paid at the airport or in advance at the Investigation Unit (☎ (2) 287-3129, ext 2204), Immigration Bureau, Room 416, 4th floor, Old Bldg, Soi Suan Plu, Sathon Tai Rd in Bangkok.

Extending a Non-Immigrant Visa very much depends on how the officials feel about you – if they like you then they will extend it. Other than the 500B extension fee, money doesn't usually come into it; neat appearance and polite behaviour count for more. Typically, one must collect a number of signatures and go through various interviews which result in a 'provisional' extension.

You may then have to report to a local immigration office every 10 to 14 days for the next three months until the actual extension comes through. Becoming a monk doesn't necessarily mean you'll get a longer visa either – again, it depends on whom you see and how they feel about you. (See also Tax Clearance below.)

Retirees 55 years of age or older may extend the 90 day Non-Immigrant Visa one year at a time. To do this you will need to bring the following documents to the Immigration Bureau: copy of passport, one photo, 500B extension fee, proof of financial status or pension. The requirement for the latter is that foreigners aged 60 or older must show proof of an income of not less than 200,000B per year (or 20,000B per month for extensions of less than a year); for those aged 55 to 59 the minimum is raised to 500,000/50,000B. According to immigration regulations, however: 'If the alien is ill, or has weak health and is sensitive to colder climates, or has resided in Thailand for a long period, and is 55-59 years of age, special considerations will be granted'.

Foreigners with Non-Immigrant Visas who have resided in Thailand continuously for three years – on one year extensions – may apply for permanent residency at Section 1, Subdivision 1, Immigration Division 1, Room 301, 3rd floor, Immigration Bureau, Soi Suan Phlu, Sathon Tai Rd (☎ (2) 287-3117/01); foreigners who receive permanent residence must carry an 'alien identification card' at all times.

### Re-Entry Permits & Multiple-Entry Visas
If you need to leave and re-enter the kingdom before your visa expires, say for a return trip to Laos or the like, apply at the immigration office on Soi Suan Phlu, Sathon Tai Rd, Bangkok. The cost is 500B; you'll need to supply one passport photo. There is no limit to the number of Re-Entry Permits you can apply for and use during the validity of your visa.

Thailand does not issue multiple-entry visas. If you want a visa that enables you to leave the country and then return, the best you can do is to obtain a visa permitting two entries; this will cost double the single-entry visa. For example, a two entry, 90 day Non-Immigrant Visa will cost US$40 and will allow you six months in the country, as long as you cross a border with immigration facilities by the end of your first three months. The second half of your visa is validated as soon as you recross the Thai border, so there is no need to go to a Thai embassy/consulate abroad. All visas acquired in advance of entry are valid for 90 days from the date of issue.

### Tax Clearance
Anyone who receives income while in Thailand must obtain a tax clearance certificate from the Revenue Department before they'll be permitted to leave the country. The Bangkok office (☎ (2) 281-5777, 282-9899) of the Revenue Department is on Chakkapong Rd not far from the Democracy Monument. There are also Revenue Department offices in every provincial capital.

Old Thai hands note: the tax clearance requirement no longer applies to those who have simply stayed in Thailand beyond a cumulative 90 days within one calendar year – this regulation was abolished in 1991. This makes it much easier for expats or other long-termers who live in Thailand on Non-Immigrant Visas – as long as they don't receive income. Hence there's no more hustling for tax clearance every time you make a visa trip to Penang or Vientiane.

### Onward Tickets
Thai immigration does not seem very concerned with whether or not you arrive with proof of onward travel. Legally speaking all holders of Tourist Visas or the no-visa 30 day stay permit are *supposed* to carry such proof. In all my years of frequent travel in and out of the kingdom, my onward travel documents haven't been checked a single time.

### Travel Insurance
A travel insurance policy to cover theft, loss and medical problems is strongly recommended. Though Thailand is generally a safe

country to travel in, sickness, accidents and theft do happen. There are a wide variety of policies and travel agents have recommendations. Check the small print to see if the policy covers any potentially dangerous sporting activities you may do, such as diving or trekking, and make sure that it adequately covers your valuables. A few credit cards offer limited, sometimes full, travel insurance to the holder. See the Health section later in this chapter for more information on health insurance.

## Driving Licence & Permits
An international driving permit is necessary for any visitor who intends to drive a motorised vehicle while in Thailand. These are usually available from motoring organisations, such as AAA (USA) or BAA (UK), in your home country. If you'd like to obtain a Thai driving licence, see the Driving Permits section of the Getting Around chapter for details.

## Hostel Card
Hostelling International (HI; formerly known as International Youth Hostel Federation) issues a membership card that will allow you to stay at Thailand's member hostels. Without such a card or the purchase of a temporary membership you won't be admitted. See the Accommodation section further on for more details on Thai hostels.

Memberships may be purchased at any member hostel worldwide or from the head office: Hostelling International, 9 Guessens Rd, Welwyn Garden City, Hertfordshire AL8 6QW, UK.

## Student Cards
The International Student Identity Card (ISIC), issued by the International Student Travel Confederation (☎ 3393-9303; fax 3393-7377), Box 9048, DK1000, Copenhagen, Denmark, can be used as identification to qualify for the rare student discount at some museums in Thailand. It's probably not worth getting just for a visit to Thailand, but if you already have one, or plan to use one elsewhere in Asia, then bring it along.

## Photocopies
It's a good idea to keep photocopies of all vital documents – passport data page, credit card numbers, airline tickets, travellers' cheque serial numbers and so on – in a separate place from the originals. In case you lose the originals, replacement will be much easier to arrange if you can provide issuing agencies with copies. You might consider leaving extra copies of these documents with someone at home or in a safe place in Bangkok or other point of entry.

## EMBASSIES
### Thai Embassies Abroad
To apply for a visa, contact the Royal Thai embassy (or consulate) in any of the following countries. In many cases, if you apply in person you may receive a Tourist or Non-Immigrant Visa on the day of application; by mail it generally takes anywhere from two to six weeks.

Australia – 111 Empire Circuit, Yarralumla, Canberra, ACT 2600 (☎ (06) 273-1149/2937)
Canada – 180 Island Park Drive, Ottawa, Ontario K1Y OA2 (☎ (613) 722-4444)
China – 40 Guanghua Lu, Beijing 100600 (☎ (010) 532-1903)
France – 8 Rue Greuze, 75116 Paris (☎ 01 47 27 80 79, 01 47 24 32 22)
Germany – Ubierstrasse 65, 53173 Bonn (☎ (0228) 355-065/8)
Hong Kong – 8th floor, Fairmont House, 8 Cotton Tree Drive, Central (☎ 2521-6481/2)
India – 56-N Nyaya Marg, Chanakyapuri, New Delhi, 110021 (☎ (11) 60-5679, 60-7289)
Indonesia – Jalan Imam Bonjol 74, Jakarta (☎ (021) 390-4052/3/4)
Italy – Via Bertoloni 26 B, 00197 Rome (☎ (06) 807-8955)
Japan – 3-14-6 Kami-Osaki, Shinagawa-ku, Tokyo 141 (☎ (03) 3441-1386/7)
Laos – Route Phonkheng, Vientiane Poste 128 (☎ (21) 214582/3)
Malaysia – 206 Jalan Ampang, Kuala Lumpur (☎ (03) 248-8222/350)
Myanmar (Burma) – 91 Pyi Rd, Yangon (☎ (01) 282471, 276555)
Nepal – Jyoti Kendra Bldg, Thapathali, Kathmandu (☎ (01) 213-910/2)
Netherlands – Buitenrustweg 1, 2517 KD The Hague (☎ (070) 345-2088/9703)
New Zealand – 2 Cook St, Karori, Wellington 5 (☎ (04) 476-8618/9)

Philippines – 107B Rada St, Legaspi Village, Makati, Metro Manila (☎ (02) 810-3833, 815-4219)

Singapore – 370 Orchard Rd (☎ 235-4175, 737-2158/3372)

Sweden – 5th floor, Sandhamnsgatan 36, Stockholm (☎ (08) 667-2160/8090)

Switzerland – 3rd floor, Eigerstrasse 60, 3007 Bern (☎ (031) 372-2281/2)

UK – 29-30 Queen's Gate, London SW7 5JB (☎ (0171) 589-0173/2944)

USA – 1024 Wisconsin Ave NW, Washington, DC 20007 (☎ (202) 944-3600)

Vietnam – 63-65 Hoang Dieu St, Hanoi (☎ (04) 235-092/94)

## Foreign Embassies in Thailand

Bangkok is a good place to collect visas for onward travel, and most countries have diplomatic representation in Bangkok. The visa sections of most embassies and consulates are open from around 8.30 to 11.30 am, Monday to Friday only (call first to be sure).

If you're heading on to India you'll definitely need a visa, and if you're going to Nepal it's highly advisable to have one even though they can be obtained on arrival.

For travel to Myanmar or Laos you'll also need a visa; Myanmar visas are available direct from the Myanmar embassy, while Lao visas usually require the services of a travel agent. However, as part of an experimental programme, Lao visas can be obtained from the Lao consulate in the North-Eastern Thai town of Khon Kaen within three days. Visas are available on arrival in Malaysia, Cambodia and Vietnam.

Countries with diplomatic representation in Bangkok include:

Argentina – 20/85 Soi 49, Sukhumvit Rd (☎ (2) 259-0401/2)

Australia – 37 Sathon Tai Rd (☎ (2) 287-2680)

Austria – 14 Soi Nantha, Sathon Tai Rd (☎ (2) 254-6970)

Bangladesh – 727 Soi 55, Sukhumvit Rd (☎ (2) 392-9437)

Belgium – 44 Soi Phiphat, Silom Rd (☎ (2) 236-0150, 233-9370)

Brazil – 239 Soi Sarasin, Lumphini (☎ (2) 262-6043/23)

Brunei – 19 Soi 26, Sukhumvit Rd (☎ (2) 260-5884)

Canada – Boonmitr Bldg, 138 Silom Rd (☎ (2) 234-1561/8, 237-4126)

Chile – 18th floor, Bangkok Bank Bldg, 333 Silom Rd (☎ (2) 233-2177)

China – 57 Ratchadaphisek Rd (☎ (2) 245-7032/49)

Colombia – c/o TTMC Ltd, Than Settakij Bldg, 222 Vibhavadi Rangsit Rd (☎ (2) 278-4386)

Denmark – 10 Soi Attakanprasit, Sathon Tai Rd (☎ (2) 213-2021)

Egypt – 49 Soi Ruam Rudi, Ploenchit Rd (☎ (2) 252-6139, 253-0161)

Finland – 16th floor, Amarin Tower, 500 Ploenchit Rd (☎ (2) 256-9306/9)

France – 35 Customs House Lane, Charoen Krung Rd (☎ (2) 234-0950/6); consular section (visas): 29 Sathon Tai Rd (☎ (2) 213-2181/4)

Germany – 9 Sathon Tai Rd (☎ (2) 286-4223/7, 213-2331/6)

Greece – 3rd floor, Thanakul Bldg, Rama IX Rd (☎ (2) 251-5111)

Hungary – 28 Soi Sukchai, Sukhumvit Rd (☎ (2) 391-2002/3)

India – 46 Soi Prasanmit (Soi 23), Sukhumvit Rd (☎ (2) 258-0300/6)

Indonesia – 600-602 Phetburi Rd (☎ (2) 252-3135/40)

Iran – 602 Sukhumvit Rd (between sois 22 and 24) (☎ (2) 259-0611/3)

Iraq – 47 Pradipat Rd (☎ (2) 278-5335/8)

Ireland – 205 United Flour Mill Bldg, Ratchawong Rd (☎ (2) 223-0876)

Israel – 31 Soi Lang Suan, Ploenchit Rd (☎ (2) 252-3131/4)

Italy – 399 Nang Linchi Rd (☎ (2) 286-4844/6)

Japan – 1674 New Phetburi Rd (☎ (2) 252-6151/9)

Kenya – 568 Soi Panit Anan, Sukhumvit Rd, Khlong Tan (☎ (2) 391-8294)

Korea (North) – 81 Soi Ari 7, Phahonyothin Rd (☎ (2) 278-5118)

Korea (South) – 23 Thiam-Ruammit Rd, Huay Khwang, Sam Saen Nok (☎ (2) 247-7537)

Laos – 193 Sathon Tai Rd (☎ (2) 254-6963, 213-2573)

Malaysia – 35 Sathon Tai Rd (☎ (2) 286-1390/2)

Mexico – 44/7-8 Convent Rd (☎ (2) 235-6367, 234-0935)

Myanmar (Burma) – 132 Sathon Neua Rd (☎ (2) 233-2237, 234-4698)

Nepal – 189 Soi Phuengsuk (Soi 71), Sukhumvit Rd (☎ (2) 391-7240)

Netherlands – 106 Withayu Rd (☎ (2) 254-7701, 252-6103/5)

New Zealand – 93 Withayu Rd (☎ (2) 251-8165)

Norway – 11th floor, Bank of America Bldg, Withayu Rd (☎ (2) 253-0390)

Pakistan – 31 Soi Nana Neua (Soi 3), Sukhumvit Rd (☎ (2) 253-0288/9)

Peru – 10 Soi 3, Seri 2 Rd, Soi Ramkhamhaeng 24, Hua Mak (☎ (2) 314-1054)

Philippines – 760 Sukhumvit Rd (☎ (2) 259-0139)

Poland – 61 Soi 23, Sukhumvit Rd (☎ (2) 258-4112/3)

Portugal – 26 Captain Bush Lane, Si Phraya Rd (☎ (2) 234-0372, 233-7610)

Russia – 108 Sathon Neua Rd (☎ (2) 234-9824/2012)

Saudi Arabia – Sathon Thani Bldg, 90 Sathon Neua Rd (☎ (2) 237-1938, 235-0875/8)

Singapore – 129 Sathon Tai Rd (☎ (2) 286-2111/1434)

South Africa – 6th floor, Park Place, 231 Soi Sarasin (☎ (2) 253-8473)

Spain – 93 Withayu Rd (☎ (2) 252-6112)

Sri Lanka – 48/3 Soi 1, Sukhumvit Rd (☎ (2) 251-2789)

Sweden – 20th floor, Pacific Place, 140 Sukhumvit Rd (☎ (2) 254-4954/55)

Switzerland – 35 Withayu Rd (☎ (2) 252-8992/4, 253-0156/60)

Taiwan – Far East Trade Office, 10th floor, Kian Gwan Bldg, 140 Withayu Rd (☎ (2) 251-9274/6)

Turkey – 153/2 Soi Mahatlekluang 1, Ratchadamri Rd (☎ (2) 251-2987/8)

UK – 1031 Ploenchit Rd (☎ (2) 253-0191/9)

USA – 95 Withayu Rd (☎ (2) 252-5040/9)

Vietnam – 83/1 Withayu Rd (☎ (2) 251-7201/3)

## CUSTOMS

Like most countries, Thailand prohibits the import of illegal drugs, firearms and ammunition (unless registered in advance with the Police Department) and pornographic media. A reasonable amount of clothing for personal use, toiletries and professional instruments are allowed in duty-free, as are one still or one movie/video camera with five rolls of still film or three rolls of movie film or videotape. Up to 200 cigarettes can be brought into the country without paying duty, or for other smoking materials a total of up to 250g. One litre of wine or spirits is allowed in duty-free.

Electronic goods like personal stereos, calculators and computers can be a problem if the customs officials have reason to believe you're bringing them in for resale. As long as you don't carry more than one of each, you should be OK. Occasionally, customs will require you to leave a hefty deposit for big-ticket items (eg a lap-top computer or midi-component stereo) which is refunded when you leave the country with the item in question. If you make the mistake of saying you're just passing through and don't plan to use the item while in Thailand, they may ask you to leave it with the Customs Department until you leave the country.

For information on currency import or export, see the Money section.

### Antiques & Art

Upon leaving Thailand, you must obtain an export licence for any antiques or objects of art you want to take with you. An antique is any 'archaic movable property whether produced by man or by nature, any part of ancient structure, human skeleton or animal carcass, which by its age or characteristic of production or historical evidence is useful in the field of art, history or archaeology'. An object of art is a 'thing produced by craftsmanship and appreciated as being valuable in the field of art'. Obviously these are very sweeping definitions, so if in doubt go to the Fine Arts Department for inspection and licensing.

Application can be made by submitting two front-view photos of the object(s) (no more than five objects to a photo) and a photocopy of your passport, along with the object(s) in question, to one of three locations in Thailand: the Bangkok National Museum, the Chiang Mai National Museum or the Songkhla National Museum. You need to allow three to five days for the application and inspection process to be completed.

Thailand has special regulations for taking a Buddha or other deity image (or any part thereof) out of the country. These require not only a licence from the Fine Arts Department but a permit from the Ministry of Commerce as well. The one exception to this are the small Buddha images (phrá phim or phrá khreûang) that are meant to be worn on a chain around the neck; these may be exported without a licence as long as the reported purpose is religious.

### Temporary Vehicle Importation

Passenger vehicles (car, van, truck or motorcycle) can be brought into Thailand for tourist purposes for up to six months. Documents needed for the crossing are a valid international driving licence, passport vehicle registration papers (in the case of a borrowed or hired vehicle, authorisation from the owner) and a cash or bank guarantee equal to the value of the vehicle plus 20%. (For entry through Khlong Toey Port or Bangkok international airport, this means a letter of bank credit; for overland crossings via Malaysia a 'self-guarantee' filled in at the border is sufficient.)

## Home Country Customs
Be sure to check the import regulations in your home country before bringing or sending back a large quantity or high valued Thailand purchases. The limit varies from country to country; the USA, for example, allows US$400 worth of foreign-purchased goods to enter without duty (with no limit on handicrafts and unset gems), while in Australia the total value is limited to A$400.

## MONEY
## Costs
Food and accommodation outside Bangkok are generally quite inexpensive and even in Bangkok they are fairly cheap, especially considering the value vis-à-vis other countries in South and South-East Asia.

Outside Bangkok, budget-squeezers should be able to get by on 200B per day if they really keep watch on their expenses. This estimate includes basic guesthouse accommodation, food, nonalcoholic beverages and local transport, but not film, souvenirs, tours, long-distance transport or vehicle hire. Add another 50 to 75B per day for every large beer (25 to 35B for small bottles) you drink.

Expenses vary, of course, from place to place; where there are high concentrations of budget travellers, for example, accommodation tends to be cheaper and food more expensive. With experience, you can travel in Thailand for even less if you live like a Thai of modest means and learn to speak the language.

Someone with more money to spend will find that for around 350 to 500B per day, life can be quite comfortable; cleaner and quieter accommodation is easier to find once you pass the 200B-a-night zone in room rates. Of course, a 50B guesthouse room with a mattress on the floor and responsive management is better than a poorly maintained 350B room with air-con that won't turn off and a noisy all-night card game next door.

In Bangkok there's almost no limit to the amount you *could* spend, but if you live frugally, avoid the tourist ghettos and ride the public bus system you can get by on only slightly more than you would spend in the provinces. Where you stay in Bangkok is of primary concern, as accommodation is generally a good deal more expensive here than upcountry. Typically, the visitor spends over 300B per day in Bangkok just for accommodation – this is generally the absolute minimum for air-con (in a twin room). On the other hand, if you can do without air-con, accommodation can be found in Bangkok for as little as 60B per person. But the noise, heat and pollution in Bangkok may drive many budget travellers to seek more comfort than they might otherwise need upcountry.

Those seeking international-class accommodation and food will spend at least 1500B a day for a room with all the modern amenities

| Living Costs in Thailand | | | |
|---|---|---|---|
| *Average Daily Cost per Person* | *Low Budget* | *Medium Budget* | *High Budget* |
| Accommodation | 60 to 100B | 250 to 500B | 600B up |
| Food | 75 to 100B | 300B | 1500B up |
| Local transport | 25B | 75 to 100B | 500B up |
| Incidentals (admission fees, personal items) | 40B | 100B | 200B up |

– IDD phone, 24 hour hot water and air-conditioning, carpeting, fitness centre and all-night room service. Such hotels are found only in the major cities and resort areas.

Food is somewhat more expensive in Bangkok than in the provinces. However, in Thonburi (Bangkok's 'Left Bank'), where I lived for some time, many dishes are often cheaper than they are upcountry, due to the availability of fresh ingredients. This is also true for the working-class districts on the Bangkok side, such as Khlong Toey or Makkasan.

Bangkok is the typical 'primate city' cited by sociologists, meaning that most goods produced by the country as a whole end up in Bangkok. The glaring exception is western food, which Bangkok has more of than anywhere else in the kingdom but charges the most for. Eat only Thai and Chinese food if you're trying to spend as little as possible. After all, why go to Thailand to eat steak and potatoes?

### Carrying Money

Give some thought in advance to how you're going to carry your financial media – whether travellers' cheques, cash, credit and debit cards, or some combination of these. Many travellers favour hidden pouches that can be worn beneath clothing. Hip-pocket wallets are easy marks for thieves. Pickpockets work markets and crowded buses throughout the country, so it pays to keep your money concealed. See Dangers & Annoyances later in this chapter for more on petty crime.

It's a good idea not to keep all your money in one place; keep an 'emergency' stash well concealed in a piece of luggage separate from other money. Long-term travellers might even consider renting a safety deposit box at a bank in Bangkok or other major cities. Keep your onward tickets, a copy of your passport, a list of all credit card numbers and some money in the box just in case all your belongings are stolen while you're on the road. It's not common, but it does happen.

### Currency

The basic unit of Thai currency is the *baht*. There are 100 *satang* in one baht; coins include 25 satang and 50 satang pieces and baht in 1B, 5B and 10B coins. Older coins exhibit Thai numerals only, while newer coins have Thai and roman numerals. At the time of writing, 1B coins came in three sizes: only the middle size works in public pay phones! Likewise, 5B coins come in three sizes: a large one with a Thai numeral only and two smaller coins that have Thai and roman numerals (one of the smaller 5B coins has nine inset edges along the circumference). The copper-and-silver 10B coin has Thai and Arabic numerals. Eventually Thailand will phase out the older coins, but in the meantime, counting out change can be confusing.

Twenty-five satang equals one *saleng* in colloquial Thai, so if you're quoted a price of six saleng in the market, say, for a very small bunch of bananas or a bag of peanuts, this means 1.50B. The term is becoming increasingly rare as ongoing inflation makes purchases of less than 1B or 2B almost extinct.

Paper currency comes in denominations of 10B (brown), 20B (green), 50B (blue), 100B (red), 500B (purple) and 1000B (beige). A 10,000B bill is on the way. The 10B bills are being phased out in favour of the relatively new 10B coin and have become rather uncommon. Fortunately for newcomers to Thailand, numerals are printed in their western as well as Thai forms. Notes are also scaled according to the amount; the larger the denomination, the larger the note. Large denominations – 500B and especially 1000B bills – can be hard to change in small towns, but banks will always change them.

### Changing Money

There is no black-market money exchange for baht, so there's no reason to bring in any Thai currency. Banks or legal money-changers offer the best exchange rate within the country. The baht is firmly attached to the US dollar and is as stable.

Exchange rates at the time of writing include:

| | | | |
|---|---|---|---|
| Australia | A$1 | = | 19.84B |
| Canada | C$1 | = | 18.62B |
| France | FF1 | = | 5.01B |
| Germany | DM1 | = | 17.07B |
| Japan | ¥100 | = | 23.49B |
| Malaysia | M$1 | = | 9.99B |
| New Zealand | NZ$1 | = | 17.27B |
| Singapore | S$1 | = | 17.98B |
| UK | UK£1 | = | 38.72B |
| USA | US$1 | = | 25.28B |

Exchange rates are given in the *Bangkok Post* and *The Nation* every day. For buying baht, US dollars are the most readily acceptable currency and travellers' cheques get better rates than cash. Since banks charge 10B commission and duty for each travellers' cheque cashed, you will save on commissions if you use larger cheque denominations (eg a US$50 cheque will only cost 10B while five US$10 cheques will cost 50B). Note that you can't exchange Indonesian rupiah, Nepali rupees, Cambodian riel, Lao kip, Vietnamese dong or Myanmar kyat into Thai currency at banks, though some Bangkok money-changers carry these currencies. The latter can in fact be good places to buy these currencies if you're going to any of these countries. Rates are comparable with black-market rates in countries with discrepancies between the 'official' and free market currency values.

Visa and MasterCard credit-card holders can get cash advances of up to US$500 (in baht only) per day through some branches of the Thai Farmers Bank, Bangkok Bank and Siam Commercial Bank (and also at the night-time exchange windows in well touristed spots like Banglamphu, Chiang Mai, Ko Samui and so on).

American Express card holders can also get advances, but only in travellers' cheques. The Amex agent is SEA Tours (☎ (2) 216-5757), Suite 88-92, Payathai Plaza, 8th floor, 128 Phayathai Rd, Bangkok.

See the Business Hours section later in this chapter for information on bank opening hours.

## ATM & Credit/Debit Cards

An alternative to carrying around large amounts of cash or travellers' cheques is to open an account at a Thai bank and request an ATM card. Most major banks in Thailand now have automatic teller machines (ATMs) in provincial capitals and in many smaller towns as well, open 24 hours. Once you have a card you'll be able to withdraw cash at machines throughout Thailand, whether those machines belong to your bank or another Thai bank. ATM cards issued by Thai Farmers Bank or Bangkok Bank can be used with the ATMs of 14 major banks – there were over 2500 machines nationwide as of 1996. A 10B transaction charge is usually deducted for using an ATM belonging to a bank with whom you don't have an account.

Debit cards (also known as cash cards or check cards) issued by a bank in your own country can also be used at several Thai banks to withdraw cash (in Thai baht only) directly from your cheque or savings account back home, thus avoiding all commissions and finance charges. You can use MasterCard debit cards to buy baht at foreign exchange booths or desks at either Bangkok Bank or Siam Commercial Bank. Visa debit cards can buy cash through Thai Farmers Bank exchange services.

These cards can also be used at many Thai ATMs, though a surcharge of around US$1 is usually subtracted from your home account each time you complete a machine transaction. As a general rule, debit cards issued under the MasterCard name work best at Bangkok Bank ATMs, while Visa debit cards work best with Thai Farmers Bank machines. Some travellers now use debit cards in lieu of travellers' cheques because they're quicker and more convenient, although it's a good idea to bring along an emergency travellers' cheque fund in case you lose your card. One disadvantage of debit card accounts, as opposed to credit card accounts, is that you can't arrange a 'charge back' for unsatisfactory purchases after the transaction is completed – once the money's drawn from your account it's gone.

Plastic money is becoming increasingly popular in Thailand and many shops, hotels and restaurants now accept credit as well as debit cards. The most commonly accepted cards are Visa and MasterCard, followed by Diner's Club and Japan Card Bureau (JCB). American Express and Carte Blanche are of much more limited use.

**Card Problems** Occasionally when you try to use a Visa or MasterCard at upcountry hotels or shops, the staff may try to tell you that only cards issued by Thai Farmers Bank or Siam Commercial Bank are acceptable. With a little patience, you should be able to make them understand that the Thai Farmers Bank will pay the merchant and that your bank will pay the Thai Farmers Bank – and that any Visa or MasterCard issued anywhere in the world is indeed acceptable.

Another problem concerns illegal surcharges on credit-card purchases. It's against Thai law to pass on to the customer the 3% merchant fee charged by banks, but almost all merchants in Thailand do it anyway. Some even ask 4% or 5%! The only exception seems to be hotels (although even a few hotels will hit you with a credit-card surcharge). If you don't agree to the surcharge they'll simply refuse to accept your card. Begging and pleading or pointing out the law doesn't seem to help. The best way to get around the illegal surcharge is to politely ask that the credit-card receipt be itemised with cost of product or service and the surcharge listed separately. Then when you pay your bill, photocopy all receipts showing the surcharge and request a 'charge back'. If a hotel or shop refuses to itemise the surcharge, take down the vendor's name and address and report them to TAT's tourist police – they may be able to arrange a refund. Not all banks in all countries will offer such refunds – banks in the UK, for example, refuse to issue such refunds, while banks in the USA usually will.

To report a lost or stolen credit/debit card, call the following telephone hotlines in Bangkok: American Express (☎ (2) 273-0022/44), Diners Club (☎ (2) 238-3660),

MasterCard (☎ (2) 299-1990), Visa (☎ (2) 273-1199/7449). See Dangers & Annoyances in this chapter for important warnings on credit-card theft and fraud.

### International Money Transfer

If you have a reliable place to take mail in Thailand, one of the safest and cheapest ways to receive money from overseas is to have an international cashier's cheque (or international money order) sent by courier. It usually takes no more than four days for courier mail to reach Thailand from anywhere in the world.

If you have a bank account in Thailand or your home bank has a branch in Bangkok, you can have money wired direct via a telegraphic transfer. This costs a bit more than having a cheque sent; telegraphic transfers take anywhere from two days to a week to arrive. International banks with branches in Bangkok include Hongkong Bank, Standard Chartered Bank, Sakura Bank, Bank of America, Banque Indosuez, Citibank, Banque Nationale de Paris, Chase Manhattan Bank, Bank of Tokyo, Deutsche Bank, Merrill Lynch International Bank, Hongkong & Shanghai Bank, United Malayan Bank and many others.

Western Union (☎ (2) 251-9201) had an office on the 3rd floor of Central Department Store at 1027 Ploenchit Rd before this branch of Central burnt down in late 1995; it should be operating again by the time you read this.

### Safety Deposit Boxes

Travellers can rent safety deposit boxes at Bangkok's Safety Deposit Centre, 3rd floor, Chan Issara Tower, 942/81 Rama IV Rd (near the Silom Rd intersection) for 150B a month plus 2000B for a refundable key deposit. The centre is open from 10 am to 7 pm Monday to Friday, and from 10 am to 6 pm Saturday, Sunday and public holidays. A few banks will rent safety deposit boxes as well, but generally you need to open an account with them first.

## Exchange Control

Legally, any traveller arriving in Thailand must have at least the following amounts of money in cash, travellers' cheques, bank draft or letter of credit, according to visa category: Non-Immigrant Visa, US$500 per person or US$1000 per family; Tourist Visa, US$250 per person or US$500 per family; Transit Visa or no visa, US$125 per person or US$250 per family. Your funds may be checked by authorities if you arrive on a one way ticket or if you look as if you're at 'the end of the road'.

According to 1991 regulations, there are no limits to the amounts of Thai or foreign currency you may bring into the country. Upon leaving Thailand, you're permitted to take no more than 50,000B per person without special authorisation; exportation of foreign currencies is unrestricted.

It's legal to open a foreign currency account at any commercial bank in Thailand. As long as the funds originate from abroad, there are no restrictions on their maintenance or withdrawal.

## Bargaining

Good bargaining, which takes practice, is another way to cut costs. Anything bought in a market should be bargained for; prices in department stores and most nontourist shops are fixed. Sometimes accommodation rates can be bargained down. One may need to bargain hard in heavily touristed areas since the one week, all air-con type of visitor often pays whatever's asked, creating an artificial price zone between the local and tourist market that the budgeter must deal with.

On the other hand the Thais aren't *always* trying to rip you off, so use some discretion when going for the bone on a price. There's a fine line between bargaining and niggling – getting hot under the collar over 5B makes both seller and buyer lose face. Some more specific suggestions concerning costs can be found in the Accommodation and Things to Buy sections of this chapter.

The cost of transportation between cities and within them is very reasonable; again,

bargaining (when hiring a vehicle) can save you a lot of baht. See the Getting Around chapter.

## Tipping

Tipping is not normal practice in Thailand, although they're getting used to it in expensive hotels and restaurants. Elsewhere don't bother. In taxis where you have to bargain the fare, it certainly isn't necessary.

## Consumer Taxes

In January 1992 Thailand instituted a 7% value-added tax (VAT) for certain goods and services. Unfortunately no-one seems to know what's subject to VAT and what's not, so the whole situation is rather confusing. It doesn't mean that consumers are to be charged 7% over retail – the tax is supposed to be applied to a retailer's cost for the product. For example, if a merchant's wholesale price is 100B for an item that retails at 200B, the maximum adjusted retail including VAT should be 207B, not 214B. In practice the tax is supposed to have caused a net decrease in prices for most goods and services since the VAT replaces a graduated business tax that averaged 9%. But this doesn't always stop Thai merchants from trying to add 'VAT' surcharges to their sales. Like the credit-card surcharge, a direct VAT surcharge is illegal and should be reported to the TAT tourist police.

Tourist hotels add a 7% to 11% hotel tax, and sometimes an 8% to 10% service charge as well, to your room bill.

## POST & COMMUNICATIONS
## Post

Thailand has a very efficient postal service and within the country postage is very cheap.

The poste restante service is also very reliable, though during high tourist months (December to February, July, August) you may have to wait in line at the Bangkok GPO. There is a fee of 1B for every piece of mail collected, 2B for each parcel. As with many Asian countries, confusion at poste restante offices is most likely to arise over given names and surnames. Ask people who are writing to you to print your surname clearly and to underline it. If you're certain a letter should be waiting for you and it cannot be found, it's always wise to check that it hasn't been filed under your given name. You can take poste restante at almost any post office in Thailand.

The American Express office (☎ (2) 216-5757), Suite 88-92, Payathai Plaza, 8th floor, 128 Phayathai Rd, will also take mail on behalf of Amex card holders. The hours are from 8.30 am to noon and 1 to 4.30 pm Monday to Friday, and 8.30 to 11.30 am on Saturday. Amex won't accept courier packets that require your signature. The mail window staff have a reputation for being less than helpful though.

Bangkok's GPO on Charoen Krung (New) Rd is open from 8 am to 8 pm Monday to Friday and from 8 am to 1 pm weekends and holidays. A 24 hour international telecommunications service (including telephone, fax, telex and telegram) is located in a separate building behind and to the right of the main GPO building.

Outside Bangkok the typical provincial GPO is open from 8.30 am to 4.30 pm Monday to Friday, 9 am to noon on Saturday.

Larger GPOs in provincial capitals may also be open for a half day on Sunday.

**Postal Rates** Air-mail letters weighing 10g or less cost 13B to Europe, Australia and New Zealand, and 16B to the Americas. Aerograms cost 10B regardless of the destination, while postcards are 9B.

Letters sent by registered mail cost 20B in addition to regular air-mail postage. International express mail (EMS) fees vary according to country of destination. Sample rates for items weighing 100 to 250g are: Japan 250B; Australia, Germany and the UK 215B; France, Canada and the USA 235B. Within Thailand, this service costs only 20B (100 to 250g) in addition to regular postage.

The rates for parcels shipped by post vary according to weight (rising in one-kg increments), country of destination and whether they're shipped by surface (takes up to two months) or air (one to two weeks). See the Parcel Postage Rates table below for sample prices.

Most provincial post offices sell do-it-yourself packing boxes (11 sizes!) costing from 5 to 35B; tape and string are provided at no charge. Some offices even have packing services, which cost from 4 to 10B

**Parcel Postage Rates**

| Destination | | 1 kg | 5 kg | 10 kg | 20 kg |
|---|---|---|---|---|---|
| Australia | surface | 270B | 430B | 610B | 1000B |
|  | air | 400B | 1400B | 2650B | 5150B |
| Canada | surface | 220B | 380B | 560B | 920B |
|  | air | 450B | 1570B | 2970B | 3770B |
| France | surface | 330B | 550B | 770B | 1210B |
|  | air | 500B | 1500B | 2750B | 5250B |
| Germany | surface | 330B | 550B | 770B | 1210B |
|  | air | 500B | 1500B | 2750B | 5250B |
| Japan | surface | 370B | 530B | 690B | 1010B |
|  | air | 400B | 920B | 1550B | 2870B |
| New Zealand | surface | 330B | 550B | 770B | 1210B |
|  | air | 500B | 1500B | 2750B | 5250B |
| UK | surface | 330B | 550B | 770B | 1210B |
|  | air | 500B | 1500B | 2750B | 5250B |
| USA | surface | 180B | 550B | 1080B | 2080B |
|  | air | 500B | 1500B | 2750B | 5250B |

per parcel depending on size. Private packing services may also be available in the vicinity of large provincial post offices.

You can insure a package's contents for 8.50B for each 1740B of the goods' value.

## Couriers

Several companies in Thailand offer courier services. The main ones, headquartered in Bangkok, include:

DHL Worldwide – 22nd floor, Grand Amarin Tower, New Phetburi Rd (☎ (2) 207-0600)
Federal Express – 8th floor, Green Tower, Rama IV Rd (☎ (2) 367-3222)
TNT Express – 599 Chong Non Sii Rd, Khlong Toeu (☎ (2) 249-0242)

## Telephone

The telephone system in Thailand, operated by the government-subsidised Telephone Organization of Thailand (TOT) under the Communications Authority of Thailand (CAT), is quite efficient and from Bangkok you can usually direct-dial most major centres with little difficulty.

The country code for Thailand is ☎ 66. See the Thai Area Codes table later in this section for listings of domestic area codes.

**Telephone Office Hours** GPO telephone centres in most provincial capitals are open daily from 7 am to 11 pm; smaller provincial phone offices may be open from 8 am to 8 or 10 pm. Bangkok's international CAT phone office at the Charoen Krung Rd GPO is open 24 hours.

**International Calls** To direct-dial an international number (other than those in Malaysia and Laos) from a private phone, simply dial ☎ 001 before the number. For operator-assisted international calls, dial ☎ 100.

The Home Direct service is available at Bangkok's GPO, at airports in Bangkok, Chiang Mai, Phuket, Hat Yai and Surat Thani, and at post office CAT centres in Bangkok, Hat Yai, Phuket, Chiang Mai, Surat Thani, Pattaya, Hua Hin and Kanchanaburi. Home Direct phones offer easy one-button connection with international operators in some 20 countries around the world. You can also direct-dial Home Direct access numbers from any private phone (most hotel phones won't work) in Thailand.

For Home Direct service, dial ☎ 001-999 followed by:

| Australia | 61-1000 |
|---|---|
| Canada | 15-1000 |
| Denmark | 45-1000 |
| Germany | 49-1000 |
| Hawaii | 14414 |
| Hong Kong | 852-1086 |
| Indonesia | 62-1000 |
| Italy | 39-1000 |
| Japan | 81-0051 |
| Korea | 82-1000 |
| Netherlands | 31-1035 |
| New Zealand | 64-1066 |
| Norway | 47-1000 |
| Philippines | 63-1000 |
| Singapore | 351-1000 |
| Taiwan | 886-1000 |
| UK | 44-1066 |
| USA | (AT&T) 1111 |
| USA | (MCI) 12001 |
| USA | (Sprint) 13877 |

Hotels generally add surcharges (sometimes as much as 30% over and above the TOT rate) for international long-distance calls; it's always cheaper to call abroad from a CAT telephone office. These offices are almost always attached to a city's GPO, often on the building's 2nd floor, around the side or just behind the GPO. There may also be a separate TOT office down the road, used only for residential or business service (eg billing or installation), not public calls; even when public phone services are offered (as at the TOT office on Ploenchit Rd in Bangkok), TOT offices accept only cash payments – reverse-charge and credit-card calls aren't permitted. Hence the CAT office is generally your best choice.

Once you've found the proper office and window, the procedure for making an international long-distance call (*thorásàp ráwàang pràthêt*) begins with filling out a

BERNARD NAPTHINE

BERNARD NAPTHINE

## Buddhism in Thailand
Top: Performing an early morning alms-round
Bottom: Congregation at Wat Phra That Doi Suthep, near Chiang Mai

BERNARD NAPTHINE

BERNARD NAPTHINE

JOE CUMMINGS

BERNARD NAPTHINE

## Festivals
Top Left: Chiang Mai's famed Flower Festival, held annually in February
Top Right: Cooling off during Songkhran
Bottom Left: Flamboyant festival float adorned with *jaofao* spirit hooks
Bottom Right: Veteran participant at Chiang Mai's Flower Festival

bilingual form with your name and details pertaining to the call's destination. Except for reverse-charge calls, you must estimate in advance the time you'll be on the phone and pay a deposit equal to the time/distance rate. There is always a minimum three minute charge, refunded if your call doesn't go through. Usually, only cash or international phone credit cards are acceptable for payment at CAT offices; some provincial CAT offices also accept American Express and a few take Visa/MasterCard.

If the call doesn't go through you must pay a 30B service charge anyway – unless you're calling reverse charges (*kèp plai-thaang*). For reverse-charge calls it's the opposite, ie you pay the 30B charge only if the call goes through. Depending on where you're calling, reimbursing someone later for a reverse-charge call to your home country may be less expensive than paying CAT/TOT charges – it pays to compare rates at source and destination. For calls between the USA and Thailand, for example, AT&T collect rates are less than TOT's direct rates.

Private long-distance telephone offices are also available in most towns, but sometimes these are only for calls within Thailand. Often they're just a desk or a couple of booths in the rear of a retail shop. These private offices typically collect a 10B surcharge for long-distance domestic calls, 50B for international calls. The vast majority of such offices accept only cash.

Whichever type of phone service you use, the least expensive time of day to make calls is from 10 pm to 7 am (66% discount from standard rates), followed by 6 to 10 pm (50% discount). You pay full price from 7 am to 6 pm.

***Malaysia & Laos*** CAT does not offer long-distance service to Malaysia or Laos. To call these countries you must go through TOT. For Vientiane, you must dial ☎ 101 to reach a TOT operator and arrange an operator-assisted call. Malaysia can be dialled direct by prefixing the Malaysian number (including area code) with the code ☎ 09.

**Domestic Calls** In most places there are two kinds of public pay phones in Thailand, 'red' and 'blue'. The red phones are for local city calls and the blue are for long-distance calls (within Thailand). Local calls from pay phones cost 1B. Although there are three different 1B coins in general circulation, only the middle-sized coin fits the coin slots. Some hotels and guesthouses have private pay phones that cost 5B per call; these take only nine-sided 5B coins.

Card phones are available at most Thai airports as well as major shopping centres and other public areas throughout urban Thailand. Phonecards come in 25B, 50B, 100B, 200B and 240B denominations, all roughly the same size as a credit card; they can be purchased at any TOT office. In airports you can usually buy them at the airport information counter or at one of the gift shops.

The newest phone booth service in Thailand – found mostly in Bangkok – is called Telepoint (formerly Fonepoint), a system which uses a one way mobile phone network operated by TOT. Such mobile phones can be used within 100m to 200m of a Telepoint location to communicate with other mobile phones and pagers. For a Telepoint account TOT charges a monthly service fee of 350B plus 1B per minute (three minute minimum) in Bangkok, or normal TOT rates for upcountry and overseas calls, plus registration fees.

***Cellular Phones*** TOT authorises use of private cell phones using two systems, NMT 470 MHZ and Cellular 900 NMT. The latter system is more common, with at least 10 dealer agencies around the country and more base stations.

It costs 1000B to register a phone and 500B per month for 'number rental'. Rates are 3B per minute within the same area code, 8B per minute to adjacent area codes and 12B per minute to other area codes. Cell phone users must pay for incoming as well as outgoing calls. Keep this in mind whenever you consider calling a number that begins with the code ☎ 01 – this means

## Thai Area Codes
The area codes for Thailand's major cities are presented below. See the relevant destination chapters for the area codes of smaller towns not listed here. Note that zeros aren't needed in area codes, whether dialling domestically or from overseas. To dial a long-distance, domestic phone number (eg to call the THAI office in Bangkok from Chiang Mai) dial ☎ (2)+ 513-0121.

| | |
|---|---|
| 2 | Bangkok, Thonburi, Nonthaburi, Pathum Thani, Samut Prakan |
| 32 | Phetburi, Cha-am, Prachuap Khiri Khan, Pranburi, Ratchaburi |
| 34 | Kanchanaburi, Nakhon Pathom, Samut Sakhon, Samut Songkhram |
| 35 | Ang Thong, Ayuthaya, Suphanburi |
| 36 | Lopburi, Saraburi, Singburi |
| 37 | Nakhon Nayok, Prachinburi, Aranya Prathet |
| 38 | Chachoengsao, Chonburi, Pattaya, Rayong, Si Racha |
| 39 | Chanthaburi, Trat |
| 42 | Loei, Chiang Khan, Mukdahan, Nakhon Phanom, Nong Khai, Sakon Nakhon, Udon Thani |
| 43 | Kalasin, Khon Kaen, Mahasarakham, Roi Et |
| 44 | Buriram, Chaiyaphum, Nakhon Ratchasima (Khorat) |
| 45 | Si Saket, Surin, Ubon Ratchathani, Yasothon |
| 53 | Chiang Mai, Chiang Rai, Lamphun, Mae Hong Son |
| 54 | Lampang, Nan, Phayao, Phrae |
| 55 | Kamphaeng Phet, Phitsanulok, Sukhothai, Tak, Mae Sot, Utaradit |
| 56 | Nakhon Sawan, Phetchabun, Phichit, Uthai Thani |
| 73 | Narathiwat, Sungai Kolok, Pattani, Yala |
| 74 | Hat Yai, Phattalung, Satun, Songkhla |
| 75 | Krabi, Nakhon Si Thammarat, Trang |
| 76 | Phang-Nga, Phuket |
| 77 | Chumphon, Ranong, Surat Thani, Chaiya, Ko Samui |

you're calling a cell phone number and will be charged accordingly. Note also that the zero in these codes needs to be dialled.

### Fax, Telex & Telegraph
GPO telephone offices throughout the country offer fax, telegraph and telex services in addition to regular phone services. There's no need to bring your own paper, as the post offices supply their own forms. A few TOT offices also offer fax services. International faxes typically cost a steep 100 to 140B for the first page, and 65 to 110B per page for the remaining pages, depending on the size of the paper and the destination.

Larger hotels with business centres offer the same telecommunication services but always at higher rates.

## BOOKS
Most books are published in different editions by different publishers in different countries. As a result, a book might be a hardcover rarity in one country while it's readily available in paperback in another. Fortunately, bookshops and libraries search by title or author, so your local bookshop or library is best placed to advise you on the availability of the following recommendations.

### Description & Travel
The earliest western literature of note on Thailand, Guy Tachard's *A Relation of the Voyage to Siam*, recounts a 1680s French expedition through parts of the country with little literary flair. Shortly after, Simon de la

Loubére's 1693 *New Historical Relation of the Kingdom of Siam* chronicled the French mission to the Ayuthaya court in great detail. Maurice Collis novelised this period with a focus on the unusual political relationship between King Narai and his Greek minister, Constantin Phaulkon, in *Siamese White*.

Frank Vincent's *The Land of the White Elephant*, first published in 1873, is a very readable account of an American merchant's travels in Siam. Carl Bock's illustrated *Temples and Elephants* covered similar territory in 1884. Tachard, Loubére, Collis, Vincent and Bock have all been republished and are readily available in Bangkok bookstores. Other reprints to look for if you're interested in pre-20th century historical detail include Ernest Young's *The Kingdom of the Yellow Robe* (1898) and the anonymous *An Englishman's Siamese Journals* (1890-93).

The infamous Anna Leonowens published *The English Governess at the Siamese Court* in 1870. Its largely inauthentic descriptions of Siamese life were later transformed into two Hollywood movies and a Broadway musical.

Joseph Conrad evoked Thailand in several of his pre-WWII novels and short stories, most notably in his 1920s *The Secret Sharer* and *Falk: A Reminiscence*. More detail from the 1920s can be found in *Teak Wallah*, by Reginald Campbell, a Briton who worked as a teak inspector in Northern Thailand.

Pierre Boulle's post-WWII novel *The Bridge over the River Kwai* dramatised the construction and destruction of the infamous Death Railway Bridge in Kanchanaburi Province. In 1957 it was made into an Academy Award-winning motion picture that remains the most internationally famous film having to do with Thailand.

Charles Nicholls' semi-fictional *Borderlines* (1992) takes the reader on a voyage to the Thai-Myanmar border in the company of a colourful group of travellers. Along the way the author weaves cultural insights into the storyline, making the book more than just a beach read.

Nicholls, Pico Iyer, Robert Anson Hall

and several other well known and not so well known authors have contributed travel essays of varying style to *Travelers' Tales Thailand* (edited by James O'Reilly & Larry Habegger, 1994). It was the first title in a relatively new series that assembles travel articles and chapters from various sources into a single anthology devoted to a particular country. Savvy travel tips are sprinkled throughout the text.

A more serious collection of literature is available in *Traveller's Literary Companion: South-East Asia*, edited by Alastair Dingwall. The Thailand chapter, edited by scholar Thomas John Hudak, is packed with hard-to-find information on the history of literature in Thailand and includes extracts from various works by Thai as well as foreign authors.

Temple buffs will find plenty to chew on in *Guide to Thailand* by Achille Clarac, edited and translated by Michael Smithies. Studded with descriptions of obscure temple ruins throughout the kingdom, Clarac's guide originally appeared in English in 1971 as *Discovering Thailand*; it hasn't been updated since 1977 but was a pioneering work in its day.

If you can get hold of a copy of *Hudson's Guide to Chiang Mai & the North* you'll learn a lot about this area that is unknown to the average traveller. Much of the information is out of date (since the book is long out of print) but it makes interesting reading and has one of the best Thai phrase sections ever published – 218 phrases *with* tone marks. (Phrase sections without tone marks are next to worthless.) In 1987, Roy Hudson also published the minuscule *Hudson's Guide to Mae Hong Son* which you may come across in the North.

For an insider's view of temple life, read Tim Ward's amusing *What The Buddha Never Taught* (Celestial Arts, Berkeley, 1993), an account of the author's sojourn as a monk at a North-Eastern forest wat.

### People, Culture & Society
*Culture Shock! Thailand & How to Survive It* by Robert & Nanthapa Cooper is an inter-

esting outline on getting along with the Thai way of life, although it's heavily oriented toward Bangkok. *Letters from Thailand* by Botan (translated by Susan Fulop Kepner) and Carol Hollinger's *Mai Pen Rai Means Never Mind* can also be recommended for their insights into traditional Thai culture. *Bangkok Post* reporter Denis Segaller's *Thai Ways* and *More Thai Ways* present yet more expat insights into Thai culture.

*Ramakian: The Thai Ramayana* by Naga Books (anonymous author) is a thorough exposition of the Thai version of Indian poet Valmiki's timeless epic.

Jack Reynolds' 1950s *A Woman of Bangkok* (republished in 1985), a well written and poignant story of a young Englishman's descent into the world of Thai brothels, remains the best novel yet published with this theme. Expat writer Christopher G Moore covers the Thai underworld in his 1990s novels *A Killing Smile, Spirit House* and *A Bewitching Smile* but with a rose-tinted view of the go-go bar scene.

For a look at Bangkok's infamous Patpong Rd from a western female's perspective, read *Patpong Sisters* (1994) by Cleo Odzer. Odzer, an American who carried out un-authorised anthropological research on Patpong in the late 1980s, comes to the unique conclusion that prostitution is em-powering work for women who grow up in Thailand with few other employment possi-bilities. Although such a conclusion flies in the face of statistics (which show that the percentage of women who make up the labour force in Thailand is greater than in either China or the USA), and generalises from atypical Patpong-style prostitution, the book nonetheless offers many insights into the world of her 'sisters'.

For books on Buddhism and how it is practised in Thailand, see Religion in the Facts about the Country chapter.

**Books By Thai Authors** For a look at rural life in Thailand, the books of Pira Sudham are unparalleled. Sudham was born to a poor family in North-Eastern Thailand and has written *Siamese Drama, Monsoon Country*

and *People of Esarn*. These books are not translations – Sudham writes in English in order to reach a worldwide audience. These fiction titles are fairly easy to find in Bangkok but can be difficult to find over-seas.

*Behind the Smile: Voices of Thailand* (1990) by Sanitsuda Ekachai is a very enlightening collection of interviews with Thai peasants from all over the country. *In the Mirror* (1985) is an excellent collection of translated modern Thai short stories from the 1960s and 1970s. The Siam Society's *Culture & Environment in Thailand* is a col-lection of scholarly papers by Thai and foreign authors delivered at a 1988 sympo-sium which examined the relationship between Thai culture and the natural world; topics range from the oceanic origins of the Thai race and nature motifs in Thai art to evolving Thai attitudes toward the environ-ment.

*Siam in Crisis* by Sulak Sivaraksa, one of Thailand's leading intellectuals, analyses modern Thai politics from Sulak's unique Buddhist-nationalist perspective. Sivaraksa has written several other worthwhile titles on Thai culture which have been translated into English. Essays by this contrary and contra-dictory character posit an ideal that neither Thailand nor any other country will likely ever achieve, and his attempts to use western-style academic argument to dis-credit western thinking can alternately be exasperating and inspiring.

*The Lioness in Bloom*, translated by Susan Fulop Kepner, is an eye-opening collection of 11 short stories written by or about Thai women.

**Hill Tribes** If you are interested in detailed information on hill tribes, seek out the hard-to-find *The Hill Tribes of Northern Thailand* by Gordon Young (Monograph No 1, The Siam Society). Young was born of third generation Christian missionaries among the Lahu people, speaks several tribal dialects and is even an honorary Lahu chief-tain with the highest Lahu title, the Supreme Hunter. The monograph covers 16 tribes, including descriptions, photographs, tables and maps.

*From the Hands of the Hills*, by Margaret Campbell, has lots of beautiful pictures. *Peoples of the Golden Triangle*, by Elaine & Paul Lewis, is also very good, very photo-oriented and expensive. Lonely Planet's *Thai Hill Tribes phrasebook* has descriptions of Thailand's major hill tribes, maps and phrases in several hill-tribe languages.

See the special Hill Tribes section in the Northern Thailand chapter for some further information.

## History & Politics
George Coedes' classic prewar work on South-East Asian history, *The Indianised States of South-East Asia*, contains ground-breaking historical material on early Thai history, as does WAR Wood's *A History of Siam*, published in the same era. One of the more readable general histories written in the latter half of the 20th century is David Wyatt's *Thailand: A Short History* (Trasvin Publications, Chiang Mai).

Concentrating on post-revolutionary Thailand, *The Balancing Act: A History of Modern Thailand* (Asia Books, 1991), by Joseph Wright Jr, starts with the 1932 revolution and ends with the February 1991 coup. Wright's semi-academic chronicle concludes that certain 'natural laws' – endemic to the culture – govern the continuous circulation of elites. Though the book is packed with detail, such deep-structure theorising brings to mind the way Anglo scholars until very recently identified all French political trends as 'Bonapartiste'. Wright's most demonstrable thesis is that, despite the 1932 revolution, democracy has never gained a firm foothold in Thai society.

The best source of information on Thailand's political scene during the turbulent 1960s and 1970s is *Political Conflict in Thailand: Reform, Reaction, Revolution* by David Morrell & Chai-anan Samudavanija.

Although it sheds no new light on the Death Railway's historical significance, WWII buffs may enjoy Clifford Kinvig's *River Kwai Railway: The Story of the Burma-Siam Railroad*, which presents lots of previously hard-to-find details on, for example, the movement of specific military regiments in South-East Asia, types and amounts of explosives used in construction of the railway and the composition of Japanese forces in Thailand.

Thailand's role in the international narcotics trade is covered thoroughly in Alfred McCoy's *The Politics of Heroin in Southeast Asia* and Francis Belanger's *Drugs, the US, and Khun Sa*.

Although it's fiction, ex-prime minister Kukrit Pramoj's 1961 *Red Bamboo* vividly portrays and predicts the conflict between the Thai communist movement and the establishment during the 1960s and 1970s. His book *Si Phaendin: Four Reigns* (1981), the most widely read novel ever published in Thailand, covers the Ayuthaya era. Both novels are available in English-language versions.

Axel Aylwen's novel *The Falcon of Siam* and its sequel *The Falcon Takes Wing* are not up to Kukrit's literary standards but nonetheless capture the feel and historical detail of 17th century Siam; Aylwen obviously read Collis, Loubére and Tachard closely (see Description & Travel above).

Although it's tough to find, *The Devil's Discus* by Rayne Kruger focuses on the circumstances surrounding the mysterious death of Rama VIII. It's banned in Thailand, of course, for its police blotter-style analysis of a taboo topic.

## Natural History
Complete with sketches, photos and maps, *The Mammals of Thailand* (Association for the Conservation of Wildlife, 1988), by Boonsong Lekagul & Jeffrey McNeely, remains the classic on Thai wildlife in spite of a few out-of-date references (it was first published in 1977). Birdlovers should seek out the *Bird Guide of Thailand* (Association for the Conservation of Wildlife, 1972) by Boonsong Lekagul & EW Cronin for comprehensive descriptions of Thailand's avian species.

Detailed summaries of 77 of Thailand's

national parks, along with an objective assessment of current park conditions, are available in *National Parks of Thailand* (Communication Resources, Bangkok, 1994) by Gray, Piprell & Graham.

### Food & Shopping

Amongst the explosion of Thai cookbooks that have appeared in recent years, one of the best remains *Thai Cooking* (formerly *The Original Thai Cookbook*) by Jennifer Brennan. For those without access to a complete range of Thai herbs and spices, *Cooking Thai Food in American Kitchens* by Malulee Pinsuvana makes reasonable substitutions. Though expensive and unwieldy, the huge, coffee-table-style *Thailand the Beautiful Cookbook* by Panurat Poladitmontri contains excellent photography and very authentic recipes.

*Shopping in Exotic Thailand* (Impact Publications, USA) by Ronald & Caryl Rae Krannich is packed with general shopping tips as well as lists of speciality shops and markets throughout Thailand.

Although it's a bit out of date, John Hoskins' 1988 *Buyer's Guide to Thai Gems & Jewellery* is a must for anyone contemplating a foray into Thailand's gem market. *Arts and Crafts of Thailand* (1994), written by William Warren and photographed by Luca Invernizzi Tettoni, makes a useful primer for delving into the world of Thai handicrafts.

### Bookshops

Bangkok probably has the largest selection of English-language books and bookshops in South-East Asia. The principal chains are Asia Books (headquarters on Sukhumvit Rd near Soi 15) and DK Book House (Siam Square); each has branch shops in half a dozen street locations around Bangkok as well as in well touristed cities like Chiang Mai, Hat Yai and Phuket. Asia and DK offer a wide variety of fiction and periodicals as well as books on Asia. Some of Thailand's larger tourist hotels also have bookshops with English-language books and periodicals.

In Chiang Mai, the independent Suriwong

Book Centre on Si Donchai Rd is especially good for books on Thailand and Asia.

In Nong Khai, Wasambe Bookshop near Mutmee Guest House has the best selection of books in North-Eastern Thailand.

See the Bookshop entries under the relevant cities for further details.

### ONLINE SERVICES

A growing number of online service providers offer information on Thailand. Many of these World Wide Web sites are commercial sites established by tour operators or hotels; the ratio of commercial to noncommercial sites is liable to increase over time if current Internet trends continue. Remember that all URL's (universal resource locators) mentioned below are subject to change without notice; a couple even changed addresses while I was compiling this section. You can of course use your own Web browser to conduct searches; there's a lot of information out there.

The Tourism Authority of Thailand (TAT) has its own World Wide Web site at http://www.tat.or.th; like many Web sites these days, it contains only basic info crowded with lots of ad-style propaganda. Thailand's Ministry of Foreign Affairs has a list of all Thai embassies and consulates and details of visa requirements at http://www.nectec.or.th/bureaux/mfa/index .html. Another Web site sourced from Thailand is one carried by Siam Net (http:// www.siam.net). Pages include general information, a list of tour operators in Thailand, a hotel directory and a golf directory. All hotel lists I have come across on the Net have been sorely incomplete, whether oriented toward budget or luxury properties.

Lonely Planet's Web site (http://www. lonelyplanet.com) contains Thailand updates from travellers, occasional author updates for this edition, and other salient info; for a direct link to Thailand-related material, go for http://www.lonelyplanet. com.au/dest/sea/thai.htm. Indochina.net (http://www.icn.net/icn/) links to many Thailand-related Web pages. Mahidol University in Bangkok maintains a very useful site (http://www.mahidol.ac.th/Thailand/Thailand-main.html) that's searchable by keyword.

The *Bangkok Post* Web site (http://www.bkk.post.co.th) runs around 60 pages of stories as well as photos. For information on Bangkok, *Bangkok Metro* magazine's site, http://www.icn.net/METRO.html shows promise (note this address is case sensitive). Utopia, a gay/lesbian centre in Bangkok, maintains an informative page at http://www.utopia-asia.com/tipsthai.htm. With all of these, links to other Thailand sites may prove useful.

Aside from the Web, another Internet resource is the ftp usenet group culture.thai. It's very uneven, as it's basically a chat outlet for anyone who thinks they have something to say about Thailand. Still it's not a bad place to start if you have a burning question that you haven't found an answer to elsewhere.

### Online in Thailand

If you're bringing computer and modem to Thailand with hopes of staying in the info highway's fast lane, keep in mind that online options are still quite limited and that baud rates are very slow – generally 9600 or less (2400 was the overall practical norm as of mid-1996). Higher baud rates are bottlenecked by low bandwidth and can be very unreliable. This will change rapidly with time, and as more global providers are allowed into the market. One big bureaucratic impasse stands in the way: the Communications Authority of Thailand (CAT), which is very much opposed to privatisation of the telecommunications industry. For the moment CAT isn't content with simply collecting normal local and long-distance phone rates, operating instead on the principle that digital telecommunications is a 'premium' service that requires extra charges. All service, so far, is thus surcharged according to baud rate.

CompuServe and IBM Global are the only 'international' providers so far that include Bangkok nodes. AT&T and MCI have promised global services soon. Rates are very high, but since it's mostly the Thai and expat elite who are plugged in, virtually no-one complains loudly about paying the prevailing price.

CompuServe is available at up to 9600 baud (2400 and occasional 7200 in everyday practice) through InfoNet World for a basic $US10 per hour charge (added to one's home account). If a CompuServe/Pacific deal currently in the works goes through it will probably be Thailand's best bet since it hopes to offer a 28.8M-baud, CIS-direct node in Thailand. IBM Global offers Net access at an advertised 9600 baud but in reality service is very slow and unreliable for any purposes except e-mail. CompuServe, incidentally, has a very dynamic travel forum with lots of member input on Thailand in its Asia section; the quality of Thailand material found on America Online – so far – suffers by comparison.

The Net is gaining in popularity in Thailand, especially as more and more local, Thai-language pages go online and folks get their Net software installed for Thai language. IBM Global operates at 9600, or you can pay a fat CAT-mandated surcharge for 28.8M service. Microsoft Network is similar. Local Internet providers (KSC, NECTEC, LoxInfo) typically charge around 1500 to 2000B per month for 28.8M service with 20 to 40 hours 'free'. Low-grade, text-only services are available for basic charges as low as 600B a month, plus per-hour charges once your online time is maxed out.

For the moment all dial-ups go through Bangkok, which means you must add long-distance charges to your online costs if you plug in outside the capital. A company called Samart Cybernet Services recently announced that it would begin operations in Chiang Mai in the near future.

RJ11 phone jacks are becoming the standard in new hotels, but in older hotels and guesthouses the phones may still be hard-wired. A pocketknife and pair of alligator clips are useful for stripping and attaching wires, or bring along an acoustic coupler.

A few guesthouses (eg the New Joe guesthouse in Banglamphu) and bars/cafes (eg the CyberPub at the Dusit Thani Hotel, Häagen

Dazs on Ploenchit Rd) in Bangkok are beginning to offer e-mail and Internet log-ons at house terminals. For the visitor who only needs to log on once in a while, these are a less expensive alternative to getting your own account – and it certainly beats lugging around a laptop. The going rate is 3 or 4B per on and offline minute. At the time of writing, the only source outside Bangkok offering such services was Wasambe Bookshop in Nong Khai in North-Eastern Thailand. To cover long-distance phone costs to Bangkok, Wasambe charges a 150B flat rate for sending e-mail that includes 30 minutes of composition time. Receipt of e-mail costs 10B per page. As these services become more popular, other places around the country where wireheads congregate will surely follow suit.

One electronic bulletin board service (BBS) worth checking out is Sala Thai (modem (2) 679-8380), which has a subscriber base of over 700. Topics are diverse. For a list of over 40 other BBS sites in Bangkok, Pattaya, Chiang Mai and Phuket, see a current issue of *Bangkok Metro* or contact Piyabute Fuangkhon at the Information Center on modem (2) 734-7301.

Loxinfo recently began offering NetAccess cards, prepaid telephone card packages with special uses for modem communications. These cards come in denominations of two hours (300B), four hours (500B) and 10 hours (1000B). Purchasers are provided with a sealed envelope containing a user name, password, local phone access number (currently Bangkok, Chiang Mai and Pattaya) and log-on procedures. Follow the latter and you'll be able to navigate the Internet, check e-mail at your online home address, and access any online services you subscribe to, such as CompuServe or America Online. Complete details about the NetAccess Card, including a list of authorised agents, can be obtained through Loxinfo's home page at http://www.loxinfo.co.th.

## FILMS

A number of classic international films have used Thailand either as a subject or as a location – more often the latter. In fact nowadays location shooting in Thailand has become something of a boom industry as Thailand's jungles, rice fields and islands find themselves backdrops for all manner of scripts set in 'exotic' tropical countries.

The first film to come out of Thailand was *Chang*, a 1927 silent picture shot entirely in Nan Province (then still a semi-independent principality with Siamese protection). Produced by American film impresarios Copper and Schoedsack – who later produced several major Hollywood hits – *Chang* contains some of the best jungle and wildlife sequences filmed in Asia to date.

Next came *Anna & the King of Siam*, a 1946 American production (filmed on Hollywood sets) starring Rex Harrison and based on the book *The English Governess at the Siamese Court* by Anna Leonowens, who cared for Rama IV's children in the 19th century. Though the movie opened to very mixed reviews, screenwriter Arthur Miller was honoured with an Academy Award. A 1956 musical remake, *The King & I*, grew from a very successful Broadway stage production starring Yul Brynner (who earned an Oscar for the film). Both films, as well as the musical, are banned in Thailand because they are seen to compromise the dignity of the monarchy.

Probably the most famous movie associated with Thailand is *The Bridge on the River Kwai*, a 1957 Academy Award-winning production stemming from Pierre Boulle's book of the same name and starring Alec Guinness. Although based on WWII events in Thailand, much of the film was shot on location in Sri Lanka (then Ceylon). Another early film of some notoriety was 1962's *The Ugly American*, a Marlon Brando vehicle based on the novel by William J Lederer. In this muddled picture Thailand stands in for the fictionalised South-East Asian nation of Sarkan. Part-time Thai politician and academic Kukrit Pramoj enjoyed a substantial film role as the fake nation's prime minister. Kukrit went on to become Thailand's prime minister in 1974.

*The Man with the Golden Gun*, a pedestrian

1974 James Bond vehicle starring Roger Moore and Christopher Lee, brought the karst islands of Ao Phang-Nga to international attention for the first time. A year later the French soft-porn movie *Emmanuelle* ('Much hazy, soft-focus coupling in downtown Bangkok', wrote *The Illustrated London News)* added to the myth of Thailand as sexual idyll and set an all-time box office record in France. A half dozen or so Emmanuel sequels, at least two of which returned to Thailand for script settings, were produced over the next decade.

Virtually every film produced with a Vietnam War theme has been shot either in the Philippines or in Thailand, with the latter ahead by a long shot as the location of choice due to relative logistical ease. The first Vietnam-themed movie to use Thailand as a location was *The Deer Hunter*, which starred Robert DeNiro and relative newcomer Meryl Streep; it won the 1978 Academy Award for best picture. Oliver Stone's *Heaven and Earth* (1993) is one of the more recent pictures to paint Vietnam on a Thai canvas.

*The Killing Fields* (1984) skilfully used Thailand as a stand-in for Cambodia in a story about the Khmer Rouge takeover of Phnom Penh. In a 1987 spin-off of this movie, *Swimming to Cambodia*, monologist Spalding Gray recounts behind-the-scenes anecdotes of the Thailand shooting of the film.

Jean-Claude Van Damme's *The Kickboxer* brought Thai boxing to the big screen with a bit more class than the average martial arts flick; more than a few foreign pugilists have packed their bags for Bangkok after viewing the movie's exotic mix of ring violence and Thai Buddhist atmospherics. Sly Stallone's 1980s *Rambo* movies (Rambos II & III used Thailand locations) did little for Thailand, but the success of *Good Morning Vietnam* (1988), a Robin Williams comedy widely publicised as having been shot in Bangkok and Phuket, helped generate a tourism boom for the country. Also in the 1980s, two very forgettable comedy flicks were filmed in Mae Hong Son: *Volunteers*, a Tom Hanks and John Candy vehicle about a couple of

Peace Corps workers falling afoul of Reds and dope peddlers, and *Air America* with a dashing Mel Gibson falling afoul of more Reds and dope peddlers. In 1994 *Mortal Kombat* leapt from the world of video games to the silver screen with help from Thai locations; other movies of the 1990s have included *Operation Dumbo Drop* and *The Phantom*, both directed by Australian Simon Wincer of *The Man from Snowy River* fame.

Thailand now maintains a substantial contingent of trained production assistants and casting advisors who work continuously with foreign companies on location shoots – many of them from Japan, Hong Kong and Singapore.

# MEDIA
## Newspapers
Thailand's 1991 constitution guarantees freedom of the press, though the National Police Department reserves power to suspend publishing licences for national security reasons. Editors nevertheless exercise self-censorship in certain realms, particularly with regard to the monarchy. Monarchical issues aside, Thailand is widely considered to have the freest print media in South-East Asia. In a recent survey conducted by the Singapore-based Political and Economic Risk Consultancy, 180 expatriate managers in 10 Asian countries ranked Thailand's English-language press the highest in Asia. Surprisingly, these expats cited the *Bangkok Post* and *The Nation* more frequently as their source of regional and global news than either the *Asian Wall Street Journal* or the *Far Eastern Economic Review*.

These two English-language newspapers are published daily in Thailand and distributed in most provincial capitals throughout the country – the *Bangkok Post* in the morning and *The Nation* in the afternoon. *The Nation* is almost entirely staffed by Thais and presents, obviously, a Thai perspective, while the *Post*, which was Thailand's first English daily (established 1946), has a mixed Thai and international staff and represents a more international view. For international news, the *Post* is the better of the two papers and is in fact regarded by many journalists as the best English daily in the region. *The Nation*, on the other hand, has better regional coverage – particularly with regard to Myanmar and former Indochina, and the paper is to be commended for taking a harder anti-NPKC stance during the 1991 coup.

A third English-language daily, the less widely available *Thailand Times*, is owned by an investment company with obvious biases regarding growth and development.

The Singapore edition of the *International Herald Tribune* is widely available in Bangkok, Chiang Mai and heavily touristed areas like Pattaya and Phuket.

The most popular Thai-language newspapers are *Thai Rath* and *Daily News*, but they're mostly full of blood-and-guts stories. The best Thai journalism is found in the somewhat less popular *Matichon* and *Siam Rath* dailies. Many Thais read the English-language dailies as they consider them better news sources. The *Bangkok Post* also publishes a Thai-language version of the popular English daily.

Outside Thailand one can subscribe to the *Bangkok Post Weekly*, a recapitulation of all the major *Post* news stories of the week printed on Bible-thin paper and sent by air mail round the world.

## Magazines

English-language magazine publishing continues to grow, although the lifespan of individual titles tends to be short. Though mostly devoted to domestic and regional business, the English-language *Manager* occasionally prints very astute, very up-to-date cultural pieces. *Bangkok Metro*, a slick lifestyle magazine introduced in 1995, brings a new sophistication to Bangkok publications concerned with art, culture and music.

Many popular magazines from the UK, USA, Australia and Europe – particularly those concerned with computer technology, autos, fashion, music and business – are

available in bookstores which specialise in English-language publications (see Bookshops under Books earlier in this chapter).

## Radio

Thailand has more than 400 radio stations, with 41 FM and 35 AM stations in Bangkok alone. Bangkok's national public radio station, Radio Thailand (Sathãanii Wíthãyú Hàeng Pràthêt Thai), broadcasts English-language programmes at 97 FM from 6 am to 11 pm. Most of the programmes comprise local, national and international news, sports, business and special news-related features. For up-to-date news reports this is the station to listen to. An official news bulletin (national news sponsored by the government) is broadcast at 7 am, and 12.30 and 7 pm. The station hosts musical programmes between 9.15 and 11 am, and from 8.30 pm on.

Another public radio station is 107 FM, which is affiliated with Radio Thailand and Channel 9 on Thai public television. It broadcasts Radio Thailand news bulletins at the same hours as Radio Thailand (7 am, and 12.30 and 7 pm). Between 5 pm and 2 am daily, 107 FM features some surprisingly good music programmes with British, Thai and American DJs. Another station with international pop and English-speaking DJs is Radio Bangkok, 95.5 FM. Looking for Thai music? A station 87.5 FM broadcasts classic Thai pop, including old *lûuk thûng* styles played on accordion.

Close by at 95 FM, Digital Classic plays classical and instrumental sounds. Chulalongkorn University broadcasts classical music at 101.5 FM from 9.30 pm to midnight nightly, jazz from 4 to 5 pm. A schedule of the evening's programmes can be found in the *The Nation* and *Bangkok Post* newspapers.

In the evenings between 6 and 8 pm, several FM stations provide soundtracks in English for local and world satellite news on television Channel 3 (105.5 FM), Channel 7 (103.5 FM), Channel 9 (107 FM) and Channel 11 (88 FM).

The Voice of America, BBC World Service, Radio Canada, Radio New Zealand, Singapore Broadcasting Company and Radio Australia all have English and Thai-language broadcasts over short-wave radio from about 6 am to midnight. The radio frequencies and schedules, which change hourly, also appear in the *Post* and *The Nation*. Radio listeners without short-wave receivers can listen to VOA on 95.5 FM, and BBC World Service on 105 FM from midnight to 6 am.

Radio France Internationale and Deutsche Welle carry short-wave programmes in French and German respectively. Deutsche Welle also broadcasts 50 minutes of English programming three times daily.

**Television**

Thailand has five TV networks based in Bangkok. Following the 1991 coup the Thai government authorised an extension of telecast time to 24 hours and networks have been scrambling to fill air time ever since. As a result, there has been a substantial increase in English-language telecasts – mostly in the morning hours when Thais aren't used to watching TV.

Channel 5 is a military network (the only one to operate during coups) and broadcasts from 6 am to midnight: between 6 and 10 am this network presents a mix of ABC, CNN International and English-subtitled Thai news programmes; English-language news at noon and 7 pm; then CNN headlines again at 11.37 pm. Channel 9, the national public television station, broadcasts from 6 am until midnight. An English-language soundtrack is simulcast with Channel 9's evening news programme Monday to Friday at 7 pm on radio station FM 107.

Channel 3 is privately owned; broadcast hours vary but there's an English-language news simulcast at 7 pm on FM 105.5. Channel 7 is military owned but broadcast time is leased to private companies; the channel offers an English-language news simulcast via FM 103.5 at 7 pm. Channel 11 is run by the Ministry of Education and features educational programmes from 5.30 am to 11 pm, including TV correspondence classes from Ramkhamhaeng and Sukhothai Thammathirat open universities. An English-language news simulcast comes over FM 88 at 8 pm.

Upcountry cities will generally receive only two networks – Channel 9 and a local private network with restricted hours.

**Satellite & Cable TV** As elsewhere in Asia, satellite and cable television services are swiftly multiplying in Thailand, and competition for the largely untapped market is keen. Of the many regional satellite operations aimed at Thailand, the most successful so far is Satellite Television Asian Region (STAR), beamed from Hong Kong via AsiaSat 1 & 2. STAR offers five free 24 hour channels, including Music TV Asia (a tie-in with America's MTV music-video channel), Prime Sports (international sports coverage), BBC World Service Television (news) and two channels showing movies in Chinese and English. AsiaSat 1 & 2 also supply Channel V (a Hong Kong-based music video telecast), Zee TV (Hindi programming), Deutsche Welle (German government network), Pakistan TV and Myanmar TV.

Thailand has launched its own ThaiCom 1 & 2 as an uplink for AsiaSat and as carriers for the standard Thai networks as well as for International Broadcasting Corporation (IBC – news and entertainment), Vietnam Television and Thai Sky. The latter includes five channels offering news and documentaries, Thai music videos, Thai variety programmes, the BBC World Service and MTV-Asia.

Turner Broadcasting (CNN International), ESPN, HBO and various telecasts from Indonesia, Malaysia, the Philippines, Brunei and Australia are available in Thailand via Indonesia's Palapa C1 satellite. Other satellites tracked by dishes in Thailand include China's Apstar 1 and soon-to-be-launched Apstar 2.

Tourist-class hotels in Thailand often have one or more satellite TV channels (plus in-house video), including a STAR 'sampler' channel that switches from one STAR offering to another.

## PHOTOGRAPHY & VIDEO
### Film & Equipment
Print film is fairly inexpensive and widely available throughout Thailand. Japanese print film costs 65 to 70B per 36 exposures, US print film 75 to 90B. Fujichrome Velvia and Provia slide films cost around 160B per roll, Kodak Ektachrome Elite is 140B and Ektachrome 200 about 200B. Slide film, especially Kodachrome, can be hard to find outside Bangkok and Chiang Mai, so be sure to stock up before heading upcountry. Film processing is generally quite good in the larger cities in Thailand and also quite inexpensive. Kodachrome must be sent out of the country for processing, so it can take up to two weeks to get it back. Dependable E6 processing is available at several labs in Bangkok and Chiang Mai.

Pack some silica gel with your camera to prevent mould growing on the inside of your lenses. A polarising filter could be useful to cut down on tropical glare at certain times of day, particularly around water or highly polished glazed-tile work.

### Video
The predominant video format in Thailand is PAL, a system compatible with that used in most of Europe (France's SECAM format is a notable exception) as well as in Australia. This means if you're bringing videotapes from the USA or Japan, which use the NTSC format, you'll have to bring your own VCR to play them! Some video shops (especially those which carry pirated or unlicensed tapes) sell NTSC as well as PAL and SECAM tapes. A 'multisystem' VCR has the capacity to play both NTSC and PAL, but not SECAM.

### Photographing People
Hill-tribe people in some of the regularly visited areas expect money if you photograph them, while certain Karen and Akha will not allow you to point a camera at them. Use discretion when photographing villagers anywhere in Thailand as a camera can be a very intimidating instrument. You may feel better leaving your camera behind when visiting certain areas.

### Airport Security
The X-ray baggage inspection machines at Thailand's airports are all deemed film safe. Nevertheless if you're travelling with high-speed film (ISO 400 or above), you may want to have your film hand-inspected rather than X-rayed. Security inspectors are usually happy to comply. Packing your film in see-through plastic bags generally speeds up the hand inspection process. Some photographers pack their film in lead-lined bags to ward off potentially harmful rays.

## TIME
### Time Zone
Thailand's time zone is seven hours ahead of GMT/UTC (London). Thus, noon in Bangkok is 3 pm in Sydney, 1 pm in Perth, 6 am in Paris, 5 am in London, 1 am in New York and 10 pm the previous day in Los Angeles.

### Thai Calendar
The official year in Thailand is reckoned from 543 BC, the beginning of the Buddhist Era, so that 1997 AD is 2540 BE.

## ELECTRICITY
Electric current is 220V, 50 cycles. Electrical wall outlets are usually of the round, two pole type; some outlets also accept flat, two bladed terminals, and some will accept either flat or round terminals. Any electrical supply shop will carry adapters for any international plug shape as well as voltage converters.

## Thai Time

There are three ways of expressing time in Thailand: the common 12 hour system (eg 11 am is 12 hours distant from 11 pm); 'official' *(râatchakaan)* time, based on the 24 hour clock (eg 11 pm is the same as 2300 hours); and the traditional six hour system.

From dusk to dawn, most Thais tell time using the traditional six hour method. In this system, times are expressed the same way as in the 12 hour clock until 6 pm, but from 7 pm to midnight Thais use *thûm* (the sound of a drumstroke), counting from one to six – eg 7 pm is *nèung thûm* or 'one thum', 11 pm is *hâa thûm* or 'five thum'. After midnight *(thîang khêun)*, it's back to one again with the hours referred to as *tii* (the sound of wooden clackers), so that 3 am is *tii sǎam* or 'three tii' (the word order is reversed for tii). After 6 am Thai speakers revert to thum with the addition of the word *cháo* (morning), eg *sǎwng thûm cháo* is 'two thum chao' or 8 am.

At one time drums and wooden clackers were used throughout Thailand to mark the hours during these respective times of day. Today the wooden clackers are often replaced by steel bars, which neighbourhood watchmen clank together on the hour while guarding residential districts. If the neighbourhood's inhabitants don't hear the comforting clanks or clacks throughout the night they become alarmed. ■

## WEIGHTS & MEASURES

Dimensions and weight are usually expressed using the metric system in Thailand. The exception is land measure, which is often quoted using the traditional Thai system of *waa*, *ngaan* and *râi*. Old-timers in the provinces will occasionally use the traditional Thai system of weights and measures in speech, as will boat-builders, carpenters and other craftspeople when talking about their work. Here are some conversions to use for such occasions:

| | | |
|---|---|---|
| 1 sq *waa* | = | 4 sq m |
| 1 *ngaan* (100 sq waa) | = | 400 sq m |
| 1 *râi* (4 ngaan) | = | 1600 sq m |
| 1 *bàht* | = | 15g |
| 1 *taleung* or *tamleung* | | |
| (4 bàht) | = | 60g |
| 1 *châng* (20 taleung) | = | 1.2 kg |
| 1 *hàap* (50 chang) | = | 60 kg |
| 1 *níu* | = | about 2 cm |
| | | (or 1 inch) |
| 1 *khêup* (12 niu) | = | 25 cm |
| 1 *sàwk* (2 kheup) | = | 50 cm |
| 1 *waa* (4 sawk) | = | 2m |
| 1 *sén* (20 waa) | = | 40m |
| 1 *yôht* (400 sen) | = | 16 km |

## LAUNDRY

Virtually every hotel and guesthouse in Thailand offers a laundry service. Rates are generally geared to room rates; the cheaper the accommodation, the cheaper the washing and ironing. Cheapest of all are public laundries, where you pay by the kg.

Many Thai hotels and guesthouses also have laundry areas where you can wash your clothes at no charge; sometimes there's even a hanging area for drying. In accommodation where there is no laundry, do-it-yourselfers can wash their clothes in the sink and hang clothes out to dry in their rooms – see What to Bring in this chapter for useful laundry tools. Laundry detergent is readily available in general mercantile shops and supermarkets.

For dry-cleaning, take clothes to a dry-cleaner. Laundries that advertise dry-cleaning often don't really dry-clean (they just boil everything!) or do it badly. Luxury hotels usually have dependable dry-cleaning services.

Two reliable dry-cleaners in Bangkok are Erawan Dry Cleaners (basement of Landmark Plaza, Sukhumvit Rd) and Spotless Dry Cleaning & Laundry (166 Soi 23, Sukhumvit Rd). Both of these companies can dry-clean large items like sleeping bags as well as clothes.

# Thailand's Highlights

T hailand's travel scene has many faces and exploring all the country has to offer is a lifetime endeavour. Time and money constraints will compel most of us to decide – either in advance or as we go along – which parts we're going to see and which parts will have to be left out. In Thailand it usually pays to be a little under-ambitious with one's travel plans; don't try to see too much in too short an interval or your travels may quickly become a chore.

Your recreational and aesthetic inclinations will largely determine which direction you take. The basic threads most visitors are interested in following include islands and beaches, historic temple architecture, trekking, handicrafts and performing arts. These travel aspects are not necessarily mutually exclusive, though it's hard to find one place that has them all! In Songkhla, for example, you'll find handicrafts and beaches, while many places in the North-East offer temple ruins and handicrafts.

One of the main highlights of Thailand travel is just soaking up the general cultural ambience, which can be done just about anywhere in the country. You won't obtain much in terms of Thai culture if you spend most of your time sitting around in guesthouse cafes, hanging out on the beach or trekking with your own kind. At least once during your trip, try going to a small to medium-sized town well off the main tourist circuit, staying at a local hotel and eating in Thai curry shops and noodle stands. It's not as easy as going with the crowd but you'll learn a lot more about Thailand.

## Islands & Beaches

Thailand's coastline boasts some of the finest islands and beaches in Asia. Head to Southern Thailand if you have a week or more to spare and will be using ground transportation. Which side of the peninsula you choose – the Gulf of Thailand (for Prachuap Khiri Khan, Ko Samui, Songkhla) or the Andaman Sea (Phuket, Krabi, Trang) – might be determined by the time of year. Both sides are mostly rain-free from March to May, both are somewhat rainy from June to November, while the Gulf side is drier than the Andaman side from November to January.

For shorter beach excursions, check out the islands and beaches along the eastern Gulf coast of Central Thailand (Pattaya, Ko Samet, Ko Chang) or upper Gulf coast (Cha-am, Hua Hin). Or, if you can afford it, plan to fly to one of the airports in the Southern beach resort areas (eg Ko Samui, Phuket).

### Ko Chang                                        *Central, p 384*
An archipelago, with national marine park status in some areas, near the Cambodian border. The main island, Ko Chang, has coastal zones where development is permitted but so far high-profile development has been kept at bay by its distance from Bangkok and mountainous geography. Attracts those looking for quiet, economical beach stays. Accessible by boat only.

### Ko Samet                                        *Central, p 368*
Only three hours from Bangkok by road and boat on the eastern Gulf coast, this small island can be quite overrun on weekends and holidays. The fine white sand and clear waters attract a cross-section of expats, Thais and tourists. Some snorkelling at nearby islets. Accessible by boat only.

### Pattaya
*Central, p 356*

Golf, go-karting, parasailing, wave-running, sailboarding, high-style dining and a notorious nightlife attract those interested in an active, urbanised beach vacation on Thailand's eastern Gulf coast. The bay is less than clean – nearby Jomtien is a bit better – though there is fair snorkelling and diving at nearby islands (including shipwrecks).

### Prachuap Khiri Khan
*Central, p 403*

This province along the upper Gulf coast offers sandy beaches of medium quality along much of its length, from the well touristed Hua Hin in the north to little known Thai resorts near Ao Manao and Bang Saphan. Not much in the way of diving, but its seafood is superb and economical.

### Ko Pha-Ngan
*Southern, p 737*

Just north of Ko Samui in the Gulf, this is the main backpackers' headquarters at the moment since beach accommodation is the least expensive in the country; some more up-market places are emerging, too. Good snorkelling and diving in some parts of the island. Very little in the way of nightlife except at Hat Rin on the south-east tip, famous for its full moon parties (now on the wane). Accessible by boat only.

### Ko Samui
*Southern, p 720*

Off the coast of Surat Thani, this is Thailand's third largest island and undergoing very rapid development. Once a haven for backpackers on the Asian trail, it now mainly given over to middle-class hotels and guesthouses. Snorkelling and diving are fair. Accessible by boat and air.

### Ko Tao
*Southern, p 747*

A small island north of Ko Pha-Ngan with the best diving in the area. Development here has outpaced Ko Pha-Ngan for the most part due to the diving industry. Accessible by boat only.

### Ko Surin, Ko Similan & Ko Tarutao
*Southern, pp 683-6, 813*

These Andaman island groups are separate national marine parks that enjoy some of the best protection in Thailand (although not perfect by any means). Fantastic diving and snorkelling. Accommodation is limited to park bungalows and camping, except for one private island in Tarutao. Accessible by boat only, and only during the non-monsoon months (November to April).

### Phuket
*Southern, p 689*

On the Andaman coast, this is Thailand's largest island and the first to develop a tourist industry. Nowadays it has become a fairly sophisticated international resort destination, albeit one with the highest number of 'green' hotel developments as well as some highly regarded national parks. Good diving at nearby islands and reefs and Ao Phang-Nga. Best Thai cuisine of any of the islands. Accessible by air and road (via a causeway).

### Krabi
*Southern, p 778*

This province facing Ao Phang-Nga opposite Phuket on the Andaman coast offers a range of beaches and islands ringed with striking limestone formations. Rock-climbing, snorkelling, diving, boating and beach camping are the main activities. Generally quiet, though accommodation tends to book out from December to February, while it can be nearly deserted during May, June, September and October. Islands, and some beaches, accessible by boat only.

**Trang**                                                      *Southern, p 801*
A largely undiscovered province on the lower Andaman coast, though
the islands and beaches aren't as pretty as neighbouring Krabi's.
Good diving though you'll need your own gear. Islands accessible by
boat only.

**Songkhla, Pattani & Narathiwat**          *Southern, pp 764, 823, 827*
These deep south provinces on the lower Gulf coast near Malaysia
offer hundreds of km of deserted beach. During the north-east monsoon (November to March) the water tends to be murky due to cross-
currents.

## Historic Temple Architecture

The former Thai capitals of Ayuthaya, Lopburi, Kamphaeng Phet,
Sukhothai, Si Satchanalai and Chiang Mai offer a wide range of
Buddhist temple architecture, most of it from the 11th to 17th centuries. The Thai government has developed several of these sites into
historical parks, complete with on-site museums and impressive
temple restorations. For Khmer and Lao temple architecture, head to
Isaan (North-Eastern Thailand). Hundreds of Khmer ruins dating from
the 8th to 13th centuries – including many Angkor-period monuments
– dot the Isaan countryside.

See the special section on Thai Arts & Architecture in the Facts about
the Country chapter for more details on art styles and archaeological
sites.

**Ayuthaya**                                                *Central, p 300*
Just an hour or two north of Bangkok by road, this former royal capital
harbours 14th to 18th century temple ruins on an 'island' created by two
rivers and a canal. Although the surrounding urban environment
detracts a bit from the World Heritage-designated monuments, the
Ayuthaya Historical Park is perfect for those with limited time or a milder
interest in Thai temple ruins.

**Lopburi**                                                 *Central, p 312*
Because it features a mix of Khmer and Thai monuments, this central
Thai city is another noteworthy stop. The former palace of King Narai
(17th century), whose chief advisor was the Greek adventurer Constantin
Phaulkon, is particularly impressive.

**Chiang Mai & Lampang**                        *Northern, pp 423, 475*
These thoroughly Northern Thai cities contain many older wooden
temples built in the Shan, Burmese and Lanna styles. Wat Phra That
Lampang Luang in Lampang Province, thought to be Thailand's oldest
surviving wooden temple, makes an interesting side trip from Chiang
Mai.

**Sukhothai & Si Satchanalai**                  *Northern, pp 493, 497*
Both these former royal cities in lower Northern Thailand have been
made into historical parks that feature temple ruins dating to Thailand's
'Golden Age', the Sukhothai era (13th to 15th century). These two World
Heritage parks are well maintained; the one at Si Satchanalai is less
visited and hence offers more of an off-the-beaten-track atmosphere.

The secluded caves and coves of Krabi's striking limestone formations once presented ideal hide-outs for Asian pirates. Today, visitors can explore some of these rocky outcrops via sea canoe.

SARA JANE CLELAND

Wat Si Sawai, with its well preserved corncob-shaped prangs, was one of the earliest temples constructed in the former royal city of Sukhothai. The whole area, consisting of over 70 sites within a five km radius, has been declared a World Heritage historical park.

MARK KIRBY

Thousands of boats ply the seas in and around the islands of Southern Thailand, throwing out lines of fishing nets or transporting people and cargo. Boat-owners often decorate their boats with coloured ribbons to placate the spirits who inhabit the sea.

RICHARD NEBESKY

Thailand is essentially a country of rural villages, each with their own enduring local crafts. The village of Baw Sang, near Chiang Mai, produces these delicate hand-painted umbrellas.

RICHARD I'ANSON

SARA JANE CLELAND

Weaving techniques are traditionally passed down from generation to generation in the remote societies of the mountainous North. Designs differ significantly, depending on the region and village as well as the age and status of the wearer.

JOE CUMMINGS

Dr Thawi's Folk Museum in Phitsanulok displays many of the utensils that are used in everyday life in the North: earthenware pots, woven bamboo baskets and ladles for cooking and serving.

The small provincial capital of Kamphaeng Phet, once a royal fortress of the Sukhothai kingdom, has a little-visited historical park featuring the slender forms of weather-beaten Buddhas.

JOE CUMMINGS

The cascades of Nong Rong in Khao Yai National Park in the North-East form part of one of the largest intact monsoon forests in mainland Asia.

BERNARD NAPTHINE

Richly coloured and elaborately carved religious motifs traditionally adorned the entrances and porticoes of Thai temples in the North.

SARA JANE CLELAND

**Kamphaeng Phet**                                  *Northern, p 482*
Another World Heritage site in lower Northern Thailand and featuring
Sukhothai-era temple ruins, this is a smaller historical park but also well
maintained.

**Isaan**                                  *North-Eastern, pp 585, 590*
The most impressive sites are those at Prasat Hin Phimai in Nakhon
Ratchasima Province and Prasat Hin Khao Phanom Rung (abbreviated
to Phanom Rung) in Buriram Province, but don't neglect some of the
smaller, out-of-the-way spots if you have the time and inclination. Dozens
of famous Lao temples – both ruins and operating wats – can be found along
the Maekhong River from Loei Province to Ubon Ratchathani Province.

# Handicrafts
Thailand's ethnic diversity means that a wide range of handicrafts is
available for study or purchase throughout the country.

**Chiang Mai**                                  *Northern, p 423*
As the cultural and business capital of Northern Thailand, Chiang Mai
has been the North's main handicrafts centre for over 30 years. Here
you'll find virtually every type of craft produced in the region, as well as
materials from Myanmar (Burma) and Laos. Northern specialities
include silverwork, woodcarving, painted umbrellas, hill-tribe crafts,
leather, ceramics and antique furniture.

**Nakhon Ratchasima & Surrounds**  *North-Eastern, pp 575, 598, 607*
The best selection of handmade cotton and silk textiles is found in the
central North-Eastern capitals of Nakhon Ratchasima (Khorat), Khon
Kaen, Roi Et and Udon Thani. Visit some of these silk-weaving towns to
experience first-hand Thai weaving techniques.

**Ubon Ratchathani**                                  *North-Eastern, p 649*
In Thailand's north-eastern corner, this provincial capital offers a good
selection of crafts from nearby Cambodia and Laos, plus locally produced silver and ceramics.

**Nakhon Si Thammarat**                                  *Southern, p 754*
This provincial town on the lower Gulf coast is a busy centre for many
indigenous handicrafts: nielloware, silverware, shadow-play cutouts and
intricate basketry.

**Songkhla & Surrounds**                *Southern, pp 764, 819, 823, 827*
For cotton prints, sarongs and batik (with Malay-Indonesian design
influences), visit the Southern provinces of Songkhla, Yala, Pattani and
Narathiwat near the Malaysian border.

# Museums
Thailand's Fine Arts Department maintains a good national museum
system with regional branches throughout the country, and there are also
a few idiosyncratic collections sponsored by other public as well as
private organisations. The better ones are listed on the following page.

### National Museum                                 *Bangkok, p 228*
Housed in a former vice-regal palace, the country's most well endowed museum contains pottery, sculpture, furniture, clothing and musical instruments from many other places in South-East Asia as well as Thailand. Phutthaisawan (Buddhaisawan) Chapel, a temple building on the grounds, contains some of the country's finest Buddhist mural paintings.

### Chao Sam Phraya Museum & Palace        *Central, p 303*
Ayuthaya's 500 year history is the source of an extensive display of art and artefacts distributed among two separate national museums.

### Nan National Museum                          *Northern, p 564*
This is the best place in Thailand to view art objects from the little known Nan kingdom in the far north, including pieces of Lao and Thai Lü provenance.

### Phimai National Museum                 *North-Eastern, p 585*
A relatively new and well designed museum in the small town of Phimai containing exhibits of Khmer art from the Angkor period as well as earlier Dvaravati-style art.

### Dr Thawi's Folk Museum                      *Northern, p 487*
The nation's best preserved collection of Northern Thai folk utensils, including everything from basketry and ceramics to coconut graters, can be found in this museum in Phitsanulok.

### Ko Yo Folklore Museum                      *Southern, p 769*
Near Songkhla, this is a newer museum sponsored by the Institute of Southern Thai Studies, with an impressive array of Southern Thai religious and folk art.

## National Parks
Thailand boasts nearly 80 national parks, a number expected to exceed 100 by the end of the century. See the Ecology & Environment section in the Facts about the Country chapter for general information about the country's protected areas, and the destination chapters for complete details on each of the parks covered in this guidebook. The book *National Parks of Thailand*, by Denis Gray, Colin Piprell & Mark Graham, is the most comprehensive source of English-language material on the parklands.

### Kaeng Krachan National Park                    *Central, p 399*
Thailand's largest and least explored park covers almost 3000 sq km of evergreen and mixed deciduous forests along the Myanmar border in Phetburi Province. Bisected by the Tenasserim Range, the park serves as a major watershed for upper Southern Thailand, feeding the huge Kaeng Krachan Reservoir. For hikers and campers who venture into the interior, wildlife viewing – especially gibbons and hornbills – can be superb. Guides and accommodation are available. Best visited November to April.

### Doi Inthanon National Park                    *Northern, p 464*
This 482 sq km park near Chiang Mai surrounds Thailand's tallest peak. The misty upper slopes support a profusion of orchids, lichens, mosses and epiphytes as well as nearly 400 bird varieties – more than any other habitat in Thailand. Can be enjoyed all year round, though the summit is quite cold (by South-East Asian standards) from November to February.

**Thung Salaeng Luang Wildlife Sanctuary**  *Northern, p 493*
Formerly a major base for communist insurgents, 1,262 sq km Thung
Salaeng Luang encompasses vast meadows and dipterocarp forests –
good hiking territory. The Siamese fireback pheasant is one of its most
famous feathered residents. Limited facilities. Best visited in the cool
season, November to February.

**Khao Yai National Park**  *North-Eastern, p 587*
The kingdom's oldest and third largest national park, in Nakhon
Ratchasima Province, is considered one of the best in the world in terms
of wildlife variation and scope of protection – it was recently designated
as an ASEAN National Heritage Site. Its 2172 sq km encompasses one
of the largest intact monsoon forests in South-East Asia, and is home to
a sizeable herd of wild elephants. Limited accommodation is available
again after a brief hiatus, and there are hotels and guesthouses in nearby
Pak Chong. Best visited October to June.

**Nam Nao National Park**  *North-Eastern, p 636*
Wide expanses of dry dipterocarp forest, bamboo groves and rolling
sandstone hills combine to provide excellent hiking potential in this park,
which borders Chaiyaphum Province. There's plenty of wildlife as the park
abuts Phu Khiaw Wildlife Sanctuary. Accommodation is very limited, both
inside and outside the park. Can be visited all year round, though the forest
is most lush May to November.

**Phu Kradung National Park**  *North-Eastern, p 629*
This flat-topped, bell-shaped mountain park in Loei Province is a favourite
with Thais for its pine forests and sweeping views. The well marked, nine
km ascent offers benches and shelters along the way; tents can be rented
at the summit. Elephants are occasionally seen. Best visited October to
December; during the rainy season ascents can become very difficult.

**Khao Sok National Park**  *Southern, p 719*
Limestone crags, rainforests and jungle streams provide the perfect environment for the remnants of Thailand's threatened tiger and clouded leopard,
as well as two species of Rafflesia in the western part of Surat Thani
Province. Treehouse-style accommodation protects the forest floor and
offers visitors an opportunity to experience one of the country's most
important ecosystems. Best visited December to February.

**Similan Islands National Marine Park**  *Southern, p 685*
Although relatively small, this remote nine-island archipelago off the
upper Andaman coast has become one of Thailand's better known dive
destinations due its profusion of hard corals growing on huge rock reefs.
Sea turtles are known to nest here. Camping and bungalows found on
one island only. Best visited November to April.

**Thaleh Ban National Park**  *Southern, p 818*
White meranti forest, waterfalls, limestone formations, a natural lake and
highly varied birdlife make up the attractions of this little visited 196 sq
km park, which straddles the Thai-Malaysian border in Satun Province.
Camping and bungalows available. Best visited December to March.

## HEALTH

Travel health depends on your predeparture preparations, your day-to-day health care while travelling and how you handle any medical problem or emergency that does develop. While the list of potential dangers can seem quite frightening, with a little luck, some basic precautions and adequate information few travellers experience more than upset stomachs.

### Travel Health Guides

There are a number of books on travel health:

*Staying Healthy in Asia, Africa & Latin America* – Moon Publications, 1994. Probably the best all-round guide to carry, as it's compact but very detailed and well organised.

*Travellers' Health* – Dr Richard Dawood, Oxford University Press, 1995. Comprehensive, easy to read, authoritative and also highly recommended, although it's rather large to lug around.

*Where There is No Doctor* – David Werner, Macmillan, 1994. A very detailed guide intended for someone (such as a Peace Corps volunteer) going to work in an undeveloped country, rather than for the average traveller.

*Travel with Children* – Maureen Wheeler, Lonely Planet Publications, 1995. Includes basic advice on travel health for younger children.

*Guide to Healthy Living in Thailand* – published jointly by the Thai Red Cross Society and US embassy. Available from the 'Snake Farm' (Queen Saovabha Memorial Institute) for 100B, this booklet is rich in practical health advice on safe eating, child care, tropical heat, immunisations and local hospitals. Contains wise tidbits with a literary flair, including 'Bangkok is a stopping point for many travellers and restless souls. Acute psychiatric emergencies, including alcohol and drug abuse, are, unfortunately, not rare' and 'Bangkok's traffic poses a far greater danger than snakes and tropical diseases combined.'

There are also a number of excellent travel health sites on the Internet. From the Lonely Planet home page at http://www.lonely planet.com, there are links, at http://www.lonelyplanet.com/health/health.htm/h-links.htm, to the World Health Organisation (WHO), Centers for Diseases Control & Prevention in Atlanta (Georgia) and Stanford University Travel Medicine Service.

### Predeparture Preparations

**Health Insurance** A travel insurance policy to cover theft, loss and medical problems is a wise idea. There is a wide variety of policies and your travel agent will have recommendations. Some policies offer lower and higher medical-expense options but the higher ones are chiefly for countries like the USA which have extremely high medical costs. Check the small print:

- Some policies specifically exclude 'dangerous activities' which can include scuba diving, motorcycling, even trekking. If such activities are on your agenda you don't want that sort of policy. A locally acquired motorcycle licence may not be valid under your policy.
- You may prefer a policy which pays doctors or hospitals direct rather than one which requires you to pay on the spot and claim later. If you have to claim later, make sure you keep all documentation. Some policies ask you to call back (reverse charges) to a centre in your home country where an immediate assessment of your problem is made.
- Check if the policy covers ambulances or an emergency flight home. If you have to stretch out you will need two seats and somebody has to pay for them!

**Medical Kit** A small, straightforward medical kit is a wise thing to carry. A possible kit list includes:

- Aspirin or paracetamol (acetaminophen in the USA) – for pain or fever.
- Antihistamine (such as Benadryl) – useful as a decongestant for colds and allergies, to ease the itch from insect bites or stings and to help prevent motion sickness. There are several antihistamines on the market, all with different pros and cons, so it's worth discussing your requirements with a pharmacist or doctor. Antihistamines may cause sedation and interact with alcohol so care should be taken when using them.
- Antibiotics – useful if you're travelling well off the beaten track, but they must be prescribed and you should carry the prescription with you.
- Loperamide (eg Imodium) or Lomotil – for diarrhoea. Antidiarrhoea medication should not be given to children under the age of 12.

- Rehydration mixture – for treatment of severe diarrhoea. This is particularly important if travelling with children, but is recommended for everyone.
- Antiseptic such as povidone-iodine (eg Betadine), which comes as a solution, ointment, powder and impregnated swabs – for cuts and grazes.
- Multivitamins – are a worthwhile consideration, especially for long trips when dietary vitamin intake may be inedequate. Men, women and children each have different vitamin requirements so obtain multivitamin tablets which are specific to age and gender.
- Calamine lotion or Stingose spray – to ease irritation from bites or stings.
- Bandages and Band-aids – for minor injuries.
- Scissors, tweezers and a thermometer (note that mercury thermometers are prohibited by airlines).
- Cold and flu tablets and throat lozenges.
- Insect repellent, sunscreen, chap stick and water purification tablets.
- A couple of syringes, in case you need injections. Ask your doctor for a note explaining why they have been prescribed.

Ideally, antibiotics should be administered only under medical supervision and should never be taken indiscriminately. Take only the recommended dose at the prescribed intervals and continue using the antibiotic for the prescribed period, even if the illness seems to be cured earlier. Antibiotics are quite specific to the infections they can treat. Stop immediately if there are any serious reactions and don't use the antibiotic at all if you are unsure that you have the correct one.

In Thailand medicine is generally available over the counter and the price will be much cheaper than in the west. However, be careful when buying drugs, particularly where the expiry date may have passed or correct storage conditions may not have been followed. Bogus drugs are not uncommon and it's possible that drugs which are no longer recommended, or have even been banned, in the west are still being dispensed in Thailand.

**Health Preparations** Make sure you're healthy before you start travelling. If you are embarking on a long trip make sure your teeth are OK; there are lots of places where a visit to the dentist would be the last thing you'd want to do.

If you wear glasses, take a spare pair and your prescription. Losing your glasses can be a real problem, although in many places you can get new spectacles made up quickly, cheaply and competently.

If you require a particular medication take an adequate supply, as it may not be available locally. Take the prescription or, better still, part of the packaging showing the generic rather than the brand name (which may not be locally available), as it will make getting replacements easier. It's a wise idea to have a legible prescription with you to show you legally use the medication – it's surprising how often over-the-counter drugs from one place are illegal without a prescription or even banned in another.

**Immunisations** Vaccinations provide protection against diseases you might meet along the way. However, there are no health requirements for Thailand in terms of required vaccinations unless you are coming from an infected area (eg Africa). Smallpox has now been wiped out worldwide, so immunisation is no longer necessary.

Any vaccinations that you do have should be recorded on an International Health Certificate, which is available from your physician or government health department.

Plan ahead for getting your vaccinations: some of them require an initial shot followed by a booster, while some vaccinations should not be given together. It is recommended you seek medical advice at least six weeks prior to travel.

Most travellers from western countries will have been immunised against various diseases during childhood but your doctor may still recommend booster shots against measles or polio. The period of protection offered by vaccinations differs widely and some are contraindicated if you are pregnant.

In Thailand immunisations are available from a number of sources, including both public hospitals and private clinics. Bangkok is your best bet in terms of locating less common or more expensive vaccines.

Vaccinations you should consider having for Thailand are:

*Tetanus & Diphtheria* – Boosters are necessary every 10 years and protection is highly recommended.

*Typhoid* – Available either as an injection or oral capsules. Protection lasts from one to five years and is useful if you are travelling for long in rural, tropical areas. You may get some side effects such as pain at the injection site, fever, headache and a general unwell feeling. A new single-dose injectable vaccine (Typhim Vi), which appears to have few side effects, is now available but is more expensive. Side effects are unusual with the oral form but occasionally an individual will have stomach cramps.

*Hepatitis A* – The most common travel-acquired illness which can be prevented by vaccination. Protection can be provided in two ways – either with the antibody gamma globulin or with a vaccine called Havrix 1440.

Havrix 1440 provides long-term immunity (possibly more than 10 years) after an initial injection and a booster at six to 12 months. It may be more expensive than gamma globulin but certainly has many advantages, including length of protection and ease of administration. It is important to know that, being a vaccine, it will take about three weeks to provide satisfactory protection – hence the need for careful planning prior to travel.

Gamma globulin is not a vaccination but a ready-made antibody which has proven very successful in reducing the chances of hepatitis infection. Because it may interfere with the development of immunity, it should not be given until at least 10 days after administration of the last vaccine needed; it should also be given as close as possible to departure because it is at its most effective in the first few weeks after administration and the effectiveness tapers off gradually between three and six months.

*Hepatitis B* – Travellers at risk of contact are strongly advised to be vaccinated, especially if they are children or will have close contact with children. The vaccination course comprises three injections given over a six month period then boosters every three to five years. The initial course of injections can be given over as short a period as 28 days then boosted after 12 months if more rapid protection is required.

*Rabies* – Pretravel rabies vaccination involves having three injections over 21 to 28 days and should be considered by those who will spend a month or longer in an area where rabies is common, especially if they are cycling, handling animals, caving, travelling to remote areas, or children (who may not report a bite). If someone who has been vaccinated is bitten or scratched by an animal they will require two booster injections of vaccine.

*Japanese Encephalitis* – A good idea for those who think they may be at moderate or high risk while in Thailand.

See the relevant entries later on in this section for further information.

## Basic Rules

Care in what you eat and drink is the most important health rule; stomach upsets are the most likely travel health problem (between 30% and 50% of travellers in a two week stay experience this) but the majority of these upsets will be relatively minor. Don't become paranoid; trying the local food is part of the experience of travel, after all.

**Water** If you don't know for certain that the water is safe always assume the worst. Reputable brands of Thai bottled water or soft drinks are generally fine, although in some places bottles refilled with tap water are not unknown. Only use water from containers with a serrated seal – not tops or corks. Take care with fruit juice, particularly if water may have been added. Chinese tea served in most restaurants is safe.

Ice is produced from purified water under hygienic conditions and is therefore theoretically safe. During transit to the local restaurant, however, conditions are not so hygienic (you may see blocks of ice being dragged along the street), but it's very difficult to resist in the hot season. The rule of thumb is that if it's chipped ice, it probably came from an ice block (which may not have been handled well) but if it's ice cubes or 'tubes', it was delivered from the ice factory in sealed plastic. In rural areas, villagers mostly drink collected rainwater. Most travellers can drink this without problems, but some people can't tolerate it.

In Thailand, virtually no-one bothers with filters, tablets or iodine since bottled water is so cheap and readily available. Try to purchase the water bottles, however, as these are recyclable (unlike the plastic disposable ones).

**Food** Salads and fruit should be washed with

purified water or peeled where possible. Ice cream is usually OK if it is a reputable brand name, but beware of street vendors and of ice cream that has melted and been refrozen. Thoroughly cooked food is safest but not if it has been left to cool or if it has been reheated. Uncooked shellfish such as mussels, oysters and clams should be avoided as well as undercooked meat, particularly in the form of mince. Steaming does not make shellfish safe for eating.

If a place looks clean and well run and if the vendor also looks clean and healthy, then the food is probably safe. In general, places that are packed with travellers or locals will be fine, while empty restaurants are questionable. Busy restaurants mean the food is being cooked and eaten quite quickly with little standing around and is probably not being reheated.

**Nutrition** If your food is poor or limited in availability, if you're travelling hard and fast and therefore missing meals, or if you simply lose your appetite, you can soon start to lose weight and place your health at risk.

Make sure your diet is well balanced. Eggs, tofu, beans, lentils and nuts are all safe ways to get protein. Fruit you can peel (eg bananas, oranges or mandarins) is usually safe and a good source of vitamins. Try to eat plenty of grains (rice) and bread. Remember that although food is generally safer if it is cooked well, overcooked food loses much of its nutritional value. If your diet isn't well balanced or if your food intake is insufficient, it's a good idea to take vitamin and iron pills.

In hot weather make sure you drink enough – don't rely on feeling thirsty to indicate when you should drink. Not needing to urinate or very dark yellow urine is a danger sign. Always carry a water bottle with you on long trips. Excessive sweating can lead to loss of salt and therefore muscle cramping. Salt tablets are not a good idea as a preventative, but in places where salt is not used much adding salt to food can help.

**Everyday Health** A normal body temperature is 37°C (or 98.6°F); more than 2°C (4°F)

higher is a 'high' fever. A normal adult pulse rate is 60 to 100 per minute (children 80 to 100, babies 100 to 140). You should know how to take a temperature and a pulse rate. As a general rule the pulse increases about 20 beats per minute for each °C (2°F) rise in fever.

Respiration (breathing) rate is also an indicator of illness. Count the number of breaths per minute: between 12 and 20 is normal for adults and older children (up to 30 for younger children, 40 for babies). People with a high fever or serious respiratory illness (like pneumonia) breathe more quickly than normal. More than 40 shallow breaths a minute usually means pneumonia.

Clean your teeth with purified water rather than straight from the tap. Avoid climatic extremes: keep out of the sun when it's hot, dress warmly when it's cold. Avoid potential diseases by dressing sensibly. You can get worm infections through walking barefoot or dangerous coral cuts by walking over coral without shoes. You can avoid insect bites by covering bare skin when insects are around, by screening windows or beds or by using insect repellents. Seek local advice: if you're told the water is unsafe due to jellyfish, crocodiles or bilharzia, don't go in. In situations where there is no information, discretion is the better part of valour.

It is important for people travelling in areas of poor sanitation to adjust their personal hygiene habits.

### Medical Problems & Treatment

Self-diagnosis and treatment can be risky, so wherever possible seek qualified help. Although we do give treatment dosages in this section, they are for emergency use only. Medical advice should be sought where possible before administering any drugs.

An embassy or consulate can usually recommend a good place to go for such advice. So can five-star hotels, although they often recommend doctors with five-star prices. (This is when that medical insurance really comes in useful!) In some places standards of medical attention are so low that for some ailments the best advice is to get on a plane and go somewhere else.

### AIDS in Thailand

Because HIV infections are often associated with sexual contact and Thailand has an international reputation for illicit night-time activities, rumours regarding the status of AIDS in the country vary wildly. Some think the threat is greatly exaggerated while others are convinced the Thai government is involved in a massive cover-up of the epidemic. The risks of contracting the disease are very real but should be placed in perspective.

For the record, as of January 1996 the World Health Organisation (WHO) estimated there were approximately 600,000 HIV-positive cases in Thailand (the country's total population is approximately 61 million), a number also supported by the country's Ministry of Public Health research. An estimated 6% of these are thought to be full-blown AIDS cases but the number will undoubtedly have increased by the time you read this. Thirty-three percent of all reported infections are thought to be associated with intravenous drug injection, most of the remainder from sexual transmission. Thai women and their children are now the highest risk group, as infection has moved from the homosexual population in the early 1980s to intravenous drug users mid-decade and then from prostitutes in the late 1980s to the general population. In Thailand, homosexual/bisexual males now have the lowest incidence of infection next to blood-transfusion recipients, dispelling the myth that AIDS is a 'gay disease'. Statistics show one HIV-positive male homosexual for every 100 HIV-positive female prostitutes.

Thus the main risk to the casual male visitor is HIV transmission via sexual contact with prostitutes or any Thai female whose HIV infection status is unknown. According to AIDS researchers, the percentage of HIV-positive prostitutes is much higher in rural areas than in Bangkok, especially in Northern Thailand – which, for Thai males, is the 'capital' of Thai prostitution. A 1993 provincial health investigation, for example, found that 70% of prostitutes tested in Chiang Rai Province were HIV-positive; Northern Thailand in general accounts for about 75% of all infections reported. The apparent reason for this is that Bangkok sex workers are much more likely to insist on condom use than their provincial counterparts. Thai male customers, on the other hand, are much less likely to use condoms than farang customers, which explains why even Pattaya – the capital for sex services to foreigners – shows a lower rate of infection than anywhere in the North. Of the estimated 210,000 full-time sex workers in the country, the vast majority are patronised by Thai customers, and since Thai males visit prostitutes an average of twice a month the virus is now finding its way to their wives and girlfriends. A recent American study concluded that 12% of military draftees stationed outside Bangkok were HIV-infected.

For female visitors the main risk is having sexual contact with any male – Thai or farang – known to have had intercourse with Thai prostitutes since the mid-1980s. For both genders, the second highest risk activity would be any use of unsterilised needles, especially in illicit intravenous drug use.

### Environmental Hazards

**Sunburn** In the tropics you can get sunburnt surprisingly quickly, even through cloud. Use a sunscreen and take extra care to cover areas which don't normally see sun – eg your feet. A hat provides added protection, and you should also use zinc cream or some other barrier cream for your nose and lips. Calamine lotion is good for mild sunburn.

Remember that too much sunlight, whether its direct or reflected (glare) can damage your eyes. If your plans include being near water or sand, then good sunglasses are doubly important. Good quality sunglasses are treated to filter out ultraviolet radiation, but poor quality sunglasses provide limited filtering, allowing more ultraviolet light to be absorbed than if no sunglasses were worn at all. Excessive ultraviolet light will damage the surface structures and lens of the eye.

**Prickly Heat** Prickly heat is an itchy rash caused by excessive perspiration trapped under the skin. It usually strikes people who

The Thai government is not involved in covering up the epidemic and is in fact very keen to make HIV/AIDS statistics public and to educate the public about the disease and how to prevent transmission. Even the Tourism Authority of Thailand addresses the issue in their annual reports. WHO officials report that Thailand has done more than any other country in South-East Asia to combat the AIDS threat, including following a WHO-approved national AIDS-prevention campaign since 1988. Radio and TV ads, public billboards and AIDS-awareness marches became everyday occurrences much sooner in Thailand than in Europe or the USA relative to the occurrence of the country's first known AIDS-related death (1984). The ministry is also establishing outpatient centres at provincial hospitals around the nation to provide medical care, counselling and psycho-social support for HIV carriers.

On a local level, Ministry of Public Health offices are undertaking intensive public awareness programmes, conducting regular blood tests in brothels, massage parlours and coffee houses and distributing free condoms at their office locations as well as at sex service locations (including hotels). But health officials don't have the power to close sex service operations; even if they could, officials say this would only force prostitution underground where it would be even more difficult to monitor and educate sex workers.

As with their success in sharply reducing population growth in the 1970s, the ministry's aggressive AIDS campaign in the 1980s and 1990s seems to be having a positive effect. A survey conducted by Thailand's Epidemiology Department during 1993 revealed that the HIV infection rate (the frequency with which new infections develop) among sex workers had dropped 60% over the previous four years. This has been confirmed by long-term Population & Community Development Association (PDA) studies, which note that in the mid to late 1980s HIV figures in Thailand were doubling every six months, a rate which soon slowed to doubling every year, and is now doubling every two years. Between 1991 and 1994 Thailand's overall infection rate dropped 77%, an achievement that earned PDA director Mechai Viravaidya the prestigious Magsaysay Award in 1994. Since the 1970s, when Mechai initiated a vigorous national programme aimed at educating the public about contraception, the most common Thai nickname for 'condom' has been 'Mechai'. At last report an estimated 82 new infections per day were occurring, down from 600 only three years ago; Thai health officials are confident the country can cut this rate in half by the end of the 1990s.

Although the following comparisons shouldn't be taken to mean that precautions aren't absolutely mandatory, WHO officials estimate Thailand has a lower per-capita HIV infection rate than Australia, Switzerland or the USA. Among Asian countries, WHO reports the infection rate and projected vulnerability for AIDS are now higher in India, Pakistan, Bangladesh, Myanmar, Cambodia and the Philippines. As of the end of 1995 WHO reported that 70% of all HIV/AIDS cases were found in Africa, 18% in the Americas, 6% in Asia, 4% in Europe and 1% in Oceania. As elsewhere around the globe, however, absolute numbers will only increase with time until/unless a cure is discovered.

In May 1994 the Ministry of Public Health – in a somewhat controversial move – authorised a US biomedical company to begin testing a new AIDS vaccine in Thailand, the results of which won't be available for several years to come. In the meantime, behaviour modification is the best strategy available for combating the spread of the disease.

One of Thailand's chief accomplishments in the war against HIV transmission is that the medical blood supply is now considered safe, thanks to vigorous screening procedures. ■

have just arrived in a hot climate and whose pores have not yet opened sufficiently to cope with greater sweating. Keeping cool but bathing often, using a mild talcum powder or even resorting to air-conditioning may help until you acclimatise.

**Heat Exhaustion** Dehydration or salt deficiency can cause heat exhaustion. Take time to acclimatise to high temperatures and make sure you get sufficient liquids. Salt deficiency is characterised by fatigue, lethargy, head-aches, giddiness and muscle cramps and in this case salt tablets may help. Vomiting or diarrhoea can deplete your liquid and salt levels.

Anhydrotic heat exhaustion, caused by an inability to sweat, is quite rare. Unlike the other forms of heat exhaustion it is likely to strike people who have been in a hot climate for some time, rather than newcomers.

**Heat Stroke** This serious, sometimes fatal, condition can occur if the body's heat-regulating mechanism breaks down and the body temperature rises to dangerous levels. Long, continuous periods of exposure to high temperatures can leave you vulnerable to heat stroke. You should avoid excessive alcohol or strenuous activity when you first arrive in a hot climate.

The symptoms are feeling unwell, not sweating very much or at all and a high body temperature (39°C to 41°C, or 102°F to 106°F). Where sweating has ceased the skin becomes flushed and red. Severe, throbbing headaches and lack of coordination will also occur, and the sufferer may be confused or aggressive. Eventually the victim will become delirious or convulse. Hospitalisation is essential, but meanwhile get victims out of the sun, remove their clothing, cover them with a wet sheet or towel and then fan continually.

**Fungal Infections** Hot-weather fungal infections are most likely to occur on the scalp, between the toes or fingers (athlete's foot), in the groin (jock itch or crotch rot) and on the body (ringworm). You get ringworm (which is a fungal infection, not a worm) from infected animals or by walking on damp areas, like shower floors.

To prevent fungal infections wear loose, comfortable clothes, avoid artificial fibres, wash frequently and dry carefully. If you do get an infection, wash the infected area daily with a disinfectant or medicated soap and water, and rinse and dry well. Apply an antifungal powder like the widely available Tinaderm. Try to expose the infected area to air or sunlight as much as possible and wash all towels and underwear in hot water as well as changing them often.

**Cold** Too much cold is just as dangerous as too much heat, particularly if it leads to hypothermia. If you are trekking at high altitudes or simply taking a long bus trip over mountains, particularly at night, be prepared. In Thailand this is usually only a potential problem in the North and North-East.

Hypothermia occurs when the body loses heat faster than it can produce it and the core temperature of the body falls. It is surprisingly easy to progress from very cold to dangerously cold due to a combination of wind, wet clothing, fatigue and hunger, even if the air temperature is above freezing. It is best to dress in layers; silk, wool and some of the new artificial fibres are all good insulating materials. A hat is important, as a lot of heat is lost through the head. A strong, waterproof outer layer is essential, as keeping dry is vital. Carry basic supplies, including food containing simple sugars to generate heat quickly and lots of fluid to drink.

Symptoms of hypothermia are exhaustion, numb skin (particularly toes and fingers), shivering, slurred speech, irrational or violent behaviour, lethargy, stumbling, dizzy spells, muscle cramps and violent bursts of energy. Irrationality may take the form of sufferers claiming they are warm and trying to take off their clothes.

To treat hypothermia, first get the person out of the wind and/or rain, remove their clothing if it's wet and replace it with dry, warm clothing. Give them hot liquids – not alcohol – and some high-kilojoule, easily digestible food. This should be enough for the early stages of hypothermia, but if it has gone further it may be necessary to place victims in warm sleeping bags and get in with them. Do not rub victims but place them near a fire. If possible, place a sufferer in a warm (not hot) bath.

**Motion Sickness** Eating lightly before and during a trip will reduce the chances of motion sickness. If you are prone to motion sickness try to find a place that minimises disturbance – near the wing on aircraft, close to midships on boats, near the centre on buses. Fresh air usually helps, reading or cigarette smoke don't. Commercial antimotion-sickness preparations, which can cause drowsiness, have to be taken before the trip commences; when you're feeling sick it's too late. Ginger (available in capsule form) and peppermint (including mint-flavoured sweets) are natural preventives.

## Infectious Diseases

**Diarrhoea** A change of water, food or climate can all cause the runs; diarrhoea caused by contaminated food or water is more serious. Despite all your precautions you may still get a bout of mild travellers' diarrhoea but a few rushed toilet trips with no other symptoms is not indicative of a serious problem. Moderate diarrhoea, involving half a dozen loose movements in a day, is more of a nuisance. Dehydration is the main danger with any diarrhoea, particularly for children where dehydration can occur quite quickly. Fluid replacement remains the mainstay of management. Weak black tea with a little sugar, soda water, or soft drinks allowed to go flat and diluted 50% with water, are all good. With severe diarrhoea a rehydrating solution is necessary to replace minerals and salts. Commercially available ORS (oral rehydration salts) is very useful; add the contents of one sachet to a litre of boiled or bottled water. In an emergency you can make up a solution of eight teaspoons of sugar to a litre of boiled water and eat salted cracker biscuits at the same time. You should stick to a bland diet as you recover.

Lomotil or Imodium can be used to bring relief from the symptoms, although they do not actually cure the problem. Only use these drugs if absolutely necessary – eg if you *must* travel. For children under 12 years, Lomotil and Imodium are not recommended. Under all circumstances fluid replacement is the main message. Do not use these drugs if the person has a high fever or is severely dehydrated.

In certain situations the need for antibiotics may be indicated by: diarrhoea with blood and mucous (gut-paralysing drugs like Imodium or Lomotil should be avoided in this situation); watery diarrhoea with fever and lethargy; persistent diarrhoea for more than five days; severe diarrhoea, if it is logistically difficult to stay in one place.

The recommended drugs (adults only) are either norfloxacin 400 mg twice daily for three days or ciprofloxacin 500 mg twice daily for three days.

The drug bismuth subsalicylate has also been used successfully. It is not available in some countries. The dosage for adults is two tablets or 30 ml; for children it is one tablet or 10 ml. This dose can be repeated every 30 minutes to one hour, with no more than eight doses in a 24 hour period.

The drug of choice for children is co-trimoxazole (Bactrim, Septrin, Resprim) with dosage dependent on weight. A five day course is given.

**Giardiasis** The parasite causing this intestinal disorder is present in contaminated water. The symptoms are stomach cramps, nausea, a bloated stomach, watery and foul-smelling diarrhoea and frequent gas. Giardiasis can appear several weeks after you have been exposed to the parasite. The symptoms may disappear for a few days and then return; this can go on for several weeks. Tinidazole (known as Fasigyn) or metronidazole (Flagyl) are the recommended drugs for treatment. Either can be used in a single treatment dose. Antibiotics are of no use.

**Dysentery** This serious illness is caused by contaminated food or water and is characterised by severe diarrhoea, often with blood or mucous in the stool. There are two kinds of dysentery. Bacillary dysentery is characterised by a high fever and rapid onset; headache, vomiting and stomach pains are also symptoms. It generally does not last longer than a week, but it is highly contagious. Amoebic dysentery is often more gradual in the onset of symptoms, with cramping abdominal pain and vomiting less likely; fever may not be present. It is not a self-limiting disease: it will persist until treated and can recur and cause long-term health problems.

A stool test is necessary to diagnose which kind of dysentery you have, so you should seek medical help urgently. In case of an emergency the drugs norfloxacin or ciprofloxacin can be used as presumptive treatment for bacillary dysentery, and metronidazole (Flagyl) for amoebic dysentery. For bacillary dysentery, norfloxacin 400 mg twice daily for seven days or ciprofloxacin 500 mg twice daily for seven days are the recommended dosages.

If you're unable to find either of these drugs then a useful alternative is co-trimoxazole 160/800 mg (Bactrim, Septrin, Resprim) twice daily for seven days. This is a sulpha drug and must not be used in people with a known sulpha allergy.

In the case of children, a reasonable first-line treatment is the drug co-trimoxazole.

For amoebic dysentery, the recommended adult dosage of metronidazole (Flagyl) is one 750 mg to 800 mg capsule three times daily for five days. Children aged between eight and 12 years should have half the adult dose; the dosage for younger children is one-third the adult dose.

An alternative to Flagyl is Fasigyn, taken as a two gram daily dose for three days. Alcohol must be avoided during treatment and for 48 hours afterwards.

**Cholera** Cholera vaccination is not very effective. The bacteria responsible for this disease are waterborne, so attention to the rules of eating and drinking should protect the traveller.

Outbreaks of cholera are generally widely reported, so you can avoid such problem areas. The disease is characterised by a sudden onset of acute diarrhoea with 'rice water' stools, vomiting, muscular cramps and extreme weakness. You need medical help – but treat for dehydration, which can be extreme, and if there is an appreciable delay in getting to hospital then begin taking tetracycline. The adult dose is 250 mg four times daily. It is not recommended in children aged eight years or under nor in pregnant women. An alternative drug would be Ampicillin, though people allergic to penicillin should not take this drug. Remember that while antibiotics might kill the bacteria, it is a toxin produced by the bacteria which causes the massive fluid loss. Fluid replacement is by far the most important aspect of treatment.

**Viral Gastroenteritis** This is caused not by

bacteria but, as the name suggests, by a virus. It is characterised by stomach cramps, diarrhoea and sometimes by vomiting and/or a slight fever. All you can do is rest and drink lots of fluids.

**Hepatitis** Hepatitis A is a very common problem amongst travellers to areas with poor sanitation, such as Thailand. With good water and adequate sewage disposal in most industrialised countries since the 1940s, very few young adults now have any natural immunity and must be protected.

The disease is spread by contaminated food or water. The symptoms are fever, chills, headache, fatigue, feelings of weakness and aches and pains, followed by loss of appetite, nausea, vomiting, abdominal pain, dark urine, light coloured faeces, jaundiced skin and the whites of the eyes may turn yellow. In some cases you may feel unwell, tired, have no appetite, experience aches and pains and be jaundiced. You should seek medical advice, but in general there is not much you can do apart from rest, drink lots of fluids, eat lightly and avoid fatty foods. People who have had hepatitis must forego alcohol for six months after the illness, as hepatitis attacks the liver and it needs that amount of time to recover.

Hepatitis B, which used to be called serum hepatitis, is spread through contact with infected blood, blood products or bodily fluids, eg through sexual contact, unsterilised needles and blood transfusions. Other risk situations include having a shave or tattoo in a local shop, or having your body pierced. The symptoms of type B are much the same as type A except that they are more severe and may lead to irreparable liver damage or even liver cancer. Although there is no treatment for hepatitis B, an effective prophylactic vaccine is readily available in most countries. The immunisation schedule requires two injections at least a month apart followed by a third dose five months after the second. Persons who should receive a hepatitis B vaccination include anyone who anticipates contact with blood or other bodily secretions, either as a health care worker or through sexual contact with the local population, particularly those who intend to stay in the country for a long period.

Hepatitis Non-A Non-B is a blanket term formerly used for several different strains of hepatitis, which have now been separately identified. Hepatitis C is similar to B but is less common. Hepatitis D (the 'delta particle') is also similar to B and always occurs in concert with it; its occurrence is currently limited to IV drug users. Hepatitis E, however, is similar to A and is spread in the same manner, by water or food contamination. Hepatitis E is common in Thailand.

Tests are available for these strands, but are very expensive. Travellers shouldn't be too paranoid about this apparent proliferation of hepatitis strains; following the same precautions as for A and B should be all that's necessary to avoid them.

**Typhoid** Typhoid fever is another gut infection that travels the faecal-oral route – ie contaminated water and food are responsible. Vaccination against typhoid is not totally effective and it is one of the most dangerous infections, so medical help must be sought.

In its early stages typhoid resembles many other illnesses: sufferers may feel like they have a bad cold or flu on the way, as early symptoms are a headache, a sore throat and a fever which rises a little each day until it is around 40°C (104°F) or more. The victim's pulse is often slow relative to the degree of fever present and gets slower as the fever rises – unlike a normal fever where the pulse increases. There may also be vomiting, diarrhoea or constipation.

In the second week the high fever and slow pulse continue and a few pink spots may appear on the body; trembling, delirium, weakness, weight loss and dehydration are other symptoms. If there are no further complications, the fever and other symptoms will slowly dissipate during the third week. However you must get medical help before this because pneumonia (acute infection of the lungs) or peritonitis (perforated bowel) are common complications, and because typhoid is very infectious. The fever should

be treated by keeping the victim cool and dehydration should also be watched for.

The drug of choice is ciprofloxacin at a dose of one gram daily for 14 days. It is quite expensive and may not be available. The alternative, chloramphenicol, has been the mainstay of treatment for many years. In many countries it is still the recommended antibiotic but there are fewer side effects with Ampicillin. The adult dosage is two 250 mg capsules, four times a day. Children aged between eight and 12 years should have half the adult dose; younger children should have one-third the adult dose.

People who are allergic to penicillin should not be given Ampicillin.

**Worms** These parasites are most common in rural, tropical areas and a stool test when you return home is not a bad idea. They can be present on unwashed vegetables or in undercooked meat and you can pick them up through your skin by walking in bare feet. Infestations may not show up for some time, and although they are generally not serious, if left untreated they can cause severe health problems. A stool test is necessary to pinpoint the problem and medication is often available over the counter.

**Schistosomiasis (Bilharzia)** Also known as 'blood flukes', this disease is caused by tiny flatworms that burrow their way through the skin and enter the bloodstream. Humans contact the worms when swimming or bathing in contaminated fresh water (the flukes can't survive in salt water).

The worm enters through the skin, and the first symptom may be a tingling and sometimes a light rash around the area where it entered. Weeks later, when the worm is busy producing eggs, a high fever may develop. A general feeling of being unwell may be the first symptom; once the disease is established abdominal pain and blood in the urine are other signs. The infection often causes no symptoms until the disease is well established (several months to years after exposure) and damage to internal organs irreversible.

The overall risk for this disease is quite

low, but it's highest in the southern reaches of the Maekhong River and in the lakes of North-Eastern Thailand – avoid swimming or bathing in these waterways. If submersion is for some reasons unavoidable, vigorous towel-drying reduces the risk of penetration. If schistosomiasis symptoms appear, consult a physician; the usual treatment is a regimen of praziquantel (often sold as Biltricide). The recommended dosage is 40 mg per kg in divided doses over one day. Niridazole is an alternative drug.

**Opisthorchiasis** Also called 'liver flukes', these are tiny worms that are occasionally present in freshwater fish. The main risk comes from eating raw or undercooked fish. Travellers should in particular avoid eating *plaa ráa* (sometimes called *paa daek* in North-Eastern Thailand), an unpasteurised fermented fish used as an accompaniment for rice in the North-East. Plaa ráa is not commonly served in restaurants, but is common in rural areas of the North-East, where it's considered a great delicacy. The Thai government is currently trying to discourage North-Easterners from eating plaa ráa or other uncooked fish products. A common roadside billboard in the region these days reads *isãan mâi kin plaa dìp* or 'North-Eastern Thailand doesn't eat raw fish'.

Liver flukes *(wiwâat bai tàp* in Thai) are endemic to villages around Sakon Nakhon Province's Nong Han, the largest natural lake in Thailand. Don't swim in this lake! (As with blood flukes, liver flukes can bore into the skin.) A much less common way to contract liver flukes is through swimming in rivers. The only other known area where the flukes might be contracted by swimming in contaminated waters is in the southern reaches of the Maekhong River.

The intensity of symptoms depends very much on how many of the flukes get into your body. At low levels, there are virtually no symptoms at all; at higher levels, an overall fatigue, low-grade fever and swollen or tender liver (or general abdominal pain) are the usual symptoms, along with worms

or worm eggs in the faeces. Persons suspected of having liver flukes should have a stool sample analysed by a competent doctor or clinic. The usual medication is 25 mg per kg of body weight of praziquantel (Biltricide) three times daily after meals for two days.

**Tetanus** This potentially fatal disease is found in undeveloped tropical areas. It is difficult to treat but is preventable with immunisation. Tetanus occurs when a wound becomes infected by a germ which lives in soil and in the faeces of horses and other animals, so clean all cuts, punctures or animal bites. Tetanus is also known as lockjaw, and the first symptom may be discomfort in swallowing, or stiffening of the jaw and neck; this is followed by painful convulsions of the jaw and whole body.

**Rabies** Rabies is found in many countries, including Thailand, and is caused by a bite or scratch by an infected animal. Dogs are noted carriers as are monkeys and cats. Any bite, scratch or even lick from a warm-blooded, furry animal should be cleaned immediately and thoroughly. Scrub with soap and running water, and then clean with an alcohol solution. If there is any possibility that the animal is infected medical help should be sought immediately. Even if the animal is not rabid, all bites should be treated seriously as they can become infected or can result in tetanus. A rabies vaccination is now available and should be considered if you are in a high-risk category – eg if you intend to explore caves (bat bites could be dangerous) or work with animals.

**Tuberculosis (TB)** There is a world-wide resurgence of TB. It is a bacterial infection which is usually transmitted from person to person by coughing but may be transmitted through consumption of unpasteurised milk. Milk that has been boiled is safe to drink, and the souring of milk to make yoghurt or cheese also kills the bacilli. Typically many months of contact with the infected person are required before the disease is passed on.

The usual site of the disease is the lungs, although other organs may be involved. Most infected people never develop symptoms. In those who do, especially infants, symptoms may arise within weeks of the infection occurring and may be severe. In most, however, the disease lies dormant for many years until, for some reason, the infected person becomes physically run down. Symptoms include fever, weight loss, night sweats and coughing.

**Diphtheria** Diphtheria can be a skin infection or a more dangerous throat infection. It is spread by contaminated dust contacting the skin or by the inhalation of infected cough or sneeze droplets. Frequent washing and keeping the skin dry will help prevent skin infection. Treatment needs close medical supervision.

**Sexually Transmitted Diseases** Sexual contact with an infected sexual partner spreads these diseases. While abstinence is the only 100% preventative, using latex condoms is also effective. In Thailand gonorrhoea, non-specific urethritis (NSU) and syphilis are the most common of these diseases; sores, blisters or rashes around the genitals, discharges or pain when urinating are common symptoms. In some STDs, such as wart virus and chlamydia, symptoms may be less marked or not observed at all in women. Syphilis symptoms eventually disappear completely but the disease continues and can cause severe problems in later years. The treatment of gonorrhoea and syphilis is by antibiotics.

There are numerous other sexually transmitted diseases, for most of which effective treatment is available. However, there is no cure for herpes and there is also currently no cure for AIDS (Acquired Immune Deficiency Syndrome).

**HIV/AIDS** HIV, the Human Immunodeficiency Virus, could develop into AIDS. HIV is a major health problem in Thailand although the overall incidence of infection has slowed over recent years. Any exposure to blood, blood products or bodily fluids may put the individual at risk. In Thailand transmission is predominantly through heterosexual sexual activity (40%); the second most common source of HIV infection is intravenous injection by drug addicts who share needles (33%). Apart from abstinence, the most effective preventative is always to practise safe sex using condoms. It is impossible to detect the HIV-positive status of an otherwise healthy-looking person without a blood test.

The Thai phrase for 'condom' is *thŭng anaamai*. Latex condoms are more effective than animal-membrane condoms in preventing disease transmission; to specify latex condoms ask for *thŭng yaang anaamai*. Good-quality latex condoms are distributed free by offices of the Ministry of Public Health throughout the country – they come in numbered sizes, like shoes! Condoms can also be purchased at any pharmacy, but those issued by the Ministry of Public Health are considered the most effective; a recent ministry survey found that around 11% of commercial Thai condoms were damaged, mostly due to improper storage.

HIV/AIDS can also be spread through infected blood transfusions although in Thailand this risk is virtually nil due to vigorous blood-screening procedures. It can also be spread by dirty needles – vaccinations, acupuncture, tattooing and body piercing can potentially be as dangerous as intravenous drug use if the equipment is not clean. If you do need an injection, ask to see the syringe unwrapped in front of you, or better still, take a needle and syringe pack with you overseas – it is a cheap insurance package against infection with HIV.

Fear of HIV infection should never preclude treatment for serious medical conditions. Although there may be a risk of infection, it is very small indeed.

### Insect-Borne Diseases
**Malaria** This serious disease is spread by mosquito bites. If you are travelling in endemic areas it is extremely important to take malarial prophylactics. Symptoms

include headaches, fever, chills and sweating which may subside and recur. Without treatment malaria can develop more serious, potentially fatal effects. Antimalarial drugs do not prevent you from being infected but kill the parasites during a stage in their development.

There are a number of different types of malaria. The one of most concern is falciparum malaria, which is responsible for the very serious cerebral malaria. Malaria risk exists throughout the year in rural Thailand, especially in forested and hilly areas. At the moment Thailand's high-risk areas include northern Kanchanaburi Province (especially Thung Yai Naresuan National Park) and parts of Trat Province along the Cambodian border (including Ko Chang). According to the CDC and to Thailand's Ministry of Public Health, there is virtually no risk of malaria in urban areas or the main tourist areas (eg Bangkok, Phuket, Pattaya and Chiang Mai).

The problem in recent years has been the emergence of increasing resistance to commonly used antimalarials like chloroquine, maloprim and proguanil. Newer drugs such as mefloquine (Lariam) and doxycycline (Vibramycin, Doryx) are often recommended for chloroquine and multidrug resistant areas, though in Thailand most strains are also resistant to these. However, doxycycline is recommended by the WHO for travel to areas near the Cambodian and Myanmar borders and mefloquine for other parts of Thailand.

Expert advice should be sought, as there are many factors to consider when deciding on the type of antimalarial medication, including the area to be visited, the risk of exposure to malaria-carrying mosquitoes, your current medical condition and your age and pregnancy status. It is also important to discuss the side-effect profile of the medication, so you can work out some level of risk-versus-benefit ratio. It is also very important to be sure of the correct dosage of the medication prescribed to you. Some people have inadvertently taken weekly medication (chloroquine) on a daily basis,

with disastrous effects. While discussing dosages for prevention of malaria, it is often advisable to include the dosages required for treatment, especially if your trip is through a high-risk area that would isolate you from medical care.

All commonly prescribed malarial suppressants (eg chloroquine) have the potential to cause side effects. Mefloquine may affect motor skills and cause bad dreams. There is some resistance to mefloquine, but it is still a useful drug.

In Thailand, where malaria tends to be resistant to most if not all the previously mentioned prophylactics, the Chinese herb *qinghao* – or its chemical derivative artemether – has proven to be very effective. Its use in Thailand (and other mainland South-East Asian countries) has recently been endorsed by the UN Tropical Disease Programme as well as the WHO director-general. Many doctors in Thailand are now recommending halofantrine, marketed under the name HalFan, as the latest and greatest cure.

The main messages are:

- Primary prevention must always be in the form of mosquito avoidance measures. The mosquitoes (Anopheles) that transmit malaria bite from dusk to dawn and during this period travellers are advised to: wear light-coloured clothing, long pants and long-sleeved shirts; use mosquito repellents containing the compound DEET on exposed areas (commercial repellents containing no more than 35% DEET can be purchased at well-stocked Thai pharmacies); avoid highly scented perfumes or aftershave; and use a mosquito net (it may be worth taking your own).
- While no antimalarial is 100% effective, taking the most appropriate drug significantly reduces the risk of contracting the disease.
- No-one should ever die from malaria. It can be diagnosed by a simple blood test. Symptoms range from fever, chills and sweating, headache and abdominal pains to a vague feeling of ill-health – so seek examination immediately if there is any suggestion of malaria.

Contrary to popular belief, once a traveller contracts malaria they do not have it for life. One of the parasites may lie dormant in the liver but this can also be eradicated using a specific medication. Malaria is curable, as long as the traveller seeks medical help when symptoms occur.

For those with an allergy or aversion to synthetic repellents, citronella makes a good substitute. Mosquito coils *(yaa kan yung bàep jùt)* do an excellent job of repelling mosquitoes in your room and are readily available in Thailand. Day mosquitoes do not carry malaria, so it is only in the night that you have to worry – peak biting hours are a few hours after dusk and a few hours before dawn.

Like many other tropical diseases, malaria is frequently mis-diagnosed in western countries. If you should develop the symptoms after a return to your home country, be sure to seek medical attention immediately and inform your doctor that you may have been exposed to malaria.

**Dengue Fever** In some areas of Thailand there is a risk, albeit low, of contracting dengue fever via mosquito transmission. This time it's a day variety (Aedes) you have to worry about. Like malaria, dengue fever seems to be on the increase throughout tropical Asia in recent years. Dengue is found in urban as well as rural areas, especially in areas of human habitation (often indoors) where there is standing water.

Unlike malaria, dengue fever is caused by a virus and there is no chemical prophylactic or vaccination against it. The symptoms come on suddenly and include high fever, severe headache and heavy joint and muscle pain (hence its older name 'breakbone fever'), followed a few days later by a rash that spreads from the torso to the arms, legs and face. Various risk factors such as age, immunity and viral strain may mitigate these symptoms so that they are less severe or last only a few days. Even when the basic symptoms are short-lived, it can take several weeks to recover fully from the resultant fatigue.

In rare cases dengue may develop into a more severe condition known as dengue haemorrhagic fever (DHF), or dengue toxic shock syndrome, which is often fatal. DHF is most common among Asian children under 15 years who are undergoing a second dengue infection, so the risk of DHF for most international travellers is very low.

Not all mosquito bites are infectious. The mosquito which carries the disease tends to bite during the day and lives around houses. The best way to prevent dengue, as with malaria, is to take care not to be bitten at all.

The only treatment for dengue is bed rest, constant rehydration and acetaminophen (Tylenol, Panadol). Avoid aspirin, which increases the risk of haemorrhaging. Hospital supervision is necessary in severe cases.

**Japanese Encephalitis** Although long endemic to tropical Asia (as well as China, Korea and Japan), rainy-season epidemics in Northern Thailand and Vietnam during the last decade have increased the risk for travellers. The Culex mosquito is the carrier for this disease and the risk is said to be greatest in rural zones near areas where pigs are raised or rice is grown, since pigs and certain wild birds, whose habitat may include rice fields, serve as reservoirs for the virus.

Persons who may be at risk in Thailand are those who will be spending long periods of time in rural areas during the rainy season (July to October). If you belong to this group, you may want to get a Japanese encephalitis vaccination. As the vaccine itself can occasionally have serious side effects it is only recommended for people going to high exposure areas for long periods. People vaccinated should be accessible to urgent medical care for 10 days after each injection as breathing difficulties and facial swelling may occur during this time. Vaccination consists of three injections at zero, one and four weeks.

Immunity lasts about a year, at which point it's necessary to get a booster shot; then it's every three years after that.

The symptoms of Japanese encephalitis are sudden fever, chills and headache, followed by vomiting and delirium, a strong aversion to bright light and sore joints and muscles. Advanced cases may result in

## Traditional Thai Medicine

Western medical practices are for the most part restricted to modern hospitals and clinics in Thailand's towns and cities. In villages and rural areas a large number of Thais still practise various forms of traditional healing which were codified in Thailand over 500 years ago. Clinics and healers specialising in traditional Thai medicine can also be found in urban areas; many Thai doctors in fact offer a blend of international medicine – a term ethno-medical scholars prefer to 'western medicine' – and indigenous medical systems.

Traditional Thai medical theory features many parallels with India's Ayurvedic healing tradition as well as Chinese medicine. In practice, however, Thai diagnostic and therapeutic techniques may differ significantly. Obviously influenced to some degree by these traditions, Thai medicine in turn has been the predominant influence on traditional medicine in Cambodia, Laos and Myanmar.

Most Thai medicine as practised today is based on two surviving medical texts from the Ayuthaya era, the *Scripture of Diseases* and the *Pharmacopoeia of King Narai*. Presumably many more texts were available before the Burmese sacked Ayuthaya in 1767 and destroyed the kingdom's national archives. A coexisting oral tradition passed down from healer to healer conforms to the surviving texts; other materia medica developed in the Ratanakosin (or old Bangkok) era are founded on both these texts and the oral tradition.

Like medical practitioners elsewhere in the world, traditional Thai physicians perform diagnoses by evaluating the pulse, heartbeat, skin colour/texture, body temperature, abnormal physical symptoms and bodily excretions (eg blood, urine, faeces) of their patients. Unlike orthodox western doctors, Thai healers favour a holistic approach that encompasses internal, external and psycho-spiritual conditions. Thus, once diagnosed, patients may be prescribed and issued treatments from among three broad therapeutic categories.

**Herbal Medicines** Traditional pharmacological therapy employs prescribed herbs, either singly or in combination, from among 700 plant varieties (plus a limited number of animal sources) which are infused, boiled, powdered or otherwise rendered into a consumable form. Common household medicines *(yaa klaang bâan* in Thai) include the root and stem of *baw-ráphét (Tinospora rumphii*, a type of woodclimber) for fever reduction, *râak cha-phluu* (Piper roots) for stomach ailments, and various *yaa hǎwm* (fragrant medicines) used as medicinal balms for muscle pain or headaches. Medicines of this type are readily available over the counter at traditional medicine shops and to a lesser extent in modern Thai pharmacies.

More complex remedies called *yaa tamráp luāng* (royally approved/recorded medicine) are prepared and administered only by herbalists skilled in diagnosis, as the mixture and dosage must be adjusted for each patient. One of the most well known *yaa tamráp luāng* is *chanthá-lîilaa*, a powerful remedy for respiratory infections and influenza-induced fevers.

As in the Chinese tradition, many Thai herbs find their way into regional cuisine with the intent of enhancing health as well as taste. *Phrík thai* (black pepper, *Piper nigrum*), *bai krà-phaw* (stomach leaf) and *bai maeng-lák* (a variety of basil) are common curry ingredients which have proven antacid/carminative properties. Thais eat soups containing *mará* (bitter melon) – a known febrifuge – to bring down a fever.

convulsions and coma. It is fatal in 25% of cases and leaves residual neuropsychiatric damage in 50% of the time. Researchers estimate there's near universal exposure by adulthood in endemic areas. Most people develop asymptomatic resistance, ie most of those who contract the virus exhibit no symptoms whatsoever (symptoms occur in only 0.5% of infections – 1 in 200 cases). It most affects the elderly and children under 10.

As with other mosquito-borne diseases, the best way to prevent Japanese encephalitis (outside of the vaccine) is to avoid being bitten.

## Cuts, Bites & Stings

**Cuts & Scratches** Skin punctures can easily become infected in hot climates and may be difficult to heal. Treat any cut with an antiseptic such as Betadine. Where possible avoid bandages and Band-Aids, which can keep wounds wet. Coral cuts are notoriously

**Massage** The second and most internationally famous type of Thai medical therapy is *ráksăa thaang nûat* (massage treatment). The extensive and highly refined Thai massage system combines characteristics of massage (stroking and kneading the muscles), chiropractice (manipulating skeletal parts) and acupressure (applying deep, consistent pressure to specific nerves, tendons or ligaments) in order to balance the functions of the four body elements *(thâat tháng sìi)*. These four elements are: earth *(din –* solid parts of the body, including nerves, skeleton, muscles, blood vessels, tendons and ligaments); water *(náam –* blood and bodily secretions); fire *(fai –* digestion and metabolism); and air *(lom –* respiration and circulation). Borrowing from India's Ayurvedic tradition, some practitioners employ Pali-Sanskrit terms for the four bodily elements: *pathavidhatu, apodhatu, tecodhatu* and *vayodhatu.*

From the Ayuthaya period until early this century, the Thai Ministry of Public Health included an official massage division *(phanâek măw nûat).* Under the influence of international medicine and modern hospital development, responsibility for the national propagation/maintenance of Thai massage was eventually transferred to Wat Pho in Bangkok, where it remains today. Traditional massage therapy has persisted most in the provinces, however, and has recently enjoyed a resurgence of popularity throughout the country.

Within the traditional Thai medical context, a massage therapist *(măw nûat,* literally, 'massage doctor') usually applies Thai massage together with pharmacological and/or psycho-spiritual treatments as prescribed for a specific medical problem. Nowadays many Thais also use massage as a tool for relaxation and disease prevention, rather than for specific medical problems. Massage associated with Bangkok's Turkish baths *(àap òp nûat* or 'bathe-steam-massage' in Thai) is for the most part performed for recreational or entertainment purposes only (or as an adjunct to prostitution); the techniques used are loosely based on traditional Thai massage.

For problems affecting the nerves rather than the muscular or skeletal structures, many Thais resort to *nûat jàp sên* (nerve-touch massage), a Chinese-style massage technique that works with the body's nerve meridians, much like acupuncture.

**Psycho-Spiritual Healing** A third aspect of traditional Thai medicine called *ráksăa thaang nai* (inner healing) or *kâe kam kaò* (literally, 'old karma repair') includes various types of meditation or visualisation practised by the patient, as well as shamanistic rituals performed by qualified healers. These strategies represent the psycho-spiritual side of Thai medical therapy, and like massage are usually practised in conjunction with other types of treatment. With the increasing acceptance of meditation, hypnosis and biofeedback in Occidental medicine, anthropologists nowadays are less inclined to classify such metaphysical therapy as 'magico-religious', accepting them instead as potentially useful adjunct therapies.

As in the west, psycho-spiritual techniques are most commonly reserved for medical conditions with no apparent physical cause or those for which other therapies have proved unsuccessful. In Thailand they are also occasionally employed as preventive measures, as in the *bai sĭi* ceremony popular in North-Eastern Thailand and Laos. This elaborate ceremony, marked by the tying of string loops around a subject's wrists, is intended to bind the 32 *khwăn* or personal guardian spirits – each associated with a specific organ – to the individual. The ritual is often performed before a person departs on a long or distant journey, based on the reasoning that one is more susceptible to illness when away from home. ■

slow to heal, as the coral injects a weak venom into the wound. Avoid touching and walking on fragile corals in the first place, but if you are near coral reefs, then wear shoes and clean any cut thoroughly with hydrogen peroxide if available.

**Bites & Stings** Bee and wasp stings are usually painful rather than dangerous. Calamine lotion will give relief and ice packs will reduce the pain and swelling. There are some

spiders with dangerous bites but antivenenes are usually available. Scorpion stings are notoriously painful. Scorpions often shelter in shoes or clothing.

There are various fish and other sea creatures which can sting or bite dangerously or which are dangerous to eat. Local advice is the best prevention.

**Snakes** To minimise your chances of being bitten always wear boots, socks and long trousers when walking through undergrowth where snakes may be present. Don't put your hands into holes and crevices, and be careful when collecting firewood.

Snake bites do not cause instantaneous death and antivenenes are usually available. Keep the victim calm and still, wrap the bitten limb tightly, as you would for a sprained ankle, and then attach a splint to immobilise it. Then seek medical help, if possible taking along the dead snake for identification. Don't attempt to catch the snake if there is even a remote possibility of being bitten again. Tourniquets and sucking out the poison are now comprehensively discredited.

Snakebite antivenene is available at Chulalongkorn Hospital (☎ (2) 252-8181/9), Rama IV Rd, Bangkok.

**Jellyfish** Local advice is the best way of avoiding contact with these sea creatures with their stinging tentacles. Dousing in vinegar will de-activate any stingers which have not 'fired'. Calamine lotion, antihistamines and analgesics may reduce the reaction and relieve the pain.

**Bedbugs & Lice** Bedbugs live in various places, but particularly in dirty mattresses and bedding. Spots of blood on bedclothes or on the wall around the bed can be read as a suggestion to find another hotel. Bedbugs leave itchy bites in neat rows. Calamine lotion may help.

All lice cause itching and discomfort. They make themselves at home in your hair (head lice), your clothing (body lice) or your pubic hair (crabs). You catch lice through direct contact with infected people or by sharing combs, clothing and the like. Powder or shampoo treatment will kill the lice and infected clothing should then be washed in very hot water.

**Leeches & Ticks** Leeches may be present in damp rainforest conditions; they attach themselves to your skin to suck your blood. Trekkers often get them on their legs or in their boots. Salt or a lighted cigarette end will

make them fall off. Do not pull them off, as the bite is then more likely to become infected. An insect repellent may keep them away.

You should always check your body if you have been walking through a potentially tick-infested area as ticks can cause skin infections and other more serious diseases. If a tick is found attached, press down around the tick's head with tweezers, grab the head and gently pull upwards. Avoid pulling the rear of the body as this may squeeze the tick's gut contents through the attached mouth parts into the skin, increasing the risk of infection and disease. Smearing chemicals on the tick will not make it let go and is not recommended.

## Women's Health
**Gynaecological Problems** Poor diet, lowered resistance due to the use of antibiotics for stomach upsets and even contraceptive pills can lead to vaginal infections when travelling in hot climates. Keeping the genital area clean, and wearing skirts or loose-fitting trousers and cotton underwear, will help to prevent infections.

Yeast infections, characterised by a rash, itch and discharge, can be treated with a vinegar or even lemon-juice douche or with yoghurt. Nystatin, miconazole or clotrimazole suppositories are the usual medical prescription. Trichomonas and gardnerella are more serious infections; symptoms are a smelly discharge and sometimes a burning sensation when urinating. Male sexual partners must also be treated, and if a vinegar-water douche is not effective medical attention should be sought. Metronidazole (Flagyl) is the prescribed drug.

**Pregnancy** Most miscarriages occur during the first three months of pregnancy, so this is the most risky time to travel as far as your own health is concerned. Miscarriage is not uncommon, and can occasionally lead to severe bleeding. The last three months should also be spent within reasonable distance of good medical care. A baby born as early as 24 weeks stands a chance of survival, but only in a good modern hospital.

Pregnant women should avoid all unnecessary medication, but vaccinations and malarial prophylactics should still be taken where possible. Additional care should be taken to prevent illness and particular attention should be paid to diet and nutrition. Alcohol and nicotine, for example, should be avoided.

Women travellers often find that their periods become irregular or even cease while they're on the road. Remember that a missed period in these circumstances doesn't necessarily indicate pregnancy. There are health posts or family planning clinics in many small and large urban centres, where you can seek advice and have a urine test to determine whether you are pregnant or not.

### Hospitals & Clinics

Thailand's most technically advanced hospitals are in Bangkok. In the North, Chiang Mai has the best medical care; in the North-East it's Khon Kaen and in the South Hat Yai or Phuket. Elsewhere in the country, every provincial capital has at least one hospital of varying quality as well as several public and private clinics. The best emergency health care, however, can usually be found at military hospitals (*rohng phayaabaan tha-hāan* in Thai); they will usually treat foreigners in an emergency. See the respective destination chapters for information on specific health-care facilities.

Should you need urgent dental care, suggested contacts in Bangkok include:

Bumrungrad Medical Centre – 33 Soi 3, Sukhumvit Rd (☎ (2) 253-0250)
Dental Polyclinic – 2111/2113 New Phetburi Rd (☎ (2) 314-5070)
Ploenchit Clinic – Maneeya Bldg, Ploenchit Rd (☎ (2) 251-1567/8902)
Siam Dental Clinic – 412/11-2 Soi 6, Siam Square (☎ (2) 251-6315)

For urgent eye care, the best choices are in Bangkok. Try the Rutnin Eye Hospital (☎ (2) 258-0442) at 80/1 Soi Asoke or the Pirompesuy Eye Hospital (☎ (2) 252-4141) at 117/1 Phayathai Rd.

### Counselling Services

Qualified professionals at Community Services of Bangkok (☎ (2) 258-4998), 15 Soi 33, Sukhumvit Rd, offer a range of counselling services to foreign residents and newcomers to Thailand.

Members of Alcoholics Anonymous who want to contact the Bangkok group or anyone needing help with a drinking problem can call AA at ☎ (2) 253-6305 from 6 am to 6 pm or ☎ (2) 256-6578 from 6 pm to 6 am for information. Meetings are held daily at Holy Redeemer Catholic Church, 123/19 Soi Ruamrudee. There are also regular meetings in Chiang Mai and Pattaya.

## TOILETS & SHOWERS

### Toilets

In Thailand, as in many other Asian countries, the 'squat toilet' is the norm except in hotels and guesthouses geared toward tourists and international business travellers. Instead of trying to approximate a chair or stool like a modern sit-down toilet, a traditional Asian toilet sits more or less flush with the surface of the floor, with two footpads on either side of the porcelain abyss. For travellers who have never used a squat toilet it takes a bit of getting used to. If you find yourself feeling awkward the first couple of times you use one, you can console yourself with the knowledge that, according to those who study such matters, people who use squat toilets are much less likely to develop haemorrhoids than people who use sit toilets.

Next to the typical squat toilet is a bucket or cement reservoir filled with water. A plastic bowl usually floats on the water's surface or sits nearby. This water supply has a two-fold function; toilet-goers scoop water from the reservoir with the plastic bowl and use it to clean the nether regions while still squatting over the toilet. Since there is usually no mechanical flushing device attached to a squat toilet, a few extra scoops must be poured into the toilet basin to flush waste into the septic system. In larger towns, mechanical flushing systems are becoming increasingly common, even with squat toilets. More rustic toilets in rural areas may simply consist of a few planks over a hole in the ground.

Even in places where sit-down toilets are installed, the plumbing may not be designed to take toilet paper. In such cases the usual washing bucket will be standing nearby or there will be a waste basket where you're supposed to place used toilet paper.

Public toilets are common in cinema houses, department stores, bus and train stations, larger hotel lobbies and airports. While on the road between towns and villages it is perfectly acceptable to go behind a tree or bush or even to use the roadside when nature calls.

## Bathing

Some hotels and most guesthouses in the country do not have hot water, though places in the larger cities will usually offer small electric shower heaters in their more expensive rooms. Very few boiler-style water heaters are available outside larger international-style hotels.

Many rural Thais bathe in rivers or streams. Those living in towns or cities may have washrooms where a large jar or cement trough is filled with water for bathing purposes. A plastic or metal bowl is used to sluice water from the jar or trough over the body. Even in homes where showers are installed, heated water is uncommon. Most Thais bathe at least twice a day.

If ever you find yourself having to bathe in a public place you should wear a phâakhamãa or phâasîn (the cotton wraparounds); nude bathing is not the norm.

## WOMEN TRAVELLERS
### Attitudes toward Women

Chinese trader Ma Huan noted in 1433 that among the Thais 'All affairs are managed by their wives, all trading transactions large or small'. In rural areas female family members typically inherit land and throughout the country they tend to control family finances. The UNDP Human Development Report for 1995 noted that on the gender-related development index (GDI) Thailand ranks 31st of 130 countries, thus falling into the 'progressive' category. The nation's GDI increase was greater than that of any country in the world over the past 20 years. According to the report, Thailand 'has succeeded in building the basic human capabilities of both women and men, without substantial gender imparity'.

Thailand's workforce is 44% female, ranking it 27th on a worldwide scale, just ahead of China and the USA. So much for the good news. The bad news is that although women generally fare well in the labour force and in rural land inheritance, their cultural standing is a bit further from parity. An oft-repeated Thai saying reminds us that men form the front legs of the elephant, women the hind legs (at least they're pulling equal weight). Thai Buddhism commonly holds that women must be reborn as men before they can attain nirvana, though many Thai dharma teachers point out that this presumption isn't supported by the *suttas* (discourses of the Buddha) or by the commentaries. But it is a common belief, supported by the availability of a fully ordained Buddhist monastic status for men and a less prestigious eight precept ordination for women.

On a purely legal level, men enjoy more privilege. Men may divorce their wives for committing adultery, but not vice versa, for example. Men who take a foreign spouse continue to have the right to purchase and own land, while Thai women who marry foreign men lose this right.

### Safety

Around 38% of all foreign visitors to Thailand are women, a ratio equal to the worldwide average as measured by the World Tourism Organisation, and on an even par with Singapore and Hong Kong (for all other Asian countries the proportion of female visitors runs lower than 35%). This ratio is growing year by year; the overall increase for visitors between 1993 and 1994, for example, was 2.3% while the number of women visitors jumped 13.8%.

Everyday incidents of sexual harassment are much less common in Thailand than in India, Indonesia or Malaysia and this may lull women who have recently travelled in these countries into thinking that Thailand travel is safer than it is. Over the past seven years, several foreign women have been attacked while travelling alone in remote areas. If you're a woman travelling alone, try to pair up with other travellers when travelling at night or in remote areas. Urban areas seem relatively safe; the exceptions are Chiang Mai and Ko Pha-Ngan, where there have been several reports of harassment (oddly, we've had no reports from Bangkok). Make sure hotel and guesthouse rooms are secure at night – if they're not, demand another room or move to another hotel or guesthouse.

**Jii-Khōh** Small upcountry restaurants are sometimes hang-outs for drunken *jii-khōh*, an all-purpose Thai term that refers to the teenage playboy-hoodlum-cowboy who gets his kicks by violating Thai cultural norms. These oafs sometimes bother foreign women (and men) who are trying to have a quiet meal ('Are you married?' and 'I love you' are common conversation openers). It's best to ignore them rather than try to make snappy comebacks – they won't understand them and will most likely take these responses as encouragement. If the jii-khōhs persist, find another restaurant. Unfortunately restaurant proprietors will rarely do anything about such disturbances.

## GAY & LESBIAN TRAVELLERS
Thai culture is very tolerant of homosexuality, both male and female. The nation has no laws that discriminate against homosexuals and there is a fairly prominent gay/lesbian scene around the country. Hence there is no 'gay movement' in Thailand as such since there's no anti-gay establishment to move against. Whether speaking of dress or mannerism, lesbians and gays are generally accepted without comment.

Public displays of affection – whether heterosexual or homosexual – are frowned upon. As the guide *Thai Scene* (Gay Men's Press, Box 247, London N6 4AT, UK) has written, 'For many gay travellers, Thailand

is a nirvana with a long established gay bar scene, which, whilst often very Thai in culture, is particularly welcoming to tourists. There is little, if any, social approbation toward gay people, providing Thai cultural mores are respected. What people do in bed, whether straight or gay, is not expected to be a topic of general conversation nor bragged about'.

Utopia (☎ (2) 259-1619; fax 258-3250), at 116/1 Soi 23, Sukhumvit Rd, Bangkok, is a gay and lesbian multipurpose Bangkok centre consisting of a guesthouse, bar, cafe, gallery and gift shop. It maintains an Internet site called the Southeast Asia Gay and Lesbian Resources (or 'Utopia Homo Page') at http://www.utopia-asia.com/tipsthai.htm., as well as an e-mail address (utopia@ksc9.th.).

Gay men may be interested in the services of the Long Yang Club (☎ /fax (2) 679-7727) at PO Box 1077, Silom Post Office, Bangkok 10504 – a 'multicultural social group for male-oriented men who want to meet outside the gay scene' with branches in London, Amsterdam, Toronto, Canberra, Ottawa and Vancouver.

## DISABLED TRAVELLERS
Thailand presents one large, ongoing obstacle course for the mobility-impaired. With its high curbs, uneven sidewalks and nonstop traffic, Bangkok can be particularly difficult – many streets must be crossed via pedestrian bridges flanked with steep stairways, while buses and boats don't stop long enough for even the mildly disabled. Rarely are there any ramps or other access points for wheelchairs.

Hyatt International (Bangkok, Pattaya, Chiang Mai), Novotel (Bangkok, Chiang Mai, Phuket), Sheraton (Bangkok, Phuket), Holiday Inn (Bangkok, Phuket) and Westin (Chiang Mai) are the only hotel chains in the country that make consistent design efforts to provide disabled access for each of their properties. Because of their high employee-to-guest ratios, home-grown luxury hotel chains such as those managed by Dusit, Amari and Royal Garden Resorts are usually very good about making sure that the mobility-impaired are well accommodated in terms of providing staff help where architecture fails. For the rest you're pretty much left to your own resources.

For wheelchair travellers, any trip to Thailand will require a good deal of advance planning; fortunately a growing network of information sources can put you in touch with those who have wheeled through Thailand before. There is no better source of information than someone who's done it. A reader recently wrote with the following tips:

- The difficulties you mention in your book are all there. However, travel in the streets is still possible, and enjoyable, providing you have a strong, ambulatory companion. Some obstacles may require two carriers; Thais are by nature helpful and could generally be counted on for assistance.
- Don't feel you have to rely on organised tours to see the sights – these often leave early mornings at times inconvenient to disabled people. It is far more convenient (and often cheaper) to take a taxi or hired car. It's also far more enjoyable as there is no feeling of holding others up.
- Many taxis have an LPG tank in the boot (trunk) which may make it impossible to get a wheelchair in and close it. You might do better to hire a private car and driver (this usually costs no more – and sometimes less – than a taxi).
- A tuk-tuk is far easier to get in and out of and to carry two people and a wheelchair than a taxi. Even the pedicabs can hang a wheelchair on the back of the carriage.
- Be ready to try anything – in spite of my worries, riding an elephant proved quite easy.

Three international organisations which act as clearing houses for information on world travel for the mobility-impaired are: Mobility International USA (☎ (541) 343-1284), PO Box 10767, Eugene, OR 97440, USA; Access Foundation (☎ (516) 887-5798), PO Box 356, Malverne, NY 11565, USA; and Society for the Advancement of Travel for the Handicapped (SATH) (☎ (718) 858-5483), 26 Court St, Brooklyn, NY 11242, USA.

*Abilities* magazine (☎ (416) 766-9188; fax 762-8716), PO Box 527, Station P, Toronto, ON, Canada M5S 2T1, carries a new column called 'Accessible Planet' which offers tips on foreign travel for people with disabilities. One story described how two French wheelchair travellers trekked around Northern Thailand. The book *Exotic Destinations for Wheelchair Travelers* by Ed Hansen & Bruce Gordon (Full Data Ltd, San Francisco) contains a useful chapter on seven locations in Thailand. Others books of value include *Holidays and Travel Abroad – A Guide for Disabled People* (RADAR, London) and *Able to Travel* (Rough Guides, London, New York).

Accessible Journeys (☎ (610) 521-0339), 35 West Sellers Ave, Ridley Park, Pennsylvania, USA, specialises in organising group travel for the mobility-impaired. Occasionally the agency offers Thailand trips.

In Thailand you can also contact:

Association of the Physically Handicapped of Thailand – 73/7-8 Soi 8 (Soi Thepprasan), Tivanon Rd, Talaat Kawan, Nonthaburi 11000 (☎ (2) 951-0569; fax 580-1098 ext 7)
Disabled Peoples International (Thailand) – 78/2 Tivanon Rd, Pak Kret, Nonthaburi 11120 (☎ (2) 583-3021; fax 583-6518)
Handicapped International – 87/2 Soi 15 Sukhumvit Rd, Bangkok 10110
Thai Disability Organisations – David Lambertson, Ambassador (☎ /fax (2) 254-2990)

## SENIOR TRAVELLERS

Senior discounts aren't generally available in Thailand, but the Thais more than make up for this in the respect they typically show for the elderly. In traditional Thai culture status comes with age; there isn't as heavy an emphasis on youth as in the western world. Deference for age manifests itself in the way Thais will go out of their way to help older people in and out of taxis or with luggage, and – usually but not always – in waiting on them first in shops and post offices.

Nonetheless some cultural spheres are reserved for youth. Cross-generational entertainment in particular is less common than in western countries. There is a strict stratification among discos and nightclubs, for example, according to age group. One place will cater to teenagers, another to people in their early 20s, one for late 20s and 30s, yet another for those in their 40s and 50s, and once you've reached 60 you're considered to old to go clubbing! Exceptions to this rule include the more traditional entertainment venues, such as rural temple fairs and other wat-centred events, where young and old will dance and eat together. For men, massage parlours are another place where old and young mix.

## TRAVEL WITH CHILDREN

Like many places in South-East Asia, travelling with children in Thailand can be a lot of fun as long as you come well prepared with the right attitudes, equipment and the usual parental patience. Lonely Planet's *Travel with Children* by Maureen Wheeler contains useful advice on how to cope with kids on the road and what to bring along to make things go more smoothly, with special attention paid to travel in developing countries.

Thais love children and in many instances will shower attention on your offspring, who will find ready playmates among their Thai counterparts and a temporary nanny service at practically every stop.

For the most part parents needn't worry too much about health concerns though it pays to lay down a few ground rules – such as regular hand-washing – to head off potential medical problems. All the usual health precautions apply (see Health earlier for details); children should especially be warned not to play with animals since rabies is relatively common in Thailand.

## DANGERS & ANNOYANCES
### Precautions

Although Thailand is in no way a dangerous country to visit, it's wise to be a little cautious, particularly if you're travelling alone. Solo women travellers should take special care on arrival at Bangkok international airport, particularly at night. Don't take one of Bangkok's often very unofficial taxis (black-and-white licence tags) by yourself – better a licensed taxi (yellow-and-black tags) or even the public bus. Both men and women should ensure their rooms are securely

locked and bolted at night. Inspect cheap rooms with thin walls for strategic peepholes.

Take caution when leaving valuables in hotel safes. Many travellers have reported unpleasant experiences with leaving valuables in Chiang Mai guesthouses while trekking. Make sure you obtain an itemised receipt for property left with hotels or guesthouses – note the exact quantity of travellers' cheques and all other valuables.

On the road, keep zippered luggage secured with small locks, especially while travelling on buses and trains.

### Credit Cards

On return to their home countries, some visitors have received huge credit-card bills for purchases (usually jewellery) charged to their cards in Bangkok while the cards had, supposedly, been secure in the hotel or guesthouse safe. It's said that over the two peak months that this first began occurring, credit-card companies lost over US$20 million in Thailand – one major company had 40% of their worldwide losses here! You might consider taking your credit cards with you if you go trekking – if they're stolen on the trail at least the bandits won't be able to use them. Organised gangs in Bangkok specialise in arranging stolen credit-card purchases – in some cases they pay 'down and out' foreigners to fake the signatures.

When making credit-card purchases, don't let vendors take your credit card out of your sight to run it through the machine. Unscrupulous merchants have been known to rub off three or four or more receipts with one credit-card purchase; after the customer leaves the shop, they use the one legitimate receipt as a model to forge your signature on the blanks, then fill in astronomical 'purchases'. Sometimes they wait several weeks – even months – between submitting each charge receipt to the bank, so that you can't remember whether you'd been billed at the same vendor more than once.

### Druggings

On trains and buses, particularly in the South, beware of friendly strangers offering

## Scams

Thais are generally so friendly and laid-back that some visitors are lulled into a false sense of security that makes them particularly vulnerable to scams and con schemes of all kinds. Scammers tend to haunt areas where first-time tourists go, such as Bangkok's Grand Palace area. Though you could meet them anywhere in Thailand, the overwhelming majority of scams take place in Bangkok, with Chiang Mai a very distant second.

Most scams begin the same way: a friendly Thai male approaches a lone visitor – usually newly arrived – and strikes up a seemingly innocuous conversation. Sometimes the con man says he's a university student, other times he may claim to work for the World Bank or a similarly distinguished organisation (some conners even carry cellular phones). If you're on the way to Wat Pho or Jim Thompson's House, for example, he may tell you it's closed for a holiday. Eventually the conversation works its way around to the subject of the scam – the better con men can actually make it seem like *you* initiated the topic. That's one of the most bewildering aspects of the con – afterwards victims remember that the whole thing seemed like their idea, not the con artist's.

The scam itself almost always involves either gems or card playing. With gems, the victims find themselves invited to a gem and jewellery shop – your new-found friend is picking up some merchandise for himself and you're just along for the ride. Somewhere along the way he usually claims to have a connection – often a relative – in your home country (what a coincidence!) with whom he has a regular gem export-import business. One way or another, victims are convinced (usually they convince themselves) that they can turn a profit by arranging a gem purchase and reselling the merchandise at home. After all, the jewellery shop just happens to be offering a generous discount today – it's a government or religious holiday, or perhaps it's the shop's 10th anniversary, or maybe they just take a liking to you!

There is a seemingly infinite number of variations on the gem scam, almost all of which end up with the victim making a purchase of small, low-quality sapphires and posting them to their home countries. (If they let you walk out with them, you might return for a refund after realising you've been taken.) Once you return home, of course, the cheap sapphires turn out to be worth much less than what you paid for them (perhaps one-tenth to one-half). One jeweller in Perth, Australia, says he sees about 12 people a week who have been conned in Thailand.

Many have invested and lost virtually all their savings; some admit they had been scammed even after reading warnings in this guidebook or those posted by the Tourism Authority of Thailand (TAT) around Bangkok. As one letter-writer concluded his story: 'So now I'm US$500 poorer and in possession of potentially worthless sapphires – a very expensive lesson into human nature'.

Even if you were somehow able to return your purchase to the gem shop in question (I knew one fellow who actually intercepted his parcel at the airport before it left Thailand), chances are slim to none they'd give a full refund. The con artist who brings the mark into the shop gets a commission of 10% to 50% per sale – the shop takes the rest.

cigarettes, drinks or sweets (candy). Several travellers have reported waking up with a headache sometime later to find that their valuables have disappeared. One traveller was offered what looked like a machine-wrapped, made-in-England Cadbury's chocolate. His girlfriend spat it out immediately; he woke up nine hours later in hospital having required emergency resuscitation after his breathing nearly stopped. This happened on the Surat Thani to Phuket bus.

Travellers have also encountered drugged food or drink from friendly strangers in bars and from prostitutes in their own hotel rooms. Thais are also occasional victims, especially at the Moh Chit bus terminal and Chatuchak Park, where young girls are drugged and sold to brothels. Conclusion – don't accept gifts from strangers.

## Assault

Robbery of travellers by force is very rare in Thailand, but it does happen. Statistically Thailand claims only 15 violent crimes – including murder and armed robbery – per 100,000 population per year, some distance behind Malaysia (42), Australia (57.5), UK (97), Hong Kong (208) and the USA (282) as of 1991. Isolated incidences of armed

The Thai police are usually no help whatsoever, believing that merchants are entitled to whatever price they can get. The main victimisers are a handful of shops who get protection from certain high-ranking government officials. These officials put pressure on police not to prosecute or to take as little action as possible. Even TAT's tourist police have never been able to prosecute a Thai jeweller, even in cases of blatant, recurring gem fraud. A Thai police commissioner was recently convicted of fraud in an investigation into a jewellery theft by Thais in Saudi Arabia which resulted in the commissioner replacing the Saudi gems with fakes!

The card-playing scam starts out much the same – a friendly stranger approaches the lone traveller on the street, strikes up a conversation and then invites them to the house or apartment of his sister (or brother-in-law etc) for a drink or meal. After a bit of socialising a friend or relative of the con arrives on the scene; it just so happens a little high-stakes card game is planned for later that day. Like the gem scam, the card-game scam has many variations, but eventually the victim is shown some cheating tactics to use with help from the 'dealer', some practice sessions take place and finally the game gets under way with several high rollers at the table. The mark is allowed to win a few hands first, then somehow loses a few, gets bankrolled by one of the friendly Thais, and then loses the Thai's money. Suddenly your new-found buddies aren't so friendly anymore – they want the money you lost. Sometimes the con pretends to be dismayed by it all. Sooner or later you end up cashing in most or all of your travellers' cheques. Again the police won't take any action – in this case because gambling is illegal in Thailand so you've broken the law by playing cards for money.

The common denominator in all scams of this nature is the victims' own greed – the desire for an easy score. Other minor scams involve tuk-tuk drivers, hotel employees and bar girls who take new arrivals on city tours; these almost always end up in high-pressure sales situations at silk, jewellery or handicraft shops. In this case greed isn't the ruling motivation – it's simply a matter of weak sales resistance.

Follow TAT's number one suggestion to tourists: disregard all offers of free shopping or sightseeing help from strangers – they invariably take a commission from your purchases. I would add to this: beware of deals that seem too good to be true – they're usually neither good nor true. You might also try lying whenever a stranger asks how long you've been in Thailand – if it's only been three days, say three weeks! The con artists rarely prey on anyone except new arrivals. Or save your Bangkok sightseeing until after you've been upcountry.

Whether they're able to take any action or not, the TAT now has 'regulatory' powers over shops catering to tourists – you should contact the tourist police if you have any problems with consumer fraud. The tourist police headquarters (☎ (2) 255-2964) is located at 29/1 Soi Lang Suan, Ploenchit Rd in Bangkok; you can also contact them through the TAT office (☎ (2) 226-0060/72) on Bamrung Meuang Rd. There is also a police unit that deals specifically with gem swindles (☎ (2) 254-1067, 235-4017). Telephone hotline number ☎ 1699 connects with the tourist police from any phone in Thailand. ■

robbery have tended to occur along the Thai-Myanmar and Thai-Cambodian borders and on remote islands.

The safest practice in remote areas is not to go out alone at night and, if trekking in Northern Thailand, always walk in groups.

## Touts

Touting – grabbing newcomers in the street or in train stations, bus terminals or airports to sell them a service – is a longtime tradition in Asia, and while Thailand doesn't have as many as touts, say, India, it has its share. In the popular tourist spots it seems like everyone – young boys waving flyers, tuk-tuk drivers, samlor drivers, schoolgirls – is touting something, usually hotels or guest-houses. For the most part they're completely harmless and sometimes they can be very informative. But take anything a tout says with two large grains of salt. Since touts work on commission and get paid just for delivering you to a guesthouse or hotel (whether you check in or not), they'll say anything to get you to the door.

Often the best (most honest and reliable) hotels and guesthouses refuse to pay tout commissions – so the average tout will try to steer you away from such places. Hence don't believe them if they tell you the hotel or guesthouse you're looking for is 'closed', 'full', 'dirty' or 'bad'. Sometimes (rarely) they're right but most times it's just a ruse to get you to a place that pays more commission. Always have a careful look yourself before checking into a place recommended by a tout. Tuk-tuk and samlor drivers often offer free or low-cost rides to the place they're touting; if you have another place you're interested in, you might agree to go with a driver only if he or she promises to deliver you to your first choice after you've had a look at the place being touted. If drivers refuse, chances are it's because they know your first choice is a better one.

This type of commission work isn't limited to low-budget guesthouses. Taxi drivers and even airline employees at Thailand's major airports – including Bangkok and Chiang Mai – reap commissions from the big hotels as well. At either end of the budget spectrum, the customer ends up paying the commission indirectly through raised room rates. Bangkok international airport employees are notorious for talking newly arrived tourists into staying at badly located, overpriced hotels.

**Insurgent Activity**

Since the 1920s and 1930s several insurgent groups have operated in Thailand: the Communist Party of Thailand (CPT) with its tactical force, the People's Liberation Army of Thailand (PLAT), in rural areas throughout the country; Hmong guerrillas in the North hoping to overthrow the communist regime in Laos; and Malay separatists and Muslim revolutionaries in the extreme South. These groups have been mainly involved in propaganda activity, village infiltration and occasional clashes with Thai government troops. Very rarely have they had any encounters with foreign travellers. Aside from sporadic terrorist bombings – mostly in train stations in the South and sometimes at upcountry festivals – 'innocent' people have not been involved in the insurgent activity.

In 1976, the official government estimate of the number of active communist guerrillas in Thailand was 10,000. By the end of the 1970s, however, many CPT followers had surrendered under the government amnesty programme. In the 1980s new military strategies, as well as political measures, reduced the number to around two to three thousand. Another cause for the CPT's severely curtailed influence stems from the 1979 split between the CPT and the Chinese Communist Party over policy differences regarding Indochinese revolution (eg Chinese support for the Khmer Rouge against Vietnamese communists). Before the split, CPT cadres received training in Kunming, China; afterwards they were isolated.

Only a few dozen CPT guerrillas are still active in Thailand, and these are mainly involved in local extortion rackets under the guise of 'village indoctrination'. New highways in previously remote provinces such as Nan and Loei have contributed to improved communications, stability and central (Bangkok) control. This means that all routes in these provinces that were closed to foreigners in the 1970s are now open for travel (eg Phitsanulok to Loei via Nakhon Thai). Travellers can also travel from Nan to Loei by bus, and from Chiang Rai to Nan via Chiang Muan, routes that formerly ran through hotbeds of rebel activity. A new road between Phattalung and Hat Yai – a route considered 'insecure' until the mid-1980s – cut travel time between those two cities considerably.

In the North and North-East, the government claims that armed resistance has been eliminated and this appears to be verified by independent sources as well as by my experiences through former CPT strongholds. One area that supposedly remains active is a pocket of eastern Nan Province on the Laos border – the Thai military in fact doesn't allow visitors or even its own citizens into this area. Smaller, militarily inactive pockets reportedly still exist in parts of Sakon Nakhon, Tak and Phetburi provinces.

In the South, traditionally a hot spot, communist forces have been all but limited to Camp 508 in a relatively inaccessible area along the Surat Thani-Nakhon Si Thammarat provincial border. The Betong area of Yala Province on the Thai-Malaysian border was until six years ago the tactical headquarters for the armed Communist Party of Malaya (CPM). Thai and Malaysian government troops occasionally clashed with the insurgents, who from time to time hijacked trucks along the Yala to Betong road. But in December 1989, in exchange for amnesty, the CPM agreed 'to terminate all armed activities' and to respect the laws of Thailand and Malaysia. It appears that this area is now safe for travel.

Cynics note that it's in the Thai army's best interests to claim that communist insurgency still exists and that this notion is used to justify a larger standing army, higher military budgets and continuing political involvements in Bangkok. Most observers do not expect communist guerrilla activity to flare again any time in the foreseeable future. This seems especially true in light of the great economic strides Thailand has made during the last decade, which have simply made Marxism a less compelling alternative for most of the population. The softening of socialism in adjacent Myanmar, Cambodia and Laos has also greatly reduced the possibility of 'infiltration'.

**PULO** One continuing thorn in the side of the Thai government is the small but militant Malay-Muslim movement in the South. The Pattani United Liberation Organisation (PULO) was formed in 1957, trained in Libya and reached its peak in 1981 with a guerrilla strength of around 1800. The PULO refers to Thailand's three predominantly Muslim, Malay-speaking provinces of Pattani, Yala and Narathiwat – collectively known as 'Pattani'; their objective is to create a separate, sovereign state or, at the very least, to obtain annexation to Malaysia. Intelligence sources claim the rebels are supported by PAS, Malaysia's main opposition party, which is dedicated to making Malaysia a more Islamic state than it already is.

A group of 111 Muslim separatists belonging to the PULO, Barisan Revolusi Nasional (BRN, or National Revolutionary Front) and Barisan Nasional Pembebasan Pattani (BNPP, or National Front for the Freedom of Pattani) surrendered in late 1991, but PULO remnants persist in Southern Thailand's villages and jungles. This was its fourth mass surrender in five years – only a few dozen guerrillas are still active, mainly involved in propaganda and extortion activities plus the occasional attack on Thai government vehicles. PULO members collect regular 'protection' payments, for example, from rubber plantations.

Things may be heating up again, however. In August 1992 a powerful bomb exploded in the Hat Yai station, killing three and injuring 75; a PULO-signed letter was found in the station. This was the first bombing of this nature since the early 1980s. A second bombing occurred along the Bangkok-Sungai Kolok train line in Songkhla Province on 30 March; there were no serious injuries this time. In August 1993 a coordinated terrorist effort set fire to 35 government schools in Pattani, Yala and Narathiwat. Since the fire incident, law enforcement efforts in the South have intensified and the area has stayed relatively quiet.

**Other Hot Spots** Probably the most sensitive areas in Thailand nowadays are the Cambodian and Myanmar border areas. Most dangerous is the Thai-Cambodian border area, where Cambodia's former Vietnamese-backed regime sealed the border against the Khmer Rouge (KR) with heavy armament, land mines and booby traps. Most but not all of the latter are planted inside Cambodian territory, so it is imperative that you stay away from this border – it will be at least 10 years before the mines are cleared. Armed Khmer bandits or guerrillas are occasionally encountered in the vicinity of Aranya Prathet (but not in Aranya Prathet itself), still considered a risky area for casual travel.

The Khao Phra Wihaan ruins just inside Cambodia near Ubon Ratchathani have been closed to visitors from the Thai side for nearly two years now due to heavy skirmishes between KR and Phnom Penh troops. Dry-season offensives against KR strongholds tend to push KR troops all along the Thai-Cambodian border; during such periods gun and mortar fire can be heard from just about every Thai settlement in the area on a daily basis. Stray bullets and rockets do manage to find their way across national boundaries, so be sure to make security enquiries in the provincial capitals of Surin, Si Saket or Ubon before taking a trip along the border.

The Myanmar border between Um Phang and Mae Sariang occasionally receives shelling from Burmese troops in pursuit of Karen or Mon rebels. Karen rebels are trying to maintain an independent nation called Kawthoolei along the border with Thailand. If you cross illegally and are captured by the Burmese, you may automatically be suspected of supporting the Karen. If you are captured by the Karen you will probably be released, though they may demand money. The risks of catching a piece of shrapnel are substantially lower if you keep several km between yourself and the Thai-Myanmar border in this area – fighting can break out at any time. Mae Sot itself is quite safe these days, though you can still occasionally hear mortar fire in the distance.

In the Three Pagodas Pass area, there is also occasional fighting between Myanmar, Karen and Mon armies, who are competing for control over the smuggling trade between Myanmar and Thailand. Typically, the rebels advance in the rainy season and retreat in the dry; lately this area has been fairly quiet.

Along the Myanmar-Thai border in northern Mae Hong Song, the presence of Shan and Kuomintang armies make this area dangerous if you attempt to travel near opium trade border crossings – obviously these are not signposted, so take care anywhere along the border in this area. In late 1992 Thai rangers moved in on the Mae Hong Son border to force opium warlord Khun Sa and his Muang Tai Army (MTA) camp further back from the frontier – his headquarters at the time was only a km inside Burmese territory. Although the Thai rangers have delivered an ultimatum that the MTA remain at least two km away from the border, a definite risk of firefights continues. In early 1996 Khun Sa and 10,000 of his troops surrendered to Yangon, taking most of the punch out the MTA. However, as many as 8000 MTA remnants, split among four armies, are still active in the area bordering Mae Sai south to Mae Hong Son, so the area is not much safer than when Khun Sa was still around.

There is also a potential of hostilities breaking out between Myanmar government troops and the Thai army over a disputed Thai-Myanmar border section near Doi Lang, south-west of Mae Sai in Mae Ai district. The territory under dispute amounts to 32 sq km; at the moment the two sides are trying to work things out peaceably according to the 1894 Siam-Britain Treaty, which both countries recognise. The problem is that British mapping of the time made geographical naming errors that unintentionally seem to favour the Burmese side. Burmese and Thai troops will remained poised for action on either side of the border until the matter is resolved.

Although Bangkok has generally been safe from terrorist activity, a couple of large truck bombs bound for the Israeli embassy have been intercepted in the city since 1991. The district known as Little Arabia (Soi Nana Neua, off Sukhumvit Rd) is a known 'hideaway' for Muslim terrorists on the run from other parts of the world.

### Drugs

Opium, heroin and marijuana are widely used in Thailand, but it is illegal to buy, sell or possess these drugs in any quantity. (The possession of opium for consumption – but not sale – among hill tribes is legal.) A lesser known narcotic, kràtom (a leaf of the Mitragyna speciosa tree), is used by workers and students as a stimulant – similar to Yemen's qat. A hundred kratom leaves sell for around 50B, and are sold for 3 to 5B each; the leaf is illegal and said to be addictive.

In the South, especially on the rainy Gulf

of Thailand islands, mushrooms (in Thai *hèt khîi khwai*, 'buffalo-shit mushrooms', or *hèt mao*, 'drunk mushrooms') which contain the hallucinogen psilocybin are sometimes sold to or gathered by foreigners. The legal status of mushroom use or possession is questionable; police have been known to hassle Thais who sell them. Using such mushrooms is a risky proposition as the dosage is always uncertain; I've heard one confirmed story of a foreigner who swam to his death off Ko Pha-Ngan after a 'special' mushroom omelette.

Although in certain areas of the country drugs seem to be used with some impunity, enforcement is arbitrary – the only way not to risk getting caught is to avoid the scene entirely. Every year perhaps dozens of visiting foreigners are arrested in Thailand for drug use or trafficking and end up doing hard time. A smaller but significant number die of heroin overdoses.

Penalties for drug offences are stiff; if you're caught using marijuana, you face a fine and/or up to one year in prison, while for heroin, the penalty for use can be anywhere from six months to 10 years imprisonment.

## BUSINESS HOURS

Most government offices are open from 8.30 am to 4.30 pm Monday to Friday, but close from noon to 1 pm for lunch. Regular bank hours in Bangkok are 10 am to 4 pm Monday to Friday, but several banks have special foreign-exchange offices in tourist-oriented areas which are open longer hours (8.30 am until 8 pm) and every day of the week. Note that all government offices and banks are closed on public holidays (see Public Holidays & Special Events for details).

Businesses usually operate between 8.30 am and 5 pm Monday to Friday and sometimes Saturday morning as well. Larger shops usually open from 10 am to 6.30 or 7 pm but smaller shops may open earlier and close later.

## PUBLIC HOLIDAYS & SPECIAL EVENTS

The number and frequency of festivals and fairs in Thailand is incredible – there always seems to be something going on, especially during the cool season between November and February.

Exact dates for festivals may vary from year to year, either because of the lunar calendar – which isn't quite in sync with the solar calendar – or because local authorities decide to change festival dates. The TAT publishes an up-to-date *Major Events & Festivals* calendar each year that is useful for anyone planning to attend a particular event.

A major upcoming event not listed below, the *13th Asian Games*, will be held at the National Stadium in Bangkok in 1998. For information on either event contact a TAT office in Thailand or abroad.

---

### Drug Penalties

| Drug | Quantity | Penalty |
|---|---|---|
| **Marijuana** | | |
| Smuggling | any amount | 2 to 15 years imprisonment |
| Possession | less than 10 kg | up to 5 years imprisonment |
| Possession | 10 kg + | 2 to 15 years imprisonment |
| **Heroin** | | |
| Smuggling | any amount | life imprisonment |
| Smuggling | any amount with intent to sell | execution |
| Possession | 10g + | imprisonment or execution |

*\* Note: 'Smuggling' refers to any drug possession at a border or airport customs check.*

---

Last week of January
> *That Phanom Festival* – an annual week-long homage to the North-East's most sacred Buddhist stupa (Wat Phra That Phanom) in Nakhon Phanom Province. Pilgrims from all over the country, as well as from Laos, attend.

Late January

*Don Chedi Monument Fair* – held at the Don Chedi memorial in Suphanburi Province, this event commemorates the victory of King Naresuan of Ayuthaya over Burmese invaders in 1592. The highlight of the fair is dramatised elephant-back duelling.

February

*Magha Puja (Makkha Buchaa)* – held on the full moon of the third lunar month to commemorate the preaching of the Buddha to 1250 enlightened monks who came to hear him 'without prior summons'. A public holiday throughout the country, it culminates with a candle-lit walk around the main chapel at every wat.

1st week of February

*Chiang Mai Flower Festival* – colourful floats and parades exhibit Chiang Mai's cultivated flora.

*Phra Nakhon Khiri Diamond Festival* – week-long celebration of Phetburi's history and architecture focused on Phra Nakhon Khiri (also known as Khao Wang), a hill topped by a former royal palace overlooking the city. Features a sound & light show on Khao Wang, temples festooned with lights and Thai classical dance-drama.

Late February to early March

*Chinese New Year* – called *trùt jiin* in Thai, Chinese populations all over Thailand celebrate their lunar new year (the date shifts from year to year) with a week of house-cleaning, lion dances and fireworks. The most impressive festivities take place in the Chinese-dominated province capital of Nakhon Sawan.

1st week of March

*ASEAN Barred Ground Dove Fair* – large dove-singing contest held in Yala that attracts dove-lovers from all over Thailand, Malaysia, Singapore and Indonesia.

1st or 2nd week of March

*Phra Phutthabaat Festival* – annual pilgrimage to Wat Phra Buddhabat (Temple of the Holy Footprint) at Saraburi, 236 km north-east of Bangkok. Quite an affair, with music, outdoor drama and many other festivities. If you're in the area, the shrine is worth visiting even in the 'off season'.

3rd week of March

*Bangkok International Jewellery Fair* – held in several large Bangkok hotels, this is Thailand's most important annual gem and jewellery trade show. Runs concurrently with the Department of Export Promotion's Gems & Jewellery Fair.

Last week of March

*Phanom Rung Festival* – a newly established festival to commemorate the restoration of this impressive Angkor-style temple complex in Buriram Province. Involves a daytime procession up Phanom Rung Hill and spectacular sound & light shows at night. Be prepared for very hot weather.

6 April

*Chakri Day* – a public holiday commemorating the founder of the Chakri Dynasty, Rama I.

13 to 15 April

*Songkhran Festival* – the New Year's celebration of the lunar year in Thailand. Buddha images are 'bathed', monks and elders receive the respect of younger Thais by the sprinkling of water over their hands, and a lot of water is generously tossed about for fun. Songkhran generally gives everyone a chance to release their frustrations and literally cool off during the peak of the hot season. Hide out in your room or expect to be soaked; the latter is a lot more fun.

May (Full Moon)

*Visakha Puja (Wisakha Buchaa)* – a public holiday which falls on the 15th day of the waxing moon in the sixth lunar month. This is considered the date of the Buddha's birth, enlightenment and *parinibbana*, or passing away. Activities are centred around the wat, with candle-lit processions, much chanting and sermonising.

5 May

*Coronation Day* – public holiday. The king and queen preside at a ceremony at Wat Phra Kaew in Bangkok, commemorating their 1946 coronation.

Mid-May to mid-June

*Royal Ploughing Ceremony* – to kick off the official rice-planting season, the king participates in this ancient Brahman ritual at Sanam Luang (the large field across from Wat Phra Kaew) in Bangkok. Thousands of Thais gather to watch, and traffic in this part of the city comes to a standstill.

*Rocket Festival* – all over the North-East, villagers craft large skyrockets of bamboo which they then fire into the sky to bring rain for rice fields. This festival is best celebrated in the town of Yasothon, but is also good in Ubon Ratchathani and Nong Khai. Known in Thai as Bun Bang Fai.

*Bun Prawet Festival* – a unique celebration held in Loei's Dan Sai district (nowadays also in the provincial capital) in which revellers dress in garish 'spirit' costumes and painted masks of coconut wood. The festival commemorates a Buddhist legend in which a host of spirits (*phii*) appeared to greet the Buddha-to-be upon his return to his home town, during his penultimate birth. Commemorates the first sermon preached by the Buddha.

Mid to late July

*Khao Phansaa* – a public holiday and the beginning of Buddhist 'lent' (*phansāa*), this is the traditional time of year for young men to enter the monkhood for the rainy season and for all monks to station themselves in a monastery for the three months. It's a good time to observe a Buddhist ordination.

BERNARD NAPTHINE

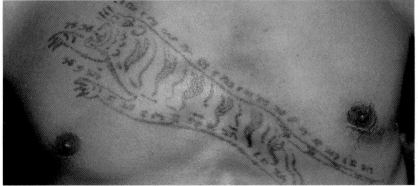

BERNARD NAPTHINE

SARA JANE CLELAND

### Street markets

Top: Taking a break from the frantic world of commerce
Middle: Tattoos – a popular form of body art in Thailand
Bottom: Eat-in or take-away, street-market style

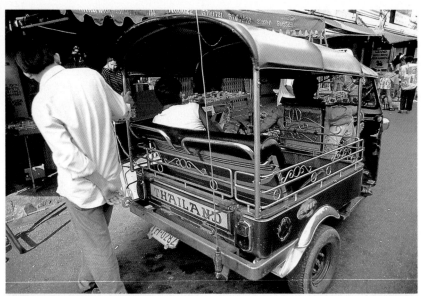

RICHARD NEBESKY

RICHARD NEBESKY

RICHARD NEBESKY

## Getting around
Top: Tuk-tuk for hire, Khao San Rd, Bangkok
Bottom Left: Decorated songthaew, Ko Samui
Bottom Right: Boats for charter, Saphaan Plaa, near Ranong

*Candle Festival* – Khao Phansaa is celebrated in the North-East by carving huge candles and parading them on floats in the streets. This festival is best celebrated in Ubon Ratchathani.

12 August

*Queen's Birthday* – public holiday. In Bangkok, Ratchadamnoen Klang Rd and the Grand Palace are festooned with coloured lights.

Mid-September

*Thailand International Swan-Boat Races* – these take place on the Chao Phraya River in Bangkok near the Rama IX Bridge.

Last week of September

*Narathiwat Fair* – an annual week-long festival celebrating local culture in Narathiwat Province with boat races, dove-singing contests, handicraft displays, traditional Southern Thai music and dance. The king and queen almost always attend.

Late September to early October

*Vegetarian Festival* – a nine day celebration in Trang and Phuket during which devout Chinese Buddhists eat only vegetarian food. There are also various ceremonies at Chinese temples and merit-making processions that bring to mind Hindu Thaipusam in its exhibition of self-mortification. Smaller towns in the South such as Krabi and Phang-Nga also celebrate the veggie fest on a smaller scale.

Mid-October to mid-November

*Thâwt Kathin* – a one month period at the end of the Buddhist lent during which new monastic robes and requisites are offered to the Sangha. In Nan Province longboat races are held on the Nan River.

23 October

*Chulalongkorn Day* – a public holiday in commemoration of King Chulalongkorn (Rama V).

November

*Loi Krathong* – on the proper full-moon night, small lotus-shaped baskets or boats made of banana leaves containing flowers, incense, candles and a coin are floated on Thai rivers, lakes and canals. This is a peculiarly Thai festival that probably originated in Sukhothai and is best celebrated in the North. In Chiang Mai, where the festival is called Yi Peng, residents also launch hot-air paper balloons into the sky. At the Sukhothai Historical Park there is an impressive sound & light show.

Third weekend in November

*Surin Annual Elephant Roundup* – Thailand's biggest elephant show is pretty touristy these days. If you ever wanted to see a lot of elephants in one place, though, here's your chance.

Late November to early December

*River Khwae Bridge Week* – sound & light shows every night at the Death Railway Bridge in Kanchanaburi, plus historical exhibitions and vintage train rides.

5 December

*King's Birthday* – this is a public holiday which is celebrated with some fervour in Bangkok. As with the queen's birthday, it features lots of lights along Ratchadamnoen Klang Rd. Some people erect temporary shrines to the king outside their homes or businesses.

10 December

*Constitution Day* – public holiday.

31 December to 1 January

*New Year's Day* – a rather recent public holiday in deference to the western calendar.

## ACTIVITIES
### Diving & Snorkelling

Thailand's two coastlines and countless islands are popular among divers for their mild waters and colourful marine life. The biggest diving centre – in terms of the number of participants, but not the number of dive operations – is still Pattaya, simply because it's less than two hours drive from Bangkok. There are several islands with reefs within a short boat ride from Pattaya and the little town is packed with dive shops.

Phuket is the second biggest jumping-off point – or largest if you count dive operations – and has the advantage of offering the largest variety of places to choose from, including small offshore islands less than an hour away, Ao Phang-Nga (a one to two hour boat ride) with its unusual rock formations and clear green waters, and the world-famous Similan and Surin islands in the Andaman Sea (about four hours away by fast boat). Reef dives in the Andaman are particularly rewarding – some 210 hard corals and 108 reef fish have so far been catalogued in this under-studied marine zone, where probably thousands more species of reef organisms live.

In recent years dive operations have multiplied rapidly on the palmy islands of Ko Samui, Ko Pha-Ngan and Ko Tao in the Gulf of Thailand off Surat Thani. Chumphon Province, just north of Surat Thani, is another up-and-coming area where there are a dozen or so islands with undisturbed reefs. Newer frontiers include the so-called Burma Banks (north-west of Ko Surin), Khao Lak and islands off the coast of Krabi and Trang provinces.

All of these places, with the possible exception of the Burma Banks, have areas that are suitable for snorkelling as well as scuba diving, since many reefs are no deeper than two metres.

Masks, fins and snorkels are readily available for rent not only at dive centres but also through guesthouses in beach areas. If you're particular about the quality and condition of the equipment you use, however, you might be better off bringing your own mask and snorkel – some of the stuff for rent is second-rate. And people with large heads may have difficulty finding masks that fit since most of the masks are made or imported for Thai heads.

**Dive Centres** Most dive shops rent equipment at reasonable rates and some also offer basic instruction and NAUI or PADI qualification for first-timers – PADI is by far the most prevalent. The average four day, full-certification course goes for around 5000 to 8000B, including all instruction, equipment and several open-water dives. Shorter, less expensive 'resort' courses are also available.

It's a good idea to shop around at several dive companies, not just to compare prices but to suss out the types of instruction, the condition of the equipment and the personalities of the instructors. German and English are the most common media of instruction, but French and Italian courses are also available at a lesser number of places. See the relevant destination sections of this book for names and locations of established diving centres.

**Dive Seasons** Generally speaking, the Gulf of Thailand has a year-round dive season, although tropical storms sometimes blow out the visibility temporarily. On the Andaman coast the best diving conditions occur between December and April; from May to November monsoon conditions prevail. Whale sharks and manta rays in the offshore Andaman (eg Similan and Surin island groups) are a major bonus during planktonic blooms in March and April.

**Dive Medicine** Due to the overall lack of medical facilities oriented toward diving injuries, great caution should be exercised when diving anywhere in Thailand. Recompression chambers are located at two permanent facilities:

Department of Underwater & Aviation Medicine – Somedej Phra Pinklao Naval Hospital, Taksin Rd, Thonburi, Bangkok (☎ (2) 460-0000/19, ext 341, 460-1105); open 24 hours
Apakorn Kiatiwong Naval Hospital – Sattahip, Chonburi (☎ (38) 601185); 26 km east of Pattaya; urgent care available 24 hours

A third recompression facility is under development in Phuket; contact any Phuket dive shop for the latest information. The Thai naval base at Thap Lamu (north of Phuket) may also restore recompression services in the near future.

**Dive Guidebooks** *Diving in Thailand* (Asia Books, 1994), by Colin Piprell & Ashley J Boyd, contains well researched, well organised information on diving throughout the country. *ScubaGuide Thailand* (1994), published by *Asian Diver* magazine, is also helpful. Both guides are illustrated with colour photos; *Diving in Thailand* has many more maps.

**Other Water Sports**

With countless islands and thousands of km of coastline along the Gulf of Thailand and Andaman Sea, just about any water-related activity imaginable can be enjoyed.

**Windsurfing** The best combinations of rental facilities and wind conditions are found on Pattaya and Jomtien beaches in Chonburi Province, on Ko Samet, on the west coast of Phuket and on Chaweng Beach on Ko Samui. To a lesser extent you'll also find rental equipment on Hat Khao Lak (north of Phuket), Ko Pha-Ngan, Ko Tao and Ko Chang.

Rental windsurfing gear found at Thai resorts is generally not the most complete and up-to-date. Original parts may be missing, or may have been replaced by improvised, Thai-made parts. For the novice windsurfer this probably won't matter, but hot-doggers may be disappointed in the selection. Bring your own if you can. In Thailand's year-round tropical climate, wetsuits aren't necessary.

If you have your own equipment you can set out anywhere you find a coastal breeze. If you're looking for something undiscovered, you might check out the cape running north from Narathiwat's provincial capital in Southern Thailand. In general the windier months on the Gulf of Thailand are mid-February to April. On the Andaman Sea side of the Thai-Malay peninsula winds are strongest from September to December.

**Surfing** This sport has never really taken off in Thailand, not least because there doesn't seem to be any sizeable, annually dependable breaks (write to me if you find any). Phuket's west coast occasionally kicks up some surfable waves during the south-west monsoon (May to November). I have also seen some fair surf action on the west coast of Ko Chang during the same time of year, and on the east coast of Ko Samet during the dry season (November to February). I'd be willing to bet there's decent surf on Ko Chang's east coast during these months.

Low-quality boards can be rented in Pattaya and on Phuket's Patong Beach (but bigger surf is usually found on Laem Singh and Hat Surin). Coastal Trang is historically reputed to receive large waves during the south-west monsoon, but I've never heard of anyone surfing there.

**Sea Canoeing** Touring the islands and coastal limestone formations around Phuket and Ao Phang-Nga by inflatable canoe has become an increasingly popular activity over the last five years. The typical sea canoe tour seeks out half-submerged caves called 'hongs' (hâwng, Thai for 'room'), timing their excursions so that they can paddle into the caverns at low tide. Several outfits in Phuket and Krabi offer equipment and guides – see the relevant sections for details.

You might also consider bringing your own craft. Inflatable or folding kayaks make the most sense from a transport perspective though hardshell kayaks track better. In Thailand's tropical waters an open-top or open-deck kayak – whether hardshell, folding or inflatable – is a more comfortable and practical choice than the closed-deck type with a spray skirt and other sealing paraphernalia, which would only transform your kayak into a floating sauna.

### River & Canal Excursions
Numerous opportunities for boat travel along Thailand's major rivers and canals are available through the extensive public boat system and aboard a small number of tourist boat services. So far only the lower Chao Phraya River and a few rivers in Northern Thailand have been introduced to regular leisure boating. A variety of watercraft are available, from air-conditioned tourist boats along the Chao Phraya River around Bangkok to rustic bamboo rafts on the Kok River and sturdy whitewater kayaks on the Pai River.

The Maekhong River, until the late 1980s considered perilous due to regional hostilities, has enormous potential. During the last six years or so short-distance boat trips have been offered in Chiang Rai, Loei and Nong Khai provinces, and in early 1994 an experimental tour service between Chiang Saen and China was inaugurated. Central Thailand's vast network of canals, centred around the Chao Phraya Delta and fanning out for hundreds of km in all directions, offers innumerable boating opportunities. Because of the sometimes imposing motorised boat traffic along these waterways, so far very few foreign visitors have tried canoeing or kayaking this grid; for the adventurous, the potential is tremendous. By public and chartered long-tail boat one can piece together canal journeys of several days duration.

For more information on river and canal travel possibilities, see the relevant destination chapters later in the book.

### Trekking
Wilderness walking or trekking is one of Northern Thailand's biggest draws. Typical

Northern Thailand trekking programmes run for four or five days (though it is possible to arrange everything from one to 10 day treks) and feature daily walks through forested mountain areas coupled with overnight stays in hill-tribe villages to satisfy both ethno and ecotourism urges. See the special Trekking section in the Northern Thailand chapter for more detail.

Other trekking opportunities are available in Thailand's larger national parks (including Khao Yai, Kaeng Krachan, Khao Sam Roi Yot, Doi Phu Kha, Khao Sok, Thap Lan and Phu Reua) where park rangers may be hired as guides and cooks for a few days at a time. Rates are reasonable. For more information, see the respective park descriptions later in this book.

### Cycling

Details on pedalling your way around Thailand can be found in the Getting Around chapter.

## COURSES
### Thai Language Study

Several language schools in Bangkok, Chiang Mai and other places where foreigners congregate offer courses in Thai language. Tuition fees average around 250B per hour. Some places will let you trade English lessons for Thai lessons; if not, you can usually teach English on the side to offset tuition costs.

If you have an opportunity to 'shop around' it's best to enrol in programmes that offer plenty of opportunity for linguistic interaction rather than rote learning or the passé 'natural method', which has been almost universally discredited for the over-attention paid to teacher input.

Schools in Bangkok with the best reputations include:

Union Language School – CCT Building, 109 Surawong Rd (☎ (2) 233-4482). Generally recognised as the best and most rigorous course (many missionaries study here). Employs a balance of structure-oriented and communication-oriented methodologies in 80 hour, four week modules. Private tuition is also available.

AUA Language Center – 179 Ratchadamri Rd (☎ (2) 252-7067/9). American University Alumni (AUA) runs one of the largest English-language teaching institutes in the world, so this is a good place to meet Thai students. Some foreigners who study Thai here complain that there's not enough interaction in class because of an emphasis on the so-called 'natural approach', which focuses on teacher input rather than student practice; others find the approach useful.

Nisa Thai Language School – YMCA Collins House, 27 Sathon Tai Rd (☎ (2) 286-9323). This school has a fairly good reputation, though teachers may be less qualified than at Union or AUA language schools. In addition to all the usual levels, Nisa offers a course in preparing for the Baw Hok or Grade 6 examination, a must for anyone wishing to work in the public school system.

AUA also has branches in Chiang Mai, Lampang, Phitsanulok, Khon Kaen, Udon, Mahasarakham, Ubon, Songkhla and Phuket. Most of these are housed on Thai college or university campuses. Not all AUAs offer regularly scheduled Thai classes, but study can usually be arranged on an ad hoc basis. Teaching methodologies in upcountry AUAs tends to be more flexible than at the Bangkok unit.

The YWCA's Siri Pattana Thai Language School (☎ (2) 286-1936), 13 Sathon Tai Rd, Bangkok, gives Thai-language lessons as well as preparation for the Baw Hok exam. Siri Pattana has a second branch at 806 Soi 38, Sukhumvit Rd.

### Language & Cultural Study

Chulalongkorn University in Bangkok, the most prestigious university in Thailand, offers an intensive Thai studies course called 'Perspectives on Thailand'. The eight week programme includes classes in Thai language, culture, history, politics and economics, plus a 10 day upcountry field trip. Classes meet six hours a day, six days a week (Saturday is usually a field trip) and are offered once a year from the first Monday in July to the last Friday in August. Students who have taken the course say they have found the quality of instruction excellent. Tuition is around US$2400, including meals, transport and accommodation on the 10 day field trip. Room and board on campus are available, though it's much less expensive to live off campus. For further information write to: Perspectives on Thailand, Continuing Education Center, 5th floor, Vidhyabhathan Bldg, Soi Chulalongkorn 12 (2), Chulalongkorn University, Bangkok 10330 (☎ (2) 218-3393; fax 214-4515).

## Meditation Study

Thailand has long been a popular place for western students of Buddhism, particularly those interested in a system of meditation known as *vipassana* (Thai: *wí-pàt-sa-nāa*), a Pali word which roughly translated means 'insight'. Foreigners who come to Thailand to study vipassana can choose among dozens of temples and meditation centres (*sãmnák wípàtsanāa*) which specialise in these teachings. Teaching methods vary from place to place but the general emphasis is on learning to observe mind-body processes from moment to moment. Thai language is usually the medium of instruction but several places also provide instruction in English.

Details on some of the more popular meditation-oriented temples and centres are given in the relevant sections. Instruction and accommodation are free of charge at temples, though donations are expected.

Short-term students will find that the two month Tourist Visa is ample for most courses of study. Long-term students may want to consider a three or six month Non-Immigrant Visa. A few westerners are ordained as monks or nuns in order to take full advantage of the monastic environment. Monks and nuns are generally (but not always) allowed to stay in Thailand as long as they remain in robes.

Places where English-language instruction is usually available include:

International Buddhist Meditation Centre – Wat Mahathat, Maharat Rd, Tha Phra Chan, Bangkok (☎ (2) 222-6011)

Wat Asokaram – Bang Na-Trat Highway (32 km south of Bangkok), Samut Prakan (☎ (2) 395-0003)

Wiwekasom Vipassana Centre – Ban Suan, Chonburi (☎ (38) 283766)

Sorn-Thawee Meditation Centre – Bangkla, Chachoengsao 24110

Boonkanjanaram Meditation Centre – Jomtien Beach, Pattaya, Chonburi (☎ (38) 231865)

Wat Tapotaram (Wat Ram Poeng) – Chiang Mai (☎ (53) 278620)

Wat Suan Mokkhaphalaram – Chaiya, Surat Thani

Wat Khao Tham – Ko Pha-Ngan, Surat Thani

Before visiting one of the above centres, it's a good idea to call or write to make sure space and instruction are available. Some places require that lay persons staying overnight wear white clothes. For even a brief visit, wear clean and neat clothing (ie long trousers or skirt and sleeves which cover the shoulder).

For a detailed look at vipassana study in Thailand, including visa and ordination procedures, read *The Meditation Temples of Thailand: A Guide* (Spirit Rock Center, PO Box 909, Woodacre, CA 94973, USA, or Silkworm Publications, Chiang Mai) or *A Guide to Buddhist Monasteries & Meditation Centres in Thailand* (available from the World Federation of Buddhists in Bangkok).

Useful premeditation course reading includes Jack Kornfield's *Living Buddhist Masters*, which contains short biographies and descriptions of the teaching methods of 12 well known Theravada teachers, including six Thais (Ajaans Buddhadasa, Jamnien, Thammatharo, Naep, Chaa and Maha Bua). Half these teachers have passed away since the book's publication but their teaching methods have been preserved and propagated by younger teachers around the country. Serious meditators will want to study *The Path of Purification (Visuddhi Magga)*, a classic commentary that reveals every detail of canonical Buddhist practice and includes a Pali-English glossary defining all the tricky terms like *kasina, jhana, nimitta, vibhaka* and so on. These books are available at bookstores in Bangkok (see Books earlier).

## Martial Arts Training

Many westerners have trained in Thailand (especially since the release of Jean-Claude Van Damme's martial arts flick, *The Kickboxer*, which was filmed on location in Thailand), but few last more than a week or two in a Thai camp – and fewer still have gone on to compete on Thailand's pro circuit.

The *Modern Gladiator Journal* (fax (312) 201-9399), PO Box 5619, Chicago, IL 60680, USA, is a homespun quarterly devoted to Thai martial arts training and competition. In Thailand you can also pick up copies of *Muay Thai World*, a biannual periodical published by Bangkok's World Muay Thai Council.

**Thai Boxing (Muay Thai)** An Australian, Patrick Cusick, occasionally directs *muay thai* seminars for foreigners. Contact him at Thai Championship Boxing (☎ (2) 234-5360; fax 237-6303) at Box 1996, Bangkok. The Pramote Gym (☎ (2) 215-8848) at 210-212 Phetburi Rd, Ratthewi, offers training in Thai boxing as well as other martial arts (judo, karate, tae kwon do, krabi-krabong) to foreigners as well as locals.

Those interested in training at a traditional muay thai camp might try the Sityodthong-Payakarun Boxing Camp in Naklua (north of Pattaya) or Fairtex Boxing Camp outside Bangkok (c/o Bunjong Busarakamwongs, Fairtex Garments Factory, 734-742 Trok Kai, Anuwong Rd, Bangkok). The newer Lanna Boxing Camp (☎ /fax (53) 273133) at 64/1 Soi 1 (Soi Chang Kian), Huay Kaew Rd, Chiang Mai 50300 and Patong Boxing Club (☎ (01) 978-9352; fax (76) 292189) at 59/4 Muu 4, Na Nai Rd, Patong Beach, Phuket, specialise in training for foreigners. Be forewarned, though: muay thai training is gruelling and features full-contact sparring, unlike tae kwon do, kenpo, kung fu and other East Asian martial arts.

For more information about Thai boxing, see the Spectator Sports section later in this chapter.

**Krabi-Krabong** A traditional Thai martial art, *kràbìi-kràbong* (literally, 'sword-staff') is taught at several Thai colleges and universities, but the country's best training venue is the Buddhai Sawan Fencing School of Thailand, at 5/1 Phetkasem Rd, Thonburi, where Ajaan Samai Mesamarna carries on the tradition as passed down from Wat Phutthaisawan. Several foreigners have trained here, including one American who became the first foreigner to attain *ajaan* (master) status. Pramote Gym (see Thai Boxing earlier) also provides krabi-krabong training. See the Spectator Sports section in this chapter for more details.

**Thai Massage**
Thailand offers ample opportunities to study its unique tradition of massage therapy. Wat Pho in Bangkok is considered the master source for all Thai massage pedagogy, although Northern Thailand boasts its own 'softer' version. For details see Massage under the Bangkok and Chiang Mai sections.

**Thai Cooking Schools**
More and more travellers are coming to Thailand just to learn how to cook. While passing through Thailand, I often meet foreign chefs seeking out recipe inspirations for the 'East-West' sort of cuisine that seems to be taking the world by storm. You, too, can amaze your friends back home after attending a course in Thai cuisine at one of the following places:

Modern Housewife Centre – 45/6-7 Sethsiri Rd, Bangkok (☎ (2) 279-2834)

Oriental Hotel Cooking School – Soi Oriental, Charoen Krung Rd, Bangkok (☎ (2) 236-0400/39); features a five day course under the direction of well known chef Chali (Charlie) Amatyakul

UFM Food Centre – 593/29-39 Soi 33/1, Sukhumvit Rd, Bangkok (☎ (2) 259-0620/33); most classes offered in Thai – you need at least four people for an English-language class

Chiang Mai Thai Cookery School – 1-3 Moon Meuang Rd (☎ (53) 206388); receives raves for its well organised courses, which include market and garden visits

The Boathouse – Kata Yai Beach, Phuket (☎ (76) 330557; fax 330561; ☎ (2) 438-1123 in Bangkok); the chefs at this outstanding Phuket beach restaurant offer occasional weekend workshops

**WORK**
Thailand's steady economic growth has provided a variety of work opportunities for

foreigners, although in general it's not as easy to find a job as in the more developed countries. The one exception is English teaching; as in the rest of East and South-East Asia, there is a high demand for English speakers to provide instruction to Thai citizens. This is not due to a shortage of qualified Thai teachers with a good grasp of English grammar, but rather to the desire to have native speaker models in the classroom.

### Teaching English

Those with academic credentials such as teaching certificates or degrees in English as a second language get first crack at the better-paying jobs, such as those at universities and international schools. But there are perhaps hundreds of private language teaching establishments that hire noncredentialed teachers by the hour throughout the country. Private tutoring is also a possibility in the larger, wealthier cities such as Bangkok, Chiang Mai, Phuket, Lampang, Khon Kaen, Phitsanulok, Hat Yai and Songkhla. International oil companies pay the highest salaries for English instructors but are also quite picky.

If you're interested in looking for such teaching work, start with the English-language *Yellow Pages of the Greater Bangkok Metropolitan Telephone Directory*, which contains many upcountry as well as Bangkok listings. Check all the usual headings – Schools, Universities, Language Schools (over 75 listings in Bangkok alone) and so on. Organisations such as Teachers of English to Speakers of Other Languages (TESOL; 1600 Cameron St, Suite 300, Alexandria, Virginia 22314, USA) and International Association of Teachers of English as a Foreign Language (IATEFL; 3 Kingsdown Chamber, Kingsdown Park, Whitstable, Kent CT52DJ, UK) publish newsletters with lists of jobs in foreign countries, including Thailand.

### Other Jobs & Volunteer Positions

Voluntary and paying positions with organisations that provide charitable services in education, development or public health are available for those with the right educational and/or experiential backgrounds. Contact the usual prospects such as: Voluntary Service Overseas (☎ (0181) 780-2266) in London; Volunteers in Overseas Cooperative Assistance (VOCA; ☎ (202) 383-4961) in Washington; Overseas Service Bureau (OSB; ☎ (03) 9279-1788) in Melbourne; or Volunteer Service Abroad (☎ (04) 472-5759) in Wellington.

The United Nations supports a number of ongoing projects in the country. In Bangkok interested people can try contacting: United Nations Development Programme (☎ (2) 282-9619); UN World Food Programme (☎ (2) 280-0427); World Health Organisation (☎ (2) 2829700); Food & Agriculture Organisation (☎ (2) 281-7844); UNICEF (☎ (2) 280-5931); or UNESCO (☎ (2) 391-0577).

Mon, Karen and Burmese refugee camps along the Thailand-Myanmar border can use volunteer help. Since none of the camps is officially sanctioned by the Thai government, few of the big non-government organisations or multilateral organisations are involved here. This means the level of overall support is low but the need for volunteers is definitely there. If this interests you, travel to the relevant areas (primarily Sangkhlaburi and Mae Sot) and ask around for the 'unofficial' camp locations.

### ACCOMMODATION

Places to stay are abundant, varied and reasonably priced in Thailand.

However, just a word of warning about touts: don't believe them if they say a place is closed, full, dirty or crooked. Sometimes they're right but most times it's just a ruse to get you to a place that pays them more commission. (See Dangers & Annoyances earlier for more information about touts.)

### Guesthouses & Hostels

Guesthouses are generally the cheapest accommodation in Thailand and are found in most areas where travellers go in Central, Northern and Southern Thailand; they are spreading slowly to the East and North-East as well. Guesthouses vary quite a bit in facilities and are particularly popular in Bangkok and Chiang Mai where stiff competition keeps rates low. Some are especially good value, while others are mere flophouses. Many serve food, although there tends to be a bland sameness to meals in guesthouses wherever you are in Thailand.

There is a Thai branch of Hostelling International (HI; ☎ (2) 282-0950; fax 281-6834), formerly International Youth Hostel Federation, at 25/2 Phitsanulok Rd, Sisao Thewet, Dusit, Bangkok 10300, with member hostels in Bangkok (two), Ayuthaya (one), Chiang Mai (two), Chiang Rai (one) and Phitsanulok (one). From time to time there have been others in Kanchanaburi, Ko Phi Phi and Nan but at the time of writing these were closed. Thai youth hostels range in price from 50B for a dorm bed to 250B for an air-con room. Since 1992, only HI card holders are accepted as guests in Thai hostels; membership costs 300B per year or 50B for a temporary (one night) membership.

### YMCA/YWCAs

A YMCA or YWCA costs a bit more than a guesthouse or hostel (an average of 400B and above) and sometimes more than a local hotel, but they are generally good value. There are Ys in Bangkok, Chiang Mai and Chiang Rai.

### Chinese-Thai Hotels

The standard Thai hotels, often run by Chinese-Thai families, are the easiest accommodation to come by and generally have very reasonable rates (average 80 to 100B for rooms without bath or air-con, 120 to 250B with fan and bath, 250 to 500B with air-con). They may be located on the main street of the town and/or near bus and train stations.

The most economical hotels to stay in are those without air-con; typical rooms are clean and include a double bed and a ceiling fan. Some have attached Thai-style bathrooms (this will cost a little more). Rates may or may not be posted; if not, they

maybe increased for *faràngs* (foreigners of European descent), so it is worthwhile bargaining. It is best to have a look around before agreeing to check in, to make sure the room *is* clean, that the fan and lights work and so on. If there is any problem, request another room or a good discount. If possible, always choose a room off the street and away from the front lounge to cut down on ambient noise.

For a room without air-con, ask for a *hâwng thammádaa* (ordinary room) or *hâwng phát lom* (room with fan). A room with air-con is *hâwng ae*. Sometimes farangs asking for air-con are automatically offered a 'VIP' room, which usually comes with air-con, hot water, fridge and TV and is about twice the price of a regular air-con room.

Some Chinese-Thai hotels may double as brothels; the perpetual traffic in and out can be a bit noisy but is generally bearable. Unaccompanied males are often asked if they want female companionship when checking into inexpensive hotels. Even certain middle-class (by Thai standards) hotels are reserved for the 'salesman' crowd, meaning travelling Thai businessmen who frequently expect extra night-time services.

The cheapest hotels may have their names posted in Thai and Chinese only, but you will learn how to find and identify them with experience. Many of these hotels have restaurants downstairs; if they don't, there are usually restaurants and noodle shops nearby.

### Tourist-Class, Business & Luxury Hotels

These are found only in the main tourist and business destinations: Bangkok, Chiang Mai, Chiang Rai, Kanchanaburi, Pattaya, Ko Pha-Ngan, Ko Samui, Phuket, Songkhla, Hat Yai and a sprinkling of large provincial capitals such as Nakhon Ratchasima (Khorat), Khon Kaen, Yala, Phitsanulok, Udon Thani and Ubon Ratchathani. Prices start at around 600B outside Bangkok and Chiang Mai and proceed to 2000B or more – genuine tourist-class hotels in Bangkok start at 1000B or so and go to 2500B for standard rooms, and up to 5000 or 10,000B for a suite. The Oriental in Bangkok, rated as the number one hotel in the world by several executive travel publications, starts at 3100B for a standard single and tops off at 20,000B for a deluxe suite. These will all have air-con, TV, western-style toilets and restaurants. Added to room charges will be an 11% government tax, and most of these hotels will include an additional service charge of 8% to 10%.

In addition to the international hotel management chains of the Hyatt, Sheraton, Accor, Hilton and Westin, Thailand has several respectable home-grown chains of some standing, including Dusit, Amari and Royal Garden. Of the internationals, Accor is expanding the most rapidly, introducing moderately priced tourist/business hotels in provincial capitals under the Ibis and Mercure brands to complement their more upscale Sofitel/Novotel properties. Among the local chains, Amari is the most active in terms of managing new or newly acquired hotels.

**Resorts** In most countries 'resort' refers to hotels which offer substantial recreational facilities (eg tennis, golf, swimming, sailing etc) in addition to accommodation and dining. In Thai hotel lingo, however, the term simply refers to any hotel that isn't located in an urban area. Hence a few thatched beach huts or a cluster of bungalows in a forest may be called a 'resort'. Several places in Thailand fully deserve the name under any definition – but it pays to look into the facilities before making a reservation.

## National Park Camping & Accommodation Facilities

Thailand has 79 national parks and nine historical parks. All but 10 of the national parks have bungalows for rent that sleep as many as 10 people for rates of 500 to 1500B, depending on the park and the size of the bungalow. During the low seasons you can often get a room in one of these park bungalows for 100B per person. A few of the historical parks have bungalows with rates

comparable to those in the national parks, mostly for use by visiting archaeologists.

Camping is allowed in all but four of the national parks (Nam Tok Phliu in Chanthaburi Province, Doi Suthep/Doi Pui in Chiang Mai Province, Hat Jao Mai in Trang Province and Thap Lan in Prachinburi Province) for only 5 to 10B per person per night. A few parks also have *reuan tháew* (longhouses) where rooms are around 150 to 200B for two. Some have tents for rent at 50 to 60B a night, but always check the condition of the tents before agreeing to rent one. It's a good idea to take your own sleeping bag or mat and other basic camping gear. You should also take a torch (flashlight), rain gear, insect repellent, a water container and a small medical kit. Finally, if you bring your own tent it's only 5 to 10B per person – almost every park has at least one camping area.

Advance bookings for accommodation are advisable at the more popular parks, especially on holidays and weekends. Most parks also charge a small entry fee to visit (typically 3 to 5B for Thais, 15 to 25B for foreigners). See National Parks under Ecology & Environment in the Facts about the Country chapter for more information.

## Universities/Schools

College and university campuses may be able to provide inexpensive accommodation during the summer vacation (March to June). There are universities in Chiang Mai, Phitsanulok, Nakhon Pathom, Khon Kaen, Mahasarakham and Songkhla. Outside Bangkok there are also teachers' colleges (*wítháyálai khruu*) in every provincial capital which may offer accommodation during the summer vacation. The typical teachers' college dorm room lets for 35 to 75B per night during holiday periods.

## Temple Lodgings

If you are a Buddhist or can behave like one, you may be able to stay overnight in some temples for a small donation. Facilities are very basic, though, and early rising is expected. Temple lodgings are usually for men only, unless the wat has a place for lay

## Prostitution

Thais generally blame 19th century Chinese immigrants for bringing prostitution to Thailand, but in reality Thailand was fertile ground because of its long-standing concubinary tradition. The first known literary references to this tradition were recorded by Chinese visitors in the early 1400s. Dutch merchants visiting Pattani in 1604 commented that 'when foreigners come there from other lands to do their business...men come and ask them whether they do not desire a woman' and that in Ayuthaya most of their peers 'had concubines or mistresses, in order (so they said) to avoid the common whores'. Seventeenth century Ayuthaya, in fact, had an official Thai government office in charge of operating a corps of 600 concubines at large.

Until 1934 Siam had no laws forbidding polygamy – or even a word for this Judaeo-Christian concept. Most men of wealth counted among their retinue at least one sŏhphenii (from the Sanskrit term for a woman trained in the kama sutra and other amorous arts), a word often translated as 'prostitute' in English today but which might better be translated as 'courtesan'. In addition, the traditional Thai mia yài mia nói (major wife, minor wife) system made it socially permissible for a man to keep several mistresses – all Thai kings up to Rama IV had mia nói, as did virtually any Thai male who could afford them until recent times. Even today talk of mia nói hardly raises an eyebrow in Thailand as the tradition lives on among wealthy businessmen, jâo phâw (organised crime 'godfathers') and politicians.

The first brothel district in Thailand was established by Chinese immigrants in Bangkok's Sampeng Lane area in the mid-19th century. In the beginning, only Chinese women worked as prostitutes here; when Thai women became involved at the turn of the century, they usually took Chinese names. Prostitution eventually spread from Sampeng's 'green-lantern district' to Chinese neighbourhoods throughout Thailand and is now found in virtually every village, town and city in the kingdom. Ethnic Chinese still control most of the trade, although the prostitutes themselves now come from almost every ethnic background. In the last few years Bangkok has even seen an influx of Russian women – most on Tourist Visas – participating in the sex trade through escort services. Women from nearby countries, particularly Myanmar and China, have also found their way – both willingly and unwillingly – into the trade.

The first true prostitutes – non-cohabiting women who accepted cash for sex services – to appear outside the Chinese districts came along soon after King Rama VII's 1934 decree banning polygamy. During WWII the Thai government stationed large numbers of Thai troops in the North to prevent Bangkok from becoming a military target. At the beginning of the war Chiang Mai had only two known prostitutes but by 1945 there were hundreds servicing the soldiers. Prostitution wasn't declared illegal until the 1950s when Field Marshal Phibun bullied his way into the prime minister's seat. In the 1960s and 1970s the Vietnam War brought unprecedented numbers of foreign soldiers to Bangkok and Pattaya on 'rest & recreation' tours, creating a new class of prostitutes who catered to foreigners rather than Thais.

Current estimates of the number of Thai citizens directly involved in offering sex services vary from the Ministry of Public Health's conservative 100,000 to wild bar-stool estimates of 500,000. After an intensive two-year study into the prostitution industry, Chulalongkorn University's Population Institute came up with a reasoned estimate of 200,000 to 210,000, a figure now widely considered the most realistic. This number is thought to include around 10,000 male and child prostitutes. Although often portrayed as Asia's sex capital, Thailand actually ranks third (behind Taiwan and the Philippines) in per-capita number of sex workers, according to international human rights reports.

An East-West Center study noted that 'As throughout most of South and South-East Asia, men in Thailand have greater freedom in their sexual activities than women, who are expected to arrive at the marriage altar as virgins and to refrain from extramarital affairs'. The Center concluded that this attitude 'creates a sexual imbalance in which large numbers of males are seeking casual sexual contact, but few females are available. The resulting active and well-attended commercial sex industry, catering largely to indigenous demand, has created a reservoir of...sex workers and clients'. Sociologists estimate that as many as 75% of single Thai males engage the services of a prostitute at an average of two times a month. In highly urban Bangkok attitudes are changing steadily as non-paid extramarital sex is becoming increasingly common and hence the percentage of Thai clients is significantly lower than elsewhere in the country.

women to stay. Neat, clean dress and a basic knowledge of Thai etiquette are mandatory. See Meditation Study under Courses earlier for information on wats in Thailand which will accommodate long-term lay students.

## ENTERTAINMENT

See the special Thai Arts & Architecture section in the Facts about the Country chapter for a rundown on the types of traditional arts that can be enjoyed in Thailand.

Today the highest per-capita concentration of sex workers is found in the North – Chiang Mai, for example, has an estimated 3000 sex workers in two brothel districts. Brothels are less common in the Southern provinces, except in Chinese-dominated Phuket, Hat Yai and Yala, and in Thai-Malaysian border towns, where the clientele is almost exclusively Malay.

Most of the country's sex industry is invisible to the visiting foreigner. A typical mid-level coffee house/brothel will offer girls ranked in price according to their beauty or supposed skills; prices are denoted by coloured tags the women wear on their dresses. Back-alley places service low-wage earners for as little as 40B. At the other end of the spectrum, Thai businessmen and government officials entertain in private brothels and member clubs where services average 1000 to 5000B.

Unlike western prostitution, there are few 'pimps' (people who manage one or more prostitutes) in Thailand. Instead, a network of procurers/suppliers and brothel owners control the trade, taking a high proportion (or all) of the sex service fees. At its worst, the industry takes girls sold or indentured by their families, sometimes even kidnapped, and forces them to work in conditions of virtual slavery. A few years ago a Phuket brothel of the type rarely patronised by farangs caught fire; several young women who were chained to their beds by the management died in the fire.

In the Patpong-style bar catering to foreigners, most bar girls and go-go dancers are freelance agents; they earn their income from taking a percentage of drinks bought on their behalf and from sex liaisons arranged outside the premises – usually after closing (if they leave during working hours, a customer usually pays a 'bar fine' on their behalf). The average Patpong type bar girl earns 6000 to 7000B per month directly from the bar she works in; fees for extracurricular services are negotiated between customer and prostitute and can run anywhere from 800 to 2000B per assignation.

Most prostitutes – male and female – are young, uneducated and from village areas. Researchers estimate they have a maximum working life of 10 to 12 years – if they haven't saved up enough money to retire by then (few do), they're often unemployable due to mental and physical disabilities acquired during their short working life. Various Thai volunteer groups are engaged in counselling Thailand's sex workers – helping them to escape the industry or to educate them to the dangers of STDs, particularly AIDS.

Officially prostitution is illegal, but the government has been either powerless or unwilling to enforce the laws. In 1992 the Thai cabinet introduced a bill to decriminalise prostitution in the hope that it would make it easier for prostitutes to seek counselling or STD testing without fear of prosecution. So far no such bill has been enacted, but in June 1993 then-prime minister Chuan Leekpai ordered a crackdown on prostitutes under 18, an act which has had quantifiable results but has by no means banished under-18s from the trade. A recent US State Department human rights report of the same year found that the percentage of prostitutes in Thailand under the age of 18 falls well below that found in India, Bangladesh, Sri Lanka or the Philippines. According to End Child Prostitution in Asian Tourism (ECPAT), as of 1996 the main centres for child prostitution are India, Cambodia and the Philippines.

In July 1994 the government strengthened child prostitution laws by making clients of under-age sex workers subject to fines and jail terms. A Prostitution Prevention and Suppression Bill introduced in 1996 expands the punishment arena to include procurers and brothel operators; under the latest law, a jail term of two to 20 years and/or a fine of 200,000 to 400,000B can be imposed on anyone caught having sex with prostitutes under 15 years of age (the age of consent in Thailand). If the child is under 13, the sentence could be life imprisonment. Parents or patrons who conspire with others to supply underage prostitutes face similar punishment. Many western countries have also instituted extra-territorial legislation whereby citizens can be charged for child prostitution offences committed abroad. The Thai government is also encouraging people to assist in the eradication of child prostitution by reporting child sexual abuses to the relevant authorities. In the first instance, travellers visiting Thailand can contact the tourist police.

Experts suggest these laws will have little effect on the indigenous market, though they may frighten away potential foreign clients and procurers. Thai men visit prostitutes an estimated aggregate of 18 million times each year, hence the economics of the industry are quite far-reaching and difficult to regulate. Realists point out that if Thailand has 200,000 prostitutes, each of whom works 25 days a month and earns an average 1000B a day for themselves and their employers, the resultant revenue is about 50% higher than the national budget. ■

These are also covered in more detail in the destination chapters.

## Cinema

Movie theatres are found in towns and cities throughout the country. Typical programmes include US and European shoot-em-ups mixed with Thai comedies and romances. Violent action pictures are always a big draw; as a rule of thumb, the smaller the town, the more violent the film offerings. English-language films are only shown with their original soundtracks in a handful of theatres in Bangkok, Chiang Mai and Hat Yai; elsewhere all foreign films are dubbed in Thai. Ticket prices range from 10 to 70B. Every film in Thailand begins with a playback of the royal anthem, accompanied by projected pictures of the royal family. Viewers are expected to stand during the anthem.

### Bars & Member Clubs

Urban Thais are night people and every town of any size has a selection of nightspots. For the most part they are male-dominated, though the situation is changing rapidly in the larger cities, where young couples are increasingly seen in bars.

Of the many types of bars, probably the most popular continues to be the 'old west' style, patterned after Thai fantasies of the 19th century American west – lots of wood and cowboy paraphernalia. Another favoured style is the 'Thai classic' pub, which is typically decorated with old black & white photos of Thai kings Rama VI and Rama VII, along with Thai antiques from Northern and Central Thailand. The old west and Thaiclassic nightspots are cosy, friendly and popular with couples as well as singles.

The 'go-go' bars seen in lurid photos published by the western media are limited to a few areas in Bangkok, Chiang Mai, Pattaya and Phuket's Patong Beach. These are bars in which girls typically wear swimsuits or other scant apparel. In some bars they dance to recorded music on a narrow raised stage. To some visitors it's pathetic, to others an apparent source of entertainment.

'Member clubs,' similar to old-style Playboy clubs, provide a slinky, James Bond atmosphere of feigned elegance and savoir faire in which women clad in long gowns or tight skirts entertain suited men in softly-lit sofa groups. A couple of drinks and a chat with the hostesses typically costs around US$50, including membership charges. These clubs are thinly scattered across the Soi Lang Suan and Sukhumvit Rd areas in Bangkok.

Under a new law passed in 1995, all bars and clubs which don't feature live music or dancing are required to close by 1 am. Many get around the law by bribing local police.

### Coffee Houses

Aside from the western-style cafe, which is becoming increasingly popular in Bangkok, there are two other kinds of cafes or coffee shops in Thailand. One is the traditional Hokkien-style coffee shop (*ráan kaa-fae*) where thick, black, filtered coffee is served in simple, casual surroundings. These coffee shops are common in the Chinese quarters of Southern Thai provincial capitals, less common elsewhere. Frequented mostly by older Thai and Chinese men, they offer a place to read the newspaper, sip coffee and gossip about neighbours and politics.

The other type, called *kaa-feh* (cafe) or 'coffee house', is more akin to a nightclub, where Thai men consort with a variety of Thai female hostesses. This is the Thai counterpart to farang go-go bars, except girls wear dresses instead of swimsuits. A variation on this theme is the 'sing-song' cafe in which a succession of female singers take turns fronting a live band. Small groups of men sit at tables ogling the girls while putting away prodigious amounts of Johnnie Walker, J&B or Mekong whisky. For the price of a few house drinks, the men can invite one of the singers to sit at their table for a while. Some of the singers work double shifts as part-time mistresses, others limit their services to singing and pouring drinks.

Cafes which feature live music are permitted to stay open till 2 am.

### Discos

Discotheques are popular in larger cities; outside Bangkok they're mostly attached to tourist or luxury hotels. The main disco clientele is Thai, though foreigners are welcome. Some provincial discos retain female staff as professional dance partners for male entertainment, but for the most part discos are considered fairly respectable nightspots for couples.

Thai law permits discotheques to stay open till 2 am.

## SPECTATOR SPORTS
### Thai Boxing (Muay Thai)

Almost anything goes in this martial sport, both in the ring and in the stands. If you don't mind the violence (in the ring), a Thai boxing match is worth attending for the pure spectacle – the wild musical accompaniment, the ceremonial beginning of each match and the frenzied betting around the stadium.

Thai boxing is also telecast on Channel 7 every Sunday afternoon; if you're wondering where everyone is, they're probably inside watching the national sport.

**History**  Most of what is known about the early history of Thai boxing comes from Burmese accounts of warfare between Myanmar and Thailand during the 15th and 16th centuries. The earliest reference (1411 AD) mentions a ferocious style of unarmed combat that decided the fate of Thai kings. A later description tells how Nai Khanom Tom, Thailand's first famous boxer and a prisoner of war in Myanmar, gained his freedom by roundly defeating a dozen Burmese warriors before the Burmese court. To this day, many martial art aficionados consider the Thai style the ultimate in hand-to-hand fighting. Hong Kong, China, Singapore, Taiwan, Korea, Japan, the USA, Netherlands, Germany and France have all sent their best and none of the challengers have been able to defeat top-ranked Thai boxers. On one famous occasion, Hong Kong's top five kung fu masters were dispatched in less than 6½ minutes cumulative total, all knock-outs.

King Naresuan the Great (1555-1605) was supposed to have been a topnotch boxer himself, and he made muay thai a required part of military training for all Thai soldiers. Later another Thai king, Phra Chao Seua (the 'tiger king'), further promoted Thai boxing as a national sport by encouraging prize fights and the development of training camps in the early 18th century. There are accounts of massive wagers and bouts to the death during this time. Phra Chao Seua himself is said to have been an incognito participant in many of the matches during the early part of his reign. Combatants' fists were wrapped in thick horsehide for maximum impact with minimum knuckle damage. They also used cotton soaked in glue and ground glass and later hemp. Tree bark and seashells were used to protect the groin from lethal kicks.

**Modern Thai Boxing**  The high incidence of death and physical injury led the Thai government to institute a ban on muay thai in the 1920s, but in the 1930s the sport was revived under a modern set of regulations based on the international Queensberry rules. Bouts were limited to five three minute rounds separated with two minute breaks. Contestants had to wear international-style gloves and trunks (always either in red or blue) and their feet were taped – to this day no shoes are worn.

There are 16 weight divisions in Thai boxing, ranging from mini-flyweight to heavyweight, with the best fighters said to be in the welterweight division (67 kg maximum). As in international-style boxing, matches take place on a 7.3 sq m canvas-covered floor with rope retainers supported by four padded posts, rather than the traditional dirt circle.

In spite of these concessions to safety, today all surfaces of the body are still considered fair targets and any part of the body except the head may be used to strike an opponent. Common blows include high kicks to the neck, elbow thrusts to the face and head, knee hooks to the ribs and low crescent kicks to the calf. A contestant may even grasp an opponent's head between his hands and pull it down to meet an upward knee thrust. Punching is considered the weakest of all blows and kicking merely a way to 'soften up' one's opponent; knee and elbow strikes are decisive in most matches.

The training of a Thai boxer and particularly the relationship between boxer and trainer is highly ritualised. When a boxer is considered ready for the ring, he is given a new name by his trainer, usually with the name of the training camp as his surname. For the public, the relationship is perhaps best expressed in the *ram muay* (boxing dance) that takes place before every match.

The ram muay ceremony usually lasts about five minutes and expresses obeisance to the fighter's guru *(khruu)*, as well as to the guardian spirit of Thai boxing. This is done through a series of gestures and body movements performed in rhythm to the ringside musical accompaniment of Thai oboe *(pìi)* and percussion. Each boxer works out his own dance, in conjunction with his trainer and in accordance with the style of his particular camp.

The woven headbands and armbands worn into the ring by fighters are sacred ornaments which bestow blessings and divine protection; the headband is removed after the ram muay ceremony, but the armband, which actually contains a small Buddha image, is worn throughout the match. After the bout begins, the fighters continue to bob and weave in rhythm until the action begins to heat up. The musicians continue to play throughout the match and the volume and tempo of the music rise and fall along with the events in the ring.

As Thai boxing has become more popular among westerners (both spectators and participants) there are increasing numbers of bouts staged for tourists in places like Pattaya, Phuket and Ko Samui. In these, the action may be genuine but the judging below par. Nonetheless, dozens of authentic matches are held every day of the year at the major Bangkok stadiums and in the provinces (there are about 60,000 full-time boxers in Thailand), and these are easily sought out.

Several Thai *nák muay* have gone on to win world championships in international-style boxing. Khaosai Galaxy, the greatest Asian boxer of all time, chalked up 19 WBA bantamweight championships in a row before retiring undefeated in December 1991. As of 1995 Thailand had five concurrent international boxing champions – all in the flyweight and bantamweight categories.

Meanwhile in some areas of the country a pre-1920s version of muay thai still exists. In North-Eastern Thailand *muay boraan* is a very ritualised form that resembles tai qi chuan or classical dance in its adherence to set moves and routines. In pockets of Southern Thailand, fighters practicing *muay katchii* still bind their hands in hemp. And each year around the lunar new year (Songkhran) in April, near the town of Mae Sot on the Thai-Myanmar border, a top Thai fighter challenges a Burmese fighter of similar class from the other side of the Moei River to a no-holds barred, hemp-fisted battle that ends only after one of the opponents wipes blood from his body.

**International Muay Thai** In Thailand an English-language periodical called *Muay Thai World* appears annually in Bangkok, Chiang Mai and Phuket bookshops that sell English-language material. It includes features on muay thai events abroad as well as in Thailand, and contains current rankings for Bangkok's Lumphini and Ratchadamnoen stadiums. The World Muay Thai Council (WMTC), a newly recognised organisation sanctioned by Thailand's Sports Authority and headquartered at the Thai Army Officers Club in Bangkok, has begun organising international muay thai bouts in Bangkok stadiums and elsewhere. The WMTC tracks training facilities as well as ranked fighters. So far the largest number of WMTC-affiliated muay thai training facilities is found in the USA, followed by Australia, the Netherlands, Canada, Japan and France. Dutch fighter Ivan Hippolyte took the middleweight WMTC championship in November 1995 at Lumphini Stadium, reportedly the first foreigner ever to win a Lumphini fight. International participation portends a new era for Thai boxing; some observers think it will upgrade the martial art by reconcentrating the focus on fight technique rather than ringside betting.

**Krabi-Krabong**

Another traditional Thai martial art still practised in Thailand is kràbìi-kràbong. This tradition focuses on hand-held weapons techniques, specifically the *kràbìi* (sword), *plông* (quarter-staff), *ngao* (halberd), *dàap sãwng meu* (a pair of swords held in each hand) and *mái sun-sàwk* (a pair of clubs).

Although for most Thais krabi-krabong is a ritual artefact to be displayed during festivals or at tourist venues, the art is still solemnly taught according to a 400 year old tradition handed down from Ayuthaya's Wat Phutthaisawan. The king's elite bodyguard are trained in krabi-krabong; many Thai cultural observers perceive it as a 'purer' tradition than muay thai.

Like muay thai of 70 years ago, modern krabi-krabong matches are held within a marked circle, beginning with a *wâi khruu* ceremony and accompanied throughout by a musical ensemble. Thai boxing techniques and judo-like throws are employed in conjunction with weapons techniques. Although sharpened weapons are used, the contestants refrain from striking their opponents – the winner is decided on the basis of stamina and the technical skill displayed. Although an injured fighter may surrender, injuries do not automatically stop a match.

For information on muay thai and krabi-krabong training courses in Thailand, see Martial Arts Training in the Courses section of this chapter.

### Takraw

*Tàkrâw*, sometimes called Siamese football in old English texts, refers to games in which a woven rattan ball about 12 cm in diameter is kicked around. The rattan (or sometimes plastic) ball itself is called a *lûuk tàkrâw*. Takraw is also popular in several neighbouring countries; it was originally introduced to the South-East Asian Games by Thailand and international championships tend to alternate between the Thais and Malays. The traditional way to play takraw in Thailand is for players to stand in a circle (the size of the circle depends on the number of players) and simply try to keep the ball airborne by kicking it soccer-style. Points are scored for style, difficulty and variety of kicking manoeuvres.

A popular variation on takraw – and the one used in intramural or international competitions – is played with a volleyball net, using all the same rules as in volleyball except that only the feet and head are permitted to touch the ball. It's amazing to see the players perform aerial pirouettes, spiking the ball over the net with their feet. Another variation has players kicking the ball into a hoop 4.5m above the ground – basketball with feet, but without a backboard!

### THINGS TO BUY

Many bargains await you in Thailand if you have the space to carry them back. Always haggle to get the best price, except in department stores. And don't go shopping in the company of touts, tour guides or friendly strangers as they will inevitably – no matter what they say – take a commission on anything you buy, thus driving prices up.

### Textiles

Fabric is possibly the best all-round buy in Thailand. Thai silk is considered the best in the world – the coarse weave and soft texture of the silk means it is more easily dyed than harder, smoother silks, resulting in brighter colours and a unique lustre. Silk can be purchased cheaply in the North and North-East where it is made or, more easily, in Bangkok. Excellent and reasonably priced tailor shops can make your choice of fabric into almost any pattern. A Thai silk suit should cost around 4000 to 6500B. Chinese silk is available at about half the cost – 'washed' Chinese silk makes inexpensive, comfortable shirts or blouses.

Cottons are also a good deal – common items like the phâakhamãa (reputed to have over a hundred uses in Thailand) and the phâasîn (the slightly larger female equivalent) make great tablecloths and curtains. Good ready-made cotton shirts are available, such as the *mâw hâwm* (Thai work shirt) and the *kúay hâeng* (Chinese-style shirt). See the sections on Pasang in the Northern Thailand chapter and Ko Yo in the Southern Thailand chapter for places to see cotton-weaving.

In recent years, cotton-weaving has become very popular in the North-East and there are fabulous finds in Nong Khai, Roi-Et, Khon Kaen and Mahasarakham. The *mãwn khwãan*, a hard, triangle-shaped pillow made in the North-East, makes a good

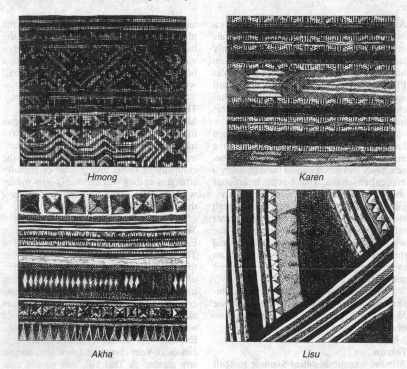

Hmong

Karen

Akha

Lisu

Thai hill-tribe embroideries are characterised by intricate geometric patterns and brocade borders.

souvenir and comes in many sizes. The North-East is also famous for its *mát-mìi* cloth, thick cotton or silk fabric woven from tie-dyed threads – similar to Indonesia's ikat fabrics.

In the North you can find Lanna-style textiles based on intricate Thai Lü patterns from Nan, Laos and China's Sipsongpanna (Xishuangbanna).

Fairly nice batik *(pa-té)* is available in the South in patterns that are more similar to the batik found in Malaysia than in Indonesia.

## Clothing

Tailor-made and ready-made clothes are relatively inexpensive. If you're not particular about style you could pick up an entire wardrobe of travelling clothes at one of Bangkok's many street markets (eg Pratunam) for what you'd pay for one designer shirt in New York or Paris.

You're more likely to get a good fit if you resort to a tailor but be wary of the quickie 24 hour tailor shops; the clothing is often made of inferior fabric or the poor tailoring means the arms start falling off after three weeks wear. It's best to ask Thai or longtime foreign residents for a tailor recommendation and then go for two or three fittings.

## Shoulder Bags

Thai shoulder bags *(yâam)* are generally quite well made. They come in many varieties, some woven by hill tribes, others by

Northern Thai cottage industry. The best are made by the Lahu hill tribes, whom the Thais call 'Musoe'. The weaving is more skilful and the bags tend to last longer than those made by other tribes. For an extra-large yaam, the Karen-made bag is a good choice, and is easy to find in the Mae Sot and Mae Hong Son areas. These days many hill tribes are copying patterns from tribes other than their own.

Overall, Chiang Mai has the best selection of standard shoulder bags, but Bangkok has the best prices – try the Indian district, Pahurat, for these as well as anything else made of cloth. Roi-Et and Mahasarakham in the North-East are also good hunting grounds for locally made shoulder bags. Prices range from 50B for a cheaply made bag to 200B for something special.

### Antiques

Real antiques cannot be taken out of Thailand without a permit from the Fine Arts Department. No Buddha image, new or old, may be exported without permission – again, refer to the Fine Arts Department, or, in some cases, the Department of Religious Affairs, under the Ministry of Education. Too many private collectors smuggling and hoarding Siamese art (Buddhas in particular) around the world have led to strict controls. See Customs earlier in this chapter for more information on the export of art objects and antiques.

Chinese and Thai antiques are sold in Bangkok's Chinatown in two areas: Wang Burapha (the streets which have Chinese 'gates' over the entrance) and Nakhon Kasem. Some antiques (and many fakes) are sold at the Weekend Market in Chatuchak Park. Objects for sale in the tourist antique shops are fantastically overpriced, as can be expected. In recent years Northern Thailand has become a good source of Thai antiques – prices are about half what you'd typically pay in Bangkok.

### Jewellery

Thailand is one of the world's largest exporters of gems and ornaments, rivalled only by India and Sri Lanka. The International Colorstones Association (ICA) relocated from Los Angeles to Bangkok's Chan Issara Tower a few years ago, and the World Federation of Diamond Bourses (WFDB) has established a bourse in Bangkok – two events that recognise that Thailand has become the world trade and production centre for precious stones. The biggest importers of Thai jewellery are the USA, Japan and Switzerland.

Although rough stone sources in Thailand itself have decreased dramatically, stones are now imported from Australia, Sri Lanka and other countries to be cut, polished and traded here. There are over 30 diamond-cutting houses in Bangkok alone. One of the results of this remarkable growth of the gem industry – in Thailand the gem trade has increased nearly 10% every year for the last 15 years – is that the prices are rising rapidly.

If you know what you are doing you can make some really good buys in both unset gems and finished jewellery. Gold ornaments are sold at a good rate as labour costs are low. The best bargains in gems are jade, rubies and sapphires. Buy from reputable dealers only, unless you're a gemologist.

The biggest gem centres in Thailand are Kanchanaburi, Mae Sot, Mae Sai and Chanthaburi – these areas are where the Bangkok dealers go to buy their stones. The Asian Institute of Gemological Sciences (☎ (2) 513-2112; fax 236-7803), 484 Ratchadaphisek Rd (off Lat Phrao Rd in the Huay Khwang district, north-east Bangkok), offers short-term courses in gemology as well as tours of gem mines for those interested. You can bring gems here for inspection but they don't assess value, only authenticity and grading. John Hoskin's book *Buyer's Guide to Thai Gems & Jewellery*, available at Bangkok bookshops, is a useful introduction to Thai gems.

**Warning** Be wary of special 'deals' that are offered for one day only or which set you up as a 'courier' in which you're promised big money. Many travellers end up losing big. Shop around and *don't be hasty*. Remember:

there's no such thing as a 'government sale' or a 'factory price' at a gem or jewellery shop; the Thai government does not own or manage any gem or jewellery shops.

See Dangers & Annoyances earlier in this chapter for detailed warnings on gem fraud.

### Hill-Tribe Crafts

Interesting embroidery, clothing, bags and jewellery from the North can be bought in Bangkok at Narayan Phand, Lan Luang Rd, at branches of the Queen's Hillcrafts Foundation, and at various tourist shops around town. See Things to Buy in the Bangkok chapter for details.

In Chiang Mai there are shops selling handicrafts all along Thaphae Rd and there is a shop sponsored by missionaries near Prince Royal College. There is a branch of the Queen's Hillcrafts Foundation in Chiang Rai. It's worth shopping around for the best prices and bargaining. The all-round best buys of Northern hill-tribe crafts are at the Chiang Mai Night Bazaar – if you know how to bargain.

### Lacquerware

Thailand produces some good lacquerware, much of it made in Myanmar and sold along the northern Myanmar border. Try Mae Sot, Mae Sariang and Mae Sai for the best buys.

Styles available today originated in 11th century Chiang Mai; in 1558 Myanmar's King Bayinnaung captured a number of Chiang Mai lacquer artisans and brought them to Bago in central Myanmar to establish the incised lacquerware tradition. Lacquer comes from the *Melanorrhea usitata* tree (not to be confused with 'lac', which comes from an insect), and in its most basic form is mixed with paddy-husk ash to form a light, flexible, waterproof coating over bamboo frames.

To make a lacquerware object, the craftsperson first weaves a bamboo frame. If the item is first-quality, only the frame is bamboo; horse or donkey hairs will be wound round the frame. In lower-quality lacquerware the whole object is made from bamboo. The lacquer is then coated over the framework and allowed to dry. After several days it is sanded down with ash from rice husks, and another coating of lacquer is applied. A high-quality item may have seven layers of lacquer altogether.

The lacquerware is engraved and painted, then polished to remove the paint from everywhere except in the engravings. Multi-coloured lacquerware is produced by repeated engraving, painting and polishing. From start to finish it can take five or six months to produce a high-quality piece of lacquerware which may have as many as five colours. Flexibility is one characteristic of good lacquerware. A top-quality bowl can have its rim squeezed together until the sides meet without suffering damage. The quality and precision of the engraving is another thing to look for.

Lacquerware is made into bowls, trays, plates, boxes, containers, cups, vases and many other everyday items. Octagonal-topped folding tables are another popular lacquerware item.

### Nielloware

This art came from Europe via Nakhon Si Thammarat and has been cultivated in Thailand for over 700 years. Engraved silver is inlaid with niello – an alloy of lead, silver, copper and sulphur – to form striking black-and-silver jewellery designs. Nielloware is one of Thailand's best buys.

### Ceramics

Many kinds of hand-thrown pottery, old and new, are available throughout the kingdom. Most well known are the greenish Thai celadon products from the Sukhothai-Si Satchanalai area and Central Thailand's *bencharong* or 'five colour' style. The latter is based on Chinese patterns while the former is a Thai original that has been imitated throughout China and South-East Asia. Rough, unglazed pottery from the North and North-East can also be very appealing.

### Other Crafts

Under Queen Sirikit's Supplementary Occupations & Related Techniques (SUPPORT) foundation, a number of regional crafts from around Thailand have been successfully revived. *Málaeng tháp* collages and sculptures are made by the artful cutting and assembling of the metallic, multicoloured wings and carapaces of female wood-boring beetles *(Sternocera aequisignata)*, harvested after they die at the end of their reproductive cycle between July and September each year. Hailing mostly from the North and North-East, they can nonetheless be found in craft shops all over Thailand.

For 'Damascene ware' (known as *kràm* in Thai), gold and silver wire is hammered into a cross-hatched steel surface to create exquisitely patterned bowls and boxes. Look for them in more upscale Bangkok department stores and craft shops.

*Yaan lipao* is a type of intricately woven basket made from a hardy grass in Southern Thailand. Ever since the queen and other female members of the royal family began carrying delicate yaan lipao purses, they've been a Thai fashion staple. Basketry of this type is most easily found in the Southern provincial capitals, or in Bangkok shops that specialise in regional handicrafts.

### Furniture
Rattan and hardwood furniture items are often good buys and can be made to order. Bangkok and Chiang Mai have the best selection of styles and quality. Teak furniture has become relatively scarce and expensive; rosewood is a more reasonable buy.

### Fake or Pirated Goods
In Bangkok, Chiang Mai and all the tourist centres, there is black-market street trade in fake designer goods; particularly Benneton pants and sweaters, Lacoste (crocodile) and Ralph Lauren polo shirts, Levi's jeans, and Rolex, Dunhill and Cartier watches. Tin-Tin T-shirts are also big. No-one pretends they're the real thing, at least not the vendors themselves. The European and American manufacturers are applying heavy pressure on the Asian governments involved to get this stuff off the street, so it may not be around for much longer.

In some cases foreign name brands are legally produced under licence in Thailand and represent good value. A pair of legally produced Levi's 501s, for example, typically costs US$10 from a Thai street vendor, and US$30 to US$40 in Levi's home town of San Francisco! Careful examination of the product usually reveals tell-tale characteristics that confirm or deny the item's legality.

Prerecorded cassette tapes are another illegal bargain in Thailand. The tapes are 'pirated', that is, no royalties are paid to the copyright owners. Average prices are from 25 to 35B per cassette for amazingly up-to-date music. Word has it that these will disappear from the streets, too, under pressure from the US music industry.

In 1991 four of the major tape piraters (including market leaders Peacock and Eagle) agreed to stop producing unlicensed tapes, but only on condition that the police prosecute the myriad smaller companies doing business. As of 1996 it was becoming quite difficult to find pirated tapes anywhere in the country except on Bangkok's Khao San Rd. Licensed tapes, when available, cost 70 to 110B each (average price 90B); Thai music tapes cost the same.

### Other Goods
Bangkok is famous the world over for its street markets – Pratunam, Chatuchak Park, Khlong Toey, Sampeng (Chinatown), Banglamphu and many more – where you'll find things you never imagined you wanted but once you see, you feel you can't possibly do without. Even if you don't want to spend any money, they're great places to wander around.

For top-end shopping, the two main centres in Bangkok are the area around the Oriental Hotel off Charoen Krung (New) Rd and the River City shopping complex on the river next to the Royal Orchid Sheraton Hotel. At the other end, Thailand's two big department store chains, Robinson and Central, offer reasonably priced clothing, electronics and houseware at several branches in Bangkok as well as in the larger towns.

# THAI CUISINE

In a 1991 study that surveyed 1450 travel agencies in 26 countries, Thailand ranked fourth after France, Italy and Hong Kong in the perceived excellence of cuisine. As with other well developed world cuisines, it can be categorically divided into several regional variations. One can also distinguish between high and low cuisine – or in Thai terms 'royal' and 'common' cooking – a distinction historically arising from the difference between recipes reserved for court palates and those enjoyed by non-royals. Nowadays court recipes may mingle with ordinary ones in the same restaurants – such as Bangkok's Thanying, which specialises in the former. However the overall spirit of the cuisine – and a majority of the ingredients – are shared across all class and regional boundaries.

## Food

Some people take to the food in Thailand immediately while others don't; Thai dishes can be pungent and spicy – lots of garlic and chillies are used, especially *phrík khîi nǔu* (literally, 'mouse-shit peppers' –

*Thailand's rich abundance of fresh ingredients and spices form the basis of its fragrant soups, aromatic curries, tangy salads and spicy rice and seafood dishes.*

## Table Etiquette

Using the correct utensils and eating gestures will garner much respect from the Thais, who are of the general opinion that western table manners are rather coarse.

Thais eat most dishes with a fork and tablespoon except for noodles, which are eaten with chopsticks (tà-kìap); noodle soups are eaten with spoon and chopsticks. Another exception to the fork-and-spoon routine is sticky rice, which is rolled into balls and eaten with the right hand, along with the food accompanying it.

The fork (sáwm) is held in the left hand and used as a probe to push food onto the spoon (cháwn); you eat from the spoon. To the Thais, pushing a fork into one's mouth is as uncouth as putting a knife into the mouth is in western countries.

When serving yourself from a common platter, put no more than one or two spoonfuls onto your own plate at a time. Thais do not scoop large portions onto their plates, as westerners tend to do. It's customary at the start of a shared meal to eat a spoonful of plain rice first – a gesture that recognises rice as the most important part of the meal. If you're being hosted by Thais, they'll undoubtedly encourage you to eat less rice and more curries, seafood, etc as a gesture of their generosity (since rice costs comparatively little). The humble guest, however, takes rice with every spoonful.

Always leave some food on the serving platters as well as on your plate. To clean your plate and leave nothing on the serving platters would be a grave insult to your hosts. This is why Thais tend to 'over-order' at social meal occasions – the more food is left on the table, the more generous the host appears. ■

these are the small torpedo-shaped devils which can be pushed aside if you are timid about red-hot curries). Almost all Thai food is cooked with fresh ingredients, including vegetables, poultry, pork and some beef. Plenty of lime juice, lemon grass and fresh coriander leaf are added to give the food its characteristic tang, and fish sauce (náam plaa, generally made from anchovies) or shrimp paste (kà-pì) to make it salty.

Other common seasonings include 'laos' or galanga root (khàa), black pepper, three kinds of basil, ground peanuts (more often a condiment), tamarind juice (náam makhãam), ginger (khĩng) and coconut milk (kà-tí). The Thais eat a lot of what could be called Chinese food (there has always been a large Chinese migrant population), which is generally, but not always, less spicy.

Rice (khâo) is eaten with most meals; 'to eat' in Thai is literally 'eat rice' or kin khâo. Thais can be very picky about their rice, insisting on the right temperature and cooking times. Ordinary white rice is called khâo jâo and there are many varieties and grades. The finest quality Thai rice is known as khâo hãwm máli or 'jasmine fragrant rice' for its sweet, inviting smell when cooked. In the North and North-East 'sticky' or glutinous rice (khâo nĩaw) is common.

## Where to Eat

Many smaller restaurants and foodstalls do not have menus, so it is worthwhile memorising a standard 'repertoire' of dishes. Most provinces have their own local specialities in addition to the standards and you might try asking for 'whatever is good', allowing the proprietors to choose for you. Of course, you might get stuck with a large bill this way, but with a little practice in Thai social relations you may also get some very pleasing results.

The most economical places to eat – and the most dependable – are noodle shops *(ráan kŭaytĭaw)*, curry-and-rice shops *(ráan khâo kaeng)* and night markets *(talàat tôh rûng)*. Most towns and villages have at least one night market and several noodle and/or curry shops. The night markets in Chiang Mai have a slight reputation for overcharging (especially for large parties), but this is usually not the case in Thailand. It helps if you speak Thai as much as possible. Curry shops are generally open for breakfast and lunch only, and are a very cheap source of nutritious food. Another common food venue in larger cities is the *ráan khâo tôm*, literally 'boiled rice shop', a type of Chinese-Thai restaurant that offers not just boiled rice soups *(khâo tôm)* but an assortment of *aahăan taam sàng*, 'food according to order'. In the better places cooks pride themselves in being able to fix any Thai or Chinese dish you name. One attraction of the ráan khâo tôm is that they tend to stay open late – some are even open 24 hours.

Sponsored by the Shell oil company, Thai food critic Thanad Sri bestows his favourite dishes at restaurants around Thailand with a sign bearing the outline of a green bowl next to the familiar Shell symbol outside the restaurant. It's not a foolproof guarantee however; some restaurants hang onto their signs long after the kitchen has lowered its standards.

# What to Eat

Thai food is served with a variety of condiments and sauces, including ground red pepper *(phrík bon)*, ground peanuts *(thùa bon)*, vinegar with sliced chillies *(náam sôm phrík)*, fish sauce with chillies *(náam plaa phrík)*, a spicy orange-red sauce called *náam phrík sĭi raachaa* (from Si Racha, of course) and any number of other dipping sauces *(náam jîm)* for particular dishes. Soy sauce *(náam sĭi-yú)* can be requested, though this is normally used as a condiment for Chinese food only.

Except for the 'rice plates' and noodle dishes, Thai meals are usually ordered family-style, ie two or more people order together, sharing different dishes. Traditionally, the party orders one of each kind of dish, eg one chicken, one fish, one soup etc. One dish is generally large enough for two people. One or two extras may be ordered for a large party. If you come to eat at a Thai restaurant alone and order one of these 'entrées', you had better be hungry or know enough Thai to order a small portion. This latter alternative is not really very acceptable socially; Thais generally consider eating alone in a restaurant unusual – but then as a farang you're an exception anyway.

A cheaper alternative is to order dishes 'over rice' or *râat khâo*. Curry *(kaeng)* over rice is called *khâo kaeng*; in a standard curry shop khâo kaeng is only 8 to 15B a plate.

Another category of Thai food is called *kàp klâem* – dishes meant to be eaten while drinking alcoholic beverages. On some menus these are translated as 'snacks' or 'appetisers'. Typical kàp klâem include *thùa thâwt* (fried peanuts), *kài săam yàang* (literally 'three kinds of chicken'; a plate of chopped ginger, peanuts, mouse-shit peppers and bits of lime – to be mixed and eaten by hand) and various kinds of *yam*, Thai style salads made with lots of chillies and lime juice.

**Vegetarian** Those visitors who wish to avoid eating meat and seafood while in Thailand can be accommodated with some effort. Vegetarian restaurants are increasing in number throughout the country, thanks largely to Bangkok's ex-Governor Chamlong Srimuang, whose strict vegetarianism has inspired a nonprofit chain of vegetarian restaurants *(ráan aahăan mangsàwírát)* in Bangkok and several provincial capitals. Many of these are sponsored by the Asoke Foundation, an ascetic (some would say heretic) Theravada Buddhist sect that finds justification for vegetarianism in the Buddhist *suttas*. Look for the green sign out the front of shops depicting large Thai numerals – each restaurant is numbered according to the order in which it was established. The food at these restaurants is usually served buffet-style and is very inexpensive – typically 5 to 8B per dish. Most are open only from 7 or 8 am until noon. At an Asoke lecture I attended in Chiang Mai last year, a spokesperson for the foundation said their objective is to *lose* money at these restaurants.

Other easy, though less widespread, venues for vegetarian meals include Indian restaurants, which usually feature a vegetarian section on the menu. Currently these are most prevalent in Bangkok, Chiang Mai, Pattaya and Phuket's Hat Patong. Chinese restaurants are also a good bet since many Chinese Buddhists eat vegetarian food during Buddhist festivals, especially in Southern Thailand.

More often than not, however, visiting vegetarians are left to their own devices at the average Thai restaurant. In Thai the magic words are *phŏm kin jeh* (for men) or *dii-chăn kin jeh* (women). Like other Thai phrases, it's important to get the tones right – the key word, *jeh*, should rhyme with the English 'jay' without the 'y'. Loosely translated this phrase means 'I eat only vegetarian food'. It might also be necessary to follow with the explanation *phŏm/dii-chăn kin tàe phàk* ('I eat only vegetables'). Don't worry – this won't be interpreted to mean no rice, herbs or fruit.

In Thai culture, 'brown' (unpolished) rice is said to be reserved for pigs and prisoners! Look for it at the local feed store.

Those interested in tapping into the Thai vegetarian movement can phone the Vegetarian Society of Bangkok (☎ (2) 254-5444/3502) for information on the group's activities. The society usually meets monthly to share a vegetarian feast, swap recipes and discuss the whys and wherefores of vegetarianism.

# Food Glossary

The following list gives standard dishes in Thai script with a transliterated pronunciation guide, using the system outlined in the Language section of the Facts about the Country chapter.

## Soups *(súp)* ซุป

mild soup with vegetables & pork
  *kaeng jèut*
  แกงจืด

mild soup with vegetables, pork & bean curd
  *kaeng jèut tâo-hûu*
  แกงจืดเต้าหู้

soup with chicken, galanga root & coconut
  *tôm khàa kài*
  ต้มข่าไก่

prawn & lemon grass soup with mushrooms
  *tôm yam kûng*
  ต้มยำกุ้ง

fish-ball soup
  *kaeng jèut lûuk chín*
  แกงจืดลูกชิ้น

rice soup with fish/chicken/shrimp
  *khâo tôm plaa/kài/kûng*
  ข้าวต้มปลา/ไก่/กุ้ง

Mangosteen – Round, purple fruit with juicy white flesh shaped like orange segments; has a sweet-sour flavour often likened to a combination of strawberries and grapes (April to September).

## Egg *(khài)* ไข่

hard-boiled egg
*khài tôm*
ไข่ต้ม

fried egg
*khài dao*
ไข่ดาว

plain omelette
*khài jiaw*
ไข่เจียว

omelette with vegetables
& pork
*khài yát sài*
ไข่ยัดไส้

scrambled egg
*khài kuan*
ไข่กวน

## Noodles *(kũaytĩaw/bà-mii)* ก๋วยเตี๋ยว/บะหมี่

wide rice noodle soup with
vegetables & meat
*kũaytĩaw náam*
ก๋วยเตี๋ยวน้ำ

wide rice noodles with vegetables
& meat
*kũaytĩaw hâeng*
ก๋วยเตี๋ยวแห้ง

wide rice noodles with gravy
*râat nâa*
ราดหน้า

thin rice noodles fried with tofu,
vegetables, egg & peanuts
*phàt thai*
ผัดไทย

fried thin noodles with
soy sauce
*phàt sii-yíw*
ผัดซีอิ๊ว

wheat noodles in broth with
vegetables & meat
*bà-mii náam*
บะหมี่น้ำ

wheat noodles with vegetables
& meat
*bà-mii hâeng*
บะหมี่แห้ง

## Rice Dishes *(khâo râat nâa)* ข้าวราดหน้า

*Custard-apple – Ready to
eat when the nobbly green
outer covering looks slightly
off; creamy white flesh has
a thirst-quenching flavour
with a hint of lemon (July to
October).*

fried rice with pork/chicken/shrimp
*khâo phàt mũu/kài/kûng*
ข้าวผัดหมู/ไก่/กุ้ง

boned, sliced Hainan-style chicken
with marinated rice
*khâo man kài*
ข้าวมันไก่

chicken with sauce over rice
*khâo nâa kài*
ข้าวหน้าไก่

roast duck over rice
*khâo nâa pèt*
ข้าวหน้าเป็ด

'red' pork with rice
*khâo mũu daeng*
ข้าวหมูแดง

curry over rice
*khâo kaeng*
ข้าวแกง

## Curries *(kaeng)* แกง

hot Thai curry with chicken/beef/pork
*kaeng phèt kài/néua/mǔu*
แกงเผ็ดไก่/เนื้อ/หมู

'green' curry with fish/chicken/beef
*kaeng khǐaw-wǎan plaa/kài/néua*
แกงเขียวหวานปลา/ไก่/เนื้อ

rich & spicy, Muslim-style curry with chicken/beef & potatoes
*kaeng mátsàman kài/néua*
แกงมัสมั่นไก่/เนื้อ

savoury curry with chicken/beef
*kaeng phánaeng kài/néua*
แกงพะแนงไก่/เนื้อ

mild, Indian-style curry with chicken
*kaeng kari kài*
แกงกะหรี่ไก่

chicken curry with bamboo shoots
*kaeng kài nàw mái*
แกงไก่หน่อไม้

hot & sour, fish & vegetable ragout
*kaeng sôm*
แกงส้ม

catfish curry
*kaeng plaa dùk*
แกงปลาดุก

## Seafood *(aahǎan tháleh)* อาหารทะเล

steamed crab
*puu nêung*
ปูนึ่ง

steamed fish
*plaa nêung*
ปลานึ่ง

steamed crab claws
*kâam puu nêung*
ก้ามปูนึ่ง

grilled fish
*plaa phǎo*
ปลาเผา

shark-fin soup
*hǔu chalǎam*
หูฉลาม

whole fish cooked in ginger, onions & soy sauce
*plaa jǐan*
ปลาเจี๋ยน

crisp-fried fish
*plaa thâwt*
ปลาทอด

sweet & sour fish
*plaa prîaw wǎan*
ปลาเปรี้ยวหวาน

fried prawns
*kûng thâwt*
กุ้งทอด

cellophane noodles baked with crab
*wûn-sên òp puu*
วุ้นเส้นอบปู

batter-fried prawns
*kûng chúp pâeng thâwt*
กุ้งชุบแป้งทอด

spicy fried squid
*plaa mèuk phàt phèt*
ปลาหมึกผัดเผ็ด

grilled prawns
*kûng phǎo*
กุ้งเผา

roast squid
*plaa mèuk yâang*
ปลาหมึกย่าง

*Pomelo – Large citrus fruit; flesh often has a purplish tinge and a flavour quite similar to a grapefruit, though the texture is tougher and drier (year-round).*

oysters fried in egg batter
*hãwy thâwt*
หอยทอด

squid
*plaa mèuk*
ปลาหมึก

shrimp
*kûng*
กุ้ง

fish
*plaa*
ปลา

catfish
*plaa dùk*
ปลาดุก

freshwater eel
*plaa lãi*
ปลาไหล

saltwater eel
*plaa lòt*
ปลาหลด

tilapia
*plaa nin*
ปลานิล

spiny lobster
*kûng mangkon*
กุ้งมังกร

green mussel
*hãwy malaeng phùu*
หอยแมลงภู่

scallop
*hãwy phát*
หอยพัด

oyster
*hãwy naang rom*
หอยนางรม

## Miscellaneous

stir-fried mixed vegetables
*phàt phàk lãi yàang*
ผัดผักหลายอย่าง

spring rolls
*pàw-pía*
เปาะปี๊ย

beef in oyster sauce
*néua phàt náam-man hãwy*
เนื้อผัดน้ำมันหอย

duck soup
*pèt tũn*
เป็ดตุ๋น

roast duck
*pèt yâang*
เป็ดย่าง

fried chicken
*kài thâwt*
ไก่ทอด

chicken fried in holy basil
*kài phàt bai kà-phrao*
ไก่ผัดใบกะเพรา

grilled chicken
*kài yâang*
ไก่ย่าง

chicken fried with chillies
*kài phàt phrík*
ไก่ผัดพริก

chicken fried with cashews
*kài phàt mét*
*má-mûang*
ไก่ผัดเม็ดมะม่วง

morning-glory vine fried in
garlic, chilli & bean sauce
*phàk bûng fai daeng*
ผักบุ้งไฟแดง

'satay' or skewers of
barbecued meat
*sà-té*
สะเต๊ะ

spicy green papaya salad
(North-Eastern speciality)
*sôm-tam*
ส้มตำ

*Durian – Infamous for its smell, this is a large, oval fruit with a hard, spiny shell; though held in high esteem by the Thais, the pale white-green flesh is definitely an acquired taste – the nearest approximation is onion-flavoured ice cream. There are several varieties and seasons, so keep trying.*

noodles with fish curry
*khănom jiin náam yaa*
ขนมจีนน้ำยา

prawns fried with chillies
*kûng phàt phrík phăo*
กุ้งผัดพริกเผา

chicken fried with ginger
*kài phàt khĭng*
ไก่ผัดขิง

fried wonton
*kíaw kràwp*
เกี๊ยวกรอบ

cellophane noodle salad
*yam wún sên*
ยำวุ้นเส้น

spicy chicken or beef salad
*lâap kài/néua*
ลาบไก่/เนื้อ

hot & sour, grilled beef salad
*yam néua*
ยำเนื้อ

chicken with bean sprouts
*kài sàp thùa ngâwk*
ไก่สับถั่วงอก

fried fish cakes with
cucumber sauce
*thâwt man plaa*
ทอดมันปลา

## Vegetables *(phàk)* ผัก

angle bean
*thùa phuu*
ถั่วภู

bitter melon
*márá-jiin*
มะระจีน

brinjal (round eggplant)
*mákhĕua pràw*
มะเขือเปราะ

cabbage
*phàk kà-làm*
    (or *kà-làm plii*)
ผักกะหล่ำ   กะหล่ำปลี

cauliflower
*dàwk kà-làm*
ดอกกะหล่ำ

Chinese radish
*phàk kàat hŭa*
ผักกาดหัว

corn
*khâo phôht*
ข้าวโพต

cucumber
*taeng kwaa*
แตงกวา

eggplant
*mákhĕua mûang*
มะเขือม่วง

garlic
*kràtiam*
กระเทียม

lettuce
*phàk kàat*
ผักกาด

long bean
*thùa fák yao*
ถั่วฝักยาว

okra ('ladyfingers')
*krà-jíap*
กระเจี๊ยบ

onion (bulb)
*hŭa hăwm*
หัวหอม

*Jackfruit – Similar in appearance to the durian but much easier to develop a taste for; has a large number of bright orange-yellow segments with a slightly rubbery texture (year-round).*

onion (green, 'scallions')
*tôn hǎwm*
ต้นหอม

peanuts (ground nuts)
*tùa lísõng*
ถั่วลิสง

potato
*man faràng*
มันฝรั่ง

### Fruit *(phõn-lá-mái)* ผลไม้

banana – over 20 varieties
(year-round)
*klûay*
กล้วย

coconut (year-round)
*máphráo*
มะพร้าว

custard-apple
*náwy naa*
น้อยหน่า

durian
*thúrian*
ทุเรียน

guava (year-round)
*fa-ràng*
ฝรั่ง

jackfruit
*kha-nũn*
ขนุน

lime (year-round)
*má-nao*
มะนาว

longan – 'dragon's eyes'; similar
to rambutan (July to October)
*lam yài*
ลำไย

mandarin orange (year-round)
*sôm*
ส้ม

pumpkin
*fák thawng*
ฟักทอง

taro
*pheùak*
เผือก

tomato
*mákhẽua thêt*
มะเขือเทศ

mango – several varieties & seasons
*má-mûang*
มะม่วง

mangosteen
*mang-khút*
มังคุด

papaya (year-round)
*málákaw*
มะละกอ

pineapple (year-round)
*sàp-pàrót*
สับปะรด

pomelo
*sôm oh*
ส้มโอ

rambeh – small, reddish-brown
and apricot-like (April to May)
*máfai*
มะไฟ

rambutan
*ngáw*
เงาะ

rose-apple – apple-like texture;
very fragrant (April to July)
*chom-phûu*
ชมพู่

tamarind – sweet and tart varieties
*mákhãam*
มะขาม

*Rambutan – Red, hairy-skinned fruit with lychee-like interior – cool and mouth-watering flesh around a central stone (July to September).*

sapodilla – small and oval; sweet
but pungent (July to September)
*lámút*
สะพุด

watermelon (year-round)
*taeng moh*
แตงโม

## Sweets *(khāwng wāan)* ของหวาน

Thai custard
*sāngkha-yaa*
สังขยา

fried, Indian-style banana
*klûay khàek*
กล้วยแขก

coconut custard
*sāngkha-yaa ma-phráo*
สังขยามะพร้าว

sweet palm kernels
*lûuk taan chêuam*
ลูกตาลเชื่อม

sweet shredded egg yolk
*fãwy thawng*
ฝอยทอง

Thai jelly with coconut cream
*ta-kôh*
ตะโก้

egg custard
*mâw kaeng*
หม้อแกง

sticky rice with coconut cream
*khâo nĭaw daeng*
ข้าวเหนียวแดง

banana in coconut milk
*klûay bùat chii*
กล้วยบวชชี

sticky rice in coconut cream with
ripe mango
*khâo nĭaw má-mûang*
ข้าวเหนียวมะม่วง

## Useful Food Words

(For 'I' men use phõm; women use
*dii-chãn*)

I eat only vegetarian food.
*phõm/dii-chãn kin jeh*
ผม/ดีฉัน  กินเจ

I can't eat pork.
*phõm/dii-chãn kin mŭu mâi dâi*
ผม/ดีฉัน  กินหมูไม่ได้

I can't eat beef.
*phõm/dii-chãn kin néua mâi
dâi*
ผม/ดีฉัน  กินเนื้อไม่ได้

(I) don't like it hot & spicy.
*mâi châwp phèt*
ไม่ชอบเผ็ด

(I) like it hot & spicy.
*châwp phèt*
ชอบเผ็ด

(I) can eat Thai food.
*kin aahãan thai pen*
กินอาหารไทยเป็น

What do you have that's special?
*mii a-rai phí-sèt?*
มีอะไรพิเศษ?

I didn't order this.
*nîi phõm/dii-chãn mâi dâi sàng*
นี้  ผม/ดีฉัน  ไม่ได้สั่ง

Do you have ...?
*mii ... mãi?*
มี...ไหม?

*Coconut – Grated for cook-
ing when mature, eaten from
the shell with a spoon when
young; juice is sweetest and
most plentiful in young coconuts (year-round).*

# Drinks

## Non-alcoholic Drinks

**Fruit Juices & Shakes** The incredible variety of fruits in Thailand means a corresponding availability of nutritious juices and shakes. The all-purpose term for fruit juice is *náam phŏn-lá-mái*. Put *náam* (water or juice) together with the name of any fruit and you can get anything from *náam sôm* (orange juice) to *náam taeng moh* (watermelon juice). When a blender or extractor is used, fruit juices may be called *náam khán* or 'squeezed juice' (eg *náam sàppàrót khán* – pineapple juice). When mixed in a blender with ice the result is *náam pon* (literally, 'mixed juice') as in *náam málákaw pon*, a papaya 'smoothie' or 'shake'. Night markets will often have vendors specialising in juices and shakes.

Thais prefer to drink most fruit juices with a little salt mixed in. Unless a vendor is used to serving farangs, your fruit juice or shake will come slightly salted. If you prefer unsalted fruit juices, specify *mâi sài kleua* (without salt).

Sugar cane juice *(náam âwy)* is a Thai favourite and a very refreshing accompaniment to curry-and-rice plates. Many small restaurants or food stalls that don't offer any other juices will have a supply of freshly squeezed náam âwy on hand.

**Coffee** Over the last 10 years or so, Nescafé and other instant coffees have made deep inroads into the Thai coffee culture at the expense of freshly ground coffee. The typical Thai restaurant – especially those in hotels, guesthouses and other tourist-oriented establishments – serves instant coffee with packets of artificial, non-dairy creamer on the side. Up-market hotels and coffee shops sometimes also offer filtered and espresso coffees at premium prices.

Traditionally, coffee in Thailand is locally grown (mostly in the hilly areas of Northern and Southern Thailand), roasted by wholesalers, ground by vendors and filtered just before serving. Thai-grown coffee may not be as full and rich-tasting as gourmet Sumatran, Jamaican or Kona beans but to my palate it's still considerably tastier than Nescafé or other instant products.

Sometimes restaurants or vendors with the proper accoutrements for making traditional filtered coffee will keep a supply of Nescafé just for foreigners (or moneyed Thais, since instant always costs a few baht more per cup than filtered). To get real Thai coffee ask for *kafae thŭng* (literally, 'bag coffee'), which refers to the traditional method of preparing a cup of coffee by filtering hot water through a bag-shaped cloth filter. Thailand's best coffee of this sort is served in Hokkien-style cafes in the Southern provinces. Elsewhere in Thailand, outdoor morning markets are the best place to find kafae thŭng.

The usual kafae thŭng is served mixed with sugar and sweetened condensed milk – if you don't want either, be sure to specify *kafae dam* (black coffee) followed with *mâi sài náam-taan* (without sugar). Kafae thŭng is often served in a glass instead of a ceramic cup – to pick a glass of hot coffee up, grasp it along the top rim.

**Tea** Both Indian-style (black) and Chinese-style (green or semi-cured) teas are commonly served in Thailand. The latter predominates in Chinese restaurants and is the usual ingredient in *náam chaa*, the weak, often lukewarm tea-water traditionally served in Thai restaurants for free. The aluminium teapots seen on every table in the average restaurant are filled with náam chaa; ask for a plain glass *(kâew plào)* and you can drink as much as you like at no charge. For iced náam chaa ask for a glass of ice (usually 1B) and pour your own; for fresh, undiluted Chinese tea request *chaa jiin*.

Black tea, both imported and Thai-grown, is usually available in the same restaurants or foodstalls that serve real coffee. An order of *chaa ráwn* (hot tea) almost always results in a cup (or glass) of black tea with sugar and condensed milk. As with coffee you must specify as you order if you want black tea without milk and/or sugar.

**Water** Water purified for drinking purposes is simply called *náam dèum* (drinking water), whether boiled or filtered. *All* water offered to customers in restaurants or to guests in an office or home will be purified, so you needn't fret about the safety of taking a sip (for more information on water safety, see the Health section earlier in this chapter). In restaurants you can ask for *náam plào* (plain water), which is always either boiled or taken from a purified source; it's served by the glass at no charge or you can order by the bottle. A bottle of carbonated water (soda) costs about the same as a bottle of plain purified water but the bottles are smaller.

# Drinks Glossary
The following list gives the Thai words and script for some of the more standard, non-alcoholic beverages. Refer to the following section for Thai words for alcoholic drinks.

## Beverages *(khreûang dèum)* เครื่องดื่ม

plain water
*náam plào*
น้ำเปล่า

hot water
*náam ráwn*
น้ำร้อน

boiled water
*náam tôm*
น้ำต้ม

cold water
*náam yen*
น้ำเย็น

ice
*náam khǎeng*
น้ำแข็ง

Chinese tea
*chaa jiin*
ชาจีน

weak Chinese tea
*náam chaa*
น้ำชา

iced Thai tea with milk & sugar
*chaa yen*
ชาเย็น

iced Thai tea with sugar only
*chaa dam yen*
ชาดำเย็น

no sugar (command)
*mâi sài náam-taan*
ไม่ใส่น้ำตาล

hot Thai tea with sugar
*chaa dam ráwn*
ชาดำร้อน

hot Thai tea with milk & sugar
*chaa ráwn*
ชาร้อน

hot coffee with milk & sugar
   *kafae ráwn*
กาแฟร้อน

traditional filtered coffee with milk
& sugar
   *kafae thŭng* (ko-píi in the South)
กาแฟถุง/โกปี๊

iced coffee with sugar, no milk
   *oh-liang*
โอเลี้ยง

Ovaltine
   *oh-wantin*
โอวันติน

orange soda
   *náam sôm*
น้ำส้ม

plain milk
   *nom jèut*
นมจืด

iced lime juice with sugar (usually
with salt too)
   *náam manao*
น้ำมะนาว

no salt (command)
   *mâi sài kleua*
ไม่ใส่เกลือ

soda water
   *náam sôh-daa*
น้ำโซดา

bottled drinking water
   *náam dèum khùat*
น้ำดื่มขวด

bottle
   *khùat*
ขวด

glass
   *kâew*
แก้ว

# Alcoholic Drinks

Drinking in Thailand can be quite expensive in relation to the cost of other consumer activities. The Thai government has placed increasingly heavy taxes on liquor and beer, so that now about 30B out of the 50 to 70B that you pay for a large beer is tax. Whether this is an effort to raise more tax revenue (the result has been a sharp decrease in the consumption of alcoholic beverages for perhaps a net decrease in revenue) or to discourage consumption, drinking can wreak havoc with your budget. One large bottle (630 ml) of Singha beer costs more than half the minimum daily wage of a Bangkok worker.

According to the UN's Food & Agriculture Organisation (FAO), Thailand ranks fifth worldwide in consumption of alcohol, behind South Korea, the Bahamas, Taiwan and Bermuda, and well ahead of Portugal, Ireland and France.

**Beer** Three brands of beer are brewed in Thailand by Thai-owned breweries: Singha, Amarit and Kloster. Singha (pronounced 'Sĭng' by the Thais) is by far the most common beer in Thailand, with some 66% of the domestic market. The original recipe was formulated in 1934 by nobleman Phya Bhirom Bhakdi and his son Prachuap, who was the first Thai to earn a brewmaster's diploma from Munich's Doemens Institute. Singha is a strong, hoppy-tasting brew thought by many to be the best beer produced in Asia. The barley for Singha is grown in Thailand, the hops are imported from Germany and the rated alcohol content is 6%. Singha is sometimes available on tap in pubs and restaurants.

Kloster is quite a bit smoother and lighter than Singha and generally costs about 5B more per bottle, but it is a good-tasting brew often favoured by western visitors, expats and upwardly mobile Thais who

PAUL BEINSSEN

Chilli peppers, an integral part of Thai cuisine today, were originally introduced to Thailand by Portuguese traders. Numerous in size and colour, the smallest chillies are generally the hottest.

RICHARD I'ANSON

Evening in Bangkok and small-time traders set up food stalls piled high with trays of freshly fried snacks. The Thai tendency to snack through the day and well into the night is more than catered for by the plethora of vendors lining any busy urban street.

BERNARD NAPTHINE

Bite-sized savoury appetisers, marinated and lightly grilled, neatly laid out for hungry passers-by.

Crispy fried fish prepared in the traditional way with a chilli and shallot garnish on a bed of banana leaves.

BERNARD NAPTHINE

Home-made curries stored in steel pots at a streetside stall. Unlike Indian curries, which are usually cooked for hours, Thai curries have relatively short cooking times; the preparation of the actual ingredients is often the more time-consuming task.

JOE CUMMINGS

Thai meals, usually made up of a combination of four or five different dishes shared among participants, draw on the country's diverse and abundant array of fresh, seasonal vegetables.

BERNARD NAPTHINE

view it as somewhat of a status symbol. Amarit NB (the initials stand for 'naturally brewed', though who knows whether it is or not) is similar in taste to Singha but a bit smoother, and is brewed by Thai Amarit, the same company that produces Kloster. Like Kloster it costs a few baht more than the national brew. Together Amarit and Kloster claim only 7% of Thailand's beer consumption. Alcoholic content for each is 4.7%.

Boon Rawd Breweries, makers of Singha, also produce a lighter beer called Singha Gold which only comes in small bottles; most people seem to prefer either Kloster or regular Singha to Singha Gold, which is a little on the bland side. Better is Singha's new canned 'draught beer' – if you like cans.

Carlsberg, jointly owned by Danish and Thai interests, is a strong newcomer to Thailand. As elsewhere in South-East Asia, Carlsberg has used an aggressive promotion campaign (backed by the makers of Mekong whisky) to grab around 25% of the Thai market in only two years. The company adjusted its recipe to come closer to Singha's 6% alcohol content, which may be one reason they've surpassed Kloster and Amarit so quickly.

Singha has retaliated in advertisements suggesting that drinking Carlsberg is unpatriotic. Carlsberg responded by creating 'Beer Chang' (Elephant Beer), which matches the hoppy taste of Singha but ratchets the alcohol content up to 7%. Dutch giant Heineken opened a plant in Nonthaburi in 1995, so look for more sparks to fly.

The Thai word for beer is *bia*. Draught beer is *bia sòt* (literally, 'fresh beer').

**Spirits** Rice whisky is a big favourite in Thailand and somewhat more affordable than beer for the average Thai. It has a sharp, sweet taste not unlike rum, with an alcoholic content of 35%. The two major liquor manufacturers are Suramaharas Co and the Surathip Group. The first produces the famous Mekong (pronounced 'Mâe-khõng') and Kwangthong brands, the second the Hong (swan) labels including Hong Thong, Hong Ngoen, Hong Yok and Hong Tho. Mekong and Kwangthong cost around 120B for a large bottle *(klom)* or 60B for the flask-sized bottle *(baen)*. An even smaller bottle, the *kòk*, is occasionally available for 30 to 35B. The Hong brands are less expensive.

In the late 1980s, the two liquor giants met and formed a common board of directors to try to end the fierce competition brought about when a 1985 government tax increase led to a 40% drop in Thai whisky sales. The meeting has resulted in an increase in whisky prices but probably also in better distribution – Mekong and Kwangthong have generally not been available in regions where the Hong labels are marketed and vice versa. A third company, Pramuanphon Distillery in Nakhon Pathom, markets a line of cut-rate rice whisky under three labels: Maew Thong (Gold Cat), Sing Chao Phraya (Chao Phraya Lion) and Singharat (Lion-King).

More expensive Thai whiskies appealing to the pre-Johnnie Walker set include Singharaj blended whisky (240B a bottle) and VO Royal Thai whisky (260B), each with 40% alcohol.

One company in Thailand produces a true rum, that is, a distilled liquor made from sugar cane, called Sang Thip (formerly Sang Som). Alcohol content is 40% and the stock is supposedly aged. Sang Thip costs several baht more than the rice whiskies, but for those who find Mekong and the like unpalatable, it is an alternative worth trying.

**Other Liquor** A cheaper alternative is *lâo khão*, or 'white liquor', of which there are two broad categories: legal and contraband. The legal kind is generally made from sticky rice and is produced for regional consumption. Like Mekong and its competitors, it is 35% alcohol, but sells for 50 to 60B per klom, or roughly half the price. The taste is sweet and raw and much more aromatic than the amber stuff – no amount of mixer will disguise the distinctive taste.

The illegal kinds are made from various agricultural products including sugar palm sap, coconut milk, sugar cane, taro and rice. Alcohol content may vary from as little as 10% or 12% to as much as 95%. Generally this *lâo thèuan* ('jungle liquor') is weaker in the South and stronger in the North and North-East. This is the choice of the many Thais who can't afford to pay the heavy government liquor taxes; prices vary but 10 to 15B worth of the stronger concoctions will intoxicate three or four people. These types of home-brew or moonshine are generally taken straight with pure water as a chaser. In smaller towns, almost every garage-type restaurant (except, of course, Muslim restaurants) keeps some under the counter for sale. Sometimes roots and herbs are added to jungle liquor to enhance flavour and colour.

Herbal liquors are somewhat fashionable throughout the country and can be found at roadside vendors, small pubs and in a few guesthouses. These liquors are made by soaking various herbs, roots, seeds, fruit and bark in *lâo khão* to produce a range of concoctions called *yàa dong*. Many of the yàa dong preparations are purported to have specific health-enhancing qualities. Some of them taste fabulous while others are rank.

**Wine**  Thais are becoming increasingly interested in wine-drinking, but still manage only a minuscule one glass per capita average consumption per year. Various enterprises have attempted to produce wine in Thailand, most often with disastrous results. The latest is a winery called Chateau de Loei, near Phu Reua in Loei Province. Dr Chaiyut, the owner, spent a lot of money and time studying western wine-making methods; his first vintage, a Chenin Blanc, is quite a drinkable wine. It's available at many of the finer restaurants in Bangkok, Chiang Mai and Phuket.

Imported wines from France, Australia and the USA are also widely available in western restaurants and supermarkets.

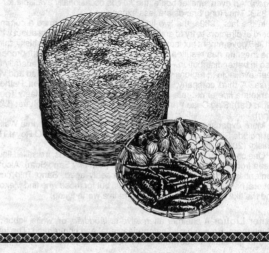

# Getting There & Away

## AIR

The expense of getting to Bangkok per air km varies quite a bit depending on your point of departure. However, you can take heart in the fact that Bangkok is one of the cheapest cities in the world to fly out of, due to the Thai government's loose restrictions on airfares and the close competition between airlines and travel agencies. The result is that with a little shopping around you can come up with some real bargains. If you can find a cheap one way ticket to Bangkok, take it, because you are virtually guaranteed to find one of equal or lesser cost for the return trip once you get there.

From most places around the world your best bet will be budget, excursion or promotional fares – when speaking to airlines ask for the various fares in that order. Each carries its own set of restrictions and it's up to you to decide which set works best in your case. Fares fluctuate, but in general they are cheaper from September to April (northern hemisphere) and from March to November (southern hemisphere).

Fares listed here should serve as a guideline – don't count on them staying this way for long (they may go down!).

### Airports & Airlines

Thailand has four international airports, one each in Bangkok, Chiang Mai, Phuket and Hat Yai. Chiang Rai and Sukhothai are both designated as 'international', but at the time of writing they did not actually field any international flights.

Three domestic carriers, Thai Airways International (commonly known as THAI), Bangkok Airways and Orient Express Air, make use of international and domestic airports in 26 cities around the country.

See the following Getting Around chapter for a list of the Thai offices of the domestic airlines and the Getting There & Away section of the Bangkok chapter for the Bangkok offices of all the international airlines.

For information on arrival and departure procedures in Bangkok, as well as details on getting to/from the international and domestic airports, see the Air section of the Getting Around chapter.

### Tickets

Although other Asian centres are now competitive with Bangkok for buying discounted airline tickets, Bangkok is still a good place for shopping around.

Travellers should note, however, that some Bangkok travel agencies have a shocking reputation. Taking money and then delaying or not coming through with the tickets, as well as providing tickets with limited validity periods or severe use restrictions are all part of the racket. There are a large number of perfectly honest agents, but beware of the rogues.

Some typical discount fares being quoted from Bangkok include:

| Around Asia | Fare |
|---|---|
| Calcutta | 3100 to 3500B |
| Colombo | 3100 to 4000B |
| Delhi | 4100B |
| Hong Kong | 3150B |
| Jakarta | 5800B |
| Kathmandu | 3900B |
| Kuala Lumpur | 2750B |
| Penang | 2500 to 3300B |
| Singapore | 1850 to 3000B |
| Yangon (Rangoon) | 1900 to 3150B |
| Tokyo | 4800B |

| Australia & New Zealand | Fare |
|---|---|
| Sydney, Brisbane, Melbourne | 10,400B |
| Darwin, Perth | 7400B |
| Auckland | 12,000 to 13,200B |

| Europe | Fare |
|---|---|
| Athens, Amsterdam, Frankfurt, London, Paris, Rome or Zurich | 9200 to 9700B |

| USA | Fare |
|---|---|
| San Francisco, Los Angeles | 11,200B |
| via Australia | 25,000B |
| New York | 13,200B |

## Air Travel Glossary

**Apex** Apex, or 'advance purchase excursion' is a discounted ticket which must be paid for in advance. There are penalties if you wish to change it.

**Baggage Allowance** This will be written on your ticket: usually one 20 kg item to go in the hold, plus one item of hand luggage.

**Bucket Shop** An unbonded travel agency specialising in discounted airline tickets.

**Bumped** Just because you have a confirmed seat doesn't mean you're going to get on the plane – see Overbooking.

**Cancellation Penalties** If you have to cancel or change an Apex ticket there are often heavy penalties involved; insurance can sometimes be taken out against these penalties. Some airlines impose penalties on regular tickets as well, particularly against 'no show' passengers.

**Check In** Airlines ask you to check in a certain time ahead of the flight departure (usually 1½ hours on international flights). If you fail to check in on time and the flight is overbooked the airline can cancel your booking and give your seat to somebody else.

**Confirmation** Having a ticket written out with the flight and date you want doesn't mean you have a seat until the agent has checked with the airline that your status is 'OK' or confirmed. Meanwhile you could just be 'on request'.

**Discounted Tickets** There are two types of discounted fares – officially discounted (see Promotional Fares) and unofficially discounted. The lowest prices often impose drawbacks like flying with unpopular airlines, inconvenient schedules, or unpleasant routes and connections. A discounted ticket can save you other things than money – you may be able to pay Apex prices without the associated Apex advance booking and other requirements. Discounted tickets only exist where there is fierce competition.

**Full Fares** Airlines traditionally offer first-class (coded F), business-class (coded J) and economy-class (coded Y) tickets. These days there are so many promotional and discounted fares available from the regular economy class that few passengers pay full economy fare.

**Lost Tickets** If you lose your airline ticket an airline will usually treat it like a travellers' cheque and, after inquiries, issue you with another one. Legally, however, an airline is entitled to treat it like cash and if you lose it then it's gone forever. Take good care of your tickets.

**No Shows** No shows are passengers who fail to show up for their flight, sometimes due to unexpected delays or disasters, sometimes due to simply forgetting, sometimes because they made more than one booking and didn't bother to cancel the one they didn't want. Full-fare passengers who fail to turn up are sometimes entitled to travel on a later flight. The rest of us are penalised (see Cancellation Penalties).

**Booking Problems** The booking of flights in and out of Bangkok during the high season (December to March) can be difficult. For air travel during these months you should book as far in advance as possible. THAI is finally loosening its stranglehold on air routes in and out of Thailand, so the situation has improved since the late 1980s when the national carrier refused to allow additional airlines permission to add much needed services through Bangkok. The addition of a second international terminal in Bangkok has also been a boon.

Also, be sure to reconfirm return or ongoing tickets when you arrive in Thailand. Failure to reconfirm can mean losing your reservation.

### USA

If you fly from the West Coast, you can get some great deals through the many bucket shops (who discount tickets by taking a cut

**On Request** An unconfirmed booking for a flight (see Confirmation).

**Open Jaws** A return ticket where you fly out to one place but return from another. If available, this can save you backtracking to your arrival point.

**Overbooking** Airlines hate to fly empty seats and since every flight has some passengers who fail to show up (see No Shows) airlines often book more passengers than they have seats. Usually the excess passengers balance those who fail to show up, but occasionally somebody gets bumped. If this happens guess who it is most likely to be? The passengers who check in late.

**Promotional Fares** Officially discounted fares like Apex fares which are available from travel agents or direct from the airline.

**Reconfirmation** At least 72 hours prior to departure time of an onward or return flight you must contact the airline and 'reconfirm' that you intend to be on the flight. If you don't do this the airline can delete your name from the passenger list and you could lose your seat. You don't have to reconfirm the first flight on your itinerary or if your stopover is less than 72 hours. It doesn't hurt to reconfirm more than once.

**Restrictions** Discounted tickets often have various restrictions on them – advance purchase is the most usual one (see Apex). Others are restrictions on the minimum and maximum period you must be away, such as a minimum of 14 days or a maximum of one year (see Cancellation Penalties).

**Standby** A discounted ticket where you only fly if there is a seat free at the last moment. Standby fares are usually only available on domestic routes.

**Tickets Out** An entry requirement for many countries is that you have an onward or return ticket – or in other words, a ticket out of the country. If you're not sure what you intend to do next, the easiest solution is to buy the cheapest onward ticket to a neighbouring country or a ticket from a reliable airline which can later be refunded if you do not use it.

**Transferred Tickets** Airline tickets cannot be transferred from one person to another. Travellers sometimes try to sell the return half of their ticket, but officials can ask you to prove that you are the person named on the ticket. This is unlikely to happen on domestic flights; on an international flight tickets may be compared with passports.

**Travel Agencies** Travel agencies vary widely and you should ensure you use one that suits your needs. Some simply handle tours while full-service agencies handle everything from tours and tickets to car rental and hotel bookings. A good one will do all these things and can save you a lot of money but if all you want is a ticket at the lowest possible price, then you really need an agency specialising in discounted tickets. A discounted ticket agency, however, may not be useful for other things, like hotel bookings.

**Travel Periods** Some officially discounted fares, Apex fares in particular, vary with the time of year. There is often a low (off-peak) season and a high (peak) season. Sometimes there's an intermediate or shoulder season as well. At peak times, when everyone wants to fly, not only will the officially discounted fares be higher but so will unofficially discounted fares or there may simply be no discounted tickets available. Usually the fare depends on your outward flight – if you depart in the high season and return in the low season, you pay the high-season fare. ∎

in commissions) and consolidators (agencies that buy airline seats in bulk) operating in Los Angeles and San Francisco. Through agencies such as these a return (round trip) airfare to Bangkok from any of 10 different West Coast cities starts at around US$750.

One of the most reliable discounters is Avia Travel (☎ (800) 950-AVIA toll-free, (415) 668-0964; fax (415) 386-8519) at 5429 Geary Blvd, San Francisco, CA 94121. Avia specialises in custom-designed around-

the-world fares, eg San Francisco-London -Delhi-Bangkok-Seoul-San Francisco for US$1486 or San Francisco-Tokyo-Kuala Lumpur-Bangkok-Amsterdam/Rome/Madrid/Athens/Paris (choice of one)-London-San Francisco for US$1512, as well as 'Circle Pacific' fares such as San Francisco-Hong Kong-Bangkok-Singapore-Jakarta-Denpasar-Los Angeles for US$1230. The agency sets aside a portion of its profits for Volunteers in Asia, a nonprofit organisation that sends grassroots volunteers to work in South-East Asia.

Another agency that works hard to get the cheapest deals is Air Brokers International (☎ (800) 883-3273 toll-free, (415) 397-1383; fax (415) 397-4767) at 323 Geary St, Suite 411, San Francisco, CA 94102. One of their 'Circle Pacific' fares, for example, offers a Los Angeles-Hong Kong-Bangkok-Denpasar-Los Angeles ticket for US$975 plus tax during the low season; you can add Honolulu, Singapore, Jakarta or Yogyakarta to this route for US$50 each stop. San Francisco/Los Angeles-Hong Kong-Bangkok-Delhi-Bombay-Rome/London-San Francisco/Los Angeles costs US$1449, or you could go New York-Los Angeles-Bali-Singapore-Bangkok-Hong Kong-New York for US$1399.

While the airlines themselves can rarely match the prices of the discounters, they are worth checking if only to get benchmark prices to use for comparison. Tickets bought directly from the airlines may also have fewer restrictions and/or less strict cancellation policies than those bought from discounters (though this is not always true).

Cheapest from the West Coast are: THAI, China Airlines, Korean Air and CP Air. Each of these has a budget and/or 'super Apex' fare that costs around US$900 to US$1200 return from Los Angeles, San Francisco or Seattle. THAI is the most overbooked of these airlines from December to March and June to August and hence their flights during these months may entail schedule delays (if you're lucky enough to get a seat at all). Several of these airlines also fly out of New York, Dallas, Chicago and Atlanta – add another US$150 to US$250 to their lowest fares.

TAROM, the Romanian carrier, offers one way excursion fares from New York to Bangkok for US$500.

### Canada

Canadian Pacific flies from Vancouver to Bangkok at fares beginning at around C$850 return for advance purchase excursion fares. Travellers living in eastern Canada will usually find the best deals out of New York or San Francisco, adding fares from Toronto or Montreal (see the USA section above).

### Australia

The full economy fare from Australia to Bangkok is around A$4000 from Sydney, Melbourne or Brisbane and A$3330 from Perth. However, tickets discounted either by travel agents or airlines are much cheaper. None of these are advance purchase nowadays, but they tend to sell out early – the airlines only allocate a limited number of these super-cheap seats to each flight. Prices start at about A$575 (one way) and A$799 (return) from Melbourne or Sydney on the cheaper carriers (eg Olympic and Alitalia), and get more expensive the better the airline's 'reputation'.

From Australia to most Asian destinations, including Bangkok, the airlines have recently introduced new seasons: the peak is December to 15 January, school holiday periods are 'shoulder' seasons, and the rest of the year is low season. Fares now also vary depending on how long you want to stay away – a fare valid for 35 days travel is about A$50 to A$60 cheaper than one valid for 90 days. This rule varies a lot, so check with individual airlines for the best deal.

At the time of writing, fares available through agents specialising in discount fares on the better known airlines (eg THAI, Qantas and British Airways) are: A$1049/1129/1239 (low/shoulder/peak season) from Sydney, Melbourne or Brisbane and A$899/949/1089 from Perth. Garuda Indonesia have cheap fares via Bali or Jakarta to Bangkok, which continue to London, for around A$929 one way, A$1579 return.

### New Zealand

THAI flies from Auckland to Bangkok daily. Fares start at NZ$1499 return for advance purchase and excursion fares.

### The UK & Continental Europe

London 'bucket shops' offer quite a range of cheap tickets to Bangkok: a student fare on Kuwait Airways is UK£215 one way and

UK£355 return and on THAI its UK£275 and UK£459. KLM offers a fare for UK£350 one way and UK£580 return.

It's also easy to stop over in Bangkok between London and Australia, with return fares for around UK£689 on THAI to the Australian east coast, UK£550 on Royal Brunei to Brisbane or Perth, UK£730 on KLM to Sydney. Good travel agencies to try for these sorts of fares are Trailfinders on Kensington High St (☎ (0171) 938-3939) and Earls Court Rd (☎ (0171) 938-3366), or STA Travel (☎ (0171) 937-9962) on Old Brompton Rd and at the universities of London, Kent, Birmingham and Loughborough. Or you can simply check the travel ads in *Time Out*, *Evening Standard* and *TNT*. For discounted flights out of Manchester or Gatwick, check with Airbreak Leisure (☎ (0171) 712-0303) at South Quay Plaza 2, 193 Marsh Wall, London, E14 92H.

One of the cheapest deals going is on TAROM (Romanian Air Transport), which has Brussels-Bangkok-Brussels fares valid for a year. Uzbekistan Airways does a London to Bangkok flight via Tashkent. Other cheapies are Lauda Air from London (via Vienna) and Czechoslovak Airlines from Prague (via London, Frankfurt and Zurich).

## Asia

**To Bangkok** There are regular flights to Bangkok international airport from every major city in Asia and it's not so difficult dealing with inter-Asia flights as most airlines offer about the same fares. Here is a sample of current estimated one way fares:

| From | Fare |
|---|---|
| Singapore | US$110-195 |
| Hong Kong | US$140-200 |
| Kuala Lumpur | US$110-195 |
| Taipei | US$220-373 |
| Calcutta | US$170 |
| Kathmandu | US$210-276 |
| Colombo | US$236 |
| New Delhi | US$236 |
| Manila | US$200-231 |
| Kunming | US$250 |
| Vientiane | US$100 |
| Phnom Penh | US$150 |

ASEAN promotional fares (return from any city, eg a Bangkok-Manila-Jakarta fare allows you to go between Manila, Jakarta, Bangkok and Manila; or Jakarta, Bangkok, Manila and Jakarta; or Bangkok, Manila, Jakarta and Bangkok) include:

| Route | Fare |
|---|---|
| Bangkok-Manila-Jakarta | US$545 |
| Bangkok-Singapore-Manila | US$440 |
| Bangkok-Jakarta-Kuala Lumpur | US$410 |
| Bangkok-Manila-Brunei-Jakarta-Singapore-Kuala Lumpur | US$580 |
| Bangkok-Singapore-Jakarta-Yogyakarta-Denpasar | US$580 |

**To Other Thai International Airports** Air travellers heading for Southern or Northern Thailand can skip Bangkok altogether by flying directly to these areas. THAI has regular flights to Phuket and Hat Yai from Singapore, to Phuket from Perth and to Chiang Mai from Singapore, Kuala Lumpur, Hong Kong, Beijing, Kunming, Yangon, Mandalay and Vientiane. During the winter, German carrier LTU offers direct flights to Phuket from Düsseldorf and Munich.

A fourth international airport has been established in Chiang Rai. Although this airport only services flights to/from Bangkok so far, THAI hopes to establish international routes to/from other Asian capitals over the next few years.

Bangkok Airways has tentative plans to use a new airport in Sukhothai as a hub for flights to Mandalay, Kunming, Luang Prabang and Siem Reap at some point in the future. At the moment their only route to/from Sukhothai services Bangkok. Likewise Bangkok Airways hopes to expand its Ko Samui service to Medan, Langkawi and Singapore someday.

**Regional Services** Thailand's Ministry of Transport allows several international air carriers to provide regional air services to Myanmar (Burma), Vietnam, Laos and Cambodia. Routes to/from Thailand by foreign carriers include Yunnan Airways and China Southwest flights from Kunming to Bangkok; Silk Air between Singapore and Phuket;

Dragonair between Hong Kong and Phuket; Malaysia Airlines between Ipoh, Malaysia, and Hat Yai; Royal Air Cambodge between Bangkok and Phnom Penh; Lao Aviation between Bangkok and Vientiane; Vietnam Airlines between Bangkok and Ho Chi Minh City; and Air Mandalay between Chiang Mai and Mandalay.

## LAND
### Malaysia
Hat Yai is the major transport hub in Southern Thailand. See that section in the Southern Thailand chapter for more details on land transport to Malaysia.

You can cross the west coast border by taking a bus to one side and another bus from the other side, the most obvious direct route being between Hat Yai and Alor Setar. This is the route used by taxis and buses but there's a long stretch of no-man's land between the Thai border control at Sadao (also known as Dan Nok) and the Malaysian one at Changlun.

It's much easier to go to Padang Besar, where the train line crosses the border. Here you can get a bus right up to the border, walk across and take another bus or taxi on the other side. On either side you'll most likely be mobbed by taxi and motorcycle drivers wanting to take you to immigration. It's better to walk over the railway by bridge into Thailand, and then ignore the touts until you get to 'official' Thai taxis who will take you all the way to Hat Yai, with a stop at the immigration office (2.5 km from the border), for 30 to 40B. A new immigration/customs office and bus/train station complex has been constructed on the Thai side, making the whole transition smoother.

There's a daily bus running between Alor Setar, Hat Yai and Kota Baru and reverse.

There's also a border crossing at Keroh (Thai side – Betong), right in the middle between the east and west coasts. This may be used more now that the Penang to Kota Baru road is open. For more information on Betong, see the Yala Province section in the Southern Thailand chapter.

See the Sungai Kolok & Ban Taba sections in the Southern Thailand chapter for crossing the border on the east coast.

Riding the rails from Singapore to Bangkok via Butterworth, Malaysia, is a great way to travel to Thailand – as long as you don't count on making a smooth change between the Kereta Api Tanah Melayu (KTM) and State Railway of Thailand (SRT) trains. The Thai train almost always leaves on time; the Malaysian train rarely arrives on time. Unfortunately the Thai train leaves Padang Besar even if the Malaysian railway express from Kuala Lumpur (or the 2nd class connection from Butterworth) is late. To be on the safe side, purchase the Malaysian and Thai portions of your ticket with departures on consecutive days and plan a Butterworth/Penang stopover.

**Bangkok to Butterworth/Penang** The daily special express No 11 leaves from Bangkok's Hualamphong station at 3.15 pm, arriving in Hat Yai at 7.04 am the next day and terminating at Padang Besar at 8 am. Everyone disembarks at Padang Besar, proceeds through immigration, then boards 2nd class KTM train No 99 for a Butterworth arrival at 12.40 pm Malaysian time (one hour ahead of Thai time). The fare to Padang Besar is 694B for 1st class, 326B for 2nd, plus a 50B special express charge, 100B for air-con. There is no 3rd class seating on this train.

For a sleeping berth in 2nd class add 100B for an upper berth, 150B for a lower. In 1st class it's 400B per person.

**Bangkok to Kuala Lumpur & Singapore** For Kuala Lumpur, make the Thai and Malaysian rail connections to Butterworth as described above, changing to an express or limited express from Butterworth. There are early morning, noon and evening services to Kuala Lumpur, and the trip takes from six to seven hours.

There are daily services running between Kuala Lumpur and Singapore – early morning, early afternoon and evening – which take from 6½ to 9 hours, depending on what type of train you take.

KTM fares from Butterworth to Kuala

## Eastern & Oriental Express

In 1991 the State Railway of Thailand (SRT), the Kereta Api Tanah Melayu (KTM; Malaysia's state railway) and Singapore's Eastern & Oriental Express Co (E&O) purchased the rights from Paris' Venice Simplon to operate the new *Eastern & Oriental Express* between Singapore and Bangkok. Finally, an Orient Express that actually begins and ends in the Orient! The original *Orient Express* ran between Paris and Constantinople in the 1880s and was considered the grandest train trip in the world; an updated version along the same route was resurrected around 20 years ago and has been very successful.

The *E&O* travels at an average speed of 50 km/h, completing the 1943 km Singapore to Bangkok journey in 41 hours, with a two hour Butterworth stopover and tour of Georgetown, Penang. As in Europe, this new train offers cruise-ship luxury on rails. Passengers dine, sleep and entertain in 22 railway carriages imported from New Zealand and refurbished using lots of brass, teak and old-world tapestry, fitted in 1930s style by the same French designer who remodelled the *Orient Express* in Europe. Aside from the locomotive(s), sleeping coaches, staff coach and luggage cars, the train features two restaurant cars, a saloon car and a bar car, with a combination bar car and open-air observation deck bringing up the rear. All accommodation is in deluxe private cabins with shower, toilet and individually controlled air-con; passengers are attended by round-the-clock cabin stewards (nearly two-thirds of the front-line staff are Thai) in the true pukka tradition.

Tariffs begin at (brace yourself) US$1400 per person for the full route in the bunk style sleeper and US$1950 in a more spacious state room; half-car presidential suites are available for a mere US$3620. These fares include four complimentary hotel nights at the Oriental Bangkok and Oriental Singapore (two nights each at either end). Half routes from Bangkok or Singapore to Butterworth or vice versa are available for a bit more than half fare, no hotel included. Honeymoon couples comprise a significant part of the clientele.

*E&O* has just announced the expansion of its services within Thailand – it will now be possible to journey all the way from Chiang Mai (with side trips to Sukhothai and Kanchanaburi) to Singapore.

The train can be booked in Singapore through Eastern & Oriental Express Co (☎ 227-2068; fax 224-9265; or (2) 251-4862 in Bangkok) at Carlton Bldg No 14-03, 90 Cecil St, Singapore 0106. Elsewhere, *E&O* reservations and information can be obtained by calling the following numbers: Australia (☎ (02) 9232-7499); France (☎ 01 45 62 00 69); Germany (☎ (0211) 162-106/7); New Zealand (☎ (09) 379-3708); Switzerland (☎ (022) 366 42 22); UK (☎ (0171) 928-6000); USA (☎ (800) 524-2420). ■

---

Lumpur on the air-con express trains (1st and 2nd class only; overnight sleepers also available) are M$19 for 3rd class, M$34 for 2nd class and M$67 for 1st class. On the limited express trains (which don't always have 1st class) the fares are M$14.40 for 3rd class, M$25.40 for 2nd and M$58.50 for 1st. Butterworth to Singapore fares on the express are M$34, M$60 and M$127 respectively; M$29.90, M$51.40 and M$118.50 on the limited express.

The information offices at the train terminals in Butterworth (☎ (04) 334-7962) and Kuala Lumpur (☎ (03) 274-7435) can provide more information about schedules, fares and seat availability on the Malayasian and Singaporean services.

For those interested in taking a more uninterrupted, luxurious journey through the Thai and Malay peninsulas, see the boxed aside on the *Eastern & Oriental Express*.

### Laos

**By Road** Since April 1993 a land crossing from Champasak Province in Laos to Chong Mek in Thailand's Ubon Ratchathani Province has been open to foreign visitors. To use this crossing you'll need a visa valid for entry via Chong Mek and Pakse – this must usually be arranged in advance through a Lao consulate or sponsoring agency. See the Chong Mek section in the North-Eastern Thailand chapter for more information on this border crossing.

A 1174m Australian-financed bridge across the Maekhong near Nong Khai opened in April 1994. Called the Thai-Lao Friendship Bridge (Saphan Mittaphap Thai-Lao), it spans a section of the river between Ban Jommani on the Thai side to Tha Na Leng on the Lao side – very near the old vehicle ferry. The next step in the plan is to build a parallel rail bridge in order to extend the Bangkok-Nong Khai railway into Vientiane. See the Nong Khai Getting There & Away section in the North-Eastern Thailand chapter for more information on this border crossing.

Construction began in early 1996 on a second Maekhong bridge to span the river between Thailand's Chiang Khong and Laos' Huay Xai. If all goes as planned, this one should be operational by early 1998 and will link Thailand with China by road via Laos' Bokeo and Luang Nam Thai provinces.

A third span is planned for either Nakhon Phanom (opposite Laos' Tha Khaek) or Mukdahan (opposite Savannakhet).

**By River** It is now legal for non-Thai foreigners to cross the Maekhong River by ferry between Thailand and Laos at the following points: Nakhon Phanom (opposite Tha Khaek), Chiang Khong (opposite Huay Xai) and Mukdahan (opposite Savannakhet).

Thais are permitted to cross at all of the above checkpoints plus at least a half-dozen others from Thailand's Loei and Nong Khai provinces, including Pak Chom, Chiang Khan, Beung Kan, Ban Pak Huay, Ban Nong Pheu and Ban Khok Phai. For the most part these checkpoints are only good for day crossings (Thai and Lao only). In the future one or more of these may become available for entry by foreign visitors as well.

## Myanmar

Several border crossings between Thailand and Myanmar are open to day-trippers or short excursions in the vicinity. As yet none of these link up with routes to Yangon or Mandalay or other cities of any size. Nor are you permitted to enter Thailand from Myanmar, at least not yet.

**Mae Sai-Tachilek** The infamous bridge, Lo Hsing-han's former 'Golden Triangle' passageway for opium and heroin, spans the Sai River between Thailand's northernmost town and the border boom town of Tachilek. Depending on the current situation in Myanmar's Shan State, where Shan rebels continue to battle Yangon troops despite warlord Khun Sa's 1996 surrender, border permits for up to five days may be obtained from the Burmese immigration at the border for excursions to Tachilek and beyond as far north as Kengtung.

Travel west to Taunggyi remains off limits; you must leave the way you came, via Tachilek. During parts of 1994 and 1995 this border crossing closed for a few months due to fighting between Khun Sa's Shan armies and the Burmese.

Rumour has it that an overland route all the way to China via Kengtung will soon open here, but so far Kengtung's the end of the line. The road continuing west from Kengtung to Taunggyi is in usable condition, although this runs through the opium poppy harvesting area of the Golden Triangle, a common site for Shan army skirmishes with the Yangon military, and is most definitely off limits to non-Burmese. It is 163 km on from Tachilek to Kengtung, and another 450 km from Kengtung to Taunggyi.

Further to the south, in Thailand's Mae Chan district, it is possible to cross the border almost everywhere – with a local and reliable guide. This is opium country and Sunday strollers are not welcome.

**Three Pagodas Pass** A gateway for invading armies and a major smuggling route for many centuries, this is one of the most interesting and accessible of the border crossing points.

Now that the Burmese have wrested control from Mon and Karen armies, there is also much legal trade going on at Three Pagodas Pass. The settlement on the Burmese side, called Payathonzu (Three Pagodas), is open to foreign tourists for day trips. Travellers have been allowed to go as far as a dozen or so km inside Myanmar from this point, but the roads are so bad that almost no-one makes it even that far.

From Kanchanaburi (the site of the 'Bridge on the River Kwai') you can get a minibus or rent a motorcycle and drive the 150 km along dusty, winding mountain roads to Sangkhlaburi. The trip takes about half a day. The road is OK as far as Thong Pha Phum, but deteriorates somewhat after that little town.

Pickup trucks make regular trips to Three Pagodas Pass from Sangkhlaburi. Along the way you must stop at a Thai military checkpoint and at the Myanmar border checkpoint you're required to sign your name and present your passport to the Burmese. The pass itself is unreal – three little pagodas standing on a crest.

Payathonzu itself is not that interesting, just a collection of wooden tea shops, a cinema, a couple of markets and several souvenir shops. The nearby Kloeng Thaw Falls take a couple of hours by motorcycle from Payathonzu. The road to the falls is only open in the dry season – reportedly the Karen control the waterfall area during the rainy season. No-one actually stops you from going to the falls then, though many people will try to wave you back. Even in good weather, the two-rut track is very rugged; not recommended for motorcycle novices.

**Mae Sot-Myawaddy** This crossing begins a route from Myawaddy to Mawlamyine (Moulmein) via Kawkareik along a rough road that has long been off limits to foreigners due to Mon and Karen insurgent activity in the area. There are regular buses from Tak to Mae Sot in the North's Tak Province. In 1994 the Myanmar government signed an agreement with Thailand to build a bridge across the Moei River between Myawaddy and Mae Sot, but although the project was begun in earnest it soon stalled due to international bickering over reclamation of the river banks. If this is resolved we can look for a possible opening up of this route sometime in the near future. It's possible to go right to the border on the Thai side of the Moei River, about six km beyond the town of Mae Sot.

Just north of Myawaddy is Wangkha, and just to the south is Phalu (Waley on the Thai side), former Karen and Mon smuggling posts now controlled by Yangon. Between Mae Sot and Tha Song Yang, south of Mae Sariang on the Thai side, are several Karen refugee camps (at last report 12 camps with a total of about 100,000 refugees) populated by civilians who have fled Burmese-Karen armed conflicts, as well as political dissidents from Yangon. The fighting was particularly bad in 1995 when dissident Karen Buddhists, backed by Burmese troops, routed the leading Christian faction; this area continues to be a military hotspot.

**Chiang Dao** A dirt track turns left 10 km north of Chiang Dao in Chiang Mai Province and leads through the small town of Meuang Ngai to Na Ok at the border. This was the most popular opium route from Myanmar 25 years ago, but the main trading items now are water buffalo and lacquer. It's wise to be very careful in this area though.

**Prachuap Khiri Khan** Not only is there a road over the Mawdaung Pass between Ban Huay Yang and Taninyarthi, there is a major business smuggling timber in from Myanmar. The 'toll gate', formerly controlled by Karen guerrillas from the Karen National Union/Karen National Liberation Army, is now once again controlled by Yangon forces. If you can find a local who knows the area well, it's possible to visit near the border crossing point of Dan Singkon.

### Cambodia

In general, there is no legal land passage between Cambodia and Thailand, and the Cambodian border won't be safe for land crossings until mines and booby traps left over from the conflict between the Khmer Rouge and the Vietnamese are removed or detonated. Travellers can sometimes cross to Cambodia by sea via Hat Lek, but it's very much an on and off situation.

### China

**By Road** The governments of Thailand, Laos, China and Myanmar recently agreed to the construction of a four-nation ring road through all four countries. The western half of the loop will proceed from Mae Sai,

Thailand, to Jinghong, China, via Myanmar's Tachilek (opposite Mae Sai) and Kengtung (near Dalau on the China-Myanmar border), while the eastern half will extend from Chiang Khong, Thailand, to Jinghong via Huay Xai, Laos (opposite Chiang Khong), and Boten, Laos (on the Yunnanese border south of Jinghong).

The stretch between Tachilek and Dalau is now under construction but it's possible to arrange one to three day trips as far as Kengtung in Myanmar's Shan State (see the Mae Sai section in the Northern Thailand chapter for details). A road between Huay Xai and Boten already exists (built by the Chinese in the 1960s and 1970s) but needs upgrading. Once the roads are built and the visa formalities have been worked out, this loop will provide alternative travel connections between China and South-East Asia, in much the same way as the Karakoram Highway has forged new links between China and South Asia. It's difficult to predict when all the logistical variables will be settled, but progress so far points to a cleared path by the end of the decade.

**By River** A third way to reach China's Yunnan Province from Thailand is by boat along the Maekhong River. Several surveys of the waterway have been completed and a specially constructed express boat made its inaugural run between Sop Ruak, Chiang Rai Province, and China's Yunnan Province in early 1994. For the moment, permission for such travel is restricted to private tour groups, but it's reasonable to assume that in the future – if demand is high enough – a scheduled public service may become available. The boat trip takes six hours – considerably quicker than any currently possible road route.

### Future Rail Possibilities

At a 1995 summit meeting in Bangkok, representatives of the Association of South-East Asian Nations (ASEAN) proposed the completion of a regional rail network linking Singapore with China via Malaysia, Thailand, Laos and Vietnam. In all but Laos and Cambodia, railbeds for such a circuit already exist. Current plans call for the extension of a rail line across the Maekhong River from Thailand to Laos via the existing Thai-Lao Friendship Bridge. If completed this line may someday connect with a proposed north-south line from Vientiane to Savannakhet in Laos and then with a west-east line from Savannakhet to Dong Ha, Vietnam.

### SEA

There are several ways of travelling between Thailand's southern peninsula and Malaysia by sea. Simplest is to take a long-tail boat between Satun, right down in the south-west corner of Thailand, and Kuala Perlis. The cost is about M$4, or 40B, and boats cross over fairly regularly. You can also take a ferry to the Malaysian island of Langkawi from Satun. There are immigration posts at both ports so you can make the crossing quite officially.

From Satun you can take a bus to Hat Yai and then arrange transport to other points in the south or further north. It's possible to bypass Hat Yai altogether by heading directly for Phuket or Krabi via Trang.

You can also take a ferry to Ban Taba on the east coast of Thailand from near Kota Baru – see the Sungai Kolok and Ban Taba sections in the Southern Thailand chapter.

See the Phuket section in the Southern Thailand chapter for information on yachts to Penang and other places.

On-again, off-again passenger ferry services also run between Pulau Langkawi and either Satun or Phuket, Thailand. None ever seems to last longer than nine months or so; your best bet is to make enquiries through local travel agents to find out the latest on sea transport to/from Langkawi.

### WARNING

The information in this chapter is particularly vulnerable to change: prices for international travel are volatile, routes are introduced and cancelled, schedules change, special deals come and go and rules and visa requirements are amended. Airlines and governments seem to take a perverse pleasure in making price structures and regulations as complicated as possible. You should check directly with the airline or a travel agent to make sure you understand how a fare (and ticket you may buy) works. In addition, the travel industry is highly competitive and there are many lurks and perks.

The upshot of this is that you should get opinions, quotes and advice from as many airlines and travel agents as possible before you part with your hard-earned cash. The details given in this chapter should be regarded as pointers and are not a substitute for your own careful, up-to-date research.

# Getting Around

## AIR
### Thai Airways International
Most domestic air services in Thailand are operated by Thai Airways International (THAI), which covers 22 airports throughout the kingdom. On certain southern routes, domestic flights through Hat Yai continue on to Malaysia (Penang, Kuala Lumpur), Singapore and Brunei (Bandar Seri Begawan). THAI operates Boeing 737s or Airbus 300s on its main domestic routes.

The accompanying chart shows some of the fares on more popular routes. Note that through fares are generally less than the combination fares – Chiang Rai to Bangkok, for example, is less than the addition of Chiang Rai to Chiang Mai and Chiang Mai to Bangkok fares. This does not always apply to international fares, however. It's much cheaper to fly from Bangkok to Penang via Phuket or Hat Yai than direct, for example.

**Air Passes** THAI offers special four-coupon passes – available only outside Thailand for foreign currency purchases – in which you can book any four domestic flights for one fare of US$259 as long as you don't repeat the same leg. Unless you plan carefully this isn't much of a saving since it's hard to avoid repeating the same leg in and out of Bangkok.

If you were to buy separate tickets from Bangkok to Hat Yai, then Hat Yai to Phuket, Phuket to Bangkok and finally Bangkok to Chiang Mai you'd spend 6625B (US$265), a savings of only US$6. However, if you were to fly from Bangkok to Phuket, Phuket to Bangkok, Bangkok to Chiang Mai – then continue overland to Sakon Nakhon and fly back to Bangkok from there, you'd save approximately US$60 over the total of the individual fares.

For information on the four-coupon deal, known as the 'Discover Thailand fare', enquire at any THAI office outside Thailand.

**THAI Offices** Offices for THAI's domestic services can be found throughout Thailand:

Bangkok – (head office) 89 Vibhavadi Rangsit Rd (☎ (2) 513-0121)
485 Silom Rd (☎ (2) 234-3100/19)
6 Lan Luang Rd (☎ (2) 280-0060, 628-2000)
Asia Hotel, 296 Phayathai Rd (☎ (2) 215-2020/1)
Grand China Tower, 3rd floor, 215 Yaowarat Rd (☎ (2) 223-9745/50)
Bangkok international airport, Don Muang (☎ (2) 535-2081/2, 523-6121)
Chiang Mai – 240 Phra Pokklao Rd (☎ (53) 211044/7, 210043/5)
Chiang Rai – 870 Phahonyothin Rd (☎ (53) 711179, 715207)
Hat Yai – 166/4 Niphat Uthit 2 Rd (☎ (74) 245851, 246165, 233433)
190/6 Niphat Uthit 2 Rd (☎ (74) 231272, 232392)
Khon Kaen – 183/6 Maliwan Rd (☎ (43) 236523, 239011, 238835)
Lampang – 314 Sanambin Rd (☎ (54) 217078, 218199)
Loei – 22/15 Chumsai Rd (☎ (42) 812344/355)
Mae Hong Son – 71 Singhanat Bamrung Rd (☎ (53) 611297/194)
Mae Sot – 76/1 Prasat Withi Rd (☎ (55) 531730/440)
Nakhon Ratchasima (Khorat) – 14 Manat Rd (☎ (44) 257211/5)
Nakhon Si Thammarat – 1612 Ratchadamnoen Rd (☎ (75) 342491)
Nan – 34 Mahaphrom Rd (☎ (54) 710377/498)
Narathiwat – 322-324 Phupapugdee Rd (☎ (73) 511161, 513090/2)
Nong Khai – 453 Prajak Rd (☎ (42) 411530)
Pattani – 9 Prida Rd (☎ (73) 349149)
Pattaya – Royal Cliff Beach Resort, Cliff Rd (☎ (38) 250286/7, 250804)
Phitsanulok – 209/26-28 Borom Trailokanat Rd (☎ (55) 258020, 251671)
Phrae – 42-44 Ratsadamnoen Rd (☎ (54) 511123)
Phuket – 78 Ranong Rd (☎ (76) 211195, 212499/946)
41/33 Montri Rd (☎ (76) 212400/644/880)
Sakon Nakhon – Sukkasem Rd (☎ (42) 712259/60)
Songkhla – 2 Soi 4, Saiburi Rd (☎ (74) 311012)
Surat Thani – 3/27-28 Karunarat Rd (☎ (77) 273710/355)
Tak – 485 Taksin Rd (☎ (55) 512164)
Trang – 199/2 Visetkul Rd (☎ (75) 218066)
Ubon Ratchathani – 364 Chayangkun Rd (☎ (45) 313340/4)
Udon Thani – 60 Mak Khaeng Rd (☎ (42) 246697, 243222)

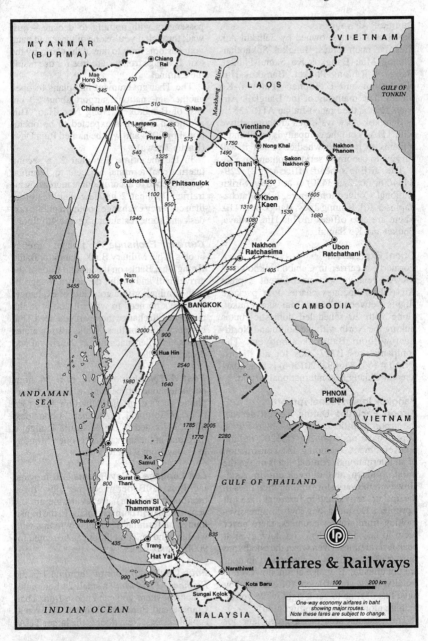

**Airfares & Railways**

One-way economy airfares in baht
showing major routes.
Note these fares are subject to change.

## Bangkok Airways

Bangkok Airways, owned by Sahakol Air, flies five main routes: Bangkok-Sukhothai-Chiang Mai, Bangkok-Ko Samui-Phuket, Bangkok-Ranong-Phuket, Bangkok-Hua Hin-Samui and U Taphao (Pattaya)-Ko Samui. The mainstay of the Bangkok Airways fleet is the Franco-Italian ATR-72.

Bangkok Airways' fares are competitive with THAI's but the company is small and it remains to be seen whether or not it will survive to become a serious contender.

The airline's head office (☎ (2) 229-3434/56; fax 229-3450) is at Queen Sirikit National Convention Centre, New Ratchadaphisek Rd, Khlong Toey, Bangkok 10110. There are also offices in Hua Hin, Pattaya, Phuket and Ko Samui.

## Orient Express Air

Formerly a carrier in Cambodia known as SK Air, relative newcomer Orient Express Air (OEA) operates charter tour package flights between Chiang Mai and Phuket, along with 20 scheduled domestic routes linking the North with the South and North-East without Bangkok stopovers. The company uses B727-200s for all flights. OEA (☎ (53) 818092, 201566) is headquartered at Chiang Mai international airport.

## Bangkok International Airport

**Airport Facilities** During the last decade, the airport facilities at Bangkok international airport have undergone a US$200 million redevelopment, including the construction of an international terminal that is one of the most modern and convenient in Asia. However, the very slow immigration lines in the upstairs arrival hall in Terminal 1 are still a problem. Despite a long row of impressive-looking immigration counters, there never seem to be enough clerks on duty, even at peak arrival times. Even when the booths are fully staffed, waits of 45 minutes to an hour are not unusual. Baggage claim, however, is usually quick and efficient (of course, they have lots of time to get it right while you're inching along through immigration).

The customs area has a green lane for passengers with nothing to declare – just walk through if you're one of these and hand your customs form to one of the clerks by the exit. Baggage trolleys are free for use inside the terminal.

The Thai government has plans to open another international airport about 20 km east of Bangkok at Nong Ngu Hao. This additional airport is expected to be operational by 2004 and will be named Raja Deva (Racha Thewa).

In the meantime Terminal 2, a second international terminal adjacent to Terminal 1, has opened to accommodate increasing air traffic. Terminal 2 has few facilities other than currency exchange booths, a public taxi desk and some restaurants on the 4th floor.

**Currency Exchange** The foreign currency booths (Thai Military Bank, Bangkok Bank, Krung Thai Bank) on the ground floor of the arrival hall and in the departure lounge of both terminals give a good rate of exchange, so there's no need to wait till you're in the city centre to change money if you need Thai currency. Each of these banks also operates automatic teller machines in the arrival and departure halls.

**Post & Telephone** There is a 24 hour post/telephone office with a Home Direct phone service in the departure hall (3rd floor) of Terminal 1. Another 24 hour post office is located in the departure lounge; a third one in the arrival hall is open Monday to Friday from 9 am to 5 pm.

**Left Luggage & Day Rooms** Left-luggage facilities (20B per piece per day, three months maximum) are available in the departure hall in both terminals. In the transit lounge of Terminal 1, clean day rooms with washing and toilet facilities can be rented for 900B per six hours.

**Food** On the 4th floor of Terminal 1 is the *Rajthanee Food Mall*, a small 24 hour cafeteria area where you can choose from Thai, Chinese and European dishes at fairly reasonable prices. Next door is the larger THAI restaurant with more expensive fare. On the 2nd level above the arrival area is a coffee shop which is open from 6 am to 11 pm, and there is also a small snack bar in the waiting area on the ground floor. The departure lounge has two snack bars which serve beer and liquor.

On the 4th floor of Terminal 2 is a cluster of new fast-food-style places, including *Swenson's, John Bull Pub, Burger King* and *Pizza Hut*. Opposite these is a posh Chinese restaurant. On the arrival floor of this terminal there's also a *KFC*.

The *Airbridge Cafe*, a European-style coffee shop on the enclosed bridge between Terminal 1 and the Amari Airport Hotel, provides a quiet alternative to the airport places.

**Shopping** There are several newsstands and souvenir shops in the arrival and departure areas of Terminal 1. Duty-free shopping is available in the departure lounge as well. The books and magazine selection at the airport newsstands is spotty; if you have enough time to walk across the enclosed footbridge from Terminal 1 to the Amari Airport Hotel, you'll find a much better bookshop in the hotel's shopping arcade (south of reception).

**Near the Airport** If you leave the airport building area and cross the expressway on the pedestrian bridge (just north of the passenger terminal), you'll find yourself in the Don Muang town area where there are all sorts of shops, a market, lots of small restaurants and food stalls, even a wat, all within 100m or so of the airport.

The modern and luxurious Amari Airport Hotel (☎ (2) 566-1020/1) has its own air-conditioned, enclosed footbridge from Terminal 1 and 'special mini-stay' daytime rates (8 am to 6 pm) for stays of up to a maximum of three hours for around 500B for singles/doubles, including tax and service. Longer daytime rates are available on request. For additional information on overnight accommodation in the Don Muang area, see Places to Stay in the Bangkok chapter.

The Amari also has a selection of decent restaurants serving Italian, Japanese and Thai food.

**To/From the Airport** Bangkok international airport is located in Don Muang district, approximately 25 km north of Bangkok. You have a choice of transport modes from the airport to the city ranging from 3.50 to 300B.

**THAI Minibus** THAI has a minibus service to major hotels (and minor ones if the driver feels like it) for 100B per person. THAI touts in the airport arrival hall will try to get you into the 350B limo service first, then the 100B minibus.

**To Pattaya** THAI operates direct air-con buses to Pattaya from the airport thrice daily at 9 am, 11 am and 7 pm; the fare is 200B one way. Private sedans cost 1500B per trip.

**Airport Bus** In mid-1996 a new airport express bus service began operating from Bangkok international airport to three different Bangkok districts for 70B per person. Buses run every 15 minutes from 5 am to 11 pm. A map showing the designated stops is available at the airport; each route makes approximately six stops in each direction. A great boon to travellers on a budget, these new buses mean you can avoid hassling with taxi drivers to get a reasonable fare as well as forgo the slow pace of the regular bus routes.

Since this service is quite new, the routes, fares and hours could change during the first year or two of operation. So far few airport arrivals seem to be using the service – one hopes it won't be cancelled as a result.

The Airport Bus counter stands around 200m to the left (with your back to Terminal 1) of the city taxi counter.

*A-1* – to the Silom Rd business district via Pratunam and Ratchadamri Rd, stopping at big hotels like the Indra, Grand Hyatt Erawan, Regent Bangkok and Dusit Thani

A-2 – to Sanam Luang via Phayathai, Lan Luang, Ratchadamnoen Klang and Tanao Rds; this is the one you want if you're going to the Siam Square or Banglamphu areas

A-3 – to the Phrakhanong district via Sukhumvit Rd

**Public Bus** Cheapest of all are the public buses to Bangkok which stop on the highway in front of the airport. There are two non-air-con bus routes and four air-con routes that visitors find particularly useful for getting into the city. The ordinary buses, however, no longer accept passengers carrying luggage.

Air-con bus No 29 costs 16B and plies one of the most useful, all-purpose routes from the airport into the city as it goes to the Siam Square and Hualamphong areas. After entering the city limits via Phahonyothin Rd (which turns into Phayathai Rd), the bus passes Phetburi Rd (where you'll want to get off to change buses for Banglamphu), then Rama I Rd at the Siam Square/Mahboonkrong intersection (for buses out to Sukhumvit Rd, or to walk to Soi Kasem San 1 for various lodgings) and finally turns right on Rama IV Rd to go to the Hualamphong district (where the main train station is located). You'll want to go the opposite way on Rama IV Rd for the Soi Ngam Duphli lodging area. No 29 runs only from 5.45 am to 8 pm, so if you're arriving on a late-night flight you'll miss it.

Air-con bus No 13 (16B; 5.45 am to 8 pm) also goes to Bangkok from the airport, coming down Phahonyothin Rd (like No 29), turning left at the Victory Monument to Ratchaprarop Rd, then south to Ploenchit Rd, where it goes east out Sukhumvit Rd all the way to Bang Na. This is definitely the one to catch if you're heading for the Sukhumvit Rd area.

Air-con bus No 4 (16B; 5.45 am to 8 pm) begins with a route parallel to that of the No 29 bus – down Mitthaphap Rd to Ratchaprarop and Ratchadamri Rds (Pratunam district), crossing Phetburi, Rama I, Ploenchit and Rama IV Rds, then down Silom, left on Charoen Krung, and across the river to Thonburi.

No backpacks or large luggage are allowed onto the non-air-con, ordinary buses. Ordinary bus No 59 costs only 3.50B (5B between 11 pm to 5 am) and operates 24 hours – it zigzags through the city to Banglamphu (the Democracy Monument area) from the airport, a trip that can take up to 1½ hours or more in traffic.

Ordinary bus No 29 (3.50B; or 5B from 11 pm to 5 am; 24 hours) plies much the same route as air-con bus No 29. Green bus No 2 (16B; 5.30 am to 8 pm) has a similar route to the air-con No 4; first it goes through Pratunam, then direct to Ratchadamri, Silom and Chareon Krung Rds.

Unless you're really strapped for baht, it's worth the extra 12.50B for the air-con and almost guaranteed seating, especially in the hot season, since the trip to central Bangkok by bus usually takes an hour or more. Even better is the 70B Airport Bus, described above.

**Train** You can also get into Bangkok from the airport by train. Just after leaving Terminal 1, turn right (north), cross the highway via the pedestrian bridge, turn left and walk about 100m towards Bangkok. Opposite the big Amari Airport Hotel is the small Don Muang station from where trains depart regularly to Bangkok. The 3rd class fare from Don Muang is only 10B on the ordinary and commuter trains if you buy your ticket on the platform, 20B if purchased on the train. Tickets for rapid or express trains cost 50B.

There are trains every 15 to 30 minutes between 5 am and 8 pm and it takes about 45 minutes to reach Hualamphong, the main station in central Bangkok. In the opposite direction trains run frequently between 4.20 am and 8 pm. From the Hualamphong station you can walk to bus stop almost opposite Wat Traimit for bus No 23 to Banglamphu, if that's your destination.

**Taxi** As reported in previous editions, hassles with airport taxi drivers continue to plague Bangkok international airport. The taxis which wait near the arrival area of the airport are supposed to be airport-regulated. Ignore all the touts waiting like sharks near the customs area and buy a taxi ticket from the public taxi booth at the southern end of the arrival hall (to the far left as you leave customs). Fares are set according to city destination and no haggling should be necessary; most destinations in central Bangkok are 200B (eg Siam Square) or 300B (eg Banglamphu). Taxis using this system are not required to use their meters. Two, three, or even four passengers (if they don't have much luggage) can split the fare.

Sometimes unscrupulous drivers will approach you before you reach the desk and try to sell you a ticket for 350 or 400B – ignore them and head straight for the desk. A few touts from the old taxi mafia that used to prowl the arrival area are still around and may approach you with fares of around 150B. Their taxis have white-and-black plates and are not licensed to carry passengers, hence you have less legal recourse in the event of an incident than if you take a licensed taxi (yellow-and-black plates).

The real hassle begins if you decide you'd prefer to take a metered taxi rather than pay the rather high 250B most drivers want. You're *supposed* to be able to take a metered taxi from the airport if you so choose, but the reality from 1994 to 1996 was that once you got in the cab most drivers refused to run the meters – in clear violation of the regulations printed on sheets given to all passengers in advance – and asked for 250B. Drivers complain that it really doesn't pay for them to queue up for passengers at the current metered rates. In mid-1996 the Ministry of Transport authorised drivers of metered taxis from the airport to collect a 100B surcharge over the meter reading. With surcharge included you shouldn't have to pay more than 210 to 240B for most destinations in Bangkok. One hopes the new surcharge – if actually followed – will result in fewer arguments between passenger and driver.

Going to the airport from the city, a metered taxi costs from 115B (eg from Siam Square) to 140B (from Banglamphu or the Silom Rd area). The occasional driver will refuse to use his meter and quote a flat rate of 150 to 200B.

On a metered taxi trip to/from the airport, passengers are responsible for the 10B or 20B (depending on which entrance the driver chooses) expressway toll. If you take a flat-rate taxi, the driver should pay. During heavy traffic you can save money by staying on the surface (non-expressway) streets – which are just as speedy as (if not speedier than) the expressway during heavy commuter hours.

One way to get an unsurcharged metered taxi is to go upstairs to the departure area and get an incoming city taxi, one that has just dropped passengers off. These will usually take you to Bangkok on the meter. The downstairs taxi mafia frowns on this practice, however, and you may be hassled.

Metered taxis flagged down on the highway in front of the airport (turn left from the arrival hall) are even cheaper – 100 to 120B for central Bangkok. When the queue at the public taxi desk is particularly long, it's sometimes faster to go upstairs or walk out to the highway and flag one down.

***THAI Limousine*** THAI offers an airport limousine, which is really just a glorified air-con taxi service, for 400B to central Bangkok, 300B to the Northern Bus Terminal or 500B to the Southern Bus Terminal.

***Terminal Shuttle*** THAI operates a free shuttle bus between the international and domestic terminals every 15 minutes between 6 am and 11.20 pm.

***Boat*** The Riverjet (☎ (2) 585-9120) is a fast hydrofoil that operates in conjunction with a bus service from the airport to a pier near the Rama VII Bridge in northern Bangkok for service to the following hotels along the river: Oriental, Shangri-La, Royal Orchid Sheraton and the Marriott Royal Garden Riverside. Tickets are a steep 700B; although the Riverjet boat/bus service is quicker during peak traffic periods (6.30 to 9.30 am, 3.30 to 8 pm), the rest of the time it's faster to take a taxi. Hours of operation are 7 am to 10 pm.

*Helicopter* The Shangri-La Hotel (☎ (2) 236-7777) continues its own helicopter service – introduced for the World Bank/ IMF meeting in 1991 – from Bangkok international airport to the hotel rooftop for 3500B per person, minimum three passengers. The flight takes only 10 minutes but is reserved for Shangri-La guests only. If you can afford the copter flight you can certainly afford this hotel, which has one of Bangkok's best river locations.

*Warning* Beware of airport touts – this means anyone trying to steer you away from the city taxi counter or asking where you plan to stay while you're in Bangkok. A legion of touts – some in what appear to be airport or airline uniforms – are always waiting for new arrivals in the arrival area, and will begin their badgering as soon as you clear customs. Posing as helpful tourist information agents, their main objective is to get commissions from overpriced taxi rides or hotel rooms. If you're foolish enough to mention the hotel or guesthouse you plan to stay at, chances are they'll tell you it's full and that you must go to another hotel (which will pay them a commission, though they may deny it). Sometimes they'll show you a nice collection of photos; don't get sucked in, as these touted hotels are often substandard and badly located.

The hotel reservation desks operated by the Thai Hotels Association (THA) at the back of the arrival hall in both terminals also take a commission on every booking, but at least they have a wide selection of accommodation. There have been reports that the THA desks occasionally claim a hotel is full when it isn't, just to move you into a hotel that pays higher commissions. If you protest, the staff may ask you to speak to the 'reservations desk' on the phone – usually an accomplice who confirms the hotel is full. Dial the hotel yourself if you want to be certain.

Now that the TAT supposedly has regulatory powers, one of its first acts should be to clean the touts out of the airport arrival area, as the present situation gives many visitors a rather negative first impression of Thailand.

Then again, some see it as part of the challenge of Asian travel!

## Don Muang Domestic Airport

Bangkok's Don Muang airport stands a few hundred metres south of Bangkok international airport. Facilities include a post and telephone office on the ground floor, a snack bar in the departure lounge and a restaurant on the 2nd floor. THAI operates a free shuttle bus between the international and domestic terminals every 15 minutes between 6 am and 11.20 pm.

See the previous section for information on transport options to/from the city centre.

## Departure Tax

Airport departure tax is 250B for international flights departing from Bangkok international airport, 200B for international departures from Phuket and Chiang Mai and 30B for domestic flights. Children under two are exempt.

## BUS
## Government Bus

Several different types of buses ply the roads of Thailand. The cheapest and slowest are the ordinary government-run buses *(rót tham daa)* that stop in every little town and for every waving hand along the highway. For some destinations – smaller towns – these orange-painted buses are your only choice, but at least they leave frequently. The government also runs faster, more comfortable, but less frequent air-conditioned buses called *rót ae* or *rót pràp aakàat*; these are painted with blue markings. If these are available to your destination, they are your very best choice since they don't cost that much more than the ordinary stop-in-every-town buses. The government bus company is called Baw Khaw Saw, an abbreviation of Borisàt Khõn Sòng (literally, Transportation Company). Every city and town in Thailand linked by bus transportation has a Baw Khaw Saw terminal, even if it's just a patch of dirt by the roadside.

The service on the government air-con buses is usually quite good and includes beverage service and video. On longer routes (eg Bangkok to Chiang Mai, Bangkok to Nong Khai), the air-con buses even distribute claim checks (receipt dockets) for your baggage. Longer routes may also offer two classes of air-con buses, regular and 1st class; the latter buses have toilets. 'VIP' buses have fewer seats (30 to 34 instead of 44; some routes have Super VIP, with only 24 seats) so that each seat reclines more. Sometimes these are called *rót nawn* or sleepers. For small to medium-sized people they are more comfortable, but if you're big in girth you may find yourself squashed on the 34-seaters when the person in front of you leans back. Occasionally you'll get a government air-con bus in which the air-con is broken or the seats are not up to standard, but in general I've found them more reliable than the private tour buses.

See Getting There & Away in the Bangkok chapter for information on the main bus terminals in Bangkok.

**Private Bus**
Private buses are available between major tourist and business destinations: Chiang Mai, Surat, Ko Samui, Phuket, Hat Yai, Pattaya, Hua Hin and a number of others. To Chiang Mai, for example, several companies run daily buses out of Bangkok. These can be booked through most hotels or any travel agency, although it's best to book directly through a bus office to be assured that you get what you pay for.

Fares may vary from company to company, but usually not by more than a few baht. However, fare differences between the government and private bus companies can be substantial. Using Surat Thani as an example, state-run buses cost 158B for the ordinary bus or 285B (1st class) for the air-con, while the private companies charge up to 385B. On the other hand, to Chiang Mai the private buses often cost less than the government buses, although those that charge less offer inferior service. Departures for some private companies are more frequent than for the equivalent Baw Khaw Saw route.

There are also private buses running between major destinations within the various regions, eg Nakhon Si Thammarat to Hat Yai in the South, and Chiang Mai to Sukhothai in the North. New companies are cropping up all the time. The numbers seemed to reach a peak in the 1980s, but are now somewhat stabilised because of a crackdown on licensing. Minibuses are used on some routes, eg Surat to Krabi and Tak to Mae Sot.

The private air-con buses are usually no more comfortable than the government air-con buses and feature similarly narrow seats and a hair-raising ride. The trick the tour companies use to make their buses seem more comfortable is to make you think you're not on a bus by turning up the air-con until your knees knock, handing out pillows and blankets and serving free soft drinks. On overnight journeys the buses usually stop somewhere en route and passengers are awakened to get off the bus for a free meal of fried rice or rice soup. A few companies even treat you to a meal before a long overnight trip.

Like their state-run equivalents, the private companies offer VIP (sleeper) buses on long hauls. In general private bus companies that deal mostly with Thais are good, while tourist-oriented ones – especially those connected with Khao San Rd – are the worst as the agents know they don't need to deliver good service because very few customers will be returning.

Out of Bangkok, the safest, most reliable private bus services are the ones which operate from the three official Baw Khaw Saw terminals rather than from hotels or guesthouses. Picking up passengers from any points except these official terminals is actually illegal, and services promised are often not delivered. Although it can be a hassle getting out to the Baw Khaw Saw terminals, you're generally rewarded with safer, more reliable and punctual service.

**Service**
Although on average the private companies charge more than the government does on the same routes, the service does not always

match the higher relative cost. In recent years the service on many private lines has in fact declined, especially on the Bangkok to Chiang Mai, Bangkok to Ko Samui, Surat to Phuket and Surat to Krabi routes.

Sometimes the cheaper lines – especially those booked on Khao San Rd in Bangkok – will switch vehicles at the last moment so that instead of the roomy air-con bus advertised, you're stuck with a cramped van with broken air-con. One traveller recounted how his Khao San Rd bus stopped for lunch halfway to Chiang Mai and then zoomed off while the passengers were eating – leaving them to finish the journey on their own! To avoid situations like this, it's always better to book bus tickets directly at a bus office – or at the government Baw Khaw Saw station – rather than through a travel agency.

Another problem with private companies is that they generally spend more time cruising the city for passengers before getting under way, meaning that they rarely leave at the advertised departure time.

A recent reader's letter opined:

[Your] guide offers good advice vis-à-vis travel within Thailand. Only once did I take a private bus from Khao San Rd. The service was poor; there was no free food or drink, one-setting air conditioning and negligible leg room. The bus to Chiang Mai was packed and I was forced to sit right at the front. The ride was terrifying, a roller coaster nightmare journey which saw the driver overtake blindly around sharp corners at speeds of around 100 km/h. During the journey the bus was stuck in a traffic jam so the driver decided to take a cross-country short cut; the mud track we were driven along was barely the width of the bus. At one stage we were inconvenienced by a tree blocking our path – no problem. It was chopped down.

My advice would be to take a train or public bus and if this fails then sit at the back of the bus. The public bus journeys I took were far superior; two free meals, plenty of leg room and drivers who had at least a modicum of respect for human life.

## Safety

Statistically, private buses meet with more accidents than government air-con buses. Turnovers on tight corners and head-on collisions with trucks are probably due to the inexperience of the drivers on a particular route. This in turn is probably a result of the companies opening and folding so frequently and because of the high priority given to making good time – Thais buy tickets on a company's reputation for speed.

As private bus fares are typically higher than government bus fares, the private bus companies attract a better heeled clientele among the Thais, as well as among foreign tourists. One result of this is that a private bus loaded with money or the promise of money is a temptation for upcountry bandits. Hence, private buses occasionally get robbed by bands of thieves. These incidents are diminishing, however, due to increased security under provincial administration.

In an effort to prevent druggings and robbery in Southern Thailand, which peaked in the 1980s, Thai police now board buses plying the southern roads at unannounced intervals, taking photos and videotapes of the passengers and asking for IDs. Reported incidents are now on the decrease.

Large-scale robberies never occur on the ordinary government buses, very rarely on the government air-con buses and rarely on the trains. Accidents, however, are not unknown on the government buses either, so the train still comes out the safest means of transport in Thailand.

Robberies and accidents are relatively infrequent (though more frequent than they should be) considering the number of buses taken daily, and I've never been on a bus that's suffered either mishap – the odds are on your side. Travellers to Thailand should know the risk of private bus travel against the apparent convenience, especially when there are alternatives. Some travellers really like the tour buses, though, so the private companies will continue to do good business.

Keep an eye on your bags when riding buses – pilfering by stealth is still the most popular form of robbery in Thailand, though again the risks are not that great – just be aware. Most pilfering seems to take place on the private bus runs between Bangkok and Chiang Mai, especially on buses booked on Khao San Rd. Keep zippered bags locked and well secured.

## TRAIN

The railway network in Thailand, run by the Thai government through the State Railway of Thailand (SRT), is surprisingly good. After travelling several thousand km by train and bus, I have to say that the train wins hands down as the best form of public transport in the kingdom. It is not possible to take the train everywhere in Thailand, but if it was that's how I'd go. If you travel 3rd class, it is often the cheapest way to cover a long distance; by 2nd class it's about the same as a private tour bus but much safer and more comfortable. Trains take a bit longer than chartered buses on the same journey but are worth the extra travel time, on overnight trips especially.

The trains offer many advantages: there is more space and more room to breathe and stretch out (even in 3rd class) than there is on even the best buses. The windows are big and usually open, so that there is no glass between you and the scenery (good for taking photos) and more to see. The scenery itself is always better along the train routes compared to the scenery along Thai highways – the trains regularly pass small villages, farmland, old temples etc. The pitch-and-roll of the railway cars is much easier on the bones, muscles and nervous system than the quick stops and starts, the harrowing turns and the pothole jolts endured on buses. The train is safer in terms of both accidents and robberies. Last, but certainly not least, you meet a lot more interesting people on the trains, or so it seems to me.

### Rail Routes

Four main rail lines cover 4500 km along the northern, southern, north-eastern and eastern routes. There are several side routes, notably between Nakhon Pathom and Nam Tok (stopping in Kanchanaburi) in the western Central region, and between Tung Song and Kantang (stopping in Trang) in the South. The southern line splits at Hat Yai, one route going to Sungai Kolok on the Malaysian east coast border, via Yala, and the other route going to Padang Besar in the west, also on the Malaysian border.

A new Bangkok to Pattaya spur, inaugurated in 1991, has not been as popular as expected. Within the next few years, a southern spur may well be extended from Khiriratnikhom to Phuket, establishing a rail link between Surat Thani and Phuket. A spur from Den Chai to Chiang Rai in the North is also under discussion. The SRT may also renovate the Japanese line that was built with forced POW and coolie labour during WWII between Nam Tok and Sangkhlaburi in Kanchanaburi Province.

Closer at hand, the SRT is surveying an unused rail extension between Aranya Prathet in Thailand and Poi Pet in Cambodia with the intention to resume international rail services between the two countries.

**Bangkok Terminals** Most long-distance trains originate from Bangkok's Hualamphong station. Before a railway bridge was constructed across the Chao Phraya River in 1932, all southbound trains left from Thonburi's Bangkok Noi station. Today this station services commuter and short-line trains to Kanchanaburi/Nam Tok, Suphanburi, Ratchaburi and Nakhon Pathom (Ratchaburi and Nakhon Pathom can also be reached by train from Hualamphong). A slow night train to Chumphon and Lang Suan, both in Southern Thailand, leaves nightly from Thonburi (Bangkok Noi) station but it's rarely used by long-distance travellers.

### Classes

The SRT operates passenger trains in three classes – 1st, 2nd and 3rd – but each class varies considerably depending on whether you're on an ordinary, rapid or express train.

**Third Class** A typical 3rd class car consists of two rows of bench seats divided into facing pairs. Each bench seat is designed to seat two or three passengers, but on a crowded upcountry line nobody seems to care about design considerations. On a rapid train (which carries 2nd and 3rd class cars only), 3rd class seats are padded and reasonably comfortable for shorter trips. On ordinary 3rd class only trains in the East and North-East, seats are sometimes made of hard wooden slats, and are not recommended for more than a couple of hours at a time. Express trains do not carry 3rd class cars at all. Commuter trains in the Bangkok area are all 3rd class and the cars resemble modern subway or rapid transit trains, with plastic seats and ceiling hand-straps for standing passengers.

**Second Class** In a 2nd class car, seating arrangements are similar to those on a bus, with pairs of padded seats all facing towards the front of the train. Usually the seats can be adjusted to a reclining angle, and for some people this is good enough for overnight trips. In a 2nd class sleeper, you'll find two rows of facing seat pairs; each pair is separated from the next by a dividing wall. A table folds down between each pair and at night the seats convert into two fold-down berths, one over the other. Curtains provide a modicum of privacy and the berths are fairly comfortable, with fresh linen for every trip. A toilet stall is located at one end of the car and washbasins at the other. Second class cars are found only on rapid and express trains; some routes offer air-con 2nd class as well as ordinary 2nd class.

**First Class** First class cars provide private cabins for singles or couples. Each private cabin has individually controlled air-con, an electric fan, a fold-down washbasin and mirror, a small table and a long bench seat (or two in a double cabin) that converts into a bed. Drinking water and towels are provided free of charge. First class cars are available only on express and special express trains.

**Bookings**

The disadvantage of travelling by rail, in addition to the time factor mentioned earlier, is that trains can be difficult to book. This is especially true around holiday time, eg the middle of April approaching the Songkhran Festival, since many Thais prefer the train. Trains out of Bangkok should be booked as far in advance as possible – a minimum of a week for popular routes such as the northern line to Chiang Mai and southern line to Hat Yai, especially if you want a sleeper. For the north-eastern and eastern lines a few days will suffice.

Advance bookings may be made one to 90 days before your intended date of departure. If you want to book tickets in advance, go to Hualamphong station in Bangkok, walk through the front of the station house and go straight to the back right-hand corner where a sign says 'Advance Booking' (open 8.30 am to 4 pm Monday to Friday, 8.30 am to noon weekends and holidays). The other ticket windows, on the left-hand side of the station, are for same-day purchases, mostly 3rd class.

Reservations are now computerised in the Advance Booking office. Instead of having to stop at three different desks as in previous years, you simply take a queue number, wait until your number appears on one of the electronic marquees, report to the correct desk (one for the southern line, one for the north and north-eastern) and make your ticket arrangements. Only cash baht is acceptable here.

Note that buying a return ticket does not necessarily guarantee you a seat on the way back, it only means you do not have to buy a ticket for the return. If you want a guaranteed seat reservation it's best to make that reservation for the return immediately upon arrival at your destination.

Booking trains back to Bangkok is generally not as difficult as booking trains out of Bangkok; however, at some stations this can be quite difficult (eg buying a ticket from Surat Thani to Bangkok).

Tickets between any station in Thailand can be purchased at Hualamphong station (☎ (2) 223-3762, 225-6964, 224-7788; fax 225-6068). You can also make advance bookings at Don Muang station (across from Bangkok international airport) and at the Advance Booking offices at train stations in the larger cities. Advance reservations can be made by phone from anywhere in Thailand. Throughout Thailand SRT ticket offices are *generally* open from 8.30 am to 6 pm on weekdays, 8.30 am to noon on weekends and public holidays. Train tickets can also be purchased at certain travel agencies in Bangkok (see the Travel Agencies section in the Bangkok chapter). It is much simpler to book trains through these agencies than to book them at the station; however, they usually add a surcharge of 50 to 100B to the ticket price.

## Charges & Surcharges

There is a 50B surcharge for express trains *(rót dùan)* and 30B for rapid trains *(rót raew)*. These trains are somewhat faster than the ordinary trains, as they make fewer stops. On the northern line during the day there is a 70B surcharge for 2nd class seats in air-con cars. For the special express trains *(rót dùan phísèt)* that run between Bangkok and Padang Besar or between Bangkok and Chiang Mai there is a 70B surcharge.

The charge for 2nd class sleeping berths is 100B for an upper berth and 150B for a lower berth (or 130B and 200B respectively on a special express). The difference between upper and lower is that there is a window next to the lower berth and a little more headroom. The upper berth is still quite comfortable. For 2nd class sleepers with air-con add 250/320B per upper/lower ticket. No sleepers are available in 3rd class.

All 1st class cabins are air-con. A two bed cabin costs 520B per person; single cabins are no longer available.

Following significant fare hikes in the mid-1980s, train travel is not quite the bargain it once was, especially considering that the charge for 2nd class berths is as high as the cost of cheaper hotel rooms outside Bangkok. You can figure on 500 km costing around 180B in 2nd class (not counting the surcharges for rapid/express services), twice that in 1st class and less than half in 3rd. Surprisingly, fares have hardly changed since the 1987 edition, in spite of an overall inflation rate in Thailand of 5% to 8% per annum, although supplemental charges have increased steadily. Although the government continues to subsidise train travel to some extent, I predict that fares will be taking a significant jump in the next two to three years, say around 10% to 15%. (I said the same thing four years ago but it hasn't happened yet!)

## Eating Facilities

Meal service is available in dining cars and at your seat in 2nd and 1st class cars. Menus change as frequently as the SRT changes catering services. For a while there were two menus, a 'special food' menu with 'special' prices (generally given to tourists) and a cheaper, more extensive menu. Nowadays all the meals seem a bit overpriced (75 to 200B on average) – if you're concerned with saving baht, bring your own.

Train staff sometimes hand out face wipes, then come by later to collect 10B each for them – a racket since there's no indication to passengers that they're not complimentary. (On government buses they're free, and they're available in the station for 1B.) Drinking water is provided, albeit in plastic bottles; sometimes it's free, sometimes it costs 5 to 10B per bottle.

Several readers have written to complain about being overcharged by meal servers on trains. If you do purchase food on board, be sure to check prices on the menu rather than trusting server quotes. Also check the bill carefully to make sure you haven't been overcharged.

## Station Services

Accurate, up-to-date information on train travel is available at the Rail Travel Aids counter in Hualamphong station. There you can pick up timetables or ask questions about fares and scheduling – one person behind the counter usually speaks a little English. There are two types of timetable available: two condensed English timetables (one for the south, another for the northern, north-eastern and eastern lines) with fares, schedules and routes for rapid, express and special express trains on the four trunk lines; and four complete, separate Thai timetables for each trunk line, with side lines as well. These latter timetables give fares and schedules for all trains – ordinary, rapid and express. The English timetables only display a couple of the ordinary routes; for example, they don't show the wealth of ordinary trains that go to Ayuthaya and as far north as Phitsanulok.

All train stations in Thailand have baggage storage services (sometimes called the 'cloak room'). The rates and hours of operation vary from station to station. At Hualamphong station the hours are from 4 am to 10.30 pm and left luggage costs 20B per piece per day. Hualamphong station also has a 5B shower service in the rest rooms.

All stations in provincial capitals have restaurants or cafeterias as well as various snack vendors. These stations also offer an advance-booking service for rail travel anywhere in Thailand. Although Hat Yai station is the only one with a hotel attached, there are usually hotels within walking distance of other major stations.

Hualamphong station has a travel agency where other kinds of transport can be booked. This station also has a post office that's open from 7.30 am to 5.30 pm from Monday to Friday, 9 am to noon on Saturday and holidays; it's closed on Sunday.

### Rail Passes

Eurotrain International (St Kongensgade 40h, DK-1264 Copenhagen, Denmark) issues a Thailand Explorer Pass that may save on fares if you plan to ride Thai trains extensively within a relatively short interval. To be eligible for the pass you must hold a valid International Student Identity Card (ISIC) or International Teacher Identity Card (ITIC) or be under 26 years of age; accompanying spouses and children are also eligible. The pass must be purchased outside Thailand and is available from most places that issue Eurail passes and ISICs/ITICs. See the Visas & Documents section of the Facts for the Visitor chapter.

The cost for seven days of unlimited 2nd class rail travel is US$33, for 14 days US$40 and for 21 days US$48. This includes all rapid or express surcharges but does not include sleeping berths or air-con charges, which cost extra according to the standard

SRT schedule. Passes must be validated at a local station before boarding the first train. The price of the pass includes seat reservations which, if required, can be made at any SRT ticket office. The pass is valid until midnight on the last day of the pass. However, if the journey is commenced before midnight on the last day of validity, the passenger can use the pass until that train reaches its destination.

Do the passes represent a true savings over buying individual train tickets? According to my calculations, the answer is yes only if you can average more than 117 km by rail per day for the 21 day pass, 150 km per day for the 14 day pass or 255 km a day for the seven day pass. If you travel at these levels (or less), then you'll be paying the same amount (or more) as you would if you bought ordinary train tickets directly. On less crowded routes where there are plenty of available 2nd class seats they save time that might otherwise be spent at ticket windows, but for high-demand routes (eg from Bangkok to Chiang Mai or Hat Yai) you'll still need to make reservations.

## CAR & MOTORCYCLE
### Roadways

Thailand has over 170,000 km of roadways, of which around 16,000 km are classified 'national highways' (both two lane and four lane), which means they're generally well maintained. Route numberings are fairly consistent: some of the major highways have two numbers, one under the national system and another under the optimistic 'Asia Highway' system which indicates highway links with neighbouring countries. Route 105 to Mae Sot on the Myanmar border, for example, is also called 'Asia 1', while Highway 2 from Bangkok to Nong Khai is 'Asia 12'. For the time being, the only border regularly crossed by noncommercial vehicles is the Thai-Malaysian border.

Kilometre stones are placed at regular intervals along most larger roadways, but place names are usually printed on them in Thai script only. Highway signs in both Thai and roman script showing destinations and distances are becoming increasingly common.

## Road Rules

Thais drive on the left-hand side of the road – most of the time. Other than that just about anything goes, in spite of road signs and speed limits – the Thais are notorious scofflaws when it comes to driving. Like many places in Asia, every two-lane road has an invisible third lane in the middle that all drivers feel free to use at any time. Passing on hills and curves is common – as long as you've got the proper Buddhist altar on the dashboard, what could happen?

The main rule to be aware of is that right of way belongs to the bigger vehicle; this is not what it says in the Thai traffic law, but it's the reality. Maximum speed limits are 60 km/h within city limits, 80 km/h on highways – but on any given stretch of highway you'll see vehicles travelling as slowly as 30 km/h or as fast as 150 km/h. Speed traps are becoming more common; they seem especially common along Highway 4 in the South and Highway 2 in the North-East.

Indicators are often used to warn passing drivers about oncoming traffic. A flashing left indicator means it's OK to pass, while a right indicator means someone's approaching from the other direction.

The principal hazard to driving in Thailand besides the general disregard for traffic laws is having to contend with so many different types of vehicles on the same road – bullock carts, 18-wheelers, bicycles, tuk-tuks and customised racing bikes. In village areas the vehicular traffic is lighter but you have to contend with stray chickens, dogs, water buffaloes, pigs, cats and goats. Once you get used to the challenge, driving in Thailand is very entertaining, but first-time drivers tend to get a bit unnerved.

**Checkpoints** Military checkpoints are common along highways throughout Northern and North-Eastern Thailand, especially in border areas. Always slow down for a checkpoint – often the sentries will wave you through without an inspection, but occasionally you will be stopped and briefly questioned. Use common sense and don't act belligerent or you're likely to be detained longer than you'd like.

## Rental

Cars, jeeps and vans can be rented in Bangkok, Chiang Mai, Chiang Rai, Mae Hong Son, Pattaya, Phuket, Ko Samui and Hat Yai. A Japanese sedan (eg Toyota Corolla) typically costs from around 1000 to 1500B per day; minivans (eg Toyota Hi-Ace, Nissan Urvan) go for around 1800B a day. Hertz rents Mitsubishi 1.3l Champs for 800B a day plus 4B per km or unlimited kms for 1200 to 1400B a day, slightly larger Toyota Coronas or Mitsubishi Lancers for 1100 to 1500B a day plus 4 to 5B per km, or 1500 to 1600B a day unlimited. The best deals are usually on 4WD Suzuki Caribians (sic) or Daihatsu Miras, which can be rented for as low as 700 to 800B per day with no per-km fees for long-term rentals or during low seasons. Unless you absolutely need the cheapest vehicle, you might be better off with a larger vehicle (eg the Toyota 4WD Mighty X Cab, if you absolutely need 4WD); Caribians are notoriously hard to handle at speeds above 90 km/h and tend to crumple dangerously in collisions. Cars with automatic shift are uncommon. Drivers can usually be hired with a rental for an additional 300 to 400B per day.

Check with travel agencies or large hotels for rental locations. It is advisable always to verify that a vehicle is insured for liability before signing a rental contract; you should also ask to see the dated insurance documents. If you have an accident while driving an uninsured vehicle you're in for some major hassles.

Motorcycles can be rented in major towns as well as many smaller tourist centres like Krabi, Ko Samui, Ko Pha-Ngan, Mae Sai, Chiang Saen, Nong Khai etc (see Motorcycle Touring below). Rental rates vary considerably from one agency to another and from city to city. Since there is a glut of motorcycles for rent in Chiang Mai and Phuket these days, they can be rented in these towns for as little as 80B per day. A substantial deposit is usually required to rent a car;

motorcycle rental usually requires that you leave your passport.

## Driving Permits

Foreigners who wish to drive motor vehicles (including motorcycles) in Thailand need a valid international driving permit. If you don't have one, you can apply for a Thai driver's licence at the Police Registration Division (PRD) (☎ (2) 513-0051/5) on Phahonyothin Rd in Bangkok. Provincial capitals also have PRDs. If you present a valid foreign driver's licence at the PRD you'll probably only have to take a written test; other requirements include a medical certificate and three passport-sized colour photos. The forms are in Thai only, so you'll also need an interpreter.

## Fuel & Oil

Modern petrol (gasoline) stations with electric pumps are in plentiful supply everywhere in Thailand where there are paved roads. In more remote off-road areas petrol (ben-sin or náam-man rót yon) is usually available at small roadside or village stands – typically just a couple of ancient hand-operated pumps fastened to petrol barrels. The Thai phrase for 'motor oil' is náam-man khrêuang.

As this book went to press, regular (thamádaa) petrol cost about 10B per litre, super (phísèt) a bit more. Diesel (dii-soen) fuel is available at most pumps for around 8.50 to 9B.

## Motorcycle Touring

Motorcycle travel is becoming a popular way to get around Thailand, especially in the North. Dozens of places along the guest-house circuit, including many guesthouses themselves, have set up shop with no more than a couple of motorbikes for rent. It is also possible to buy a new or used motorbike and sell it before you leave the country – a good used 125cc bike costs around 20,000B.

Daily rentals range from 80B a day for an 80cc or 100cc step-through (eg Honda Dream, Suzuki Crystal) to 400B a day for a good 250cc dirt bike. The motorcycle industry in Thailand has stopped assembling dirt bikes,

so many of the rental bikes of this nature are getting on in years – when they're well maintained they're fine. When they're not well maintained, they can leave you stranded if not worse. The latest trend in Thailand is for small, heavy racing bikes that couldn't be less suitable for the typical farang body.

The legal maximum size for motorcycle manufacture in Thailand is 150cc, though in reality few bikes on the road exceed 125cc. Anything over 150cc must be imported, which means an addition of up to 600% in import duties. The odd rental shop specialises in bigger motorbikes (average 200 to 500cc) – some were imported by foreign residents and later sold on the local market but most came into the country as 'parts' and were discreetly assembled, and licensed under the table.

A number of used Japanese dirt bikes are available, especially in Northern Thailand. The 250cc, four-stroke, water-cooled Honda AX-1 combines the qualities of both touring and off-road machines, and features economical fuel consumption. If you're looking for a more narrowly defined dirt bike, check out the Honda XL 250.

While motorcycle touring is undoubtedly one of the best ways to see Thailand, it is also undoubtedly one of the easiest ways to cut your travels short, permanently. You can also run up very large repair and/or hospital bills in the blink of an eye. However, with proper safety precautions and driving conduct adapted to local standards, you can see parts of Thailand inaccessible by other modes of transport and still make it home in one piece. Some guidelines to keep in mind:

- If you've never driven a motorcycle before, stick to the smaller 100cc step-through bikes with automatic clutches. If you're an experienced rider but have never done off-the-road driving, take it slowly the first few days.

- Always check a machine over thoroughly before you take it out. Look at the tyres to see if they still have tread, look for oil leaks, test the brakes. You may be held liable for any problems that weren't duly noted before your departure. Newer bikes cost more than clunkers, but are generally safer and more reliable. Street bikes are more comfortable and ride more smoothly on paved roads than dirt bikes; it's silly to rent an expensive dirt bike if most of your riding is going to be along decent roads. A two-stroke bike suitable for off-roading generally uses twice the fuel of a four-stroke bike with the same engine size, thus lowering your cruising range in areas where roadside pumps are scarce (eg the 125cc Honda Wing gives you about 300 km per tank while a 125cc Honda MTX gets about half that).

- Wear protective clothing and a helmet (most rental places will provide a helmet with the bike if asked). Without a helmet, a minor slide on gravel can leave you with concussion, cuts or bruises. Long pants, long-sleeved shirts and shoes are highly recommended as protection against sunburn and as a second skin if you fall. If your helmet doesn't have a visor, then wear goggles, glasses or sunglasses to keep bugs, dust and other debris out of your eyes. Gloves are also a good idea, to prevent blisters from holding on to the twist-grips for long periods of time. It is practically suicidal to ride on Thailand's highways without taking these minimum precautions for protecting your body.

- For distances of over 100 km or so, take along an extra supply of motor oil, and if riding a two-stroke machine carry two-stroke engine oil. On long trips, oil burns fast.

- You should never ride alone in remote areas, especially at night. There have been incidents where farang bikers have been shot or harassed while riding alone, mostly in remote rural areas. When riding in pairs or groups, stay spread out so you'll have room to manoeuvre or brake suddenly if necessary.

- In Thailand the de facto right of way is determined by the size of the vehicle, which puts the motorcycle pretty low in the pecking order. Don't fight it and keep clear of trucks and buses.

- Distribute whatever weight you're carrying on the bike as evenly as possible across the frame. Too much weight at the back of the bike makes the front end less easy to control and prone to rising up suddenly on bumps and inclines.

- Get insurance with the motorcycle if at all possible. The more reputable motorcycle rental places insure all their bikes; some will do it for an extra charge. Without insurance you're responsible for anything that happens to the bike. If an accident results in a total loss, or if the bike is somehow lost or stolen, you can be out 25,000B plus. To be absolutely clear about your liability, ask for a written estimate of the replacement cost for a similar bike – take photos as a guarantee. Some agencies will only accept the replacement cost of a new bike. Health insurance is also a good idea – get it before you leave home and check the conditions in regard to motorcycle riding.

## BICYCLE

Bicycles can be hired in many locations; guesthouses often have a few for rent at only 20 to 30B per day. Just about anywhere outside Bangkok, bikes are the ideal form of local transport because they're cheap, non-polluting and keep you moving slowly enough to see everything. Carefully note the condition of the bike before hiring; if it breaks down you are responsible and parts can be very expensive.

Many visitors are bringing their own touring bikes to Thailand these days. Grades in most parts of the country are moderate; exceptions include the far north, especially Mae Hong Son and Nan provinces, where you'll need iron thighs. There is plenty of opportunity for dirt-road and off-road pedalling, especially in the North, so a sturdy mountain bike would make a good alternative to a touring rig. Favoured touring routes include the two-lane roads along the Maekhong River in the North and the North-East – the terrain is mostly flat and the river scenery is inspiring.

No special permits are needed for bringing a bicycle into the country, although bikes may be registered by customs – which means if you don't leave the country with your bike you'll have to pay a huge customs duty. Most larger cities have bike shops – there are several in Bangkok and Chiang Mai – but they often stock only a few Japanese or locally made parts. All the usual bike trip precautions apply – bring a small repair kit with plenty of spare parts, a helmet, reflective clothing and plenty of insurance.

Thailand Cycling Club, established in 1959, serves as an information clearing-house on biking tours and cycle clubs around the country; call ☎ (2) 243-5139 and ☎ (2) 241-2023 in Bangkok. One of the best shops for cycling gear in Thailand is the Bike Shop in Bangkok, which has branches on New Phetburi Rd opposite Wat Mai Chonglom (☎ (2) 314-6317); at Soi 62, Sukhumvit Rd (☎ (2) 332-3538); and on Si Ayuthaya Rd near Phayathai Rd (☎ (2) 247-7220).

## HITCHING

Hitching is never entirely safe in any country in the world, and we don't recommend it. Travellers who decide to hitch should understand that they are taking a small but serious risk. You may not be able to identify the local rapist/murderer before you get into their vehicle. However, many people do choose to hitch, and the advice that follows should help to make the journey as fast and safe as possible.

People have mixed success with hitch-hiking in Thailand; sometimes it's great and at other times no-one wants to pick you up. It seems easiest in the more touristed areas of the North and South, most difficult in the Central and North-Eastern regions where farangs are a relatively rare sight. To stand on a road and try to flag every vehicle that passes by is, to the Thais, something only an uneducated village dweller would do.

If you're prepared to face this perception, the first step is to use the correct gesture used for flagging a ride – the thumb-out gesture isn't recognised by the average Thai. When Thais want a ride they stretch one arm out with the hand open, palm facing down, and move the hand up and down. This is the same gesture used to flag a taxi or bus, which is why some drivers will stop and point to a bus stop if one is nearby.

In general, hitching isn't worth the hassle as ordinary buses (no air-con) are frequent and fares are cheap. There's no need to stand at a bus terminal – all you have to do is stand on any road going in your direction and flag down a passing bus or songthaew (pickup truck).

The exception is in areas where there isn't any bus service, though in such places there's not liable to be very much private vehicle traffic either. If you do manage to get a ride it's customary to offer food or cigarettes to the driver if you have any.

## BOAT

As any flight over Thailand will reveal, there is plenty of water down there and you'll probably have opportunities to get out on it sometime during your trip. The true Thai river transport is the 'long-tail boat' (reua hang yao), so called because the propeller is mounted at the end of a long drive shaft extending from the engine. The engine, which varies from a small marine engine to a large car engine, is mounted on gimbals and the whole unit is swivelled to steer the boat. Long-tail boats can travel at a phenomenal speed.

Between the mainland and islands in the Gulf of Thailand or Andaman Sea, all sorts of larger ocean-going craft are used. The standard is an all-purpose wooden boat eight to 10m long with a large inboard engine, a wheelhouse and a simple roof to shelter passengers and cargo. Faster, more expensive hovercraft or jetfoils are sometimes available in tourist areas.

## LOCAL TRANSPORT

The Getting Around section in the Bangkok chapter has more information on various forms of local transport.

### Bus

In most larger provincial capitals, there are extensive local bus services, generally operating with very low fares (2 to 5B).

### Taxi

Many regional centres have taxi services, but although there may well be meters, they're never used. Establishing the fare before departure is essential. Try to get an idea from a third party what the fare should be and be prepared to bargain. In general, fares are reasonably low. With the recent success of metered taxis in Bangkok, look for meters to appear in larger upcountry towns like Chiang Mai, Khon Kaen or Hat Yai.

### Samlor/Tuk-Tuk

Samlor means 'three wheels' (săam láw), and that's just what they are – three-wheeled vehicles. There are two types of samlors, motorised and non-motorised. You'll find motorised samlors throughout the country. They're small utility vehicles, powered by a horrendously noisy two-stroke engine – if the noise and vibration doesn't get you, the fumes will. These samlors are more commonly known as *túk-túks* from the noise they make. The non-motorised version, on the other hand, are bicycle rickshaws, just like you find, in various forms, all over Asia. There are no bicycle samlors in Bangkok but you will find them elsewhere in the country. In either form of samlor the fare must be established, by bargaining if necessary, before departure.

A bicycle rickshaw, the less noisy alternative.

## Songthaew

A songthaew *(săwng tháew*, literally 'two rows') is a small pickup truck with two rows of bench seats down the sides, very similar to an Indonesian *bemo* and akin to a Filipino *jeepney*. Songthaews sometimes operate fixed routes, just like buses, but they may also run a share-taxi type of service or even be booked individually just like a regular taxi.

## ORGANISED TOURS

Many tour operators around the world can arrange guided tours of Thailand. Most of them simply serve as brokers for tour companies based in Thailand; they buy their trips from a wholesaler and resell them under various names in travel markets overseas. Hence, one is much like another and you

might as well arrange a tour in Thailand at a lower cost – there's so many available. Two of Thailand's largest tour wholesalers in Bangkok are: World Travel Service (☎ (2) 233-5900; fax 236-7169) at 1053 Charoen Krung Rd; and Deithelm Travel (☎ (2) 255-9150; fax 256-0248) at Kian Gwan Bldg II, 140/1 Withayu Rd.

Several Bangkok-based companies specialise in ecologically oriented tours, including: Friends of Nature Eco-Tours (☎ (2) 642-4426; fax 642-4428), 133/21 Ratchaprarop Rd, Ratthewi; and Khiri Travel (☎ (2) 629-0491; fax 629-0493), Viengtai Hotel, 42 Thani Rd, Banglamphu.

The better overseas tour companies build their own Thailand itineraries from scratch and choose their local suppliers based on which ones best serve these itineraries. Of these, several specialise in adventure and/or ecological tours, including those listed below. Bolder Adventures, for example, offers trips across a broad spectrum of Thai destinations and activities, from Northern Thailand trekking to sea canoeing in the Phuket Sea, plus tour options that focus exclusively on North-Eastern Thailand. The average trip runs 14 to 17 days.

Ms Kasma Loha-Unchit (☎ (510) 655-8900); 4119 Howe St, Oakland, California 94611, USA), a Thai native living in California, offers highly personalised, 26 day 'cultural immersion' tours of Thailand.

Backroads – 801 Cedar St, Berkeley, CA 94710, USA (☎ (800) 462-2848, (510) 527-1555; fax (510) 527-1444)

Bolder Adventures – PO Box 1279, Boulder, CO 80306, USA (☎ (800) 642-2742, (303) 443-6789; fax (303) 443-7078)

Exodus – 9 Weir Rd, London SW12 OLT, UK (☎ (0181) 673-5550; fax 673-0779)

Intrepid Travel – 246 Brunswick St, Fitzroy, Victoria 3065, Australia (☎ (03) 9416-2655; fax 9419-4426)

Mountain Travel-Sobek – 6420 Fairmount Ave, CA 94530, USA (☎ (800) 227-2384, (510) 527-8100; fax (510) 525-7710)

# Bangkok

The very epitome of the modern, steamy Asian metropolis, Bangkok (560 sq km; population six million) has a surplus of attractions if you can tolerate the traffic, noise, heat (in the hot season), floods (in the rainy season) and somewhat polluted air. The city is incredibly urbanised, but beneath its modern veneer lies an unmistakable Thainess. To say that Bangkok is not Thailand, as has been superciliously claimed by some, is tantamount to saying that New York is not the USA, Paris is not France, or London not England.

The capital of Thailand was established at Bangkok in 1782 by the first king of the Chakri dynasty, Rama I. The name Bangkok comes from *bang makok*, meaning 'place of olive plums', and refers to the original site, which is only a very small part of what is today called Bangkok by foreigners. The official Thai name is quite a tongue twister:

Krungthep mahanakhon bowon rattanakosin mahintara ayuthaya mahadilok popnopparat ratchathani burirom udomratchaniwet mahasathan amonpiman avatansathir sakkathatitya visnukamprasit

Fortunately this is shortened to Krung Thep (City of Angels) in everyday usage. Metropolitan Krung Thep includes Thonburi, the older part of the city (and predecessor to Bangkok as the capital), which is across the Chao Phraya River to the west.

Bangkok caters to diverse interests: there are temples, museums and other historic sites for those interested in traditional Thai culture; an endless variety of good restaurants, clubs, international cultural and social events; movies in several different languages; and discos, heavy metal pubs, folk cafes, even modern art galleries for those seeking contemporary Krung Thep. As William Warren, the dean of expat authors in Thailand, has said, 'The gift Bangkok offers me is the assurance I will never be bored'.

## HIGHLIGHTS

- Wat Phra Kaew with its tiny Emerald Buddha, colourful mosaics and glittering spires
- National Museum for an impressive display of the country's sculptural and decorative arts
- Views of Bangkok from atop the peaceful Wat Arun, on the bank of the Chao Phraya River
- Elegant Vimanmek Teak Mansion – one of the world's largest golden teak buildings
- Khŏn performances of dance-drama at the Art-Deco Chalermkrung Royal Theatre or shrine dancing at Lak Meuang and Erawan shrines
- Trips up Bangkok's huge canal system for a glimpse of water life and floating markets
- Rambling Wat Pho housing Thailand's largest reclining Buddha
- Raucous Thai boxing bouts at Lumphini and Ratchadamnoen stadiums
- Walking tours of Chinese and Indian market districts – temples, bazaars, shophouses and alleys

### Orientation

The east side of the Chao Phraya River, Bangkok proper, can be divided into two by

SARA JANE CLELAND

RICHARD I'ANSON

RICHARD I'ANSON

### Bangkok
Top: Taking an early morning stroll, Grand Palace
Middle: Caught in traffic, bustling Chinatown
Bottom: Wat Arun from across the busy waterways of the Chao Phraya River

RICHARD I'ANSON

GLENN BEANLAND

RICHARD NEBESKY

RICHARD NEBESKY

## Bangkok

Top Left: Serene face of a gilded Buddha image, Wat Pho
Top Right: Intricate lotus-bud patterns and lacquered panels, Wat Phra Kaew
Bottom Left: Mythical *kinnari* figure, Wat Phra Kaew
Bottom Right: Mosaic-encrusted columns, Wat Phra Kaew

## Bangkok Primacy

Bangkok has dominated Thailand's urban hierarchy since the late 18th century and is today considered Asia's quintessential 'primate city' by sociologists. A primate city is one that is demographically, politically, economically and culturally dominant over all other cities in the country. Approximately 70% of Thailand's urban population (and 10% of the total population) lives in Bangkok, as compared with 30% in Manila and 27% in Kuala Lumpur (the second and third most primate in the region). More statistics: 79% of the country's university graduates, 78% of its pharmacists and 45% of its physicians live in the capital; 80% of the nation's telephones and 72% of all passenger cars registered in the country (30% of all motor vehicles) are found in Bangkok. ■

the main north-south train line. The portion between the river and the train line is old Bangkok (often called Ko Ratanakosin), where most of the older temples and the original palace are located, as well as the Chinese and Indian districts. That part of the city east of the railway, which covers many times more area than the old districts, is 'new' Bangkok. It can be divided again into the business/tourist district wedged between Charoen Krung (New) and Rama IV Rds, and the sprawling business/residential/ tourist district stretching along Sukhumvit and New Phetburi Rds.

This leaves the hard-to-classify areas below Sathon Tai (South) Rd (which includes Khlong Toey, Bangkok's main port), and the area above Rama IV Rd between the train line and Withayu (Wireless) Rd (which comprises an infinite variety of businesses, several movie theatres, civil service offices, the shopping area of Siam Square, Chulalongkorn University and the National Stadium). The areas along the east bank of the Chao Phraya River are undergoing a surge of redevelopment and many new buildings, particularly condos, are going up.

On the opposite (west) side of the Chao Phraya River is Thonburi, which was Thailand's capital for 15 years before Bangkok was founded. Few tourists ever set foot on the Thonburi side except to visit Wat Arun, the Temple of Dawn. Fang Thon (Thon Bank), as it's often called by Thais, seems an age away from the glittering high-rises on the river's east bank, although it is an up-and-coming area for condo development.

**Finding Addresses** Any city as large and unplanned as Bangkok can be tough to get around. Street names often seem unpronounceable to begin with, compounded by the inconsistency of romanised Thai spellings. For example, the street often spelt as Rajadamri is pronounced Ratchadamri (with the appropriate tones), or in abbreviated form Rat'damri. The 'v' in Sukhumvit should be pronounced like a 'w'. The most popular location for foreign embassies is known both as Wireless Rd and Withayu Rd (*wítháyú* is Thai for 'radio').

Many street addresses show a string of numbers divided by slashes and hyphens; for example, 48/3-5 Soi 1, Sukhumvit Rd. This is because undeveloped property in Bangkok was originally bought and sold in lots. The number before the slash refers to the original lot number; the numbers following the slash indicate buildings (or entrances to buildings) constructed within that lot. The pre-slash numbers appear in the order in which they were added to city plans, while the post-slash numbers are arbitrarily assigned by developers. As a result numbers along a given street don't always run consecutively.

The Thai word *thanŏn* means road, street or avenue. Hence Ratchadamnoen Rd (sometimes referred to as Ratchadamnoen Ave) is always called Thanon Ratchadamnoen in Thai.

A *soi* is a small street or lane that runs off a larger street. In our example, the address referred to as 48/3-5 Soi 1, Sukhumvit Rd will be located off Sukhumvit Rd on Soi 1. Alternative ways of writing the same address

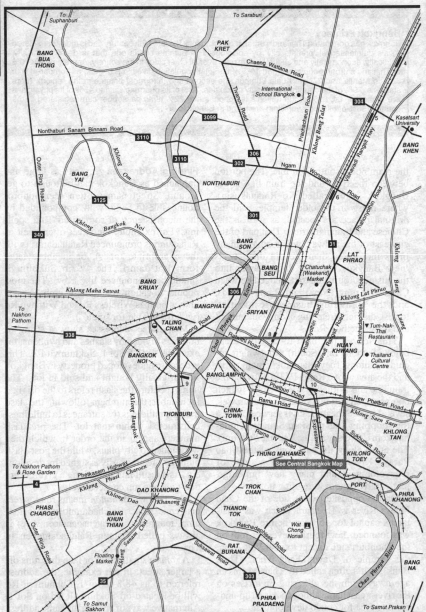

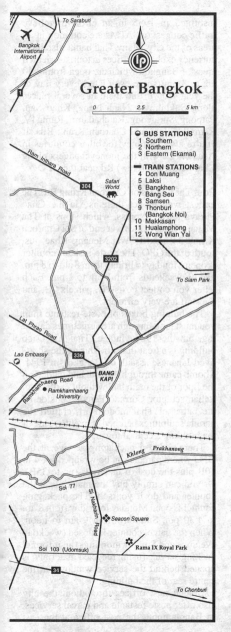

**Greater Bangkok**

0    2.5    5 km

**BUS STATIONS**
1  Southern
2  Northern
3  Eastern (Ekamai)

**TRAIN STATIONS**
4  Don Muang
5  Laksi
6  Bangkhen
7  Bang Seu
8  Samsen
9  Thonburi
   (Bangkok Noi)
10 Makkasan
11 Hualamphong
12 Wong Wian Yai

To Saraburi

Bangkok International Airport

Ram Inthara Road

Safari World

To Siam Park

Lat Phrao Road

Lao Embassy

BANG KAPI

Ramkhamhaeng Road

Ramkhamhaeng University

Khlong  Prakhanong

Soi 77

Si Nakharin Road

Seacon Square

Soi 103 (Udomsuk)

Rama IX Royal Park

To Chonburi

include 48/3-5 Sukhumvit Rd Soi 1, or even just 48/3-5 Sukhumvit 1. Some Bangkok sois have become so large that they can be referred to both as thanŏn and soi, eg Soi Sarasin/Sarasin Rd and Soi Asoke/Asoke Rd.

Smaller than a soi is a *tràwk* (usually spelt 'trok') or alley. Well known alleys in Bangkok include Chinatown's Trok Itsanuraphap and Banglamphu's Trok Rong Mai.

**Maps**  A map is essential for finding your way around Bangkok, and the best one, because it clearly shows all the bus routes (and some walking tours), is the *Bangkok Bus Map* published by Bangkok Guide Co. The map costs 35 to 40B and although it's regularly updated, some bus routes will inevitably be wrong, so take care. Other companies put out similar maps called *Tour'n Guide Map to Bangkok Thailand* and *Latest Tour's Map to Bangkok & Thailand* that will also do the job. For more detail on bus routes you'll have to get the *Bus Guide*, a booklet published by Bangkok Guide for 35B. It contains maps and a listing of all the public bus routes in Bangkok as well as a Bangkok train schedule. To use it properly takes some patience since much of the guide is in Thai and the English is horrendous. However these bus maps are necessary if you intend to spend a lot of time in Bangkok and want to use the very economical bus system.

Another map to consider is *Nancy Chandler's Map of Bangkok*, which costs 70B. This map has a whole host of information on out-of-the-way places, including lots of stuff on where to buy unusual things around the city. The Fine Arts Commission of the Association of Siamese Architects produces a pack of four unusual maps showing temples and important places of cultural interest. The maps are *Bangkok*, *Grand Palace*, *Canals of Thonburi* and *Ayuthaya*. The Tourism Authority of Thailand (TAT) issues a *Sightseeing & Shopping Map* of Bangkok that has lively three-dimensional drawings of popular tourist spots along Ratchadamri, Rama IV, Rama I and Phayathai Rds.

## Information

**Tourist Offices** The TAT has a desk in the arrivals area at Bangkok international airport that's open from 8 am to midnight. The TAT's main office (☎ 226-0060/72) is in a large government compound on the corner of Bamrung Meuang and Worachak Rds. English-speaking staff dispense information from a small round building in the centre of the compound. The TAT produces the usual selection of colourful brochures, but they're also one of the best tourist offices in Asia for putting out useful hard facts – on plain but quite invaluable duplicated sheets. This main office is open daily from 8.30 am to 4.30 pm.

Smaller TAT offices with fewer materials can be found at Chatuchak (Weekend) Market and opposite Wat Phra Kaew on Na Phra Lan Rd; these two are open daily from 8.30 am to 7.30 pm.

The TAT also maintains a Tourist Assistance Centre (TAC; ☎ 282-8129, 281-5051) in the main compound for matters relating to theft and other mishaps; it's open from 8 am to midnight. The paramilitary arm of the TAT, the tourist police, can be quite effective in dealing with such matters, particularly 'unethical' business practices – which sometimes turn out to be cultural misunderstandings. Note that if you think you've been overcharged for gems (or any other purchase), there's very little the TAC can do.

**Foreign Embassies** See the Facts for the Visitor chapter for a list of embassies in Bangkok.

**Immigration Department** For visa extensions or applications, you'll need to visit the Immigration Department office (☎ 287-1774) on Soi Suan Phlu, off Sathon Tai Rd. It's open Monday to Friday from 8.30 am to 4.30 pm (with limited staff noon to 1 pm), Saturday from 8.30 am to noon. Most applications/extensions require two photos and a photocopy of the photo page of your passport.

**Money** Regular bank hours in Bangkok are now 10 am to 4 pm – a new schedule was instituted in 1995 in an effort to relieve traffic congestion. ATMs are common in all areas of the city. Many Thai banks also have currency exchange offices in tourist-oriented areas of Bangkok which are open from 8.30 am to 8 pm (some even later) every day of the year. You'll find them in several places along Sukhumvit, Nana Neua, Khao San, Patpong, Surawong, Ratchadamri, Rama IV, Rama I, Silom and Charoen Krung Rds. If you're after currency for other countries in Asia, check with the moneychangers along Charoen Krung (New) Rd near the GPO.

**Post** The GPO is on Charoen Krung Rd. The easiest way to get there is via the Chao Phraya River Express, which stops at Tha Meuang Khae at the river end of Soi Charoen Krung 34, next to Wat Meuang Khae, just south of the GPO. The poste-restante counter is open Monday to Friday from 8 am to 8 pm, and on weekends from 8 am to 1 pm. Each letter you collect costs 1B, parcels 2B, and the staff are very efficient.

The bulging boxes of poste-restante mail you must look through are sometimes daunting, but the 1927 vintage, Thai Art Deco building is a treat in itself. During the short-lived Japanese assault on Bangkok in 1941, a bomb came through the roof and landed on the floor of the main hall without exploding. Italian sculptor Corrado Feroci, considered the father of Thai modern art, crafted the garuda sculptures perched atop either side of the building's central tower.

There's also a packaging service at the GPO where parcels can be wrapped for 4 to 10B plus the cost of materials (up to 35B). Or you can simply buy the materials at the counter and do it yourself. The packaging counter is open Monday to Friday from 8 am to 4.30 pm, Saturday from 9 am to noon. When the parcel counter is closed (weekday evenings and Sunday mornings) an informal packing service (using recycled materials) is opened behind the service windows at the centre rear of the building.

Branch post offices throughout the city also offer poste restante and parcel services. In Banglamphu, the post office at the east end of Trok Mayom Rd near Nat II Guest House is very conveniently located; packaging services are available here as well.

**Telephone & Fax** The CAT international telephone office, around the corner from the main GPO, is open 24 hours. At last count, 16 different countries had Home Direct service, which means you can simply enter a vacant Home Direct booth and get one-button connection to an international operator in any of these countries (see the Posts & Communications section in the Facts for the Visitor chapter for a country list). Other countries (except Laos and Malaysia) can be reached via IDD phones. Faxes can also be sent from the CAT office.

Other Home Direct phones can be found at Queen Sirikit National Convention Centre, World Trade Centre, Sogo Department Store and at the Banglamphu and Hualamphong post offices.

You can also make long-distance calls and faxes at the TOT office on Ploenchit Rd, but this office accepts cash only, no reverse charge or credit card calls. Calls to Laos and Malaysia can only be dialled from the TOT office or from private phones.

Bangkok's area code is ☎ (2).

**Travel Agencies** Bangkok is packed with travel agencies of every manner and description, but if you're looking for cheap airline tickets it's wise to be cautious. In the past three or four years, at least two agencies on Khao San Rd closed up shop and absconded with payments from more than 30 tourists who never received their tickets. The really bad agencies change their names frequently, so ask other travellers for advice. Wherever possible, try to see the tickets before you hand over the money.

STA Travel maintains reliable offices specialising in discounted yet flexible air tickets at Wall Street Tower (☎ 233-2582), 33 Surawong Rd, and in the Thai Hotel (☎ 281-5314), 78 Prachatipatai Rd, Banglamphu. Another reliable, long-running agency is Vieng Travel (☎ 280-3537), Trang Hotel, 99/8 Wisut Kasat Rd, in Banglamphu.

Some agencies will book Thai train tickets and pick them up by courier – a service for which there's usually a 100B surcharge. Four agencies permitted to arrange direct train bookings (without surcharge) are:

Airland – 866 Ploenchit Rd (☎ 255-5432)
SEA Tours – Suite 414, 4th floor, Siam Center, Rama I Rd (☎ 251-4862, 255-2080)
Songserm Travel Center – 121/7 Soi Chalermla, Phayathai Rd (☎ 255-8790) and 172 Khao San Rd (☎ 282-8080)
Thai Overland Travel & Tour – 407 Sukhumvit Rd, between sois 21 and 23 (☎ 635-0500; fax 635-0504)

The following agencies specialise in arranging tourist visas to Laos and Vietnam:

Diethelm Travel – Kian Gwan Bldg II, 140/1 Withayu Rd (☎ 255-9150; fax 256-0248)
Exotissimo Travel – 21/17 Soi 4, Sukhumvit Rd (☎ 253-5250; fax 254-7683)
MK Ways – 57/11 Withayu Rd (☎ 254-3390; fax 254-5583)
Skyline Travel Services – 27th floor, Ocean Tower II Bldg, 75/62-63 Sukhumvit Rd, Soi 21 (☎ 260-5525; fax 260-5534)

There are also several brokers on Khao San Rd who arrange visa packages for Thailand's socialist neighbours, but none are authorised for direct sales – they must work through other agencies.

If you are heading onto Europe and need a Eurail Pass, Dits Travel Ltd (☎ 255-9205) at Kian Gwan House, 140 Withayu Rd, is one agency authorised to issue them.

**Magazines & Newspapers** Several ad-laden giveaways contain tourist information, but the best all-around source for straight info is the *Bangkok Metro* magazine, a lifestyle monthly packed with listings on health, entertainment, events, social services, travel tips and consumer-oriented articles. *The Nation* and the *Bangkok Post* also contain useful articles and listings of events.

**Bookshops** Bangkok has many good bookshops, with possibly the best selection in South-East Asia.

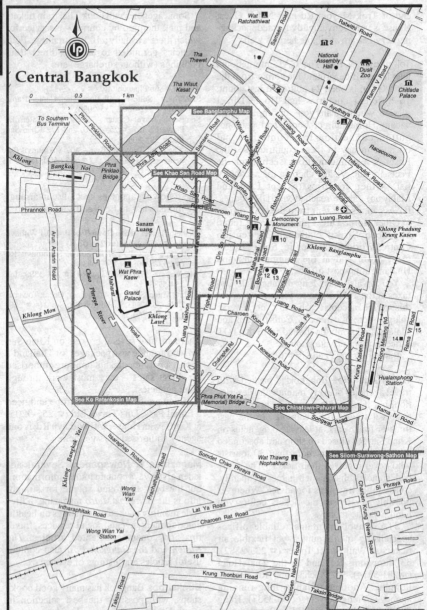

# Central Bangkok

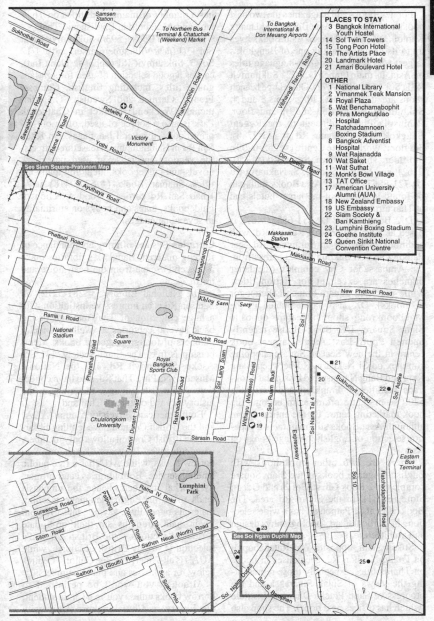

PLACES TO STAY
3   Bangkok International
    Youth Hostel
14  Soi Twin Towers
15  Tong Poon Hotel
16  The Artists Place
20  Landmark Hotel
21  Amari Boulevard Hotel

OTHER
1   National Library
2   Vimanmek Teak Mansion
3   Royal Plaza
5   Wat Benchamabophit
6   Phra Mongkutklao
    Hospital
7   Ratchadamnoen
    Boxing Stadium
8   Bangkok Adventist
    Hospital
9   Wat Rajanadda
10  Wat Saket
11  Wat Suthat
12  Monk's Bowl Village
13  TAT Office
17  American University
    Alumni (AUA)
18  New Zealand Embassy
19  US Embassy
22  Siam Society &
    Ban Kamthieng
23  Lumphini Boxing Stadium
24  Goethe Institute
25  Queen Sirikit National
    Convention Centre

For new books and magazines the two best bookshop chains are Asia Books and Duang Kamol (DK) Book House. Asia Books lives up to its name by having one of Bangkok's largest selections of English-language titles on Asia. Its main branch is at 221 Sukhumvit Rd at Soi 15 (☎ 252-7277). Other large branch shops are at: Landmark Plaza, sois 3 and 4, Sukhumvit Rd (☎ 253-5839); 2nd floor, Peninsula Plaza, adjacent to the Regent Bangkok on Ratchadamri Rd (☎ 253-9786); 3rd floor, World Trade Centre (☎ 255-6209); 3rd floor, Thaniya Plaza, Silom Rd (☎ 250-0162); and Seacon Square, Si Nakharin Rd (☎ 721-8867). Smaller Asia Books stalls can be found in several of the larger hotels and at Thai airports.

DK Book House (☎ 251-6335/1467) is based at Siam Square, off Rama I Rd, with additional branches on Surawong Rd near Patpong and on Sukhumvit Rd across from the Ambassador City complex (the latter branches are excellent for fiction titles, while the Siam Square branch is better for textbooks). DK also has a branch in the Mahboonkrong shopping centre opposite Siam Square. DK Book House recently opened South-East Asia's largest book centre in the new Seacon Square shopping complex on Si Nakharin Rd between Bang Kapi and Bang Na. Inspired by similar book-trade facilities in Frankfurt and Paris, the 5200 sq m centre promises to become the book marketing centre for the entire region, although Asia Books still maintains a superior selection of English-language books on Asia.

There are two other bookshops with English-language books in the Siam Square complex: the Book Chest (Soi 2) and Odeon Store (Soi 1). In the Silom Rd area, The Bookseller at 81 Patpong 1 has a wide selection, in particular art, photography, design and architecture.

Suksit Siam, opposite Wat Ratchabophit on Fuang Nakhon Rd, specialises in books on Thai politics, especially those representing the views of Sulak Sivaraksa and the progressive Santi Pracha Dhamma Institute (which has offices next door). The shop also has a number of mainstream titles on Thailand and Asia, both in English and Thai.

Elite Used Books, 593/5 Sukhumvit Rd at Soi 33/1 (near Villa supermarket) and at 1/12 Soi 3, Sukhumvit Rd (opposite Nana Inn), carries a good selection of used foreign-language titles, including English, Chinese, French, German and Swedish. The Chatuchak (Weekend) Market in Chatuchak Park is also a source of used, often out-of-print books in several languages. On Khao San Rd in Banglamphu, at least three streetside vendors specialise in used paperback novels and guidebooks, including many LP titles. Shaman Books (☎ 629-0418) at 71 Khao San Rd carries a good selection of guidebooks, maps and books on spirituality in several languages.

**Libraries** Besides offering an abundance of reading material, Bangkok's libraries make a peaceful escape from the heat, noise and traffic.

The National Library (☎ 281-5212) on Samsen Rd is an impressive institution with a huge collection of Thai material dating back several centuries as well as smaller numbers of foreign-language books. Membership is free. The Siam Society, 131 Soi Asoke, Sukhumvit Rd, and the National Museum, Na Phra That Rd, also have collections of English-language materials on the history, art and culture of Thailand.

Both American University Alumni (AUA) and the British Council have lending libraries; the British Council allows only members (residents over 16 years of age only) to borrow books, while AUA has a free public lending service. Both libraries cater primarily to Thai members, hence the emphasis tends to be on English-language teaching materials rather than, say, the latest fiction. Their main strengths are their up-to-date periodical sections – the British Council's selection is strictly British of course, while AUA's is all-American. See Cultural Centres below for addresses and phone numbers.

Although you won't be permitted to borrow books unless you're a Chula student, the library in Chulalongkorn University (south of Siam Square) is a good place to hang out – quiet and air-conditioned.

In a class all its own, the Neilson Hays Library (☎ 233-1731), at 193 Surawong Rd next to the British Club, is a historical monument as well as a good, all-purpose lending library. Built in 1921 by Dr Heyward Hays as a memorial to his wife Jennie Neilson Hays, the classic colonial Asian edifice is operated by the 100 year old Bangkok Library Association and is the oldest English-language library in Thailand. It has well over 20,000 volumes, including a good selection of children's books and titles on Thailand. The periodical section offers a few Thai magazines, and you can even borrow jigsaw puzzles. Although the building has only one air-con reading room, the ancient ceiling fans do a good job keeping the other sitting areas cool. The library's Rotunda Gallery hosts monthly art exhibitions and occasional art sales. Membership rates are 1300B per adult per year, 800B for children or 1700B per family. Opening hours are Monday to Saturday from 9.30 am to 4 pm, Sunday from 9.30 am to 12.30 pm. Free parking for members is available at the library's small car park near the corner of Surawong and Naret Rds.

The Foreign Correspondents Club of Thailand (see Cultural Centres below) also has a small selection of books on South-East Asian affairs, as well as current copies of the *International Herald Tribune* and other periodicals. Nonmembers are welcome to browse as long as they buy something at the bar or restaurant.

**Cultural Centres** Various Thai and foreign associations organise and support cultural events of a wide-ranging nature. They can be good places to meet Bangkok residents and Thais with an international outlook. Some of the more active organisations include:

Alliance Française – 29 Sathon Tai Rd (☎ 213-2122, 286-3841); French-language courses; translation services; monthly bulletin; French films; small library and bookshop; French and Thai cafeteria; music, arts and lecture programmes

American University Alumni (AUA) – 179 Ratchadamri Rd (☎ 252-7067/9); English and Thai-language courses; monthly newsletter; American films; TOEFL testing; Thai cafeteria; library; music, art and lecture programmes

British Council – 428 Soi 2, Siam Square, Rama I Rd (☎ 252-6136/8); English-language classes; monthly calendar of events; British films; music, art and drama programmes

Foreign Correspondents Club of Thailand – 12th floor, Jewelry Trade Center, Silom Rd (☎ 630-0043); home to wayward journalists and anyone else interested in keeping up with current Thai news, the FCCT meets every Wednesday at 8 pm for a talk by a local or visiting media personality; special events are often staged, and films with a news slant such as *Beyond Rangoon* are occasionally shown; bar and restaurant provide sweeping views of Central Bangkok

Goethe Institute (Thai-German Cultural Centre) – 18/1 Soi Attakanprasit, between Sathon Tai Rd and Soi Ngam Duphli (☎ 286-9002); German-language classes; monthly calendar of events; German restaurant; German films; art exhibits

Thailand Cultural Centre (TCC) – Ratchadaphisek Rd, Huay Khwang (☎ 247-0028); important centre hosting a variety of local and international cultural events, including musical and theatrical performances, art exhibits, cultural workshops and seminars

The TCC also sponsors the Cultural Information Service Centre, an information clearing house that issues a bimonthly calendar of notable cultural events throughout the country. Many of the events listed are held in Bangkok at foreign culture associations, universities, art galleries, film societies, theatres and music centres. This is the best single source for cultural happenings in Thailand; it even keeps track of obscure provincial festivals like Utaradit's Langsat Fair and Buriram's Sombat Isan Tai Festival. The calendar is available at the TCC as well as at the TAT office on Bamrung Meuang Rd.

**Religious Services** More than one reader has written to point out that not everyone who comes to Thailand is either an atheist or a Buddhist. For those seeking houses of worship in the Judaeo-Christian-Muslim tradition:

Anglican/Episcopal – Christ Church, 11 Convent Rd (☎ 234-3634)

Catholic – Assumption Cathedral, 23 Oriental Lane, Charoen Krung Rd (☎ 234-8556)
  Holy Redeemer Church, 123/19 Soi Ruam Rudi (behind US embassy) (☎ 253-6305)
  St Louis Church, Soi St Louis, Sathon Tai Rd (☎ 211-0220)
Jewish – Jewish Association of Thailand, 121/3 Soi 22, Sukhumvit Rd (☎ 258-2195)
Muslim – Haroon Mosque, Charoen Krung Rd (near GPO)
  Darool Aman Mosque, Phetburi Rd (near Ratthewi Circle)
Protestant – Calvary Baptist Church, 88 Soi 2, Sukhumvit Rd (☎ 251-8278, 234-3634)
  International Church of Bangkok, Student Christian Centre, 328 Phayathai Rd (☎ 215-0628/9)
Seventh-Day Adventist – Bangkok Ekamai Church, 57 Soi Charoenchai, Ekamai Rd (☎ 391-3593)
  Bangkok Chinese Church, 1325 Rama IV Rd (☎ 215-4529)

**Medical Services** Bangkok is Thailand's leading health care centre, with three university research hospitals, 12 public and private hospitals and hundreds of medical clinics. The Australian, US and UK embassies usually keep up-to-date lists of doctors who can speak English; for doctors who speak other languages, contact the relevant embassy.

Several store-front clinics in the Ploenchit Rd area specialise in lab tests for sexually transmitted diseases. According to *Bangkok Metro* magazine, Bangkok General Hospital has the most sophisticated HIV blood testing programme. Bangkok's better hospitals include:

Bangkok Adventist (Mission) Hospital – 430 Phitsanulok Rd (☎ 281-1422, 282-1100)
Bangkok Christian Hospital – 124 Silom Rd (☎ 233-6981/9, 235-1000)
Bangkok General Hospital – Soi 47, New Phetburi Rd (☎ 318-0066)
Bangkok Nursing Home – 9 Convent Rd (☎ 233-2610/9)
Bumrumgrad Hospital – 33 Soi 3, Sukhumvit Rd (☎ 253-0250)
Chao Phraya Hospital – 113/44 Pinklao Nakhon-Chaisi Rd, Bangkok Noi (☎ 434-6900)
Phayathai Hospital – 364/1 Si Ayuthaya Rd (☎ 245-2620) 943 Phahonyothin Rd (☎ 270-0780)
Samitivej Hospital – 133 Soi 49, Sukhumvit Rd (☎ 392-0010/9)
Samrong General Hospital – Soi 78, Sukhumvit Rd (☎ 393-2131/5)
St Louis Hospital – 215 Sathon Tai Rd (☎ 212-0033/48)

There are plenty of Chinese doctors and herbal dispensaries in Bangkok's Sampeng district, in the vicinity of Ratchawong, Charoen Krung, Yaowarat and Songwat Rds. The Pow Tai Dispensary at 572-574 Charoen Krung Rd has been operating since 1941.

**Emergency** All of the hospitals listed above offer 24 hour service. Bangkok does not have an emergency phone system staffed by English-speaking operators. Between 8 am and midnight, your best bet for English-speaking assistance is the Tourist Assistance Centre (☎ 281-5051, 282-8129). After midnight you'll have to rely on your own resources or on English-speaking hotel staff.

If you can find a Thai to call on your behalf, here are the city's main emergency numbers:

| | |
|---|---|
| Police | ☎ 191 or 123 |
| Fire | ☎ 199 |
| Ambulance | ☎ 252-2171/5 |

**Dangers & Annoyances** Bangkok's most heavily touristed areas, especially around Wat Phra Kaew and Khao San Rd, are favourite hunting grounds for Thai con artists of every ilk. They also tend to hang out near Soi Kasem San 1 and Soi Kasem San 2, opposite Mahboonkrong shopping centre and near Jim Thompson's House, and typically dress in Thai business suits and carry cellular phones. The Chao Phraya River Express piers between Tha Tien and Tha Phra Athit also attract cons who may try to intercept tourists as they get off the boats – the favourite line is 'Wat Pho (or Wat Phra Kaew, or Wat Arun) is closed today for repairs, government holiday etc'. Don't believe anyone on the street who tells you Wat Pho, Jim Thompson's House or some other attraction is closed for a holiday; check for yourself. More obvious are the tuk-tuk drivers who are out to make a commission by dragging you to a local silk or jewellery shop, even though you've requested an entirely different destination. In either case, if you accept an invitation for 'free' sightseeing or shopping, you're quite likely to end up wasting an afternoon or – as happens all too often – losing a lot of money.

For full details on common scams, see the Dangers & Annoyances section in the Facts for the Visitor chapter.

**Tourist Police** Under the Crime Suppression Division of the National Police Department, the tourist police are a separate force established in 1982 to deal with tourist problems. In Bangkok, some 500 English-speaking officers are stationed in tourist areas – their kiosks, cars and uniforms are clearly marked. If you have any problems related to criminal activity, try contacting the tourist police first. When they can't solve the problem, or if it's out of their jurisdiction, they can act as a bilingual liaison with the regular police. The head tourist police office (☎ 255-2964) at 29/1 Soi Lang Suan, Ploenchit Rd, deals with tourism-related crime, particularly gem fraud; they can be reached by dialling the special number ☎ 1699. The tourist police also have a branch at the TAT compound on Bamrung Meuang Rd.

### Wat Phra Kaew & Grand Palace
วัดพระแก้วและพระที่นั่งจักรี

Also called the Temple of the Emerald Buddha (official name: Wat Phra Si Ratana Satsadaram), this wat adjoins the Grand Palace on common ground which was consecrated in 1782, the first year of Bangkok rule. The 945,000 sq m grounds encompass over 100 buildings that represent 200 years of royal history and architectural experimentation. Most of the architecture, royal or sacred, can be classified Ratanakosin or old Bangkok style, with lots of minor variation.

The wat structures are extremely colourful, comprising gleaming, gilded *chedis* (stupas), polished orange and green roof tiles, mosaic-encrusted pillars and rich marble pediments. Extensive murals depicting scenes from the *Ramakian* (the Thai version of the Indian epic *Ramayana)* line the inside walls of the compound. Originally painted during Rama I's reign (1782-1809),

the murals have undergone several restorations, including a major one finished in time for the 1982 Bangkok/Chakri dynasty bicentennial. Divided into 178 sections, the murals illustrate the epic in its entirety, beginning at the north gate and moving clockwise around the compound.

Except for an anteroom here and there, the **Grand Palace** (Phra Borom Maharatchawong), is today used by the king only for certain ceremonial occasions such as Coronation Day (his current residence is Chitlada Palace in the northern part of the city), and is closed to the public. The exteriors of the four buildings are worth a swift perusal, however, for their royal bombast.

**Borobiman Hall** (east end), a French-inspired structure that served as a residence for Rama VI, is occasionally used to house visiting foreign dignitaries. In April 1981 General San Chitpatima used it as headquarters for an attempted coup. Next west is **Amarindra Hall**, originally a hall of justice but used today for coronation ceremonies.

Largest of the palace buildings is the triple winged **Chakri Mahaprasat**, literally 'Great Holy Hall of Chakri' but usually translated as 'Grand Palace Hall'. Built in 1882 by British architects using Thai labour, the exterior shows a peculiar blend of Italian Renaissance and traditional Thai architecture, a style often referred to as *faràng sài chá-daa* or 'European wearing a Thai classical dancer's headdress' because each wing is topped by a *mondòp*, a layered, heavily ornamented spire representing a Thai adaptation of the Hindu *mandapa* or shrine. The tallest of the mondóps, in the centre, contains the ashes of Chakri kings; the flanking mondóps enshrine the ashes of Chakri princes who never inherited the throne. Thai kings traditionally housed their huge harems in the mahaprasat's inner palace area, which was guarded by combat-trained female sentries.

Last from east to west is the Ratanakosin-style **Dusit Hall**, which initially served as a venue for royal audiences and later as a royal funerary hall.

Admission to the Wat Phra Kaew/Grand

## Emerald Buddha

The so-called Emerald Buddha or Phra Kaew, 60 to 75 cm high (depending on how it is measured), is actually made of a type of jasper or perhaps nephrite (a type of jade), depending on whom you believe. A definite aura of mystery surrounds the image, enhanced by the fact that it cannot be examined closely (it sits in a glass case, on a pedestal high above the heads of worshippers) and photography within the bòt is forbidden. Its mystery further adds to the occult significance of the image, which is considered the 'talisman' of the Thai kingdom, the legitimator of Thai sovereignty.

It is not known for certain where the image originated or who sculpted it, but it first appeared on record in 15th century Chiang Rai. Legend says it was sculpted in India and brought to Siam by way of Ceylon, but stylistically it seems to belong to the Chiang Saen or Lanna period (13th to 14th centuries). Sometime in the 15th century, the image is said to have been covered with plaster and gold leaf and placed in Chiang Rai's own Wat Phra Kaew (literally, 'Temple of the Jewel Holy Image'). While being transported elsewhere after a storm had damaged the chedi in which the image had been kept, the image supposedly lost its plaster covering in a fall. It next appeared in Lampang where it enjoyed a 32 year stay (again at a Wat Phra Kaew) until it was brought to Wat Chedi Luang in Chiang Mai.

Laotian invaders took the image from Chiang Mai in the mid-16th century and brought it to Luang Prabang in Laos. Later it was moved to Wiang Chan (Vientiane). When Thailand's King Taksin waged war against Laos 200 years later, the image was taken back to the Thai capital of Thonburi by General Chakri, who later succeeded Taksin as Rama I, the founder of the Chakri dynasty. Rama I had the Emerald Buddha moved to the new Thai capital in Bangkok and had two royal robes made for it, one to be worn in the hot season and one for the rainy season. Rama III added another to the wardrobe to be worn in the cool season. The three robes are still solemnly changed at the beginning of each season by the king himself. The huge bòt at Wat Phra Kaew in which it is displayed was built expressly for the purpose of housing the diminutive image. ∎

Palace compound is 125B, and opening hours are from 8.30 to 11.30 am and 1 to 3.30 pm. The admission fee includes entry to the Royal Thai Decorations & Coins Pavilion (on the same grounds) and to both Vimanmek ('the world's largest golden teak-wood mansion') and Abhisek Dusit Throne Hall, near the Dusit Zoo. (See the later Vimanmek/Abhisek entries for more details.)

Since wats are sacred places to Thai Buddhists, this one particularly so because of its monarchical associations, visitors should dress and behave decently. If you wear shorts or sleeveless shirts you may be refused admission; sarongs and baggy pants are sometimes available on loan at the entry area. For walking in the courtyard areas you must wear shoes with closed heels and toes – thongs aren't permitted. As in any temple compound, shoes should be removed before entering the main chapel (bòt) or sanctuaries (wihāan) of Wat Phra Kaew.

The most economical way of reaching Wat Phra Kaew and the Grand Palace is by air-con bus No 8 or 12. You can also take the Chao Phraya River Express, disembarking at Tha Chang.

## Wat Pho (Wat Phra Chetuphon)

A long list of superlatives for this one: the oldest and largest wat in Bangkok, it features the largest reclining Buddha and the largest collection of Buddha images in Thailand and was the earliest centre for public education. As a temple site Wat Pho dates back to the 16th century, but its current history really begins in 1781 with the complete rebuilding of the original monastery.

Narrow Chetuphon Rd divides the grounds in two, with each section surrounded by huge whitewashed walls. The most interesting part is the northern compound, which includes a very large bòt enclosed by a gallery of Buddha images and four wihāan, four large chedis commemorating the first three Chakri kings (Rama III has two chedis), 91 smaller chedis, an old tripitaka (Buddhist scriptures) library, a sermon hall, a large wihãan which houses the reclining Buddha and a school building for classes in Abhidhamma (Buddhist philosophy), plus several less important structures. The temple is currently undergoing a 53 million baht renovation.

Wat Pho is the national headquarters for the teaching and preservation of traditional Thai medicine, including Thai massage. A massage school convenes in the afternoons at the eastern end of the compound; a massage costs 180B per hour, 100B for a half hour. You can also study massage here in seven to 10 day courses.

The tremendous reclining Buddha, 46m long and 15m high, illustrates the passing of the Buddha into nirvana. The figure is modelled out of plaster around a brick core and finished in gold leaf. Mother-of-pearl inlay ornaments the eyes and feet of this colossal image, the feet displaying 108 different auspicious *laksanas* or characteristics of a Buddha. The images on display in the four wihãan surrounding the main bòt in the eastern part of the compound are interesting. Particularly beautiful are the Phra Jinnarat and Phra Jinachi Buddhas, in the west and south chapels, both from Sukhothai. The galleries extending between the four chapels feature no less than 394 gilded Buddha images. Rama I's remains are interred in the base of the presiding Buddha image in the bòt.

The temple rubbings for sale at Wat Pho and elsewhere in Thailand come from the 152 *Ramakian* reliefs, carved in marble and obtained from the ruins of Ayuthaya, which line the base of the large bòt. The rubbings are no longer taken directly from the panels but are rubbed from cement casts of the panels made years ago.

You may hire English, French, German or Japanese-speaking guides for 150B for one visitor, 200B for two, 300B for three. Also on the premises are a few astrologers and palmists.

The temple is open to the public from 8 am to 5 pm daily; admission is 10B. The ticket booth is closed from noon to 1 pm. Air-con bus Nos 6, 8 and 12 stop near Wat Pho. The nearest Chao Phraya River Express pier is Tha Tien.

## Wat Mahathat
วัดมหาธาตุ

Founded in the 1700s, Wat Mahathat is a national centre for the Mahanikai monastic sect and houses one of Bangkok's two Buddhist universities, Mahathat Rajavidyalaya. The university is the most important place of Buddhist learning in mainland South-East Asia today; the Lao, Vietnamese and Cambodian governments send selected monks to further their studies here.

Mahathat and the surrounding area have developed into an informal Thai cultural centre of sorts, though this may not be obvious at first glance. A daily open-air market features traditional Thai herbal medicine, and out on the street you'll find a string of shops selling herbal cures and offering Thai massage. On weekends, a large produce market held on the temple grounds brings people from all over Bangkok and beyond. Opposite the main entrance on the other side of Maharat Rd is a large religious amulet market.

The monastery's International Buddhist Meditation Centre offers meditation instruction in English on the second Saturday of every month from 2 to 6 pm in the Dhamma Vicaya Hall. Those interested in more intensive instruction should contact the monks in Section 5 of the temple compound.

The temple complex is officially open to visitors from 9 am to 5 pm every day and on *wan phrá*, Buddhist holy days (the full and new moons every fortnight). Admission is free.

Wat Mahathat is right across the street from Wat Phra Kaew, on the west side of Sanam Luang (Royal Field). Air-con bus Nos 8 and 12 both pass by it, and the nearest Chao Phraya River Express pier is Tha Maharat.

## Wat Traimit
วัดไตรมิตร

The attraction at the Temple of the Golden Buddha is, of course, the impressive three-metre-tall, 5.5-tonne, solid-gold Buddha image, which gleams like no other gold artefact I've ever seen.

Sculpted in the graceful Sukhothai style, the image was 'rediscovered' some 40 years ago beneath a stucco or plaster exterior when it fell from a crane while being moved to a new building within the temple compound. It has been theorised that the covering was added to protect it from 'marauding hordes', either during the late Sukhothai period or later in the Ayuthaya period when the city was under siege by the Burmese. The temple itself is said to date from the early 13th century.

The golden image can be seen every day from 8 am to 5 pm, and admission is 10B. Nowadays lots of camera-toting tour groups haunt the place (there's even a moneychanger on the premises), so it pays to arrive in the early morning if you want a more traditional feel. Wat Traimit is near the intersection of Yaowarat and Charoen Krung Rds, near Hualamphong station.

## Wat Arun
วัดอรุณ

The striking Temple of Dawn, named after the Indian god of dawn, Aruna, appears in all the tourist brochures and is located on the Thonburi side of the Chao Phraya River. The present wat was built on the site of 17th century Wat Jang, which served as the palace and royal temple of King Taksin when Thonburi was the Thai capital; hence, it was the last home of the Emerald Buddha before Rama I brought it across the river to Bangkok.

The 82m *prang* (Khmer-style tower) was constructed during the first half of the 19th century by Rama II and Rama III. The unique design elongates the typical Khmer prang into a distinctly Thai shape. Its brick core has a plaster covering embedded with a mosaic of broken, multihued Chinese porcelain, a common temple ornamentation in the early Ratanakosin period when Chinese ships calling at Bangkok used tonnes of old porcelain as ballast. Steep stairs reach a lookout point about halfway up the prang from where there are fine views of Thonburi and the river. During certain festivals, hundreds of lights illuminate the outline of the prang at night.

Also worth a look is the interior of the bòt.

The main Buddha image is said to have been designed by Rama II himself. The murals date to the reign of Rama V; particularly impressive is one that depicts Prince Siddhartha encountering examples of birth, old age, sickness and death outside his palace walls, an experience which led him to abandon the worldly life. The ashes of Rama II are interred in the base of the bòt's presiding Buddha image.

The temple looks more impressive from the river than it does from up close, though the peaceful wat grounds make a very nice retreat from the hustle and bustle of Bangkok. Between the prang and the ferry pier is a huge sacred banyan tree.

Wat Arun is open daily from 8.30 am to 5.30 pm; admission is 10B. To reach Wat Arun from the Bangkok side, catch a cross-river ferry from Tha Tien at Thai Wang Rd. Crossings are frequent and cost only 1B.

## Wat Benchamabophit
วัดเบญจมบพิตร

This wat of white Carrara marble (hence its tourist name, 'Marble Temple') was built at the turn of the century under Chulalongkorn (Rama V). The large cruciform bòt is a prime example of modern Thai wat architecture. The base of the central Buddha image, a copy of Phitsanulok's Phra Phuttha Chinnarat, contains the ashes of Rama V. The courtyard behind the bòt exhibits 53 Buddha images (33 originals and 20 copies) representing famous figures and styles from all over Thailand and other Buddhist countries – an education in itself if you're interested in Buddhist iconography.

Wat Ben is on the corner of Si Ayuthaya and Rama V Rds, diagonally opposite the south-west corner of Chitlada Palace; it's open daily and admission is 10B. Bus Nos 2 (air-con) and 72 stop nearby.

## Wat Saket
วัดสระเกศ

Wat Saket is an undistinguished temple except for the Golden Mount (Phu Khao Thong) on the western side of the grounds

which provides a good view out over Bangkok rooftops. This artificial hill was created
when a large chedi under construction by
Rama III collapsed because the soft soil
beneath would not support it. The resulting
mud-and-brick hill was left to sprout weeds
until Rama IV built a small chedi on its crest.

Frank Vincent, a well travelled American
writer, describes his 1871 ascent in *The Land
of the White Elephant*:

From the summit...may be obtained a fine view of the
city of Bangkok and its surroundings; though this is
hardly a correct statement, for you see very few of the
dwelling-houses of the city; here and there a wat, the
river with its shipping, the palace of the King, and a
waving sea of cocoa-nut and betel-nut palms, is about
all that distinctly appears. The general appearance of
Bangkok is that of a large, primitive village, situated
in and mostly concealed by a virgin forest of almost
impenetrable density.

Rama V later added to the structure and
housed a Buddha relic from India (given to
him by the British government) in the chedi.
The concrete walls were added during WWII
to prevent the hill from eroding. Every
November there is a big festival on the
grounds of Wat Saket, which includes a
candle-lit procession up the Golden Mount.

Admission to Wat Saket is free except for
the final approach to the summit of the
Golden Mount, which costs 5B. The temple
is within walking distance of the Democracy
Monument; air-con bus Nos 11 and 12 pass
nearby.

### Wat Rajanadda (Ratchanatda)
วัดราชนัดดา

Across Mahachai Rd from Wat Saket and
behind the old Chalerm Thai movie theatre,
this temple dates from the mid-19th century.
It was built under Rama III and is an unusual
specimen, possibly influenced by Burmese
models.

The wat has a well known market selling
Buddhist amulets or magic charms (*phrá
phim*) in all sizes, shapes and styles. The
amulets not only feature images of the
Buddha, but also famous Thai monks and
Indian deities. Full Buddha images are also

---

### Buddha Amulets

In the Thai language, Buddhas or *phrá phim*
are never 'bought' or 'sold', they are 'rented'.
The images are purported to protect the wearer
from physical harm, though some act as 'love
charms'. Amulets that are considered to be
particularly powerful tend to cost thousands of
baht and are worn by soldiers, taxi drivers and
other Thai believers working in high-risk professions. ■

---

for sale. Wat Rajanadda is an expensive place
to purchase a charm, but a good place to look.

### Wat Bovornives (Bowonniwet)
วัดบวรนิเวศ

Wat Bowon, on Phra Sumen Rd in Banglamphu, is the national headquarters for the
Thammayut monastic sect, the minority sect
in Thai Buddhism. King Mongkut, founder
of the Thammayuts, began a royal tradition
by residing here as a monk – in fact he was
the abbot of Wat Bowon for several years.
King Bhumibol and Crown Prince Vajiralongkorn, as well as several other males in the royal
family, have been temporarily ordained as
monks here. The temple was founded in
1826, when it was known as Wat Mai.

Bangkok's second Buddhist university,
Mahamakut University, is housed at Wat
Bowon. India, Nepal and Sri Lanka all send
selected monks to study here. Across the
street from the main entrance to the wat are
an English-language Buddhist bookshop and
a Thai herbal clinic.

Because of its royal status, visitors should
be particularly careful to dress properly for
admittance to this wat – no shorts or sleeveless shirts.

### Lak Meuang (City Pillar)
ศาลหลักเมือง

The City Pillar is across the street from the
eastern wall of Wat Phra Kaew, at the southern
end of Sanam Luang. This shrine encloses a
wooden pillar erected by Rama I in 1782 to

## Walking Tour – Ratanakosin Temples & River

This walk covers the area of Ko Ratanakosin (Ratanakosin Island), which rests in a bend of the river in the middle of Bangkok and contains some of the city's most historic architecture – Wat Phra Kaew, the Grand Palace, Wat Pho, Wat Mahathat and Wat Suthat (each described in detail in the main text) – and prestigious universities. The river bank in this area is dotted with piers and markets, worthwhile attractions in themselves. Despite its name, Ko Ratanakosin is not an island at all, though in the days when Bangkok was known as the 'Venice of the East', Khlong Banglamphu and Khlong Ong Ang – two lengthy adjoining canals that run parallel to the river to the east – were probably large enough for the area to seem like an island.

This circular walk (one to three hours depending on your pace) begins at **Lak Meuang** (City Pillar), a shrine to Bangkok's city spirit. At the intersection of Ratchadamnoen Nai and Lak Meuang Rds, opposite the southern end of Sanam Luang, the shrine can be reached by taxi, by air-con bus Nos 3, 6, 7 and 39, by ordinary bus Nos 39, 44 and 47 or on foot if you're already in the Royal Hotel area. (If the Chao Phraya River Express is more convenient, you can start this walk from Tha Tien). By tradition, every city in Thailand must have a foundation stone which embodies the city spirit *(phĭi meuang)* and from which intercity distances are measured. This is Bangkok's most important site of animistic worship; believers throng the area day and night, bringing offerings of flowers, incense, whisky, fruit and even cooked food.

From Lak Meuang, walk south across Lak Meuang Rd and along Sanamchai Rd with the Grand Palace/Wat Phra Kaew walls to your right until you come to Chetuphon Rd on the right (the second street after the palace walls end, approximately 500m from Lak Meuang). Turn right onto Chetuphon Rd and enter **Wat Pho** through the second portico. Officially named Wat Phra Chetuphon, this is Bangkok's oldest temple and is famous for its huge reclining Buddha and for its massage school, the oldest in Thailand. After you've done the rounds of the various sanctuaries within the monastery grounds, exit through the same door and turn right onto Chetuphon Rd, heading towards the river.

Chetuphon Rd ends at Maharat Rd after 100m or so; turn right at Maharat and stroll north, passing the **market** area on your left. At the northern end of this block, Maharat Rd crosses Thai Wang Rd. On the south-western corner is an older branch of the **Bangkok Bank**; turn left on Thai Wang to glimpse a row of rare early Ratanakosin-era shophouses. The city has plans to renovate and preserve this area. If you continue along Thai Wang Rd to the river you'll arrive at **Tha Tien**, one of the pier stops for the Chao Phraya River Express. From an adjacent pier you can catch one of the regular ferries across the Chao Phraya to **Wat Arun**, which features one of Bangkok's most striking prangs, a tall Hindu/Khmer-style pagoda.

Stroll back along Thai Wang Rd to Maharat Rd and turn left to continue the walking tour. On the left along Maharat Rd are two government buildings serving as headquarters for the departments of internal trade and public welfare. On the right are the whitewashed west walls of the Grand Palace. Two air-con city buses, Nos 8 and 12, stop along this stretch of Maharat – something to keep in mind when you've had enough walking. About 500m from the Thai Wang Rd intersection, Maharat Rd crosses Na Phra Lan Rd; turn left to reach **Tha Chang**, another express boat stop.

The entrance to the **Grand Palace/Wat Phra Kaew** is on the right (south) side of Na Phra Lan Rd less than 100m from Maharat Rd. The Grand Palace has been supplanted by Chitlada Palace as the primary residence of the royal family, but it is still used for ceremonial occasions. Wat Phra Kaew is a gleaming example of Bangkok temple architecture at its most baroque. Note that all visitors to the palace and temple grounds must be suitably attired. Temple staff can provide wraparound sarongs for bare legs. Shops opposite the main entrance to the complex offer film, cold drinks, curries and noodles; there is also a small post office.

After you've had enough of wandering around the palace and temple grounds, exit via the same doorway and turn left towards the river again. On the right you'll pass the entrance to **Silpakorn University**, Thailand's premier university for fine arts studies. Originally founded as the School of Fine Arts by Italian artist Corrado Feroci, the university campus includes part of an old Rama I palace. A small bookshop inside the gate to the left offers a number of English-language books on Thai art. At Maharat Rd, turn right (past the Siam City Bank on the corner) and almost immediately you'll see vendor tables along the street. On the tables are cheap amulets representing various Hindu and Buddhist deities. Better quality religious amulets are found a bit farther north along Maharat Rd in the large **amulet market** between the road and the river. Walk back into the market area to appreciate how extensive the amulet trade is. Opposite the amulet market on Maharat Rd is **Wat Mahathat**, another of Bangkok's older temples and the headquarters for the country's largest monastic sect.

If you're hungry by now, this is an excellent place on the circuit to take time out for a snack or meal. Head back along Maharat Rd from the amulet market just a few metres and turn right at Trok Thawiphon (the romanised sign reads 'Thawephon'). This alley leads to **Tha Maharat**, yet another express boat stop; on either side of the pier is a riverside restaurant – *Maharat* to the left and *Lan Theh* to the right. Although the food at both is quite adequate, most local residents head past the Lan Theh (no roman script sign) and into a warren of smaller restaurants and food vendors along the river. The food here is very good and extremely inexpensive – to order, all you'll need is a pointing index finger. Rumour has it that these vendor stalls may soon be forced to leave to accommodate the planned Ko Ratanakosin restoration project.

Renewed and refuelled, start walking north again along Maharat past the amulet market and Wat Mahathat to Phra Chan Rd, around 80m from Trok Thawiphon. Turn left to reach Tha Phra Chan if you want to catch an express boat north or south along the river, or turn right to reach Sanam Luang, the end of the tour. If you take the latter route, you'll pass **Thammasat University** on the left. Thammasat is known for its law and political science faculties; it was also the site of the bloody October 1976 demonstrations in which hundreds of Thai students were killed or wounded by military troops. Opposite the university entrance are several very good noodle shops. ■

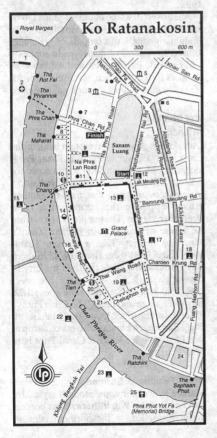

**Ko Ratanakosin**

| | |
|---|---|
| 1 | Thonburi (Bangkok Noi) Station |
| 2 | Siriraj Hospital |
| 3 | National Museum |
| 4 | National Theatre |
| 5 | National Gallery |
| 6 | Royal Hotel |
| 7 | Thammasat University |
| 8 | Amulet Market |
| 9 | Wat Mahathat |
| 10 | Siam City Bank |
| 11 | Silpakom University |
| 12 | Lak Meuang (City Pillar) |
| 13 | Wat Phra Kaew |
| 14 | No 8 Bus |
| 15 | Wat Rakhang Khositaram |
| 16 | No 12 Bus |
| 17 | Wat Ratchapradit |
| 18 | Wat Ratchabophit |
| 19 | Wat Pho (Wat Phra Chetuphon) |
| 20 | Bangkok Bank |
| 21 | Market |
| 22 | Wat Arun |
| 23 | Wat Kalayanimit |
| 24 | Pak Khlong Market |
| 25 | Santa Cruz Church |

represent the founding of the new Bangkok capital. Later, during the reign of Rama V, five other idols were added to the shrine. The spirit of the pillar is considered the city's guardian deity and receives the daily supplications of countless Thai worshippers, some of whom commission classical Thai dancers to perform *lákhon chatrii* at the shrine. Some of the offerings include severed pigs' heads with sticks of incense sprouting from their foreheads.

## Maha Uma Devi Temple
วัดมหาอุมาเทวี (วัดแขก)

This small Hindu temple sits alongside busy Silom Rd (near the Pan Rd intersection) in Bangrak, a district with a high concentration of Indian residents. The principal temple structure, built in the 1860s by Tamil immigrants, features a six metre facade of intertwined, full-colour Hindu deities, topped by a gold-plated copper dome. The temple's main shrine contains three main deities: Jao Mae Maha Umathewi (Uma Devi, also known as Shakti, Shiva's consort) at the centre; her son Phra Khanthakuman (Khanthakumara or Subramaniam) on the right; and her elephant-headed son Phra Phikhkanesawora (Ganesha) on the left. Along the left interior wall sit rows of Shivas, Vishnus and other Hindu deities, as well as a few Buddhas, so that just about any non-Muslim, non-Judaeo-Christian Asian can worship here – Thai and Chinese devotees come to pray along with Indians. Bright yellow marigold garlands are sold at the entrance for this purpose.

An interesting ritual takes place in the temple at noon on most days, when a priest brings out a tray carrying an oil lamp, coloured powders and holy water. He sprinkles the water on the hands of worshippers who in turn pass their hands through the lamp flame for purification; then they dip their fingers in the coloured powder and daub prayer marks on their foreheads. On Fridays at around 11.30 am, *prasada* (blessed vegetarian food) is offered to devotees.

Thais call this temple Wat Khaek – *khàek* is a Thai colloquial expression for people of Indian descent. The literal translation is 'guest', an obvious euphemism for a group of people you don't particularly want as permanent residents; hence most Indians living permanently in Thailand don't appreciate the term.

## Wat Thammamongkhon
วัดธรรมมงคล

East of Bangkok on Sukhumvit Soi 101, this 95m-high chedi resulted from a monk's vision. While meditating in 1991, Phra Viriyang Sirintharo saw a giant jade boulder; at around the same time a 32 tonne block of solid jade was discovered in a Canadian riverbed. Viriyang raised funds to purchase the block (US$560,000) and commissioned a 14 tonne Buddha sculpture (carried out by Carrara sculptors) to go in a pavilion at Thammamongkhon; an image of this magnitude deserved a massive chedi. The chedi, which contains a hair of the Buddha presented to Thailand by Bangladesh's Sangharaja (head of a Theravada monastic order), features a lift so you can ride to the top. The chedi's grand opening ceremony was held in 1993.

A leftover 10 tonne chunk of jade is to be carved into a figure of Kuan Yin (the Chinese Buddhist goddess of compassion). Smaller leftovers – a total of nearly eight tonnes – will be made into amulets and sold to worshippers for US$20 each, to raise money for 5000 day care centres throughout Thailand.

## Wat Phailom
วัดไผ่ล้อม

Outside Bangkok, on the eastern bank of the Chao Phraya River in Pathum Thani Province, this old, wooden Mon wat is noted for the tens of thousands of open-billed storks *(Anastomus oscitans)* that nest in bamboo groves opposite the temple area from December to June. The temple is 51 km from the centre of Bangkok in Pathum Thani's Sam Kok district. Take a Pathum Thani-bound bus (10B) from Bangkok's Northern Bus Terminal and cross the river by ferry to the wat grounds.

Bus No 33 from Sanam Luang goes all the way to Phailom and back. The Chao Phraya River Express tours from Tha Maharat to Bang Pa-In each Sunday also make a stop at Wat Phailom – see River & Canal Trips later in this chapter.

## Other Temples & Shrines

Marked by its enormous, modern-style 32m standing Buddha, **Wat Intharawihan** borders Wisut Kasat Rd, at the northern edge of

Banglamphu. Check out the hollowed-out air-con stupa with a lifelike image of Luang Phaw Toh. Entry to Wat In is by donation.

**Wat Suthat**, begun by Rama I and completed by Rama II and Rama III, boasts a wihãan with gilded bronze Buddha images (including Phra Si Sakayamuni, one of the largest surviving Sukhothai bronzes) and colourful *jataka* murals depicting scenes from the Buddha's life. Wat Suthat holds a special place in the Thai national religion because of its association with Brahman priests who perform important annual ceremonies, such as the Royal Ploughing Ceremony in May. These priests perform rites at two Hindu shrines near the wat – the Thewa Sathaan (Deva Sthan) across the street to the north-west and the smaller Saan Jao Phitsanu to the east. The former contains images of Shiva and Ganesha while the latter is dedicated to Vishnu. The wat holds the rank of Rachavoramahavihan, the highest royal temple grade; the ashes of Rama VIII (Ananda Mahidol, the current king's deceased older brother) are contained in the base of the main Buddha image in Suthat's wihãan.

At nearby **Sao Ching-Cha**, the Giant Swing, a spectacular Brahman festival in honour of the Hindu god Shiva used to take place each year until it was stopped during the reign of Rama VII. Participants would swing in ever-heightening arcs in an effort to reach a bag of gold suspended from a 15m bamboo pole – many died trying. The Giant Swing is a block south of the Democracy Monument.

**Wat Chong Nonsii**, off Ratchadaphisek Rd near the Bangkok side of the river, contains notable jataka murals painted between 1657 and 1707. It is the only surviving Ayuthaya-era temple in which both the murals and architecture are of the same period with no renovations. As a single, 'pure' architectural and painting unit, it's considered quite important for the study of late Ayuthaya art; the painting style is similar to that found in the Phetburi monasteries of Wat Yai Suwannaram and Wat Ko Kaew Sutharam.

There are also numerous temples on the Thonburi side of the river which are less visited. These include **Wat Kalayanimit** with its towering Buddha statue and, outside, the biggest bronze bell in Thailand; **Wat Pho Bang-O** with its carved gables and Rama III-era murals; **Wat Chaloem Phrakiat**, a temple with tiled gables; and **Wat Thawng Nophakhun** with its Chinese-influenced *uposatha* (bòt). See the Fine Arts Commission's *Canals of Thonburi* map, available from TAT, for more information and the locations of these wats. **Wat Yannawa**, on the Bangkok bank of the river near Tha Sathon, was built during Rama II's reign and features a building resembling a Chinese junk.

Just off Chakraphet Rd in the Pahurat district is a **Sikh Temple** (Sri Gurusingh Sabha) where visitors are welcome to walk around. Basically it's a large hall, somewhat reminiscent of a mosque interior, devoted to the worship of the Guru Granth Sahib, the 16th century Sikh holy book which is itself considered the last of the religion's 10 great gurus or teachers. Prasada is distributed among devotees every morning around 9 am.

On the corner of Ratchaprarop and Ploenchit Rds, next to the Grand Hyatt Erawan Hotel, is a large shrine, Saan Phra Phrom (also known as the **Erawan Shrine**), which was originally built to ward off bad luck during the construction of the first Erawan Hotel (torn down to make way for the Grand Hyatt Erawan some years ago). The four-headed deity at the centre of the shrine is Brahma (Phra Phrom in Thai), the Hindu god of creation. Apparently the developers of the original Erawan (named after Brahma's three-headed elephant mount) first erected a typical Thai spirit house but decided to replace it with the more impressive Brahman shrine after several serious mishaps delayed the hotel construction. Worshippers who have a wish granted may return to the shrine to commission the musicians and dancers who are always on hand for an impromptu performance.

Since the success of the Erawan Shrine, several other flashy Brahman shrines have been erected around the city next to large hotels and office buildings. Next to the **World Trade Centre** on Ploenchit Rd is a large shrine containing a standing Brahma, a rather unusual posture for Thai Brahmans.

Another hotel shrine worth seeing is the lingam (phallus) shrine behind the **Hilton International** in tiny Nai Loet Park off Withayu Rd. Clusters of carved stone and wooden lingam surround a spirit house and shrine built by millionaire businessman Nai Loet to honour Jao Mae Thapthim, a female deity thought to reside in the old banyan tree on the site. Someone who made an offering shortly thereafter had a baby, and the shrine has received a steady stream of worshippers – mostly young women seeking fertility – ever since. Nai Loet Park is fenced off so you must wind your way through the Hilton complex to visit the shrine. Or come via the Khlong Saen Saep canal taxi; ask to get off at Saphaan Withayu (Radio Bridge) – look for the TV3 building on the north side of the canal.

### Churches

Several Catholic churches were founded in Bangkok in the 17th to 19th centuries. Worth seeing is the **Holy Rosary Church** (known in Thai as Wat Kalawan, from the Portuguese 'Calvario') in Talaat Noi near the River City shopping complex. Originally built in 1787 by the Portuguese, the Holy Rosary was rebuilt by Vietnamese and Cambodian Catholics around the turn of the century, hence the French inscriptions beneath the stations of the cross. This old church has a splendid set of Romanesque stained-glass windows, gilded ceilings and a very old Christ statue that is carried through the streets during Easter celebrations. The alley leading to the church is lined with old Bangkok shophouse architecture.

The **Church of the Immaculate Conception** near Krungthon Bridge (north of Phra Pinklao Bridge) was also founded by the Portuguese and later taken over by Cambodians fleeing civil war. The present building is an 1837 reconstruction on the church's 1674 site. One of the original church buildings survives and is now used as a museum

housing holy relics. Another Portuguese-built church is 1913 vintage **Santa Cruz** (Wat Kuti Jiin) on the Thonburi side near Phra Phut Yot Fa (Memorial) Bridge (sometimes also called Saphaan Phut). The architecture shows Chinese influence, hence the Thai name 'Chinese monastic residence'.

**Christ Church**, at 11 Convent Rd next to Bangkok Nursing Home, was established as English Chapel in 1864. The current Gothic-style structure, opened in 1904, features thick walls and a tiled roof braced with teak beams; the carved teak ceiling fans date to 1919.

### National Museum
พิพิธภัณฑ์แห่งชาติ

On Na Phra That Rd, the west side of Sanam Luang, the National Museum is the largest museum in South-East Asia and an excellent place to learn something about Thai art before heading upcountry. All periods and styles are represented from Dvaravati to Ratanakosin, and English-language literature is available. Room 23 contains a well maintained collection of traditional musical instruments from Thailand, Laos, Cambodia and Indonesia. Other permanent exhibits include ceramics, clothing and textiles, woodcarving, royal regalia, Chinese art and weaponry.

The museum buildings were originally built in 1782 as the palace of Rama I's viceroy, Prince Wang Na. Rama V turned it into a museum in 1884.

In addition to the exhibition halls, the museum grounds contain the restored **Buddhaisawan (Phutthaisawan) Chapel**. Inside the chapel (built in 1795) are some well preserved original murals and one of the country's most revered Buddha images, Phra Phut Sihing. Legend says the image came from Ceylon, but art historians attribute it to 13th century Sukhothai.

Free English tours of the museum are given by National Museum volunteers on Wednesday (Buddhism) and Thursday (Thai art, religion and culture), starting from the ticket pavilion at 9.30 am. These guided

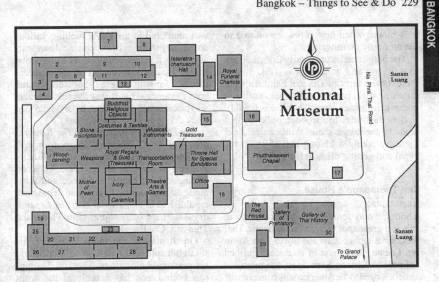

National
Museum

1  Sukhothai Art
2  Sukhothai Art
3  Lanna Art
4  Lanna Art
5  Buddha Images
6  Coins
7  Chao Phraya Yommarat
   Memorial Building
8  Chinese House
9  Ayuthaya Art
10  Ayuthaya Art
11  Decorative Arts
12  Ratanakosin (Bangkok
   Period) Art
13  Toilets
14  Coffee Shop
15  Pavilion (Sala)
16  Pavilion (Sala)
17  Pavilion (Sala)
18  Pavilion (Sala)
19  Lopburi Art
20  Hindu Gods
21  Lopburi Art
22  Director's Office
23  Toilets
24  Asian Art
25  Srivijaya Art
26  Java Art
27  Dvaravati Art
28  Dvaravati Art
29  Toilets
30  Baggage Check, Telephone
   & Museum Shop

tours are excellent and many people have written to recommend them. The tours are also conducted in German (Thursday), French (Wednesday) and Japanese (Wednesday). For more information on the tours, contact the volunteers on ☎ 215-8173. The museum is open from 9 am to 4 pm Wednesday to Sunday; admission is 20B.

### Royal Barges
เรือพระที่นั่ง

The royal barges are long, fantastically ornamented boats used in ceremonial processions on the river. The largest is 50m long and requires a rowing crew of 50 men, plus seven umbrella bearers, two helmsmen, two navigators, as well as a flagman, rhythm-keeper and chanter.

The barges are kept in sheds on the Thonburi side of the river. They're on Khlong Bangkok Noi, near the Phra Pinklao Bridge. *Suphannahong*, the king's personal barge, is the most important of the boats. One of the best times to see the fleet in action on the river is during the royal *kathin* ceremony at the end of *phansãa* (the Buddhist Rains Retreat, ending with an October or November new moon) when new robes are offered to the monastic contingent.

The barge shed is open daily from 8.30 am to 4.30 pm and admission is 10B. To get there, take a ferry to Tha Rot Fai, then walk down the street parallel to the tracks until you come to a bridge over the *khlong* (canal). Follow the bridge to a wooden walkway that leads to the barge sheds. You can also get there by taking a khlong taxi (5B) up the canal and getting off near the bridge.

### Jim Thompson's House
บ้านจิมทอมสัน

Though it may sound corny when described, this is a great spot to visit for authentic Thai residential architecture and South-East Asian art. Located at the end of an undistinguished soi next to Khlong Saen Saep, the premises once belonged to the American silk entrepreneur Jim Thompson, who deserves most of the credit for the current worldwide popularity of Thai silk.

Born in Delaware in 1906, Thompson was a New York architect who briefly served in the Office of Strategic Services (OSS, forerunner of the CIA) in Thailand during WWII. After the war he found New York too tame and moved to Bangkok. Thai silk caught his connoisseur's eye; he sent samples around to fashion houses in Milan, London and Paris, gradually building a steady worldwide clientele for a craft that had been in danger of dying out.

A tireless promoter of traditional Thai arts and culture, Thompson collected parts of various derelict Thai homes in central Thailand and had them reassembled in the current location in 1959. Although for the most part assembled in typical Thai style, one striking departure from tradition is the way each wall has its exterior side facing the house's interior, thus exposing the wall's bracing system to residents and guests.

While out for an afternoon walk in the Cameron Highlands of west Malaysia in 1967, Thompson disappeared under quite mysterious circumstances; he has never been heard from since. That same year his sister

was murdered in the USA, fuelling various conspiracy theories to explain the disappearance. Was it a man-eating tiger? Communist spies? Business rivals? The most recent theory – for which there is apparently some hard evidence – has it that the silk magnate was accidentally run over by a Malaysian truck driver who hid his remains.

*The Legendary American – The Remarkable Career & Strange Disappearance of Jim Thompson* (Houghton Mifflin, 1970), by William Warren, is an excellent book on Thompson, his career, residence and intriguing disappearance. In Thailand, it has been republished as *Jim Thompson: The Legendary American of Thailand* (Jim Thompson Thai Silk Co, Bangkok).

On display in the main house are his small but splendid Asian art collection and his personal belongings. The Jim Thompson Foundation has a table at the front where you can buy prints of old Siam maps and Siamese horoscopes in postcard and poster form.

The house, on Soi Kasem San 2, Rama I Rd, is open Monday to Saturday from 9 am to 5 pm. Admission is 100B (proceeds go to Bangkok's School for the Blind) but you may wander around the grounds for free. Students under 25 years get in for 40B. The rather sleazy khlong at the end of the soi is one of Bangkok's most lively. Beware of well dressed touts in the soi who will tell you Thompson's house is closed – it's just a ruse to take you on a buying spree.

### Wang Suan Phakkard (Phakkat)
วังสวนผักกาด

The Lettuce Farm Palace, once the residence of Princess Chumbon of Nakhon Sawan, is a collection of five traditional wooden Thai houses containing varied displays of art, antiques and furnishings. The landscaped grounds are a peaceful oasis complete with ducks and swans and a semi-enclosed garden reminiscent of Japanese gardens.

The diminutive **Lacquer Pavilion** at the back of the complex dates from the Ayuthaya period (the building originally sat in a monastery compound on the Chao Phraya River, just south of Ayuthaya) and features gold-leaf jataka and *Ramayana* murals as well as scenes from daily Ayuthaya life. Larger residential structures at the front of the complex contain displays of Khmer Hindu and Buddhist art, Ban Chiang ceramics and a nice collection of historic Buddhas, including a beautiful late U Thong-style image. In the noise and confusion of Bangkok, the gardens offer a tranquil retreat.

The grounds are open daily except Sundays from 9 am to 4 pm and admission is 150B (students 30B). It's on Si Ayuthaya Rd, between Phayathai and Ratchaprarop Rds; air-con bus No 3 passes by right in front.

## Vimanmek Teak Mansion (Phra Thii Nang Wimanmek)
พระที่นั่งวิมานเมฆ

Originally constructed on Ko Si Chang in 1868 and moved to the present site in the Dusit Palace grounds in 1910, this beautiful L-shaped, three-storey mansion contains 81 rooms, halls and anterooms and is said to be the world's largest golden teak building. Teak was once one of Thailand's greatest natural resources (it has since all but disappeared) and makes an especially good wood for building houses because it's so durable. A special oil contained in the wood makes teak resistant to heavy rain and hot sun and also repels insects. A solid piece of teak can easily last 1000 years.

### Rama V Cult

Since 1991 a new spirit cult has swept the Thai public, involving the veneration of the spirit of Rama V (1868-1910; also known as King Chulalongkorn or, to the Thais, as Chula Chom Klao). The cult is particularly strong in Bangkok and other large urban centres, since its members tend to be middle-class and nouveau riche Thais with careers in commerce or the professions.

In Bangkok the most visible devotional activities are focused on a bronze statue of Rama V standing in Royal Plaza, opposite the south-east corner of the Vimanmek/Abihisek throne hall compound from where the venerated king once ruled the kingdom as absolute monarch. Although originally intended as mere historical commemoration, the statue has quite literally become a religious shrine, where every Tuesday evening thousands of Bangkokians come to offer candles, flowers (predominantly pink roses), incense and bottles of whisky to the newly ordained demigod. Worship of the statue begins at around 9 pm and continues till early in the morning.

All over Thailand Rama V portraits are selling briskly. Some devotees place the portraits at home altars, while others wear tiny, coloured porcelain likenesses of the king on gold chains around their necks in place of the usual Buddhist amulet. In some social circles Rama V amulets are now more common than any other phrá phim.

No single event occurred to ignite the Rama V movement; rather, its growth can be traced to a series of events beginning with the 1991 military coup – which caused the intelligentsia to once again lose faith in the constitutional monarchy – on top of the 1990-92 economic recession. Along with worsening traffic and a host of other problems, these events brought about an unfocused, general mistrust of modern politics, technology and affluence among many Thais, who began looking for a new spiritual outlet with some historical relevancy. They seized on Rama V, who without the help of a parliament or the military had brought Thai nationalism to the fore while fending off European colonialisation. He is also considered a champion of the common person for his abolition of slavery and corvée (the requirement that every citizen be available for state labour when called).

Ironically few Rama V cultists realise that the much revered Rama V conceded substantial Thai territory to French Indochina and British Malaya during his reign – for a total loss of land greater than any Thai king had allowed since before the Sukhothai era. Rama V also deserves more of the blame for 'westernisation' than any other single monarch. He was the first king to travel to Europe, which he did in 1897 and again in 1907. After seeing Europeans eating with forks, knives and spoons, he discouraged the Thai tradition of taking food with the hands; he also introduced chairs to the kingdom (before his reign Thais sat on the floor or on floor cushions). Following one European visit he asked his number one concubine to grow her hair long after the European fashion; by custom Thai women had kept their hair cropped short since the Ayuthaya period. ∎

Vimanmek was the first permanent building on the Dusit Palace grounds. It served as Rama V's residence in the early 1900s, was closed in 1935 and reopened in 1982 for the Ratanakosin bicentennial. The interior of the mansion contains various personal effects of the king, and a treasure trove of early Ratanakosin art objects and antiques.

English-language tours leave every half hour beginning at 9.45 am, with the last one at 3.15 pm. The tours cover around 30 rooms and last an hour. Smaller adjacent buildings display historic photography documenting the Chakri dynasty. Traditional Thai classical and folk dances are performed in the late morning and early afternoon in a pavilion off the canal side of the mansion.

Vimanmek is open from 9.30 am to 4 pm daily; admission is 50B for adults, 20B for children. It's free if you've already been to the Grand Palace/Wat Phra Kaew and kept the entry ticket for Vimanmek/Abhisek. As this is royal property, visitors wearing shorts or sleeveless shirts will be refused entry.

Vimanmek and Abhisek (see below) lie towards the northern end of the Dusit Palace grounds, off U-Thong Nai Rd (between Si Ayuthaya and Ratwithi Rds), across from the western side of the Dusit Zoo. An air-con No 3 (Si Ayuthaya Rd), air-con No 10 (Ratwithi Rd) or red microbus No 4 (Ratwithi Rd) will drop you nearby.

### Abhisek Dusit Throne Hall
### (Phra Thii Nang Aphisek Dusit)
อภิเศกดุสิต

This hall is a smaller wood, brick-and-stucco structure completed in 1904 for Rama V. Typical of the finer architecture of the era, the Victorian-influenced gingerbread and Moorish porticos blend to create a striking and distinctly Thai exterior. The hall now houses an excellent display of regional handiwork crafted by members of the Promotion of Supplementary Occupations & Related Techniques (SUPPORT) foundation, an organisation sponsored by the queen. Among the exhibits are mát-mìi cotton and silk, málaeng tháp collages (made from

metallic, multicoloured beetle wings), Damascene ware, neilloware and yaan lipao basketry.

Abhisek is open from 10 am to 4 pm daily and admission is 50B (or free with a Wat Phra Kaew/Grand Palace ticket). There is a souvenir shop on the premises. As at Wat Phra Kaew and Vimanmek, visitors must be properly dressed.

### Siam Society & Ban Kamthieng
สยามสมาคมบ้านคำเที่ยง

At 131 Soi Asoke, Sukhumvit Rd, the Siam Society is the publisher of the renowned Journal of the Siam Society and its members are valiant preservers of traditional Thai culture. The society headquarters is a good place to visit for those with a serious interest in Thailand. A reference library is open to visitors and Siam Society monographs are for sale. Almost anything you'd want to know about Thailand (outside the political sphere, since the society is sponsored by the royal family) can be researched here. An ethnological museum of sorts exhibiting Thai folk art is located on the Siam Society grounds in the Northern-style Kamthieng House. Ban Kamthieng is open Tuesday to Saturday from 9 am to 5 pm. Admission is 25B. For information call ☎ 258-3491.

### Other Museums
The **Museum of the Department of Forensic Medicine**, on the ground floor of the Forensic Medicine Building, Siriraj Hospital, in Thonburi (Phrannok Rd, near the Thonburi (Bangkok Noi) railway station), is the most famous of 10 medical museums on the hospital premises. Among the grisly displays are the preserved bodies of famous Thai murderers. Open Monday to Friday, 9 am to 4 pm; free admission.

The **Hall of Railway Heritage**, just north of Chatuchak Park, displays steam locomotives, model trains and other artefacts related to Thai railroad history. It's open Sundays only from 5 am to noon, and admission is free. Call the Thai Railfan Club (☎ 243-2037) for further information.

The **Bangkok Doll Factory & Museum** (☎ 245-3008) at 85 Soi Ratchataphan (Soi Mo Leng), off Ratchaprarop Rd in the Pratunam district, houses a colourful selection of traditional Thai dolls, both new and antique. Dolls are also available for purchase. It's open Monday to Saturday from 8 am to 5 pm; admission is free.

Military aircraft aficionados shouldn't miss the **Royal Thai Air Force Museum**, on Phahonyothin Rd near Wing 6 of the Don Meuang airport. Among the world-class collection of historic aircraft is the only existing Japanese Tachikawa trainer, along with a Spitfire and several Nieuports and Breguets. The museum is open from 8.30 am to 4.30 pm Monday to Friday and on the first weekend of each month; admission is free.

Bangkok also has a **Museum of Science** and a **planetarium**, both on Sukhumvit Rd between sois 40 and 42.

### Art Galleries

Opposite the National Theatre on Chao Fa Rd, the **National Gallery** (☎ 281-2224) displays traditional and contemporary art, mostly by artists who receive government support; the general consensus is that it's not Thailand's best, but the gallery is worth a visit for die-hard art fans or if you're in the vicinity. The gallery is closed Monday and Tuesday, and open from 9 am to 4 pm on other days. Admission is 10B.

At the forefront of the contemporary Buddhist art movement is the **Visual Dhamma Art Gallery** (☎ 258-5879) at 44/28 Soi Asoke (Soi 21, Sukhumvit Rd). Works by some of Thailand's most prominent muralists are sometimes displayed here, along with the occasional foreign exhibition. The gallery is open Monday to Friday from 1 to 6 pm, Saturday from 10 am to 5 pm, or at other times by appointment. Although the address is Soi Asoke, the gallery is actually off Asoke – coming from Sukhumvit Rd, take the second right into a small lane opposite Singha Bier Haus.

Bangkok's latest trend in public art consumption is the 'gallery pub', an effort to place art in a social context rather than leaving it to sterile galleries and museums. **Why Art? Pub & Gallery**, behind Cool Tango in the Royal City Avenue complex (Soi Sunwichai, Rama IX Rd) has a pub on the first two floors with copies of Michaelangelo and Botticelli murals executed by Silpakorn University art students, and an art display space on the 3rd floor. **Seri Art Gallery**, at Premier entertainment complex, is similar in concept. The place that actually initiated this trend, **Ruang Pung Art Community**, opposite section 13 in Chatuchak (Weekend) Market, has been in business around 12 years. It's open weekends from 11 am to 6 pm and features rotating exhibits. Also in Chatuchak Market is the very active **Sunday Gallery** (Sunday Plaza), which contrary to its name is open Monday, Wednesday and Friday from 10 am to 5 pm, Saturday and Sunday from 7 am to 7 pm.

**Utopia Gallery**, a gallery-pub-social centre opposite Tia Maria Restaurant at 116/1 Soi 23, Sukhumvit Rd, specialises in gay and lesbian art and is open daily from noon to 10 pm.

**Silpakorn University** (near Wat Phra Kaew) is Bangkok's fine arts university and has a gallery of student works; it's open weekdays from 8 am to 7 pm, weekends and holidays from 8 am to 4 pm. The **Thailand Cultural Centre** on Ratchadaphisek Rd (in the Huay Khwang district, between Soi Tiam Ruammit and Din Daeng Rd) has a small gallery with rotating contemporary art exhibits, as does the **River City** shopping complex next to the Royal Orchid Sheraton on the river.

Bangkok's foreign cultural centres hold regular exhibits of foreign and local artists – check the monthly bulletins issued by AUA, Alliance Française, the British Council and the Goethe Institute (see Cultural Centres under Information earlier in this chapter).

Several of Bangkok's luxury hotels display top-quality contemporary art in their lobbies and other public areas. The **Grand Hyatt Erawan** (on the corner of Ratchadamri and Ploenchit Rds) and the **Landmark Hotel** (Sukhumvit Rd) have the best collections of contemporary art in the country. The Erawan alone has over 1900 works exhibited on a rotating basis.

The **Neilson Hays Library** at 193 Surawong Rd occasionally hosts small exhibitions in its Rotunda Gallery.

### Chinatown (Sampeng)
เยาวราช (สำเพ็ง)

Bangkok's Chinatown, off Yaowarat and Ratchawong Rds, comprises a confusing and crowded array of jewellery, hardware, wholesale food, automotive and fabric shops, as well as dozens of other small businesses. It's a good place to shop since goods here are cheaper than almost anywhere else in Bangkok and the Chinese proprietors like to bargain, especially along Soi Wanit 1 (also known as Sampeng Lane). Chinese and Thai antiques in various grades of age and authenticity are available in the so-called Thieves' Market (Nakhon Kasem), but it's better for browsing than buying these days.

During the annual Vegetarian Festival, celebrated fervently by Thai Chinese for the first nine days of the ninth lunar month (September-October), Bangkok's Chinatown becomes a virtual orgy of vegetarian Thai and Chinese food. The festivities are centred around **Wat Mangkon Kamalawat (Neng Noi Yee)**, one of Chinatown's largest temples, on Charoen Krung Rd. All along Charoen Krung Rd in this vicinity, as well as on Yaowarat Rd to the south, restaurants and noodle shops offer hundreds of different vegetarian dishes.

A Chinese population has been living in this area ever since the Chinese were moved here from Bang Kok (today's Ko Ratanakosin) by the royal government in 1782 to make room for the new capital. A census in the area taken exactly 100 years later found 245 opium dens, 154 pawnshops, 69 gambling establishments and 26 brothels. Pawnshops, along with myriad gold shops, remain a popular Chinatown business, while the other three vices have gone underground; brothels continue to exist under the guise of 'tea halls' (*róhng chaa*), back-street heroin vendors have replaced the opium dens and

illicit card games convene in the private upstairs rooms of certain restaurants. Four Chinese newspapers printed and distributed in the district have a total circulation of over 160,000.

At the south-eastern edge of Chinatown stands **Hualamphong station**, built by Dutch architects and engineers just before WWI. One of the city's earliest and most outstanding examples of the movement toward Thai Art Deco, the vaulted iron roof and neoclassical portico demonstrate engineering that was state-of-the-art in its time, while the patterned, two-toned skylights exemplify pure de Stijl-style Dutch modernism.

Fully realised examples of Thai Deco from the 1920s and 1930s can be found along Chinatown's main streets, particularly Yaowarat Rd. Vertical towers over the main doorways are often surmounted with whimsical Deco-style sculptures – the Eiffel Tower, a lion, an elephant, a Moorish dome. Atop one commercial building on Songwat Rd near Tha Ratchawong is a rusting model of a WWII vintage Japanese Zero warplane, undoubtedly placed there by the Japanese during their brief 1941 occupation of Bangkok; in style and proportion it fits the surrounding Thai Deco elements.

### Pahurat
พาหุรัต

At the edge of Chinatown, around the intersection of Pahurat (Phahurat) and Chakraphet (Chakkaphet) Rds, is a small but thriving Indian district, generally called Pahurat. Here dozens of Indian-owned shops sell all kinds of fabric and clothes. This is the best place in the city to bargain for such items, especially silk. The selection is unbelievable, and Thai shoulder bags (*yâams*) sold here are the cheapest in Bangkok, perhaps in Thailand.

Behind the more obvious storefronts along these streets, in the 'bowels' of the blocks, is a seemingly endless Indian bazaar selling not only fabric but household items, food and other necessities. There are some good, reasonably priced Indian restaurants in this area, too, and a Sikh temple off Chakraphet Rd (see Other Temples & Shrines).

## Dusit Zoo (Suan Sat Dusit)
สวนสัตว์ดุสิต (เขาดิน)

The collection of animals at Bangkok's 19 hectare zoo comprises over 300 mammals, 200 reptiles and 800 birds, including relatively rare indigenous species such as banteng, gaur, serow and rhinoceros. Originally a private botanical garden for Rama V, it was converted to a zoo in 1938 and is now one of the premier zoological facilities in South-East Asia. The shady grounds feature trees labelled in English, Thai and Latin, plus a lake in the centre with paddle boats for rent. There's also a small children's playground.

If nothing else, the zoo is a nice place to get away from the noise of the city and observe how the Thais amuse themselves – mainly by eating. A couple of lakeside restaurants serve good, inexpensive Thai food. Entry to the zoo is 20B for adults, 5B for children, 10B for those over 60; it's open daily from 9 am to 6 pm. A small circus performs on weekends and holidays between 11 am and 2 pm. Sundays can be a bit crowded – if you want the zoo mostly to yourself, go on a weekday.

The zoo is in the Dusit district between Chitlada Palace and the National Assembly Hall; the main entrance is off Ratwithi Rd. Buses that pass the entrance include the ordinary Nos 18 and 28 and the air-con No 10.

## Queen Saovabha Memorial Institute (Snake Farm)
สวนเสาวภา

At this research institute (☎ 252-0161), formerly known as the Pasteur Institute, on Rama IV Rd (near Henri Dunant Rd), venomous snakes are milked daily to make snake-bite antidotes, which are distributed throughout the country. The milking sessions – at 10.30 am and 2 pm weekdays, 10.30 am only on weekends and holidays – have become a major Bangkok tourist attraction. Unlike other 'snake farms' in Bangkok,

this is a serious herpetological research facility; a very informative half-hour slide show on snakes is presented before the milking sessions. This will be boring to some, fascinating to others. Feeding time is 3 pm. Admission is 70B.

A booklet entitled *Guide to Healthy Living in Thailand*, published jointly by the Thai Red Cross and the US embassy, is available here for 100B. You can also get common vaccinations against such diseases as cholera, typhoid, hepatitis A and smallpox.

## Monk's Bowl Village
บ้านบาตร

This is the only one remaining of three such villages established in Bangkok by Rama I for the purpose of handcrafting monk's bowls (*bàat*). The black bowls, used by Thai monks to receive alms-food from faithful Buddhists every morning, are still made here in the traditional manner. Due to the expense of purchasing a handmade bowl, the 'village' has been reduced to a single alley in a district known as Ban Baht (*bâan bàat*; Monk's Bowl Village). About half a dozen families still hammer the bowls together from eight separate pieces of steel representing the eight spokes of the wheel of dharma (which in turn symbolise Buddhism's Eightfold Path). The joints are fused in a wood fire with bits of copper, and the bowl is polished and coated with several layers of black lacquer. A typical bowl-smith's output is one bowl per day.

To find the village, walk south on Boriphat Rd south of Bamrung Meuang Rd, then left on Soi Baan Baht. The artisans who fashion the bowls are not always at work, so it's largely a matter of luck whether you'll see them in action. At any of the houses which make them, you can purchase a fine quality alms bowl for around 400 to 500B. To see monks' robes and bowls on sale, wander down Bamrung Meuang Rd in the vicinity of Sao Ching Cha.

## Lumphini Park
สวนลุมพินี

Named after the Buddha's birthplace in Nepal, this is Bangkok's largest and most

BANGKOK

## Walking Tour – Chinatown & Pahurat

This route meanders through Bangkok's busy Chinese and Indian market districts – best explored on foot since vehicular traffic in the area is in almost constant gridlock. Depending on your pace and shopping intentions, this lengthy route could take from 1½ to three hours. You can also do this tour in reverse, beginning from the Pahurat fabric market.

Be forewarned that the journey should only be undertaken by those who can withstand extended crowd contact as well as the sometimes unpleasant sights and smells of a traditional fresh market. The reward for tolerating this attack on the senses consists of numerous glimpses into the 'real' day-to-day Bangkok, away from the glittering facade of department stores and office buildings along Bangkok's main avenues – not to mention the opportunity for fabulous bargains. (If you plan to buy anything, you'd better bring along either a phrasebook or an interpreter as very little English is spoken in these areas.)

Start at **Wat Mangkon Kamalawat (Neng Noi Yee)**, one of Chinatown's largest and liveliest temples (the name means Dragon Lotus Temple), on Charoen Krung Rd between Mangkon Rd and Trok Itsaranuphap. A taxi direct to the temple is recommended over taking a bus, simply because the district is so congested and street names don't always appear in roman script. If you're determined to go by bus, Nos 1, 4, 7, 25, 35, 40, 53 and 73 pass the temple going east (the temple entrance will be on the left), or you could take air-con bus No 1, 7 or 8 and get off near the Mangkon Rd intersection on Yaowarat Rd, a block south of Charoen Krung. Yet another alternative is to arrive by Chao Phraya River Express at Tha Ratchawong, then walk four blocks north-east along Ratchawong Rd to Charoen Krung Rd, turn right and walk one and a half blocks to the temple.

Whichever approach you choose, to help pinpoint the right area on Charoen Krung Rd look for neighbouring shops selling fruit, cakes, incense and ritual burning paper for offering at the temple. Inscriptions at the entrance to Wat Mangkon Kamalawat are in Chinese and Tibetan, while the labyrinthine interior features a succession of Buddhist, Taoist and Confucian altars. Virtually at any time of day or night this temple is packed with worshippers lighting incense, filling the ever-burning altar lamps with oil and praying to their ancestors.

Leaving the temple, walk left along Charoen Krung Rd about 20m to the nearest crosswalk (a policeman is usually directing traffic here), then cross the road and head down the alley on the other side. You're now heading south-west on **Trok Itsaranuphap**, one of Chinatown's main market lanes. This section is lined with vendors purveying ready-to-eat or preserved foodstuffs, including cleaned chickens, duck and fish; though not for the squeamish, it's one of the cleanest looking fresh markets in Bangkok.

One hundred metres or so down Trok Itsaranuphap you'll cross **Yaowarat Rd**, a main Chinatown thoroughfare. This section of Yaowarat is lined with large and small gold shops; for price and selection, this is probably the best place in Thailand to purchase a gold chain (sold by the *baht*, a unit of weight equal to 15g). From the trok entrance, turn right onto Yaowarat Rd, walk 50m to the crosswalk and, using a couple of savvy-looking Chinese crones as screens, navigate your way across the avenue.

Trok Itsaranuphap continues southward on the other side. Down the lane almost immediately on your left is the Chinese-ornamented entrance to **Talaat Kao (Old Market)**. This market section off Trok Itsaranuphap has been operating continuously for over 200 years. All manner and size of freshwater and saltwater fin and shellfish are displayed here, alive and filleted – or sometimes half alive and half filleted.

About 100m farther on down Itsaranuphap, past rows of vendors selling mostly dried fish, you'll come to a major Chinatown market crossroads. Running perpendicular to Itsaranuphap in either direction is famous **Sampeng Lane (Soi Wanit 1)**. Turn right onto Sampeng. This is usually the most crowded of Chinatown's market sois – a traffic jam of pedestrians, pushcarts and the occasional annoying motorbike twisting through the crowds. Shops along this section of Sampeng sell dry goods, especially shoes, clothing, fabric, toys and kitchenware.

About 25m west, Sampeng Lane crosses Mangkon Rd. On either side of the intersection are two of Bangkok's oldest commercial buildings, a Bangkok Bank and the venerable **Tang To Kang** gold shop, both over 100 years old. The exteriors of the buildings are classic early Ratanakosin (or Bangkok), showing lots of European influence; the interiors are heavy with hardwood panelling. Continue walking another 60m or so to the Ratchawong Rd crossing (a traffic cop is usually stationed here to part the vehicular Red Sea for pedestrians), cross and re-enter Sampeng Lane on the other side.

At this point, **fabric shops** – many of them operated by Indian (mostly Sikh) merchants – start dominating the selection as the western edge of Chinatown approaches the Indian district of Pahurat. If you're looking for good deals on Thai textiles you're in the right place. But hold off buying until you've had a chance to look through at least a dozen or more shops – they get better the farther you go. After about 65m is the small Mahachak Rd crossing and then, after another 50m or so, the larger Chakrawat (Chakkawat) Rd crossing, where yet another traffic cop assists. Along Chakrawat Rd in this vicinity, as well as farther ahead along Sampeng Lane on the other side of Chakrawat, there are many gem and jewellery shops.

If you were to follow Chakrawat Rd north from Soi Wanit, you could have a look around the

Chinese-Thai antique shops of **Nakhon Kasem** (also known as the Thieves' Market since at one time stolen goods were commonly sold here) between Yaowarat and Charoen Krung Rds. After you re-enter Soi Wanit on the other side of Chakrawat Rd the jewellery shops are mixed with an eclectic array of houseware and clothing shops until you arrive, after another 50m, at the **Saphaan Han** market area, named after a short bridge *(saphāan)* over Khlong Ong Ang. Clustered along the khlong on either side of the bridge is a bevy of vendors selling noodles and snacks. On the other side of the bridge, Sampeng Lane ends at Chakraphet Rd, the eastern edge of the Pahurat district.

**Chakraphet Rd** is well known for its Indian restaurants and shops selling Indian sweets. One of the best eateries in the area is the *Royal India Restaurant*, which serves north Indian cuisine and is justly famous for its tasty selection of Indian breads. To get there, turn left onto Chakraphet and walk about 70m along the east (left) side of the road; look for the Royal India sign pointing down an alley on the left. On the opposite side of Chakraphet Rd from the Royal India is a Chinese temple. North of this temple, in a back alley on the west side of the road, is a large **Sikh temple** – turn left before the ATM Department Store to find the entrance. Visitors to the temple – reportedly the second largest Sikh temple outside of India – are welcome but they must remove their shoes. If you arrive on a Sikh festival day you can partake of the *langar* or communal Sikh meal served in the temple.

Several inexpensive Indian food stalls are found in an alley alongside the department store. Behind the store, stretching westward from Chakraphet Rd to Triphet Rd, is the **Pahurat Market**, devoted almost exclusively to textiles and clothing. Pahurat Rd itself runs parallel to and just north of the market.

If you're ready to escape the market hustle and bustle, you can catch city buses on Chakraphet Rd (heading north and then east to the Siam Square and Pratunam areas) or along Pahurat Rd (heading west and then north along Tri Thong Rd to the Banglamphu district). Or walk to the river and catch a Chao Phraya River Express boat from Tha Saphaan Phut, which is just to the north-west of Phra Phut Yot Fa (Memorial) Bridge. If you're doing this route in reverse, you can arrive by Chao Phraya River Express at Tha Saphaan Phut. ■

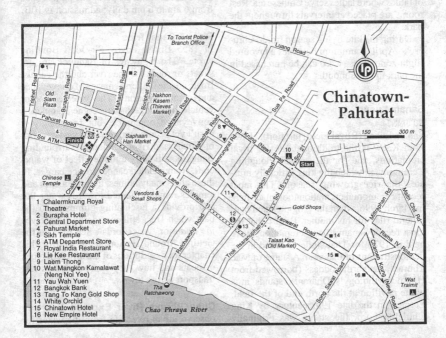

1  Chalermkrung Royal Theatre
2  Burapha Hotel
3  Central Department Store
4  Pahurat Market
5  Sikh Temple
6  ATM Department Store
7  Royal India Restaurant
8  Lie Kee Restaurant
9  Laem Thong
10  Wat Mangkon Kamalawat (Neng Noi Yee)
11  Yau Wah Yuen
12  Bangkok Bank
13  Tang To Kang Gold Shop
14  White Orchid
15  Chinatown Hotel
16  New Empire Hotel

Chinatown-Pahurat

popular park. It is bordered by Rama IV Rd to the south, Sarasin Rd to the north, Withayu Rd to the east and Ratchadamri Rd to the west, with entrance gates on all sides. A large artificial lake in the centre is surrounded by broad, well tended lawns, wooded areas and walking paths – in other words, it's the best outdoor escape from Bangkok without leaving town.

One of the best times to visit the park is in the early morning before 7 am when the air is fresh (well, relatively so for Bangkok) and legions of Chinese are practising t'ai chi. Also in the morning, vendors set up tables to dispense fresh snake blood and bile, considered health tonics by many Thais and Chinese. Rowboats and paddle boats can be rented at the lake for 20B per half hour. A weight lifting area in one section becomes a miniature 'muscle beach' on weekends. Other facilities include a snack bar, an asphalt jogging track, several areas with tables and benches for picnics and a couple of tables where ladies serve Chinese tea. Rest rooms are placed at intervals throughout the park.

During the kite flying season (mid-February to April), Lumphini becomes a favoured flight zone; kites (*wâo*) can be purchased in the park in these months.

## Sanam Luang
สนามหลวง

Sanam Luang (Royal Field) just north of Wat Phra Kaew is the traditional site for royal cremations, and for the annual Ploughing Ceremony, in which the king officially initiates the rice-growing season. The most recent ceremonial cremation took place here in March 1996, when the king presided over funeral rites for his mother. Before that the most recent Sanam Luang cremations were held in 1976 for Thai students killed in the demonstrations of that year. A statue of Mae Thorani, the earth goddess (borrowed from Hindu mythology's Dharani), stands in a white pavilion at the north end of the field. Erected in the late 19th century by King Chulalongkorn, the statue was originally

attached to a well that provided drinking water to the public.

Before 1982, Bangkok's famous Weekend Market was regularly held at Sanam Luang (it's now at Chatuchak Park). Nowadays the large field is most popularly used as a picnic and recreational area. A large kite competition is held here during the kite-flying season.

## Rama IX Royal Park
สวนพระรามที่

Opened in 1987 to commemorate King Bhumibol's 60th birthday, Bangkok's newest green area covers 81 hectares and includes a water park and botanical gardens. Since its opening, the latter has developed into a significant horticultural research centre. A museum with an exhibition on the life of the king sits at the centre of the park. Take bus No 2 or 23 to Soi Udomsuk (Soi 103), off Sukhumvit Rd in Phrakhanong district, then a green minibus to the park. The park is open from 6 am to 6 pm daily; admission is 10B.

## River & Canal Trips

In 1855 British envoy Sir John Bowring wrote, 'The highways of Bangkok are not streets or roads but the river and the canals. Boats are the universal means of conveyance and communication'. The wheeled motor vehicle has long since become Bangkok's conveyance of choice, but fortunately it hasn't yet become universal. A vast network of canals and river tributaries surrounding Bangkok still carry a motley fleet of watercraft, from paddled canoes to rice barges. In these areas many homes, trading houses and temples remain oriented towards water life and provide a fascinating glimpse into the past, when Thais still considered themselves *jâo nâam* or 'water lords'. See Boat in the Getting Around section at the end of this chapter for descriptions of the different types of boats and how they can be used as fast transport across town.

**Chao Phraya River Express** You can observe urban river life from the water for

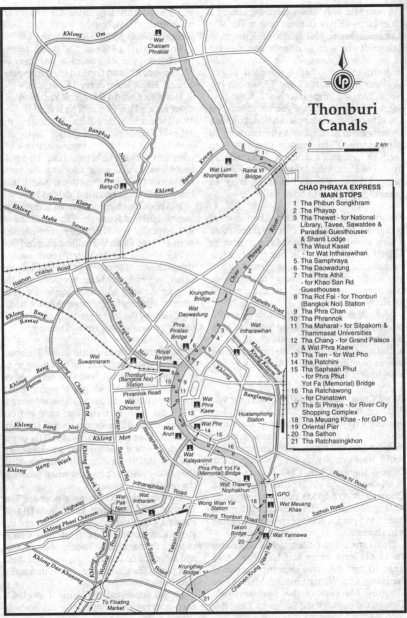

# Thonburi Canals

0        1        2 km

**CHAO PHRAYA EXPRESS MAIN STOPS**

1  Tha Phibun Songkhram
2  Tha Phayap
3  Tha Thewet - for National Library, Tavee, Sawatdee & Paradise Guesthouses & Shanti Lodge
4  Tha Wisut Kasat - for Wat Intharawihan
5  Tha Samphraya
6  Tha Daowadung
7  Tha Phra Athit - for Khao San Rd Guesthouses
8  Tha Rot Fai - for Thonburi (Bangkok Noi) Station
9  Tha Phra Chan
10  Tha Phrannok
11  Tha Maharat - for Silpakorn & Thammasat Universities
12  Tha Chang - for Grand Palace & Wat Phra Kaew
13  Tha Tien - for Wat Pho
14  Tha Ratchini
15  Tha Saphaan Phut - for Phra Phut Yot Fa (Memorial) Bridge
16  Tha Ratchawong - for Chinatown
17  Tha Si Phraya - for River City Shopping Complex
18  Tha Meuang Khae - for GPO
19  Oriental Pier
20  Tha Sathon
21  Tha Ratchasingkhon

BANGKOK

1½ hours for only 7B by climbing aboard a Chao Phraya River Express boat at Tha Wat Ratchasingkhon, just north of Krungthep Bridge. If you want to ride the entire length of the express route all the way to Non-thaburi, this is where you must begin. Ordinary bus Nos 1, 17 and 75, air-con bus No 4 and red microbus No 2 Kaw pass Ratchasingkhon pier. Or you could board at any other express boat pier in Bangkok for a shorter ride to Nonthaburi to the north; eg 20 minutes from Tha Phayap (the first stop north of Krungthon Bridge), or 30 minutes from Tha Phra Athit (near the Phra Pinklao Bridge). Express boats run about every 15 minutes from 6 am to 6 pm daily.

**Khlong Bangkok Noi Taxi** Another good boat trip is the Bangkok Noi canal taxi route which leaves from Tha Maharat next to Silpakorn University. The fare is only a few baht and the farther up Khlong Bangkok Noi you go, the better the scenery becomes, with teak houses on stilts, old wats and plenty of greenery.

Stop off at Wat Suwannaram to view 19th century jataka murals painted by two of early Bangkok's foremost religious muralists. Art historians consider these the best surviving temple paintings in Bangkok. One way fare anywhere is 10B.

**Other Canal Taxis** From Tha Tien near Wat Pho, get a canal taxi along **Khlong Mon** (leaving every half hour from 6.30 am to 6 pm; 5B) for more typical canal scenery, including orchid farms. A longer excursion could be made by making a loop along khlongs Bangkok Noi, Chak Phra and Mon, an all-day trip. An outfit called Chao Phraya Charters (☎ 433-5453) runs a tour boat to Khlong Mon from Tha Tien each afternoon from 3 to 5 pm for 300B per person including refreshments.

Boats from Tha Chang to **Khlong Bang Yai** (10B) leave every half hour from 6.15 am to 10 pm – this is the same trip that passes the Bang Khu Wiang Floating Market (see Floating Markets in the next section). Though the market itself is over by 7 am, this trip is worthwhile later in the day as it passes a number of interesting wats, traditional wooden homes and the Royal Barges.

From the Tha Phibun Songkram pier in Nonthaburi you can board a boat taxi up picturesque **Khlong Om** and see durian plantations. Boats leave every 15 minutes.

Boats to **Khlong Bangkok Yai**, available from either Tha Tien or Tha Ratchini, pass Wat Intharam, where a chedi contains the ashes of Thonburi's King Taksin. Taksin was assassinated by his own ministers in 1782 after they decided he'd gone mad. Fine gold and black lacquerwork adorning the main bòt doors depicts the mythical *naariiphõn* tree, which bears beautiful girls as fruit.

It is possible to go as far from Bangkok as Suphanburi and Ratchaburi by boat, though this typically involves many boat connections (see the Central Thailand chapter).

For details on boat transport on the Bangkok side of the river, where four lengthy canal routes have been revived, see the Getting Around section at the end of this chapter. Although they provide quick transport, none of the four right-bank canal routes can be recommended for sightseeing.

**Boat Charters** If you want to see the Thonburi canals at your own pace, the best thing to do is charter a long-tail boat – it need not be expensive if you can get a small group together to share the costs. The usual price is 300B per hour and you can choose from among eight different canals in Thonburi alone. Beware of 'agents' who will try to put you on the boat and rake off an extra commission. Before travelling by boat, establish the price – you can't bargain when you're in the middle of the river!

The best piers for hiring a boat are **Tha Chang, Tha Saphaan Phut** and **Tha Si Phraya**. Close to the latter, to the rear of the River City complex, the Boat Tour Centre charges the same basic hourly price (300B) and there are no hassles with touts. Of these four piers, Tha Chang usually has the largest selection of boats.

Those interested in seeing Bangkok's deep-water port can hire long-tail boats to

Khlong Toey or as far downriver as Pak Nam, which means 'river mouth' in Thai. It's about two hours each way by boat, or a bit quicker if you take a bus or taxi one way.

Finally, if you're really a canal freak, look for *50 Trips Through Siam's Canals* (Editions Duang Kamol, 1979) by Geo-Ch Veran (translated from French into English by Sarah Bennett). The book contains 25 detailed maps and clear instructions on how to take the various trips, some of which are very time-consuming. The prolific William Warren has recently written *Bangkok's Waterways*, which may be easier to find but is more photo-oriented and less detailed.

**Dinner Cruises** A dozen or more companies in Bangkok run regular cruises along the Chao Phraya for rates ranging from 40 to 700B per person, depending on how far they go and whether dinner is included with the fare. Most require advance phone reservations.

The less expensive, more casual boats allow you to order as little or as much as you want from moderately priced menus; a modest charge of 40 to 70B per person is added to the bill for the cruise. It's a fine way to dine outdoors when the weather is hot, away from city traffic and cooled by river breezes. Several of the dinner boats cruise under the illuminated Rama IX Bridge, the longest single-span cable-suspension bridge in the world. This engineering marvel supports the elevated expressway joining Bangkok's Thanon Tok district with Thonburi's Ratburana district. Those dinner cruises offering an à-la-carte menu plus surcharge include:

Ban Khun Luang Restaurant – Ban Khun Luang Restaurant to Oriental pier; Thursday, Friday, Saturday (☎ 243-3235)
Khanap Nam Restaurant – Krungthon Bridge to Sathon Bridge; twice daily (☎ 433-6611)
Riverside Company – Krungthon Bridge to Rama IX Bridge; daily (☎ 434-0090)
River Sight-Seeing Ltd – Tha Si Phraya to Wat Arun or Rama IX Bridge (depending on current); daily (☎ 437-4047)
Yok Yor Restaurant – Yok-Yor Restaurant (Tha Wisut Kasat) to Rama IX Bridge; daily (☎ 281-1829, 282-7385)

More swanky dinner cruises charge a set price of 300 to 750B per person for the cruise and dinner; beer and liquor cost extra. They include:

Loy Nava Co – Tha Si Phraya to Tha Wasukri; twice daily (☎ 437-4932/7329)
Manohra Cruises – Marriott Royal Garden Riverside Hotel to Krungthep Bridge; nightly (☎ 476-0021)
Oriental Hotel –Oriental pier to Nonthaburi; Wednesday only (☎ 236-0400/9)
Wanfah Cruise – River City to Krungthon Bridge; twice daily (☎ 433-5453, 424-6218)

**Sunset Cruise** Before its regular 2½ hour 7.30 pm dinner cruise, the *Manohra* sails at 5.30 pm from the Marriott Royal Garden Riverside Hotel for an hour-long sunset cocktail cruise. Boarding is free; passengers are only charged for drinks purchased from the well stocked bar on board. A free river taxi operates between the River City pier and the Royal Garden pier at 5 pm, just in time for the 5.30 pm cruise departure. Call ☎ 476-0021 for more information.

**Longer Cruises** All-day and overnight cruises on the river are also available. The Chao Phraya River Express Boat Co (☎ 222-5330, 225-3002/3) does a reasonably priced tour on Sundays only, starting from Tha Maharat at 8 am and returning at 5.30 pm, that includes visits to the Royal Folk Arts & Handicrafts Centre in Bang Sai, Bang Pa-In Palace near Ayuthaya and the bird sanctuary at Wat Phailom in Pathum Thani Province. The price is 180B per person lower deck, 250B upper deck, not including lunch, which you arrange on your own in Bang Pa-In.

Mit Chao Phraya Express Boat Co (☎ 225-6179) operates another moderately priced programme through several Thonburi canals, with stops at Wat Arun, the Royal Barges, an orchid farm and the Crocodile Farm. The tour departs from Tha Maharat at 8.30 am and returns at 6 pm. The programme is 150B, not including admission fees to the aforementioned attractions.

The Oriental Hotel's luxurious all air-con *Oriental Queen* (☎ 236-0400/9) also does a cruise to Bang Pa-In that leaves at 8 am from the Oriental pier and returns by air-con bus at 5 pm. The *Oriental Queen* cruise costs 1300B including lunch and guided tour. Note that neither of the cruises that visit Ban Pan-In really allows enough time for you to see Ayuthaya properly, so if that's your primary intention, go on your own. On the other hand I've had letters from history-weary readers who thought 15 to 30 minutes was plenty of time to see the ruins! Two other companies running similar Bang Pa-In/Ayuthaya tours for 1000 to 1200B per person are Horizon Cruise (☎ 538-3491) and River Sun Cruise (☎ 237-7608).

Royal Garden Resorts and Siam Exclusive Tours maintain three restored 50-year-old teak rice barges that have been transformed into four and 10 cabin cruisers. Decorated with antiques and Persian carpets, these craft represent the ultimate in Chao Phraya River luxury, the nautical equivalent of the *Eastern & Oriental Express* train. These barges – two

named *Mekhala*, one called *Manohra Song* – typically leave Bangkok in the afternoon and head upriver towards Ayuthaya (or downriver towards Bangkok). In the evening they anchor at Wat Praket, where a candle-lit dinner is served. The next morning passengers offer food to the monks from the wat, and then the barge moves on to Bang Pa-In. After a tour of the Summer Palace, a long-tail boat takes passengers on a tour of the ruins of Ayuthaya. At present four Ayuthaya cruises per week are scheduled. The cost for the two day cruise is variable depending on which barge is used, starting at around 3000B per person for the *Mekhala*, from 7000B per person for the super-deluxe, four cabin *Manohra Song* depending on time of year; prices include all meals and nonalcoholic beverages, accommodation, guide services, admission fees in Ayuthaya and hotel transfers. Shorter cruises are available by charter. Call ☎ 476-0021 at the Marriott Royal Garden for details.

## Floating Markets
ตลาดน้ำ

Among the most heavily published photo images of Thailand are those that depict wooden canoes laden with multicoloured fruits and vegetables, paddled by Thai women wearing indigo-hued clothes and wide-brimmed straw hats. Such floating markets *(talàat náam)* do exist in various locations throughout the huge canal system that surrounds Bangkok – but if you don't know where to go you may end up at a very inauthentic tourist-show scene.

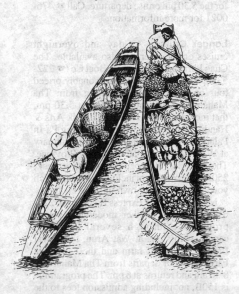

Floating markets – testimony to the busy water trade that characterised old Bangkok.

**Bang Khu Wiang Floating Market** At Khlong Bang Khu Wiang in Thonburi a small floating market operates between 4 and 7 am. Boats to the Khu Wiang Market (Talaat Naam Khuu Wiang) leave from the Tha Chang pier near Wat Phra Kaew every morning between 6.15 and 8 am; take the earliest one to catch the market before it's over, or arrange to charter a long-tail boat at an earlier hour.

**Damnoen Saduak Floating Market** There is a larger if somewhat more commercial floating market on Khlong Damnoen Saduak in Ratchaburi Province, 104 km south-west of Bangkok, between Nakhon Pathom and Samut Songkhram. You can get buses from the Southern Bus Terminal on Charan Sanitwong Rd in Thonburi to Damnoen Saduak starting at 6 am. Get there as early in the morning as possible to escape the hordes. See the Ratchaburi section in the Central Thailand chapter for more details.

**Wat Sai Floating Market** In recent years, visitors to the floating market near Wat Sai on Khlong Sanam Chai (off Khlong Dao Khanong) have outnumbered vendors to the point that opinions are now virtually unanimous – don't waste your time at this so-called market. Go to Bang Khu Wiang or Damnoen Saduak instead, or find your own.

If you're set on doing the Wat Sai trip, take one of the floating market tours that leave from the Oriental pier (Soi Oriental) or Tha Maharat near Silpakorn University – your only alternative is to charter a whole boat (at the Oriental pier), which can be quite expensive. Floating market tours cost from 50B, and give you only 20 minutes or so at the market (probably more than enough for this non-event). Most tours charge 300 to 400B for 1½ hours. Be prepared for a very touristy experience.

**Theme & Amusement Parks**
Just outside Bangkok are a host of artificial tourist attractions that provide either the 'see the whole country in an hour' theme or the standard western-style amusement park. If these attractions appeal to you, it's often worth booking tickets through travel agencies when such a booking includes return transport from your lodgings.

**West** Thirty-two km west of Bangkok, on the way to Nakhon Pathom, the **Rose Garden Country Resort** (☎ 253-0295), encompasses a canned Thai 'cultural village' (with demos of handicrafts, dancing, traditional ceremonies and martial arts), resort hotel, swimming

pools, tennis courts, a three hectare lake, elephant rides and a golf course. Admission to the 24 hectare garden area, which boasts 20,000 rose bushes, is 10B; it's another 220B for the 11 am and 2.45 pm performances in the cultural village. The resort and rose garden are open from 8 am to 6 pm daily, while the cultural village is open from 10.30 am to 5 pm. Shuttle buses run between the resort and major Bangkok hotels.

Just one km north of the Rose Garden, at the nine hectare **Samphran Elephant Ground & Zoo** (☎ 284-1873), you can see elephant 'roundups' and crocodile shows; a number of other animals can also be observed in zoo-like conditions. Kids generally like this place. It's open daily from 8.30 am to 6 pm, with crocodile wrestling shows at 12.45, 2.20 and 4.30 pm, elephant shows at 1.45 and 3.30 pm weekdays, plus additional shows on weekends and holidays at 11.30 am. Admission is 220B for adults, 120B children.

**North-East** In Minburi, 10 km north-east of Bangkok, **Siam Park** (☎ 517-0075) at 101 Sukhaphiban 2, is a huge recreational park with pools, water slides, a wave pool and the like. It's highly recommended for a splash. Admission is 200B for adults, 100B for children. Saturdays are less crowded than Sundays. Get there on bus No 26 or 27 from the Victory Monument or bus No 60 from the Democracy Monument.

Also in Minburi is **Safari World** (☎ 518-1000), 99 Ramindra 1 – a 69 hectare wildlife park said to be the largest 'open zoo' in the world. It's divided into two portions, the drive through Safari Park and the walk through Marine Park. The five km Safari Park drive (aboard air-con coaches or your own vehicle) intersects eight habitats with an assortment of giraffes, lions, zebras, elephants, orang-utans and other African and Asian animals (75 mammal species and 300 bird species in all). A Panda House displays rare white pandas. The Marine Park focuses on trained animal performances by dolphins. Safari World is open daily from 10 am to 6 pm; admission is 250B for adults, 150B for children aged three to 12, under three free.

It's 45 km east of central Bangkok; for public transport catch a No 26 bus from the Victory Monument to Minburi, then a songthaew to the park.

**South** Two attractions, Ancient City and the Crocodile Farm, in nearby Samut Prakan Province are often included on lists of Bangkok sights. See the Samut Prakan Province section in the Central Thailand chapter.

### Athletic Facilities

The first and grandest of the city's sports facilities is the **Royal Bangkok Sports Club** (RBSC) between Henri Dunant and Ratchadamri Rds (the green oval marked 'Turf' on the Bangkok bus maps). Facilities include a horse track, polo grounds (located elsewhere off Withayu Rd), a swimming pool, a sauna, squash and tennis courts (both hard and grass) and an 18-hole golf course. There's a waiting list for membership, so the only way you're likely to frolic at this prestigious club is to be invited there by a lucky RBSC member.

Membership at the **British Club** (☎ 234-0247), 189 Surawong Rd, is open to citizens of Australia, Canada, New Zealand and the UK or to others by invitation; membership fees are very costly. Among the sports facilities are a pool, golf drive range, squash and tennis courts.

The least expensive swimming facility in Bangkok is the one operated by the **Department of Physical Education** (☎ 215-1535) at the National Stadium on Rama I Rd, next to Mahboonkrong shopping centre; membership costs just 200B per year plus 20B per hour.

**Hollywood Gym** (☎ 208-9298), 420 Hollywood Street Center, Phetburi Rd (opposite Asia Hotel), offers a fully equipped gym, sauna and lounge; this is where many of Thailand's champion weight lifters work out. It's open daily from 10 am to midnight, and English, French, Spanish and Italian are spoken. Drop-in fees are 150B per session or you can pay heavily discounted fees in one week, one month, three month, six month and year-long increments. The top-class

**Clark Hatch Physical Fitness Centres**, with weight machines, pool, sauna and massage, can be found at the Hilton International, Amari Watergate and DeVille Palace hotels; non-hotel guests are welcome.

Other sports clubs open to the public include:

Amorn & Sons – 8 Soi Amorn 3, Soi 39, Sukhumvit Rd (☎ 392-8442); tennis, squash, badminton

Asoke Sports Club – 302/80-81 Asoke-Din Daeng Rd (☎ 246-2260); tennis, swimming

Bangkhen Tennis Court – 47/2 Vibhavadi Rangsit Hwy (☎ 579-7629); tennis

The Bangkok Gym – 9th floor, Delta Grand Pacific Hotel, 259 Sukhumvit Soi 19 (☎ 255-2440); weights, sauna, swimming, aerobics

Central Tennis Court – 13/1 Soi Atakanprasit, Sathon Tai Rd (☎ 213-1909); tennis

Gold Health & Fitness Club – 40th floor, 408 Phahonyothin Place (☎ 619-0460); weights, sauna, swimming, aerobics

Kanpaibun Tennis Court – 10 Soi 40, Sukhumvit Rd (☎ 391-8784, 392-1832); tennis

NTT Sports Club – 612/32 Soi Laoladda, Arun Amarin Rd, Thonburi (☎ 433-4623); swimming, weights, aerobics

Saithip Swimming Pool – 140 Soi 56, Sukhumvit Rd (☎ 331-2037); tennis, badminton, swimming

Santhikham Court – 217 Soi 109, Sukhumvit Rd (☎ 393-8480); tennis

Sivalai Club Tennis Court & Swimming Pool – 168 Soi Anantaphum, Itsaraphap Rd, Thonburi (☎ 411-2649); tennis, swimming

Soi Klang Racquet Club – 8 Soi 49, Sukhumvit Rd (☎ 391-0963, 382-8442); squash, tennis, racquetball, swimming, aerobics

Sukhavadee Swimming Pool – 107/399 Gp 6, Soi 91 Lat Phrao Rd (☎ 538-6879); swimming

Swim & Slim Family Club – 918 Soi 101/1, Sukhumvit Rd (☎ 393-0889); badminton, swimming, weights

### Meditation Study

Although at times Bangkok may seem like the most un-Buddhist place on earth, there are several places where foreigners can learn about Theravada Buddhist meditation. (See the Religion section in the Facts about the Country chapter for background information on Buddhism in Thailand.)

**Wat Mahathat** This 18th century wat opposite Sanam Luang provides meditation instruction several times daily at Section 5, a building near the monks' residences. Some of the Thai monks here speak English and there are often western monks or long-term residents available to interpret. There is also a special Saturday session for foreigners at the Dhamma Vicaya Hall. Instruction is based on the Mahasi Sayadaw system of *satipatthana* or mindfulness. Air-con bus Nos 8 and 12 both pass near the wat; the nearest Chao Phraya River Express pier is Tha Maharat.

**Wat Pak Nam** This very large wat, where hundreds of monks and nuns reside during the Buddhist Rains Retreat, has hosted many foreigners (especially Japanese) over the years. The meditation teacher, Phra Khru Phawana, speaks some English and there are usually people around who can interpret. The emphasis is on developing concentration through *nimittas* (acquired mental images), in order to attain trance-absorption states. A small English library is available. Pak Nam is on Thoet Thai Rd, Phasi Charoen, Thonburi. Take bus Nos 4, 9 or 103; the wat can also be reached by chartered long-tail boat from Tha Chang or Tha Saphaan Phut along the river and Thonburi canals.

**Wat Rakhang Khositaram** Only a few foreigners have studied at this temple, but the meditation teacher, Ajaan Mahathawon from Ubon Province in the North-East, has quite a good reputation. The teaching tradition at Wat Rakhang is strongly Abhidhamma-based, with much emphasis given to Buddhist psychology. Vipassana is considered attainable without strong concentration by means of a dialectic process similar to Krishnamurti's 'choiceless awareness'. To study here, one ought to be able to speak Thai fairly well; otherwise, an interpreter will have to be arranged. Wat Rakhang is on Arun Amarin Rd, Thonburi. Cross-river ferries leave frequently from Tha Chang on the opposite bank of the Chao Phraya River.

**Wat Cholaprathan Rangsarit** The teachers here, Ajaan Pañña (the abbot) and Ajaan Khao, employ a modified version of the

Mahasi Sayadaw system of satipatthana. Occasionally there's someone around who can interpret; otherwise it will be necessary to arrange in advance for interpreting. This wat also serves as a Bangkok headquarters for monks from Wat Suanmok (see Chaiya in the Southern Thailand chapter). Wat Cholaprathan is in Pak Kret, Nonthaburi Province (although not actually part of Bangkok, Nonthaburi is so connected to Bangkok's urban sprawl you can hardly tell the difference).

**World Fellowship of Buddhists** The WFB, at 33 Sukhumvit Rd, is a clearing house for information on Theravada Buddhism as well as dialogue between various schools of Buddhism. The centre hosts meditation classes from 2 to 5.30 pm on the first Sunday of every month.

**Other Courses**
For more information about cooking, language, martial arts and meditation courses in Bangkok, see under Courses in the Facts for the Visitor chapter.

**Places to Stay – bottom end**
Bangkok has perhaps the best variety and quality of budget places to stay of any Asian capital – which is one of the reasons it's such a popular destination for roving world travellers. Because of the wide distribution of places, your choice actually depends on what part of the city you want to be in – the tourist ghettos of Sukhumvit Rd and Silom-Surawong Rds, the backpackers' ghetto of Banglamphu, the centrally located Siam Square area, Chinatown or the old travellers' centre around Soi Ngam Duphli, off Rama IV Rd.

Chinatown (around Hualamphong station) and Banglamphu are the best all-round areas for seeing the real Bangkok, and are the cheapest districts for eating and sleeping. The Siam Square area is also well located, in that it's more or less in the centre of Bangkok – this, coupled with the good selection of city buses that pass through the Rama I and Phayathai Rd intersection, makes even more of the city accessible. In addition, this area has good bookshops, several banks, shopping centres, excellent mid-range restaurants, travel agencies and eight movie theatres within 10 to 15 minutes walk.

In Bangkok, bottom-end accommodation will be taken to mean places costing from 60 to 500B per night; mid-range from roughly 500 to 1500B per night, and top end from 2000B up.

**Banglamphu** If you're really on a tight budget head for the Khao San Rd area, near the Democracy Monument, parallel to Ratchadamnoen Klang Rd – ordinary bus Nos 2, 15, 17, 44, 56 and 59 will get you there, also air-con bus Nos 11 and 12. This is the main travellers' centre these days and new guesthouses are continually springing up.

Rates in Banglamphu are generally the lowest in Bangkok and although some of the places are barely adequate (bedbugs are sometimes a problem), a few are excellent value if you can afford just a bit more. At the bottom end, rooms are quite small and the

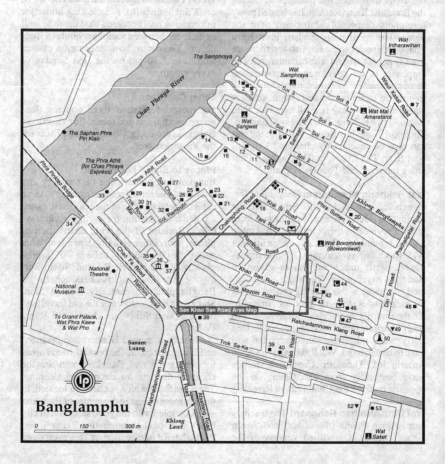

Banglamphu

walls dividing them are thin – in fact most are indistinguishable from one another. Some places have small attached cafes with limited menus. Bathrooms are usually down the hall or out the back somewhere; mattresses may be on the floor.

The least expensive rooms are 80/120B (60/100B with haggling in the low season) for singles/doubles, though these are hard to come by due to the hordes of people seeking them out. More common are the 100/140B rooms. Occasionally, triple rooms are available for as low as 160B and dorm beds for 50B. During most of the year, it pays to visit several guesthouses before making a decision, but in the high season (December to February, when Khao San Rd is bursting with life), you'd better take the first vacant bed you come across. The best time of day to find a vacancy is from around 9 to 10 am.

A decade or so ago there were only two Chinese-Thai hotels on Khao San Rd, the Nith Jaroen Suk (now called New Nith Jaroen Hotel) and the Sri Phranakhon (now the Khao San Palace Hotel). Now there are close to 100 guesthouses in the immediate vicinity, too many to list here. If you haven't already arrived with a recommendation in hand, you might best use the Banglamphu and Khao San Rd area maps and simply pick a place at random for your first night. If you're not satisfied you can stow your gear and explore the area till something better turns up. A tip: the guesthouses along Khao San Rd tend to be cubicles in modern shophouses, while those in Banglamphu's quieter lanes and alleys are often housed in old homes, some of them with a lot of character.

At the cheaper places it's not worth calling ahead, since the staff usually won't hold a room for you unless you pay in advance. For places that *may* take phone reservations I've included phone numbers.

***Central Banglamphu*** Simple, adequate places with rooms for 60 to 100B a single,

| PLACES TO STAY | | |
|---|---|---|
| 1 Home & Garden Guest House | 23 Super Siam Guest House | 47 Sweety Guest House |
| 2 Clean & Calm Guest House | 24 My House | 48 Prasuri Guest House |
| 3 River House | 25 Merry V Guest House | 51 Hotel 90 |
| 4 Villa Guest House | 26 Green Guest House | |
| 5 Truly Yours Guest House | 27 New Siam Guest House | PLACES TO EAT |
| 6 AP Guest House | 28 New Merry V | 14 Roti-Mataba |
| 7 Trang Hotel & Vieng Travel | 29 Beer & Peachy Guesthouses | 34 Wang Ngar Restaurant |
| 8 Vimol Guest House | 30 Apple Guest House | 49 Vijit Restaurant |
| 9 New World House Apartments & Guest House | 31 Rose Garden Guest House | 52 Arawy Restaurant |
| 11 Banglamphu Square Guest House | 32 Mango Guest House | OTHER |
| 12 Gipsy Guest House | 35 Chai's House | 10 Siam Commercial Bank |
| 13 PS Guest House | 37 Charlie's House | 17 New World Shopping Centre |
| 15 Apple Guest House II | 38 Royal Hotel | 18 Banglamphu Department Store |
| 16 KC Guest House | 39 P Guest House | 19 Post Office |
| 20 Canalside Guest House | 40 Palace Hotel | 33 UNICEF |
| 21 Sawasdee House/Terrace Guest House | 41 Central Guest House | 36 National Gallery |
| 22 Chusri Guest House | 42 PC Guest House | 44 Mosque |
| | 43 Srinthip Guest House | 45 Post Office |
| | 46 Nat II Guest House | 50 Democracy Monument |
| | | 53 City Hall |

80 to 120B a double on or just off Khao San Rd include:

*Chada Guest House* (plus air-con for 250B), *CH 1 Guest House* (dorm available for 40B), *Classic Place* (plus air-con 380/480B), *Siri Guest House, Marco Polo Guest House* (also called *160 Guest House*), *Good Luck Guest House, VIP Guest House* (all rooms 80B), *Tong Guest House, Nat Guest House, Bonny Guest House* (dorm beds for 60B), *Top Guest House, Dior Guest House, Grand Guest House, PB Guest House* (dorm beds for 40B, snooker hall & gym), *Khao San Guest House, Buddy Guest House, Lek Guest House, Mam's Guest House, Hello Restaurant & Guest House, Prakorp's House & Restaurant* (highly recommended), *Chart Guest House* (plus air-con for 450B), *NS Guest House, Thai Guest House, Sitdhi Guest House & Restaurant* and *Ploy Guest House.*

The *Khao San Palace Hotel* (☎ 282-0578), set off down an alley at 139 Khao San Rd, has had a face-lift; rooms cost 250/350B single/double with ceiling fan and private bath, 450/500B with air-con and hot water. Down a parallel alley, the *New Nith Jaroen Hotel* (☎ 281-9872) has similar rates and rooms to the Khao San Palace, but slightly better service. The new *Nana Plaza Inn* (☎ 281-6402), near the Siri Guest House towards Khao San's east end, is a large, hotel-like enterprise built around a restaurant; air-con/hot water rooms go for 400/500B a single/double.

Two narrow alleys between Khao San and Rambutri Rds feature a string of cramped places that nonetheless manage to fill up. The alley farthest west off Khao San sports *Doll, Suneeporn, Leed, Jim's, AT* and *Green House* (☎ 281-0323). Except for Green House, all feature small, luggage-crammed lobbies with staircases leading to rooms layered on several floors and which cost around 60 to 100B. Green House is a bit more expansive, with a pleasant restaurant downstairs and rooms with fan and private bath for 150 to 200B. East down Khao San is a wider alley that's a bit more open, with the small, Indian-run *Best Aladdin Guest House & Restaurant* (90/160B) and the hotel-like *Marco Polo Hostel* (120 to 250B, most rooms with private bath). Farther south-east another alley has only one guest-

house, *New Royal* with nothing-special rooms from 100/150B with shared bath, 200 to 250B with attached bath. A final, very narrow alley just before you come to Tanao Rd has three standard-issue places, the *Harn, Nisa* and *VS*.

Parallel to Khao San Rd but much quieter is Trok Mayom, an alley reserved for mostly pedestrian traffic. *J & Joe* (☎ 281-2949; fax 281-1198) is an old teak home with pleasant rooms for 90 to 160B; not surprisingly, it's almost consistently full. There's also a *New Joe* (☎ 281-2948) on Trok Mayom, a new rather modern-looking place set off the alley a bit with an outdoor cafe downstairs. Rooms cost 170/250B a single/double with private bath, 350B air-con; e-mail and fax services are available. Farther east, towards Tanao Rd, *Ranee Guest House* charges 90/160B for singles/doubles with shared bath.

*Orchid House* (☎ 280-2691), a rather spiffy guesthouse near the Viengtai Hotel on Rambutri Rd (north of Khao San Rd), offers clean apartment-style rooms for 300B a single with fan and bath, 350/400B a single/double with air-con or 450B for larger air-con rooms.

**West Banglamphu** Several long-running guesthouses are on sois between Chakraphong Rd and the Chao Phraya River, putting them within walking distance of Tha Phra Athit where you can catch express boats. This area is also close to the Thonburi (Bangkok Noi) station across the river, the National Museum and the National Theatre.

West of Chakraphong on Soi Rambutri, *Sawasdee House* (☎ 281-8138) follows the trend towards hotel-style accommodation in the Khao San Rd area, with a large restaurant downstairs and small to medium-sized rooms on several floors upstairs, all with private bath in the 120 to 300B range. Next along Soi Rambutri are the *Chusri* and *Terrace* guesthouses, all of which have adequate rooms for 50 to 60B per person but are nothing special. Right where Soi Rambutri makes a sharp turn to the south-west, the newish *Super Siam* catches the overflow from the more popular guesthouses in the area.

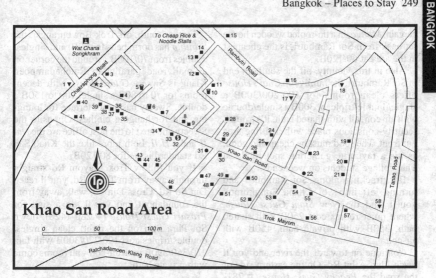

# Khao San Road Area

0    50    100 m

## PLACES TO STAY
- 3 Siam Guest House
- 4 Sitdhi Guest House
- 7 Mam's Guest House
- 8 Lek Guest House
- 9 Buddy Guest House
- 11 Doll Guest House & Others
- 12 Suneeporn Guest House
- 13 AT, Leed & Jim's Guesthouses
- 14 Green House
- 15 Viengtai Hotel
- 16 Orchid House
- 19 VS Guest House
- 20 Nisa Guest House
- 21 Harn Guest House
- 23 New Royal Guest House
- 24 Marco Polo Hostel
- 26 Nat Guest House
- 27 New Nith Jaroen Hotel
- 28 Khao San Palace Hotel
- 29 Grand Guest House
- 30 Dior Guest House
- 33 PB Guest House
- 35 Chart Guest House
- 36 Hello Guest House
- 37 Prakorp's House & Restaurant
- 38 NS Guest House
- 39 Thai Guest House
- 40 Ploy Guest House
- 41 J Guest House
- 42 Joe Guest House
- 43 Ranee Guest House
- 44 New Joe Guest House
- 45 Kaosarn Privacy Guest House
- 46 Thai Massage GH
- 47 Bonny & Top Guesthouses
- 48 Marco Polo (160 Guest House)
- 49 Good Luck Guest House
- 50 VIP Guest House
- 51 Tong Guest House
- 52 Neo Guest House
- 53 Nana Plaza Inn
- 54 Siri Guest House
- 55 CH Guest House
- 56 7-Holder Guest House
- 57 Chada Guest House

## PLACES TO EAT
- 1 Gaylord Indian Restaurant
- 6 Hello Pub
- 17 Chabad House
- 18 Pizza Hut
- 25 Best Aladdin Restaurant & Guest House
- 34 Royal India Restaurant
- 58 Arawy Det

## OTHER
- 2 Chana Songkhram Police Station
- 5 Paradise, No-Name & Hole in the Wall
- 10 Artsy Fartsy Bar & Art Gallery
- 22 Central Minimart
- 31 Shops
- 32 Krung Thai Bank

Right around the bend along Soi Rambutri is the popular *Merry V Guest House* (☎ 282-9267) with rooms from 100 to 160B; the cosy, similarly priced *Green* is next door. At *My House* on the same soi the Thai-style downstairs sitting area looks nice, but the guest rooms upstairs are bare cubicles with open transoms – at 150B not much of a bargain. *Mango*, in a tin-roofed wooden house set back from Soi Rambutri, is the cheapest in the area at 60/120B.

Also in this vicinity, off the southern end of Soi Rambutri, the family run *Chai's House* offers clean rooms for 100/200/300B a single/double/triple, or 300B a single/double with air-con, all with shared bath. It's a quiet, security-conscious place with a sitting area out front. The food must be cheap and good, as it's a favourite gathering spot for local Thai college students on weekends.

Backtracking along Soi Rambutri and turning left into Soi Chana Songkhram, you'll find the *New Siam Guest House*, where quiet rooms cost 250B with shared bath, 350B with private bath, 450B with air-con.

Continue on towards the river and you'll reach Phra Athit Rd. On the eastern side of the road the *Peachy Guest House* (☎ 281-6471) and *New Merry V* are more like small hotels than family-type guesthouses. Peachy has a pleasant garden restaurant and singles/doubles cost 85/130B, 250/320B with air-con. The New Merry V, a bit north from Peachy, has comfortable rooms with private hot water showers for 260B, or with shared bath for 140B. Both are quite popular.

Parallel to Soi Chana on Trok Rong Mai, off Phra Athit Rd, are a few old-timers, most with only two-bed rooms. The *Apple Guest House*, at 10/1 Trok Rong Mai, may not look like much, but it's popular with rooms at 70/100B, plus dorm beds for 50B. There's also an *Apple Guest House II* out on Trok Kai Chae Rd (off Phra Sumen Rd), for 100/120B, which one traveller recommended as being better.

**East Banglamphu**  There are several guesthouses clustered in the alleys east of Tanao Rd. In general, rooms are bigger and quieter here than at places around Khao San Rd. *Central Guest House* (☎ 282-0667) is just off Tanao Rd on Trok Bowonrangsi – look for the rather inconspicuous signs. This is a very pleasant guesthouse, with clean, quiet rooms for 60B per person. There are some more spacious doubles for 120B.

Farther south, off Trok Bowonrangsi, the *Srinthip* has dorm beds for 50B, and singles/doubles from 70/100B. Around the corner on a small road parallel to Ratchadamnoen Klang is *Sweety Guest House* with decent rooms for 70 to 80B a single, 100 to 150B a double. Sweety has a roof terrace for lounging and for hanging clothes. Opposite the Sweety and next to the post office are the *Nat II* and *CH II*, both more like the Khao San Rd standard issue for 80/120B.

If you follow Trok Mayom Rd straight through, away from Tanao Rd, you'll reach Din So Rd. Cross Din So, walk away from the roundabout and you'll see a sign for *Prasuri Guest House* (☎ 280-1428), down Soi Phra Suri on the right; clean singles/doubles/triples cost 190/220/300B with fan, 330/360/390B with air-con – all rooms come with private bath.

**South Banglamphu**  On the other side of Ratchadamnoen Klang, south of the Khao San Rd area, are a couple of independent hotels and at least one guesthouse worth investigating. If you walk south along Tanao Rd from Ratchadamnoen Klang, then left at the first soi, you'll come to *Hotel 90* (☎ 224-1012). It's mostly a short-time place but large, clean rooms with fan and private bath are 200/250B, 400B with air-con and TV.

Return west on this soi to Tanao Rd, turn left and then take the right at Trok Sa-Ke towards the upper mid-range Royal Hotel, and after 50m or so you'll come to the *Palace Hotel* (☎ 224-1876), an all air-con version of Hotel 90 with singles/doubles at 330/400B. The friendly *P Guest House* is nearby at 80/120B.

**North Banglamphu**  Up on Phra Sumen Rd, opposite the north entrances to Wat Bowon, is the *Canalside Guest House* which, as its name suggests, overlooks a khlong. Basic rooms are 100B a single/double – nothing to get excited about – but at least the guesthouse is away from the Khao San ghetto.

At 11/1 Soi Surao, off Chakraphong Rd towards the Banglamphu Department Store and market, the friendly *BK Guest House*

☎ 281-3048) offers clean rooms with shared bath for 120/150B with fan, 300/350B with air-con. *PS Guest House* (☎ 282-3932), a Peace Corps favourite, is all the way at the end of Phra Sumen Rd towards the river, off the south side of Khlong Banglamphu; its well kept rooms go for 110 to 160B. Next door is the similar *Gipsy Guest House* and, farther south-east, the more modern-looking *Banglamphu Square Guest House*, which has a coffee shop downstairs. On the opposite side of Phra Sumen in this area is an alley with a couple of cheapies, including the friendly *KC*.

Facing the north side of Khlong Banglamphu off Samsen Rd (the northern extension of Chakraphong Rd), the *New World House Apartments & Guest House* (☎ 281-5596) does both short and long-term room rentals starting at 400B per night. Rooms come with private hot water shower, air-con and a small balcony.

Also off Samsen Rd, farther north of Khlong Banglamphu, is a small cluster of guesthouses in convenient proximity to the Tha Samphraya river express landing. On Soi 1 Samsen, just off Samsen Rd, the Khao San Rd-style *Truly Yours* (☎ 282-0371) offers 100/160B rooms over a large downstairs restaurant. A bit farther on along Soi 1, *Villa Guest House* is a quiet, leafy, private home with 10 rooms from 200 to 450B; it's often full. Up on Soi 3 Samsen (also known as Soi Wat Samphraya), are the *River House* (☎ 280-0876), *Home & Garden* (☎ 280-1475) and *Clean & Calm*, each with small but clean rooms with shared bath for 60 to 120B. Note that Soi 3 zigs left, then zags right before reaching these three guesthouses, a good 10 minute walk from Samsen Rd. River House is the best of the three. *Vimol Guest House* on Soi 4 (east of Samsen Rd) rounds out the Samsen Rd offerings with rooms in a wooden house for 60 to 80B a single, 100 to 120B a double, 150 to 200B a triple.

Out on noisy Samsen Rd itself, the grungy *Sukwawasdi (Suksawat) Hotel* offers air-con rooms for 350 to 450B with private bath. Prostitutes are also known to hang around here. Farther north along Samsen, turn east on Soi 6 Samsen, and find *Nakhon Pink Hotel*, *Mitr Paisarn Hotel* and *Vorapong Guest House*, all places with overpriced rooms and a penchant for short-time trade. Continue along the zigzag soi almost all the way to the end and you'll come to the *AP*, a 70/140B guesthouse near Wat Mai Amaratarot.

The next river express stop north, and the last in the Banglamphu district, is next to Wisut Kasat Rd, where there are a couple of decent choices. The *MD Guest House* (☎ 280-3069), near Wat Intharawihan at 12 Wisut Kasat Rd (actually on a trok off Wisut Kasat), has very comfortable rooms with fan for 150B; the staff are very lax. The comfortable, mid-range *Trang Hotel* (☎ 282-2141), at 99/8 Wisut Kasat Rd has air-con rooms from 1150B a single/double, 1350B a triple. Both are east of Samsen Rd, so they're a good walk from the river.

**Thewet & National Library Area** The district north of Banglamphu near the National Library is another little travellers' enclave. Heading north up Samsen Rd from Wisut Kasat Rd, you'll come to *TV Guest House* (☎ 282-7451) at 7 Soi Phra Sawat, just off Samsen Rd to the east. It's clean, modern and good value at 40B for a dorm bed, 80B a double.

Continue for another half a km or so and cross the canal to the place where Phitsanulok Rd finishes on Samsen Rd and where Si Ayuthaya Rd crosses Samsen Rd. Just beyond this junction is the National Library. On two parallel sois off Si Ayuthaya Rd towards the river (west from Samsen) are five guesthouses run by various members of the same extended family: *Tavee Guest House* (☎ 282-5983), *Sawatdee Guest House* (☎ 282-5349), *Backpacker's Lodge* (☎ 282-3231), *Shanti Lodge* (☎ 281-2497) and *Original Paradise Guest House* (☎ 282-8673). All are clean, well kept, fairly quiet and cost 50B for a dorm bed, from 100/150B for singles/doubles.

A fifth, independently run place on the same soi as Paradise is *Little Home Guest*

*House* (☎ 282-1574), which is similar to the others in this area except that it has a busy travel agency in front. There's a good market across the road from both sois, and a few small noodle and rice shops along Krung Kasem Rd, south of and parallel to Si Ayuthaya (and west of Samsen Rd), which leads to Tha Thewet, a Chao Phraya River Express pier which provides good access to the National Library area; from the pier walk east along Krung Kasem Rd to Samsen Rd, turn left, cross the canal and then take another left into Si Ayuthaya Rd. Ordinary bus Nos 16, 30 and 53, and air-con bus Nos 56 and 6 pass Si Ayuthaya Rd while going up and down Samsen Rd; ordinary bus No 72 terminates on the corner of Phitsanulok and Samsen Rds, a short walk from Si Ayuthaya. Air-con bus No 10 from the airport also passes close to the area along Ratwithi Rd to the north, before crossing Krungthon Bridge.

East of Samsen Rd, the *Bangkok International Youth Hostel* (☎ 282-0950, 281-0361) is at 25/2 Phitsanulok Rd. A bed in the fan dorm costs 70B a night, while in the air-con dorm it's 80B. Rooms with fan and bath are 200B, while air-con singles/doubles with hot water are 250/300B. The rooms with fan are larger than the air-con rooms, and there's a cafeteria downstairs. In 1992 the hostel stopped accepting nonmembers as guests. Annual Hostelling International (formerly IYHF) membership costs 300B, or you can purchase a temporary membership for 50B. This hostel gets mixed reports – the rooms seem nice enough but the staff can be quite rude.

If you want to be close to Ratchadamnoen Boxing Stadium, or simply away from the river guesthouse scene, have a look at *Venice House* (☎ 281-8262) at 548-546/1 Krung Kasem Rd. This friendly, well maintained guesthouse is next to Wat Somanat, just around the corner from Ratchadamnoen Nok Rd (walk north on Ratchadamnoen Nok from the stadium, turn right on Krung Kasem and walk about 80m till you see a sign for Venice House). Rooms are air-con and cost 300/350B. It's about a 15 minute walk from the Tha Thewet landing.

**Soi Ngam Duphli** This area off Rama IV Rd is where most budget travellers used to come on their first trip to Bangkok. With a couple of notable exceptions, most of the places here are not especially cheap or even good value any more, and the area has taken on a rather seedy atmosphere. Overall, the Banglamphu area has better-value accommodation, although some travellers still prefer less crowded Soi Ngam Duphli. Several countries (Canada, Australia, Germany, Singapore, CIS, Korea, Laos, Myanmar) maintain embassies on nearby Sathon Rd, so it's also a convenient location for those with visa/passport business at these embassies.

The entrance to the soi is on Rama IV Rd, near the Sathon Tai Rd intersection, and within walking distance of verdant Lumphini Park and the Silom Rd business district. Ordinary bus Nos 4, 13, 14, 22, 45, 47, 74, 109 and 115, and air-con bus No 7 all pass by the entrance to Soi Ngam Duphli along Rama IV Rd.

At the northern end of Soi Ngam Duphli near Rama IV Rd is *ETC Guest House* (☎ 286-9424, 287-1478), an efficiently run, multistorey place with a travel agency downstairs. Rooms are small and uninspiring but clean; rates are 120B with shared bath, 160/200B for singles/doubles with private bath. All room rates include a breakfast of cereal, fruit, toast and coffee or tea.

Just south of ETC an alley leads left to the Quality Hotel Lumphini (see Places to Stay – top end). The cheerless *Tokyo Guest House* is farther south down Ngam Duphli; rooms are 100/140B for singles/doubles with shared bath.

Next south on the left is the *Anna Guest House* above the Anna Travel Agency. The odd place on the block, it reeks of cloying incense and has dilapidated rooms with shared bath for 100 to 180B; not recommended unless all else is full.

Farther down from here, the *Malaysia Hotel* (☎ 286-3582/7263), at 54 Soi Ngam Duphli, was once Bangkok's most famous travellers' hotel. Its 120 air-con, hot water rooms cost from 498B for a standard single

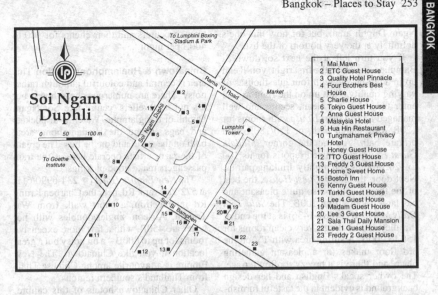

## Soi Ngam Duphli

0  50  100 m

To Lumphini Boxing
Stadium & Park

Rama IV Road

Market

Lumphini
Tower

To Goethe
Institute

1 Mai Mawn
2 ETC Guest House
3 Quality Hotel Pinnacle
4 Four Brothers Best House
5 Charlie House
6 Tokyo Guest House
7 Anna Guest House
8 Malaysia Hotel
9 Hua Hin Restaurant
10 Tungmahamek Privacy Hotel
11 Honey Guest House
12 TTO Guest House
13 Freddy 3 Guest House
14 Home Sweet Home
15 Boston Inn
16 Kenny Guest House
17 Turkh Guest House
18 Lee 4 Guest House
19 Madam Guest House
20 Lee 3 Guest House
21 Sala Thai Daily Mansion
22 Lee 1 Guest House
23 Freddy 2 Guest House

Soi Ngam Duphli

Soi Si Bamphen

or double, 586B with a TV and small fridge and 700B with a TV, larger fridge and carpet. The Malaysia has a swimming pool which may be used by visitors for 50B per day (it's free for guests of course). Since the 1970s, the Malaysia has made a conscious effort to distance itself from the backpackers' market; for a while it seemed to be catering directly to the lonely male hired-sex market. There seem to be fewer prostitutes around the lobby than in the old days – at least before midnight. After the Patpong bars close, bar girls who didn't pick up an outside customer earlier in the evening tend to congregate in the hotel coffee shop.

The *Tungmahamek Privacy Hotel* (☎ 286-2339/8811), across the road to the south of the Malaysia, is also fully air-con and costs 300 to 400B for a double. Many 'short-time' residents here give the place a sleazy feel, though it's less of a 'scene' than the Malaysia. In the other direction from the Malaysia is the *LA Hotel* (the English sign just says 'Hotel'), which generally refuses western guests unless brought there by a prostitute.

Turn left (east) from Ngam Duphli into Soi Si Bamphen and before you reach the Boston Inn take the alley to the right. Near the end of the alley, *TTO Guest House* (☎ 286-6783; fax 287-1571) offers clean air-con rooms with private bath for 350 to 400B, plus a few fan rooms for 250B. Though it isn't cheap, it's well managed with spacious rooms and reasonably friendly staff.

Across Soi Si Bamphen in another alley is the *Home Sweet Home Guest House*, a friendly place with singles/doubles for 120/150B. Rooms facing Si Bamphen are newer, nicer and noisier; rooms on the alley are quieter. Farther down Si Bamphen is another alley on the right with guesthouses on both corners that change their names on average every other year; at the moment they're called *Kenny* and *Turkh*. Both have dingy rooms upstairs for 150 to 250B; don't be fooled by the OK looking restaurants downstairs – the rooms are quite shabby. Down this same alley on the right is the even more miserable looking *Freddy 3 Guest House* with basic accommodation for 80 to 100B. Let's not mince words; this alley has a reputation for harbouring junkies.

The notorious *Boston Inn* is still a blight on Soi Si Bamphen. Rumour has it the owner was planning to renovate (at one time the Boston was one of the better places in the Soi

Ngam Duphli area), but for now this one's definitely at the very bottom of the list.

If you turn left at the next soi down Si Bamphen, then take the first right, you'll end up in a cul-de-sac with four guesthouses of varying quality. First up on the right as you enter the soi is the clean, secure and well managed *Lee 4 Guest House* with rooms for 120B with shared bath, or 150/180B with private bath. Around the corner, *Madam Guest House* gets mixed reports for its 100 to 120B rooms and nightly drinking parties. Next door, the *Lee 3 Guest House*, the best of the three Lees, is also quite pleasant and has large rooms from 100B. The *Sala Thai Daily Mansion* (☎ 287-1436) is at the end of the alley and has large, very clean rooms for 150 to 200B. A sitting area with TV on the 3rd floor makes for a pleasant gathering place, and there is a breezy rooftop terrace. The owner speaks English and her design background is evident in the tasteful furnishings. Many repeat or long-term guests fill the rooms here.

If you continue north along the main soi that passes the previously mentioned guesthouses you'll come to a left turn which dead-ends at Soi Saphan Khu (parallel to Soi Ngam Duphli). Turn right and you'll come to two guesthouses on your left, *Charlie House* and *Four Brothers Best House*. Well run Charlie House (☎ 679-8330; fax 679-7308) aims for a slightly more upscale market with carpeted rooms with air-con, phone and TV starting at 450B. Smoking is prohibited; a sign reads 'Decently dressed ladies, gentlemen and their children are welcome'. Four Brothers (☎ 678-8822) costs 400B per day for air-con rooms; the game arcade downstairs can be a bit noisy.

Back out on Soi Si Bamphen heading south-east are two more guesthouses. First on the left is the original *Lee 1 Guest House*, with decaying rooms from 80B, followed by the better *Freddy 2*, a clean, well run place with rooms for 80/150B and a contingent of resident Thai bar girls.

South of the Privacy on Soi Ngam Duphli is *Honey*, an apartment building with tiny, cheap rooms which mostly cater to prosti-tutes, procurers and their clients for 100 to 400B per night.

**Chinatown & Hualamphong Station** This area is central and colourful although rather noisy. There are numerous cheap hotels but it's not a travellers' centre like Soi Ngam Duphli or Banglamphu. Watch your pockets and bags around the Hualamphong area, both on the street and on the bus. The cream of the razor artists operate here as the train passengers make good pickings.

The *New Empire Hotel* (☎ 234-6990/6) is at 572 Yaowarat Rd, near the Charoen Krung Rd intersection, a short walk from Wat Traimit. Air-con singles/doubles with hot water are 450B, with a few more expensive rooms for up to 800B – a bit noisy but a great location if you like Chinatown. The New Empire is a favourite among Chinese Thais from Thailand's southern regions.

Other Chinatown hotels of this calibre, most without English signs out the front, can be found along Yaowarat, Chakraphet and Ratchawong Rds. The *Burapha Hotel* (☎ 221-3545/9), at the intersection of Mahachai and Charoen Krung Rds, on the edge of China-town, is a notch better than the Empire and costs 500B single/double, and up to 1000B for a deluxe room. Likewise for the *Somboon Hotel* (☎ 221-2327), at 415 Yaowarat Rd.

Straddling the bottom and mid-range is the *River View Guest House* (☎ 234-5429, 235-8501) at 768 Soi Phanurangsi, Songwat Rd in the Talaat Noi area south of Chinatown – wedged between Bangrak (Silom) and Chinatown. The building is behind the Jao Seu Kong Chinese shrine, about 400m from the Royal Orchid Sheraton, in a neigh-bourhood filled with small machine shops. To get there, turn right from the corner of Si Phraya Rd (facing the River City shopping complex), take the fourth left, then the first right. Large rooms are 450B with fan and private bath, 700 to 800B with air-con and hot water. As the name suggests, many rooms have a Chao Phraya River view; the view from the 8th floor restaurant is superb, even if you have to wake up the staff to get a meal. If you call from the River City complex, someone from the guesthouse will pick you up.

Not far from the River View Guest House on Songwat Rd, the *Chao Phraya Riverside Guest House* has less expensive rooms for 250/300B single/double.

Along the eastern side of Hualamphong station is Rong Meuang Rd which has several dicey Chinese hotels. The *Sri Hualamphong Hotel*, at No 445, is one of the better ones – all rooms are 120B with fan. The *Sahakit (Shakij) Hotel* is a few doors down towards Rama IV Rd and is quite OK too. Rooms are from 100B; if you stay here, try to get a room on the 4th floor which has a terrace with a view and the occasional breeze.

Out towards the front of the station, after Rong Meuang Rd makes a sharp curve, is the *Station Hotel*, a classic Third World dive. A room with torn curtains, dim sheets and crusty attached bath costs an astounding 150B.

The market area behind the Station Hotel is full of cheap food stalls, and on a small soi parallel to Rong Meuang Rd is the *Hoke Aan Hotel*, yet another 100/120B Chinese hole-in-the-wall (but at least it's away from the Rong Meuang traffic). Also off Rong Meuang Rd next to the Chinese market is the noisy but adequate *Nam Ia Hotel* for only 100B.

At least four other cheap Chinese hotels can be found west of the station along Maitrichit Rd, all in the 70 to 100B range.

Also convenient to Hualamphong station, and more suitable for stays of more than a night or two, are the TT guesthouses. The somewhat easier-to-find *TT 2 Guest House* (☎ 236-2946) is at 516-518 Soi Sawang, Si Phraya Rd near the Mahanakhon Rd intersection. Rooms here are 180B. To find the TT 2 from the train station, turn left onto Rama IV, right on Mahanakhon, left on Soi Kaew Fa and then right on Soi Sawang. Or from Si Phraya Rd (take Microbus 6) turn directly onto Soi Sawang. To find the more hidden *TT 1 Guest House* (☎ 236-3053), at 138 Soi Wat Mahaphuttharam off Mahanakhon Rd from the station, cross Rama IV Rd, walk left

down Rama IV, then right on Mahanakhon and follow the signs for TT 1. It's only about a 10 minute walk from the station. Dorm beds are just 40B; singles/doubles go for 150B. Baggage storage and laundry service are available; both TTs enforce a strict midnight curfew.

*FF Guest House* has a similar setup for 120B a single, 150B a double. From Hualamphong station, walk east on Rama IV Rd 200m and look for a small sign pointing down an alley to the guesthouse.

**Silom & Surawong Rds** Several of the cheaper mid-range guesthouses and hotels can be found in and around the Silom and Surawong Rds area.

The *Madras Lodge* (☎ 235-6761), in Vaithi Lane off Silom Rd, not far from the Maha Uma Devi Temple, has rooms with fan starting at 220B. The proprietor is a friendly Indian man from Madras (a retired gem dealer) and his kitchen serves delicious south Indian food. Also off Silom Rd is *Bangkok Christian Guest House* (☎ 253-3353) at 123 Sala Daeng Soi 2, Convent Rd. It has very nice air-con rooms from 650B including breakfast.

Opposite the GPO, on Charoen Krung Rd, are a couple of guesthouses catering mostly to middle-class north Indians, Pakistanis and Bangladeshis – *Naaz* and *Kabana Inn*, each charging a reasonable 400 to 500B for air-con rooms. Just a bit more expensive but offering better service is the *Woodlands Inn*, on the soi that runs along the northern side of the GPO. Clean, air-con rooms with hot water, TV and fridge are 600B for singles/doubles. Downstairs is an air-con Indian restaurant, the Cholas.

**Siam Square** Several good places can be found in this central area, which has the additional advantage of being on the Khlong Saen Saep canal taxi route.

There are several lower mid-range places on or near Soi Kasem San 1, off Rama I Rd near Jim Thompson's House and the National Stadium. The eight-storey *Muangphol (Muangphon) Mansion* (☎ 215-0033) on the

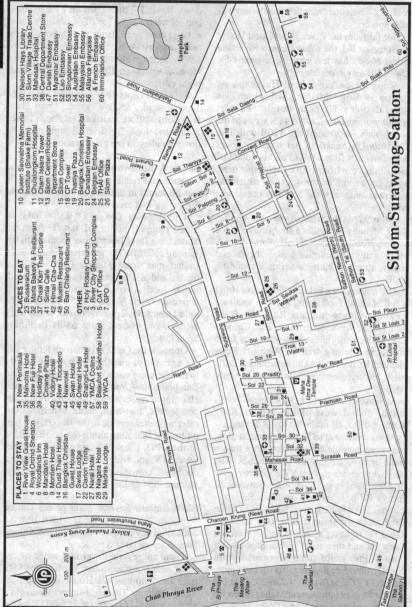

## Silom-Surawong-Sathon

**PLACES TO STAY**
1  River View Guest House
4  Royal Orchid Sheraton
6  Woodlands Inn
8  Mandarin Hotel
9  Montien Hotel
14  Dusit Thani Hotel
16  Bangkok Christian
    Guest House
17  Swiss Lodge
22  Clarion Trinity
27  Narai Hotel
28  Niagara Hotel
29  Madras Lodge
34  New Peninsula
35  Manohra Hotel
36  New Fuji Hotel
39  Holiday Inn
    Crowne Plaza
40  Victory Hotel
43  New Trocadero
44  Newrotel
45  Swan Hotel
46  Oriental Hotel
49  Shangri-La Hotel
57  YMCA Collins
58  Beaufort Sukhothai Hotel
59  YWCA

**PLACES TO EAT**
23  Bussaracum
32  Mahà Bakèn & Restaurant
37  Chaai Karr Thai Cuisine
41  Simla Cafe
42  Himali Cha-Cha
48  Muslim Restaurant
50  Ban Chiang Restaurant

**OTHER**
2  Holy Rosary Church
3  River City Shopping Complex
5  CAT Office
7  GPO
10  Queen Saovabha Memorial
    Institute (Snake Farm)
11  Chulalongkorn Hospital
12  Sham Issara Tower
13  Central/Robinson
    Department Store
15  Silom Complex
18  CP Tower
19  Thaniya Plaza
20  Bangkok Christian Hospital
21  Canadian Embassy
24  Belgian Embassy
25  THAI Office
26  Silom Plaza
30  Neilson Hays Library
31  Silom Village Trade Centre
33  Mahesak Hospital
38  Central Department Store
47  Danish Embassy
51  Myanmar Embassy
52  Lao Embassy
53  Singaporean Embassy
54  Australian Embassy
55  Malaysian Embassy
56  Alliance Française
    & French Embassy
60  Immigration Office

corner of Soi Kasem San 1 and Rama I Rd (931/8 Rama I Rd) has singles/doubles for 450/550B. It's good value, with air-con, hot water, a 24 hour restaurant and good service. Behind the Muangphol, off this soi, is the apartment-style *Pranee Building* (☎ 216-3181), which has one entrance next to the Muangphol and another on Rama I Rd. Fan-cooled rooms with private bath are 300 to 350B; air-con rooms with hot water start at 400B. There are no lifts. The Pranee also does long-term rentals at a 10% discount.

*White Lodge* (☎ 216-8867/8228), at 36/8 Soi Kasem San 1, past the more expensive Reno Hotel on the left, offers clean if some-what small rooms at 400B for singles/doubles. There's a pleasant terrace cafe out front. The next one down on Soi Kasem San 1 is the three-storey *Wendy House* (☎ 216-2436), where small but clean rooms with air-con, hot shower and TV go for 400/450B. If you're carrying unusually heavy bags, note there's no lift. A small restaurant is on the ground floor.

Next up the soi is the ancient *Star Hotel* (☎ 215-3381) at 36/1 Soi Kasem San 1, a classic sort of mid-1960s Thai no-tell motel, with fairly clean, comfortable, air-con rooms with bath and TV for 550 to 650B a double, depending on the room – a bit steep for this area. Perhaps the higher rate is due to the curtained parking slots next to the ground floor rooms, which hide cars belonging to guests from casual passers-by.

Opposite the Star is *A-One Inn* (☎ 215-3029; fax 216-4771) at No 25/12-15, a friendly and pleasant place that gets a lot of return business. Fair-sized air-con doubles with bath and hot water are 400B; spacious triples are 500B (rates may drop 100B in low season). The similar *Bed & Breakfast Inn* diagonally opposite the A-One has room rates that fluc-tuate from 350 to 500B depending on demand; air-con rooms are substantially smaller than the A-One's but rates include a European breakfast.

Over on Soi Kasem San 2 (same soi as Jim Thompson's House) the efficient, 54-room *MP Villa* (☎ 214-4495) offers good 500B single/double rooms with air-con, phone, TV and fridge, plus a downstairs restaurant.

**Sukhumvit Rd** Staying in this area puts you in the newest part of Bangkok and the far-thest from old Bangkok near the river. Taxis take longer to get here because of the one way street system. The majority of the hotels in this area are in the middle-price range.

The oldest hostelry in the Sukhumvit area is the historic *Atlanta Hotel* (☎ 252-1650/6069), at 78 Soi 2 (Soi Phasak), Sukhumvit Rd. Owned since its construction in the 1950s by Dr Max Henn, a former secretary to the maharajah of Bikaner and owner of Bangkok's first international pharmacy, the Atlanta is a simple but reliable stand-by with clean, comfortable rooms in several price categories. Rooms with private shower, fan, balcony and one large double bed cost 300/400B a single/double, while similar rooms with twin beds (no balcony) go for 300/400/500B a single/double/triple. Air-con rooms with hot showers and built-in safe boxes go for 450/550/605B a single/double/triple on the 3rd floor, 50B extra for lower floors. Monthly stays paid in advance warrant a 10% discount; children under 12 can stay with parents for 50B above the single or double room rate.

The Atlanta's 1954 vintage swimming pool was the first hotel pool in Thailand; the original 1950s-era hotel lobby is occasion-ally used as a backdrop for Bangkok fashion shoots. The subdued, simply decorated coffee shop – formerly part of the Continen-tal, a restaurant that once served royalty and foreign diplomats – features a heavily anno-tated menu (itself a crash course in Thai cuisine), a selection of British, German and French newspapers, a sound system playing Thai, classical and jazz (including an hour of King Bhumibol's compositions beginning at noon) and evening video selections which include film classics with Thailand themes (eg *Chang, Bridge on the River Kwai*). A map room and letter-writing lounge round out the offerings at this Bangkok institution.

The *Golden Palace Hotel*, at 15 Soi 1, Sukhumvit Rd, has a swimming pool, is well situated and costs 400 to 500B for a double with air-con and bath. The clientele here are mostly middle-class tourists 'on a budget',

BANGKOK

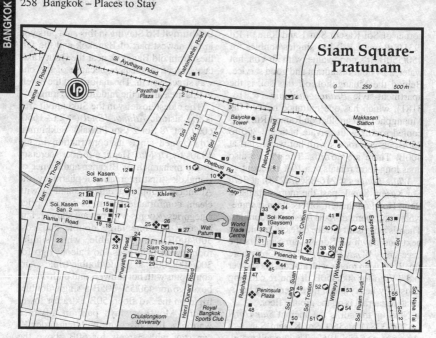

# Siam Square-Pratunam

PLACES TO STAY
1   Siam City Hotel
2   Florida Hotel
5   Indra Regent Hotel
6   Mercure Bangkok
    Hotel
7   Borarn House
9   Amari Watergate
    Hotel
12  Asia Hotel
14  A-One Inn
15  Star Hotel & Bed
    & Breakfast Inn
16  White Lodge &
    Wendy House
17  Reno Hotel
18  Pranee &
    Muangphol
    Buildings
19  Krit Thai Mansion
20  MP Villa
27  Siam Intercontinental
    Hotel
30  Novotel Bangkok
33  Felix Arnoma
    Swissotel
35  Siam Orchid Inn

36  Le Meridien
    President Hotel
41  Hilton International
    Bangkok
43  Golden Palace Hotel
47  Grand Hyatt Erawan
48  Regent Bangkok
53  Imperial Hotel
55  Atlanta Hotel

PLACES TO EAT
28  Hard Rock Cafe
50  Whole Earth
    Restaurant

OTHER
3   Wang Suan
    Phakkard
4   Post Office
8   Pratunam Market
10  Phanthip Plaza
11  Indonesian Embassy
13  Tha Ratchathewi
    (Canal Taxis)
21  Jim Thompson's
    House
22  National Stadium

23  Mahboonkrong
    Shopping Centre
24  Scala Cinema
25  Siam Center
26  Post Office
29  British Council
31  Gaysorn Plaza
32  Narayana Phand
34  Robinson
    Department Store
37  Central Department
    Store
38  TOT Office
39  UK Embassy
40  Norwegian
    Embassy
42  Swiss Embassy
44  Maneeya Building
45  Sogo Department
    Store
46  Erawan Shrine
    (Saan Phra Phrom)
49  Israeli Embassy
51  Netherlands
    Embassy
52  Spanish Embassy
54  Vietnam Embassy

but the Golden Palace has seen better days. On the next soi east, the quiet *Best Inn* (☎ 253-0573) at 75/5-6 Soi 3, Sukhumvit Rd, provides smallish rooms with fan for 350B and air-con rooms for 450B. Also in the inner Sukhumvit area is *Thai House Inn* (☎ 255-4698; fax 253-1780), between sois 5 and 7. Rooms with air-con and hot water are 500B a single or double; facilities include a safety-deposit service and a coffee shop. Back on the other side of Sukhumvit Rd, the newish *Uncle Rey* (☎ 252-5565) at 7/10 Soi 4, offers simple air-con lodging for 400B.

Moving farther out on Sukhumvit Rd, the *Miami Hotel* (☎ 252-5140/4759/5036), at Soi 13, Sukhumvit Rd, dates back to the 1960s and 1970s R&R period. The room and service quality seems to seesaw every three years or so but recent reports reckon it's decent value at 500/550B a single/double for air-con rooms and a swimming pool. The *Crown Hotel* (☎ 258-0318), at Soi 29, Sukhumvit Rd, is in decline and gets mostly short-term traffic these days.

*Disra House* (☎ 258-5102), on the access street to Villa Theatre between sois 33 and 33/1, has similar rooms to the Crown for 80 to 120B.

**Thonburi** *The Artists Place* (☎ 852-0056; fax 862-0074), at 63 Soi Thiam Bunyang off Soi Krung Thonburi 1 (near Wong Wian Yai), was recently opened by Thai artist Charlee Sodprasert as a place for visiting artists to congregate and work. Singles and doubles cost 80 to 120B, while more expensive rooms go for 350B. Studio space is available. It's a bit difficult to find, so call for directions first. Very few farangs or other tourists stay on the Thonburi side of the river, so this is a good choice for people who want to be in the Bangkok milieu while getting away from the tourist scene.

**Places to Stay – middle**
Bangkok is saturated with small and medium-sized hotels in this category. The clientele are a very mixed bunch of Asian business travellers, western journalists on slim expense accounts, economy-class tour groups, along

with a smattering of independent tourists who seem to have chosen their hotels at random. Not quite 'international class', these places often offer guests a better sense of being in Thailand than the luxury hotels.

During the late 1980s, when there was a shortage of tourist accommodation, many mid-range hotels doubled their rates in a grab for short-term profit over long-term goodwill. In the off-season (March to November) you may be able to get a low-occupancy discount off the rates listed below.

**Banglamphu** Before Khao San Rd was 'discovered', the most popular Banglamphu hotel was the *Viengtai Hotel* (☎ 280-5434; fax 281-8153) at 42 Rambutri Rd. Over the last decade or so the Viengtai has continually raised its prices (not always concomitant with an upgrading of facilities) until it now sits solidly in the middle-price range of Bangkok hotels; singles/doubles are 1400B.

On Phra Athit Rd, close to the Tha Phra Athit riverboat stop, the apartment-style *Phra Athit Mansion* offers rooms with air-con, TV, hot water showers and fridge for 650B a single/double, 850B a triple.

Besides the Oriental and the Atlanta, the oldest continually operating hotel in the city is the *Royal Hotel* (☎ 222-9111/20), still going strong on the corner of Ratchadamnoen Klang and Atsadang Rds about 500m from the Democracy Monument. The Royal's 24 hour coffee shop is a favourite local rendezvous; this is one of the few upper mid-range places where there are as many Asian as non-Asian guests. Singles/doubles start at 960B; during the low season this can sometimes be negotiated down to around 700B. Incidentally, most of the taxi drivers know this hotel as the 'Ratanakosin' (as the Thai sign on top of the building reads), not as the Royal. During the bloody May 1992 protests against General Suchinda's appointment as prime minister, the Royal served as a makeshift hospital for injured demonstrators. A place of similar vintage and atmosphere, the *Majestic Hotel* (☎ 281-5000; fax 280-0965) can be found right around the corner at 97 Ratchadamnoen Klang Rd near the

Democracy Monument. Here rooms start at 1200B.

Another mid-range place in this area is the *Thai Hotel* (☎ 282-2833), at 78 Prachatipatai Rd, which has singles/doubles for 1100/1250B.

**Chinatown** Mid-range hotels in Chinatown are tough to find. Best bets are the 80-room *Chinatown* (☎ 226-1267), at 526 Yaowarat Rd, which has rooms for 700 to 1200B, and the *Miramar Hotel* (☎ 222-4191), 777 Mahachai Rd, where standard singles/doubles cost 780 to 1800B.

**Silom & Surawong Rds** This area is packed with upper mid-range places; discounts are often dispensed from April to October. Bangkok's YMCA and YWCA are both in this area. The *YMCA Collins International House* (☎ 287-1900/2727; fax 287-1996), at 27 Sathon Tai (South) Rd, has air-con rooms with TV, telephone and private bath from 1377B. Guests may use the Y's massage room, gym, track and swimming pool. The *YWCA* (☎ 286-1936) is at 13 Sathon Tai Rd and has cheaper air-con rooms starting at 567B.

On the south side of Silom Rd is Soi Suksavitthaya (Seuksa Withaya), with the mid-range *Niagara Hotel* (☎ 233-5783/4) at 26 Soi Suksavitthaya, where clean air-con rooms with hot water and telephone are a bargain at 550 to 600B.

A decent upper mid-range choice is the *Newrotel* (☎ 237-1094; fax 237-1102) at 1216/1 Charoen Krung Rd, near the GPO and the river. Air-con singles/doubles cost 1200B.

The two hotels nearest Patpong Rd – the *Suriwong* and the *Rose* – are in the 700 to 800B range. They can't really be recommended for light sleepers as they suffer from heavy people-traffic from the Patpong bars. The Rose has a primarily gay clientele.

Classic mid-range hotels on Surawong Rd include the *New Fuji* (☎ 234-5364) at No 299-310 with rooms from 1124 to 1338B, and the *New Trocadero Hotel* (☎ 234-8920/9) at No 34, where singles/doubles cost

from 770 to 1400B. Because both hotels offer good service and amenities for under 1500B, they are favourites among journalists. A fair number of package tours stop here as well. The recently refurbished, Thai-style *Manohra Hotel* (☎ 234-5070) at No 412 offers singles/doubles starting at 2600B. A newer entry at No 173/8-9, *La Residence* (☎ 235-4795; fax 233-3301), is an intimate 23-room place with rates from 750 to 1550B.

**Siam Square/Hualamphong** This area tends to offer either upper-end budget or top-end luxury hotels, with little in the middle. *Krit Thai Mansion* (☎ 215-3042), out on busy Rama I Rd opposite the National Stadium, costs 700 to 800B for rooms with air-con, hot water, private bath, telephone, colour TV/video, fridge and security parking. The coffee shop downstairs is open 24 hours. Reports are mixed – some seem to like the hotel, some don't. An old Siam Square stand-by, the *Reno Hotel* (☎ 215-0026) on Soi Kasem San 1 is a veteran from the Vietnam War days when a spate of hotels opened in Bangkok with the names of US cities. Singles/doubles/triples with air-con and hot water cost 550 to 990B; there's a pool on the premises.

The *Siam Orchid Inn* (☎ 255-2119; fax 255-3144), off Soi Gaysorn close to Le Meridien President Hotel, offers well appointed rooms with all the amenities for around 1500B.

For anyone who wants to be near the Royal Orchid Sheraton, the River City complex and the river (Tha Si Phraya landing), the *Orchid Inn* (☎ 234-8934; fax 234-4159) at 719/1 Si Phraya Rd provides decent mid-range value at 750/900B (discounts of 100 to 150B are often available) for tidy air-con rooms with TV and mini-fridge. Another advantage here is that the ordinary No 36 bus and Microbus No 6 each terminate almost directly opposite the hotel. The downside is the high number of touts and big-spending tourists in the neighbourhood.

The multistorey *Tong Poon Hotel* (☎ 216-0020; fax 215-0450), at 130 Soi 8, Rama VI (formerly called Soi 4, Rong Meuang), is a mid-price place favoured for low-budget conventions and Asian tour groups. Although rack rates (room rates quoted to walk-ins) for large rooms with air-con, colour TV and phones are 1800/2000B a single/double, discounts of around 1000 to 1500B are sometimes available. The Tong Poon has a coffee shop and pool, and it's a short tuk-tuk ride from Hualamphong station.

**Pratunam** The *Opera Hotel* (☎ 252-4031; fax 253-5360), at 16 Soi Somprasong 1, Phetburi Rd, is very near the heart of Pratunam and features air-con doubles with hot water from 550 to 800B. The Opera also has a swimming pool and coffee shop.

*Bangkok Noorie* (☎ 252-3340), at 178/7 Soi Wuttiphan, Ratchaprarop Rd near the Indra Regent Hotel, charges 650 to 850B for reasonable air-con rooms. The nearby *Classic Inn* (☎ 208-0496) off Ratchaprarop Rd costs around 400B for decent air-con rooms. A long walk east along the soi opposite the Indra (off Ratchaprarop Rd) leads eventually to *Borarn House* (☎ 246-4525; fax 253-3639), a Thai-style apartment building at 487/48 Soi Wattanasin, with singles/doubles for 850/950B with air-con and TV. The adequate *Siam Hotel* (☎ 252-5081), at 1777 Phetburi Rd, has 120 rooms; singles/doubles cost 880/1060B.

**Sukhumvit Rd** This area is choked with hotels costing 800 to 1500B. Stick to the lower numbered sois to save crosstown travel time.

The *Federal Hotel* (☎ 253-0175), at 27 Soi 11, Sukhumvit Rd, is a favourite among Vietnam War and Peace Corps vets but I've found the accommodation overpriced at 700 to 1050B, especially for the added-on rooms at ground level; these occasionally flood in the rainy season, when they're available for 550B. The modest pool and coffee shop are the main attractions. The well run *Parkway Inn*, on Sukhumvit Rd at Soi 4, next to the Landmark Hotel is better value at 800 to 1000B a night; amenities include a rooftop pool.

Moving farther east along Sukhumvit Rd, the well run *Carlton Inn* (☎ 258-0471; fax 258-3717), at 22/2-4 Soi 21, Sukhumvit Rd, has decent rooms from 750B. A bit nicer are the two *City Lodges* on sois 9 (☎ 253-7680) and 19 (☎ 254-4783). Rooms at either location are 1016B for a single or double, and include air-con, telephone, TV/video and minibar. Other mid-range hotels in the Sukhumvit Rd area include:

*Asoke Place* – 4/49 Soi 21, Sukhumvit Rd (☎ 258-3742); 20 rooms, singles/doubles 650 to 850B
*Business Inn* – 155/4-5 Soi 11, Sukhumvit Rd (☎ 254-7981); 70 rooms, singles/doubles 500 to 700B
*China Inn* – 19/27-28 Soi 19, Sukhumvit Rd (☎ 255-7571); 27 rooms, singles/doubles 650 to 750B
*Comfort Inn* – 153/11 Soi 11, Sukhumvit Rd (☎ 651-1470); 60 rooms, singles/doubles 810 to 1300B
*Dynasty Inn* – 5/4-5 Soi 4, Sukhumvit Rd (☎ 250-1397); 55 rooms, singles/doubles 850 to 950B
*Euro Inn* – 249 Soi 31, Sukhumvit Rd (☎ 259-9480); 82 rooms, singles/doubles 1100 to 1570B
*Fortuna Hotel* – 19 Sukhumvit Rd (☎ 251-5121); 110 rooms, singles/doubles 900/1100B
*Grace Hotel* – 12 Nana Neua (Soi 3), Sukhumvit Rd (☎ 253-0651); 542 rooms, 760 to 1507B
*Grand Inn* – 2/7-8 Soi 3, Sukhumvit Rd (☎ 254-9021); 24 rooms, 800 to 1200B
*Manhattan* – Soi 15, Sukhumvit Rd (☎ 252-7141/9); 206 rooms, from 1400B
*Nana Hotel* – 4 Nana Tai, Sukhumvit Rd (☎ 255-0122); 224 rooms, 960 to 1500B
*Rajah Hotel* – 18 Soi 4, Sukhumvit Rd (☎ 255-0040); 450 rooms, singles/doubles from 1287B
*Rex Hotel* – 762/1 Soi 32; Sukhumvit Rd (☎ 259-0106); 131 rooms, singles/doubles 1100 to 1310B
*White Inn* – 41 Soi 4, Sukhumvit Rd (☎ 251-1662); 11 rooms, singles/doubles from 750B

**Victory Monument Area** Just north of Siam Square, in the Victory Monument area, are several hotels, including the decent *Century Hotel* (☎ 246-7800) at 9 Ratchaprarop Rd. This hotel has 96 rooms at 972B for singles or doubles. At the more up-market *Continental Hotel* (☎ 278-1596/8), 971/16 Phahonyothin Rd, singles cost from 1200 to 2400B. The Indochina War-era *Florida Hotel* (☎ 247-0990), at 43 Phayathai Square, Phayathai Rd, has singles/doubles at 700/800B.

**Airport Area** Finding decent, moderately priced accommodation in the airport area is difficult. Most of the hotels in this area charge nearly twice as much as comparable hotels in the city. Typical is *Don Muang Mansion* (☎ 566-3095), at 118/7 Soranakom Rd, Don Muang, which looks classy on the outside but asks 1000 to 1200B for a small, stuffy room that in Bangkok would cost at the most 500 to 750B. It's possible to negotiate a lower rate of 800B with some discussion.

If you can spend a bit more, a better choice is the 150-room *Comfort Inn Airport* (☎ 552-8929; fax 552-8920), about five minutes south of the airport by car at 88/117 Vibhavadi (Wiphaawadi) Rangsit Highway. Large rooms with all the amenities (satellite TV, air-con, hot water bath/shower) cost 1500 to 1800B if you book through a Bangkok travel agent, 2500 to 2800B for walk-ins. Best of all, the hotel provides a free shuttle to and from the airport every hour. Other facilities include a coffee shop, pool, sauna and health club. About the only drawback is that you can hear planes landing and taking off until around midnight.

For quite a bit less you could stay at the well run *We-Train Guest House* (☎ 566-1774/2288; fax 566-3481), at 501/1 Mu 3, Dechatung Rd, Sikan, Don Muang. Simple but very clean fan rooms with two beds and private bath cost 450B a single/double or 770B with air-con (extra beds cost 150B). You can also get a bed in a fan-cooled dorm for 150B, air-con 200B. To these rates add the usual 10% service charge but no tax since it's operated by a nonprofit women's organisation (male guests are welcome). Facilities include a pool, Thai massage, laundry service, a coffee shop and beauty salon. One major drawback to the We-Train is its distance from the airport – you must get a taxi to cross the highway and railway, then go about three km west along Dechatung Rd to the Thung Sikan school (*rohng rian thûng sĩi-kan*). If you don't have much luggage, walk across the airport pedestrian bridge to reach Don Muang, then get a taxi – it's much cheaper that way because you avoid the high taxi-desk fees. From the guesthouse there are usually no taxis in the area when you're ready to return to the airport or continue on to Bangkok, but transportation to and from the airport can be arranged on request (for which We-Train charges a steep 200B one way).

**Other Areas** North of central Bangkok in Nonthaburi – about 40 minutes away by Chao Phraya River Express – *Thai House* (☎ 280-0740; fax 280-0741), at 3677/4 Muu 8 Tambon Bang Meuang, Amphoe Bang Yai, is popular with repeat visitors for its traditional Thai decor and for the cooking courses taught on the premises. Rates are 900B a single, 1200B a double. Thai House maintains a separate reservation office in Banglamphu at 22 Phra Athit Rd.

*Aquarius Guest House* (☎ /fax 286-217), at 243 Soi Hutayan, Soi Suan Phlu, off Sathon Tai Rd, is a quiet Thai-style place that courts a gay male clientele. It has satellite TV, a shady courtyard and rooms which cost 750B per night.

Medium-price hotels in other areas of the city include:

*Baron Hotel* – 544 Soi Huay Khwang, Ratchadaphisek Rd, Huay Khwang (☎ 246-4525); 155 rooms, singles/doubles 600/650B
*Golden Dragon* – 20/21 Ngam Wongwan Rd (10 km from the airport) (☎ 588-4414/5); 114 rooms, 770 to 1320B
*Golden Horse Hotel* – 5/1 Damrongrak Rd (☎ 281-6909); 130 rooms, 600 to 1800B
*Liberty Hotel* – 215 Pratipat Rd, Saphan Khwai (☎ 271-0880); 209 rooms, singles/doubles 475 to 871B
*Royal Lake View* – 649/1-76 Asoke-Din Daeng Rd (☎ 246-3327); 176 rooms, 1200B

## Places to Stay – top end
Bangkok has all sorts of international-standard tourist hotels, from the straightforward package places to some of Asia's classic hotels. Three of Bangkok's luxury hotels, in fact, consistently make Condé Nast *Traveler*'s annual worldwide top 25 list: the Oriental, the Regent and the Shangri-La. Although there's no single area for top-end hotels you'll find quite a few around the Siam

Square area, along the parallel Surawong and Silom Rds, and along the river, while many of the slightly less expensive 'international standard' places are scattered along Sukhumvit Rd.

From 1988 to 1991, luxury-class hotels in Bangkok raised their rates more than any other class of hotel in Thailand, capitalising on the 90%-plus occupancy rates of the late 1980s. When a hotel construction boom collided with the 1990-91 Gulf War and recession, many of the price-gougers were humbled. At all but the top-rated places such as the Oriental, Regent Bangkok or Grand Hyatt Erawan, rates quoted in 1996 were often lower than those from 1994, yet you should still be able to negotiate discounts of up to 40% on the rates listed. Booking through a travel agency almost always means lower rates, or try asking for a hotel's 'corporate' discount. Several luxury hotels have even lowered their rack rates since the last edition of this book.

A welcome trend in Bangkok hotels in the past few years has been the appearance of several European-style 'boutique' hotels – small, business-oriented places of around 100 rooms or less with rates in the 2000 to 3000B range, like Mansion Kempinski, the Royal Princess and the Swiss Lodge (see later in this section for details). Many experienced Bangkok business travellers prefer this type of hotel because they get personal service for about 1000B less than the bigger hotels; also these smaller hotels don't accept tour groups, so regular guests don't have to wade through crowds in the lobby.

Newer hotel standouts include the *Chateau de Bangkok* (☎ 290-0125; fax 290-0167), at 25 Soi Ruam Rudi, Ploenchit Rd, behind the US embassy. Owned by the French hotel group Accor, it offers 139 serviced studios – one and two bedroom apartments, each with walk-in closet, IDD phone and fax – for 2500B a night.

The less expensive, tastefully decorated *Hotel Rembrandt* (☎ 261-7100; fax 261-7107), at Soi 18, Sukhumvit Rd, has 406 large rooms that were 2700B in 1996 though rack rates were listed at 3000B or more.

Facilities include a swimming pool and the best Mexican restaurant in Bangkok, Señor Pico's of Los Angeles. Another advantage is the Rembrandt's proximity to Queen Sirikit National Convention Centre, off Soi 16.

All of the hotels in this category will add a 10% service charge plus 7% tax to hotel bills.

**On the River** The 118 year old *Oriental Hotel* (☎ 236-0400/39), 48 Oriental Ave, on the Chao Phraya River, is one of the most famous hotels in Asia, right up there with the Raffles in Singapore or the Peninsula in Hong Kong. What's more it's also rated as one of the very best hotels in the world, as well as being just about the most expensive in Bangkok. The hotel management prides itself on providing highly personalised service through a staff of 1200 (for 398 rooms) – once you've stayed here they'll remember your name, what you like to eat for breakfast, even what type of flowers you prefer in your room.

Nowadays the Oriental is looking more modern and less classic – the original Author's Wing is dwarfed by the Tower (built in 1958) and River (1976) wings. Authors who have stayed at the Oriental and had suites named after them include Joseph Conrad, Somerset Maugham, Noel Coward, Graham Greene, John Le Carré, James Michener, Gore Vidal and Barbara Cartland. Room rates start at 6500B, suites are as much as 10 times that. It's worth wandering in, if only to see the lobby (no shorts, sleeveless shirts or thongs allowed).

On the Thonburi bank of the Chao Phraya River, a bit south of central Bangkok, the tastefully appointed, 420-room *Marriott Royal Garden Riverside Hotel* (☎ 476-0021; fax 460-1805), at 257/1-3 Charoen Nakhon Rd, near Krungthep Bridge, is highly valued for its serene atmosphere and expansive, airy public areas. The grounds encompass a large swimming pool, lush gardens, two lighted tennis courts and a world-class health club. Trader Vic's and Benihana are among the hotel's six restaurants; the *Manohra*, a luxury rice-barge dinner cruiser, is also moored here. A free water taxi service shuttles guests back and forth to the Oriental and River City piers every hour from 7 am to 11 pm. Rack rates for very spacious rooms are 4200B, or 4800B with a river view.

Two other luxury gems along the river are the *Shangri-La* (☎ 236-7777; fax 236-8570) at 89 Soi Wat Suan Phlu, Charoen Krung Rd; and the *Royal Orchid Sheraton* (☎ 266-0123; fax 236-8320), 2 Captain Bush Lane, Si Phraya Rd. The Shangri-La has 694 rooms starting from 5265B, and its own helicopter transport from the airport, while the Sheraton (776 rooms, from 5649B) is known for crisp, efficient service (the business centre is open 24 hours).

The *Menam* (☎ 289-1148/9; fax 291-9400), towering over the river at 2074 Charoen Krung Rd, Yannawa, has 718 rooms from 4237B. The *Royal River* (☎ 433-0300; fax 433-5880), at 670/805 Charan Sanitwong Rd, Thonburi, has 458 rooms from 2300B; the latter receives lots of tour groups.

### Siam Square, Ploenchit Rd & Pratunam

People accustomed to heady hotels claim the plush *Regent Bangkok* (☎ 251-6127; fax 253-9195), at 155 Ratchadamri Rd, tops the Oriental in overall quality for the money; it's also one of the city's top choices for business travellers because of its efficient business centre and central location (local calls are free at the Regent, probably the only luxury hotel in the city to offer this courtesy). The hotel also offers (for 1650B an hour) an 'office on wheels', a high-tech, multi-passenger van equipped with computers, cell phones, fax machines, TVs/VCRs and swivelling leather seats so that small conferences can be held while crossing town in Bangkok's turgid traffic. The Regent's 415 rooms start at 5885B.

Another top executive choice is the *Hilton International Bangkok* (☎ 253-0123; fax 253-6509) on Withayu Rd, where you won't find tour groups milling around in the lobby; its 343 rooms start at 4400B. The expansive grounds are a major plus; only Bangkok's older hotel properties are so fortunate.

Another of this generation, the 400-room

*Siam Intercontinental* (☎ 253-0355; fax 253-0355), ensconced in spacious grounds at 967 Rama I Rd (near Siam Square), takes in a mix of well heeled pleasure and business travellers. Standard rooms start at 5179B.

The *Grand Hyatt Erawan* (☎ 254-1234; fax 2253-5856), at the intersection of Ratchadamri and Ploenchit Rds, was raised on the site of the original Erawan Hotel (built at the same time as the Royal) five years ago and has obvious ambitions to become the city's number one hotel. The neo-Thai architecture has been well executed; inside is the largest collection of contemporary Thai art in the world. Adding to the elite atmosphere, rooms in the rear of the hotel overlook the Bangkok Royal Sports Club racetrack. For most visitors – whether for business or leisure – it vies with the Novotel Bangkok on Siam Square for having the best location of all the city's luxury hotels vis-à-vis transport and proximity to shopping.

During the 1991 opening of the Grand Hyatt, 99 monks ('nine' is considered a lucky number in Thai culture, hence number 99 doubles the good luck) offered Buddhist chants in the lobby and received a sumptuous alms dinner. A Brahman ceremony was performed at the adjacent Erawan Shrine, and at an astrologically auspicious moment, 510 balloons and 99 doves were simultaneously released into the air. Huge rooms start at 5000B.

Thailand's own Amari Hotels & Resorts opened the 34-storey *Amari Watergate* (☎ 267-653-9000; fax 653-9045) at the end of 1994 right in the centre of Bangkok's busiest district, Pratunam. The neoclassical interior design blends Thai and European motifs, guest rooms are large and facilities include a 900 sq m Clark Hatch fitness centre, free-form pool, two squash courts, Thai massage, a 24 hour business centre, an American-style pub and very highly rated Cantonese and Italian restaurants. The hotel is on Phetburi Rd near the Ratchaprarop Rd intersection. Tour groups check in via a separate floor and lobby while individually booked guests use the main lobby, a boon to business travellers. Huge rooms cost

4200/4600B a single/double; the top three floors contain more luxuriously appointed executive rooms at 5200/5800B. Other brand new Amari hotels in central Bangkok include the *Amari Atrium* (☎ 318-5295; fax 319-0789) on Phetburi Tat Mai Rd east of Soi Asoke (3000/3200B a single/double) and the *Amari Boulevard* (☎ 255-2930; fax 255-2950) at Soi 5, Sukhumvit Rd (3000 to 4200B). Amari also has an airport hotel – see Airport Area below.

Another extremely well located hotel for business or leisure is the 429-room *Novotel Bangkok* (☎ 366-8666; fax 366-8699) in Siam Square. Just steps away from one of Bangkok's most vibrant shopping and entertainment districts, the Novotel boasts a full business centre, bakery, pool and various restaurants. Huge rooms are 4100/4500B.

Other top-notch hotels in the Siam Square area include:

*Asia Hotel* – 296 Phayathai Rd (☎ 215-0808; fax 215-4360); 640 rooms, from 2600B; it's in a good location, but often full of tour groups and conventioneers

*Felix Arnoma Swissotel* – 99 Ratchadamri Rd (☎ 255-3410; fax 255-3456); 400 rooms, from 2400B

*Mercure Hotel Bangkok* – 1091/336 New Phetburi Rd (☎ 253-0500; fax 253-0556); 678 rooms, 2825B; contains several lounges, coffee shops and massage parlours oriented towards the East Asian visitor

*Imperial Hotel* – Withayu Rd (☎ 254-0023; fax 253-3190); 370 rooms, from 2719B

*Indra Regent* – Ratchaprarop Rd (☎ 208-0033; fax 208-0388); 500 rooms, from 3400B

*Le Meridien President* – 135/26 Gaysorn Rd (☎ 253-0444; fax 253-7565); 387 rooms, from 3531B

*Sol Twin Towers Hotel* – 88 Soi Rong Muang, New Rama VI Rd (near Hualamphong station) (☎ 216-9555; fax 216-9544); 660 rooms, from 3178B

**Silom, Surawong & Sathon Rds** There are many hotels with similar amenities to the Regent, Hilton and Sheraton, but which are a step down in price because of their location or smaller staff-to-guest ratios. In the Silom and Surawong areas these include: the *Montien* (☎ 234-8060; fax 234-8060) at 54 Surawong Rd (500 rooms, from 4680B), a very Thai hotel; the *Dusit Thani* (☎ 233-1130;

fax 2366400) at Rama IV Rd (520 rooms, from 6120B), a great hotel in a busy location; the *Narai* (☎ 237-0100; fax 236-7161) at 222 Silom Rd (520 rooms, from 3200B); and the *Holiday Inn Crowne Plaza* (☎ 238-4300/34; fax 238-5289) at 981 Silom Rd (662 rooms, from 3200B).

Another entry in the luxury/executive market is the 190-room *Beaufort Sukhothai* (☎ 287-0222; fax 287-4980) at 13/3 Sathon Tai Rd. The Sukhothai features an Asian minimalist decor, including an inner courtyard with lily ponds; the same architect and interior designer created Phuket's landmark Amanpuri. Standard rooms start at 5297B.

New to the scene is the ultra-modern *Westin Banyan Tree* (☎ 679-1200; fax 679-1199), which towers over Sathon Tai Rd with 216 business suites. The hotel is ensconced on the lower two and top 28 floors of the 60-storey Thai Wah Tower II, the tallest building in Thailand. The Westin Banyan Tree's huge rooms feature separate work and sleep areas, two-line speaker phones and data ports and two TV sets along with all the other amenities expected of lodgings that cost over 6000B a night. The spa/fitness centre spans four floors.

Other top-end hotels in this area include:

*Clarion Trinity* – 150 Soi 5, Silom Rd (☎ 231-5333; fax 231-5417); 109 rooms, 2400 to 3100B

*Mandarin Hotel* – 662 Rama IV Rd (☎ 233-4980/9; fax 237-1620); 343 rooms, 3178 to 8828B

*New Peninsula* – 295/3 Surawong Rd (☎ 234-3910; fax 236-5526); 102 rooms, 2225 to 3895B

*Silom Plaza* – 320 Silom Rd (☎ 236-8441/84; fax 236-7566); 209 rooms, from 2589B

*Swiss Lodge* – 3 Convent Rd (☎ 233-5345; fax 236-9425); 57 rooms, from 2419B

**Sukhumvit Rd** Top-end hotels in this area include:

*Ambassador Hotel* – Soi 11, Sukhumvit Rd (☎ 254-0444; fax 253-4123); 1050 rooms, from 2119B; an amazing conglomeration of restaurants, food centres, nightclubs and cocktail lounges

*Bel-Aire Princess* – 16 Soi 5, Sukhumvit Rd (☎ 253-4300; fax 255-8850); 160 rooms, from 2800B

*Delta Grand Pacific Hotel* – Soi 17-19, Sukhumvit Rd (☎ 233-2922/7; fax 237-5740); easy access to Queen Sirikit National Convention Centre; 400 rooms, from 4914B

*Impala Hotel* – Soi 24, Sukhumvit Rd (☎ 258-8612/6; fax 259-2896); 200 rooms, from 2314B

*Landmark* – 138 Sukhumvit Rd (☎ 254-0404; fax 255-8419); 415 rooms, 4826 to 9416B; has a Videotex in every room and a very good business centre

*Mansion Kempinski* – 75/23 Soi 11, Sukhumvit Rd (☎ 255-7200; fax 253-2329); 127 rooms, from 2750B

*Novotel Lotus Bangkok* – 1 Soi Daeng Udom, Soi 33, Sukhumvit Rd (☎ 261-0111; fax 262-1700); 219 rooms, from 4826B

*Park Hotel* – 6 Soi 7, Sukhumvit Rd (☎ 255-4300; fax 255-4309); 128 rooms, 2000 to 6000B

*Windsor Hotel* – 3 Soi 20, Sukhumvit Rd (☎ 258-0160; fax 258-1491); 235 rooms, 2589 to 9416B

**Airport Area** The 434-room *Amari Airport Hotel* (☎ 566-1020; fax 566-1941), directly across from the airport, has undergone recent renovations and is quite well appointed. The executive floor features huge suites and 24 hour butler service. Rates start at 4200B for a standard double. Another luxury-class hotel towards the airport is the *Central Plaza Bangkok* (☎ 541-1234; fax 541-1087) at 1695 Phahonyothin Rd, overlooking the Railway Golf Course and Chatuchak Park. There are 600 rooms, starting at 3955B for a standard room. Or stay five minutes from the airport at the less expensive *Comfort Inn Airport* (see Places to Stay – middle).

A new top-end project, the *Asia Airport Hotel*, is due to open nearby in late 1997.

**Other Areas** Top-end hotels in other areas include:

*The Emerald* – 99/1 Ratchadaphisek Rd, Huay Khwang (☎ 276-4567; fax 276-4555); 640 rooms, from 2600B

*Quality Hotel Lumphini* – 17 Soi Ngam Duphli, Rama IV Rd (☎ 287-3411; fax 287-3420); 170 rooms, 2590/2825B

*Rama Gardens* – 9/9 Vibhavadi Rangsit Rd (☎ 561-0022; fax 561-1025); 380 rooms, from 3800B

*Royal Princess Hotel* – 269 Lan Luang Rd (☎ 281-3088; fax 280-1314); 170 rooms, from 3300B

*Siam City Hotel* – 477 Si Ayuthaya Rd (☎ 247-0130; fax 247-0178); 535 rooms, from 4300B

## Places to Eat

No matter where you go in Bangkok, you're almost never more than 50m away from a restaurant or sidewalk food vendor. The variety of places to eat is simply astounding and defeats all but the most tireless food samplers in their quest to say they've tried everything. As with seeking a place to stay, you can find something in every price range in most districts – with a few obvious exceptions. Chinatown is naturally a good area for Chinese food, while Bangrak and Pahurat (both districts with high concentrations of Indian residents) are good for Indian and Muslim cuisine. Some parts of the city tend to have higher priced restaurants than others (eg Siam Square, and Silom, Surawong and Sukhumvit Rds) while other areas are full of cheap eats (eg Banglamphu and the river area around Tha Maharat).

As transport can be such a hassle in Bangkok, most visitors choose to eat in a district most convenient to reach (rather than seeking out a specific restaurant); this section has therefore been organised by area, rather than cuisine.

**Banglamphu & Thewet** This area near the river and old part of the city is one of the best for cheap eating establishments. Many of the guesthouses on Khao San Rd have open-air cafes, which are packed with travellers from November to March and July to August. The typical cafe menu has a few Thai and Chinese standards plus traveller favourites like fruit salads, muesli and yoghurt. None of them are particular standouts, though the side-by-side *Orm* and *Wally House* produce fair Thai, western and vegetarian meals, while *Prakorp's House & Restaurant* makes good coffee. *Arawy Det*, an old Hokkien-style noodle shop on the corner of Khao San and Tanao Rds, has somehow managed to stay authentic amidst the cosmic swirl.

*Gaylord Indian Restaurant*, hidden away in the rear upstairs of a building on Chakraphong Rd opposite the west entrance to Khao San Rd, has decent Indian food. *Royal India* on the south side of Khao San Rd used to be good but has slid downhill since it moved across the street (the original Royal India in the Pahurat district is still worth trying). *Chabad House*, a Jewish place of worship on Rambutri Rd, serves Israeli-style kosher food downstairs.

For more authentic (and cheaper) Thai food check out other places on Rambutri Rd. At the western end are several open-air restaurants serving excellent Thai food at low prices. A good spot for Southern Thai food is a no-name food shop at 8-10 Chakraphong, south of Khao San Rd and two doors south of the Padung Cheep mask shop. In the mornings it serves khâo mòk kài (Thai chicken biryani) as well as khâo yam, a kind of rice salad which is a traditional breakfast in Southern Thailand. Nearby at No 22 is a cheap and efficient Chinese noodle (bàmìi) and wonton (kíaw) shop; No 28 offers tasty Thai curries.

A small shop called *Roti-Mataba* (no English sign) on the corner of Phra Athit and Phra Sumen Rds near the river offers delicious kaeng mátsàman (Thai Muslim curry), chicken kurma, chicken or vegetable mátàbà (a sort of stuffed crepe) and a bilingual menu; look for a white sign with red letters. There are several unassuming Chinese dim sum and noodle places along Phra Athit Rd north of the New Merry V guesthouses, plus a couple of Thai curry shops. The *Raan Kin Deum* (no English sign), a few doors down from New Merry V, is a nice two-storey cafe with wooden tables and chairs, traditional Thai food and live folk music nightly; the laid-back atmosphere reaches its acme in the evenings when Thais and farangs crowd the place.

Farther north of Khao San Rd, in the heart of Banglamphu's market, are two shopping complexes with food centres, fast-food vendors and supermarkets. At the high-rise *New World* shopping centre, the ground floor features donut shops and meatball vendors, the 5th floor has a supermarket and on the 8th is a brilliant food centre with city and river views. Centre vendors offer seafood, vegetarian, coffee, noodles, curries and more. The 6th floor of *Banglamphu Department Store*, between Krai Si and Rambutri Rds, also has a supermarket and small food centre. The department store has been condemned by the Bangkok Metropolitan Authority (BMA) for noncompliance with building codes, so who knows how long it will be before it either closes or collapses.

Many of the Khao San Rd guesthouse cafes offer vegetarian dishes. For an all-veggie menu at low prices, seek out the *Vegetarian Restaurant* at 117/1 Soi Wat Bowon, near Srinthip Guest House. To find this out-of-the-way spot, turn left on Tanao Rd at the eastern end of Khao San Rd, then cross the street and turn right down the first narrow alley, then left at Soi Wat Bowon – an English sign reads 'Vegetarian'. The fare is basically western veggie, with wholemeal breads, salads and sandwiches; it's open from 8 am until around 10 pm. A very good Thai vegetarian place is *Arawy* (no English sign), which is south of Khao San Rd, across Ratchadamnoen Klang at 152 Din So Rd (opposite the City Hall) near a 7-Eleven. This was one of Bangkok's first Thai vegetarian restaurants, inspired by ex-Bangkok Governor Chamlong Srimuang. It's open daily from 7 am to 7 pm.

Good curry-and-rice is available for around 15B at the outdoor dining hall at *Thammasat University* near the river; it's open for lunch only. Opposite the southern entrance of the university there are several good noodle and rice shops. For North-Eastern Thai food, try the restaurants next to the boxing stadium on Ratchadamnoen Nok Rd, near the TAT office.

At the Tha Wisut Kasat pier in north-western Banglamphu, there's a very good floating seafood restaurant called *Yok Yor*. Especially good at Yok Yor is the hàw mòk (fish curry). Yok Yor also offers inexpensive evening dining cruises – you order from the regular menu and pay a nominal 50B charge for the boat service. Nearby is the similar *Chawn Ngoen*; it has no English sign, but there is an English menu. *Wang Ngar*, in west Banglamphu next to the Phra Pinklao Bridge, is another decent waterfront place.

At the Democracy Monument circle on Ratchadamnoen Klang Rd, there are a few air-con Thai restaurants, including the *Vijit* and the *Sorn Daeng*, which have reasonable prices considering the food and facilities. At lunchtime on weekdays they're crowded with local government office workers. Both stay open until 11 pm or so.

For authentic, sit-down Thai cuisine, try the long-running *Yod Kum* (Yawt Kham) opposite Wat Bowon on Phra Sumen Rd. Specialities include phàt phèt plaa dùk (catfish stir-fried in basil and curry paste), kaeng khĭaw-wăan (green curry) and seafood.

For those in the mood for continental food, *Kanit's* at 68 Tee Thong Rd is just south of the Sao Ching-Cha (Giant Swing) and is another worthwhile semi-splurge. The lasagne and pizza are probably the best you can find in this part of Bangkok.

**Silom & Surawong Rds** This area represents the heart of the financial district so it features a lot of pricey restaurants, along with cheaper ones that attract both office workers and the more flush. Many restaurants are found along the main avenues but there's an even greater number tucked away in sois and alleys. The river end of Silom and Surawong Rds towards Charoen Krung Rd (the Bangrak district) is a good hunting ground for Indian food.

***Thai & Other Asian*** The *Soi Pracheun (20) Night Market*, which assembles each evening off Silom Rd in front of the municipal market pavilion, is good for cheap eats. During the day there are also a few food vendors in this soi. At lunchtime and early evening a batch of food vendors – everything from noodles to raw oysters – set up on Soi 5 next to Bangkok Bank's main branch.

The area to the east of Silom Rd off Convent Rd and Soi Sala Daeng is a Thai gourmets' enclave. Most of the restaurants tucked away here are very good, but a meal for two will cost 600 to 800B. One such up-market spot is *Bussaracum* (☎ 235-8915), pronounced 'boot-sa-ra-kam', at 35 Soi Phipat off Convent Rd. Bussaracum specialises in 'royal Thai' cuisine, that is, recipes that were created for the royal court

in days past; these recipes were kept secret from 'commoners' until late this century. Every dish is supposedly prepared only when ordered, from fresh ingredients and freshly ground spices. Live classical Thai music, played at a subdued volume, is also provided. This is a fancy place, recommended for a splurge. Two can eat for around 650 to 850B; call ahead to be sure of a table.

Another great place for traditional Thai, at moderate prices, is *Ban Chiang* (☎ 236-7045), a restored wooden house in a verdant setting at 14 Soi Si Wiang, Pramuan Rd (off Silom Rd west of Wat Khaek). Owned by a Thai movie star, *Thanying* (☎ 236-4361) at 10 Soi Pramuan off Silom Rd features an elegant decor and very good, moderately expensive royal Thai cuisine. It's open daily from 11 am to 10.30 pm; there's another branch at the World Trade Centre on Ploenchit Rd.

*Mango Tree* (☎ 236-2820), at 37 Soi Anuman Ratchathon, opposite the Tawana Ramada Hotel between Silom and Surawong, offers classic Thai cuisine and live traditional Thai music amidst a decor of historical photos and antiques. Recommended dishes include plaa sămlii dàet diaw (half-dried, half-fried cottonfish with spicy mango salad) and kài bai toei (chicken baked in pandanus leaves). Prices are moderate and it's open daily for lunch and dinner.

Moving towards the river, just west of Soi 9 at 160 Silom Rd, you'll find the open-air *Isn't Classic* (the Thai name is 'Isaan Classic'), a popular restaurant specialising in North-Eastern Thai food. Prices are very reasonable for the good quality sticky rice, kài yâang (spicy grilled chicken), lâap (meat salad), sôm-tam (spicy green papaya salad) and other Isaan delights. Over on Surawong Rd at No 173/8-9, *All Gaengs* is a medium-priced, modern, air-con place specialising in Thai curries and spicy Thai-style salads (yam).

A good one-stop eating place with a lot of variety is the Silom Village Trade Centre, an outdoor shopping complex at Soi 24. Though it's basically a tourist spot with higher than average prices, the restaurants are of high quality and plenty of Thais dine here as well. The centrepiece is *Silom Village*, a place with shaded outdoor tables where the emphasis is on fresh Thai seafood, sold by weight. The menu also has extensive Chinese and Japanese sections. Prices are moderate to high by Thai standards. For the quick and casual, *Silom Coffee Bar* in the trade centre makes a good choice. At night *Ruen Thep* offers one of the city's better Thai classical dance-and-dinner venues. During the daytime, vendors dressed in traditional Thai clothing sell a variety of traditional snacks like khanŏm khrók (steamed coconut pastries) and mîang kham (savoury titbits wrapped in wild tea leaves) – more than a little corny, but again the food quality is high.

*Chaai Karr* (☎ 233-2549), on Silom Rd across from the Holiday Inn and a few shops east of Central Department Store, is simply decorated with Thai antiques. The medium-price menu is mostly Thai, with a few farang dishes, plus 19 varieties of brewed coffee; the Thai mango salad and spicy seafood soup are very good. Thai folk music plays in the background. Chaai Karr is open daily from 10.30 am to 9.30 pm.

Towards the eastern end of Surawong Rd, about a 10 minute walk west of Montien Hotel, is the famous *Somboon Seafood* (open from 4 pm to midnight), a good, reasonably priced seafood restaurant known for having the best crab curry in town. Soy-steamed seabass (plaa kràphong nêung sii-yíu) is also a speciality. Somboon has a second branch called *Somboon Seafood* farther north, across Rama IV Rd near Chulalongkorn University at Soi Chulalongkorn 8 (711-717 Chula Soi 8, Ban That Thong Rd).

Toward the west end of Surawong Rd at No 311/2-4 (on the corner of Soi Pramot), the economic *Maria Bakery & Restaurant* is well known for its fresh Vietnamese and Thai food as well as French pastries, pizza and vegetarian food. A newer Maria branch can be found at 909-911 Silom Rd opposite Central Department Store. Both are clean, with air-con and have reasonable prices.

*Mizu's Kitchen* on Patpong Rd 1 has a loyal Japanese and Thai following for its

inexpensive but good Japanese food, including Japanese-style steak. Another very good Japanese place, especially for sushi and sashimi, is *Goro* at 399/1 Soi Siri Chulasewok off Silom; prices are reasonable.

**Indian & Muslim** Towards the western end of Silom and Surawong Rds, an area known as Bangrak, Indian eateries begin making an appearance. Unlike at Indian restaurants elsewhere in Bangkok, the menus in Bangrak don't necessarily exhibit the usual, boring predilection toward north Indian Moghul-style cuisine. For authentic south Indian food (dosa, idli, vada etc), try the *Madras Cafe* (☎ 235-6761) in the Madras Lodge at 31/10-11 Vaithi Lane (Trok 13), off Silom Rd near the Narai Hotel (open daily 9 am to 10 pm). Another place serving south Indian (and north Indian) food is the very basic *Simla Cafe* at 382 Soi Tat Mai (opposite Borneo & Co) off Silom Rd, in an alley behind the Victory Hotel. Across from the Narai Hotel, near the Maha Uma Devi Temple, street vendors sometimes sell various Indian snacks.

*India Hut* (☎ 237-8812), a new place on Surawong Rd opposite the Manohra Hotel, specialises in Nawabi (Lucknow) cuisine; it's quite good, friendly and moderate to medium-high in prices (45 to 100B per dish). The vegetarian samosas and fresh prawns cooked with ginger are particularly good. It's three flights of steps off the street, with a modern Indian decor.

*Himali Cha-Cha* (☎ 235-1569), at 1229/11 Charoen Krung Rd, features good north Indian cuisine at slightly higher prices. Founder Cha-Cha reportedly worked as a chef for India's last Viceroy; his son has taken over the kitchen here. It is open daily for lunch and dinner.

The *Cholas*, a small air-con place downstairs in the Woodlands Inn on Soi Charoen Krung 32 just north of the GPO, serves decent, no-fuss north Indian food for 50 to 80B a dish. The open-air *Sallim Restaurant*, next door to the Woodlands, is a cheaper place with north Indian, Malay and Thai-Muslim dishes – it's usually packed.

Around the corner on Soi Phuttha Osot is the very popular but basic-looking *Naaz* (Naat in Thai), often cited as having the richest khâo mòk kài (chicken biryani) in the city. The milk tea is also very good, and daily specials include chicken masala and mutton kurma. For dessert, the house speciality is firni, a Middle Eastern pudding spiced with coconut, almonds, cardamom and saffron. Naaz is open from 7.30 am to 10.30 pm daily. There are several other Arab/Indian restaurants in this area.

Down near the intersection of Charoen Krung and Silom Rds, at 1356 Charoen Krung Rd, is the *Muslim Restaurant*, one of the oldest in the area. The faded yellow walls and chrome chairs aren't inspiring, but you can fill yourself on curries and roti for 40B or less.

On Soi Pracheun (Soi 20) off Silom Rd there's a mosque, Masjid Mirasuddeen, so Muslim food vendors are common.

**Vegetarian** *Rabianthong Restaurant*, in the Narai Hotel on Silom Rd, offers a very good vegetarian section in its luncheon buffet, on wan phrá (full moon days) only, for 260B.

The *Hare Krishna Centre* at 139 Soi Phuttha Osot, off Charoen Krung Rd and opposite the GPO (near the Naaz restaurant), offers free Indian vegetarian meals on Sunday at around 7.45 pm (following chanting and a reading of the *Bhagavad Gita*).

**Other Cuisines** If you crave German or Japanese food, there are plenty of places serving these cuisines on and around Patpong Rd. *Bobby's Arms*, an Aussie-British pub on Patpong 2 (through a garage), has good fish & chips. The *Brown Derby*, also on Patpong 1, is recommended for American-style deli sandwiches. Authentically decorated *Delaney's Irish Pub* (☎ 266-7160), at 1-4 Sivadon Bldg, Convent Rd in the Silom Rd district, serves a set lunch menu for 130 to 160B from Monday to Friday, plus other pub grub daily. Irish bands play nightly.

Wedged between the go-go bars on Patpong 2 are several fast-food chicken joints, including *KFC, Chicken Divine* and *Magic Grill*. Probably the best Patpong find of all is the *Cafi de Paris* (☎ 237-2776) on Patpong 2, an air-con spot popular with French expats for its decent approximations of Parisian-style bistro fare; it's open daily from 11 am to 1 am. Yet another branch of the *Little Home Bakery & Restaurant* does a booming business serving farang and Filipino food on Soi Thaniya (one soi east of Patpong 2, or two sois east if you're walking along Silom Rd).

In the CP Tower building on Silom Rd are a cluster of air-con American and Japanese-style fast-food places: *McDonald's, Pizza Hut, Chester's Grilled Chicken, Suzuki Coffee House* and *Toplight Coffee House*. Several are open late to catch the night-time Patpong traffic.

The tiny *Harmonique* (☎ 237-8175), on Soi Charoen Krung 34, around the corner from the GPO, is a refreshing oasis in this extremely busy, smog-filled section of Charoen Krung. European-managed and unobtrusive, the little shop serves a variety of teas, fruit shakes and coffee on Hokkien-style marble-topped tables – a pleasant spot to read poste-restante mail while quenching your thirst. Well prepared if pricey (60 to 150B per dish) Thai food is also available. The shop discreetly sells silk, silverwork and antiques. It's open daily from 10 am to 10 pm.

**Siam Square** This shopping area is interspersed with several low and medium-priced restaurants as well as American fast-food franchises. Chinese food seems to predominate, probably because it's the well-off Chinese Thais that most frequent Siam Square. The square's Soi 1 has three shark-fin places: *Scala, Penang* and *Bangkok*. At the other end of Siam Square, on Henri Dunant Rd, the big noodle restaurant called *Coca Garden* (open from 10.30 am to 10.30 pm) is good for Chinese-style sukiyaki.

Can't decide what kind of Asian or farang food you're in the mood for? Then head for *S&P Restaurant & Bakery* on Soi 12. The extensive menu features Thai, Chinese,

Japanese, European and vegetarian specialities, plus a bakery with pies, cakes and pastries – all high-quality fare at low to moderate prices.

On the square's Soi 11, the Bangkok branch of London's *Hard Rock Cafe* serves good American and Thai food; prices are about the same as at other Hard Rocks around the world. Look for the tuk-tuk captioned 'God is my co-pilot' coming out of the building's facade. The Hard Rock stays open till 2 am, a bit later than many Siam Square eateries.

Just to the right of the Siam Square's Scala cinema, plunge into the alley that curves behind the Phayathai Rd shops to find a row of cheap, good food stalls. A shorter alley with food stalls also leads off the north end of Siam Square's Soi 2.

On both sides of Rama I Rd in Siam Square and Siam Center you'll find a battery of American fast-food franchises, including *Mister Donut, Dunkin Donuts, Burger King, Pizza Hut, Swensen's Ice Cream, McDonald's, Shakey's Pizza, A&W Root Beer* and *KFC*. Prices are close to what you would pay in the USA. Siam Center contained a bevy of good Thai coffee shops on its upper floors, but the whole complex save McDonald's and Pizza Hut on the ground floor closed following the Center's disastrous 1995 fire; eight months later they still hadn't re-opened.

If you're staying on or nearby Soi Kasem San 1, you don't have to suck motorcycle fumes crossing Rama I and Phayathai Rds to find something to eat. Besides the typical hotel coffee shops found on the soi, there are also two very good, inexpensive curry-and-rice vendors with tables along the east side of the soi. No need to be fluent in Thai, they're used to the 'point-and-serve' system. Two outdoor cafes on either side of the White Lodge serve more expensive Thai and European food, burgers, pastries, coffees and breakfast. Right around the corner on Rama I Rd, next to the liquor dealer with the vintage British and US motorcycles out the front, is *Thai Sa Nguan* (no English sign), a fairly clean shop with khâo kaeng (curry-and-rice) for 12B (two toppings 17B), fried

duck with noodles (kŭaytĭaw pèt yâang) and Hainanese-style chicken and rice (khâo man kài).

**Mahboonkrong Shopping Centre** Another building studded with restaurants, MBK is directly across from Siam Square at the intersection of Phayathai and Rama I Rds. A section on the ground floor called Major Plaza contains two cinemas and a good food centre. An older food centre is on the 7th floor; both places have vendors serving tasty dishes from all over Thailand, including vegetarian, at prices averaging 20 to 25B per plate. Hours are 10 am to 10 pm, but the more popular vendors run out of food as early as 8.30 or 9 pm – come earlier for the best selection. A beer garden on the terrace surrounding two sides of the 7th floor food centre, with good views of the Bangkok nightscape, is open in the evening.

Scattered around other floors, especially the 3rd and 4th, are a number of popular medium-price places, including *Little Home Bakery* (an American-style pancake house with a few Filipino dishes), *13 Coins* (steak, pizza and pasta), *Kobune Japanese Restaurant, Chester's Grilled Chicken, Pizza Hut* and many others.

**World Trade Centre** This relatively new office and shopping complex on the corner of Ploenchit and Ratchadamri Rds contains a few up-market restaurants and the city's trendiest food centre. Located on the ground floor of this huge glossy building are *Kroissant House* (coffees, pastries and gelato) and *La Fontana* (bistro-style Italian). The 6th floor of the centre features *Lai-Lai* and *Chao Sua*, two sumptuous Chinese banquet-style places, plus the elegant traditional Thai *Thanying* and the more casual *Narai Pizzeria*. There are also two food centres on the 7th floor with standard Thai and Chinese dishes, which are only a little more expensive than the usual Bangkok food centre.

The basement of Zen Department Store contains a Thai deli with many curries, a good Japanese sushi and noodle bar (a sizeable plate of sushi costs 60 to 120B), a bakery, sandwich/coffee bar and western deli. The basement food centre has very few seats, encouraging takeaways.

**Soi Lang Suan** East from Siam Square and off Ploenchit Rd, Soi Lang Suan offers a number of medium-price eating possibilities. Despite its farang name, *Sarah Jane* (☎ 252-6572), on an alley off the west side of Lang Suan about a block and a half south of Ploenchit, serves very good Isaan food in a modest air-con dining room. It's open from 11 am to 10 pm.

*Thang Long* (☎ 251-3504), 82/5 Soi Lang Suan, is favoured by Thais as well as expats for its reasonable prices and Thai-Vietnamese menu; open daily for lunch and dinner.

The Italian-owned *Pan Pan* (☎ 252-7501) at 45 Soi Lang Suan is very popular with western residents for wood-fired pizza (takeaway orders accepted), pastas, salads, gelato (the best in Thailand) and pastries. A low-calorie vegetarian menu is available on request. A second Pan Pan (☎ 258-5071) is on Soi 33.

The *Whole Earth Restaurant* (☎ 252-5574), at 93/3 Soi Lang Suan, is a good Thai and Indian vegetarian restaurant (non-veg dishes are also served) with service to match, but is a bit pricey if you're on a tight budget. The upstairs room features low tables with floor cushions. A second branch (☎ 258-4900) has opened at 71 Soi 26, Sukhumvit Rd.

*Nguan Lee Lang Suan*, on the corner of Soi Lang Suan and Soi Sarasin, is a semi-outdoor place specialising in Chinese-style seafood and kài lâo daeng (chicken steamed in Chinese herbs).

**Sukhumvit Rd** This avenue stretching east all the way to the city limits has hundreds of Thai, Chinese and western restaurants to choose from.

***Thai & Other Asian*** The ground floor of the *Ambassador Hotel* between sois 11 and 13 has a good food centre. It offers several varieties of Thai, Chinese, Vietnamese, Japanese, Muslim and vegetarian food at 20 to 40B per dish – you must buy coupons first and exchange them for dishes you order.

*Cabbages & Condoms* at No 10 Soi 12, is run by the Population & Community Development Association (PDA), the brainchild of Mechai Viravaidya who popularised condoms in Thailand, first for birth-control and now as STD prevention. The restaurant offers not only an extensive selection of condoms, but great Thai food at very reasonable prices. The tôm khàa kài (chicken and coconut soup) is particularly tasty; the restaurant is open from 11 am to 10 pm. The *Mandalay* (☎ 255-2893), at 23/7 Soi Ruam Rudi (along with a second branch on Surawong Rd), is supposedly the only Burmese restaurant in town; it's good but not cheap.

The *Yong Lee Restaurant* at Soi 15, near Asia Books, has excellent Thai and Chinese food at reasonable prices and is a longtime favourite among Thai and farang residents alike. There is a second Yong Lee between sois 35 and 37.

The famous *Djit Pochana* (☎ 258-1578) has a branch on Soi 20 and is one of the best-value restaurants in town for traditional Thai dishes. The all-you-can-eat lunch buffet is 90B. This central section of Sukhumvit Rd is loaded with medium-priced Thai restaurants which feature modern decor but real Thai food. *Baan Kanitha* (☎ 258-4181), 36/1 Soi 23, Sukhumvit Rd, offers traditional decor and authentic Thai food; the sea-bass in lime sauce (plaa kràphong nêung mánao) and chicken in coconut-galangal broth (tôm khàa kài) are tops.

For nouvelle Thai cuisine, you can try the *Lemongrass* (☎ 258-8637) at 5/21 Soi 24, which has an atmospheric setting in an old Thai house decorated with antiques. The food is exceptional; try the yam pèt (Thai-style duck salad). It is open from 11 am to 2 pm and 6 to 11 pm.

Another restaurant with an inventive kitchen is *L'Orangery* at 48/11 Soi Ruam Rudi (close to where Ploenchit Rd becomes Sukhumvit Rd). Billed as Pacific Rim cuisine, the food shows the dual influences of Californian and Asian cooking; sometimes it works, sometimes it doesn't.

Yet another hidden gem down Sukhumvit Rd is *Laicram* (Laikhram) at Soi 33 (☎ 238-2337) and at Soi 49/4 (☎ 392-5864). The food at Laicram is authentic gourmet Thai, but not outrageously priced. One of the house specialities is hàw mòk hãwy, an exquisite thick fish curry steamed with mussels inside the shell. Sôm-tam (spicy green papaya salad) is also excellent here, usually served with khâo man, rice cooked with coconut milk and bai toei (pandanus leaf). Opening hours are from 10 am to 9 pm Monday to Saturday, 10 am to 3 pm Sunday.

There are many restaurants around the major hotels on Sukhumvit Rd with mixed Thai, Chinese, European and American menus – most of average quality and slightly above-average prices.

The upscale *Le Dalat* (☎ 258-0290), at 47/1 Soi 23, Sukhumvit Rd, has the most celebrated Vietnamese cuisine in the city. A house speciality is nãem meuang, grilled meatballs which you place on steamed rice-flour wrappers, then add chunks of garlic, chilli, ginger, starfruit and mango along with a tamarind sauce, and finally wrap the whole thing into a lettuce bundle before popping it in your mouth. There are two other branches at Patpong Business Centre, 2nd floor, Surawong Rd (☎ 234-0290) and Premier Shopping Village, Chaeng Wattana Rd (☎ 573-7017). Also good for a stylish Vietnamese meal is *Pho* (☎ 252-5601) on the 3rd floor of Sukhumvit Plaza, Soi 12, Sukhumvit Rd. A second branch can be found in the Alma Link Bldg, 25 Soi Chitlom, Ploenchit Rd; both branches are open daily for lunch and dinner.

**Indian & Muslim** *Mrs Balbir's* (☎ 253-2281) at 155/18 Soi 11 (behind the Siam Commercial Bank) has a good variety of moderately priced vegetarian and non-veg Indian food (mostly north Indian). Mrs Balbir has been teaching Indian cooking for many years and has her own Indian grocery store as well.

The splurge-worthy *Rang Mahal* (☎ 261-7100), a rooftop restaurant in the Rembrandt Hotel on Soi 18, offers very good north and south Indian 'royal cuisine' with cityscape views. On Sundays the restaurant puts on a sumptuous Indian buffet from 11.30 am to 3 pm. Another decent Indian place is *Bangkok Brindawan* (☎ 258-8793) at 15 Soi 35 near the Fuji supermarket. This one specialises in south Indian food; an all-you-can-eat 120B lunch buffet is offered Monday to Friday, 11 am to 3 pm.

A few medium to expensive restaurants serving Pakistani and Middle Eastern food can be found in the 'Little Arabia' area of Soi 3 (Soi Nana Neua). The best value in the whole area is *Al Hossain*, a roofed outdoor cafe on the corner of a lane (Soi 3/5) off the east side of Soi Nana Neua. A steam table holds a range of vegetarian, chicken, mutton and fish curries, along with dal (curried lentils), aloo gobi (spicy potatoes and cauliflower), nan and rice. Dishes cost 20 to 40B each. *Shiraz* on the same soi is a slightly pricier indoor place that provides hookahs for Middle Eastern gentlemen who while away the afternoon smoking out the front. Similar places in the vicinity include *Mehmaan, Akbar's, Al Hamra* and *Shaharazad*.

**Vegetarian** *Vegetarian House International* (☎ 254-7357), in an alley off the west side of Soi Nana Neua, serves meatless Indian, Thai and Italian dishes in a 3rd floor walkup; open from noon to 11 pm.

**Western Cuisine** Homesick Brits need look no farther than *Jool's Bar & Restaurant* at Soi 4 (Soi Nana Tai), past Nana Plaza on the left walking from Sukhumvit Rd. The British-style bar downstairs is a favourite expat hangout while the dining room upstairs serves decent English food.

Several rather expensive West European restaurants (Swiss, French, German etc) are also found on touristy Sukhumvit Rd. *Bei Otto*, between sois 12 and 14, is one of the most popular German restaurants in town and has a comfortable bar. *Haus München* (☎ 252-57776), 4 Soi 15, Sukhumvit Rd, serves large portions of good German and Austrian food; prices are reasonable and there are recent German-language newspapers on hand. It's open daily for breakfast, lunch and dinner

Nostalgic visitors from the USA, especially those from southern USA, will appreciate the well run *Bourbon St Bar & Restaurant* on Soi 22 (behind the Washington Theatre). The menu here emphasises Cajun and Creole cooking; some nights there is also free live music.

One of the top French restaurants in the city, and probably the best not associated with a luxury hotel, is *Le Banyan* (☎ 253-5556) at 59 Soi 8 in a charming early Ratanakosin-style house. The kitchen is French-managed and the menu covers the territory from ragout d'escargot to canard maigret avec foie gras. It has a superb wine list. This is definitely a splurge experience, although the prices are moderate when compared with other elegant French restaurants in the city.

*Giverny* (☎ 391-1126), at 342 Soi 63, Sukhumvit Rd, is also considered one of the better French restaurants. The menu includes all the French standards, and the well selected wine list is long. Figure on spending 400 to 500B per person for three courses.

*Pomodoro* (☎ 252-9090), a place with floor-to-ceiling windows on the ground floor of the Nai Lert Building on Sukhumvit Rd (between sois 3 and 5), specialises in Sardinian cuisine. The menu includes over 25 pasta dishes, and special set lunch menus are available for 180 to 240B, while the wine list encompasses vintages from nine regions in Italy, along with others from France, Australia and the USA. Pomodoro is open daily from 10 am to 11 pm.

If you're looking for Mexican food, the city's best can be found at *Señor Pico's of Los Angeles* (☎ 261-7100), on the 2nd floor of the Rembrandt Hotel, Soi 18, Sukhumvit Rd. This brightly decorated, festive restaurant offers reasonably authentic Tex-Mex cuisine, including fajitas, carnitas, nachos and combination platters. Expect to spend around 200 to 300B for two.

For American-style pizza, there's a *Pizza Mall* on the corner of Soi 33 and Sukhumvit Rd (the *Uncle Ray's Ice Cream* next door has the best ice cream in Bangkok) and a *Pizza Hut* at Soi 39.

The *Little Home Bakery & Restaurant* (☎ 390-0760), at 413/10-12 Soi 55, has an extensive western menu along with a few Filipino items – this place has a very loyal Thai following. Unless you're already out this far on Sukhumvit Rd, the Little Home in Mahboonkrong shopping centre would be more convenient to most Bangkok locations.

**Chinatown, Hualamphong & Pahurat** Some of Bangkok's best Chinese and Indian food is found in these adjacent districts, but because few tourists stay in this part of town (for good reason – it's simply too congested) they rarely make any eating forays into the area. A few old Chinese restaurants have moved from Chinatown to locations with less traffic, the most famous being *Hoi Tien Lao*, now the excellent *Hoi Tien Lao Rim Nam* and located adjacent to River House Condominium on the Thonburi bank of the Chao Phraya River, more or less opposite the Portuguese embassy and River City shopping complex. But many places are still hanging on to their venerable Chinatown addresses, where the atmosphere is still part of the eating experience.

Most specialise in southern Chinese cuisine, particularly that of coastal Guangdong and Fujian provinces. This means seafood, rice noodles and dumplings are often the best choices. The large, banquet-style Chinese places are mostly found along Yaowarat and Charoen Krung Rds, and include *Lie Kee* (on the corner of Charoen Krung and Bamrungrat Rds, a block west of Ratchawong Rd), *Laem Thong* (on Soi Bamrungrat just off Charoen Krung Rd) and *Yau Wah Yuen* (near the Yaowarat and Ratchawong Rds intersection). Each of these has an extensive menu, including dim sum before lunchtime.

The best noodle and dumpling shops are hidden away on smaller sois and alleys. At No 54 on Soi Bamrungrat is the funky *Chiang Kii*, where the 100B khâo tôm plaa (rice soup with fish) belies the casual surroundings – no place does it better. *Kong

*Lee*, at 137/141 Ratchawong, has a very loyal clientele for its dry-fried wheat noodles (bàmìi hâeng in Thai) – again it's reportedly the best in Bangkok. Another great noodle place, *Pet Tun Jao Thaa*, is on the southeastern edge of Chinatown in the direction of the GPO, at 945 Soi Wanit 2 opposite the Harbour Department building. The restaurant's name means 'Harbour Department Stewed Duck' – the speciality is rice noodles (kǔaytǐaw) served with duck or goose, either roasted or stewed.

All-night *food hawkers* set up along Yaowarat Rd at the Ratchawong Rd intersection, opposite Yaowarat Market and near the Cathay Department Store; this is the least expensive place to dine out in Chinatown. The city reportedly has plans to relocate all the vendors from this area to a new 'Chinatown Night Plaza' around the corner on Ratchawong Rd in order to reduce traffic on Yaowarat Rd.

*Suki Jeh Yuu Seu* (the English sign reads 'Health Food'), a Chinese vegetarian restaurant just 70m down Rama IV Rd from Hualamphong station, serves excellent if a bit pricey vegetarian food in a clean, air-con atmosphere. The fruit shakes are particularly well made; this is a great place to fortify yourself with food and drink while waiting for a train at Hualamphong.

Over in Pahurat, the Indian fabric district, most places serve north Indian cuisine, which is heavily influenced by Moghul or Persian flavours and spices. For many people, the best north Indian restaurant in town is the *Royal India* at 392/1 Chakraphet Rd in Pahurat. It can be very crowded at lunchtime, almost exclusively with Indian residents, so it might be better to go there after the standard lunch hour or at night. The place has very good curries (both vegetarian and non-vegetarian), dal, Indian breads (including six kinds of paratha), raita, lassi etc, all at quite reasonable prices. Royal India also has a branch in Khao San Rd in Banglamphu but it's not as good.

The *ATM Department Store* on Chakraphet Rd near the pedestrian bridge has a food centre on the top floor that features several Indian vendors – the food is cheap and tasty and there's quite a good selection. Running alongside the ATM building on Soi ATM are several small teahouses with very inexpensive Indian and Nepali food, including lots of fresh chapatis and strong milk tea. For a good choice of inexpensive vegetarian food, try the Sikh-operated *Indrathep* on Soi ATM. In the afternoons, a Sikh man sets up a pushcart on the corner of Soi ATM and Chakraphet Rd and sells vegetarian samosas often cited as the best in Bangkok.

Wedged between the western edge of Chinatown and the northern edge of Pahurat, the three-storey *Old Siam Plaza* shopping centre houses a number of Thai, Chinese and Japanese restaurants. The most economical places are on the 3rd floor, where a food centre serves inexpensive Thai and Chinese meals from 10 am to 5 pm. The 3rd floor also has several reasonably priced, Thai-style coffee shops. Attached to the adjacent Chalermkrung Royal Theatre is a branch of the highly efficient, moderately priced *S&P Restaurant & Bakery*, where the extensive menu encompasses everything from authentic Thai to well prepared Japanese, European and vegetarian dishes, along with a selection of pastries and desserts.

**Vegetarian** During the annual Vegetarian Festival (centred around Wat Mangkon Kamalawat on Charoen Krung Rd in September-October), Bangkok's Chinatown becomes a virtual orgy of vegetarian Thai and Chinese food. Restaurants and noodle shops in the area offer hundreds of different dishes. One of the best spreads is at *Hua Seng Restaurant*, a few doors west of Wat Mangkon on Charoen Krung Rd.

**Soi Ngam Duphli** *Hua Hin Restaurant*, on Soi Atakanprasit (off Soi Ngam Duphli south-west of the Malaysia Hotel), serves decent western breakfasts, including fresh brewed coffee, for 35 to 50B; open daily from 7.30 am. On the 11th floor of *Lumphini Tower* on busy Rama IV Rd is a cafeteria-style food centre open from 7 am to 2 pm.

Opposite Lumphini Tower on the same road is a warren of food vendors with cheap eats.

Air-con *Mai Mawn* (look for a green sign with Thai script and a small English sign reading 'Restaurant – Thai, Chinese, Seafood') on Soi Ngam Duphli itself, serves good Thai noodle dishes at lunchtime for around 25B, and excellent Thai and Chinese food for dinner starting at 40B.

Another restaurant in the Soi Ngam Duphli area worth mentioning is *Ratsstube* (☎ 287-2822) in the Thai-German Cultural Centre (Goethe Institute), also on Soi Atakanprasit. Home-made sausages and set meals from 120B attract a large and steady clientele; open daily from 10 am to 10 pm.

**Other Dining Options** Bangkok also offers the opportunity to try something new – whether that's dining at one of Bangkok's huge outdoor restaurants or more intimately onboard a sunset dinner cruise.

*Mega-Restaurants Tum-Nak-Thai (Tamnak Thai)* (☎ 276-7810), 131 Ratchadaphisek Rd, is one of several large outdoor restaurants built over boggy areas of Bangkok's Din Daeng district north of Phetburi Rd. Built on four hectares of land and water, it can serve up to 3000 diners at once. The menu exceeds 250 items and includes Thai, Chinese, Japanese and European food. All orders are computer coordinated and some of the waiters glide by on roller skates. One section of the restaurant offers while-you-dine Thai classical dance performances. Two can eat here for under 400B including beer.

Tum-Nak-Thai was billed as the largest outdoor restaurant in the world – as verified by the Guinness record book – until *Mang Gorn Luang (Royal Dragon) Seafood Restaurant* (☎ 398-0037) opened recently at Km 1 on the Bangna-Trat expressway. Around 1200 roller-skating servers in traditional Thai costumes, along with waitresses paddling along artificial canals in 'happy boats', serve up to 10,000 diners per day. Other loony touches include soundproof karaoke pavilions and a dining area housed in a seven-storey pagoda. House specialities on the 440 item menu (not including drinks or desserts) include hàw mòk (thick seafood curry steamed in banana leaves) and yam yong (sweet and salty banana shoot salad). Figure 300 to 500B for two diners.

**Dinner Cruises** There are a number of companies that run cruises during which you eat dinner. Prices range from 40 to 700B per person depending on how far they go and whether dinner is included in the fare. For more information, see Dinner Cruises under River & Canal Trips earlier in this chapter.

**Hotel Restaurants** For splurge-level food, many of Bangkok's grand luxury hotels provide memorable – if expensive – eating experiences. With western cuisine, particularly, the quality usually far exceeds anything found in Bangkok's independent restaurants. Some of the city's best Chinese restaurants are also located in hotels. If you're on a budget, check to see if a lunchtime buffet is available on weekdays; usually these are the best deals, ranging from 150 to 300B per person (up to 490B at the Oriental). Also check the *Bangkok Post* and *The Nation* for weekly specials presented by visiting chefs from far-flung corners of the globe – Morocco, Mexico City, Montreal, no matter how obscure, they've probably done the Bangkok hotel circuit.

The Oriental Hotel has six restaurants, all managed by world-class chefs, and buffet lunches are offered at several. The hotel's *China House* (☎ 236-0400, ext 3378), set in a charming wooden house opposite the hotel's main wing, has one of the best Chinese kitchens in Bangkok, with an emphasis on Cantonese cooking. The lunchtime dim sum is superb and is a bargain by luxury hotel standards at 50B or less per plate or all you can eat for 250B. The Oriental's *Lord Jim's* is designed to imitate the interior of a 19th century Asian steamer, with a view of the river; the menu focuses on seafood (lunch buffet available).

The new *Bai Yun* (☎ 679-1200), on the 50th floor of the Westin Banyan Tree, specialises in

---

**High Tea**

Although Thailand was never a British colony (or anyone's colony for that matter), influences from nearby Kuala Lumpur and Singapore have made afternoon tea (or high tea) a custom at the more ritzy hotels. One of the best spreads is afternoon tea in the *Regent Bangkok* lobby from 2 to 5.30 pm on weekdays. The cost is 190B for a selection of herbal, fruit, Japanese, Chinese and Indian teas plus a variety of hot scones, Devonshire cream, jam, cakes, cookies and sandwiches. A live string quartet provides atmosphere.

At the Authors Lounge of the *Oriental Hotel* high tea costs 275B (plus tax and service) for a range of sweet and savoury delights and one of the best tea assortments in Bangkok, all taken in the quasi-colonial atmosphere enjoyed by Maugham, Coward and Greene. Tea is served daily from 2 to 6 pm.

Amidst the Asian minimalism of the *Sukhothai Hotel's* lobby salon, the usual sandwiches, pastries and tea selections go for just 180B. Add champagne to the afternoon's knosh for 420B. Served daily from 2.30 to 6 pm.

Afternoon tea in the lobby-lounge of the *Shangri-La Hotel* costs 220B weekdays, 2 to 6 pm, for a variety of teas, sandwiches and cakes; on weekends the Shangri-La does a more lavish 40-item 'high tea buffet' for 250B. ■

---

nouvelle Cantonese – an east-west fusion – and is the highest restaurant in Thailand.

Dusit Thani's *Chinatown* (☎ 236-0450) was probably the inspiration for the Oriental's China House, though here the menu focuses on Chiu Chau (Chao Zhou) cuisine as well as Cantonese. Dim sum lunch is available, but it's a bit more expensive than the Oriental's. As at the Oriental, service is impeccable. Dusit also has the highly reputed *Mayflower*, with pricey Cantonese cuisine, and the Vietnamese *Thien Duong*.

For hotel dim sum almost as good as that at the Dusit or Oriental – but at less than a third the price – try the *Jade Garden* (☎ 233-7060) at the Montien Hotel. Though not quite as fancy in presentation, the food is nonetheless impressive.

For French food, the leading hotel contenders are *Ma Maison* (☎ 253-0123) at the Hilton International, *Normandie* (☎ 236-0400, ext 3380) at the Oriental and *Regent Grill* (☎ 251-6127) at the Regent Bangkok. All are expensive but the meals and service are virtually guaranteed to be of top quality. The Regent Bangkok also offers the slightly less formal *La Brasserie*, specialising in Parisian cuisine.

One of the best Italian dining experiences in the city can be found at the very posh *Grappino Italian Restaurant* (☎ 653-9000)

in the Amari Watergate Hotel, on Phetburi Rd in the busy Pratunam district. All pasta and breads are prepared fresh on the premises daily, and the small but high-tech wine cellar is one of Bangkok's best – the grappa selection is, of course, unmatched. Grappino is open daily for lunch and dinner; reservations are recommended.

The minimalist *Colonnade Restaurant* (☎ 287-0222) at the Beaufort Sukhothai Hotel lays out a huge 500B brunch, including made-to-order lobster bisque, from 11 am to 3 pm on Sundays. A jazz trio supplies background music. Reservations are recommended.

*Caviar Corner*, in The Promenade, a small but posh shopping mall in front of the Hilton International on Withayu Rd, offers a variety of Persian caviars. Platters start at 275B for two kinds of caviar, salmon, toast and mascarpone; larger amounts of caviar start at 750B. Vodka, wine and champagne are also available, by the glass or by the bottle.

Finally, if eating at one of the above would mean spending your life savings, try this pauper's version of dining amidst the bright hotel lights of Bangkok. Go to the end of the soi in front of the Shangri-La Hotel and take a ferry (1B) across the river to the wooden pier immediately opposite. Next to this pier is the riverside *Prom*, where you can enjoy an inexpensive Thai seafood meal outdoors with impressive night-time views of the Shangri-La and Oriental hotels opposite. The ferry runs till Prom closes, around 2 am.

**Vegetarian** One of the oldest Thai vegetarian restaurants, operated by the Buddhist ascetic *Asoke Foundation*, is the branch at Chatuchak (Weekend) Market off Kamphaeng Phet Rd (near the main local bus stop, a pedestrian bridge and a Chinese shrine – look for a sign reading 'Vegetarian' in green letters). It's open only on weekends from 8 am to noon. Prices are almost ridiculously low – around 7 to 12B per dish. The *cafeteria* at the Bangkok Adventist Hospital at 430 Phitsanulok Rd also serves inexpensive veggie fare. All the Indian restaurants in town also have vegetarian selections on their menus.

## Entertainment

In their round-the-clock search for *khwaam sa-nùk* (fun), Bangkokians have made their metropolis one that literally never sleeps. To get an idea of what's available, check the entertainment listings in the daily *Bangkok Post* and *The Nation*, the free tourist-oriented weeklies *This Week* and *Angel City*, or the relatively new monthly *Bangkok Metro*.

Possibilities include classical music performances, rock concerts, videotheque dancing, Asian music/theatre ensembles on tour, art shows and international buffets. Boredom should not be a problem in Bangkok, at least not for a short-term visit; however, save some energy and money for your upcountry trip!

**Nightlife** Bangkok's overpublicised, naughty nightlife image is linked to the bars, coffee houses, nightclubs and massage parlours left over from the days when the City of Angels was an R&R stop for GIs serving in Vietnam. By and large these throwbacks are seedy, expensive and cater to men only. Then there is the new breed of S&S (sex & sin) bar, some merely refurbished R&R digs, that are more modest, classy and welcome females and couples. Not everybody's cup of tea, but

they do a good business. More recently, other places have appeared which are quite chic and suitable for either gender.

All the major hotels have flashy nightclubs too. Many feature live music – rock, country & western, Thai pop music and jazz. Hotels catering to tourists and businesspeople often contain up-to-date discos. You'll find the latest recorded music in the smaller neighbourhood bars as well as in the megadiscos.

All bars and clubs are supposed to close at 1 or 2 am (the latter closing time is for places with dance floors and/or live music), but in reality only a few obey the law.

**Live Music** Bangkok's live music scene has expanded rapidly over the past decade or so, with a multiplicity of new, extremely competent bands and new clubs. The three-storey *Saxophone Pub Restaurant* (☎ 246-5472), south-east of the Victory Monument circle at 3/8 Victory Monument, Phayathai Rd, has become a Bangkok institution for musicians of several genres. On the ground floor is a bar/restaurant featuring jazz from 9 pm to 1.30 am; the next floor up has a billiards hall with recorded music; the top floor has live bands playing reggae, R&B, jazz or blues from 10.30 pm to 4 am, and on Sundays there's an open jam session. There's never a cover charge at Saxophone and you don't need to dress up.

Another very casual spot to hear music is the open-air bar operated by *Ruang Pung Art Community* next to Chatuchak (Weekend) Market. Thai rock, folk, blues and jam sessions attract an artsy Thai crowd.

Bars with regular live jazz include *Why Art?* in the Royal City Avenue complex, off New Phetburi Rd (nightly 10 pm to 2 am), the strangely named *Imageries by the Glass* on No 2 Soi 24, Sukhumvit Rd (Monday and Tuesday nights only; see also below), and *Blues/Jazz* (☎ 258-7747) at Soi 53 Sukhumvit Rd. The Oriental's famous *Bamboo Bar* has live jazz from 5 to 8.30 pm nightly in an elegant but relaxed atmosphere; other hotel jazz bars include *Entrepreneur* at the Asia Hotel (Saturday night only), the Grand Hyatt's

*Garden Lounge* (Tuesday through Sunday), the Beaufort Sukhothai Hotel's *Colonnade* (Tuesday through Sunday) and the Hilton's *The Lounge* (Friday night only).

The imaginatively named *Rock Pub*, opposite the Asia Hotel on Phayathai Rd, offers up Thai heavy metal – with plenty of hair-throwing and lip-jutting – nightly. Regulars include Kaleidoscope, Wizard, Uranium and the Olarn Project. The *Hollywood Rock Place* on Phayathai Rd near the MacKenna Cinema is similar.

**Eclectic** Bangkok's better-than-average *Hard Rock Cafe*, Siam Square, Soi 11, features live rock music most evenings from around 10 pm to 12.30 am, including the occasional big name act (Chris Isaak's incendiary 1994 performance left bootnail dents in the bar top).

Not to be overlooked on Sarasin Rd, the *Old West* (Thailand's original old-west-style pub) books good Thai folk and blues groups – look for a rockin' outfit called D-Train here. Down the road a bit, *Blue's Bar* is similar. The *Magic Mushroom* at 212/33 Sukhumvit Road (next to Soi 12) hires a variety of rock and blues acts nightly, including some of Bangkok's biggest names. The *Front Page*, Soi Sala Daeng, off Rama IV Rd, hosts journeyman folk and blues groups on Monday, Tuesday and Saturday nights.

Elegant *Spasso* in the Grand Hyatt Erawan features imported pop/dance bands from Europe, the USA and Australia. *Imageries By The Glass*, owned by Thai composer-musician Jirapan Ansvananada, boasts a huge sound board and closed circuit TV for its stage shows, which welcome local as well as foreign bands of all genres. It's at No 2 Soi 24, Sukhumvit Rd.

**Bars** Bangkok has definitely outgrown the days when the only bars around catered to male go-go oglers. Trendy among Bangkok Thais these days are bars which strive for a more sophisticated atmosphere, with good service and choice music. The Thais call them pubs but they bear little resemblance to any traditional English pub. Some are

'theme' bars, conceived around a particular aesthetic. All the city's major hotels feature western-style bars as well.

One of the main hotspots in town for young Thais is a huge bar and dance club complex called *Royal City Avenue* (Soi Sunwichai, north off New Phetburi Rd). Originally designed a few years back as a shopping centre, RCA has been taken over by a 2.5 km horizontal strip of high-tech bars with names like *Absolute Zero, Baby Hand Pub, Bar Code, Chit, Cool Tango, Exit, Fahrenheit, Jigsaw, Radio Underground, Relax, Route 66, Shit Happens, Why Art?* and *X Symbol*. Most have recorded music – everything from soul to techno to Thai pop – but a few also feature local bands. *Cool Tango*, operated by the original owners of the now-defunct Brown Sugar on Sarasin Rd, has the best live music and most international ambience; bands from overseas play here regularly. The three-storey *Casper's Palace* features live as well as recorded music and has somehow been able to sidestep the national 2 am closing law (staying open as late as 5 am). Although it is the most happening place at the moment, the scene at RCA changes almost week to week.

RCA was immensely popular in 1995 and early 1996 until a police crackdown on under-18 drinkers stifled things a bit. Such enforcement is a first for Thailand, a country where any six year old child can walk into a market and buy a beer. Most of the RCA clientele are in their teens and early 20s; some bars are owned by loose collectives of 20 or more university students who just want a place to hang out with their friends and possibly make a little extra money while others are serious high-roller clubs.

A similarly youthful scene can be found at another new complex called *Premier*. Aesthetically this one has a more interesting layout, as the bars and restaurants are centred around a fountain pool. Post-modern pubs here include *Pool Side, Talk of the Town, Zeal, Tied Up, Vintage Special, Sanggasi, Le Mans* and *La Dee Da*, each with an artsy decor. The *Nude Bar* even sports Robert Mapplethorpe prints, while the *Seri Art*

*Gallery* doubles as a pub and Thai art gallery. Premiere's *One Dollar Music Room* is a sans-bar disco where you dance to recorded music as long as you like for a 25B cover. There's also a *beer garden* open during the cool season only, and nearly a dozen restaurants serving Thai, American and French food. Premier is on New Rama IX Rd, past Ramkhamhaeng Rd, near Soi 24 (Soi Seri) just before New Rama IX Rd intersects Si Nakarin Rd.

Bangkok is a little short on plain neighbourhood bars without up-market pretensions or down-market sleaze. One that's close to fitting the bill is the *Front Page*, a one-time journalists' hangout (before the nearby *Bangkok Post* offices moved to Khlong Toey) on Soi 1, Sala Daeng (off Silom and Rama IV). Two low-key, British-style taverns include *Jool's* on Soi 4 near Nana Plaza, *Bull's Head* on the ground floor of Angus Steak House, Soi 33/1, Sukhumvit Rd, and the *Witch's Tavern* at 306/1 Soi 55, Sukhumvit Rd. The latter features live music on weekends.

*Delaney's Irish Pub* (☎ 266-7160), a new place at 1-4 Sivadon Bldg, Convent Rd in the Silom Rd district, is so far the only place in Bangkok that serves Guinness on tap; the interior wood panels, glass mirrors and bench seating were all custom-made and imported from Ireland. Delaney's features a daily happy hour and live Irish music Tuesday through Saturday.

*Henry J Bean's Bar & Grill* in the basement of the Amari Watergate Hotel (there's a separate entrance so that you don't have to walk through the hotel) on Phetburi Rd in Pratunam is a relaxed spot with an American-style 1950s and 1960s decor. Performing bartenders flip bottles and glasses while serving and there's an early evening happy hour daily. A house band called the Nighthawks plays roots rock and reggae most nights; other live bands occasionally appear.

*Wong's Place*, at 27/3 Si Bamphen, is a low-key hangout for local residents and visitors staying in the Soi Ngam Duphli area and sports a good collection of music videos. The *Hole in the Wall* and *No Name* bars on a short, dead-end soi toward the west end of Khao San Rd are cheap places to drink and chat with Khao San Rd denizens.

The guitar-shaped bar at Bangkok's *Hard Rock Cafe* (☎ 251-0792), Siam Square, Soi 11, features a full line of cocktails and a small assortment of local and imported beers. The crowd is an ever-changing assortment of Thais, expats and tourists. From 10 pm on there's also live music.

For slick aerial city views, the place to go is the *Sky Lounge*, in the Baiyoke Tower on Ratchaprarop Rd in Pratunam. It's 43 floors above the city and open 24 hours. The *Compass Rose*, a new bar on the 59th floor of the Westin Banyan Tree on Sathon Tai Rd, is even higher but is only open 11.30 am to 1 am. TV jocks can keep up with their favourite teams via big-screen satellite TV at *Champs* (☎ 252-7651), a huge American-style sports bar in the Nai Lert Building on Sukhumvit Road, near Soi 5.

*CM²*, a new complex attached to the Novotel in Siam Square, contains a number of ultra-modern bars, including one where 'virtual reality machines' will soon be installed.

Wireheads can check their e-mail or skim the Net at the new *CyberPub* (☎ 236-0450 ext 2971) in the Dusit Thani Hotel on the corner of Silom and Rama IV Rds. Booze and food are available, along with a bank of 10 up-to-date computer stations. Charges are 5B per online minute; you pay for food, beverages and online time using a 'smart card' issued by CyberPub. This is surely only the first of many such cybercafes Bangkok will see over the next few years.

**Discos & Dance Clubs** All the major hotels have international-style discotheques but only a small number – those at the Dusit Thani, the Shangri-La, the Grand Hyatt and the Regent – can really be recommended as attractions in themselves. Cover charges are pretty uniform: around 150 to 200B on weekday nights, including one drink, and around 300 to 350B on weekends, including two drinks. Most places don't begin filling up till after 11 pm.

Bangkok is famous for its huge high-tech discos that hold up to 5000 people and feature mega-watt sound systems, a giant-screen video and the latest in light-show technology. The clientele for these dance palaces is mostly an aggro crowd of young, moneyed Thais experimenting with life-styles of conspicuous affluence, plus the occasional Bangkok celebrity. The most 'in' disco of this nature at the moment is *Phoebus Amphitheatre Complex* on Ratchadapisek Rd. Other biggies include *Paradise* on Arun Amarin Rd in Thonburi and the *Palace* on Vibhavadi Rangsit Highway towards the airport. A mega-disco that gets older as well as younger Thais is the *Galaxy* on Rama IV Rd, from which WBA world boxing champions Khaosai Galaxy and his brother Khaokor have taken their surname. The Galaxy is also popular with some Japanese visitors who patronise the 'no-hands' section of the club, where hostesses feed the customers so they never have to lift their hands.

Well heeled Thais and Thai celebrities frequent the more exclusive, high-tech *Narcissus* (☎ 258-2549) at 112 Soi 23 Sukhumvit Rd. *FM 228* (☎ 231-1228), in the United Center Building, 323 Silom Rd, tries to cover all the bases with separate rooms featuring videotheque dancing, live music, and karaoke, plus an American restaurant and bar.

Dance clubs sprinkled throughout the Royal City Avenue and Premier entertainment complexes have become very popular very quickly, especially among young (late teens and early 20s) Thais – see Bars above for details.

A string of small dance clubs on Soi 2 and Soi 4 (Soi Jaruwan), both parallel to Patpong 1 and 2, off Silom Rd, attracts a more mixed crowd in terms of age, gender, nationality and sexual orientation than either the hotel discos or the RCA/Premier entertainment complexes. The norm for recorded music here includes techno, trance, hip-hop and other current dance trends. Main venues – some of which are small and narrow – include on Soi 2 *Disco Disco (DD)* and *DJ Station*, and on Soi 4 *Hyper, Divine, Deeper,*

*Rome Club* and *Sphinx*. The larger places collect cover charges of around 100 to 300B depending on the night of the week; the smaller ones are free. The clientele at these clubs was once predominantly gay but has become more mixed as word got around about the great dance scene. Things don't get started here till relatively late – around midnight; in fact on most nights the Soi 2/Soi 4 dance clubs serve more as 'after hours' hangouts since they usually stay open past the official 2 am closing time.

*Star Bar*, on the rooftop of the building opposite the police station at the intersection of Khao San and Chakraphong Rds, is a casual dance scene that attracts the tie-dyed world travellers who frequent the area. In spite of its proximity to the police, Star Bar often manages to stay open past official closing times. Near the end of a dead-end soi on the north side of Khao San Rd, the *Paradise* offers a similar ambience with a touch of 1960s black-light retro-ism.

*Temptations*, at the Novotel Bangkok in Siam Square, provides big band music for *lii-lâat* (ballroom dancing). Every night of the week a dressed-to-the-nines crowd of Bangkok Thais cha-cha, foxtrot, tango and rumba across the glazed dance floor. In addition to serving drinks, waiters and waitresses will lead novices through the steps. The cover charge of 400B includes one drink and all the instruction necessary to turn you into a *nák lii-lâat*.

**Gay/Lesbian Scene** See the information on the sois 2 and Soi 4, Silom Rd dance club scene under Discos & Dance Clubs for places that attract mixed gay/straight/bi clientele. In general the Soi 2 clubs are more gay than the Soi 4 bars, though Soi 4's *Telephone* is more exclusively gay then other bars on this street. The hottest gay dance scene on Soi 2 is currently *DJ Station*. *Khrua Silom*, in Silom Alley off Soi 2, attracts a young Thai gay and lesbian crowd. There's a cluster of seedier gay bars off Soi Anuman Ratchathon, off Silom Rd opposite the Tawana Ramada Hotel – more or less the gay equivalent of Patpong.

*Utopia* (☎ 259-9619), at 116/1 Soi 23, Sukhumvit Rd is a combination bar, gallery, cafe and information clearing house for the local gay and lesbian community – the only such facility in South-East Asia. Friday nights are designated women's night, and there are regular film nights as well as Thai lessons. Special events, such as Valentine's Day candlelit dinners, are held from time to time. Utopia is open daily from noon to 2 am.

Other lesbian venues include: *By Heart Pub* (☎ 570-1841), at 117/697, Soi Sainanikhom 1, Bang Kapi; *Be My Guest*, around the corner from Utopia on Soi 31; and *Obsession*, in the Royal City Avenue complex.

*Babylon Bangkok* (☎ 213-2108), at 50 Soi Atakanprasit, off Sathon Tai Rd, is a four-storey gay sauna which *Thai Scene* called one of the top 10 gay saunas in the world. Facilities include a bar, roof garden, gym, massage room, steam and dry saunas and Jacuzzi baths. It's open daily from 5 to 11 pm. Other gay-oriented saunas include *The Obelisks* (☎ 662-4377) at 39/3 Soi 53, Sukhumvit Rd, *The Colony* (☎ 391-4393) at 117 Soi Charoensuk (off Soi 55, Sukhumvit Rd) and *V Club* (☎ 279-3322) at 541 Soi Aree (Soi 7), Phahonyothin Rd. All of these facilities charge a cover of around 150B weekdays, 250 to 300B weekends.

*Jet Set* at 32/19 Soi 21, Sukhumvit Rd is a karaoke lounge patronised by young gay Thais. The *Long Yang Club* (☎ 679-7727), GPO Box 1077, Silom, Bangkok 10504, organises members-only activities for gay men in Bangkok on a regular basis.

**Go-Go Bars**  These are concentrated along Sukhumvit Rd (between sois 21 and 23), off Sukhumvit Rd on Soi Nana Tai and in the world-famous Patpong Rd area, between Silom and Surawong Rds.

Patpong's neon-lit buildings cover roughly four acres standing on what was once a banana plantation owned by the Bank of Indochina, which sold the land to the Hainanese-Thai Patpongphanit family for 60,000B (US$2400) just before WWII. The typical bar measures four by 12m deep; the Patpongphanit family collects a total of 10 million baht (US$400,000) rent per month from Patpong tenants. According to the Patpongphanit patriarch himself, who was recently interviewed in *Bangkok Metro* magazine, it wasn't American GIs who originally supported the Patpong bar business but rather airline staff from some 15 airline offices which established themselves in the area after WWII. Bangkok's first massage parlour, Bangkok Onsen, was established here in 1956 to serve Japanese expats and senior Thai police officers. By the 1960s Soi Patpong had a flourishing local nightclub scene that was further boosted by the arrival of US and Australian soldiers in the early 1970s. (See the information on prostitution in the Entertainment section of the Facts for the Visitor chapter.)

Patpong has calmed down a bit over the years. These days it has more of an open-air market feel as several of the newer bars are literally on the street, and vendors set up shop in the evening hawking everything from roast squid to fake designer watches. On Patpong's two parallel lanes there are around 38 go-go bars, plus a sprinkling of restaurants and cocktail bars. The downstairs clubs, with names like *King's Castle* and *Pussy Galore*, feature go-go dancing while upstairs the real raunch is kept behind closed doors. The 1 am closing law is strictly enforced on Patpong 1 and 2.

Another holdover from the R&R days is *Soi Cowboy*, a single lane strip of 25 to 30 bars off Sukhumvit Rd between sois 21 and 23. *Nana Entertainment Plaza*, off Soi 4 (Soi Nana Tai) Sukhumvit Rd, is a three-storey complex which has surged in popularity among resident and visiting oglers. Nana Plaza comes complete with its own guest-houses in the same complex, used almost exclusively by Nana Plaza's female bar workers for illicit assignations. There are 18 bars in the whole complex.

Soi Tantawan (Soi 6) and Thaniya Rd, on either side of and parallel to Patpong 1, 2 and 4, feature expensive Japanese-style hostess bars (which non-Japanese are usually barred from entering) as well as a handful of gay bars that feature male go-go dancers and 'bar boys'.

Transvestite cabarets are big in Bangkok and several are found in the Patpong area. *Calypso Cabaret* (☎ 261-6355), in the Ambassador Hotel at Soi 11, has the largest regularly performing transvestite troupe in town, with nightly shows at 8.30 and 10 pm. Some of the gay bars on sois 2 and 4 off Silom Rd also feature short drag shows during intermissions between dance sets.

**Massage Parlours** Massage parlours have been a Bangkok attraction for many years now, though the TAT tries to playdown the city's reputation in this respect. Massage as a healing art is a centuries-old tradition in Thailand, and it is possible to get a really legitimate massage in Bangkok, despite the commercialisation of recent years (see Traditional Massage below). That many of the city's modern massage parlours (*àap òp nûat* or 'bathe-steam-massage') also deal in prostitution is well known; less well known is the fact that many (but by no means all) of the girls working in the parlours are bonded labour – they are not necessarily there by choice. There is a definite AIDS presence in Thailand (see the information on this and other sexually transmitted diseases under Health in the Facts for the Visitor chapter).

All but the most insensitive males will be saddened by the sight of 50 girls/women behind a glass wall with numbers pinned to their dresses. Often the bank of masseuses is divided into sections according to skill and/or appearance. Most expensive is the 'superstar' section, in which the women try to approximate the look of fashion models or actresses. A smaller section is reserved for women who are actually good at giving massages, and who offer nothing extra.

*Traditional Massage* Traditional Thai massage, also called 'ancient' massage, is now widely available in Bangkok as an alternative to the red-light massage parlours. One of the best places to experience a traditional massage is at *Wat Pho*, Bangkok's oldest temple. Massage here costs 180B per hour or 100B for half an hour. For those interested in studying massage, the temple also offers two 30 hour courses – one on general Thai massage, the other on massage therapy – which you can attend three hours per day for 10 days, or two hours per day for 15 days. Tuition is 4500B. You must also pay the regular 10B per day admission fee for Wat Pho whether you are a student or massagee.

Next to Wat Mahathat (toward Thammasat University at the south-east corner of Maharat and Phra Chan Rds) is a strip of Thai herbal medicine shops offering good massage for a mere 80B an hour.

A more commercial area for Thai massage – still legit – as well as Thai herbal saunas is Surawong Rd. Here you'll find *Marble House* (☎ 235-3519) at 37/18-19 Soi Surawong Plaza, Surawong Rd; *SL* (☎ 237-5690) on the 10th floor of Silom-Surawong Condos, 176 Soi Anuman Ratchathon off Soi 6, Silom Rd; *Vejakorn* (☎ 237-5576), 37/25 Soi Surawong Plaza, Surawong Rd; and *Eve House* (☎ 266-3846), 18/1 Surawong Rd, opposite Thaniya Plaza. Eve House charges 150B per hour and accepts women only. The rest of these charge 200 to 300B per hour and offer Thai herbal sauna as well as massage. *Arima Onsen* (☎ 235-2142) at 37/10-11 Soi Surawong Plaza specialises in Japanese-style massage and reflexology.

Out on Sukhumvit Rd you can find traditional Thai massage at *Buathip Thai Massage* (☎ 255-1045) at 4/13 Soi 5, Sukhumvit Rd; and at *Winwan* (☎ 251-7467) between sois 1 and 3, Sukhumvit Rd.

Fees for traditional Thai massage should be no more than 300B per hour, though some places have a 1½ hour minimum. Be aware that not every place advertising traditional or ancient massage offers a really good one; sometimes the only thing 'ancient' about the pummelling is the age of the masseuse or masseur. Thai massage aficionados say that the best massages are given by blind masseurs (available at Marble House).

Most hotels also provide a legitimate massage service either through their health clubs or as part of room service. The highly praised *Oriental Hotel Spa* offers a 40 minute 'jet lag massage' designed to alleviate body-clock time differences.

**Thai Dance-Drama** Thailand's most traditional *lákhon* and *khõn* performances are held at the *National Theatre* (☎ 224-1342) on Chao Fa Rd near Phra Pinklao Bridge. The theatre's regular public roster schedules six or seven performances per month, usually on weekends. Admission fees are very reasonable at around 20 to 200B depending on the seating. Attendance at a khõn performance (masked dance-drama based on stories from the *Ramakian)* is highly recommended.

Occasionally, classical dance performances are also held at the *Thailand Cultural Centre* (☎ 245-7711) on Ratchadaphisek Rd and at the *College of Dramatic Arts* (☎ 224-1391), near the National Theatre.

For more information on Thai classical dance see the special Thai Arts & Architecture section in the Facts about the Country chapter.

A classical Thai dancer wearing the *chadok* –the traditional royal headdress.

**Chalermkrung Royal Theatre** The 1993 renovation of this Thai Deco building at the edge of the city's Chinatown-Pahurat district provides a striking new venue for khõn performance in Thailand. When originally opened in 1933, the royally funded Chalermkrung was the largest and most modern theatre in Asia, with state-of-the-art motion picture projection technology and the first chilled-water air-con system in the region. Prince Samaichaloem, a former student of the École des Beaux-Arts in Paris, designed the hexagonal building.

The reborn theatre's 80,000 watt audio system, combined with computer-generated laser graphics, enable the 170 member dance troupe to present a technologically enhanced version of traditional khõn. Although the special effects are reasonably impressive, the excellent costuming, set design, dancing and music are reason enough to attend.

The khõn performance lasts about two hours with intermission; performances are generally held twice a week (usually every Tuesday and Thursday at 8 pm), but this schedule changes from time to time as the theatre feels its way through the Bangkok

cultural market. Other Thai performing arts may also be scheduled at the theatre.

Khõn tickets cost a steep 500, 700, 800 and 1000B. Theatre members can obtain a 200 to 300B discount on these rates; only Bangkok residents are eligible, although for once this includes foreigners as well as Thais. For ticket reservations, call ☎ 222-0434 or visit the box office in person. The theatre requests that patrons dress respectfully, which means no shorts or thongs. Bring a wrap or long-sleeved shirt in case the air-con is running full blast.

The Chalermkrung Royal Theatre is on the corner of Charoen Krung and Triphet Rds, adjacent to the Old Siam Plaza complex and only a block from the Pahurat fabric market. Air-con bus Nos 8, 48 and 73 pass the theatre (going west on Charoen Krung). You can also comfortably walk to the theatre from the western terminus of the Saen Saep canal ferry. Taxi drivers may know the theatre by its original name, Sala Chalerm Krung, which is spelt out in Thai in the lighted sign surmounting the front of the building.

**Dinner Theatres** Most tourists view performances put on solely for their benefit at one of the several Thai classical dance/dinner theatres in the city (see list below). Admission prices at these evening venues average 200 to 500B per person and include a 'typical' Thai dinner (often toned down for farang palates), a couple of selected dance performances and a martial arts display.

The historic *Oriental Hotel* has its own dinner theatre (the Sala Rim Namon) on the Thonburi side of the Chao Phraya River opposite the hotel. The admission is well above average but so is the food and the performance; the river ferry between the hotel and restaurant is free. The much less expensive dinner performance at Silom Village's *Ruen Thep* restaurant on Silom Rd is recommended because of the relaxed, semi-outdoor setting.

Baan Thai Restaurant – 7 Soi 32, Sukhumvit Rd (☎ 258-5403)
Maneeya Lotus Room – 518/5 Ploenchit Rd (☎ 251-0382)
Phiman Restaurant – 46 Soi 49, Sukhumvit Rd (☎ 258-7866)
Ruen Thep – Silom Village, Silom Rd (☎ 233-9447)
Sala Norasing – Soi 4, Sukhumvit Rd (☎ 251-5797)
Sala Rim Nam – opposite Oriental Hotel, Charoen Nakhon Rd (☎ 437-6221/3080)
Suwannahong Restaurant – Si Ayuthaya Rd (☎ 245-4448/3747)
Tum-Nak-Thai Restaurant – 131 Ratchadaphisek Rd (☎ 277-3828)

**Shrine Dancing** Free performances of traditional lákhon chatrii dance can be seen daily at the *Lak Meuang* and *Erawan* shrines if you happen to arrive when a performance troupe has been commissioned by a worshipper. Although many of the dance movements are the same as those seen in classical lákhon, these relatively crude performances are specially choreographed for ritual purposes and don't represent true classical dance forms. But the dancing is colourful – the dancers wear full costume and are accompanied by live music – so it's worth stopping by to watch a performance if you're in the vicinity.

**Thai Boxing** *Muay thai* (Thai boxing) can be seen at two boxing stadiums, *Lumphini*

(on Rama IV Rd near Sathon Tai (South) Rd) and *Ratchadamnoen* (on Ratchadamnoen Nok Rd, next to the old TAT office). Admission fees vary according to seating: the cheapest seats in Bangkok are now around 170B and ringside seats cost 500B or more. Monday, Wednesday, Thursday and Sunday the boxing is at Ratchadamnoen, while Tuesday, Friday and Saturday it's at Lumphini. The Ratchadamnoen matches begin at 6 pm, except for the Sunday shows which start at 5 pm, and the Lumphini matches all begin at 6.20 pm. Aficionados say the best-matched bouts are reserved for Tuesday nights at Lumphini, and Thursday nights at Ratchadamnoen. The restaurants on the north side of Ratchadamnoen stadium are well known for their delicious kài yâang and other North-Eastern dishes.

**Cinema** Dozens of movie theatres around town show Thai, Chinese, Indian and western movies. The majority of films shown are comedies and shoot-em-ups, with the occasional drama slipping through. These theatres are air-con and quite comfortable, with reasonable rates (40 to 80B). All movies in Thai theatres are preceded by the Thai royal anthem. Everyone in the theatre is expected to stand quietly and respectfully for the duration of the anthem (which was written by the king).

The main theatres showing commercial English-language films are *Scala, Lido 1, 2 & 3* and *Siam* at Siam Square; *Major 1 & 2* at Mahboonkrong shopping centre; *Hollywood* at Hollywood Street Center, Phetburi Rd; *Metro*, Phetburi Rd; *World Trade Center 1, 2 & 3*, Ratchadamri Rd; *Century 1 & 2* and *MacKenna* on Phayathai Rd; and the *Washington 1 & 2* at Soi 24, Sukhumvit Rd. Movie ads appear daily in both *The Nation* and the *Bangkok Post*; listings in *The Nation* include addresses and programme times.

Foreign films are often altered before distribution by Thailand's board of censors; usually this involves obscuring nude sequences. Some distributors also edit films they consider to be too long; occasionally Thai narration is added to explain the storyline (when *The*

*Omen* was released in Thailand, distributors chopped off the ambiguous ending and added a voice-over, giving the film a 'new' ending).

Film buffs may prefer the weekly or twice weekly offerings at Bangkok's foreign cultural clubs. French and German films screened at the cultural clubs are almost always subtitled in English. Admission is sometimes free, sometimes 30 to 40B. For addresses and phone numbers see the Cultural Centres section earlier in this chapter.

**Video** Video rentals are very popular in Bangkok; not only are videos cheaper than regular film admissions, but many films are available on video that aren't approved for theatre distribution by Thailand's board of censors. For those with access to a TV and VCR, the average rental is around 20 to 50B. Sukhumvit Rd has the highest concentration of video shops; the better ones are found in the residential area between sois 39 and 55. Blockbuster, the world's largest video chain, has opened a branch on Soi 33/1, Sukhumvit Rd and plans to open many more branches throughout the capital.

TVs and VCRs (both PAL and NTSC) can be rented at *Silver Bell* (☎ 236-2845), 113/1-2 Surawong Centre, Surawong Rd.

**Things to Buy**

Regular visitors to Asia know that, in many ways, Bangkok beats Hong Kong and Singapore for deals on handicrafts, textiles, gems, jewellery, art and antiques – nowhere else will you find the same combination of selection, quality and prices. The trouble is finding the good spots, as the city's intense urban tangle makes orientation sometimes difficult. *Nancy Chandler's Map of Bangkok* makes a very good buying companion, with annotations on all sorts of small, out-of-the-way shopping venues and markets (called *tàlàat* in Thai).

Be sure to read the introductory Things to Buy section in the Facts for the Visitor chapter before setting out on a buying spree. Amidst all the bargains are a number of cleverly disguised rip-off schemes – *caveat emptor*!

**Weekend Market** Also known as Chatuchak Market, this is the Disneyland of Thai markets; on weekends 8672 vendor stalls cater to an estimated 200,000 visitors a day. Everything is sold here, from live chickens and snakes to opium pipes and herbal remedies. Thai clothing such as the *phâakhamāa* (sarong for men) and the *phâasîn* (sarong for women), *kaang keng jiin* (Chinese pants) and *sêua mâw hâwm* (blue cotton farmer's shirt) are good buys. You'll also find musical instruments, hill-tribe crafts, religious amulets, antiques, flowers, clothes imported from India and Nepal, camping gear and military surplus. The best bargains of all are household goods like pots and pans, dishes, drinking glasses etc. If you're moving to Thailand for an extended period, this is the place to pick up stuff for your kitchen. Don't forget to try out your bargaining skills. There is plenty of interesting and tasty food for sale if you're feeling hungry, and live music in the early evening. And if you need some cash, a couple of banks have ATMs and foreign-exchange booths at the Chatuchak Park offices, near the north end of the market's sois 1, 2 and 3. Plan to spend a full day, as there's plenty to see and eat, even live music in the early evening in Thai folk music cafes. And leave time for getting lost!

An unfortunate footnote is that Chatuchak Park remains an important hub of Thailand's illegal exotic wildlife trade – in spite of occasional police raids – as well as a conduit for endangered species from surrounding countries. Some species are sold for their exotic food value, eg barking deer, wild boar, crocodiles and pangolins, while some are sold for their supposed medicinal value, eg rare leaf-monkeys. Thai laws protect most of these species, but Thais are notorious scofflaws. Not all wildlife trade here is illicit though; many of the birds sold, including the hill mynah and zebra dove, have been legally raised for sale as pets.

The main part of the Weekend Market is open on Saturday and Sunday from around 8 am to 8 pm. There are a few vendors out on weekday mornings and a daily vegetables/plants/flowers market opposite the market's

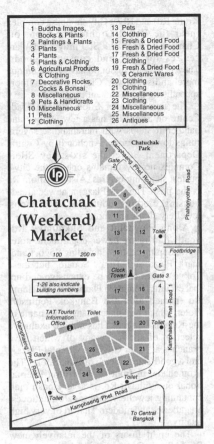

| 1 | Buddha Images, Books & Plants | 13 | Pets |
|---|---|---|---|
| 2 | Paintings & Plants | 14 | Clothing |
| 3 | Plants | 15 | Fresh & Dried Food |
| 4 | Plants | 16 | Fresh & Dried Food |
| 5 | Plants & Clothing | 17 | Fresh & Dried Food |
| 6 | Agricultural Products & Clothing | 18 | Clothing |
| 7 | Decorative Rocks, Cocks & Bonsai | 19 | Fresh & Dried Food & Ceramic Wares |
| 8 | Miscellaneous | 20 | Clothing |
| 9 | Pets & Handicrafts | 21 | Clothing |
| 10 | Miscellaneous | 22 | Miscellaneous |
| 11 | Pets | 23 | Clothing |
| 12 | Clothing | 24 | Miscellaneous |
| | | 25 | Miscellaneous |
| | | 26 | Antiques |

**Chatuchak (Weekend) Market**

*1-26 also indicate building numbers*

Chatuchak Market directors may construct a huge three-storey building with parking lots and modern vendor stalls on the existing 70 *rai* plot of land (one rai equals 1600 sq m), which is leased from the Railway Authority of Thailand. Opponents of the plan point out that around 75% of Chatuchak market-goers currently arrive by public transport, hence the construction of a huge parking facility will worsen traffic and change the character of the market by catering to the more affluent.

**Flower Markets & Nurseries** A good selection of tropical flowers and plants is available at the Thewet Market near the Tha Thewet pier on Krung Kasem Rd to the north-west of Banglamphu. The city's largest wholesale flower source is Pak Khlong Market on the right bank of the Chao Phraya River at the mouth of Khlong Lawt, between Atsadang Rd and Phra Phut Yot Fa (Memorial) Bridge. Pak Khlong is also a big market for vegetables. The newest and largest plant market is opposite the south side of Chatuchak (Weekend) Market, near the Northern Bus Terminal off Phahonyothin Rd; unlike Chatuchak it's open all week. It's sometimes called Talaat Phahonyothin (Phahonyothin Market).

The best area for nursery plants, including Thailand's world-famous orchid varieties, is Thonburi's Phasi Charoen district, which is accessible via the Phetkasem Highway north of Khlong Phasi Charoen itself. The latter is linked to the Chao Phraya River via Khlong Bangkok Yai. Two places with good selections are Eima Orchid Co (☎ 454-0366; fax 454-1156) at 999/9 Mu 2, Bang Khae, Phasi Charoen, and Botanical Gardens Bangkok (☎ 467-4955) at 6871 Kuhasawan, Phasi Charoen. Ordinary bus Nos 7 and 80, plus air-con bus No 9, stop in the Phasi Charoen district.

**Other Markets** Under the expressway at the intersection of Rama IV and Narong Rds in the Khlong Toey district is the Khlong Toey Market, possibly the cheapest all-purpose market in Bangkok (best on Wednesday).

south side. One section of the latter, known as the Aw Taw Kaw Market, sells organically grown (no chemical sprays or fertilisers) fruits and vegetables.

The Weekend Market lies at the southern end of Chatuchak Park, off Phahonyothin Rd and across from the Northern Bus Terminal. Air-con bus Nos 2, 3, 9, 10 and 13, and a dozen other ordinary city buses (including No 3 from Phra Athit Rd in Banglamphu), all pass the market – just get off before the Northern Bus Terminal. The air-con bus No 12 and ordinary bus No 77 conveniently terminate right next to the market.

South of the Khlong Toey Market, closer to the port, is the similar Penang Market, so called because a lot of the goods 'drop off' cargo boats from Penang (and Singapore, Hong Kong etc). Both markets are in danger of being demolished under current urban renewal plans.

Pratunam Market, at the intersection of Phetburi and Ratchaprarop Rds, runs every day and is very crowded, but has great deals in new, cheap clothing. You won't see it from the street; you must look for one of the unmarked entrances that lead back behind the main storefronts.

The huge Banglamphu Market spreads several blocks over Chakraphong, Phra Sumen, Tanao and Rambutri Rds, a short walk from the Khao San Rd guesthouse area. The Banglamphu Market area is probably the most comprehensive shopping district in the city as it encompasses everything from street vendors to up-market department stores. Also in this part of Bangkok you'll find the Thewet flower market (see Flower Markets & Nurseries above).

The Pahurat and Chinatown districts have interconnected markets selling tonnes of well priced fabrics, clothes and household wares, as well as a few places selling gems and jewellery. The Wong Wian Yai Market in Thonburi, next to the large roundabout directly south-west of Phra Phut Yot Fa (Memorial) Bridge, is another all-purpose market – but this one rarely gets tourists.

### Shopping Centres & Department Stores

The growth of large and small shopping centres has accelerated over the last few years into a virtual boom. Central and Robinson department stores, the original stand-bys, have branches in the Sukhumvit and Silom areas with all the usual stuff (designer clothes, western cosmetics etc) plus supermarkets and Thai delis, cassette tapes, fabrics and other local products that might be of interest to some travellers. Typical opening hours are 10 am to 8 pm. The Central branch on Ploenchit Rd suffered a major fire in 1995 and is under reconstruction.

Oriental Plaza (Soi Oriental, Charoen

Krung Rd) and River City shopping complex (near the Royal Orchid Sheraton, off Charoen Krung and Si Phraya Rds) are centres for high-end consumer goods. They're expensive but do have some unique merchandise; River City has two floors specialising in art and antiques.

The much smaller Silom Village Trade Centre on Silom Rd has a few antique and handicraft shops with merchandise several rungs lower in price. Anchored by Central Department Store, the six-storey Silom Complex nearby remains one of the city's busiest shopping centres. Also on Silom Rd is the posh Thaniya Plaza, a newer arcade housing clothing boutiques, bookshops, jewellery shops and more.

Along Ploenchit and Sukhumvit Rds you'll find many newer department stores and shopping centres, including Sogo, Landmark Plaza and Times Square, but these Tokyo clones tend to be expensive and not that exciting. Peninsula Plaza on Ratchadamri Rd (named after the Bangkok Peninsula Hotel, which has since changed its name to the Regent Bangkok) has a more exclusive selection of shops – many of which have branches at River City and Oriental Plaza – and a good-sized branch of Asia Books. The Promenade, in front of the Hilton International on Withayu Rd, is a very posh mall containing jewellery shops, cafes, antiques, art galleries and modern Thai art of very high quality.

The eight floors of the relatively new World Trade Centre near the intersection of Ploenchit and Phayathai Rds seem to go on and on. The main focus is the Zen Department Store, which has clothing shops reminiscent of Hong Kong's high-end boutiques. On the 8th floor is Bangkok's premier antidote to the tropics, the World Ice Skating Center. If you're looking for clothing or toys for kids, ABC Babyland on WTC's 2nd floor has just about everything. Asia Books has a branch in the WTC and more shops are opening as a new wing is being added, including a new Thailand Duty Free Shop on the 7th floor (passport and airline ticket required for purchases).

Siam Square, on Rama I Rd near Phayathai Rd, is a network of some 12 sois lined with shops selling mid-price designer clothes, books, sporting goods and antiques. On the opposite side of Rama I stands Thailand's first shopping centre, the four-storey, 20 year old Siam Center. Before a 1995 fire (four Bangkok department stores in all suffered fires that year), it was big on designer clothing shops – Benetton, Chaps, Esprit, Chanel, Jaspal, Anne Cole, Guy Laroche and Paul Smith to name a few – as well as coffee shops, travel agencies, banks and airline offices. At the time of writing Siam Center was still closed for repairs.

One of the most varied shopping centres to wander around is the Mahboonkrong (MBK) shopping centre near Siam Square. It's all air-con, but there are many small, inexpensive vendors and shops in addition to the flashy Tokyu Department Store. Bargains can be found here if you look. The Travel Mart on MBK's 3rd floor stocks a reasonable supply of travel gear and camping equipment – not the highest quality but useful in a pinch.

North of Siam Square on Phetburi Rd, Phanthip Plaza specialises in shops selling computer equipment and software. Until 1992 or so bootleg software was abundant here; some of the shops still knock off a few pirated programmes under the counter.

Old Siam Plaza, bounded by Charoen Krung, Burapha, Pahurat and Triphet Rds, is the first new development of any significance in the Chinatown-Pahurat area in over a decade. Along with the renovation and reopening of the adjacent Chalermkrung Royal Theatre, this old Bangkok-style shopping centre represents a minor renaissance for an otherwise shabby and congested district. Most of the shops purvey Thai-style goods or services; one whole side is devoted to gun dealers, another to gem and jewellery stores, the rest to Thai handicrafts, furniture, restaurants and coffee shops.

South-East Asia's largest shopping centre/mall is Seacon Square, out on Si Nakharin Rd. It encompasses practically every type of shop mentioned in this section, including huge branches of DK Books and Asia Books, plus a cinema multiplex and a number of cafes.

**Antiques & Decorative Items** Real Thai antiques are rare and costly. Most Bangkok antique shops keep a few antiques around for collectors, along with lots of pseudo-antiques or traditionally crafted items that look like antiques. The majority of shop operators are quite candid about what's really old and what isn't. As Thai design becomes more popular abroad, many shops are now specialising in Thai home decorative items.

Reliable antique shops (using the word 'antique' loosely) include Elephant House (☎ 286-2780) at 67/12 Soi Phra Phinit, Soi Suan Phlu; Peng Seng, on the corner of Rama IV and Surawong Rds; Asian Heritage (☎ 258-4157) at 57 Soi 23, Sukhumvit Rd; Thai House (☎ 258-6287), 720/6 Sukhumvit Rd, near Soi 28; and Artisan's in the Silom Village Trade Centre, Silom Rd. The River City and Oriental Plaza shopping complexes also have several good, if pricey, antique shops.

**Gems & Jewellery** Recommending specific shops is tricky, since to the average eye one coloured stone looks as good as another, so the risk of a rip-off is much greater than for most other popular shopping items. One shop that's been a longtime favourite with Bangkok expats for service and value in set jewellery is Johnny's Gems (☎ 222-1756) at 199 Fuang Nakhon Rd (off Charoen Krung Rd). Another reputable jewellery place is Merlin et Delauney (☎ 234-3884), with a large showroom and lapidary at 1 Soi Pradit, Surawong Rd and a smaller shop at the Novotel Bangkok, Soi 6, Siam Square. Both have unset stones as well as jewellery. Three other dependable places that specialise in unset stones are Lambert International (☎ 236-4343) at 807 Silom Rd, Gemexpert (☎ 236-2638) at 50/29 Pan Rd and Thai Lapidary (☎ 214-2641) at 277/122 Rama I Rd.

**Bronzeware** Thailand has the oldest bronze-working tradition in the world and there are several factories in Bangkok producing bronze sculpture and cutlery. Two factories that sell direct to the public (and where you may also be able to observe the bronze-working process) are Siam Bronze Factory (☎ 234-9436), at 1250 Charoen Krung Rd, and SN Thai Bronze Factory (☎ 215-7743), at 157-33 Phetburi Rd. Make sure any items you buy are silicon-coated, otherwise they'll tarnish. To see the casting process for Buddha images, go to the Buddha Casting Foundry next to Wat Wiset Khan on Phrannok Rd, Thonburi (take a river ferry from Tha Phra Chan or Tha Maharat on the Bangkok side to reach the foot of Phrannok Rd).

Many vendors at Wat Mahathat's Sunday market sell old and new bronzeware – haggling is imperative.

**Handicrafts** Bangkok has excellent buys in Thai handicrafts, though for Northern hill-tribe materials you might be able to do better in Chiang Mai. Narayana Phand (☎ 252-4670) on Ratchadamri Rd is a bit on the touristy side but has a large selection and good marked prices – no haggling is necessary. Central Department Store on Ploenchit Rd has a Thai handicrafts section with marked prices.

International School Bangkok (ISB) (☎ 583-5401/28) puts on a large charity sale of Thai handicrafts every sixth Saturday or so (except during ISB's summer holiday, June to August). Sometimes you can find pieces at the ISB craft sales that are practically unavailable elsewhere. At other times it's not very interesting; it all depends on what the sale managers are able to collect during the year. Call for the latest sale schedule. ISB is north of the city proper, towards the airport, off Route 304 (Chaeng Wattana Rd) on the way to Pak Kret, inside the Nichada Thani condo/townhouse complex; the address is 39/7 Soi Nichadathani Samakhi.

Perhaps the most interesting places to shop for handicrafts are the smaller, independent handicraft shops, each of which has its own style and character. Quality is high at Rasi Sayam (☎ 258-4195), 32 Soi 23, Sukhumvit Rd; many of the items they carry,

including wall-hangings and pottery, are made specifically for this shop. Another good one for pottery as well as lacquerware and fabrics (especially the latter) is Vilai's (☎ 391-6106) at 731/1 Soi 55 (Thong Lor), Sukhumvit Rd.

Nandakwang (☎ 258-1962), 108/3 Soi 23 (Soi Prasanmit) Sukhumvit Rd, is a branch of a factory shop of the same name in Pasang, Northern Thailand; high-quality woven cotton clothing and household wares (table-cloths, napkins etc) are their speciality. Prayer Textile Gallery (☎ 251-7549), a small shop on the edge of Siam Square facing Phayathai Rd, stocks a nice selection of new and antique textiles, in both ready-to-wear original fashions or in traditional rectangular lengths, from Thailand, Laos and Cambodia.

Lao Song Handicrafts (☎ 261-6627), at 2/56 Soi 41, Sukhumvit Rd, is a nonprofit place that sells village handicrafts to promote village cottage industries.

Khŏn masks of intricately formed wire and papier mâché can be purchased at Padung Chiip (no English sign) on Chakraphong Rd just south of the Khao San Rd intersection.

For quality Thai celadon, check Thai Celadon (☎ 229-4383) at 8/6-8 New Ratchadaphisek Rd. Inexpensive places to pick up new Thai pottery of all shapes and sizes at wholesale prices include two places on Soi On Nut, off Soi 77, Sukhumvit Rd: United Siam Overseas (☎ 721-6320) and Siamese Merchandise (☎ 333-0680). Overseas shipping can be arranged.

**Tailor Shops** Bangkok abounds in places where you can have shirts, trousers, suits and just about any other article of clothing designed, cut and sewn by hand. Workmanship ranges from shoddy to excellent, so it pays to ask around before committing yourself. Shirts and trousers can be turned around in 48 hours or less with only one fitting. But no matter what a tailor may tell you, it takes more than one or two fittings to create a good suit, and most reputable tailors will ask for three to five sittings. A custom-made suit, no matter what the material is, should cost less than US$200. An all-cashmere suit can be had for as little as US$160 to US$180 with a little bargaining; bring your own fabric and it will cost even less.

Bangkok tailors can be particularly good at copying your favourite piece of clothing. Designer-made shirts costing upward of US$100 at home can be knocked off for not much more than a tenth of the designer price. The one area where you need to be most careful is in fabric selection. If possible, bring your own personally selected fabric from home or abroad, especially if it's 100% cotton you want. Most of the so-called 'cotton' offered by Bangkok tailors is actually a blend of cotton and a synthetic; more than a few tailors will actually try to pass off full polyester or dacron as cotton. Good quality silk, on the other hand, is plentiful. Tailor-made silk shirts should cost no more than US$12 to US$20, depending on the type of silk (Chinese silk is cheaper than Thai).

Virtually every tailor working in Bangkok is of Indian or Chinese descent. Generally speaking the best shops are those found along the outer reaches of Sukhumvit Rd (out beyond Soi 20 or so) and on or off Charoen Krung Rd. Silom Rd also has some good tailors. The worst tailor shops tend to be those in tourist-oriented shopping areas in inner Sukhumvit Rd, Khao San Rd, the River City Shopping Complex and other shopping malls. 'Great deals' like four shirts, two suits, a kimono and a safari suit all in one package almost always turn out to be of inferior materials and workmanship.

Recommended tailor shops include: Marzotto at 3 Soi Wat Suan Phlu, off Charoen Krung Rd; Julie at 1279 Charoen Rd, near Silom Centre; Marco Tailor at three locations at Amarin Plaza, Silom Complex and Siam Square; and Macway's Exporters at 248/3-4 Silom Rd, near the Narai Hotel. If Siam Center ever re-opens, Siam Emporium (3rd floor) can also be recommended.

**Camera Supplies, Film & Processing** For a selection of camera supplies across a wide range of models and brand names, two of the best shops are Sunny Camera at 1267/1 Charoen Krung Rd (☎ 233-8378), at 134/5-6 Soi 8 Silom Rd (☎ 237-2054) and on the 3rd floor of the Mahboonkrong shopping centre (☎ 217-9293), and Niks (☎ 235-2929) at 166 Silom Rd.

Film prices in Bangkok are generally lower than anywhere else in Asia, including Hong Kong. Both slide and print films are widely available, although the highest concentration of photo shops can be found along Silom and Surawong Rds. In Mahboonkrong shopping centre, FotoFile on the ground floor has the best selection of slide films, including refrigerated pro films.

Quick, professional quality processing of most film types is available at: E6 Processing Centre (☎ 259-9573), 59/10 Soi 31, Sukhumvit Rd; IQ Lab at 60 Silom Rd (☎ 238-4001) or at 9/34 Thana Arcade, Soi 63, Sukhumvit Rd (☎ 391-4163); Eastbourne Professional Color Laboratories (☎ 236-1156), 173/4-5 Surawong Rd; and Supertouch (☎ 235-4711/6415), 35/12 Soi Yommarat, Sala Daeng Rd.

## Getting There & Away

**Air** Bangkok is a major centre for international flights throughout Asia, and Bangkok's international airport is a busy one. Bangkok is also a major centre for buying discounted airline tickets (see the Getting There & Away chapter for details), but be warned that the Bangkok travel agency business has more than a few crooked operators. Domestic flights operated by THAI and Bangkok Airways also fan out from Bangkok all over the country (see the Getting Around chapter). Addresses of airline offices in Bangkok are:

Aeroflot – 7 Silom Rd (☎ 233-6965)
Air France – Ground floor, Chan Issara Tower, 942/51 Rama IV Rd (☎ 234-1330/9; reservations ☎ 233-9477)
Air India – 16th floor, Amarin Tower, Ploenchit Rd (☎ 256-9620; reservations ☎ 256-9614/8)
Air Lanka – Chan Issara Tower 942/34-5 Rama IV Rd (☎ 236-4981, 235-4982)
Air New Zealand – 1053 Charoen Krung Rd (☎ 233-5900/9, 237-1560/2)
Alitalia – 8th floor, Boonmitr Bldg, 138 Silom Rd (☎ 233-4000/4)

All Nippon Airways (ANA) – 2nd floor, CP Tower, 313 Silom Rd (☎ 238-5121)

American Airlines – 518/5 Ploenchit Rd (☎ 254-1270)

Asiana Airlines – 14th floor, BB Bldg, 54 Soi Asoke (☎ 260-7700/4)

Bangkok Airways – Queen Sirikit National Convention Centre, New Ratchadaphisek Rd, Khlong Toey (☎ 229-3434/56, 253-4014)
1111 Ploenchit Rd (☎ 254-2903)

Bangladesh Biman – Chongkolnee Building, 56 Surawong Rd (☎ 235-7643/4, 234-0300/9)

British Airways – Chan Issara Tower, Rama IV Rd (☎ 236-0038)

Canadian Airlines International – Maneeya Bldg, 518/5 Ploenchit Rd (☎ 251-4521, 254-8376)

Cathay Pacific Airways – 11th floor, Ploenchit Tower, Ploenchit Rd (☎ 263-0606)

China Airlines – Peninsula Plaza, 153 Ratchadamri Rd (☎ 253-5733; reservations ☎ 253-4242)

China Southern Airlines – 1st floor, Silom Plaza Bldg, Silom Rd (☎ 266-5688)

Delta Air Lines – 7th floor, Patpong Bldg, 1 Surawong Rd (☎ 237-6855; reservations ☎ 237-6838)

Druk Air – see Thai Airways International

Egypt Air – 3rd floor, CP Tower, 313 Silom Rd (☎ 231-0504/8)

Eva Air – 3656/4-5 2nd floor, Green Tower, Rama IV Rd (☎ 367-3388; reservations ☎ 240-0890)

El Al Israel Airlines – 14th floor, Manorom Bldg, Rama IV Rd (☎ 671-6145, 249-8818)

Finnair – 175 Sathorn City Tower, Sathon Rd (☎ 679-6671; reservations ☎ 251-5075)

Garuda Indonesia – 27th floor, Lumphini Tower, 1168 Rama IV Rd (☎ 285-6470/3)

Gulf Air – Maneeya Bldg, 518/5 Ploenchit Rd (☎ 254-7931/40)

Japan Airlines – 254/1 Ratchadaphisek (☎ 274-1400, 274-1435)

KLM Royal Dutch Airlines – Maneeya Bldg, 518/5 Ploenchit Rd (☎ 254-8834; reservations 254-8325)

Korean Air – Kongboonma Bldg, 699 Silom Rd (☎ 235-9221)

Kuwait Airways – Bangkok international airport (☎ 523-6993)

Lao Aviation – Silom Plaza, 491/17 Silom Rd (☎ 236-9821/3)

Lauda Air – 33/33-4 Wall Street Tower, Surawong Rd (☎ 233-2565)

LOT Polish Airlines – 485/11-12 Silom Rd (☎ 235-2223/7092)

Lufthansa – Bank of America Bldg, 2/2 Withayu Rd (☎ 255-0385)
Asoke Bldg, Soi 21, Sukhumvit Rd (☎ 264-2400)

LTU International Airlines – Rama Gardens, Vibhavadi Rangsit Rd (☎ 561-3784)

Malaysia Airlines – 98-102 Surawong Rd (☎ 236-5871; reservations ☎ 236-4705/9)
20th floor, Ploenchit Tower, Ploenchit Rd (☎ 263-0565)

Myanmar Airways International – Chan Issara Tower, Rama IV Rd (☎ 267-5078)

Northwest Airlines – Peninsula Plaza, 153 Ratchadamri Rd (☎ 254-0789)

Pakistan International Airlines – 52 Surawong Rd (☎ 234-2961, 266-4548)

Philippine Airlines – Chongkolnee Bldg, 56 Surawong Rd (☎ 234-2483, 233-2350/2)

Qantas – Chan Issara Tower, 942/51 Rama IV Rd (☎ 267-5188, 236-0307)

Royal Air Cambodge – see Malaysia Airlines

Royal Brunei Airlines – 2nd floor, Chan Issara Tower, 942/52 Rama IV Rd (☎ 233-0506, 235-4764)

Royal Jordanian Airlines – Yada Bldg, 56 Silom Rd (☎ 236-0030)

Royal Nepal Airlines – Sivadon Bldg, 1/4 Convent Rd (☎ 233-3921/4)

Sabena Airlines – 3rd floor, CP Tower, 313 Silom Rd (☎ 238-2201/4/5)

Saudi Arabian Airlines – ground floor, CCT Bldg, 109 Surawong Rd (☎ 236-9400/3)

Scandinavian Airlines – Soi 25, Sukhumvit Rd (☎ 260-0444)

Silk Air – 12th floor, Silom Centre Bldg, Silom Rd (☎ 236-0303; reservations ☎ 236-0440)

Singapore Airlines – 12th floor, Silom Centre Bldg, 2 Silom Rd (☎ 236-0303; reservations ☎ 236-0440)

South African Airways – Maneeya Bldg, 518/5 Ploenchit Rd (☎ 254-8206)

Swissair – 1 Silom Rd (☎ 233-2930/4; reservations ☎ 233-2935/8)

TAROM – 89/12 Bangkok Bazaar, Ratchadamri Rd (☎ 253-1681)

Thai Airways International (THAI) – (head office) 89 Vibhavadi Rangsit Rd (☎ 513-0121)
485 Silom Rd (☎ 234-3100/19)
6 Lan Luang Rd (☎ 288-0060, 628-2000)
Asia Hotel, 296 Phayathai Rd (☎ 215-2020/1)
Bangkok international airport, Don Muang (☎ 535-2081/2, 523-6121)

United Airlines – 9th floor, Regent House, 183 Ratchadamri Rd (☎ 253-0558)

Vietnam Airlines (Hang Khong Vietnam) – 3rd floor, 572 Ploenchit Rd (☎ 251-4242)

**Bus** Bangkok is the centre for bus services that fan out all over the kingdom. There are basically three types of long-distance bus. First there is the ordinary public bus, then the air-con public bus. The third choice is the many private air-con services which leave from various offices and hotels all over the city and provide a deluxe service for those people for whom simple air-con isn't enough!

**Public Bus** There are three main public bus (Baw Khaw Saw) terminals. The Northern Bus Terminal (☎ 279-4484/7. 271-2961) is on Phahonyothin Rd on the way out to the airport. It's also commonly called the Moh Chit station *(sathăanii măw chít)*. Buses depart here for North and North-Eastern destinations like Chiang Mai and Nakhon Ratchasima (Khorat), as well as places closer to Bangkok such as Ayuthaya and Lopburi. Buses to Aranya Prathet also go from here, not from the Eastern Bus Terminal as you might expect. Air-con city buses Nos 2, 3, 9, 10, 12, 29 and 39, along with a dozen or more ordinary city buses and red microbus Nos 2 and 8, all pass the terminal.

The Eastern Bus Terminal (☎ 391-2504 ordinary; ☎ 391-9829 air-con), the departure point for buses to Pattaya, Rayong, Chanthaburi and other points east, is a long way out along Sukhumvit Rd, at Soi 40 (Soi Ekamai) opposite Soi 63. Most folks call it Ekamai station *(sathăanii èk-amai)*. Air-con bus Nos 1, 8, 11 and 13 all pass this station, along with red microbus No 6.

The Southern Bus Terminal (☎ 434-5558 ordinary; ☎ 391-9829 air-con) for buses south to Phuket, Surat Thani and closer centres to the west like Nakhon Pathom and Kanchanaburi, has one Thonburi location for both ordinary and air-con buses at the intersection of Highway 338 (Nakhon Chaisi Rd) and Phra Pinklao Rd. A convenient way to reach the station is by air-con city bus No 7, which terminates here; red microbus Nos 4 and 8 also pass the terminal.

When travelling on night buses take care of your belongings. Some of the long-distance buses leaving from Bangkok now issue claim checks for luggage stored under the bus, but valuables are still best kept on your person or within reach.

Allow an hour to reach the Northern Bus Terminal from Banglamphu or anywhere along the river, over an hour to reach the Southern Bus Terminal. The Eastern Bus Terminal takes 30 to 45 minutes under most traffic conditions. During occasional gridlock, eg Friday afternoons before a holiday, it can take up to three hours to get across town to the terminals by public transport.

**Private Bus** The more reputable and licensed private tour buses leave from the public terminals listed above. Some private bus companies arrange pick-ups at Khao San Rd and other guesthouse areas – these pickups are illegal since it's against municipal law to carry passengers within the city limits except en route to or from an official terminal. This is why the curtains on these buses are sometimes closed when picking up passengers.

Although fares tend to be lower on private buses, the incidence of reported theft is far greater than on the Baw Khaw Saw buses. They are also generally – but not always – less reliable, promising services (such as air-con or VIP seats) that they don't deliver. For safer, more reliable, and more punctual service, stick to buses which leave from the official Baw Khaw Saw terminals.

See the Getting Around chapter for more information about bus travel in Thailand. Also, for details on bus fares to/from other towns and cities in Thailand, see the Getting There & Away sections under each place.

**Train** Bangkok is the terminus for rail services to the South, North, North-East and East. There are two main train stations. The big Hualamphong station on Rama IV Rd handles services to the North, North-East and some of the Southern services. The Thonburi (Bangkok Noi) station handles a few services to the South. If you're heading down to Southern Thailand, make sure you know which station your train departs from. See the Train section in the Getting Around chapter for further details.

### Getting Around
Getting around in Bangkok may be difficult at first for the uninitiated but once you're familiar with the bus system the whole city is accessible. The main obstacle is traffic, which moves at a snail's pace during much

## Future Traffic Alternatives

At times, Bangkok's traffic situation seems quite hopeless. An estimated three million vehicles (a figure rising by 1000 per day) crawl through the streets at an average of 13 km/h during commuter hours, and nearly half the municipal traffic police are undergoing treatment for respiratory ailments! It's estimated that the typical Bangkok motorist spends a cumulative 44 days per year in traffic; petrol stations throughout the capital sell the Comfort 100, a portable potty that allows motorists to relieve themselves in their own vehicles during traffic jams. Cellular phones, TVs and food warmers are other commonplace auto accessories among wealthier drivers.

The main culprit, in addition to the influx of motor vehicles, is the lack of road surface, which represents only 8.5% of Bangkok's mass; to reach international standards the road surface needs to be increased to at least 20%. Privately owned automobiles aren't the gridlock's mainstay; only 25% of the city's population use personal cars. Motorcycles, buses, trucks and taxis make up the bulk of Bangkok traffic. In 1996 the government established an excise tax on products and services that harm the environment, beginning with two-stroke motorcycles, a major polluter. Buses are in dire need of attention, as they make up less than 1% of the vehicles on city roads but account for as much as half the pollutants found in the air.

Several mass transit systems (which are either in the planning or very early construction phases) promise much needed 'decongestion'. The one most likely to be completed first is the Bangkok Metropolitan Authority's (BMA) light rail system, about two-thirds of which will be elevated (Khlong Toey to Lat Phrao via Ratchadaphisek) and a third underground (Hualamphong to Khlong Toey). This project has undergone so many reroutings (initially the north-south leg was to run parallel to Ratchaprarop, Ratchadamri and Sathon Tai Rds) that it's difficult to say with any certainty whether it will ever actually get off the ground. The BMA also plans to add several more elevated expressways; sceptics say building more roadways will simply encourage Bangkokians to buy more cars.

The much ballyhooed Skytrain network, a more extensive elevated rail project that was proposed in 1986, has gone from contractor to contractor and finally began construction in 1994. The US$1.3 billion project will initially consist of two lines, the Phrakhanong-Bang Seu (23 km) and Sathon-Lat Phrao (11 km) routes, plus two more lines in each direction to follow later. If all goes as planned, this one should be operating by 1999. A second project, the US$3.2 billion Hopewell Bangkok Elevated Road and Train System (BERTS), is supposed to offer 60 km of light rail and 48 km of expressways; the project is designed so that the railways will be stacked on top of the expressways, both of which are in turn stacked atop existing roadways. Five thousand piles for BERTS have already been driven throughout Bangkok, but this plan, too, has fallen victim to interdepartmental squabbles and problems with the Hong Kong contractor. BERTS may be taken over by the optimistically named Metropolitan Rapid Transit Authority (MRTA). Finally there's the MRTA's own US$3.2 billion underground rail, to consist of one 42 km north-east to south-west main line, with a separate loop around central Bangkok. This one hasn't begun construction yet, though a 2003 completion is projected. As if all these plans weren't enough, there has also been serious talk of a monorail loop around outer Bangkok, with a feeder line for the Skytrain.

The problem with every one of these projects is the lack of coherent coordination. With separate contracts and separate supervision, it's doubtful any can remain on schedule. The main villains in all this appear to be BMA principals, who want inflexible control over every project brought to the table even where there are clear conflicts of interest. In 1993 the BMA shot down a reasonable proposal put before the Interior Ministry to split the 560 sq km city into five to eight separate townships for ease of traffic administration.

The investments involved in these rail and road projects are enormous, but as current traffic congestion costs the nation over 14 billion baht per year in fuel bills, the potential savings far exceed the outlay. Bangkok lost out to Singapore in a recent bid to be named the site of the new Asia-Pacific Economic Cooperation (APEC) secretariat largely because of the city's appalling traffic congestion.

One cheaper alternative which the government is seriously considering is a toll zone or traffic control zone within the central business district. City planners from the Massachusetts Institute of Technology, hired as consultants by BMA, concur that this would be the best approach for quick and lasting traffic congestion relief. This sort of plan has worked very well in nearby Singapore but it remains to be seen whether such a system would work in Bangkok, where even enforcement of traffic lights, parking and one way streets is shaky.

While you're stuck in a Bangkok traffic jam you can take comfort in knowing that average rush-hour traffic flows are worse in Hong Kong (12.2 km/h), Taipei (11.5 km/h), Bombay (10.4 km/h) and Manila (7.2 km/h). Dirty air? Bangkok didn't even make UNEP/WHO's list of Asia's five worst cities for air pollution – the honours were captured by Delhi, Xian, Beijing, Calcutta and Shenyang. Ambient noise ratios are equal to those measured in Seoul, Chongqing and Saigon. ∎

of the day. This means advance planning is a must when you are attending scheduled events or arranging appointments.

If you can travel by river or canal from one point to another, it's always the best choice. Bangkok was once called the 'Venice of the East', but much of the original canal system has been filled in for road construction. Larger canals, especially on the Thonburi side, remain important commercial arteries but many of the smaller canals are hopelessly polluted and would probably have been filled in by now if it weren't for their important drainage function.

**Bus**  You can save a lot of money in Bangkok by sticking to the public buses, which are 2.50B for any journey under 10 km on the ordinary blue or smaller green buses, 3.50B on the red buses or 6B for the first eight km on the air-con lines. The fare on ordinary buses is 4B for longer trips (eg from Chulalongkorn University to King Mongkut's Institute of Technology in Thonburi on bus No 21) and as high as 16B for air-con buses (eg from Silom Rd to Bangkok's airports on air-con bus No 4). The air-con buses are not only cooler, but are usually less crowded (all bets are off during rush hours).

One air-con bus service that's never overcrowded is the new red Microbus, which stops taking passengers once every seat is filled. They collect a 30B flat fare – you deposit the money in a box at the front of the bus rather than wait for an attendant to come around and collect it. Newspapers (usually Thai papers only, occasionally a *Thailand Times*) are available on the Microbus. A couple of useful Microbus lines include: the No 6, which starts on Si Phraya Rd (near the River City complex) and proceeds to the Mahboonkrong-Siam Square area, then out to Sukhumvit Rd (and vice versa); and the No 1, which runs between the Victory Monument area and Banglamphu district.

**Bus Maps**  To do any serious bus riding you'll need a Bangkok bus map – the easiest to read is the *Bangkok Bus Map (Walking Tours)* published by Bangkok Guide Co, or

Thaveepholcharoen's *Bangkok Thailand Tour'n Guide Map*. If you plan to do a lot of bus riding, the Bangkok Bus Map is the more accurate, but the Tour'n Guide Map also has a decent map of the whole country on the flip side. The bus numbers are clearly marked in red, with air-con buses in larger type. Don't expect the routes to be 100% correct, a few will have changed since the maps last came out, but they'll get you where you're going most of the time. These maps usually retail for around 35B. A more complete 113-page *Bus Guide* is available in some bookshops and newsstands for 35B, but it's not as easy to use as the bus maps.

**Bus Safety**  Be careful with your belongings while riding Bangkok buses. The place you are most likely to be 'touched' is on the crowded ordinary buses. Razor artists abound, particularly on buses in the Hualamphong station area. These dexterous thieves specialise in slashing your backpack, shoulder bag or even your trouser pockets with a sharp razor and slipping your valuables out unnoticed. Hold your bag in front of you, under your attention, and carry money in a front shirt pocket, preferably (as the Thais do) maintaining a tactile and visual sensitivity to these areas if the bus is packed shoulder to shoulder. Seasoned travellers don't need this advice, as the same precautions are useful all over the world – the trick is to be relaxed but aware.

**Taxi**  Metered taxis (called *tháeksii miitôe* in Thai) were finally introduced in Bangkok in 1993, and they now outnumber the old no-meter taxis. The ones with meters have signs on top reading 'Taxi Meter', the others 'Taxi Thai' or just 'Taxi'. Fares for metered taxis are always lower than for nonmetered, the only problem being that they can be a little harder to flag down during peak commuter hours. Demand often outstrips supply from 8 to 9 am and 6 to 7 pm, also late at night when the bars are closing (1 to 2 am). Because metered-taxi drivers use rented vehicles and must return them at the end of their shifts, they sometimes won't take longer fares as quitting time nears.

Metered taxis charge 35B at flagfall for the first two km, then 2B for each half km increment thereafter when the cab travels at six km/h or more; at speeds under five km/h, a surcharge of 1B per minute kicks in. Freeway tolls – 10 to 20B depending where you start – must be paid by the passenger. Since the introduction of metered cabs, the average passenger fare has dropped considerably. An airport trip from Siam Square, for example, previously cost 150 to 250B (depending on your negotiation skills) in a nonmetered cab; the typical meter fare for the same trip is now around 115 to 120B. A jaunt to Silom Rd from the same area that previously cost 50 or 60B is now in the neighbourhood of 40B.

A 24 hour 'phone-a-cab' service (☎ 319-9911) is available for an extra 20B over the regular metered fare. This is only really necessary if you're in an area where there aren't a lot of cabs; residents who live down long sois are the main clientele. Previously such residents had to catch a motorcycle taxi or 'baht bus' to the *pàak soi* ('soi mouth', where a soi meets a larger street).

For certain routes it can be very difficult to find a taxi driver who's willing to use the meter. One such instance is going from the Southern Bus Terminal across the river to Bangkok proper – most drivers will ask for a flat 300B but settle for 200B. In the reverse direction you can usually get them to use the meter. Another route is from Bangkok's airports into town; in this case drivers want a flat 200 or 250B, even if you hired them through the airport taxi desk. Of course in either case it's illegal, but it can be very difficult to persuade them to take you otherwise.

For those times when you're forced to use a nonmetered cab, you'll have to negotiate the fare. It's no use telling nonmetered cab drivers what a comparable metered trip would cost – they know you wouldn't be wasting your time with them if a metered cab were available. Fares to most places within central Bangkok are 60 to 80B and you should add 10B or so if you're using it during rush hour or after midnight. For airport trips

the nonmeter guys still want 150 to 200B. Perhaps sometime in the future there won't be any nonmetered cabs left on the street – until that time you'll probably be forced to use them occasionally.

You can hire a taxi all day for 1000 to 1500B depending on how much driving is involved. A better option – in terms of the quality of both car and driver – would be to hire through J&J Car Rent (☎ 531-2262), an agency that specialises in car/driver combos at competitive rates.

A useful *Taxi Guide* brochure distributed by TAT to both tourists and taxi drivers lists Thai and English addresses of hotels, guesthouses, embassies, airlines, shopping centres, temples and various tourist attractions. The guide can be of considerable help in communication between non-English-speaking drivers and non-Thai-speaking passengers.

**Tuk-Tuk** In heavy traffic, tuk-tuks are usually faster than taxis since they're able to weave in and out between cars and trucks. This is the main advantage to taking a tuk-tuk for short hops. On the down side, tuk-tuks are not air-conditioned, so you have to breathe all that lead-soaked air (at its thickest in the middle of Bangkok's wide avenues), and they're also more dangerous since they easily flip when braking into a fast curve. The typical tuk-tuk fare nowadays offers no savings over a metered cab – around 40B for a short hop (eg Siam Square to Soi 2 Sukhumvit).

Tuk-tuk drivers tend to speak less English than taxi drivers, so many new arrivals have a hard time communicating their destinations. Although some travellers have complained about tuk-tuk drivers deliberately taking them to the wrong destination (to collect commissions from certain restaurants, gem shops or silk shops), others never seem to have a problem with tuk-tuks, and swear by them. Beware of tuk-tuk drivers who offer to take you on a sightseeing tour for 10 or 20B – it's a touting scheme designed to pressure you into purchasing overpriced goods.

## Tuk-Tuk Wars

In 18th century Bangkok, residents got around on foot, by canal or in human-drawn rickshaws, called *rót chék* or 'Chinese vehicles' by the Thais. During the early 20th century the rickshaw gave way to the three-wheeled pedicab or *samlor*, which then added inexpensive Japanese two-stroke engines after WWII to become the onomatopoeic *túk-túk*.

These small three-wheeled taxicabs sound like power saws gone berserk and commonly leave trails of blue smoke whenever they rev up. Objecting Bangkokians have been trying for years to enact a ban on tuk-tuks. Several years ago the city supposedly forbade the further production of any new three-wheeled taxis, but every time I go to Bangkok I see hordes of brand new ones. It's a bit of a moral dilemma actually, since the tuk-tuk drivers are usually poor North-Easterners who can't afford to rent the quieter, less polluting Japanese autotaxis. You can buy one for around US$1200 from Tuk-Tuk Industry Thailand (☎ 437-6983), 463-465 Prachathipok Rd, Bangkok. ■

**Motorcycle Taxi** As passengers become more desperate in their attempts to beat rush-hour gridlocks, motorcycle taxis have moved from the sois to the main avenues. Fares for a motorcycle taxi are about the same as tuk-tuks except during heavy traffic, when they may cost a bit more.

Riding on the back of a speeding motorcycle taxi is even more of a kamikaze experience than riding in a tuk-tuk. Keep your legs tucked in – the drivers are used to carrying passengers with shorter legs than those of the average farang and they pass perilously close to other vehicles while weaving in and out of traffic.

**Car & Motorcycle** Cars and motorbikes are easily rented in Bangkok, if you can afford to and have steel nerves. Rates start at around 1200B per day for a small car, much less for a motorcycle, not including insurance. For long-term rentals you can usually arrange a discount of up to 35% off the daily rate. An International Driving Permit and passport are required for all rentals.

For long, cross-country trips, you might consider buying a new or used motorcycle and reselling it when you leave – this can end up being cheaper than renting, especially if you buy a good used bike. See the Getting Around chapter for more details.

Here are the names and addresses of a few car-rental companies:

Avis Rent-a-Car – 2/12 Withayu Rd (☎ 255-5300/4; fax 253-3734); branch offices at the Amari Airport, Dusit Thani and Grand Hyatt Erawan hotels

Central Car Rent – 24 Soi Tonson, Ploenchit Rd (☎ 251-2778)

Grand Car Rent – 233-5 Asoke-Din Daeng Rd (☎ 248-2991)

Hertz – Don Muang airport (☎ 535-3004) 1620 New Phetburi Rd (☎ 251-7575)

Highway Car Rent – 1018/5 Rama IV Rd (☎ 266-9393)

Inter Car Rent – 45 Sukhumvit Rd, near Soi 3 (☎ 252-9223)

Krung Thai Car Rent – 233-5 Asoke-Din Daeng Rd (☎ 246-0089/1525)

Lumpinee Car Rent – 167/4 Withayu Rd (☎ 255-1966/3482)

Petchburee Car Rent – 23171 New Phetburi Rd (☎ 319-1393)

SMT Rent-a-Car – 931/11 Rama I Rd (☎ 216-8020)

Toyota Metro Rent-A-Car – 7th floor, Koolhiran Bldg, 1/1 Vibhavadi Rangsit Rd, Chatuchak (☎ 216-2181)

Toyota Rental & Leasing – Vibultnani Bldg, 3199 Rama IV Rd (☎ 637-5050))

Sathorn Car Rent – 6/8-9 Sathon Neua Rd (☎ 633-8888)

Thongchai Car Rent – 58/117 Si Nakharin Rd (☎ 322-3313)

## Know Your Boats

**Chao Phraya River Express** The main boats that you'll want to use are the rapid Chao Phraya River Express boats *(reua dùan)*, a sort of river bus service. These cost 5 to 10B (depending on the distance) and follow a regular route up and down the river; a trip from Banglamphu to the GPO, for example, costs 6B. They may not necessarily stop at each pier if there are no people waiting, or if no-one wants to get off. You buy your tickets on the boat. Chao Phraya River Express boats are big, long boats with numbers on their roofs; the last boat from either end of the route departs at 6 pm.

*Chao Phraya River Express*

This company has a new competitor called Laemthong Express which for the most part serves outlying areas to the north and south of central Bangkok. Hence it stops at some of the same piers but not necessarily at all. It also runs less frequently than Chao Phraya River Express. The latter boats usually feature white bodies with red stripes, while Laemthong have blue or red bodies; if you're heading for one of the Chao Phraya River Express piers listed in this book, be sure not to get on the wrong boat.

**Cross-River Ferry** From the main Chao Phraya stops and also from almost every other jetty, there are slower cross-river ferries *(reua khâam*

*fâak)* which simply shuttle back and forth across the river. The standard fares are 1B and you usually pay this at the entrance to the jetty. Be careful – there will probably be a pay window at the jetty and also a straight-through aisle for people taking other boats.

**Long-Tail Taxi** Finally there are the long-tail boats *(reua hang yao)* which operate a share taxi system off the main river and up the smaller khlongs. Fares usually start from 5B – you've really got to know where you're going on these. There are also river charter taxis where you really do take the whole boat – you'll find them at certain jetties (primarily Tha Chang, Tha Si Phraya), and you can charter them for trips around the river-canal system for a standard 300B per hour.

One of the most useful canal services for most visitors runs along Khlong Saen Saep. This one provides a quicker alternative to road transport between the river and eastern Bangkok (ie outer Sukhumvit and Bang Kapi). The boat from Banglamphu to the Ramkhamhaeng University area, for example, costs 10B and takes only 40 minutes. A bus would take at least an hour under Bangkok's normal traffic conditions. The main detraction of this route is the seriously polluted canal – passengers typically hold newspapers over their clothes and faces to prevent being splashed by the stinking black water. Not the best choice of transport if you're dressed for a formal occasion.

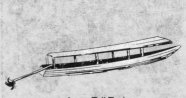

*Long-Tail Taxi*

A handy little run along this route is by long-tail boat (5B) from the Siam Square area (from Tha Ratchathewi by the bridge next to the Asia Hotel) to the Banglamphu pier near Wat Saket and the Democracy Monument. At its western end, this route intersects a north-south boat route along Khlong Banglamphu and Khlong Phadung Krung Kasem. Along this route you can catch a boat from the Khlong Banglamphu pier near the corner of Phra Sumen and Chakraphong Rds (north side of the canal) all the way to Hualamphong station in 15 minutes for 5B. ■

*Cross-River Ferry*

There are more car-rental agencies along Withayu and New Phetburi Rds. Some also rent motorcycles, but you're better off renting or leasing a bike at a place that specialises in motorcycles. Here are three:

Big Bike Rentals – Soi 55, Sukhumvit Rd (☎ 391-5670), hires 250 to 750cc bikes
Chusak Yont Shop – 1400 New Phetburi Rd (☎ 251-9225)
Visit Laochaiwat – 1 Soi Prommit, Suthisan Rd (☎ 278-1348)

**Boat** Although many of Bangkok's canals (khlongs) have been paved over, there is still plenty of transport along and across the Chao Phraya River and up adjoining canals. River transport is one of the nicest ways of getting around Bangkok as well as, quite often, being much faster than any road-based alternatives. For a start you get quite a different view of the city; secondly, it's much less of a hassle than tangling with the polluted, noisy, traffic-crowded streets. Over the last five years the Bangkok Metropolitan Authority has revived four lengthy and very useful canal routes:

Khlong Saen Saep (Banglamphu to Bang Kapi), Khlong Phrakhanong (Sukhumvit to Sinakarin campus), Khlong Bang Luang/Khlong Lat Phrao (New Phetburi Rd to Phahonyothin Bridge) and Khlong Phasi Charoen in Thonburi (Kaset Bang Khae port to Rama I Bridge). Although the canal boats can be crowded, the service is generally much faster than either an auto taxi or bus. (See the Thonburi Canals map in the River & Canal Trips section earlier in this chapter.)

**Walking** At first glance Bangkok doesn't seem like a great town for walking – its main avenues are so choked with traffic that the noise and thick air tend to drive one indoors. However, quiet spots where walks are rewarding do exist, eg Lumphini Park or neighbourhoods off the main streets. And certain places are much more conveniently seen on foot, particularly the older sections of town along the Chao Phraya River where the roads are so narrow and twisting that bus lines don't go there.

# Central Thailand

Twenty-four provinces make up Central Thailand, stretching north to Lopburi, south to Prachuap Khiri Khan, west to Kanchanaburi and east to Trat. The rain-fed network of rivers and canals in the central region makes this the most fertile part of Thailand, supporting vast fields of rice, sugar cane, pineapples and other fruit, and cassava.

Linguistically, the people of Central Thailand share a common dialect which is considered 'standard' Thai simply because Bangkok happens to be in the middle of the region. High concentrations of Chinese are found throughout the central provinces since this is where a large number of Chinese immigrants started out as farmers and merchants. Significant numbers of Mon and Burmese live to the west, and Lao and Khmer to the east due to immigration from bordering lands over hundreds of years.

Many places in Central Thailand can be visited on day trips from Bangkok, but in most cases they make better stepping stones to places farther afield. You can, for example, pause in Ayuthaya on the way north to Chiang Mai, or in Phetburi if you're heading south.

## Ayuthaya Province

### AYUTHAYA
พระนครศรีอยุธยา
• ☎ *(35)* • *pop 60,300*
Approximately 86 km north of Bangkok, Ayuthaya served as the Siamese royal capital from 1350 to 1767 and by all accounts it was a splendid city. Prior to 1350, when the capital moved here from U Thong, it was a Khmer outpost. The city was named after Ayodhya (Sanskrit for 'unassailable' or 'undefeatable'), the home of Rama in the Indian epic *Ramayana*. Its full Thai name is Phra Nakhon Si Ayuthaya (Sacred City of Ayodhya).

Although the Sukhothai period is often

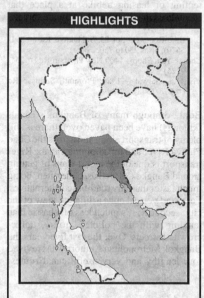

## HIGHLIGHTS

- World Heritage ruins of Ayuthaya, a former royal capital – take a day's trip by boat from Bangkok
- Popular beach resorts of Ko Samet, Pattaya, Cha-am and Hua Hin – easy travelling from Bangkok
- Floating markets and coconut plantations of Damnoen Saduak and Samut Songkhran districts
- WWII monuments of Kanchanaburi – the Death Railway, the River Khwae bridge and Hellfire Pass
- The large and little explored Kaeng Krachan National Park near Myanmar in Phetburi Province
- Remote Ko Chang island group – rainforest tracts, waterfalls, coastal walks, diving and coral reefs
- Frontier outpost town of Three Pagodas Pass
- Busy gem trading towns of Trat and Aranya Prathet along the Cambodian border

referred to as Thailand's 'golden age', in many ways the Ayuthaya era was the kingdom's true historical apex – at least this was so in terms of geographic rule (sovereignty extended well into present-day Laos, Cambodia and Myanmar), dynastic endurance

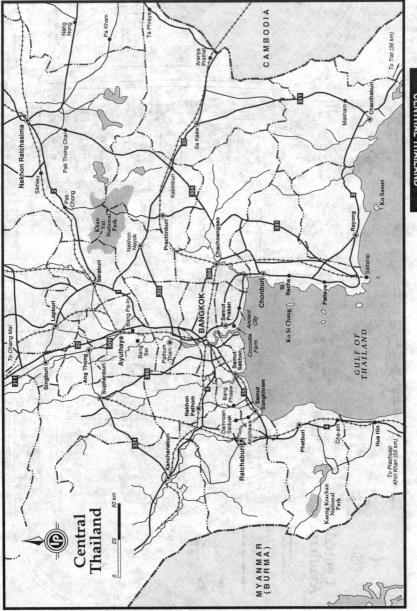

Central Thailand

CENTRAL THAILAND

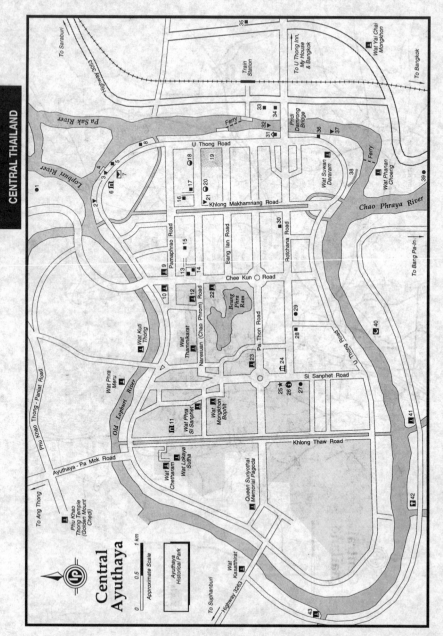

CENTRAL THAILAND

| PLACES TO STAY | | PLACES TO EAT | | 22 | Wat Phra Mahathat |
|---|---|---|---|---|---|
| 5 | U Thong Hotel | 2 | Hua Raw Night Market | 23 | Wat Phra Ram |
| 8 | Cathay Hotel | 3 | Night Market | 24 | Chao Sam Phraya |
| 13 | Thongchai Guest | 21 | Duangporn Restaurant | | National Museum |
| | House | 32 | Floating Restaurants | | & TAT Office |
| 14 | New BJ Guest House | 37 | Phae Krung Kao | 25 | Tourist Police |
| 15 | Thai Thai Bungalow | | | 26 | Future TAT |
| 16 | Ayuthaya & Old BJ | OTHER | | 27 | City Hall |
| | Guest Houses | 1 | Elephant Kraal | 29 | Ayuthaya Historical |
| 17 | Sri Smai (Samai) Hotel | 4 | Pier (Boat Landing) | | Study Centre |
| 28 | Suan Luang (Royal | 6 | Chan Kasem Palace | 38 | Phom Phet Fortress |
| | Garden) Hotel | 7 | GPO | 39 | Ayuthaya Historical |
| 30 | Wieng Fa Hotel | 9 | Chinese Shrine | | Study Centre |
| 31 | Ayuthaya Youth Hostel | 10 | Wat Suwannawat | | (Annex) |
| 33 | Tevaraj Tanrin Hotel | 11 | Royal Palace | 40 | Mosque |
| 34 | Krungsri River Hotel | 12 | Wat Ratburana | 41 | Wat Phutthaisawan |
| 35 | Ayuthaya Grand Hotel | 18 | Air-Con Minivans to | 42 | St Joseph's |
| 36 | Pai Thong Guest | | Bangkok | | Cathedral |
| | House (Under | 19 | Chao Phrom Market | 43 | Wat Chai |
| | Reconstruction) | 20 | Bus Terminal | | Wattanaram |

(over 400 years) and world recognition. Thirty-three kings of various Siamese dynasties reigned in Ayuthaya until it was conquered by the Burmese. During its heyday, Thai culture and international commerce flourished in the kingdom and Ayuthaya was courted by Dutch, Portuguese, French, English, Chinese and Japanese merchants. By the end of the 17th century Ayuthaya's population had reached one million – virtually all foreign visitors claimed it to be the most illustrious city they had ever seen.

### Orientation & Information

The present-day city is located at the confluence of three rivers, the Chao Phraya, the Pa Sak and the smaller Lopburi. A wide canal joins them and makes a complete circle around the town. Long-tail boats can be rented from the boat landing across from Chan Kasem Palace for a tour around the river/canal; several of the old wat ruins (Wat Phanan Choeng, Wat Phutthaisawan, Wat Kasatthirat and Wat Chai Wattanaram) may be glimpsed from the canal, along with picturesque views of river life. Apart from the historic ruins and museums, Ayuthaya is not particularly interesting. It's also one of three cities in Thailand known for 'gangster' activity.

**Tourist Office** TAT (☎ 246076) has a temporary information office (open from 8.30 am to 4.30 pm daily) next to the Chao Sam Phraya National Museum. It plans eventually to open a permanent office across the street next to the tourist police office on Si Sanphet Rd.

### National Museums
พิพิธภัณฑ์แห่งชาติ

There are two museums, the main one being the **Chao Sam Phraya National Museum**, which is near the intersection of Rotchana Rd (the city centre's main street, connecting with the highway to Bangkok) and Si Sanphet Rd, near the centre of town. It features a basic roundup of Thai Buddhist sculpture with an emphasis, naturally, on Ayuthaya pieces. A selection of books on Thai art and archaeology are on sale at the ticket kiosk. The museum is open daily 9 am to 4 pm; entry is 10B.

The second museum building, **Chao Sam Palace** (Phra Ratchawong Chan Kasem), is a museum piece in itself, built by the 17th king of Ayuthaya, Maha Thammarat, for his son Prince Naresuan. Among the exhibits is a collection of gold treasures from Wat Phra Mahathat and Wat Ratburana. Chan Kasem Palace is in the north-east corner of town, near the river. Hours are the same as at Chao Sam Phraya. Entry here is also 10B.

CENTRAL THAILAND

# Ayuthaya Historical Park

อุทยานประวัติศาสตร์พระนครศรีอยุธยา

**R**ecently declared a UNESCO World Heritage Site, Ayuthaya's historic temples are scattered throughout this once magnificient city and along the encircling rivers. Several of the more central ruins – Wat Phra Si Sanphet, Wat Mongkhon Bophit, Wat Phra Meru, Wat Thammikarat, Wat Ratburana and Wat Phra Mahathat – can easily be visited on foot if you avoid the hottest part of the day (11 am to 4 pm). Or you could add more temples and ruins to your itinerary by touring the city on rented bicycle. An ideal transport combination for visitors who want to 'do it all' would be bicycle for the central temples, and chartered long-tail boat for the outlying ruins along the river. See under Getting Around in the Ayuthaya section for details on modes and rates of transport and the preceding Central Ayuthaya map for actual temple locations. At many of the ruins a 10 to 20B admission fee is collected between 8 am to 4.30 pm.

## Wat Phra Si Sanphet

วัดพระศรีสรรเพชญ์

This was the largest temple in Ayuthaya in its time, and it was used as the royal temple/palace for several Ayuthaya kings. Built in the 14th century, the compound once contained a 16m standing Buddha covered with 250 kg of gold, which was melted down by the Burmese conquerors. It is mainly known for the line of three large *chedis* (stupas) erected in the quintessential Ayuthaya style, which has come to be identified with Thai art more than any other single style. Admission is 20B.

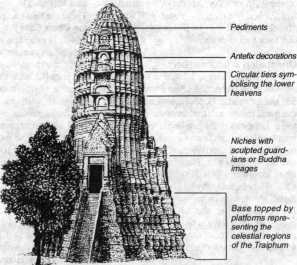

Pediments

Antefix decorations

Circular tiers symbolising the lower heavens

Niches with sculpted guardians or Buddha images

Base topped by platforms representing the celestial regions of the Traiphum

*The central prang of Wat Chai Wattanaram displays the basic features of Ayuthaya-style architecture.*

BERNARD NAPTHINE

The people of modern-day Ayuthaya show their reverence for the Buddha images in the compound of Wat Chai Mongkhon by swathing them in sacred cloth.

JOE CUMMINGS

Many Buddha images and other religious art at Ayuthaya were damaged or destroyed by the Burmese during their 1765-67 invasion. Art thieves have also left many Buddhas, such as this one at Wat Phanan Choeng, headless.

The grand Khmer-style prang of Ayuthaya's Wat Phra Mahathat stands over an expanse of spires and crumbling pillars, once a magnificent temple compound.

RICHARD I'ANSON

Standing on the banks of the Chao Phraya River, Wat Phanan Choeng with its arched stone walkways and Buddha images is one of the best sited of Ayuthaya's temples.

JOE CUMMINGS

*The French naturalist and explorer, Henri Mouhot, travelled widely through Thailand in the mid-19th century. This etching of an Ayuthaya Buddha statue was published in Mouhot's Travels in Siam, Cambodia and Laos 1858-60.*

## Wat Mongkhon Bophit

วัดมงคลบพิตร

This monastery near Si Sanphet contains one of Thailand's largest Buddha images, a blackened 15th century bronze casting. The present *wihāan* (Buddhist image sanctuary) was built in 1956.

## Wat Phra Mahathat

วัดพระมหาธาตุ

This wat, on the corner of Chee Kun and Naresuan (Chao Phrom) Rds, dates back to the 14th century and was built during the reign of King Ramesuan. Despite extensive damage – not much was left standing after the Burmese hordes – the *prang* (Khmer-style tower) is still impressive. It was one of the first prangs built in the capital. Admission is 20B.

## Wat Ratburana

วัดราชบูรณะ

The Ratburana ruins are the counterpart to Wat Phra Mahathat across the road; the chedis, however, contain murals of the early Ayuthaya period and are not quite as dilapidated. Admission is 20B.

CENTRAL THAILAND

*This etching shows a view of Ayuthaya temples from across a canal, as reproduced in Mouhot's book of his travels in the region.*

## Wat Thammikarat

วัดธรรมิกราช

To the east of the old palace grounds, inside the river loop, Wat Thammikarat features overgrown chedi ruins and lion sculptures.

## Wat Phanan Choeng

วัดพนัญเชิง

South-east of town on the Chao Phraya River, this wat was built before Ayuthaya became a Siamese capital. It's not known who built the temple, but it appears to have been constructed in the early 14th century so it's possibly Khmer. The main wihāan contains a highly revered 19m sitting Buddha image from which the wat derives its name.

The easiest way to get to Wat Phanan Choeng is by ferry from the pier near Phom Phet fortress, inside the south-east corner of the city centre. For a few extra baht you can take a bicycle with you on the boat.

## Wat Phra Meru (Phra Mehn/Mane)

วัดพระเมรุ

Across from the old royal palace grounds is a bridge which can be crossed to arrive at Wat Phra Meru. This temple is notable because it escaped destruction from the Burmese in 1767, though it has required restoration over the years. The main *bòt* (central sanctuary) was built in 1546 and features fortress-like walls and pillars. During the Burmese invasion, Myanmar's Chao Along Phaya chose this site from which to fire cannon at the palace; the cannon exploded and the king was fatally injured, thus ending the sacking of Ayuthaya.

The bòt interior contains an impressive carved wooden ceiling and a splendid Ayuthaya-era, crowned sitting Buddha, six metres high. Inside a smaller wihāan behind the bòt is a green-stone, European-pose (sitting in a chair) Buddha from Ceylon, said to be 1300 years old. The walls of the wihāan show traces of 18th or 19th century murals.

Admission to Wat Phra Meru is 10B.

## Wat Yai Chai Mongkhon

วัดใหญ่ชัยมงคล

Wat Yai, as the locals call it, is south-east of the town proper, but can be reached by minibus for 3 to 4B. It's a quiet, old place that was once a famous meditation wat, built in 1357 by King U Thong. The compound contains a very large chedi from which the wat takes its popular name (yài means 'big'), and there is a community of mâe chii (Buddhist nuns) residing here. Admission is 20B.

## Other Temples

Just north of Wat Ratburana, to the west of a colourful Chinese shrine, are the smaller ruins of **Wat Suwannawat**. The 400-year-old brick remains of eight chedis, a bòt and a wihãan are arranged in a circle – a typical early Ayuthaya layout.

The ruined Ayuthaya-style prang and chedis of **Wat Chai Wattanaram**, on the west bank of the Chao Phraya River south-west of the city centre, have been restored. These ruins can be reached by boat, or by bicycle via a nearby bridge. If you go by road, you'll pass **Wat Kasatthirat** on the way. Admission to Wat Chai Wattanaram costs 20B.

A short boat ride north along the Lopburi River will bring you to modern **Wat Pa Doh**. In front of the bòt, a unique Sukhothai-style walking Buddha image strides over a narrow arch, symbolising the crossing from samsara to nirvana.

An etching of an Ayuthaya temple and the encroaching jungle, as published in Henri Mouhot's Travels in Siam, Cambodia and Laos 1858-60.

## Ayuthaya Historical Study Centre
ศูนย์ศึกษาประวัติศาสตร์อยุธยา

Funded by the Japanese government, this US$6.8 million historical research institute (☎ 245125) is opposite Chao Sam Phraya National Museum. There are actually two buildings, the main one on Rotchana Rd and an annex just south of Wat Phanan Choeng on the south bank of the Pa Sak/Chao Phraya river junction, in a district that housed a Japanese community during Ayuthaya's heyday. The high-tech exhibit area in the main building covers five aspects of Ayuthaya's history: city development, port, administration, lifestyles and traditions. The annex contains on exhibit on foreign relations with Ayuthaya. The centre is open Wednesday to Sunday from 9 am to 4.30 pm. Admission, good for both buildings, costs 100B or 50B for students; groups of five or more can obtain a 20% discount.

**Elephant Kraal** This is a restored version of the wooden stockade once used for the annual roundup of wild elephants. A huge fence of teak logs planted in the ground at 45 degree angles kept the elephants in; the king had a special raised pavilion from which to observe the thrilling event.

### Places to Stay – bottom end
**Guesthouses & Hostels** For budgeters, there are five guesthouses and one hostel in Ayuthaya to choose from. All rent bicycles for around 50B per day. Four are on or off Naresuan Rd, not far from the bus terminal. As elsewhere in Thailand, tuk-tuk and samlor drivers will tell you anything to steer you towards guesthouses that pay commissions (up to 35B per head in this city).

Near the end of a *soi* (lane) off Naresuan Rd (not far from the Sri Smai Hotel), *Ayuthaya Guest House* charges 100B for singles/doubles in an old house. Next door, a branch of the same family runs the *Old BJ Guest House* (☎ 251526) at 80/100B a single/double, or 60B per bed in a multi-bed room; the Ayuthaya Guest House is cleaner. Both offer minimal food service. Yet another BJ relative operates the *New BJ Guest House*

### Ayuthaya Festivals
Ayuthaya holds one of the country's largest Loi Krathong festivals on the full moon of the 12th lunar month (usually November). Celebrations are held at several spots in the city: the largest spectacle takes place at **Beung Phra Ram**, the large lake in the centre of the city between Wat Phra Ram and Wat Phra Mahathat. Thousands of Thais, many of them from Bangkok, flock to the event to crowd around four or five different outdoor stages offering *lí-khe* (folk dance-drama), Thai pop, cinema and *lákhon chatrii* (classical dance-drama) – all at the same time (the din can be deafening)! Fireworks are a big part of the show, and there are lots of food vendors on the site.

More low-key and traditional is the celebration at the **Chan Kasem pier**, where families launch their *krathongs* (small lotus-shaped floats topped with incense and candles) onto the Lopburi-Pa Sak river junction. Although kids throw fireworks here, the overall atmosphere is much closer to the heart of Loi Krathong than the festival at Beung Phra Ram. Krathongs can be purchased at the pier (or you can make your own from materials for sale); for a few baht you can board one of the many waiting canoes at the pier and be paddled out to launch your krathong in the middle of the river. Thai tradition says that any couple who launch a krathong together are destined to be lovers – if not in this lifetime then the next.

Another large Loi Krathong festival takes place at the **Royal Folk Arts & Crafts Centre** in Bang Sai, about 24 km west of Ayuthaya (see the Around Ayuthaya section). The emphasis is on traditional costumes and handmade krathongs. If you can put together a small group, any of the hotels or guesthouses in Ayuthaya can arrange a trip to the Bang Sai Loi Krathong for around 250B or less per person.

During the 10 days leading to the Songkran Festival, in mid-April, there is a sound & light show with fireworks over the ruins within the moat. Every day between 10.30 am and 1.30 pm the local government runs boat tours from the Chan Kasem pier for 50B per person. ■

(☎ 244046) at 19/29 Naresuan Rd. Rooms cost 100B a single/double, dorm beds 60B and there's a simple dining area in front. One drawback is that, as it's right on Naresuan Rd, traffic noise may be distracting.

*Thongchai Guest House* (☎ 245210), on a back road parallel to Naresuan Rd and off Chee Kun Rd, has a choice of rooms available in bungalows or in a row house for 120B without bath, 200 to 250B with fan and bath or 300 to 350B for air-con and bath. The staff tends to be a bit unruly; a woman friend said she was hassled here.

Almost directly across the river from the train station in an old teak house is the *Ayuthaya Youth Hostel* (☎ 241978), also known as Reuan Derm, at 48/2 U Thong Rd. Plain rooms with ceiling fans and shared bath cost 200B for smaller rooms, 250B for larger ones. A very good floating restaurant extends from the river side of the house; it is open from 10 am till 11 pm. If you can put up with some ambient noise from the restaurant and from the traffic on busy U Thong Rd, it's not a bad choice. No-one seems to care whether you show a Hostelling International card or not – if you have one, it wouldn't hurt to ask for a discount.

*Pai Thong Guest House*, right on the river within walking distance of the train station, has recently been torn down for total reconstruction.

**Hotels** Two standard Thai-Chinese-style hotels at the junction of the Lopburi and Pa Sak rivers have been accommodating Ayuthaya visitors for two decades now. The *U Thong Hotel* (☎ 251136), on U Thong Rd near Hua Raw Night Market and Chan Kasem Palace, has adequate one bed/two bed rooms with fan for 180/250B, air-con for 300/400B. TV is 30B extra. A little southeast of the U Thong Hotel, the *Cathay Hotel* (☎ 251562) at 36/5-6 U Thong Rd costs 150/270B for a one bed/two bed room with fan, 300B for a single/double with air-con. Both hotels back up to the river.

The *Thai Thai Bungalow* (☎ 244702), at 13/1 Naresuan Rd, set well off the road between the bus terminal and the road to Wat Phra Meru, has large, semi-clean but run-down rooms from 120 to 300B with air-con. It's obviously the type of place to rely on short-time traffic but is otherwise OK.

*Sri Smai (Si Samai) Hotel* (☎ 252249), 12 Thetsaban Soi 2, just off Naresuan Rd, is a more up-market place that charges 400B for rooms with fan and bath, 550B with air-con, 600B with air-con and hot water.

**Places to Stay – middle & top end**
The *Wieng Fa Hotel* (☎ 241353) at 1/8 Rotchana Rd is a friendly, cosy place with clean, relatively quiet rooms around a garden courtyard for 400B. All rooms come with TV and air-con; English is spoken.

*Suan Luang (Royal Garden) Hotel* (☎ /fax 245537) is a new five-storey hotel training facility beside the Ayuthaya Historical Study Centre. Decent air-con rooms with fridge and TV cost a moderate 500B; a couple of six bed air-con rooms are available for 600B.

*My House* (☎ 335493), on Rotchana Rd out toward Ratchathani Hospital, has decent rooms for 500B; the isolated location is a definite drawback.

Moving towards the top end, the *U-Thong Inn* (☎ 242618) offers comfortable air-con rooms for 950 to 1400B. Facilities include a pool, sauna and massage room. It's out on Rotchana Rd past the turn-off for the train station. The newer six-storey *Ayuthaya Grand Hotel* (☎ 335483; fax 335492), out towards U-Thong Inn at 75/5 Rotchana Rd, features rooms with all the mod cons for 1100 to 1500B. There's a large swimming pool.

Ayuthaya's flashiest digs are the 202-room, eight-storey *Krungsri River Hotel* (☎ 244333; fax 243777) at 27/2 Rotchana Rd, where decked-out lodgings cost 1600 to 2000B. Facilities include a pub/coffee house, fitness centre, pool, bowling alley and snooker club.

Next door to the Krungsri, the 102-room *Tevaraj Tanrin Hotel* (☎ /fax 244139) has similar rooms in the 1000 to 2500B range (includes breakfast), a floating restaurant and beer garden.

## Places to Eat

The most dependable and least expensive places to eat are the *Hua Raw Night Market*, on the river near Chan Kasem Palace, and the *Chao Phrom Market*, opposite the ferry piers along the east side of the island. The *Chainam* opposite Chan Kasem Palace next to the Cathay Hotel has tables on the river, a bilingual menu and friendly service; it's also open for breakfast.

The artsy *Moon Cafe*, a tiny spot on the same soi as Ayuthaya Guest House, serves Thai and farang food for 30 to 50B per dish, also beer and espresso. *Duangporn* on Naresuan Rd near the main bus terminal is an indoor air-con place with Thai and Chinese food in the 40 to 80B range. There's also a modern *KFC* on this street near the Sri Smai (Samai) Hotel.

Quite a few restaurants can be found on Rotchana Rd, and there are four floating restaurants on the Pa Sak River, three on either side of the Pridi Damrong Bridge on the west bank, and one on the east bank north of the bridge. Of these, the *Phae Krung Kao* – on the south side of the bridge on the west bank – has the better reputation. There's no English sign – look for Thai flags and a topiary at the entrance. North of the bridge on the west bank, *Ruenpae* is similar. The floating *Reuan Doem*, in front of the Ayuthaya Youth Hostel, is also quite good and has the most intimate atmosphere of the riverside places.

Off Chee Khun Rd near the Thongchai Guest House, *Ruay Jaroen* is a huge wooden place specialising in seafood and duck dishes – medium to moderately high prices. It's open 11 am to 11 pm.

In the evenings a very choice night market comes to life near the pier opposite Chan Kasem Palace.

For something a little fancier, try the air-con *Rodeo Saloon* on U Thong Rd. Despite the name and old-west decor, the food is mostly Thai (an English menu is available); it's only open at night, when a small band plays Thai and international folk music.

## Getting There & Away

**Bus** Ordinary buses run between the Northern Bus Terminal in Bangkok and Ayuthaya's main terminal on Naresuan Rd every 20 minutes between 5 am and 7 pm. The fare is 22B and the trip takes around two hours. Air-con buses operate along the same route every half hour from 6 am to 6.30 pm and cost 36B; the trip takes 1½ hours when traffic north of Bangkok is light, two hours otherwise. There is also a minivan service for 30B that runs every 20 minutes from 5 am to 5 pm.

If you're arriving in Ayuthaya by bus from some place other than Bangkok or cities nearby, you may be dropped off at the long-distance bus station, five km east of the Pridi Damrong Bridge at the Highway 32 junction.

Songthaews to/from Bang Pa-In leave from the same area on Naresuan Rd and cost 8B; it's about a half hour away.

**Train** Trains to Ayuthaya leave Bangkok's Hualamphong station every hour or so between 4.20 am and 10 pm. The 3rd class fare is 15B for the 1½ hour trip; it's hardly worth taking a more expensive class, rapid or express, for this short trip. Train schedules are available from the information booth at Hualamphong station.

After getting off at Ayuthaya's train station, the quickest way to reach the old city is to walk straight west to the river, where you can take a short ferry ride across to the Chao Phrom pier for 1B.

Upon arrival at Bangkok international airport, savvy repeat visitors to Thailand sometimes choose to board a northbound train direct to Ayuthaya rather than head south into the Bangkok maelstrom. This only works if you arrive by air during the day or early evening, as local trains to Ayuthaya cease running around 9 pm. There are frequent 3rd class trains throughout the day between Don Muang station (opposite Bangkok international airport) and Ayuthaya.

**Boat** There are no scheduled or chartered boat services between Bangkok and Ayuthaya.

Several companies in Bangkok operate luxury cruises to Bang Pa-In with side trips by bus to Ayuthaya for around 1000 to 1200B per person, including a lavish luncheon. Longer two day trips in converted rice barges start at 3000B. See River & Canal Trips in the Bangkok chapter for more details.

### Getting Around

Songthaews and shared tuk-tuks ply the main city roads for 3 to 5B per person depending on distance. A tuk-tuk from the train station to any point in old Ayuthaya should be around 30B; on the island itself figure no more than 20B per trip.

For touring the ruins, you're most economical and ecological option is to rent a bicycle from one of the guesthouses (40 to 50B a day) or walk. You can hire a samlor, tuk-tuk or songthaew by the hour or by the day to explore the ruins but the prices are quite high by Thai standards (150B per hour for anything with a motor in it, 400B all day when things are slow).

It's also interesting to hire a boat from the Chan Kasem Palace pier to do a semicircular tour of the island and see some of the less accessible ruins. A long-tail boat that will take up to eight people can be hired for 300B for a three hour trip with stops at Wat Phutthaisawan, Wat Phanan Choeng and Wat Chai Wattanaram.

### AROUND AYUTHAYA
### Bang Pa-In
บางปะอิน

Twenty km south of Ayuthaya is Bang Pa-In, which has a curious collection of palace buildings in a wide variety of architectural styles. It's a nice boat trip from Bangkok if you're taking one of the cruise tours, although in itself it's not particularly noteworthy. The palace is open from 8.30 am to 3.30 pm daily. Admission is 50B.

**Palace Buildings** The postcard stereotype here is a pretty little Thai pavilion in the centre of a small lake by the palace entrance. Inside the palace grounds, the Chinese-style **Wehat Chamrun Palace** is the only building open to visitors. The **Withun Thatsana** building looks like a lighthouse with balco-

nies. It was built to give a fine view over gardens and lakes. There are various other buildings, towers and memorials in the grounds plus an interesting topiary where the bushes have been trimmed into the shape of a small herd of elephants.

**Wat Niwet Thamaprawat** Across the river and south from the palace grounds, this unusual wat looks much more like a Gothic Christian church than anything from Thailand. It was built by Rama V (Chulalongkorn). You get to the wat by crossing the river in a small trolley-like cable car. The crossing is free.

**Getting There & Away** Bang Pa-In can be reached by minibus (it's really a large songthaew truck) from Ayuthaya's Chao Phrom Market on Naresuan Rd, for 8B. From Bangkok there are buses every half hour or so from the Northern Bus Terminal and the fare is 17B ordinary, 25B air-con. You can also reach Bang Pa-In by train from Bangkok for 12B in 3rd class.

The Chao Phraya River Express Boat Co does a tour every Sunday, from the Tha Maharat pier in Bangkok, that goes to Wat Phailom in Pathum Thani (November to June) or Wat Chaloem Phrakiat (July to October) as well as Bang Pa-In and Bang Sai's Royal Folk Arts & Crafts Centre (see below). The trip leaves from Bangkok at 8 am and returns at 5.30 pm. The price is 180B (or 250B on the upper deck) not including lunch, which you arrange in Bang Pa-In. For more expensive river cruises to Bang Pa-In which include tours of old Ayuthaya, see River & Canal Trips in the Bangkok chapter.

### Bang Sai Royal Folk Arts & Crafts Centre

This 115 hectare facility in Beung Yai, Bang Sai district, is an important training centre for craftspeople from the central provinces and beyond. Under the auspices of Queen Sirikit's Promotion of Supplementary Occupations & Related Techniques (SUPPORT) foundation, handicraft experts teach craft techniques to novices while at the same time demonstrating them for visitors. The centre is open daily from 8.30 am to 4 pm; admission is 20B. Call ☎ 366092 (☎ (2) 225-8265 in Bangkok) for additional information.

The Loi Krathong festival here is considered one of the more traditional versions in Central Thailand. You can easily book a Loi Krathong trip to Bang Sai from Ayuthaya – see the earlier boxed aside on Ayuthaya Festivals for details.

# Lopburi Province

## LOPBURI
อ.เมืองลพบุรี
• ☎ (36) • pop 40,000
Approximately 154 km north of Bangkok, the town of Lopburi has been inhabited since at least the Dvaravati period (6th to 11th centuries AD), when it was called Lavo. Nearly all traces of Lavo culture were erased by Khmer and Thai inhabitants following the 10th century, but many Dvaravati artefacts found in Lopburi can be seen in the Lopburi National Museum. Ruins and statuary in Lopburi span a remarkable 12 centuries.

The Khmers extended their Angkor empire to include Lavo in the 10th century. It was during this century that they built the Prang Khaek (Hindu Shrine), San Phra Kan (Kala Shrine) and Prang Sam Yot (Three Spired Shrine) as well as the impressive prang at Wat Phra Si Ratana Mahathat.

Power over Lopburi was wrested from the Khmers in the 13th century as the Sukhothai kingdom to the north grew stronger, but the Khmer cultural influence remained to some extent throughout the Ayuthaya period. King Narai fortified Lopburi in the mid-17th century to serve as a second capital when the kingdom of Ayuthaya was threatened by a Dutch naval blockade. His palace in Lopburi was built in 1665 and he died there in 1688.

### Orientation & Information
The new town of Lopburi was begun in 1940. It is some distance east of the old fortified town and is centred around two large roundabouts.

There is really nothing of interest in the new section, so try to stay at a hotel in the old town if you're interested in the palace and temple ruins. All the historical sites in Lopburi can be visited on foot in a day or two.

**Tourist Office** There's a TAT office (☎ 422-768) in the Sala Jangwat (Provincial Hall) in new Lopburi. The staff distribute the usual brochures and can be of assistance with any problems you may encounter during your visit. This office may move to a more permanent location in the next couple of years.

### Phra Narai Ratchaniwet
พระนารายณ์ราชนิเวศน์
King Narai's palace is probably the best place to begin a tour of Lopburi. After King Narai's death in 1688, the palace was used only by King Phetracha (Narai's successor) for his coronation ceremony and was then abandoned until King Mongkut ordered restoration in the mid-19th century.

The palace took 12 years to build (1665-77). French architects contributed to the design and Khmer influence was still strong in Central Thailand at that time. It's hardly surprising then that the palace exhibits an unusual, striking blend of Khmer and European styles.

The main gate into the palace, **Pratu Phayakkha**, is off Sorasak Rd, opposite the Asia Lopburi Hotel. The grounds are well kept, planted with trees and shrubbery, and serve as a kind of town park for local children and young lovers. Immediately on the left as you enter are the remains of the king's elephant stables, with the palace water reservoir in the foreground. In the adjacent quadrangle to the left is the royal reception hall and the **Phra Chao Hao**, which probably served as a wihāan for a valued Buddha image. Passing through more stables, you come to the southwest quadrangle with the **Suttha Sawan** pavilion in the centre. The north-west quadrangle contains many ruined buildings which were once an audience hall, various sāalaa (sala; an open-sided covered meeting hall or resting place), and residence quarters for the king's harem.

CENTRAL THAILAND

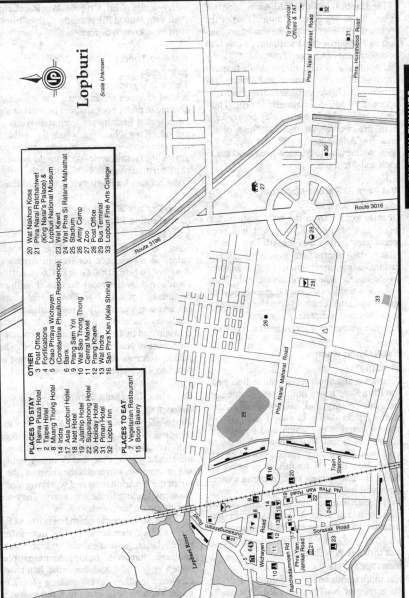

# Lopburi

Scale Unknown

To Provincial
Offices & TAT

**PLACES TO STAY**
1 Rama Plaza Hotel
2 Taipei Hotel
8 Muang Thong Hotel
14 Indra
17 Asia Lopburi Hotel
18 Nett Hotel
19 Julathip Hotel
22 Suparaphong Hotel
30 Holiday Hotel
31 Pimarn Hotel
32 Lopburi Inn

**PLACES TO EAT**
7 Vegetarian Restaurant
15 Boon Bakery

**OTHER**
3 Post Office
4 Fortifications
5 Chao Phraya Wichayen
  (Constantine Phaulkon Residence)
6 Bank
9 Prang Sam Yot
10 Wat Sao Thong Thong
11 Central Market
12 Prang Khaek
13 Wat Indra
16 San Phra Kan (Kala Shrine)
20 Wat Nakhon Kosa
21 Phra Narai Ratchaniwet
  (King Narai's Palace) &
  Lopburi National Museum
23 Wat Kawit
24 Wat Phra Si Ratana Mahathat
25 Stadium
26 Army Camp
27 Zoo
28 Post Office
29 Bus Terminal
33 Lopburi Fine Arts College

Route 3195

Route 3016

Phra Narai Maharat Road

Phra Horathibodi Road

Phra Narai Maharat Road

Lopburi River

Surasongkhram Road

Ratchadamnoen Rd

Wichayen Road

Na Phra Kan Road

Sorasak Road

Phra Yam Jamkat Road

Train Station

The **Lopburi National Museum** is located here in three separate buildings. Two of the museum buildings house an excellent collection of Lopburi-period sculpture, as well as an assortment of Khmer, Dvaravati, U Thong and Ayuthaya art. The third building features traditional farm implements and dioramas of farm life. *A Guide to Ancient Monuments in Lopburi* by MC Subhadradis Diskul, Thailand's leading art historian, may be available from the counter on the 2nd floor of the museum. Admission is 10B; the museum is open Wednesday to Sunday from 8.30 am to noon and 1 to 4 pm.

## Wat Phra Si Ratana Mahathat
วัดพระศรีรัตนมหาธาตุ
Directly across from the train station, this large 12th century Khmer wat has been recently restored by the Fine Arts Department. A very tall laterite prang still stands and features a few intact lintels, as well as some ornate stucco. A large wihāan added by King Narai also displays a ruined elegance. Several chedis and smaller prangs dot the grounds – some almost completely restored, some a little the worse for wear. Admission is 20B.

## Wat Nakhon Kosa
วัดนครโกษา
This wat is just north of the train station, near San Phra Kan. It was built by the Khmers in the 12th century and may originally have been a Hindu shrine. U Thong and Lopburi images found at the temple and now in the Lopburi National Museum are thought to have been added later. There's not much left of this wat, though the foliage growing on the brick ruins makes an interesting image. However, half-hearted attempts to restore it with modern materials and motifs detract from the overall effect. A recent excavation has uncovered a larger base below the monument.

## Wat Indra & Wat Racha
วัดอินทราและวัดราชา
Wat Indra stands on Ratchadamnoen Rd near the corner of Na Phra Kan Rd. Practically nothing is known of its history and it's now merely a pile of brick rubble. Wat Racha, off Phra Yam Jamkat Rd, is another pile of bricks with little known history.

## Wat Sao Thong Thong
วัดเสาธงทอง
This wat is north-west of the palace centre, behind the central market. The buildings here are in pretty poor shape. The wihāan and large seated Buddha are from the Ayuthaya period; King Narai restored the wihāan (changing its windows to an incongruous but intriguing Gothic style) so it could be used as a Christian chapel. Niches along the inside walls contain Lopburi-style *naga* Buddhas.

## Chao Phraya Wichayen (Constantine Phaulkon Residence)
บ้านวิชาเยนทร์
King Narai built this eclectic Thai-European palace as a residence for foreign ambassadors, of whom the Greek Constantine Phaulkon was the most famous. Phaulkon became one of King Narai's principal advisers and was eventually a royal minister. In 1688, as Narai lay dying, Phaulkon was assassinated by Luang Sorasak, who wanted the power of Narai's throne for himself. The palace is across the street and north-east of Wat Sao Thong Thong; admission is 20B.

## San Phra Kan (Kala Shrine)
ศาลพระกาฬ
To the north of Wat Nakhon Kosa, near the train tracks, this unimpressive shrine contains a crude gold-leaf laden image of Kala, the Hindu god of time and death. A virtual sea of monkeys surrounds the shrine, falling out of the tamarind trees and scurrying along the steps leading to the sanctuary. They are getting fat on hand-outs.

In late November Lopburi holds a feast for the resident monkeys, laying out buffet tables laden with peanuts, watermelon, cabbage, bananas, pumpkin, pineapple, boiled eggs and cucumbers; the latter two items are monkey faves, causing plenty of spats. Thousands of Thais turn out to watch the spectacle.

## Prang Sam Yot
ปรางค์สามยอด

Opposite the San Phra Kan, near the Muang Thong Hotel, this shrine represents classic Khmer-Lopburi style and is another Hindu turned Buddhist temple. Originally, the three prangs symbolised the Hindu *trimurti* of Shiva, Vishnu and Brahma. Now two of them contain ruined Lopburi-style Buddha images. Some Khmer lintels can still be made out, and some appear unfinished.

A rather uninteresting U Thong-Ayuthaya imitation Buddha image sits in the brick sanctuary in front of the linked prangs. At the back, facing the Muang Thong Hotel, are a couple of crudely restored images, probably once Lopburi style. The grounds allotted to Prang Sam Yot are rather small and are virtually surrounded by modern buildings. The best view of the monument would probably be from one of the upper floors of the Muang Thong. The monument is lit up at night.

## Activities
Those interested in Thai classical music and dance should stop by the **Lopburi Fine Arts College** (Withayalai Kalasilpa Lopburi) in the new town – any tuk-tuk driver will know it. Here you can watch young dancers practising the rudiments of classical dance with live musical accompaniment.

A small **zoo** north-east of the first roundabout (coming from the old town) is a quiet place to spend a couple of hours. It's open from 8 am to 6 pm; entry is 10B.

## Places to Stay
**Old Lopburi** Lopburi can be visited as a day trip en route to the North, but if you want to stay overnight there are a number of hotels in the older part of the city you can try. *Asia Lopburi Hotel* (☎ 411892), on the corner of Sorasak and Phra Yam Jamkat Rds and overlooking King Narai's palace, is clean and comfortable with good service. It has two Chinese restaurants. Rooms are 130/180B for singles/doubles with fan and bath, or up to 250/350B with air-con. Ask for a room off the street if traffic noise is bothersome.

*Muang Thong Hotel* (☎ 411036), across from Prang Sam Yot, has noisy and not-so-clean rooms for 100 to 120B with fan and bath. Rooms without bath are also available for 80B, or air-con rooms for 200B. Better is the *Taipei Hotel* (☎ 411624), at 24/6-7 Surasongkhram Rd north of the palace area. Clean rooms with private bath cost 120/180B one/two beds; air-con rooms are available for 200/260B one/two beds.

The newish *Rama Plaza Hotel*, farther north out Surasongkhram Rd, offers clean medium-price rooms for 200/300B a single/double with fan and bath, 320/450B with air-con. Popular with business travellers, it's often full.

The *Indra*, on Na Phra Kan Rd across from Wat Nakhon Kosa, continues under new – and better – management. It costs 120B for clean, spacious rooms with fan and bath, 260B with air-con. Also on Na Phra Kan Rd, the *Julathip Hotel* is near the Indra but closer to the train station, and has no English sign. This one has also cleaned up a bit (although it still doubles as a brothel) and rooms with fan and bath now cost 100B; it's a good idea to ask to see a room first.

The similar *Suparaphong Hotel*, also on Na Phra Kan Rd, is not far from Wat Phra Si Ratana Mahathat and the train station. Rooms cost 100B and are much the same as at the Julathip and Indra hotels.

The *Nett Hotel* (☎ 411738), at 17/1-2 Ratchadamnoen Rd, is actually on a soi between Ratchadamnoen and Phra Yam Jamkat Rds, parallel to Sorasak Rd. Clean, quiet rooms with fan and bath cost 140/240/280B for one/two/three bed rooms or 280/380B for air-con one/two bed rooms.

**New Lopburi** If you get stuck in the new part of town for some reason, you can choose from *Piman* at Soi Ekathot, Phra Horathibodi Rd, *Holiday* at Soi Suriyothai 2, Phra Narai Maharat Rd, or *Lopburi Inn* (☎ 412300; fax 411917) at 28/8 Phra Narai Maharat Rd. The first two are mostly middle-class short-time places with rates around 250B a night. The Lopburi Inn features very nice rooms with all the amenities from 600B.

At the top end is the new *Lopburi Inn Resort* (☎ 420777; fax 412010) at 144 Tambon Tha Sala, where rooms with all the modern amenities – including a fitness centre and swimming pool – cost 2200/2400B.

## Places to Eat
Several Chinese restaurants operate along Na Phra Kan Rd, parallel to the train line, especially near the Julathip and Indra hotels. The food is good but a bit overpriced. Restaurants on the side streets of Ratchadamnoen and Phra Yam Jamkat Rds can be better value. The Chinese-Thai restaurant next to the Asia Lopburi Hotel on Sorasak Rd, across from the main gate to King Narai's palace, is a good standby. There are also plenty of cheap curry vendors down the alleys and along the smaller streets in old Lopburi.

The market off Ratchadamnoen and Surasongkhram Rds (just north of the palace) is a great place to pick up food to eat in your hotel room – kài thâwt or kài yâang (fried or roast chicken) with sticky rice, hàw mòk (fish and coconut curry steamed in banana leaves), klûay khàek (Indian-style fried bananas), a wide selection of fruit, satay, khâo krìap (crispy rice cakes), thâwt man plaa (fried fish cakes) and other delights.

At 26/47 Soonkangkha Manora, near the Australian Education Placement Centre, is *Sala Mangsawirat* (Vegetarian Pavilion) with inexpensive Thai veggie food; like most Thai vegetarian restaurants, it's only open from around 9 am to 2 pm.

*Boon Bakery*, next to the Indra Hotel on Na Phra Kan Rd, serves western breakfasts, coffee and pastries. In the evenings a night market sets up along Na Phra Kan Rd.

## Getting There & Away
**Bus** Buses leave for Lopburi every 10 minutes from Ayuthaya, or, if you're coming from Bangkok, about every 20 minutes (5.30 am to 8.30 pm) from the Northern Bus Terminal. It's a three hour ride which costs 40B (72B air-con) from Bangkok, about half that from Ayuthaya.

Lopburi can also be reached from the west via Kanchanaburi or Suphanburi. If you're coming from Kanchanaburi, you'll have to take a bus (No 411) first to Suphanburi. The trip lasts about 2½ hours, costs 25B, and there's great scenery all the way. In Suphanburi, get off the bus in the town's main street, Malaimaen Rd (it has English signs), at the intersection which has an English sign pointing to Sri Prachan. From here you can catch a direct bus (No 464) to Lopburi for 25B, a trip of around three hours.

If you happen to miss the direct bus, you can also hopscotch to Lopburi by catching a bus first to Singburi or Ang Thong, across the river from Lopburi. The Suphanburi to Singburi leg takes about 2½ hours for 25B and the scenery gets even better – you'll pass many old, traditional Thai wooden houses (late Ayuthaya style), countless cool rice paddies and small wats of all descriptions. Finally, at the Singburi bus station, catch one of the frequent buses to Lopburi for 10B (45 minutes). The Singburi bus makes a stop in front of Prang Sam Yot in old Lopburi – if you get off here, you won't have to backtrack from the new city. An alternative to the Suphanburi to Singburi route is to take a bus to Ang Thong (10B) and then a share taxi (20B) or bus (15B) to Lopburi. This is a little faster but not quite as scenic.

From the North-East, Lopburi can be reached via Nakhon Ratchasima (Khorat) for 50B.

**Train** Ordinary trains depart Bangkok's Hualamphong station, heading north, every hour or so between 4.20 am and 8 pm, and take only 20 to 30 minutes longer to reach Lopburi than the rapid or express. Only two ordinary trains, the 7.05 am and the 8.30 am, have 2nd class seats; the rest are 3rd class only. Rapid trains leave at 6.40 am, 3, 6.10, 8 and 10 pm and take about 2½ hours to reach Lopburi. Fares are 57B in 2nd class and 28B in 3rd class, not including surcharges for rapid or express trains.

There are also regular trains from Ayuthaya to Lopburi which take about one hour and cost 13B in 3rd class. It is possible to leave Bangkok or Ayuthaya in the morning, have a look around Lopburi during the day

CENTRAL THAILAND

(leaving your bags in the Lopburi train station) and then carry on to Chiang Mai on one of the night trains (departure times are at 5.28 and 8.24 pm, and 12.22 am).

### Getting Around
Songthaews run along Wichayen and Phra Narai Maharat Rds between the old and new towns for 3B per passenger. Samlors will go anywhere in the old town for 20B.

# Ang Thong & Saraburi Provinces

## ANG THONG
อ.เมืองอ่างทอง
• ☎ (35) • pop 10,000
There are some places of interest outside small Ang Thong, which lies between Lopburi and Suphanburi, including **Wat Pa Mok** with its 22m-long reclining Buddha. The village of **Ban Phae** is famous for the crafting of Thai drums or *klawng*. Ban Phae is behind the Pa Mok Market on the banks of the Chao Phraya River.

### Places to Stay
Refurbished rooms with fan and private bath start at 140B, air-con for 380B, in the *Bua Luang* (☎ 611116) on Ayuthaya Rd. Rooms at the *Ang Thong Hotel & Bungalows* (☎ 611767/8) at 19 Ang Thong Rd cost 150/220B a single/double with fan, 260/300B with air-con.

### Getting There & Away
A bus from the Northern Bus Terminal in Bangkok costs 25B. See the Lopburi Getting There & Away section for details on transport to Ang Thong from Suphanburi.

## SARABURI & AROUND
อ.เมืองสระบุรี
• ☎ (36) • pop 64,000
There's nothing of touristic interest in Saraburi, a nondescript industrial centre, but between Lopburi and here you can turn off to **Wat**

**Phra Buddhabat** (Wat Phra Phutthabaat), one of six royal temples in the country bestowed with the kingdom's highest temple rank, Ratchavoramahavihan. A small and delicately beautiful *mondòp* (square shrine) houses a revered Buddha footprint *(phútthábàat)* that was 'discovered' during the reign of King Song Tham (1610-28). Like all genuine Buddha footprints, it is massive and identified by its 108 auspicious distinguishing marks. The original Ayuthaya-era mondòp perished in a fire; the current one dates to the reign of Rama I (1782-1809). Twice yearly, in early February and mid-March, Phra Buddhabat is the focus of a colourful pilgrimage festival.

Also outside Saraburi is the 784 acre **Samnak Song Tham Krabawk** (Bamboo Pipe Cave Monastery), a famous opium and heroin detoxification centre. Originally begun by Mae-chii Mian, a Buddhist nun, the controversial programme has been administered by Luang Phaw Chamrun Panchan since 1959. The programme employs a combination of herbal treatment, counselling and Dhamma to cure addicts and claims a 70% to 80% success rate. Thousands of addicts have come to Tham Krabawk to seek treatment, which begins with a rigorous 10 day session involving the ingestion of emetic herbs to purify the body of intoxicants. After anywhere from 30 days to six months at the centre, graduating patients swallow a piece of sacred paper inscribed with a vow to stay drug free; if they break the vow, they are told, the spirit world will come down hard on them. In 1975, by which time he had treated 57,000 addicts, Phra Chamrun was awarded the Magsaysay Prize for his work. Visitors are welcome at the centre.

Tham Krabawk has come under fire from government officials in recent years for allegedly harbouring large numbers of Hmong guerrillas – up to 9000 at a time – who hope to overthrow the communist government in Laos.

### Places to Stay
Try the *Thanin* (120 to 300B) or the *Suk San* (100 to 160B) at Amphoe Phra Buddhabat.

In Saraburi there's the recently renovated *Kyo-Un (Kiaw An)* (☎ 222022) on Phahonyothin Rd where rooms with fan cost from 420B, or from 800B with air-con.

Other hotels include the *Saraburi* (☎ 211-646/500) opposite the bus stop, where fan rooms are 180/200B a single/double, air-con 270/350B, or the cheaper *Saen Suk* (☎ 211104) on Phahonyothin Rd, a typical Thai-Chinese place with fan rooms for 150/180B for one bed/two beds.

### Getting There & Away

Ordinary buses from Bangkok's Northern Bus Terminal cost 31B to Saraburi, a two to three hour trip. Songthaews from Saraburi to Phra Buddhabat or Tham Krabawk cost around 5B per person.

# Suphanburi Province

## SUPHANBURI
อ.เมืองสุพรรณบุรี
• ☎ (35)  • *pop 26,000*

Almost 70 km north-east of Kanchanaburi, Suphanburi is a very old Thai town that may have had some connection with the semi-mythical Suvannabhumi (Suphannaphumi in Thai) mentioned in early Buddhist writings. During the Dvaravati period (6th to 10th centuries) it was called Meuang Thawarawadi Si Suphannaphumi. Today the town is a prosperous, typical Central Thai town along the Suphanburi River with a high proportion of Chinese among the population. There are some noteworthy Ayuthaya-period chedis and one Khmer-style prang. If you're passing through Suphan on a trip from Kanchanaburi to Lopburi, you might want to stop off for a couple of hours, see the sights, eat and rest.

### Temples

Entering Suphan from the direction of Kanchanaburi, you'll see **Wat Paa Lelai** on the right at the town limits. Several of the buildings, originally built during the U

Thong period, are old and the bòt is very distinctive because of its extremely high whitewashed walls. Looking inside, you'll realise the building was designed that way in order to house the gigantic (24.5m) late U Thong or early Ayuthaya-style 'European-pose' Buddha image inside. Devotees have gilded the figure's feet and ankles with squares of one baht gold leaf. Exotic-looking goats roam the grounds of this semi-abandoned wat.

Farther in towards the town centre, on the left side of Malaimaen Rd, is **Wat Phra Si Ratana Mahathat** (this must be the most popular name for wats in Thailand). Set back off the road a bit, this quiet wat features a fine Lopburi-style Khmer prang on which much of the stucco is still intact. There is a staircase inside the prang leading to a small chamber in the top.

Two other wats this side of the Suphanburi River, the late U Thong **Wat Phra Rup** and **Wat Chum**, have venerable old Ayuthaya chedis. Wat Phra Rup also contains an impressive reclining Buddha locally known as 'Nen Kaew' and the only wooden Buddha footprint in the country.

Fifteen km north-east, off the road to Ang Thong, is **Wat Sai Ngam**, a famous vipassana monastery under the direction of the 80 year old abbot, Ajaan Dhammadharo. Dhammadharo is the originator of an intricate system of developing insight by observing one's own hand and arm movements. As with all meditation wats, only serious meditators or would-be meditators should visit Wat Sai Ngam; an interpreter will be necessary as English isn't spoken at this temple.

### Don Chedi
อนุสรณ์ดอนเจดีย์

Seven km west of Suphanburi, off Route 324 on the way to Kanchanaburi, is the road to Don Chedi, a very famous battle site and early war memorial. It was here that King Naresuan, then a prince, defeated the prince of Myanmar on elephant back in the late 16th century. In doing so he freed Ayuthaya from domination by the Bago (Pegu) kingdom.

The chedi itself was built during Naresuan's lifetime but was neglected in the centuries afterwards. By the reign of Rama V (Chulalongkorn) at the beginning of this century, its location had been forgotten. Rama V began a search for the site but it wasn't until three years after his death in 1913 that Prince Damrong, an accomplished archaeologist, rediscovered the chedi in Suphanburi Province.

The chedi was restored in 1955 and the area developed as a national historic site. Every year during the week of January 25 (Thai Armed Forces Day), there is a week-long Don Chedi Monument Fair which features a full-costume re-enactment of the elephant battle that took place four centuries ago.

During the fair there are regular buses to Don Chedi from Suphanburi, the nearest place to stay. Transport from Bangkok can also be arranged through the bigger travel agencies there.

### U Thong National Museum
Seven km west of Suphanburi on Route 321 (Malaimaen Rd), this museum houses a collection of art and artefacts collected in Suphanburi Province, from stone and bronze culture tools to Buddhist sculpture of several eras. Dvaravati and U Thong styles are well covered, and there is an exhibit of Lao Song culture and handicrafts. The Lao Song are a local ethnic minority who have all but assimilated with Central Thai culture. The museum is open Wednesday to Sunday from 9 am to 4 pm; admission is 10B.

### Chaloem Phattharatchanini Park
This new recreation facility off Nan Phim Rd occupies 15 *rai* (one rai is equal to 1600 sq m) near the centre of town features a tall, space-needle-like tower containing a restaurant, gift shop and small museum chronicling local history. Down on the ground is a children's playground and a swimming pool attached to water slides. The park is open Tuesday to Friday from 10 am to 7 pm, weekends till 8.30 pm. Admission to the park

grounds is 10B adults, 5B children. There's a 30B charge to enter the tower; after 6 pm the price rises to 40B.

### Places to Stay
Hotel rooms in Suphanburi are very moderately priced. The *King Pho Sai* (☎ 522412) at 678 Nen Kaew Rd has good one bed/two bed fan rooms for 140/180B or from 280/300B with air-con. It's set back from the road a bit so is quieter than some of hotels in the city centre and is very good value overall. Near the clock tower, behind a warehouse, *KAT* (☎ 521619/639) at 433 Phra Phanwasa has decent rooms for 150/190B with fan, from 230B air-con. The hotel compound has a pleasant garden sitting area.

*Suk San* (☎ 521668) at 1145 Nang Phim Rd, opposite the new post office, is a typical Thai-Chinese hotel with restaurant downstairs; fan rooms are 150/240B, air-con 280/350B. The *Si Meuang*, 331-6 Phra Phanwasa Rd, is a slightly noisy Chinese hotel with rooms from 120B.

If you're looking for something a little fancier, comfortable air-con rooms are available at the *Kalapreuk Hotel* (☎ 522555), 135/1 Prachathipotai Rd, starting at 680B. The newest and most luxurious hotel in town is the *Khum Suphan Hotel* (☎ /fax 523553) at 28/2 Meunhan Rd, where rooms with all the amenities start at 1200B. On the premises are a swimming pool and coffee shop.

### Places to Eat
There is a string of good, inexpensive Thai restaurants along both sides of Meunhan Rd near the Khum Suphan Hotel.

### Getting There & Away
See the Getting There & Away information for Lopburi. A bus from the Northern Bus Terminal in Bangkok costs 35B (42B air-con).

### Getting Around
White songthaews ply a loop circuit round the town for 3B per person.

# Nakhon Pathom Province

CENTRAL THAILAND

## NAKHON PATHOM
อ.เมืองนครปฐม
• ☎ (34) • pop 45,000

Only 56 km west of Bangkok, Nakhon Pathom is regarded as the oldest city in Thailand – the name is derived from the Pali 'Nagara Pathama', meaning 'First City'. It was the centre of the Dvaravati kingdom, a loose collection of city states that flourished between the 6th and 11th centuries AD in the Chao Phraya River valley. The area may have been inhabited before India's Ashokan period (3rd century BC), as it is theorised that Buddhist missionaries from India visited Nakhon Pathom at that time.

Today's Nakhon Pathom is a typical provincial Thai city whose only visible link to its glorious past is the Phra Pathom Chedi.

## Phra Pathom Chedi
พระปฐมเจดีย์

The central attraction in Nakhon Pathom is the famous Phra Pathom Chedi, the tallest Buddhist monument in the world, rising to 127m. The original monument, buried within the massive orange-glazed dome, was erected in the early 6th century by Theravada Buddhists of Dvaravati, but in the early 11th century the Khmer king, Suryavarman I of Angkor, conquered the city and built a Brahman prang over the sanctuary. The Burmese of Bagan, under King Anuruddha, sacked the city in 1057 and the prang lay in ruins until King Mongkut had it restored in 1860. The king built a larger chedi over the remains according to Buddhist tradition, adding four wihāans, a bòt, a replica of the original chedi, sala (open-sided pavilions) and assorted prangs and other embellishments. There is even a Chinese temple attached to the outer walls of the chedi, next to which outdoor lí-khe is sometimes performed.

On the eastern side of the monument, in the bòt, is a Dvaravati-style Buddha seated in a European pose similar to the one in Wat Phra Meru in Ayuthaya. It may, in fact, have come from Phra Meru.

The wat surrounding the chedi enjoys the kingdom's highest temple rank, Ratchavoramahavihan, one of only six temples so honoured in Thailand. Rama VI's ashes are interred in the base of the Sukhothai-era Phra Ruang Rochanarit, a large standing Buddha image in the wat's northern wihāan.

Opposite the bòt is a museum, open Wednesday to Sunday from 9 am to 4 pm, which contains some interesting Dvaravati sculpture.

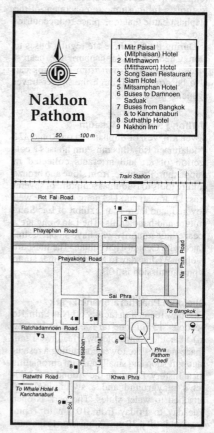

Nakhon Pathom

0   50   100 m

1 Mitr Paisal (Mitphaisan) Hotel
2 Mitrthaworn (Mitthawon) Hotel
3 Song Saen Restaurant
4 Siam Hotel
5 Mitsamphan Hotel
6 Buses to Damnoen Saduak
7 Buses from Bangkok & to Kanchanaburi
8 Suthathip Hotel
9 Nakhon Inn

## Other Attractions

Besides the chedi, the other focuses of the town are **Silpakorn University**, west of the chedi off Phetkasem Highway, and **Sanam Chan**, adjacent to the university. Sanam Chan, formerly the grounds of Rama VI's palace, is a pleasant park with a canal passing through it. The somewhat run-down palace still stands in the park but entrance is not permitted.

South-east of the city towards Bangkok, between the districts of Nakhon Chaisi and Sam Phran, is the recently completed **Phra Phutthamonthon** (from the Pali 'Buddha-mandala'). This 40.7m Sukhothai-style standing Buddha is reportedly the world's tallest; it's surrounded by a 2500 rai landscaped park containing replicas of important Buddhist pilgrimage spots in India and Nepal. All Bangkok to Nakhon Pathom buses pass the access road to the park (signposted in English as well as Thai); from there you can walk, hitch or flag one of the frequent songthaews into the park itself.

The **Thai Human Imagery Museum** (☎ (01) 211-6261), a bit out of town at Km 31, Pinklao-Nakhon Chaisi Rd (the highway to Bangkok), contains exhibits of lifelike sculptures. A group of Thai artists reportedly spent 10 years studying their subjects and creating the figures, which fall into four sections: famous Buddhist monks of Thailand, former kings of the Chakri dynasty, Thai lifestyles, and chess playing. It's open weekdays from 9 am to 5.30 pm, weekends from 8.30 am to 6 pm; admission is 140B.

## Places to Stay – bottom end

Budget accommodations in Nakhon Pathom can be a bit on the dreary side. The *Mitrthaworn Hotel* or Mitthawon (☎ 243115) is on the right as you walk directly down the street opposite the train station. It costs 200/220B for one/two bed rooms with fan and bath, 300B with air-con. The *Mitphaisan Hotel* (☎ 242422) – the English sign reads 'Mitr Paisal' – is farther down the alley to the right from the Mitthawon. Rooms here are 250B for fan and bath, 350B with air-con. Near the west side of Phra Pathom Chedi, next

to a furniture store on Lang Phra Rd, the *Mitsamphan* (☎ 242422) offers clean rooms with fan and bath for 150B. All three of the 'Mit' hotels are owned by the same family. Price differences reflect differences in cleanliness and service. My budget vote stays with Mitphaisan.

West of the chedi a few blocks from Mitsamphan on Thetsaban Rd is the *Siam Hotel* (☎ 241754). The staff here remain curt at best and rooms cost 140/180B for one/two beds with fan and bath or up to 250/280B with air-con. A bit farther south at 24/22 to 44/1 Thetsaban Rd, is the *Suthathip Hotel* (☎ 242242), with a boisterous Chinese restaurant downstairs. Rooms seem like an afterthought here and cost 150/200B for one/two beds with fan and bath, 300B for air-con.

## Places to Stay – top end

The *Nakhon Inn* (☎ 242265, 251152) at 55 Ratwithi Rd, Soi 3 is a pleasant 70-room air-con hotel where Thai guests are charged 400B per room, and farangs double that for the same accommodation! Since this is a private establishment (not government subsidised), this is simple racial discrimination. If you speak Thai well enough, you might be able to get the Thai price.

The newer *Whale Hotel* (☎ 251020; fax 253864), 151/79 Ratwithi Rd (south-west of the monument), offers good air-con rooms in four separate buildings starting at 480B. Facilities and services include a coffee shop, restaurant, karaoke, disco, snooker club, golf driving range, sauna and massage.

## Places to Eat

Nakhon Pathom has an excellent fruit market along the road between the train station and the Phra Pathom Chedi; the khâo lǎam (sticky rice and coconut steamed in a bamboo joint) is reputed to be the best in Thailand. There are many good, inexpensive food vendors and restaurants in this area.

*Song Saen*, on Ratchadamnoen Rd a few blocks directly west of Phra Pathom Chedi, offers a pleasant Thai sala setting with good, medium-priced Thai food.

## Getting There & Away

**Bus** Buses for Nakhon Pathom leave the Southern Bus Terminal in Bangkok every 10 minutes from 5.45 am to 9.10 pm; the fare is 16B for the one hour trip. Air-con buses are 28B and leave about every 20 minutes between 6 am and 10.30 pm. There are two bus routes; be sure to take the *sãi mài* or 'new route' buses, as the 'old route' buses take a half hour longer.

Buses to Kanchanaburi leave throughout the day from the east side of the Phra Pathom Chedi – get bus No 81. Buses to Damnoen Saduak Floating Market (see the Around Ratchaburi section) leave from the south-west side of the chedi.

**Train** Ordinary trains (3rd class only) leave Thonburi (Bangkok Noi) station daily at 7.20 and 7.50 am, 12.35, 1.45, 5.40, 7.15 and 8.20 pm, arriving in Nakhon Pathom in about an hour and 10 minutes. The fare is 14B.

There are also rapid and express trains to Nakhon Pathom from Hualamphong station roughly hourly between 1.30 and 9.55 pm. The 2nd class fare is 28B and 1st class 54B (add 20B and 30B respectively for rapid and express service). While rapid trains from Hualamphong take 1½ hours, the express is only 10 minutes faster. There are no longer any ordinary trains to Nakhon Pathom from Hualamphong station.

# Ratchaburi Province

## RATCHABURI
ราชบุรี
• ☎ *(32)* • *pop 46,000*

Ratchaburi (City of Kings, more commonly abbreviated to Rat'buri) is the first major town you reach on the way south from Nakhon Pathom. Like Suphanburi and Nakhon Pathom, its history dates back to the early Dvaravati period. Legend says it was also part of mythic Suvannabhumi, the pre-Dvaravati 'Land of Gold' that stretched from Myanmar's Irrawaddy delta all the way to Cambodia.

The city lies on the banks of the Mae Klong River and is connected to the rest of Central Thailand by canal. Chom Bung district, in a north-west section of the province, is the site for a large 'holding centre' (a Thai government euphemism for refugee camp) for Burmese and Karens fleeing political persecution in Myanmar.

The town itself isn't overly impressive, though the main market near the clock tower and the town's river setting make a stop not entirely unpleasant. Some people spend the night here to get an early start on Damnoen Saduak floating market.

### Information
**Money** The First Bangkok City Bank at 250/18 Kraiphet Rd has an exchange facility, and is open weekdays from 8.30 am to 3.30 pm.

**Post Office** The post and international telephone office is on the corner of Samutsadarak and Amarin Rds. The phone office upstairs is open daily from 7 am to 10 pm.

### Things to See & Do
In the north-western part of town near the Mae Klong River, the historical **Wat Phra Si Ratana Mahathat** is known for its prang, which is said to be styled after the main prang at Angkor Wat. It is doubtful that it was constructed by the Khmers in the 10th or 11th century as local literature suggests – most likely it was erected during the Ayuthaya period. The wat is a 20 minute walk from the municipal market or a 15 to 20B samlor ride (30B by tuk-tuk) from the clock tower near the market.

Two km south-west of the town centre is the abandoned hill monastery **Khao Wang**. Originally built as a palace for Rama V, who only used it once in 1877, it was later converted to Wat Khao Wang by Rama VII. The main wihãan has been restored.

Along the Ratchaburi-Suan Phung Rd, about seven km west of town via Route 3087, is a **hermit cave** *(thãm reusĩi)* containing a famous Dvaravati-period stone Buddha image. Roughly 20m high, the gilded image represents the preaching of the first sermon. Monkeys have taken the figure over and have plenty of fun running along the top of it. To get to the cave, known as Phra Phutthachai Tham Reusii Khao Ngu, take one of the numerous minibuses departing from the market near the clock tower. The fare is 4B, and the journey takes about 12 minutes.

**Ratchaburi Ceramics** Ratchaburi is very well known amongst Thais for its ceramics industry, particularly the large brown-glazed water jars etched with cream-coloured dragon motifs (from whence they get their common farang name, 'dragon jars').

To see dragon jars being made, visit Rong Ong Tao Heng Tai Factory at 234 Chedihak Rd, a 20B samlor or 25 to 30B tuk-tuk ride from the clock tower.

The province also boasts beautiful *benjarong* ceramics, small porcelain jars with intricate multicoloured (traditionally five hues) patterns. Ratanakosin Factory, about three km north of town on the highway to Bangkok, is your best bet for viewing or shopping.

**Places to Stay**
*Kuang Hua Hotel* (☎ 337119), at 202 Amarin Rd, has reasonable basic rooms for 120B with fan and bath, or 100B with shared facilities. The *Hong Fa Hotel* (☎ 337484) at 89/13 Rat Yindi Rd has rooms with fan and bath from 150B. Other hotels include the *Araya* (☎ 337781/2) at 187/1-2 Kraiphet Rd, with not-so-clean rooms for 250B with fan, or 350B with air-con and TV. Almost opposite is the best value in town, the *Namsin Hotel* (☎ 337551) at 2/16 Kraiphet Rd, where good rooms are 220B with fan and 350B with air-con.

**Places to Eat**
There are plenty of food stalls at the market on the bank of the Mae Klong River. Stalls spread out through the streets all the way to Rotfai Rd, along which runs the train line. This is also a good area for all types of shopping, with a variety of shops lining the streets.

The friendly *Arharnthai* at 142 Katathon Rd, in front of the train station, serves a wide variety of Thai dishes from 40 to 120B.

**Getting There & Away**
**Bus** The ordinary buses to/from Bangkok are stationed on Rotfai Rd, just around the corner from Kraiphet Rd. The fare is 34B and the trip takes 1½ hours. Air-con buses to Bangkok (54B) arrive and depart from in front of the Namsin Hotel on Kraiphet Rd.

Minibuses to Damnoen Saduak depart from Rotfai Rd, near the corner of Kraiphet Rd, and cost 20B. Buses to Phetburi cost 16B and take an hour.

**Train** Ratchaburi is on the southern line from Bangkok, with nine daily trains passing through. Train can be faster than bus since trains don't have to fight Bangkok traffic to reach the city limits. The fare to/from Bangkok is 25B in 3rd class and 52B in 2nd class (plus rapid or express surcharges for the latter); the trip takes about two hours no matter which train you choose.

Ordinary trains between Ratchaburi and Phetburi cost 11B for 3rd class and take about 40 minutes.

**Getting Around**
Samlors around town cost 10 to 15B, or to the outskirts of town 25B. Tuk-tuks are 20 to 30B. This must be one of the only towns in Thailand which prohibits motorcycle taxis from the centre of town, to protect the samlor service (and the urban environment).

**AROUND RATCHABURI**
**Damnoen Saduak Floating Market**
If the commercialisation of Bangkok's floating markets puts you off, there is a much more lively floating market *(talàat náam)* on Khlong Damnoen Saduak in Ratchaburi Province, 104 km south-west of Bangkok, between Nakhon Pathom and Samut Songkhram.

**Talaat Ton Khem** is the main, hundred year old market on Khlong Damnoen Saduak Canal, while **Talaat Hia Kui**, just south on the parallel Khlong Hia Kui, gets the most tourists – one area in fact has been set aside especially for tourists, with a large open shop with souvenirs for bus tours as well as souvenir-laden boats. There is a third, less crowded

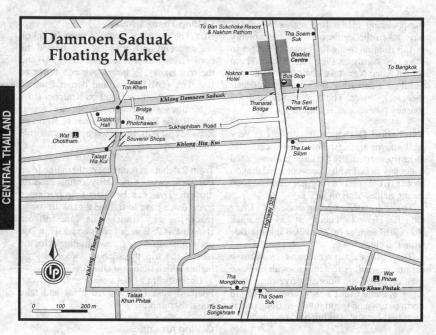

**Damnoen Saduak Floating Market**

market on a smaller canal, a bit south of Damnoen Saduak, called **Talaat Khun Phitak**. To get there, take a water taxi going south from the pier on the east side of Khlong Thong Lang Canal, which intersects Damnoen Saduak near the larger floating market, and ask for Talaat Khun Phitak. You can rent a boat to tour the canals and all three markets for 150 to 200B per hour (300B if you stay till the markets close around 11 am) depending on your bargaining skills. Try to arrive by 8 am at the latest – by 9 am the package tours are in full evidence.

Less touristed floating markets can be reached by boating south from Damnoen Saduak to Amphawa district in Samut Songkhram Province – see the Samut Songkhram section for details.

**Places to Stay** One sure way to beat the tour buses from Bangkok is to spend the night in Damnoen Saduak itself and get up before the hordes of tourists arrive. There's enough to

see to justify spending a night and a day, perhaps longer. Try the clean and quiet *Noknoi (Little Bird)*, where rooms cost 100 to 140B with fan, 170 to 250B with air-con. Noknoi is just a five minute walk from the Talaat Ton Khem.

*Ban Sukchoke Resort* (☎ (32) 253044; fax 254301) offers comfortable bungalows set over the canal from 250B. Ban Sukchoke is 1.5 km north-west of Damnoen's market area.

**Getting There & Away** Bus No 78 goes direct from Bangkok's Southern Bus Terminal to Damnoen Saduak every 20 minutes, beginning at 6.20 am, but you'll have to get one of the first few buses to arrive in Damnoen Saduak by 8 or 9 am, when the market's at its best. Air-con buses start at 6 am. The trip lasts just short of two hours under normal road conditions. The fare is 49B for air-con or 30B for an ordinary bus.

From the pier nearest the bus station (Thai

Seri Khani Kaset), take a 20B water taxi to the floating market (talàat náam) or simply walk 10 minutes west and south from the station along the canal until you come to the Hia Kui market area, where most of the rental boats are found.

Some people spend the night in Nakhon Pathom and catch an early morning bus to Samut Songkhram, asking to be let out at Damnoen Saduak.

It is also possible to get to Damnoen Saduak by bus (6B) from Samut Songkhram, a trip of around 25 minutes; Samut Songkhram is much closer to Damnoen Saduak (20 minutes by bus), and some people find it a better place to stay. A minibus to or from Ratchaburi costs 20B.

One interesting way to return to Bangkok from Damnoen Saduak is by boat via Samut Sakhon. From Khlong Damnoen Saduak, take a 30 km trip by long-tail boat (reua haang yao) to Bang Yang lock, where you can catch a ferry up the Tha Chin River, getting off at Tha Angton pier on the river's right bank. From Tha Angton you can catch a bus or songthaew to Samut Sakhon (you may have to change in Kratum Baen along the way). The total boat fare is around 16B and includes a boat change halfway at Ban Phaew – worth it for what is considered one of Thailand's most beautiful stretches of waterway.

### Wat Khongkharam

This 200 year old Mon monastery used to be called Wat Klang or Phia To. The main hall has a large Buddha image and several other smaller images. Surrounding them on the walls are some beautiful frescoes, half of which are rain-damaged and faded with age. To see inside, ask one of the monks to open the wihāan.

**Getting There & Away**  Take a bus from the corner of Kraiphet and Rotfai Rds in Ratchaburi to Klong Ta Kot. The trip costs 11B and takes about 40 minutes. Once in Klong Ta Kot, take a motorcycle taxi to the wat for 10 or 30B return.

# Samut Sakhon & Samut Songkhram Provinces

## SAMUT SAKHON
• ☎ (34)  • pop 55,800
Twenty-eight km south-west of Bangkok, Samut Sakhon (Ocean City) is popularly known as Mahachai because it straddles the confluence of the Tha Chin River and Khlong Mahachai. Just a few km from the Gulf of Thailand, this busy port features a lively market area and a pleasant breezy park around the crumbling walls of **Wichian Chodok Fort**. A few rusty cannon pointing towards the river testify to the fort's original purpose of guarding the mouth of the Chao Phraya River from foreign invaders. Before the 17th century arrival of European traders, the town was known as Tha Jiin (Chinese Pier) because of the large number of Chinese junks that called here.

A few km west of Samut Sakhon, along Highway 35 is the Ayuthaya-period **Wat Yai Chom Prasat**, which is known for the finely carved wooden doors on its bòt. You can easily identify the wat from the road by the tall Buddha figure standing in front. To get here from Samut Sakhon, take a westbound bus (3B) heading towards Samut Songkhram; the wat is only a 10 minute ride from the edge of town.

In Ban Phaew district, around 30 km north-west of Samut Sakhon via Highway 35 (west) and Route 3079 (north), the **Khlong Pho Hak Floating Market** (talàat náam khlawng phoh hàk) convenes daily except on wan phrá (full and new moon days) from 4 to 7.30 or 8 am. To get there, take a songthaew or bus to Ban Phaew (around 10B) and then catch a long-tail boat taxi along Khlong Pho Hak to the market eight km away – if you share with a group of Thais going to the market the fare should be no more than 10B apiece. It may also be possible to reach this market by chartered long-tail boat from Samut Sakhon through a network of canals. The market is also known as talàat náam làk 5 (Km 5 Floating Market).

CENTRAL THAILAND

## Places to Stay & Eat

Inland from the park, Samut Sakhon is basically a gritty urban satellite of Bangkok. The selection of places to stay is pretty downbeat and I don't recommend an overnight here. Nonetheless if you're stuck, you can try the *Wiang Thai Hotel* (☎ 411151) at 821/5 Sukhonthawit Rd; OK rooms cost 180B with fan, 220B with air-con.

Towards the harbour, Norasing Rd (off Sethakit Rd) fills with food stalls at night, making it a great spot for inexpensive dinners. *Tarua (Thaa Reua) Restaurant*, on the 1st floor of the ferry terminal building at the harbour end of Sethakit Rd, is a good seafood place with an English-language menu and seafood dishes ranging from 50 to 100B. *New Sathip* and *Wang Nam Khem* at 927/42 and 927/179 Sethakit Rd serve standard Thai and Chinese dishes at reasonable prices.

## Getting There & Away

Ordinary buses to Samut Sakhon (22B) depart from Bangkok's Southern Bus Terminal all day long. The trip takes about an hour. Buses between Samut Sakhon and Samut Songkhram cost 11B and take about half an hour.

Samut Sakhon is nearly midway along the 3rd class, short-line train route that runs between Thonburi (Bangkok Noi) station and Samut Songkhram. The fare to/from either Thonburi or Samut Songkhram is 8B; there are only four departures a day.

## Getting Around

Samlors and motorbike taxis around town cost 10 to 20B depending on the distance.

## SAMUT SONGKHRAM

• ☎ (34) • pop 34,000

Wedged between Ratchaburi, Samut Sakhon and Phetburi, 416 sq km Samut Songkhram is Thailand's smallest province. Commonly known as 'Mae Klong', the capital lies along a sharp bend in the Mae Klong River, 74 km south-west of Bangkok and just a few km from the Gulf of Thailand. Due to flat topography and abundant water sources, the area surrounding the capital is well suited for the steady irrigation needed to grow guava, lychee and grapes. Along the highway from Thonburi, visitors will pass a string of artificial sea lakes used in the production of salt. A profusion of coconut palms makes the area look unusually lush, considering its proximity to Bangkok.

Samut Songkhram would make a good jumping-off point for early morning forays to Damnoen Saduak Floating Market, 20 minutes away by bus. It does have some decent floating markets of its own, however.

## Information

The Thai Farmers Bank at 125/5 Prasitphatthana Rd offers foreign exchange services weekdays from 10 am to 4 pm.

## Things to See

The capital itself is a fairly modern city with a large market area between the train line and bus terminal. The sizeable **Wat Phet Samut Worawihaan** in the centre of town near the train station and river contains a renowned Buddha image called Luang Phaw Wat Baan Laem – named after the *phrá sàksìt* (holy monk) who dedicated it, thus transferring mystical powers to the image.

At the mouth of the Mae Klong River, not far from town, is the province's most famous tourist attraction, a bank of fossilised shells known as **Don Hoi Lot**. The type of shells embedded in the bank come from *hǎwy làwt*, clams with a tube-like shell. The shell bank is best seen late in the dry season (typically April and May) when the river surface has receded to its lowest height. Many seafood restaurants have been built at the edge of Don Hoi Lot, encroaching on a crab-eating macaque habitat. About 200 remaining simians are threatened by the development. To get to Don Hoi Lot you need to charter a boat from the Mae Klong Market pier *(thâa talàat mâe klawng)*. The trip takes about 45 minutes.

Another local attraction is the **Orchid Farm**, four km north of town on the road to Damnoen Saduak. In spite of its basic commercial function – and side function as a tourist trap – the farm is really quite impressive for its colour. A bus to the farm costs 3B and takes about 10 minutes.

Some of the most picturesque countryside I've seen this close to Bangkok lies along Highway 325 between Damnoen Saduak and Samut Songkhram. Coconut plantations interspersed with small wooden houses line the road and add to the laid-back atmosphere.

**Floating Markets** Samut Songkhram Province is crisscrossed with canals intersecting the lazy bends of the Mae Khlong River, creating the perfect environment for traditional Thai floating markets. Three of the better ones are held in Amphawa district, about seven km north-west of the Samut Songkhram city via the Mae Klong River. The **Amphawa Floating Market** *(talàat náam ampháwaa)* convenes daily in front of Wat Amphawa from 6 to 8 am but is best on weekends. The other two meet only six days a month following the traditional lunar calendar: **Bang Noi Floating Market** takes place in nearby Bang Noi from 6 to 11 am on the third, eighth and 13th days of both the waxing and waning moons, while the **Tha Kha Floating Market** meets on the second, seventh and 12th days of the waxing and waning moons. The latter convenes along an open, breezy khlong lined with greenery and older wooden houses – worth seeking out.

Any common Thai calendar, available for a few baht in a housewares market, will show you which days of the solar month coincide with this lunar schedule. These floating markets can be visited by chartered long-tail boat from the Mae Klong Market pier – figure on 150 to 200B per hour depending on negotiation, 300B for all morning.

**Places to Stay & Eat**
There are four hotels in the centre of the city, none of them very quiet. The cheapest is the *Thai Sawat* (☎ 711205) at 524 Phet Samut Rd, where basic rooms with fan cost 100 to 150B. Also inexpensive is the nearby *Mae Klong Hotel* (☎ 711150) at 546/10-13 Phet Samut Rd, opposite Wat Phet Samut Worawihaan. The owners are pleasant, speak some English and can provide information

on the area. The rooms are fairly clean and cost 120 to 150B with a fan or 350B with air-con.

Somewhat better, the *Alongkorn 1 Hotel* (☎ 711017) at 541/15 Kasem Sukhum Rd and *Alongkorn 2 Hotel* (☎ 711709) at 540 Pomkaew Rd are only separated by the cinema on busy Kasem Sukhum Rd. They have very similar rooms and standards at 120B with fan and 170/220B with air-con.

In front of Wat Phet Samut, along Phet Samut Rd, are several food stalls open all day and evening. There is also a lively night market in the square near the bus and taxi stands along Prasitphatthana Rd. *Tang Khai Hong* at 526/4 Phet Samut Rd is a very good Chinese place. *Suan Aahaan Tuk*, on the river off Soi Laem Yai, is a pleasant outdoor spot with an extensive Thai and Chinese menu.

On weekends the more adventurous might try *Jungle Home Pub*, a Thai-folk-style cafe set in a rambling garden at the end of Soi Thanai Khong, off Ekachai Rd. It's hard to find on your own, but a tuk-tuk from the market should only cost 15B. It's run by a Bohemian Thai couple and is a good spot to enjoy a beer or herbal liquor at the end of the day. It's only open Friday, Saturday and Sunday evenings from 4 pm.

**Getting There & Away**
Buses and taxis park at the intersection of Ratchayat Raksa and Prasitphatthana Rds. Buses to/from Bangkok depart and arrive here, but some buses from Bangkok may drop you off on the main highway, from where you can either walk or take a samlor or a songthaew (5B). The fare is 22B in an ordinary bus or 40B in an air-con one; either takes about 1½ hours. There are also many daily buses to Samut Sakhon for 11B, taking about an hour.

Samut Songkhram is the southernmost terminus of a 70 km train line that originates at Thonburi (Bangkok Noi) station, a journey of about an hour. The all 3rd class train to/from Bangkok costs 16B (8B to/from Samut Sakhon), and there are four departures per day. The train station is a five minute walk from the bus station, where Kasem Sukhum Rd terminates at Prasitphatthana Rd near the river.

CENTRAL THAILAND

# Kanchanaburi Province

The town of Kanchanaburi was originally established by Rama I as a first line of defence against the Burmese, who might use the old invasion route through the Three Pagodas Pass on the Thailand-Myanmar border. It's still a popular smuggling route into Myanmar today.

During WWII, the Japanese occupation used Allied prisoners of war to build the infamous Death Railway along this same invasion route, in reverse, along the Khwae

Noi River to the pass. Thousands of prisoners died as a result of brutal treatment by their captors, their experiences chronicled by Pierre Boulle in his book *The Bridge Over the River Kwai* and popularised by the movie of the same name. The bridge is still there (still in use, in fact) and so are the graves of the Allied soldiers.

West and north-west of Kanchanaburi city are several of Thailand's largest waterfalls and most extensive wildlife sanctuaries. Most of the province, in fact, remains sparsely populated and wild.

## KANCHANABURI
อ.เมืองกาญจนบุรี
• ☎ *(34)* • *pop 37,000*

Kanchanaburi lies 130 km west of Bangkok in the slightly elevated valley of the Mae Klong River amidst hills and sugar cane plantations. The weather here is slightly cooler than in Bangkok and the evenings can be especially pleasant by contrast. Kan (as the locals call it; also Kan'buri) receives enough tourists to warrant its own tourist office but as a proportion of total visitation, not that many western visitors make it here. Most tourists are Thai, Japanese, or Hong Kong and Singapore Chinese, who blaze through on air-con buses, hitting the River Khwae Bridge, the cemetery on Saengchuto Rd, the war museum, and then hurry off to the nearby sapphire mines or one of the big waterfalls before heading north to Chiang Mai or back to Bangkok.

The Mae Klong River itself is a focus for much weekend and holiday activity among the Thais. In recent years the city has given the waterfront area a face-lift, planting casuarina trees and moving most of the floating restaurants offshore. A new bridge spanning the river, another bridge on the way and a new highway bypass north-east of town signify that development has arrived in what was previously a provincial backwater.

You may notice the fish-shaped street signs in Meuang Kan – they represent *plaa yisok*, the most common food fish in the Mae Klong River and its tributaries.

### Information
**Tourist Office** The TAT office (☎ 511200) is on Saengchuto Rd, on the right before the police station as you enter town from Bangkok. A free map of the town and province is available, as well as comprehensive information on accommodation and transport. Hours are from 8.30 am to 4.30 pm daily. The office now has a contingent of tourist police – any problems with theft or other criminal occurrences should be reported to both the tourist police and the regular provincial police.

**Money** All the major Thai banks are represented and offer both foreign exchange services and ATMs. The highest concentration of banks is found on and off Saengchuto Rd in the vicinity of the market and bus terminal.

Punnee Cafe (☎ /fax 513503) on Ban Neua Rd has a moneychanging service that's useful on weekends and holidays.

**Post & Communications** The GPO on Saengchuto Rd is open weekdays from 8.30 am to 4.30 pm, Saturday from 9 am to 12 pm; international telephone service is available daily from 7 am to 11 pm. There is also a small post office on Lak Meuang Rd towards the river, close to the Lak Meuang Shrine.

### Death Railway Bridge
สะพานข้ามแม่น้ำแคว

The so-called Bridge Over the River Kwai may be of interest to war historians but really looks quite ordinary. It spans the Khwae Yai River, a tributary of the Mae Klong River, three km from Kanchanaburi's *làk meuang* (town pillar/phallus). Khwae Yai literally translates as 'large tributary'. It is the story behind the bridge that is dramatic. The materials for the bridge were brought from Java by the Imperial Japanese Army during their occupation of Thailand. In 1945 the bridge was bombed several times and was only rebuilt after the war – the curved portions of the bridge are original. The first version of the bridge, completed in February 1943, was all wood. In April of the same year a second bridge of steel was constructed.

It is estimated that 16,000 POWs died while building the Death Railway to Myanmar, of which the bridge was only a small part. The strategic objective of the railway was to secure an alternative supply route for the Japanese conquest of Myanmar and other Asian countries to the west. Construction of the railway began on 16 September 1942 at existing terminals in Thanbyuzayat, Myanmar and Nong Pladuk, Thailand. Japanese engineers at the time estimated that it would take five years to link Thailand and Myanmar by rail, but the Japanese army forced the POWs to complete the 415 km, one metre gauge

CENTRAL THAILAND

railway (of which roughly two-thirds ran through Thailand) in 16 months. Much of the railway was built in difficult terrain that required high bridges and deep mountain cuttings. The rails were finally joined 37 km south of Three Pagodas Pass; a Japanese brothel train inaugurated the line. The River Khwae Bridge was in use for 20 months before the Allies bombed it in 1945. Only one POW is known to have escaped, a Briton who took refuge among pro-British Karen guerrillas.

Although the number of POWs who died during the Japanese occupation is horrifying, the figures for the labourers, many from Thailand, Myanmar, Malaysia and Indonesia, are even worse. It is thought that 90,000 to 100,000 coolies died in the area.

Today little remains of the original railway. West of Nam Tok, Karen and Mon carried off most of the track to use in the construction of local buildings and bridges.

Train nuts may enjoy the **railway museum** in front of the bridge, with engines used during WWII on display. Every year during the first week of December there is a nightly sound & light show at the bridge, commemorating the Allied attack on the Death Railway in 1945. It's a pretty big scene, with the sounds of bombers and explosions, fantastic bursts of light, and more. The town gets a lot of Thai tourists during this week, so book early if you want to witness this spectacle.

There are a couple of large outdoor restaurants near the bridge, on the river, but these are for tour groups that arrive en masse throughout the day. If you're hungry, you can save money by eating with the tour bus and songthaew drivers in the little noodle places at the northern end of Pak Phraek Rd.

**Getting There & Away** The best way to get to the bridge from town is to catch a songthaew along Pak Phraek Rd (parallel to Saengchuto Rd towards the river) heading north. Regular songthaews are 5B and stop at the bridge, which is about three km from the làk meuang. You can also take a train from the Kanchanaburi train station to the bridge for 2B.

## Allied War Cemeteries
สุสานทหาร

There are two cemeteries containing the remains of Allied POWs who died in captivity during WWII; one is north of town off Saengchuto Rd, just before the train station, and the other is across the Mae Klong River west of town, a few km down the Khwae Noi (Little Tributary) River.

The **Kanchanaburi Allied War Cemetery** is better cared for, with green lawns and healthy flowers. It's usually a cool spot on a hot Kanchanaburi day. It's only a 15 minute walk from the River Kwai Hotel or you can catch a songthaew anywhere along Saengchuto Rd going north – the fare is 5B. Jump off at the English sign in front of the cemetery on the left, or ask to be let off at the *sùsăan* (Thai for cemetery). Just before the cemetery on the same side of the road is a very colourful Chinese cemetery with burial mounds and inscribed tombstones.

To get to the **Chung Kai Allied War Cemetery**, take a 2B ferry boat from the pier at the west end of Lak Meuang Rd across the Mae Klong, then follow the curving road through picturesque corn and sugar cane fields until you reach the cemetery on your left. This is a fairly long walk, but the scenery along the way is very pleasant. You can also easily take a bicycle over the new bridge here. Like the more visited cemetery north of town, the Chung Kai burial plaques carry names, military insignia and short epitaphs for Dutch, British, French and Australian soldiers.

About a km south-west of the Chung Kai cemetery is a dirt path that leads to **Wat Tham Khao Pun**, one of Kanchanaburi's many cave temples. The path is approximately one km long and passes through thick forest with a few wooden houses along the way. This wat became notorious in late 1995 when a drug-addicted monk living at the wat murdered a British tourist and disposed of her corpse in a nearby sinkhole. Kan residents – like the rest of Thailand – were absolutely mortified by the crime and many now refer to the cave as 'Johanne's Cave' in memory of the victim. The monk was de-frocked and sentenced to death (commuted to life imprisonment without parole by the king in 1996).

## JEATH War Museum
พิพิธภัณฑ์สงคราม

This odd museum next to Wat Chaichumphon (Wat Tai) is worth visiting just to sit on the cool banks of the Mae Klong. Phra Maha Tomson Tongproh, a Thai monk who devotes much energy to promoting the museum, speaks some English and can answer questions about the exhibits, as well as supply information about what to see around Kanchanaburi and how best to get there. If you show him this book, he'll give you a 5B discount off the usual 20B admission. The museum itself is a replica example of the bamboo-atap huts used to house Allied POWs during the occupation. The long huts contain various photographs taken during the war, drawings and paintings by POWs, maps, weapons and other war memorabilia. The acronym JEATH represents the fated meeting of Japan, England, Australia/America, Thailand and Holland at Kanchanaburi during WWII.

The war museum is at the end of Wisuttharangsi (Visutrangsi) Rd, near the TAT office. The common Thai name for this museum is *phíphítháphan sŏngkhram wát tâi*. It's open daily from 8.30 am to 4.30 pm.

## WWII Museum
พิพิธภัณฑ์สงครามที่

Also called Art Gallery & War Museum, this new, somewhat garish structure just south of the famous bridge on the river looks like a Chinese temple on the outside. The larger, more lavishly built of the two buildings has nothing to do with WWII and little to do with art unless you include the garish murals throughout. The bottom floor contains Burmese-style alabaster Buddhas and a *phrá khreûang* (sacred amulets) display. Upper floors exhibit Thai weaponry from the Ayuthaya period and a fair collection of historic and modern ceramics. Brightly painted portraits of all the kings in Thai history fill the 4th floor. Finally, on the 5th and uppermost floor

– above the royal portraits (flirting with lese-majesty) – is the history of the Chinese family who built the museum, complete with a huge portrait of the family's original patriarch in China.

A smaller building opposite contains WWII relics, including photos and sketches made during the POW period and a display of Japanese and Allied weapons. Along the front of this building stand life-size sculptures of historical figures associated with the war, including Churchill, MacArthur, Hitler, Einstein, de Gaulle and Hirohito. The English captions are sometimes unintentionally amusing or disturbing – a reference to the atomic bomb dropped on Hiroshima, for example, reads 'Almost the entire city was destroyed in a jiffy'. Inside, a glass case contains 106 skeletons unearthed in a mass grave of Asian labourers. The gossip around town says these remains were stolen from a municipal excavation. The museum is open from 9 am to 4.30 pm daily. Entry is 30B.

## Lak Meuang Shrine
ศาลหลักเมือง

Like many other older Thai cities, Kanchanaburi has a làk meuang (town pillar/phallus) enclosed in a shrine at what was originally the town centre. Kanchanaburi's Lak Meuang Shrine is appropriately located on Lak Meuang Rd, which intersects Saengchuto Rd two blocks north of the TAT office.

The bulbous-tipped pillar is covered with gold leaf and is much worshipped. Unlike Bangkok's Lak Meuang you can get as close to this pillar as you like – no curtain.

Within sight of the pillar, towards the river, stands Kanchanaburi's original **city gate**.

## Wat Tham Mongkon Thong
วัดถ้ำมังกรทอง

The Cave Temple of the Golden Dragon is well known because of the 'floating nun' – a *mâe chii* who meditates while floating on her back in a pool of water. If you are lucky you might see her, but she seems to be doing this less frequently nowadays (try a Sunday). A nun now in her late 70s began the floating tradition and has passed it on to a younger disciple. Thais come from all over Thailand to see the younger nun float and to receive her blessings. A sizeable contingent of young Thai nuns stay here under the old nun's tutelage.

A long and steep series of steps with dragon-sculpted handrails lead up the craggy mountainside behind the main bòt to a complex of limestone caves. Follow the string of light bulbs through the front cave and you'll come out above the wat with a view of the valley and mountains below. One section of the cave requires crawling or duck-walking, so wear appropriate clothing. Bats squeak away above your head and the smell of guano permeates the air.

Another cave wat is off this same road about one or two km from Wat Tham Mongkon Thong towards the pier. It can be seen on a limestone outcrop back from the road some 500m or so. The name is **Wat Tham Khao Laem**. The cave is less impressive than that at Wat Tham Mongkon Thong, but there are some interesting old temple buildings on the grounds.

**Getting There & Away** Heading south-east down Saengchuto Rd from the TAT office, turn right on Chukkadon Rd (marked in English – about halfway between the TAT and GPO), or take a songthaew (3B) from the town centre to the end of Chukkadon Rd. A bridge has replaced the river ferry that used to cross here; wait for any songthaew crossing the bridge and you can be dropped off in front of the temple for 5B.

The road to the wat passes sugar cane fields, karst formations, wooden houses, cattle and rock quarries. Alternatively you could ride a bicycle from town – the road can be dusty in the dry season but at least it's flat.

**Wat Tham Seua & Wat Tham Khao Noi**
วัดถ้ำเสือและวัดถ้ำเขาน้อย
These large hill-top monasteries about 15 km south-east of Kanchanaburi are important local pilgrimage spots, especially for Chinese Buddhists. Wat Tham Khao Noi

(Little Hill Cave Monastery) is a Chinese temple monastery similar in size and style to Penang's Kek Lok Si. Adjacent is the half-Thai, half-Chinese-style Wat Tham Seua (Tiger Cave Monastery). Both are built on a ridge over a series of small caves. Wat Tham Khao Noi isn't much of a climb, since it's built onto the side of the slope. Seeing Wat Tham Seua, however, means climbing either a steep set of naga stairs or a meandering set of steps past the cave entrance.

A climb to the top is rewarded with views of the Khwae River on one side, rice fields on the other. Wat Tham Seua features a huge sitting Buddha facing the river, with a conveyor belt that carries money offerings to a huge alms bowl in the image's lap. The easier set of steps to the right of the temple's naga stairs leads to a cave and passes an aviary with peacocks and other exotic birds. The cave itself has the usual assortment of Buddha images.

**Getting There & Away** By public transport, you can take a bus to Tha Meuang (12 km south-east of Kan), then a motorcycle taxi (30B) from near Tha Meuang Hospital directly to the temples.

If you're travelling by motorcycle or bicycle, take the right fork of the highway when you reach Tha Meuang, turn right past the hospital onto a road along the canal and then across the dam (Meuang Dam). From here to Wat Tham Seua and Khao Noi is another four km. Once you cross the dam, turn right down the other side of the river and follow this unpaved road 1.4 km, then turn left towards the pagodas, which can easily be seen in the distance at this point. The network of roads leading to the base of the hill offers several route possibilities – just keep an eye on the pagodas and you'll be able to make the appropriate turns.

By bicycle, you can avoid taking the highway by using back roads along the river. Follow Pak Phraek Rd in Kan south-east and cross the bridge towards Wat Tham Mongkon Thong, then turn left on the other side and follow the gravel road parallel to the river. Eventually (after about 14 km) you'll see the

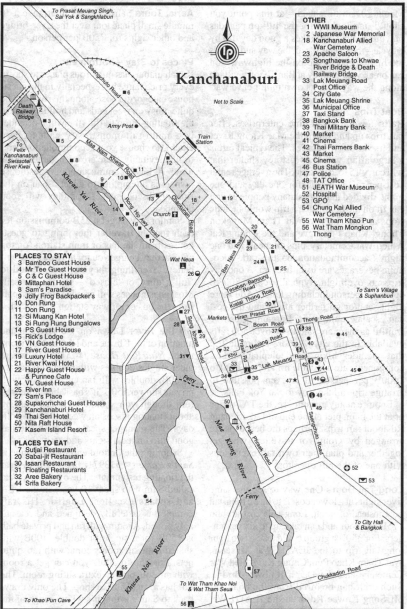

# Kanchanaburi

Not to Scale

**OTHER**
1 WWII Museum
2 Japanese War Memorial
18 Kanchanaburi Allied
   War Cemetery
23 Apache Saloon
26 Songthaews to Khwae
   River Bridge & Death
   Railway Bridge
33 Lak Meuang Road
   Post Office
34 City Gate
35 Lak Meuang Shrine
36 Municipal Office
37 Taxi Stand
38 Bangkok Bank
39 Thai Military Bank
40 Market
41 Cinema
42 Thai Farmers Bank
43 Market
45 Cinema
46 Bus Station
47 Police
48 TAT Office
51 JEATH War Museum
52 Hospital
53 GPO
54 Chung Kai Allied
   War Cemetery
55 Wat Tham Khao Pun
56 Wat Tham Mongkon
   Thong

**PLACES TO STAY**
3 Bamboo Guest House
4 Mr Tee Guest House
5 C & C Guest House
6 Mittaphan Hotel
8 Sam's Paradise
9 Jolly Frog Backpacker's
10 Don Rung
11 Don Rung
12 Si Muang Kan Hotel
13 Si Rung Rung Bungalows
14 PS Guest House
15 Rick's Lodge
16 VN Guest House
17 River Guest House
19 Luxury Hotel
21 River Kwai Hotel
22 Happy Guest House
   & Punnee Cafe
24 VL Guest House
25 River Inn
27 Sam's Place
28 Supakornchai Guest House
29 Kanchanaburi Hotel
49 Thai Seri Hotel
50 Nita Raft House
57 Kasem Island Resort

**PLACES TO EAT**
7 Sutjai Restaurant
20 Sabai-jit Restaurant
30 Isaan Restaurant
31 Floating Restaurants
32 Aree Bakery
44 Srifa Bakery

To Prasat Meuang Singh,
Sai Yok & Sangkhlaburi

Death
Railway
Bridge

To Felix
Kanchanaburi
Swissotel
River Kwai

Saengchuto Road

Mae Nam Khwae Road

Rong Hip Awy Road

Chaokunen Road

Ban Neua Road

Army Post

Train Station

Khwae Yai River

Church

Wat Neua

Tesaban Bamrung Road

Kratai Thong Road

Hiran Prasat Road

Bovon Road

U Thong Road

Song Khwae Road

Prasat Rd

Khu Meuang Road

Lak Meuang Road

Saengchuto Road

Pak Phraek Road

Mae Klong River

Ferry

To Sam's Village
& Suphanburi

To City Hall
& Bangkok

Khwae Noi River

Chukkadon Road

To Wat Tham Khao Noi
& Wat Tham Seua

To Khao Pun Cave

CENTRAL THAILAND

Meuang Dam up ahead – at this point you should start looking for the hill-top pagodas on your right. This makes a good day trip by bicycle – the road is flat all the way and avoids the high-speed traffic on the highway. You can break your journey at Ban Tham, a village along the way with its own minor cave wat.

## Boat Trips

**Rafts** Several small-time enterprises offer raft trips up and down the Mae Klong River and its various tributaries. The typical raft is a large affair with a two-storey shelter that will carry 15 to 20 people. The average rental cost per raft is 2000B for one day and one night, divided among as many people as you can fit on the boat. Such a trip would include stops at Hat Tha Aw, Wat Tham Mongkon Thong, Khao Pun Cave and the Chung Kai Allied War Cemetery, plus all meals and one night's accommodation on the raft. Alcoholic beverages are usually extra. A one day trip, no overnight, typically costs 300 to 400B per person including lunch. Add more nights and/or go farther afield and the cost can escalate quite a bit. Bargaining can be fruitful as there are said to be over 500 rafts available in the city. A more elaborate trip that includes hiking and elephant riding components are available for around 1100 to 1400B per person. It is even possible to arrange trips all the way to Sai Yok Falls.

Enquire at any guesthouse, the TAT office or at the main pier at the end of Lak Meuang Rd about raft trips. Perhaps the best trips are arranged by groups of travellers who get together and plan their own raft excursions with one of the raft operators.

**Long-Tail Boats** One way to see the same river sights at a lower cost is to hire a long-tail boat instead of a raft. Long-tails cost around 175B per hour and can take up to six passengers. For 350B a group could take a two hour long-tail trip to the JEATH War Museum, Wat Tham Khao Pun, Chung Kai Allied War Cemetery and the Death Railway Bridge. Such craft can be hired from the boat pier off Song Khwae Rd or at the JEATH War Museum.

**Aerial Tours** Sam's Place can arrange a 30 minute small plane tour over the river, bridge and other sights for 750B per person.

## Places to Stay – bottom end

Kanchanaburi has numerous places to stay in every price range but especially in the guesthouse category. Those along the river can be quite noisy on weekends and holidays due to the floating disco traffic (the worst offender is a multi-raft monstrosity called Disco Duck), so choose your accommodation carefully. Inevitably, there are even karaoke rafts now! A local commission of guesthouse owners is attempting to enact a ban on the floating discos, so perhaps they will soon disappear.

Samlor drivers get a 25B commission for each foreign traveller they bring to guesthouses from the bus or train station (on top of what they charge you for the ride), so don't believe everything they say with regard to 'full', 'dirty' or 'closed' – see for yourself. Most guesthouses will provide free transport from the bus or railway station if you call.

**On the River** Down on the river, at the junction of the Khwae and Khwae Noi rivers, is the *Nita Raft House* (☎ 514521), where older singles/doubles with mosquito net are 40/60B, doubles with fan are 100B, or with private shower 150B. It's basic but quite well run, though you should heed the warning about floating discos on weekends and holidays. The manager speaks English and has good info on local sights and activities.

Spanning the bottom end to mid-range is *Sam's Place* (☎ 513971; fax 512023), near the riverside restaurants. The owner is a local called Sam who spent 10 years in the USA and speaks excellent English. His raft complex is tastefully designed and reasonably priced. A room with fan and private bath is 150B for a single or double, 100B with shared bath; all rooms come with mosquito nets. For 250 to 300B you can get a room with air-con, plus an extra sitting room. The raft has a small coffee shop. The only drawback to Sam's is that it's within range of the floating discos.

If you want to stay out near the River Khwae Bridge (and away from the floating discos), the *Bamboo House* (☎ 512532) at 3-5 Soi Vietnam, on the river about a km before the Japanese war memorial off Mae Nam Khwae Rd, costs 100B per room with shared bath, 200B with fan and private bath, 450B with air-con. The owners are very friendly and the setting is peaceful.

Two popular places a little closer to the city centre (but also distant from Disco Duck) are the *River Guest House* (☎ 512491) and the *VN Guest House* (☎ 514082) where small, basic rooms in bamboo raft houses are 50 to 70B, 100 to 130B with bath. Both are in the same vicinity on the river, not far from the train station. They tend to get booked out in the high season. A bit farther north on the river is the similar *PS Guest House*, also a good choice at the same rates.

North of the VN, River and PS is the *Jolly Frog Backpacker's* (☎ 514579), a comparatively huge, 45-room 'bamboo motel' with a popular but nothing-special restaurant. Singles/doubles with shared bath are 50/90B; doubles with private bath are 130B. For samlor transport to any guesthouse in this vicinity, you shouldn't pay more than 10B from the train station, or 20 to 25B from the bus station.

A bit farther north-west along the river, at the end of Laos Rd, is *Mr Tee* (☎ (01) 948-2163), another two-storey thatched bamboo place. Rooms upstairs are 100B without bath, while downstairs rooms are 150B with private bath.

The latest additions to the riverside guesthouse scene are just south of Mr Tee. *C & C River Kwai Guest House* (☎ 624547), 265/2 Mae Nam Khwae Rd, Soi Angkrit (Soi England), offers clean rooms in quiet, semi-landscaped grounds for 100 to 150B with fan and private bath. You can also rent tents for 30 to 50B a night. The restaurant serves fish farmed in adjacent ponds. A bit farther south, below the bridge that crosses over to Sutjai Restaurant, *Sam's Paradise* is under construction. When finished it will feature 16 rooms in six bungalows built over the water for 100B with shared bath, 200B with private bath, 350B with air-con. As at the original Sam's Place, a terrace restaurant will be attached.

**In Town** On Pak Phraek Rd in the oldest section of town, just a block off the river, stands the ageing *Kanchanaburi Hotel*. With a little fixing up this classic could be turned into a real gem. For now, quite plain rooms cost 60/80B for one/two beds with shared bath only.

*Happy Guest House* (☎ 620848) sits next to Punnee Cafe and Valentine's Bar on Ban Neua Rd. Small but clean rooms cost 100 to 120B a single, 150B for a double with fan or 250 to 350B with air-con; some rooms come with attached bath, while others don't. Happy could be a bit noisy due to street and bar traffic.

### Places to Stay – middle

*Rick's Lodge* (☎ 514831) is along the river between the cheaper VN and PS guesthouses. Tastefully decorated bamboo accommodation with fan and private bath costs 280B on the river, 250B back from the river. Very near Sam's Place is *Supakornchai Guest House*, which is similar in scope but not quite as nice. Rooms with fan and bath are 150 to 200B for a large bed, or 300 to 350B for two beds.

One of the better places in this price range is the three-storey *VL Guest House*, across the street from the River Kwai Hotel. A clean, spacious room with fan and hot water bath is 150B for a single or double. Larger rooms sleeping four to eight people go for 50B per person. A double with air-con and hot water is 300B. The VL has a small dining area downstairs, and you can rent bicycles (20B per day) and motorcycles (from 200B). Another plus is the generous 2 pm checkout.

South of the River Kwai Hotel on Saengchuto, on the site of what once held an earlier version of the same hotel, the *River Inn* (☎ 511184) has decent air-con rooms for 450/700B a single/double.

The family that owns Sam's Place on the river has recently opened a good-value midrange place called *Sam's Village* just east of the city centre, next to a large lotus pond in a quiet housing development. Rooms in sturdy modern houses are 150B with two beds, ceiling fan and attached shower, 250B with air-con and hot water shower, or 350B with air-con, hot water bath and shower, and fridge. Bicycles and motorcycles are available for rent. To reach Sam's Village, head east on U Thong Rd over the train tracks and turn right just before the power station. Continue alongside the lotus pond till you see Sam's ahead.

Other hotels in town include the *Si Muang Kan* (☎ 511609), at 313/1-3 Saengchuto Rd (the north end), with clean singles/doubles with fan and bath for 100 to 170B, 350B with air-con; and the *Thai Seri Hotel* at the southern end of the same road, near the Visutrangsi Rd intersection and the TAT office, with somewhat dilapidated but adequate rooms from 120B.

*Wang Thong Bungalows* (☎ 511046) at 60/3 Saengchuto Rd, and *Boon Yang Bungalows* (☎ 512598) at 139/9 Saengchuto Rd, offer OK rooms in sturdy bungalows for 160 to 240B. In case you haven't figured this out on your own, bungalows (not the beach kind) are the upcountry equivalent of Bangkok's short-time hotels. They're off the road for the same reason that their Bangkok counterparts have heavy curtains over the carports – makes it difficult to spot license plate numbers. Still, they function well as tourist hotels too.

The bungalow-style *Luxury Hotel* (☎ 511-168) at 284/1-5 Saengchuto Rd is a couple of blocks north of the River Kwai Hotel, and not as centrally located, but good value. Clean one/two bed rooms with fan and bath start at 100/150B, 200 to 300B with air-con. Similar *Si Rung Rung Bungalows* (☎ 511087) has fan rooms with bath for 150B, with air-con for 250B. *Don Rung* (☎ 513755), up the street toward the bridge, has more of the same in buildings on both sides of the road.

**Places to Stay – top end**
Kanchanaburi's original first-class hotel, the *River Kwai Hotel* (☎ 511184/269) at 284/3-16 Saengchuto Rd offers semi-deluxe rooms with air-con, hot water, telephone and TV from

1400B. Facilities include a coffee shop, disco and swimming pool. Next door is the huge River Paradise massage parlour, bearing a sign on the door which reads 'No women allowed' (working masseuses are exempted of course).

Farther north along Saengchuto Rd, past the train station, is the new four-storey *Mittaphan Hotel* (☎ 514498; (2) 291-9953 in Bangkok). Standard rooms with all the amenities run 700 to 2000B. A large massage parlour and snooker club are next door.

The luxurious *Felix Kanchanaburi Swissotel River Kwai* (☎ 515061, fax 515095; ☎ (2) 255-3410, fax 255-5769 in Bangkok) sits on the west bank of the river, about two km north of the new one lane bridge. The very nicely landscaped grounds include two swimming pools. Spacious rooms with IDD phones, cable TV, minibar and personal safe cost 2300 to 3500B.

**River Resorts** The *Kasem Island Resort* (☎ 513359; (2) 255-3604 in Bangkok) sits on an island in the middle of the Mae Klong River just a couple of hundred metres from Tha Chukkadon pier. The tastefully designed thatched cottages and house rafts are cool, clean, quiet and go for 700 to 2000B. There are facilities for swimming, fishing and rafting as well as an outdoor bar and restaurant. The resort has an office near Tha Chukkadon pier where you can arrange for a free shuttle boat out to the island; shuttle service stops at 10 pm.

In the vicinity of the Death Railway Bridge are several river resorts of varying quality, most featuring standard wooden bungalows in the 800B range. Just above the bridge, two km before the turn-off for Highway 323, are the *Prasopsuk Garden Resort* (☎ 513215) with air-con town house doubles for 800B, air-con bungalows with two bedrooms for 1200B and large bungalows for 10 people for 2400B per night; and *River Kwai Lodge* (☎ 513657; (2) 251-4377 in Bangkok), where a large room for two is 600B with fan and bath or 800B with air-con. Just beyond the latter is *River Kwai Honeywell Resort* (☎ 515413), where bungalows with private bath on the river bank cost 800B.

JOE CUMMINGS

RICHARD NEBESKY

RICHARD NEBESKY

## Central Thailand
Top: Vendors at Amphawa Floating Market, Samut Songkhram
Middle: Caravan of woven mats bound for market, Aranya Prathet, Cambodian border
Bottom: Traditional teak homes along the Chanthaburi River

JOE CUMMINGS

RICHARD NEBESKY

## Central Thailand
Top: Three Pagodas Pass – for centuries a relay point for Burmese-Thai trade
Bottom: The riverways and lush tropical interior of Trat Province's Ko Chang

On the river, opposite Wat Tham Mongkon Thong to the south, the *Boon Sri River Kwai Resort* (☎ (01) 939-4185) offers more of the same for 400 to 800B a night.

## Places to Eat

The greatest proliferation of inexpensive restaurants in Kanchanaburi is along the northern end of Saengchuto Rd near the River Kwai Hotel. From here south, to where U Thong Rd crosses Saengchuto, are many good Chinese, Thai and Isaan-style restaurants. As elsewhere in Thailand, the best are generally the most crowded.

For years, one of the most popular has been the *Isaan*, on Saengchuto Rd between Hiran Prasat and Kratai Thong Rds. The Isaan still serves great kài yâang (whole spicy grilled chicken), khâo niāw (sticky rice), sôm-tam (spicy green papaya salad) as well as other Thai and local specialities and inexpensive, ice-cold beer. The kài yâang is grilled right out front and served with two sauces – the usual sweet and sour (náam jîm kài) and a roast red pepper sauce (náam phrík phâo).

Good, inexpensive eating places can also be found in the markets along Prasit Rd and between U Thong and Lak Meuang Rds east of Saengchuto Rd. In the evenings, a sizeable night market convenes along Saengchuto Rd near the Lak Meuang Rd intersection.

The *Sabai-jit Restaurant*, north of the River Kwai Hotel on Saengchuto Rd, has an English menu. Beer and Mekong whisky are sold here at quite competitive prices and the food is consistently good. Other Thai and Chinese dishes are served apart from those listed on the English menu. If you see someone eating something not listed, point.

*Punnee Cafe & Bar* (☎ 513503) on Ban Neua Rd serves Thai and European food according to expat tastes and advertises the coldest beer in town. Lots of info on Kanchanaburi is available here; there are also used paperback books for sale or trade.

Down on the river there are several large floating restaurants where the quality of the food varies but it's hard not to enjoy the atmosphere. Most of them are pretty good according to locals, but if you go, don't expect western food or large portions – if you know what to order, you could have a very nice meal here. Recommended are the *Thongnatee* and the *Mae Nam*. Across from the floating restaurants, along the road, are several restaurants that are just as good but less expensive; the best on this row is *Jukkru* (no English sign – look for blue tables and chairs). Although it's a little out of the way, one of the better riverside restaurants in town is *Sutjai*, a garden-style place on the west bank of the river next to the one lane bridge.

There are also food vendors on both sides of Song Khwae Rd along the river near the new park where you can buy inexpensive takeaways and picnic on mats along the riverbank. This is a festive and prosperous town and people seem to eat out a lot.

Two bakeries handle most of the pastry and bread business in Kan. *Srifa Bakery* on the north side of the bus terminal is the more modern of the two, with everything from French-style pastries to Singapore-style curry puffs. The *Aree Bakery* on Pak Phraek Rd around the corner from the Lak Meuang post office is less fancy but has coffee, tea, breakfast, ice cream and sandwiches plus tables and chairs for a sit-down break. Aree has great chicken curry puffs and very tasty young coconut pie.

## Entertainment

If the floating discos/karaoke bars on the river or the disco at the River Kwai Hotel don't appeal to you, try the *Apache Saloon* opposite the Sabai-jit Restaurant on Saengchuto Rd. This large, old-west-style bar/restaurant offers live folk-rock music nightly. *The Raft*, in front of the River Kwai Hotel, also features live Thai bands.

The *Beer Barrel Bar*, a couple of hundred metres south of C & C Guest House on Mae Nam Khwae Rd, is a nicely done outdoor beer garden with good prices.

## Getting There & Away

**Bus** Buses leave Bangkok from the Southern Bus Terminal in Thonburi every 20 minutes daily (beginning at 5 am, last bus at 10 pm)

CENTRAL THAILAND

338 Kanchanaburi Province – Kanchanaburi

for Kanchanaburi. The trip takes about three hours and costs 34B. Buses back to Bangkok leave Kanchanaburi between the same hours.

Air-con buses leave Bangkok's Southern Bus Terminal every 15 minutes from 5.30 am to 10 pm for 62B. These same buses depart Kanchanaburi for Bangkok from opposite the police station on Saengchuto Rd, not from the bus station. Air-con buses only take about two hours to reach Bangkok. The first bus out is at 5 am; the last one to Bangkok leaves at 7 pm.

There are frequent buses throughout the day from nearby Nakhon Pathom. Bus No 81 leaves from the east side of the Phra Pathom Chedi, costs 20B, and takes about 1½ hours. For travellers heading south, Nakhon Pathom makes a good connecting point – this way you avoid having to go back to Bangkok. Other frequent direct bus services are available to/from Ratchaburi (No 461, 26B, 2½ hours) and Suphanburi (No 411, 25B, 2½ to three hours).

**Train** Ordinary trains leave Thonburi (Bangkok Noi) station at 7.50 am and 1.45 pm, arriving at 10.55 am and 4.26 pm. Only 3rd class seats are available and the fare is 25B. Trains return to Bangkok from Kanchanaburi at 7.31 am and 3.21 pm, arriving at 10.35 am and 6.10 pm. Ordinary train tickets to Kanchanaburi can be booked on the day of departure only. There are no trains between Bangkok's Hualamphong station and Kanchanaburi.

You can also take the train from the Kanchanaburi station out to the Death Railway Bridge, a three minute ride for 2B. There are two trains per day at 6.10 am (No 353) and 10.55 am (No 171).

The same trains go on to the end of the train line at Nam Tok, which is near Sai Yok Falls. You can catch the train in Kanchanaburi at 6.10 or 10.55 am or at the bridge at 6.16 or 11 am; the fare is the same (17B). Nam Tok is eight km from Khao Pang Falls and 18 km from Hellfire Pass and the River Khwae village. A third train (No 197) makes the trip to Nam Tok daily, leaving Kan-

chanaburi at 4.26 pm. The trip to Nam Tok takes about two hours. Coming back from Nam Tok, there are trains at 5.25 am, 1.15 and 3.10 pm. The early morning trains between Kanchanaburi and Nam Tok (6.10 am) do not run on weekends and holidays.

**Tourist Train** The State Railway of Thailand (SRT) has a special tourist train from Bangkok's Hualamphong station on weekends and holidays which departs around 6.30 am and returns at 7.30 pm. The return fare is 250B for adults, 120B for children. It includes an hour-long stop in Nakhon Pathom to see the Phra Pathom Chedi, an hour at the Death Railway Bridge, a minibus to Prasat Meuang Singh Historical Park for a short tour, a walk along an elevated 'Death Railway' bridge (no longer in use), a three hour stop at the river for lunch and a bat cave visit, before returning to Bangkok with a one hour stopover at one of the war cemeteries. Also on weekends and holidays there's a direct train to Nam Tok, no stops, for 100B each way. These tickets should be booked in advance, although it's worth trying on the day even if you're told it's full. The SRT changes the tour itinerary and price from time to time.

**Share Taxi & Minivan** You can also take a share taxi from Saengchuto Rd to Bangkok for 50B per person. Taxis leave throughout the day whenever five passengers accumulate at the taxi stand. These taxis will make drops at Khao San Rd or in the Pahurat district. Kanchanaburi guesthouses also arrange daily minivans to Bangkok for 80B per person. Passengers are dropped at Khao San Rd.

### Getting Around
Don't even consider letting a samlor driver show you around, as they want big money. The town is not large, so getting around on foot or bicycle is easy. A samlor or motorcycle taxi to anywhere in Kanchanaburi should cost 10 to 15B for one person. Songthaews run up and down Saengchuto Rd for 3B per passenger.

Bicycles and motorcycles can be rented at

some guesthouses, at the Suzuki dealer near the bus station, at the Punnee Cafe and at the motorcycle repair shop near Sam's Place. Expect to pay about 200B per day for a motorbike (more for a dirt bike), 30 to 40B a day for bicycles. Punnee Cafe also rents mountain bikes for 80B per 24 hours.

The river ferry across the Mae Klong costs 2B per person. Sometimes there's an extra few baht charge for bikes (motor or push) taken on the ferry, though usually it's included in the 2B fare.

## AROUND KANCHANABURI

Most of the interesting places around Kanchanaburi are to the north and west of the capital, heading towards Three Pagodas Pass. For around 500B per person the PS, River, VN and Rick's Lodge guesthouses can arrange two day trips to Three Pagodas Pass with stops at Hellfire Pass, various waterfalls and hot springs, with an overnight in Sangkhlaburi.

### Waterfalls

Kanchanaburi Province has seven major waterfalls, all north-west of Kanchanaburi. They are Erawan, Pha Lan, Trai Trang, Khao Pang, Sai Yok, Pha That and Huay Khamin. Of these, the three most worth visiting – if you're looking for grandeur and swimming potential – are Erawan, Sai Yok and Huay Khamin. The Erawan Falls are the easiest to get to from Kanchanaburi, while Sai Yok and Huay Khamin are best visited only if you are able to spend the night in the vicinity of the falls.

Any of these waterfalls could be visited by motorcycle. Many of the guesthouses in town will rent bikes – offer 150B per day for a 80 to 100cc bike, more for a dirt bike.

### Erawan National Park

This 550 sq km park is the most visited national park in Thailand and one of the most beautiful.

Once in the park, you'll have to walk two km from the trail entrance to the end of seven levels of waterfalls (the first step is reached 700m from the visitors' centre), which feed into the Khwae Yai River. The trails weave in and out of the numerous pools and falls, sometimes running alongside the water, sometimes leading across footbridges. Wear good walking shoes or sneakers. Also, bring a bathing suit as several of the pools beneath the waterfalls are great for swimming. The shape of the topmost fall is said to resemble Erawan, the three-headed elephant of Hindu-Buddhist mythology.

The waterfalls here, as elsewhere in Kanchanaburi, are best visited during the rainy season or in the first two months of the cool season, when the pools are full and the waterfalls most impressive. The peak crowds at Erawan come in mid-April around the time of the Songkran Festival (when there's not much water); weekends can also be crowded. The park is open from 6 am to 6 pm; admission is 25B.

Two limestone caves in the park worth visiting are **Tham Phra That** (12 km northwest of the visitors' centre via a very rough road) and **Tham Wang Badan** (to the west). **Thung Naa Dam** appears 28 km before Erawan.

*Places to Stay & Eat* Official park bungalows that sleep up to 15 people cost 400 to 1000B per night. The park staff can also make less expensive arrangements in unofficial housing from 50 to 100B per person. You can pitch a tent for 5B. *Erawan Resort Guest House*, off the highway before the park entrance, has small, solid bungalows with attached bath on the river for 200 to 350B.

There are food stalls near the park entrance and at the bus station/market, outside the park. To cut down on rubbish, food is not allowed beyond the second level of the falls.

*Getting There & Away* The first bus to Erawan leaves the Kanchanaburi bus station at 8 am, takes two hours and costs 19B per person. Ask for *rót thammádaa pai náam tòk eh-raawan* (ordinary bus going to Erawan Falls). Take this first bus, as you need a full day to appreciate Erawan, and the last bus back to Kanchanaburi leaves Erawan at 4 pm. During the high season (November to January), minibuses go by all the river

CENTRAL THAILAND

guesthouses in Kan around 9 am daily to take visitors to the falls (one hour) for 60B per person. The return trip leaves at 4.30 pm.

**Huay Khamin Falls** Part of little visited **Si Nakharin National Park**, Huay Khamin (Turmeric Stream) has what are probably Kanchanaburi Province's most powerful waterfalls. The pools under the waterfalls are large and deep and this is an excellent place for swimming. Explorations farther afield in the park can be rewarding for self-contained campers. Elephants and other wildlife are not uncommon.

**Getting There & Away** Getting to Huay Khamin can be difficult. The 45 km road from Erawan is in very bad condition and takes at least two hours by motorcycle or rugged 4WD (you must bring your own transport). The falls can also be reached by a similarly rugged – and much longer – dirt road from Route 323 north of Thong Pha Phum.

An alternative is to charter a boat at Tha Reua Khun Phaen, a pier on the south-east shore of Si Nakharin Reservoir in the village of Mongkrathae. The price varies – according to your bargaining skills and the mood of the boat pilots – from 1000 to 3000B; this need not be as expensive as it sounds if you can bring a group, since the boats can hold up to 20 people. A good price for a long-tail boat holding five to 10 people would be 1200B return. If you can afford it, boat is a much better option than road.

Infrequent Si Sawat buses from Kanchanaburi pass Mongkrathae.

**Sai Yok National Park** About 100 km northwest of Kanchanaburi, scenic Sai Yok Falls are part of 500 sq km Sai Yok National Park. In addition to the park's two falls, Sai Yok and Sai Yok Noi, other attractions include the limestone caves of **Tham Sai Yok, Tham Kaew** and **Tham Phra**, the remains of a **Death Railway bridge** and Japanese cookstoves (actually little more than piles of brick), and a network of clear streams which bubble up from springs in the park. There are estab-

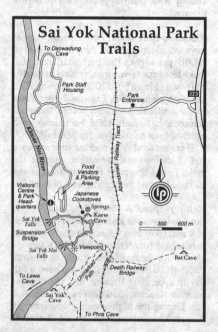

**Sai Yok National Park Trails**

To Daowadung Cave

Park Staff Housing

Park Entrance

323

Khwae Noi River

Abandoned Railway Track

Food Vendors & Parking Area

Visitors' Centre & Park Headquarters

Japanese Cookstoves

Springs

Kaew Cave

Sai Yok Falls

Suspension Bridge

Sai Yok Noi Falls

To Lawa Cave

Sai Yok Cave

Viewpoint

Unmarked Path

Death Railway Bridge

Bat Cave

To Phra Cave

0   300   600 m

Sai Yok National Park offers sanctuary to a number of wildlife, including the wreathed hornbill.

lished footpaths and trails between the falls, caves, railway bridge and the bat cave.

It was at Sai Yok that the famous Russian roulette scenes in the movie *The Deer Hunter* were filmed. The area is well known for overnight raft trips that leave from here along the Khwae Noi River; the waterfalls empty directly into the Khwae Noi. The trips are not cheap, but those who have gone say they're worth the money.

The eight-room **Tham Daowadung**, one of Thailand's prettiest limestone caves, is farther north in the park while **Tham Lawa** is in the park's far south-eastern corner; both are best visited by taking boat trips to an access point along the Khwae Noi River, then hiking in. **Hin Daat Hot Springs** is 40 minutes north of Tham Daowadung by boat. The hot springs *(bàw náam ráwn)* are looked after by a Buddhist monastery, so only men are permitted to bathe there.

Notable wildlife in the park includes Kitti's hog-nosed bat (the world's smallest mammal), regal crab, barking deer, blue pittas, wreathed hornbill, gibbons, Malayan porcupines, slow loris and serow. Wild elephants occasionally cross over from Myanmar. Admission is 25B per person.

**Places to Stay & Eat** Forestry Department bungalows are available at Sai Yok for 500 to 1000B per night; they sleep up to six people. On the river near the suspension bridge, *Saiyok View Raft* rents tidy rooms on floating rafts with private bath and air-con for 400 to 600B. During the week you may be able to get these rafthouse rooms for as low as 300B. There is a row of permanent food stalls next to the parking lot near the visitors' centre. Food vendors here can arrange rooms for 100B per person.

**Getting There & Away** Sai Yok can be reached by direct bus from Kanchanaburi for 28B and the trip takes a little over an hour. You can also get there by boarding a bus bound for Thong Pha Phum. Tell the driver you're going to Sai Yok Yai and he'll let you off at the road to the falls, on the left side of Route 323. From there you can get local transport to Sai Yok. This method takes about two hours in all and costs about the same as the direct bus.

If the water level is cooperative (it often isn't), you can also try chartering a boat that can take up to 20 people from Kanchanaburi to Sai Yok for about 600B per person.

### Si Nakharin Reservoir & Si Sawat
เขื่อนศรีนครินทร์และศรีสวัสดิ์

Route 3199 passes Erawan National Park and continues on to Si Sawat (106 km from Kanchanaburi), a town largely inhabited by North-Eastern Thais who came to work on the Si Nakharin dam years ago. On the south-east bank of the huge Si Nakharin Reservoir is a string of rustic lakeside resorts costing from 200 to 700B a night for individual thatched bungalows. Long-tail boats can be hired at the village of Mongkrathae for tours around the lake or across to Huay Khamin Falls.

### Prasat Meuang Singh Historical Park
อุทยานประวัติศาสตร์ปราสาทเมืองสิงห์

Approximately 43 km from Kanchanaburi are the remains of an important 13th century Khmer outpost of the Angkor empire called Meuang Singh (Lion City). Located on a bend in the Khwae Noi River, the recently restored city ruins cover 460 rai (73.6 hectares) and were declared a historical park under the administration of the Fine Arts Department in 1987. Originally this location may have been chosen by the Khmers as a relay point for trade along the Khwae Noi River.

All the Meuang Singh shrines are constructed of laterite bricks and are situated in a huge grassy compound surrounded by layers of laterite ramparts. Sections of the ramparts show seven additional layers of earthen walls, suggesting cosmological symbolism in the city plan. Evidence of a sophisticated water system has also been discovered amid the ramparts and moats.

The town encompasses four groups of ruins, though only two groups have been excavated and are visible. In the centre of the complex is the principal shrine, Prasat Meuang Singh, which faces east (towards Angkor). Walls surrounding the shrine have gates in each of the cardinal directions. An original sculpture of Avalokitesvara stands on the inside of the northern wall and establishes Meuang Singh as a Mahayana Buddhist centre. The shrine was apparently built during the reign of Jayavarman VII in the 12th century.

To the north-east of the main prasat are the remains of a smaller shrine whose original contents and purpose are unknown. Near the main entrance to the complex at the north gate is a small outdoor museum, which contains various sculptures of Mahayana Buddhist deities and stucco decorations.

Clear evidence that this area was inhabited before the arrival of the Khmers can be seen in another small museum to the south of the complex next to the river. The shed-like building contains a couple of prehistoric human skeletons which were found in the area, and that's it. A more complete exhibit of local neolithic remains is at the Ban Kao Neolithic Museum (see below).

Entry to the historical park is 20B and it's open daily from 8 am to 5 pm.

## Ban Kao Neolithic Museum
พิพิธภัณฑ์บ้านเก่า
During the construction of the Death Railway along the Khwae Noi River, a Dutch POW named Van Heekeren uncovered neolithic remains in the village of Ban Kao (Old Town), about seven km south-east of Meuang Singh. After the war, a Thai-Danish team retraced Van Heekeren's discovery and announced that Ban Kao was a major neolithic burial site. Archaeological evidence suggests that this area may have been inhabited as far back as 10,000 years ago.

A small but well designed museum, displaying 3000 to 4000 year old artefacts from the excavation of Ban Kao, has been established near the site. Objects are labelled and include a good variety of early pottery and other utensils, as well as human skeletons. Hours are from 8 am to 5 pm, Wednesday to Sunday.

**Places to Stay & Eat** Guest bungalows were once available for rent near the south gate of the historical park for 500B, but of late it

seems they're reserved for visiting archaeologists. If you have your own gear, you could probably camp safely by the river. There are a couple of small restaurants at the north gate to the park.

The *River Khwae Farm (Suan Mae Nam Khwae)* is 3.5 km from the Ban Kao (Tha Kilen) train station. Bungalows and raft houses here start at 800B, including all meals.

**Getting There & Away** Ban Kao and Meuang Singh are best reached by train from Kanchanaburi via Ban Kao (Tha Kilen) station, which is only one km south of Meuang Singh. Walk west towards the river and follow the signs to Meuang Singh. Trains leave Kanchanaburi daily at 6.10 and 10.31 am, arriving at Tha Kilen in about an hour. The fare is 10B. To get to Ban Kao, you may have to walk or hitch six km south along the road that follows the Khwae Noi River, though the occasional songthaew passes along this road, too. Motorcycle taxis are sometimes available at Tha Kilen station for 20B to either Ban Kao or Prasat Meuang Singh.

It's possible to get from Kanchanaburi to Meuang Singh and back in one day by catching the 6.10 or 10.31 am train there and the 3 or 4.30 pm train back.

If you have your own transport, Ban Kao and/or Meuang Singh would make convenient rest stops on the way to Hellfire Pass or Sangkhlaburi.

Coming from the Erawan National Park area, there's no need to backtrack all the way to Kanchanaburi before heading north on Route 323. A new paved road heads west from Route 3199 at Km 25, then proceeds 16 km to meet Route 323 between Km 37 and 38 – thus cutting half a day's travel from the old loop. This winding, scenic, lightly trafficked short cut is tremendous for cycling.

## Chaloem Ratanakosin (Tham Than Lot) National Park
อุทยานแห่งชาติเฉลิมรัตนโกสินทร์
This 59 sq km park, 97 km north of Kanchanaburi, is of interest to speleologists because of two caves, **Tham Than Lot Yai** and **Tham**

**Than Lot Noi**, and to naturalists for its waterfalls and natural forests. Three waterfalls – **Trai Trang**, **Than Ngun** and **Than Thong** – are within easy hiking distance of the bungalows and campground. Bungalows cost from 500 to 1000B per night and sleep 10 to 12 people. Pitch your own tent for 5B per person.

**Getting There & Away** Take a bus from Kanchanaburi to Ban Nong Preu for around 35B (a two to three hour trip) and then catching a songthaew to the park. Most visitors arrive by car, jeep or motorcycle.

### Hellfire Pass/Burma-Thailand Railway Memorial

The Australian-Thai Chamber of Commerce completed the first phase of the Hellfire Pass memorial project in 1988. The purpose of the project is to honour the Allied POWs and Asian conscripts who died while constructing some of the most difficult stretches of the Burma-Thailand Death Railway, 80 km north-west of Kanchanaburi. 'Hellfire Pass' was the name the POWs gave to the largest of a 1000m series of mountain cuttings through soil and solid rock, which were

accomplished with minimal equipment (3.5 kg hammers, picks, shovels, steel tap drills, cane baskets for removing dirt and rock, and dynamite for blasting).

The original crew of 400 Australian POWs was later augmented with 600 additional Australian and British prisoners, who worked round the clock in 12 to 18 hour shifts for 12 weeks. The prisoners called it Hellfire Pass because of the way the largest cutting at Konyu looked at night by torch light. By the time the cuttings were finished, 70% of the POW crew had died, and were buried in the nearby Konyu Cemetery.

The memorial consists of a trail that follows the railway remains through the 110m Konyu cutting, then winds up and around the pass for an overhead view. At the far end of the cutting is a memorial plaque fastened to solid stone, commemorating the death of the Allied prisoners. There are actually seven cuttings spread over 3.5 km – four smaller cuttings and three larger ones.

The Australian-Thai Chamber of Commerce also has plans to clear a path to the Hin Tok trestle bridge south-east of the Konyu cutting. This bridge was called the 'Pack of Cards' by the prisoners because it collapsed

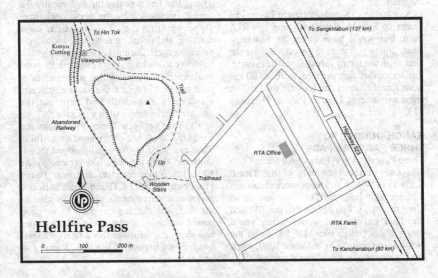

**Hellfire Pass**

0    100    200 m

To Hin Tok

Konyu Cutting

Viewpoint    Down

Trail

Abandoned Railway

Up

Wooden Stairs

Trailhead

To Sangkhlaburi (137 km)

RTA Office

Highway 323

RTA Farm

To Kanchanaburi (80 km)

three times during construction. Eventually some of the track may be restored to exhibit rolling stock from the WWII era. A museum containing artefacts from the era is be constructed on the site by the end of 1997.

**Getting There & Away** Access to Hellfire Pass is via the Royal Thai Army (RTA) farm on Route 323, between Kanchanaburi and Thong Pha Phum. Proceeding north-west along Highway 323, the farm is 80 km from Kanchanaburi, 18 km from the Nam Tok train terminus, and 11 km from the River Kwai Village Hotel. A small roman-script sign near Km 66 marks the turn-off (look for two RST rail coaches on the west side of the highway). Once you arrive at the RTA farm, take one of the dirt roads on either side of the RTA offices about 400m around to the posted trailhead. From the trailhead, it's about 340m up and down a steep walkway and along the rail bed to reach the pass.

After walking through the pass and viewing the plaque, you can follow another trail/walkway on the right to get a view of the cutting from above. Then you can either double back the way you came or continue on this trail until it wraps around and meets the trailhead.

Any bus from Kanchanaburi to Thong Pha Phum or Sangkhlaburi will pass the RTA farm, but you'll have to let the bus crew know where you want to get off – ask for the *sŭan thahăan* (army farm). If you're driving, just remember that the farm is about 80 km from Kanchanaburi and look for the English signs announcing Hellfire Pass on Highway 323.

## KANCHANABURI TO THREE PAGODAS PASS

Three Pagodas Pass (Phra Chedi Saam Ong) was one of the terminals of the Death Railway in WWII, and for centuries has been a major relay point for Thai-Burmese trade. Until recently it was a place that the TAT and the Thai government would rather you'd forget about (much like Mae Salong in the North some years ago), but since 1989, when the Myanmar government took control of the

Myanmar side of the border from insurgent armies, it's been promoted as a tourist destination. There's really not much to see at the pass – the attraction lies in the journey itself and the impressive scenery along the way.

It's an all day journey and will require you to spend at least one night in Sangkhlaburi, which is a somewhat interesting off-the-track destination in itself. The distance between Kanchanaburi and Sangkhlaburi alone is about 200 km, so if you take a motorcycle it is imperative that you fill up before you leave Kanchanaburi and stop for petrol again in Thong Pha Phum, the last town before Sangkhlaburi. By bicycle this would be a very challenging route, but it has been done.

The paved highway used to end in Thong Pha Phum, but now the roads from Thong Pha Phum to Sangkhlaburi and from Sangkhlaburi to Three Pagodas Pass are paved as well. The best time to go is during the mid to late part of the cool season (January to February). During the rainy season nearly the whole of Sangkhlaburi district is under water and travel can be difficult.

The road between Kanchanaburi and Thong Pha Phum passes through mostly flat terrain interrupted by the occasional limestone outcropping. This is sugar cane country, and if you're travelling by bicycle or motorcycle during harvest times you'll have to contend with huge cane trucks overloaded with cut cane, which strew pieces of cane and dust in their wake – take extra care. Cassava is also cultivated here but the cassava trucks aren't such a nuisance.

The road between Thong Pha Phum and Sangkhlaburi is one of the most beautiful in Thailand, winding through limestone mountains and along the huge lake created by the Khao Laem hydroelectric dam near Thong Pha Phum. North of Thong Pha Phum is a major teak reforestation project. In spite of the fact that the road surface is in good condition during the dry season, steep grades and sharp curves make this a fairly dangerous journey, especially the last 25 km or so before Sangkhlaburi.

Recently there has been talk in Kanchanaburi of rebuilding the train connection between Nam Tok and Sangkhlaburi, using the old Japanese rail bed. If it ever happens, this will be a spectacular train trip.

Another pipe dream is the construction of a road between Sangkhlaburi and Um Phang in Tak Province, approximately 120 km to the north. A very bad dirt road exists now, but it crosses the Thailand-Myanmar border in a couple of places and passes through Karen rebel territory, so it's not really legal. At the moment it's used mostly by trucks carrying ore from Korean-owned antimony mines near the border on the Thai side. During the rainy season it's often impassable due to deep streams which cross the road.

## Thong Pha Phum
ท้องผาภูมิ

Surrounded by scenic karst topography, the area around the small town of Thong Pha Phum is slowly changing from a simple way station along Route 323 to a destination in itself. Many of its inhabitants – mainly Mon or Burman – originally congregated here to work on Khao Laem Dam.

The Khwae Noi River runs along the east side of town, and it's possible to raft downriver as far as Sai Yok or even all the way to Kanchanaburi. There are some interesting walks and day trips in the area. You can, for example, ford the river over a footbridge close to town to climb a prominent limestone cliff topped by a wat. Farther afield are **Dai Chong Thong Falls** (35 km north via Route 323), **Kroeng Krawia Falls** (33 km north), **Phaa Taat Falls** (30 km south at Km 105) and **Hin Daat Hot Springs** (32 km south at Km 107). All are easily accessed from the highway.

A more difficult to find waterfall, discovered in 1995 by a forest monk, is **Tung Nang Khruan**, a nine-level cascade about 15 km north of Thong Pha Phum on the way to Sangkhlaburi. It's about five km off the road but you'll need a guide from nearby Ban Tung Nang Khruan and sturdy legs to find it. Eventually a signposted road to the falls

will probably be constructed; ask in Thong Pha Phum if you're interested in checking it out.

Between Km 32 and Km 33 (some 32 km north of Thong Pha Phum, 42 km before Sangkhlaburi) is the entrance to the **Sunyataram Forest Monastery** (Samnak Paa Sunyataram), a 45 hectare forest meditation retreat centre affiliated with one of Thailand's most famous living monks, Ajaan Yantra. Yantra was accused of sexual improprieties in 1993 (the religious establishment absolved him for lack of evidence) and the monastery is now very touchy about visitors.

**Places to Stay & Eat** *Somjaineuk Hotel*, on the left side of the town's main street off the highway, has basic but clean rooms with fan and attached bath around a shaded courtyard for 150B. A newer, all air-con building offers large, comfortable rooms with hot water showers for 600B. *Si Thong Pha Phum Bungalows* farther down the road has large private bungalows for 130B with fan, 240B with air-con, but it's next to a noisy primary school. Better is *Saw Bunging Bungalows*, which has 120B fan rooms similar to those at Somjaineuk, plus air-con rooms for 240B; since it's a bit farther off the street it tends to be quieter.

Out on the highway the *Barnchaidaen Phu Pha Phum Hotel* (☎ 599035; fax 599088) is a 49-room hotel with up-market rooms listing for 1000B (often available for as low as 550B); rooms come with satellite TV, fridge and other amenities.

*Green World Hot Spring Resort & Golf Club*, 33 km south of town near Km 108, is a huge resort with posh rooms costing 1200 to 2000B. The nearby *Thong Pha Phum River Hills* is similar. Just beyond the dam west of town are nine rustic lakeside resorts, including *Bangkok Flower, Taweechaiphaphum, Wang Phai, Phae VIP, Kho Laem, Phae Rim Kheuan, Bangkok Camping, Weekend Garden* and *Chao Kheuan*. It's mostly a Thai scene, with thatched bungalows in the 300 to 800B range.

In typical Mon style, several shops and vendors along the main street proffer long rows of curry pots; instead of two or three curry choices more typical of Thai vendors, the Mon vendors lay out eight or more – all delicious. The best variety is at a shop called *Rawy Maw* (Hundred Pots); a branch of the same shop can be found in a new shophouse on the highway just south of town.

A small night market convenes near the centre of town each evening with the usual rice and noodle dishes. A riverside restaurant near the highway bridge, *Saep-i-lii*, serves good Isaan food. A new spot just south of the bridge, *U-Biet*, is a thatched-roof outdoor place with decent Thai food and a view of the river.

**Getting There & Away** Ordinary buses leave the Kanchanaburi bus terminal for Thong Pha Phum every half hour from 6.45 am until 6 pm; the fare is 40B and the trip takes about three hours. Buses to Sangkhlaburi also stop in Thong Pha Phum – see the Sangkhlaburi Getting There & Away section for details.

## SANGKHLABURI
สังขละบุรี
• ☎ *(38)* • *pop 10,000*

This small but important Kanchanaburi outpost is inhabited by a mixture of Burman, Karen, Mon and Thai, but is mostly Karen and Mon. You'll find very little English spoken out this way – in fact, you may hear as much Burmese, Karen and Mon as Thai.

Hundreds of former residents of Myanmar have moved to the Sangkhlaburi area during the last few years because of fighting in the Three Pagodas Pass area between the Karen and Mon insurgent armies and between Myanmar government forces and the Karen. These Burmese are also escaping being pressganged as porters for the Myanmar army.

The distance between Kanchanaburi and Sangkhlaburi is about 227 km; from Thong Pha Phum it's 74 km.

### Money
A Siam Commercial Bank in the city centre near the market and Phornphalin Hotel offers foreign exchange services from 8.30 am to 3.30 pm.

### Things to See & Do
Sangkhlaburi sits at the edge of the huge lake formed by Khao Laem Dam. The town was in fact created after the dam flooded out an older village near the confluence of the three rivers that now feed the reservoir. There's not much to do in the town itself except explore the small **markets** for Burmese handicrafts such as checked cotton blankets, *longyi* (Burmese sarongs) and cheroots. The town comes alive on Mon National Day, celebrated during the last week of July.

Thailand's longest wooden bridge leads over a section of the lake near town to a friendly **Mon settlement** of thatched huts and dirt paths. A market in the village purveys goods smuggled from Myanmar, China and India; there are also a few food vendors with pots of rich Mon curry. The village can be reached in five or 10 minutes by boat from either of the guesthouses or by walking/cycling over the bridge.

**Wat Wang Wiwekaram** Also called Wat Mon since most of the monks here are Mon, this monastery is about three km north of the town on the edge of the reservoir. A tall and much revered stupa, Chedi Luang Phaw Utama, is the centrepiece of the wat. Constructed in the style of the Mahabodhi stupa in Bodhgaya, India, the chedi is topped by 400 *bàht* (about six kg) of gold. An earlier chedi is located some distance behind the tall one and is 300 to 400 years old. From the edge of the monastery grounds is a view of the tremendous lake and the three rivers that feed into it.

A new section of the Mon temple built across the road features a flashy, multiroofed wihāan with stainless steel-plated pillars, heavy carved wooden doors and marble banisters. It's surrounded by a carp-filled moat. Local rumour has it that it was built from profits made selling weapons and other supplies to the Mon and Karen armies; the wildest stories even claim that a huge weapons cache is stashed beneath the wihāan. A more likely source of support for the wat is the black-market tax collected by the Mon rebel soldiers on all goods smuggled through their territory.

**Khao Laem Lake & Mon Refugee Camps**
This huge lake was formed when a dam was erected across the Khwae Noi River near Thong Pha Phum in 1983. The lake submerged an entire village at the confluence of the Khwae Noi, Ranti and Sangkhalia rivers. The spires of the village's **Wat Sam Prasop** (Three Junction Temple) can be seen protruding from the lake in the dry season.

Canoes can be rented for exploring the lake, or for longer trips you can hire a long-tail boat and pilot. Lake boating is a tranquil pastime, best early in the morning with mist and birdlife – early evening is also good for birdwatching. Two hours across the lake and up the Pikri River by boat from Sangkhlaburi is a huge **Mon refugee camp** (population 50,000). On the way to the camp you'll pass through a flooded Ayuthaya-period mountain pass marked by a decrepit Buddha image seated under a small tin-roofed sala. This pass was part of the Thailand-Myanmar border before the border was moved south-east following WWII. During the dry season the camp can only be reached by road. Contact P Guest House or the Burmese Inn for details.

There are at least four other Mon refugee camps along the border between Three Pagodas Pass and the mining village of Pilok. North-east of Three Pagodas Pass are several Karen refugee settlements but they are very difficult to reach. If you do visit one of the camps, don't go empty-handed; bring blankets, clothes and food for the refugees.

A branch meditation centre of Kanchanaburi's Sunyataram Forest Monastery is found on the lake's **Ko Kaew Sunyataram** (Sunyataram Jewel Isle). Permission to visit must first be obtained from the Sunyataram Forest Monastery, 42 km before Sangkhlaburi.

**Boat Trips** P Guest House and Burmese Inn can arrange bamboo-raft or long-tail boat trips on the lake (one of the most popular such trips is a journey by raft along the Sangkhalia River, taking in a Mon resettlement camp along the way), elephant riding and jungle trekking. Day trips to nearby waterfalls are also a possibility. Rates depend on how many people go on a trip together, but are very reasonable.

**Places to Stay**
Sangkhlaburi has one hotel, the *Phornphalin Hotel* (formerly Sri Daeng; ☎ 595088), which is on the southern edge of town near an army camp and the central market. Rooms are 160/180B for one/two beds with fan and bath or 350B with air-con; there are also a couple of 'VIP' rooms with TV and hot water showers for 700B. The rooms are fairly clean and comfortable.

Down on the lake behind the town, an enterprising Mon-Karen family operates the *P Guest House* (☎ 595061; fax 595139). Bungalows with verandahs are placed along a slope overlooking the lake; singles/doubles with shared bath are a bargain at 30 to 50B; larger doubles with private bath cost 120B. There's a comfortable dining area with a sunset view of the lake and the chedi at Wat Mon. An information board has maps and suggestions for things to see and do in the area. Canoes can be rented for 10B per hour and there are also bicycles and motorcycles for rent. The guesthouse is about 1.2 km from the bus stop in town.

The newer *Burmese Inn* (☎ 595146) is perched in a stream gorge near the wooden bridge that crosses to the Mon village, about 800m from the Sangkhlaburi bus terminal. Run by an Austrian-Thai couple, it offers wooden bungalows with thatched roofs for 60/80B a single/double with shared bath, 120B with private bath and fan, 250B for larger rooms. Trips to local waterfalls and to Thung Yai Naresuan National Park can be arranged – there is a good, hand-drawn wall map of the area in the dining area.

A motorcycle taxi from the bus stop in Sangkhlaburi to either guesthouse costs 10B; if you come by minivan from Kanchanaburi you can ask the driver to take you to either guesthouse (it's supposed to be door-to-door service).

A couple of km north of Sangkhlaburi on the way to Wat Mon, right on the Sangkhalia River where it meets the lake, is *Songkalia River Huts* (☎ 595023; (2) 427-4936 in Bangkok). Somewhat run-down floating bungalows that will sleep two to 10 people cost 200 to 600B per night. Above the lake

CENTRAL THAILAND

CENTRAL THAILAND

near the bridge, a much better choice is *Samprasop Bungalows* (☎ 595050), where rooms with private bath cost 300B, more for air-con.

Next to P Guest House, the *Ponnatee Resort* (☎ 595134; fax 595270) is a slightly up-market place with the familiar hillside layout. Plain fan rooms are overpriced at 500B; nicer air-con rooms with more furniture are 700B. Nearby *Forget Me Not House* (☎ 595015) has nicer chalet-style accommodation for 500B. More places are sprouting up on hillsides along the lake. So far, all are resorts oriented towards Thai tourists in the 300 to 800B range. For now, Sangkhlaburi is very peaceful – one hopes that local entrepreneurs won't turn it into another Kanchanaburi river scene with all-night floating discos.

## Places to Eat

The *Phornphalin Hotel* has a decent restaurant downstairs. The *Rung Arun* restaurant, opposite the Phornphalin, has an extensive menu and is also good, and there are three or four other places to eat down the street. The day market in the centre of town sometimes has a couple of vendor stalls offering Indian nan and curry. The garden restaurant at *Samprasop Bungalows* is the nicest looking place in the area and has a good reputation locally. Food service at *P Guest House* is also commendable.

## Getting There & Away

Ordinary bus No 8203 leaves the Kanchanaburi bus terminal for Sangkhlaburi at 6.45, 9, 10.45 am and 1.15 pm and takes four to six hours, depending on how many mishaps occur on the Thong Pha Phum to Sangkhlaburi road. The fare is 70B.

A *rót tûu* (minivan) service to Sangkhlaburi leaves 10 times daily, from 6.30 am to 4.30 pm, from an office on the east side of the Kan bus terminal. The trip takes 3½ hours and costs 100B; if you want to stop off in Thong Pha Phum it's 70B (then from Thong Pha Phum to Sangkhlaburi by van it is 50B). Arriving from Kan, the van driver can drop you off at either of the guesthouses or the Phornphalin Hotel on request. In Sangkhlaburi the vans depart from a spot near the market. From either end it's usually best to reserve your seat a day in advance.

If you go by motorcycle or car, you can count on about five hours to cover the 217 km from Kanchanaburi to Sangkhlaburi, including three or four short rest stops. Alternatively, you can make it an all day trip and stop off in Ban Kao, Muang Singh and Hellfire Pass. Be warned, however, that this is not a trip for an inexperienced motorcycle rider. The Thong Pha Phum to Sangkhlaburi section of the journey (74 km) requires sharp reflexes and previous experience on mountain roads. This is also not a motorcycle trip to do alone as stretches of the highway are practically deserted – it's tough to get help if you need it and easy to attract the attention of would-be bandits.

## AROUND SANGKHLABURI

### Three Pagodas Pass/Payathonzu
พระเจดีย์สามองค์

The pagodas themselves are rather small, but it is the remote nature of this former black-market outpost that draws a trickle of visitors. Control of the Myanmar side of the border once vacillated between the Karen National Union and the Mon Liberation Front, since Three Pagodas was one of several 'toll gates' along the Thailand-Myanmar border where insurgent armies collected a 5% tax on all merchandise that passed. These ethnic groups used the funds to finance armed resistance against the Myanmar government, which has recently increased efforts to regain control of the border area.

The Karen also conduct a huge multimillion dollar business in illegal mining and logging, the products of which are smuggled into Thailand by the truckload under cover of night – not without the palms-up cooperation of the Thai police, of course. Pressure for control of these border points has increased since the Thai government enacted a ban on all logging in Thailand in 1989, which has of course led to an increase in teak smuggling.

CENTRAL THAILAND

In late 1988, heavy fighting broke out between the Karen and the Mon for control of the 'toll gate' here. Since this is the only place for hundreds of km in either direction where a border crossing is geographically convenient, this is where the Mon army (which has traditionally controlled this area) has customarily collected the 5% tax on smuggling. The Karen insurgents do the same at other points north along the Thailand-Myanmar border. Myanmar government pressure on the Karen farther north led to a conflict between the Karen and the Mon over Three Pagodas trade and the village on the Myanmar side was virtually burnt to the ground.

In 1989 the Myanmar government wrested control of the town from both the Karen and Mon, and the Burmese seem firmly established at the border for the time being. The Burmese have renamed the town Payathonzu and filled it with shops catering to an odd mix of occupation troops and tourists.

Foreigners are now allowed to cross the border here for day trips for 130B or US$5 cash. Payathonzu lies 470 km by road from Yangon but is considered '75% safe' by the Myanmar military. Apparently insurgent Mon and Karen forces are still in the area and there are occasional firefights.

A true frontier town, Payathonzu has seven Burmese teahouses (a couple with nam-bya – the Burmese equivalent to Indian nan bread), one cinema, several mercantile shops with Burmese longyis, cheroots, jade, clothes and a few general souvenir shops with Mon-Karen-Burmese handicrafts. Bargaining is necessary (some English is spoken, also Thai) but in general goods are well priced. About 20 Thai merchants operate in town – the Myanmar government offers them free rent to open shops. A new temple, **Wat Suwankhiri**, is under construction on a bluff near the town.

**Kloeng Thaw Falls**, 12 km from the border, take a couple of hours by motorcycle to reach from Payathonzu. The road to the falls is only open in the dry season – reportedly the Karen control the waterfall area during the rainy season. Even in good weather, the two rut track is very rugged, not recommended for motorcycle novices. Lately a Myanmar military checkpoint at the edge of town has barred all visitors from leaving the town limits.

The border is open from 6 am to 6 pm daily. When the border first opened in 1991 cameras had to be left at the border gate but photography is now permitted anywhere in the area.

**Places to Stay** The only place to stay here is at *Three Pagodas Pass Resort* (☎ (34) 595316; (2) 412-4159 in Bangkok), where large wooden bungalows cost 300 to 600B. Most visitors stay in nearby Sangkhlaburi.

**Getting There & Away** The 19 km paved road to Three Pagodas Pass begins four km before you reach Sangkhlaburi off Route 323. At this intersection is a Thai police checkpoint where you may have to stop for minor interrogation, depending on recent events in the Three Pagodas Pass area. Along the way you'll pass a couple of villages inhabited entirely by Mon or Karen; at one time there was a branch of the All Burma Students Democratic Front here, where self-exiled Yangon students had set up an opposition movement with the intention of ousting the Ne Win government from Myanmar. The students have since moved north to Tak Province.

If you don't have your own wheels, songthaews to Three Pagodas Pass leave about every 50 minutes between 6 am and 5 pm from Sangkhlaburi's central market area. The fare is 30B; the last songthaew back to Sangkhlaburi leaves Three Pagodas Pass at around 4.30 pm.

The border is only a short walk from the songthaew stop in Three Pagodas Pass.

**National Parks**
Along the highway between Thong Pha Phum and Sangkhlaburi are several natural attractions. Those nearest to Thong Pha Phum – south of Km 36 on Route 323 – are described in the earlier Thong Pha Phum section.

Approximately 34 km south of Sang-khlaburi between Km 39 and 40, you'll find a turn-off on the east side of the highway for the 3200 sq km **Thung Yai Naresuan National Park**, Thailand's largest protected land parcel. This rough dirt road leads to **Takien Thong Falls**, where pools are suitable for swimming nearly year-round. There are at least two other tracks off the highway into the sanctuary, but to find anything of interest you really should go with a guide – check with the Burmese Inn or P Guest House in Sangkhlaburi. Thung Yai Naresun is one of the last natural habitats in Thailand for the tiger, whose total numbers nationwide are estimated to be less than 500, perhaps no more than 250.

On the opposite side of the highway near the Thung Yai Naresuan turn-off is a paved road into the recently established **Khao Laem National Park**. As yet there are no facilities to speak of, but presumably the park was created to protect the riverine habitats near the lake.

**Tham Sukho** is a large limestone cave shrine just off the highway at Km 42.

# Samut Prakan Province

## SAMUT PRAKAN
• ☎ (2) • pop 71,500

This large city/small province lies at the mouth of the Chao Phraya River where it empties into the Gulf of Thailand just 30 km south of Bangkok. The city's name means 'Ocean Wall', a reference to the 1893 vintage **Phra Chula Jawm Klao Fort** seven km south of the provincial hall. Today it's one of Thailand's most densely populated provincial capitals, with over 70,000 people packed into 7.3 sq km.

The province's two major attractions, Ancient City and the Crocodile Farm, are popular day trips from Bangkok. In fact, Samut Prakan is best visited as a day trip, as overnight it differs little from spending the night in Bangkok.

### Ancient City (Muang Boran)
Billed as the largest open-air museum in the world, the Ancient City covers more than 80 hectares and presents scaled-down facsimiles of many of the kingdom's most famous monuments. The grounds follow Thailand's general geographical outline, with the monuments placed accordingly. The main entrance places visitors at the country's southern tip, from where you work your way to the 'northernmost' monuments. A sculpture garden focusing on episodes from the *Ramakian* was added recently. Although the entire facility is in dire need of a face-lift, for students of Thai architecture it's worth a day's visit (it takes an entire day to cover the area). It's also a good place for long, undistracted walks, as it's usually quiet and never crowded.

The Ancient City Co (☎ 226-1936/7, 224-1057, 222-8143) also publishes a lavish bilingual periodical devoted to Thai art and architecture called *Muang Boran*. The journal is edited by some of Thailand's leading art historians. The owner of both the journal and park is Bangkok's largest Mercedes Benz dealer, who has an avid interest in Thai art.

Ancient City (☎ 323-9252) is 33 km from Bangkok along the Old Sukhumvit Highway. Opening hours are 8 am to 5 pm; admission to the site is 50B for adults, 25B children. Public bus Nos 25 (3.50B) or air-con bus Nos 7, 8 or 11 (12 to 16B) to the Samut Prakan terminal can take up to two hours depending on traffic; from the terminal get a 10 minute songthaew to Muang Boran for another 5B. Transport can also be arranged through the Bangkok office at 78 Democracy Monument circle, Ratchadamnoen Klang Rd.

### Samut Prakan Crocodile Farm & Zoo
In the same area as the Ancient City is Samut Prakan Crocodile Farm & Zoo (☎ 387-0020), where you can even see crocodile wrestling! There are over 30,000 crocs here (including the largest known Siamese croc, a boy named Yai who's six metres long and weighs 1114 kg) as well as elephants, monkeys and snakes. Many of the crocs escaped

during the tempestuous floods of 1995. The farm is open from 7 am to 6 pm daily with trained animal shows – including croc wrestling – every hour between 9 and 11 am and between 1 and 4 pm daily. Elephant shows take place at 9.30 and 11.30 am, while the reptiles usually get their dinner between 4 and 5 pm. Admission is a steep 300B for adults, 200B for children (50/30B for Thais). CITES-certified items – handbags, belts, shoes – made from crocodile hide are available from the farm's gift shop. You can reach the crocodile farm via air-con bus Nos 7, 8 or 11, changing to songthaew Nos S1 to S80.

### Other Attractions
The Ayuthaya-era **Phra Samut Chedi**, popularly known as Phra Chedi Klang Nam (Chedi in the Middle of the River) for its original location on an island in the Chao Phraya River, now sits on the river bank in front of the Provincial Hall. Beginning on the fifth day of the waning moon in the 11th lunar month each year (usually in October), the chedi is the site of a nine day festival with lots of food vendors, music and lights.

The port area of the city, **Pak Nam** (River Mouth), is worth a visit for those interested in international ports. Samut Prakan as a whole is commonly referred to as Meuang Pak Nam.

### Places to Stay & Eat
In Pak Nam, five minutes walk from the bus station, the *Pak Num Hotel* at 101/2-3 Naraiprapsuk Rd has a gruff staff, windowless rooms with grotty walls for 200B with fan and shower, 300B with air-con. Of similar price but better quality – due to recently painted lobby and rooms – is the nearby *Nithra Swan (Nit Sawan)*, which charges 200B for rooms with fan, 320B for air-con.

The Pak Nam market is a good place for cheap food all day long. At 19/17-18 Naraiprapsuk Rd, the *Wall's* ice cream restaurant has decent Thai food.

*Bang Pu Seaside Resort*, a landscaped garden restaurant in nearby Bang Pu Mai district (10 km south-east of Samut Prakan via Highway 3), is a local favourite for long, leisurely meals.

### Getting There & Away
Ordinary bus No 25 (3.50B) and air-con buses Nos 7, 8 and 11 (12 to 16B) each ply regular routes between central Bangkok and Pak Nam. The journey can take up to two hours depending on traffic.

### Getting Around
The bus station is on Srisamut Rd in front of the harbour and market. Songthaews depart from the market area to Ancient City and the Crocodile Farm for 3B each. To get from the Crocodile Farm to Ancient City, turn right from the farm and walk for 10 minutes to Sukhumvit Rd or catch a songthaew or a motorcycle taxi. On Sukhumvit Rd, hail a songthaew or a minibus (3B) which will take 10 minutes to get to Ancient City.

# Chachoengsao Province

### CHACHOENGSAO
จ.เมืองฉะเชิงเทรา
• ☎ (38) • *pop 43,000*
This provincial town, divided by the wide Bang Pakong River, is hardly visited by foreign tourists, probably because it's not on any of the major road or rail lines out of Bangkok. As a short day trip, however, it's a good way to escape Bangkok and experience provincial Thai life without encountering the tourists and touts of Ayuthaya or Nakhon Pathom.

The main attraction is **Wat Sothon Wararam Worawihaan**, which houses Phra Phuttha Sothon, one of the most sacred Buddha images in the country. The origins of the 198-cm-high image are cloaked in mystery, the only point of agreement being that the image is associated with a famous monk named Luang Phaw Sothon. Sothon was considered a *phrá sàksìt*, a monk with holy powers, and Buddha amulets modelled on the Phuttha Sothon are thought to be particularly effective protectors if blessed by the monk. Luang Phaw Sothon supposedly predicted the exact moment of his own death

CENTRAL THAILAND

– thousands gathered at the temple to watch him die while sitting in meditation posture. The temple sits along the bank of the river about two km south of the provincial hall. Major temple festivals are held in the middle of the fifth and 12th lunar months.

In the centre of the city, opposite City Hall, is the 90 rai **Somdet Phra Si Nakharin Park** with shade trees and a large pond.

The **Sorn-Thawee Meditation Centre** (Samnak Vipassana Sonthawi), about 17 km north of the city, offers 20 to 50 day meditation courses in the style of Myanmar's late Mahasi Sayadaw. Two German monks can provide instruction in English or German. If you are interested in taking the course, write in advance to Sorn-Thawee Meditation Centre, Bangkla, Chachoengsao 24110.

### Places to Stay

Should you want to stay overnight in Chachoengsao, you'll find several hotels along Phanom Sarakham Rd, including the *Happy Inn* (270B air-con), *Panom Garden* (160B fan, 300B air-con) and *Phanom* (150B fan, 230B air-con). The cheaper *Kitchai Hotel* at 28-34 Kuekoon Rd has OK fan rooms for 60 to 100B. The *River Inn* (☎ 511921), next to the river on Naruphong Rd, has good air-con rooms starting at 370B.

### Getting There & Away

The best way to visit Chachoengsao by public transport is via the eastern railway line. Ten trains a day leave Bangkok's Hualamphong station between 6 am and 6.05 pm; in the reverse direction trains depart between 5.30 am and 7.05 pm. The fare – 3rd class only – is 13B and the trip takes around 1½ hours each way.

Buses to Chachoengsao leave hourly between 6 am and 6 pm from Bangkok's Eastern Bus Terminal, at Soi 40, Sukhumvit Rd. The fare is 22B on the ordinary bus (around two hours) or 45B on the air-con bus (1½ hours). There are also buses to Chachoengsao from the Northern Bus Terminal for 21B (ordinary) and 29B (air-con); the latter buses take two and 2½ hours respectively to reach Chachoengsao.

# Chonburi Province

## SI RACHA
ศรีราชา
• ☎ *(38)* • *pop 23,000*
About 105 km from Bangkok on the east coast of the Gulf of Thailand is the small town of Si Racha, home of the famous spicy sauce *náam phrík sīi raachaa*. Some of Thailand's best seafood, especially the local oysters, is served here accompanied by this sauce.

On **Ko Loi**, a small rocky island which is connected to the mainland by a long jetty, there is a Thai-Chinese Buddhist temple. Farther offshore is a large island called Ko Si Chang, flanked by two smaller islands – Kham Yai to the north and Khang Kao to the south. As this provides a natural shelter from the wind and sea, it is used as a harbour by large incoming freighters. Smaller boats transport goods to the Chao Phraya Delta some 50 km away.

The motorised samlors in this fishing town and on Ko Si Chang are unlike those seen anywhere else in Thailand – huge motorcycles powered by auto engines, with the passenger seating at the rear.

### Places to Stay

For most people Si Racha is more of a transit point than an overnight stop. The best places to stay in Si Racha are the rambling wooden hotels built on piers over the waterfront. The *Siriwatana Hotel*, across from Tessaban 1 Rd and the Bangkok Bank, is the cleanest of the lot and has the best service. There are rustic sitting areas with tables outside the rooms along the piers. Their basic fan-cooled rooms with attached shower cost 140B, while rooms with shared shower are 120B. Simple, inexpensive meals can be prepared on request or you're free to bring your own food and use the tables provided.

The *Siwichai*, next to the Siriwatana, has similar rooms for 200B, plus its own pier restaurant. The *Samchai*, on Soi 10, across from Surasakdi 1 Rd, has reasonable rooms

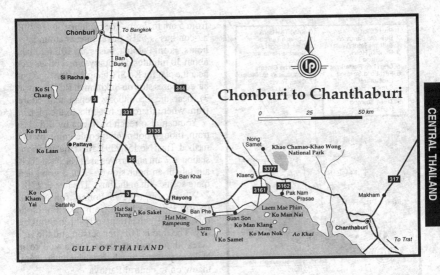

**Chonburi to Chanthaburi**

0          25          50 km

for 170B and some air-con rooms (350B) as well. All three are open and breezy, with outdoor tables where you can bring food in the evening from nearby markets.

On Soi 18, the *Grand Bungalows* rent bungalows of various sizes, built off the pier, for 400 to 1100B. Each one sleeps several people and they are very popular among holidaying Thais and Chinese.

There are several new top-end hotels in town, including the 20-storey *Laemthong Residence Hotel* (☎ /fax 322888) in the centre of town, just off Sukhumvit Rd (Highway 3). Comfortable rooms with all the amenities start at 900B; on the premises are a swimming pool and tennis courts.

The *City Hotel* (☎ 322700; fax 322739), a classy place at 6/126 Sukhumvit Rd, offers capacious rooms for 2293 to 3440B. An escalator leads from the pavement to the 2nd floor reception; facilities include a pub, coffee shop, fitness centre and business centre.

**Places to Eat**

There is plenty of good seafood in Si Racha, but you have to watch the prices. Best known is the Chinese owned *Chua Lee* on Jermjompol (Choemchomphon) Rd next to Soi 10, across

from the Krung Thai Bank. The seafood is great but probably the most expensive in town. Next door and across the street are several seafood places with similar fare at much more reasonable prices, such as the *Fast Food Seafood Restaurant* opposite the Chua Lee at 81/26-27.

*Jarin*, on the Soi 14 pier, has very good one plate seafood dishes, especially seafood curry steamed with rice (khâo hàw mòk thaleh) and Thai-style rice noodles with fresh shrimp (kūaytīaw phàt thai kûng sòt). It's a great place to kill time while waiting for the next boat to Ko Si Chang; prices are low to moderate.

At the end of the pier at Soi 18 is the large *Seaside Restaurant* – now just about the best all-round seafood place in town for atmosphere, service and value. The full-colour bilingual menu includes a tasty grilled seafood platter stacked with squid, mussels, shrimp and cockles. Last time I was there they even had Häagen Dazs ice cream.

The most economical place to eat is in the market near the clock tower at the southern end of town. In the evenings the market offers everything from noodles to fresh seafood, while in the daytime it's mostly an ordinary

CENTRAL THAILAND

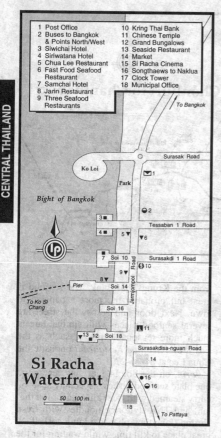

1 Post Office
2 Buses to Bangkok & Points North/West
3 Siwichai Hotel
4 Siriwatana Hotel
5 Chua Lee Restaurant
6 Fast Food Seafood Restaurant
7 Samchai Hotel
8 Jarin Restaurant
9 Three Seafood Restaurants
10 Kring Thai Bank
11 Chinese Temple
12 Grand Bungalows
13 Seaside Restaurant
14 Market
15 Si Racha Cinema
16 Songthaews to Naklua
17 Clock Tower
18 Municipal Office

To Bangkok

Surasak Road

Ko Loi

Park

Bight of Bangkok

Tessaban 1 Road

Surasakdi 1 Road

Soi 10

Soi 14

Pier

To Ko Si Chang

Soi 16

Soi 18

Surasakdisa-nguan Road

Si Racha Waterfront

0  50  100 m

To Pattaya

food and clothing market with some noodle and snack stands.

Outside town, off Sukhumvit Rd (Highway 3) on the way to Pattaya, there are a couple of cheap, but good, fresh seafood places. Locals favour a place near Laem Chabang, about 10 km south of Si Racha, called *Sut Thang Rak* or 'End of Love Rd'. Closer to town is Ao Udom, a small fishing bay where there are several open-air seafood places.

### Getting There & Away

Buses to Si Racha leave the Eastern Bus Terminal in Bangkok every 25 minutes or so

from 5 am to 7 pm. The ordinary bus is 29B, air-con bus is 52B; travel time is around 1¾ hours. From Pattaya, buses are 10B and take about 30 minutes. Ordinary direct buses stop near the pier for Ko Si Chang, but through and air-con buses stop on Sukhumvit Rd (Highway 3), near the Laemthong Department Store, from where there are tuk-tuks to the pier.

You can also reach Si Racha by 3rd class train, though not many people come by this method. Train No 151/239 leaves Hualamphong station at 7 am and arrives at Si Racha at 10.15 am (about an hour slower – but a good deal more scenic – than the bus). The fare is 28B.

White songthaews bound for Naklua (North Pattaya) leave from near the clock tower in Si Racha frequently throughout the day. The fare is 10B per person and the ride takes about half an hour. Once you're in Naklua you can easily catch another song-thaew on to central Pattaya.

Boats to Ko Si Chang leave from the Soi 14 pier.

### Getting Around

In Si Racha and on Ko Si Chang there are fleets of huge motorcycle taxis, many powered by Nissan engines, that will take you any-where in town or on the island for 10 to 20B.

### KO SI CHANG
เกาะสีชัง
• ☎ (38) • *pop 4000*

Ko Si Chang makes a nifty one or two day getaway from Bangkok. There is only one town on the island, facing the mainland; the rest of the island is practically deserted and fun to explore. The small population is made up of fisherfolk, retired and working mari-ners and government workers who are stationed with the customs office or with one of the aquaculture projects on the island. Although there has been talk of building a deep-water port on the island, so far Ko Si Chang has remained free of industry.

A branch of Thai Farmer's Bank in town – on the main road to the right as you walk up from the pier – does foreign exchange on weekdays.

## Things to See & Do

The meditation hermitage, **Yai Phrik Vipass-ana Centre**, is ensconced in limestone caves and palm huts along the island's centre ridge. The hermit caves make an interesting visit but should be approached with respect – monks and mâe chiis from all over Thailand come here to take advantage of the peaceful environment for meditation. Be careful that you don't fall down a limestone shaft; some are almost completely covered with vines.

On the opposite side of the island, facing out to sea, are some beaches with decent swimming – take care with the tide and the sea urchins, though. Don't come here looking for perfect white sand and turquoise waters, as the island's proximity to shipping lanes and fishing grounds means its shores are less than tidy. Depending on sea currents and time of year, the shoreline can be relatively clean or cluttered with flotsam. For beaches you're better off heading farther south-east to Ko Samet.

Secluded **Hat Tham** (also called Hat Sai), can be reached by following a branch of the ring road on foot to the back of the island. During low tide there's a strip of sand here; when the tide comes in it disappears. A partially submerged cave can be visited at the east end of the little bay. There is also a more public – and generally less clean – beach at the western end of the island (about two km from the pier) near the old palace grounds, called **Hat Tha Wang**. Thai residents and visitors from the mainland come here for picnics.

The palace was once used by King Chulalongkorn (Rama V) in the summer months, but was abandoned when the French briefly occupied the island in 1893. Little remains of the various palace buildings, but there are a few ruins to see. The main throne hall – a magnificent golden teak structure called Vimanmek – was moved to Bangkok in 1910, but the stairs leading up to it are still there; if you follow these stairs to the crest of the hill overlooking Tha Wang, you'll come to a stone outcropping wrapped in holy cloth. The locals call it 'Bell Rock' because if struck with a rock or heavy stick it rings like a bell. Flanking the rock are what appear to be two ruined chedis. The large chedi on the left actually contains **Wat Atsadangnimit**, a small consecrated chamber where King Chulalongkorn used to meditate. The unique Buddha image inside was fashioned 50 years ago by a local monk who now lives in the cave hermitage. There are attempts to rebuild this palace and some work was going on at the time of writing.

Not far from Wat Atsadangnimit is a large limestone cave called **Tham Saowapha**, which appears to plunge deep into the island. If you have a torch, the cave might be worth exploring.

To the east of town, high on a hill overlooking the sea, is a large Chinese temple called **San Jao Phaw Khao Yai**. During Chinese New Year in February, the island is overrun with Chinese visitors from the mainland. This is one of Thailand's most interesting Chinese temples, with shrine-caves, several different temple levels and a good view of Si Chang and the ocean. It's a long and steep climb from the road below.

Like most islands along Thailand's eastern seaboard, Ko Si Chang is best visited on weekdays; on weekends and holidays the island can get crowded.

## Places to Stay

The cheapest place is the rather characterless *Tiewpai Guest House* (☎ 216084) in town, not far from the main piers. They have one basic room that costs 100B; the remaining nine rooms, arrayed around a courtyard area behind the restaurant and reception area, range from 160B for a simple double with shared facilities to nicer rooms with private shower for 250B and air-con rooms for 500B. Perhaps because they have the lowest prices on the island and send touts to the pier to meet arriving visitors, the place is often full and the staff can be rather cold.

Out near the gate to Hat Tha Wang, *Benz Bungalow* (☎ 216091) offers clean rooms facing the sea in a basic hotel-style building or in one of its unique stone bungalows for 300 to 500B with fan and bath, 600B with air-con.

Near Hat Tham at the back of the island is *Si Phitsanu Bungalow* (☎ 216024). Rooms in a row house cost 300 to 500B per night, or you can get a one bedroom bungalow overlooking the small bay for 700B, or a two bedroom one for 1000B. *Top Bungalow* (☎ 216001), off the road on the way to Si Phitsanu, is similar in price but has no sea view; the buildings are decaying badly. To reach this area from town, take the first right past the Tiewpai Guest House, then follow the road straight past the Yai Phrik Vipassana Centre. A motorcycle samlor costs 20B.

The *Green House 84* (☎ 216024), off the ring road towards the Chinese temple, costs 150/300B for somewhat dark and dingy singles/doubles in a 10-room row house.

Also in the vicinity of the Chinese temple is the rather new *Sichang View Resort* (☎ 216-210), with 10 tidy apartment-style bungalows on nicely landscaped grounds for 800 to 1100B.

*Sichang Palace* (☎ 216276; fax 21630) is a new three-storey, 62-room hotel in the middle of town on Atsadang Rd. Clean, comfortable rooms facing the swimming pool cost 1000/1200B a single/double, while those with sea views are 1400/1600B. During the week the staff may knock 100 to 200B off these prices.

You can camp anywhere on the island without any hassle, including in Rama V's abandoned palace at Hat Tha Wang.

### Places to Eat

The town has several small restaurants, but nothing special, with all the Thai and Chinese standard dishes. Along the road that leads to the public beach are a couple of rustic seafood places.

*Sichang Palace* and *Sichang View Resort* each have their own restaurants serving good seafood at medium-high prices. *Tiewpai Guest House* offers reasonably priced Thai and western food.

### Getting There & Away

Boats to Ko Si Chang leave hourly from the pier in Si Racha at the end of Soi 14, Jermjompol Rd. The fare is 20B each way; the first boat leaves at about 5 am and the last at 7 pm. The last boat back to Si Racha from Si Chang is at 5 pm. As you approach Ko Si

Chang by boat, check out the dozens of barges anchored in the island's lee. Their numbers have multiplied from year to year as shipping demands by Thailand's booming import and export business have increased.

### Getting Around

There are fleets of huge motorcycle taxis that will take you anywhere in town for 10 to 20B. You can also get a complete tour of the island for 100 to 150B per hour. Asking prices for any ride tend to be outrageous; the supply of taxis is plentiful, however, and you can usually get the local price after talking to several drivers.

## PATTAYA
พัทยา

• ☎ (38) • pop 55,000

On Sukhumvit Rd through Pattaya, before Pattaya Beach (Hat Pattaya), the bus from Bangkok passes a number of prosperous sign-making businesses. Upon arrival at Pattaya Beach, the reason for their prosperity is immediately apparent – the place is lit up like Miami Beach at night. In fact this is Thailand's closest equivalent to Miami Beach – minus the chic. Many travellers will find Pattaya lacking in culture as well as good taste, since much of the place seems designed to attract the worst kind of western tourist. Budget travellers, in particular, would do well to scratch it from their itineraries. Pattaya Beach is not such a great beach to begin with and its biggest businesses – water sports and street sex – have driven prices for food and accommodation beyond Bangkok levels. Pattaya has recently begun experiencing a steady decline in tourist visitation. In response, local authorities and travel suppliers have been trying to upgrade Pattaya's image as well as clean the place up. Still, it continues to attract a loyal following of Bangkok expats, conventioneers and package tourists. According to recent TAT statistics, an average one-third of all foreign tourists coming to Thailand visits Pattaya; in a typical November to March season Pattaya receives around a million visitors.

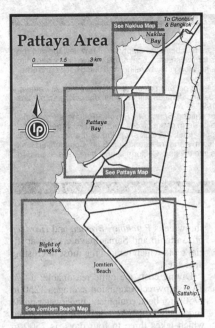

**Pattaya Area**

0    1.5    3 km

To Chonburi
& Bangkok

See Naklua Map

Naklua
Bay

Pattaya
Bay

See Pattaya Map

Bight of
Bangkok

Jomtien
Beach

To
Sattahip

See Jomtien Beach Map

Pattaya got its start as a resort when American GIs from a base in Nakhon Ratchasima began visiting the one-time fishing village in 1959. US navy men from nearby Sattahip added to the military influx during the Indochina War years. Nowadays there are still plenty of sailors around, but of many nationalities. National and international convention goers make up another large segment of the current market, along with Asian golfers seeking out the 12 local golf courses, including courses designed by names such as Robert Trent Jones and Jack Nicklaus.

Pattaya is acclaimed for its seafood, but it's generally way overpriced by national (but not international) standards. That part of South Pattaya known as 'the village' attracts a large number of *ka-toeys* (Thai transvestites), who pose as hookers and ply their trade among the droves of well heeled European tourists, as well as a prominent gay scene.

The one thing the Pattaya area has going

for it is diving centres. There are over a dozen nice islands off Pattaya's shore, although they can be expensive to reach. If you're a snorkelling or scuba enthusiast, equipment can be booked at any of the several diving shops/schools at Pattaya Beach. Ko Laan, the most popular of the offshore islands, even has places to stay.

For beach enthusiasts, if you can't get to one of the better beaches in Southern Thailand, the best in the immediate Pattaya area is six-km-long Jomtien Beach (Hat Jomtien), a couple of km south of Pattaya. Here the water is clean and you're well away from the noisy Pattaya bar scene.

Hat Naklua, north of Pattaya, is also quiet and fairly tastefully developed. Jomtien and Naklua are where visiting families tend to stay, as Pattaya/South Pattaya is pretty much given over to single male tourists or couples on package tours. The glitziest digs are at North Pattaya and Cliff beaches (between South Pattaya and Jomtien).

### Information

**Tourist Office** The TAT office (☎ 427667), at the midpoint of Pattaya Beach Rd, keeps an up-to-date list of accommodation in the Pattaya area, and is very helpful. The tourist police (☎ 429371) has moved to a new location on Pattaya 2 Rd.

**Post & Communications** The GPO and international telephone office are together in South Pattaya on Soi 15 (Soi Post Office). There are also several private long-distance phone offices in town, but calls from the government office at the GPO are always less expensive.

**Radio** Pattaya has a radio station with English-language broadcasts at FM 107.7 MHz. American and British announcers offer a mix of local news and music.

**Magazines & Newspapers** *Explore Pattaya*, a free monthly magazine distributed around town, contains information on current events, sightseeing and advertisements for hotel and restaurant specials. *Pattaya Mail*, a weekly

CENTRAL THAILAND

### Water Quality

One of Pattaya's main problems during recent years has been the emptying of raw sewage into the bay, a practice that has posed serious health risks for swimmers. Local officials have finally begun to take notice and are now taking regular bacteria counts along the shoreline, and fining hotels and other businesses found to be releasing untreated sewage.

The Thai government has allocated US$60 million for pollution clean-up and prevention at Pattaya. By 1995, water treatment plants in Pattaya, Naklua and Jomtien will be in full operation; authorities claim the coastal waters will be pollution-free by 1997.

In the meantime, according to a TAT pamphlet entitled *Striving to Resolve Pattaya's Problems*, beach areas considered safe for swimming (with a coliform count of less than 1000 MPN per 100 ml) include those facing Wong Amat Hotel, Dusit Resort Hotel, Yot Sak shopping centre and the Royal Cliff Hotel. Shoreline areas found to exceed the coliform standard extend from Siam Commercial Bank in South Pattaya to where Khlong Pattaya empties into the sea. Coliform counts here have exceeded 1700 MPN per 100 ml. ■

newspaper, publishes articles on political, economic and environmental developments in the area as well as the usual ads.

### Water Sports

Pattaya and Jomtien have some of the best water sports facilities in Thailand. Water-skiing costs 800 to 1000B per hour including equipment, boat and driver. Parasailing is 200 to 300B a shot (about 10 to 15 minutes) and windsurfing 500B an hour. Game-fishing is also a possibility; rental rates for boats, fishing guides and tackle are quite reasonable.

Jomtien Beach is the best spot for windsurfing, not least because you're a little less likely to run into parasailors or jet skiiers. Surf House on Jomtien Beach Rd rents equipment and offers instruction.

**Scuba Diving** Pattaya is the most convenient dive location to Bangkok, but it is far from being the best Thailand has to offer. Recent reports say the fish population has dwindled considerably and visibility is often poor due to heavy boat traffic. Although nearby Ko Laan, Ko Sak and Ko Krok are fine for beginners, accomplished divers may prefer the 'outer islands' of Ko Man Wichai and Ko Rin which have more visibility. In most places expect three to nine metres of visibility under good conditions, or in more remote sites five to 12m. Farther south-east,

shipwrecks *Petchburi Bremen* and *Hardeep* off Sattahip and Samae have created artificial reefs which remain the most interesting dive sites.

Diving costs are quite reasonable: a two dive shipwreck excursion averages 1250 to 1750B for boat, equipment, underwater guide and lunch. Full NAUI or PADI certification, which takes three to four days, is 7500 to 10,000B for all instruction and equipment.

Some shops do trips to nearby islands for as low as 500B, and to islands a bit farther out for 650B; these prices include lunch, beverages, transport and dive master but not equipment rental. Average rental rates are: mask, fins and snorkel 125B; regulator w/SPG 250B; buoyancy compensation device 200 to 250B; weightbelt 100B; tank 125B; and wetsuit 200B. Airfills typically cost 80B.

Shops along Pattaya Beach Rd advertise trips, and several Pattaya hotels also arrange excursions and equipment.

Dave's Diver Den – Central Pattaya Rd (☎ 420411)
Diver's World – Soi Yamato, South Pattaya (☎ 426517)
Mermaid's Dive School – Mermaid Beach Resort Hotel, Jomtien Beach (☎ 232219; fax 232221)
Paradise Scuba Divers – Siam Bayview Resort (☎ 710587)
Scuba Tek Dive Center – Weekender Hotel, Pattaya 2 Rd (☎ 361616)
Seafari Sports Center – Soi 5, North Pattaya (☎ 429253; fax 424708)
Steve's Dive Shop – Soi 4, North Pattaya (☎ 428392)

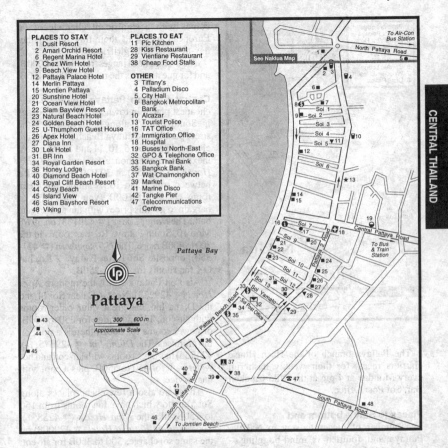

**PLACES TO STAY**
1 Dusit Resort
2 Amari Orchid Resort
6 Regent Marina Hotel
7 Chez Wim Hotel
9 Beach View Hotel
12 Pattaya Palace Hotel
14 Merlin Pattaya
15 Montien Pattaya
20 Sunshine Hotel
21 Ocean View Hotel
22 Siam Bayview Resort
23 Natural Beach Hotel
24 Golden Beach Hotel
25 U-Thumphorn Guest House
26 Apex Hotel
27 Diana Inn
30 Lek Hotel
31 BR Inn
34 Royal Garden Resort
36 Honey Lodge
40 Diamond Beach Hotel
43 Royal Cliff Beach Resort
44 Cosy Beach
45 Island View
46 Siam Bayshore Resort
48 Viking

**PLACES TO EAT**
11 Pic Kitchen
28 Kiss Restaurant
29 Vientiane Restaurant
38 Cheap Food Stalls

**OTHER**
3 Tiffany's
4 Palladium Disco
5 City Hall
8 Bangkok Metropolitan
   Bank
10 Alcazar
13 Tourist Police
16 TAT Office
17 Immigration Office
18 Hospital
19 Buses to North-East
32 GPO & Telephone Office
33 Krung Thai Bank
35 Bangkok Bank
37 Wat Chaimongkhon
39 Market
41 Marine Disco
42 Tangke Pier
47 Telecommunications
   Centre

Pattaya Bay

**Pattaya**

0    300    600 m
Approximate Scale

## Karting

One of the legacies left behind by American GIs is karting, the racing of miniature autos (go-karts) powered by five to 15 hp engines. Karting has since turned into an international sport often described as the closest approximation to Formula One racing available to the average driver.

Pattaya Kart Speedway (☎ 423062), at 248/2 Thepprasit Rd, boasts Asia's only track sanctioned by the Commission Internationale de Karting (CIK), a 1080m loop that meets all CIK safety and sporting standards, plus a beginner track and an off-road (unpaved)

track. It's open daily from 9.30 am to 9.30 pm (except when international kart races are hosted). Prices range from 150B for 10 minutes of racing in a five hp kart (oriented toward children) to 250B for a 10 to 15 hp kart.

## Other Sports

Other recreational activities available include golf, bowling, snooker, archery, target shooting, horse riding and tennis. Among the several gyms and fitness centres around town is Gold's Gym in South Pattaya's Julie Complex. Gold's has a second branch in North Pattaya just past Soi 1 on Naklua-Pattaya Rd.

CENTRAL THAILAND

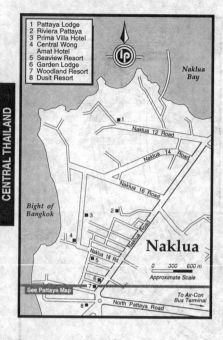

1 Pattaya Lodge
2 Riviera Pattaya
3 Prima Villa Hotel
4 Central Wong
  Amat Hotel
5 Seaview Resort
6 Garden Lodge
7 Woodland Resort
8 Dusit Resort

Naklua
Bay

Bight of
Bangkok

Naklua

Naklua 12 Road

Naklua 14 Road

Naklua 16 Road

Naklua 18 Rd

0    300    600 m
Approximate Scale

See Pattaya Map

North Pattaya Road

To Air-Con
Bus Terminal

The Pattaya branch of the Hash House Harriers meets for their weekly hash run every Monday at 4 pm at the Wild Chicken Bar, Soi Post Office.

### Places to Stay – bottom end

The number of places to stay in Naklua, Pattaya and Jomtien is mind-boggling – close to 200 hotels, guesthouses and bungalows with the total number of rooms over 13,000. Because of low occupancy rates, some hotels offer special deals, especially mid-week; bargaining for a room may also net a lower rate. On weekends and holidays the cheaper rooms tend to book out.

In Pattaya itself, North Pattaya and Naklua are quieter and better places to stay if you want to avoid the full-on nightlife of South Pattaya. Overall Jomtien Beach is much better, with clean water and beach, and no obvious sex scene. No place in the area is entirely immune from sex tourism, however; almost every place from Naklua to Jomtien

comes with a significant clientele of fat European men and their tiny rent-by-the-day-or-week Thai girlfriends.

The average hotel ranges from 350 to 2000B, and for guesthouses the range is 200 to 450B.

**Central & South Pattaya** You'll find the cheapest places in town are the guesthouses in South Pattaya along Pattaya 2 Rd, the street parallel to Pattaya Beach Rd. Most are clustered near sois 6, 10, 11 and 12. The most inexpensive guesthouse I found was *Lucky House* (☎ 428955) at 397/20 Pattaya 2 Rd between sois 8 and 10. A simple but clean room costs just 100B (you may have to bargain to get this price) with fan and private bath. The *Honey Lodge* (☎ 429133) on 597/8 Moo 10, South Pattaya Rd, has rooms in the 300 to 400B range. The *U-Thumphorn* (☎ 421-350), opposite Soi 10 on Pattaya 2 Rd, has OK fan rooms for 150 to 250B.

Also on Pattaya 2 Rd, the modern *Apex Hotel* (☎ 429233), No 216/2 near Soi 11 and the Diana Inn, has great value older rooms with air-con, TV and fridge for 250 to 300B, or newer rooms for 500B; there's a pool on the premises. The *Diana Inn* (☎ 429675; fax 424566) has large rooms with air-con and hot water bath for 450 to 550B, plus a pool with bar service.

There are also a few cheap places along Soi Yamato which have fan rooms from 150 to 250B, like the *Nipa House* (☎ 425851). The *Meridian Pattaya Hotel* (☎ 429008) on the same soi charges 300 to 350B for air-con rooms – check first if you want a room with a window.

In a lane south of Soi 12 the *BR Inn* (☎ 426-449) offers 35 reasonably clean rooms for 200B with fan, 300B air-con. On Soi 13, the *Malibu Guest House* (☎ 423180) has 250B air-con rooms that include breakfast. The rest of the many guesthouses on Soi 13 are in the 200 to 350B range, but rooms are usually cramped and without windows. An exception is *Ma Maison* (☎ 429318), which offers chalet-style air-con rooms around a swimming pool for 600B; as the name suggests, it's French managed and there's a French restaurant on the premises.

Down in South Pattaya on Soi Viking, the *Viking* (☎ 423164; fax 425964) has been a long-time favourite for its quiet 250 to 350B rooms and pool.

**North Pattaya/Naklua** Quiet Soi 1 in North Pattaya features the charming *Chez Wim* (☎ 429044), where bargain rooms cost 250B with fan or 350B with air-con. Wedged between North and Central Pattaya on North Pattaya Beach Rd, *BJ Guest House* (☎ 421147) sits right across from the beach and rents air-con rooms for 350B, fan rooms from 200B.

In North Pattaya the *German Garden Hotel* (☎ 225612; fax 225932) on Soi 12, Naklua Rd, is a bit far from the beach but it's quiet and rooms range from 400B. Another German-oriented North Pattaya place that has been recommended is *Welkom Inn* (☎ 422589; fax 361193), Soi 3, where air-con doubles cost 350 to 500B; a large pool, Thai garden restaurant and Franco-Belgian restaurant are pluses.

**Jomtien** At Jomtien Beach, the bottom end consists of several places around the mid-range Surf House International Hotel at the north end of the beach. The *AA Guest House* (☎ 231183) has 350B rooms with air-con and TV. Right behind AA is the flashier *Moonshine Place* (☎ 231956) at 380B; the popular bar-restaurant downstairs could make it noisy at night. Next to Surf House is *Sunlight* (☎ 429108) with similar 350 to 400B air-con rooms.

The *DD Inn* (☎ 232995) is also at the north end of the beach, where the road turns towards Pattaya; very clean rooms cost 300B with fan, 400B air-con; showers for beach going nonguests cost 10B.

Nearby *JB Guest House* (☎ 231581) takes the prize, with very decent fan rooms for 200/250B a single/double, simple air-con rooms for 300B, air-con rooms with sea view for 400B and larger rooms for 500B. *Seaview Villa* (☎ 422766) has seven fan-cooled bungalows for 300 to 400B. *Maisonette Guest*

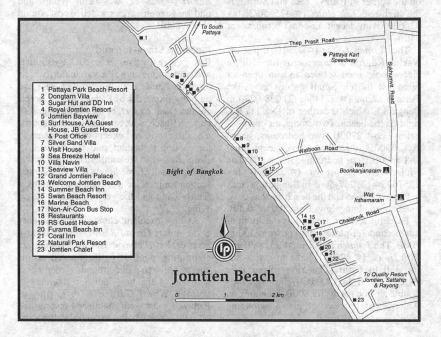

1 Pattaya Park Beach Resort
2 Dongtarn Villa
3 Sugar Hut and DD Inn
4 Royal Jomtien Resort
5 Jomtien Bayview
6 Surf House, AA Guest House, JB Guest House & Post Office
7 Silver Sand Villa
8 Visit House
9 Sea Breeze Hotel
10 Villa Navin
11 Seaview Villa
12 Grand Jomtien Palace
13 Welcome Jomtien Beach
14 Summer Beach Inn
15 Swan Beach Resort
16 Marine Beach
17 Non-Air-Con Bus Stop
18 Restaurants
19 RS Guest House
20 Furama Beach Inn
21 Coral Inn
22 Natural Park Resort
23 Jomtien Chalet

To South Pattaya

Thep Prasit Road

Pattaya Kart Speedway

Sukhumvit Road

Watboon Road

Wat Boonkanjanaram

Bight of Bangkok

Wat Inthamaram

Chaiapruk Road

To Quality Resort Jomtien, Sattahip & Rayong

**Jomtien Beach**

0        1        2 km

CENTRAL THAILAND

*House* (☎ 231835; fax 232676) has the usual 400B rooms attached to a French restaurant.

One of the cheapest places to stay is the tidy *RS Guest House* (☎ 231867/8), which sits at the southern end of the beach, near Chalapruk Rd. Reasonable smallish rooms cost 250B with fan or 350B with air-con.

You can also find unnamed *rooms for rent* in 'condotels' along Jomtien Beach for about 200 to 400B a night with fan, 400 to 600B with air-con.

## Places to Stay – middle

Good mid-range places can be found in Naklua, North Pattaya and Jomtien. In Pattaya the *Sunshine Hotel* (☎ 429247; fax 421302) is tucked away at 217/1 Soi 8, and all their fine rooms cost 550B. The hotel also has a pool. On Soi 11 the 70-room *Natural Beach Hotel* (☎ 429239; fax 429650) overlooks the beach with good air-con rooms from 400 to 700B, plus a seedier section of 180B fan rooms at the back. Farther south, on the corner of Pattaya 2 Rd and Soi 13, is the high-rise *Lek Hotel* (☎ 425550/2; fax 426629) with decent air-con/TV rooms for 640B.

The *Garden Lodge* (☎ 429109), just off Naklua Rd, has air-con rooms for 650B, a clean pool, good service and an open-air breakfast buffet. Small groups may like *Pattaya Lodge* (☎ 225464; (2) 238-0230 in Bangkok), which is farther off Naklua Rd, right on the beach. Two-storey, air-con bungalows cost 2700B (two bedrooms, sleeps six), 3500B (three bedrooms, sleeps nine) and 3800B (four bedrooms, sleeps 12). The *Riviera Hotel Pattaya* (☎ 225230; fax 225764; ☎ (2) 252-5068 in Bangkok) stands between the road and the beach and has cosy, quiet air-con bungalows from 380 to 2000B.

Peaceful Jomtien Beach has mostly mid-range condotel places ranging from 500 to 700B. The *Jomtien Bayview* (☎ 251889) and *Visit House* (☎ 426331) have air-con rooms for 350 to 650B. The *Silver Sand Villa* (☎ 231288/9; fax 231030) has spacious double air-con rooms for 800B, including an American-style breakfast, plus a swimming pool.

The friendly *Surf House International Hotel* (☎ 231025/6) has air-con rooms for 400B, 500B with sea view; all rooms come with TV and fridge. The *Marine Beach Hotel* (☎ 231031) and the well run *Sea Breeze* (☎ 231057; fax 231059) are just a bit more expensive at 500 to 700B per air-con room but the latter is very good value at this rate. Another good-value place is the friendly *Summer Beach Inn* (☎ /fax 231777), near the Marine Beach, where new rooms cost 650B, including satellite TV and minibar in all rooms. Another good deal is the new *Furama Beach Inn* (☎ 231545), where standard rooms cost 655 to 700B a day, deluxe rooms 1200B.

Jomtien also has several more expensive places that rent bungalows in the 1000 to 2000B range (see Places to Stay – top end). The high-rise development of Pattaya and Cliff Beach is spreading fast to Jomtien.

At the time of writing there was only one place to stay on Ko Laan. The *Ko Laan Resort* (☎ 428422) was being rebuilt and mid-range rooms are expected to cost around 600 to 800B.

## Places to Stay – top end

Pattaya is really a resort for package tourists and conventioneers so the vast majority of its accommodation is in this bracket. The two reigning monarchs of Pattaya luxury hotels are the *Dusit Resort*, at the northern end of Pattaya Beach, with two pools, tennis courts, a health centre and exceptional dim sum in the rooftop restaurant, and the *Royal Cliff Beach Resort*, at the southern end of Pattaya, which is really three hotels in one: a central section for package tours and conventions, a family wing and the very up-market Royal Wing.

Another excellent choice in this category is the *Amari Orchid Resort*, set on 10 lush acres in North Pattaya, with an Olympic-size swimming pool, two illuminated tennis courts, children's playground, garden chess and one of the best Italian restaurants in Pattaya. *Royal Garden Resort*, one of Pattaya's most well established resorts, sits on eight acres of palms in central Pattaya and has lotus ponds and Thai-style pavilions. It's attached to a new four-storey shopping centre as well as a Ripley's Believe It or Not Museum; also on the premises are a fitness centre, two tennis courts, two cinemas and a pool.

All of the hotels listed below have air-con rooms and swimming pools (unless otherwise noted). In most cases the upper end of the price range represents suites, while the lower end are standard doubles. Many of the top-end hotels have lowered rates on standard singles and doubles so it's worth asking if anything cheaper is available when requesting a rate quote. Rooms are also often cheaper when booked through a Bangkok travel agency.

## Hat Naklua

*Central Wong Amat Hotel* – Naklua Rd (☎ 426990/9; fax 428599; Bangkok ☎ (2) 547-1234); 207 rooms, from 1600B

*Garden Beach Resort* – Mu 5, Soi Wong Amat, Pattaya-Naklua Rd (☎ 411940; fax 411949; Bangkok ☎ (2) 254-5220); 419 rooms, 2100 to 5800B

*Loma Hotel* – 193 Mu 5, Naklua Rd (☎ 426027; fax 421501); 120 rooms, 850 to 2100B

*Woodlands Resort* – Naklua Rd (☎ 421707; fax 425663); 80 rooms, 1600 and 2000B

## North Pattaya

*Amari Orchid Resort* – North Pattaya (☎ 428161; fax 428165; Bangkok ☎ (2) 267-9708); 234 rooms, 1800 to 4400B

*Beach View* – 389 Soi 2, Beach Rd (☎ 422660; fax 422664); 104 rooms, 590 to 850B (discounted from 850 to 1290B)

*Dusit Resort* – Mu 5, Pattaya-Naklua Rd (☎ 428541; fax 428239; Bangkok ☎ (2) 236-0450); 408 rooms, from 3500B

*Merlin Pattaya* – Beach Rd (☎ 428755/9; fax 421673; Bangkok ☎ (2) 253-2140); 360 rooms, 1800B

*Montien Pattaya* – Beach Rd (☎ 428155/6; fax 423155; Bangkok ☎ (2) 233-7000); 320 rooms, singles/doubles 2500 to 3000B

*Pattaya Palace Hotel* – Beach Rd (☎ 428319; fax 428026; Bangkok ☎ (2) 252-4926); 261 rooms, 1600 to 3600B

*Regent Marina Hotel* – North Pattaya Rd (☎ 429298; fax 423296; Bangkok ☎ (2) 390-2511); 208 rooms, from 1800B

*Thai Garden Resort* – North Pattaya Rd (☎ 424356; fax 426198); 170 rooms, 1200 to 2300B

## Central & South Pattaya

*Baiyoke Pattaya* – Pratamnak Rd (☎ 423300; fax 426124; Bangkok ☎ (2) 255-0155); 136 rooms, 1521 to 1755B

*Beverly Plaza* – Pratamnak Rd (☎ 421278; fax 429718; Bangkok ☎ (2) 254-4221); 200 rooms, 1200 to 1800B

*Golden Beach Hotel* – 519/29 Pattaya 2 Rd (☎ 428891; fax 425935); 1700 and 2000B

*Royal Century* – Central Pattaya Rd (☎ 427800; fax 428069; Bangkok ☎ (2) 254-5220); 272 rooms, 1200 to 2000B

*Royal Garden Resort* – Beach Rd (☎ 428122/6/7; fax 429926; Bangkok ☎ (2) 476-0021); 300 rooms, from 2600B

*Siam Bayshore Resort* – South Pattaya Rd (☎ 428678/81; fax 428730; Bangkok ☎ (2) 221-1004); 270 rooms, 1600B

*Siam Bayview Resort* – Beach Rd (☎ 423871/7; fax 423879; Bangkok ☎ (2) 221-1004); 370 rooms, from 2236B up

*Town in Town* – Central Pattaya Rd (☎ 426350; fax 426351; Bangkok ☎ (2) 529-8358); 360 rooms, 1600 to 2000B

## Hat Cliff

*Asia Pattaya Beach Hotel* – Cliff Rd (☎ 250602; fax 259496; Bangkok ☎ (2) 215-0808); 314 rooms, from 2119B

*Cosy Beach* – Cliff Rd (☎ 428818; fax 422818); 160 rooms, 1600 to 1800B

*Golden Cliff House* – Cliff Rd (☎ 231590; fax 231259; Bangkok ☎ (2) 258-8452); 50 rooms, 1000 to 3500B

*Island View* – Cliff Rd (☎ 250813; fax 250818; Bangkok ☎ (2) 249-8941); 150 rooms, 1200 to 1452B

*Royal Cliff Beach Resort* – Cliff Rd (☎ 250421/30; fax 250522; Bangkok ☎ (2) 282-0999); 650 rooms, from 3600B

## Hat Jomtien

*Ban Suan* – (☎ 231072); 36 rooms, 800 to 1500B

*Coral Inn* – (☎ 231283/7); 36 rooms, 850B

*Dongtarn Villa* – (☎ 231049); 23 bungalows, 1500 to 3000B

*Grand Jomtien Palace* – (☎ 231405/8; fax 231404; Bangkok ☎ (2) 271-3613); 356 Jomtien Beach Rd; 252 rooms, 1300 to 1500B

*Natural Park Beach Resort* – 412 Jomtien Beach Rd (☎ 231561; fax 231567; Bangkok ☎ (2) 247-2825); 122 rooms, from 1500B

*Pattaya Park Beach Resort* – 345 Jomtien Beach Rd (☎ 251201; fax 251209; Bangkok ☎ (2) 511-0717); 270 rooms, 1800 to 3600B

*Quality Resort Jomtien* – (☎ 231490; fax 231495; Bangkok ☎ (2) 254-8753); 137 rooms, 1500 to 2000B

CENTRAL THAILAND

*Royal Jomtien Resort* – 408 Mu 12 Jomtien Beach Rd (☎ 231350; fax 231369; Bangkok ☎ (2) 254-1865); 400 rooms, from 1800B

*Swan Beach Resort* – (☎ 231464; fax 231266); 126 rooms, 1350 to 1584B

*Welcome Jomtien Beach* – (☎ 231701/16; fax 232716; Bangkok ☎ (2) 252-0594); 382 rooms, from 1900B

## Places to Eat

Most food in Pattaya is expensive, but good Thai food is available in shops along Pattaya's back street (Pattaya 2 Rd), away from the beach. The front signs outside the many snack bars reveal that bratwurst mit brot is far more readily available than khâo phàt.

Arabs and South Asians have been coming to Pattaya for many years now, so there are plenty of Indian, Pakistani and Middle Eastern restaurants in town, some with fairly moderate prices.

The best seafood restaurants are in South Pattaya, where you pick out the sea creatures yourself and are charged by weight. Prices are sky-high.

One moderately priced yet well appointed Pattaya restaurant is the *PIC Kitchen* on Soi 5 (second entrance on Soi 4). The Thai-style salas have low wooden tables and cushions for dining and the emphasis is on Thai food with a limited selection of western dishes. The upstairs bar area occasionally features live jazz. Another interesting place to eat is *Vientiane Restaurant* (☎ 411298) at 485/18 Pattaya 2 Rd, opposite Soi Yamato. The over 500-item menu includes mostly Thai and Lao dishes ranging from 60 to 120B, plus lunch specials for 30 to 50B. The 24 hour *Kiss* on Pattaya 2 Rd, near the Diana Inn, has reasonably priced American and European breakfasts, Thai dishes, snacks and drinks.

Opposite the bus station on the corner of Jomtien Beach and Chalapruk Rds are a few basic and cheap restaurants serving the usual Thai/Chinese dishes.

*San Domenico's* (☎ 426871), on Jomtien Rd between South Pattaya and Jomtien Beach, is operated by the same Italian family that started Pan Pan in Bangkok. The Italian menu is superb and though regular meals are

pricey there is also an excellent buffet for just under 200B stocked with antipasti, pasta, seafood and Luciano Pantieri's famous desserts.

*Moonshine Place* on Jomtien Beach specialises in Mexican and Southern Thai food; you can also buy a picnic lunch here.

*Alt Heidelberg* at 273 Beach Rd, South Pattaya, is one of the more established German restaurants. It opens at 9 am for breakfast and stays open till 2 am. The Royal Garden Plaza shopping centre, attached to Royal Garden Resort, contains several fast-food franchise restaurants, including *KFC, Pizza Hut, McDonald's, Swensen's* and *Mister Donut*.

## Entertainment

Eating, drinking and making merry are the big pastimes once the sun goes down. Making merry in Pattaya, aside from the professional sex scene, means everything from hanging out in a video bar to dancing all night at one of the discos in South Pattaya. Two transvestite palaces, *Alcazar* and *Tiffany's*, offer complete drag-queen shows; the Alcazar (☎ 428746), at 78/14 Pattaya 2 Rd, is the best and puts on three shows nightly at 6.30, 8 and 9.30 pm.

Among the several discos in town, the very glitzy *Palladium* has a capacity of 6000 customers, reportedly the largest disco in Thailand. It's close to the Alcazar at 78/33-35 Pattaya 2 Rd. 'Pattaya Land', encompassing sois 1, 2 and 3 in South Pattaya, is one of the most concentrated bar areas. The many gay bars on Soi 3 are announced by signs over the soi reading 'Boys Town'.

Actually, one of the best things to do in the evening is just to stroll down Beach Rd and check out the amazing variety of bars – there's one for every proclivity, including a couple of outdoor Thai boxing bars featuring local talent. Truly the Garden of Earthly Delights, in the most Boschean sense.

## Getting There & Away

**Air** Bangkok Airways has a daily flight between U-Taphao and Ko Samui for 1660B each way.

At the moment there is no regularly scheduled air service to Pattaya from Bangkok. Two airlines, Tropical Sea Air and Bangkok Airways, have each operated flights from Bangkok to Pattaya or nearby U-Taphao at one time or another, but due to a lack of profitability neither lasted.

**Bangkok International Airport** If you've just flown into Bangkok and need to get to Pattaya right away, there are airport minibuses that go directly to Pattaya at 9 am, noon and 7 pm daily for 200B one way. In the reverse direction, the THAI minibus leaves from the Royal Cliff Resort in Pattaya at 6 am, 12.30 and 6 pm; it takes around 2½ hours to reach the airport. Some hotels in Pattaya also run their own buses to Bangkok for fares ranging from 160 to 300B one way.

**Bus** Ordinary buses from Bangkok's Eastern Bus Terminal cost 37B one way and leave at 30 minute intervals from 5.20 am to 9 pm daily. In Pattaya they leave from the depot on Sukhumvit Rd, where it meets Central Pattaya Rd. Count on around three hours for this trip.

Air-con buses from the same station in Bangkok leave at similar intervals for 66B (or 126B return) between 6.30 am and 8 pm. Air-con buses to Pattaya are also available from Bangkok's Northern Bus Terminal for 67B. In Pattaya the air-con bus stop is on North Pattaya Rd, near the intersection with Sukhumvit Rd. The air-con route takes around 2½ hours. Several hotels and travel agencies in Bangkok also run thrice-daily air-con tour buses to Pattaya for around 100 to 150B. Cramped minivans from Khao San Rd typically cost 170B per person. These buses take around two hours in either direction.

From Si Racha you can grab a public bus on Sukhumvit Rd to Pattaya for 10B.

There are also buses between Pattaya and several North-Eastern towns, including Khon Kaen (225B air-con), Nong Khai (165B ordinary, 297B air-con) and Ubon Ratchathani (160B ordinary, 290B air-con).

Pattaya has a separate bus stop for buses to the North-East on Central Pattaya Rd a couple of blocks east of Pattaya 2 Rd.

**Train** A No 151/239 train goes from Hualamphong station to Pattaya via Chachoengsao daily at 7 am, arriving at 10.45 am. In the opposite direction train No 240 departs Pattaya at 1.47 pm and arrives at Hualamphong at 5.15 pm. The trip costs 31B one way. Although this is an hour longer than the typical bus ride from Bangkok, it beats biting your nails in traffic jams along the highway from Bang Na to Trat. The Pattaya train station is just north of the T-intersection of Central Pattaya Rd and Sukhumvit Rd.

### Getting Around
**Songthaew** Songthaews cruise up and down Pattaya Beach and Pattaya 2 Rds frequently – just hop on and when you get out pay 5B anywhere between Naklua and South Pattaya, 10B as far as Jomtien. Don't ask the fare first as the driver may interpret this to mean you want to charter the vehicle. A chartered songthaew to Jomtien should be 30B. It's usually easier to get a share songthaew from Jomtien to central Pattaya rather than vice versa.

Many readers have complained about riding the 5B songthaews with local passengers and then being charged a high charter price of 50B or more when they get off. In some instances drivers have threatened to beat farang passengers when they wouldn't pay this exorbitant fare. It's little use complaining to the tourist police unless you can give them the licence plate number of the offending driver's vehicle. A refund is highly unlikely but perhaps if the tourist police receive enough complaints, they'll take some action to reduce or eliminate the rip-offs. As of 1996 this seemed to be less of a problem.

**Boat** The ferry to Ko Laan leaves from Tangke Pier in South Pattaya, takes 40 minutes and costs 100B. For 250B the ferry service will throw in lunch. They depart in the morning around 9 am and return at 4 pm. Boat charters cost around 1000 to 1500B per day depending on the size of the boat.

**Car & Jeep** Jeeps can be hired for around 600 to 800B per day, and cars start at 1200B (as low as 800B for a 4WD Suzuki in the low season) depending on size and model; insurance and tax cost up to 160B more. All rentals in Pattaya are on a 24 hour basis. Avis has offices at the Dusit Resort (☎ 429901) and Royal Cliff Beach Resort (☎ 422421); Hertz is at the Royal Garden Resort (☎ 428-122). For lower rates try Via (☎ 423293) and Pop Eye (☎ 429631), both on Pattaya 2 Rd.

**Motorcycle** Motorcycles cost 150 to 200B per day for an 80 or 100cc; a 125cc will cost 250B and you'll even see a few 750 to 1000cc machines for hire for 500 to 700B. There are several motorcycle hire places along Pattaya Beach Rd and a couple on Pattaya 2 Rd. Pattaya is a good place to purchase a used motorcycle – check the rental shops.

## AROUND PATTAYA

Farther south and then east from Pattaya are more beaches and more resorts. In fact, the more up-market places may, in the future, be restructuring themselves in favour of more middle-class tourists and conventioneers.

*Bang Saray Villa* (☎ (38) 436070), in Bang Saray, has 24 air-con bungalows for a reasonable 300B, while the *Bang Saray Fishing Inn* (☎ (38) 436095) and *Bang Saray Fishing Lodge* (☎ (38) 436757) are small hotels with air-con rooms for 550 to 850B. *Nong Nooch Village* (☎ (38) 429342) has a choice of rooms from 300B or bungalows from 1600B. *Sea Sand Club* (☎ (38) 435163; fax 435166) has 46 air-con bungalows that cost 749B from Sunday to Thursday, and 856B on Friday and Saturday.

There are still some good seafood restaurants for local Thais in Bang Saray – something Pattaya hasn't seen for years.

Still farther south is Sattahip, a vacation spot for the Thai military – some of the best beaches in the area are reserved for their use. There are several Thai navy and air force bases in the vicinity.

# Rayong Province

## RAYONG & AROUND
จ.เมืองระยอง
• ☎ (38) • pop 45,000

Rayong lies on the Gulf coast 220 km from Bangkok by the old highway (Highway 3) or 185 km on Highway 36. The province produces fine fruit (especially durian and pineapple) and *náam plaa* (fish sauce). Rayong itself is not really worth visiting, but nearby beaches are fair and Ko Samet is a favourite island getaway for Bangkokians. Except for Ko Samet, this area has not received many foreign visitors yet, although it has been popular with Thai tourists for several years.

Estuarial beaches at **Laem Chareon**, a couple of km south of the provincial capital of Rayong, aren't that great but there are some reasonable seafood restaurants. Better are the beaches near **Ban Phe**, a seaside town around 25 km south-east of Rayong (this is also the departure point for Ko Samet). If sun and sand are what you've come to Rayong for, head straight for Ban Phe. Then pick out a beach or board a boat bound for Samet.

Another much smaller island near Rayong is **Ko Saket**, which is a 20 minute boat ride from the beach of Hat Sai Thong (turn south off Highway 3 at Km 208).

The **Suan Son Pine Park**, five km farther down the highway from Ban Phe, is a popular place for Thai picnickers and has white sand beaches as well.

**Suan Wang Kaew** is 11 km east of Ban Phe and has more beaches and rather expensive bungalows. **Ko Thalu**, across from Wang Kaew, is said to be a good diving area – the proprietors of Suan Wang Kaew, a private park, can arrange boats and gear. Other resort areas along the Rayong coast include **Laem Mae Phim** and **Hat Sai Thong**. **Hat Mae Rampeung**, a 10 km strip of sand between Ban Taphong and Ban Kon Ao (11 km east of Rayong), is part of Laem Ya-Ko Samet National Park. See the Ko Samet section for more information on the park.

CENTRAL THAILAND

**Khao Chamao-Khao Wong National Park** is inland about 17 km north of Km 274 off Highway 3. Though less than 85 sq km, the park is famous for limestone mountains, caves, high cliffs, dense forest, waterfalls, and freshwater swimming and fishing. The park service here rents bungalows, long houses and tents. To get here from Ban Phe take a songthaew to Km 274 for 20B, and another songthaew to the park.

Many more resort-type places are popping up along Rayong's coastline. Bangkok developers envisage a string of Thai resorts all the way to Trat along the eastern seaboard, banking on the increasing income and leisure time of Bangkok Thais.

One non-resort development along the coast is the new deep-water port at **Maptaphut** which, along with Chonburi's Laem Chabang Port, is charted to catch the large shipping overflow from Bangkok's Khlong Toey Port.

### Information
**Money** The Bangkok Bank at 56/1 Sukhumvit Rd, between the cinema and Tawan Ok Hotel, has an exchange window open daily from 7 am to 10 pm.

### Places to Stay & Eat
**Rayong** There are three inexpensive hotels near the bus station off Sukhumvit Rd. The *Rayong Hotel*, at 65/3 Sukhumvit Rd, and the *Rayong Otani*, at 69 Sukhumvit, both have fan rooms from 150B, air-con from 350B. The *Tawan Ok*, at 52/3 Sukhumvit, has fan-cooled rooms for 100B without bath, 150B with bath.

For cheap food check the market near the Thetsabanteung cinema, or the string of restaurants and noodle shops on Taksin Maharat Rd just south of Wat Lum Mahachaichumphon. If you have plenty of time, take a songthaew (3B) south from Sukhumvit road to the mouth of the Rayong River at Laem Charoen, where the well established *Laem Charoen* and *Ocha Rot* serve moderately priced seafood.

**Ban Phe** There are several hotels in Ban Phe near the central market and within walking distance of the pier. *TN Place*, about 100m

from the pier, has rooms with fan for 200B or with air-con for 300B. The owners are friendly and provide plenty of information, but the hotel can get a bit noisy. The *Queen* is up the lane from the pier, near the central market, and has rooms for 150B (no bath), 250B with bath, or 350/450B a single/double with air-con; painted ladies on hand testify to its mainly short-time clientele though it's basically an OK place. Also close to the pier is the mid-range, six-storey *Hotel Diamond Phe* (☎ 651826; fax 424888), with air-con rooms for 500B.

The *Thale Thawng* restaurant, where the tour bus from Bangkok stops, has good Thai seafood dishes – especially recommended is the kũaytĩaw tha-leh, a seafood noodle soup. The shop across the street is a good place to stock up on food, mosquito coils and the like to take to Ko Samet. You'll most likely be spending some time in this spot, waiting either for the boat to leave the nearby pier for Ko Samet or for the bus to arrive from Bangkok.

**Nearby Islands** Three small islands off the coast of Rayong offer accommodation packages that include boat transport from the nearest pier along with three or four meals a day. These are best arranged by phone in advance through Bangkok reservation numbers. On **Ko Saket**, opposite Hat Sai Thong (11 km west of amphoe meuang Rayong), the *Ko Saket Phet* (☎ (01) 319042; (2) 319-9929 in Bangkok) has 15 bungalows and 10 'tourist houses' for 1300 to 2500B a night, including boat transport and all meals. *Ko Nok Resort* (☎ (2) 255-0836 in Bangkok) has a similar setup on **Ko Man Nok**, 15 km off Pak Nam Prasae (53 km east of Ban Phe).

Eight km off Laem Mae Phim (27 km east of Ban Phe) on **Ko Man Klang**, the *Raya Island Resort* (☎ (2) 316-6717 in Bangkok) offers bungalows for 900B with boat transport and meals. Ko Man Klang and Ko Man Nok, along with Ko Man Nai to their immediate west, are part of Laem Ya-Ko Samet National Park. As with Ko Samet, this official designation has not kept away all development, only moderated it. The islands

**Rayong Vicinity**

0    5    10 km

*Approximate Scale*

GULF OF THAILAND

Ko Samet

are in fair condition ecologically, the main threat to surrounding corals being the arrival of jet skis.

### Getting There & Away

Public transport to the pier departure points for the three small islands off Rayong can be arranged in Ban Phe. On weekends and holidays there may be share taxis (or songthaews) out to the piers; otherwise you'll have to charter a vehicle from the market for 50 to 100B one way – be sure to make a pickup appointment for your return.

See the Ko Samet Getting There & Away section for details on transport to and from Rayong.

### KO SAMET

เกาะเสม็ด

This T-shaped island earned a permanent place in Thai literature when classical Thai poet Sunthorn Phu set part of his epic *Phra Aphaimani* on its shores. The story follows the travails of a prince exiled to an undersea kingdom ruled by a lovesick female giant. A mermaid aids the prince in his escape to Samet where he defeats the giant by playing

a magic flute. Formerly Ko Kaew Phitsadan or 'Vast Jewel Isle' – a reference to the abundant white sand – this island became known as Ko Samet or 'Cajeput Isle' after the cajeput tree which grows in abundance here and which is very highly valued as firewood throughout South-East Asia. Locally, the *samet* tree has also been used in boat building.

In the early 1980s, the 13.1 sq km Ko Samet began receiving its first visitors interested in more than cajeput trees and sand – young Thais in search of a retreat from city life. At that time there were only about 40 houses on the island, built by fisherfolk and Ban Phe locals. Rayong and Bangkok speculators saw the sudden interest in Ko Samet as a chance to cash in on an up-and-coming Phuket and began buying up land along the beaches. No-one bothered with the fact that Ko Samet, along with Laem Ya and other nearby islands, was part of a national park (now one of seven marine parks in Thailand) and had been since 1981.

When farangs started coming to Ko Samet in greater and greater numbers, spurred on by rumours that Ko Samet was similar to Ko Samui '10 years ago' (one always seems to

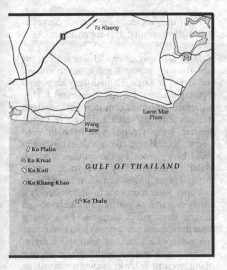

To Klaeng

3

Laem Mae
Phim

Wang
Kaew

⃝ Ko Platin
⃝ Ko Kruai
⃝ Ko Kuti
⃝ Ko Khang Khao
⃝ Ko Thalu

*GULF OF THAILAND*

modation on Samui and Pha-Ngan is better value overall, though of course these islands are much more expensive and time-consuming to reach from Bangkok.

In spite of the fact that the island is supposedly under the protection of the National Parks Division, on recent trips to Ko Samet I have been appalled at the runaway growth in the Na Dan and Hat Sai Kaew areas. Piles of rubbish and construction materials spoil the island's charm at the northern end. Once you get away from this end of the island, however, things start looking a bit better.

Ko Samet can be very crowded during Thai public holidays: early November (Loi Krathong Festival); 5 December (King's Birthday); 31 December to 1 January (New Year); mid to late February (Chinese New Year); and mid-April (Songkran Festival). During these times there are people sleeping on the floors of beach restaurants, on the beach, everywhere. September gets the lowest number of visitors (average 2500), March the most (around 40,000, approximately 36,000 of them Thai). Thais in any month are more prevalent than foreigners but many are day visitors; most stay at White Sand or Wong Deuan in the more up-market accommodation.

The Forestry Department has temporarily closed the park to all visitors a couple of times in an effort to halt encroachment on national park lands; so far they've always reopened the island within a month or less in response to protests by resort operators. Developers reasonably objected that if Ko Samet is to be closed then so must Ko Phi Phi. Court hearings continue; until a decision is reached, a permanent moratorium on new developments remains in place in order to preserve the island's forested interior.

## Information

Near Na Dan and on Hat Sai Kaew and Ao Wong Deuan are several small travel agencies that can arrange long-distance phone calls as well as bus and train reservations – they even do air ticketing. A small post office next to Naga Bungalows has poste restante. It's open weekdays from 8.30 am to 12.30

miss it by a decade, eh?), the National Parks Division stepped in and built a visitors' office on the island, ordered that all bungalows be moved back behind the tree line and started charging a 5B admission into the park.

This entry fee has since risen to 50B. Other more recent changes have included the introduction of several vehicles to the island, more frequent boat services from Ban Phe and a much improved water situation. Ko Samet is a very dry island (which makes it an excellent place to visit during the rainy season). Before they started trucking water to the bungalows you had to bathe at often muddy wells. Now most of the bungalow places have proper Thai-style bathrooms and Ko Samet is a much more comfortable place to visit, though it sometimes becomes overcrowded. Because of a ban on new accommodation (except where it replaces old sites), bungalows are spread thinly over most of the island, with the north-east coast being the most crowded. The beaches really are lovely, with the whitest, squeakiest sand in Thailand. There is even a little surf occasionally (best months are December to January). However, I still think the accom-

CENTRAL THAILAND

**Ko Samet**

0    0.5    1 km

pm and from 2 to 4 pm, Saturday from 8 am to noon.

Ko Samet phone numbers are on the cellular system so a ☎ (01) code is necessary before dialling the number. Some places maintain telephone numbers in Rayong, where the area code is ☎ (38).

An excellent guide to the history, flora and fauna of Ko Samet is Alan A Alan's 94-page *Samet*, published by Asia Books. Instead of writing a straightforward guidebook, Alan has woven the information into an amusing fictional travelogue involving a pair of Swedish twins on their first trip to the island.

The foreigner entry fee for Ko Samet is now 50B for adults, 35B for children.

**Malaria** A few years ago, if you entered the park from the northern end near the village, you'd see a large English-language sign warning visitors that Ko Samet was highly malarial. The sign is gone now but the island still has a bit of malaria. If you're taking malarial prophylactics you have little to worry about. If not, take a little extra care to avoid being bitten by mosquitoes at night. Malaria is not that easy to contract, even in malarial areas, unless you allow the mosquitoes open season on your flesh. It's largely a numbers game – you're not likely to get malaria from just a couple of bites (that's what the experts say anyway), so make sure you use repellent and mosquito nets at night.

There is a public health clinic on the island, located halfway between the village harbour and the park entrance. Go there for a blood test if you develop a fever while on Ko Samet, or for any other urgent health problems such as attacks from poisonous sea creatures or snakes.

### Activities

Several bungalows on the island can arrange boat trips to nearby reefs and uninhabited islands. Ao Phutsa, Naga Beach (Ao Hin Khok), Hat Sai Kaew and Ao Wong Deuan each have windsurfing equipment rental places that do boat trips as well. Typical day trips to Ko Thalu, Ko Kuti etc cost 150 to 210B per person, including food and beverages (minimum of 10 people). Sailboards rent for around 150B per hour or 600 to 700B per day. Jaray Windsurfing School on Hat Sai Kaew offers one hour lessons for 80B.

Dutch-run Hat Wasahn Divers on the west side of the island offers dive trips for 500B, full open-water certification for 6250B.

### Places to Stay

The two most developed (overdeveloped) beaches are Hat Sai Kaew and Ao Wong Deuan. All of the other spots are still rather peaceful. Every bungalow operation on the island has at least one restaurant and most

**A Request**
The Rayong tourist police request that visitors refrain from hiring jet skis on Samet beaches as they are harmful to coral and dangerous to swimmers. They're hard on the aural environment, too. The local police won't do anything about them even though they're illegal – either because they're afraid of beach developers or are in their pockets. You'll be doing Ko Samet a big favour by avoiding the use of these polluters. ■

now have running water and electricity. Most places have electric power from 5 or 6 pm till 6 am; only the more up-market places have 24 hour power.

On less popular beaches you may come across abandoned bungalow sites, and some of the most expensive places even during the high season offer discounts for accommodation to attract customers. Very basic small huts with a hard mattress on the floor cost in the 50 to 80B range, similar huts with bath start from 80 to 120B, and those including a bed and a fan average 150 to 200B. Bungalows with furniture and air-con start at 600B. Most places offer discounts for stays of four or more days, while on weekends and public holidays most will raise their rates to meet the demand.

Since this is a national park, camping is allowed on any of the beaches. In fact, this is a great island to camp on because it hardly ever rains. There is plenty of room; most of the island is uninhabited and, so far, tourism is pretty much restricted to the north-eastern and north-western beaches.

**Places to Stay – east coast**
**Hat Sai Kaew** Samet's prettiest beach, 'Diamond Sand', is a km or so long and 25 to 30m wide. The bungalows here happen to be the most commercial on the island, with video in the restaurants at night and lots of lights. They're all very similar and offer a range of accommodation from 80B (in the low season) for simple huts without fan or

bath, 400 to 500B for one with fan, mosquito net and private bath, or as high as 2500B with air-con. All face the beach and most have outdoor restaurants serving a variety of seafood. Like elsewhere in Thailand, the daily rate for accommodation can soar suddenly with demand. The more scrupulous places don't hike rates by much, though:

*Coconut House* – (☎ (01) 651661); 250 to 600B fan, 800 to 1500B air-con
*Diamond Hut* – (☎ (01) 321-0814); 350B fan, 700B air-con, 1200B air-con and three beds
*Golden Sand* – 100 to 120B
*Ploy Talay* – (☎ (01) 321-1109); 300 to 600B
*Saikaew Villa* – 450 to 4500B all air-con; the top-end place on the prettiest part of the beach
*Sinsamut* – 150 to 250B
*White Sand* – (☎ (01) 321734); 200 to 400B

**Ao Hin Khok** The beach here is about half the size of Sai Kaew but nearly as pretty – the rocks that give the beach its name add a certain character. Hin Khok is separated from Sai Kaew by a rocky point surmounted by a mermaid statue, a representation of the mermaid that carried the mythical Phra Aphaimani to Ko Samet in the Thai epic of the same name. Ao Kin Kok and Ao Phai, the next inlet south, offer the advantage of having among the least expensive huts on the island along with reasonably priced restaurants with good food.

Two of Samet's original bungalow operations still reign here – *Naga* (☎ (01) 353-2575) and *Little Hut* (☎ (01) 323-0264). Naga offers simple bungalows set on a hill overlooking the sea for 80B and decent ones with a good mattress from 120B. The restaurant at Naga sells great bread (which is distributed to several other bungalows on the island), cookies, cakes, pizzas and other pastries, baked under the supervision of Englishwoman Sue Wild. Water is wisely rationed here.

The bungalows at Little Hut are a little more solid and go for 150B; the restaurant here is also quite good. At the end of the beach is *Jep's Inn*, with very sturdy, clean bungalows for 300 to 350B.

Farther down the beach you may see what

CENTRAL THAILAND

looks like a Thai 'gathering of the tribes' – a colourful outpost presided over by Chawalee, a free-spirited Thai woman who has lived on this beach since long before the bungalows came.

**Ao Phai** Around the next headland is another shallow bay with the friendly *Ao Phai Hut* (☎ (01) 353-2644), which has bungalows with bath and fan from 150/200B a single/double and air-con ones for 600B; weekends and holidays add 200B. They organise tours around the island and have an international telephone service, as well as basic postal services. The next place is *Sea Breeze* (☎ (01) 321-1397), with a variety of rather closely spaced bungalows from 100 to 500B; the restaurant is good. Next is *Silver Sand* (☎ (01) 211-0974), with good bungalows for 150 to 250B; there's a disco on weekends.

The Swiss-run *Samed Villa* (☎ (01) 494-8090) has very clean, well maintained bungalows from 350/400B a single/double – and these rates don't shoot up on weekends.

**Ao Phutsa** After Ao Phai, the remaining beaches south are separated from one another by steep headlands. To get from one to the next, you have a choice of negotiating rocky paths over the hilly points or walking east to the main road that goes along the centre of the island, then cutting back on side roads to each beach. This is also where the cross-island trail to Ao Phrao starts.

On Ao Phutsa, also known as Ao Thap Thim, you'll find *Pudsa Bungalow*, where basic huts cost 200B and newer ones 300B, and the larger *Tub Tim*, where older huts are 200 to 300B, newer wooden bungalows 400 to 500B. At both places, the more expensive huts have private showers.

**Ao Nuan** If you blink, you'll miss this one. Huts at *Ao Nuan* – some lamplit for the sake of *thammachâat* (natural) ambience – rent for 100 to 300B. This is one of the more secluded places to stay without having to go to the far south of the island. The food is another reported highlight. It's a five minute walk over the headland from Ao Phutsa.

**Ao Cho (Chaw)** A five minute walk across the next headland from Ao Nuan, this bay has its own pier and can be reached directly from Ban Phe on the boat, *White Shark*, or aboard the supply boat. *Lung Wang (Wonderland Resort)* has basic, rather unkempt bungalows with attached shower and toilet for 100 to 250B. Huts at *Tantawan* are OK but a bit pricey for what you get at 300B.

**Ao Wong Deuan** This area is now mostly given over to more expensive resort-type bungalows. The cheaper bungalows that were here a few years ago have nearly all disappeared and those that remain can't be recommended – the whole bay is too crowded with buildings and people. The best of the lot is *Wong Deun Resort* (☎ (38) 651777) with bungalows for 600 to 900B, complete with running water, flush toilet and fan. The air-con ones cost 1100 to 1200B. *Vongduern Villa* (☎ (38) 651742; fax 651741) is similar but all air-con, ranging from 600 to 2500B.

The *Malibu Garden Resort* (☎ (01) 321-0345, (38) 651292) has cheaper bungalows with fan for 400 to 700B, air-con for 900 to 1200B; the more expensive rooms have TVs. The *Seahorse I & II* (☎ (01) 323-0049, 353-3072) has practically taken over the beachfront with two restaurants, a travel agency and fan rooms in a longhouse for 100B, or 300 to 750B for bungalows depending on whether they feature fans or air-con. Three boats go back and forth between Ao Wong Deuan and Ban Phe – the *Malibu, Seahorse* and *Vongduern Villa*.

**Ao Thian** This is better known by its English name, 'Candlelight Beach'. Far removed from the more active beaches to the north, this is the place to come for a little extra solitude, though the bungalow operations here, *Candle Light Beach* and *Lung Dam* (☎ (38) 651810), are no great shakes. Food, I'm told, is a definite minus here too. You can bring your own from the village on the northern tip of the island. Rates are 150 to 350B during the high season or on weekends and holidays, 70 to 150B other times.

**Other Bays**  You really have to be determined to get away from it all to go farther south on the east coast of Samet – not a bad idea. Water is only available for an hour or so in the mornings and evenings. Lovely **Ao Wai** is about a km from Ao Thian but can be reached by the boat *Phra Aphai* from Ban Phe. There's only one bungalow operation here, the very private *Sametville Resort* (☎ (01) 321-1284), where two bed bungalows with attached bath cost 700 to 900B inclusive of all meals. Larger bungalows with more beds are available, including an eight bed one for 2600B. Most bookings are done in Bangkok, but you can try your luck by contacting someone on the *Phra Aphai* at the Ban Phe pier. Finding a vacant bungalow – even in the peak season – usually isn't a problem.

A 20 minute walk over the rocky shore from Ao Wai, **Ao Kiu Na Nok** also had only one place to stay at the time of writing, the friendly and clean *Ao Kiu Coral Beach* (☎ (01) 321-1231, (38) 652561). Bamboo huts are 200/300B a single/double while rather uninviting cement huts cost 300/400B, or 600B and 1200B for nicer one bedroom and two bedroom bungalows. The beach here is fairly long and, because so few people use it, quite clean. Just a bit farther is rocky **Ao Karang**, where rustic *Pakarang* charges 100B per wooden hut (no electricity, no running water – just rainwater from ceramic jars). Sometimes this place closes down during the week. You'll find good coral in this area.

### Places to Stay – west coast
**Ao Phrao** is the only beach on the west side of the island, and has nice sunset views. In Thai the name means 'Coconut Bay Beach' but for incomprehensible marketing reasons bungalow operators tend to use the cliched 'Paradise Beach' moniker. So far there are no jet skis on this side of the island, so it tends to be quieter than the island's east coast. Local bungalow operators also do a good job of keeping the beach clean.

At the northern end of the beach is *Ao Phrao Resort* (☎ (38) 651814; (2) 438-9771 in Bangkok), where well designed, screened bungalows with fan and attached bath cost 850B during the week, 1100B on weekends and holidays; similar air-con bungalows cost 1800 to 2500B depending on size and whether it's a weekday or weekend or holiday.

In the middle of the beach is *Dome Bungalows* (☎ (2) 713-0046 in Bangkok), with nice huts built with private facilities on the hillside for 300 to 600B, 150/200B for small huts or 1000B for four in a 'VIP' bungalow; the more expensive huts feature screened windows. At the southern end near the cross-island trail is the very tidy *Hat Sawahn Paradise Beach* (☎ (01) 438-4916), where bamboo huts with fan and attached bath cost 350B (up to 500B weekends and holidays). There's also a large 15 bed bungalow that goes for 1500B.

There is a daily boat between Ban Phe and Ao Phrao for 50B per person.

### Places to Stay – Na Dan area
To the west of Samet's main pier is a long beach called Ao Wiang Wan where several rather characterless bungalows are set up in straight lines facing the mainland. Here you get neither sunrise (maybe a little) nor sunset. The cheapest place is *SK Bungalows* where accommodation is from 80 to 350B. There are several other places with rates in the 200 to 600B range.

Between Na Dan and Hat Sai Kaew, along the north-east corner of the island, are a couple of small beach-bays with bungalow operations. Hardly anyone seems to stay here, and it was only *Pineapple Bungalow* at Laem Yai beach which showed any sign of life. The asking rate of 400B per bungalow was definitely not worth it.

### Places to Eat
All bungalows except Pakarang at Ao Karang have restaurants offering mixed menus of Thai and farang travellers food; prices are typically around 30 to 40B per dish. Fresh seafood is almost always available and costs around 60 to 100B per dish. The pleasant *Bamboo Restaurant* at Ao Cho offers inexpensive but tasty food and good service. It's open for breakfast, lunch and dinner. *Naga*

on Ao Hin Khok has a very good bakery with all kinds of breads and cakes. *Nop's Kitchen*, attached to Ao Phai Hut, is also recommended for good food at decent prices, as is the restaurant at *Ao Nuan*. Ao Wong Deuan has a cluster of restaurants serving western and Thai food: *Roti Bar, Nice & Easy, Ton's Restaurant*.

On Hat Sai Kaew, the *White Sands Restaurant* has good seafood in the 100B range. For cheaper fare on this beach, try the popular *Toy Restaurant*.

### Getting There & Away
**Bus** Many Khao San Rd agencies in Bangkok do transport to Ko Samet, including boat, for 150 to 160B (250B return). This is more expensive than doing it on your own, but for travellers who don't plan to go anywhere else on the east coast it's convenient.

For those who want the flexibility and/or economy of arranging their own travel, the way to go is to take a bus to Ban Phe in Rayong Province, then catch a boat out to Ko Samet. There are regular buses to Rayong throughout the day from the Eastern Bus Terminal, but if your destination is Ban Phe (for Ko Samet) you'd do better to take one of the direct Ban Phe buses, which only cost 5B more; a songthaew to Ban Phe from Rayong is 10B. The Bangkok to Rayong air-con bus is 85B, Bangkok to Ban Phe is 90B. Cheaper still is the ordinary bus to Rayong (50B) and then a local bus to Ban Phe. Buses from Bangkok stop in Ban Phe about 300m from the pier. Air-con buses between Rayong and Bangkok's Eastern Bus Terminal take around 3½ hours, ordinary buses about an hour longer.

Ordinary buses to Chanthaburi or Pattaya from Rayong cost 30B and take about 1½ hours in either direction. To get one of these, you need to catch a motorcycle taxi (10B) to the bus stop on Sukhumvit Rd (Highway 3).

**Boat** There are various ways to get to and from the island by boat.

***To Ko Samet*** There are three piers in Ban Phe: Saphaan Nuan Tip for the regularly scheduled passenger boats, Saphaan Mai for supply boats and Saphaan Sri Ban Phe for tour groups. Saphaan Nuan Tip is usually the only one you'll need, but if you arrive between passenger boat departures you can try for a ride aboard one of the cargo boats from Saphaan Mai (for which you must still pay the regular passenger fare).

Passenger boats to Ko Samet leave at regular intervals throughout the day starting at around 8 am and finishing at around 5 pm. How frequently they depart mostly depends on whether they have enough passengers and/or cargo to make the trip profitable, so there are more frequent boats in the high season (December to March). Still, there are always at least three or four boats a day going to Na Dan and Ao Wong Deuan.

It can be difficult to find the boat you need, as agents and boat owners want you to go with them rather than with their competitors. In most cases they'll be reluctant to tell you about another boat if they will not be making any money from you. Some travellers have reported being hassled by 'agents' who present photo albums of bungalows on Samet, claiming that they must book a bungalow for several days in order to get onto the island. This is false; ignore such touts and head straight for the boats. Report any problems to the TAT office in Rayong.

For Hat Sai Kaew, Ao Hin Khok, Ao Phai and Ao Phutsa, take one of the regular Na Dan boats (operated by Samet Tour, Suriya Tour and Thepmongkonchai) for 30B. Ignore touts or ticket agents who claim the fare is 100B; simply climb into one of these boats and wait to pay the ticket collector directly. From Na Dan you can either walk to these beaches (10 to 15 minutes) or take one of the trucks that go round the island. See the Getting Around section below for standard fares.

The boat *White Shark* also goes directly to Ao Cho from Ban Phe for 30B – have a look around the Ban Phe pier to see if it's available.

The *Seahorse*, *Malibu* and *Wong Deuan Villa* all go to Ao Wong Deuan for 30B. There's no jetty here, so passengers are pulled to shore on a raft or in long-tail boats. You can also get a truck-taxi here from Na Dan, but the fare could be as high as 200B if you're alone. For Ao Thian, you should get either the *White Shark* to Ao Cho or one of the Ao Wong Deuan boats.

The *Phra Aphai* makes direct trips to Ao Wai for 40B. For Ao Kiu or Ao Karang, get the *Thep Chonthaleh* (30B).

For Ao Phrao, you can taxi from Na Dan or possibly get a direct boat from Ban Phe for 30B. The boat generally operates from December to May, but with the increase in passengers this service may soon go all year.

If you arrive in Ban Phe at night and need a boat to Samet, you can usually charter a one way trip at the Ban Phe pier for 250 to 300B (to Na Dan).

**From Ko Samet** Samet Tour seems to run a monopoly on return trips from Na Dan and they leave only when they're full – a minimum of 18 people for some boats, 25 for others – unless someone contributes more to the passage. The usual fare is 30B.

These days it is so easy to get boats back from the main beaches to Ban Phe that few tourists go to Na Dan to get a boat. There are four daily boats each from Ao Wong Deuan and Ao Cho, plus at least one daily boat from Ao Wai, Ao Kiu and Ao Phrao.

While waiting for a boat back to the mainland from Na Dan, you may notice a shrine not far from the pier. This *sāan jâo phâw* is a spirit shrine to Puu Dam (Grandfather Black), a sage who once lived on the island. Worshippers offer statues of *reusī* (hermit sages), flowers, incense and fruit.

### Getting Around

If you take the boat from Ban Phe to the village harbour (Na Dan), you can easily walk to Hat Sai Kaew, Ao Phai or Ao Phutsa. Don't believe the taxi operators who say these beaches are a long distance away. If you're going farther down the island, or have a lot of luggage, you can take the taxi (a truck or a three-wheeled affair with a trailer) as far as Ao Wong Deuan.

Set fares for transport around the island

from Na Dan are posted on a tree in the middle of the square in front of the Na Dan harbour: 10B per person to Hat Sai Kaew (100B to charter); 20B to Ao Phai or Ao Phutsa (150B to charter); 30B to Ao Wong Deuan or Ao Phrao (200B to charter); 40B to Ao Thian or Ao Wai (300B and 400B to charter); and 50B to Ao Kiu (500B to charter). Exactly how many people it takes to constitute 'public service' rather than a 'charter' is not a hard and fast number. Figure on 20B per person for six to eight people for anywhere between Na Dan and Ao Cho. If they don't have enough people to fill the vehicle, they either won't go, or passengers will have to pay up to 200B to charter the vehicle.

There are trails from Ao Wong Deuan all the way to the southern tip of the island, and a few cross-island trails as well. Taxis will make trips to Ao Phrao when the road isn't too muddy.

# Chanthaburi Province

### CHANTHABURI
อ.เมืองจันทบุรี
• ☎ *(39)* • *pop 39,700*

Situated 330 km from Bangkok, the 'City of the Moon' is a busy gem trading centre, particularly noted for sapphires and rubies from all over South-East Asia and farther afield. Chanthaburi (Chan'buri) is also renowned for tropical fruit (rambutan, durian, langsat and mangosteen) and rice noodles – Chanthaburi noodles are in fact exported all over the world.

A significant proportion of the local population are Vietnamese Christians who fled religious or political persecution in Vietnam years ago. The first wave arrived in the 19th century as refugees from anti-Catholic persecution in Cochin China (southern Vietnam); the second came between the 1920s and 1940s, fleeing French rule; and the third wave arrived after the 1975 communist takeover of southern Vietnam. From

1893 to 1905, while negotiating with the Siamese over where to draw the borders for Laos and Cambodia, the French occupied the town.

Chanthaburi's most recent claim to fame arose in 1993 when 1500 tonnes of war materiel was found cached in 12 warehouses throughout the province. The arms were thought to have been destined for the Khmer Rouge communist rebels who hold parts of western Cambodia. Although the allegations were never proven, it is almost certain the arms were in the control of certain factions within the Thai military.

### Things to See & Do
Because of the Vietnamese-French influence, Chanthaburi has some interesting shophouse architecture, particularly along the river. The French-style **cathedral** here is the largest in Thailand. Originally, a small missionary chapel was built on this site in 1711; four reconstructions between 1712 and 1906 (the last carried out by the French) transformed the structure into its current form.

The gem dealers in town are found mostly along Si Chan Rd and along Trok Kachang and Thetsaban 4 Rd, off Si Chan Rd in the south-east quarter. All day long buyers and sellers haggle over little piles of blue and red stones. During the first week of June every year there is a gem festival and Chanthaburi can get very crowded. Most of the gems bought and sold here come from places other than Chan'buri – chiefly Cambodia, Vietnam, Myanmar and Australia. Sapphires and rubies are very good buys if (and only if) you know what you're buying.

**King Taksin Park** is a large public park with gazebos and an artificial lake near the centre of town – nice for an evening stroll. A few km north of town off Route 3249 is **Khao Phloi Waen**, or 'Sapphire-Ring Mountain', which is only 150m high but features a Sri Lankan-style chedi on top, built during the reign of King Mongkut. Tunnels dug into the side of the hill were once gem-mining shafts.

**Wat Khao Sukim**, a reasonably well known meditation centre, is 16 km north of

Chanthaburi off Route 3322. Another meditation centre is at **Wat Sapchan**, 27 km west of Chanthaburi in Tha Mai district; Wat Sapchan is a branch of defrocked Ajaan Yantra's Sunyataram Forest Monastery in Kanchanaburi.

### Places to Stay
At 98/1 Benchamarachutit Rd, the three-storey *Kasemsan I Hotel* (☎ 312340) has large, clean rooms with fan, private shower and toilet for 150 to 180B, or 250B with air-con. As usual, rooms off the street are quieter than those on it, but it's the best deal in town and very convenient to the city centre.

Down by the river at a nice spot on Rim Nam Rd, is the smaller *Chantha Hotel* (☎ 312310), with rooms without bath for 80B, with bath for 100/120B. Some of the rooms have a view of the river. It's a bit run-down and has a slightly sleazy feel, but it's the cheapest place in town and rooms with windows on the river catch a breeze.

In the municipal market area is the *Kasemsan II* on Rong Meuang Rd. It has slightly cheaper rooms than the Kasemsan I (120 to 190B with fan only) but it's not as clean and is noisier. The nearby *Chai Lee Hotel* (no English sign) on Khwang Rd has large, clean rooms for 120/160B a single/double with fan, 220/250B with air-con. In the same area, the *Chanthaburi Hotel* on Tha Chalaep Rd is OK if a little pricey for local standards at 200B with fan and bath, 370B with air-con.

On Si Chan Rd you'll find the friendly *Muang Chan Hotel*, with adequate fan rooms for 150B, air-con for 300B. Out on Tha Luang Rd at the north end of town, away from everything, is the *Kiatkachorn (Kiat Khachon) Hotel* (☎ 311212) with comfortable fan-cooled rooms for 150/160B, air-con 250B, VIP air-con 450B. The latter includes TV, phone and fridge; all rooms have private baths.

*Mark's Travelodge* (☎ 311531/647), 14 Raksakchamun Rd, was once a popular hotel with business travellers, but has become rather run-down. Large, if musty, rooms range from 250 to 450B with air-con, private bath and TV.

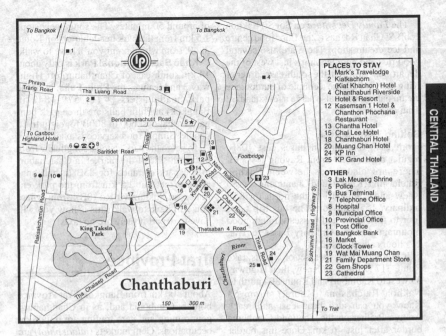

To Bangkok
To Bangkok

Phraya
Trang Road

Tha Luang Road

Benchamarachutit Road

To Caribou
Highland Hotel

Saritidet Road

Footbridge

Raksakchamun Road

Thetsaban 1 & 2

Kwaeng Road

Si Chan Road

Rim Nam Road

King Taksin
Park

Thetsaban 4 Road

River

Chanthaburi

Chanthaburi

Sukhumwit Road (Highway 3)

Trirat Road

0    150    300 m

To Trat

**PLACES TO STAY**
1  Mark's Travelodge
2  Kiatkachorn
   (Kiat Khachon) Hotel
4  Chanthaburi Riverside
   Hotel & Resort
12 Kasemsan 1 Hotel &
   Chanthon Phochana
   Restaurant
13 Chantha Hotel
15 Chai Lee Hotel
18 Chanthaburi Hotel
20 Muang Chan Hotel
24 KP Inn
25 KP Grand Hotel

**OTHER**
3  Lak Meuang Shrine
5  Police
6  Bus Terminal
7  Telephone Office
8  Hospital
9  Municipal Office
10 Provincial Office
11 Post Office
14 Bangkok Bank
16 Market
17 Clock Tower
19 Wat Mai Muang Chan
21 Family Department Store
22 Gem Shops
23 Cathedral

Business travellers – at least the gem-buying types – have switched to the 18-storey *KP Grand Hotel* (☎ 323201/13; fax 323214/5) at 35/200-201 Trirat Rd. Modern rooms with all the amenities start at 1000B. Across the street is the *KP Inn* (☎ 311756), a condo-style place with rooms for 550B a single/double with air-con and hot water showers.

The new six-storey, 120-room *Caribou Highland Hotel* (☎ 323431), west of the town centre on Chawan Uthit Rd, offers the best accommodation in town – large air-con rooms with TV, IDD phone and minibar – for 2000B. In 1996 the hotel was offering a discounted rate of 1188B including breakfast. One and two bedroom suites are available starting at 4000B (discounted to 2508B).

A 20 to 25B taxi ride from town is the *Chanthaburi Riverside Hotel & Resort* (☎ 311726) at 63 Muu 9, Chanthanimit 5 Rd, between Sukhumvit Rd (Highway 3) and the east bank of the Chanthaburi River. Origi-

nally planned to be super luxurious, the hotel must have run out of development money as it has turned out to be no more than a four-star establishment on 42 rai, rather unkempt grounds. On the premises are a swimming pool, coffee shop, nightclub and conference facilities. Rates are 700B in the hotel section, from 800B for lodgings in separate single, double and triple Thai-style cottages.

**Places to Eat**
For those famous Chanthaburi noodles, head for the Chinese/Vietnamese part of town along the Chanthaburi River and you'll see variations on the basic rice noodle theme, including delicious crab-fried noodles. The popular *Chanthon Phochana* restaurant beneath the Kasemsan I Hotel has a good variety of Thai and Chinese dishes.

*Khrua Rabiang*, beside the Caribou Highlands at Chawan Uthit 3, is a very nice, medium-high priced open-air restaurant serving mostly Thai food.

The *Family Dept Store* on Soi Sri Sakhon 1, off Si Chan Rd, has a 2nd floor food centre and ice cream shop. There are also several good rice and noodles shops just west of the department store. On the south-east corner of King Taksin Park are a couple of outdoor ice cream parlours that also serve a few standard Thai dishes.

### Getting There & Away
From Bangkok, air-con buses cost 108B, regular buses 60B. From Rayong it's 30B. There are also buses between Nakhon Ratchasima (Khorat) and Chanthaburi via Sa Kaew and Kabinburi to the north for 85B ordinary, 155B air-con. The bus trip takes four to five hours and passes through good mountain scenery. Ordinary buses to Trat, 1½ hours away, cost 22B.

If you have your own set of wheels, take Route 317 north to Sa Kaew, then Highway 33 west to Kabinburi and Route 304 north to Nakhon Ratchasima (Khorat). From Sa Kaew you can also head east and reach Aranya Prathet on the Thailand-Cambodia border after just 46 km. Once this border crossing is open you'll be able to take a train straight from Poipet on the Cambodian side of the border to Phnom Penh or stop off at Sisaphon (for buses to Siem Reap/Angkor Wat).

### AROUND CHANTHABURI
Two small national parks are within an hour's drive of Chanthaburi. Both are malarial, so take the usual precautions. **Khao Khitchakut National Park** is about 28 km north-east of town off Route 3249 and is known for the **Krathing Falls**. There's a series of trails to the falls but no established trails or footpaths in the rest of the park.

Across the road from park headquarters (☎ 431983) are bungalows ranging from 600B for six people to 1200B for 14 people. Camping costs 40B in a hired tent or 5B if you bring your own. A basic restaurant sells snacks and a few rice dishes.

To get to Khao Khitchakut by public transport, take a songthaew from the north side of the market in Chanthaburi for 15B, a jaunt

of around 50 minutes. The songthaew stops 1.5 km from the park headquarters on Route 3249, from which point you'll have to walk.

**Khao Sabap National Park** is only about 14 km south-east of Chanthaburi off Highway 3 and features the **Phliu Falls**. Near the park headquarters (☎ (2) 579-4842 in Bangkok) at Phliu Falls are three park bungalows that cost 600 to 800B for eight to 10 people. Simple food service is available.

To get to the park, catch a songthaew from the north side of the market in Chanthaburi to the park entrance for 25B (a half-hour ride), or get out 2.5 km from the park entrance on Sukhumvit Rd (8B), from where you will have to walk (this is how you will have to depart if there are no taxis).

# Trat Province

About 400 km from Bangkok, Trat Province borders Cambodia and, as in Chanthaburi, gem mining and gem trading are important occupations. Gem markets (*talàat phloi*) are open intermittently at the **Hua Thung** and **Khlong Yaw** markets in the Bo Ria district, about 40 km north of Trat on Route 3389. A smaller market is sometimes open all day in **Khao Saming** district only 20 km north-west of Trat.

Recently, there have been reports of a drop in activity in the gem markets due to the dwindling supply of local gem stock. A sad byproduct of gem mining has been the destruction of vast tracts of land – the topsoil is stripped away, leaving acres of red-orange mud.

If the gem business doesn't interest you, another attraction Bo Rai district offers is **Salak Tai Falls** (15 km north-west of Bo Rai). In late 1993 and early 1994 travel in the region was restricted due to Khmer Rouge activity – enquire in amphoe meuang Trat for the latest.

The other big industry in Trat is the smuggling of consumer goods between Cambodia and Trat. For this reason, travelling alone along the border, or around the offshore islands

**Wiw** (View-Admiring Point), where you can get a panorama of the surrounding area, including Cambodia. Trat Province's south-easternmost point is at **Hat Lek**, which is also a semi-legal jumping-off point for boat trips to the Cambodian coast. Although there are Thai military checkpoints between Trat and Hat Lek (two at last count), they seem to be getting less strict about allowing foreigners through. From time to time the Trat provincial government and its counterpart on the Cambodian side of the border allows foreigners to cross by boat to Cambodia's Ko Kong.

## TRAT & AROUND

อ.เมืองตราๆ

• ☎ (39) • *pop 14,000*

The provincial capital of Trat has little to offer except as a jumping-off point for the Ko Chang island group or forays into outlying gem and Cambodian markets. The locals are friendly, however, and there are certainly worse places to spend a few days. Market fans will note Trat seems to have more markets for its size than almost any other town in Thailand – again partly due to Cambodian coastal trade.

### Information

A few of Trat's guesthouses can arrange local day trips to gem markets or the Trat River estuary. The estuary trips go by boat from the canal in town to the Trat estuary to gather clams (when in season) for 100B or less per person for an all day outing – the exact price depends on the number of people.

Information on Ko Chang National Marine Park is available at the park headquarters in Laem Ngop, a small town 20 km south-west of Trat. This is also where you get boats to Ko Chang.

**Immigration** There is no immigration office in Trat – you must go to the provincial offices in Khlong Yai or Laem Ngop for visa extensions or other immigration matters. If Cambodian border crossings from Trat by land or sea are permitted in the future, Khlong Yai is where you'll have to go to have

which serve as conduits for sea smuggling, requires caution. More and more people have discovered the beaches and islands of Trat, however, and as the locals and the police have begun to see the benefits of hospitality to outsiders, security has apparently improved. One relatively safe spot for observing the border trade is at the Thai-Cambodian market in **Khlong Yai**, near the end of Route 318/Highway 3 south of Trat. As much as 10 million baht changes hands in these markets daily.

As Route 318 goes east and then south from Trat on the way to Khlong Yai district, the province thins to a narrow sliver between the Gulf of Thailand and Cambodia. Along this sliver are a number of little known beaches, including **Hat Sai Si Ngoen**, **Hat Sai Kaew**, **Hat Thap Thim** and **Hat Ban Cheun**. Ban Cheun has a few bungalows, but there was no accommodation at the other beaches at the time of writing.

At Km 70, off Route 318, is **Jut Chom**

CENTRAL THAILAND

CENTRAL THAILAND

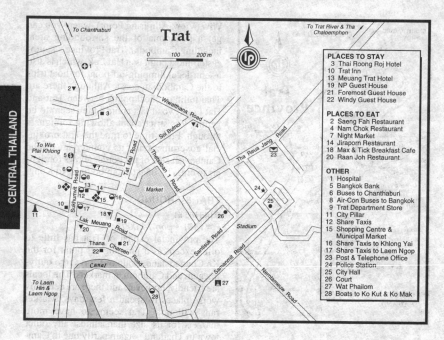

**Trat**

PLACES TO STAY
3 Thai Roong Roj Hotel
10 Trat Inn
13 Meuang Trat Hotel
19 NP Guest House
21 Foremost Guest House
22 Windy Guest House

PLACES TO EAT
2 Saeng Fah Restaurant
4 Nam Chok Restaurant
7 Night Market
14 Jiraporn Restaurant
18 Max & Tick Breakfast Cafe
20 Raan Joh Restaurant

OTHER
1 Hospital
5 Bangkok Bank
6 Buses to Chanthaburi
8 Air-Con Buses to Bangkok
9 Trat Department Store
11 City Pillar
12 Share Taxis
15 Shopping Centre &
    Municipal Market
16 Share Taxis to Khlong Yai
17 Share Taxis to Laem Ngop
23 Post & Telephone Office
24 Police Station
25 City Hall
26 Court
27 Wat Phailom
28 Boats to Ko Kut & Ko Mak

your passport stamped upon return from Cambodia.

**Money** Bangkok Bank on Sukhumvit Rd has a foreign exchange window open daily from 8.30 am to 5 pm. In Laem Ngop, a Thai Farmers Bank (near Chut Kaew Guest House) has an exchange counter open weekdays from 8.30 am to 3.30 pm.

**Post & Communications** The main post office is a long walk from the city centre on Tha Reua Jang Rd. It's open from 8.30 am to 4.30 pm weekdays, 9 am to noon Saturday. The attached international phone office is open daily from 7 am till 10 pm.

**Malaria** Rates of infection for malaria are significantly higher for rural Trat (including Ko Chang) than for much of the rest of Thailand, so take the usual precautions. There is a malaria centre on the main road through Laem Ngop (20 km south-west of

Trat); here you can get the latest information on the disease. This office can also assist with testing and/or treatment for malaria.

### Things to See & Do

Trat town's older homes and shophouses are along the canal – you may be able to rent a canoe from one of the guesthouses for a water-level look. During high tide it's possible to boat from the canal to the Trat estuary on the Gulf. This can also be done from the Trat River, north of the city; enquire at Tha Chaloemphon (also known simply as *thâa reua* or 'boat pier').

**Wat Plai Khlong** (Wat Bupharam), two km west of the city centre, is over 200 years old and worth a visit if you're looking to kill an hour or so. Several of the wooden buildings date to the late Ayuthaya period, including the wihãan, bell tower and *kutis* (monk's quarters). The wihãan contains a variety of sacred relics and Buddha images dating from the Ayuthaya period and earlier.

Trat is famous for 'yellow oil' *(náam-man lĕuang)*, a herb-infused liquid touted as a remedy for everything from arthritis to stomach upsets. It's produced by a local resident, Mae Ang-kii (Somthawin Pasananon), using a secret pharmaceutical recipe that has been handed down through her Chinese-Thai family for generations. The Thais say that if you leave Trat without a couple of bottles of Mae Ang-kii's yellow oil, then you really haven't been to Trat. The stuff is available direct from her house at No 5 Rat Uthit Rd (☎ 511935) or from the Max & Tick Breakfast Cafe (see Places to Eat); Tick is Mae Ang-kii's daughter.

Farther afield, **Ban Nam Chiaw** – about eight km from Trat – is a mostly Muslim village where one of the main industries is the handweaving of hemispherical straw hats called *ngôp*, the traditional Khmer rice farmer's hat.

**Markets** Of Trat's several markets, the largest are the new day market beneath the municipal shopping centre off Sukhumvit Rd, the old day market off Tat Mai Rd and the day market next to the air-con bus office; the latter becomes a night market in the evening. Look for eccentricities like deep-fried lizards.

**Places to Stay**

**Trat** The friendly *NP Guest House* (☎ 512564) has moved from its former location on the outskirts of town to a more central spot at 1-3 Soi Luang Aet, Lak Meuang Rd (in a lane which is a south-west continuation of Tat Mai Rd); it's a short walk from the main day and night markets as well as local bus stops. It's basically an old wooden shophouse with a glassed-in downstairs; a bed in the clean three bed dorm costs 50B or you can get a private room for 80/100B a single/double with shared bath.

*Foremost Guest House* (☎ 511923), at 49 Thana Charoen Rd near the canal, offers rooms upstairs in an old shophouse; bathrooms are shared but clean, and a hot shower is available. Rates are 60/80/100B for a single/double/triple. The same family runs the *Windy Guest House* across the road on the canal; here prices are 40B in a dorm, 60/80B a single/double. Bicycles and motorcycles are also available for rent for 20B and 180 to 250B per day. Ask about renting canoes for exploring the canal (20B per day) – it depends on who's managing the guesthouse at the time and whether canoes are available.

Any of the guesthouses can arrange boat trips along the Trat River or to Ko Chang if enough people are interested.

Most of the hotels in Trat are along or just off Sukhumvit Rd. The *Trat Inn* (☎ 511208) at 66-71 Sukhumvit Rd has rooms from 110 to 200B. The *Thai Roong Roj (Rung Rot)* (☎ 511141) in a lane off Sukhumvit Rd has rooms with fan from 140B or with air-con from 250B. At 234 Sukhumvit Rd is *Sukhumvit Inn* (☎ 512151) with 140 to 180B rooms.

More comfortable is the renovated *Meuang Trat* (☎ 511091), off Sukhumvit Rd next to the market, which has standard fan rooms for 220 to 300B, air-con from 340B. This is the only hotel in town with a lift.

Eleven km south-east of town at Laem Sok, the *Ban Pu Resort* (☎ /fax 512400) has opened adjacent to Suan Puu, a famous seafood restaurant/crab farm. Large, well appointed wooden bungalows connected by a boardwalk surrounding a large crab pond start at 1200B for a one bedroom unit with two beds; a larger one bedroom unit with six beds costs 2600B. There are also deluxe two bedroom bungalows with TVs, VCRs and stereos for 2400 to 3400B. It's a 20B, 15 minute mini-songthaew ride from town. Ban Pu can arrange speedboat transport to Ko Chang and other Trat islands.

**Laem Ngop** There's usually no reason to stay here, since most boats to Ko Chang leave in the morning and early afternoon and it's only 20 km from Trat. However, there are a couple of good accommodation choices. A five minute walk from the harbour on the right is the *Chut Kaew Guest House*, which is run by a nurse, teacher and university student – local, somewhat dated information (including hiking info for Ko Chang) is available in thick notebooks compiled by guests. Rooms cost 60B per person and are relatively clean. Food is available as are bike rentals for just 10B a day.

The next place on the right, about 100m from the road, is *PI Guest House*, a new, clean place with large rooms in a Thai house; it's usually closed during the June to November rainy season. All rooms have one double bed for 60/120B a single/double. The *Laem Ngop Inn* (☎ 597044) is farther up again, but 300m from the road, with rooms with fan for 200B, and air-con ones for 300 to 450B. The *Paradise Inn* (☎ 512831) near the police station has similarly priced rooms.

A Bangkok development company is constructing a new pier and commercial site called Koh Chang Centre Point at Laem Ngop.

**Khlong Yai** The *Suksamran Hotel*, an old-fashioned Thai-Chinese-style place on a street between the market and the highway, offers rooms with fan from 120B, or 250B with air-con. Out of town a bit off Highway 3, *Bang In Villa* has nicer rooms, but with less character, starting at 150B.

**Places to Eat**
With all the markets in Trat, you're hardly ever more than 50m away from something good to eat. The indoor municipal market beneath the shopping centre has a food section with cheap, good noodle and rice dishes from early morning to early evening. Another good spot for cheap breakfasts is the ancient coffee stand in the old day market on Tat Mai Rd.

In the evenings, there's a good night market next to the air-con bus station. On the Trat River in the northern part of town is a small but atmospheric night market – a good choice for long, leisurely meals. Trat is a good city for seafood, which is cheaper here than in Bangkok or in more well touristed cities (it's not the international tourists who drive up the seafood prices but the Thais, who spend huge sums of money on eating out).

The best place in the whole province for seafood is *Suan Puu* (Crab Farm) in Ban Laem Hin, on the way to Laem Sok 11 km south-east of town (a 20B mini-songthaew ride each way). Tables are atmospherically arranged on wooden piers over Ao Meuang Trat (Trat Bay). All seafood is served fresh; crab, raised on the premises, is of course the house speciality and prices are moderate to medium high (still considerably cheaper than in Bangkok). The menu is in Thai only, so bring along a Thai friend to translate.

*Max & Tick Breakfast Cafe* (☎ 520799), at 1-3 Soi Luang Aet, Lak Meuang Rd (in a lane which is a south-west continuation of Tat Mai Rd), offers good coffee and western breakfasts from 6.30 to 11 am. This is also a good spot for local info; Max and Tick are a friendly young Thai couple who speak excellent English and they know the area well. Their collection of music tapes/CDs is one of the best around.

One of the longest running Thai-Chinese restaurants in town is the *Jiraporn*, a small cafe-style place a few doors from the Meuang Trat Hotel where a small crowd of older regulars hang out over tea and coffee every morning. As it's mostly a breakfast place, the main menu offerings here are toast and eggs with ham, jók and khâo tôm, but they can also do fried rice or noodles.

The *Nam Chok* outdoor restaurant on the corner of Soi Butnoi and Wiwatthana Rd is another local institution. Around lunchtime a good place is *Raan Joh* (no English sign) at 90 Lak Meuang Rd. The number is next to impossible to see, just look for the only place making khanom beûang, a Khmer veggie crepe prepared in a wok. They also do other local specialities – it's very inexpensive and open lunchtime only.

A good mid-range restaurant, the air-con *Saeng Fah* (☎ 511222) at 156-7 Sukhumvit Rd, has a large menu with Thai specialities between 50 and 100B. The food is good, and there are plenty of seafood dishes. They also serve breakfast, when you might (or might not) want to try the house speciality – rice with curdled pig's blood.

At the Laem Ngop pier are two good

seafood restaurants. The *Saengchan Restaurant*, on the right in front of the pier, doesn't have great food but many travellers wait here for minibuses to Trat which connect with air-con buses to Bangkok.

### Getting There & Away
**Bangkok** Buses cost 140B air-con or 78B ordinary and leave from the Eastern Bus Terminal. The trip takes five to six hours one way by air-con bus, or about eight hours by ordinary bus. Three bus companies operate a Trat to Bangkok service: Sahamit, on Sukhumvit Rd near the Trat Hotel and night market, has the best and most frequent (12 trips a day) air-con buses.

**Chanthaburi** Ordinary buses between Chanthaburi and Trat are 22B and take about 1½ hours for the 66 km trip.

You can also take the quicker share taxis between Trat and Chanthaburi for 40B per person – these take around 45 minutes. During the middle of the day, however, it may take up to an hour to gather the seven passengers necessary for a departure; try to schedule your departure between 7 and 9 am or 4 and 6 pm for the shortest wait.

**Laem Ngop** Share taxis to Laem Ngop leave Trat from a stand on Sukhumvit Rd next to the municipal market; these cost 10B per person shared or 100B to charter. They depart regularly throughout the day, but after dark you will have to charter.

**Khlong Yai, Hat Lek & Bo Rai** Songthaews and share taxis to Khlong Yai cost 25B per person and take about 45 minutes. The songthaew fare from Khlong Yai to Hat Lek is 10B for the 16 km trip; these taxis leave from the back of the municipal market. Motorcycle taxis are also available between Khlong Yai and Hat Lek for 50B. A door-to-door minibus to Bo Rai is 35B.

### Getting Around
Samlors around town should cost 10B per person. Small songthaews cost 5B per person on a share basis or 20B for the whole vehicle.

## HAT LEK TO CAMBODIA
The small Thai border outpost of Hat Lek is the southernmost point on the Trat mainland. Untaxed goods ply back and forth between Cambodia and Thailand here; at the small market just before the border crossing itself, next to the pier for boats to Cambodia, American Budweiser beer is often available for 20B per can. Opposite Hat Lek on Cambodian turf, a cockfighting arena is under construction; when it's finished, presumably residents from both sides of the border will be able to convene here visa-free for weekend cockfights.

Until recently there were as many as five military checkpoints along Highway 3 between Trat town and Hat Lek to slow the flood of Cambodian refugees; the checkpoints have been reduced to two.

Small boats are available from Hat Lek to Pak Khlong on the island of Ko Kong (on the Cambodian side of the border) for 100B per person or 800B charter. If you plan to continue farther, you can take a passenger ferry from Pak Khlong to Sao Thong for 10B, then change to a three hour speedboat ride (500B per boat) to Sihanoukville. From Sihanoukville it's a three hour, 40B share taxi ride to Phnom Penh. You may also be able to catch the once daily bus all the way to Phnom Penh.

A Cambodian visa is necessary, and obtainable in Bangkok, not at the border. As far as the Thai authorities are concerned this is semi-illegal and while in Cambodia, you are technically in Thailand! You need to do the trip with a valid Thai visa on which you can return to Thailand. Some foreign expats in the Trat/Ko Chang area use the Trat-Cambodia route for Thai visa renewals.

If this option is not available or you just feel like getting a taste of Cambodian border life, it's easy to visit Ko Kong, an island on the Cambodian side of the border, by boat as described above. Though not a particularly exciting destination in itself, Ko Kong is an important relay point for goods imported from Singapore into Cambodia, which is now Singapore's largest trade entrepôt in Indochina. Contact the Foremost or Windy guesthouses in Trat for the latest information about entering Cambodia.

CENTRAL THAILAND

**Warning** Travel into Cambodia is potentially dangerous and many embassies advise against it. You may like to check with your embassy in Thailand first before making extensive plans for Cambodian travel. Although many Khmer Rouge have switched sides, the situation is still volatile with ongoing internal conflict as well as skirmishes with the government forces.

### Khlong Yai

Khlong Yai consists of a cluster of older wooden buildings west of the highway, surrounded by modern structures on both sides of the highway. There's a large market in the centre of town, as well as the moderately priced *Suksamlan Hotel* and two banks with foreign exchange services. Just south of town is a large shrimp farm.

See the Trat Getting There & Away section for information on public transport to Khlong Yai and Hat Lek.

### Beaches

The sliver of Trat Province that extends south-eastward along the Cambodia border is fringed by several Gulf of Thailand beaches. **Hat Sai Si Ngoen** (Silver Sand Beach), lies just north of Km 41 off Highway 3; a billboard says a resort will be constructed here but so far there's no sign of development. Nearby at Km 42 is **Hat Sai Kaew** (Crystal Sand Beach) and at Km 48 **Hat Thaptim** (Sapphire Beach); neither quite lives up to their fanciful names, though they're basically OK places to walk along the water's edge or picnic in the shade of casuarina and eucalyptus trees.

The most promising beach is **Hat Ban Cheun**, a very long stretch of clean sand near Km 63. The partially paved, six km road (currently being upgraded) that leads to the beach passes the leftover foundation pillars of a defunct Cambodian refugee camp. There are the usual casuarina and eucalyptus trees, a small restaurant and four unattractive huts (200B) set on swampy land behind the beach. Camping on the beach would be a far better choice; you could have the restaurant proprietors hold onto you valuables for security's sake.

## KO CHANG NATIONAL MARINE PARK
อุทยานแห่งชาติทางทะเลหมู่เกาะช้าง

Forty-seven of the islands off Trat's coastline belong to a national park named after **Ko Chang** (Elephant Island), which at 492 sq km is the second largest island in Thailand after Phuket. Ko Chang itself is about 70% undisturbed island rainforest – the best preserved in Thailand, perhaps in all South-East Asia – with steep hills and cliffs reaching as high as 744m Khao Jom Prasat. Beach forest and mangrove are also found in abundance. Notable wildlife includes the stump-tailed macaque, small Indian civet, Javan mongoose, monitor lizard, water monitor, Burmese and reticulated pythons, king cobra, barking deer and wild pig. Avian species (61 resident species, plus 12 migratory) include Pacific reef egret, nightjar, green imperial pigeon, white-winged tern, blue-winged pitta, hooded pitta and three hornbill species. An endemic amphibian, the Ko Chang frog (*Rana kohchang*) is also found here.

Other major islands in the park include Ko Kut and Ko Mak. Ko Chang is ringed with small bays and beaches, among them Ao Khlong Son, Hat Sai Khao, Hat Khlong Phrao, Hat Kaibae, Ao Bang Bao and Ao Salak Phet. Near each of these beaches are small villages.

Ko Chang National Marine Park's wildlife includes species such as the barking deer.

Until very recently there wasn't a single paved road on Ko Chang, only red dirt roads between Khlong Son and Hat Kaibae on the west coast of the island, and between Khlong Son and Ban Salak Phet on the east side, plus walking trails passable by motorcycle from Kaibae to Bang Bao and Salak Kok to Salak Phet. Road crews are working to extend the road on the west side (a paved section now exists between Khlong Son/Ao Sapparot and Hat Sai Khao), however, and Trat authorities say the island will have a paved ring road – or at least the beginnings of one – within the next two or three years. The province has plans to 'civilise' Ko Chang further by stringing power lines around the island right behind the paved road.

In 1995 Ko Chang received around 60,000 visitors, most of whom were Thai. Thai visitors tend to arrive on weekends and holidays only, stay for 24 hours or less, and stay in the more expensive accommodation. The average stay for non-Thai visitors is around five days; a small number of visitors take up residence for weeks on end.

A combination of steep terrain and year-round streams creates several scenic waterfalls. A series of three falls along the stream of Khlong Mayom in the interior of the island, **Than Mayom Falls**, can be reached via Tha Than Mayom or Ban Dan Mai on the east coast. The waterfall closest to the shore can be climbed in about 45 minutes via a well marked footpath. The view from the top is quite good and there are two inscribed stones bearing the initials of Rama VI and Rama VII nearby. The second waterfall is about 500m farther east along Khlong Mayom and the third is about three km from the first. At the third waterfall is another inscribed stone, this one with the initials of Rama V. At the lower levels are public picnic areas.

A smaller waterfall on the west coast, **Khlong Phu Falls**, can be visited from Ao Khlong Phrao (45 minutes) or from Hat Kaibae (one hour) by following Khlong Phrao two km inland. Or pedal a bicycle along the main dirt road until you see the sign on the eastern side of the road. Ride up to the restaurant near the falls, from where it is only a 15 minute walk to the falls themselves. A pool beneath the falls is a good spot for a refreshing swim, and it is possible to stay in the bungalows or camp here.

On **Ko Kut** you'll find beaches mostly along the west side, at Hat Tapho, Hat Khlong Chao and Hat Khlong Yai Kii. A dirt road runs between Ban Khlong Hin Dam, the island's main village on the west coast, and Ao Salat along the north-east shore. Other villages on the island include Ban Ta Poi, Bang Ao Salat, Ban Laem Kluai, Bang Khlong Phrao and Ban Lak Uan. The nearby small islands of Ko Rang and Ko Rayang have good coral in spots. Ko Kut is best reached from Khlong Yai on the mainland.

**Ko Mak**, the smallest of the three main islands, has a beach along the north-west bay and possibly others as yet undiscovered. Monsoon forest covers 30% of the island while coconut plantations take up another 60%. A few tractors or jeeps travel along the single paved road which leads from the pier to the main village. It is possible to rent motorbikes and organise diving trips from the resorts on the island.

**Ko Wai** has some of the best coral and is excellent for snorkelling and diving. The island has one bungalow operation. **Ko Kham** is also recommended for underwater explorations; accommodation is available. **Ko Lao-ya** has natural attributes similar to those at Ko Wai, with one rather expensive place to stay. The tiny **Ko Rang** archipelago, south-west of Ko Chang, is a primary nesting ground for the endangered hawksbill sea turtle.

Ko Chang National Marine Park officially encompasses 192 sq km of land surface, and 458 sq km of sea. As with other national marine parks in Thailand, park status versus resort development is a hot issue. On Ko Chang, so far, everyone seems to be in agreement about what is park land and what isn't. Any land that was planted before the conferral of park status in 1982 can be privately deeded, bought, sold and developed – this includes many beach areas used for coconut plantations, or about 15% of the island. The Forestry Department makes regular flights

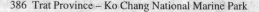

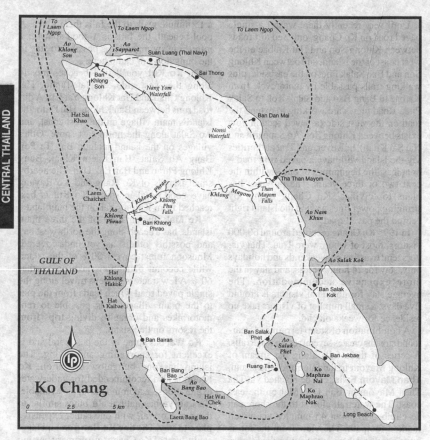

**Ko Chang**

0    2.5    5 km

*GULF OF THAILAND*

over the island to check for encroachment on the 85% belonging to the national park – mostly in the interior – and they are said to be very strict with interlopers.

### Information

There is no bank on Ko Chang, but money-changers will change US dollars and travellers' cheques at very unfavourable rates. The only post office is near the pier at Khlong Son, where there is a telegram service but no international phones. On Hat Sai Khao and Hat Kaibae, a few places offer international telephone service at very high rates.

There is a health clinic at Khlong Son; the nearest hospital is in Laem Ngop on the mainland. A two-room jail at Ban Salak Phet sometimes contains visitors caught smoking dope on the island.

### Walking on Ko Chang

In general the more interesting hikes can be found in the southern half of the island where there are fewer roads. At the northern end you can walk from Khlong Son to Hat Sai Khao in about 1½ to two hours; from Hat Sai Khao to Hat Khlong Phrao in about two hours; and from Hat Khlong Phrao to Hat

Kaibae in about two hours. All three are straightforward walks along the main road. If you're looking for more of a grunt, just head for the interior – the steep, forested hills will have you sweating in no time. A footpath connects Khlong Phrao on the west coast with Khlong Mayom on the east, but this all day cross-island route shouldn't be undertaken without a local guide.

Down south a challenging walk is to hike from Kaibae to Ao Bang Bao through coconut and rubber plantations – this takes about three to four hours and you may have to ask directions from villagers along the way as there are several interconnecting trails.

Bang Bao to Salak Phet? Don't try it unless you're an experienced tropical hiker with moderate orienteering skills – there's a lot of up-and-down and many interconnecting trails. A Swede who hiked the entire perimeter of the island suggested that for this part of the island you carry a note in Thai reading 'I would like to go to Salak Phet. I like very much to walk in the jungle and have done it before. Please show me the start of this trail'. If you don't get lost, this hike will take four to six hours; should you decide to attempt it, carry enough food and water for an overnight, just in case. If you do get lost, climb the nearest hilltop and try to locate the sea or a stream to get a bearing on where you are. Following any stream will usually take you either to a village or to the sea. Then you can either follow the coast or ask directions. This advice is also good for hiking anywhere across the island, as it is very easy to get lost on the many intersecting, unmarked trails. At the south-east end of Ao Bang Bao, around a headland that leads to Ao Salak Phet, is a beautiful and secluded beach, Hat Wai Chek.

On the east side of the island it's a one hour walk between Dan Mai and Than Mayom, two hours between Dan Mai and Sai Thong (or Khlong Son and Sai Thong). Salak Kok to Salak Phet is straightforward and takes around three hours. The estuary at Ao Salak Kok's western end boasts one of the best mangrove systems in Thailand, though like other coastal wetlands it's threatened by increased shrimp farming.

A hike around the entire island can be done at a comfortable pace in a week to 10 days. Remember to carry plenty of water and watch out for snakes – a few poisonous varieties live on the island.

## Diving

Ko Chang and its vicinity is a new frontier relative to other marine locales in Thailand. Climate-wise, November to April is the main diving season. The best dive sites are off the south-western tip of the island and include Hin Luuk Bat and Hin Laap, both seamounts with depths of around 18 to 20m. Nearby Ko Rang gets scenic around 25m, while Hin Phrai Nam has whitetip and reef sharks to around 20m. Near the mouth of Ao Salak Phet, at the south-eastern tip of the island, lies the wreck of a Thai warship at a depth of 15m; the ship was supposedly sunk by the French in 1941 during a dispute over whether these islands belonged to Thailand or to French-colonised Cambodia. According to Thai history there should be a second wreck nearby but divers have yet to report on it.

Ko Chang Divers at Haad Sai Khao specialises in PADI certification for novice divers. Dive trips typically include two dives with all guiding, transport and equipment for 1200B; snorkellers are welcome to join for 250B per day. Ko Chang Divers offers a free half-hour, one tank introduction at beachside, or a full PADI course for 6000B; instructors speak German, English, French and Thai. The only other full-time dive guiding/instruction centre on the island so far is the Dive Centre at Hat Kaibae, between Nangnuan Bungalows and Porn's.

## Other Activities

Some of the guesthouses at Hat Sai Khao rent kayaks and sailboards. Rooks Ko Chang Resort at Ao Khlong Phrao also offers water sport equipment and instruction, eg waterskiing for 1500B per hour or you can rent a mask and snorkel for 100B per hour. Mountain bikes can be rented at several places on Ko Chang, including Muk Hut Restaurant at Hat Sai Khao, and Palm Beach Resort at Hat Kaibae.

Several bungalow operations along Ko Chang's west coast beaches offer boat trips to nearby islands, eg 150B per person to Ko Yuak or Ko Man; 300B to Ko Rang, Ko Wai, Ko Khlam or Ko Mak; and 1000B to Ko Kut.

## Places to Stay – Ko Chang

Many beach huts on the island have only been open about five years and standards vary quite a bit. Some are only open during the dry season (November to May), but this may change as the island becomes more popular year-round and boat service becomes more regular. During the rainy season, boats usually only go as far as Ao Sapparot, Dan Mai and Than Mayom – the surf farther south along the west coast can be impassable during heavy rains.

Even during dry months, the trend now is for boats to drop off at Ao Sapparot so that visitors can continue on to the beaches by songthaew. When boats ply the west coast, remember that you can ask the boat pilots to drop you off at almost any bungalow operation on any beach, so if you know where you are going ask the pilot in Laem Ngop. It is also possible to get picked up from any bungalow on any beach – skiffs or long-tail boats take people to the boat if there is no pier. At Hat Sai Khao the boatmen have been known to charge 5B per person to relay passengers from the ferry to the beach.

**West Coast** As the island's better beaches are along the west coast, this is where most of the beach accommodation is. Most huts and bungalows feature one double mattress on the floor or on a raised platform. If you are staying longer than a few days all places will discount their rates, even in peak season. Most of the island has limited electricity or no electricity at all; on the popular beaches most restaurants use generators between 6 pm and midnight, otherwise sites are lit by kerosene or gas lanterns. Only a few places have music and, blessedly, even fewer have videos.

At the northern tip of the island is the largest village, Khlong Son, which has a network of piers at the mouth of the khlong,

a wat, a school, several noodle shops, a health clinic and one basic friendly bungalow operation on stilts, *Manee Guest House* near the piers is just 40 to 70B a night. Few people stay here any more since most passenger boats now moor at the Ao Sapparot pier rather than in Khlong Son. A few longtimers like staying here for village life, however.

From Khlong Son to Hat Sai Khao (White Sand Beach) is five km. At the lower end of the beach, well off the road and separated from other Hat Sai Khao bungalow developments by a couple of small rocky points, is the nicely landscaped *White Sand Beach Resort* where solid huts go for 100/150B for singles/doubles, and more up-market ones with bath cost 300 to 400B; roofs are tarped so that they don't leak in the rain.

Next south are a couple of less isolated spots beginning with the *Rock Sand*, which has a few rustic wooden huts on a rocky outcrop surrounded by beach on both sides for 100B per hut with nicer ones for up to 500B. The similarly priced grass mat huts at *KC* are better but the recent addition of electric power probably means this one is about to rebuild as a more upscale resort. *Yaka Bungalows* is a small place with inflatable kayaks for rent.

Farther south is a string of cheapies with basic huts for 100 to 200B (only 40 to 100B in the off season), and more solid ones from 300B. All are very similar in style and layout; if you get off the boat anywhere along this beach, you can walk from one to the other before deciding. This is one of the island's more 'social' beaches, where long-termers stoke their bongs with Cambodian herb while watching the sun set. Starting from the north you'll find *Tantawan* and *Bamboo*, which – like several other bungalow operations along this coast – organise trips to other islands. A newer place, *Ban Rung Rong* (☎ (39) 597184), offers flashier huts for 120 to 200B and nicer ones with bath for 300B; techno parties are another draw or turn-off, depending on your disposition. They also offer money exchange (5% commission) and rent mountain bikes for 120B per day. Next is *Cookie*, with basic huts for 100B, and motorbike rental for 60B per hour or 400B per day. Then there is *Mac* and *Nut Hut*, both with nicer bungalows for 300 to 450B, including bath.

The well run *Haad Sai Khao* has simple thatched huts from 100B along the back row, 120B middle rows, 150B front row, and a couple of flash bungalows with private bath facing the front for 900B; telephone and mail service are available. When full, Haad Sai Khao rents tents for 100B. *Apple* and *Sunsai* finish off this stretch with decent huts in the 150 to 200B range.

The German-owned *Plaloma Cliff Resort* is a bit south of Sunsai on the other side of a rocky headland, spread over a rocky cliff. Large tile and cement bungalows – shades of Ko Samui – cost 600B and 900B per night. On the cliff's highest point Plaloma has some very nice bamboo and thatch huts with private bath for 250B a night; the interspersed coconut palms and sea view are additional pluses.

About four km south of Hat Sai Khao (nine km from Khlong Son) is Ao Khlong Phrao (Coconut Bay). It stretches south of Laem Chaichet and encompasses the canal Khlong Phrao as well as its namesake village Ban Khlong Phrao (12 km from Khlong Son). On the north side of the canal is *Chaichet Bungalows* starting at 80 to 200B for separate bungalows with private bath. The bungalows are strung out along Laem Chaichet, a gently curving cape, though there's no beach to speak of. Also on the north bank of Khlong Phrao, *Klong Plow Resort* has modern wooden bungalows in a semicircle around a lagoon for 700B. Near Ban Chaichet south of Ao Khlong Phrao is *Coconut Beach Bungalows*, where typical thatched-roof-style bungalows cost 100B for singles/doubles or you can pay 400B for bamboo or concrete bungalows with bath. The bungalows are well kept and the pleasant beach has its own pier. Chaichet shares a pier with Coconut Beach Bungalows.

About a 10 minute walk farther south along the beach is the pricey *Rooks Ko Chang Resort* (☎ (01) 329-0434; (2) 277-5256 in Bangkok). Up-market bungalows here cost 1766 to 2943B and include all the usual comforts with air-con and colour TV. Most of the guests are Thai businesspeople on vacation, many on incentive travel packages.

It is possible to cross the river in a long-tail boat but you need to call for one on the south bank. If you are staying at *PSS Bungalow* the service is only 5B but if staying anywhere else it's 10B. The PSS huts cost 120B. About a 10 minute walk farther south near Wat Ban Khlong Phrao is *KP Bungalows*, where basic thatched huts cost 60/100B, larger and nicer ones with bath cost 300B. The food here is good, but the restaurant closes at 8 pm and the lights are out by 9 pm. The service could be a little friendlier; they are closed during the rainy season.

About 700m past the turn-off for Khlong Pliu Falls, off the main road in Ban Khlong Phrao, is the secluded *Hobby Hut* (☎ (01) 213-7668). A favourite with Thais associated with the music business, Hobby Hut has only four simple but large wooden cottages that rent for 1500B per month (shorter rentals may be possible if there's a vacancy). It's 300m to the nearest beach; a small inland lagoon offers canoeing possibilities. There's live music Wednesday to Friday evenings.

Around another headland to the south are two beach areas separated by a canal, Hat Khlong Makok and Hat Kaibae (15 km south of Khlong Son). These beaches tend to disappear during high tide but they're OK – lots of coconut palms. *Erawan* and *Magic* have bungalows for 80B but they're none too clean, while the better bungalows with bath cost from 150 to 300B. Magic has a pier, telephone service and scuba-diving tours. The owner has a boat monopoly from Laem Ngop so is able to funnel many passengers directly to this beach. Magic's best feature is its restaurant built over the bay. Next door is *Good Luck* (Chokdee), with cleaner, nicer thatched huts for 50B or concrete bungalows for 300B, set amidst coconut palms – a drawback is that it has no beach to speak of.

Next south on Hat Kaibae proper is an area that has become quite developed, with a new pier and bungalows with generator-powered electricity. Starting in the north, the first place you come to is the German-run *Palm Beach Resort*, where basic huts start at 50B, up to 350B for large bungalows. The food here is reportedly good; mountain bikes rent for 150B per day.

*Coral Resort* is set amidst a bumper crop of coconut palms and costs 50B for basic huts or 450B for larger bungalows with private bath. They also have an international telephone service. A khlong separates the similar *Nang Nual Resort*; this area is a bit trashed in places and the adjacent shrimp farm is a definite detraction.

*Kaibae Hut*, on the south side of the khlong, has a nicely laid out restaurant and fair bungalows, plus a bit of a beach even at high tide; rates are the usual 80B for basic huts and 200 to 250B for nicer bungalows with bath. It's quiet, too, and features a security gate that's locked at night.

There is more of a beach down towards the southern end of Hat Kaibae. *Porn's* has basic 80B huts while the large *Seaview Resort* has similar huts for 100B and nice large bungalows from 800B. Seaview Resort, which sits just opposite Ko Man Nai, charters boats from 150 to 5000B depending on the destination and trip length. A boat charter to Laem Ngop costs 3000B. The last place on the beach is the secluded and friendly *Siam Bay Resort* with huts for 80 to 100B, bungalows with private bath from 200B and more expensive fancier huts up to 1000B.

**South Coast** None of the following places is typically open during the rainy season (May to November) when regular transport is difficult. Ao Bang Bao has the *Nice Beach Bang Bao* with average bungalows with attached bath for 250 to 300B, and the cheaper *Bang Bao Blue Wave* and *Bang Bao Lagoon* for 80 to 300B. You may also be able to rent rooms cheaply in the village (Ban Bang Bao). At the moment you can walk between Bang Bao and Hat Kaibae in about three hours; eventually a road will connect the two. During the rainy season the only way here is on foot.

The next bay along the coast, Ao Salak

Phet, features the on-again, off-again *Ban Salakpetch Bungalow* with typical thatched huts for 40 to 60B. A couple of as yet unnamed bungalow places rent huts for 50 to 100B a night near the fishing villages of Ruang Tan and Ban Salak Phet. As at Ao Bang Bao, you may be able to rent a room or house in Ban Salak Phet. Rumours that bungalows are under construction farther south-east along the bay at Ban Jekbae have yet to bear fruit.

The very secluded *Long Beach Bungalows*, near the end of the long cape to the south-east of Ao Salak Phet, has well made huts with electricity for 100/120B a night. They are closed between July and December. Farther on, right at the rocky tip of the cape, is the friendly *Tantawan House* with only seven huts costing 70/100B. The beach is only a two minute swim away. To get here take a boat from Ao Salak Phet for 30B.

A dirt road leads from Ao Sapparot all the way to Ban Salak Phet; songthaews meet the Ao Sapparot boats. The village itself is very spread out; the main road terminates at Wat Salak Phet, from where there are smaller tracks along the southern coast. Power lines also terminate in Ban Salak Phet.

**East Coast** There are a couple of mediocre places to stay near the nicely landscaped national park headquarters at Than Mayom. Privately managed, unnamed *bungalows* opposite the park offices cost 200B; they're not in very good condition and hardly anyone ever seems to stay here. A couple of km north, *Thanmayom Resort* rents A-frame huts for 100B a night; there is a pier but no beach to speak of, and since the huts are on the other side of a dusty road from the sea, it's not very inviting. If you have camping gear, it might be better to hike up and camp near Than Mayom Falls.

The visitors' centre contains faded photo displays with English labels and useful info. At the end of a small pier is a very casual restaurant with rice and noodles dishes.

### Places to Stay – other islands
**Ko Kut** At Hat Tapho on the west coast, the aptly named *First* has expensive bungalows

for up to 1000B, plus a few basic huts for 100B, with outside bath. If this one's closed when you arrive, try village homes in nearby Ban Hin Dam.

**Ko Mak** On the west bay, amidst a coconut and rubber plantation, is the Israeli-managed *Lazydays Resort* (☎ (2) 281-3412 in Bangkok), where huts with verandahs cost 100B a night. *Ao Kok Resort* (☎ (39) 425263) offers comfortable bungalows with fan and private bath for 500B a night in the low season, 700B high season. *TK Huts*, a new place, reportedly has nice bungalows for 300B. Diving equipment and instruction are available from Ao Kok Resort. The boat fare from Laem Ngop is 150B.

**Ko Kradat** The *Ko Kradat* has air-con bungalows for 600B. Mr Chumpon in Bangkok (☎ (2) 311-3668) can arrange accommodation at Ko Kradat and transport to the island in advance.

**Ko Kham** *Ko Kham Resort*, run by a friendly ex-cop, offers bamboo bungalows for 80 to 120B. A resort-sponsored boat leaves the main Laem Ngop pier daily at 1 pm, November to April only.

### Places to Eat
Menus at all the bungalows on Ko Chang are pretty similar, with highest marks going to Kaibae Hut (Hat Kaibae), Sunsai Bungalows (Hat Sai Khao) and Tantawan (Hat Sai Khao).

Several small eateries have opened up along the east side of the main road in Hat Sai Khao. *AM/PM Restaurant*, an upstairs place where you sit on cushions, is good for Thai lunches and dinner and western breakfasts, while the *Muk Hut* next door does pizza and other western dishes. The latter also offers moneychanging and mountain bike rental services.

*Sandalwood*, off the road a bit farther south opposite Sunsai Bungalows, is a larger indoor/outdoor place with Thai food, seafood barbecues and occasional live music. On opening night in 1996, the lead composer/singer of Caravan, Phii Surachai, performed here. Nearby *Aloha Bakery* is popular for items like banana bread and chocolate chip cookies.

The food is also quite good at *KP* on Ao Khlong Phrao and at the *Beach Restaurant* at Hat Kaibae. *Rim Saphan* is a decent seafood restaurant on the Laem Ngop pier.

### Getting There & Away
**Ko Chang** Take a songthaew (10B, 25 minutes) from Trat to Laem Ngop on the coast, then a ferry to Ko Chang. In Laem Ngop there are now two piers serving Ko Chang – the main one at the end of the road from Trat, and a newer one called Ko Chang Centrepoint, which is operated by Rooks Ko Chang Resort, four km north-west of Laem Ngop.

At the first pier you have a choice of several different ferries, depending on the

## Ferry Timetable

| Destination | Fare | Departures | Trip Length | Return |
|---|---|---|---|---|
| Ao Sapparot | 40B** | 9 am, noon, 1 pm , 4 pm | 45 minutes | 9 am, noon, 4 pm |
| Hat Sai Khao (White Sand)* | 70B | 11 am & 3 pm | 1½ hours | 7 to 8 am & 2 pm |
| Khlong Phrao* | 70B | 11 am & 3 pm | 2 hours | 6.30 am & 1.30 pm |
| Hat Kaibae* | 70B | 11 am & 3 pm | 2½ hours | 6 am & 1 pm |
| Ao Bang Bao* | 70B | 1 & 3 pm | 3½ hours | 7 am & 1 pm |
| Ao Salak Phet* | 50B | 1 & 3 pm | 4 hours | 6 am and noon |
| Than Mayom | 35B | 1 pm | 45 minutes | 7 am |
| Ao Salak Kok | 35B | 1 pm | 2 hours | 6.30 to 7 am |

*Boats to these beaches may not run in the rainy season*
** *70B with songthaew fare to west coast beaches*

destination and time of day. Only Ao Sapparot on Ko Chang is able to dock boats year-round; even in the dry season this is where most people disembark. See the Ferry Timetable on the previous page for the kinds of departures available; in many cases the same boat makes two or three stops. All times are approximate and depend on weather, number of passengers and any number of other factors. You should check on fares in advance – sometimes the boat crews overcharge farangs. During the wet season the boat service is erratic and most boats will only go to Ao Sapparot (Pineapple Bay), where it will be necessary to go to the beaches by pickups or motorbike. Boat fares to Ao Sapparot usually include the taxi fare on to one of the beaches, although you can insist on paying only the boat fare if you have your own transport waiting on the island. Otherwise it's simpler just to pay the whole thing; it's 70B with taxi, 40B without.

From the gleaming Ko Chang Centrepoint pier, there's so far only one boat per day, at 7 am for 80B. The boat drops passengers off at Ao Sapparot and the fare includes a songthaew ride to one of the beaches. The problem with using the Centrepoint pier is that there's no accommodation or restaurants nearby, so the 7 am departure means an even earlier wake-up in Ban Laem Ngop or Trat.

If you get enough people together, the Foremost Guest House in Trat can arrange boat trips from the canal in town all the way to Ko Chang (destination of choice, except in high swells when the west coast may be unnavigable) for 100B per person.

There are direct minivans from Khao San Rd in Bangkok to Laem Ngop for 250B per person. Although it's no longer the case that the minivans necessarily miss the last boat to Ko Chang, it's better to take a regular bus, spend the night in Trat or Laem Ngop and take your time choosing a boat the next day. Or start out earlier in the day by government tour bus to Trat from Bangkok's Eastern Bus Terminal, then in Trat catch a songthaew to Laem Ngop in time for the afternoon boats. You can make the last boat to Ko Chang at 3 pm if you catch the 140B air-con bus to Trat at 8.30 am from Bangkok's Eastern Bus Terminal. This will arrive in Trat around 1.30 pm, leaving plenty of time to get a songthaew to Laem Ngop in time for the boat departure.

**Ko Kut** Two or three fishing boats a week go to Ko Kut from the pier of Tha Chaloemphon on the Trat River towards the east side of Trat. They'll take passengers for 80B per person. Similar boats leave slightly less frequently (six to eight times a month) from Ban Nam Chiaw, a village about halfway between Trat and Laem Ngop. Departure frequency and times from either pier depend on the weather and the fishing season – it's best to enquire ahead of time. The boats take around six hours to reach Ko Kut.

Coconut boats go to Ko Kut once or twice a month from a pier next to the slaughterhouse in town – same fare and trip duration as the fishing boats.

If you want to charter a boat to Ko Kut, the best place to do so is from Ban Ta Neuk, near Km 68 south-east of Trat, about six km before Khlong Yai off Highway 318. A longtail boat, capable of carrying up to 10 people, can be chartered here for 1000B. Travel time is about one hour. During the rainy season these boats may suspend service.

**Ko Mak** During the November to May dry season boats to Ko Mak leave daily from the Laem Ngop pier at 3 pm (7 to 7.30 am in the reverse direction); the fare is 150B per person and the trip takes around three to 3½ hours. During the rainy season the departure schedule is cut back to every other day – except in high surf when boats may be cancelled altogether for several days.

Coconut boats also go to Ko Mak from the pier near the slaughterhouse in Trat twice a month. The trip takes five hours and costs around 100B per person.

**Other Islands** Daily boats to Ko Kham depart around 3 pm (arriving at 6 pm) for 150B. A boat to Ko Wai leaves at 3 pm and arrives at 4.30 pm, costing 70B. Both boats return the next day at around 7.30 am.

CENTRAL THAILAND

## Getting Around

To get from one part of Ko Chang to another you have a choice of motorbike taxi, Japanese pickup, jeep, boat and foot (see the earlier Walking on Ko Chang section).

**Motorcycle & Truck** Songthaews meeting the boats at Ao Sapparot charge 30B per person to any beach along the west coast.

The motorcycle taxi mafia on the island charges 40B from Ao Sapparot to Hat Sai Khao, then from Sai Khao south it's 40B to Laem Chaichet and Khlong Phrao (or 70B from Ao Sapparot) and 60B to Hat Kaibae (100B from Khlong Son). The main motorcycle taxi stand is opposite the north end of Hat Sai Khao; you can also rent one of their motorcycles to drive yourself for 400B a day. Other bungalow operations in Khlong Son and Hat Sai Khao also charge 400 to 600B per day for motorbike hire; elsewhere on the island rental bikes are scarce. The owners claim they have to charge these rates because the island roads are so hard on the bikes.

**Jeep** Between Ao Salak Kok and Ao Salak Phet there's a daily jeep service that costs 10B per person. The jeep leaves Ao Salak Kok around 4.30 pm, returning from Ao Salak Phet the following day at 6 am.

**Boat** The regular boat to Ao Phrao and Hat Kaibae usually stops first at Hat Sai Khao and Ao Phrao; you can catch a ride from one area to the other along the west coast for 30B. Boat rides up Khlong Phrao to the falls cost 50B per person and can be arranged through most bungalows.

On the east coast, there is a daily boat service between Than Mayom and Ao Salak Kok farther south for 20B per person. On the southern end, you can charter a boat between Salak Phet and Long Beach Bungalows for around 150B.

Charter trips to nearby islands average 500B for a half-day. Make sure that the charter includes all user 'fees' for the islands – sometimes the boatmen demand 200B on top of the charter fee for using the beach.

# Prachinburi & Sa Kaew Provinces

Lying roughly halfway between Bangkok and the Cambodian border, the largely rural provinces of Prachinburi and Sa Kaew are peppered with many small, unexcavated, unrestored Dvaravati and Khmer ruins. The latter province's name, in fact, means 'Jewel Pool', a reference to various Mon-Khmer reservoirs in the area. Little more than loose collections of laterite blocks, most will be of little interest to the casual visitor. The provincial capitals and larger towns lie next to the banks of the Prachin River – now paralleled by the eastern railway line and Highway 33 – in the midst of a rice-growing region crossed by canals. The eastern districts of Prachinburi centred around amphoe Sa Kaew attained separate provincial status in January 1994.

## National Parks

North of Prachinburi, Route 3077 leads to Khao Yai National Park (see Nakhon Ratchasima Province in the North-Eastern Thailand chapter). North and north-east of Kabinburi, along the southern escarpment of the Khorat Plateau, are the contiguous Thap Lan National Park and Pang Sida National Park. Together these parks encompass 3084 sq km, one of the largest protected natural areas in Thailand.

**Thap Lan National Park** is well known as a habitat for the abundant *tôn lan*, or talipot palm, the leaves of which were once used for palm leaf Buddhist manuscripts. Wildlife seen in the park includes elephants, gaur, tigers, sambar, barking deer, palm civets, hornbills and gibbons. Lowland bird varieties are particularly well represented here. This area was an important refuge for Thailand's communist guerrillas during the 1960s and 1970s, and remnants of their camps can be seen along the streams Khlong Nam Brang and Khlong Sam Son. Facilities in the park are minimal; anyone who would like to explore the interior should contact the rangers at park headquarters in Thap Lan village, amphoe Na Di. The rangers can arrange for a tour of the park and provide camping permits. There is no public transport to the park entrance, which is around 32 km north of Kabinburi via Route 304 (the road to Nakhon Ratchasima).

**Pang Sida National Park**, centred around 30 km south-east of Thap Lan near Sa Kaew, is smaller but hillier than Thap Lan. Streams that cut through the park form several scenic waterfalls, including **Pang Sida** and **Na Pha Yai Falls** near the park headquarters, and the more difficult to reach **Suan Man Suan Thong** and **Daeng Makha Falls**.

### Historical Ruins

South-east of amphoe meuang Prachinburi via Routes 319 and 3070, in the village of Ban Sa Khoi (between Khok Pip and Sa Maha Pho on Route 3070), is the Angkor-period **Sa Morakot**. Thai for 'Emerald Pool', this was an important Khmer reservoir during the reign of Angkor's Jayavarman VII. Original laterite-block sluices next to the dam, along with assorted *semas* (boundary stones), naga sculptures, pedestals and a sandstone lingam, can still be seen here. Water from this reservoir is still considered sacred and has been used in Thai coronation ceremonies.

**Sa Kaew** or 'Jewel Pool', another historic reservoir site, is just south of Khok Pip off Route 3070. This one features a Dvaravati-period laterite quarry with some surviving bas-relief on the walls. There are a number of other Dvaravati and Angkor laterite foundations in the area.

### ARANYA PRATHET
อรัญประเทศ
• ☎ (37) • *pop 55,000*

This district next to the Thailand-Cambodia border has long been an important trade and transport centre. After the Khmer Rouge took over Cambodia in 1975, and again when the Vietnamese invaded Cambodia in 1979, Aranya Prathet became a major recipient of Cambodian refugees. Today, random skirmishes between Khmer Rouge guerrillas and the Phnom Penh government continue to send Cambodian citizens scurrying over the border from time to time.

There isn't a lot to see around town; the refugee camp business changed its relatively sleepy nature seemingly forever, and a slow increase in border trade has surrounded the older town centre with a smattering of modern auto dealers and office buildings. Convoys of shining Toyota land cruisers flying UN flags ply the main streets on their way to and from Cambodia.

**Talaat Rong Kleua**, a large market consisting of rows of warehouse-like sheds at the northern edge of town, attracts a ragtag crowd of Cambodians who sell gems, textiles, basketry, brass and other handcrafted merchandise to the Thais. It's a fascinating spot to visit just to observe the steady stream of Cambodians coming across the border with hand-pulled carts piled high with market goods. Those who can afford it pay workers to pull up to six passengers at a time in little roofed wooden carts. There are several simple restaurants serving Thai food in the market.

Theft and banditry are common in the area, so take care with night travel. Although it's relatively safe to cross the border directly to Poipet (with permission), areas to the north and south of the district seat are heavily mined. Audible firefights these days are not uncommon, and Khmer Rouge guerrillas have been known to cross the border into Thailand, especially north of Aranya Prathet towards Buriram Province. One-legged Ta Mok, deputy commander-in-chief of the Khmer Rouge, commands an area just a km from the border near Anlong Veng, Cambodia. A huge army base on the Thai side of Aranya Prathet houses a battalion of Thailand's 3rd Infantry.

### Places to Stay & Eat

The *Aran Garden 1*, 59/1-7 Rat Uthit Rd, is an older, somewhat seedy central hotel with OK fan rooms with attached bath for 120B. Further up the road, the newer and larger *Aran Garden 2* (110 Rat Uthit Rd) offers clean, quiet rooms with fan for 160B a night, air-con rooms for 270 to 400B.

Two new places cater to visiting, comparatively wealthy border traders and NGO employees. *Inn Pound* (☎ 232588; fax 232115) on the main highway leading into Aranya Prathet from the west offers clean, modern rooms with air-con, phone, satellite TV and minibar for 350 to 600B. The new and better located (for anyone who wants to see the town on foot) *Inter Hotel* is tucked away in a quiet residential area near the town centre. Nice rooms with satellite TV and private hot water bathrooms cost 400B; 450B with fridge.

The air-con *Little Home Restaurant*, in the town centre, serves pizza, salads, sandwiches, ice cream and Thai and Chinese food from 7.30 am to 9.30 pm. A block south-east of Little Home is a small night market with a cluster of food vendors.

### Getting There & Away
Ordinary buses from Bangkok's Northern Bus Terminal cost 74B, leave hourly from 5.30 am to 4.30 pm and take around five hours to reach Aranya Prathet. Air-con buses (133B) leave hourly from 5.30 to 10.30 am and from noon to 5 pm. Buses to/from Prachinburi cost 31B and 55B for ordinary and air-con buses respectively.

The 3rd class only eastern railway line between Bangkok and Aran leaves Bangkok's Hualamphong station twice daily at 6 am and 1.10 pm, arriving in Aran 5½ hours later. The one way fare is 48B.

If you have your own wheels you could also reach Aran from Chanthaburi Province to the south via Route 317, or from Buriram Province to the north via Route 3068. Before taking the latter road in either direction, check the current security situation with a reliable local; Khmer Rouge activity in the area may precipitate the temporary closing of the road.

### Crossing to Cambodia
The SRT train continues another half hour east of Aran to the border for 5B. From Poipet on the Cambodian side you can catch a train all the way to Phnom Penh (420 km) or as far as Sisaphon (49 km), the jumping-off point for buses north to Siem Reap/Angkor Wat.

It's legal to enter Cambodia at Poipet with special permission (usually given to people working for NGOs who are active in the area). Whether or not it's legal to exit Thailand here is another story. Some people have been denied an exit stamp from Thai immigration authorities; others have had no problem. If you're not planning to return to Thailand in the near future, ie you're on your way to Vietnam and then onward from there, it hardly matters.

*Warning* Travel into Cambodia via this route is dangerous and many embassies advise against it. You may like to check with your embassy in Thailand first before making any extensive plans. Although many Khmer Rouge have defected, the situation remains highly volatile.

# Phetburi Province

### PHETBURI
อ.เมืองเพชรบุรี
• ☎ *(32)* • *pop 35,000*
Situated 160 km south of Bangkok, Phetburi (or Phetchaburi, also known as Meuang Phet) is worth a stopover for its many old temples spanning several centuries. Six or seven temples can be seen via a circular walk of two or three hours through the city. These temples have made very few concessions to the 20th century and thus provide a glimpse of the traditional Siamese urban wat.

Also noteworthy is Khao Wang, just west of the city, which has the remains of a King Mongkut palace and several wats, plus a good aerial view of the city. The underground Buddhist shrine at the Khao Luang Caves, north of the city, is also worth seeing.

### Orientation & Information
If you arrive at the train station, follow the road south-east of the tracks until you come to Ratchadamnoen Rd, then turn right.

CENTRAL THAILAND

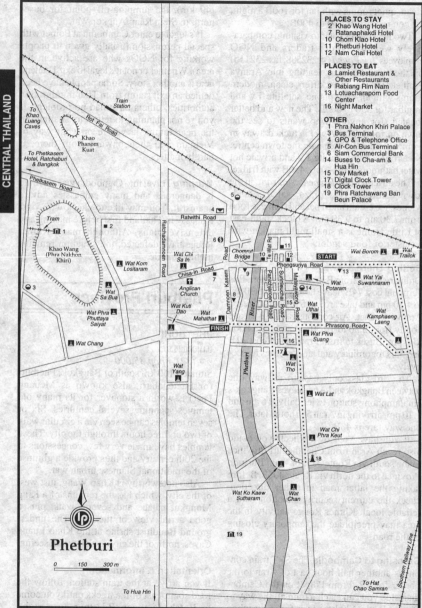

PLACES TO STAY
2  Khao Wang Hotel
7  Ratanaphakdi Hotel
10  Chom Klao Hotel
11  Phetburi Hotel
12  Nam Chai Hotel

PLACES TO EAT
8  Lamiet Restaurant &
   Other Restaurants
9  Rabiang Rim Nam
13  Lotuacharaporn Food
    Center
16  Night Market

OTHER
1  Phra Nakhon Khiri Palace
3  Bus Terminal
4  GPO & Telephone Office
5  Air-Con Bus Terminal
6  Siam Commercial Bank
14  Buses to Cha-am &
    Hua Hin
15  Day Market
17  Digital Clock Tower
18  Clock Tower
19  Phra Ratchawang Ban
    Beun Palace

To Khao
Luang
Caves

To Phetkasem
Hotel, Ratchaburi
& Bangkok

Train Station

Rot Fai Road

Khao
Phanom
Kuat

Phetkasem Road

Tram

Khao Wang
(Phra Nakhon
Khiri)

Wat Kom
Lositaram

Wat Sa Bua

Wat Phra
Phuttaya
Saiyat

Wat Chang

Ratchadamnoen Road

Wat Chi
Sa In

Chisa-In Road

Anglican
Church

Wat Kuti
Dao

Wat
Mahathat

Wat Yang

Ratwithi Road

Damnoen Kasem Road

Wat Chi
Sa In

Chomruot
Bridge

Ta Wat Rd

START

Phongsuriya Road

Pchiboon Road

Surinrchit Road

Matayawong Road

Wat Borom

Wat Trailok

Wat Yai
Suwannaram

Wat
Potaram

Wat
Uthai

Wat
Kamphaeng
Laeng

FINISH

River

Phetburi

Phrasong Road

Wat Phra
Suang

Wat Tho

Wat Lat

Wat Chi
Phra Keut

Wat Ko Kaew
Sutharam

Wat
Chan

Phetburi

0    150    300 m

To Hua Hin

To Hat
Chao Samran

Southern Railway Line

## Walking Tour – Phetburi Temples

### Wat Yai Suwannaram
วัดใหญ่สุวรรณาราม
After you've crossed the Phetburi River by Chomrut Bridge and passed the Nam Chai Hotel on the left, walk about 300m farther along Phongsuriya Rd until you see a big temple on the right. This is Wat Yai, originally built in the 17th century and renovated during the reign of King Chulalongkorn (1868-1910). The main bòt is surrounded by a cloister filled with sober Buddha images. The murals inside the bòt date to the 1730s and are in good condition. Next to the bòt, in the middle of a pond, is a beautifully designed old haw trai, or tripitaka library.

### Wat Borom & Wat Trailok
วัดบรมและวัดไตรโลก
These two wats are next to one another on the opposite side of Phongsuriya Rd from Wat Yai, a little to the east. They are distinctive for their monastic halls and long, graceful, wooden 'dormitories' on stilts. Turn right onto the road heading south from Wat Trailok and follow this road down past a bamboo fence on the right to the entrance for Wat Kamphaeng Laeng.

### Wat Kamphaeng Laeng
วัดกำแพงแลง
This is a very old (13th century) Khmer site with five prangs and part of the original wall still standing. The prang in front contains a Buddha footprint. Of the other four, two contain images dedicated to famous lŭang phâw (venerable elderly monks), one was in ruins (but is being restored) and the last has recently been uncovered from a mound of dirt. The Khmers built these as Hindu monuments, so the Buddhist symbols are late additions.

### Wat Phra Suang & Wat Lat
วัดพระสวงและวัดลาด
Follow the road (Phrasong Rd) beside Wat Kamphaeng Laeng, heading west back towards the river until you pass Wat Phra Suang on the left, undistinguished except for one very nice Ayuthaya-style prasat. Turn left immediately after this wat, heading south again until you come to the clock tower at the southern edge of town. You'll have passed Wat Lat on the left side of the street along the way, but it's not worth breaking your momentum for; this is a long walk.

### Wat Ko Kaew Sutharam
วัดแก้วสุตธาราม
Turn right at the clock tower and look for signs leading to the Ayuthaya-period Wat Ko. Two different sois on the left lead to the wat, which is behind the shops along the curving street. The bòt features early 18th century murals that are among the best conceived in Thailand. One mural panel depicts what appears to be a Jesuit priest wearing the robes of a Buddhist monk, while another shows other foreigners undergoing Buddhist conversions. There is also a large wooden monastic hall on stilts similar to the ones at Wat Borom and Wat Trailok, but in much better condition.

### Wat Mahathat
วัดมหาธาตุ
Follow the street in front of Wat Ko north (back towards central Phetburi), and walk over the first bridge you come to on the left, which leads to Wat Mahathat. Alternatively, you can cross the river at Wat Ko, near the clock tower, and take the street on the other side of the river around to Wat Mahathat. The large white prang of this wat can be seen from a distance – a typical late Ayuthaya/early Ratanakosin adaptation of the Khmer prangs of Lopburi and Phimai. This is obviously an important temple in Phetburi, judging from all the activity here. ■

Follow Ratchadamnoen Rd south to the second major intersection and turn left towards central Phetburi to begin the walking tour (see the previous page). Or take a samlor from the train station to Chomrut Bridge (Saphaan Chomrut) for 10B. If you've come by bus, you'll be getting off very near Khao Wang, and will have to take a samlor into the centre of town.

**Money** The Siam Commercial Bank has an exchange office at 2 Damnoen Kasem Rd, just south of the post office. Several other banks in the vicinity offer foreign exchange, as well as ATMs.

**Post & Communications** The post office is on the corner of Ratwithi and Damnoen Kasem Rds. An international telephone office, upstairs in the same building, is open daily from 7 am to 10 pm.

### Khao Wang & Phra Nakhon Khiri Historical Park
เขาวัง/อุทยานประวัติศาสตร์พระนครคีรี

Just west of the city, a 10B samlor ride from the bus station, is Khao Wang. Cobblestone paths lead up and around the hill, which is studded with wats and various components of King Mongkut's palace on Phra Nakhon Khiri (Holy City Hill). The views are great, especially at sunset. The walk up looks easy but is fairly strenuous. Fat monkeys loll about in the trees and on the walls along the main paths. In 1988 Phra Nakhon Khiri was declared a national historical park, so there is an entry fee of 20B. A tram has been installed to save you walking up to the peak (10B per person one way). The park is open Monday to Friday from 8 am to 5.30 pm and on weekends till 6 pm.

### Khao Luang Caves
ถ้ำเขาหลวง

Five km north of Phetburi is the cave sanctuary of Khao Luang (Great Hill). Concrete steps lead down into an anteroom then into the main cavern, which is filled with old Buddha images, many of them put in place

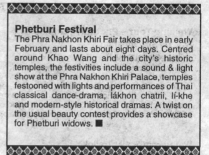

**Phetburi Festival**
The Phra Nakhon Khiri Fair takes place in early February and lasts about eight days. Centred around Khao Wang and the city's historic temples, the festivities include a sound & light show at the Phra Nakhon Khiri Palace, temples festooned with lights and performances of Thai classical dance-drama, lákhon chatrii, lí-khe and modern-style historical dramas. A twist on the usual beauty contest provides a showcase for Phetburi widows. ■

by King Mongkut. Sunlight from two holes in the chamber ceiling spray light on the images, which are a favourite subject for photographers. To the rear of the main cavern is an entrance to a third, smaller chamber. On the right of the entrance is Wat Bunthawi, with a sala designed by the abbot himself and a bòt with impressively carved wooden door panels.

Admission to the caves is free (donations are accepted). A samlor from the city centre to Khao Luang costs 50B, a motorcycle taxi 25 to 30B.

### Places to Stay
On the eastern side of Chomrut Bridge, on the right bank of Phetburi River, is the *Chom Klao Hotel* (☎ 425398), an ordinary, fairly clean Chinese hotel with friendly staff. It costs 100B for rooms with fan and shared bath, or 130B with private bath.

The *Nam Chai Hotel* (no English sign) is a block farther east from the Chom Klao Hotel, and has rooms for 100B with shared bath, 140/150B with attached bath, but is not as good value as the Chom Klao. Another cheapie is the *Ratanaphakdi Hotel* on Chisa-In Rd, where clean rooms with private bath cost 200B a single/double. Behind the Nam Chai is the *Phetburi Hotel* (☎ 425315), another divey sort of place, with grotty and overpriced rooms for 150B with fan and bath.

The *Khao Wang Hotel* (☎ 425167), opposite Khao Wang used to be my favourite in

Phet, but the rooms have gone downhill a bit in recent years. A fairly clean room with fan and bath costs 200/300B for one/two beds. Air-con rooms are 300/550B. Most rooms have TV.

The best hotel in town is the friendly and clean *Phetkasem Hotel* (☎ 425581), 86/1 Phetkasem Rd, which is on the highway north to Bangkok on the edge of town. Rooms are 180 to 220B with fan and bath, 280 to 320B with air-con and 350 to 450B with hot water.

### Places to Eat

There are several good restaurants in the Khao Wang area, with a range of standard Thai and Chinese dishes. A variety of cheap eats is available at the night market at the southern end of Surinleuchai Rd, under the digital clock tower.

Other good eating places can be found in the town centre along the main street to the clock tower. Across from Wat Mahathat, *Lamiet* sells really good khanŏm mâw kaeng (egg custard) and fāwy thawng (sweet shredded egg yolk) – which they also ship to Bangkok. This shop also has a branch near Khao Wang, where a whole group of egg custard places serve tourists.

Near Wat Yai Suwannaram on Phongsuriya Rd, the *Lotuacharaporn Food Center* is managed by a family who grow their own vegetables and breed their own animals without the use of chemicals. The menu covers a wide variety of Thai and Chinese dishes, and no MSG.

The *Rabiang Rim Nam*, on the south side of Chisa-In Rd near Chomrut Bridge, features a Thai and English menu of over 100 items, including seafood and 30 kinds of yam; most non-seafood dishes cost around 25 to 50B, seafood and some soups 70B or more.

### Getting There & Away

**Bus** From Bangkok, buses leave regularly from the Southern Bus Terminal in Thonburi for 36B (ordinary) on the new road, 31B on the old road (via Ratchaburi and Nakhon Pathom), or 65B air-con. The bus takes about 2½ hours.

Buses to Phetburi from Cha-am and Hua Hin are 15 and 20B and take 60 and 90 minutes respectively. Other ordinary bus fares are: Ratchaburi 16B (45 minutes), Nakhon Pathom 25B (two hours), Prachuap Khiri Khan 40B (three hours) and Phuket 180B (12 hours). The main bus terminal in Phetburi is just south-west of Khao Wang.

**Train** Trains leave Bangkok's Hualamphong station at 1.30 pm (rapid), 1.40 pm (ordinary 3rd class), 2.25 pm (special express), 3.15 pm (special express), 3.50 pm (rapid), 6.30 pm (rapid), 7.20 pm (express), 7.45 pm (rapid) and 9.55 pm (special express). All of these trains offer 1st and 2nd class seating (no 3rd class) and take about 3½ hours to reach Phetburi. Fares are 78B and 153B, not including rapid or express surcharges. The bus is cheaper and faster.

There is no longer an ordinary train between Hualamphong and Phetburi, but there are still two ordinary 3rd class trains daily from Thonburi (Bangkok Noi) station at 7.20 am and 7.15 pm (34B).

### Getting Around

Samlors go anywhere in the town centre for 10B; you can charter one for the whole day for 100B. Share mini-songthaews cost 5B around town, including to and from the train station.

## KAENG KRACHAN NATIONAL PARK

อุทยานแห่งชาติแก่งกระจาน

This 3000 sq km park is Thailand's largest, covering nearly half of Phetburi Province along the Myanmar border. In spite of its size and proximity to Bangkok, Kaeng Krachan doesn't seem to get many visitors (or perhaps its huge size just swallows them up). Because this part of Phetburi receives some of the heaviest rainfall in Thailand, the rainforest is particularly abundant in places. There are also areas of savanna-like grasslands, mountains, steep cliffs, caves, waterfalls, long-distance hiking trails and two rivers, the Phetburi and the Pranburi, which are suitable for rafting. Above the **Kaeng Krachan Dam** is a large reservoir stocked with fish. Animals living in Kaeng Krachan include wild elephants, deer, tigers, bears, gibbons, boars, hornbills, bantengs, dusky leaf langurs, gaurs and wild cattle. Small Karen settlements here have taken their toll on the park via illegal farming and poaching. According to Piprell & Graham's latest *National Parks of Thailand*, 'Kaeng Krachan...could become one of the world's premier reserves if properly managed in the future'.

Hiking and camping are excellent as long as you have your own food, water and camping gear. Forestry officials at the park headquarters can sometimes be hired as guides for overnight trekking in the park. The standard guide fee is 200B per day. Very little English is spoken so this option is best for those who know some Thai or who don't need any commentary. Eighteen-tiered **Tho Thip Falls** is a three hour hike from Km 33 on the road into the park; longer hikes can reach the headwaters of the Phetburi River or the summit of **Phanoen Thung**, the park's highest point. Deeper into the park, near La-U Reservoir, are the twin waterfalls of **Paa La-U Yai** and **Paa La-U Noi**; reaching the heights of this cascade requires several days of trekking for which an experienced guide is necessary. There is a Karen village near the latter. The best hiking and camping months are November to April.

You can rent boats on Kaeng Krachan Reservoir for 300B per hour or 700B for three hours. Admission to the park is 25B.

### Places to Stay & Eat
The 11 bungalows near the park headquarters cost 100B per person. You can also set up your own tent for 5B per person per night. Near the visitors' centre is a modest restaurant.

*Kaeng Krachan Resorts* (☎ (2) 513-3238 in Bangkok) offers expensive 'floatel' accommodation at the La-U Reservoir.

As malaria is a definite risk in the park, be sure to take precautions against mosquito bites at evening and at night.

### Getting There & Around
Kaeng Krachan is about 60 km from Phetburi, off Route 3175. The turn-off for Route 3175 is at Tha Yang on Highway 4, about 18 km south

of Phetburi. The park headquarters is eight km past the dam, where the road ends. There is no regular transport all the way to the park, but you can get a songthaew from Phetburi as far as the village of Ban Kaeng Krachan (also known as Fa Prathan), four km from the park. The songthaews leave from near the digital clock tower in Phet every half hour between 7 am and 4 pm and cost 20B; there's a half-hour stopover in Tha Yang. From Ban Kaeng Krachan you should be able to hitch or charter a pickup ride from the locals.

If you have your own wheels, you can explore the park by means of several dirt roads.

## CHA-AM
ชะอำ
• ☎ (32) • *pop 22,000*
A tiny town 178 km from Bangkok, 38 km from Phetburi and 25 km from Hua Hin, Cha-am is known for its long, casuarina-lined beach, good seafood and, on weekends and school holidays, its party atmosphere – sort of a Palm Beach or Fort Lauderdale for Thai students. During the week the beach is virtually deserted.

Beach umbrellas and sling chairs are available for hire. The jet skis are a definite minus but not that common yet; if the local tourism promoters want to lure visitors away from fast-developing Hua Hin, the first thing they should do is get rid of the jet skis. There are public bathhouses where you can bathe in fresh water for 5 to 7B.

Near the beach there's not much of a town to speak of – the old centre is on the opposite side of Phetkasem Highway, where you'll find the post office, market, train station and government offices. Inland from the beach (follow the signs) at **Wat Neranchararama** is a fat, white, six-armed Buddha statue; the six hands cover the nine bodily orifices in a symbolic gesture denying the senses.

### Information
A TAT office (☎ 471005/8) has been established on Phetkasem Highway just 500m south of town. The staff are very helpful;

they distribute information on Cha-am, Phetburi and Hua Hin. The office is open daily from 6 am to 8 pm

**Money** Several banks maintain foreign exchange booths along the beach strip, typically open from 10 am to 8 pm. In the town centre, west of Highway 4, are a number of banks with exchange services and ATMs.

**Places to Stay – bottom end & middle**

Cha-am Beach has three basic types of accommodation: charming, old-style, spacious wooden beach bungalows on stilts, set back from the road; tacky apartment-style hotels built of cheap materials with faulty plumbing, right on the beach road; and more expensive 'condotel' developments. New places are going up all the time at the northern and southern ends. Expect a 20% to 50% discount on posted rates for weekday stays.

One main road leads to the beach area from the highway; if you turn right you'll find the places listed under 'South' below; turn left and you'll see those listed under 'North'.

**South** Near the air-con bus terminal, a couple of *guesthouses* which change name from time to time can be found in a row of modern shophouses similar to the scourge of Pattaya, Hua Hin and Phuket's Patong Beach – they all look the same. Rooms here run from 200B with fan and shared bath, 500B with air-con.

South of the air-con bus terminal, the *Anantachai Guest House* (☎ 433396) has nice rooms with a beach view, air-con, TV, shower and toilet for 500 to 800B. They also provide information about the area and have a cheap Thai restaurant.

Cheaper rooms are available at *Som's Guest House* (☎ 433753), where clean basic rooms with shared bath cost 200 to 250B.

*Santisuk Bungalows & Beach Resort* (☎ 471212) is a long-time favourite, with both the early Cha-am-style wooden cottages and a newer, equally tasteful section. A room in a hotel-style section with bath is 300B with fan, 400B air-con. Larger two bedroom cottages with bath and sitting area are 1000B, and 2000B for a three bedroom,

two bath place. The *Nirandorn Resort* (☎ 471893) has similar cottages for 350B with fan, 500 to 700B with air-con.

*Saeng Thong Condominiums* (☎ 471466) costs 800 to 2000B per night, less in the rainy season. The *White Hotel* (☎ 471118), an air-con apartment-style place, costs 300 to 400B for a fan room with private bath, 500 to 600B with air-con, 700B for larger rooms with carpet, tub and TV.

**North** *JJ Hotel* and *Somkheat Villa* (☎ 471-229; fax 471229) are adjacent apartment-style hotels with rooms from 300 to 600B at the former, and from 500 to 800B at the latter.

*Thiptari Place* (☎ /fax 471879) is a fairly reasonable place, with air-con rooms from 500 to 800B. Farther up, *Rua Makam Villa* (☎ 471073) has old-style wooden cottages, spacious and off the road, for 400/700B a single/double with fan, 600/1200B with air-con. *Happy Home* has older-style wooden cottages from 250B with fan, from 500B with air-con.

The *Kaen-Chan Hotel* (☎ 471314) has a variety of accommodation – bungalows are 200 to 250B with fan, 300 to 350B with air-con; air-con rooms in the hotel are 700 to 900B. There is a pool on the grounds.

The next cheapest places are the *Jitravee Resort* (☎ 471382) and *Cha-am Villa* (☎ 471-010/241), which will let you have rooms for 200B midweek (300B on weekends); air-con rooms cost 400 to 500B. Better value again is the new *Prathonchok House* (☎ 471215), which has clean fan rooms with shared facilities for 150B, air-con rooms with attached bath for 250B and fancier air-con rooms with TV and fridge for 400B.

*Top House* (☎ 433307) is a big place with 193 rooms for 400B with fan and private bath, 600 to 1200B with air-con, TV and hot water. *Jolly Jumper* (☎ 433887), operated by a Dutch couple at 274/3 Ruamjit Rd, features fan rooms for 150 to 250B, plus air-con rooms for 450 to 600B.

At the northern end of the beach are the closely clustered bungalows of *Paradise Bungalow* which cost from 250B with fan, from 600B with air-con and TV.

**Inthira Plaza** This complex off the main road (Narathip Rd) running to the beach from the highway is striving to become a Pattaya-style bar centre ('entertainment centre' in the jargon of the moment). A couple of the bars have apartment-style rooms upstairs for 250 to 300B with fan and bath, 350 to 400B with air-con. They could be noisy at night.

### Places to Stay – top end
Many places in Cha-am call themselves 'resorts' but only two places in the central area come close to the term. First is *Cha-am Methavalai Hotel* (☎ 471580; fax 471590); it has well kept, modern rooms with flowers spilling from every balcony, plus a pool and a small beach area of its own. Walk-in rates are 2691B including tax but during the week an automatic 40% discount applies.

For roughly the same price, the seven-storey *Novotel Gems Cha-am* (☎ 434003; fax 434002) is a resort-style hotel in which all 105 rooms have ocean views and all the amenities from satellite TV to IDD phones; there's also a business centre. Rates start at 2100/2300B per room plus tax and service.

Nearby *Long Beach Cha-am Hotel* (☎ 472442; fax 472287) offers luxury rooms for 2600B weekends, 1530B weekdays.

North of town a bit, the *Regent Cha-am Beach Resort* (☎ 471480/91; fax 471491) has rooms starting at 3000B; they advertise a 30% to 40% discount for weekdays. Facilities include a swimming pool, squash and tennis courts and a fitness centre.

Also on the beach north of town is the posh *Dusit Resort & Polo Club* (☎ 520009; fax 520296), where rates start at 3872B. The Dusit offers a fitness centre, minigolf, horse riding, pool, tennis and squash courts and, of course, polo.

### Places to Eat
Vendors on the beach sell fair chow. Opposite the beach are several good seafood restaurants which, unlike the bungalows, are reasonably priced.

Moderately priced *Khan Had Restaurant* has an extensive menu. *Anantachai Guest House* is a good place for inexpensive to moderately priced Thai and seafood dishes, while the *Jolly Jumper* does reasonable western food.

The luxury hotels have generally fine Thai, seafood and western cuisine at the standard high prices. Seafood and Thai cuisine are especially good at the Methavalai Hotel's *Sorndaeng Restaurant*, a branch of the famous Bangkok restaurant of the same name.

### Getting There & Away
Buses from Phetburi and Hua Hin each cost 15B. From Hua Hin, take a Phetburi-bound bus and ask to be let off at Hat Cha-am (Cha-am Beach); the fare is 10B.

Ordinary buses from Bangkok's Southern Bus Terminal to Cha-am cost 50B (92B air-con). In Cha-am ordinary buses stop on Phetkasem Highway, from where you can take a motorbike taxi (10B) or a share taxi (5B) out to the beach. A few hundred metres south of the corner of Narathip and Ruamjit Rds, a private bus company operates six daily air-con buses to Bangkok for 83B.

The train station is on Narathip Rd, west of Phetkasem Highway and a 10B motor-cycle ride to/from the beach. Trains depart Hualamphong station at 9.25 am and 1.40 pm, and return at 6.25 am, 12.12 and 2.49 pm. The train is slower than the bus by one hour (taking about four hours) and costs 36B.

### Getting Around
Standard prices for motorbike taxi and public songthaew are 10B and 5B (30B to charter) respectively. You can rent motorcycles for a steep 200 to 300B a day.

### AROUND CHA-AM
Sandy Hat Peuktian between Cha-am and Phetburi has the usual casuarina trees and food vendors favoured by Thai beach goers, and hardly a farang in sight. Three rocky islets are within wading distance of shore, one with a sala for shade. Also standing knee-deep just offshore is a six metre statue of Phi Seua Samut, the undersea female

deity that terrorised the protagonist of *Phra Aphaimani*. A statue of the prince himself sits on a nearby rock playing a flute.

A tasteless two-storey, town house-style development has recently been built off the beach. Designed in the pseudo-classical style prevalent in modern city blocks all over Thailand, it looks rather incongruous with the natural beach surroundings.

# Prachuap Khiri Khan Province

Pineapples and fishing are the main livelihoods of the Thais living in this narrow province along the upper part of the Gulf peninsula. Along the Gulf coast are a variety of small seaside resorts, most of them very low-key.

## HUA HIN
หัวหิน
• ☎ *(32)* • *pop 34,500*
The beaches of Hua Hin first came to the country's attention when Rama VII built Klai Kangwon, a seafront summer palace just north of what was then a small fishing village, in 1928. Rama VII learned of Thailand's first coup d'état in 1932 while playing golf at the Royal Hua Hin Golf Course. Once endorsed by the royal family, Hua Hin remained a traditional favourite among the Thais long after the beaches of Pattaya and Phuket had been taken over by foreign tourists. The palace is still used from time to time by the royal family.

During the last five years or so, the secret has got out: Hua Hin is a fairly quiet and fairly economical place to get away from it all, yet it's less than four hours by train from Bangkok. The local private sector has been promoting Hua Hin tourism, and developers have moved in. The resort now attracts a mix of Thais and older farang tourists who are seeking a comfortable beach holiday near Bangkok but don't want the sleaziness of Pattaya. French, German and Italian tourists dominate the scene.

CENTRAL THAILAND

Prachuap Khiri Khan Province

0    10    20 km

PHETBURI PROVINCE

To Ratchaburi

Hua Hin
Khao Takiap
Khao Tao
Ko Singtoh

Pranburi

Pranburi Dam

Khao Sam Roi Yot National Park

Kuiburi

MYANMAR (BURMA)

Dan Singkhon

Ao Khan Kradai
Ao Noi
Prachuap Khiri Khan
Ao Prachuap
Ao Manao

Huay Yang Falls

Hat Wanakon
Ko Phing
Ko Phang

Thap Sakae

Ban Krut

GULF OF THAILAND

Bang Saphan Yai
Hat Baw Thawng Lang
Hat Sombun
Ao Bang Saphan
Hat Suan Luang
Bang Saphan Noi
Ko Thalu
Ko Sing
CHUMPHON PROVINCE   To Chumphon   Ko Sang

CENTRAL THAILAND

Unfortunately Hua Hin may go the way of Pattaya unless the local community and the interlopers start planning now. Already appearing are a lot of the same kind of cheap, unsightly shophouse-apartment buildings with plumbing problems seen in Pattaya and Phuket's Patong Beach, as well as a recent invasion of girlie bars. Hua Hin has almost entirely lost its fishing village atmosphere – the fishing fleet is being moved out and the town's infamous squid-drying piers have been replaced by hotels.

On the bright side, a new sewage treatment plant and municipal sewer system have been constructed and the beach is cleaner than ever. The main swimming beach still has thatched umbrellas and long chairs; vendors from the nearby food stalls will bring loungers steamed crab, mussels, beer etc and there are pony rides for the kids. The Sofitel Central Hua Hin Hotel has successfully campaigned to have the vendors removed from the beach fronting the hotel – a minus for atmosphere but a plus for cleanliness. They are now restricted to a small area near the public entrance to the beach, and to another short string south of the Sofitel. Beer, soft drinks and seafood are reasonably cheap and there's no charge for umbrellas and sling chairs if you order food.

### Information

Tourist information on Hua Hin and the surrounding area is available at the municipal office on the corner of Phetkasem and Damnoen Kasem Rds, a couple of hundred metres east of the train station. Their brochure 'Welcome to Hua Hin' contains a lot of useful info on hotels, restaurants and transport. It's open daily from 8.30 am to 4.30 pm.

The home-grown *Hua Hin Observer*, an expat-published newsletter with short features in English and German, contains snippets on eating out, culture and entertainment.

**Money** There are several banks around town. Most convenient to the beach is the Bank of Ayudhya's exchange booth on Naretdamri Rd, near the corner of Damnoen Kasem Rd.

**Post & Communications** The post office is on Damnoen Kasem Rd near the corner of Phetkasem Rd. The attached CAT office offers Home Direct international phone service daily from 6 am to 10 pm.

### Ao Takiap
อ่าวตะเกียบ

Eight to 13 km south of Hua Hin along Ao Takiap (Chopsticks Bay) are the beaches of **Hat Khao Takiap**, **Suan Son** and **Khao Tao**, all of which are undergoing resort development. Two hill-top temples can be visited here. **Wat Khao Thairalat** is well off the beach on a rocky hill and is nothing special. At the end of the bay is the more well endowed **Wat Khao Takiap**; climb the steps for a good bay view.

The southern end of the bay is now one big construction site as one high-rise after another goes up, blocking the sea view from all points inland. North along the bay, however, are several quiet, wooded spots with cabins and beachhouses.

If you're driving, the turn-off for Ao Takiap is four km south of Hua Hin. There are regular songthaews back and forth from town.

### Places to Stay – bottom end

Prices are moving up quickly for places near the beach. Hotels in town are still reasonable and it's only a five or 10 minute walk to the beach from most of them.

**Guesthouses** Near – but not on – the beach, the cheapest places are found along or just off Naretdamri Rd. A room glut has kept rates low. Several small hotels and guesthouses in this area have rooms for 150 to 200B a night for rooms with fan and attached bath, 300 to 400B with air-con. Rooms at *Dang's House (Khun Daeng House)* on Naretdamri Rd cost 100 to 150B with private bath. *Parichart Guest House* (☎ 513863), next to Dang's House, is a more up-market, modern, multi-storey place with rooms for 350B with fan and private bath, 450 to 550B with air-con.

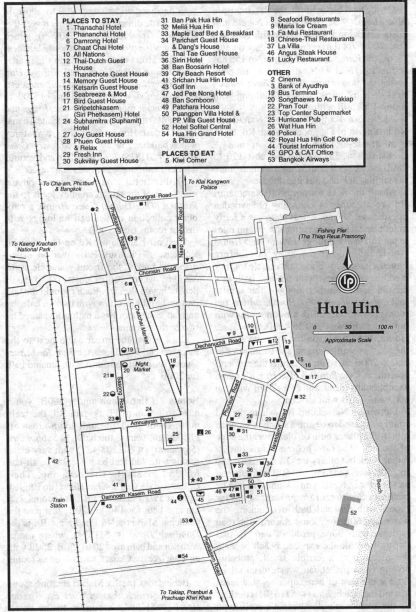

**PLACES TO STAY**
1 Thanachai Hotel
4 Phananchai Hotel
6 Damrong Hotel
7 Chaat Chai Hotel
10 All Nations
12 Thai-Dutch Guest House
13 Thanachote Guest House
14 Memory Guest House
15 Ketsarin Guest House
16 Seabreeze & Mod
17 Bird Guest House
21 Siripetchkasem (Siri Phetkasem) Hotel
24 Subhamitra (Suphamit) Hotel
27 Joy Guest House
28 Phuen Guest House & Relax
29 Fresh Inn
30 Sukvilay Guest House
31 Ban Pak Hua Hin
32 Meliá Hua Hin
33 Maple Leaf Bed & Breakfast
34 Parichart Guest House & Dang's House
35 Thai Tae Guest House
36 Sirin Hotel
38 Ban Boosarin Hotel
39 City Beach Resort
41 Srichan Hua Hin Hotel
43 Golf Inn
47 Jed Pee Nong Hotel
48 Ban Somboon
49 Patchara House
50 Puangpen Villa Hotel & PP Villa Guest House
52 Hotel Sofitel Central
54 Hua Hin Grand Hotel & Plaza

**PLACES TO EAT**
5 Kiwi Corner
8 Seafood Restaurants
9 Maria Ice Cream
11 Fa Mui Restaurant
18 Chinese-Thai Restaurants
37 La Villa
46 Angus Steak House
51 Lucky Restaurant

**OTHER**
2 Cinema
3 Bank of Ayudhya
19 Bus Terminal
20 Songthaews to Ao Takiap
22 Pran Tour
25 Top Center Supermarket
25 Hurricane Pub
26 Wat Hua Hin
40 Police
42 Royal Hua Hin Golf Course
44 Tourist Information
45 GPO & CAT Office
53 Bangkok Airways

To Cha-am, Phetburi & Bangkok

To Klai Kangwon Palace

Damrongrat Road

To Kaeng Krachan National Park

Phetkasem Road

Naep Kehat Road

Chomsin Road

Fishing Pier (Tha Thiap Reua Pramong)

Chatchai Market

**Hua Hin**

0    50    100 m
Approximate Scale

Dechanuchit Road

Night Market

Sasong Road

Phunsuk Road

Naretdamri Road

Amnuaysin Road

Beach

Train Station

Damnoen Kasem Road

Phetkasem Road

To Takiap, Pranburi & Prachuap Khiri Khan

On the next block north, the Pakistani-run *Moti Mahal* (☎ 513769) at 152/1 Naretdamri costs 150B for a small room with bath and fan, 200B for larger rooms. Also on this block, the *Europa* (☎ 513235) at No 158 has rooms for 150B with bath, and a European restaurant downstairs. *Sunee Guest House*, next door, is an old wooden building with rooms for 150B with shared bath.

Along Soi Kanjanomai, off Naretdamri Rd just north of Damnoen Kasem Rd, is the comfortable-looking *Maple Leaf Bed & Breakfast* (☎ 533757). Rooms cost 120 to 180B, some with bath. On the same soi are the similar *MP* and *SM* guesthouses.

Along the next soi north off Naretdamri Rd are a couple of charming old wooden guesthouses. *Phuen Guest House* is a fairly quiet place with a nice atmosphere and rates in the 150 to 200B range. *Relax Guest House* (☎ 513585), down an alley just before Phuen, charges 150B a single/double for four medium-size rooms with fan and bath in a private home. Farther along is the similar looking *Sukvilay Guest House*, where fan rooms cost 150 to 180B, air-con rooms with hot water showers 380 to 400B. *Joy Guest House* (☎ 512967), on the opposite side of the soi, has similar charm and room rates of 150 to 200B. Also on this soi is the modern, apartment-style *Ban Pak Hua Hin*; it's quiet, exceptionally clean, and costs 200B with fan and bath, 300B with air-con.

Farther up Naretdamri Rd, where the old squid piers used to be, are a string of wooden motel-like places built on piers over the edge of the sea. *Mod (Mot) Guest House* has 29 rather small but otherwise OK rooms for 150 to 250B with fan, 350 to 450B with air-con and hot water, 650B with TV and fridge. The next door *Seabreeze (Sirima)* costs 250B for rooms with fan and bath overlooking the water, or 160B for rooms closer to the road without bath. One problem here is that during low tide the exposed beach beneath the piers emits a terrible smell, probably arising from inadequate waste disposal. A little south-east of here, up a soi that leads toward the beach, *Bird* (☎ 511630) is the best of the seaside guesthouses; it's well kept,

well designed and charges 200 to 500B. In the opposite direction is the rather motel-like *Ketsarin Guest House* (☎ 513999), which combines the pier-style guesthouse business with a seafood restaurant, as do the nearby *Thanachote Guest House* and *Karoon Hut*. Both offer the same basic restaurant/guesthouse combo with fan rooms for 200 to 350B, fancier rooms with air-con, fridge and TV for 400 to 700B. Almost opposite Thanachote Guest House, in a long two-storey white building, is the new *Memory Guest House* (☎ 511816). It's super clean and features a locked entrance gate; rates start at 200B.

Farther north along Naretdamri on the same side of the street, an alley leads to the *Pattana (Thai-Dutch) Guest House*, a rambling collection of wooden buildings with decent rooms from 200B.

West off Naretdamri Rd on Dechanuchit Rd (east of Phunsuk Rd), over an expat-managed pub, is the friendly and clean *All Nations*, where rooms cost 200 to 300B depending on the size. Each room in the tall, narrow building comes with its own balcony and fan; each floor has a bathroom shared by two or three rooms.

Back across the street again next to the more top-end Sirin Hotel, the *Thai Tae (Thae) Guest House* offers rooms with fan and bath for 200B.

**Hotels** To find hotels under 300B, you'll have to go up to Phetkasem Rd, the main north-south road through town. Just off Phetkasem, behind the bank, is *Subhamitra (Suphamit)* (☎ 511208/487) with very clean rooms with fan and bath for 250B, air-con for 350 to 800B. The decaying, Thai-Chinese-style *Chaat Chai Hotel* (no English sign) at 59/1 Phetkasem Rd has rooms with fan and bath for 140 to 220B. Just past the Chatchai Market at 46 Phetkasem Rd is the *Damrong Hotel* (☎ 511574), where rooms with fan and bath are 120 to 150B, 350B with air-con; like the Chaat Chai, this one's fading fast.

Behind the Chatchai Market area on Sasong Rd, the *Siripetchkasem (Siri Phetkasem) Hotel* (☎ 511394) is similar to the hotels along Phetkasem Rd. Rooms with fan are 200B and air-con rooms are 400B. South of here on the same side of the road, the new *Srichan Hua Hin Hotel* (☎ 513130) charges 280B for cement-floor rooms with fan and private bath, 450B with carpet and air-con – a bit overpriced for this location.

Finally, north at 11 Damrongrat Rd, is *Thanachai* (☎ 511755), a good upper bottom-end place for 250B with fan and bath, 500B for air-con. The Thanachai accepts credit cards.

### Places to Stay – middle

Hua Hin's mid-range places are typically small, sedate, modern hotels with air-con rooms and such luxuries as telephones. The forerunner of this trend, *Ban Boosarin* (☎ 512076), calls itself a 'mini-deluxe hotel' and although it's 670B a night, all rooms come with air-con, hot water, telephone, colour TV, fridge and private terrace. It's super clean and rates don't rise on weekends. There's a 10% discount for stays of a week or more.

Along Soi Kasem Samphan next to the Jed Pee Nong Hotel are a couple of Ban Boosarin clones. *Patchara House* (☎ 511787) costs 300B for rooms with fan or 550/610B for singles/doubles with air-con, TV/video, telephone, hot water and fridge. Also on this soi is the similar *Ban Somboon*, where nicely decorated rooms are 300B with fan and hot showers, 550B with air-con; all rates include breakfast and there is a pleasant sitting garden on the premises. On the corner of Soi Kasem Samphan and Damnoen Kasem Rd are the relatively new *Puangpen Villa Hotel* and the *PP Villa Guest House* (☎ 533785; fax 511216), which share a garden and pool; clean, air-con rooms cost 840B with hot water, TV and fridge in the former, 600B with hot water in the latter. These hotels, as well as the Jed Pee Nong and City Beach described below, are only a couple of hundred metres from the beach.

The popular *Jed Pee Nong* (☎ 512381) is on Damnoen Kasem Rd. Modern, clean but otherwise unimpressive rooms cost 400B with fan and bath, 500B with air-con or 600 to 800B for air-con rooms by the new swimming pool behind the hotel.

On Naretdamri Rd, the modern *Fresh Inn* (☎ 511389) has all air-con rooms for 700 to 875B; this pleasant tourist-class hotel would have had a sea view if not for the construction of the high-rise Meliá Hua Hin between it and the sea. Downstairs is an Italian restaurant, Lo Stivale.

Running north-east from Chomsin Rd (the road leading to the main pier) is Naep Khehat Rd. At No 73/5-7, the *Phananchai Hotel* (☎ 511707) has air-con rooms for 350 to 600B. It's a bit of a walk from the swimming beaches but all rooms come with air-con, hot water, TV and telephone.

### Places to Stay – top end

The air-con *Sirin Hotel* (☎ 511150; fax 513571) is on Damnoen Kasem Rd towards the beach, down from the City Beach Hotel. The rooms here are well kept and come with hot water and fridge. The semi-outdoor restaurant area is pleasant. Double rooms are 850B during the week and 1200B on weekends and holidays. Nearby, the old Hua Hin Raluk Hotel has been rebuilt and resurrected as the *City Beach Resort* (☎ 512870/75; fax 51244) at 16 Damnoen Kasem Rd. Quiet, semi-luxurious rooms with the usual service and extras cost from 1600B.

Near the train station, off Damnoen Kasem Rd near the Royal Hua Hin Golf Course, is the *Golf Inn* (☎ 512473), where air-con rooms are 700 to 1290B.

Hua Hin has several super-luxury hotels. *Hotel Sofitel Central Hua Hin* (☎ 512021/40; (2) 233-0974/80 in Bangkok), formerly the Hua Hin Railway Hotel, is a magnificent two-storey colonial-style place on the beach at the end of Damnoen Kasem Rd. Rooms in the original L-shaped colonial wing cost 3100B; rooms in the new wing are more expensive. Across the road is the Sofitel's former Villa Wing, now called *Mercure Resort Hua Hin* (☎ 512036; fax 511014), a collection of charming one and two bedroom wooden beach bungalows for 3100 to 5000B. From 20 December to 20 February there's a 700B peak-season supplement on all room charges at both the Mercure and the Sofitel.

The plush *Meliá Hua Hin* (☎ 512879; fax

CENTRAL THAILAND

## Hua Hin Railway Hotel

In 1922 the State Railway of Thailand (then the Royal Thai Railway) extended the national rail network to Hua Hin to allow easier access to the Hua Hin summer palace. The area proved to be a popular vacation spot among non-royals too, so in the following year they built the Hua Hin Railway Hotel, a graceful colonial-style inn on the sea, with sweeping teak stairways and high-ceilinged rooms. When I researched the first edition of this guide in 1981, a double room was still only 90B and the service was just as unhurried as it had been when I first stayed here in 1977. It probably hadn't changed much since 1923, except for the addition of electric lighting and screened doors and windows. Big-bladed ceiling fans stirred the humid sea air and in the dining room one ate using State Railway silverware and thick china from the 1920s. Unfortunately, when Bangkok's Central Department Store took over the management of the hotel they floundered in their attempt to upgrade the facilities, failing to take advantage of the hotel's original ambience.

In 1986 the French hotel chain Sofitel became part of a joint venture with Central and together they restored the hotel to most of its former glory. It now bears the awkward name *Hotel Sofitel Central Hua Hin*, but if you've been looking for a historic South-East Asian hotel to spend some money on, this might well be it. All of the wood panelling and brass fixtures throughout the rooms and open hallways have been restored. While the old railway silverware and china have been retired to antique cabinet displays, the spacious, lazy ambience of a previous age still remains. Even if you don't want to spend the money to stay here, it's well worth a stroll through the grounds and open sitting areas for a little history. It's more interesting in terms of atmosphere than either the Raffles in Singapore or the Oriental in Bangkok (neither of which have eight hectare grounds), and somewhere in between in terms of luxury.

Incidentally, in 1983 this hotel was used as Hotel Le Phnom for the filming of *The Killing Fields*. Also, the State Railway of Thailand still owns the hotel; Sofitel/Central are just leasing it. ■

511135; ☎ (2) 271-0205 in Bangkok), off Nar-etdamri Rd, is part of the Spanish-owned Meliá hotel chain and is Hua Hin's first high-rise (also the first to mar the skyline, unfortunately). Rooms with all the amenities cost 3700 to 4400B, more for suites. From 20 December to 10 January there's a 900B peak-season supplement on all room charges. There's not much of a beach in front of the hotel at high tide, but the adjacent free-form pool area is well designed to encompass sea views. Other facilities include two tennis courts, two air-con squash courts, a fitness centre, sauna and massage facilities.

Along Hua Hin's southern beach at 107/1 Phetkasem Beach Rd, the *Royal Garden Resort* (☎ 511881; fax 512422) offers 220 rooms and suites, all with sea views, in a modern high-rise-style complex. Spacious rooms start at 3400B and go up to 13,000B for penthouse suites with Jacuzzis and private rooftop gardens. The more laid-back *Royal Garden Village* (☎ 520250; fax 520259) at 41/1 Phetkasem Beach Rd north of town features 162 rooms and suites in Thai-style

villas on 14 landscaped acres from 3600B. Both Royal Garden resorts offer tennis courts and swimming pools, nearby golf course privileges, Thai massage services and water sport activities; the Royal Garden Resort also has a golf driving range.

The US$26 million *Chiva-Som International Health Resort* (☎ 536536; fax 511154), at 74/4 Phetkasem Highway, is a new concept featuring 40 ocean-view rooms and 17 Thai-style pavilions on seven beachside acres south of town (before Nong Khae and Ao Takiap). The name means 'Haven of Life' in Thai-Sanskrit. The staff of 200 fuses eastern and western approaches to health with planned nutrition, step and aqua aerobics, Thai, Swedish or underwater massage, t'ai chi, dance and the usual round of mudpacks, saunas (including a multilevel steam room), Jacuzzis and hydrotherapy. Flotation tanks containing tepid saltwater are on hand for sensory deprivation sessions. You can pick up a life membership with unlimited use of the facilities for US$18,000 (so far 250 members have signed up), or pay US$400 a single, US$600 a double per day, a rate that includes three meals (with wine only, and only at dinner) along with health and fitness consultations, massage and all other activities. One week, 10 day and two week packages are also available.

There are a few more top-end places on beaches just north and south of town. Some add peak-season (November to April) supplements, others offer 40% discounts in the off season:

*Hua Hin Grand Hotel & Plaza* – 222/2 Phetkasem Rd (☎ 511391/499; fax 511765; ☎ (2) 254-7675 in Bangkok); 1900 to 2800B
*Hua Hin Sport Villa* – 1085 Phetkasem Rd (☎ 511453); 1800B
*Majestic Creek Country Club* – Klai Kangwon Beach (☎ 520162; fax 520477); 3060B
*Sailom Hotel* – 29 Phetkasem Rd (☎ 511890/1; fax 512047; ☎ (2) 258-0652 in Bangkok); 1690 to 3500B

### Places to Stay – out of town

In Hat Takiap, the *Fangkhlun Guest House* (☎ 512402) has five fan-cooled rooms from 500 to 600B. The *Ta-kiab Beach Resort* (☎ 512639; fax 515899) is south of Khao Takiap, and has air-con rooms and a pool from 1500B a night. The *Sri Pathum Guest House* (☎ 512339) is cheaper and has 11 rooms from 250B with fan, 350B with air-con, and the *Vegas Hotel* (☎ 512290) has 32 rooms from 600B for a small room, 1000B for something larger.

In a forested area called Nong Khae at the north end of Ao Takiap are the quiet *Rung Arun Guest House* (☎ 511291), with cabins ranging from 200 to 700B, and the deluxe low-rise *Nern Chalet* (☎ 513588; fax 511288), with 14 air-con rooms for 1500B each. Between Nong Khae and Takiap, *Hua Hin Bluewave Beach Resort* (☎ 511036) is a condotel-style place with rooms for 1800 to 2000B; on the grounds are a pool and fitness centre.

In Hat Khao Tao, the *Nanthasuda Guest-house (Nanthasuda Restaurant)* has rooms from 300B, while Hat Suan Son has the modern *Suan Son Padiphat* (☎ 511239) with fan-cooled rooms for 250B (600B on the sea) or air-con rooms for 500 to 1000B.

In low-key Pranburi, the *Pransiri Hotel* (☎ 621061), at 283 Phetkasem Rd, and *Pranburi Hotel* (☎ 621942), at 283 Phetkasem Rd, each have rooms starting at 150B. More expensive resort-style accommodation starting at around 1000B is available at *Club Aldiana* (☎ 611701; (2) 233-3871 in Bangkok) and *Bor Kaeo Resort* (☎ 621713; (2) 246-5242 in Bangkok).

### Places to Eat

The best seafood in Hua Hin is found in three main areas. Firstly, there are some medium-priced restaurants along Damnoen Kasem Rd near the Jed Pee Nong and City Beach hotels, and off Damnoen Kasem, on Phunsuk and Naretdamri Rds. Secondly, there's excellent and inexpensive food in the Chatchai night market, off Phetkasem Rd on Dechanuchit Rd, and in the nearby Chinese-Thai restaurants. The third area is next to Tha Thiap Reua Pramong, the big fishing pier at the end of Chomsin Rd. The fish is, of course, fresh off the boats but not necessarily the cheapest in town. One of the places near the pier, *Saeng Thai*, is the oldest seafood restaurant in Hua Hin and quite reliable if you know how to order. The best value for money can be found in the smaller eating places on and off Chomsin Rd and in the Chatchai night market. There is also a night market on Chomsin Rd.

The best seafood to order in Hua Hin is plaa sămlii (cotton fish or kingfish), plaa kapŏng (perch), plaa mèuk (squid), hăwy malaeng phùu (mussels) and puu (crab). The various forms of preparation include:

| | |
|---|---|
| dìp | raw |
| nêung | steamed |
| phǎo | grilled |
| phàt | sliced, filleted and fried |
| râat phrík | smothered in garlic and chillies |
| thâwt | fried whole |
| tôm yam | in a hot and tangy broth |
| yâang | roast (squid only) |

Chinese-Thai seafood places along Phetkasem Rd include *Khuang Seng, Supharot* and *Thara Jan*, none of which bear English signs; all are fairly good value. The least expensive place to eat seafood is an out-of-the-way spot west of Phetkasem Highway called *Phae Mai*. It's a very simple outdoor restaurant built over a pond with a steady following among local Thais who can't afford the central city tourist places. It's a 10B samlor ride from the centre of town – samlor drivers all know where it is. Virtually no English is spoken.

Chatchai Market is excellent for Thai breakfasts – they sell very good jók and khâo tôm (rice soups). Fresh-fried paa-thông-kö (in the Hua-Hin-style – small and crispy, not oily), are 2B for three. A few vendors also serve hot soy milk in bowls (4B) – break a few paa-thông-kö into the soy milk and drink free náam chaa – a very tasty and filling breakfast for 10B if you can eat nine paa-thông-kö.

*Gee Cuisine*, next to the Jed Pee Nong, caters mostly to farangs but the Thai food is generally good. The nonstop video in the evenings, however, is a curse one hopes won't spread to other restaurants in town. *Lucky Restaurant*, next to PP Villa nearby, is very similar to Gee Cuisine.

*Moti Mahal Restaurant & Guest House* on Naretdamri Rd serves decent Indian and Pakistani food; it's open daily 8 am to 11 pm.

*Fa Mui*, on Dechanuchit Rd near All Nations, is a cosy, atmospheric place serving Thai and seafood cuisine to a hip crowd of local and visiting Thais; prices are inexpensive to moderate.

Phunsuk and Naretdamri Rds are becoming centres for farang-oriented eateries. On Naretdamri Rd, the *Beergarden* is just what it sounds like – an outdoor pub with western food. The *Headrock Cafe* (not a misspelling but a pun on the name Hua Hin – 'head rock') is more of a drinking place, but also has Thai and western food. On Phunsuk Rd is the Italian *La Villa*, with pizza, spaghetti, lasagne and so on. The new *Le Paris Bangkok* restaurant at 54/2 Dechanuchit Rd specialises in French cuisine, with dishes starting from 100B. *Kiwi Corner* at 21 Chomsin serves western breakfasts, while *Bob's German Bakery* at 120/2 Naretdamri Rd offers German rye bread, whole grain breads, pastries, cakes and cured meats.

*Maria Ice Cream*, at 54/2 Dechanuchit Rd, offers fabulous home-made ice cream, including flavours like papaya, watermelon and coconut. Steak lovers can get their fill at *Angus Steak House* on Damnoen Kasem Rd, just near the post office.

### Entertainment

Several farang bars under German, Swiss, Italian, French and New Zealand management can be found in and around Naretdamri and Phunsuk Rds. Most offer the familiar Thai hostess atmosphere. One that dares to be different is the *All Nations Bar* at 10-10/1 Dechanuchit Rd, which successfully re-creates a pub atmosphere and has quite a collection of flags and other memorabilia from around the world.

*Stone Town*, an old-west-style pub next to Jed Pee Nong Hotel on Damnoen Kasem Rd, features live folk and country music nightly. For rock 'n' roll, check out the semi-outdoor *Hurricane Pub* off Phetkasem Rd, where a live Thai band plays Thai and western pop nightly. There's no cover charge and drinks are no more expensive than at any of the town's farang bars.

### Getting There & Away

**Air** Bangkok Airways (☎ 512083 in Hua Hin; (2) 253-8942 in Bangkok; (77) 420133 on Ko Samui) flies daily between Bangkok, Hua Hin and Ko Samui for 900B (Bangkok-Hua Hin) and 1640B (Hua Hin-Ko Samui) each way; the flights take a half hour and an hour respectively. The Hua Hin airport is 10 km north of the city.

The Bangkok Airways office, on Phetkasem Rd a couple of blocks south of the tourist information office, is open daily from 8 am to 5 pm.

**Bus** Buses from Bangkok's Southern Bus Terminal are 92B air-con, 51B ordinary. The trip takes 3½ to four hours. Pran Tour on Sasong Rd near the Siripetchkasem Hotel in Hua Hin runs air-con buses to Bangkok every half hour from 3 am to 9.20 pm, for 63B 2nd class air-con or 92B 1st class air-con. Pran Tour air-con buses to Phetburi are 60B.

CENTRAL THAILAND

MP Travel, at Nana Plaza Inn (☎ (2) 281-5954) on Khao San Rd in Bangkok, operates minivans to Hua Hin for 150B per person.

Ordinary buses for Hua Hin leave Phetburi regularly for 20B. The same bus can be picked up in Cha-am for 15B. Other ordinary buses from the main terminal in Hua Hin go to/from Prachuap Khiri Khan (25B), Chumphon (66B), Surat Thani (112B), Phuket (163B, seven a day), Krabi (158B, two a day) and Hat Yai (178B, three a day).

**Train** The same trains south apply here as those described in the Phetburi Getting There & Away section. The train trip takes 3¾ hours from Bangkok; 1st class fare is 182B (express only), 2nd class 92B (rapid and express only), and 3rd class 44B.

You can also come by train from any other station on the southern railway line, including Phetburi (3rd class, 13B), Nakhon Pathom (2nd/3rd class, 52/33B), Prachuap (3rd class, 19B), Surat Thani (2nd/3rd class, 116/74B) and Hat Yai (2nd/3rd class, 183/116B). The 1st and 2nd class fares do not include rapid or express surcharges.

### Getting Around
Local buses/songthaews from Hua Hin to the beaches of Khao Takiap, Khao Tam and Suan Son cost 5B per person though farangs are sometimes charged 10B. These buses run from around 6 am until 5.50 pm; the ones to Hat Takiap leave from opposite the main bus terminal on Sasong Rd, while the latter two leave from Chomsin Rd opposite the wat. Buses to Pranburi are 7B and leave from the same area on Chomsin Rd.

Samlor fares in Hua Hin have been set by the municipal authorities so there shouldn't be any haggling. Here are some sample fares: the train station to the beach, 20B; the bus terminal to Naretdamri Rd, 20 to 25B; Chatchai Market to the fishing pier, 20 to 30B; and the train station to the Royal Garden Resort, 40B.

Motorcycles and bicycles can be rented from a couple of places on Damnoen Kasem Rd near the Jed Pee Nong Hotel. Motorcycle rates are reasonable: 150 to 200B per day for

100cc, 200 to 300B for 125cc. Occasionally larger bikes – 400 to 750cc – are available for 500 to 600B a day. Bicycles are 30 to 70B per day.

At the fishing pier you can hire boats out to Ko Singtoh for 800B a day. On Hat Takiap you can get boats for 700B.

## KHAO SAM ROI YOT NATIONAL PARK
อุทยานแห่งชาติเขาสามร้อยยอด
This 98 sq km park (established in 1966) has magnificent views of the Prachuap coastline if you can stand a little climbing. Khao Daeng is only about a half-hour walk from the park headquarters, and from here you can see the ocean as well as some brackish lagoons. If you have the time and energy, climb the 605m **Khao Krachom** for even better views. If you're lucky, you may come across a serow (Asian goat-antelope) while hiking. The lagoons and coastal marshes are great places for birdwatching. Along the coast you may see the occasional pod of Irrawaddy dolphins (*plaa lohmaa hǔa bàat* in Thai) passing by.

Be sure to bring insect repellent along for any park visits. Rama IV (King Mongkut) and a large entourage of Thai and European guests convened here on 18 August 1868 to observe a total solar eclipse – predicted, so the story goes, by the monarch himself – and enjoy an elaborate feast prepared by a French chef. Two months later the king expired from malaria, contracted via mosquito bites inflicted here. The risk of malaria in the park is relatively low, but mosquitoes can be quite pesky.

### Fauna
Notable wildlife around Khao Sam Roi Yot (Three Hundred Peaks) includes crab-eating macaque, dusky langur (the park is considered one of the best spots in the world for viewing dusky langurs), barking deer, slow loris, Malayan pangolin, fishing cat, palm civet, otter, serow, Javan mongoose and monitor lizard.

Because the park lies at the intersection of the East Asian and Australian flyways, as many

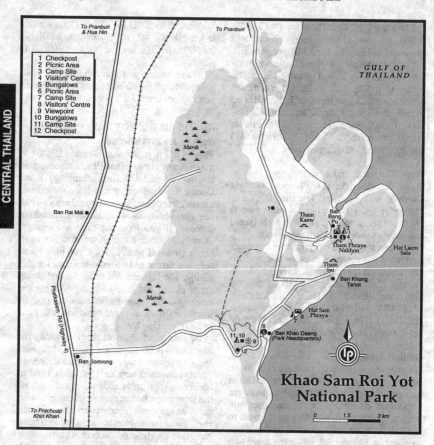

1 Checkpost
2 Picnic Area
3 Camp Site
4 Visitors' Centre
5 Bungalows
6 Picnic Area
7 Camp Site
8 Visitors' Centre
9 Viewpoint
10 Bungalows
11 Camp Site
12 Checkpost

To Pranburi & Hua Hin

To Pranburi

GULF OF THAILAND

Marsh

Ban Rai Mai

Tham Kaew

Ban Bang Pu

Tham Phraya Nakhon

Hat Laem Sala

Tham Sai

Ban Khung Tanot

Marsh

Phetkasem Rd (Highway 4)

Hat Sam Phraya

Ban Somrong

Ban Khao Daeng (Park Headquarters)

To Prachuap Khiri Khan

Khao Sam Roi Yot National Park

0    1.5    3 km

as 300 migratory and resident bird species have been recorded, including yellow bittern, cinnamon bittern, purple swamp hen, water rail, ruddy-breasted crake, bronze-winged jacana, grey heron, painted stork, whistling duck, spotted eagle and black-headed ibis. The park protects Thailand's largest freshwater marsh (along with mangroves and mudflats), and is one of only three places in the country where the purple heron breeds.

Waterfowl are most commonly seen in the cool season. Encroachment by shrimp farmers in the vicinity has sadly destroyed substantial portions of mangroves and other wetlands, thus depriving the birds of an important habitat.

### Beaches, Canals & Marshes

A sandy beach flanked on three sides by dry limestone hills and casuarinas, **Hat Laem Sala** is the location for a small visitors' centre, restaurant, bungalows and camping area. Boats with a capacity of up to 10 people can be hired from Bang Pu to the beach for 150B return. You can also reach the beach from Bang Pu via a steep trail, about a 20 minute walk.

**Hat Sam Phraya**, five km south of Hat

Laem Sala, is a km long beach with a restaurant and washrooms. The park headquarters is located just past the village of Khao Daeng, about four km south-west of Hat Sam Phraya. A larger visitors' centre at the headquarters features well curated exhibits. Binoculars or telescopes can be rented for birdwatching; there are several bird blinds nearby on the nature trails. September to March are the best birding months for waterfowl.

A four km canal trip in a 10-person boat along **Khlong Khao Daeng** can be arranged in Khao Daeng for 200B. The trip lasts about 1½ hours and passes mangrove remnants and waterfowl habitats. The birds are most active in early morning or late afternoon. You might also spot monitor lizards and monkeys.

### Caves
The other big attraction at Sam Roi Yot are the three caves of Tham Kaew, Tham Sai and Tham Phraya Nakhon. **Tham Phraya Nakhon** is the most visited and can be reached by boat or on foot. The boat trip only takes about half an hour there and back, while it's half an hour each way on foot along a steep, rocky trail. There are actually two large caverns, both with sinkholes that allow light in. In one cave is a royal sala built for King Chulalongkorn, who would stop off here when travelling back and forth between Bangkok and Nakhon Si Thammarat.

**Tham Kaew**, two km from the Bang Pu turn-off, features a series of chambers connected by narrow passageways; you enter the first cavern by means of a permanent ladder. Stalactites and other limestone formations, some of which glitter with calcite crystals as if diamond encrusted (hence the cave's name, 'Jewel Cave'), are plentiful. Lamps can be rented for 100B, but Tham Kaew is best visited in the company of a park guide because of the dangerous footing.

**Tham Sai** is ensconced in a hill near Ban Khrun Tanot, about 2.5 km from the main road between Ale Sala and Sam Phraya beaches. Villagers rent lamps for around 30B at a shelter near the cave mouth. A 280m trail

leads up the hillside to the cave, which features a large single cavern. Be careful of steep drop-offs in the cave.

Guides can be hired at the park office for 100B per hike; not much English is spoken but they're accustomed to leading non-Thai as well as Thai visitors.

### Places to Stay
The Forestry Department hires out large bungalows near the visitors' centre as well as at Hat Laem Sala for 500 to 1000B per night or 100B per person; they sleep eight to 20 people. Three person tents are available for 40B a night. You can also pitch your own tent for 10B per person at camp sites at the park headquarters, Hat Laem Sala or Hat Sam Phraya. There are restaurants at all three places. Bring insect repellent as the park is rife with mosquitoes.

For accommodation reservations, contact the Forestry Department in Bangkok on ☎ (2) 561-4292 (ext 747).

### Getting There & Away
The park is 37 km south of Pranburi. Catch a bus or train to Pranburi (8B or 7B from Hua Hin) and then a songthaew to Bang Pu for 20B – these run between 6 am and 4 pm. From Bang Pu you must charter a vehicle, hitch or walk.

You can save the hassle of finding a ride in Bang Pu by chartering a songthaew for 250B or a motorcycle taxi for 150B from Pranburi all the way to the park. Be sure to mention you want to go the national park (*ùthayaan hàeng châat*) rather than the village of Khao Sam Roi Yot.

Most convenient of all would be to rent a car or motorbike in Hua Hin. If you're coming by car or motorcycle from Hua Hin, it's about 25 km to the park turn-off, then another 38 km to park headquarters.

If you're coming straight from Bangkok, another option is to catch an air-con bus bound for Prachuap Khiri Khan. Ask to get off at Ban Somrong (Km 286.5) and then hitch a ride 13 km to the park headquarters at Ban Khao Daeng.

CENTRAL THAILAND

# PRACHUAP KHIRI KHAN
อ.เมืองประจวบศีรีขันธ์

• ☎ *(32)* • *pop 14,500*

Roughly 80 km south of Hua Hin, Prachuap
Khiri Khan serves as the capital of the province of the same name, though it is somewhat
smaller than Hua Hin. There are no real
swimming beaches in town, but the eight-
km-long bay of Ao Prachuap is pretty
enough. Better beaches can be found north
and south of town. The seafood here is fantastic, however, and cheaper than in Hua Hin.
Fishing is still the mainstay of the local
economy.

## Information
Prachuap has its own city-run tourist office
in the centre of town. The staff are very
friendly and they have maps and photos of
all the attractions in the area.

Local resident Pinit Ounope has been recommended for his inexpensive day tours to
Khao Sam Roi Yot National Park, Dan Singkhon and to nearby beaches, other national
parks and waterfalls. He lives at 144 Chai
Thaleh Rd near the beach in town and invites
travellers to visit him. His house is rather
difficult to find, so take a tuk-tuk or a motorcycle taxi. The typical day tour is 200B for
two people, plus 50B for each extra person.

## Things to See & Do
At the northern end of Ao Prachuap is **Khao
Chong Krajok** (Mirror Tunnel Mountain –
named after the hole through the side of the
mountain which appears to reflect the sky).
At the top is **Wat Thammikaram**, established by Rama VI. You can climb the hill for
a view of the town and bay – and entertain
the hordes of monkeys who live here. A
metal ladder leads into the tunnel from the
wat grounds.

If you continue north from Prachuap Khiri
Khan around Ao Prachuap to the headland
you'll come to a small boat-building village
on **Ao Bang Nang Lom** where they still
make wooden fishing vessels using traditional Thai methods. It takes about two
months to finish a 12m boat, which will sell

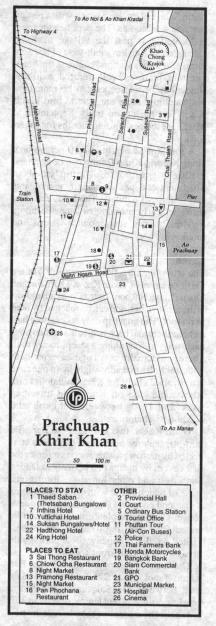

Prachuap Khiri Khan

0    50    100 m

| PLACES TO STAY | OTHER |
|---|---|
| 1 Thaed Saban | 2 Provincial Hall |
| (Thetsaban) Bungalows | 4 Court |
| 7 Inthira Hotel | 5 Ordinary Bus Station |
| 10 Yuttichai Hotel | 9 Tourist Office |
| 14 Suksan Bungalows/Hotel | 11 Phuttan Tour |
| 22 Hadthong Hotel | (Air-Con Buses) |
| 24 King Hotel | 12 Police |
| | 17 Thai Farmers Bank |
| PLACES TO EAT | 18 Honda Motorcycles |
| 3 Sai Thong Restaurant | 19 Bangkok Bank |
| 6 Chiow Ocha Restaurant | 20 Siam Commercial |
| 8 Night Market | Bank |
| 13 Pramong Restaurant | 21 GPO |
| 15 Night Market | 23 Municipal Market |
| 16 Pan Phochana | 25 Hospital |
| Restaurant | 26 Cinema |

for around 400,000B without an engine. West of the beach at Ao Bang Nang Lom is a canal, **Khlong Bang Nang Lom**, lined with picturesque mangroves. A few km north of Ao Prachuap is another bay, **Ao Noi**, the site of a small fishing village with a few rooms to let.

South of Ao Prachuap, around a small headland, is the scenic **Ao Manao**, a bay ringed by a clean white-sand beach with small islands offshore. Because a Thai air force base is near the bay, the beach was closed to the public until 1990, when the local authorities decided to open the area to day visitors. The beach is two or three km from the base entrance. There are several salas along the beach, a hotel, one restaurant, toilets and a shower. Beach vendors offer chairs, umbrellas and inexpensive seafood and beverages. You must leave your passport at the gate and sign in; the beach closes at 6.30 pm except for military and guests at the hotel (see Places to Stay – Ao Manao).

Each year around late March/early April the Thai air force sponsors an international skydiving competition at Ao Manao – it's free and fun to watch.

### Places to Stay
**Prachuap Khiri Khan** The *Yuttichai Hotel* (☎ 611055) at 35 Kong Kiat Rd has fair rooms with fan and shared bath for 100/150B one bed/two beds, or 150/200B with attached bath; the latter are quieter since they're towards the back of the hotel. Around the corner on Phitak Chat Rd is the *Inthira Hotel* with similar rooms in the 100 to 200B range; it's currently under renovation so these rates may change. Both these hotels are quite near the night market and tourist office.

The *King Hotel* (☎ 611170), farther south on the same street, has larger fan-cooled rooms at 200 to 250B. Facing Ao Prachuap is the *Suksan* (☎ 611145), with fan-cooled rooms for 200 to 240B and air-con bungalows from 250 to 350B, but it's very much one big brothel in the evenings.

Also facing the bay are the plain but well kept *Thaed Saban Bungalows* (Thetsaban Bungalows, meaning 'Municipal Bungalows' but also known as the 'Mirror Mountain Bungalows'), which are owned by the city.

A one-room bungalow (sleeps two) is 300B with fan and bath or 400B for air-con; a two-room (sleeps four) is 600B; a three-room (sleeps six) is 800B; and a four-room (sleeps eight) is 1800B. There are also a couple of newer three-room bungalows for 1200B.

The slightly up-market *Hadthong Hotel* (☎ 601050; fax 601057) next to the bay in town has modern air-con rooms with balconies for 600B (mountain view) and 728B (sea view), plus a 200B surcharge from 20 December to 31 January. A pool is on the premises.

North of the city, on the road to Ao Noi, *Rimhad Bungalow* (☎ 601626) offers tiny fan-cooled rooms for 250B, larger rooms with air-con for 500B. The bungalows face scenic Khlong Bang Nang Lom and mangroves. *Happy Inn* nearby has the same prices and similar accommodation.

**Ao Manao** *Ahkan Sawadii Khan Wing 53* (☎ 611017) is a new place operated by the Thai air force near the centre of the beach. There are 92 units in all, each with a sea view; a room with TV, phone and private shower costs 500B a single/double, while larger town houses in a separate wing cost 1000B and include bathtubs and hot water.

**Ao Noi** In Ao Noi there are several rooms and small 'weekend inns', most catering to Thais. *Aow Noi Beach Bungalows* (☎ (2) 510-9790 in Bangkok) offers well kept cottages for 300 to 600B a night with breakfast; farangs – particularly Germans – make up a large percentage of the clientele. Facilities include a small bar and restaurant with Thai and western food, plus a clean, secluded beach.

### Places to Eat
Because of its well deserved reputation for fine seafood, Prachuap has many restaurants for its size. The best place for the money is the night market that convenes near the government offices in the middle of town. On Chai Thaleh Rd near the Hadthong Hotel is a smaller night market that's also quite good; tables set up along the sea wall sometimes get a good breeze.

Of the many seafood restaurants, the best

CENTRAL THAILAND

are the *Pan Phochana* on Sarachip Rd and the *Sai Thong* on Chai Thaleh Rd near the Thaed Saban Bungalows. Both serve great-tasting seafood at reasonable prices. The Pan Phochana is famous for its hàw mòk hǎwy, ground fish curry steamed in mussels on the half-shell. One of the seafood specialities of Prachuap that you shouldn't miss is plaa sǎmlii tàet dìaw, whole cottonfish that's sliced lengthways and left to dry in the sun for half a day, then fried quickly in a wok. It's often served with mango salad on the side. It may sound awful, but the taste is sublime. Just south of the Pan Phochana is a good night market with many seafood stalls.

Other good restaurants include the *Chiow Ocha* (a bit higher priced – this is where the Thai tour buses stop), the *Pramong* and the *Chao Reua*. The *Phloen Samut Restaurant*, adjacent to Hadthong Hotel, is a good outdoor seafood place though it doesn't have everything that's listed on the menu.

Several good seafood restaurants can also be found along the road north of Ao Prachuap on the way to Ao Noi. *Rap Lom* (literally, 'breeze-receiving') is the most popular – look for the Green Spot sign.

The *Hadthong Hotel* dining room offers a bargain Thai buffet lunch on weekdays for just 65B. Across from the Inthira Hotel is a small morning market with tea stalls that serve cheap curries and noodles.

### Getting There & Away
**Bus** From Bangkok, ordinary buses are 72B; they leave the Southern Bus Terminal frequently between 3 and 9.20 pm. Air-con buses cost 130B from the Southern Bus Terminal. In the opposite direction, air-con buses to Bangkok leave from Phuttan Tour (☎ 611411) on Phitak Chat Rd every two hours from 6.15 am to 6.30 pm. In either direction the trip takes four to five hours.

From Hua Hin buses are 25B and leave from the bus station on Sasong Rd every 20 minutes from 7 am to 3 pm, taking 1½ to two hours.

From Prachuap you can catch ordinary buses to Chumphon (50B), Surat Thani (100B), Nakhon Si Thammarat (125B), Krabi (140B) and Phuket (145B).

The air-con bus from Bangkok to Samui stops on the highway in Prachuap at 12.30 am – if seats are available you can buy a through ticket to Samui for 190B. It's a five minute, 10B motorcycle taxi ride from the town centre to the highway bus stop.

**Train** For departure details from Bangkok, see the earlier Phetburi Getting There & Away section: the same services apply. Fares from Bangkok are 122B for 2nd class and 58B for 3rd class. Ordinary trains between Hua Hin and Prachuap are 19B; from Hua Hin they leave at 10.30 and 11.47 am, and 6.25 pm, arriving in Prachuap 1½ hours later. There are also a couple of rapid trains between the two towns, but the time saved is only about 20 minutes. A 3rd class ticket on to Chumphon is 34B.

### Getting Around
Prachuap is small enough to get around on foot, or you can hop on a tuk-tuk for 5B anywhere on the main roads.

A tuk-tuk to Ao Noi costs 25B. The Honda dealer on Sarachip Rd rents 100cc motorcycles for 200B a day.

A motorbike taxi to Ao Manao costs 20 to 25B. They aren't permitted past the gate, from where it is necessary to walk the three km to the beach.

## AROUND PRACHUAP KHIRI KHAN
### Wat Khao Tham Khan Kradai
วัดเขาถ้ำคันกระได
About eight km north of town, following the same road beyond Ao Noi, is this small cave wat at one end of **Ao Khan Kradai** (also known as Ao Khan Bandai – a long, beautiful bay.

A trail at the base of the limestone hill leads up and around the side to a small cavern and then to a larger one which contains a reclining Buddha. If you have a torch you can proceed to a larger second chamber also containing Buddha images. From this trail you get a good view of Ao Khan Kradai. The beach here is suitable for swimming and is virtually deserted. It's not far from Ao Noi, so you could stay in Ao Noi and walk to the beach. Or you could stay in town, rent a motorcycle and make a day trip to Ao Khan Kradai.

## Dan Singkhon
ด่านสิงขร

Just south of Prachuap is a road leading west to Dan Singkhon on the Myanmar border. This is the narrowest point in Thailand between the Gulf of Thailand and Myanmar – only 12 km across. The Myanmar side changed from Karen to Yangon control following skirmishes in 1988-89. The border is closed; on the Thai side is a small frontier village and a Thai police camp with wooden semi-underground bunkers built in a circle.

Off the road on the way to Dan Singkhon are a couple of small cave hermitages. The more famous one at **Khao Hin Thoen**, surrounded by a park of the same name, has some interesting rock formations and sculptures – but watch out for the dogs. The road to Khao Hin Thoen starts where the paved road to Dan Singkhon breaks left. **Khao Khan Hawk** (also known as Phutthakan Bang Kao) is a less well known cave nearby where an elderly monk, Luang Phaw Buaphan Chatimetho, lives. Devotees from a local village bring him food each morning.

## THAP SAKAE & BANG SAPHAN
ทับสะแกและบางสะพาน

• ☎ (32)

These two districts lie south of Prachuap Khiri Khan and together they offer a string of fairly good beaches that get hardly any tourists.

The town of Thap Sakae is set back from the coast and isn't much, but along the seashore there are a few places to stay (see below). The beach opposite Thap Sakae isn't anything special either, but north and south of town are the beaches of **Hat Wanakon** and **Hat Laem Kum**. There is no private accommodation at these beaches at the moment, but you could ask permission to camp at Wat Laem Kum, which is on a prime spot right in the middle of Hat Laem Kum. Laem Kum is only 3.5 km from Thap Sakae and at the northern end is the

fishing village of Ban Don Sai, where you can buy food. Hat Wanakon was recently declared part of Hat Wanakon National Marine Park, which covers 22.6 sq km of coastline and 15.4 sq km of marine resources.

Bang Saphan (Bang Saphan Yai) is no great shakes as a town either, but the long beaches here are beginning to attract some speculative development. In the vicinity of Bang Saphan you'll find the beaches of **Hat Sai Kaew, Hat Ban Krut, Hat Khiriwong, Hat Ban Nong Mongkon, Hat (Ao) Baw Thawng Lang, Hat Pha Daeng** and **Hat Bang Boet**, all of which are worth looking up. Getting around can be a problem since there isn't much public transport between these beaches.

There are also islands off the coast, including **Ko Thalu** and **Ko Sing**, where there is good snorkelling and diving from the end of January to mid-May.

### Places to Stay & Eat

**Thap Sakae** The *Chaowarit (Chawalit)*, right off the highway near the south end of town, has simple but clean rooms for 120B with shared bath, 150 to 200B with fan and bath – good value overall. Around the corner less than 100m from Chaowarit, the *Sukkasem* features very basic rooms for 70 to 120B.

A new place at the north end of town on the highway is *Thap Sakae Hotel* (☎ 671273), offering 10 clean fan rooms for 300/400B a double, air-con for 400/500B.

On the coast opposite Thap Sakae are a couple of concrete block-style bungalows for 200 to 400B, eg *Chan Reua*. Much more congenial and economical – if it's open – is the *Talay Inn* (☎ 671417), a cluster of neglected bamboo huts on a lake fed by the Huay Yang waterfall, but back from the beach a bit in the fishing village. Accommodation in thatched bungalows costs 100B per person; there is also one new air-con bungalow for 300B. The place changed hands recently, so it may close or take a new direction. It's about one km east of the Thap Sakae train station, which is about 1.5 km from Thap Sakae. Talay Inn is within easy walking distance of the sea.

CENTRAL THAILAND

**Hat Sai Kaew** Between Thap Sakae and Bang Saphan on the beach of Hat Kaew (Km 372, Highway 4) is *Haad Kaeo Beach Resort*. It's actually just 200m from the Ban Koktahom train station, which can only be reached by ordinary train from the Hua Hin, Prachuap, Thap Sakae, Bang Saphan Yai or Chumphon terminals. Pretty, white, air-con bungalows are 900 to 1200B per day on weekends, 20% less weekdays.

**Hat Ban Krut** *Reun Chun Seaview* (☎ (01) 215-1857; (2) 424-8364 in Bangkok) has one bedroom bungalows for 800B, two bedroom, two bath ones for 1800B, all air-con and not bad for families. Nearby *Ban Rim Haad* (☎ (01) 216-7926) is similar.

The most economic place on this beach is *Long Samut* (☎ 695045), which rents air-con bungalows for 400B, larger ones for 500 to 1200B.

The new *Ban Klang Aow Beach Resort* (☎ 695086; (2) 463-7908 in Bangkok) is an up-market place on the beach with a nice pool. Standard bungalows costs 2000B, larger ones 3000B, all with air-con, TV and fridge. *Suan Ban Krut Resort* (☎ 695103; (2) 576-0238 in Bangkok) is a similar affair with 26 bungalows for 1250B as well as a number of beach homes for sale or rent.

**Hat Khiriwong** *Tawee Beach Resort* (also *Tawees*, *Tawee Sea*) has simple thatched bungalows with private scoop showers for 70/120B a single/double, plus a few concrete bungalows with fans for 200/300B. Or you can pitch a tent for 10B.

*Sai-Eak Beach Resort* (☎ (01) 213-0317; (2) 321-4543 in Bangkok) opened in 1996 and is the nicest resort in the area. It's right on the beach, and features a variety of bungalows with satellite TV and fridge ranging from 2000 to 3000B, depending on whether they face pool or sea. Low season discounts of 30% to 50% are available May to November.

Take a train or bus to the nearby town of Ban Krut, then a motorcycle taxi (30B daytime, 50B night) to Hat Khiriwong.

**Bang Saphan** Along the bay of Ao Bang Saphan are several beach hotels and bungalows. At Hat Somboon, the *Hat Somboon Sea View* is 480 to 580B per room with private hot water bath and air-con. The cheaper *Boonsom Guest House* (☎ 691273) has rooms with fan for 200 and 300B. *Van Veena Bungalows* (☎ 691251), also in this area, offers rooms with fan for 200B or air-con for 550B, including TV and video. Bungalows are also available for 200 and 400B. The same management also handles *Bangsaphan Resort* (☎ 691152/3), which has similarly priced rooms.

*Karol L's* (☎ 691058), operated by an American and his Thai wife, has 80 and 100B bungalows in the old Samui-style six km south of Bang Saphan Yai. If you call from the train or bus terminal, they'll provide free transport. Meals here are very reasonably priced as well. Karol L's can arrange trips to nearby islands and caves; they have lots of info about the area.

The fairly new *Suan Luang Resort* (☎ (01) 212-5687; fax 691054), at 97 Muu 1, is 600m from the beach, just up from Karol's. They also will pick up customers from the train station if you give them a call. The resort is run by a friendly and helpful Thai-Italian couple, a combination also reflected in their dining room menu. New and spacious bungalows with mosquito proofing cost 200B for wooden ones, 350B for concrete. There are discounts for longer stays. If you have your own tent, camping is free, and they have four motorbikes for rent as well as windsurfing, diving and sailing equipment. They can organise boat trips to nearby islands, or motorbike trips to surrounding areas, including Myanmar if the border is open. The going rate for a half-day snorkel trip to Ko Sing is 300B, or full day to Ko Thalu 400B, including lunch. An overnight camping trip to Ko Thalu with meals costs 1200B.

*Bang Saphan Coral Hotel*, under construction near Suan Luang, will offer two bedroom suites for 1400B, single/double rooms for 970B.

The *Krua Klang Ao* restaurant, right near the centre of Ao Bang Saphan, is a good place for seafood. Because of an Italian-staffed development project nearby, many of the local hotel and restaurant staff speak a smattering of Italian.

**Hat Bo Kaew** Eight km south of Hat Bang Saphan Yai (15 km south of Bang Saphan town), this up and comer boasts two places to stay. *Suan Annan Resort* has 10 bungalows around 300m from the beach costing 500B a night with air-con, TV and fridge. A half km south, *Haad Boa Kaew* offers six fan-cooled bungalows for 300B and an air-con one for 600B; it's not as good value as Suan Annan.

### Getting There & Away
Buses from Prachuap to Thap Sakae are 12B and from Thap Sakae to Bang Saphan Yai, 8B. If you're coming from farther south, buses from Chumphon to Bang Saphan Yai are 25B.

You can also get 3rd class trains between Hua Hin, Prachuap, Thap Sakae, Ban Koktahom, Ban Krut and Bang Saphan Yai for a few baht each leg, as all of them have train stations (the rapid and express lines do not stop in Thap Sakae, Ban Krut or Bang Saphan). Each of these train stations is around four km from the beach, with motorcycle taxis the only form of public transport available. It's possible to rent 100cc motorbikes in Bang Saphan for 150B per day.

CENTRAL THAILAND

# Northern Thailand

The first true Thai kingdoms (Lanna, Suk-hothai, Nan, Chiang Mai and Chiang Saen) arose in what is now Northern Thailand, hence this region is endowed with a wide range of traditional culture and architecture, including the country's most majestic temple ruins. It is also the home of most of the Thai hill tribes, whose cultures are dissolving rapidly in the face of Thai modernisation and foreign tourism. Despite this, the scenic beauty of the North has been fairly well preserved, and Chiang Mai is still probably Thailand's most livable city.

The Northern Thai people (who call themselves *khon meuang)* are known for their relaxed, easy-going manner, which shows up in speech – the Northern dialect *(kham meu-ang)* has a rhythm which is slower than that of Thailand's other three main dialects. Northern Thais are very proud of their local customs, considering Northern ways to be part of Thailand's 'original' tradition and culture. Symbols expressing cultural solidarity are frequently displayed by Northern Thais and include clay water jars placed in front of homes, *kalae* (a carved wooden 'X' motif) which decorate house gables, Shan or hill-tribe-style shoulder bags and the ubiquitous *sêua mâw hâwm* (indigo-dyed rice farmers' shirt) worn on Fridays at many banks, universities and other institutions throughout the North.

Northern Thailand also has its own cuisine, featuring a large variety of vegetables (the region's mountain slopes are well suited to vegetable cultivation). Sticky rice is preferred over the Central and Southern Thai-style white rice and, as in North-Eastern Thailand and Laos, it is eaten with the hands. *Sôm-tam,* a tart and spicy salad usually made with green papaya (the Northern Thais also use a variety of other fruits and vegetables to make this dish), is very popular in the North but, unlike North-Eastern Thais, khon meuang tend to eat it as a between-meals snack rather than as part of a main meal.

## HIGHLIGHTS

- World Heritage historical parks at Sukhothai and Si Satchanalai-Chaliang – Thailand's finest collection of monuments from its 'golden age'
- Vibrant Northern capital of Chiang Mai – with its 300 temples, celebrated arts and crafts and courses in massage, cooking and boxing
- Misty Doi Inthanon National Park, featuring Thailand's tallest peak, is home to 400 bird species
- Traditional Lampang – known for its horsecarts and Thailand's oldest surviving wooden temple
- Crossroads province of Mae Hong Son – ethnic minorities, dense forests, trekking and rafting trips
- Remote and rural provinces of Phrae, with its old teak mansions and quiet lanes, and Nan, with its fertile river valleys and Thai Lü communities
- Crossborder trips to Myanmar's historic Kengtung – crumbling Buddhas and colonial architecture
- Large limestone caves of Tham Lot and Tham Nang Lang near Soppong in Mae Hong Son

The mountainous North also contains the infamous 'Golden Triangle', the region where Myanmar, Laos and Thailand meet and where most of the world's illicit opium poppies are

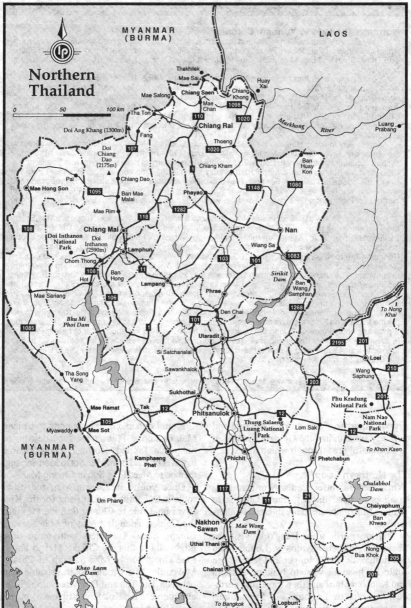

## Northern Thailand to Yunnan, China

It's finally possible to travel from Thailand to China's Yunnan Province by road via Laos, a land route which ties together the Golden Triangle and Yunnan's Sipsongpanna district in south-western China. The Thais, Shan and Lao all consider Sipsongpanna (called Xishuangbanna in China) to be a cultural homeland.

One can now cross into Laos from Thailand at least six legal border crossings. Once in Laos, head to Luang Nam Tha or Udomxai, then proceed north to the Lao village of Boten on the Chinese border, close to the Sipsongpanna town of Mengla. From Mengla, an existing road leads to Jinghong. To reach Luang Nam Tha from Northern Thailand you may cross by ferry (and soon bridge) from Chiang Khong on the Thai side to Huay Xai on the Lao side. This crossing is already operational; foreigners may enter Laos here with the proper visa. The Boten crossing is now also legal for all nationalities.

Another way to reach Boten is via Pakbeng in Laos' Udomxai Province. Pakbeng is midway along the Maekhong River route between Huay Xai and Luang Prabang; from Pakbeng a Chinese-built road system continues all the way to Boten. To facilitate trade and travel between China and Thailand, the Chinese have offered to build a new road directly south to the Thai border (Nan Province) from the river bank opposite Pakbeng. For now Thai authorities are not too happy about this proposed road extension, which is seen as a push towards an 'invasion' of Thailand. During the years of Thai communist insurgency, CPT cadres used the Pakbeng road to reach Kunming, China, for training in revolutionary tactics.

Another land route to China begins at the Burmese border town of Thakhilek (opposite Mae Sai on the Thai side) and proceeds 164 km northward to Myanmar's Kengtung (known as Chiang Tung to the Thais), Shan State. At present this road is a rough track that takes all day to cover when road conditions are good; permission to cross here can be arranged in Mae Sai on the Thai side. From Kengtung the road continues another 100 km north to Myanmar's Mong La (opposite Daluo on the Chinese border); at the moment this latter section isn't approved for tourist travel although its opening is imminent. The Chinese have agreed to finance the Daluo to Kengtung section of the road in return for limited mineral and logging rights in Myanmar. From Daluo it's 300 km to Jinghong, capital of Sipsongpanna. Since Thai immigration authorities hold your passport in Mae Sai while allowing you to travel north into the Shan State, it's not yet legal to cross the Chinese border by land from Myanmar.

In the long term, the river route is also promising. Chinese barges weighing up to 100 tonnes now ply the Maekhong River eight months a year; from the Chinese border to Chiang Khong, Thailand, the trip takes about five days. During the drier months, however, river transport north of Luang Prabang is hampered by rocks and shallows. Blasting and dredging could make way for boats of up to 500 tonnes to travel year-round. A new express ferry service promises to deliver passengers to China from the Chiang Saen area in one day. ■

grown. Apart from the air of adventure and mystery surrounding the Golden Triangle, it is a beautiful area through which to travel.

## The Northern Loop

While the straightforward way of travelling north is to head directly from Bangkok to Chiang Mai, there are many interesting alternatives.

Starting north from Bangkok, visit the ancient capitals of Ayuthaya, Lopburi and Sukhothai, or take a longer and less beaten route by heading west to Nakhon Pathom and Kanchanaburi and then travelling northeast by bus to Lopburi via Suphanburi (backtracking to Ayuthaya if desired).

From Lopburi, either head north to Chiang Mai, or stop at Phitsanulok for side trips to Sukhothai, Tak and Mae Sot. It is now possible to travel by road from Mae Sot to Mae Sariang, then on to Mae Hong Son or Chiang Mai.

Once you're in Chiang Mai, the usual route is to continue on to Fang for the Kok River boat ride to Chiang Rai, then on into the Golden Triangle towns of Mae Sai and Chiang Saen. Travellers with more time might add to this the Chiang Mai to Pai to Mae Hong Son to Mae Sariang to Chiang Mai circle. A very rough but traversable road between Tha Ton and Doi Mae Salong is an alternative to the Kok River trip once you get to the Fang area.

From Chiang Mai, proceed to North-Eastern Thailand via Phitsanulok and Lom Sak, entering the North-East proper at either Loei or Khon Kaen. From there, Nong Khai, Udon Thani and Khon Kaen are all on the train line back to Bangkok, but there are several other places in the area worth exploring before heading back to the capital.

The old Laotian loop – from Bangkok to Vientiane, Luang Prabang and Huay Xai, then back into Thailand to Chiang Rai and eventually Chiang Mai – has become possible again with the opening of Laos to individual tourism. This loop can also be done in the reverse, starting with the crossing of the Maekhong River at Chiang Khong, Chiang Rai Province, to Huay Xai, and then continuing by river to Luang Prabang and Vientiane. From Vientiane you can loop back into North-Eastern Thailand or continue on to Vietnam or China by road or air.

# Chiang Mai Province

## CHIANG MAI
อ.เมืองเชียงใหม่
• ☎ (53) • *pop 154,777*

More than 700 km north-west of Bangkok, Chiang Mai has over 300 temples (121 within the *thêtsabaan* or municipal limits) – almost as many as Bangkok – making it visually striking. Doi Suthep rises 1676m above and behind the city, providing a nice setting for this fast-developing centre.

Thai King Mengrai took over a Mon settlement to develop Nopburi Si Nakhon Ping Chiang Mai (shortened to Chiang Mai, 'New City') in 1296. Historically, Chiang Mai succeeded King Mengrai's Chiang Rai kingdom after he conquered the post-Dvaravati kingdom of Hariphunchai (modern Lamphun) in 1281. Mengrai, reportedly a prince from Nam Chao, a Thai kingdom in south-west China, built Chiang Mai's original city walls in 1296; traces of these earthen ramparts can still be seen today along Kamphaeng Din Rd.

Later, in the 13th and 14th centuries, Chiang Mai became a part of the larger kingdom of Lan Na Thai (literally, 'million Thai rice fields'), which extended as far south as Kamphaeng Phet and as far north as Luang Prabang in Laos. During this period Chiang Mai became an important religious and cultural centre – the 8th world synod of Theravada Buddhism was held there in 1477.

The Burmese capture of the city in 1556 was the second time the Burmese had control of Chiang Mai Province: before King Mengrai's reign, King Anuruddha of Pagan (present-day Bagan) had ruled the area in the 11th century. The second time around, the Burmese ruled Chiang Mai for over 200 years.

In 1775 Chiang Mai was recaptured by the Thais under King Taksin, who appointed Chao Kavila, a *jâo meuang* (lord) from nearby Lampang principality, as viceroy of Northern Thailand. In 1800 Kavila built the monumental brick walls around the inner city, and expanded the city in southerly and easterly directions, establishing a river port at the end of what is today Tha Phae Rd (*thâa phae* means pier). Under Kavila, Chiang Mai became an important regional trade centre. Many of the later Shan and Burmese-style temples seen around the city were built by wealthy teak merchants who emigrated from Burma during the 19th century.

The completion of the northern railway line to Chiang Mai in 1921 finally linked the North with Central Thailand. Word soon spread among the Thais and foreign visitors that the quaint Northern capital was a great place for shopping and recreation. Tourism has since replaced commercial trade as Chiang Mai's number one source of outside revenue. Close behind is the manufacture and sale of handicrafts. Long before tourists began visiting the region, Chiang Mai was an important centre for handcrafted pottery, weaving, umbrellas, silverwork and woodcarving. If you visit arts and craft shops anywhere in Thailand today, chances are at least someone working in the shop hails from the Chiang Mai area.

NORTHERN THAILAND

NORTHERN THAILAND

Many visitors stay in Chiang Mai longer than planned because of the high quality of accommodation, food and shopping, the cool nights (in comparison to Central Thailand), the international feel of the city and the friendliness of the people. Also, the city is small enough to get around by bicycle. And with the increasing number of cultural and spiritual learning experiences available in Chiang Mai these days – Thai massage, Thai cooking, Thai language, yoga, *vipassana* (meditation) and t'ai chi – the city has become much more than just a quick stop on the Northern Thailand tourist circuit.

Not all the foreign faces you see in Chiang Mai are tourists – many live in Chiang Mai part-time or all year round. Chiang Mai residents often comment that living here has all the cultural advantages of being in Bangkok, but fewer of the disadvantages such as traffic jams and air pollution. In recent years, however, traffic has increased and the city's main avenues have became noisy and polluted, particularly around the reconstructed Tha Phae Gate.

To preserve the city's character, it has been proposed that a 'twin city' be built nearby to channel development away from the old city – possibly at San Kamphaeng to the east. Conservation measures include a 1991 ban on the building of any high-rise construction within 93m of a temple, thereby protecting about 87% of all lands within municipal limits. This law is designed to halt any future condo developments along the Ping River – the existing condos have already contributed to water pollution and spoiled the city's skyline. As usual, unscrupulous developers have found a loophole – hotels are exempt from the ban, so many condo-type developments are applying for hotel licences. Others are setting their sights on Chiang Rai farther north, where there are no such legal barriers.

Development in the last four years has reached an apparent plateau due to a regional recession in the North. One positive development was the 1992 dredging of the formerly polluted city moat and installation of an automatic filtering system. Although not the most pristine of waterways, the moat now contains lots of fish and turtles. Another boon has been the recent establishment of a one-way traffic system that allowed the city to extinguish many traffic lights and improve overall traffic flow considerably. The city also has the most comprehensive municipal recycling programme in the country; recycling bins on roadsides around town accept glass, plastic and paper.

### Orientation

The old city of Chiang Mai is a neat square bounded by moats. Moon Meuang Rd, along the east moat, is the centre for cheap accommodation and places to eat. Tha Phae Rd runs straight from the middle of this side and crosses the Ping River where it changes to Charoen Meuang Rd.

The train station and the GPO are farther down Charoen Meuang Rd, a fair distance from the centre. There are several bus stations around Chiang Mai, so make sure you're going to the right one.

Several of Chiang Mai's important temples are within the moat area, but there are others to the north and west. Doi Suthep rises up to the west of the city and its temples give you a fine view over the city.

**Maps** Finding your way around Chiang Mai is fairly simple, although a copy of Nancy Chandler's *Map of Chiang Mai* is a worthwhile investment for 70B. It shows all the main points of interest, bus routes and innumerable oddities which you'd be most unlikely to stumble upon by yourself. Similar in scope are *DK's Chiang Mai Tourist Map* published by DK Book House (this has more emphasis on local transport information but very shaky transliteration) and P&P's *Tourist Map of Chiang Mai*. TAT also puts out a sketchy city map that's free.

### Information

**Tourist Office** Chiang Mai has a friendly TAT office (☎ 248604/07) on the Chiang Mai-Lamphun Rd near Nawarat Bridge. It's open daily from 8 am to 5 pm. This is also the headquarters for the city's tourist police, who have a good reputation for honesty and efficiency.

**Foreign Consulates** Chiang Mai has several foreign consular posts where you may be able to arrange visas. The Indian consulate here is a familiar stopping-off point for travellers on their way to India; it takes about four days to process a visa here.

Austria – 15 Muu 1, Huay Kaew Rd (☎ 400231)
Canada – 151 Chiang Mai-Lamphun Rd (☎ 850147)
China – 111 Chang Law Rd (☎ 276135)
France – 138 Charoen Prathet Rd (☎ 215719)
India – 344 Faham (Charoenrat) Rd, Faham, (☎ 243066, 242491)
Japan – Na Watket Rd Soi 1 (☎ 302042)
Sweden – International Hotel, Chiang Mai, 11 Soemsuk Rd (☎ 222356)
UK – 139/2 3rd floor, IBM Bldg, Huay Kaew Rd (☎ 894189/40)
USA – 387 Wichayanon Rd (☎ 252629/31)

**Immigration** The immigration office (☎ 277-510) is off Route 1141 near the airport (bus No 6 will take you there).

**Money** All major Thai banks have several branches throughout Chiang Mai; most are open 8.30 am to 3.30 pm. In the well touristed areas – Tha Phae Rd, Moon Meuang Rd, Night Bazaar etc – the banks also operate foreign exchange booths that are open after bank hours as late as 8 pm.

**Post** The GPO is near the train station on Charoen Meuang Rd. It's open Monday to Friday from 8.30 am to 4.30 pm, Saturday and Sunday from 9 am to noon. Bus Nos 1 and 3 pass in front of the GPO.

More convenient to visitors staying west of the river toward the old city, the new Mae Ping post office is open Monday to Friday 8.30 am to 4.30 pm, Saturday 9 am to noon. The old Mae Ping post office across the street now houses the Chiang Mai Philatelic Museum (open weekends and holidays only, 9 am to 4 pm).

Other useful branch post offices can be found at Praisani, Samlan, Phra Pokklao, Chotana, Mahidon, Chang Pheuak and Chang Khlan Rds, and at Chiang Mai University and Chiang Mai international airport.

Mail Boxes Etc on Chang Khlan Rd near the Chiang Mai Night Bazaar offers the usual private mail services, including rental boxes, mailing supplies, stationery and a courier service. They also do passport photos and photocopies.

**Communications** Overseas telephone calls, telexes, faxes and telegrams can be arranged 7 am to 10 pm in the telecommunications office around the side and upstairs from the GPO on Charoen Meuang Rd. International calls can also be made from larger hotels for a service charge (up to 30%) and at the international telephone office at 44 Si Donchai Rd from 9 am to 10.30 pm.

Home Direct phones, with easy one-button connection with foreign operators in a number of countries around the world, are available at: Chiang Inn Plaza, 100/1 Chang Khlan Rd, behind the Night Bazaar; Chiang Mai international airport; the GPO on Charoen Meuang Rd; the THAI office on 240 Phra Pokklao Rd; and the TAT office.

**Bookshops** Chiang Mai has several bookshops, the best being DK Book House on Kotchasan Rd and Suriwong Book Centre on Si Donchai Rd. DK has a second branch at Chiang Mai University. DK's large size is deceptive; they stack the books face out so there are really not as many titles to choose from as it seems at first glance. Suriwong, overall, has a better selection.

The USIS/AUA library on Ratchadamnoen Rd inside the east gate has a large selection of English-language newspapers and magazines. The library is open Monday to Friday from noon to 6 pm. The British Council on Bamrungrat Rd also has a small English-language library. The Chiang Mai University library has a collection of foreign-language titles.

The Library Service at 21/1 Ratchamankha Rd Soi 2, not far from Tha Phae Gate, is a small bookshop-cum-cafe with used paperbacks for sale or trade. The shop is open Monday to Saturday from 9 am to 6 pm.

**Media** Several free publications are distributed at tourist spots throughout the city.

NORTHERN THAILAND

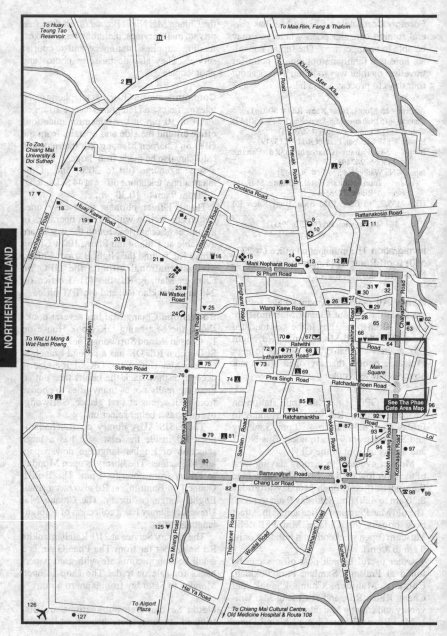

NORTHERN THAILAND

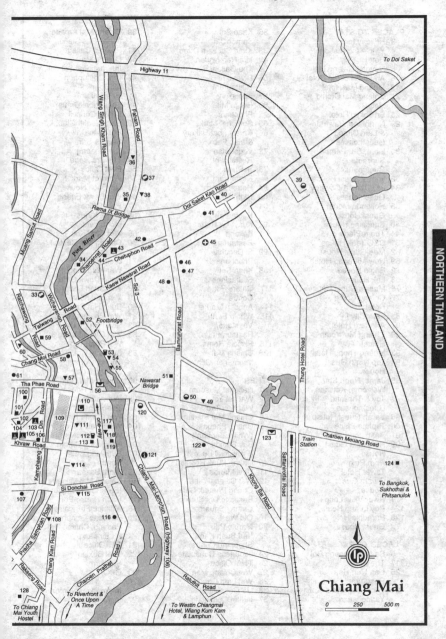

Chiang Mai

0    250    500 m

To Doi Saket

Highway 11

Wang Singh Kham Road

Faham Road

36

37

34

38

35

Rama IX Bridge

Doi Saket Kao Road

40

Muang Samut Road

Ratchawong Road

Ping River

Charoenrat Road

43

34

44

Chetuphon Road

41

42

45

46

47

Kaew Nawarat Road

Sol 3

48

33

Wichayanon Road

Taiwang Road

52    Footbridge

59

60

Chang Moi Road

58

61

Tha Phae Road

100

101

102

104    103

105    106

109

Khraw Road

110

111

117

112    118

113    119

Kamphaeng Road

114

Si Donchai Road

107

115

108

116

Prach Samphan Road

Chang Klan Road

Ratakeng Road

128

To Chiang Mai Youth Hostel

To Riverfront & Once Upon A Time

Charoen Prathet Road

Chiang Mai-Lamphun Road (Highway 106)

To Westin Chiangmai Hotel, Wiang Kum Kam & Lamphun

Ratuhit Road

Khong Sai Road

Sattaniotia Road

Bamrungrat Road

53

54

55

51

57

56

Nawarat Bridge

50    49

120

121

122

123

Train Station

Charoen Meuang Road

Thung Hotel Road

124

To Bangkok, Sukhothai & Phitsanulok

**NORTHERN THAILAND**

**PLACES TO STAY**
3 Holiday Inn
4 YMCA International Hotel
6 Novotel Chiang Mai
18 Amari Rincome Hotel
19 Muang Mai Hotel
21 Chiang Mai Orchid Hotel
23 Sri Tokyo Hotel
29 Northland, Sawatdee & Lam Chang Guesthouses
30 Libra, SK, Peter & Supreme Guesthouses
32 Tanya Guest House
34 Je t'Aime & Cowboy Guesthouses
35 Hollanda Montri Guest House
40 Sunshine House
44 The rePlace
51 C&C Teak House
52 Mee Guest House
59 New Mitrapap Hotel
62 Eagle House
63 Lek House
75 Manit's Guest House
77 Chiang Come Hotel
83 Felix City Inn
87 Anodard Hotel
89 Chiang Mai Youth Hostel
93 Muang Thong Hotel
94 Top North Guest House
95 Jame, North Star, Welcome, Kritsada, Toy & Thailand Guesthouses
96 Sarah Guest House
100 Taphae Place
101 Baan Jongcome
102 Ratchada Guest House
113 Porn Ping Tower Hotel
117 Galare Guest House
119 River View Lodge
124 Poy Luang Hotel
128 Paradise Hotel & Guest House

**PLACES TO EAT**
5 Sa-Nga Choeng Doi
17 The Pub
25 Uan Heh-Haa Restaurant
31 Wira Laap Pet & Kai Yaang Isaan
36 Khao Soi Samoe Jai
38 Khao Soi Lam Duan
49 Lim Han Nguan
54 The Gallery
55 Riverside Bar & Restaurant
57 Bacco
60 Ruam Mit Phochana
65 Somphet Market
66 Crusty Loaf Bakery & Irish Pub
72 Vegetarian Restaurant
73 Si Phen Restaurant
84 Heuan Phen
86 Night Market
91 Mitmai Restaurant
92 Kuaytiaw Reua Koliang Restaurant
99 Si Donchai Phochana
108 Khao Soi Suthasinee 2
111 Galare Food Centre
114 Anusan Market
115 Whole Earth Vegetarian Restaurant
118 Piccola Roma
125 Chiang Mai Vegetarian Centre

**OTHER**
1 National Museum
2 Wat Jet Yot
7 Wat Kuu Tao
8 Chiang Mai Stadium
9 Chang Pheuak (White Elephant) Bus Station (Provincial Buses)
10 Chang Puek Hospital
11 Devi Mandir
12 Wat Chiang Yuen
13 Chang Pheuak Gate
14 Buses to Doi Suthep
15 Cathay Square
16 Old West
20 Marble Pub
22 Kad Suan Kaew Shopping Centre
24 Japanese Consulate
26 THAI Office
27 Wat Chiang Man
28 Wat Lam Chang
33 US Consulate
37 Indian Consulate
39 Chiang Mai Arcade (New) Bus Station
41 Phayap College
42 Chiang Mai International School
43 Wat Chetuphon
45 McCormick Hospital
46 Thai Tribal Crafts
47 British Council
48 Sara Health Club
50 Buses to Baw Sang & San Kamphaeng
53 The Brasserie
56 Post Office
58 Warorot Market
61 DK Book House
64 Wat Dawk Euang
67 Post Office
68 Three Kings Monument
69 Wat Chai Kiat
70 Chiang Mai Central Prison
71 District Offices
74 Wat Phra Singh
76 Suan Dawk Gate
78 Wat Suan Dawk
79 Mengrai Kilns
80 Buak Hat Park
81 Wat Pheuak Hong
82 Suan Prung Gate
85 Wat Chedi Luang & Wat Phan Tao
88 Buses to Hot, Chom Thong, Doi Inthanon & Hang Dong
90 Chiang Mai Gate
97 DK Book House
98 International Telephone Offices
103 Wat Chang Khong
104 Wat Phan Thong
105 Wat Loi Khraw
106 Hangdong Rattan
107 Suriwong Book Centre
109 Night Bazaar
110 Chiang Mai Mosque (Ban Haw Mosque)
112 Hash House Pub
116 Alliance Française
120 Buses to Lamphun, Pasang, Chiang Rai & Lampang
121 TAT Office
122 Thai Boxing Stadium
123 GPO
126 Chiang Mai International Airport
127 Immigration

*Trip Info* is a very useful monthly booklet with extensive listings of government agencies, banks, churches, apartments, condos and current bus, train and plane schedules. The monthly *Chiang Mai Newsletter* runs articles on local culture and politics as well as a listing of local events.

The tourism-oriented *Chiang Mai Guidelines* and *Welcome to Chiangmai & Chiangrai* contain the usual assortment of brief, rather shallow cultural essays embedded among stacks of advertisements for bars, restaurants and antique shops. The amateurish *Siam Chiangmai News* is a one-person show produced by local developer Udom Surin.

Radio Thailand Chiang Mai offers English-language broadcasts – a mix of news and music – from 6 to 8.30 am and 6 to 8.30 pm daily at FM 93.25.

**Cultural Centres** Several foreign cultural centres in Chiang Mai host film, music, dance, theatre and other events of a socio-cultural nature.

Alliance Française – 138 Charoen Prathet Rd (☎ 275277). French films (subtitled in English) are held every Tuesday at 4.30 pm, Friday at 8 pm; admission is free to members, 10B students, 20B general public. French-language courses are also offered. Opposite is a branch research library for the Ecôle Française d'Extrême Orient housed in an impressive old Chiang Mai house. Permission from the director for research here is needed.
USIS/AUA – 24 Ratchadamnoen Rd (☎ 278407, 211377). USIS shows US films every second and fourth Saturday at 2 and 7 pm; admission is free. AUA also offers English and Thai-language courses (see the Activities section later in this section for details on Thai language study).
British Council – 198 Bamrungrat Rd (☎ 242103). Free British movies are held every Thursday evening at 7 pm.

**Medical Services** McCormick Hospital (☎ 241107) on Kaew Nawarat Rd is recommended over Chiang Mai Hospital because they are more geared to foreigners, speak better English and won't keep you waiting for as long. Another good one is the newer, modern Chang Puek Hospital (☎ 220022; fax 218120) at 1/7 Chang Pheuak Rd Soi 2.

Other medical facilities include Ariya-wongse Clinic on Chang Moi Rd, Chiang Mai Hospital on Suan Dawk Rd, Lanna Hospital on Highway 11 (Super Highway) and the Malaria Centre on 18 Bunreuangrit Rd.

Alcoholics Anonymous (☎ 282627) meets several times weekly at McCormick Hospital, Room 133.

**Film & Processing** Outside of Bangkok, Chiang Mai has the best supply of quality photographic film in the country. Broadway Photo (☎ 251253), on Tha Phae Rd about 100m east of Tha Phae Gate, has a good selection of slide film, including hard-to-find Fujichrome Pro 400 and Velvia 50. For slide processing many professionals in the area use Champ Photo on Phra Pokklao Rd, opposite the Three Kings Monument.

**Other** The tourist police (☎ 248974) have an office next to TAT on the Chiang Mai-Lamphun Rd. They are open from 6 am until midnight; their after-hours number is ☎ 491420.

Oriented toward expatriate residents of Chiang Mai, the relatively new Raintree Community Services offers information, enrichment classes, support groups, massage and children's programmes. The group's Info Line (☎ 306317) is open Monday to Friday 9 am to 1 pm, while the 24 hour Movie Line (☎ 306447) features a recorded listing of English-language films playing at local cinemas.

The Network Talks convene at 7.30 pm on the second Saturday of each month at the Crusty Loaf Bakery & Irish Pub (☎ 271131). It's a loose affiliation of various NGO (non-governmental organisation) staff working in Chiang Mai and others interested in human development, organised by the local Raja Yoga Centre.

### Wat Chiang Man
วัดเชียงมั่น
The oldest wat in the city, Wat Chiang Man was founded by King Mengrai in 1296 and features typical Northern Thai architecture

NORTHERN THAILAND

**Chiang Mai Festivals**
The week-long Winter Fair in late December and early January is a great occasion, as is the April Songkran Water Festival which is celebrated here with great enthusiasm. In late January the Baw Sang Umbrella Festival features a colourful umbrella procession during the day and a night-time lantern procession. Although it sounds touristy the festival is actually a very Thai affair; one of the highlights is the many Northern Thai music ensembles that perform in shopfronts along Baw Sang's main street.

Perhaps Chiang Mai's best celebrated festival is the Flower Festival, also called the Flower Carnival, which is held annually in February (actual dates vary from year to year). Events occur over a three day period and include displays of flower arrangements, a long parade of floats decorated with hundreds and thousands of flowers, folk music, cultural performances and the Queen of the Flower Festival contest. Most activities are centred at Buak Hat Park in the south-west corner of the city moats. People from all over the province and the rest of the country turn out for this occasion, so book early if you want a room in town.

In May the Intakin Festival, held at Wat Chedi Luang and centred around the city làk meuang, propitiates the city's guardian deity to assure that the annual monsoon will arrive on time. Also in May – when the mango crop is ripe – a Mango Fair is celebrated in Buak Hat Park with lots of mango eating and the coronation of the Mango Queen. ■

with massive teak columns inside the *bòt* (central sanctuary), which in Northern Thailand is called a *sīm*. Two important Buddha images are kept in a glass cabinet in the smaller *wihăan* (Buddhist image sanctuary) to the right of the *sīm*.

The Phra Sila is a marble bas-relief Buddha standing 20 to 30 cm high. It's supposed to have come from Sri Lanka or India 2500 years ago, but since no Buddha images were produced anywhere before around 2000 years ago it must have arrived later. The well known Phra Satang Man, a crystal seated Buddha image, was shuttled back and forth between Thailand and Laos like the Emerald Buddha. It's thought to have come from Lavo (Lopburi) 1800 years ago and stands just 10 cm high. A very interesting silver Buddha sits in front of the cabinet among a collection of other images.

The *sīm* containing the venerated images is open daily 9 to 5. Wat Chiang Man is off Ratchaphakhinai Rd in the north-east corner of the old city.

## Wat Phra Singh
วัดพระสิงห์

Started by King Pa Yo in 1345, the *wihăan* which houses the Phra Singh image was completed between 1385 and 1400. It is an example of the classic Northern-Thai style found during this period from Chiang Mai to Luang Prabang. The Phra Singh Buddha supposedly comes from Sri Lanka, but it is not particularly Sinhalese in style. As it is identical to two images in Nakhon Si Thammarat and Bangkok, and has quite a travel history (Sukhothai, Ayuthaya, Chiang Rai, Luang Prabang – the usual itinerary for a travelling Buddha image, involving much royal trickery), no-one really knows which image is the real one, nor can anyone document its place of origin. The *bòt* was finished in about 1600.

Wat Phra Singh is at the end of Phra Singh Rd near Suan Dawk Gate.

## Wat Chedi Luang
วัดเจดีย์หลวง

This temple complex, on the corner of Phra Pokklao and Phra Singh Rds, contains a very large and venerable *chedi* (stupa) dating from 1441. It's now in partial ruins, damaged either by a 16th century earthquake or by the cannon fire of King Taksin in 1775 during the recapture of Chiang Mai from the Burmese. It's said that the Emerald Buddha was placed in the eastern niche here in 1475. The *làk meuang* (guardian deity post) for the city is within the wat compound in the small building to the left of the main entrance.

There are also some impressive dipterocarp trees on the grounds.

A restoration of the great chedi, financed by UNESCO and the Japanese government, is almost finished. Since no-one knows for sure how the original superstructure looked, Thai artisans are designing a new spire for the chedi. New Buddha images have been placed in the four directional niches, but the new porticoes and *naga* (dragon-headed serpent) guardians lack the charm of the originals. Cement elephants in the pediment replace the original brick and stucco ones.

### Wat Phan Tao
วัดพันเต้า

Adjacent to Wat Chedi Luang, this wat has a wooden wihăan and some old and interesting monks' quarters. Across Ratchadamnoen Rd from here, at the Phra Pokklao Rd intersection, is an uninteresting monument marking the spot where King Mengrai was struck by lightning!

### Wat Jet Yot
วัดเจ็ตยอต

Out of town on the northern highway loop near the Chiang Mai National Museum, this wat was built in the mid-15th century to host the 8th World Buddhist Council in 1477. Based on the design of the Mahabodhi Temple in Bodhgaya, India, the proportions for the Chiang Mai version are quite different from the Indian original, so it was probably modelled from a small votive tablet depicting the Mahabodhi in distorted perspective. The seven spires represent the seven weeks Buddha was supposed to have spent in Bodhgaya after his enlightenment.

On the outer walls of the old wihăan is some of the original stucco relief. There's an adjacent stupa of undetermined age and a very glossy wihăan. The entire area is surrounded by well kept lawns. It's a pleasant, relaxing temple to visit, although curiously it's not very active in terms of worship.

Wat Jet Yot is a bit too far from the city centre to reach on foot; by bicycle it's easy or you can take a No 6 city bus (red).

### Wat Suan Dawk (Dok)
วัดสวนดอก

Built in 1383, the large open wihăan was rebuilt in 1932. The bòt contains a 500-year-old bronze Buddha image and vivid *jataka* (Buddha life-story) murals. Amulets and Buddhist literature printed in English and Thai can be purchased at quite low prices in the wihăan.

There is an interesting group of white-washed stupas, framed by Doi Suthep. The large central stupa contains a Buddha relic which supposedly self-multiplied. One relic was mounted on the back of a white elephant (commemorated by Chiang Mai's White Elephant Gate), which was allowed to wander until it 'chose' a site on which a wat could be built to shelter the relic. The elephant stopped and died at a spot on Doi Suthep, where Wat Phra That Doi Suthep was built.

### Wat Kuu Tao
วัดกู่เต้า

North of the moat, near the Chiang Mai Stadium, Wat Kuu Tao dates from 1613 and has a unique chedi which looks like a pile of diminishing spheres, said to be of possible Yunnanese design. Note the amusing sculptures on the outer wall of the wat.

### Wat U Mong
วัดอุโมงค์

This forest wat was first used during King Mengrai's rule in the 14th century. Brick-lined tunnels here were supposedly built around 1380 for the clairvoyant monk Thera Jan. The monastery was abandoned at a later date and wasn't reinstated until a local Thai prince sponsored a restoration in the late 1940s. The late Ajaan Buddhadasa, a well known monk and teacher at Southern Thailand's Wat Suanmok, sent several monks to re-establish a Sangha (Buddhist brotherhood) at U Mong in the 1960s. One building contains modern artwork by various monks who have resided at U Mong, including some foreigners. A marvellously grisly image of the fasting Buddha – ribs, veins and all – can be seen on the grounds.

A small library/museum with English-language books on Buddhism is also on the premises.

To get there, travel west on Suthep Rd for about two km and turn left past Wang Nam Kan, then follow the signs for another couple of km to Wat U Mong. Songthaews to Doi Suthep and city bus No 1 also pass the Wang Nam Kan turn-off.

## Wat Ram Poeng
วัตร่ำเปิง

Not far from Wat U Mong, this large monastery supports the well known Northern Insight Meditation Centre (☎ 211620), where many foreigners have studied vipassana. One month individual courses are taught by a Thai monk (Ajaan Thong or Luang Paw Banyat) with western students or bilingual Thais acting as interpreters. As of mid-1996 courses were temporarily suspended and at the time of writing I don't know when they'll resume.

A large *tripitaka* (Buddhist scriptures) library has recently been completed and houses versions of the Theravada Buddhist canon in Pali, Thai, Chinese, English and other languages.

The formal name for this wat is Wat Tapotaram. To get there, take city bus No 1 or a songthaew west on Suthep Rd to Phayom Market (Talaat Pha-yawm). From here, take a songthaew south to the wat entrance (4B).

## Wiang Kum Kam
เวียงกุมกำ

These excavated ruins are near the Ping River, five km south of the city via Highway 106 (the Chiang Mai-Lamphun Rd). Apparently this was the earliest historical settlement in the Chiang Mai area, established by the Mon in the 11th or 12th century (well before King Mengrai's reign, though the city's founding is often mistakenly attributed to Mengrai) as a satellite town for the Hariphunchai kingdom. The walled city was abandoned in the early 18th century due to

massive flooding, and visible architectural remains are few – only the Mon-style chedi of Wat Chedi Si Liam and the layered brick pediments and stupa of Wat Kan Thom (the Mon name; in Thai the temple was known as Wat Chang Kham) are left.

Altogether over 1300 inscribed stone slabs, bricks, bells and stupas have been excavated at the site – all are currently undergoing translation at Chiang Mai University. So far, the most important archaeological discovery has been a four-piece inscribed stone slab now on display in the Chiang Mai National Museum. These early 11th century inscriptions indicate that the Thai script actually predates King Ramkhamhaeng's famous Sukhothai inscription (introduced in 1293) by 100 or more years.

The stones display writing in three scripts of varying ages; the earliest is Mon, the latest is classical Sukhothai script, while the middle-period inscription is proto-Thai. Historical linguists studying the slabs now say that the Thai script was developed from Mon models, later to be modified by adding Khmer characteristics. This means Ramkhamhaeng was not the 'inventor' of the script as previously thought, but more of a would-be reformer. His reformations appear on only one slab and weren't accepted by contemporaries – his script in fact died with him.

An ideal way of getting to Wiang Kum Kam is to hire a bicycle; follow the Chiang Mai-Lamphun Rd south about three km and look for a sign to the ruins on the right. From this junction it's another two km to the ruins. You could also hire a tuk-tuk to take you there for 30 or 40B (one way). Once you're finished looking around you can walk back to the Chiang Mai-Lamphun Rd and catch a No 2 city bus back into the city.

## Other Temples, Shrines & Mosques

Temple freaks looking for more wat energy can check out **Wat Pheuak Hong**, behind Buak Hat Park off Samlan Rd. The locally revered **Chedi Si Pheuak** is over 100 years old and features the 'stacked spheres' style seen only here and at Wat Kuu Tao. Another unique local temple is the Burmese-built **Wat Chiang Yuen** on the north side of the moat (across Mani Nopharat Rd), between Chang Pheuak Gate and the north-eastern corner of the old city. Besides the large Northern-style chedi here, the main attraction is an old Burmese colonial gate and pavilion on the east side of the school grounds attached to the wat. It looks like it dropped out of the sky from Yangon or Mandalay.

Three wats along Tha Phae Rd, **Jetawan, Mahawan** and **Bupharam**, feature highly ornate wihãans and chedis designed by Shan or Burmese artisans; most likely they were originally financed by Burmese teak merchants who immigrated to Chiang Mai 100 years ago or more. Evidence of Burmese influence is easily seen in the abundant peacock symbol (a solar symbol common in Burmese and Shan temple architecture) and the Mandalay-style standing Buddhas found in wall niches. At Wat Mahawan no two guardian deity sculptures are alike; the whimsical forms include monkeys or dogs playing with lions and various mythical creatures.

**Wat Lokmoli**, hidden away on an abandoned lot near Cathay Square shopping centre, was built in 1541 to commemorate the death of local prince Phra Meuang Ket Klao. The large main chedi, restored by the Fine Arts Department in 1959, is a very large brick tower in stepped, geometric Lanna style – like a smaller version of Chedi Luang except that the superstructure on this one is intact. The Buddha niches are now empty, but there's some final stucco ornamentation remaining. **Wat Chai Kiat**, on Ratchaamnoen Rd east of Wat Phra Singh, contains a huge bronze Buddha cast by order of a Burmese military commander in 1565.

Of the 12 mosques in Chiang Mai, the oldest and most interesting is **Matsayit Chiang Mai** (Chiang Mai Mosque, sometimes called 'Ban Haw Mosque') on Charoen Prathet Soi 1, between Chang Khlan and Charoen Prathet Rds, not far from the Night Bazaar. Founded by *jiin haw* or Yunnanese Muslims over a hundred years ago, it still primarily caters to this unique ethnic group; you'll hear Yunnanese almost as often as Thai within the compound. Along this *soi* (lane) are several Yunnanese Muslim restaurants.

The most colourful of Chiang Mai's two Hindu temples is the brightly painted, traditional mandir and sikhara **Devi Mandir Chiang Mai** on Ratanakosin Rd, opposite Chiang Mai Stadium. At **Siri Guru Singh Sabha**, a Sikh temple at 134 Charoenrat Rd (behind Wat Kat Gate), free *prasada* (blessed vegetarian food) is distributed to templegoers on Friday mornings.

### Chiang Mai National Museum
พิพิธภัณฑ์แห่งชาติ

The museum has a good selection of Buddha images in all styles on display, including a very large bronze Buddha downstairs. Pottery is also displayed downstairs (note the 'failed' jar on the stairs), while upstairs there are household and work items. Look for the amusing wooden 'dog' used for spinning thread.

The museum is open Wednesday to Sunday from 9 am to 4 pm. Admission is 10B. The museum is close to Wat Jet Yot on Highway 11 which curves around the city; city bus No 6 stops nearby.

### Chiang Mai Central Prison
คุกเชียงใหม่

Near the centre of town, off Ratwithi Rd, this is where dozens of farangs have been incarcerated on drug charges. Chiang Mai is notorious for samlor and tuk-tuk drivers who sell dope and then inform the police about their customers. Fines for even the smallest amounts of ganja are very high – 50,000B for a couple of grams is not unusual. Those who cannot afford to buy out of this dangerous game go to jail.

### Night Bazaar

An extensive night market sprawls over the area between Loi Khraw, Tha Phae and Chang Klan Rds. This market is made up of several different roofed concession areas and

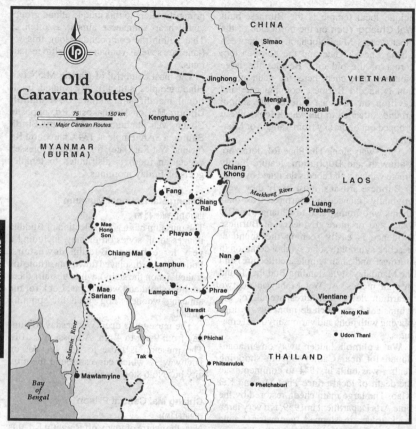

**Old Caravan Routes**

0    75    150 km

···· Major Caravan Routes

CHINA

Simao

VIETNAM

Jinghong

Mengla

Phongsali

Kengtung

MYANMAR
(BURMA)

Chiang
Khong

LAOS

Fang

Chiang
Rai

Maekhong River

Luang
Prabang

Mae
Hong
Son

Phayao

Chiang Mai

Lamphun

Nan

Lampang

Mae
Sariang

Phrae

Vientiane

Nong Khai

Utaradit

Udon Thani

Phichai

Salawin River

Tak

Phitsanulok

THAILAND

Mawlamyine

Bay
of
Bengal

Phetchaburi

dozens of street vendors displaying a variety of Thai and Northern Thai goods, as well as designer goods (both fake and licensed, look carefully) at very low prices – if you bargain well. Actually, many importers buy here because the prices are so good, especially when buying in quantity. The Night Bazaar is in fact the legacy of the original Yunnanese trading caravans that stopped over here along the ancient trade route between Simao (China) and Mawlamyine (on Myanmar's Gulf of Martaban coast). Most items sold here are made in Thailand but you'll also see goods from India, Nepal and China.

Good buys include Phrae-style *sêua mâw hâwm* (farmers' shirts), Northern and North-Eastern handwoven fabrics, *yâams* (shoulder bags), hill-tribe crafts (many tribespeople set up their own concessions here), opium scales, hats, silver jewellery, lacquerware and many other items.

If you're in need of new travelling clothes, this is a good place to look. A light cotton dress, trousers or yâams can be bought for less than 100B, and work shirts cost between 50 and 80B, depending on size.

You must bargain patiently but mercilessly. The fact that there are so many different

NORTHERN THAILAND

## Caravans of Northern Thailand

Dating from at least the 15th century, Chinese-Muslim caravans from Yunnan Province used Chiang Mai as a 'back door' entry and exit for commodities transported between China and the port of Mawlamyine in Myanmar for international seagoing trade. British merchant Ralph Fitch, the first to leave an English-language chronicle of South-East Asian travel, wrote of his 1583 to 1591 journey through Thailand: 'To the town of Jamahey (Chiang Mai) come many merchants out of China, and bring a great store of Muske, Gold, Silver, and many other things of China worke'.

The main means of transport for the Yunnanese caravaneers were mules and ponies, beasts of burden which contrasted with the South-East Asian preference for oxen, water buffalo and elephants. The Chinese Muslims who dominated the caravan traffic owed their preferred mode of conveyance, as well as their religious orientation, to mass conversions effected during the Mongol invasions of Yunnan in the 13th century. The equestrian nature of the caravans led the Thais to call the Yunnanese *jiin haw* or 'galloping Chinese'.

Three main routes emanated from the predominantly Thai Sipsongpanna region in southern Yunnan into Northern Thailand, and onward to the Gulf of Martaban via Mawlamyine. The western route proceeded south-west from Simao to Chiang Rung (now known as Jinghong), then on through Chiang Tung (Kengtung) to Fang or Chiang Rai. The middle route went south to Mengla near the Chinese-Lao border, crossed Laos via Luang Nam Tha, and entered what is today Thailand at Chiang Khong (at the time an independent principality) on the Maekhong River. At this point the middle route merged with the western route at Chiang Rai, and formed a single route through Chiang Mai to Mae Sariang, a line that continued along the Salawin River to Mawlamyine. The third route went from Simao to Phongsali in northern Laos then through Luang Prabang, crossing the Maekhong to Meuang Nan and Meuang Phrae (now Nan and Phrae provinces) before curving north-westward to Chiang Mai.

Principal southward exports along these routes included silk, opium, tea, dried fruit, lacquerware, musk, ponies and mules, while northward the caravans brought gold, copper, cotton, edible bird's nests, betelnut, tobacco and ivory. By the end of the 19th century many artisans from China, northern Burma and Laos had settled in the area to produce crafts for the steady regional trade. The city's original transhipment point for such trade movements was a market district known as Ban Haw, a stone's throw from today's Night Bazaar in Chiang Mai. ■

concessions selling the same items means that competition effectively keeps prices low, if you haggle. Look over the whole bazaar before you begin buying. If you're not in the mood or don't have the money to buy, it's still worth a stroll, unless you don't like crowds – most nights it's elbow to elbow. Several restaurants and many food trolleys feed the hungry masses.

### Tribal Research Institute
ศูนย์ศึกษาชาวเขา

This research institute (☎ 221933) is on Chiang Mai University campus, five km west of the city. A No 1 bus goes by the university. The institute features a small hill-tribes museum, and literature on hill tribes is available. It's open Monday to Friday from 8.30 am to 4.30 pm.

### Other Attractions
The **Old Chiang Mai Cultural Centre** (☎ 275-097) on Route 108 south of town is a tourist centre where Northern Thai and hill-tribe dances are performed nightly from 7 to 10 pm. Performances include a *khan tòk* dinner (Northern-style food eaten from small round tables) and cost 250B per person. It's a touristy affair but done well.

**Three Kings Monument** (Anusaowali Saam Kasat) on Phra Pokklao Rd towards the THAI office, is a set of three bronze sculptures depicting Phaya Ngam Meuang, Phaya Mantra and Phaya Ruing Haw Hun Ramkhamhaeng, the three Northern Thai-Lao kings most associated with early Chiang Mai history.

**Buak Hat Park**, in the south-western corner of the moat, is Chiang Mai's miniature counterpart to Bangkok's Lumphini Park, with very pleasant grass expanses, fountains and palms; many people jog here. The **Chiang Mai University** campus is another

NORTHERN THAILAND

quiet place to wander around. It's also interesting in the evenings, with a busy night bazaar of its own.

Out towards Doi Suthep, six km from the town centre, are the shady, nicely landscaped, hilly **Chiang Mai Zoo** (take city bus No 3) and the nearby **Chiang Mai Arboretum**. Zoo admission is 10B adults, 5B children; you can drive a vehicle through the zoo grounds for 40B per car or truck, 5B for a motorcycle or bicycle. Except for the name of each species, most signs are in Thai only; reportedly over 5000 birds (150 species) fly about the zoo's Nakhon Ping Birdwatching Park. A few snack vendors scattered around the park offer simple rice and noodle dishes. It's open daily 9 am to 5.30 pm. The quiet, lush arboretum is a favourite local jogging spot.

Along the same road nearby are the **Huay Kaew Fitness Park** and **Huay Kaew Falls**.

## Thai Massage Study

Over the years Chiang Mai has become a centre for Thai massage studies. Not all the places purporting to teach massage are equally good. The oldest and most popular place to study is the Old Medicine Hospital (OMH; ☎ 275085) on Soi Siwaka Komarat off Wualai Rd, opposite the Old Chiang Mai Cultural Centre. The 11 day course runs daily from 9 am to 4 pm and costs around 2500B, including all teaching materials. There are two courses per month year-round, except for the first two weeks of April. The OMH curriculum is very traditional, with a Northern Thai slant (the Thai name for the institute actually means Northern Traditional Healing Hospital). Classes tend to be large during the months of December to February. You can also receive a 1½ hour massage here (a requisite for admission to the course) for 160B.

Chaiyuth Priyasith's School of Thai Remedial Massage (no phone), at 52 Soi 3 Tha Phae Rd, offers a course similar to OMH's; Chaiyuth, in fact, taught at OMH for many years and is said to have taught most of the massage instructors working today in Chiang Mai. He charges 200B per hour for both massage and instruction.

International Training Massage (☎ 218632) at 171/7 Morakot Rd in Santitham features another OMH-inspired curriculum with a five day, 1500B course. Founder Chongkol Setthakorn was head teacher at OMH for several years.

A unique, one-on-one course is available at Baan Nit, Soi 2, Chaiyaphum Rd. The teacher is Nit, an older woman who is a specialist in deep-tissue, nerve and herbal massages. Her methods were handed down to her from a long line of ancestral Chinese healers. Length of study and payment for Nit tutelage is up to the individual – according to what you can afford – but all studies begin with an offering of nine flowers to nine Chinese deities. Nit doesn't speak English so you must know some Thai, though much of the teaching is unspoken. Most students live in and eat meals with Nit and her family while studying. If you want to try Nit's massage talents, you have to pay a minimum of 9B to the same deities; most massagees pay 100B an hour.

The rePlace (☎ 248838) at 1 Chetuphon Rd (next to Wat Chetuphon) offers a more modern course based on traditional methods taught by a Thai-Swiss couple. A variety of study packages is available, starting at 1350B for a five day workshop to 2500B for a 10 day workshop.

Sunshine House at 24 Soi 4, Kaew Nawarat Rd, offers a unique all-in-one course that combines yoga, vipassana and Thai massage under the tutelage of a German who calls himself Asokananda.

## Thai Language Study

The basic Thai course at AUA (☎ 278407, 211377), 24 Ratchadamnoen Rd, consists of 60 hours of instruction at three levels; there are also 30 hour classes in 'small talk', reading and writing. Costs range from 2500B for the conversation course to 3300B per level for the 60 hour courses. Private tutoring is also available at 200B per hour.

The Australia Centre (☎ 894547; fax 894549), 7th floor, Kad Suan Kaew, has recently established a new Thai-language programme; rates hadn't yet been set as we went to press.

## Raja Yoga

Brahma Kumari's Raja Yoga (☎ 214904) has a centre at 218/6 Chotana Rd in northern Chiang Mai. Raja Yoga (kingly yoga, or Hindu meditation) teaches a seven-step course involving the topics of self, god, karma, cycles, lifestyles and powers. Founded in northern India earlier this century, it's basically a simplified adaptation of Upanishad-inspired Hinduism. 'Creative meditation', held every Wednesday evening, mixes group therapy, visualisation, inquiry and other non-contemplative activities.

## Cooking Classes

The Chiang Mai Thai Cookery School (☎ 206388, 490456), at 1-3 Moon Meuang Rd opposite Tha Phae Gate, offers one, two and three day courses in Thai cooking starting at 700B. The classes come highly recommended and include an introduction to Thai herbs and spices, a local market tour, cooking instructions and a recipe booklet. Of course you get to eat the delicious Thai food as well, everything from Chiang Mai-style chicken curry to steamed banana cake.

Raintree Community Services (☎ 306317) sponsors a two hour cooking class on Saturday mornings; call for information or to register (required at least three days in advance).

## Informal Northern Thai Group

The 12 year old INTG meets every second Tuesday of the month at 7.30 pm at the Alliance Française, 138 Charoen Prathet Rd. The usual evening format involves a lecture from a resident or visiting academic on some aspect of Thailand or South-East Asia, followed by questions and answers and an informal drink afterwards at a local bar or restaurant. Admission is 20B.

## Muay Thai

Lanna Muay Thai (☎ /fax 273133), at 64/1 Soi Chiang Khian, off Huay Kaew Rd, is a boxing camp that offers kickboxing instruction to foreigners as well as Thais. For non-resident boxers, training is held from 4 to 8 pm daily, while resident trainees also have morning sessions. Rates run 100B a day or 2500B a month; simple camp accommodation is available for 50B per day or 1200B per month. According to the camp management, 'Foreign boxers are much sought after and we offer match-ups with local boxers for all levels of competition'.

## Swimming

Landlocked Chiang Mai can get very hot, particularly from March to July. Fortunately, local opportunities for a refreshing swim – providing an alternative to the usual tourist solution (vegetating in refrigerated rooms most of the day) – are many.

**City Pools** Chiang Mai has several swimming pools for public use; you can pay on a per-day basis, or buy an annual membership. Typical per-use fees range from 5 to 40B (public pools are cheaper than hotel or private pools), while annual memberships start at around 200 to 300B.

Amari Rincome Hotel – Huay Kaew Rd at Nimanhaemin Rd (☎ 221044); 10 am to 6.30 pm
Chiang Mai University – Faculty of Education, Huay Kaew Rd (☎ 221699, ext 3050); 9 to 10.45 am and 1 to 5.45 pm, closed Mondays
Padungsilpa Sports Club – Padungsilpa School, Rat Uthit Rd (☎ 241254); 8.30 am to 8.30 pm
Physical Education College – Chiang Mai Stadium, Sanam Kila Rd (☎ 213629); 5 am to 7 pm weekdays, 9 am to 5 pm weekends
Pongpat Swimming Pool – 73/2 Chotana Rd (☎ 212812); 9 am to 7 pm
Sara Health Club – 109 Bunreuangrit Rd (☎ 244371); 8 am to 6 pm
Suandok Hospital – Faculty of Medicine, Suthep Rd (☎ 221699); 9 am to 8 pm (closed Thursday)
Top North Guest House – 15 Soi 2, Moon Meuang Rd (☎ 278900); 9 am to 8 pm

**Huay Teung Tao Reservoir** This sizeable lake about 12 km north-west of the city is a great place for an all-day swim and picnic, especially during the hotter months. Windsurfing equipment can be rented for around 100B an hour. By car or motorcycle you can get there by driving 10 km north on Route 107 (follow signs towards Mae Rim), then west two km past an army camp to the reservoir.

On public transport, you could take a city bus No 2 until it terminates at the army camp, then walk to the reservoir.

Cyclists would do best to pedal to the reservoir via the canal road (Jon Phra Than). Head west on Huay Kaew Rd, then turn right on an unmarked road just past the Chiang Mai Home for Boys just before the canal. Follow the canal road until it ends at the unpaved road between the reservoir and the highway; turn left here and you'll reach the lake after another km or so of pedalling. From the north-west corner of the moat, the bike ride takes about an hour.

If you don't bring your own, food is available from vendors at the lake, who spread mats out for people to sit on. Fishing is permitted if you'd like to try your luck at hooking lunch.

### Tennis

Anantasiri Tennis Courts, off the expressway and opposite the National Museum, is the best public tennis facility in Chiang Mai. The eight courts are illuminated at night, and you can hire a 'knocker' (tennis opponent) for a reasonable hourly fee in addition to the regular court fee. Other places with public tennis courts include:

Gymkhana Club – Rat Uthit Rd (☎ 241035)
Lanna Sports Club – Chotana Rd (☎ 221911)
SL Courts – opposite the National Museum

There are also public courts at the Amari Rincome Hotel and Padungsilpa Sports Club, listed under Swimming Pools.

### Jogging

Top spots for joggers are Buak Hat Park, the Chiang Mai Arboretum and the fitness park at Maharaj Hospital. Tracks are available at Chiang Mai Stadium and at Chiang Mai University.

**Hash House Harriers** The Chiang Mai Harriers meet weekly at the Hash House Pub on Soi 6, Charoen Prathet Rd, and organise a 'hash' (foot race) every Saturday at various locations in the Chiang Mai area. Afterwards

all the calories burned in the race are reinstated through copious beer consumption.

### Boat Cruise

At a small pier on the Ping River behind Wat Chaimongkhon, you can rent a roofed boat to tour the river for around 200B an hour. If you get a small group of people together it's not expensive as the boats can take up to 15 people. For an extra fee, meals can be arranged.

### Places to Stay – bottom end

At any one time there are about 300 hotels and guesthouses operating in Chiang Mai. Hotels range from 40B for a dorm room at Banana Guest House to 3750B for a double room at the Westin Chiangmai, with an average room costing from 200 to 400B per night. Guesthouses range from 40B per person for a dorm bed to 300B for a room. At the cheaper hotels, 'single' means a room with one large bed (big enough for two) while 'double' means a room with two beds; the number of people staying in the room is irrelevant.

**Hotels** In Chiang Mai's small Chinatown, the basic *Sri Ratchawongse* (☎ 235864) at 103 Ratchawong Rd, between the east moat and the Ping River, has singles/doubles with fan and bath for 120/180B. Nearby at 94-98 Ratchawong Rd is the nicer *New Mitrapap* (☎ 235436), where rooms are 130 to 200B. Both hotels are close to several good, inexpensive Chinese restaurants, as well as the Warorot Market.

*Sri Santitham* (☎ 221585) at 15 Soi 4 Chotana Rd, near Chang Pheuak (White Elephant) bus station, has singles with fan and bath from 130B, or from 200B with air-con. A better alternative in this area is *Chiang Mai Phu Viang Hotel* (☎ 221632/532) at 5-9 Soi 4, Chotana Rd. Clean, spacious rooms are 200B with fan and bath, up to 500B with air-con.

The funky, old Thai-style *Muang Thong* (☎ 278438) at 5 Ratchamankha Rd, a good location inside the city moats, has singles with fan and bath from just 100B, and

**Rip-Offs**

Upon arrival in Chiang Mai – whether by bus, plane or train – you'll quite likely be crowded by touts trying to get you to a particular hotel or guesthouse. As elsewhere in Thailand, the touts get a commission for every prospective guest they bring to a guesthouse or hotel. Commissions run as high as 150B per head; call guesthouses from the bus or train station and they will be delighted to give you a ride to avoid paying such exorbitant commissions.

At the train station, ignore the official-looking table with uniformed attendants who will try to funnel you into hotels and guesthouses paying commissions – they'll say that anything not on their list is either full, dirty, or closed.

Another scam to be aware of is the bus or minivan services from Khao San Rd in Bangkok, which often advertise a free night's accommodation in Chiang Mai if you buy a Bangkok-Chiang Mai ticket. What usually happens on arrival is that the 'free' guesthouse demands you sign up for one of the hill treks immediately; if you don't, the guesthouse is suddenly 'full'. Sometimes they levy a charge for electricity or hot water. The better guesthouses don't play this game.

The old gem scam has also reached Chiang Mai. The same modus operandi used in Bangkok is employed here: a well-dressed Thai man strikes up a seemingly harmless conversation that ends with you buying worthless sapphires at inflated prices in a local gem shop. ■

doubles for 150 to 170B. Near the train station at 46 Sathani Rotfai Rd, the *Settakit Hotel* (☎ 242765) has simple rooms for 120 to 250B.

*Miami* (☎ 235240), another reasonable hotel at 119 Chaisiphum Rd, has singles/doubles for 150 to 220B, and *Nakhorn Ping* (☎ 236024), a long-time favourite at 43 Taiwang Rd, offers similar but cheaper accommodation from 120B per room.

*Roong Ruang Hotel* (☎ 232017/8), also spelt 'Roong Raeng', is situated in a prime location at 398 Tha Phae Rd, near Tha Phae Gate, on the eastern side of the city moat. The service is good and the rooms, which face an inner courtyard and are therefore quiet, have been renovated with the addition of pleasant sitting areas. Singles/doubles with fan and bath are 270B; with air-con and hot shower they are 370B. The Roong Ruang also has some larger rooms with fan or air-con for a slightly higher cost. This is a good place to stay for the Flower Festival in early February as the Saturday parade passes right by the entrance. Another entrance is on Chang Moi Kao Rd.

*YMCA International Hotel* (☎ 221819, 222366; fax 215523) is at 2/4 Mengrairasmi Rd, above the north-west corner of the moat. Singles/doubles in the old wing with fan and shared bath are 140/200B, 220B with fan and

private bath or 250/350B with air-con. Dorm beds in the old wing are 75B. In the fully air-con new wing, singles/doubles with private bath, telephone and TV are 530/630B. Facilities include a travel agency, handicraft centre and cafeteria.

The *Montri Hotel* (☎ 211069/70), on the corner of Moon Meuang and Ratchadamnoen Rds, has overpriced singles with fan and bath for 350B, 500B with air-con. The fan rooms are especially poor value, as they're bombarded by noise from Moon Meuang Rd which reflects off Tha Phae wall.

*Nice Apartment* (☎ 218290), behind the Montri Hotel, at 15 Soi 1, Ratchadamnoen Rd, has clean, simple rooms with private bath for 150 to 200B single/double depending on the room; monthly rates of around 2500B are also available. On Soi 7 off Moon Meuang Rd are a couple of other good apartment-style places, *SP Hotel* and *CM Apartment*, each with rooms in the 200 to 300B range, with monthly rates of 2500 to 3000B. *Veerachai Court* (☎ 251047; fax 252402), on Soi Tha Phae 2, features a nine-storey building on the east side of the soi, and a four-storey one on the west side. Clean, quiet if smallish rooms with air-con and hot water showers cost 350B a night here, with monthly rates of 3500B.

NORTHERN THAILAND

**Guesthouses** Guesthouses are clustered in several areas: along Charoenrat Rd east of the Ping River, which is far from the centre of the city but near buses to Chiang Rai, Lamphun and the train station; along Moon Meuang Rd (the inside of the east moat) and on streets off Moon Meuang Rd; along several sois running south off Tha Phae Rd; and along Charoen Prathet Rd, parallel to Charoenrat but west of the Ping River. Several others are scattered elsewhere around the western side of Chiang Mai.

Guesthouses come and go with frequency in Chiang Mai. The best are owned and managed by local families. The worst are those opened by Bangkok Thais who fiddle with your stored belongings while you're off on a trek. There are basically two kinds of budget guesthouse accommodation – old family homes converted into guest rooms (these usually have the best atmosphere though the least privacy) and hotel or apartment-style places with rows of cell-like rooms. In both the furnishings are basic – a bed and few sticks of furniture. Usually you must supply your own towel and soap; the rooms are cleaned only after guests leave. You can assume that rooms under 100B will not have a private bath but will probably have a fan.

The cheaper guesthouses make most of their money from food service and hill-tribe trekking rather than from room charges. Many of the guesthouses can arrange bicycle and motorcycle rental. If you phone a guesthouse, most will collect you from the train or bus station for free if they have a room (this saves them having to pay a commission to a driver).

The following list is not exhaustive but covers most of the more reliable, long-running places. Guesthouses which belong to the Chiangmai Northern Guest House Club (☎ 217513) are probably more secure in terms of theft than those which are not. As members pay government taxes, they are generally more interested in long-term operation. Members also meet regularly to discuss tourism issues, accommodation standards and room rates. The TAT office on the Chiang Mai-Lamphun Rd can provide an up-to-date list of members, which at last count was limited to 45.

*Warning* Lonely Planet has received many letters from travellers who have left their valuables in a guesthouse safe while they were trekking. Unfortunately, upon their return, they discovered that their property had been removed from the safe and that items such as travellers' cheques, Swiss army pocket knives and sunglasses were missing. One Australian traveller discovered that A$2500 had been spent on her MasterCard which had been left in a safe while she had been trekking. An Irish couple had £6000 worth of goods charged to their credit cards in Bangkok while they were on a three day trek! If you leave your valuables in a safe, make sure you obtain a fully itemised receipt before departing on a trek.

*Inner Moat Area Banana Guest House* (☎ 206285), at 4/9 Ratchapakhinai Rd (near Chiang Mai Gate), is a small place with dorm beds for just 40B, plus single rooms with shared facilities for 60B and doubles with private bath for 120B. *Nat Guest House* (☎ 212878), at 7 Soi 6, Phra Pokklao Rd, is a comfortable, long-established place with 24 rooms for 100/150B. *Pha Thai* (☎ 278-013), at 48/1 Ratchphakhinai Rd in the south-east of the inner moat area, has clean rooms in a modest three-storey building with private solar-heated showers for 100 to 150B a night.

*Manit's Guest House* (☎ 213771) is a one-person show at 81/1 Arak near Suan Dawk Gate, in a large off-the-street house inside the city moat. Large rooms with fan and bath cost 100B in the low season, 150B in the high. Manit handles every aspect of this business himself. *Visaj Guest House* (☎ 214016), a new place at 104 Ratchadamnoen Rd, near Wat Phra Singh, shows promise. Rooms with private shower and toilet cost 90B single/double, or 120B including breakfast; the guesthouse rooftop affords an interesting view of Wat Phra Singh.

The friendly *Chiangmai Garden Guest*

*House* (☎ 210881) at 82-86 Ratchamankha Rd, formerly Racha Guest House, has clean rooms and good food. Singles/doubles cost 100/120B with fan and bath, 250B single/ double with air-con.

Near the Library Service off Soi 2 Moon Meuang Rd, the *New Saitum* (☎ 211575) offers separate, clean bungalows with private bath and balconies in a garden setting for a bargain 80 to 90B. Almost opposite on the same soi, *Somwang Guest House* (☎ 278505) features rooms in an older buildings for 60B with shared hot shower, 80B with private bath, plus rooms in a newer two-storey building for 150B with private hot shower.

There are plenty of other guesthouses inside the old city, especially down the little side lanes off Moon Meuang Rd. Soi 9, off Moon Meuang near the north-east corner of the moat, is a particularly good area to look if you're having trouble finding a vacant room during festivals such as Songkran and the Flower Festival. Several tacky, newer buildings here contain cheap guesthouses. On this soi the clean and friendly *Libra* (☎ 210687) has decent rooms for 80/100B single/double; *SK House* is also pretty good. Turn right off Soi 9 onto Soi 1, Sriphum Rd to reach the smaller *Money Guest House*. Directly opposite is a vegetarian restaurant, then off the roadside a bit on your right you'll see *Tanya Guest House* (☎ 210675), which offers rooms in an old wooden house for 40B per dorm bed, 120B per room. Others on or off Soi 9 Moon Muang Rd include *Supreme House, SUP Court, PT* and *Peter*, all very similar with 80 to 100B rooms with shared bath, 150 to 180B with private bath.

Parallel Soi 7 has the similar apartment-style *Northland House, CM Apartments* and *SP Hotel* along with the more atmospheric *Sawatdee House* and *Lam Chang*; the latter two offer a wide range of rooms from 80B single with fan to 250B for air-con.

On Soi 5 off Moon Muang, *Rama House* has clean rooms with private facilities in a secure three-storey building for 150/200B single/double.

Bridging the gap between bottom-end and middle-range places are a couple of comfort-able guesthouses in the 175 to 400B range. *Gap House* (☎ /fax 278140) on Soi 4 Ratcha-damnoen (behind the AUA Thai Language Centre) has Northern Thai-style houses built around a quiet garden. All rooms have carpet, air-con and private hot showers; rates are 175/350B for singles/doubles and include a filling breakfast.

On the other side of Ratchadamnoen at Soi 5, *Rendezvous Guest House* (☎ 213763) is a stylish inn costing 100B for a single with fan, 120 to 150B in a twin room with fan or 280B for an air-con room; add 30B to all rates for hot water service. Facilities include a video bar. Farther north along the same soi as Rendezvous are a short string of three and four-storey apartment-style places: *Kavil House* (120 to 150B a night), *Amphawan House* (120B up) and *Kristi House* (180 to 250B). The main advantage to these three is their quiet location.

The hotel-style *Moon Muang Golden Court* (☎ 212779), off Moon Meuang Rd north of Tha Phae Gate, features clean doubles with fan and hot shower for 150B, air-con for 280B.

See under Chang Pheuak Gate Area later in this section for places just inside the moat at the northern end of the old city.

*Chiang Mai Youth Hostel* (☎ 272169) at 63A Bamrungburi Rd behind Chiang Mai Gate has single rooms with shared facilities for 80B, doubles with fan and bath for 120B. A Hostelling International membership is required to stay here; a temporary member-ship valid for one night costs 50B.

*Top North Guest House* (☎ 278900), at 15 Soi 2, Moon Meuang Rd, is a popular, effi-ciently run place where rooms cost 300B with fan, 400B with air-con, 500B with TV and bathtub; all rooms come with private hot shower. Facilities include a pretty swimming pool. Also on this soi are the inexpensive *Jame House, Toy House, Welcome House, Thailand Guest House, North Star House* and *Kritsada*, all in the 150 to 300B range.

Just inside the northern moat on Si Phum Rd, opposite Chang Pheuak Gate, the friendly *Mountain View Guest House* (☎ 212866) has large rooms and hot showers.

NORTHERN THAILAND

NORTHERN THAILAND

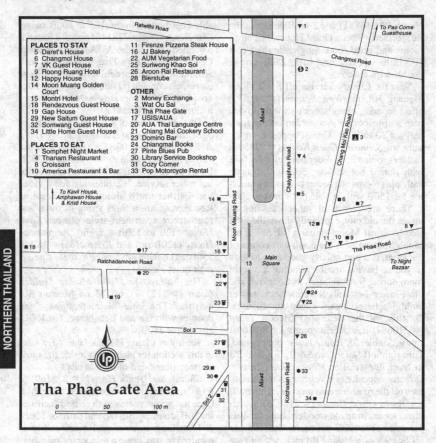

**PLACES TO STAY**
5 Daret's House
6 Changmoi House
7 VK Guest House
9 Roong Ruang Hotel
12 Happy House
14 Moon Muang Golden
   Court
15 Montri Hotel
18 Rendezvous Guest House
19 Gap House
29 New Saitum Guest House
32 Somwang Guest House
34 Little Home Guest House

**PLACES TO EAT**
1 Somphet Night Market
4 Thanam Restaurant
8 Croissant
10 America Restaurant & Bar

11 Firenze Pizzeria Steak House
16 JJ Bakery
22 AUM Vegetarian Food
25 Suriwong Khao Soi
26 Aroon Rai Restaurant
28 Bierstube

**OTHER**
2 Money Exchange
3 Wat Ou Sai
13 Tha Phae Gate
17 USIS/AUA
20 AUA Thai Language Centre
21 Chiang Mai Cookery School
23 Domino Bar
24 Chiangmai Books
27 Pinte Blues Pub
30 Library Service Bookshop
31 Cozy Corner
33 Pop Motorcycle Rental

**Tha Phae Gate Area**

A dorm bed is 50B, rooms with fan and bath are 150 to 250B, and air-con rooms 250 to 350B. Tables and chairs along the balconies add a nice touch.

***Tha Phae Gate Area*** *Changmoi House* (☎ 233184) on Chang Moi Kao Rd, a half block north of Tha Phae Rd, replaces an old favourite on this soi destroyed by fire in 1994. Simple, clean rooms in a narrow shop-house cost 50B for dorm bed, 60B single, 80 to 100B double, 120 to 150B triple, all with fan and hot shower except for the dorm. Down an alley off Chang Moi Kao Rd is the

basic but adequate *VK Guest House* with singles/doubles for 50/70B; a triple room with bath is available for 40B per person.

Another Chiang Mai original is *Lek House* at 22 Chaiyaphum Rd, near the Chang Moi Kao Rd intersection on the soi to Wat Chompu. It's quiet and has a pleasant garden, but I've had mixed reports about service. Rooms with fan and bath are 80/100B downstairs, 100/120B in the larger, newer rooms upstairs. Near Lek House is the equally pleasant standby *Pao Come* at 9 Chang Moi Kao Rd. Singles/doubles cost 50/70B.

A bit farther north on Soi 3 Chang Moi

Kao Rd is *Eagle House* (☎ 235387; fax 216368), which offers dorm beds for 30B or simple rooms with private bath for 80 to 100B a double, 70B a single. The multi-lingual staff boast French, German, English and Spanish-language skills. *Chiang Mai Inn* (☎ 251400), a three-storey place off Chaiyaphum Rd not far from Eagle House, offers clean, quiet fan rooms with hot bath for 150B, or with air-con for 250B.

In the other direction towards Tha Phae Rd is the hotel-like *Happy House* (☎ 234969) at 11 Chang Moi Kao Rd, towards Tha Phae Gate. Big rooms with hot shower range from 150B with fan, 200 to 250B with air-con.

The Daret Restaurant has moved from its original Moon Meuang Rd location and now operates another restaurant and a rather crowded guesthouse across the moat at 4/5 Chaiyaphum Rd, called *Daret's House*. Basic rooms cost 80 to 100B with a shared bath, 150B with private bath. The large sidewalk cafe in front serves cheap if somewhat uninspired food.

Soi 4, farther east (towards the river) along Tha Phae Rd, has several newer, two-storey brick guesthouses with downstairs sitting areas: *Midtown House, Tapae, Thana, Sarah, Flamingo* and *Baan Jongcome* (☎ 274823), each with good rooms in the 80 to 200B range.

*Fang Guest House* (☎ 282940, 272505) is nearby at 46-48 Soi 1 Kamphaeng Din Rd in a newer four-storey building well away from traffic. Clean rooms with fan and bath are 200B a single or double, 250B for triples, and 300B with air-con and carpet. All rooms have solar-heated hot showers; the system is very weak, however, and hot water is available in the afternoon only. Farther down this soi, right where it connects with Tha Phae Rd Soi 3, you'll find *Nice Place Inn* (☎ 272919), a newish multi-storey spot with small rooms with hot water, fridge, TV and fan for 400B, or with air-con 500B. Prices are inflated since it relies excessively on budget tour groups; the public areas are not very clean. Much better value is available just opposite at *Ratchada Guest House* (☎ 275556) on Tha Phae Rd Soi 3, where quiet rooms with

fan and shower cost 80 to 120B. Over on Soi 5, Tha Phae Rd, *Living House* (☎ 275370) has rooms in a newer building for 200 to 400B with private facilities.

Towards the middle range, *Little Home Guest House* (☎ 273662), a well run spot at 1/1 Soi 3, Kotchasan Rd, offers large, comfortable rooms in a modern Thai-style building for 270 to 300B per night or 250B a night for more than three days.

**East of the River** *C&C Teak House* (☎ 246-966), at 39 Bamrungrat Rd between the train station and the Ping River, has quiet, comfortable rooms in a 100 year old teak house for 50B single or 60/80B single/double with fan downstairs, 120B double with fan upstairs. Bathroom facilities are shared; the upstairs shower has hot water.

There are a string of guesthouses along Charoenrat Rd, paralleling the river – a bit far from the centre of town but recommended for those who are seeking a quiet atmosphere. The long-running *Je t'Aime* (☎ 241912), 247-9 Charoenrat Rd, has a variety of bungalow-style accommodation on landscaped grounds for 70 to 150B. *Cowboy Guest House* (☎ 241314), at 233 Charoenrat Rd just before Je t'Aime, is run by a Thai nicknamed Cowboy (with a son named Banjo and daughter named Guitar!) who speaks good English – he once ran a Thai restaurant in the Philippines. Bungalows at Cowboy are 100B with private bath, 60/80B with shared bath. On the same road is *Mee Guest House*, at No 193/1, where doubles with bath cost 60B, and *Pun Pun* (☎ 243362), at No 321, where fan rooms are 130B, upgraded air-con rooms 250B.

Farther north along Charoenrat (just about where it turns into Faham Rd) at No 365 is the Dutch-run *Hollanda Montri* (☎ 242450), with clean rooms and hot showers from 160 to 240B. The same family owns the Riverside Bar & Restaurant farther downriver.

*The rePlace* (☎ 248838) at 1 Chetuphon Rd (next to Wat Chetuphon) is a Thai/Swiss-run place in a Northern Thai-style compound. Rooms with fan and shared hot water bath range from 70 to 180B single, 230 to 250B double with private bath, or 280 to 350B for a private cottage. Many of the residents participate in the Thai massage workshops available here.

South of Nawarat Bridge at 4/11 Soi 2, Chiang Mai-Lamphun Rd, *Ben's Guest House* (☎ 244103) has quiet rooms in a garden setting for 150B a night. Although it's on the east side of the river, Ben's is within walking distance of the Night Bazaar.

***Chang Pheuak Gate Area*** Several guesthouses have sprung up north of the city walls, far from the Tha Phae action but near the Chang Pheuak bus station (for Chiang Dao, Fang and Tha Ton). *Camp of Troppo Guest House* (☎ 279360) at 83/2 Ling Kok Rd, off Chotana Rd, has a relaxed atmosphere and costs from 60 to 80B per room. Farther up Chotana Rd at No 129 is *Chawala Guest House* where rooms range between 120 and 220B with a fan and bath.

***Chang Khlan & Wualai Rds*** A nicer branch of the *Chiang Mai Youth Hostel* (☎ 277737; fax 279043) at 21/8 Chang Khlan Rd has single/double rooms for 120/150B with fan and bath; with air-con 250/300B.

South of the city at 92 Wualai Rd Soi 2 is the *Srisupan Guest House* (☎ 252811) which has fan-cooled and air-con rooms from 180 to 250B, including private hot shower.

### Places to Stay – middle
Some of the places in this price range really blur the line between 'hotel' and 'guesthouse', the difference often being in name only. The well managed *Galare Guest House* (☎ 273885; fax 279088), for example, at 7/1 Charoen Prathet Rd Soi 2, is fully air-con and has rooms from 300 to 500B. It's popular with repeat visitors for its Ping River location and proximity to both the Night Bazaar and post office. Another good one on the river is *The Riverfront* (☎ 275125), a large, old teak house at 43/3 Chang Khlan Rd with a very good Thai restaurant on the veranda. Rooms with fan and private bath cost 250 to 350B, air-con rooms are 400 to 650B.

Also good is the old standby *Anodard*

*Hotel* (☎ 270755) at 5 Ratchamankha Rd in the inner city area. Well kept rooms here cost 260B with fan, 360B air-con and there's a pool on the premises.

In this range you can expect daily room cleaning, the option of air-con (some places have rooms with fan also) and – in the hotels – TV and telephone. If anything marks a guesthouse, it's the absence of these latter appliances.

Because of a room glut since 1991, room rates for many top-end places have been lowered to the middle range; for example, you can sometimes get 1000B rooms for 500B. Other guesthouses and hotels in this range, with similar facilities, include:

*Baan Kaew* – 142 Charoen Prathet Rd (☎ 271606); 300 to 400B
*Chang Pheuak Hotel* – 133 Chotana Rd (☎ 221755); 350 to 500B
*Chatree Guest House* – 11/10 Suriyawong Rd (☎ 279085); 280 to 400B
*Chiang Come Hotel* – 7/35 Suthep Rd (☎ 222237); 300 to 800B
*Chiang Mai Phucome Hotel* – 21 Huay Kaew (☎ 211026); 505 to 750B
*Chiang Mai Travel Lodge* – 18 Kamphaeng Din Rd (☎ 271572); 335 to 500B
*Chomdoi House* – 33/3 Huay Kaew Rd (☎ 210111, 222749); 250 to 400B
*Diamond Riverside Hotel* – 33/10 Charoen Prathet Rd (☎ 270080; fax 273947); 749B
*Dragon House* – 2/1-2 Chang Khlan Rd (☎ 282305, 279172); 350 to 450B
*Grand Apartment* – 24/1 Ratchaphakhinai Rd (☎ 217291); 350 to 600B
*Iyara Hotel* – 126 Chotana Rd (☎ 222723); 390 to 690B
*Lai Thai Guest House* – 111/4 Kotchasan Rd (☎ 271725/534); 300 to 400B
*Lanna Thai Guest House* – 41/8 Soi 6, Loi Khraw Rd (☎ 282421, 275563); 280 to 380B
*New Asia Hotel* – 55 Ratchawong Rd (☎ 235288; fax 252427); 416 to 520B
*Northern Inn Hotel* – 234/12 Mani Nopharat Rd (☎ 210002; fax 215828); 668 to 860B
*Northern Palace* – 7/9 Huay Kaew Rd (☎ 221549); 250 to 700B
*Prince Hotel* – 3 Taiwang Rd (☎ 236396); from 700B
*The Providence* – 99/9 Huay Kaew Rd (☎ 221750, 222122); 530 to 781B
*Sri Tokyo Hotel* – 6 Bunreuangrit Rd (☎ 213899; fax 211102); 577B
*Taphae Place* – 2 Soi 3, Tha Phae Rd (☎ 270841); 700 to 800B

## Places to Stay – top end

Chiang Mai has plenty of more expensive hotels, several of which are along Huay Kaew Rd, towards Doi Suthep. In general, hotel rates for luxury hotels are lower in Chiang Mai than in Bangkok. Top properties at the moment are the *Holiday Inn Green Hills, Amari Rincome, Chiang Mai Orchid* and *Westin Chiangmai*.

Top-enders, all of which have air-con, TV, IDD telephone and swimming pool, include the following:

- *Amari Rincome Hotel* – 301 Huay Kaew Rd (☎ 221044; fax 221915); 154 rooms, 2000/2200B, plus 400B during peak season (20 December to 9 January)
- *Chiang Inn Hotel* – 100 Chang Khlan Rd (☎ 272070; fax 274299); 170 rooms, 1600 to 2100B
- *Chiang Mai Garden Hotel* – 330 Super Highway (Highway 11) (☎ 210240; fax 218650); 900 to 1400B
- *Chiang Mai Orchid* – 100 Huay Kaew Rd (☎ 222099; fax 221625); 267 rooms, from 2825B
- *Chiang Mai Plaza* – 92 Si Donchai Rd (☎ 252050; fax 272230); 444 rooms, from 2000B
- *Chiang Mai President* – 226 Wichayanon Rd (☎ 251025; fax 251032); 57 rooms, from 819B
- *Empress Hotel* – 199 Chang Khlan Rd (☎ 270240; fax 272467); 373 rooms, 1883 to 2236B
- *Felix City Inn* – 154 Ratchamankha Rd (☎ 270710; fax 270709); 124 rooms, 1400 to 1600B
- *Holiday Inn Green Hills* – 24 Chiang Mai-Lampang Rd (☎ 220100; fax 221602); 200 rooms, 2100 to 2500B
- *Mae Ping* – 153 Si Donchai Rd (☎ 270160; fax 270181); 374 rooms, from 1647B
- *Novotel Chiang Mai* – 183 Chang Pheuak Rd (☎ 225500; fax 410277); 163 rooms, 1800/2200B
- *Porn Ping Tower Hotel* – 46-48 Charoen Prathet Rd (☎ 270100; fax 270119); 325 rooms, from 1124B
- *Poy Luang Hotel* – 146 Super Highway (Highway 11) (☎ 242633; fax 242490); 227 rooms, 1340 to 2340B
- *Quality Chiang Mai Hills* – 18 Huay Kaew Rd (☎ 211101; fax 210035); 150 rooms, 1600 to 1900B
- *River View Lodge* – 25 Charoen Prathet Rd Soi 2 (☎ 271101; fax 279019); 36 rooms, 1170 to 1400B, with discounts May to August
- *Royal Princess* – 122 Chang Khlan Rd (☎ 281033; fax 281044); 198 rooms, from 2400B
- *Suriwong Zenith Hotel* – 110 Chang Khlan Rd (☎ 236789; fax 271604); 169 rooms, 1900 to 2100B
- *Westin Chiangmai* – 324/11 Chiang Mai-Lamphun Rd (☎ 275300; fax 275299); 526 rooms, from 3750B

**Out of Town** North of the city in the Mae Rim/Mae Sa area are a string of countryside plush resorts. Most offer free shuttle vans back and forth from the city. The *crème de la crème* of these, *The Regent Chiang Mai* (☎ 298181; fax 298190), features 64 vaulted pavilion suites (each around 75 sq m) plus two and three bedroom residences spread amidst 20 acres of landscaped gardens and rice terraces worked by water buffalo. On the premises are a health club, Thai herbal steam rooms, massage facilities, a pool, two illuminated tennis courts and a gym. Rates start at 5250B for a garden room.

*Chiangmai Sports Club* (☎ 298327; fax 297897), seven km from town on Mae Rim Rd, has 45 rooms and three two-storey luxury suites on 71 *rai* (one rai equals 1600 sq m). Living up to its name, the resort boasts air-con squash courts, a badminton hall, grass and hardcourt tennis, fitness centre, sauna, gym and pool; you have to pay extra for the badminton, squash and tennis facilities, while all else is free for guests. Room rates are 2400B for a single/double or 6500B for a suite, plus a 400B peak season surcharge on holidays.

About the same distance south of town, in Ban Kong Sai village on Soi 5/6 off Chiang Mai-Lamphun Rd, *Teak Villa* (☎/fax 321439) offers several rustic teak homes decorated with Thai textiles and antiques for 625B a night including breakfast.

## Places to Eat

Chiang Mai has the best variety of restaurants of any city in Thailand, apart from Bangkok. Most travellers seem to have better luck here than in Bangkok though, simply because it's so much easier to get around and experiment.

Chiang Mai's guesthouses serve a typical menu of western food along with a few pseudo-Thai dishes.

**Thai** One of Chiang Mai's most famous restaurants is the large, open-air *Aroon Rai*, across the moat on Kotchasan Rd near Tha Phae Gate. Aroon Rai specialises in Northern Thai dishes and has a huge menu; prices are

NORTHERN THAILAND

inexpensive to moderate. Look for Chiang Mai specialities like kaeng hang-leh, kaeng awm and kaeng khae. Despite the Thai word kaeng in these dish names, only the first is a curry by the usual definition, that is, made from a thick spicy paste; the latter two dishes are more like stews and rely on local roots and herbs for their distinctive, bitter-hot flavours.

The smaller and super-clean *Thanam Restaurant* on Chaiyaphum Rd, north from Tha Phae Gate, specialises in both Northern and Central Thai cuisine. Hallmark dishes include phàk náam phrík (fresh vegetables in chilli sauce), plaa dùk phàt phèt (spicy fried catfish), kaeng sôm (hot and sour vegetable ragout with shrimp), as well as local dishes like khâo soi (Burmese chicken curry soup with noodles) and khanŏm jiin náam ngiáw (Chinese noodles with spiced chicken curry). Thanam has a small English sign inside. It closes at about 8 pm, doesn't serve alcohol and won't serve people wearing beach clothes (such as tank tops).

The highly regarded *Si Phen* (no English sign), at 103 Inthawarorot Rd near Wat Phra Singh, specialises in both Northern and North-Eastern-style dishes. The kitchen prepares some of the best sôm-tam in the city, including a variation made with pomelo. The kài yâang-khâo nĭaw combo (grilled chicken and sticky rice) is also very good, as is the khâo sòi and khanŏm jiin (with either náam yaa or náam ngíaw) – always incredible. Si Phen is open 9 am to 5 pm only. Another great place for Northern Thai food is the popular *Heuan Phen*, east of the Felix City Inn at 112 Ratchamankha Rd. Among the house specialities here are Chiang Mai and jiin haw dishes such as khanŏm jiin náam ngíaw, khâo sòi, lâap khua, náam phrík num, kaeng hang-leh, kaeng awm, kaeng khae, and other aahăan phéun meuang. There's no English sign, but it's almost opposite a school.

A good place for Isaan (North-Eastern Thai) food is *Wira Laap Pet*, in the north-east corner of the old city on Si Phum Rd, inside the moat; it's cheap and open from noon to 9 pm. The house speciality here is lâap pèt

(duck salad). Just west of Wira Laap Pet is *Kai Yaang Isaan* (the roman script sign reads 'SP Chicken'), which specialises in tasty Isaan-style grilled chicken and is only open 4 to 9 pm.

If you tire of Northern and North-Eastern Thai cuisines or just want a little coconut in your curry, check out *Khrua Phuket Laikhram* (Classical Phuket Kitchen), a small family-run restaurant at 1/10 Suthep Rd near Chiang Mai University. It's worth hunting down for the delicious, cheap, yet large portions of authentic home-style Southern Thai cooking. If there are no seats downstairs, try the upstairs dining room. Specialities include yâwt phráo phàt phèt kûng (spicy stir-fried shrimp with coconut shoots), hèt hŭu nŭu phàt khài (eggs stir-fried with mouse-ear mushrooms) and yam phukèt laikhram (a delicious salad of cashew nuts and squid). The restaurant has daily specials, too.

The long-established *Si Donchai Phochana* on Si Donchai Rd near Suriwong Book Centre is famous for the kitchen's ability to prepare virtually any Thai or Chinese dish. It's usually open late.

If you happen to be in the vicinity of the YMCA, there are two small Santitham district places worth trying. *Sa-Nga Choeng Doi* on Charoensuk Rd, a five minute walk from the Y, has probably the best khâo mòk kài (Thai chicken biryani) and mátàbà (martabak) in town; it's only open from around 10 am to 2 pm. On the same street, *Noi Muu Bang* has excellent sôm-tam. Neither restaurant has a roman-script sign – just look for the appropriate dishes on the tables.

Chiang Mai University campus has a very good and inexpensive Thai restaurant called *Busaya*, open from 7 am to 9 pm daily.

On the small lane leading to DK Book House off Kotchasan Rd are two modest establishments serving regional cuisines: *Rot Awng* (North-Eastern Thai) and *Chai Pak Tai* (Southern Thai).

Several good splurge places for Thai food are found along the Ping River east of the city centre. *River Ping Palace* (☎ 274932) is set amidst a traditional teak-wood residence and gardens at 385/2 Charoen Prathet Rd. The menu is excellent and includes several Northern Thai dishes; dishes average around 80B. Another elegant eatery along the river on Charoenrat Rd is *The Gallery* (☎ 248601), a converted Chinese temple that's half art gallery, half restaurant; it's owned by Dutch painter Theo Meier's widow.

Over the years, the most consistent riverside place has been the *Riverside Bar & Restaurant* (☎ 243239), on Charoenrat Rd, 200m north of Nawarat Bridge. The food is almost always superb (try the kài bai hàw toei – chunks of chicken grilled in pandanus leaves). The atmosphere is convivial and there's good live music nightly. *The Riverfront (Tha Nam) Restaurant* (☎ 275125) on Chang Khlan Rd along the west bank of the Ping River is housed in an old Northern Thai-style building and is also quite good; a live Northern Thai folk ensemble performs in the evenings.

Although it's a little away from the town centre, *Baan Khun Yai* (☎ 246589), at 114 Muu 8, San Phii Seua Soi 1, does very good Chiang Mai cuisine and is open 11 am to 11 pm; if you telephone the restaurant, they will pick up groups of five or more. A local ensemble plays Northern Thai music alternating with a Thai and farang group that plays American folk/bluegrass. It's three km north of town near the Mae Jo intersection *(sāam yâek mâe joh)* and the Lanna Villa subdivision off Chiang Mai-Mae Rim Rd.

**Chinese** Chiang Mai has a small Chinatown in an area centred around Ratchawong Rd north of Chang Moi Rd. Here you'll find a whole string of Chinese rice and noodle shops, most of them offering variations on Tae Jiu (Chao Zhou) and Yunnanese cooking. Many of the Chinese living in Chiang Mai are Yunnanese immigrants or direct descendants of Yunnanese immigrants who the Thais call jiin haw (literally 'galloping Chinese'). This could be a reference to their migratory ways or to the fact that many brought pack horses from Yunnan.

*Han Yang Hong Kong* (Hong Kong Roast Goose) next to the New Mitrapap Hotel on Ratchawong Rd does succulent roast duck, pork and goose, as well as dim sum. There are several other inexpensive Chinese restaurants along this street.

An old stand-by for Yunnanese food is *Ruam Mit Phochana* (an English sign reads 'Yunnanese Restaurant'), across from the public playground on Sithiwong Rd (one block west of Ratchawong). The food is as good as anything you'll find in Kunming, the capital of China's Yunnan Province; specialities include plaa thâwt náam daeng (whole fried fish in a red sauce, cooked with large, semi-hot Yunnanese red peppers), mūu sāam cham jîm sĭi-yúu (shredded white pork served with a chilli, garlic and soy sauce), mūu tôm khēm (salty, boiled pork or 'Yunnanese ham') and tâo hûu phàt phrík daeng (braised bean curd and red peppers). Apart from a rice accompaniment, you can order mantou, which are plain Chinese steamed buns, similar to the Thai salabao but without stuffing. The restaurant is medium-priced and is open daily 10 am to 9 pm.

Another authentic Yunnanese spot, the clean, simple and spacious *Mitmai Restaurant* (no roman-script sign), specialises in delicious vegetable soups made with pumpkin, taro, Chinese mushrooms, snowpeas or other Chinese vegetables. Especially tasty is the tôm sôm plaa yâwt máphráo (hot and sour fish soup with coconut shoots). The very complete bilingual menu also includes yam made with Chinese vegetables, Yunnanese steamed ham, Chinese medicine chicken and many vegetarian dishes. Prices are moderate, no MSG is used in the cooking and it's open daily 9 am to 9 pm. The Mitmai is on Ratchamankha Rd diagonally opposite the Napoleon Karaoke Club.

For a quick Chinese breakfast, try the food stall opposite JJ Bakery on Ratchadamnoen Rd. It has held out against Tha Phae Gate development for many years and still serves cheap jók (rice congee), paa-thông-kō (Chinese 'doughnuts') and náam tâo-hûu (hot soy milk). This is one of the few places in the Tha Phae Gate area that opens early for breakfast – around 6 am. You can also get great jók from the vendor next to the Bangkok Bank on Chang Moi Rd, with a choice of chicken, fish, shrimp or pork.

*Lim Han Nguan* (no English sign), east of the river on Charoen Meuang Rd near the Bangkok Bank (about midway between the river and the train station), is famous for its 30 kinds of khâo tôm (rice soup), including the traditional khâo tôm kuay – plain boiled rice soup with side dishes of salted egg, salt pork etc. Other assets include the 1950s Chinese shophouse decor and the fact that it's open until 3 am.

Probably the best total splurge Chinese place in town is the Westin Chiangmai's *China Palace*, which specialises in excellent if pricey Cantonese cuisine.

**Markets** Chiang Mai is full of interesting day and night markets stocked with very inexpensive and very tasty foods. The *Somphet Market* on Moon Meuang Rd, north of the Ratwithi Rd intersection, sells cheap takeaway curries, yam, lãap, thâwt man (fish cakes), sweets and seafood. On the opposite side of the moat, along Chaiyaphum Rd north of Lek House, is a small but thriving night market where you can get everything from noodles and seafood to Yunnanese specialities. A lot of travellers eat here, so prices are just a bit higher than average, but the food is usually good.

Another good hunting ground is the very large night market near Chiang Mai Gate along Bamrungburi Rd. People tend to take their time here, making an evening of eating and drinking – there's no hustle to vacate tables for more customers. Over on the east side of the city, a large fruit and vegetable market assembles nightly along Chang Moi Rd near the Charoen Prathet intersection; several rice and noodle vendors co-exist alongside fruit stalls.

In the upstairs section of *Warorot Market* (on the corner of Chang Moi and Wichayanon Rds) are a number of great stalls for khâo tôm, khâo man kài, khâo mũu daeng ('red' pork with rice), jók and khâo sòi (curried chicken and noodle broth), with tables overlooking the market floor. It's not

the best cooking in Chiang Mai by a long shot but it's cheap. A set of vendors on the ground floor specialise in inexpensive noodles – this area is particularly popular. The market is open from 6 am to 5 pm daily.

*Anusan Market*, near the Night Bazaar, used to be one of the best places to eat in the city, but many of the stalls have gone downhill during the last few years. If you wander over here, look for the stalls that are crowded – they're usually the best. Several vendors do kũaytĩaw râat nâa thaleh (braised seafood and rice noodles). The large khâo tôm place near the market entrance, *Uan Heh-Haa*, still packs in the customers; the most popular dish is the khâo tôm plaa (fish and rice soup). (Uan Heh-Haa has established an additional branch on Arak Rd next to the west moat.) *Sanpakhoi Market*, midway between the river and the train station on Charoen Meuang, has a better selection and lower prices than Anusan.

**Noodles** Noodles in Chiang Mai are wonderful and the variety astounding. Khâo sòi – a Shan-jiin haw (Yunnanese Muslim) concoction of chicken, spicy curried broth and flat, squiggly, wheat noodles – is one of the most characteristic Northern Thai noodle dishes. The oldest area for khâo sòi is Ban Haw, the jiin haw (Yunnanese Muslim) area around the Ban Haw Mosque on Soi 1, Charoen Prathet Rd, around the corner from the Diamond Riverside Hotel and Galare Guest House and not far from the Night Bazaar; in fact this is where the jiin haw caravans of yore used to tie up. Yunnanese-run *Khao Soi Fuang Fah* and *Khao Soi Islam*, both on this soi near Ban Haw Mosque, serve khâo soi (20 to 25B) as well as Muslim curries and khâo mòk kài. *Suriwong Khao Soi*, on Kotchasan Rd opposite Tha Phae Gate, is a convenient spot for those staying in the Tha Phae Gate vicinity. Most khâo sòi places are open from around 10 am till 3 or 4 pm, although Khao Soi Islam and Khao Soi Fuang Fah are open 5 am to 5 pm (prime caravan time?).

Most locals say the city's best khâo sòi is found at *Khao Soi Lam Duan* on Faham Rd, just north of Rama IX Bridge opposite Hollanda Montri Guest House. The cook has prepared khâo sòi for no less a personage than King Bhumiphol. Large bowls of beef, pork or chicken khâo sòi cost 20B. Also on the menu are kâo lao (soup without noodles), mŭu saté (grilled spiced pork on bamboo skewers), khâo sòi with beef or pork instead of chicken, khanŏm rang pheûng (literally, 'beehive pastry', a coconut-flavoured waffle), Mekong rice whisky and beer. Two more very good Khao Soi places along this same stretch of Faham Rd are *Khao Soi Samoe Jai* and *Khao Soi Haw*.

Inside the old city, *Khao Soi Suthasinee*, on Soi 1 Inthawarorot opposite the district office, also serves exemplary khâo sòi. Suthasinee has another branch at 164/10 Chang Khlan Rd near Lanna Commercial College and yet a third at 267-9 Chang Khlan Rd. Other khâo sòi places can be found around the city – just look for the distinctive noodle shape and orange broth.

Unassuming *Rot Sawoei*, on Kotchasan Rd near DK Book House, is famous for very delectable kŭaytĭaw kài tŭn yaa jiin, (Chinese herb-steamed rice noodles). A normal bowl costs 25B, while a phîsèht (special) order with extra chicken costs 35B. Khâo nâa kài (sliced chicken over rice) is also good. In addition Rot Sawoei serves wonderful juices made from fresh toddy palm, coconut, orange or guava. It's open daily 11 am to 2.30 am, and makes the perfect late night spot for a snack.

*Kuaytiaw Reua Koliang*, on the corner of Ratchamankha and Moon Meuang Rd, has been serving authentic kŭaytĭaw reua ('boat noodles' – rice noodles served in a dark broth seasoned with ganja leaves) for many years now.

Every evening a vendor sets up in the alley just east of the Roong Ruang Hotel, off Tha Phae Rd, and serves exemplary – and cheap – phàt thai.

**Indian & Muslim** Along Charoen Prathet Soi 1, between Chang Khlan and Charoen Prathet Rds and near the Chiang Mai (Ban Haw) Mosque, are a number of simple restaurants and alley vendors selling inexpensive Muslim curries and khâo sòi. *Sophia*, on the opposite side of the soi from Khao Sai Islam and Khao Soi Fuang Fah (described in the Noodles section), serves good curries and khâo mòk kài, the Thai-Muslim version of chicken biryani. *Mataam Islam* on this soi is similar. Néua òp hãwm ('fragrant' Yunnanese Muslim-style dried beef), a speciality of Chiang Mai, is also sold along the lane.

*Shere Shiraz* (☎ 276132), on Charoen Prathet Rd Soi 6, serves mostly north Indian food with a few south Indian dishes. The extensive menu includes many vegetarian dishes. It's open daily 9.30 am to 11.30 pm. Although the food is quite OK service can be so slow and at times rude that one wonders whether it's simply a money-laundering operation!

One well established vendor in the *Galare Food Centre* off Chang Khlan Rd in the Night Bazaar area does very good Indian curries and chapatis. A couple of very simple foodstalls in Chinatown, off Chang Moi Rd, serve rice, dal and Indian curry; look for chalkboard signs.

**Western** The amazing *JJ Bakery*, on the corner of Moon Meuang and Ratchadamnoen Rds, offers a very diverse menu of western, Thai and Chinese dishes. JJ has very good coffee, inexpensive cocktails and a great selection of pies, cakes, croissants and cookies – a personal fave is the toddy palm pie. JJ Coffeeshop has a second branch at Chiang Inn Plaza, off Chang Khlan Rd near the Night Bazaar. Both are open daily 6.30 am to 11.30 pm.

For something European in the morning, try *Croissant*, next to Wat Jetawan on Tha Phae Rd. Besides its namesake, the cafe has a variety of other breakfast pastries, plus full lunch and dinner menus and free nightly videos.

Yet another hotspot for western breakfasts is the mellow *Kafé* at 127-129 Moon Meuang (at Soi 5 near Somphet Market); in addition to breakfasts, the menu here features decent Thai, Chinese and European food at very good prices. It's open 8 am to midnight; in

NORTHERN THAILAND

the evening there's live jazz and blues. The slightly more expensive *Crusty Loaf Bakery & Irish Pub* (the main sign merely reads 'Irish Pub') on Ratwithi Rd offers baked goods, good coffee, yoghurt, muesli, sandwiches, pasta, vegetarian dishes, baked potatoes, ice cream, some Thai food, beer on tap, fruit and vegetable juices and a two-for-one paperback swap. The homey indoor section is decorated with Irish kitsch and there's pleasant garden seating out the back.

The *American Restaurant & Bar* on Tha Phae Rd near the Roong Ruang Hotel, specialises in pizza, burgers, deli sandwiches, breakfast (including breakfast burritos) and Tex-Mex; for the latter the Yank-supervised cooks grind locally grown corn to make the necessary tortillas. It's open 8 am to 11 pm. *Firenze Pizzeria Steak House*, an air-con place with wooden booths in a narrow shopfront next to the American Restaurant & Bar on Tha Phae Rd, does good pizzas, pastas, steak, fruit juices and espresso drinks at moderate prices. *Pizzeria La Villa*, at 145 Ratchadamnoen Rd, serves pizzas baked in a wood-fired oven.

*The Pub*, 88 Huay Kaew Rd, is one of the oldest restaurants in Chiang Mai serving European food and beer on tap. It's not cheap, but *Newsweek* magazine did name it 'one of the world's best bars' in 1986 and it's still got class.

The clean and friendly *Dara Steak Shop*, next to Queen Bee Car Rental and the Muang Thong Hotel on the corner of Moon Meuang and Ratchamankha Rds, has an extensive Thai and western menu and low prices.

Two Italian places worth trying include the luxurious *Piccola Roma* (☎ 271256), at 3/2-3 Charoen Prathet Rd, and the more casual and diminutive *Pum Pui Italian Restaurant* near Top North Guest House. Both are operated by Italian expats and prepare reasonably authentic Italian food. Pum Pui's low-key garden setting and low prices are particularly welcome in Chiang Mai; the menu features good olive paté and other antipasti, along with salads, Italian wines, several vegetarian selections, ice cream, breakfast and espressos. Piccola Roma is

more of a splurge setting, with subdued lighting, sharp service and great attention to culinary details; it's open for lunch and dinner only.

Popular among German expats and visitors are the *Bierstube* at 33/6 Moon Meuang Rd (near Tha Phae Gate) and *Haus München* at 115/3 Loi Khraw Rd (opposite the Suriwong Zenith Hotel in the Night Bazaar area).

*Chez Daniel Brasserie Garden Grill* (☎ 248-840), at 68-68/1 Chiang Mai-Lamphun Rd, serves the best country French cuisine in town at fairly moderate prices. The attached wine shop carries the best selection of wines in Northern Thailand. More expensive and formal, long-standing *Le Coq d'Or* (☎ 282-024) serves French haute cuisine in a lavishly decorated mansion at 68/1 Ko Klang Rd, off Chiang Mai-Lamphun Rd east of the river. It's open for lunch and dinner only; reservations are suggested.

The main fast-food district in Chiang Mai runs along Chang Khlan Rd, just north of the Night Bazaar area. This strip now features *Swensen's Ice Cream, McDonald's, Burger King, Pizza Hut, KFC, 7-Eleven, Mister Donut, Baskin Robbins* and other culinary exotica from the west. Similar franchise-style places can be found in the new Kad Suan Kaew shopping centre on Huay Kaew Rd and at Airport Plaza near the airport.

**Vegetarian Food** Chiang Mai is blessed with several vegetarian restaurants, most of them very inexpensive. One of the most popular with travellers is *AUM Vegetarian Food*, on Moon Meuang Rd near Tha Phae Gate. The all-veggie menu features a varied list of traditional Thai and Chinese dishes, including Northern and North-Eastern Thai dishes, prepared without meat or eggs. Although it's looking a little shopworn, there is an upstairs eating area with cushions on the floor and low tables. It is open daily from 8 am to 9 pm.

On Soi 1 Inthawarorot Rd, a few doors down from Khao Soi Suthasinee toward Chiang Mai Central Prison, is another good – and very cheap – Thai vegetarian place.

The cooks put out 15 to 20 pots of fresh vegetarian dishes daily between 8 am and early afternoon (till everything's sold). The dishes feature lots of bean curd, squash, peas, pineapples, sprouts and potato and the desserts are good. There's no sign; look for a cluster of stainless steel pots.

The Asoke Foundation-sponsored *Chiang Mai Vegetarian Center* (☎ 271262) operates a dirt-cheap Thai vegetarian restaurant on Om Muang Rd south of the south-west corner of the city walls; it's open Sunday through Thursday from 6 am to 2 pm only. From Thursday afternoon through Saturday it's closed so that the staff can visit a Santi Asoke retreat centre in the *amphoe* (district) of Mae Taeng.

*Sabianboon* at 21/2 Suthep Rd is another good one for Thai/Chinese vegetarian and unlike most others in town it's open 7 am to 7 pm. Most dishes cost just 10 to 15B.

Out along Si Donchai Rd, past the Chang Khlan Rd intersection, is the *Whole Earth Vegetarian Restaurant*, associated with a Transcendental Meditation centre. The food is Thai and Indian and the atmosphere is suitably mellow, although the food may be a bit overpriced. *The Cafeteria* at 27-29 Chang Khlan also serves Arabic and Indian food in vegetarian variations; these days it's looking none too clean.

Other veggie spots include a no-name place opposite Money Guest House on Soi 1 Sri Phum Rd and a small vegetarian restaurant on Chiang Mai University campus; both are open limited daytime hours only.

**Garden Restaurants** If you like garden restaurants (*sūan aahāan*), Chiang Mai has plenty. Several are along Highway 11 near Wat Jet Yot and the National Museum. The food can be very good, but it is the *ban-yaakàat* (atmosphere) that is most prized by Thais.

Inside the moat, *Ta-Krite (Ta-Khrai)*, on Samlan Rd Soi 1 (the soi that runs along the south side of Wat Phra Singh), is a nice indoor-outdoor place with ironwork chairs in a garden setting. The kitchen focuses on Central Thai food for the most part, and

prices are very reasonable. Náam phrík is a house speciality, along with khâo tang nâa tâng (sticky rice with meat, shrimp and coconut). It's open daily from 10 am to 11 pm; there are at least four other Ta-Krite branches around town.

**Food Centres** A new food centre on the 3rd floor of the Kad Suan Kaew shopping centre on Huay Kaew Rd gathers together vendors selling all kinds of Thai and Chinese dishes at reasonable prices. *Galare Food Centre*, opposite the main Night Bazaar building on Chang Khlan Rd, is also good; free Thai classical dancing is featured on some evenings.

### Entertainment
**Cinema** Movies with English soundtracks are frequently shown at the *Vista* chain of cinemas at the shopping centres of Airport Plaza (Om Muang Rd), Kad Suan Kaew (Huay Kaew Rd) and Vista Chotana Mall (Chang Pheuak Rd). Occasionally an original soundtrack film may also be shown at *Saeng Tawan Cinema* on Chang Khlan Rd.

**Theatre** Kad Suan Kaew's state-of-the-art Kad Performing Arts Centre seats 1550 people in its main hall and 500 in the smaller Kad Playhouse. As a venue for live theatre it's just getting off the ground; so far it has hosted productions of *Grease, South Pacific, Cabaret, Hello Dolly, Cats, West Side Story* and a few other American and British shows. Tickets cost a steep (for Thailand) 1600 to 1800B; these prices mean that most of the theatre's clientele fly in from Bangkok. There are plans to add an art library, exhibition hall, symphony orchestra and repertory theatre.

**Live Music** Anybody who's anybody makes the scene at the *Riverside Rim Ping*, a restaurant-cafe on Charoenrat Rd, on the Ping River. It has good food, fruit shakes, cocktails and live music nightly – mostly Eagles and Beatles covers. It's usually packed with both foreigners and Thais on weekends, so arrive early to get a table on the outdoor

NORTHERN THAILAND

veranda overlooking the river. There are two indoor bars, both packed with regulars. It usually stays open till 2 or 3 am.

A few doors north of the Rim Ping at 37 Charoenrat Rd, *The Brasserie* has become a favourite late night spot (11.15 pm to 2 am) to listen to a talented Thai guitarist named Took play energetic versions of Pink Floyd, Hendrix, Cream, Dylan, Marley and other 1960s and 1970s gems. A couple of other local bands warm up the house before Took comes on. See him before he burns out.

*Old West*, near the north-west corner of the old city on Mani Nopharat Rd (west of Cathay Square Department Store), is decorated in the typical old-west style found in similar pubs throughout Thailand; most nights a live folk or country band plays after 9 pm. The *Smiling Monkey Pub*, at 40 Bamrungburi Rd (near Chiang Mai Gate), is popular with Thai students and features good Thai food and live music nightly in a garden setting. Another good spot is *Western Art* on Si Phum Rd near the north-east corner of the moat; some of Chiang Mai's best contemporary and alternative bands play here.

Jazz fans have a choice of several local spots along Huay Kaew Rd, including *The Level, Marvel* and *Marble Pub.*

**Discos**  All the flashy hotels have discos with high-tech recorded music. Currently the hottest in town are the *Stardust* (Westin Chiangmai), *Crystal Cave* (Empress Hotel), *The Wall* (Chiang Inn) and *Bubbles* (Porn Ping Tower Hotel). The cover charge at each is around 100B, which includes one drink.

The most popular non-hotel discos of the moment are *Gigi* and *Climax*, both on Chiang Mai-Lamphun Rd east of the river. All Chiang Mai discos are legally required to close at 2 am, although Gigi and Climax sometimes stay open later.

**Bars**  Along Moon Meuang Rd, between Ratchadamnoen Rd and Soi 3, are a string of small bars with low-volume music that are good for a quiet drink. The *Pinte Blues Pub*, at 33/6 Moon Meuang Rd, serves espresso and beer, and plays all pre-recorded blues.

The *Bierstube* features German grub and beer, while the *Cozy Corner* and *Cheers Pub* are pretty featureless. *Domino* has good food, draught beer, videos and English pub grub. The Blues Pub and Domino are the only bars in Tha Phae Gate vicinity where you generally see couples or farang women.

*The Hard Rock Cafe* (no legal relation to the worldwide chain), at 66/3 Loi Khraw Rd, is decorated with old LP covers and has a pool table. Co-owned by Roxanna Brown, journalist and author of *Ceramics of Southeast Asia*, the bar features a good selection of rock music tapes – the house mix is even sold on cassette in six volumes. Along with a full bar, the Hard Rock offers good Italian food.

About a dozen or so bars are tucked away in narrow alleys along either side of Night Bazaar. Each is only a few metres wide, with just a few stools and tables and a mini-component stereo system, but the bars are fully stocked and it's a friendly, hassle-free, low-cost place to tipple.

**Gay Venues**  Chiang Mai has several gay men's bars, including the relaxed *Coffee Boy Bar* in a 70 year old teak house at 248 Thung Hotel Rd, not far from the Arcade bus station. On weekends there's a cabaret show. Other popular gay meeting places include low-key *Danny's Bar* (☎ 225171), 161 Chang Phukha Rd Soi 4, and *Kra Jiap Bar & Restaurant*, at 18/1 Wualai Rd Soi 3. The three-storey *Adam's Apple*, at 132/46-47 Soi Wiang Bua, Chotana Rd, has a massage centre, go-go bar, gay pub and karaoke lounge; it's open daily 7 pm to 2 am.

**Things to Buy**
Hundreds of shops all over Chiang Mai sell hill-tribe and Northern Thai craftwork, but a lot of it is commercial and touristy junk churned out for the undiscerning. So bargain hard and buy carefully! The nonprofit outlets often have the best quality, and although the prices are sometimes a bit higher than at the Night Bazaar, a higher percentage of your money goes directly to the hill-tribe artisans.

Thai Tribal Crafts (☎ 241043) at 208

Bamrungrat Rd, near the McCormick Hospital, is run by two church groups on a nonprofit basis and has a good selection of quality handicrafts. Hill-Tribe Products Promotion Centre (☎ 277743) at 21/17 Suthep Rd, near Wat Suan Dawk, is a royally sponsored project; all profits go to hill-tribe welfare programmes. The YMCA International Hotel also operates a nonprofit handicrafts centre.

The two commercial markets with the widest selections of Northern Thai folk crafts are Warorot Market at the eastern end of Chang Moi Kao Rd and the Night Bazaar off Chang Khlan Rd. Warorot (also locally called Kaat Luang or Great Market) is the oldest market in Chiang Mai. A former royal cremation ground, it has been a marketplace site since the reign of Chao Inthawararot (1870-97). Although the huge enclosure is quite dilapidated (the escalator and lifts don't work any more), it's an especially good market for fabrics.

In the Night Bazaar there are a couple of dozen permanent shops selling antiques, handicrafts, rattan and hardwood furniture, textiles, jewellery, pottery, basketry, silverwork, woodcarving and other items of local manufacture. Prices can be very good if you bargain hard.

As Chiang Mai is Thailand's main handicraft centre, it's ringed by small cottage factories and workshops where you can watch craftspeople at work. In general, though, merchandise you see at factories outside the city will cost more than it would in Chiang Mai unless you're buying in bulk.

One shop that seems to have it all – handicrafts, antiques, textiles, ceramics, everything but jewellery – is the long-running Chiangmai Banyen (☎ 274007) at 201/1 Wualai Rd, south of the Old Chiang Mai Cultural Centre.

**Antiques** You'll see lots of these around, including opium weights (the little animal-shaped weights supposedly used to measure opium in the Golden Triangle). Check prices in Bangkok first, as Chiang Mai's shops are not always cheap. Also remember that worldwide there are a lot more instant antiques than authentic ones. The Night Bazaar area is probably the best place to look for fake antiques.

Inside the Nakhon Ping Night Bazaar building, toward the back on the second floor, are a few small shops with real antiques. Among the best are The Lost Heavens at Stall 21, specialising in Mien tribal artefacts, and Under the Bo at Stall 23, which carries many unique pieces, including woodcarvings and weavings from Africa, South Asia and South-East Asia. Under the Bo has a larger shop on Ratchamankha Rd inside the moat, just west of the Napoleon Karaoke and almost next door to Mitmai Yunnanese Restaurant. Neither is cheap, but many items are one-of-a-kind.

Many more antiques shops can be found along Tha Phae Rd and especially along Loi Khraw Rd.

**Ceramics** Thai Celadon, about six km north of Chiang Mai, turns out ceramics modelled on the Sawankhalok pottery that used to be made hundreds of years ago at Sukhothai and exported all over the region. With their deep, cracked, glazed finish some pieces are very beautiful and prices are often lower than in Bangkok. The factory is closed on Sunday.

The reliable Mengrai Kilns (☎ 272063) has recently moved operations to 9/2 Arak Rd in the south-west corner of the inner moat area near Buak Hat Park. Other ceramic stores can be found close to the Old Chiang Mai Cultural Centre.

There are also several celadon operations in the nearby town of Hang Dong.

**Clothes** All sorts of shirts, blouses and dresses, plain and embroidered, are available at very low prices, but check the quality carefully. The Night Bazaar and stores along Tha Phae and Loi Khraw Rds have good selections. Also see the following section.

**Cotton & Silk** Very attractive lengths of material can be made into all sorts of things. Thai silk, with its lush colours and pleasantly rough texture, is a particularly good bargain and is usually cheaper here than in Bangkok. Warorot Market is one of the best and least expensive places to look for fabrics, but take care as many items said to be silk are actually polyester.

Several individual shops in town focus on high-quality traditional (sometimes antique) Thai and Lao fabrics, sold by the metre or made up into original-design clothes. A list of the best places in town would have to include Sbun-Nga and Nandakwang, both in a strip of shops opposite the Amari Hotel. Naenna Studio (☎ /fax 217707), nearby on Soi 9 off Nimanhaemin Rd, is operated by Patricia Cheeseman, an expert on Thai-Lao textiles who has written extensively on the subject. The Loom, at 27 Ratchamankha Rd near Soi 3, carries very fine fabrics from North and North-Eastern Thailand, Laos and Cambodia.

If you want to see where and how the cloth is made, go to the nearby town of San Kamphaeng for Thai silk or to Pasang, south of Lamphun, for cotton.

**Lacquerware** Decorated plates, containers, utensils and other items are made by building up layers of lacquer over a wooden or woven bamboo base. Burmese lacquerware, smuggled into the North, can often be seen, especially at Mae Sai. There are several lacquerware factories in San Kamphaeng.

**Rattan** The best place in town for furniture and accessories made from this jungle vine is Hangdong Rattan (☎ 208167) at 54-55 Loi Khraw Rd. In addition to the many items on display, Hangdong takes custom orders.

**Silverwork** There are several silverwork shops on Wualai Rd close to Chiang Mai Gate. Hill-tribe jewellery, which is heavy, chunky stuff, is very nice.

**Umbrellas** At Baw Sang, the umbrella village, you'll find beautiful hand-painted paper umbrellas. You can also buy very attractive framed leaf paintings here.

**Woodcarving** Many types of carvings are available, including countless elephants. Teak salad bowls are good and very cheap. Many shops along Tha Phae Rd and in the vicinity of the Night Bazaar stock wood crafts.

**Shopping Centres & Department Stores**
Chiang Mai had 17 shopping centres with department stores at last count. Tantrapan, the city's first department store, has expanded and moved to Airport Plaza near the airport; it stocks a wide selection of ready-made clothing, electrical appliances, toiletries, stationery etc. Airport Plaza also has a branch of DK Book House.

The newer Kad Suan Kaew shopping centre on Huay Kaew Rd is centred around a branch of Bangkok's Central Department Store. There are several other up-market shops in the complex.

**Tailors** Several tailor shops are clustered off Kotchasan Rd near Aroon Rai Restaurant, including Florida, Chao Khun, Chaiyo and Progress. Prices are very reasonable, often cheaper than in Bangkok. Ask to see some finished work before choosing a shop.

### Getting There & Away

**Air** Chiang Mai international airport lands regularly scheduled international flights from Kunming (THAI), Singapore (Silk Air) Hong Kong (THAI), Kuala Lumpur (Malaysia Airlines), Yangon (Air Mandalay), Mandalay (Air Mandalay) and Vientiane (Lao Aviation), as well as domestic flights from several other cities in Thailand.

The THAI office (☎ 211044/7) is within the city moat area at 240 Phra Pokklao Rd, behind Wat Chiang Man. THAI has several daily one hour flights between Bangkok and Chiang Mai. The fare is 1940B one way in economy class.

Airfares between Chiang Mai and some other Thai cities are:

| City | Fare |
| --- | --- |
| Chiang Rai | 420B |
| Mae Hong Son | 345B |
| Mae Sot | 590B |
| Nan | 510B |
| Phitsanulok | 650B |
| Phuket | 3455B |

A new carrier, Orient Express Air (☎ 818-092/120), has its headquarters at the airport and offers five flights a week to/from Surat

Thani (2450B one way) and Hat Yai (2900B) and four days a week to/from Khon Kaen (1115B), Ubon (1950B) and Udon (2600B).

Bangkok Airways also operates three flights per week to/from Bangkok via Sukhothai for 1640B. The 30 minute flight to/from Sukhothai only costs 540B.

**Bus** From Bangkok's Northern Bus Terminal there are seven ordinary buses daily to Chiang Mai, departing from 5.30 am to 10.30 pm. The 12 hour trip costs 161B via Nakhon Sawan and 164B via Ayuthaya. Seven 1st class air-con buses leave the adjacent air-con terminal between 8.50 and 10 am and eight buses leave from 8 to 9.45 pm. These buses cost 304B one way and take from 10 to 11 hours depending on traffic. There are also five 2nd class air-con buses per day for 237B. The public buses from the Northern Bus Terminal are generally more reliable and on schedule than the private ones booked in Banglamphu and other places.

Ten or more private tour companies run air-con buses between Bangkok and Chiang Mai, departing from various points throughout both cities. Return tickets are always somewhat cheaper than one way tickets. Fares range from 180 to 320B depending on the bus. VIP buses are the most expensive as these have fewer seats per coach to allow for reclining positions; the typical VIP fare is 470B. Similar buses can be booked in the Soi Ngam Duphli area of Bangkok and near the Indra Hotel in Pratunam.

Several Khao San Rd agencies offer bus tickets to Chiang Mai for as low as 120 to 180B, including a night's free stay at a guesthouse in Chiang Mai. Sometimes this works out well, but the buses can be substandard and the 'free' guesthouse may charge you 40B for electricity or hot water, or apply heavy pressure for you to sign up for one of its treks before you can get a room. Besides, riding in a bus stuffed full of foreigners and their bulky backpacks is not the most cultural experience. Recently the bus driver on a Khao San Rd bus bound for Chiang Mai attacked a passenger with a machete when he asked why the promised air-con wasn't working.

The only advantage of the private buses is that they pick you up from where you booked your ticket (supposedly this is legal only for tour operators). If you don't have a lot of baggage it's probably better to leave from the Mo Chit terminal for government buses.

Public buses between Chiang Mai and other towns in the North and North-East have frequent departures throughout the day (at least hourly), except for the Mae Sai, Khon Kaen, Udon, Ubon and Khorat buses, which have morning and evening departures only. (See the table on the following page for public bus fares and destinations.)

For buses to destinations within Chiang Mai Province use the Chang Pheuak station, while for buses outside the province use the Chiang Mai Arcade station. City bus No 3 (yellow) goes to the Chiang Mai Arcade station; bus No 2 (yellow) goes to the Chang Pheuak terminal.

**Train** Chiang Mai-bound express trains leave Bangkok's Hualamphong station daily at 8.10 am (2nd class only), 6, 7.25 and 7.40 pm, arriving in Chiang Mai at 6.50 pm, 5.10, 6.10 and 7.55 am.

Rapid trains leave at 6.40 am, 3 (air-con 2nd class) and 10 pm (no air-con), arriving at 7.35 pm, 5 and 11.30 am respectively. There are no longer any 3rd class ordinary trains between Bangkok and Chiang Mai, although 3rd class tickets (151B including rapid surcharge) are available on the rapid trains.

The basic 2nd class fare is 281B, excluding either the special express (70B), express (50B) or rapid (30B) surcharges. Add 100B for an upper berth and 150B for a lower berth in a 2nd class sleeping car (130 and 200B respectively on the special express). For air-con 2nd class, add 70B per ticket for ordinary cars and 120B for sleepers. For example, if you take a 2nd class upper berth on a rapid train, your total fare will be 385B (255+100+30B).

The basic 1st class fare is 593B; berths are 400B per person and are available on the special express only.

Trains leave Lopburi for Chiang Mai at 9.11 am (rapid), 5.31 (rapid), 8.19 (express), 9.25 pm (special express) and 12.27 am (rapid), arriving at the times listed for the same trains from Bangkok. Fares are 267B

## Bus Destinations from Chiang Mai

| City | Fare | Duration |
|---|---|---|
| Chiang Dao* | 21B | 1½ hours |
| Chiang Khong | 91B | 6½ hours |
| (air-con) | 128B | 6 hours |
| Chiang Rai | 57B | 4 hours |
| (air-con) | 79B | 3 hours |
| (1st class) | 102B | 3 hours |
| Chiang Saen | 73B | 5 hours |
| (air-con) | 130B | 3½ hours |
| Fang* | 43B | 3½ hours |
| Khon Kaen | 192B | 12 hours |
| (air-con, Highway 12) | 268B | 12 hours |
| (1st class air-con, Highway 12) | 345B | 12 hours |
| (air-con, Highway 11) | 307B | 11 hours |
| Khorat | 180B | 12 hours |
| (air-con) | 180B | 12 hours |
| (1st class air-con) | 324B | 12 hours |
| Lampang | 29B | 2 hours |
| Lamphun* | 7B | 1 hour |
| Mae Hong Son (Route 108) | 115B | 8 hours |
| (air-con) | 206B | 8 hours |
| Mae Sai | 71B | 5 hours |
| (air-con) | 99B | 4 hours |
| (1st class air-con) | 127B | 4 hours |
| Mae Sariang | 50B | 4-5 hours |
| Mae Sot | 96B | 6½ hours |
| (air-con) | 172B | 6 hours |
| Nan | 83B | 7 hours |
| (air-con) | 115B | 6 hours |
| (1st class air-con) | 148B | 6 hours |
| Pai | 45B | 4 hours |
| Pasang* | 10B | 45 minutes |
| Phayao | 51B | 3 hours |
| (air-con) | 71B | 2½ hours |
| Phrae | 55B | 4 hours |
| (air-con) | 76B | 3½ hours |
| (1st class air-con) | 98B | 3½ hours |
| Phitsanulok | 86B | 5-6 hours |
| (air-con) | 104B | 5 hours |
| (1st class air-con) | 146B | 5 hours |
| Sukhothai | 91B | 6 hours |
| Tak | 57B | 4 hours |
| (air-con) | 82B | 4 hours |
| Tha Ton* | 50B | 4 hours |
| Ubon Ratchathani | 247B | 16 hours |
| (air-con) | 445B | 15 hours |
| Udon Thani | 170B | 12 hours |
| (1st class air-con, via Loei) | 305B | 12 hours |

*\* Leaves from White Elephant (Chang Pheuak) bus station, Chotana Rd. All other buses leave from the Chiang Mai Arcade bus station (also called New Station) off Kaew Nawarat Rd.*

2nd class express, 143B 3rd class express – 20B less for the rapid.

Berths on sleepers to Chiang Mai are increasingly hard to reserve without booking well in advance. Tour groups sometimes book entire cars. The return trip from Chiang Mai to Bangkok doesn't seem to be as difficult, except during the Songkran (mid-April) and Chinese New Year (February) holiday periods.

Chiang Mai's neat and tidy railway station has an ATM and an advance booking office open daily 5 am to 9 pm. The booking office has a computerised reservation system through which you can book train seats for anywhere in Thailand. There is also a left-luggage facility that is open from 6 am to 6 pm daily. The cost is 5B per piece for the first five days and 10B per piece thereafter.

City bus Nos 1, 3 and 6 stop in front of the train station.

### Getting Around
### To/From Chiang Mai International Airport
Two companies run taxis from Chiang Mai airport; the airport 'taxi' for 80B requires three passengers or you can pay 100B for an airport 'limousine' and not have to wait. Both modes of transport are sedan cars that can take up to four or five people with luggage. The airport is only two or three km from the city centre. The red bus No 6 goes to the airport but you must catch it somewhere on the Highway 11 loop. You can get a taxi from the centre of Chiang Mai to the airport for 50B, although a songthaew would be less again.

The airport has currency exchange counters, a post office, an international (IDD and Home Direct) phone office (open from 8.30 am to 8 pm), a tourist information counter, two snack bars (one under the trees by the car park, the other in the arrival area), a bar in an old air force transport aircraft, a THAI-operated restaurant and a duty-free shop on the departure level.

**Bus** City buses operate from 6 am to 6 pm and cost 3B in town, up to 6B for the highway loop. Nos 1, 2 and 3 (yellow) cover the whole city, No 5 (red) does a loop around the moat and No 6 (red) goes around the highway loop. Air-con versions of Nos 1, 2 and 3 are less frequent and cost 5B and 8B respectively.

**Songthaew & Samlor** Songthaews go anywhere on their route for 5B. You can also charter a samlor anywhere in the city for 50B or less. Samlors cost between 10 and 15B for most trips.

**Car Rental** Cars, jeeps and minivans are readily available at several locations throughout the city. Be sure that the vehicle you rent has insurance (liability) coverage – ask to see the documents and carry a photocopy with you while driving.

Two of the best agencies in town for service and price are Queen Bee (☎ 275525; fax 274349), next to Muang Thong Hotel on Moon Meuang Rd, and North Wheels (☎ 216189, 279554; fax 221709) at 127/2 Moon Meuang Rd near Somphet Market. Both offer hotel pickup and delivery as well as 24 hour emergency road service; North Wheel's rates include insurance, while Queen Bee charges extra for insurance. Sample rentals at North Wheels include Suzuki Caribians for 800B per 24 hour day, 4900B weekly or 18,000B monthly; or a Toyota Mighty-X 4WD for 1800B per day, 11,000 weekly, 30,000B for a month. At Queen Bee, Suzuki Caribians cost 800B per 24 hour day in high season, 700B in low season; pickup trucks cost 1000B.

By comparison, Hertz and Avis charge 1200B per day for a Caribian – plus 12% VAT, plus 150B collision damage waiver and 100B personal accident insurance. This works out to 1594B per day; a three day minimum rental is required.

Other prominent rental agencies include:

Avis – 14/14 Huay Kaew Rd (☎ 221316)
   Chiang Mai international airport (☎ 222013)
Chiang Mai MK – 59-61 Moon Meuang Rd (☎ 270961)
Erawan PUC – 211/14-15 Chang Khlan Rd (☎ 274212; fax 276548)
Hertz – 90 Si Donchai Rd (☎ 279474)
   Chiang Inn Hotel (☎ 270070)
Loong Vill Car Rent – 32/1 Muang Samut Rd (☎ 876167)
PD Express – 138/4 Phra Pokklao Rd (☎ 277876)

**Motorcycle** These can be rented for 80 to 150B (100cc Honda Dream step-throughs) or 200 to 250B (125 to 150cc Hondas or Yamahas) per day, depending on the size of the motorbike and the length of rental. Prices are very competitive in Chiang Mai because there's a real glut of motorcycles. For two people, it's cheaper to rent a small motorcycle for the day to visit Doi Suthep than to go up and back on a songthaew.

Motorcycle hire places come and go with the seasons. Many of them are lined up along the east side of the moat on Moon Meuang, Chaiyaphum and Kotchasan Rds. Among the more established ones are Pop (☎ 276014), 51 Kotchasan Rd on the moat, and Queen Bee (☎ 274349), 5 Moon Meuang Rd. These agencies offer motorcycle insurance for 50B per day, not a bad investment considering you could face a 25,000B liability if your bike is stolen. Most policies have a deductible (excess) of 300 to 1000B, so in cases of theft you're usually responsible for a third to half of the bike's value – even with insurance. A newer place that specialises in quick, easy and inexpensive rentals of 100cc bikes for around town is Mr Beer at 2 Moon Meuang Rd near the market.

Availability of bikes bigger than 100cc also varies from year to year but at the time of writing you could get a Honda XL600 (550B a day), Honda AX-1 250 (500B, 350B off season), Honda Baja 250 (500B, 350B off season) and Honda XR 250 (400B). JK Big Bike on Chaiyaphum Rd next to the Soi 2 entrance rents Honda XL 250s for 350B a day; bigger bikes are available as well. Several car-rental places also rent motorcycles. See the introductory Getting Around chapter for information on motorcycle touring.

**Bicycle** This is by far the best way to get around Chiang Mai. The city is small enough so that everywhere is accessible by bike, including Chiang Mai University, Wat U Mong, Wat Suan Dawk and the National Museum on the outskirts of town.

Bicycles can be rented for between 20 and 30B per day from several of the guesthouses or from various places along the east moat.

NORTHERN THAILAND

# Trekking in Northern Thailand

**F**or years Chiang Mai has been a centre for treks into the mountainous northern areas inhabited by hill tribes. It used to be pretty exciting to knock about the dirt roads of rural Chiang Rai Province, do the boat trip between Fang and Chiang Rai and hike into the various villages of the Karen, Hmong, Akha, Lisu and Mien tribes as well as Kuomintang (KMT) settlements. You could spend the night in rustic surroundings and get a pretty authentic insight into traditional village life.

Only a very few Thai locals living in Chiang Mai had the travel and linguistic knowledge necessary to lead adventurous foreign trekkers through this area. Booking a trip usually meant waiting for optimum conditions and adequate numbers of participants, which sometimes took quite a while.

The trips began to gain popularity in the early 1970s and now virtually every hotel and guesthouse in Chiang Mai books hill-tribe tours for countless tour organisations.

Soon the word was out that the area north of the Kok River in the Golden Triangle was being over-trekked, with treks crisscrossing the area in such a fashion that the hill-tribe villages were starting to become human zoos. With their only contact with the outside world coming through a camera lens and a flow of sweets and cigarettes, many villages faced cultural erosion. So the tours moved south of the Kok River, around Chiang Dao and Wiang Papao, then to Mae Taeng and Mae Hong Son where most of them now operate. It will be only a short time before these areas suffer from the heavy traffic as well.

Meanwhile, thousands of foreign travellers each year continue to take these treks. Most come away with a sense of adventure while a few are disillusioned. The primary ingredient in a good trek is having a good leader/organiser, followed by a good group of trekkers. Some travellers finish a tour complaining more about the other trekkers than about the itinerary, food or trek leader.

## Before Trekking

Hill-tribe trekking isn't for everyone. First, you must be physically fit to cope with the demands of sustained up and down walking, exposure to the elements and spotty food. Second, many people feel awkward walking through hill-tribe villages and playing the role of voyeur.

In cities and villages elsewhere in Thailand, Thais and other lowland groups are quite used to foreign faces and foreign ways (from TV if nothing else), but in the hills of Northern Thailand the tribes lead largely insular lives. Hence, hill-tribe tourism has pronounced effects, both positive and negative. On the positive side, travellers have a chance to see how traditional subsistence-oriented societies function. (See the special Hill Tribes section later in this chapter.) Also, since the Thai government is sensitive about the image projected by their minority groups, tourism may actually have forced it to review and sometimes improve its policies towards hill tribes. On the negative side, trekkers introduce many cultural items and ideas from the outside world that may erode tribal customs to varying degrees.

If you have any qualms about interrupting the traditional patterns of life in hill-tribe areas, you probably should not go trekking. It is undeniable that trekking in Northern Thailand is marketed like soap or any other commodity. Anyone who promises you an authentic experience is probably exaggerating at the very least, or at worst contributing to the decline of hill-tribe culture by leading foreigners into unhampered areas.

# Choosing a Company

Because of the inherent instability of the trekking business, it's difficult to make specific recommendations for particular trekking companies in Chiang Mai. Many of the trekking guides are freelance and go from one company to the next, so there's no way to predict which companies are going to give the best service at any time. Many guesthouses that advertise their own trekking companies actually act as brokers for off-site operations; they collect a commission for every guest they book into a trek.

The TAT office in Chiang Mai maintains and distributes a list of licensed agencies. It is also making efforts to regulate trekking companies operating out of Chiang Mai and recommends that you trek only with members of the Professional Guide Association of Chiang Mai or the Jungle Tour Club of Northern Thailand. Still, with more than 100 companies, it's very difficult to guarantee any kind of control. Ultimately, however, the best way to shop for a trek is to talk to travellers who have just returned from treks.

If you decide to do a trek keep these points in mind: choose your trek operator carefully, try to meet the others in the group (suggest a meeting) and find out exactly what the tour includes and does not include, as usually there are additional expenses beyond the basic rate. In the cool season, make sure sleeping bags are provided, as the thin wool blankets available in most villages are not sufficient for the average visitor. If everything works out, even an organised tour can be worthwhile. A useful check list of questions to ask are:

- How many people will there be in the group? (Six to 10 is a good maximum range.)
- Can the organiser guarantee that no other tourists will visit the same village on the same day, especially overnight?
- Can the guide speak the language of each village to be visited? (This is not always necessary, as many villagers can speak Thai nowadays.)
- Exactly when does the tour begin and end? (Some three day treks turn out to be less than 48 hours in length.)
- Do they provide transport before and after the trek or is it just by public bus (often with long waits)?

In general the trekking business has become more conscious of the need to tread carefully in hill-tribe villages then in previous decades. Most companies tend to limit the number of visits to a particular area and are careful not to overlap areas used by other companies. Everyone benefits from this consciousness: the hill tribes are less impacted, the trekkers have a more authentic experience and the companies preserve a sustainable cultural resource. Opium continues to be a problem with some companies; a few companies are now advertising drug-free treks to avoid the pitfalls of opium-addicted guides and adverse influences on young hill-tribe members.

These days there are plenty of places apart from Chiang Mai where you can arrange treks. Often these places have better and usually less expensive alternatives which originate closer to the more remote and untrekked areas. Also, they are generally smaller, friendlier operations and the trekkers are usually a more determined bunch since they're not looking for an easy and quick in-and-out trek. The treks are often informally arranged, usually involving discussions of duration, destination, cost etc.

You can easily arrange treks out of the following Northern Thai towns: Chiang Rai, Mae Hong Son, Pai, Mae Sai and Tha Ton. With a little time to seek out the right people, you can also go on organised treks from Mae Sariang, Khun Yuam, Soppong (near Pai), Mae Sot, Um Phang and various out-of-the-way guesthouses which are springing up all over the North.

The down side, of course, is that companies outside of Chiang Mai are generally subject to even less regulation than those in Chiang Mai, and there are fewer guarantees with regard to trekking terms and conditions.

## Costs

Organised treks out of Chiang Mai average from 1500B for a four day, three night trek to 2600B for a deluxe seven day, six night trek which includes rafting and/or elephant riding. Rates vary, so it pays to shop around – although these days so many companies are competing for your business that rates have remained pretty stable for the last few years. You can count on an extra 1000B for elephants or other exotic additions to a basic trek. Elephant rides actually become quite boring and even uncomfortable after an hour or two. Some companies now offer quickie day treks or one night, two day programmes.

Don't choose a trek by price alone. It's better to talk to other travellers in town who have been on treks. Treks out of other towns in the North are usually less expensive – around 300B per person per day.

The Professional Guide Association in Chiang Mai meets monthly to set trek prices and to discuss problems, and issues regular, required reports to TAT about individual treks. All trekking guides and companies are supposed to be government-licensed and bonded. As a result, a standard for trekking operators has emerged whereby you can expect the price you pay to include: transport to and from the starting/ending points of a trek (if outside Chiang Mai); food (three meals a day) and accommodation in all villages visited; basic first aid; predeparture valuables storage; and sometimes the loan of specific equipment, such as sleeping bags in cool weather or water bottles.

Not included in the price are beverages other than drinking water or tea, the sometimes available opium-smoking, lunch on the first and last days and personal porters.

## Seasons

Probably the best time to trek is November to February, when the weather is refreshing with little or no rain and poppies are in bloom everywhere. Between March and May the hills are dry and the weather is quite hot. The second-best time to trek is early in the rainy season, between June and July, before the dirt roads become too saturated.

## Safety

Every year or so there's at least one trekking robbery in Northern Thailand. Often the bandits are armed with guns, which they will use without hesitation if they meet resistance. Once they collect a load of cameras, watches, money and jewellery, many bandit gangs hightail it across the border into Myanmar. In spite of this, police have had a good arrest record so far and have created hill-country patrols. Still, gangs can form at any time and anywhere. The problem is that most people living in the rural North believe that all foreigners are very rich (a fair assumption in relation to hill-tribe living standards). Most of these people have never been to Chiang Mai and, from what they have heard about the capital, consider Bangkok to be a virtual paradise of wealth and luxury. So don't take anything that you can't afford to lose, and don't resist robbery attempts.

## Conduct

Once trekking, there are several other guidelines to minimising the negative impact on the local people:

- Always ask for permission before taking photos of tribespeople and/or their dwellings. You can ask through your guide or by using sign language. Because of traditional belief systems, many individuals and even whole tribes may object strongly to being photographed.

- Show respect for religious symbols and rituals. Don't touch totems at village entrances or any other object of obvious symbolic value without asking permission. Keep your distance from ceremonies being performed unless you're asked to participate.

- Practise restraint in giving things to tribespeople or bartering with them. If you want to give something to the people you encounter on a trek, the best thing is to make a donation to the village school or other community fund. Your guide can help arrange this.

## Opium Smoking

Some guides are very strict now about forbidding the smoking of opium on treks. This seems to be a good idea, since one of the problems trekking companies have had in the past is dealing with opium-addicted guides! Volunteers who work in tribal areas also say opium smoking sets a bad example for young people in the villages.

Opium is traditionally a condoned vice of the elderly, yet an increasing number of young people in the villages are now taking opium and heroin. This is possibly due in part to the influence of young trekkers who may smoke once and a few weeks later be hundreds of km away while the villagers continue to face the temptation every day.

Opium overdoses aren't unknown; in 1991 a 23 year old Brazilian died after smoking 18 pipes of opium while on a trek in Northern Thailand.

## Independent Trekking

You might consider striking out on your own in a small group of two to five people. Gather as much information as you can about the area you'd like to trek in from the Tribal Research Institute at Chiang Mai University. The institute has an informative pamphlet which is available at its library. Don't bother staff with questions about trekking as they are quite non-committal, either from fear of liability or fear of retribution from the Chiang Mai trekking companies. Maps, mostly distributed by guesthouses outside of Chiang Mai, pinpoint various hill-tribe areas in the North. Look for more details about launching out on a trek independently under the individual destination entries in this chapter.

Be prepared for language difficulties. Few people you meet will know any English. Usually someone in a village will know some Thai, so a Thai phrasebook can be helpful. Lonely Planet also publishes a *Thai Hill Tribes phrasebook* with phrase sections for each of the six major hill-tribe languages.

As in Himalayan trekking in Nepal and India, many people now do short treks on their own at the lower elevations, staying in villages along the way. It is not necessary to bring a lot of food or equipment, just money for food which can be bought along the way in small Thai towns and occasionally in the hill-tribe settlements. However, TAT strongly discourages trekking on your own because of the safety risk. Check with the police when you arrive in a new district so they can tell you if an area is considered safe or not. A lone trekker is an easy target.

NORTHERN THAILAND

## AROUND CHIANG MAI
### Doi Suthep
ดอยสุเทพ

Sixteen km north-west of Chiang Mai is Doi Suthep, a 1676m peak named after the hermit Sudeva, who lived on the mountain's slopes for many years. Near its summit is **Wat Phra That Doi Suthep**; first established in 1383 under King Keu Naone it is one of the North's most sacred temples. A naga staircase of 300 steps leads to the wat at the end of the winding road up the mountain. If the climb seems too much of a chore, you can take a short tram ride from the parking lot to the wat grounds for 5B. At the top, weather permitting, there are some fine aerial views of Chiang Mai. Inside the cloister is an intriguing copper-plated chedi topped by a five-tier gold umbrella.

About four km beyond Wat Phra That is **Phra Tamnak Phu Phing** (a winter palace for the royal family), the gardens of which are open on weekends and holidays. The road that passes Phu Phing Palace splits off to the left, stopping at the peak of Doi Pui. From there a dirt road proceeds for two or three km to a nearby Hmong hill-tribe village. If you won't have an opportunity to visit more remote villages, it's worth visiting this one, even though it is very well touristed. Some Hmong handiwork can be purchased, and traditional homes and costumes can be seen, although these are mostly posed situations.

If you're cycling or driving to the summit, you can stop along the way at **Monthathon Falls**, which is 2.5 km off the paved road to Doi Suthep. The trail is well marked; if you're interested in checking it out, have the songthaew driver drop you off on the way up the mountain. Pools beneath the falls hold water all year-round, though swimming is best during or just after the annual monsoon. The falls can be a little crowded on weekends.

**Doi Suthep/Doi Pui National Park** Most visitors do a quick tour of the temple, the Hmong village and perhaps the winter palace grounds, altogether missing the surrounding park. This 261 sq km preserve is home to more than 300 bird species and nearly 2000 species of ferns and flowering plants. Because of its proximity to urban Chiang Mai, development of the park has become a very sensitive issue. The west side of the park has been severely disturbed by poachers and land encroachers, including around 500 hill-tribe families. In 1986 a Bangkok company tried to establish a lengthy cable-car system through the park to the temple, but protests, petitions and marches by the Group for Chiang Mai (Chomrom Pheua Chiang Mai) stopped the plan.

There are extensive hiking trails in the park, including one that climbs 1685m Doi Pui; the summit is a favourite picnic spot. Other trails pass Hmong villages that rarely get farang visitors. Bungalow and dormitory accommodation is available near the park headquarters (past the temple car park on the right). Depending on who's on duty at the park headquarters, there are also maps available here.

A four km trail also leads to the scenic and more isolated **Sai Yoi Falls**, and connects with a trail to Monthathon Falls.

**Getting There & Away** Songthaews to Doi Suthep leave Chiang Mai throughout the day from the west end of Huay Kaew Rd in front of Chiang Mai University. The fare is 30B up, 20B down. To Phu Phing Palace add 10B and to Doi Pui add 20B in each direction.

### Baw Sang
บ่อสร้าง

Baw Sang (often spelt 'Bo Sang' or 'Bor Sang'), nine km east of Chiang Mai on Route 1006, is usually called the umbrella village because of its many umbrella manufacturers. Practically the entire village consists of craft shops selling painted umbrellas, fans, silverware, straw handiwork, bamboo and teak, statuary, china, celadon and lacquerware, along with very tacky Chiang Mai and Northern Thai souvenirs, as well as quality items.

The larger shops can arrange overseas shipping at reasonable rates. As in Chiang Mai's Night Bazaar, discounts are offered for quantity purchases. Some of the places will also

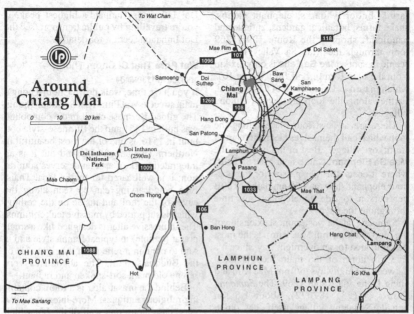

Around Chiang Mai

0    10    20 km

pack and post parasols, apparently quite reliably.

One of the best times to visit Baw Sang is during the annual Umbrella Festival.

### San Kamphaeng
สันกำแพง

Four or five km farther down Route 1006 is San Kamphaeng, which flourishes on cotton and silk weaving. Stores offering finished products line the main street, although the actual weaving is done in small factories down side streets. There are some deals to be had here, especially in silk. For cotton, you'd probably do better in Pasang, a lesser known village near Lamphun, although you may see shirt styles here not available in Pasang. A cotton shirt or blouse can cost between 80 and 250B.

**Getting There & Away** Buses to Baw Sang and San Kamphaeng leave Chiang Mai frequently during the day from the north side of Charoen Meuang Rd, east of the Ping River. The bus stop is towards the GPO and the train station and across from Sanpakhoi Market. The fare is 5B to Baw Sang and 6B to San Kamphaeng.

### Hang Dong
หางดง

Thirteen km south of Chiang Mai on Route 108 is Hang Dong, well known for ceramics, woodcarving and antiques. Many of the shops here deal in wholesale as well as retail, so prices are low. Catch a bus from Chiang Mai Gate to Hang Dong (6B fare). Most of the shops are actually about two km before Hang Dong.

### Mae Sa & Samoeng

This forested loop north-west of Chiang Mai via Mae Rim and/or Hang Dong makes a good day or overnight trip. Although dotted with tourist developments – resorts, orchid farms, butterfly parks, elephant camps, snake farms, botanical gardens, antique and handicraft shops – the Route 1096/1269 loop through the Mae Sa Valley is very scenic in spots. **Mae Sa Falls** is only six km from the Mae Rim turnoff from Route 107, which in turn is 12 km north of Chiang Mai. Farther along the loop are several Hmong villages.

There are at least four places along the loop which call themselves elephant 'camp', 'farm' or 'village'. Best of the bunch is the **Mae Sa Elephant Camp** near Mae Sa Falls, where it costs 40B per person for the one-hour elephant show at 9.30 am daily, or 50B per person to ride an elephant any time throughout the day.

Samoeng, at the westernmost extension of the loop (35 km from Mae Rim), is the most peaceful area for an overnight stay, since it's five km north of the main loop junction between the highways to/from Mae Rim and Hang Dong via Route 1269. The *Samoeng Resort* (☎ (53) 487072), about 1.5 km outside Samoeng village itself, has quiet, well designed bungalows from 300B for rooms with fan, more for air-con.

**Getting There & Away** You can get a song-thaew to Samoeng from the Chang Pheuak bus station in Chiang Mai for about 14B.

Since it's paved all the way, the winding loop road makes a good ride by bicycle or motorcycle. From Samoeng you can take a north-west detour along Route 1265 to Route 1095 for Pai and Mae Hong Son; the 148 km road (136 km unpaved, 12.2 km paved) breaks north at the Karen village of Wat Chan, where fuel is available. This is the longest unpaved road stretch remaining in Northern Thailand and is recommended for experienced off-highway bikers only (and only in the dry season). The road passes a few Hmong and Karen villages.

## CHOM THONG & AROUND
จอมทอง

Chom Thong (pronounced 'jawm thawng') is a necessary stop between Chiang Mai and Doi Inthanon, Thailand's highest peak, if you're travelling by public transport (see the Doi Inthanon section for details).

## Wat Phra That Si Chom Thong
วัดพระธาตุศรีจอมทอง

If you have time, walk down Chom Thong's main street to Wat Phra That Si Chom Thong. The gilded Burmese chedi in the compound was built in 1451 and the Burmese-style bòt, built in 1516, is one of the most beautiful in Northern Thailand. Inside and out it is an integrated work of art that deserves admiration; it is well cared for by the local Thais. Fine woodcarving can be seen along the eaves of the roof and inside on the ceiling, which is supported by massive teak columns. The impressive altar is designed like a small prasat (temple) in typical Lanna style and is said to contain a relic from the right side of the Buddha's skull. The abbot is a very serene old man, soft-spoken and radiant.

Behind the prasat-altar is a room containing religious antiques. More interesting is a glass case along one wall of the bòt which contains ancient Thai weaponry – a little out of place in a wat, maybe.

A few doors up from the wat compound, the Vegetarian Restaurant offers simple rice and noodles dishes which substitute tofu and gluten for meat.

## Wat Phra Nawn Yai
วัดพระนอนใหญ่

About halfway between Chiang Mai and Chom Thong, off the highway, you may see Wat Phra Nawn Yai (on the right heading towards Chom Thong), with its distinctive cartoonish Buddha figures (standing, sitting and reclining), as well as sculptured scenes from selected jatakas.

## Doi Inthanon National Park
อุทยานแห่งชาติดอยอินทนนท์

Doi Inthanon, Thailand's highest peak (2595m), has three impressive waterfalls cascading down its slopes. Starting from the bottom, these are **Mae Klang Falls**, **Wachiratan Falls** and **Siriphum Falls**. The first two have picnic

JOE CUMMINGS

RICHARD I'ANSON

### Northern Thailand
Top: Mahout and his elephant – their working relationship usually lasts a lifetime
Bottom: Spinning and dyeing cotton – still a traditional craft of Northern hill tribes

BERNARD NAPTHINE

DALE WAHREN

SARA JANE CLELAND

## Hill Tribes

Top: Embroidered cap frames the face of an Akha child
Bottom Left: Red Akha tribeswoman with distinctive Akha headdress
Bottom Right: Lisu woman dressed in a characteristically colourful tunic

areas and food vendors nearby. Mae Klang is the largest waterfall and the easiest to get to; you must stop there to get a bus to the top of Doi Inthanon. Mae Klang Falls can be climbed nearly to the top, as there is a footbridge leading to massive rock formations over which the water cascades. Wachiratan is also very nice and less crowded.

The views from Inthanon are best in the cool dry season from November to February. You can expect the air to be quite chilly towards the top, so bring a jacket or sweater. For most of the year a mist, formed by the condensation of warm humid air below, hangs around the highest peak. Along the 47 km road to the top are many terraced rice fields, tremendous valleys and a few small hill-tribe villages. Around 4000 Hmong and Karen tribespeople make the mountain slopes their home.

The entire mountain is a national park (482 sq km), despite agriculture and human habitation. One of the top destinations in South-East Asia for naturalists and bird-watchers, the mist-shrouded upper slopes produce a bumper crop of orchids, lichens, mosses and epiphytes while supporting nearly 400 bird varieties, more than any other habitat in Thailand. The mountain is also one of the last habitats of the Asiatic black bear, along with the Assamese macaque, Phayre's leaf-monkey and a selection of other rare and not-so-rare monkeys and gibbons, plus the more common Indian civet, barking deer and giant flying squirrel – around 75 mammalian species in all.

Most of the park's bird species are found between 1500 and 2000m; the best birding season falls February through April, and the best spots are the *beung* (bogs) toward the summit.

**Phra Mahathat Naphamethanidon**, a chedi built by the Royal Thai Air Force to commemorate the king's 60th birthday in 1989, is off the highway between Km 41 and 42, about four km before reaching the summit. In the base of the octagonal chedi is a hall containing a green stone Buddha image.

A 3B admission fee is collected for Mae Klang Falls near the foot of the mountain. At the park headquarters, 31 km from Chom Thong, you can book park bungalows for 100B per person or tents for 40B. Blankets may be hired for 10B each.

**Getting There & Away**

Buses to Chom Thong leave regularly from just inside the Chiang Mai Gate at the south moat in Chiang Mai. Some buses go directly to Mae Klang Falls and some terminate in Hot, although the latter will let you off in Chom Thong. The fare to Chom Thong, 58 km away, is 15B.

From Chom Thong there are regular songthaews to Mae Klang, about eight km north, for 10B. Songthaews from Mae Klang to Doi Inthanon leave almost hourly until late afternoon and cost 25 to 30B per person. Most of the passengers are locals who get off at various points along the road up, thus allowing a few stationary views of the valleys below. If you're travelling by private vehicle, you'll have to pay a toll of 20B per car or 5B per motorcycle at the park entrance.

For another 10B you can go from Chom Thong to Hot, where you can get buses on to Mae Sariang or Mae Hong Son. However, if you've gone to Doi Inthanon and the waterfalls, you probably won't have time to make it all the way to Mae Sariang or Mae Hong Son in one day, so you may want to stay overnight in the park or in Chom Thong. Forestry Service bungalows near the park headquarters (past the Chom Thong park entrance) cost from 300 to 1000B per night. In Chom Thong, enquire at the wat for a place to sleep.

## NORTH TO THA TON
### Mae Taeng & Chiang Dao
เชียงดาว

The mountainous area around Mae Taeng – especially south-west of the junction of Routes 107 and 1095 – has become a major trekking area because of the variety of Lisu, Lahu, Karen and Hmong villages in the region. Rafting along the Mae Taeng River is so popular these days that there's a permanent rafting centre, Maetaman Rafting, west of Route 107. For the most part, the centre handles groups on trips out of Chiang Mai.

The **Elephant Training Centre Taeng-Dao**, off Route 107 between Mae Taeng and Chiang Dao, is one of several in the area that puts on elephant shows for tourists. If you haven't seen the one in Lampang Province (Thung Kwian), this one's a reasonable alternative.

**Fang Dao Forest Monastery**, off the highway south of Chiang Dao near Km 52, is a meditation wat in the North-Eastern forest tradition.

**Tham Chiang Dao**  The main attraction along the way to Fang and Tha Ton is this cave complex five km west of Route 107 and 72 km north of Chiang Mai.

The complex is said to extend some 10 to 14 km into 2285m Doi Chiang Dao; the interconnected caverns which are open to the public include Tham Maa (7365m long), Tham Kaew (477m), Tham Phra Nawn (360m), Tham Seua Dao (540m) and Tham Naam (660m). Tham Phra Nawn and Tham Seua Dao contain religious statuary and are electrically illuminated (and thus easily explored on one's own) while Tham Maa, Tham Kaew and Tham Naam have no light fixtures. A lantern and guide can be hired for 20B per cavern or 60B for all three. Interior cave formations are quite spectacular in places – over 100 of them are named.

Local legend says this cave complex served as the home of a *reu-sii* (hermit sage) for a thousand years. As the legend goes, the sage was on such intimate terms with the deity world that he convinced some *thewadaa* (the Buddhist equivalent of angels) to create seven magic wonders inside the caverns: a stream flowing from the pedestal of a solid-gold Buddha; a storehouse of divine textiles; a mystical lake; a city of nagas; a sacred immortal elephant; and the hermit's tomb. No, you won't find any of the seven wonders created for the cave hermit; the locals say these are much deeper inside the mountain, beyond the last of the illuminated caverns. The locals also say that anyone who attempts to remove a piece of rock from the cave will forever lose their way in the cave's eerie passages.

Admission to the overall complex is 5B. There is a wat complex outside the cavern and a collection of vendors selling roots, herbs and snacks (mostly noodles).

The surrounding area is quite scenic and largely unspoiled. From the summit of Doi Chiang Dao mountain there are spectacular views. Beyond Tham Chiang Dao along the same rural road is a smaller sacred cave called **Tham Pha Plong**.

**Places to Stay**  Under Thai and German management, *Malee's Nature Lovers Bungalows* (☎ (01) 961-8387), about 1.5 km past Chiang Dao Cave on the right, has dorm beds for 80B and thatch and brick bungalows for 250B double. Malee's can arrange trekking, rafting and birding trips in the area.

*Traveller Inn Hotel*, on the highway in Mae Taeng, is a well run place with rooms in the 300 to 400B range. An old wooden hotel in Chiang Dao village, the *Pieng Dao*, has rooms for 80B.

*Chiang Dao Hill Resort* (☎ (53) 236995), off the highway between Km 100 and 101, offers good tourist bungalows for 600 to 1200B. The *Royal Ping Garden Resort*, off the highway south of Chiang Dao, has more expensive luxury rooms.

**Getting There & Away**  Buses to Chiang Dao from Chiang Mai's Chang Pheuak station cost 21B.

### Doi Ang Khang
ดอยอ่างขาง

About 20 km before Fang is the turn-off for Route 1249 to Doi Ang Khang, Thailand's 'Little Switzerland'. Twenty-five km from the highway, this 1300m peak has a cool climate year-round and supports the cultivation of flowers, as well as fruits and vegetables that are usually found only in more temperate climates.

A few hill-tribe villages (Lahu, Lisu and

Hmong) can be visited on the slopes. You can pick up a free map of the area at the main military checkpoint on Route 1249. Some interesting do-it-yourself treks can be made in the area.

The Yunnanese/KMT village of **Ban Khum** on Doi Ang Khang has some hillside bungalows for rent in the 200B range.

## FANG & THA TON
ฝาง/ท่าตอน
• ☎ (53)

The present city of Fang was founded by King Mengrai in the 13th century, although as a human settlement and trading centre for jiin haw caravans the locale dates back at least 1000 years. North from Chiang Mai along Route 107, Fang doesn't look particularly inviting, but the town's quiet back streets are lined with interesting little shops in wooden buildings. The Burmese-style **Wat Jong Paen** (near the Wiang Kaew Hotel) has a very impressive stacked-roof wihāan.

There are also Mien and Karen villages nearby which you can visit on your own, but for most people Fang is just a road marker on the way to Tha Ton, the starting point for Kok River trips to Chiang Rai (and other points along the river in between), and for guided or solo treks to the many hill-tribe settlements in the region. However, if you're planning to spend the night before catching the boat, Fang is as good a place to stay as Tha Ton. On the other hand some people prefer Tha Ton's more rural setting. Either way it's only half an hour or so by songthaew to the river from Fang or vice versa. Two banks along the main street in Fang offer currency exchange. Through the Wiang Kaew Hotel in Fang you can arrange tours to local villages inhabited by Palaung (a Karenic tribe that arrived from Myanmar around 12 years ago), Black Lahu, Akha and Yunnanese.

About 10 km west of Fang at Ban Meuang Chom, near the agricultural station, is a system of **hot springs**. Just ask for the *bàw náam ráwn* ('baw nâam hâwn' in Northern Thai), part of Doi Fang National Park. There are frequent songthaews carrying Thai picnickers from Fang on weekends.

Tha Ton is a collection of riverboats, tourist accommodation, restaurants, souvenir shops and a songthaew stand along a pretty bend in the Kok River. For something to do, climb the hill to **Wat Tha Ton** and attached Chinese shrine for good views of the surrounding area. A large temple bell, which sounds every morning at 4 am (wake-up call for monks) and again at 6 am (alms-round call), can be heard throughout the valley surrounding Tha Ton.

### Trekking & Rafting

There are some pleasant walks along the Kok River. Treks and raft trips can be arranged through Tha Ton's Thip's Travellers House, Mae Kok River Lodge or the Thaton River View. Thip's arranges economical bamboo house-rafts with pilot and cook for three days for 1200B per person (four person minimum), including all meals, lodging and rafting. The first day you'll visit several villages near the river and spend the night in a Lisu village; on the second day rafters visit hot springs and more villages, and spend the second night on the raft; and on the third day you dock in Chiang Rai.

The Mae Kok River Lodge uses a sturdy, steel-hulled raft topped with bamboo for one night, two day river trips which cost 1500B per person.

You could also pull together a small group of travellers and arrange your own house-raft with a guide and cook for a two or three day journey downriver, stopping off in villages of your own choosing along the way. A house-raft generally costs around 350B per person per day including all meals and takes up to six people – so figure on 1000 to 1200B for a three day trip with stops at Shan, Lisu and Karen villages along the way. New police regulations require that an experienced boat navigator accompany each raft – the river has lots of tricky spots and there have been some mishaps.

Near the pier you can rent inflatable kayaks to do your own paddling in the area. Upstream a few km the river flows into

NORTHERN THAILAND

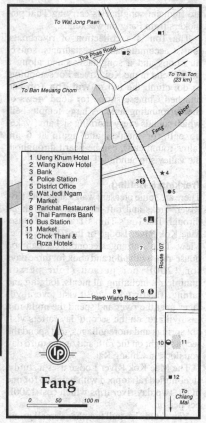

To Wat Jong Paen

Tha Phae Road

To Tha Ton
(23 km)

To Ban Meuang Chom

Fang River

1  Ueng Khum Hotel
2  Wiang Kaew Hotel
3  Bank
4  Police Station
5  District Office
6  Wat Jedi Ngam
7  Market
8  Parichat Restaurant
9  Thai Farmers Bank
10  Bus Station
11  Market
12  Chok Thani &
    Roza Hotels

Route 107

Rawp Wiang Road

**Fang**

0    50    100 m

To
Chiang
Mai

Myanmar. The Mong Tai Army occasionally clashes with Yangon troops in the area; in May 1993 two raftmen sitting next to the bridge in Tha Ton were killed by a stray K-81 rocket that dropped in from a nearby battle. Khun Sa's 1995 'surrender' to Burmese authorities has not stopped the fighting.

### Places to Stay & Eat
**Fang** A reliable choice is the friendly *Wiang Kaew Hotel*, behind the Fang Hotel off the main street. Basic but clean rooms with private bath are 110B with hot water, 80B without.

The *Ueng Khum (UK) Hotel* (☎ 451268) around the corner on Tha Phae Rd has large bungalow-style accommodation around a courtyard for 120/180B a single/double; all rooms have hot showers. More up-market digs near the market on the highway are available at the *Chok Thani* and *Roza*, both with rooms with fan from 200B, air-con from 320B.

The *Fang Restaurant* (its Thai sign reads 'Khun Pa') next to the Fang Hotel entrance has a bilingual menu and quite decent food. The clean *Parichat Restaurant*, on Rawp Wiang Rd near the highway market, serves an exemplary bowl of khâo sòi with chicken or beef, plus kuǎytǐaw, khâo phàt and other standards. Farther down this same road is a row of cheap Isaan restaurants and lâo dong (herbal liquor) bars.

A few food vendors – not quite enough to make a true 'night market' – set up near the bus terminal at night.

**Tha Ton** If you want to spend the night near the pier in Tha Ton, there are several options. Old standby *Thip's Travellers House* is a short walk from the pier, quite near the bridge where the road from Fang meets the river. Rates are 50 to 80B for rooms without bath, 80 to 100B with bath. Thip has a more atmospheric location overlooking a stream called Huay Nam Yen about three km past the bridge. Rates are 100, 200 and 400B depending on the size of the rooms. Enquire at Thip's in town for transport back and forth to Huay Nam Yen.

*Chankasem*, down near the pier, has a pleasant restaurant on the river and a variety of rooms: 60B with shared bath in the older wooden section; 80B for singles/doubles with fan and bath; 100 to 200B with hot water and 300B for a brick bungalow. Also near the pier is the *Apple Guest House*, with very basic rooms for 40/60B.

On the opposite side of the river there are three more places to choose from. The *Maekok River Lodge* (☎ 222172) has landscaped grounds, a pool and deluxe rooms overlooking the river for 625B, plus a few more basic rooms for 300B.

On the river another 100m or so north from the bridge, the tranquil *Garden Home* offers very clean thatched bungalows spaced well apart on landscaped grounds for 150B with private shower (cold water, but a hot shower is available in the restaurant). From the bridge, turn left at the Thaton River View Hotel sign to find it.

Farther on along the river, the well designed *Thaton River View Hotel* (☎ (01) 510-1781; ☎ (2) 287-0123, fax 287-3420 in Bangkok) has immaculate, spacious rooms facing the river for around 1000B. The River View's restaurant is the best in the area, with Shell Chuan Chim honours for four different dishes on the menu.

Two Thai-style resorts near the entrance to Tha Ton from Fang, *Kok Garden Resort* and *Khumphukham Garden*, have rooms with all the amenities from 650B up.

*Chao Phae*, an indoor-outdoor place opposite Thip's Travellers House, is the best non-hotel restaurant in Tha Ton. There are several rustic foodstalls near the pier and near the bridge. Downriver a bit from the Apple and Chankasem guesthouses, the *Rim Kok Restaurant* has decent Thai and Chinese food. The owners also rent a few rooms for 250B to 500B.

A local culinary speciality is lûy, a Northern Thai salad made with pig's blood.

About 15 km north-east of Tha Ton, in Lou-Ta, the nearest Lisu village, *Asa's Guest Home* offers two basic bamboo-walled rooms for 150B per person per night including two meals. The friendly family who own the house can arrange one and two day jungle trips in the area. To get there take a yellow songthaew from Tha Ton for 10B (or motorcycle taxi for 20B) and ask to get off in Lou-Ta.

### Getting There & Away
**Bus & Songthaew** Buses to Fang leave from the Chang Pheuak bus station in Chiang Mai. The three hour trip costs 43B.

From Fang it's 23 km to Tha Ton. A songthaew does the 40 minute trip for 11B; the larger orange buses from Fang leave less frequently and cost only 8B. Buses leave from near the market, or you can wait in front of the Fang Hotel for a bus or songthaew. Both operate from 5.30 am to 5 pm only.

**Mae Salong** The river isn't the only way to get to points north from Tha Ton. Yellow songthaews leave from the east side of the river in Tha Ton to Mae Salong in Chiang Rai Province several times daily between 7 am and 3 pm. The trip takes about 2½ hours and costs 60B per person. Hold tight – the road is steep and twisty.

**Mae Sai & Chiang Rai** If you'd rather not take the boat downriver, buses runs several times daily between Tha Ton and Chiang Rai for 25B. From Chiang Rai there are frequent buses on to Mae Sai. The direct bus service between Tha Ton and Mae Sai was recently discontinued.

**Pai** If you're heading to or coming from Mae Hong Son Province, it's not necessary to dip all the way south to Chiang Mai before continuing westward or eastward. At Ban Mae Malai, the junction of Route 107 (the Chiang Mai-Fang highway), you can pick up a bus to Pai for 38B; if you're coming from Pai, be sure to get off here to catch a bus north to Fang. Buses between Ban Mae Malai and Fang cost 40B.

**Motocycle** Motorcycle trekkers can also travel between Tha Ton and Doi Mae Salong, 48 km north-east along a fully paved but sometimes treacherous mountain road. There are a couple of Lisu and Akha villages along the way. The 27 km or so between Doi Mae Salong and the village of Hua Muang Ngam are very steep and winding – take care, especially in the rainy season. When conditions are good, the trip can be accomplished in 1½ hours.

For an extra charge, you can take a motorcycle on most boats to Chiang Rai.

# Hill Tribes

The headdress of an Akha woman is traditionally decorated by beads, feathers and dangling silver ornaments.

T he term 'hill tribe' refers to ethnic minorities living in the mountainous regions of Thailand's far north and west. The Thais refer to them as *chao khão* (literally 'mountain people'). Each hill tribe has its own language, customs, mode of dress and spiritual beliefs.

Most are of semi-nomadic origin, having migrated to Thailand from Tibet, Myanmar, China and Laos during the past 200 years or so, although some groups may have been in Thailand much longer. They are 'fourth world' people in the sense that they belong neither to the main aligned powers nor to the developing nations. Rather, they have crossed and continue to cross national borders without regard for recent nationhood. Language and culture constitute the borders of their world – some groups are caught between the 6th and 20th centuries, while others are gradually being assimilated into modern Thai life. Many tribespeople are also moving into lowland areas inhabited by Thais as montane lands become deforested by both traditional swidden (slash-and-burn) cultivation methods and illegal logging.

. The Tribal Research Institute in Chiang Mai recognises 10 different hill tribes in Thailand, but there may be up to 20. The Institute estimates the total hill-tribe population to be around 550,000. The largest tribes most likely to be encountered in the region can be divided into three main linguistic groups: the Tibeto-Burman (Lisu, Lahu, Akha), the Karenic (Karen, Kayah) and the Austro-Thai (Hmong, Mien). Within each major group there may also be several subgroups, eg Blue Hmong, White Hmong, Striped Hmong; these names usually refer to predominant elements of clothing.

The Shan (Thai Yai) are not included in the brief descriptions below as they are not a hill-tribe group per se – they live in permanent locations, practise Theravada Buddhism and speak a language very similar to Thai. Thai scholars consider the Shan to have been the original inhabitants (Thai Yai means 'larger' or 'majority Thais') of the area. Nevertheless, Shan villages are often common stops on hill-tribe trekking itineraries.

The following comments on ethnic dress refer mostly to the female members of each group, as hill-tribe men tend to dress like rural Thais. Population figures have been taken from 1989 estimates. For more detailed descriptions on Thailand's hill tribes, look up some of the publications listed in the Books section of the Facts for the Visitor chapter.

## Akha (Thai: *i-kaw*)

*Population:* 38,000
*Origin:* Tibet
*Present locations:* Thailand, Laos, Myanmar, Yunnan
*Economy:* rice, corn, opium
*Belief system:* animism, with an emphasis on ancestor worship
*Distinctive characteristics:* villages are along mountain ridges or on steep slopes from 1000 to 1400m in altitude. The well known Akha Swing Ceremony takes place mid-August to mid-September – between planting and harvest – and is linked to ancestor worship and spirit offerings. The Akha are amongst the poorest of Thailand's ethnic minorities and tend to resist assimilation into the Thai mainstream. Like the Lahu, they often cultivate opium for their own consumption.

## Lahu (*musoe*)

*Population:* 58,700
*Origin:* Tibet
*Present locations:* Thailand, southern China, Myanmar
*Economy:* rice, corn, opium

The Lahu people are particularly well known for their richly coloured and intricately woven shoulder bags (yâam).

*Belief system:* theistic animism; some groups are Christian
*Distinctive characteristics:* black and red jackets with narrow skirts for women, bright green or blue-green baggy trousers for men. They live in mountainous areas at about 1000m. There are five main groups – Red Lahu, Black Lahu, White Lahu, Yellow Lahu and Lahu Sheleh.

## Lisu *(lisaw)*

*Population:* 25,000
*Origin:* Tibet
*Present locations:* Thailand, Yunnan (China)
*Economy:* rice, opium, corn, livestock
*Belief system:* animism with ancestor worship and spirit possession
*Distinctive characteristics:* the women wear long multicoloured tunics over trousers and sometimes black turbans with tassels. Men wear baggy green or blue pants pegged in at the ankles. Premarital sex is said to be common, along with freedom in choosing marital partners. Lisu villages are usually in the mountains at about 1000m.

*The Lisu are traditionally organised into patrilineal clans which have pan-tribal jurisdiction – this is unique among hill-tribe groups; power normally resides with the shaman or village head-man at the village level.*

## Mien *(yao)*

*Population:* 38,000
*Origin:* central China
*Present locations:* Thailand, southern China, Laos, Myanmar, Vietnam
*Economy:* rice, corn, opium
*Belief system:* animism with ancestor worship and Taoism
*Distinctive characteristics:* women wear black jackets and trousers decorated with intricately embroidered patches and red fur-like collars, along with large dark blue or black turbans. They tend to settle near mountain springs at between 1000 and 1200m. Kinship is patrilineal and marriage is polygamous. The Mien are highly skilled at embroidery and silversmithing.

## Hmong *(meo* or *maew)*

*Population:* 87,000
*Origin:* southern China
*Present locations:* Thailand, southern China, Laos, Vietnam
*Economy:* rice, corn, opium
*Belief system:* animism
*Distinctive characteristics:* simple black jackets and indigo or black baggy trousers with striped borders or indigo skirts, and silver jewellery. Most women wear their hair in a large bun. They usually live on mountain peaks or plateaus above 1000m. Kinship is patrilineal and polygamy is permitted. They are Thailand's second-largest hill-tribe group and are especially numerous in Chiang Mai Province.

## Karen *(yang or kariang)*

*Population:* 285,000
*Origin:* Myanmar
*Present locations:* Thailand, Myanmar
*Economy:* rice, vegetables, livestock
*Belief system:* animism, Buddhism and Christianity (depending on the group)
*Distinctive characteristics:* thickly woven V-neck tunics of various colours (unmarried women wear white). Kinship is matrilineal and marriage is monogamous. They tend to live in lowland valleys and practise crop rotation rather than swidden agriculture. There are four distinct Karen groups: the White Karen (Skaw Karen), Pwo Karen, Black Karen (Pa-O) and Red Karen (Kayah). These groups combined form the largest hill tribe in Thailand, numbering about half of all hill-tribe people. Many Karen continue to migrate into Thailand from Myanmar, fleeing Burmese government persecution.

*The Mien people have been heavily influenced by Chinese traditions – Chinese characters are used to write the Mien language.*

NORTHERN THAILAND

## KOK RIVER TRIP TO CHIANG RAI

From Tha Ton you can make a half-day long-tail boat trip to Chiang Rai down the Kok River. The regular passenger boat leaves at 12.30 pm and costs 160B per person. You can also charter a boat, which between eight or 10 people works out at much the same cost per person but gives you more room to move. The trip is a bit of a tourist trap these days as most of the passengers are farangs and the villages along the way sell Coke and souvenirs, and there are lots of TV aerials – but it's still fun. The best time to do the trip is at the end of the rainy season in November when the river level is high.

To catch a boat on the same day from Chiang Mai you'd have to leave by 7 or 7.30 am at the latest and make no stops on the way. The 6 am bus is the best bet. The travel time downriver depends on river conditions and the skill of the pilot, taking anywhere from three to five hours. You could actually make the boat trip in a day from Chiang Mai, catching a bus back from Chiang Rai as soon as you arrive, but it's far better to stay in Fang or Tha Ton, take the boat trip, then stay in Chiang Rai or Chiang Saen before travelling on. You may sometimes have to get off and walk or push the boat if it gets stuck on sandbars.

Some travellers take the boat to Chiang Rai in two or three stages, stopping first in **Mae Salak**, a large Lahu village which is about a third of the distance, or **Ban Ruammit**, a Karen village about two-thirds of the way down. Both villages are well touristed these days (charter boat tours stop for photos and elephant rides), but from here you can trek to other Shan, Thai and hill-tribe villages, or do longer treks south of Mae Salak to **Wawi**, a large multi-ethnic community of jiin haw, Lahu, Lisu, Akha, Shan, Karen, Mien and Thai peoples. The Wawi area has dozens of hill-tribe villages of various ethnicities, including the largest Akha community in Thailand (Saen Charoen) and the oldest Lisu settlement (Doi Chang). A few years ago DK Book House in Chiang Mai published helpful Wawi and Kok River trekking maps which marked trails and village locations. These maps are now out of print but if you can manage to get copies they could prove very useful.

Another alternative is to trek south from Mae Salak all the way to the town of **Mae Suai**, where you can catch a bus on to Chiang Rai or back to Chiang Mai. You might also try getting off the boat at one of the smaller villages (see boat fares below) – **Jakheu** looked interesting. Another alternative is to make the trip (much more slowly) upriver from Chiang Rai – this is possible despite the rapids.

Several of the guesthouses in Tha Ton now organise raft trips down the river – see the earlier Tha Ton section.

The following table shows boat fares from Tha Ton:

| Destination | Fare |
| --- | --- |
| Ban Mai | 40B |
| Mae Salak | 50B |
| Pha Tai | 60B |
| Jakheu | 70B |
| Kok Noi | 90B |
| Pha Khwang | 90B |
| Pha Khiaw | 140B |
| Hat Wua Dam | 140B |
| Ban Ruammit | 150B |
| Chiang Rai | 160B |

### Warning

Whether travelling by raft or long-tail boat, all passengers are required to sign in at police posts three times along the river: in Tha Ton, Mae Salak and Ban Ruammit. This requirement is part of an overall attempt to improve security along the river following several armed bandit attacks on passing boats during the late 1980s. Things have been quiet for the last decade, so the system seems to be effective. Still, don't travel with any valuables you can't afford to lose.

Bring sun block and a hat (one that you can tie down once the boat reaches warp speed) or scarf, as long-tail boats provide no shelter from the sun.

# Lamphun Province

This tiny province south-east of Chiang Mai is very much one small city surrounded by farms and villages.

## LAMPHUN
อ.เมืองลำพูน
• ☎ *(53)* • *pop 14,750*
Best seen on a day trip from Chiang Mai,
along with Pasang, Lamphun was the centre
of the small Hariphunchai principality
(750-1281 AD) originally ruled by the Mon
princess Chama Thewi. Long after its pro-
genitor, Dvaravati, was vanquished by the
Khmers, Hariphunchai succeeded in remaining independent of both the Khmers and the
Chiang Mai Thais.

This provincial capital is fairly quiet but
there are a few places to stay if you want to get
away from the hustle and bustle of Chiang Mai
or want to study the temples here in depth.

The village just north of Lamphun, Nong
Chang Kheun, is known for producing the
sweetest *lam yai* (longan) fruit in the country.
During the second week of August, Lamphun
hosts the annual Lam Yai Festival, which features floats made of the fruit and, of course, a
Miss Lam Yai contest.

### Wat Phra That Hariphunchai
วัดพระธาตุหริภุญชัย
This wat, which was built on the site of Queen
Chama Thewi's palace in 1044 (1157 according to some datings), is on the left on the main
road into Lamphun from Chiang Mai. The
temple lay derelict for many years until Khrubaa
Siwichai, one of Northern Thailand's most
famous monks, made renovations in the 1930s.
It has some interesting post-Dvaravati architecture, a couple of fine Buddha images and two
old chedis of the original Hariphunchai style.
The tallest, Chedi Suwan, dates to 1418;
although not built during the Hariphunchai
period, it was styled after Hariphunchai models.
The chedi's 46m height is surmounted by a
nine-tier umbrella made of 6.5 kg of pure gold.

The world's largest bronze gong hangs in
a reddish pavilion on the grounds.

### Lamphun National Museum
พิพิธภัณฑ์แห่งชาติลำพูน
Across the street from Wat Phra That Hariphunchai, the museum's small collection includes
artefacts from the Dvaravati, Hariphunchai and

Lanna kingdoms. Opening hours are Wednesday
to Sunday from 9 to 4 pm. Entry is 10B.

### Wat Chama Thewi (Wat Kukut)
วัดจามเทวี (วัดกู่กุด)
A larger Hariphunchai chedi can be seen at Wat
Chama Thewi (popularly called Wat Kukut),
which is said to have been erected in the 8th or
9th century as a Dvaravati monument, then
rebuilt by the Hariphunchai Mons in 1218. As
it has been restored many times since then it is
now a mixture of several schools.

Each of the four sides of the chedi – known
as Chedi Suwan Chang Kot – has five rows
of three Buddha figures, diminishing in size
on each higher level. The stucco standing
Buddhas are definitely of the Dvaravati
style, though they are of recent creation.

Wat Kukut is on the opposite side of town
from Wat Hariphunchai. To get there, walk
west down Mukda Rd, perpendicular to the
Chiang Mai-Lamphun road (opposite Wat
Hari), passing over the town moat, then past
the district government offices until you
come to the wat on the left.

### Places to Stay & Eat
The easiest accommodation to find is the *Si
Lamphun Hotel*, on the town's main street,
Inthayongyot Rd, at Soi 5. Adequate singles
with grotty bathrooms cost 80 to 100B,
doubles 140B. Traffic noise is a problem.

*Tareerat Court* (☎ 560224), on Chama
Thewi Rd near Wat Mahawan, is a clean apartment-style place with rooms for 130 to 150B.
*Haw Phak Sawat Ari* on the opposite side of
this road used to be the place visiting archaeologists stayed, although nowadays Tareerat
Court is a better choice for the average visitor.
At Sawat Ari you can have an apartment with
a bedroom (mattress on the floor), bathroom
and sitting room for 80B per night or 1200B
per month. If the rooms have been vacant a long
time, they'll need a good cleaning.

*84 Motel*, a no-tell motel with curtained
garages about two km from town on the way
back to Chiang Mai, has decent rooms with
fan and bath for 200B, or with air-con, TV
and phone for 350B.

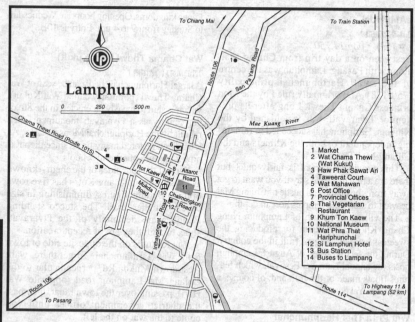

Lamphun

1 Market
2 Wat Chama Thewi
  (Wat Kukut)
3 Haw Phak Sawat Ari
4 Taweerat Court
5 Wat Mahawan
6 Post Office
7 Provincial Offices
8 Thai Vegetarian
  Restaurant
9 Khum Ton Kaew
10 National Museum
11 Wat Phra That
   Hariphunchai
12 Si Lamphun Hotel
13 Bus Station
14 Buses to Lampang

Along Inthayongyot Rd south of Wat Phra That is a string of OK noodle and rice shops. Behind the museum, housed in the former teak palace of a local prince, the all air-con *Khum Ton Kaew* offers a Thai and western menu (most dishes 50 to 150B) and is a good place to escape the heat.

The *Thai Vegetarian Restaurant*, on the same road as Khum Ton Kaew (on the next block on the opposite side) serves meatless curries and stir-fried veggies for around 10B including rice.

### Getting There & Away

Buses to Lamphun from Chiang Mai leave at 20 minute intervals throughout the day from the Chiang Mai-Lamphun Rd near the south side of Nawarat Bridge. From Lamphun in the reverse direction they leave in front of the National Museum. The 26 km bus ride (7B) goes along a beautiful country road, parts of which are bordered by tall *yang* (dipterocarp) trees.

If you're continuing on to Lampang (71 km) you can get a bus for 20B.

## PASANG
ป่าซาง

Don't confuse this village with Baw Sang, the umbrella village. In Pasang, cotton weaving is the cottage industry. The Nandakwang Laicum shop, one of many that weave and sell their own cotton, is on the right side of the main road going south and is recommended for its wide selection and tasteful designs. A cotton shirt or dress of unique Pasang design can be purchased in town for between 80 and 500B, depending on the quality. Songthaews from Lamphun to Pasang cost 5B.

### Wat Phra Phutthabaat Taak Phaa
วัดพระพุทธบาทตากผ้า

About nine km south of Pasang or 20 km south of Lamphun, off Route 106 in the subdistrict (*tambon*) of Ma-Kawk (follow

Route 1133 one km east), is this famous Mahanikai wat. A shrine to one of the North's most famous monks, Luang Puu Phromma, it contains a lifelike wax figure of the deceased monk sitting in meditation.

One of his disciples, Ajaan Thirawattho, teaches meditation to a large contingent of monks who are housed in *kuti* (meditation huts) of laterite brick. Behind the spacious grounds is a type of park and a steep hill mounted by a chedi. The wat is named after an unremarkable Buddha footprint (Phra Phutthabaat) shrine in the middle of the lower temple grounds and another spot where Buddha supposedly dried his robes (Taak Phaa).

### Getting There & Away
A songthaew will take you from Lamphun to Pasang for 5B. From Chiang Mai it costs 10B by regular bus or 12B by minibus.

If you're heading south to Tak Province under your own power, traffic is generally much lighter along Route 106 to Thoen than on Highway 11 to Lampang; a winding 10 km section of the road north of Thoen is particularly scenic. Both highways intersect Highway 1 south, which leads directly to Tak's capital.

### DOI KHUNTAN NATIONAL PARK
This park receives only 10,000 visitors a year, one of Northern Thailand's lowest park visitation rates. It's unique in that the main access is from the Khuntan train station (four daily trains from Chiang Mai; 15B; 1½ hours). Once at the Khuntan station, cross the tracks and follow a steep, marked path 1.5 km to park headquarters. By car take the Chiang Mai-Lampang highway to the Mae Tha turnoff, then follow signs along a steep unpaved road 18 km to the park. The park covers 255 sq km and ranges in elevation from 350m at the bamboo forest lowlands to 1363m at the pine-studded summit of Doi Khuntan. Wildflowers, including orchids, ginger and lillies, are abundant. Thailand's longest railway tunnel (1352m) intersects the mountain slope. In addition to a well marked trail covering the mountain's four

peaks, there's also a trail to Tat Moei Falls (a 7 km roundtrip).

Nice bungalows are available for 100B per person near park headquarters and at Camp 1 on the first peak. At the second peak or Camp 2 it's just 50B per person or you can pitch your own tent for 10B; food is available at a small shop near the park headquarters. There's an entry fee of 3B per person. The park is very popular on cool season weekends.

# Lampang Province

### LAMPANG
จ.เมืองลำปาง
• ☎ (54) • pop 43,369
One hundred km from Chiang Mai, Lampang was inhabited as far back as the 7th century in the Dvaravati period and played an important part in the history of the Hariphunchai kingdom. Legend says the city was founded by the son of Hariphunchai's Queen Chama Thewi.

Like Chiang Mai, Phrae and other older Northern cities, Lampang was built as a walled rectangle alongside a river (in this case the Wang River). At the turn of the century Lampang, along with nearby Phrae, became an important centre for the domestic and international teak trade. Because of their familiarity with the teak industry in Myanmar (at the time part of the British Raj along with India), a large British-owned local timber company brought in Burmese supervisors to train Burmese and Thai loggers in the area. These well paid supervisors, along with independent Burmese teak merchants who plied their trade in Lampang, sponsored the construction of more than a dozen impressive temples in the city. Burmese artisans designed and built the temples out of local materials, especially teak. Their legacy lives on in several of Lampang's best maintained wats, now among the city's main visitor attractions. At least four wats in town have Burmese abbots.

Many Thais visit Lampang for a taste of urban Northern Thailand without the crass commercialism of Chiang Mai. Although the central area is quite busy, the shophouses provide a more traditional feel.

## Information

The city maintains a tourist office on the second floor of the main provincial complex on the south side of Boonyawat Rd just east of Praisani Rd. It's open daily 8.30 am to 5.30 pm and handles general enquiries, as well as handing out hotel brochures and a locally printed map of the city.

## Horsecarts

Lampang is known throughout Thailand as Meuang Rot Maa (Horsecart City) because it's the only town in Thailand where horsecarts are still used as public transport. These days, Lampang's horsecarts are mainly for tourists. Trying to get a good price is more difficult than ever. A 15 minute horsecart tour around town costs at least 50 to 80B; for 100B you can get a half-hour tour that goes along the Wang River, and for 200 to 300B a one hour tour which stops at Wat Phra Kaew Don Tao and Wat Si Rong Meuang. If there's not much business you may be able to negotiate to bring the price down to 120B per half-hour or 200B per hour. The main horsecart stands are in front of the City Hall and Tipchang Hotel.

## Wat Phra Kaew Don Tao
วัดพระแก้วดอนเต้า

This wat, on the north side of the Wang River, was built during the reign of King Anantayot and housed the Emerald Buddha (now in Bangkok's Wat Phra Kaew) from 1436 to 1468. The main chedi shows Hariphunchai influence, while the adjacent mondòp was built in 1909. The mondòp, decorated with glass mosaic in typical Burmese style, contains a Mandalay-style Buddha image. A display of Lanna artefacts (mostly religious paraphernalia and woodwork) can be viewed in the wat's **Lanna Museum**.

## Other Temples

Two more wats built at the turn of century by Burmese artisans are **Wat Si Rong Meuang** and **Wat Si Chum**. Both have temple buildings constructed in the Burmese 'layered' style, with tin roofs gabled by intricate woodcarvings. The current abbots of these temples are Burmese as well.

Besides the wihāan at Wat Phra That Lampang Luang (see the following Around Lampang Province section), the mondòp at **Wat Pongsanuk Tai** is one of the few remaining local examples of original Lanna-style temple architecture, which emphasised open-sided wooden buildings.

**Wat Chedi Sao**, about six km north of town toward Jae Hom, is named for the 20 whitewashed Lanna-style chedis on its grounds (*sao* is Northern Thai for 20). It's a pretty, well endowed wat landscaped with bougainvillaea and casuarina. At one edge of the wat stands a very colourful statue of Avalokitesvara; while a pavilion in the centre features a gilded Buddha similar in style to the Phra Chinnarat in Phitsanulok. But the wat's real treasure is a solid gold 15th century seated Buddha on display in a glassed-in pavilion built over a square pond. The image weighs 1507g, stands 38 cm tall and is said to contain a piece of the Buddha's skull in its head and an ancient Pali-inscribed golden palmleaf in its chest; precious stones decorate the image's hairline and robe. A farmer reportedly found the figure next to the ruins of nearby Wat Khu Kao in 1983. Monks stationed at Wat Chedi Sao make and sell herbal medicines; the popular *yaa mong* is similar to tiger balm. The pavilion with the gold Buddha is open daily 8 am to 5 pm.

## Baan Sao Nak (Many Pillars House)
บ้านเสานัก

Built in 1896 in the traditional Lanna style, this huge teak house in the old Wiang Neua (North City) section of town is supported by 116 square teak pillars. The local *khun yïng* (a title equivalent to 'lady' in England) who owned the house died recently and left the house to the Thai government to be used as

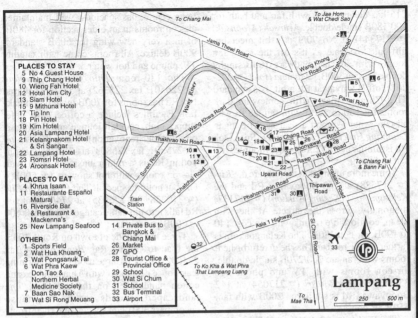

PLACES TO STAY
5 No 4 Guest House
9 Thip Chang Hotel
10 Wieng Fah Hotel
12 Hotel Kim City
13 Siam Hotel
15 9 Mithuna Hotel
17 Tip Inn
18 Pin Hotel
19 Kim Hotel
20 Asia Lampang Hotel
21 Kelangnakorn Hotel
   & Sri Sangar
22 Lampang Hotel
23 Romsri Hotel
24 Aroonsak Hotel

PLACES TO EAT
4 Khrua Isaan
11 Restaurante Español
   Maturaj
16 Riverside Bar
   & Restaurant &
   Mackenna's
25 New Lampang Seafood

OTHER
1 Sports Field
2 Wat Hua Khuang
3 Wat Pongsanuk Tai
6 Wat Phra Kaew
   Don Tao &
   Northern Herbal
   Medicine Society
7 Baan Sao Nak
8 Wat Si Rong Meuang

14 Private Bus to
   Bangkok &
   Chiang Mai
26 Market
27 GPO
28 Tourist Office &
   Provincial Office
29 School
30 Wat Si Chum
31 School
32 Bus Terminal
33 Airport

Lampang

NORTHERN THAILAND

a museum. The entire house is furnished with Burmese and Thai antiques; three rooms display antique silverwork, lacquerware, ceramics and other Northern Thai crafts. The area beneath the house is sometimes used for khan tòk ceremonial dinners.

When I was last there the house was closed while the government was preparing to convert the operation from a private to a public museum. When the house is open its hours are daily from 9.30 am to 5.30 pm; admission is 20B.

### Traditional Massage
**Samakhom Samunphrai Phaak Neua**
(Northern Herbal Medicine Society) at 149 Pratunam Rd, next to Wat Hua Khuang in the Wiang Neua area, offers traditional Northern Thai massage and herbal saunas. The massage costs 80B per hour; 1½ hours is a recommended minimum for best effect. The outdoor sauna room is pumped with herbal steam created by heating a mixture of 108

medicinal herbs; it costs 45B per use. Once you've paid, you can go in and out of the sauna as many times as you want during one visit. The massage service and sauna are open from 8 am to 8 pm daily.

### Places to Stay – bottom end & middle
The cheapest place in town is the *No 4 Guest House*, a large old teak house which has gone through at least three different managers and two different names over the last six years. The location in the pleasant residential Wang Neua area, north of the river, along with the spacious grounds, make it a good choice for long-term stays. Rooms are basic – just a mattress on the floor – and cost 80/100B single/double. The shared bathroom facilities feature hot water but aren't exceptionally clean.

There are several economical choices along Boonyawat Rd, which runs through the centre of town. The centrally located *Sri Sangar (Si Sa-Nga)* (☎ 217070) at No 213-

215 has clean rooms with fan and bath for 100/180B single/double. *Arunsak (Aroonsak)* (☎ 217344) at No 90/9 is a bit nicer but difficult to locate as it's off the road; fan rooms with attached bath are 180B single/double, air-con 300B. *9 Mithuna Hotel* (☎ 222-261), off Boonyawat Rd a bit, is a standard Thai-Chinese place with somewhat dark rooms for 160 to 220B with fan, 280B with air-con – not as good a deal as Sri Sangar. *Lampang Hotel* (☎ 227311) at 696 Suan Dok Rd is similar at 170/250B single/double with fan and bath.

Some more up-market options are the *Kim* (☎ 217588) at 168 Boonyawat Rd and the *Kelangnakorn (Keeling Nakhon)* (☎ 217137) diagonally across the street. At the Kim clean, comfortable rooms with fan cost 140 to 190B, air-con 280B. The Kelangnakorn is farther off the road and has been refurbished; rooms with fan are 200/270B single/double, air-con rooms with TV and phone are 330/410B. The *Romsri* (☎ 217054) at 142 Boonyawat Rd is similar at 200B with fan, 350B air-con.

The *Tip Inn* (☎ 221821) at 143 Talaat Kao Rd (off Thipchang Rd) is an almost hidden spot with nine quiet rooms off the street. Clean rooms are 100B for a single with shared bath, 160B double with private bath. The English-speaking Thai owners have a Thai silk shop nearby on Thip Chang Rd. It's down a small alley marked by a small green sign reading 'Hotel'.

The friendly *Siam Hotel* (☎ 217472), south-west of the clock circle on Chatchai Rd, has clean, well kept rooms for 190/250B with fan and attached bath or 350/390B with air-con, TV, phone and hot water.

### Places to Stay – top end

The long-running *Asia Lampang Hotel* (☎ 227844; fax 224436) at 229 Boonyawat Rd has good air-con rooms facing the street for 380B, and nicer rooms with TV for 400 to 500B; the latter are large suite-style rooms on the 5th floor. The Asia's pleasant street-level cafe is its best feature.

The *Pin Hotel* (☎ /fax 221509) at 8 Suan Dok Rd, right behind the Kim Hotel in the town centre, has spacious, well maintained air-con rooms in an older section for 480B, or in a very new wing for 600B standard, 900B deluxe. All rooms come with satellite TV, phone and hot water.

The 130-room *Thip Chang Lampang* (☎ 226501; fax 225362) at 54/22 Thakhrao Noi Rd has rooms for 700B including breakfast. Facilities include a coffee shop, cafe, supper club, cocktail lounge and pool (currently under renovation). *Wieng Fah Hotel* (☎ 225801; fax 225803) at 138/109 Phahonyothin Rd is a minor business hotel with air-con rooms with hot showers for 500B – OK but nothing special. The *Hotel Kim City* (☎ 310238; fax 226635) at 274/1 Chatchai Rd falls into this same category and costs 600 to 700B per room.

Three km outside of town on Route 1035, the road to Chiang Rai, *Bann Fai* (☎ /fax 224602) offers 14 large rooms in a charming teak house decorated with Thai antiques and cotton handwoven on the premises. The landscaped grounds around the house encompass 300 plant species and river frontage, plus views of nearby rice fields and mountains. Rates are 220B per double – four bathrooms are shared.

### Places to Eat

In the vicinity of the Kim and Asia hotels there are several good rice and noodle shops. Just east of the Kelangnakorn Hotel is a little row of jók and noodle shops open early morning. *Mae Hae Restaurant*, on Upparat Rd, is a diminutive but clean place with cheap and good Northern Thai food.

The outdoor *Riverside Bar & Restaurant* is in an old unrestored teak structure at 328 Thip Chang Rd on the river. It's a good choice for a sociable drink or meal, with live folk music nightly and reasonable prices considering the high quality of the food and service. Next door, the *Mackenna* also has good food and live music.

*Restaurante Español Maturaj*, between the Kim City and Wieng Fah hotels, serves moderately priced Spanish food, including paella, plus Thai food, burgers and pastries. It's open daily 9 am to 8 pm.

If you find yourself on the north bank of the river in the Wiang Neua district, *Khrua Isaan* near the bridge is a reasonably priced North-Eastern Thai place open 10 am to 4 pm.

For *New Lampang Seafood* – no English sign – follow your nose along Thip Chang Rd and you're sure to find it. You can pick out the fresh seafood yourself from ice boxes in front. Prices run from 60 to 120B per dish for seafood (20 to 30B for vegetable dishes) and portions are large. Another surprisingly good place for seafood is the *641 Restaurant* on Praisani Rd near the post office. It's very ordinary-looking but the seafood is very fresh; the owner started out as a street vendor who went to Bangkok twice a week for fresh ingredients.

### Getting There & Away

Buses to Lampang from Phitsanulok's main bus station cost 75B (113B air-con) and take four hours. From Chiang Mai, buses for Lampang leave from the Chiang Mai Arcade station about every half hour during the day and also from next to the Nawarat Bridge in the direction of Lamphun. The fare is 29B and the trip takes 1½ hours; there are also air-con buses available for 50 to 66B depending on the company and service. Buses from Lamphun are 20B. Ordinary buses to/from Bangkok leave hourly from 6 am to midnight and cost 145B. The bus station in Lampang is some way out of town – 10B by songthaew.

To book an air-con bus from Lampang to Bangkok or Chiang Mai there is no need to go out to the bus station as the tour bus companies have offices in town along Boonyawat Rd near the roundabout. Sombud, Thanjit Tour and Thaworn Farm each have 1st class air-con buses to Bangkok for 270B that leave nightly around 8 pm.

### AROUND LAMPANG PROVINCE
### Wat Phra That Lampang Luang
วัดพระธาตุลำปางหลวง
Probably the most magnificent temple in all of Northern Thailand, Wat Phra That Lampang Luang is also the best compendium of Lanna-style temple architecture.

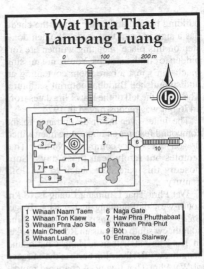

**Wat Phra That Lampang Luang**

0    100    200 m

1  Wihaan Naam Taem
2  Wihaan Ton Kaew
3  Wihaan Phra Jao Sila
4  Main Chedi
5  Wihaan Luang
6  Naga Gate
7  Haw Phra Phutthabaat
8  Wihaan Phra Phut
9  Bòt
10 Entrance Stairway

Surrounded by roofed brick cloisters, the centrepiece of the complex is the large, open-sided Wihaan Luang. Thought to have been built in 1476, the impressive building features a triple-tiered wooden roof supported by teak pillars. It's thought to be the oldest existing wooden building in Thailand. A huge gilded mondòp in the back of the wihăan contains a Buddha image cast in 1563; the faithful leave small gold-coloured Buddha figures close to the mondòp and hang Thai Lü weavings behind it.

Early 19th century jataka murals are painted on wooden panels around the inside upper perimeter of the wihăan. The tall Lanna-style chedi behind the wihăan, raised in 1449 and restored in 1496, measures 24m at its base and is 45m high. The small, simple Wihaan Ton Kaew to the right of the main wihăan was built in 1476. The oldest structure in the compound is the smaller 13th century Wihaan Phra Phut to the left (standing with your back to the main gate) of the main chedi; the wihăan to the right of the chedi (Wihaan Naam Taem) was built in the early 16th century and amazingly still contains traces of the original murals.

The Haw Phra Phutthabaat, a small white

building behind and to the left of the chedi, has a sign in front that reads 'Women don't step on this place' meaning women are forbidden to climb the steps. You're not missing much – it's just a bare room containing an undistinguished Buddha footprint sculpture. The bòt to the left of the Haw Phra dates from 1476 but was reconstructed in 1924.

The lintel over the main entrance to the compound features an impressive intertwined dragon relief – once common in Northern Thai temples but rarely seen these days. Supposedly this gate dates back to the 15th century.

Wat Phra That Lampang Luang is 18 km south-west of Lampang in Ko Kha. To get there by public transport, catch a blue songthaew south on Praisani Rd to the market in Ko Kha (8B), then a Hang Chat-bound songthaew (3B) three km north to the entrance of Wat Phra That Luang. A chartered motorcycle taxi from the Ko Kha songthaew terminal to the temple costs 20 to 30B.

If you're driving or cycling from Lampang, head south on Asia 2 and take the Ko Kha exit, then follow the road over a bridge and bear right. Note the police station on your left and continue for two km over another bridge until you see the temple on the left. If you're coming from Chiang Mai via Highway 11, turn south onto Route 1034 18 km north-west of Lampang at Km 13 – this is a 50 km short cut to Ko Kha that avoids much of Lampang.

### Young Elephant Training Centre
ศูนย์ฝึกลูกช้าง

In Hang Chat district north-west of Lampang, outside Thung Kwian at Km 37, is a camp for the training of young elephants. Also called the Thai Elephant Conservation Centre, this camp has moved from its previous location in Ngao, between Lampang and Chiang Rai; the Ngao centre will remain in use as a care facility for elderly tuskers.

In addition to the standard tourist show, the new centre will offer exhibits on the history and culture of Thai elephants as well as elephant rides through the surrounding forest. The animals appreciate a few pieces of fruit – 'feels like feeding a vacuum cleaner with a wet nozzle', reported one visitor. Training takes place daily between 7 and 11 am, with public shows at 9.30, 11 am and 2 pm except during the elephants' summer vacation from March to May. Show times seem to change from year to year.

To reach the camp, you can take a bus or

---

#### Elephants in Thailand

Current estimates put the number of wild elephants in Thailand at between 3000 and 4000. Around 1900 it was estimated that there were at least 100,000 elephants working in Thailand. In 1952 there were 13,397 domestic elephants in Thailand and until 1917 a white elephant appeared on the Thai national flag.

Elephant mothers carry their calves for 22 months. An adult can run at speeds of up to 23 km per hour and put less weight on the ground per sq cm than a deer. Elephants begin training when they're between three and five years old and the training continues for five years. Tasks they learn under the direction of their mahouts include pushing, carrying and piling logs, as well as bathing and walking in procession.

Working elephants have a career of about 50 years, hence when young they are given two mahouts, one older and one younger (sometimes a father-and-son team) who can see the animal through its lifetime. Thai law requires that elephants be retired and released into the wild at age 61. They often live for 80 years or more.

Now that logging has been banned in Thailand, one wonders if there is going to be less demand for trained elephants. Illegal logging aside, the elephant is still an important mode of jungle transport as it beats any other animal or machine for its ability to move through a forest with minimum damage – its large, soft feet distribute the animal's weight without crushing the ground. ∎

songthaew from Lampang's main bus terminal bound for Chiang Mai and get off at Km 37.

## Thung Kwian Forest Market
ตลาดป่าทุ่งเกวียน

The famous Forest Market *(talàat pàa)* at Thung Kwian in Hang Chat district (between Lampang and Chiang Mai off Highway 11) sells all manner of wild flora and fauna from the jungle, including medicinal and culinary herbs, wild mushrooms, bamboo shoots, field rats, beetles, snakes, plus a few rare and endangered species like pangolin. Officials are said to be cracking down on the sale of endangered species. The market meets every Wednesday from around 5 am till noon.

The nearby **Thung Kwian Reforestation Centre** protects a new 353 rai forest under the auspices of the state-owned Forest Industry Organisation.

## Other Attractions

North and east of Lampang are the cotton-weaving villages of **Jae Hom** and **Mae Tha**. You can wander around and find looms in action; there are also plenty of shops along the main roads.

**Pha Thai Cave** is 66 km north of Lampang, between Lampang and Chiang Rai about 500m off Highway 1. Besides the usual formations (stalagmites and stalactites), the cave has a large Buddha image.

The province is well endowed with waterfalls. Three are found within Wang Neua district, roughly 120 km north of the provincial capital via Route 1053: **Wang Kaew**, **Wang Thong** and **Than Thong** (Jampa Thong). Wang Kaew is the largest, with 110 tiers. Near the summit is a Mien hill-tribe village. This area became part of the 1172 sq km **Doi Luang National Park** in 1990; animals protected by the park include serow, barking deer, pangolin and pig-tailed macaque.

In Meuang Pan district, about halfway to Wang Neua from Lampang, is another waterfall, **Jae Sawn**, part of the 593 sq km **Jae Sawn National Park**. Elevations in the park reach above 2000m. Jae Sawn has six drops, each with its own pool; close to the falls are nine hot springs. Camping is permitted in both Jae Sawn and Doi Luang national parks.

# Nakhon Sawan Province

## NAKHON SAWAN
อ.เมืองนครสวรรค์

• ☎ *(56)* • *pop 107,000*

A fairly large town on the way north from Bangkok, Nakhon Sawan has an excellent view from the hill-top **Wat Chom Khiri Nak Phrot**. Thais and farangs both agree that Nakhon Sawan is not known for its hospitality, though it's a bustling trade centre. The population is largely Chinese and during Chinese New Year celebrations in February every hotel in town is booked. The celebrations here are reportedly the best in Thailand.

## Places to Stay

Most of the hotels in the city are located along Phahonyothin Rd (the highway from Bangkok) or along Matuli Rd. The *Anodard Hotel* (☎ 221844) at 479 Kosi Rd has very clean air-con rooms for a reasonable 280 to 320B. Other places include the *Asia* (☎ 213-752) at 956 Phahonyothin Rd, where rooms range from 100 to 200B, and the *Sawan Nakhon* (☎ 212027) at 110/1 Sawanwithi Rd, where the cost is from 200 to 260B for air-con.

*Visanu Inn* (☎ 222938), at 217-25 Matuli Rd, has air-con rooms from 250 to 400B, and down by the river *Airawan (Irawan)* (☎ 221889) at 1-5 Matuli Rd has fan rooms from 150 to 250B.

A more expensive hotel is the *Phiman* (☎ 222473; fax 221253), in front of the bus terminal at the Nakhon Sawan shopping centre, where air-con rooms range from 690 to 850B.

## Getting There & Away

The ordinary bus fare from Chiang Mai to Nakhon Sawan is 114B (160B air-con). From Bangkok, ordinary buses are 59B (107B air-con, 166B VIP).

NORTHERN THAILAND

NORTHERN THAILAND

# Kamphaeng Phet Province

## KAMPHAENG PHET
อ.เมืองกำแพงเพชร
• ☎ (55) • pop 23,750

Formerly known as Chakangrao or Nakhon Chum, Kamphaeng Phet (Diamond Wall) was once an important front line of defence for the Sukhothai kingdom but is now mostly known for producing the tastiest *klûay khài* (egg banana) in Thailand. It's a nice place to spend a day or two wandering around the ruins and experiencing a small Northern provincial capital that receives little tourism.

## Information
A privately sponsored Tourist Information Center, a block south of Chakungrao Hotel and off Thesa Rd, can answer general queries about accommodation and restaurants.

The main post office is just south of the old city on Thesa Rd.

## Old City
เมืองเก่า
Only a couple of kms off the Bangkok-Chiang Mai road are some ruins within the old city area of Kamphaeng Phet as well as some very fine remains of the long city wall.

A Kamphaeng Phet Historical Park has been established at the old city site and the area is now cared for by the Fine Arts Department. There is a 20B entry fee to the ruins within the city wall. Here you'll find **Wat Phra Kaew**, which used to be adjacent to the royal palace. The weather-corroded Buddha statues here have assumed slender, porous forms which remind many visitors of Giacometti sculptures. About 100m south-east of Wat Phra Kaew is **Wat Phra That**, distinguished by a large round-based chedi surrounded by laterite columns.

## Kamphaeng Phet National Museum
พิพิธภัณฑ์แห่งชาติกำแพงเพชร
Across the road and south 100m or so from these temples is a national museum. Down-

stairs has the usual survey of Thai art periods while upstairs has a collection of artefacts from the Kamphaeng Phet area, including terracotta ornamentation from ruined temples and Buddha images in the Sukhothai and Ayuthaya styles. The museum is open Wednesday to Sunday from 8.30 am to 4 pm. Admission is 10B.

## San Phra Isuan
ศาลพระอิศวร
Near the museum, San Phra Isuan is a shrine with a sandstone base, upon which is a Khmer-style bronze sculpture of Shiva (Isvara). This image is actually a replica: the original is in the Kamphaeng Phet National Museum.

## Wat Phra Borom Mathat
วัดพระบรมธาตุ
Across the Ping River are more neglected ruins in an area that was settled long before Kamphaeng Phet's heyday, although visible remains are post-classical Sukhothai in design. Wat Phra Borom Mathat features a few small chedis and one large chedi of the late Sukhothai period, which is now crowned with a Burmese-style umbrella added early this century.

## Other Wats
North-east of the old city walls, **Wat Phra Si Ariyabot** has the shattered remains of standing, sitting, walking and reclining Buddha images sculpted in the classic Sukhothai style.

North-west of Ariyabot, **Wat Chang Rop** (literally, 'temple surrounded by elephants') is just that – a temple with an elephant-buttressed wall.

## Places to Stay
*The Guest House* (☎ 712295), on Soi 2 Thesa Rd opposite the police station, is a new guesthouse run by a Thai-farang couple with dorm beds for 80B and rooms for 120 to 250B; the more expensive rooms have balconies. This is the closest lodging to the old

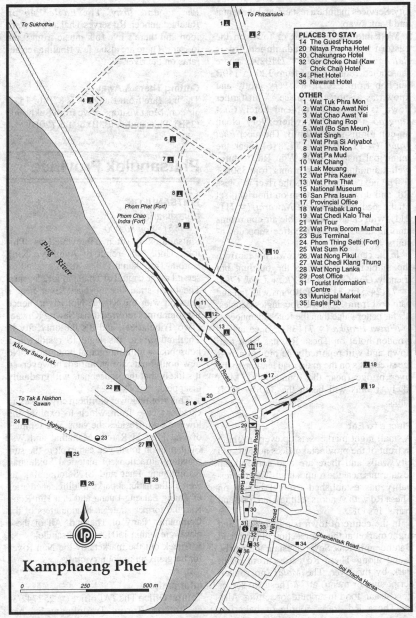

To Sukhothai

To Phitsanulok

Phom Phet (Fort)

Phom Chao Indra (Fort)

Ping River

Khlong Suan Mak

To Tak & Nakhon Sawan

Highway 1

Thesa Road

Ratchadamnoen Road

Thesa Road

Wijit Road

Charoensuk Road

Soi Pracha Hansa

**PLACES TO STAY**
14  The Guest House
20  Nitaya Prapha Hotel
30  Chakungrao Hotel
32  Gor Choke Chai (Kaw Chok Chai) Hotel
34  Phet Hotel
36  Nawarat Hotel

**OTHER**
1   Wat Tuk Phra Mon
2   Wat Chao Awat Noi
3   Wat Chao Awat Yai
4   Wat Chang Rop
5   Well (Bo San Meun)
6   Wat Singh
7   Wat Phra Si Ariyabot
8   Wat Phra Non
9   Wat Pa Mud
10  Wat Chang
11  Lak Meuang
12  Wat Phra Kaew
13  Wat Phra That
15  National Museum
16  San Phra Isuan
17  Provincial Office
18  Wat Trabak Lang
19  Wat Chedi Kalo Thai
21  Win Tour
22  Wat Phra Borom Mathat
23  Bus Terminal
24  Phom Thing Setti (Fort)
25  Wat Sum Ko
26  Wat Nong Pikul
27  Wat Chedi Klang Thung
28  Wat Nong Lanka
29  Post Office
31  Tourist Information Centre
33  Municipal Market
35  Eagle Pub

NORTHERN THAILAND

# Kamphaeng Phet

0        250        500 m

city. Services include a restaurant, bike rental and book swap.

Well into the new part of town on the eastern side of Ratchadamnoen Rd is *Ratchadamnoen Hotel* (☎ 711029), where fan-cooled rooms range from 120 to 140B (air-con from 220B); it's very grotty and known as a short-time place. A bit farther down is the town's top-end hotel, *Chakungrao* (☎ 711315), where very clean air-con rooms start at 280B. The nicer *Phet Hotel* (☎ 712810; fax 712816), near the municipal market at 99 Wijit Rd, features well maintained air-con rooms from 350B.

The next street towards the river is Thesa Rd, and down about 200m on the right, set off the road, is the *Navarat (Nawarat)* (☎ 711-211), with clean, comfortable air-con rooms starting at 350B, and a coffee shop downstairs.

In the centre of the new town, not far from the municipal market, is the bustling but friendly *Gor Choke Chai (Kaw Chok Chai)* (☎ 711247; fax 713870). Rooms with fan and bath cost from 170/190B for singles/doubles; it's far better value than the Ratchadamnoen.

*Nitaya Prapha* (☎ 711381), once an old wooden hotel on Thesa Rd, has been torn down and will reportedly be moved across the street. It's on the main road leading to the river bridge (near the roundabout). Most likely, rooms will be in the 300 to 500B range.

### Places to Eat

A small night market sets up every evening in front of the provincial offices near the old city walls and there are also some cheap restaurants near the roundabout. The municipality has established a night bazaar on Thesa Rd with vendors selling Thai food and crafts; it's OK.

In the centre of town is a larger day and night market at the intersection of Wijit and Banthoengjit Rds. Several restaurants can be found along Thesa Rd across from Sirijit Park by the river. The *Malai* (no roman-script sign or menu) at 77 Thesa Rd serves good Isaan food in an outdoor setting. Also on Thesa Rd are a couple of bakeries,

*Phayao* and *Tasty*. The *Eagle Pub* on Ratchadamnoen Rd serves Thai and western food and there's live folk music from 9 pm to 2 am. There are also a few floating restaurants on the river.

### Getting There & Away

The bus fare from Bangkok is 87B or 157B air-con. Most visitors arrive from Sukhothai (25B), Phitsanulok (35B) or Tak (20B).

# Phitsanulok Province

### PHITSANULOK
อ.เมืองพิษณุโลก
• ☎ (55) • pop 80,000

Phitsanulok is often abbreviated as 'Philok'. Under the reign of Ayuthaya King Borom Trailokanat (1448-88), Phitsanulok served as the capital of Thailand for 25 years. The town straddles the Nan River near a junction with the Khwae Noi River, hence it's sometimes referred to as 'Sawng Khwae' (Two Tributaries), and it's the only city in Thailand where it's legal to reside on a houseboat within municipal boundaries. No new houseboats are permitted, however, so it's likely that the houseboats will gradually disappear.

This vibrant lower Northern city makes an excellent base from which to explore the lower North. Besides the venerable temples of Wat Phra Si Ratana Mahathat and Wat Chulamani in town, you can explore the surrounding attractions of historical Sukhothai, Kamphaeng Phet and Si Satchanalai, as well as the national parks/wildlife sanctuaries of Thung Salaeng Luang and Phu Hin Rong Kla, the former strategic headquarters of the Communist Party of Thailand. All of these places are within 150 km of Phitsanulok.

Check out the markets by the Nan River for bargains on upcountry crafts.

### Information
**Tourist Office** The TAT office (☎ 252742/3) at 209/7-8 Borom Trailokanat Rd has

knowledgeable and helpful staff (some of TAT's best) who give out free maps of the town and a sheet that describes a suggested walking tour. The office also distributes info on Sukhothai and Phetchabun provinces. It's open daily 8.30 am to 4.30 pm.

If you plan to do the trip from Phi-lok to Lom Sak, ask for the sketch map of Highway 12 which marks several waterfalls and resorts along the way.

AUA (☎ 252970, ext 70) has a branch at Naresuan University on Sanambin Rd where Thai-language instruction may be arranged.

**Money** Several banks in town offer foreign-exchange services; only the Bangkok Bank, at 35 Naresuan Rd, has an after-hours exchange window (usually open till 8 pm).

**Post & Communications** The GPO on Phuttha Bucha Rd is open Monday to Friday from 8.30 am to 4.30 pm, Saturday and Sunday from 9 am to noon. The attached CAT phone office is open from 7 am to 11 pm daily.

### Wat Phra Si Ratana Mahathat
วัดพระศรี

The full name of this temple is Wat Phra Si Ratana Mahathat, but the locals call it Wat Phra Si or Wat Yai. The wat is next to the bridge over the Nan River (on the right as you're heading out of Phi-lok towards Sukhothai). The main wihãan contains the Chinnarat Buddha (Phra Phuttha Chinnarat), one of Thailand's most revered and copied images. This famous bronze image is probably second in importance only to the Emerald Buddha in Bangkok's Wat Phra Kaew. In terms of total annual donations collected (about 12 million baht per year), Wat Yai follows Wat Sothon in Chachoengsao.

The image was cast in the late Sukhothai style, but what makes it strikingly unique is the flame-like halo around the head and torso that turns up at the bottom to become dragon-serpent heads on either side of the image. The head of this Buddha is a little wider than standard Sukhothai, giving the statue a very solid feel.

The story goes that construction of this wat was commissioned under the reign of King Li Thai in 1357. When it was completed, King Li Thai wanted it to contain three high-quality bronze images, so he sent for well known sculptors from Si Satchanalai, Chiang Saen and Hariphunchai (Lamphun), as well as five Brahman priests. The first two castings worked well, but the third required three attempts before it was decreed the best of all. Legend has it that a white-robed sage appeared from nowhere to assist in the final casting, then disappeared. This last image was named the Chinnarat (Victorious King) Buddha and it became the centrepiece in the wihãan. The other two images, Phra Chinnasi and Phra Si Satsada, were later moved to the royal temple of Wat Bowonniwet in Bangkok. Only the Chinnarat image has the flame-dragon halo.

The walls of the wihãan are low to accommodate the low-swept roof, typical of Northern temple architecture, so the image takes on larger proportions than it might in a Central or North-Eastern wat. The brilliant interior architecture is such that when you sit on the Italian marble floor in front of the Buddha, the lacquered columns draw your vision towards the image and evoke a strong sense of serenity. The doors of the building are inlaid with mother-of-pearl in a design copied from Bangkok's Wat Phra Kaew.

Another sanctuary to one side has been converted into a museum displaying antique Buddha images, ceramics and other historic artefacts. It's open Wednesday to Sunday from 9 am to 4 pm; admission is free. Dress appropriately when visiting this most sacred of temples – no shorts or revealing tops.

Near Wat Yai, on the same side of the river, are two other temples of the same period – Wat Ratburan and Wat Nang Phaya.

### Wat Chulamani
วัดจุฬามณี

Five km south of the city (a 3B trip on bus No 4 down Borom Trailokanat Rd) is Wat Chulamani, the ruins of which date from the Sukhothai period. The original buildings

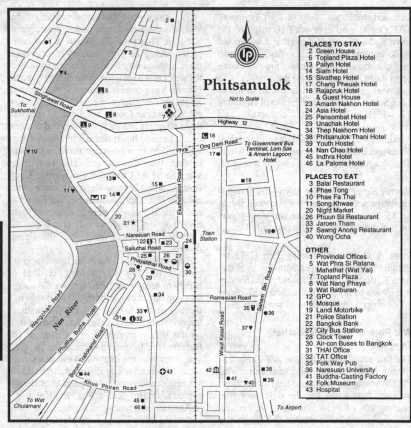

# Phitsanulok

Not to Scale

**PLACES TO STAY**
2  Green House
6  Topland Plaza Hotel
13  Pailyn Hotel
14  Siam Hotel
15  Sivathep Hotel
17  Chang Pheuak Hotel
18  Rajapruk Hotel
    & Guest House
23  Amarin Nakhon Hotel
24  Asia Hotel
25  Pansombat Hotel
29  Unachak Hotel
34  Thep Nakhorn Hotel
38  Phitsanulok Thani Hotel
39  Youth Hostel
44  Nan Chao Hotel
45  Indhra Hotel
46  La Paloma Hotel

**PLACES TO EAT**
3  Balai Restaurant
4  Phae Tong
10  Phae Fa Thai
11  Song Khwae
20  Night Market
26  Phuun Sii Restaurant
33  Jaroen Tham
37  Sawng Anong Restaurant
40  Wong Ocha

**OTHER**
1  Provincial Offices
5  Wat Phra Si Ratana
    Mahathat (Wat Yai)
7  Topland Plaza
8  Wat Nang Phaya
9  Wat Ratburan
12  GPO
16  Mosque
19  Landi Motorbike
21  Police Station
22  Bangkok Bank
27  City Bus Station
28  Clock Tower
30  Air-con Buses to Bangkok
31  THAI Office
32  TAT Office
35  Folk Way Pub
36  Naresuan University
41  Buddha-Casting Factory
42  Folk Museum
43  Hospital

must have been impressive, judging from what remains of the ornate Khmer-style *prang* (tower). King Borom Trailokanat was ordained as a monk here and there is an old Thai inscription to that effect on the ruined wihăan, dating from the reign of King Narai the Great.

The prang itself has little left of its original height, but Khmer-style door lintels remain, including a very nice one with a Sukhothai walking Buddha and a dhammachakka in the background.

Besides the prang and the wihăan, the only original structures left are the remains of the

monastery walls. Still, there is a peaceful, neglected atmosphere about the place.

## Buddha-Casting Foundry
โรงหล่อพระ

On Wisut Kasat Rd, not far from the Phitsanulok Youth Hostel, is a small factory where bronze Buddha images of all sizes are cast. Most are copies of the famous Phra Chinnarat Buddha at Wat Yai. Visitors are welcome to watch and there are even detailed photo exhibits describing step by step the lost wax method of metal casting. Some of the larger images take a year or more to complete. The foundry is owned by Dr Thawi, an artisan and nationally renowned expert on Northern Thai folklore.

There is a small gift shop at the foundry where you can purchase bronze images of various sizes. The foundry is open to the public daily from 8.30 am to 4.30 pm.

### Folk Museum
พิพิธภัณฑ์พื้นบ้าน

Across the street and a short distance north of the foundry is a folk museum established by Dr Thawi. Exhibits include items from his personal collection of traditional farm implements, cooking utensils, hunting equipment, musical instruments and other folkloric artefacts from throughout the Northern region. It's the best collection of its kind in the country and many of the objects on display are virtually nonexistent in modern Thai life. If you're lucky, Dr Thawi may be around to offer you an impromptu demonstration of rustic devices used for calling birds and other animals, including elephants! The museum is open Tuesday to Sunday 8.30 am to 4.30 pm; entrance is by donation.

### Places to Stay – bottom end
Phi-lok has good coverage in the budget accommodation category.

**Guesthouses & Hostels** The *Phitsanulok Youth Hostel* (☎ 242060) at 38 Sanam Bin Rd stands well above all other Thai hostels associated with Hostelling International. Sapachai, the owner, worked as a systems analyst in Bangkok for 10 years before giving up the rat race to return to his boyhood home. Set amidst a lush garden with aromatic jasmine vines and a spring, his 45 year old house has been converted into a restaurant featuring Thai and European food. A lofty teak-wood *sāalaa (sala;* open-sided pavilion) behind the house is built of salvaged timber from seven old Tak teak houses to create a pleasant, open-air sitting and dining area – a good place to sit back and

relax over a glass of wine or fresh-brewed locally grown coffee while listening to the cadence of frogs and crickets.

Row house rooms behind the sala, each with antique Northern Thai beds, cost 100/140/210B single/double/triple; dorm beds are 40B. A Hostelling International membership is mandatory (temporary one-night memberships are 50B; annual membership is 300B). A new three-storey building with tastefully designed rooms and the same antique touches is being added; these will come with air-con and hot water showers and start at 300B.

From the train station you can get to the hostel by samlor (20 to 30B) or on a No 4 city bus. From the airport take a tuk-tuk (30B) or a No 4 bus which passes by the hostel (on the right). From the bus terminal, take a samlor (30B) or a No 1 city bus (get off at Ramesuan Rd and walk the last 300m or so).

At 11/12 Ekathotsarot Rd, the *Green House* offers simple comfort and a casual atmosphere for 80B single, 100 to 120B double with shared bath. Take a No 5 or No 11 bus from the bus stop around the corner from the train station.

**Hotels** Near the train station are several inexpensive hotels and places to eat. An old standby on Phayalithai Rd, *Unachak Hotel* (☎ 258387) has recently been renovated and now offers decent singles with fan for 150B, or single/double air-con rooms for 300/400B.

Farther towards the river on Phayalithai Rd, the run-down *Chanprasert* has plain fan rooms for 90 to 120B.

If you turn left out of the station and then take the first right turn on to Sailuthai Rd, you'll come to *Pansombat Hotel* on the left side of the road. Rooms with private shower and shared toilet are 120/150B, or 200B with toilet. It's noisy and a bit of a brothel, however. The *Sukkit* (☎ 258876) at 20/1-2 Sailuthai Rd is a better deal at 120 to 150B for a room with fan. Although it's strictly basic and a little dark, it's centrally located a block from the river and is less noisy than hotels toward the station. Another Sailuthai

Rd cheapie, the *Chokeprasit Hotel*, has rooms with private shower and shared toilet for 120B, with toilet for 120 to 150B.

Probably the best hotel deal in this price range is the clean and friendly *Siam Hotel* (☎ 258844), an old-fashioned four-storey place at 4/8 Athitayawong Rd, a half block from the river and main post office. Large, well kept rooms, all with attached bath and ceiling fan, cost 150B single, 200B double; those towards the back are considerably quieter.

Not far from the train station on Eka-thotsarot Rd is the *Asia Hotel* (☎ 258378), with quite decent single/double rooms for 150B, air-con for 350B (single) and 450B (double). Street noise can be deafening, so ask for a room towards the back of the hotel.

## Places to Stay – middle
Behind the more up-market Rajapruk Hotel on Phra Ong Dam Rd is the *Rajapruk Guest House Hotel* (☎ 258788), where fan-cooled rooms with hot showers go for 161B (great value), air-con 530B. Guests may use the Rajapruk Hotel swimming pool.

Also good is the *Indhra Hotel* (☎ 259188/638) at 103/8 Sithamatraipidok Rd, south of Phutthachinnarat Provincial Hospital (Phitsanulok Teaching Hospital). Clean air-con singles/doubles with TV are 250 to 1000B.

The *Chang Pheuak Hotel* (☎ 252822) at 66/28 Phra Ong Dam Rd and the *Sivathep Hotel* (☎ 244933) at 110/21 Prasongprasat were once the top end in Phi-lok. Both offer clean air-con rooms for 220 to 400B; the Sivathep has a slight edge in quality.

## Places to Stay – top end
Phi-lok's upper end hotels all start at 1000B or less, making it one of Thailand's bargain provincial capitals. This is also where the main hotel growth is, so a room glut will probably keep prices stable or even slightly depressed, especially at the older places.

*Rajapruk Hotel* (☎ 258477; fax 251395) at 99/9 Phra Ong Dam Rd offers good upper-range value. All rooms come with air-con, hot showers, carpeting, TV and telephone for

800B for singles/doubles; there are also more expensive suites available.

Another good value place is the *Thep Nakhon Hotel* (☎ 244070) at 43/1 Sithama-traipidok Rd, where quiet air-con standard rooms are 570B, deluxe rooms 750B. The centrally located and swankier *Pailyn Hotel* (☎ 252411) at 38 Borom Trailokanat Rd has rooms starting at 899B. Others in this category – places that were once Phi-lok's flashiest digs but are now a little worn at the edges yet still quite comfortable – include *Nan Chao Hotel* (☎ 252510; fax 244794), from 450B and *Amarin Nakhon Hotel* (☎ 258588), 3/1 Chao Phraya Phitsanulok Rd, from 720B. The latter is undergoing renovation so rates might rise.

The 200-room *Topland Plaza Hotel* (☎ 247800; fax 247815) is connected to Topland Plaza shopping centre at the inter-section of Singhawat and Ekathotsarot Rds. It's a very luxurious place with a beauty salon, cafe, fitness centre, several restaurants and other facilities. Rates start at 1400B, though when I visited they were readily dis-pensing rooms for 850B just to get people in the hotel, a bargain compared to Bangkok or Chiang Mai prices for similar quality.

*La Paloma Hotel* (☎ 217930; fax 217937) at 103/8 Sithamatraipidok Rd, just south of the Indhra Hotel, is a 240-room luxury hotel with a family orientation – they will arrange day care with advance notice. Rooms with all the amenities start at 1200B.

*Amarin Lagoon Hotel* (☎ 214149; fax 214157) is located around eight km out of town on Highway 12. Phi-lok's best hotel boasts landscaped grounds, lush gardens, a fitness centre and a swimming pool. Rates go from 1000 to 1600B.

Under construction right next door to the Phitsanulok Youth Hostel, the *Phitsanulok Thani Hotel* (☎ 211065; fax (2) 236-6400 in Bangkok) will feature 110 air-con rooms and a beer garden. As this hotel is part of the Dusit chain you can expect rates to start at around 1400 to 1500B a night. Another deluxe place coming up is the *Golden Grand Hotel*, next to the Chang Pheuak Hotel on Ekathotsarot Rd.

## Places to Eat

Phitsanulok is a great town for eating – there must be more restaurants per capita here than in just about any other town in Thailand.

Excellent, inexpensive Thai food can be had at the *Phuun Sii* opposite the Lithai Building on Phayalithai Rd. Recommended dishes here include tôm khàa kài (chicken-coconut soup), lâap (Isaan-style minced meat salad), kaeng mátsàman kài (Muslim chicken curry) and thâwt man plaa (fried fish cakes). *Tui Phochana*, opposite Phuun Sii and operated by a cousin from the same family, makes fabulous yam khanūn (curried jackfruit) at the beginning of the cool season, plus many other outstanding Thai curries year-round. There are plenty of other cheap Thai restaurants in this area too.

Close to the Phitsanulok Youth Hostel are several small noodle and rice shops. South around the corner from the hostel a permanent vendor stand called *Wong Ocha* (no roman sign) sells delicious kài yâang, khâo nǐaw and yam phàk kràchèt (water mimosa salad). Across from the Naresuan University campus on Sanam Bin Rd is the very popular and very inexpensive *Sawng Anong* outdoor restaurant, open from 9 am to 3 pm daily. It has a great selection of curries, noodles and Thai desserts, all priced at less than 25B. Try the são náam, a mixture of pineapple, coconut, dried shrimp, ginger and garlic served over khanǒm jiin – it's delicious. Also good is the kaeng yûak, a curry made from the heart of a banana palm, and kǔaytǐaw sùkhǒthai, thin rice noodles served dry in a bowl with peanuts, barbecued pork, spices, green beans and bean sprouts.

Early risers should try the small but lively morning market next to Naresuan University. Vendors serve inexpensive khâo man kài (Hainanese chicken and rice), salabao (Chinese buns), paa-thông-kǒ (Chinese doughnuts) and jók (broken-rice soup) from 6 to 10 am daily. The bakery near the clock tower downtown makes some of the best chocolate brownies in Thailand.

The cheapest meal in town has got to be kǔaytǐaw phàt thai (Thai-style fried rice noodles) at the intersection of Phra Ong Dam Rd and Ekathotsarot Rd. The intersection is called Sii-Yaek Baan Khaek (Indian Village Crossroads) and the vendor on the north-west corner has been serving up 7B dishes of phàt thai (12B for two eggs) for many years. There's a cluster of inexpensive market-style foodstalls just west of the Chokeprasit Hotel near the cinema.

By the mosque on Phra Ong Dam Rd are several Thai-Muslim cafes. One very famous one (no English sign – look for the crowded place near the railroad crossing, with the mosque directly behind it) has thick rotis served with kaeng mátsàman, which is unusual this far north. Ask for roti kaeng to get the set plate. This small cafe also has fresh milk and yoghurt.

A small restaurant next to the Indhra Hotel offers very inexpensive vegetarian food. *Jaroen Tham*, around the corner from TAT, is similar. Both are open from 8 am to noon only.

Several restaurants along Sanam Bin Rd in the vicinity of the youth hostel serve good medium-priced Thai and Chinese dishes. They include *Feuang Fah* (air-con), *Rak* (air-con) and *Daeng* (outdoors).

If you're out past midnight, your best bet is the very good, 24 hour khâo tôm place next to the train station. There's a *KFC* at Topland Plaza.

**On the River** Floating restaurants light up the Nan River at night. Good choices include *Song Khwae, Phae Fa Thai, Phae Tong* and *Tipfy Restaurant*. Phae Fa Thai has a talented chef. South of the main string of floating restaurants is a pier where you can board a restaurant-boat, owned by Fa Thai, that cruises the Nan River every night. You pay 20B to board the boat and then order from a menu as you please – no minimum charge.

Also along the river is a popular night market area with dozens of food vendors, a couple of whom specialise in phàk bûng loi fáa (literally, 'floating-in-the-sky morning glory vine'), which usually translates as 'flying vegetable'. This food fad originated in Chonburi but has somehow taken root in Phi-lok. There are several of these places in town as well as along the river. The dish is basically morning glory vine stir-fried in soy bean sauce and garlic, but with a performance included. The cook fires up a batch in the wok and then flings it through the air to a waiting server who catches it on a plate. The eating places on the river are now so performance-oriented that the server climbs to the top of a van to catch the flying vegetable! Tour companies bring tour groups here and invite tourists to try the catch – it's just as amusing watching the tourists drop phàk bûng all over the place as it is to watch the cook. During the day this area is a sundries market.

The old and established *Balai* – just back from the river and north of Wat Phra Si – is famous for kŭaytĭaw hâwy khàa (literally, 'legs-hanging rice noodles'). The name comes from the way customers sit on a bench facing the river, with their legs dangling below. It's only open from 10 am to 4 pm daily.

*Baan Suan Vietnam*, four km north of town on the right side of Highway 11, is a pleasant garden restaurant with excellent Vietnamese food and good service.

### Entertainment
Along Borom Trailokanat Rd near the Pailyn Hotel is a string of popular Thai pubs. *Jao Samran* on this street features live Thai folk and pop. Food service starts around 5 or 6 pm and the music comes on around 8 pm. Opposite the Siam Hotel, the *Cowboy Pub* features the usual Thai renditions of old west decor and folk music.

Two Thai folk pubs worth checking out are *River Blue* and *Ketnika*. River Blue is a cluster of Thai-style pavilions and tables that spill out onto the sidewalk; Ketnika is decorated in the 'classic Thai' look from the turn of the century. The *Folk Way Pub*, north of Phitsanulok Youth Hostel and opposite the exit gate for Naresuan University, is another folk music place popular with locals.

### Getting There & Away
**Air** The THAI office (☎ 258020, 251671) is at 209/26-28 Borom Trailokanat Rd. THAI has four daily 45 minute flights to Phitsanulok from Bangkok for 950B one way. There are also flights between Phitsanulok

and Chiang Mai (daily, 650B), Lampang (daily, 485B), Mae Sot (four times weekly, 495B) and Nan (thrice weekly, 575B).

Phitsanulok's airport is just out of town. Songthaews leave the airport every 20 minutes or so and go into town for 5B, otherwise you can catch the No 4 city bus for 3B. The big hotels in town run free buses from the airport, and THAI has a door-to-door van service for 30B per person.

**Bus** Phi-lok lies about 390 km from Bangkok. Transport choices out of Phitsanulok are very good, as it's a junction for bus lines running both north and north-east. Bangkok is six hours away by bus and Chiang Mai 5½ hours. Ordinary buses leave Bangkok's Northern Bus Terminal for Phitsanulok several times daily and cost 96B (163B air-con). Be sure to get the *sǎi mài* (new route) bus via Nakhon Sawan (Route 117), as the old route via Tak Fa (Highway 11) takes six hours and costs more. Phitsanulok Yan Yon Tour and Win Tour run VIP buses between Bangkok and Phitsanulok for 180 to 210B.

Direct buses between Phitsanulok and Loei via Dan Sai cost 58B (104B air-con) and take four hours. Buses to destinations in other North and North-Eastern provinces leave several times a day from the Baw Khaw Saw (government bus terminal) just outside town, except for the air-con buses which may depart only once or twice a day:

Buses to Lom Sak cost 40B.

| City | Fare | Duration |
|---|---|---|
| Chiang Mai (via Den Chai) | 86B | 5½ hours |
| (air-con) | 155B | 5 hours |
| Chiang Mai (via Tak) | 104B | 6 hours |
| (air-con) | 146B | 6 hours |
| Chiang Rai (via Utaradit) | 104B | 6½ hours |
| (air-con) | 146B | 6 hours |
| Chiang Rai (via Sukhothai) | 115B | 7½ hours |
| (air-con) | 160B | 7 hours |
| Khon Kaen | 92B | 5 hours |
| (air-con) | 129-156B | 5 hours |
| Nakhon Ratchasima (Khorat) | 82B | 6 hours |
| (air-con) | 146B | 6 hours |
| Mae Sot | | |
| (air-con minivan) | 80B | 5 hours |
| Udon Thani | 91B | 7 hours |
| (air-con) | 164B | 7 hours |

Buses to the following nearby points leave on the hour (*), every two hours (**) or every three hours (***) from early morning until 5 or 6 pm (except for Sukhothai buses, which leave every half-hour):

| City | Fare | Duration |
|------|------|----------|
| Dan Sai** | 38B | 3 hours |
| Kamphaeng Phet* | 30B | 3 hours |
| Lom Sak* | 40B | 2 hours |
| Phetchabun*** | 47B | 3 hours |
| Sukhothai | 16B | 1 hour |
| Tak* | 36B | 3 hours |
| Utaradit* | 41B | 3 hours |

**Train** The 3rd class fare (69B) is only available on ordinary trains; the ordinary train with the most convenient arrival time is No 101, which leaves Bangkok at 7.05 am (or Ayuthaya at 8.41 am) and arrives in Phitsanulok at 2.40 pm. For most people this is a more economic and much more convenient way to reach Phi-lok from Bangkok compared to bus, since you don't have to go out to Bangkok's Northern Bus Terminal.

The 6.40 am and 3 pm rapid trains from Bangkok arrive in Phitsanulok at 12.57 and 9.26 pm. The basic fare is 159B 2nd class or 324B 1st class, plus a 30B surcharge for the rapid service. There is also an all air-con, 1st class diesel service (No 907) daily at 8.10 am that arrives in Phitsanulok at 1.13 pm, an hour quicker than the rapid service. The 290B fare includes a meal and a snack.

Trains between Phi-lok and Chiang Mai cost 65B in 3rd class, 136B in 2nd class and 276B in 1st class (not including rapid or express charges for 1st and 2nd class trains).

If you're going straight on to Sukhothai from Phitsanulok, a tuk-tuk ride from the station to the bus station four km away is 30 to 40B. From there you can get a bus to Sukhothai. Or you can catch a Sukhothai-bound bus in front of the Topland Hotel on Singhawat Rd; a tuk-tuk to Singhawat costs 20B from the train station.

**Getting Around**

Samlor rides within the town centre should cost 20 to 30B per person. City buses are 3B and there are five lines making the rounds,

so you should be able to get just about anywhere by bus. A couple of the lines also feature air-con coaches for 5B. The terminal for city buses is near the train station off Ekathotsarot Rd.

Motorcycles can be rented at Landi Motorbike (☎ 252765) at 57/21-22 Phra Ong Dam Rd (near Rajapruk Hotel). Rates are 150B a day for a 100cc and 200B for a 150cc.

## PHU HIN RONG KLA NATIONAL PARK
อุทยานแห่งชาติภูหินร่องกล้า

From 1967 to 1982, Phu Hin Rong Kla was the strategic headquarters for the Communist Party of Thailand (CPT) and its tactical arm, the People's Liberation Army of Thailand (PLAT). The remote mountain location was perfect for an insurgent army. Another benefit was that the headquarters was only 50 km from the Lao border, so lines of retreat were well guarded after 1975 when Laos fell to the Pathet Lao. China's Yunnan Province was only 300 km away and it was here that CPT cadres received their training in revolutionary tactics.

The CPT camp at Phu Hin Rong Kla became especially active after the October 1976 student uprising in Bangkok in which hundreds of students were killed by the Thai military. Many students fled here to join the CPT, setting up a hospital and a school of political and military tactics. For nearly 20 years the area around Phu Hin Rong Kla served as a battlefield for skirmishes.

In 1972, the Thai government launched an offensive against the PLAT in an unsuccessful attempt to rout them from Phu Hin Rong Kla. By 1978 the PLAT here had swelled to 4000. In 1980 and 1981, the Thai armed forces tried again and were able to recapture some parts of CPT territory. But the decisive blow to the CPT came in 1982 when the government declared an amnesty for all the students who had joined the communists after 1976. The departure of most of the students broke the spine of the movement, which had, by this time, become dependent on their membership. A final military push in 1982 effected the surrender of the PLAT

NORTHERN THAILAND

and Phu Hin Rong Kla was declared a national park in 1984.

### Orientation & Information

The park covers about 307 sq km of rugged mountains and forest. The elevation at park headquarters is about 1000m, so the park is refreshingly cool even in the hot season. The main attractions are the remains of the CPT stronghold, including a rustic meeting hall, the school of political and military tactics and the CPT administration building. Across the road from the school is a waterwheel designed by exiled engineering students.

In another area of the park is a trail that goes to Phaa Chu Thong (Flag Raising Cliff, sometimes called Red Flag Cliff), where the communists would raise the red flag to announce when they had had a military victory. Also in this area is an air-raid shelter, a lookout and the remains of the main CPT headquarters – the most inaccessible point in the territory before a road was constructed by the Thai government. The buildings in the park are made out of wood and bamboo with no plumbing or electricity – a testament to how primitive the living conditions were.

At the park headquarters is a small museum which displays relics from CPT days, including medical instruments and weapons. At the end of the road into the park is a small White Hmong village. When the CPT were here, the Hmong were their allies. Now they've undergoing 'development' at the hands of the Thai government. One wonders what would have happened if the CPT had succeeded in its revolutionary goal. Maybe the Thai army's headquarters in Phitsanulok would now be a museum instead.

If you're not interested in the history of Phu Hin Rong Kla, there are hiking trails, waterfalls and scenic views, plus some interesting rock formations – an area of jutting boulders called Laan Hin Pum (Million Knotty Rocks) and an area of deep rocky crevices where PLAT troops would hide during air raids, called Laan Hin Taek (Million Broken Rocks).

Phu Hin Rong Kla can become quite crowded on weekends and holidays; schedule a more peaceful visit for mid-week.

### Places to Stay

The Forestry Department rents out bungalows that sleep five for 600B, eight for 800B, 10 for 1000B and 14 for 1500B. You can pitch your own tent for 10B a night or sleep in park tents for 40B per person (no bedding provided except blankets for 20B per night). If you want to build a fire, you can buy chopped wood for 150B a night. You can also book accommodation in advance through the Forestry Department's Bangkok office (☎ (2) 579-0529/4842), or by calling their provincial office (☎ (55) 389002) or Golden House Tour Company (☎ (55) 259973, 389002) in Phitsanulok.

### Places to Eat

Near the campground and bungalows are some vendors. The best are *Duang Jai Cafeteria* – try their famous sôm-tam – and *Rang Thong*.

### Getting There & Away

The park headquarters is about 125 km from Phitsanulok. To get there, first take an early bus to Nakhon Thai (32B), where you can

Phu Hin Rong Kla National Park
Not to Scale

Phatcharin Ton Waterfall (800m from road)
To Nakhon Thai & Phitsanulok
Laan Hin Taek (Million Broken Rocks)
Camp Ground
Park Headquarters
Rom Klao Waterfall (250m from road)
Waterwheel
School of Politics & Military Tactics
Huay Khamin Noi Falls (100m from road)
To Hmong Village, Lom Sak & Phetchabun
Phaa Chu Thong (Flag Raising Cliff)
CPT Administration
Air-raid Shelter

catch a songthaew to the park (three times daily between 7.30 am and 4.30 pm for 20B).

A small group could also charter a pickup and driver in Nakhon Thai for about 550B for the day. This is a delightful trip if you're on a motorbike as there's not much traffic along the way. A strong engine is necessary to make it up the hills to Phu Hin Rong Kla.

**PHITSANULOK TO LOM SAK**

Along Highway 12 between Phi-lok and Lom Sak, the scenic 'gateway' to North-Eastern Thailand, there are several resorts and waterfalls. As with Phu Hin Rong Kla, the sites here tend to be more popular on weekends and holidays.

The Phitsanulok TAT office distributes a sketch map of attractions along this 130 km stretch of road which marks the resorts and three waterfalls. You may want to bypass the first two waterfalls, **Sakhunothayan Falls** and **Kaeng Sawng**, which are on the way to Phu Hin Rong Kla and hence get overwhelmed with visitors. The third, **Kaeng Sopha** at Km 72, is a larger area of small falls and rapids where you can walk from rock formation to rock formation in the midst of it all – there are more or less rocks depending on the rains and resulting river height. Food vendors provide inexpensive sôm-tam and kài yâang.

Farther east along the road is 1262 sq km **Thung Salaeng Luang Wildlife Sanctuary** (entrance at Km 80), one of Thailand's largest and most important protected areas. Thung Salaeng Luang encompasses vast meadows and dipterocarp forests and also once home to the PLAT. Among bird-watchers it's known as a habitat for the colourful Siamese fireback pheasant.

**Places to Stay & Eat**

There are several resorts just off Highway 12 west of the Route 2013 junction for Nakhon Thai. Best of the lot is the *Rainforest Resort* (☎ (55) 241185; (2) 423-0749 in Bangkok) at Km 44. Spacious, tastefully designed cottages spread over a hillside facing the Khek River cost 800 to 1000B for two people; there is also one cottage for eight to 10 people for 2400B. All cottages come with air-con and hot water.

An indoor-outdoor restaurant serves locally grown coffee and good Thai food. Other resorts in the area, *Wang Nam Yen, SP Huts* and *Thanthong*, are similarly priced.

On the way to or from Phitsanulok, stop at *Blue Mountain Coffee* at Km 42, *Rainforest Resort* at Km 44 or *Thawee Fresh Coffee* at Km 45, all on Highway 12 near Ban Kaeng Sawng (close to Kaeng Sawng Waterfall). These restaurants serve some of the best fresh coffee outside of Bangkok; the beans are all locally grown *kafae jàak râi* (literally 'coffee from the fields') but have names like Blue Mountain and Brazil. Freshly brewed coffee costs between 15 and 25B, but it's worth it for 100% Arabica or Robusta beans.

**Getting There & Away**

Buses between Phi-lok and Lom Sak cost 40B each way, so any stop along the way will cost less. During daylight hours it's easy to flag down another bus to continue your journey, but after 4 pm it gets a little chancy.

# Sukhothai Province

**SUKHOTHAI**
อ.เมืองสุโขทัย
• ☎ *(55)* • *pop 25,000*

As Thailand's first capital, Sukhothai (literally, 'rising of happiness') flourished from the mid-13th century to the late-14th century. The Sukhothai kingdom is viewed as the 'golden age' of Thai civilisation – the religious art and architecture of the Sukhothai era are considered to be the most classic of Thai styles.

The new town of Sukhothai is almost 450 km from Bangkok and is undistinguished except for its very good municipal market in the town centre. The old city *(meuang kào)* of Sukhothai features around 45 sq km of ruins – which have been made into a historical park – making an overnight stay in New Sukhothai worthwhile, although you could make a day trip to the old city ruins from Phitsanulok.

See the following Sukhothai Historical Park section for more details about the ruins.

# Sukhothai Historical Park

อุทยานประวัติศาสตร์สุโขทัย

The original capital of the first Thai kingdom was surrounded by three concentric ramparts and two moats bridged by four gateways. Today the remains of 21 historical sites and four large ponds can be seen within the old walls, with an additional 70 sites within a five km radius. The more remote ruins in the hills west of the old city walls, such as Wat Saphaan Hin, used to be considered a dangerous area, but since UNESCO and the Thai government joined in the development of the old city environs, all ruins are safe to visit with or without a guide. The Sukhothai ruins have been declared a historical park and rank as one of Thailand's World Heritage Sites. The ruins are divided into five zones – central, north, south, east and west – each of which has a 20B admission fee. The park's official hours (when admission is collected) are from 6 am to 6 pm.

Sukhothai temple architecture is most typified by the classic lotus-bud stupa, which features a conical spire topping a square-sided structure on a three-tiered base. Some sites also exhibit other rich architectural forms introduced and modified during the period – bell-shaped Sinhalese and double-tiered Srivijaya stupas.

See under Getting Away of the Sukhothai section for details on the best way to tour the park.

## Ramkhamhaeng National Museum

พิพิธภัณฑ์แห่งชาติรามคำแหง

The museum provides a good starting point for an exploration of the ruins. A replica of the famous Ramkhamhaeng inscription (see Wiang Kum Kam in the Chiang Mai section of this chapter) is kept here amongst a good collection of Sukhothai artefacts.

The museum is open daily except public holidays from 9 am to 4 pm and admission is 10B.

## Wat Mahathat

วัดมหาธาตุ

The largest in the city and built in the 13th century, Wat Mahathat is surrounded by brick walls (206m long and 200m wide) and a moat, said to represent the outer wall of the universe and the cosmic ocean, respectively. The stupa spires feature the famous lotus-bud motif and some of the original stately Buddha figures still sit among the ruined columns of the old wihǎans. There are 198 chedis within the monastery walls – a lot to explore in what many consider was the spiritual and administrative centre of the old capital.

## Wat Si Sawai

วัดศรีสวาย

Just south of Wat Mahathat, this shrine (dating from the 12th and 13th centuries) features three corncob-like prangs and a picturesque moat. It was originally built by the Khmers as a Hindu temple.

## Wat Sa Si

วัดสระศรี

Wat Sa Si, or 'Sacred Pond Monastery', sits on an island west of the bronze monument of King Ramkhamhaeng (the third Sukhothai king).

It's a simple, classic Sukhothai-style wat with one large Buddha, one chedi and the columns of the ruined wihãan.

## Wat Trapang Thong

วัดตระพังทอง

Next to the museum, this small, still inhabited wat with its fine stucco reliefs is reached by a footbridge across the large lotus-filled pond which surrounds it. This reservoir, the original site of Thailand's Loy Krathong Festival, supplies the Sukhothai community with most of its water.

## Wat Phra Pai Luang

วัดพระพายหลวง

Outside the city walls in the north zone, this somewhat isolated wat features three Khmer-style prangs, similar to those at Si Sawai but bigger, dating from the 12th century. This may have been the centre of Sukhothai when it was ruled by the Khmers of Angkor prior to the 13th century.

## Wat Si Chum

วัดศรีชุม

This wat is north-west of the old city and contains an impressive, much-photographed mondòp with a 15m, brick-and-stucco seated Buddha. Archaeologists theorise that this image is the 'Phra Atchana'

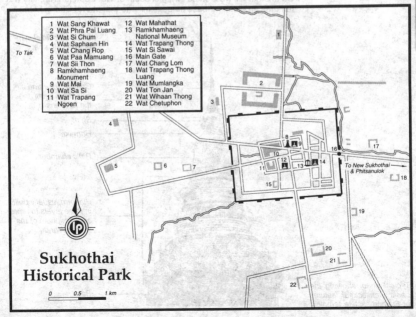

1 Wat Sang Khawat
2 Wat Phra Pai Luang
3 Wat Si Chum
4 Wat Saphaan Hin
5 Wat Chang Rop
6 Wat Paa Mamuang
7 Wat Sii Thon
8 Ramkhamhaeng Monument
9 Wat Mai
10 Wat Sa Si
11 Wat Trapang Ngoen
12 Wat Mahathat
13 Ramkhamhaeng National Museum
14 Wat Trapang Thong
15 Wat Si Sawai
16 Main Gate
17 Wat Chang Lom
18 Wat Trapang Thong Luang
19 Wat Mumlangka
20 Wat Ton Jan
21 Wat Wihaan Thong
22 Wat Chetuphon

To Tak

To New Sukhothai & Phitsanulok

## Sukhothai Historical Park

0    0.5    1 km

mentioned in the famous Ramkhamhaeng inscription. A passage in the mondòp wall which leads to the top has been blocked so that it's no longer possible to view the jataka inscriptions which line the tunnel ceiling.

## Wat Chang Lom

วัดช้างล้อม

Off Highway 12 in the east zone, Wat Chang Lom ('Elephant Circled Monastery') is about a km east of the main park entrance. A large bell-shaped chedi is supported by 36 elephants sculpted into its base.

## Wat Saphaan Hin

วัดสะพานหิน

Wat Saphaan Hin is a couple of km to the west of the old city walls in the west zone, on the crest of a hill that rises about 200m above the plain. The name of the wat, which means 'stone bridge', is a reference to the slate path and staircase leading to the temple, which are still in place. The site affords a good view of the Sukhothai ruins to the south-east and the mountains to the north and south.

All that remains of the original temple are a few chedis and the ruined wihāan, consisting of two rows of laterite columns flanking a 12.5m-high standing Buddha image on a brick terrace.

## Wat Chang Rop

วัดช้างรอบ

On another hill west of the city, just south of Wat Saphaan Hin, this wat features an elephant-base stupa, similar to that at Wat Chang Lom.

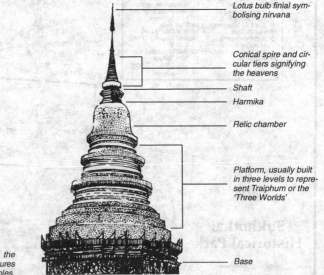

Lotus bulb finial symbolising nirvana

Conical spire and circular tiers signifying the heavens

Shaft

Harmika

Relic chamber

Platform, usually built in three levels to represent Traiphum or the 'Three Worlds'

Base

*Typical chedi showing the basic architectural features of Sukhothai-style temples.*

NORTHERN THAILAND

MARK KIRBY

*The elegant lines and tall, tapering spire of Wat Sa Si's Sinhalese-style chedi framed against Sukhothai's far hills.*

MICHAEL CLARK

*The pneumatic, 'boneless' attributes of Thai Buddhist sculpture, as portrayed here in Wat Si Chum's huge seated Buddha image, reached their peak at Sukhothai and Si Satchanalai-Chaliang.*

JOE CUMMINGS

*Artisans constructed the buildings at Sukhothai using mortared brick finished in stucco. Five centuries of neglect has caused virtually all of the stucco — including delicate bas relief work — to fall away.*

This famous prang – a corncob-shaped chedi influenced by early Khmer architecture in Thailand – stands near the Yom River at the Wat Chao Chan compound in Chaliang.

JOE CUMMINGS

In traditional Sukhothai-style temple architecture, a rectangular uposatha or sanctuary contained a large sitting Buddha at one end. Behind the uposatha stood a tiered, bell-shaped chedi. Over the years many of the sanctuary walls in the Sukhothai complex have fallen down, leaving solitary Buddha images backed by chedis.

JOE CUMMINGS

# Si Satchanalai-Chaliang Historical Park

อุทยานประวัติศาสตร์ศรีสัชนาลัย-ชะเลียง

**T**he Sukhothai period ruins in the old cities of Si Satchanalai and Chaliang, about 50 km north of Sukhothai, are in the same basic style as those in the Sukhothai Historical Park, but with some slightly larger sites. The 13th to 15th century ruins cover roughly 720 hectares, surrounded by a 12m-wide moat. Chaliang, a km to the south-east, is an older city site (dating to the 11th century) though its two temples date to the 14th century. This historical park has also been classified as a World Heritage Site.

The ruins at Si Satchanalai are set among hills and are very attractive in the sense that they're not as heavily visited as the Sukhothai ruins. Some people actually prefer the more unrestored atmosphere at Si Satchanalai over Sukhothai. Numerous in number, what's listed below represents only the more distinctive of the Si Satchanalai ruins.

Recent additions to the park, which is open 8 am to 6 pm, include a coffee shop near the ponds in the middle of the complex. Elephant rides through the park are available for 50 to 100B per person and admission to the historical park is 20B for pedestrians/cyclists, 30B for car or motorcycle. For details on getting to the park, see under Getting There & Away in the Around Sukhothai section.

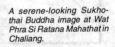

*A serene-looking Sukhothai Buddha image at Wat Phra Si Ratana Mahathat in Chaliang.*

## Wat Chang Lom

วัดช้างล้อม

This fine temple, marking the centre of the old city of Si Satchanalai, has the same name and style as the one in Sukhothai – elephants surrounding a bell-shaped stupa – but is somewhat better preserved. A stone inscription says the temple was built by King Ramkhamhaeng of Sukhothai between 1285 and 1291.

## Wat Khao Phanom Phloeng

วัดเขาพนมเพลิง

On the hill overlooking Wat Chang Lom to the right are the remains of Wat Khao Phanom Phloeng, including a large seated Buddha, a chedi and stone columns which once supported the roof of the wihãan. From this hill you can make out the general design of the once great city. The slightly higher hill west of Phanom Phloeng is capped by a large Sukhothai-style chedi – all that remains of Wat Khao Suwan Khiri.

## Wat Chedi Jet Thaew

วัดเจดีย์เจ็ดแถว

Next to Wat Chang Lom, these ruins contain seven rows of lotus-bud chedis, the largest of which is a copy of one at Wat Mahathat in Sukhothai. An interesting brick-and-plaster wihãan features barred windows designed to look like lathed wood (an ancient Indian technique used all over South-East Asia). A prasat and chedi are stacked on the roof.

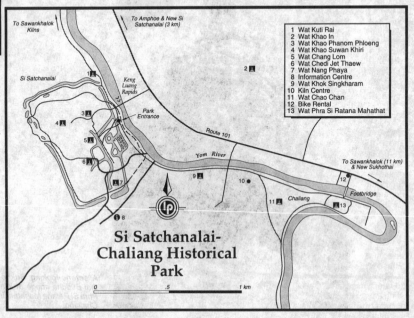

1  Wat Kuti Rai
2  Wat Khao In
3  Wat Khao Phanom Phloeng
4  Wat Khao Suwan Khiri
5  Wat Chang Lom
6  Wat Chedi Jet Thaew
7  Wat Nang Phaya
8  Information Centre
9  Wat Khok Singkharam
10  Kiln Centre
11  Wat Chao Chan
12  Bike Rental
13  Wat Phra Si Ratana Mahathat

Si Satchanalai-
Chaliang Historical
Park

NORTHERN THAILAND

In the Si Satchanalai section of the park, Wat Chang Lom is a well preserved chedi of the Sukhothai period.

# Wat Nang Phaya

วัดนางพญา

South of Wat Chang Lom and Wat Chedi Jet Thaew, this stupa is Sinhalese in style and was built in the 15th or 16th century, a bit later than other monuments at Si Satchanalai. Stucco reliefs on the large laterite wihāan in front of the stupa – now sheltered by a tin roof – date to the Ayuthaya period when Si Satchanalai was known as Sawankhalok. Goldsmiths in the district still craft a design known as *nang phaya*, modelled after these reliefs.

# Wat Phra Si Ratana Mahathat

วัดพระศรีรัตนมหาธาตุ

These ruins at Chaliang consist of a large laterite chedi (dating from 1448-88) between two wihāans. One wihāan contains a large seated Sukhothai Buddha image, a smaller standing image and a bas-relief of the famous walking Buddha, so exemplary of the flowing, boneless Sukhothai style. The other wihāan contains some less distinguished images.

There's a separate 10B admission for this wat.

# Wat Chao Chan

วัดเจ้าจันทร์

These wat ruins are about 500m west of Wat Phra Si Ratana Mahathat in Chaliang. The central attraction is a large Khmer-style prang similar to later prangs in Lopburi and probably built during the reign of Khmer King Jayavarman VII (1181-1217). The prang has been restored and is in fairly good shape. The roofless wihāan on the right contains the remains of a large standing Buddha.

## Information

The tourist police maintain an office in the
Sukhothai Historical Park directly across
from the museum. Sukhothai Travel Service
(☎ 613075), next door to Rai Im-Aim Restaurant on Charot Withithong Rd in New
Sukhothai, does domestic air booking and
ticket reconfirmations; the staff can also
provide local guides. The young proprietor
says he will be establishing a 'Travellers
Club' at the agency where travellers can
drink inexpensive beer and soft drinks, swap
information and watch videos.

**Post & Communications** The post office on
Nikhom Kasem Rd is open Monday to
Friday 8.30 am to noon, 1 to 4.30 pm on
weekends and 9 am to noon on holidays. The
attached CAT office offers international
phone services daily from 7 am to 10 pm.

## Places to Stay

**Guesthouses** Most of the guesthouses in
New Sukhothai offer reasonably priced
accommodation in family homes (dorms
and/or private rooms), and all rent bicycles
and motorcycles. Places continue to multiply, and competition keeps prices low. The
local taxi mafia has its hooks into the guesthouse proprietors, so expect lots of opinions
about where you want to go from the samlor
drivers.

*Lotus Village* (☎ 621484; fax 621463), at
170 Ratchathani Rd on the east bank of the
Yom River, is set on spacious grounds, with
a garden sitting area, and is quite suitable for
long-term stays. Some rooms are in teak
houses on stilts over a lotus pond in the back.
Rates are 100 to 150B per person depending
on room size.

*Yupa House* (☎ 612578) is near the west
bank of the Yom River at 44/10 Prawet
Nakhon Rd, Soi Mekhapatthana. The family
that runs it is friendly and helpful and often
invites guests to share family meals. They
have a 30B dorm, plus rooms of various sizes
from 60 to 80B. There's a nice view of the
city from the roof. *Somprasong Guest House*
(☎ 611709) is on the way to Yupa along the
same road, at No 32. The rooms are arranged

hotel-like on the 2nd floor of a large family
house and cost 50/80B for singles/doubles
with fan and bath. Also along this road, next
door to the Somprasong, is the newer *Ban
Thai* (☎ 610163), run by yet another friendly
family for 60/80B with shared bath, 150B for
a bungalow with private bath. Ban Thai is a
good place for reliable info on things to see
and do in the Sukhothai area.

Another relatively new entry to the guesthouse scene is *Friend House* (☎ 610172) at
52/7 Soi Nissan, off Loet Thai Rd (parallel
to Prawet Nakhon Rd). All rooms come with
private bath and cost 80B for a single/double
with fan, 150B (one room only) with air-con
and 60B for a dorm bed. Discounts for more
than a two night stay are available. The
guesthouse has a small garden dining area,
free bikes and motorcycles for rent. The proprietor teaches English to Thais so it's a good
place to meet students.

*Anasukho Guest House* (☎ 611315) is in a
large house at 234/6 Charot Withithong Rd,
Soi Panitsan, near the Rajthanee Hotel. It's
an OK place but a bit noisy due to the local
barking dog population. Rooms cost from 50
to 80B, or 40B for a dorm bed.

*O-2 Guest House* (☎ 612982), standing
for 'Original Two Teachers', is at 26/4 Rat
Uthit Rd, a five minute walk from the bus
stop outside Win Tour (about 100m past the
Thai Military Bank and down a soi). It's a
very casual, self-serve kind of place with OK
rooms for 70/100B single/double with
attached bath, 80B double with shared bath.

A bit out of the way out on Route 101,
about two km north-west of the town centre,
the hotel-like *Sky House* (☎ 612237) has
decent rooms with fan and private bath for
120 to 150B single, 340 to 400B double;
discounts for stays of more than one night
are available. An attached restaurant has
good coffee (including espresso) along with
Thai, Chinese and European food.

Out on Charot Withithong Rd, about 30m
from the bus stop for the historical park, *Bi
Bi Guest House* (☎ 610425) offers simple
rooms with shared bath in a wooden house
for 60 to 80B. Street noise can be a problem.

*No 4 Guest House*, the first guesthouse in

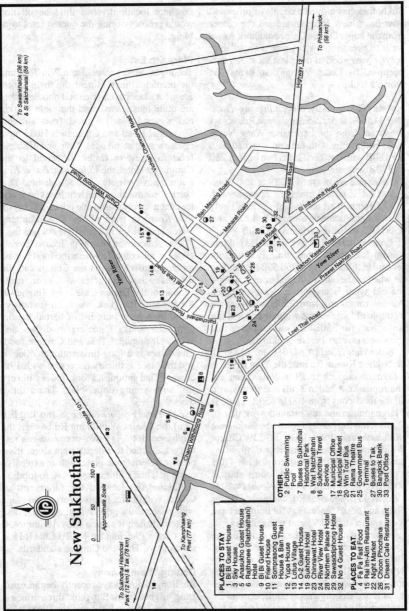

**New Sukhothai**

To Sawankhalok (36 km)
& Si Satchanalai (56 km)

To Phitsanulok
(56 km)

Highway 12

To Sukhothai Historical
Park (12 km) & Tak (78 km)

To Kamphaeng
Phet (77 km)

Route 101

Yom River

Yom River

Vichian Chamnong Road

Charot Withithong Road

Rai Uthit Road

Ratchathani Road

Ban Meuang Road

Maharat Road

Singhawat Road

Singhawat Road

Nikhon Kasem Road

Prawet Nakhon Road

Si Intharathit Road

Loet Thai Road

Charot Withithong Road

0        50      100 m
Approximate Scale

**PLACES TO STAY**
1  Bi Bi Guest House
3  Sky House
5  Anasukho Guest House
6  Rajthanee (Ratchathani)
   Hotel
9  Bi Bi Guest House
10 Friend House
11 Somprasong Guest
   House & Ban Thai
12 Yupa House
13 Lotus Village
14 O-2 Guest House
23 Chinnawat Hotel
24 River View Hotel
28 Northern Palace Hotel
29 Sawasddiphong Hotel
32 No 4 Guest House

**PLACES TO EAT**
4  Fa Fa Fast Food
15 Rai Im-Aim Restaurant
22 Night Market
26 Choon Phochana
31 Dream Cafe Restaurant

**OTHER**
2  Public Swimming
   Pool
7  Buses to Sukhothai
   Historical Park
8  Wat Ratchathani
16 Sukhothai Travel
   Service
17 Municipal Office
18 Municipal Market
20 Win Tour Bus
21 Rama Theatre
25 Government Bus
   Terminal
27 Buses to Tak
30 Bangkok Bank
33 Post Office

Sukhothai, has moved a couple of times and now has a new location around the corner from the larger Dream Cafe restaurant. As we went to press room rates weren't available; service was good at their last location (now occupied by Lotus Village), so it may be worth a look.

**Hotels** The friendly *Sawaddiphong Hotel* (☎ 611567), at 56/2-5 Singhawat Rd, across the street from the expensive Wang Neua, has good rooms with fan and attached bath for 180B with one bed, 250B two beds or 280 to 370B with air-con.

*Sukhothai Hotel* (☎ 611133), at 15/5 Singhawat Rd, is an old travellers' favourite with lots of room to sit around downstairs. Fairly clean singles/doubles with fan and bath cost 150/180B and air-con rooms are 350B.

*Chinnawat Hotel* (☎ 611385), at 1-3 Nikhon Kasem Rd, needs renovating. Rooms with fan and bath cost from 80 to 150B, depending on whether they are in the old or new wing – the old wing is cheaper and a bit quieter. Air-con rooms cost from 250B, and there are a couple of large rooms with air-con and hot water bath for 350B. Be sure to check that the air-con works before booking in.

*River View Hotel* (☎ 611656; fax 613373), on Nikhon Kasem Rd near the Yom River, is a favourite among small traders. Clean air-con rooms cost 320 to 370B and rooms with all the mod-cons from 400 to 650B. There is a large lounge and restaurant downstairs.

Once the top hotel in town, the *Rajthanee (Ratchathani)* (☎ 611031), at 229 Charot Withithong Rd, has seen better days. Standard rooms with fan are overpriced at 470B a single/double and air-con rooms start at 600B. *Northern Palace (Wang Neua)* (☎ 611-193), at 43 Singhawat Rd, charges 475B for Thais and 650B for farangs for unimpressive rooms with small TVs and refrigerators.

About eight km from the city centre on the road between the old and new cities of Sukhothai, the huge *Pailyn Sukhothai* (☎ 613-310; fax 613317) caters mostly to tour groups and has a disco, health centre and several restaurants. Rooms start at 800B; occupancy has been quite low since opening (due to the

nowhere location), so a little negotiation would probably bring the quoted rates tumbling.

**Places to Eat**
The night market across from Win Tour and the municipal market near the town centre are great places to eat; rice and noodle dishes are quite inexpensive and the night market has a vendor with good fruit shakes. Sukhothai Hotel and Chinnawat Hotel have restaurants that prepare Thai and Chinese food for western tastes. Attached to the Chinnawat Hotel, the *Chinnawat Bar & Restaurant* has a variety of noodle dishes, Thai curries, sandwiches, western breakfasts and ice cream at very reasonable prices. *Sukhothai Suki-Koka*, in front of the Sawaddiphong Hotel, specialises in Thai-style sukiyaki.

One street over near Win Tour is *Dream Cafe*, an air-con cafe where the food is a bit more expensive than at the Chinnawat, but the place has character. A larger, nicer version of the Dream Cafe is on Singhawat Rd opposite Bangkok Bank. The extensive menu includes a long list of herbal liquors ('stamina drinks'), ice-cream dishes and very well prepared Thai and Chinese food. The owner is a long-time antique collector and the place is thickly decorated with 19th century Thai antiques, a look that is still very 'in' with young upper-class Thais these days.

*Fah Fah (F&F) Fast Food* (no English sign), on Charot Withithong Rd beyond the Rajthanee Hotel, is a two-storey air-con restaurant attached to a department store. It's a clean, cafeteria-style place with an extensive menu of Thai, Chinese and western foods.

*Rai Im-Aim*, toward the other end of Charot Withithong Rd, is a very clean place with moderately priced Thai, Chinese and western dishes; it's open daily 10 am to 10 pm. *Choon Phochana* at 1-5 Tri Chat Rd has inexpensive Thai and Chinese standards.

**Getting There & Away**
**Air** Bangkok Airways recently began operating flights from Bangkok three times a week; the fare is 1100B and the flight takes

and hour and 10 minutes. The flight continues on to Chiang Mai for an additional 540B. BA's offices are at the airport; there's no regular phone number as staff are only present when BA flights are arriving and departing. Any travel agency in town can issue tickets.

**Bus** Sukhothai can be reached by road from Phitsanulok, Tak or Kamphaeng Phet. If you arrive in Phitsanulok by rail or air, take a city bus No 1 (2B) to the air-con bus terminal in the centre, or to the Baw Khaw Saw (government bus) terminal, for buses out of town. The bus to Sukhothai costs 16B, takes about an hour and leaves regularly throughout the day.

From Tak, get a Sukhothai bus at the Baw Khaw Saw terminal just outside town. The fare is 23B and the trip takes about 1½ hours. Buses from Kamphaeng Phet are 23B and take from one to 1½ hours.

Ordinary Baw Khaw Saw buses to/from Chiang Mai cost 91B via Tak (the shortest, fastest route) and take from 4½ to five hours; air-con is 127B. Buses between Bangkok and Sukhothai are 106B (148B air-con) and take seven hours. Buses to Chiang Rai cost 102B (142B air-con) and take six hours; there are four departures per day of each type. Buses to Khon Kaen cost 120B (185B air-con) and take from six to seven hours.

Phitsanulok Yan Yon Tour has four daily VIP buses (with reclining seats) to Bangkok for 210B. Ordinary buses to destinations outside Sukhothai Province leave from the government bus terminal; tour buses leave from Win Tour or Phitsanulok Yan Yon Tour near the night market area. Buses to Tak leave from Ban Meuang Rd, two streets east of Singhawat Rd.

Buses to Sawankhalok (10B, 45 minutes) and Si Satchanalai (19B, one hour) leave hourly from the intersection opposite the Sukhothai Hotel, between about 6 am and 6 pm.

### Getting Around
Around New Sukhothai, a samlor ride shouldn't cost more than 15 or 20B. Songthaews run frequently between New Sukhothai and

Sukhothai Historical Park, leaving from Charot Withithong Rd near the Yom River; the fare is 5B and it takes 20 to 30 minutes from the river to the park.

The best way to get around the historical park is by bicycle; these can be rented at shops outside the park entrance for 20B per day or you could borrow or rent one at any guesthouse in New Sukhothai. If you rent a bike in town, instead of taking Highway 12 straight to the park, a more scenic if slower way to reach the ruins is to turn north off the highway two km west of the main junction of Highway 12 and Highway 101. Continue north less than a km till you cross a canal, then turn left (north-west) and follow the canal all the way to the historical park. You shouldn't get lost as long as you can keep the canal in sight. On the way you'll get a taste of village life.

The park operates a tram service through the old city for 20B per person. Local farmers sometimes offer bullock cart rides through the park for about the same rate.

## AROUND SUKHOTHAI
### Si Satchanalai-Chaliang Historical Park
See the previous special section on the historical parks for details on the major ancient sites in this 720 hectare park. The nearby town of Sawankhalok is the main supply centre for the area.

### Sawankhalok Kilns
เตาไฟสวรรคโลก
The Sukhothai-Si Satchanalai area has long been famous for its beautiful pottery, much of which was exported throughout Asia. In China – the biggest importer of Thai pottery during the Sukhothai and Ayuthaya periods – the pieces came to be called 'Sangkalok', a mispronunciation of Sawankhalok (Si Satchanalai's later name). Particularly fine specimens can be seen in the national museums of Jakarta and Pontianak, as the Indonesians of the time were keen collectors.

At one time, more than 200 huge pottery kilns lined the Yom River in this area.

Several have been carefully excavated and can be viewed at the **Si Satchanalai Centre for Study & Preservation of Sangkalok Kilns**, which opened in 1987. So far the centre has opened two phases to the public, a small museum in Chaliang with excavated pottery samples and one kiln and a larger outdoor kiln site a couple of km north-west of the Si Satchanalai ruins. The exhibits are very well presented, although there are no English labels. More phases are planned, including one that will feature a working kiln.

Sawankhalok pottery rejects, buried in the fields, are still being found. Shops in Sukhothai and Sawankhalok sell misfired, broken, warped and fused pieces. The **Sawanwaranayok Museum** near Sawankhalok's Wat Sawankhalam on the west bank of the river exhibits pottery and Buddha images unearthed by local villagers and donated to the wat. Thai Celadon near Chiang Mai is a ceramics centre producing a modern interpretation of the old craft.

### Ban Hat Siaw

This colourful village south-east of Si Satchanalai is home to the Thai Phuan, a Thai tribal group that immigrated from Xieng Khuang Province in Laos around 100 years ago when the Annamese and Chinese were causing mayhem in north-eastern Laos. The local Thai Phuan are famous for their rich handwoven textiles, known as *phâa hàat sîaw* among the Thais and characterised by patterns of horizontal stripes bordered by brocade.

Traditionally every Thai Phuan woman is taught weaving skills, which are passed on from generation to generation. Practically every stilt house in the village has a loom beneath it; cloth can be purchased at the source or from shops in Sawankhalok. Vintage Hat Siaw textiles 80 to 200 years old can be seen at the Village Old Clothes Museum in central Si Satchanalai.

Another Thai Phuan custom is the use of elephant-back processions in local monastic ordinations; these usually take place in early April.

### Places to Stay & Eat

*Wang Yom Resort*, just outside the Si Satchanalai historical park, has a number of well appointed bamboo bungalows and a 'handicraft village' set amid beautifully landscaped grounds. Depending on the location (some are on the river), bungalows here cost from 400B; there are also a few basic huts in the handicraft area that cost 200B a night. Wang Yom's large restaurant is reportedly very good. Food and drink are also available at a coffee shop in the historical park until 6 pm.

A grocery store in a large wooden house at the T-junction near the Si Satchanalai park entrance has two rooms for rent at the back. A larger room upstairs goes for 500B, while a smaller room downstairs is 300B; both rooms share a private downstairs bath. These rates may be negotiable.

**Sawankhalok** This charming town on the Yom River about 11 km south of the historical park has a couple of other possibilities for visitors wishing to explore the area in more depth. *Muang In* (☎ 642622), at 21 Kasemrat Rd, has rooms with fan for 160B, air-con for 250B and a dark sing-song cafe downstairs. The more centrally located *Sangsin Hotel* (☎ 641259), at 2 Thetsaban Damri 3 Rd (the main street through town), has clean, comfortable rooms with fan for 180B, 240 to 320B with air-con.

This isn't a big town for eating; most places serve sell noodles and khâo man kài and not much else. *Van Waw*, a noodle shop opposite Sangsin Hotel, is one of the better ones; it's open from 8 am to 3 pm only. For khâo kaeng (rice and curry), try the shop opposite the Thai Farmers Bank. There is also a night market in town along the main streets which is bigger than the one in New Sukhothai. *Ko Heng* is an old riverside Chinese restaurant that's well past its prime and is now primarily a place for old Chinese cronies to sit and drink tea.

Probably the best eating spot is *Kung Nam*, a Thai and Chinese garden restaurant on the outskirts of town toward Sukhothai, not far from the Muang In Hotel.

NORTHERN THAILAND

## Getting There & Away
**Bus** The Si Satchanalai-Chaliang Historical Park is off Route 101 between Sawankhalok and New Si Satchanalai. From New Sukhothai, take a Si Satchanalai bus (19B) and ask to get off at the old city (meuang kào). There are two places along the left side of the highway where you can get off the bus and reach the ruins in the park; all involve crossing the Yom River. The first leads to a footbridge over the Yom River to Wat Phra Si Ratana Mahathat at Chaliang; the second crossing is about two km farther north-west just past two hills and leads directly into the Si Satchanalai ruins.

**Train** Rama VI had a 60 km railway spur constructed from Ban Dara (a small town on the main northern trunk) to Sawankhalok just so that he could visit the ruins. The original small wooden railway station in Sawankhalok is one of the main local sights. One local train per day uses this spur, No 315, originating from Taphan Hin (73 km north of Nakhon Sawan). You can catch this train in Phitsanulok at 11.14 am and arrive in Sawankhalok at 1.55 pm. The 3rd class (only) fare is 14B.

## Getting Around
Bicycle is the best way to see the ruins. These can be rented from a shop at the intersection of Route 101 and the road leading to Chaliang; rates are a low 25B per day. You can also hire an elephant and mahout to tour Si Satchanalai (but not Chaliang) for 50 to 100B.

# Tak Province

Tak, like Loei, Nan, Phetchabun, Krabi and certain other provinces, has traditionally been considered a 'remote' province, that is, one which the central Bangkok government has had little control over. In the 1970s, the mountains of west Tak were a hotbed of communist guerrilla activity. Now the former leader of the local CPT movement is involved in resort hotel development and Tak is open to outsiders, but the area still has an untamed feeling

about it. The entire province has a population of only around 350,000.

Western Tak has always presented a distinct contrast with other parts of Thailand because of heavy Karen and Burmese cultural influences. The Thailand-Myanmar border districts of Mae Ramat, Tha Song Yang and Mae Sot are dotted with refugee camps, a result of recent fighting between the Karen National Union (KNU) and the Myanmar government which is driving Karen civilians across the border. As of mid-1996 there were an estimated 10,000 Burmese and Karen refugees along the border; repatriation may follow ceasefire agreements between the two armies.

The main source of income for people living on both sides of the border is legal and illegal international trade. Black-market dealings are estimated to account for at least 150 million baht per year in local income. The main smuggling gateways on the Thailand side are Tha Song Yang, Mae Sarit, Mae Tan, Wangkha, Mae Sot and Waley. On the Myanmar side, all these gateways except Mae Sot and Waley are controlled by the KNU. One important contraband product is teak, brought into Thailand from Myanmar on big tractor trailers at night. More than 100,000B in bribes per truckload is distributed among the local Thai authorities responsible for looking the other way. Some of the trade is legal since the Thai and Burmese military leaderships have started cutting deals.

Most of the province is forested and mountainous and is excellent for trekking. Organised trekking occurs, some from out of Chiang Mai farther north. There are Hmong, Musoe (Lahu), Lisu and White and Red Karen settlements throughout the west and north.

## TAK
อ.เมืองตาก
• ☎ (55) • pop 21,000
Lying along the east bank of the Ping River, Tak is not particularly interesting except as a point from which to visit the Lan Sang and Taksin Maharat national parks to the west or Phumiphon Yanhi Dam to the north. Travellers heading to Mae Sot on the Thailand-Myanmar

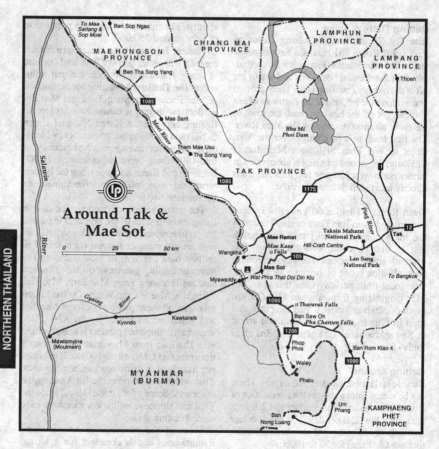

**Around Tak & Mae Sot**

border occasionally find themselves here for a few hours or occasionally overnight.

Although most of Tak exhibits nonde-script, cement-block architecture, the southern section of the city harbours a few old teak homes. Local residents are proud of the sus-pension bridge (for motorcycles, pedicabs, bicycles and pedestrians only) over the Ping River, which flows quite broadly here even in the dry season. There's also a larger highway bridge over the river.

### Information
TAT (☎ 5144341) has an office in a beautiful

new building at 193 Taksin Rd on Mahat Thai Borong Rd, where you can pick up a few tour company pamphlets and resort/hotel brochures.

### Taksin Maharat & Lan Sang National Parks
These small national parks receive a steady trickle of visitors on weekends and holidays but are almost empty during the week. Taksin Maharat (established 1981) covers 149 sq km; the entrance is two km from Km 26 on Route 105/Asia 1, the highway to Mae Sot. The park's most outstanding features are

the 30m, nine-tiered **Mae Ya Pa Falls** and a record-holding *thábàk*, a dipterocarp that is 50m tall and 16m in circumference. Bird-watching is said to be particularly good here; known resident and migrating species include the tiger shrike, forest wagtail and Chinese pond heron.

Lan Sang National Park preserves 104 sq km surrounding an area of rugged, 1000m granite peaks, part of the Tenasserim Range. A network of trails leads to several water-falls, including the park's 40m namesake. To reach the park entrance, take Route 1103 three km south off Route 105.

### Places to Stay & Eat

Most of Tak's hotels are lined up on Mahat Thai Bamrung Rd in the town centre. The biggest hotel, *Wiang Tak* (☎ 511910), at 25/3 Mahat Thai Bamrung Rd, has recently upgraded air-con rooms from 650 to 900B. A similar *Wiang Tak 2* (☎ 512508) on the Tak River costs the same. The less expensive *Racha Villa* (☎ 512361) at the intersection of Route 105 and Highway 1 is a better value for fairly well appointed fan rooms for 250B, air-con for 450B.

Back on Mahat Thai Bamrung Rd the even less expensive *Tak* (☎ 514422) has clean but basic rooms with fan and bath for 155 to 220B. It's off the road down a long alley. The *Mae Ping* (☎ 511807) is very similar but a little more worn; large rooms with fan and bath are 70 to 100B, air-con 250B. On the next street over is the *Sa-nguan Thai* (☎ 511153) at 619 Taksin Rd. Fan rooms are 170B, air-con 290B and there is a restaurant downstairs.

About 50m from the government bus ter-minal near the intersection of Highways 1 and 12, *Panasak Hotel* (☎ 511436) has basic but clean bungalows for 100 to 150B with fan and bath, air-con from 200B; it's good value if a little removed from town.

Cheap food can be bought in the market across the street from the Mae Ping Hotel.

### Getting There & Away

Tak airport, 15 km out of town towards Sukhothai on Highway 12, isn't operating at the moment; the nearest functioning airports are in Phitsanulok and Mae Sot. THAI pro-vides a free shuttle van from Phitsanulok airport to Tak daily at 8 am and 2 pm, and in the opposite direction at 6 am and noon. In Tak the vans stop at the Vieng Tak Hotel.

There are frequent buses to Tak from Sukhothai and fares are 23B for an ordinary Baw Khaw Saw bus or 34B for an air-con bus with Win Tour. The trip takes from one to 1½ hours. The Tak bus station is just outside town, but a motorised samlor will take you to the Tak Hotel (in the town centre) for 15B.

Minivans to Mae Sot leave frequently from the main terminal in Tak for 28B per person, share taxis for 38B.

## MAE SOT
แม่สอด
• ☎ (55)

Mae Sot is 80 km from Tak on the so-called Pan-Asian Highway (Asia Route 1, which would ostensibly link Istanbul and Singa-pore if all the intervening countries allowed land crossings), numbered Route 105 under the Thai highway system.

Just a few years ago, several public bill-boards in town carried the warning (in Thai): 'Have fun, but if you carry a gun, you go to jail', underscoring Mae Sot's reputation as a free-swinging, profiteering wild east town. The billboards are gone but the outlaw image lingers. The local black-market trade is booming since the Myanmar government's 1991 ban on legal border trade between Myawaddy and Mae Sot, imposed because of Myawaddy's huge trade deficit and the downward spiralling kyat (Burmese cur-rency). Most of the black-market dealings take place in the now-prospering Thai dis-tricts of Mae Ramat, Tha Song Yang, Phop Phra and Um Phang.

This Burmese-Chinese-Karen-Thai trad-ing outpost is slowly becoming a tourist destination. Local opinion is divided on just how untamed a place Mae Sot really is. Although a centralised government presence dominates provincial politics, local economics is controlled by factions which settle con-flicts extra-legally. As elsewhere in Thailand where this happens, the local police are all-powerful since they control the greatest number of armaments. So, business success often means cultivating special connections with police. As long as they stay out of the local trade in guns, narcotics, teak and gems, outsiders will experience a fascinating but basically easy-going milieu.

Mae Sot itself is small but growing, as it has become the most important jade and gem centre along the border. In recent years the local gem trade has become increasingly controlled by Chinese and Indian immigrants from Myanmar.

Walking down the streets of Mae Sot, you'll see an interesting mixture of ethnicities – Burmese men in their longyis, Hmong and Karen women in traditional hill-tribe dress, bearded Indo-Burmese men and, during the opium harvest season (January to February), the occasional Thai army ranger with M-16 and string of opium poppies around his neck. Shop signs along the streets are in Thai, Burmese and Chinese. Most of the local temple architecture is Burmese. The town's Burmese population is largely Muslim, while Burmese living outside town are Buddhist and the local Karen are mostly Christian.

The large municipal market in Mae Sot, behind the Siam Hotel, sells some interesting stuff, including Burmese clothing, Indian food and cheap takeaways.

A big Thai-Burmese gem fair is held in April. Around this time Thai and Burmese boxers meet for an annual muay thai competition held somewhere outside town in the traditional style. Matches are fought in a circular ring and go for five rounds; the first four rounds last three minutes, the fifth has no time limit. Hands bound in hemp, the boxers fight till first blood or knockout. You'll have to ask around to find the changing venue for the annual slugfest, as it's not exactly legal.

The Thai and Myanmar governments began building an international highway bridge over the Moei River a couple of years ago, then fell into disagreement over the river border and halted all work in 1995. In mid-1996 work began again but for how long

is anyone's guess. If completed, this bridge will link Mae Sot with the highway west to Mawlamyine (Moulmein) and Yangon, an exciting prospect for overland travel.

## Information
The tourist police have an office next to No 4 Guest House.

DK Book House has a branch in Mae Sot on Intharakhiri Rd. The only English-language books it stocks so far are Penguin classics, but there are a few maps of the area for sale, including a detailed Thai military-surveyed topographic map (1:250,000) of the border area entitled 'Moulmein'. This map extends as far north as Mae Ramat, to the south almost to Um Phang, west to Mawlamyine and only about 50 km east of Mae Sot.

In town, the family that operates the Myawaddy (see Places to Eat), one of the better handicraft shops, has been in the border trade for nearly 50 years. Doy, the owner, speaks excellent English and distributes information on things to see and do in the area.

SP Guest House and West Frontier Guest House can arrange trekking and rafting trips north and south of Mae Sot.

## Border Market
Songthaews frequently go to the border, six km west of Mae Sot: ask for Rim Moei (the Moei River). The trip costs 7B and the last songthaew back to Mae Sot leaves Rim Moei at 6 pm. At Rim Moei you can walk along the river and view the Union of Myanmar and its eastern outpost, Myawaddy, on the other side. Clearly visible are a school, a Buddhist temple and compounds of thatched-roof houses.

The border crossing, which consists of a footbridge and a ferry service, has been closed on and off since fighting broke out between the Karen National Union and the Myanmar government in the early 1980s. From time to time, mortar fire rocks the area, forcing Myawaddy residents to seek shelter on the Thai side. Lately things have been quite peaceful and work on an international highway bridge has re-started.

NORTHERN THAILAND

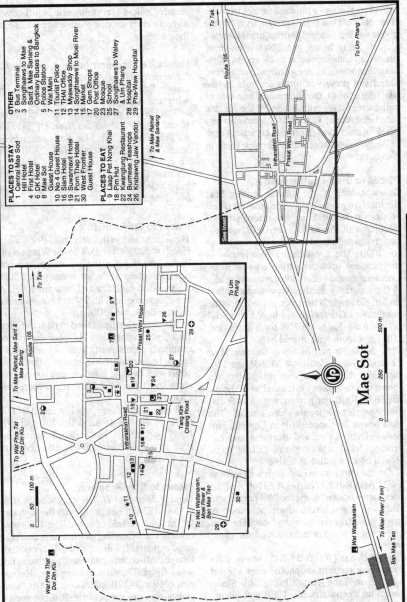

Mae Sot

**PLACES TO STAY**
1   Central Mae Sod
4   Fiill Hotel
6   DK Hotel
8   Mae Sot
    Guest House
10  No 4 Guest House
16  Siam Hotel
19  Suwannavit Hotel
21  Porn Thep Hotel
30  West Frontier
    Guest House

**PLACES TO EAT**
9   Laap Pet Nong Khai
18  Pim Hut
22  Kwangtung Restaurant
24  Burmese Teashops
26  Krabawng Jaw Vendor

**OTHER**
2   Bus Terminal
3   Songthaews to Mae
    Sant & Mae Sariang &
    Ordinary Buses to Bangkok
5   Police Station
7   Wat Mani
11  Tourist Police
12  THAI Office
13  Myawaddy Shop
14  Songthaews to Moei River
15  Market
17  Gem Shops
20  Post Office
23  Mosque
25  School
27  Songthaews to Waley
    & Um Phang
28  Hospital
29  Pha-Waw Hospital

A market about a hundred metres from the river on the Thai side legally sells Burmese goods – dried fish and shrimp, dried bamboo shoots, mung beans, peanuts, woven-straw products, teak carvings, thick cotton blankets, lacquerware, tapestries, jade and gems. Dried and preserved foods are sold by the *pan* (the pound), the Burmese/Karen unit of weight measure, rather than by the kg, the usual measure in Thailand. You can also buy black-market kyat (Burmese currency) here at very favourable rates (better than in Yangon).

### Places to Stay – bottom end

**Guesthouses** At the time of writing Mae Sot had five guesthouses. The *Mae Sot Guest House* on Intharakhiri Rd offers singles/doubles with shared bath for 100B, and air-con rooms with cold showers in a row house for 200B. The guesthouse's best feature is the pleasant open-air sitting area in front. Local maps and information are available.

Considerably farther west along Intharakhiri Rd towards the river, at No 736, is the simple *No 4 Guest House*, a large house well off the road. Rates are 30B for a dorm bed, 60B for a room with shared bath.

In the south part of town, the new *West Frontier Guest House* (☎ 532638) at 18/2 Bua Khun Rd near Pha-Waw Hospital has six rooms in a two-storey brick and wood house for 70 to 100B per person, with a 20B discount when two people share a room. The staff boasts language skills in English, Japanese, Thai, Karen and Burmese and can arrange local trekking and rafting trips. Rental bikes are also available.

On the north-western outskirts of town at 14/21 Asia Rd, *SP House* (☎ 531409) offers adequate wooden rooms for 30B per person. Although it's a bit far from the centre of town, good travel info is available. The staff can arrange various treks around the province.

*B+B House* (☎ /fax 532818) has upstairs rooms in a modern shophouse over a travel agency on Tang Kim Chiang Rd. Small rooms up steep stairs cost 150B with shared hot shower. It's not particularly recommended unless everything else is full or you have an early morning departure on one of their tours.

**Hotels** The cheapest hotel in town is the *Suwannavit Hotel* (☎ 531162) on Soi Wat Luang. Rooms with bath cost 80B in the old wing and 100B in the new building.

You can get adequate but decidedly overpriced rooms at the *Siam Hotel* (☎ 531376) on Prasat Withi Rd, Mae Sot's other main street, for 180/200B with fan, 250B with air-con, 500B with carpet and TV. Although it's basically a truckers' hotel, local rumour has it that Burmese intelligence agents hang out at the Siam.

### Places to Stay – middle

The clean and efficiently run *Porn Thep Hotel* (☎ 532590) at 25/4 Soi Si Wiang is off Prasat Withi Rd near the day market. Air-con singles/doubles with hot water cost 350B, while rooms with fan and bath are 200B. A few deluxe rooms with TV and hot water are also available for 450B.

The top digs in town used to be at the *First Hotel*, off Intharakhiri Rd near the police station. It seems pretty ordinary now, with faded but comfortable rooms starting at 160B with fan and bath; air-con rooms cost up to 450B. Like the Siam, it's favoured by Thai truckers.

A new three-storey hotel attached to DK Book House on Intharakhiri Rd, the *DK Hotel* (☎ 531699), has smallish apartment-style rooms with air-con and attached bath for 400B.

### Places to Stay – top end

*Central Mae Sod Hill Hotel* (☎ 532601/8; (2) 541-1234 in Bangkok) is on the highway to Tak, just outside of town. The 120-room hotel has a swimming pool, tennis courts, a good restaurant, a disco and a Thai cocktail lounge. All rooms come with air-con, hot water, fridge, TV, video and telephone. Rooms cost 1059 to 1412B, suites cost 2400B. Non-guests may use the pool for 20B per person per day.

**NORTHERN THAILAND**

## Places to Eat

Near the Siam Hotel are several good places to eat, including the rambling market behind it. Next door to the Siam on Prasat Withi Rd is a small Thai-Chinese food centre with several different vendors serving noodles and curry; it's open morning to afternoon only.

A Burmese-run restaurant opposite the mosque has good roti kaeng (curry and flat bread), fresh milk, curries and khâo sòi (spicy chicken broth with flat noodles). On the same side of the street, a Burmese Muslim teashop does cheap and tasty samosas, curries and nan; a meal of curry, dal, vegetables, two nan, two plates of rice, two teas and two coffees cost only 70B when last I stopped by. Another Burmese Muslim place down the street is not as clean but seems more popular.

A favourite local snack is krabawng jaw (Burmese for 'fried crispy'), a sort of vegetable tempura. The best place to eat it is at the small vendor stand between Prasat Withi Rd and the hospital, where the same family has been supplying Mae Sot residents with 'fried crispy' for many years. You can sit at a small table near the wok and order fresh chunks of squash, pumpkin or papaya fried in egg batter and dipped in a delicious sauce of peanuts, tamarind, molasses and dried chilli. If you don't want to eat it here they'll wrap for takeaways in two portion sizes, 5B or 10B. The family fires up the wok around 4.30 pm and keeps cooking until 8 pm or until they've run out of ingredients.

*Laap Pet Nong Khai*, on the ground floor of a two-storey white house just east of Mae Sot Guest House on Intharakhiri Rd, serves good duck salad and other Isaan specialities.

The best Chinese restaurant in town is the unassuming *Kwangtung Restaurant*, which specialises in Cantonese cooking. It's around the corner from the Porn Thep Hotel, south of Prasat Withi Rd.

If you're looking for an atmospheric evening out, try *Khao Mao Khao Fan* a little north of town on the road to Mae Ramat. A Thai botanist designed this open-air restaurant to make it feel as if you're dining in the forest, with lots of common and not-so-common live plants from around the North,

even a very natural-looking artificial waterfall that imitates Um Phang's Thilawsu Falls on a much smaller scale. The Thai cuisine is equally inventive, with such specialities as yam hèt khon, (a spicy salad made with forest mushrooms available in September and October only), mūu khâo mâo (a salad of home-cured sausage, peanuts, lettuce, ginger, lime and chilli) and fried ice cream with mixed fruit. It's open daily 11 am to 9 pm.

The *Myawaddy* handicraft shop on Prasat Withi Rd has a few tables out front where the proprietors serve good meals from a short menu; breakfast is especially good and includes real coffee. It's closed on Wednesdays.

A small, no-name vegetarian restaurant next to the Um Phang songthaew stop offers good, inexpensive Thai vegetarian food from around 7 am to 7 pm or until the food is sold out.

A little farang restaurant enclave has surfaced along Tang Kim Chiang Rd, where you'll find *Pim Hut* with pizza, steak, Thai and Chinese dishes, ice cream and western breakfasts at moderate prices. Opposite is the brightly lit *Fah Fah 2 Bakery*, with a very similar menu which is slightly less expensive. Both cater to tourists, foreign volunteer workers (from nearby Karen-Burmese refugee camps) and upper middle-class Thais.

Several foodstalls in the commercial centre next to DK Hotel offer inexpensive Thai and Chinese standards; one vendor also does delicious khâo mòk kài. There are also several OK food vendors at the Mae Moei border market.

## Getting There & Away

**Air** THAI flies to Mae Sot from Bangkok (1865B) four times a week via Phitsanulok (495B), and four times from Chiang Mai (590B).

The THAI office in Mae Sot (☎ 531730) is in the town centre at 76/1 Prasat Withi Rd.

**Bus** Buses to Mae Sot leave every half-hour from the Tak bus station, from 6.30 am until 6 pm. An air-con minibus costs 28B or you can share a taxi for 38B; in Mae Sot, both depart from the First Hotel car park. The trip takes 1½ hours on a beautiful winding road through forested mountains and passes several hill-tribe villages.

Ordinary buses between Bangkok and Mae Sot depart from either end four times daily and cost 125B. VIP buses (24 seats) to Bangkok leave three times daily for 345B; 1st class air-con buses leave once daily for 224B and there are two 2nd class air-con buses daily for 174B. The trip takes about 10 hours. In Mae Sot, Bangkok-bound air-con and VIP buses leave from Inthakhiri Rd near the police station; ordinary buses to Bangkok leave from the bus terminal near the market north of the police station.

Air-con minivans to Chiang Mai leave from the Siam Hotel parking lot once a day between 8 and 9 am for 150B per person.

Songthaews to destinations north of Mae Sot (such as Mae Sarit and Mae Sariang) leave from a bus terminal near the small market north of the police station. Buses to Mae Sarit cost 50B and take 2½ hours, to Mae Sariang 150B and five or six hours.

Songthaews heading to Um Phang (80B, five hours) leave frequently between 7.30 am and 3.30 pm.

**Myawaddy to Mawlamyine, Myanmar** Theoretically it's possible to cross the river to Myawaddy and catch a bus to Mawlamyine via Kawkareik. Each leg takes about two hours; the Myawaddy-Kawkareik stretch can be dicey when fighting between Yangon and KNU troops is in progress, while the Kawkareik-Mawlamyine stretch is generally safe though the road itself is quite rough. Another way to reach Mawlamyine is to get off the road at Kyondo and continue by boat along the Gyaing River. At the moment it's not legal to enter Myanmar this way, but it's very conceivable that this road will open to foreigners within the next five years.

**Getting Around**
Most of Mae Sot can be visited on foot. Jit Alai, a motorcycle dealer on Prasat Withi Rd, sometimes rents motorcycles for 150B (100cc) to 200B (125cc) a day. Make sure you

test-ride a bike before renting; some of Jit Alai's machines can be in rather poor condition.

## AROUND MAE SOT
### Ban Mae Tao
บ.แม่เต๋า
Wat Wattanaram (Phattanaram) is a Burmese temple at Ban Mae Tao, three km west of Mae Sot on the road to the border. A large alabaster sitting Buddha is in a shrine with glass-tile walls, very Burmese in style. In the main wihãan on the 2nd floor is a collection of Burmese musical instruments, including tuned drums and gongs.

### Wat Phra That Doi Din Kiu (Ji)
วัดพระธาตุดอยดินกิว(จี)
This is a forest temple 11 km north-west of Mae Sot on a 300m hill overlooking the Moei River and Myanmar. A small chedi mounted on what looks like a boulder balanced on the edge of a cliff is one of the attractions, and is reminiscent of the Kyaiktiyo Pagoda in Myanmar.

The trail that winds up the hill provides good views of thick teak forests across the river in Myanmar. On the Thai side, a scattering of smaller trees is visible. There are a couple of small limestone caves in the side of the hill on the way to the peak. The dirt road that leads to the wat from Mae Tao passes through a couple of Karen villages.

During Myanmar's dry-season offensives against the KNU, this area is sometimes considered unsafe and the road to the temple is occasionally blocked by Thai rangers. Ask in town about the current situation before heading up the road.

### Karen & Burmese Refugee Camps
ค่ายผู้หนีภัยชาวพม่า
Several refugee camps have been set up along the east bank of the Moei River in either direction from Mae Sot. Most of the refugees in these camps are Karen fleeing battles between Burmese and KNU troops across the border. The camps have been around for a decade but the Thai government

has generally kept their existence quiet, fearing the build-up of a huge refugee volunteer industry such as that which developed around the Indochinese camps in eastern Thailand in the 1970s.

Although many Thai and foreign volunteers have come to the refugees' aid, the camps are very much in need of outside assistance. Visitors are always welcome, as the refugees are starved for recognition by the international community. Donations of clothes, medicines (to be administered by qualified doctors and nurses) and volunteer English teaching are even more welcome.

Most conveniently visited from Mae Sot are those at **Mawker** (7000 refugees), a couple of hours south of Mae Sot on the road to Waley, and **Huaykalok** (4000 refugees), about an hour north of town on the road to Mae Sarit. If you can't travel to any of the camps yourself, you can leave old clothes or other donations at Mae Sot's No 4 Guest House.

For more information on the plight of the Burmese and Karen refugees, contact the Burma Project (☎ (2) 437-9445; fax 222-5788), 124 Soi Watthongnoppakhun, Somdet Chaophraya Rd, Klongsan, Bangkok 10600; or the Santi Pracha Dhamma Institute (☎ (2) 223-4915; fax 222-5188), 117 Fuang Nakhon Rd, Bangkok 10200.

### Waley
 วะเลย์

Thirty-six km from Mae Sot, Route 1206 splits south-west off Route 1090 at Ban Saw Oh and terminates 25 km south at the border town of Waley, an important smuggling point. The Burmese side was once one of the two main gateways to Kawthoolei, the Karen nation, but in 1989 the Yangon government ousted the KNU. Burmese teak is the main border trade here now; a huge lumberyard just outside Waley is stacked with piles of teak logs which have crossed at Waley. Visitors may be able to arrange a day crossing by asking nicely at the Thai military post at the Moei River bridge – the guards will radio the Burmese side to see if it's OK.

One can visit hill-tribe villages near **Ban**

**Chedi Kok** as well as the large Mawker refugee camp, both off Route 1206 on the way to Waley. Opium is cultivated extensively in this area, much to the chagrin of Thai authorities who send rangers in every year to cut down the production. There is a small hotel in Phop Phra with rooms for 50B.

**Getting There & Away** Songthaews to Waley depart frequently from a stop south-east of the mosque in Mae Sot for 32B per person. If you go by motorcycle or car, follow Route 1090 south-east towards Um Phang and after 36 km take Route 1206 south-west. From this junction it's 25 km to Waley; the last 10 km of the road are unpaved. Your passport may be checked at a police outpost before Waley.

### UM PHANG
อุ้มผาง
• ☎ (55)

Route 1090 goes south from Mae Sot to Um Phang, 150 km away. This road used to be called 'Death Highway' because of the guerrilla activity in the area which hindered highway development. Those days are past, but lives are still lost because of brake failure or treacherous turns on this steep, winding road through incredible mountain scenery. Along the way – short hikes off the highway – are two waterfalls, **Thararak Falls** (26 km from Mae Sot) and **Pha Charoen Falls** (41 km). Thararak Falls streams over limestone cliffs and calcified rocks with a rough texture that makes climbing the falls easy. It's been made into a park of sorts, with benches right in the stream at the base of the falls for cooling off and a couple of outhouse toilets nearby; on weekends food vendors set up here. The eucalyptus-lined dirt road leaves the highway between Kms 24 and 25. A side road at Km 48 leads to a group of government-sponsored hill-tribe villages (Karen, Lisu, Hmong, Mien, Lahu).

Um Phang itself is an overgrown village populated mostly by Karen at the junction of the Mae Klong and Um Phang rivers. Many Karen villages in this area are very traditional

NORTHERN THAILAND

– elephants are used as much as oxen for farm work. Elephant saddles *(yaeng)* and other tack used for elephant wrangling are a common sight on the verandas of Karen houses outside of town.

An interesting hike can be done following footpaths south-east of the village through rice fields and along a stream called Huay Um Phang to smaller Karen villages.

Opposite the Um Phang district in Myanmar (or Kawthoolei, according to the Karen) there is a large KNU base, the successor to the KNU's long-time headquarters farther north, over-run by Yangon troops in 1995. On the Thai side is a refugee village of 570 Karen who were originally from Htikabler village on the other side of border. The new settlement is called Nopadaw; it's near the Thai-Karen villages of Ban Nong Luang and Ban Huay.

Several of the guesthouses in Um Phang can arrange trekking and rafting trips in the area. Typical charges are 2500B for three nights, four days with a two person minimum, including rafting, an elephant ride, food and guide service.

## Thilawsu Falls
น้ำตกทีลอซู

In Um Phang district, you can arrange trips down the Mae Klong River to Thilawsu Falls and Karen villages for around 750B a day (enquire at any guesthouse in Um Phang). Typical three day excursions include a raft journey along the river from Um Phang to the falls, then a two day trek from the falls through the Karen villages of **Khotha** and **Palatha**, where a jeep picks trekkers up and returns them to Um Phang (25 km from Palatha by road). Some people prefer to spend two days on the river, the first night at a cave or hot springs along the river before Thilawsu and a second night at the falls. On the third day you can cross the river by elephant to one of the aforementioned villages to be met by a truck and returned to Um Phang. Or you can continue south along the road to Palatha 20 km farther to the Hmong village of **Kangae Khi**.

The scenery along the river is stunning,

especially after the rainy season (November and December), when the cliffs are streaming with water and Thilawsu Falls are at their best. There's a shallow cave behind the falls. Thilawsu Falls is now part of the recently established Um Phang Wildlife Sanctuary.

You can also drive to the falls via a rough 47 km road from Um Phang suitable for 4WD or a skilled dirt-bike rider only. Or follow the main paved road south of Um Phang to Km 19; the walk to the falls is a stiff four hours from here via **Mo Phado** village. Every two days there's a songthaew for 10 to 15B per person to Km 19; ask for *kii-lôh sìp kâo*.

## Lethongkhu & Sangkhlaburi Vicinity

From Ban Mae Khlong Mai, a few km northwest of Um Phang via the highway to Mae Sot, a dirt road heads south-west along the border to **Peung Kleung**, a Karen and Thai village where buffalo carts are more common than motorbikes. Impressive **Ekaratcha Falls** is an hour's walk away; songthaews from Um Phang usually make this trip once a day, and it's possible to put up at the village clinic or in a private home for a donation of 100B per person.

Two hours walk from here, near the Myanmar border, is the culturally singular village of **Letongkhu** (Leh Tawng Khu). The villagers are for the most part Karen in language and dress, but their spiritual beliefs are unique to this area. They will eat only the meat of wild animals and hence do not raise chickens, ducks, pigs or beef cattle. They do, however, keep buffalo, oxen and elephants as work animals. Some of the men wear their hair in long topknots. The village priests, whom the Thais call *reusii* (rishi or sage) have long hair and beards and dress in brown or white robes. The priests live apart from the village in a temple and practise traditional medicine based on herbal healing and ritual magic. Antique elephant tusks are kept as talismans. Nobody seems to know where their religion comes from, although there are indications that it may be Hindu-related. Recently an altercation between the Thai border police and Letongkhu villagers over

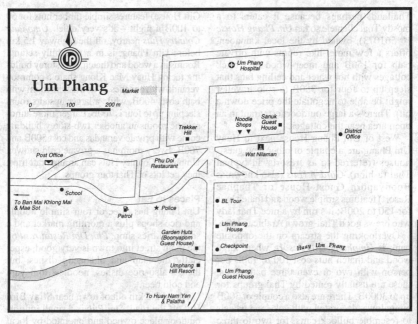

**Um Phang**

Market

0    100    200 m

Um Phang Hospital

Trekker Hill

Noodle Shops

Sanuk Guest House

District Office

Wat Nilaman

Post Office

Phu Doi Restaurant

To Ban Mai Khlong Mai & Mae Sot

School

Police

Petrol

BL Tour

Um Phang House

Garden Huts (Boonyapom Guest House)

Checkpoint

Huay Um Phang

Umphang Hill Resort

Um Phang Guest House

To Huay Nam Yen & Palatha

NORTHERN THAILAND

hunting rights resulted in the knifing deaths of five policemen. Another reusii village, Beung Khoeng, is a further three hours walk.

**Sangkhlaburi** (Kanchanaburi Province) is 90 km or four to five days walk from Peung Kleung. On the way (11 km from Peung Kleung), about 250m off the road, is the extensive cave system of **Tham Takube**. From Ban Mae Chan, 35 km on the same route, there's a dirt road branching across the border to a KNU-controlled village. You may be able to arrange guides for this trek in Peung Kleung or Um Phang.

**Organised Tours**

In Um Phang, BL Tour (☎ 561021), on the same street as Um Phang House, charges 800B per person for one day rafting on the Mae Klong River, plus 50B per person per meal; extra days can be added for 300B per person. Umphang Hills Resort, Sanuk Guest House and Trekker Hill arrange similar excursions – figure on 2500 to 3000B for a

three night trekking/rafting trip. This is significantly less expensive than companies running out of Mae Sot.

Maesot Conservation Tour (☎ 532818), attached to B+B Guest House in Mae Sot, offers four day, three night trips to Um Phang and Thilawsu Falls with camping and rafting for 8000B per person for one or two people, plus 3000B for each additional person. These rates include return transport from Mae Sot, meals and guide service. SP Tour (Mae Sot Travel Centre; ☎ 531409) at SP House in Mae Sot does Um Phang trips for about the same rates, plus trips north of Mae Sot along the Salawin River.

Um Phang Hills Resort claims to be able to arrange one week treks from Um Phang south to Sangkhlaburi in Kanchanaburi – this could be quite an interesting trip.

**Places to Stay**

Accommodation in Um Phang is a tad more expensive than elsewhere in Northern

NORTHERN THAILAND

Thailand, perhaps because it caters to a mostly Thai clientele so far. *Um Phang House* (☎ 561073), owned by the local kamnoen, offers a few motel-like rooms with private bath for 150B and nicer wood and brick cottages with hot water and ceiling fans that sleep up to four for 350B (a solo traveller might be able to negotiate the price down a bit). There's a large outdoor restaurant in an open area near the cottages.

West of Um Phang House next to Huay Um Phang are a couple of other new guesthouses (referred to as 'resorts' in typical Thai fashion). *Garden Huts* (also known as Boonyaporn Guest House or Thaphae Resort) features simple wood and thatch huts for 150 to 200B; it's run by a nice Thai lady who brews good Thai-grown Arabica coffee.

Overlooking the stream on the opposite bank is *Umphang Hill Resort*, where large wood and thatch huts cost 100 to 150B per person with two or even three bathrooms; these are usually rented by Thai groups for up to 3000B. There are also a couple of 300B bungalows, decorated with yoke and wheels to resemble bullock carts, for two to three people, and some very small huts for 150B.

A further 600m west of the checkpoint near the bridge, the atmospheric *Ban Huay Nam Yen* offers Thai-style bungalows furnished with woven mats and axe pillows with terraces overlooking a stream for 200B per person. The larger rooms sleep up to 10 people. It's quiet yet within walking distance of the village.

BL Tour, on the road to Um Phang House, is building *Um Phang Guest House* (☎ 561-021) just past Huay Um Phang on the road to Palatha. It will cost just 80B per room. *Sanuk Guest House*, in the village centre, offers bungalows with shared bath in a garden setting for 100B per night, or a dorm bed in a teak house for 50B per person

*Trekker Hill* (☎ 561090), also toward the village centre, charges 50B per person for beds in rustic thatched-roof shelters. It has the cheapest restaurant in Um Phang, with breakfast for just 15B, lunch 20B and dinner 25B.

About three km before town coming from Mae Sot, *Stray Bird's Hut* (also known as

Gift House) features simple timber huts for 60 to 100B a night – it's very quiet. *Umphang Country Huts* nearby, off the highway 1.5 km before Um Phang, is in a nice hilly setting. Rooms in a wood and thatch, two-storey building facing Huay Mae Klong share a common veranda with benches. A downstairs room with bath costs 400B, while a larger upstairs room sleeping up to four is 700B. Larger, more atmospheric rooms in another two-storey building come with private verandas and cost 500B and 700B. Every room has a private cold shower. Umphang Country Huts can arrange raft trips; they get lots of Thai tour groups.

**Places to Eat**
Um Phang has three or four simple noodle and rice shops plus a morning market and a small sundries shop. *Phu Doi Restaurant* on the main street into town is very good, especially the lâap and phanaeng dishes, but there's also rice dishes, noodles, tôm yam and cold beer.

About 2.5 km out of town near Stray Bird Hut off the road, *Sun Pub* is a small indoor-outdoor place owned and operated by local teacher Sompong Meunjit. Sompong is also a composer and performer of Thai folk music inspired by the beauty of the Um Phang area; he usually performs live on weekends. The pub serves typical Thai and Northern Thai dishes.

**Getting There & Away**
Songthaews to Um Phang cost 80B and leave several times a day from Mae Sot, starting around 7.30 am and finishing around 3.30 pm. It takes five or six hours to complete the 164 km journey. Songthaews usually stop for lunch at windy **Ban Rom Klao 4** (Um Piam is its original name) along the way. There are a few Hmong villages in the vicinity of Ban Rom Klao 4.

If you decide to try and ride a motorcycle from Mae Sot, be sure it's one with a strong engine as the road has lots of fairly steep grades. Total drive time is around 3½ to four hours. The only petrol pump along the way is in Ban Rom Klao 4, 80 km from Mae Sot, so you may want to carry three or four litres of extra fuel. The road is barely 1½ lanes wide in some spots, and the sealing is rough. The stretch between Ban Rom Klao 4 and Um Phang passes some impressive stands of virgin monsoon forest.

## MAE SOT TO MAE SARIANG

Route 1085 runs north from Mae Sot all the way to Mae Sariang in Mae Hong Son Province. The section of the road north of Tha Song Yang has finally been sealed and public transport is now available all the way to Mae Sariang (226 km), passing through **Mae Ramat, Mae Sarit, Ban Tha Song Yang** and **Ban Sop Ngao** (Mae Ngao). In Mae Ramat a temple called **Wat Don Kaew**, behind the district office, houses a large Mandalay-style marble Buddha. Other attractions on the way to Mae Sariang include **Mae Kasa Falls** between Km 13 and 14 and limestone caverns at **Tham Mae Usu** near Ban Tha Song Yang.

Instead of doing the Myanmar border run in one go, some people elect to spend the night in **Mae Sarit** (118 km from Mae Sot), then start fresh in the morning to get to Ban Tha Song Yang in time for a morning songthaew from Ban Tha Song Yang to Mae Sariang. Songthaews to Mae Sarit are 50B and leave frequently from the market north of the police station in Mae Sot. They take four hours to reach Mae Sarit. Mae Sarit to Ban Tha Song Yang is 20B and from there to Mae Sariang is 50B; this last leg takes three hours. If you miss the morning songthaew from Mae Sarit to Mae Sariang, you can usually arrange to charter a truck for 100B.

If you decide not to stay overnight in Mae Sarit you can take a direct Mae Sariang songthaew from Mae Sot for 150B. Songthaews leave four times daily between 7 am and 12.30 pm and the trip takes about six hours. Along the way you'll pass through thick forest, including a few stands of teak, Karen villages, the occasional work elephant and a Thai ranger post called the Black Warrior Kingdom.

## Places to Stay

**Mae Sarit** Someone from *Chai Doi House* (☎ (55) 531782 in Mae Sot) usually meets the first songthaew of the day from Mae Sot

and takes prospective guests to bungalows on a hill overlooking the border area. Rates are 250B a day including all meals and local trekking guide service. Treks to nearby villages and 'black' border markets can be arranged if you'd like to explore the area.

The *Mae Salid Guest House* offers rooms with meals for 120B.

**Tha Song Yang** There are no guesthouses yet in Tha Song Yang but it would probably be easy to arrange a place to stay by inquiring at the main market (where the songthaews stop) in this prosperous black-market town.

# Mae Hong Son Province

Mae Hong Son Province is 368 km from Chiang Mai by the southern route through Mae Sariang (on Route 108), or 270 km by the northern road through Pai (on Route 1095). Thailand's most north-western province is a crossroads for ethnic minorities (mostly Karen, with some Hmong, Lisu and Lahu), Shan and Burmese immigrants, and opium traders living in and around the forested Pai River valley. Reportedly 75% of the province consists of mountains and forest.

As the province is so far from the influence of sea winds and is thickly forested and mountainous, the temperature seldom rises above 40°C, while in January the temperature can drop to 2°C. The air is often misty with ground fog in the winter and smoke from slash-and-burn agriculture in the hot season.

The province has undergone a tourist mini-boom over the last seven years, with many resorts opening in the area around the capital. So far few visitors seem to leave the beaten Mae Hong Son-Soppong-Pai track.

## MAE SARIANG & KHUN YUAM
แม่สะเรียง
• ☎ *(53)* • *pop 7600*

Many of the hill-tribe settlements in Mae Hong Son Province are concentrated in the districts and towns of Khun Yuam, Mae La

Noi and Mae Sariang, which are good departure points for treks to Hmong, Karen and Shan villages. Of these three small towns, Mae Sariang is the largest and offers the most facilities for use as a base. Khun Yuam is also a good place to start from. Nearby **Mae Sam Laep**, west on the Myanmar border, can be reached by songthaew or motorcycle, and from there you can hire boats for trips down the scenic **Salawin River**.

Although there is little to see in Mae Sariang, it's a pleasant riverside town with a small travel scene. Two Burmese/Shan temples, **Wat Jong Sung (Uthayarom)** and **Wat Si Bunruang**, just off Mae Sariang's main street not far from the bus station, are worth a visit if you have time. Built in 1896, Wat Jong Sung is the more interesting of the two and features slender, Shan-style chedis and wooden monastic buildings.

The Riverside Guest House can arrange day and overnight boat trips on the Salawin River that include stops in Karen villages and Mae Sam Laep. During the dry season, a truck from the Riverside leaves every morning around 6.30 am for Mae Sam Laep, where a boat takes visitors two hours down the Salawin River to a sand beach at Sop Moei. The total cost is 100B per person. There are also songthaews from Mae Sariang to the Karen villages of **Sop Han**, **Mae Han**, and **Ban Huay Pong**.

About 36 km south-east of Mae Sariang at **Ban Mae Waen** is Pan House, where a guide named T Weerapan (Mr Pan) leads local treks. To get to Ban Mae Waen, take a Chiang Mai-bound bus east on Route 108 and get out at the Km 68 marker. Mae Waen is a five km walk south up a mountain.

On the slopes of **Doi U-Khaw**, 25 km from Khun Yuam via upgraded Route 1253, is a Hmong village (Mae U-Khaw) and the 250m **Mae Surin Falls**, reportedly Thailand's highest cataract. The area blooms with scenic sunflowers in November; this is also the best time to view the waterfall.

A **hot spring**, with an outdoor restaurant and tables beneath small pavilions, can be visited off the highway about 10 km before Mae Hong Son.

## Places to Stay

**Mae Sariang** Out on Route 108 is a combination truck stop and brothel, the *Salawin Inn*, where basic motel-like rooms with attached bath cost 100 to 150B. The much better *Ekalak Hotel* (☎ 681052) on the highway almost opposite the Salawin Inn charges 150B for a fairly clean room with ceiling fan, air-con and attached bath with hot water. It has an attached restaurant as well.

Mae Sariang's oldest hotel, *Mitaree Hotel* (☎ 681022), near the bus station on Mae Sariang Rd in town, has doubles for 120B in the old wooden wing (called the Mitaree Guest House) or for 250B with hot shower in the new wing. Air-con rooms in the new wing cost 300B. The old wing is popular with Thai truckers.

On Wiang Mai Rd near the post office is *New Mitaree Guest House* (☎ 681109), run by the same people. Rooms in the low-rise building cost 150B single with fan and hot shower, 190/200B single/double with hot shower and air-con, and similar rooms in the newer two-storey building are 200 to 250B, 200 to 300B with air-con. There is also a set of new wooden cottages at the back with sitting areas in front for 300 to 600B.

If you turn left out of the bus terminal and then take the first right you'll come to the small *Mae Sariang Guest House* on Mongkhonchai Rd, opposite the entrance to Wat Jong Sung. Decent rooms are 80/50B with/without bath but it's nothing special. Around the corner on Laeng Phanit Rd on the Yuam River is the efficiently run *Riverside Guest House* (☎ 681188), where basic rooms are 60/80B for singles/doubles, or 120B on the river. There's a pleasant sitting/ dining area overlooking the river. The guesthouse has a few quiet, thatched bungalows on the river bank opposite the main building for 150B.

The *See View Guest House* (☎ 681154), on the west side of the Yuam River away from the town centre, offers rooms with private hot shower in a row house for 120B. The management say these rates are negotiable in the low season and that they offer free transport to/from the bus terminal.

NORTHERN THAILAND

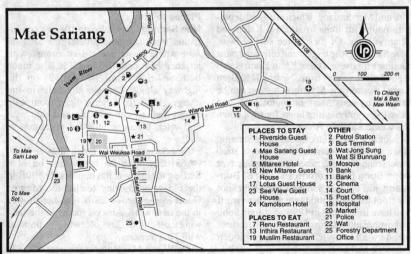

Mae Sariang

**PLACES TO STAY**
1 Riverside Guest
  House
4 Mae Sariang Guest
  House
5 Mitaree Hotel
16 New Mitaree Guest
  House
17 Lotus Guest House
23 See View Guest
  House
24 Kamolsorn Hotel

**PLACES TO EAT**
7 Renu Restaurant
13 Inthira Restaurant
19 Muslim Restaurant

**OTHER**
2 Petrol Station
3 Bus Terminal
3 Wat Jong Sung
6 Wat Si Bunruang
9 Mosque
10 Bank
11 Bank
12 Cinema
14 Court
15 Post Office
18 Hospital
20 Market
21 Police
22 Wat
25 Forestry Department
  Office

The *Kamolsorn Hotel* (☎ 681204) on Mae Sariang Rd just south of Wai Weuksa Rd is a new multi-storey place with fan rooms with attached bath and TV for 350B, with air-con for 450B or with air-con and TV for 600B.

*Lotus Guest House* (☎ 681048), at 73/5 Wiang Mai Rd, is an odd little complex in a cul-de-sac with a restaurant, karaoke, massage and barber shop. Clean rooms with attached bath cost 100B single/double.

**Khun Yuam** The *Mit Khun Yuam Hotel* (☎ 691057) is an old wooden hotel on the main road through the centre of town with rooms for 80/100B single/double with shared facilities, 120B with attached shower and toilet. A new building toward the back of the property offers comfortable rooms with fan and hot showers for 250/300B single/double.

Off the main road towards the northern end of town (look for the signs) is the superclean *Baan Farang* (☎ 622086), operated by a Frenchman and his Thai wife. Dorm beds are 50B, rooms in a row house with private facilities 200B a night, new bungalows 250B.

At the south end of town the new *Bua Thong* has plain rooms for 400B – not particularly good value.

Rustic accommodation is sometimes available at the Hmong village of Mae U-Khaw, between Khun Yuam and Mae Surin Falls.

**Places to Eat**
The *Riverside Guest House* on Laeng Phanit Rd in Mae Sariang has a pleasant restaurant area upstairs overlooking the river.

The *Inthira Restaurant*, on the left side of Wiang Mai Rd as you enter town from Chiang Mai (not far from the Mae Sariang Rd intersection), is well known for its batter-fried frogs, though you won't see them on the English menu. It's open 11.20 am to 10.30 pm and is still the best place in town. Across the street is the *Renu Restaurant*, decorated with photos of the king playing saxophone and offering such menu delights as nut-hatch curry. Both restaurants have English menus, and both are very good.

The food stall next to the bus terminal on Mae Sariang Rd serves excellent khâo sòi and khanŏm jiin for less than 10B – it's only open from morning till early afternoon. A

Muslim restaurant on Laeng Phanit Rd near the main market in the town centre serves good curries and khâo mòk kài (chicken biryani).

In Khun Yuam, your best bets are the new open-air dining area at the *Mit Khun Yuam Hotel* or the cosy restaurant at *Baan Farang*. Just west of Wat Photaram at the south end of Khun Yuam are several food booths with khâo man kài.

### Getting There & Around
Buses to Mae Sariang leave Chiang Mai's Arcade station about every two hours between 6.30 am and 9 pm. The trip takes about four hours and costs 59B. From Mae Sariang to Khun Yuam it's another 36B, or 61B to Mae Hong Son (four to five hours). An air-con bus to Mae Hong Son costs 110B but there's no way to reserve a seat – you must wait for the bus from Chiang Mai and hope there's a vacant seat. There's one daily bus between Mae Sot and Mae Sariang for 150B which takes six hours.

A bus for Bangkok leaves from near the Mae Sariang bus terminal daily at 5 pm, arriving in Bangkok at 6 am. The fare is 190B.

Local songthaews go from Mae Sariang to the following Karen villages: Sop Han (10B), Mae Han (15B) and Huay Pong (10B). By motorcycle taxi these destinations are 30, 50 and 40B respectively.

One songthaew goes to Mae Sam Laep on the Salawin River every morning. The fare is 50B or you can charter a truck for 300B.

See the Mae Sot to Mae Sariang section earlier for details on songthaew transport between Mae Sot and Mae Sariang.

**Motorcycle Rental** Next to the service station across from the bus terminal is a small motorcycle rental place.

### MAE HONG SON
อ.เมืองแม่ฮ่องสอน
• ☎ (53) • pop 6600
The provincial capital is still peaceful (boring to some), despite the intrusion of daily flights from Chiang Mai. Much of the capital's pros-

perity is due to its supply of rice and consumer goods to the drug lords across the border. It's also becoming something of a travellers' scene – there were more than 20 guesthouses at last count. Most of the town's original inhabitants are Shan. Several Karen and Shan villages in the vicinity can be visited as day trips.

Two Hollywood films were shot in the immediate area: *Volunteers*, a comedy-adventure starring Tom Hanks and John Candy about the Peace Corps, and *Air America*, a Mel Gibson vehicle loosely based on events that occurred during the secret US war in Laos during the 1960s.

Mae Hong Son is best visited between November and March when the town is at its most beautiful. During the rainy season (June to October) travel in the province can be difficult because there are few paved roads. During the hot season, the Pai River valley fills with smoke from slash-and-burn agriculture. The only problem with going in the cool season is that the nights are downright cold – you'll need at least one thick sweater and a good pair of socks for mornings and evenings and a sleeping bag or several blankets. If you're caught short, you might consider buying a blanket at the market (the Chinese acrylic blankets are cheap) and cutting a hole in the middle for use as a poncho.

The new Suun Silapaachiip (Vocational Arts Centre), a km south of the Holiday Inn on Route 108, has a small collection of local handicrafts on display.

### Information
**Tourist Police** Tourist brochures and maps can be picked up at the fledgling tourist police office (☎ 611812) on Singhanat Bamrung Rd. Open 24 hours, this is also the place to come to report mishaps such as theft or to lodge complaints against guesthouses and trek operators.

**Money** Foreign exchange services are available at Bangkok Bank, Thai Farmers Bank and Bank of Ayudhya, all located along Khunlum Praphat Rd in the centre of town. Bangkok Bank and Thai Farmers Bank have ATMs.

NORTHERN THAILAND

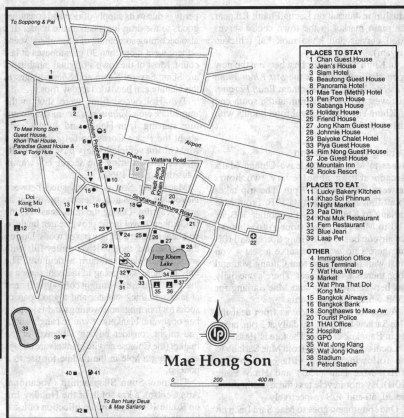

To Soppong & Pai

To Mae Hong Son
Guest House,
Khon Thai House,
Paradise Guest House &
Sang Tong Huts

Khunlum Praphat Road

Phanit

Wattana Road

Airport

Padit Jong Kham Road

Doi
Kong Mu
(1500m)

Singhanat Bamrung Road

Jong Kham
Lake

To Ban Huay Deua
& Mae Sariang

**Mae Hong Son**

0    200    400 m

NORTHERN THAILAND

**PLACES TO STAY**
1  Chan Guest House
2  Jean's House
3  Siam Hotel
6  Beautong Guest House
8  Panorama Hotel
10  Mae Tee (Methi) Hotel
13  Pen Porn House
19  Sabanga House
25  Holiday House
26  Friend House
27  Jong Kham Guest House
28  Johnnie House
29  Baiyoke Chalet Hotel
34  Piya Guest House
34  Rim Nong Guest House
37  Joe Guest House
40  Mountain Inn
42  Rooks Resort

**PLACES TO EAT**
11  Lucky Bakery Kitchen
14  Khao Soi Phinnun
17  Night Market
23  Paa Dim
24  Khai Muk Restaurant
31  Fern Restaurant
32  Blue Jean
39  Laap Pet

**OTHER**
4  Immigration Office
5  Bus Terminal
7  Wat Hua Wiang
9  Market
12  Wat Phra That Doi
    Kong Mu
15  Bangkok Airways
16  Bangkok Bank
18  Songthaews to Mae Aw
20  Tourist Police
21  THAI Office
22  Hospital
30  GPO
35  Wat Jong Klang
36  Wat Jong Kham
38  Stadium
41  Petrol Station

**Post & Communications** The Mae Hong Son GPO, towards the south end of Khunlum Praphat Rd, is open Monday to Friday from 8.30 am to 4.30 pm, Saturday from 9 am to noon. International telephone service is available at the attached CAT office from 7 am to 11 pm daily.

**Wat Phra That Doi Kong Mu**
Climb the hill west of town, Doi Kong Mu (1500m), to visit this Shan-built wat, also known as Wat Phai Doi. The view of the sea of fog which collects in the valley each morning is impressive; other times of day

you get a view of the town. Two Shan stupas, erected in 1860 and 1874, enshrine the ashes of monks from Myanmar's Shan State. Around the back of the wat you can see a tall, slender standing Buddha and catch views west of the ridge. No shorts or miniskirts are permitted in the wat grounds, but you can rent coverups.

**Wat Jong Kham & Wat Jong Klang**
วัดจองคำและวัดจองกลาง
Next to a large pond called Nong Jong Kham in the southern part of town are a couple of

semi-interesting Burmese-style wats – Wat Jong Kham and Wat Jong Klang. Jong Kham was built nearly 200 years ago by Thai Yai (Shan) people, who make up about 50% of the population of Mae Hong Son Province. Jong Klang houses 100-year-old glass jataka paintings and a small rooms full of wooden reliefs and figures depicting the Vessantara Jataka – all very Burmese in style. The wihãan containing these is open daily 8 am to 6 pm.

### Wat Hua Wiang

Although the wooden bòt itself is in an advanced state of decay, a famous bronze Buddha in the Mandalay style, called **Chao Phlalakhaeng,** can be seen in this wat on Phanit Wattana Rd, a bit east of Khunlum Praphat Rd.

### Trekking

Trekking out of Mae Hong Son can be arranged at several guesthouses and travel agencies; Mae Hong Son Guest House (see Places to Stay – bottom end) has some of the most dependable and experienced guides. Typical rates for most treks are 300 to 400B per day, with three to five days the normal trek duration. Popular routes include the Pai River Valley, Khun Yuam district and north of Soppong. A six day trek from east of Mae Hong Son to near Soppong costs 350B per

day per person. As with trekking elsewhere in Northern Thailand, be sure to clarify when a trek starts and stops or you may not get your money's worth.

Nearby Karen villages can be visited without a guide by walking one or two hours outside of town – several guesthouses in town can provide a map.

### Places to Stay – bottom end

**Guesthouses** With more than 20 guesthouses in town, the accommodation scene in Mae Hong Son is very competitive – most places are 50 to 80B with shared bath, 80 to 100B with private bath.

The original *Mae Hong Son Guest House* (☎ 612510) has a secluded spot on the north-western outskirts of town (about 700m west of Khunlum Praphat Rd). Rooms in·a wooden longhouse are 60 to 100B without bath, 200B for a bungalow with private bath. The guesthouse is a good source of information and inexpensive meals. On the corner nearby, *Khon Thai House* has new, rather closely spaced thatched-roof and cement block bungalows for 100B each. *Paradise Guest House* farther up the road has larger huts for 200B single/double.

In the hills nearby are the equally secluded *Sang Tong Huts*, which have panoramic views. The setting is pretty but it's not cheap at 150B for an older hut with shared facilities

NORTHERN THAILAND

---

### Mae Hong Son Festivals

Wat Jong Klang and Wat Jong Kham are the focal point of the Poi Sang Long Festival in March when young Shan boys are ordained as novice monks *(bùat lûuk kâew)* during the school holidays. Like elsewhere in Thailand, the ordinands are carried on the shoulders of friends or relatives and paraded around the wat under festive parasols, but in the Shan custom the boys are dressed in ornate costumes (rather than simple white robes) and wear flower headdresses and facial make-up. Sometimes they ride on ponies.

Another important local event is the Jong Para Festival held at the end of the Buddhist Rains Retreat in October (actually three days before the full moon of the 11th lunar month – so it varies from year to year). The festival begins with local Shan bringing offerings to monks in the temples in a procession marked by the carrying of castle models on poles. An important part of the festival is the folk theatre and dance performed on the wat grounds, some of which is unique to north-west Thailand.

During Loi Krathong – a national holiday usually celebrated by floating *krathongs* (small lotus floats) on the nearest pond, lake or river – Mae Hong Son residents launch balloons called *krathong sawăn* (heaven krathongs) from Doi Kong Mu. ■

and up to 300B for a hut with hot shower; service is rather indifferent.

Also at this end of town is the friendly *Jean's House* (☎ 611662) at 6 Pracha Uthit Rd, with rates at 80B for rooms with bath. From here turn left and go north toward the airport and just over a little bridge you'll come to the *Chan Guest House* (☎ 620432), a large house with a few smallish but clean rooms with attached cold shower, plus one common hot shower, for 100B; the high ratio of bathrooms to guest rooms and fairly quiet location are pluses.

Back on Khunlum Praphat Rd, south of the bus terminal on the right and set back off the road a bit, is *Beautong Guest House*, where rustic rooms are 100B.

In the area of Jong Kham Lake are several very pleasant guesthouses. *Jong Kham Guest House* (☎ 611150) overlooks the lake from the north and has good rooms in a row house plus some newer thatched huts for 60/100B single/double. The nearby *Friend House* has large clean rooms for 100B single/double, 300B for up to four. At both places a shared hot shower is available. East of Jong Kham, also on the northern side of the lake, is *Johnnie House*, a wooden row house with clean rooms with shared facilities for 50/80B single/double or 100B for a room with attached hot shower.

On the west side of the lake, *Holiday House* has two-bed rooms with shared hot bath for 80B. Just south of Holiday House, *Piya Guest House* (☎ 611260/307) features nice rooms built around a garden, with a bar/restaurant in front; rates are 250B with fan, 350B with air-con. All rooms come with private hot showers; cleanliness and service get mixed reports, however. Around the corner on Udom Chaonithet Rd is the basic *Sabanga House*, a bamboo row house with rooms for 150B.

On the south side of the lake is *Rim Nong Guest House*, a friendly place with a little restaurant on the water's edge. Rates are a low 40B per person in multi-bed rooms, 70 to 100B in private rooms with shared hot water bath. Across the street, away from the lake, is the very basic *Joe Guest House* with

80B rooms and shared hot water bath in an old teak house and up to 230B for newer rooms with private hot shower.

On the diagonal street running south-east from Khunlum Praphat Rd to the lake is *Namrin House*, an old wooden building with basic rooms for 60 to 80B. Another inexpensive place in town is *Lanna Lodge* down an alley off Khunlum Praphat Rd, opposite the Thai Farmers Bank. Bungalows here are 80B with shared hot shower. More basic 50B rooms are available in an old Thai house on the premises.

*Pen Porn House* (☎ 611577), on the road to Wat Phra That Doi Kong Mu, sits in a residential neighbourhood on a slope on the west side of town. Rooms in a row house cost 200B a double, 400B in a four-bed room, all with private hot water bath.

**Hotels** Most of the hotels in Mae Hong Son are along the main north-south road, Khunlum Praphat. *Siam Hotel* (☎ 612148), next to the bus station, is overpriced at 170/200B for ordinary rooms with fan, 350B with air-con. Farther down at No 55, *Mae Tee (Methi) Hotel* (☎ 611141) is slightly lower priced but better; rooms with fan cost 150B while air-con rooms start at 300B.

Other less convenient places can be found around Mae Hong Son – the touts will find you at the bus terminal.

### Places to Stay – middle & top end

The three-storey *Panorama Hotel* (☎ 611-757; fax 611790) at 51 Khunlum Praphat Rd, charges 300B for a double with fan and hot shower, 700B for a simple but clean room with fridge, TV, air-con and hot shower. There's a book store downstairs. In just about any other Thai town of this size, rooms like this would go for 500B.

Towards the southern end of town, *Baiyoke Chalet Hotel* (☎ 611486) at 90 Khunlum Praphat offers all the typical amenities for 850/1030B in standard rooms, 1300 to 1500B in VIP ones. The larger *Mountain Inn* (☎ 612285; fax 612284), farther south at 112 Khunlum Praphat Rd, charges 700B single/double for clean, medium-sized air-con/hot water rooms around a courtyard, including breakfast. The Mountain Inn has well kept, nicely landscaped public areas.

A bit farther south, the 114-room *Rooks Resort* (☎ 611390; fax 611524) at 114/5-7 Khunlum Praphat definitely represents the top end in town. Rooms and bungalows cost 2000 to 3500B. Facilities include a swimming pool, tennis courts, disco, snooker club, bakery, coffee shop and restaurant.

**Out of Town** South-west of town a few km towards Ban Huay Deua and Ban Tha Pong Daeng on the river are several 'resorts', which in the Thai sense of the term means any hotel located in a rural or semi-rural area. Here you'll find the upscale *Tara Mae Hong Son Hotel* (☎ 611272; fax 611252), with doubles from 2000B. Farther off the highway, three mid-range places are worth considering: *Rim Nam Klang Doi Resort* (☎ 612142; fax 612086), with doubles from 400 to 750B; *Mae Hong Son Resort* (☎ 611504, 611406), with doubles from 650B; and *Sam Mork Villa* (☎ 611478), with doubles from 600B.

**Places to Eat**
Mae Hong Son isn't known for its food, but there are a few decent places to eat besides the guesthouses. *Khai Muk*, an outdoor restaurant just off Khunlum Praphat Rd, is one of the better Thai-Chinese restaurants in town. Another very good spot with an extensive Thai-Chinese menu is *Fern Restaurant*, south of the post office on Khunlum Praphat Rd. Most other restaurants in town pale by comparison with these two.

*Paa Dim*, diagonally opposite Khai Muk, is a warehouse-like restaurant with dishes from every region in Thailand; it's popular with Thais and foreigners alike because of its reasonable prices and good-size portions. Also in this area, the *Blue Jean*, done up saloon-style but more tasteful-looking than most 'old west' places, serves many kinds of yam and lâap, also pepper steak. It's mostly a night-time place, with a full bar.

The morning market behind the Mae Tee Hotel is a good place to buy food for trek-

king. Get there before 8 am. *Lucky Bakery Kitchen*, west of Khunlum Praphat Rd on Singhanat Bamrung Rd, does 'cowboy steak' and baked goods.

Visitors staying at Pen Porn House are close to *Khao Soi Phinnun*, a friendly neighbourhood establishment on the same street which has inexpensive khâo sòi or kũaytĩaw as well as eggs, toast and coffee. A small enclosed food centre almost opposite Pen Porn offers pizza, noodles and Shan-style chicken curry.

*Laap Pet*, just off Khunlum Praphat Rd on the road to Doi Kong Mu, is a nice open-air spot with Isaan food.

*Sunflower Café* at 7 Singhanat Bamrung Rd offers fresh-baked wholewheat breads and cakes, pizzas and coffee.

**Getting There & Away**
**Air** THAI flies to Mae Hong Son from Chiang Mai four times daily. The fare is 345B and the flight takes 40 minutes. It's possible to book a flight to Chiang Mai that links with an onward flight to Mae Hong Son for 1865B. Mae Hong Son's THAI office (☎ 611297/194) is at 71 Singhanat Bamrung Rd.

**Bus** From Chiang Mai there are two bus routes to Mae Hong Son, the northern route through Pai (90B ordinary, 175B air-con; 7 to 8 hours) and the southern route through Mae Sariang (115B ordinary, 205B air-con; 8 to 9 hours).

Although it's longer, the southern route through Mae Sariang is much more comfortable because the bus stops every two hours for a 10 to 15 minute break and larger buses – with large seats – are used. The bus to Mae Hong Son via Mae Sariang leaves Chiang Mai's Arcade bus station every two hours between 6.30 am and 9 pm.

The northern route through Pai, originally built by the Japanese in WWII, is very winding and offers spectacular views from time to time. Because the buses used on this road are smaller, they're usually more crowded and the younger passengers tend to get motion sickness. The Pai bus leaves the

**NORTHERN THAILAND**

Chiang Mai Arcade station five times a day at 7, 8.30 and 11 am, 1 and 2 pm.

Buses as far as Soppong are 25B or to Pai 40B.

### Getting Around

Most of Mae Hong Son is walkable. Motorcycle taxis within town cost 10B, to Doi Kong Mu it's 30B one way or 50B return. Motorcycle drivers will also take passengers farther afield but fares out of town are expensive; for example, it costs 500B to get to Mae Aw.

Several guesthouses in town rent bicycles and motorcycles. Hertz Rent-a-Car (☎ 612-108) has an office at Rooks Resort.

### AROUND MAE HONG SON
### Rafting

Raft trips on the nearby Pai River are gaining in popularity, as are boat trips into the Karen state (or nation, depending on your political allegiances) of Myanmar. The same guesthouses and trekking agencies that organise treks can arrange the river trips. The most common type of trip sets off from the Pai River pier in **Ban Huay Deua**, eight km south-west of town, for a day-long upriver journey of five km. From the same pier, downriver trips to the 'long-neck' village of **Kariang Padawng Kekongdu** on the Thailand-Myanmar border are also possible. Another popular raft route runs between **Sop Soi** (10 km north-west of town) and the village of **Soppong** to the west (not to be confused with the larger Shan trading village of the same name to the east). These day trips typically cost 400B per person if arranged in Ban Huay Deua, 700B or more if done through a Mae Hong Son agency.

The Pai River raft trips can be good fun if the raft holds up – it's not uncommon for rafts to fall apart or sink. The Myanmar trip, which attracts travellers who want to see the Padaung or 'long-necked' people, is a bit of a rip-off, and to some, exploitative – a four hour trip through unspectacular scenery to see a few Padaung people who are practically captives of the Karen operators involved. They fled to Mae Hong Son to escape an ethnic war and potentially worse fate in Myanmar. The brass ornaments the women

wear around their necks look like rings but are actually detachable coils that depress the collarbone, making it look as though their necks have been unnaturally stretched.

When there is fighting between the Mong Tai Army (or its various splinter armies) and Yangon troops in the area this trip may not be possible.

### Mae Aw
### แม่ออ

One of the best day trips you can do from the provincial capital is to Mae Aw, 22 km north of Mae Hong Son on a mountain peak at the Myanmar border. Mae Aw is a Chinese Kuomintang settlement, one of the last true KMT outposts in Thailand. Occasionally there is fighting along the border between the KMT and the Mong Tai Army, formerly led by the infamous opium warlord Khun Sa but now operating as four splinter units under separate leaderships. When this happens, public transport to these areas is usually suspended and you are advised against going without a guide. (See the boxed aside on Opium & the Golden Triangle in the Facts about the Country chapter.) The modern Thai name for Mae Aw is Ban Rak Thai (Thai-Loving Village).

Thatched hut accommodation is available in the Hmong village of Na Pa Paek, 7.3 km south of Mae Aw, for 40B per person or 150B including two meals (enquire at Pen Porn Guest House in Mae Hong Son for advance bookings). From Na Pa Paek a rough dirt road leads north-west to the Hmong village of Ma Khua Som (3.5 km) and the KMT village of Pang Ung La (6 km) on the Myanmar border. Pang Ung La also has a guesthouse.

Since the construction of a better road, songthaew trips to Mae Aw are easier. There are rather irregular songthaews going back and forth from Mae Hong Son for 40B per person but it's so unpredictable these days that you're better off getting a group of people together and chartering a songthaew. It will cost you 500 to 1000B (depending on whether the drivers have any paid cargo). This option lets you stop and see the sights along the way. Check Singhanat Bamrung Rd near the telephone office at around 9 am to see if there are any songthaews going. The trip takes two hours and passes Shan, Karen and Hmong villages, the **Pang Tong Summer Palace** and waterfalls

If you have your own transport, you can stop off at **Pha Sua Falls** on the way to Mae Aw. About 11 km north of Route 108, turn onto a marked dirt road. The cataract has water all year round; during the rainy season swimming can be dangerous due to swift water flow.

**Tham Plaa National Park** A trip to Mae Aw could be combined with a visit to this recently established national park centred around the animistic Tham Plaa or Fish Cave, a water-filled cavern where hundreds of soro brook carp (*tor soro*) thrive. These fish grow up to a metre in length and are found only in the provinces of Mae Hong Son, Ranong, Chiang Mai, Rayong, Chantaburi and Kanchanaburi. The fish eat vegetables and insects, although the locals believe them to be vegetarian and feed them only fruit and vegetables (which can be purchased at the park entrance). You can see the fish through a two sq m rock hole at the base of an outer wall of the cave. A statue of a Hindu rishi called Nara, said to protect the holy fish from danger, stands nearby.

A path leads from the park entrance to a suspension bridge which crosses a stream and continues to the cave. The park is a shady, cool place to hang out; picnic tables are available. Perhaps because of the spiritual nature of the cave, there is no entrance fee for this park; you are even permitted to pitch a tent for free on the grounds. The park is 17 km north-east of provincial capital (*amphoe meuang*) Mae Hong Song on the north side of Highway 1095.

### Mae La-Na
แม่ละนา

Between Mae Hong Son and Pai is an area of forests, mountains, streams and limestone caves dotted with Shan and hill-tribe villages.

Some of Mae Hong Son's most beautiful scenery is within a day's walk of the Shan villages of Mae La-Na and Soppong, both of which have accommodation. In the area you can trek to several Red and Black Lahu villages and a couple of large caves (4.5 and eight km away). It's possible to walk a 20 km half loop all the way from Mae La-Na to Tham Lot and Soppong, staying overnight in Red Lahu villages along the way. Ask for a sketch map at the Mae Lana Guest House (see Places to Stay following). Experienced riders can accomplish this route on a sturdy dirt bike – but not alone or during the rainy season.

Twenty-seven km west of Pangmapha is a short turn-off for **Wat Tham Wua Sunyata**, a peaceful forest monastery under the auspices of the famous Phra Ajaan Yantra.

The Mae La-Na junction is 55 km from Mae Hong Son, 10 km from Soppong and 56 km from Pai. The village itself is six km north of the junction. Infrequent songthaews from the highway to the village cost 20B per person – mornings are your best bet.

### Soppong
สบป่อง

Soppong is a small but relatively prosperous market village a couple of hours north-west of Pai and about 70 km from Mae Hong Son. Since the paving of Route 1095, Soppong and Tham Lot have become popular destinations for minivan tours from Mae Hong Son and Chiang Mai.

Close to Soppong are several Shan, Lisu, Karen and Lahu villages that can easily be visited on foot. Enquire at the Jungle Guest House or Cave Lodge in Soppong for reliable information. It's important to ask about the current situation as the Myanmar border area is somewhat sensitive due to the opium trade.

Soppong has a post office opposite the main market area on the highway.

The rough back road between Soppong and Mae La-Na is popular with mountain bikers and off-highway motorcyclists.

**Tham Lot** About eight km north of Soppong is Tham Lot (Tham Lawt), a large limestone cave with a wide stream running through it. Along with Tham Nam Lang farther west, it's one of the longest known caves in mainland South-East Asia (though some as yet unexplored caves in Southern Thailand may be even longer). It is possible to hike all the way through the cave (approximately 400m) by following the stream, though it requires some wading back and forth. Apart from the main chamber, there are three side chambers that can be reached by ladders – it takes two or three hours to see the whole thing.

At the park entrance you must hire a gas lantern and guide for 100B to take you through the caverns; they no longer permit visitors to tour the caves alone. The guide fee includes visits to the first and third caverns; to visit the second cavern you must cross the stream. Raftmen waiting inside the cave charge 10B per person per crossing; in the dry season you may be able to wade across. For 100B you can stay on the raft through the third cavern.

The park is open from 8 am to 5 pm every day. A restaurant outside the park entrance is notorious for overcharging foreigners who can't read the posted menus in Thai. If you decide to book a Tham Lot day tour from Mae Hong Son, ask if the tour cost includes guide, lamp and raft fees.

**Tham Nam Lang**  Near Ban Nam Khong, 30 km north-west of Soppong, this cave is nine km long and is said to be one of the largest caves in the world in terms of volume. There are many other caves in the area, some of which contain 2000-year-old wooden coffins. There is some controversy over whether these coffins were 'planted' by Shan or farang entrepreneurs to turn the caves into a tourist attraction.

## Places to Stay

There is a sprinkling of accommodation in the area, mostly concentrated around Soppong. Just off the highway near the bus stop, *Lemon Hill Guest House* features nicely designed huts with bougainvillaea tumbling over the roofs facing the Nam Lan

stream. Rates are 200B single/double with hot shower or 100B with shared hot shower.

On the opposite side of the road a narrow lane leads to *Kemarin Garden Lodge*, with nothing-special bungalows for 50/80B a single/double. If you continue along this track another km (the last half km is accessible by foot or bicycle only) and cross a footbridge over a stream you'll come to *Charming Home*. Several well designed, well spaced huts with attached bath sit on a breezy hillside backed by primary forest; rates are 100B per hut. There are many birds in this area and you can easily hike to Lisu and Lahu villages nearby.

The friendly *Jungle Guest House*, one km west on the road to Mae Hong Son, offers well designed huts for 40B per person. The restaurant serves better fare than most of the other guesthouses in the area. The nearby *Pangmapa Guest House* is similar.

**Tham Lot**  In the nearby forests and in the vicinity of Tham Lot, several guesthouses have come and gone. Over the last six years, Forestry Department officials have been cracking down on illegal accommodation encroaching on the forest. Accommodation may still be arranged in nearby villages, however.

One place to escape the Forestry Department is the *Cave Lodge* near Tham Lot; it's run by a former trekking guide from Chiang Mai and her Australian husband. They were the first to open regular accommodation in the area, starting the trend. Beds are 45B in a dorm, 100B for bungalows sleeping two, 240B for one that sleeps four. Be sure to check the condition of the huts in advance, as some are in need of repair. Guided day hikes are available for a very reasonable 200 to 350B, though recent complaints said the equipment wasn't sufficient and that charges collected for drinking water weren't announced in advance. Follow signs in Soppong to get there – it's about a 1½ hour walk to Ban Tham, the village closest to Tham Lot cave. The village headman in Ban Tham has also been known to arrange room rentals in the village for travellers.

On the banks of the stream that runs through the cave, west of the park entrance, the rather worn *River Lodge* has basic riverside huts for 50B per person.

**Mae La-Na & Vicinity** Just outside Mae La-Na village, the secluded, laid-back *Mae Lana Guest House* rents four large doubles with mosquito nets for 80B per night and a four-bed dorm for 40B per person. *Top Hill*, run by Mae La-Na's village headman, takes the overflow from Mae Lana Guest House at the same rates.

At Ban Nam Khong, the *Wilderness Lodge* is run by the same family that owns the Cave Lodge. Huts are 50B per person. The Route 108 turn-off for Wilderness Lodge is located 25 km west of Pangmapha village.

About 12 km north of Mae La-Na in the Black Lahu village of Ban Huay Hea (very close to the Myanmar border) is the *Lahu Guest House*, run by a village teacher who speaks English. Simple accommodation is 40B per person and the money goes into a community fund.

### Getting There & Around
Pai to Mae Hong Son buses stop in Soppong and there are two or three each day in either direction. From Mae Hong Son, buses take about 2½ hours and cost 25B. The trip between Pai and Soppong costs 22B and takes from 1½ to two hours.

Motorcycle taxis stationed at the bus stop in Soppong will carry passengers to Tham Lot or the Cave Lodge for 40B per person. If you have your own wheels, the road from Soppong to Ban Tham has improved; the grading now runs out about Km 7, after which it's dirt all the way to the cave.

## PAI
ปาย
• ☎ (53)
It first appears that there's not a lot to see in Pai, a peaceful crossroads town about halfway between Chiang Mai and Mae Hong Son on Route 1095. But if you stick around

a few days and talk to some of the locals, you may discover some beautiful out-of-town spots in the surrounding hills. Any of the guesthouses in town can provide information on local trekking and a few do guided treks for 200 to 400B per day. Six to seven day treks to Mae Hong Son are available for as low as 1800B per person.

Most of the town's population are Shan and Thai, but there's also a small but visible Muslim population – mostly jiin haw. Northwest of town are several Shan, Lahu, Lisu and Kuomintang villages and a waterfall that can be visited on foot. The waterfall, **Maw Paeng Falls**, is an eight km walk from town; you can cut the hike in half by taking a Mae Hong Son-bound bus north about five km and getting off at a signpost for the falls; from the highway it's only four km. A pool at the base of the falls is suitable for swimming.

Across the river and eight km south-east of town via a paved road is **Tha Pai Hot Springs**, a well kept local park one km back from the road. A scenic stream runs through the park; it mixes with the hot springs in places to make pleasant bathing areas. Or you can use the relatively new bathing rooms to which hot spring water is piped. Entry to the park is free.

### Wat Phra That Mae Yen
วัดพระธาตุแม่เย็น
Simply known as Wat Mae Yen, this is a newish temple built on a hill with a good view overlooking the valley. Walk one km east from the main intersection in town, across a stream and through a village, to get to the stairs (353 steps) which lead to the top. The monks are vegetarian, uncommon in Thai Buddhist temples.

### Traditional Massage
Pai Traditional Massage (☎ 699121), in a house near the river, has very good Northern-Thai massage for 120B an hour. The couple that do the massages are graduates of Chiang Mai's Old Medicine Hospital. They've built their own herbal sauna house where you

NORTHERN THAILAND

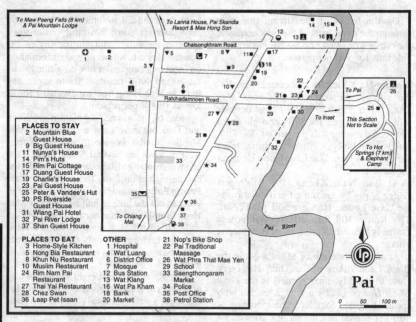

To Maw Paeng Falls (8 km) & Pai Mountain Lodge

Chaisongkhram Road

To Lanna House, Pai Skandia Resort & Mae Hong Son

Ratchadamnoen Road

To Pai

26

This Section Not to Scale

To Inset

To Hot Springs (7 km) & Elephant Camp

To Chiang Mai

Pai River

Pai

0    50    100 m

**PLACES TO STAY**
2   Mountain Blue Guest House
9   Big Guest House
11  Nunya's House
14  Pim's Huts
15  Rim Pai Cottage
17  Duang Guest House
19  Charlie's House
23  Pai Guest House
25  Peter & Vandee's Hut
30  PS Riverside Guest House
31  Wiang Pai Hotel
32  Pai River Lodge
37  Shan Guest House

**PLACES TO EAT**
3   Home-Style Kitchen
5   Nong Bia Restaurant
8   Khun Nu Restaurant
10  Muslim Restaurant
24  Rim Nam Pai Restaurant
27  Thai Yai Restaurant
28  Chez Swan
36  Laap Pet Isaan

**OTHER**
1   Hospital
4   Wat Luang
6   District Office
7   Mosque
12  Bus Station
13  Wat Klang
16  Wat Pa Kham
18  Bank
20  Market
21  Nop's Bike Shop
22  Pai Traditional Massage
26  Wat Phra That Mae Yen
29  School
33  Saengthongaram Market
34  Police
35  Post Office
38  Petrol Station

can steam yourself in *samun phrai* (medicinal herbs) for 50B per visit. A three day massage course is available for 1800B. The house is open from 4.50 to 8.50 pm Monday to Friday, 8.30 am to 8.30 pm weekends.

### Rafting & Elephant Riding

Raft trips on the nearby Pai River operate from July to December, sometimes longer in rainy years; September is usually the best month. Most outfits use flimsy bamboo rafts but it's fun anyway if you don't mind getting wet.

Thai Adventure Rafting (☎ /fax 699111), operated by Guy (Khun Kii in Thai), the French proprietor at Chez Swan, leads excellent two day trips in sturdy rubber rafts from Pai to Mae Hong Son for 1600B per person including food, rafting equipment, camping gear and dry bags. Along the way rafters visit a waterfall, a fossil reef and a hot springs; one night is spent at Guy's permanent riverside camp. Guy is fluent in Thai and uses a

carefully selected Thai crew. The main rafting season is July to December; after that the trips aren't normally run.

An elephant camp south-east of Pai near the hot springs offers jungle rides year-round. The cost is 400B for two people for 1½ hours, 800B for 2½ hours, 1500B all day. To book a ride, contact the elephant camp office (☎ 699101) near Duang Guest House in town.

### Places to Stay

Across from the bus station is the friendly *Duang Guest House* (☎ 699101), where 26 clean rooms with shared hot showers are 40 to 50B a single, 80 to 100B a double. A few rooms with private hot shower are also available at 150B. Towards the western end of this road, *Mountain Blue Guest House* (some signs read 'Blue Mountain') offers simple wood bungalows at similar rates.

On the main road through town are a string of guesthouses, some of them quite good value. The friendly *Nunya's House* (☎ 699-051) is in a newer wooden building facing a garden sitting area; rooms with private hot bath are 120B, smaller rooms without bath cost 80B. Across the road is the clean and secure *Charlie's House*, where nicer rooms around a large courtyard cost 50/80B with shared bath, 120B with hot bath and 160 to 200B in a bungalow, plus 40B for a third person or 40B per person in a dorm. Charlie's is often full during high season.

Nearby but off the main street, *Big Guest House* has small A-frame huts for 40/70B, larger rooms for 100B with shared toilet and hot shower, plus a few nicer rooms with private shower for 150B single/double. Behind the Chez Swan restaurant, Guy and his Thai wife offer a row of large rooms with private hot water showers and thick mattresses for 200B per night.

Farther south along the street, the *Wiang Pai Hotel* is a traditional wooden hotel with 15 spacious rooms. Single rooms (sleeping one or two) cost 50B; a double room is 100B. Behind the old hotel is a new wing where a plain double with a bath is 120B. Hot water is available on request.

On the southern edge of town, off the road a bit, is the *Shan Guest House* (☎ 699162), run by Boonyang, an outgoing Shan who has worked in Bangkok and Saudi Arabia. The atmosphere and food are good and Boonyang tries hard to please. Shan-style bungalows with private hot showers and comfortable beds cost 150 to 200B.

Along the Pai River east of town are four bungalow operations. The *Pai Guest House* offers basic bungalows near the Rim Nam Pai Restaurant for 50/70B. Just off the road to Wat Mae Yen and next to the bridge is the *PS Riverside Guest House*, which has places to sit along the river and huts at 50/70B for singles/doubles, 80B with private bath. Farther down the river, the *Pai River Lodge* has nice huts arranged in a large circle with a dining/lounge area on stilts in the middle. Rates are 50/80B for singles/doubles; because of its quiet, scenic location it's often full. The up-market (for Pai) *Rim Pai Cottage* (☎ 699133, 235931) is farther north along

the river not far from the bus station. Rim Pai's clean, quiet A-frames with bath, electricity and mosquito nets go for 150 to 200B single, 300B double, including breakfast. Just around a bend in the river the recently built *Pim's Huts* offer nice thatched huts lined up along the river for the usual 50/80B. All five places along the river have hot showers.

**Out of Town** *Peter & Vandee's Hut*, near the village of Mae Yen about two km from the bridge over the Pai River (the turn-off is only 1.2 km from the bridge), offers 15 simple thatched huts spread over a slight slope for 30B single, 50B double. A hot shower is available, and you can rent bikes here. The food is exceptional for guesthouse fare – very Thai. Tha Pai Hot Springs is 5.8 km farther down the road.

*Pai Mountain Lodge* (☎ 699068) is seven km north-west of Pai near Maw Paeng Falls and several hill-tribe villages. Spacious A-frames with hot baths and stone fireplaces sleep four for 400B – good value. In the off season (September to October, April to June) prices drop as low as 150B. In town you can book a room or arrange transport at 89 Chaisongkhram Rd, near the Northern Green bike shop.

*Pai Skandia Resort*, 4.5 km north of town on the highway to Mae Hong Son, features very nice A-frame houses for 400 to 500B a night. Closer in on the same road (2.3 km north of Pai), *Lanna House* rents large wooden bungalows at slightly lower rates. *Pai Cabana* (☎ 699190) in the same area offers quiet, spacious, landscaped grounds; one motel-like section features rooms with hot water for 300B, while smallish, over-priced wooden bungalows cost 250B.

**Places to Eat**
There are several farang-oriented cafes with the usual not-quite-the-real-thing pizza, felafel, hummus and tacos (the Thai food in these places is equally bad) along the main north-south and east-west roads in Pai. For authentic local food try the *Rim Nam Pai* (no English sign) on the river next to the bridge.

This pleasant outdoor spot serves several Northern Thai dishes including lâap (Isaan-style meat salad) and jaew (Northern-style noodle hotpot) as well as Thai standards like tôm yam and khâo phàt. A bilingual menu is available.

On Chaisongkhram Rd, the *Khun Nu* has a good variety of Thai and Chinese standards, as does *Nong Bia*. Nong Bia has long been the most popular restaurant in town among local residents; recently they started serving khâo sòi. The *Muslim Restaurant* on the main north-south street has khâo sòi and a few rice dishes.

At the south end of town near Shan Guest House, *Laap Pet Isaan* serves good lâap pèt (duck salad) and other isaan dishes at very reasonable prices.

Every evening a row of local food vendors sets up in front of the day market. During the day, takeaway food can also be purchased at the larger Saengthongaram Market on the next street west. Also on this street you'll find a row of noodle shops near the post office.

One traveller-oriented restaurant worth mentioning is *Thai Yai*, which does the best farang breakfast and lunch menu in town – wholemeal bread, real butter, good locally grown coffee, fruit salads, muesli and sandwiches, plus a few Thai dishes. The *Home-Style Kitchen*, a block west of the main drag, attempts a similar menu with less success.

Good French food – including several cheeses – is available at the nicely decorated *Chez Swan* on the main north-south strip through town. Especially tasty is the 'Caprice', slices of fresh mozzarella and tomatoes dressed in basil and olive oil.

### Getting There & Around

From Chiang Mai's Arcade bus station there are five buses a day at 7, 8.30 and 11 am, 1 and 2 pm. The distance is only 134 km but the trip takes about three hours due to the steep and winding road. The fare has dropped to 45B since the road paving was completed. From Mae Hong Son there are three buses a day at 7 and 11 am and 2 pm. This winding, 111 km stretch takes three to four hours; the fare is also 45B.

All of little Pai is accessible on foot. For local excursions you can rent bicycles or motorcycles at Nop's Bike Shop on Ratchadamnoen Rd near the river. Bicycles cost 50B a day, 100cc motorcycles are 160B, 250cc bikes 320B; you get free maps of the area with every rental. Duang Guest House also rents bicycles.

### AROUND PAI

Visitors can use Pai as a base for excursions to nearby hill-tribe villages, as described earlier in the Pai section. Farther afield, the area north-east of Pai has so far been little explored. A network of unpaved roads – some little more than footpaths – skirts a mountain ridge and the Taeng River valley all the way to the Myanmar border near **Wiang Haeng** and **Ban Piang Haeng**, passing several villages along the way. Near Ban Piang Luang is a Shan temple built by Khun Sa, the infamous opium warlord. Printing facilities for *Freedom's Way*, a propaganda journal for the Mong Tai-Shan United Army, are just across the border.

This area can also be visited by road from Chiang Dao in Chiang Mai Province.

# Chiang Rai Province

Chiang Rai, the northernmost province in Thailand, is one of the country's most rural areas. Half of its northern border, separating province and nation from Laos, is formed by the Maekhong River. Mountains form the other half, cleaving Myanmar from Thailand, with the junction of the Sai, Ruak and Maekhong rivers at Thailand's peak. The fertile Maekhong flood plains to the east support most of the agriculture in the province; to the west the land is too mountainous for most crops. One crop that thrives on steep mountain slopes is opium, and until very recently Chiang Rai was the centre for most of the poppy cultivated in Thailand.

Crop substitution and other development projects sponsored by the late Princess Mother (the king's mother), along with accelerated law enforcement, have pushed much of the opium trade over the border into Myanmar and Laos. While there are undoubtedly still pockets of the trade here and there, even a few poppy patches, Chiang Rai's Golden Triangle fame is now mostly relegated to history books and museums.

## CHIANG RAI
อ.เมืองเชียงราย
• ☎ *(53)* • *pop 36,542*

About 180 km from Chiang Mai, Chiang Rai (called 'Chiang Hai' in Northern Thai dialect) is known as the gateway to the Golden Triangle. Most visitors to the town are interested in hill-tribe trekking or a boat trip on the Kok River.

Chiang Rai was founded by King Mengrai in 1262 as part of the Lanna kingdom. It became a Thai territory in 1786 and a province in 1910. Its most historic monument, Wat Phra Kaew, once hosted the Emerald Buddha during its circuitous travels (the image eventually ended up at the wat of the same name in Bangkok). It now houses a replica of Chiang Mai's Wat Phra Singh Buddha image and a new 'Emerald Buddha' of its own.

Lots of wealthy Thais are moving to Chiang Rai and in the early 1990s the area saw a development boom as local entrepreneurs speculated on the city's future. Things have calmed down since then and a few guesthouses have even fallen by the wayside, though having an airport has increased its potential as a major tourist destination. From a tourist point of view, Chiang Rai is becoming an alternative to Chiang Mai.

### Information

**Tourist Office**  The TAT office (☎ 717433) on Singkhlai Rd, north of Wat Phra Singh, distributes maps of the city as well as useful brochures on accommodation and transport. It's open daily from 8.30 am to 5 pm.

**Post & Communications**  The GPO, on Utarakit Rd south of Wat Phra Singh, is open from 8.30 am to 4.30 pm weekdays, 9 am to 1 pm weekends and holidays.

A new CAT office at Ratchadat Damrong and Ngam Meuang Rds offers international telephone, telegram, telex and fax services from 7 am to 11 pm daily.

### Wat Phra Kaew
วัดพระแก้ว

Originally called Wat Paa Yia (Bamboo Forest Monastery) in local dialect, this is the city's most revered Buddhist temple. Legend says that in 1434 lightning struck the temple's octagonal chedi, which fell apart to reveal the Phra Kaew Morakot or Emerald Buddha (actually made of jade). (See the Bangkok chapter for more information on the Emerald Buddha.)

Around 1990 Chiang Rai commissioned a Chinese artist to sculpt a new image from Canadian jade. Named the Phra Yok Chiang Rai (Chiang Rai Jade Buddha), it was intentionally a very close but not exact replica of the Phra Kaew Morakot in Bangkok, with dimensions of 48.3 cm across the base and 65.9 cm in height (the original is 48.3 and 66 cm respectively). The image was installed at the temple in June 1991. At present, the image sits in a gilded box in front of a larger seated image in the main wihāan; eventually it will be moved to the new Lanna-style Haw Phra Kaew (Jewel Buddha Hall), soon to be completed. The Princess Mother honoured the image with the royal title of Phra Phuttha Ratanakon Nawutiwat Sanuson Mongkhon, which roughly translates as 'the ultimate blessed jewel-made Buddha image'.

The main wihāan is a medium-sized, nicely preserved wooden structure with unique carved doors. The chedi behind it dates to the late 14th century and is typical Lanna style.

### Wat Jet Yot
วัดเจ็ดยอด

The namesake for this wat is a seven-spired chedi similar to the chedi in Chiang Mai's Wat Jet Yot but without stucco ornamentation. Of more aesthetic interest is the wooden

NORTHERN THAILAND

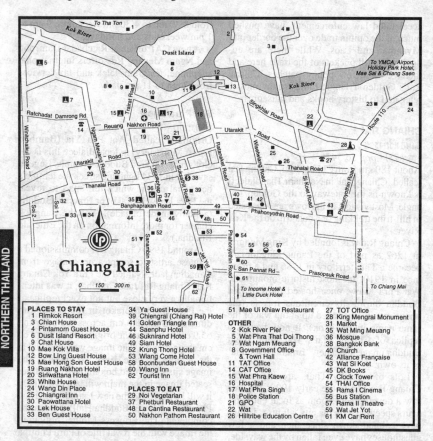

**Chiang Rai**

0    150    300 m

**PLACES TO STAY**
1  Rimkok Resort
3  Chian House
4  Pintamorn Guest House
6  Dusit Island Resort
9  Chat House
10  Mae Kok Villa
12  Bow Ling Guest House
13  Mae Hong Son Guest House
19  Ruang Nakhon Hotel
20  Siriwattana Hotel
23  White House
24  Wang Din Place
25  Chiangrai Inn
30  Paowattana Hotel
32  Lek House
33  Ben Guest House

34  Ya Guest House
39  Chiengrai (Chiang Rai) Hotel
41  Golden Triangle Inn
44  Saenphu Hotel
46  Suknirand Hotel
47  Siam Hotel
52  Krung Thong Hotel
53  Wiang Come Hotel
58  Boonbundan Guest House
60  Wiang Inn
62  Tourist Inn

**PLACES TO EAT**
29  Noi Vegetarian
37  Phetburi Restaurant
48  La Cantina Restaurant
50  Nakhon Pathom Restaurant

51  Mae Ui Khiaw Restaurant

**OTHER**
2  Kok River Pier
5  Wat Phra That Doi Thong
7  Wat Ngam Meuang
8  Government Office
   & Town Hall
11  TAT Office
14  CAT Office
15  Wat Phra Kaew
16  Hospital
17  Wat Phra Singh
18  Police Station
21  GPO
22  Wat
26  Hilltribe Education Centre

27  TOT Office
28  King Mengrai Monument
31  Market
35  Wat Ming Meuang
36  Mosque
38  Bangkok Bank
40  Church
42  Alliance Française
43  Wat Si Koet
45  DK Books
47  Clock Tower
54  THAI Office
55  Rama I Cinema
56  Bus Station
57  Rama II Theatre
59  Wat Jet Yot
61  KM Car Rent

ceiling in the front veranda of the main wihǎan; the ceiling features a unique Thai astrological fresco.

## Wat Phra Singh
วัดพระสิงห์

Yet another temple housing a copy of a famous Buddha image, this one was built in the late 14th century during the reign of Chiang Rai's King Mahaphrom. A sister temple to Chiang Mai's Wat Phra Singh, the original temple buildings are typical Northern-style wooden structures with low,

sweeping roofs. The main wihǎan houses a copy of Chiang Mai's Phra Singh Buddha.

## Other Temples
**Wat Phra That Doi Thong** is a hill-top wat north-west of Wat Phra Kaew with views of the river and an occasional river breeze. **Wat Paa Kaw**, near the entrance to the old Chiang Rai airport south of town, is a Shan-built temple with distinctive Burmese designs. Also near the old airport is **Wat Phra That Doi Phrabaat**, a Northern-style temple perched on a hillside.

## Hilltribe Education Centre
ศูนย์การศึกษาชาวเขา

The nonprofit Population & Community Development Association (PDA) operates this combination of museum and handicrafts centre at 620/25 Thanalai Rd (☎ 713410, 711475). Crafts for sale are displayed on the ground floor. The 2nd and 3rd floors of the facility serve as a museum with typical clothing for each tribe, folk implements and other anthropological exhibits. The centre also offers a slide show on Thailand's hill tribes with narration in English, French, German, Japanese and Thai. Admission to the slide show depends on the number of people who want to see it, ranging from 10B per person in a group of 10, to 50B for one person.

If you've already been to the Tribal Research Institute at Chiang Mai University, you'll have seen it all before; otherwise, it's a good place to visit before undertaking any hill-tribe treks.

## Trekking

More than 20 travel agencies, guesthouses and hotels offer trekking, typically in the Doi Tung and Chiang Khong areas. Chiang Rai's guesthouses were the first places to offer treks in the area and generally have the most experienced guides. Many of the local travel agencies merely act as brokers for guides associated with one of the local guesthouses; hence it may be cheaper to book directly through a guesthouse. As elsewhere in Northern Thailand, you're more assured of a quality experience if you use a TAT-licensed guide. Guide service and transport averages 400 to 500B per day.

From the Kok River pier, boats can take you upriver as far as Fang. (See Fang & Tha Ton in this chapter.) An hour's boat ride from Chiang Rai is **Ban Ruammit**, a fair-sized Karen village. From here you can trek on your own to Lahu, Mien, Akha and Lisu villages – all within a day's walk. Inexpensive room and board (30B per person, meals 15 to 25B) are available in many villages in the river area. Another popular area for do-it-yourself trekkers is **Wawi**, south of the

river town of Mae Salak near the end of the river route. (See the Kok River Trip to Chiang Rai section earlier.)

## Places to Stay – bottom end & middle
**Guesthouses** Near the Kok River pier (for boats from Tha Ton) is *Mae Kok Villa* (☎ 711786) at 445 Singkhlai Rd, which has dorm beds for 40B, bungalows with fan and bath for 120/150B and large singles/doubles with fan and hot bath for 140/190B. The owner keeps over 10 dachshunds on the property. Another nice place near the Kok River pier is *Chat House* (☎ 711481), at 1 Trairat Rd. It's an old Thai house with singles/doubles at 50/80B with shared bath, 100 to 150B with private hot water shower, or 40B for a dorm. There are bicycles for rent and guided treks are available.

A bit east of here in a network of sois off Singkhlai Rd are a couple of small family-run guesthouses. First is the clean and friendly *Bow Ling House* (☎ 712704), which has rooms with shared bath for 60B and rooms with private bath for 80B. A hot shower is available. Next is the very pleasant *Mae Hong Son Guest House of Chiang Rai* (☎ 715367), so named because it was once run by the same family as the original guesthouse in Mae Hong Son. Rooms are 60/80B or 70/100B with shared hot showers, 100/150B with private ones. This guesthouse has a very nice garden cafe, and also rents motorcycles and organises treks.

North of here are a couple of places on a large island separated from the city by a Kok River tributary. *Chian House* (☎ 713388) at 172 Si Bunruang Rd has simple but nicely done rooms from 80/100B with hot shower, 100 to 200B for bungalows with hot shower. Chian House lends free bikes to guests, and there's a pool on the premises, unusual for a place this inexpensive. Also on the island is *Pintamorn Guest House* (☎ 713317, 714161), where comfortable singles/doubles are 80/120B with hot water. There are also doubles with air-con in a separate house for 150/250B and a few cheaper rooms with shared facilities for 50/80B and 70/100B, plus a dorm that costs just 10B per bed. A 'sports club' on the premises has work-out rooms open to the public for 50B a day, plus a bar/restaurant and sauna.

*Lek House* (☎ 713337) at 95 Thanalai Rd near the city centre has rooms in an old house for 60/80B single/double with shared bath, or bungalows with private bath for 100B. Lek rents motorcycles and a jeep. If you follow Thanalai farther west till it becomes Ratchayotha Rd, you'll find Soi 2. Down Soi 2, just before it ends at San Khong Noi Rd, is *Chai House* (☎ 716681), a quiet spot away from everything with simple bungalows for 50B per person.

If you follow Soi 1 Ratchayotha south till it ends, then turn left, you'll come to the ambitious *Ben Guest House* (☎ 716775). Clean rooms in a new building made of salvaged teak cost 160B with fan and hot shower, 60/100B without bath. The owners speak English very well and can arrange treks with licensed guides.

In the southern part of town is the *Boonbundan Guest House* (☎ 712914) in a walled compound at 1005/13 Jet Yot Rd. The choice of accommodation here includes small rooms off the garden, in huts or in the new air-con building overlooking the garden – something to suit all budgets. Small rooms with hot bath are 60/80B. Singles/doubles in huts are 100/120B with fan and bath, and large singles/doubles with a fan in the new building are 200/250B, 250/350B with air-con. Also in this vicinity is the friendly and efficient *Tourist Inn* (☎ 714682) at 1004/5-6 Jet Yot Rd. Clean, large rooms are 150B with fan and private bath in the old house, 200B in a new building; the proprietors, who speak English, Thai and Japanese, plan to add 350B air-con rooms soon. Bikes are loaned for free and car/motorcycle rentals can be arranged.

The well run *White House* (☎ 744051) at 789/7 Phahonyothin Rd toward the river has very good rooms from 60B single with shared bath to 150B double with private bath. *Ya Guest House* (☎ 717090), nestled down a soi at the end of Banphaprakan Rd has basic rooms in a wooden building with shared facilities for 40/60B single/double, or

80B with private shower. A quiet garden and a lending library with hundreds of used paperbacks are Ya's main advantage.

**Hotels** On Suksathit Rd near the clock tower and district government building is the well run *Chiengrai Hotel* (☎ 711266), a favourite with Thai truck drivers and travelling sales-people. Clean rooms with fan and bath cost 140/190/250B a single/double/triple. Also centrally located is the *Suknirand* (☎ 711055) at 424/1 Banphaprakan Rd, between the clock tower and Wat Ming Meuang, around the corner from the Chiang Rai Hotel. Prices start at 300B for rooms with fan, 350B for air-con. Similar to the Suknirand but cheaper is *Siam* (☎ 711077) at 531/6-8 Banphaprakan, where rates are 180/240B with fan and bath.

*Ruang Nakhon* (☎ 711566) at 25 Reuang Nakhon Rd, near the hospital, allows four people to share a room with bath for 200B. Bungalows are 160B, doubles 180B and air-con doubles from 220 to 420B.

If you favour the old Thai-Chinese type of hotel, check out the *Paowattana* (☎ 711722) at 150 Thanalai Rd, which has rooms for 150 to 200B. Another cheap – but noisy – hotel is the *Siriwattana* (☎ 711466) at 485 Utarakit Rd next to the GPO, where singles/doubles cost 130 to 180B and there are a couple of bungalows at 100B.

The clean and efficient *Krung Thong Hotel* (☎ 711033; fax 711848), at 412 San-ambin Rd, has large singles/doubles with fan and bath for 200/240B; air-con rooms cost 320B.

Out of town, at 70 Phahonyothin Rd (the highway to Mae Sai), is the YMCA's *Golden Triangle International House* (☎ 713785). This is a very modern establishment with dorm beds for 70B, singles/doubles with fan and private bath for 250/280B or 300 to 500B with air-con. All rooms come with hot water and a telephone. Guests may use the Y's swimming pool.

### Places to Stay – top end
The *Golden Triangle Inn* (☎ 716996; fax 713963), at 590 Phahonyothin Rd, has 39 tastefully designed rooms with tile floors,

air-con and hot water (even bathtubs) for 600/650B single/double, including American breakfast. During the off season, April to October, the Golden Triangle knocks 100B off these rates. Also on the landscaped grounds are a cafe, a small Japanese-Thai garden and an efficient travel agency. It's a popular place, so book in advance to ensure you get in.

On the same theme, but not quite as successful, is the newer *Chiangrai Inn* (☎ 712673; fax 711483) at 661 Utarakit Rd. Large air-con rooms are a bit overpriced at 800 to 1100B for singles/doubles.

Much better value in this range is the centrally located *Saenphu Hotel* (☎ 717-300/9; fax 711372). Rooms with all the amenities – air-con, TV, phone, fridge – cost a bargain 550B for a single or double. The hotel's basement nightclub has live music and is a very popular local rendezvous spots. *Income Hotel* (☎ 717850), on Ratbamrung Rd south of the city centre, offers similar rooms for 600B and has the most popular disco in town.

The *Wiang Inn* (☎ 711543), at 893 Phahonyothin Rd, has modestly luxurious rooms priced at 1028B but readily discounted 100 to 200B. Facilities include a swimming pool, bar, restaurant, coffee shop and disco. Nearing the top of the Chiang Mai room-rate scale is *Wiang Come* (☎ 711800), at 869/90 Premawiphat Rd in the Chiang Rai Trade Centre. International-class rooms start at 1200B, complete with TV and fridge. The hotel has a disco, coffee shop, restaurant and nightclub.

A rash of new luxury hotels opened in Chiang Rai just in time for the travel recession of 1990-92. Perched on its own island in the Kok River (you can't miss seeing its stacked white facade if you arrive in Chiang Rai by boat), the 270-room *Dusit Island Resort* (☎ 715777) is an island unto itself, insulating its guests from the rigours of laid-back Chiang Rai. Rooms start at 2500B, but since occupancy rates often run below 60%, the Dusit may consider a discount to attract prospective guests.

Opposite the Dusit Island Resort on the other side of river, the Thai-style *Rimkok Resort* (☎ 716445; fax 715859; ☎ (2) 278-1154 in Bangkok) is probably Chiang Rai's most beautiful hotel. Set on lush grounds, spacious rooms with all the amenities start at 1700B. One drawback is the lack of a nearby bridge, so it's a 15 minute trip back and forth from Chiang Rai via the highway bridge at the east end of town.

Another good choice in this range is *Wang Din Place* (☎ 713363; fax 716790) at 34/1 Khae Wai Rd, in the north-east corner of town near the river. Sturdy, Thai-style bungalows with fridge, TV, air-con and private hot bath start at 800B.

The 350-room *Little Duck Hotel* (☎ 715-620), south of the city past the old airport, has picked up a regular clientele of Thai politicos and entrepreneurs in spite of its distance from the new airport and town. Tourist-class rooms start at 1600B. The original developer was indicted on drug trafficking charges, leading many to believe the hotel was built with Golden Triangle profits.

North on Phahonyothin Rd just before the road crosses the river on the way to Mae Sai, the *Holiday Park Hotel* (☎ 712243) is also new, but better located. Rooms start at 642B; facilities include an attached shopping plaza, restaurant and a garden sitting area.

### Places to Eat
**Thai** There are plenty of restaurants in Chiang Rai, especially along Banphaprakan and Thanalai Rds. Just east of the once-great (now awful) Haw Nalika Restaurant on Banphaprakan Rd are the inexpensive *Phetburi* and *Ratburi* restaurants. The Phetburi has a particularly good selection of curries and other Thai dishes. One speciality is cha-om thâwt, a type of fried quiche of cha-om greens cut in squares and served with a delicious chilli sauce.

For Northern Thai food, the best place in town is the clean *Mae Ui Khiaw* (☎ 753173) at 1064/1 Sanambin Rd, almost opposite Krung Thong Hotel. It's open from 8 am to 10 pm and the simple menu includes such classic Northern dishes as kaeng hang leh (vegetable-herb curry) and náam phrík nùm (Northern-style chilli sauce). There is an outdoor dining area as well as an indoor cushions-on-the-floor room reserved for groups of six to 10 persons. Mae's old location at 106/9 Ngam Meuang Rd now sells preserved Northern sausages and pastries. Another spot specialising in local cuisine as well as standard Thai dishes is *Khrua Mae Korn* at 10/1 Phahonyothin Rd, open from around 10 am to 10 pm.

*Nakhon Pathom*, yet another local restaurant named after a Central Thailand city, is very popular for inexpensive khâo man kài (Hainanese chicken rice) and kŭaytĭaw pèt yâang (roast duck with rice noodles). The restaurant is on Phahonyothin Rd near the Banphaprakan intersection.

*Muang Thong Restaurant*, just south of the Wiang Inn, has an extensive Thai and Chinese menu that includes a frog section. The house speciality is kaeng pà pèt, a delicious duck curry made without coconut milk.

Next to the mosque on Itsaraphap Rd is a Thai-Muslim restaurant with delicious khâo mòk kài, a Thai version of chicken biryani. Near the bus station are the usual food stalls; the night market next to the terminal and Rama I cinema is also good. There's a string of inexpensive rice and noodle restaurants along Jet Yot Rd between Thanalai Rd and Wat Jet Yot, near the Chiengrai and Wiang Come hotels.

*Noi* is a small family-run Thai vegetarian place at the corner of Utarakit and Ngam Meuang Rds – an English sign simply reads 'Vegetarian'.

*T Hut*, on Phahonyothin Rd near the second post office (about 1.5 km south of Mae U Khiaw), is a bit pricey for Thai food but is considered one of the best places to eat in the North. The restaurant at the *Little Duck Hotel* puts on a good 80B buffet Monday to Friday from 11 am to 2 pm; come early to beat the crowd.

**Western** Trapkaset (pronounced 'Sapkaset') Plaza, an L-shaped soi between Banphaprakan and Suksathit Rds, has become something of a farang food and bar centre. *La Cantina* (☎ 716808), operated by an Italian expat, offers an extensive selection of pizza, pasta, Italian regional specialities and wines; Mr Vallicelli even plays Italian opera on the sound system!

*Bierstube* (☎ 714195) on Phahonyothin Rd south of the Wiang Inn has been recommended for German food, and there are several other western-style pubs along here and on Suksathit/Jet Yot Rd near the Wiang Come Hotel. *Cafe de Paris* (☎ 716655) at 1015 Jet Yot Rd, operated by a Corsican, is good for coffee and European food.

### Entertainment

*Heuan Kao* (Old House), diagonally opposite the Chiengrai Hotel on Suksathit Rd, has live music nightly from 7 pm till midnight. The decor and atmosphere is 'Thai classic' (lots of black & white photos of Rama VII) and there's a reasonable Thai-Chinese menu for munchies, good ice cream as well.

Another popular local hang-out is the basement nightclub of the *Saenphu Hotel*, which has live Thai pop bands nightly. The indoor-outdoor *Country Nite Pub* on Banphaprakan Rd is also a rather lively spot.

Trapkaset Plaza has two go-go bars and the semi-outdoor *Easy Bar*. The Easy Bar is for video addicts – English-language videos are shown almost nonstop throughout the afternoon and evening.

Homesick Brits may enjoy the Dusit Island Resort's *Cellar Pub*, which offers pub grub, draught beer and darts; it's open 4 pm till late.

### Things to Buy

Prices for antiques and silverwork are sometimes – but not always – lower in Chiang Rai than in Chiang Mai. Several shops worth checking out for handicrafts, silver and antiques are found along Phahonyothin Rd, including Gong Ngoen at No 873/5, Silver Birch at No 891 and Chiangrai Handicrafts Center at No 273. Ego, at 869/81 Premawiphak, carries more up-market items including antique textiles.

## Getting There & Away

**Air** Chiang Rai's airport lies 10 km north of the city. THAI flies twice daily between Chiang Rai and Chiang Mai; the flight takes 30 minutes and costs 420B. Daily flights are also available to/from Bangkok (one hour and 20 minutes, 1855B). There is talk of flights from Hong Kong, Kunming, Vientiane and Mandalay, but as long as Chiang Mai's airport fields flights from these cities it's not likely.

Chiang Rai's THAI office (☎ 711179, 715207) is at 870 Phahonyothin Rd, not far from the Wiang Come Hotel.

Taxis into town from the airport cost 150B. Out to the airport you can get a tuk-tuk for 80 to 100B.

**Bus** There are two bus routes to Chiang Rai from Chiang Mai, an old and a new. The old route *(sāi kào)* heads south from Chiang Mai to Lampang before heading north through Ngao, Phayao, Mae Chai and finally to Chiang Rai. If you want to stop at any of these cities, this is the bus to catch, but the trip will take up to seven hours. In Chiang Mai the bus leaves from the Chiang Mai-Lamphun Rd, near Nawarat Bridge; the fare is 83B (ordinary only).

The new route *(sāi mài)* heads north-east along Route 1019 to Chiang Rai, stopping in Doi Saket and Wiang Papao, and takes about four hours. The fare is 57B ordinary, 79B 2nd class air-con or 102B for 1st class air-con. New-route buses leave from Chiang Mai's Arcade bus station. Chiang Mai to Chiang Rai buses are sometimes stopped for drug searches by police.

Chiang Rai's bus station is on Prasopsuk Rd, several blocks south of Phahonyothin Rd.

Other bus services from Chiang Rai include:

| City | Fare | Duration |
|---|---|---|
| Bangkok | 189B | 12 hours |
| (air-con) | 265B | 11 hours |
| (1st class) | 358B | |
| (VIP) | 525B | |
| Chiang Saen | 17B | 1½ hours |
| Chiang Khong | 39B | 3 hours |
| Khon Kaen | 189B | 12 hours |
| (air-con) | 264B | 11 hours |
| (1st class) | 339B | 11 hours |
| Mae Sai | 17B | 1¾ hours |
| Nan | 74B | 6 hours |
| Phayao | 21B | 1¾ hours |
| Phitsanulok | 104B | 6 hours |
| (air-con) | 140B | 5 hours |
| Phrae | 50B | 4 hours |

**Boat** One of the most popular ways of getting to Chiang Rai is the river trip from Tha Ton (see the Kok River Trip to Chiang Rai section earlier in this chapter).

For boats heading upriver on the Mae Kok, go to the pier in the north-western corner of town. Regular long boats from Chiang Rai stop at the following villages along the Kok (times are approximate for ideal river conditions):

| Destination | Fare | Duration |
|---|---|---|
| Ban Ruammit | 40B | 1 hour |
| Hat Yao | 60B | 2¼ hours |
| Kok Noi | 90B | 3 hours |
| Mae Salak | 130B | 4 hours |
| Phaa Khwang | 70B | 2½ hours |
| Phaa Muup | 50B | 1¾ hours |
| Phaa Tai | 120B | 3½ hours |
| Pong Nam Rawn | 45B | 1 hour 20 min |
| Tha Ton | 170B | 4½ to 5 hours |

## Getting Around

A samlor ride anywhere in central Chiang Rai should cost 15 to 20B. Tuk-tuks cost twice as much. A city songthaew system (2B fare) circulates along the main city streets; there are also route tuk-tuks that charge 5B.

Several small agencies near the Wiang Come Hotel rent cars (800 to 1200B a day), vans (1300 to 1500B) and jeeps (800 to 1200B).

Most of the guesthouses in town rent or lend bicycles, which are a good way to get around town. Daily bike rental costs 30 to 50B a day. Motorcycles are also easily rented through guesthouses. A reliable motorcycle rental and repair shop is Soon (☎ 714068), on the eastern side of Trairat Rd between Banphaprakan and Thanalai Rds; rates here start at 150B a day for a 100cc and rise to 350B for big bikes. Another place that rents motorcycles is ST Motor (☎ 713652) near the clock tower.

## MAE SALONG (SANTIKHIRI)
แม่สลอง (สันติคีรี)
• ☎ (53)

The village of Mae Salong was originally settled by the renegade KMT 93rd Regiment, which fled to Myanmar from China after the 1949 Chinese revolution. The renegades were again forced to flee in 1961 when the Myanmar government decided they wouldn't allow the KMT to remain legally in northern Myanmar (some still hide out in the hills).

Ever since the Thai government granted these renegades refugee status in the 1960s, the Thais have been trying to incorporate the Yunnanese KMT and their families into the Thai nation. Before now they weren't having much success, as the KMT persisted in involving themselves in the Golden Triangle opium trade, along with opium warlord Khun Sa and the Shan United Army (SUA).

This area is very mountainous and there are few paved roads, so the outside world has always been somewhat cut off from the goings-on in Mae Salong. Hence, for years the KMT were able to ignore attempts by Thai authorities to suppress opium activity and tame the region. Infamous Khun Sa made his home in nearby Ban Hin Taek (now Ban Theuat Thai) until the early 1980s when he was finally routed by the Thai military. Khun Sa's retreat to Myanmar seemed to signal a change in local attitudes and the Thai government finally began making progress in its pacification of Mae Salong and the surrounding area. (See the boxed aside on Opium & the Golden Triangle in the Facts about the Country chapter.)

In a further effort to separate the area from its old image as an opium fiefdom, the Thai government officially changed the name of the village from Mae Salong to Santikhiri (Hill of Peace). Until the 1980s pack horses were used to move goods up the mountain to Mae Salong, but today the 36 km road from Basang (near Mae Chan) to Santikhiri is paved

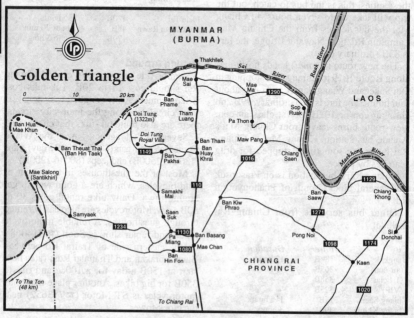

and a Thai-language elementary school has been established. There are also evening adult classes in the Thai language.

Despite government efforts to 'Thai-ise' the area, Mae Salong is unlike any other town in Thailand. The combination of pack horses, hill tribes (Akha, Lisu, Mien, Hmong) and southern Chinese-style houses conjures up images of a small town or village in Yunnan Province in China, and there is still a steady stream of illegal immigrants entering from Yunnan.

Most people in the area speak Yunnanese, except, of course, for members of the local hill tribes, who are mainly Akha and speak hill-tribe dialects. Like other villages throughout rural Thailand undergoing similar pacification programmes, Mae Salong is wired with a loudspeaker system that broadcasts official programming in the streets, starting at 6 am. The locals are reluctant to speak of their KMT past and deny that there are any KMT regulars left in the area. To the Thais, they are simply the jiin haw (galloping Chinese), a reference either to their use of horses or their migratory status.

One of the most important government programmes is the crop-substitution plan to encourage hill tribes to cultivate tea, coffee, corn and fruit trees. This seems to be somewhat successful, as there are plenty of these products for sale in the town markets, and tea and corn are abundant in the surrounding fields. There is a tea factory in town where you can taste the fragrant Mae Salong teas (originally from Taiwan), and there are many fruit wines and liquors for sale at the markets. The local illicit corn whisky is much in demand – perhaps an all too obvious substitution for the poppy. Some bottles contain large pickled centipedes.

Another local speciality is Chinese herbs, particularly the kind that are mixed with liquor (yaa dong in Thai). Thai and Chinese tourists who come to Mae Salong always take back a bag or two of assorted Chinese herbs.

The weather is always a bit cooler on Doi Mae Salong than on the plains below. During the cool and dry months, November to Feb-ruary, nights can actually get cold – be sure to bring sweaters and socks for visits at this time of year.

An interesting morning market convenes from around 4.30 to 8 am (5 to 6 am is the peak time) at the T-junction near Shin Sane Guest House and is attended by hill tribespeople from the surrounding districts.

Minivans full of Thai day-trippers begin arriving in Mae Salong around 10 am and leave by 4 pm. If you can stay overnight you'll pretty much have the place to yourself in the mornings and evenings.

### Trekking
Shin Sane Guest House has a wall map showing approximate routes to Akha, Mien, Hmong, Lisu, Lahu and Shan villages in the area. Nearby Mien, Akha and Lisu villages are less than half a day's walk away.

The best hikes are north of Mae Salong between Ban Hin Taek (Ban Theuat Thai) and the Myanmar border. Ask about political conditions before heading off in this direction (towards Myanmar), however. SUA and Wa National Army forces are competing for control over this section of the Thailand-Myanmar border and occasionally clash in the area.

It's possible to walk south from Mae Salong to Chiang Rai in three or four days, following trails which pass through fairly remote hill-tribe villages. There are also several easily reached hill-tribe villages along the highway between Ban Basang and Mae Salong, but these days they're full of day tourists from Chiang Rai.

Shin Sane Guest House arranges six hour horseback treks to four nearby villages for 500B, including lunch, or a three hour trek for 400B. Laan Tong Lodge can also arrange treks. You could also trek the 12 km to the Lahu village of Ja-Ju on your own. A basic guest house there offers rooms and two meals a day for 50B per person.

### Places to Stay
*Shin Sane (Sin Sae) Guest House* (☎ 765-026), Mae Salong's original hotel, is a wooden Chinese affair with a bit of atmos-

phere. Basic rooms are 50B per person; there are also some newer cabins in back for 100/150B single/double with private hot showers and good beds. Information on trekking is available; there is also a nice little eating area and a place for doing laundry. Calls to prayer from a mosque behind Shin Sane will bring you closer to Allah bright and early in the morning. Next to the Shin Sane, *Akha Mae Salong Guest House* (☎ 765103) offers cramped, bare rooms for 50/100B with shared bath, 150B with bath – poor value unless the Shin Sane is full (not likely).

At the top of the price range is the *Mae Salong Resort* (☎ 765014), where so-so bungalows (they look good from a distance but are none too clean) cost 2000B on weekends, as low as 500B with mid-week discounts. The Yunnanese restaurant here is very good – especially tasty are the fresh mushroom dishes.

*Mae Salong Villa* (☎ 765114) just below the town centre has bungalow-style accommodation from 600 to 800B – this is better value than the Mae Salong Resort. On the opposite side of town near the afternoon market, on the road to Tha Ton, the upscale *Khumnaiphol Resort* (☎ 765000) offers modern hotel-style rooms for 800 to 2000B.

**Out of Town** Three km from Ban Basang on the road to Mae Salong is a turn-off to *Winnipa Lodge* (☎ 712225), on a hillside overlooking the road. Bungalows are 200 to 1500B; there is also tent accommodation available for 80B a night. From here you can see Doi Tung in the distance.

If you're hiking or driving to Chiang Rai from Doi Mae Salong or Tha Ton, you could stop off in Ban Hin Fon and stay at the friendly family-run *Laan Tong Lodge* (☎ 771366 in Mae Chan), which is about 13 km west of Mae Chan or 31 km from Mae Salong (17 km east of the Mae Salong-Tha Ton road junction). Otherwise you can reach it by taking a songthaew from Mae Chan to the village (10B) and then hiking the three km to the lodge. Large, well kept and well separated huts on impressively landscaped grounds cost 80/100B without bath, up to

400B with bath. One of the activities here is tubing along the Mae Chan River. As we went to press I heard news that the Laan Tong had been sold to a Chinese entrepreneur, so changes may be in the offing.

**Places to Eat**
Don't miss the many street noodle vendors who sell khanōm jiin náam ngíaw, a delicious Yunnanese rice-noodle concoction topped with spicy chicken curry – Mae Salong's most famous local dish and a gourmet bargain at 6B per bowl.

Around town you'll find a variety of places serving simple Chinese snacks like fluffy mantou (plain steamed Chinese buns) and salabao (pork-stuffed Chinese buns) with delicious pickled vegetables. Many of the Chinese in Mae Salong are Muslims, so you'll find several Chinese-Muslim restaurants serving khâo sòi (curried chicken and noodles).

**Getting There & Away**
To get to Mae Salong by public transport, take a bus from Mae Sai or Chiang Rai to Ban Basang, which is about two km north of Mae Chan. From Ban Basang, there are songthaews up the mountain to Mae Salong for 50B per person (down again costs 40B); the trip takes about an hour. This service stops at around 5 pm; you can charter a songthaew in either direction for 400B. The bus fare from Chiang Rai to Ban Basang is 11B. You can also reach Mae Salong by road from Tha Ton. See the earlier Fang & Tha Ton section for details.

**MAE SAI**
แม่สาย
• ☎ (53)
The northernmost point in Thailand, Mae Sai is a good place from which to explore the Golden Triangle, Doi Tung and Mae Salong. It's also a good spot to observe border life, as Mae Sai is one of the few official land crossings open between Myanmar and Thailand.

Burmese authorities have spruced up Thakhilek (the town opposite Mae Sai, also

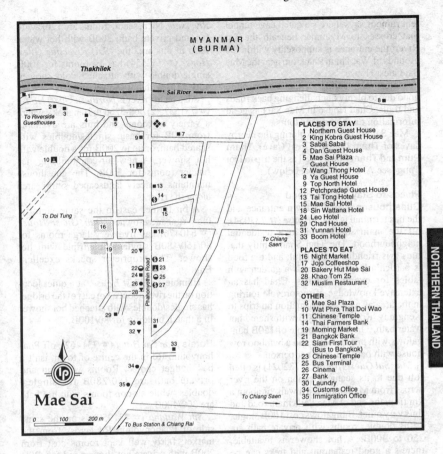

MYANMAR
(BURMA)

Thakhilek

Sai River

To Riverside
Guesthouses

To Doi Tung

To Doi Tung

To Chiang
Saen

To Chiang Saen

To Bus Station & Chiang Rai

Mae Sai

0   100   200 m

**PLACES TO STAY**
1 Northern Guest House
2 King Kobra Guest House
3 Sabai Sabai
4 Dan Guest House
5 Mae Sai Plaza
    Guest House
7 Wang Thong Hotel
8 Ya Guest House
9 Top North Hotel
12 Petchpradap Guest House
13 Tai Tong Hotel
15 Mae Sai Hotel
18 Sin Wattana Hotel
24 Leo Hotel
29 Chad House
31 Yunnan Hotel
33 Boom Hotel

**PLACES TO EAT**
16 Night Market
17 Jojo Coffeeshop
20 Bakery Hut Mae Sai
28 Khao Tom 25
32 Muslim Restaurant

**OTHER**
6 Mae Sai Plaza
10 Wat Phra That Doi Wao
11 Chinese Temple
14 Thai Farmers Bank
19 Morning Market
21 Bangkok Bank
22 Siam First Tour
    (Bus to Bangkok)
23 Chinese Temple
25 Bus Terminal
26 Cinema
27 Bank
30 Laundry
34 Customs Office
35 Immigration Office

**NORTHERN THAILAND**

spelt Tachilek) and foreigners are allowed across for one to three days as far as Kengtung, 163 km from Thailand and 100 km short of China. Within four years, the road should be open all the way to the Chinese border – already the town seems to be gearing up for Thailand-China traffic. (See Around Mae Sai below for current details on this trip.) In spite of the opening, Thai tourists are much more commonly seen in Mae Sai than farangs.

Burmese lacquerware, gems, jade and other goods from Laos and Myanmar are sold in shops along the main street in Mae Sai. Many Burmese come over during the day from Thakhilek to work or do business, hurrying back by sunset. Gem dealers from as far away as Chanthaburi frequent the **gem market** opposite the police station.

Take the steps up the hill near the border to **Wat Phra That Doi Wao**, west of the main street, for superb views over Myanmar and Mae Sai. This wat was reportedly constructed in memory of a couple of thousand Burmese soldiers who died fighting KMT here in 1965. There are also some interesting trails in the cliffs and hills overlooking the Mae Sai Guest House and the river. A persistent rumour says there's a gated cave tunnel that crosses to Myanmar beneath the Sai River; the entrance is supposedly within the grounds of Wat Tham Phaa Jom near the Mae Sai Guest House.

Motorcycle touring in the area is quite good due to plenty of challenging back roads and trails. Chad House in Mae Sai has good information on motorcycle tours.

Mae Sai is a base for exploring the nearby caves of **Tham Luang** (Great Cave), **Tham Pum** and **Tham Pla**, as well as the trip to Doi Tung (see Around Mae Sai below).

### Places to Stay – bottom end

**Guesthouses** Near the town entrance and the bus terminal is *Chad House* (☎ 732054), off the main street a bit in a residential neighbourhood. The Thai-Shan family that runs it is friendly and helpful, and the food is particularly good. There's a garden with tables for evening repasts. Chad has an extensive knowledge of motorcycle touring in the area as well as information on trips to Kengtung. Rooms are 100B with shared hot water bath. There are a couple of 150B bungalows with private bath, and a bamboo row house with beds for 50B per person.

*Mae Sai Guest House* (☎ 732021) is often full due to its scenic location on the river across from Myanmar. It's a walk of about a km from the end of Mae Sai's main road and thus very quiet. Bungalows cost 100B single, 150B double; rooms with private bath are 250 to 300B. A hot shower is available, there's a good restaurant and treks can be arranged. The staff can be rather unfriendly.

Closer to town and just back from the river is the rambling, 71-room *Mae Sai Plaza Guest House* (☎ 732230). This huge hillside bamboo and wood complex has a laid-back atmosphere and a cafe overlooking the road – good for people-watching. Singles/doubles with shared bath cost from 60 to 100B, doubles with private bath are 100B and there are larger rooms at 120B with hot shower; most rooms have a view of the river. Between Mae Sai Plaza and Mae Sai Guest House, next to the river landing for local Thai-Burmese trade, is the relatively new *Sai*

*Riverside*. Nice, secure rooms are 120B with fan and private bath, 200B with hot water. Also in this area the *(Sai) Riverside Guest House* (☎ 732554) has 17 rooms for 100B single/double with attached cold shower, 150/200B with hot shower and fan.

Also on the river is *Northern Guest House* (☎ 731537; (2) 468-3266 in Bangkok), where a variety of rooms and huts are available from 80B for basic singles/doubles with shared bath, or up to 200B for a double with hot shower. A new air-con building has fancier rooms for 500B. The guesthouse maintains a nicely landscaped sitting area along the river.

A bit farther east in the same vicinity, the Yunnanese-owned *Dan Guest House* (☎ 640476) has five very large rooms for 80/160/180B single/double/triple with hot shower. The proprietor speaks excellent English.

Humble *Ya Guest House*, at a quiet location on the river about a km east of the bridge, has singles/doubles with attached hot shower in a thatch building for 80/100B.

**Hotels** *Mae Sai Hotel* (☎ 731462), off Pha-honyothin Rd in the centre of town, isn't a bad budget choice. Rooms with fan and private bath are 180/280B for singles/doubles, while air-con rooms with hot bath are 300/400B.

*Sin Wattana* (☎ 731950) is on the same side of Phahonyothin Rd across from the market; fairly well kept rooms cost from 200B with private hot shower and fan, 30B with air-con.

### Places to Stay – middle & top end

**Guesthouses** Above Mae Sai Guest House on a hill overlooking the river, the new *Rabiengthong House* offers comfortable suites for three or four people at 500B, plus less expensive rooms in the main house for 200B. It gets a mostly Thai clientele and features a fair Thai restaurant.

*Petchpradap Guest House* (☎ 731820), on a back street east of and parallel to the main strip, rents air-con bungalows with TV and hot water for 400B.

Down on the river strip near Mae Sai Plaza Guest House, the American-run *King Kobra Guest House* (☎ 733055) features apartment-style rooms with private hot bath and fans for 150/200B single/double, or 350/400B with air-con, including breakfast. The staff do trekking and motorcycle tours, as well as Kengtung 4WD tours.

Next door the new *Sabai Sabai* (☎ 732722) offers simple rooms for 250B single/double with fan, 350B with air-con; it's not very good value.

**Hotels** *Top North Hotel* (☎ 731955), on the west side of Phahonyothin Rd towards the bridge, has comfortable singles/doubles with private bath for 250/350B, add hot water for 400B, air-con for 500B or air-con, fridge and TV for 550B. The newer *Leo Hotel* (☎ 732-064), opposite the bus terminal, has rooms for 480 to 700B including air-con, hot water, TV and fridge – good mid-range value.

*Tai Tong (Thai Thong) Hotel* (☎ 731975) at 6 Phahonyothin Rd has standard rooms at 650B, and somewhat larger rooms for up to 1000B. All come with air-con and hot water, but considering the rooms, these rates are perhaps a tad high.

The nine-storey, 150-room *Wang Thong Hotel* (☎ 733388; (2) 225-9298 in Bangkok), off Phahonyothin Rd in the northern part of town, recently opened and is entertaining brisk traffic among business travellers. Spacious, international-class rooms with all the amenities start at 1400/1600B for singles/doubles, not including tax and service; these rates drop to 800B in the low season. Facilities include a swimming pool, pub, disco and restaurant.

About a hundred metres before the turnoff for Chad Guest House is the new and somewhat gaudy-looking *Yunnan Hotel* (☎ 642169), with a beer garden in front. Nice rooms sleeping up to three people cost 480B and come with hot water and TV; VIP rooms with the same plus sofa and fridge cost 560B. A tad farther south and off the road a bit is the aptly named *Boom Hotel*, with 15 rooms and curtained carports for 300B plus nice six A-frame bungalows sleeping up to four people for 500B.

**Places to Eat**

The night market is rather small but the Chinese vendors do excellent kŭaytĭaw phàt sĭi-yúu (rice noodles stir-fried in soy sauce) and other noodle dishes. You can also get fresh paa-thông-kŏh (Chinese doughnuts) and hot soy milk.

*Jojo Coffeeshop* on Phahonyothin Rd serves very good Thai curries and Thai vegetarian dishes, plus ice cream and western snacks. You'll eat well while contemplating the collection of Lanna-style wooden Buddhas along the walls; note that it's only open 6.30 am to 4.30 pm. For late eats your best bet is *Khao Tom 25* near Chad House, open nightly 4 pm to 4 am.

*Bakery Hut Mae Sai* on the main drag has a fairly nice assortment of pastries. Down near the bridge on the river is a floating restaurant that's OK.

South of Chad House on the main road is a small Muslim restaurant with good curries and khâo mòk.

**Getting There & Away**

Buses to Mae Sai leave frequently from Chiang Rai and cost 18B for the 1½ hour trip. To/from Chiang Saen by bus costs 16B via Mae Chan. (See Getting Around in the Chiang Saen section for details on different routes between Mae Sai and Chiang Saen.)

To/from Chiang Mai it's 71B by ordinary bus (five departures a day) or 127B air-con (six a day); this trip takes about four to five hours.

There are also direct buses to Mae Sai from Fang (33B) and Tha Ton (27B) via the paved Tha Ton-Mae Chan road. Other destinations include Doi Tung (30B), Mae Chan (8B), Mae Salong (50B) and Sop Ruak (30B). Mae Sai's main bus terminal is five km south of town, a 5B shared songthaew ride.

**Bangkok** Siam First Tour operates VIP 'sleeper' buses from Mae Sai to Bangkok that leave at about 5.30 or 6 pm daily for 400 to 568B depending on the number of seats; the journey takes around 13 hours. Standard air-con buses to Bangkok cost 364B and depart the main street ten times daily between 7 am and 8 pm. There is no longer a direct non-air-

NORTHERN THAILAND

con bus service between Mae Sai and Bangkok; baht-pinchers will have to bus first to Chiang Mai and change to a Bangkok-bound ordinary bus.

### Getting Around

Songthaews around town are 10 to 15B. Most guesthouses in Mae Sai have stopped renting motorcycles, but Honda Dreams can be rented at Pornchai on Phahonyothin near the market for 150B per day.

## AROUND MAE SAI
### Tham Luang (Great Cave)
ถ้ำหลวง

About six km south of Mae Sai off Route 110 is a large cave that extends into the hills for at least a couple of km, possibly more. The first cavern is huge, and a narrow passage at the back leads to a series of other chambers and side tunnels of varying sizes. The first km is fairly easy going but after that you do some climbing over piles of rocks to get further in. At this point the roof formations become more fantastic and tiny crystals make them change colour according to the angle of the light. For 20B you can borrow a gas lantern from the caretakers in front of the cave or you can take someone along as a guide (for which there's no fixed fee; just give him whatever you want). Guides aren't always available during the week.

### Tham Pum & Tham Pla
ถ้ำปุ่มและถ้ำปลา

Only 13 km south of Mae Sai, just off Route 110 at Ban Tham, are a couple of caves with freshwater lakes inside. Bring a torch to explore the caves as there are no lights. Another attraction here is the unique cake-like chedi in front of the cave entrance. It's a very large, multi-tiered structure stylistically different from any other in Thailand.

### Doi Tung
ดอยตุง

About halfway between Mae Chan and Mae Sai on Route 110 is the turn-off west for Doi Tung. The name means 'Flag Peak', from the

Northern Thai word for 'flag' *(tung)*. King Achutarat of Chiang Saen ordered a giant flag to be flown from the peak to mark the spot where two chedis were constructed in 911 AD; the chedis are still there, a pilgrimage site for Shan Buddhists.

But the main attraction at Doi Tung is getting there. The 'easy' way is via Route 1149, which is mostly paved to the peak of Doi Tung. But it's winding, steep and narrow, so if you're driving or riding a motorcycle, take it slowly.

Along the way are Shan, Akha and Musoe (Lahu) villages. Opium is cultivated in the vicinity of Doi Tung and this can be a dangerous area to explore alone if you go far off the main roads. Travelling after 4 pm – when traffic thins out – is not advised except along the main routes.

Myanmar is a short trek from the peak and many travellers used to climb to the border to view the very large poppy fields guarded by hill tribespeople and KMT soldiers on the other side. Around 1991 the fields were moved three km away from the border to hide them from curious eyes. It is probably not safe to trek in this area without a Thai or hill-tribe guide simply because you may be mistaken for a USDEA agent (by the opium traders) or drug dealer (by the Thai army rangers who patrol the area). You may hear gunfire from time to time, which might indicate that rangers are in pursuit of MTA, Karen rebels or others caught between two hostile governments.

On the theory that local hill tribes will be so honoured by a royal presence that they will stop cultivating opium, Thailand's royal family maintains the **Doi Tung Royal Villa** on the slopes of Doi Tung near Pa Kluay Reservoir. It was meant to serve as a summer palace for the king's mother, who passed away in 1995. A beautifully landscaped flower garden at the villa is open to the public for a 20B admission fee.

At the peak, 1800m above sea level, **Wat Phra That Doi Tung** is built around twin Lanna-style chedis purportedly erected in 911 AD. The chedis were renovated by famous Chiang Mai monk Khruba Siwichai earlier this century. Pilgrims bang on the usual row of temple bells to gain merit and toss money into the large bellybutton of a fat Chinese Buddha statue. Although the wat isn't that impressive, the high forested setting will make the trip worthwhile. From the walled edge of the temple you can get an aerial view of the snaky road you've just climbed.

A walking path next to the wat leads to a spring, and there are other short walking trails in the vicinity. A bit below the peak is the smaller **Wat Noi Doi Tung**, where food and beverages are available from vendors.

**Places to Stay** *Kwan Guest House*, on the north side of the road leading to Doi Tung before the palace, offers A-frame bungalows in the 100 to 400B range, but it's very much substandard accommodation and the main attraction here seems to be a small, dark nightclub.

Out on Route 1149, the road to Doi Tung, it's possible to rent a room at the Akha village of Ban Pakha or at *Akha Guest House*, next to the village. The latter no longer officially operates because of a restriction on guesthouses in this area, but sometimes there's someone around to rent out bamboo huts. Neither the village nor the unsigned guesthouse has electricity or running water, and the food is not that good, but there are nice views of the valley below. A place to sleep costs 40B per person and guides can be hired for as little as 50 to 100B per person for a day trek.

**Getting There & Away** Buses to the turn-off for Doi Tung are 8B from either Mae Chan or Mae Sai. From Ban Huay Khrai, at the Doi Tung turn-off, a songthaew to Ban Pakha is 20B or 40B all the way to Doi Tung, 18 km away.

The road to Doi Tung has seriously deteriorated above Pakha in the last few years and this section is becoming more of a challenge to climb, whether you're in a truck, jeep or motorcycle.

You can also travel by motorcycle between Doi Tung and Mae Sai along a challenging 15 km half-paved track that starts in the Akha village of Ban Phame, eight km south of Mae Sai (four km south along Route 110, then four km west), and joins the main road about two-thirds of the way up Doi Tung. You can also pick this road up by following the dirt road that starts in front of Mae Sai's Wat Doi Wao. West of Ban Phame this route has lots of tight curves, mud, rocks, precipitous drops, passing lorries and bulldozers – figure on two to 2½ hours by motorbike or jeep from Mae Sai. Eventually this road will be paved all the way but for now it's a road for experienced bikers only. The road also runs high in the mountains along the Myanmar border and should not be travelled alone or after 4 pm. Ask first in Mae Sai about border conditions.

**Cross-Border Trips to Thakhilek & Kengtung, Myanmar**
For much of 1993 and 1994, foreigners were permitted to cross the bridge over the Sai River into Thakhilek (also pronounced Tachilek by the Burmese). Then in May 1994 Khun Sa's Mong Tai Army (MTA) bombed the Thakhilek dyke, draining the reservoir that supplied the town with water.

Following this incident the border was closed until April 1996. At the time of writing the crossing was again open to foreigners. If the security situation deteriorates, the crossing may close again. For now you can enter upon payment of a US$10 fee and the deposit of your passport at the Thai immigration post.

Besides shopping for Shan handicrafts (about the same price as on the Thai side) and eating Shan/Burmese food, there's little to do in Thakhilek. About 3000 to 4000 people cross the bridge to Thakhilek daily, most of them Thais who shop for dried mushrooms, herbal medicines, cigarettes and other cheap imports from China. Foreigners are permitted to spend the night in A-frame bungalows strung with coloured lights on the river bank facing Thailand for US$8 to US$14.

Three night, four day excursions to the town of Kengtung (called Chiang Tung by the Thais and usually spelt Kyaingtong by the Burmese), 163 km north, may be arranged through any Mae Sai guesthouse or travel agency or you can do it on your own by paying US$18 for a four day, three night permit at the border, plus a mandatory exchange of US$100 for Myanmar's Foreign Exchange Certificates. These FECs can be spent on hotel rooms or exchanged on the black market for kyat (the Burmese currency). The permit can be extended for up to three months at a cost of US$36 at the immigration office in Kengtung.

Kengtung is a sleepy but historic capital for the Shan State's Khün culture – the Khün speak a Northern Thai language related to Shan and Thai Lü and use a writing script similar to the ancient Lanna script. It's a bit more than halfway between the Thai and Chinese borders – eventually the road will be open all the way to China but for now Kengtung is the limit. Built around a small lake, and dotted with ageing Buddhist temples and crumbling British colonial architecture, it's a much more scenic town than Thakhilek, and probably the most interesting town in Myanmar's entire Shan State. About 70% of all foreign visitors to Kengtung are Thais seeking a glimpse of ancient Lanna. Few westerners are seen around town save for contract employees working for the UNDCP (United Nations Drug Control Project).

The road trip allows glimpses of Shan, Akha, Wa and Lahu villages along the way. The *Noi Yee Hotel* in Kengtung costs US$10 per person per night in multi-bed rooms. Myanmar Tours & Travel tries to steer tourists towards the more expensive, government-run *Kyainge Tong Hotel*, where rooms range from US$30 to US$42.

*Harry's Guest House & Trekking*, at 132 Mai Yang Rd, Kanaburoy Village (☎ (101) 21418), is operated by an English-speaking Kengtung native who spent many years as a trekking guide in Chiang Mai. His simple rooms go for US$5 per person, payable in US, Thai or Burmese currency.

For a complete description of Kengtung and vicinity, see Lonely Planet's *Myanmar* guidebook.

**Getting There & Beyond** As with the Thakhilek day trips, you must leave your passport at the border for trips to Kengtung. The cheapest form of transport to Kengtung is the 45B songthaew that leaves each morning from Thakhilek. You can rent jeeps on either side of the border, but Thai vehicles with a capacity of five or fewer passengers are charged a flat US$50 entry fee, US$100 for vehicles with a capacity of over five. Burmese vehicle hire is more expensive and requires the use of a driver. Whatever the form of transport, count on at least six to 10 gruelling hours (depending on road conditions) to cover the 163 km stretch between the border and Kengtung.

The road is currently being improved and will eventually be paved all the way to the Chinese border, 100 km beyond Kengtung. If the Chinese border opens, perhaps Thai immigration authorities in Mae Sai will allow visitors to travel with their passports, which would make an overland trip into China possible. For the time being foreigners are rarely given permission to travel north of Kengtung; the border area between Kengtung and China is controlled by the Eastern Shan State National Democratic Army, a rebel Shan splinter group. Neither the MTA nor the ESSNDA have ever been known to threaten or harm tourists.

If current economic and political conditions in Myanmar prevail, the road between Kengtung and Taunggyi should open to foreign travel. At the moment only Myanmar citizens are permitted to use this road. Fighting between Myanmar's Yangon government and the Shan State's splintered Mong Tai Army makes the Kengtung-Taunggyi journey potentially hazardous.

## CHIANG SAEN
เชียงแสน
• ☎ (53)

A little more than 60 km from Chiang Rai, Chiang Saen is a small crossroads town on the banks of the Maekhong River. Scattered throughout the town are the ruins of the Chiang Saen kingdom, a Lanna principality founded in 1328 by King Mengrai's nephew Saenphu. Surviving architecture includes chedis, Buddha images, wihăan pillars and earthen city ramparts. A few of the old monuments still standing predate Chiang Saen by a couple of hundred years; legend says this pre-Chiang Saen kingdom was called Yonok. Formerly loosely affiliated with various Northern Thai kingdoms, as well as 18th century Myanmar, Chiang Saen didn't really become a Siamese possession until the 1880s. A 19th century American missionary wrote that the city was:

...admirably situated for purposes of trade, at the intersection of routes leading from China, Burmah, Karenni, the Shan States, Siam, Tonquin and Annam. It forms, in fact, a centre of intercourse between all the Indo-Chinese races and the point of dispersion for caravans along the diverging trade routes.

Yunnanese trade routes extended from Simao, Yunnan, through Laos to Chiang Saen and then on to Mawlamyine in Burma, via Chiang Rai, Chiang Mai and Mae Sariang. A lesser used route proceeded through Utaradit, Phayao and Phrae.

The sleepy town hasn't changed too much in spite of Golden Triangle commercialisation, which is concentrated in nearby Sop Ruak. Practically everything in Chiang Saen closes down by 9 pm. This may change if passenger boat traffic to and from China along the Maekhong River becomes firmly established.

The Lao side of the mighty Maekhong here looks deserted, but Lao boats occasionally float by. Hill-tribe crafts can be bought in a few shops along the river.

## Information

A new TAT office near the western entrance to town offers sketch maps and information on the area. Hanging on one of the inside walls is a better area map which extends coverage all the way to Sop Ruak. The office is open daily from 8.30 am to 4.30 pm.

## National Museum
พิพิธภัณฑ์แห่งชาติ

Near the town entrance, a small national museum displays artefacts from the Lanna period as well as prehistoric stone tools from the area, and hill-tribe crafts, dress and musical instruments. It's open Wednesday to Sunday from 9 am to 4 pm and admission is 10B.

## Wat Chedi Luang
วัดเจดีย์หลวง

Behind the museum to the east, the ruins of this wat feature an 18m octagonal chedi in the classic Chiang Saen or Lanna style. Archaeologists argue about its exact construction date but agree it dates to some time between the 12th and 14th centuries.

## Wat Paa Sak
วัดป่าสัก

About 200m from the Chiang Saen Gate are the remains of Wat Paa Sak, which is undergoing restoration by the Fine Arts Department. The ruins of seven monuments are visible. The main mid-14th century stupa combines elements of the Hariphunchai and Sukhothai styles with a possible Burmese Bagan influence. Since these ruins form part of a historical park, there is a 20B admission fee.

## Wat Phra That Chom Kitti
วัดพระธาตุจอมกิตติ

About 2.5 km north of Wat Paa Sak on a hill-top are the remains of Wat Phra That Chom Kitti and Wat Chom Chang. The round chedi of Wat Phra That is thought to have been constructed before the founding of the kingdom. The smaller chedi below it belonged to Wat Chom Chang. There's nothing much to see at these chedis, but there's a good view of Chiang Saen and the river from the top of the hill.

## Maekhong River Trips

A new boat landing and customs station was recently completed alongside the Chiang Saen waterfront. Boats from China, Laos and Myanmar can be seen unloading their cargoes in the mornings.

NORTHERN THAILAND

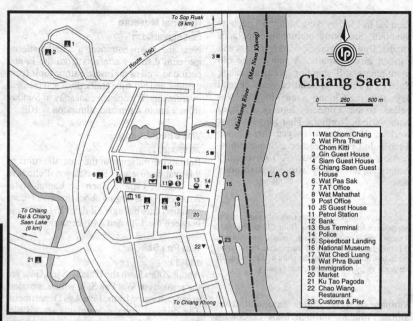

Chiang Saen

0    250    500 m

1  Wat Chom Chang
2  Wat Phra That Chom Kitti
3  Gin Guest House
4  Siam Guest House
5  Chiang Saen Guest House
6  Wat Paa Sak
7  TAT Office
8  Wat Mahathat
9  Post Office
10 JS Guest House
11 Petrol Station
12 Bank
13 Bus Terminal
14 Police
15 Speedboat Landing
16 National Museum
17 Wat Chedi Luang
18 Wat Phra Buat
19 Immigration
20 Market
21 Ku Tao Pagoda
22 Chao Wiang Restaurant
23 Customs & Pier

Six-passenger speedboats (*reua raew* in Thai) will go to Sop Ruak (half an hour) for 300B per boat one way or 400B roundtrip, or all the way to Chiang Khong (two hours) for 1200/1700B.

See the Sop Ruak section for more information on Maekhong River boat services.

**Places to Stay**

The *Chiang Saen Guest House* is the cheapest, with small singles/doubles for 60/70B, and larger rooms in the main house with private bath for 70/90B. Nicer A-frame bungalows cost 100/150B. It's on the road to Sop Ruak, opposite the river.

A bit farther along this road on the same side, *Siam Guest House* offers singles/doubles in huts with mosquito nets for 60/100B with shared bath, 100/120B with private bath. This guesthouse also has a pleasant cafe, and rents out bicycles and motorcycles.

Farther north on the edge of town (about

1.5 km from the bus terminal) is the secluded *Gin Guest House* with a variety of accommodation possibilities. Rooms in the main house cost 200 to 400B with private hot bath, 80 to 100B without; dorm beds are 40B. Bungalows behind the house are 200B. Gin rents mountain bikes for 50B a day; visas for Laos can be arranged in five days for 1800B.

The *JS Guest House* (☎ 777060) is in town about 100m off the main road near the post office. Rooms in a long concrete building cost 100B a single/double with shared bath; a solar hot shower is available in the proprietor's house. Vegetarian Thai meals are available here.

North-west of town off Route 1290, *Ban Suan* (☎ 650419) is a slightly up-market, Thai-oriented guest house with 10 bungalows with carpet, fan, fridge and hot showers for 400B, or with TV for 500B. There's also a large dorm with mattresses on the floor for 100B per person.

About five km out of town near Chiang

Saen Lake, *Yonok Lake Resort* (☎ 650364) has a few 500B bungalows with fridge and hot showers, plus a pleasant garden dining area.

Twenty km from Chiang Rai on the way to Chiang Saen via Highway 1129, in the lively Hmong village of Ban Khiu Khan, the *Hmong Guest House* offers rudimentary huts for 70B a night.

### Places to Eat

Cheap noodle and rice dishes are available in and near the market on the river road and along the main road through town from the highway.

Two open-air riverside restaurants off the river road out of Chiang Saen towards Sop Ruak, *Suan Aahaan Sawng Fang Khong* and *Suan Aahaan Rim Khong*, offer extensive menus of Thai, Chinese and Isaan food. Bring along your Thai-language eating guide though. Near the new customs station and pier, on the river, the small *Chao Wiang Restaurant* serves decent Thai and Chinese food.

Most places in town close early. An exception is the *Toh Lung* opposite the main bus stop, which stays open all night.

### Getting There & Away

There are frequent buses from Chiang Rai to Chiang Saen for 17B. The trip takes between 40 minutes and 1½ hours.

Returning from Chiang Saen, don't take a Chiang Mai bus (out of Chiang Saen directly) unless you want to travel along the old road (sǎi kào). The old road passes through Pham, Phayao, Ngao, Lampang and Lamphun before arriving in Chiang Mai, a trip that takes from seven to nine hours. To take the new road (sǎi mài), first go to Chiang Rai (on a Chiang Rai bus of course) then change to a Chiang Mai bus, a trip of about 4½ hours.

### Getting Around

A good way to see the Chiang Saen-Mae Sai area is on two wheels – bicycles and motorcycles can be rented at guesthouses in either town, though there's usually a better choice of machines in Mae Sai.

From Mae Sai to Chiang Saen there's a choice of two scenic paved roads (one from the centre of Mae Sai and one near the town entrance), or a wider, busier paved road via Route 110 to Mae Chan and then Route 1016 to Chiang Saen.

The roads out of Mae Sai are considerably more direct but there are several forks where you have to make educated guesses on which way to go (there are occasional signs). The two roads join near the village of Mae Ma, where you have a choice of going east through Sop Ruak or south through Pa Thon. The eastern route is more scenic.

### AROUND CHIANG SAEN
### Sop Ruak
สบรวก

Nine km north of Chiang Saen is Sop Ruak, the official centre of the Golden Triangle where the borders of Myanmar, Thailand and Laos meet, at the confluence of the Ruak and Maekhong rivers. In historical terms, 'Golden Triangle' actually refers to a much larger geographic area, stretching thousands of sq km into Myanmar, Laos and Thailand, within which the opium trade is prevalent. Nevertheless hoteliers and tour operators have been quick to cash in on the name by referring to the tiny village of Sop Ruak as 'the Golden Triangle', conjuring up images of illicit adventure even though the adventure quotient here is close to zero. In Northern Thai this village is pronounced 'Sop Huak'; many out-of-town Thais don't know either Thai name and simply call it 'Saam Liam Thong Kham' (Thai for 'Golden Triangle').

Tourists have replaced opium as the local source of gold. Sop Ruak has in fact become something of a tourist trap, with souvenir stalls, restaurants, a massage place and busloads of package-tour visitors during the day. In the evenings things are quieter. Good yâams can be purchased for 50B without much bargaining.

One place worth a visit is the **House of Opium**, a small museum with historical displays pertaining to opium culture. Exhibits include all the various implements used in the planting, harvest, use and trade of *Papaver* *somniferum* resin, including pipes, weights, scales and so on, plus photos and maps. Most labels are in Thai only. The museum is at Km 30, at the south-eastern end of Sop Ruak. It's open daily from 7 am to 6 pm; admission is 10B.

On the Burmese side of the river junction you may notice the construction site for the upcoming Golden Triangle Paradise Resort, a huge hotel-and-trade project financed by a wealthy Thai businessman from Suphanburi and his Japanese partners who have leased nearly 3000 rai from the Myanmar government. The site has become the man's private fiefdom – no-one enters or leaves the area without his permission (visas are superfluous). Work on the resort has been stop and go due to fighting between the MTA and Yangon forces, but the latest word is that the project's still on. In addition to the 300 hotel rooms and a trade centre, plans for the complex include an 18 hole golf course, helipad, hospital and hovercraft pier. Rumours persist that the hotel will eventually add a casino, which will not only draw business from Thailand, Laos and Myanmar but will also play host to visiting riverboats from China. Only two currencies – baht and dollars – will be accepted at the hotel.

**Maekhong River Cruises** Local long-tail or speedboat boat trips can be arranged through several local agents. The typical trip involves a two hour circuit around a large island in the river for 200B per person, with a four person minimum. Longer trips head downriver as far as Chiang Khong for 450 to 500B per person return.

Six large express ferries of German/Thai make are now docked at a massive pier on the river bank between Chiang Saen and Sop Ruak. Similar in style to the express boats that go to Ko Samui in Southern Thailand, these boats are powered by two 760 hp engines and will eventually be used to ferry passengers back and forth to China's Yunnan Province. A pilot trip was accomplished in January 1994, but regular service still hasn't been established (the latest estimate is 1997). Most likely these Thailand-China trips will

be available only as part of an expensive package that will include meals and some sightseeing. It may be a long time coming; getting the governments of Thailand, Myanmar, Laos and China to agree on regulations is a major obstacle.

Currently the 88-passenger 'jetboats' use Chiang Khong, farther south, as a terminal for Maekhong River cruises. Operator MP World Transport (☎ (53) 784071), 127/1 Muu 1 Chiang Saen, claims these boats can cruise at 35 kph on open water, but average 15 kph in challenging sections of the river. A two hour cruise to Ban Muang Mom in Laos and back costs 500B in economy class, 650B in VIP class (16 seats), including beverages on board and dinner at Ha Chiang Plaza opposite the wharf.

**Places to Stay & Eat** Most budget travellers stay in Chiang Saen these days. Virtually all the former budget places in Sop Ruak have given way to souvenir stalls and larger tourist hotels.

*MP World Villa*, at the eastern edge of Sop Ruak, offers wooden bungalows for 700B with fan, 900B air-con – about 500B more than they're worth. In the same price range but better value is *Debavalya Park Resort* (☎ (53) 784113; fax 784224), just past the 'Golden Triangle' sign. Simple clean rooms with good beds cost 500B single/double with fan, 600B with air-con; all rooms have hot showers.

In the top-end hotel category, the 73-room *Delta Golden Triangle Resort Hotel* (☎ (53) 784001; (2) 260-6108 in Bangkok) is on a hillside overlooking the river and offers first-class accommodation from 1500B.

Also at the top end, *Le Meridien Baan Boran Hotel* (☎ (53) 716678; (2) 254-8147 in Bangkok) is on a secluded hillside spot off the road between Sop Ruak and Mae Sai. Designed by Thai architect ML Tridhosyuth Devakul, the Baan Boran melds classic Northern Thai design motifs with modern resort hotel tricks like cathedral ceilings and skylights. To fit the naughty Golden Triangle image, one of the restaurants is called *Suan Fin* (Opium Field) and is decorated with poppy motifs; windows off the dining area serve up a view of Myanmar and Laos in the distance. The hotel bar is called Trafficker Rendezvous. What does it cost to stay amidst this glorification of the regional narcotics trade? Singles are 1500 to 2000B, doubles 2200 to 2500B and one-bedroom suites 5000B.

**Getting There & Away** From Chiang Saen to Sop Ruak, a songthaew/share taxi costs 10B; these leave every 20 minutes or so throughout the day. It's an easy bike ride from Chiang Saen to Sop Ruak.

### Chiang Khong
เชียงของ

At one time Chiang Khong was part of a small riverbank meuang called Juon, founded in 701 AD by King Mahathai. Over the centuries Juon paid tribute to Chiang Rai, then Chiang Saen and finally Nan before being occupied by the Siamese in the 1880s. The territory of Chiang Khong extended all the way to Yunnan Province in China until the French turned much of the Maekhong River's left bank into French Indochina in 1893.

More remote yet more lively than Chiang Saen, Chiang Khong is an important market town for local hill tribes and for trade – legal and illegal – with northern Laos. Nearby are several villages inhabited by Mien and White Hmong. Among the latter are contingents who fled Laos during the 1975 communist takeover and who are rumoured to be involved in an organised resistance movement against the current Lao government.

Today's Chiang Khong has several Northern-style wats of minor interest. **Wat Luang**, on the main road, was once one of the most important temples in Chiang Rai Province and features a chedi dating to the 13th century (restored in 1881).

On a hill overlooking the town and river

NORTHERN THAILAND

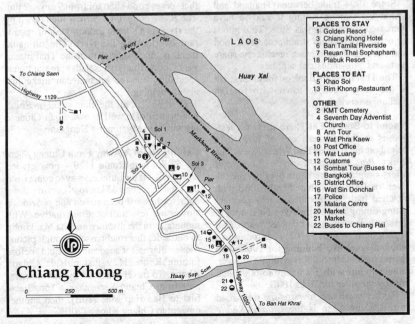

**PLACES TO STAY**
1 Golden Resort
3 Chiang Khong Hotel
6 Ban Tamila Riverside
7 Reuan Thai Sophapham
18 Plabuk Resort

**PLACES TO EAT**
5 Khao Soi
13 Rim Khong Restaurant

**OTHER**
2 KMT Cemetery
4 Seventh Day Adventist Church
8 Ann Tour
9 Wat Phra Kaew
10 Post Office
11 Wat Luang
12 Customs
14 Sombat Tour (Buses to Bangkok)
15 District Office
16 Wat Sin Donchai
17 Police
19 Malaria Centre
20 Market
21 Market
22 Buses to Chiang Rai

**Chiang Khong**

LAOS

Huay Xai

To Chiang Saen

Highway 1129

Maekhong River

Soi 1
Soi 2
Soi 3

Pier
Ferry
Pier
Pier
Pier

Huay Sop Som

Highway 1020

To Ban Hat Khrai

0    250    500 m

is a **Nationalist Chinese Soldiers Cemetery** where over 200 KMT soldiers are interred. The grave mounds are angled on the hill so that they face China. A shrine containing old photos of KMT soldiers-in-arms stands at the top of the hill.

The village of **Ban Hat Khrai**, about a km south of Chiang Khong, is famous as being one of the few places where *plaa bèuk* (giant Maekhong catfish) are still caught, probably the largest freshwater fish in the world. Locals says that these fish swim all the way from Qinghai Province (where the Maekhong originates) in northern China.

Huay Xai, opposite Chiang Khong on the Lao side of the river, is a legal point of entry for Laos. Anyone with a valid Laos visa may cross by ferry, but a new international bridge is being built across the Maekhong River to establish a road link between Chiang Khong and Huay Xai. From Huay Xai it's 250 km to Luang Nam Tha, a short distance from Boten, a legal border crossing to/from China. See Crossing to Laos below for details.

Since 1994 trade between Thailand and China via Chiang Khong is said to have increased by as much as 80%. Thai goods going north include dried/processed food and beverages, cosmetics, machinery, spare parts and agro-industrial supplies.

The Thai Farmers Bank on the main street is the only place in town with foreign exchange services.

**Places to Stay & Eat**  There are two guesthouses at the northern end of town in a neighbourhood called Ban Wiang Kaew. The funky *Ban Tamila Riverside Bungalows* offers simple thatched huts overlooking the river for 100B with shared bath, 200B with attached bath; there's also a very pleasant sitting/dining area by the river. Next door to the south, the newer and fancier *Reuan Thai Sophapharn* (☎ (53) 791023) has rooms in a wooden hotel-like building for 100B with shared bath, 150 to 200B with hot shower, fancier rooms with TV for up to 600B and huts by the river for 70 to 100B.

Farther north and towards the river road from Chiang Saen is the *Chiang Khong*

*Hotel* (☎ (53) 791182). Plain but nicely kept singles/doubles with hot shower and fan are 120/150B, 300B with air-con.

On the southern outskirts of town on the river and towards the bus terminal, the *Plabuk Resort* (☎ (53) 791281; (2) 258-0423 in Bangkok) features 16 spacious rooms with air-con, hot water and comfortable beds for 500B a single/double. A restaurant and bar are well separated from the guest rooms.

Next to the KMT cemetery, high on a hill overlooking Chiang Khong, the river and Huay Xai, is the *Golden Resort* (☎ (53) 791350). Large, well appointed rooms with air-con and private hot bath cost 650B; the resort's entrance is off Highway 1129, the road to Chiang Saen. The only drawback is that the resort is so high up that noise from vehicles and from diesel boats on the Maekhong beams straight into the rooms.

There are a number of rice and noodle shops along the main street, none of them particularly good. Just north-west of Ban Tamila Riverside Bungalows is a foodstall that serves good khâo sòi from 9 am to 2 pm. The *Rim Khong*, on a narrow road down by the river, is a simple indoor/outdoor restaurant overlooking the river. The bilingual menu is much shorter than the Thai menu; yam (spicy Thai-style salads) are the house speciality, but the kitchen can make just about anything.

*Lawt Tin Lu*, off the main street on Soi 2, is a branch of a well known Shan-Chinese restaurant in Myanmar's Kengtung.

**Getting There & Away**  From Chiang Saen, the 52-km-long Route 1129 – now graded and paved – is the quickest way to come from the west. A second 65 km road curving along the river has just been paved and provides a slower but less trafficked alternative. With mountains in the distance and the Maekhong to one side, this road passes through picturesque villages, tobacco and rice fields before joining Route 1129 just outside Chiang Khong. To travel this road by public transport from Chiang Saen, take a songthaew first to Ban Hap Mae (20B), then another onward to Chiang Khong (20B).

Buses from Chiang Rai and beyond use roads from the south (primarily Route 1020) to reach Chiang Khong. The Chiang Rai bus (No 2127, red) costs 31B and takes about three hours; there are departures approximately every 15 minutes from 4.45 am to 5.45 pm daily.

Air-con buses to/from Bangkok cost 370B and take around 13 hours.

Boats taking up to 10 passengers can be chartered up the Maekhong River from Chiang Khong to Chiang Saen for 800B. Boat crews can be contacted near the customs pier behind Wat Luang, or farther north at the pier for ferries to Laos.

**Crossing to Laos** Ferries to Huay Xai, Laos, leave frequently from a pier at the northern end of Chiang Khong for 20B each way. As long as you hold a visa valid for Laos, there should be no problem crossing. If you don't already have a visa, Ann Tour (☎/fax (53) 791218) on the main road in town near Ban Tamila Guest House can arrange one in one day for 1700B; if you submit your passport to the office at 8 am, they'll have it back to you, complete with visa, by 3 pm – in time to get across the river and start your Laos journey.

Once on the Lao side you can continue on by road to Luang Nam Tha and Udomxai or by boat down the Maekhong to Luang Prabang and Vientiane. Lao Aviation flies from Huay Xai to Vientiane a couple of times a week.

Close to the Maekhong River ferry pier in Huay Xai is the basic *Manilat Hotel* with clean, very adequate rooms for 6000 kip (162B) single/double. For more information on Huay Xai, see Lonely Planet's *Laos* guide.

# Phrae Province

Phrae Province is probably most famous for the distinctive sêua mâw hâwm, the indigo-dyed cotton farmer's shirt seen all over Thailand. 'Made in Phrae' has always been a sign of distinction for these staples of rural Thai life, and since the student-worker-farmer political solidarity of the 1970s, even Thai university professors like to wear them. The cloth is made in Ban Thung Hong outside the town of Phrae.

The annual Rocket Festival kicks off the rice-growing season in May. In Phrae the biggest celebrations take place in **Long** and **Sung Men** districts. Look for launching towers in the middle of rice fields for the exact location.

Sung Men district is also known for **Talaat Hua Dong**, a market specialising in carved teak wood. Phrae was, and still is, an important teak centre. Along Route 101 between Phrae and Nan you'll see a steady blur of teak forests (thickest around Km 25). Since the 1989 national ban on logging, these forests are all protected by law. Most of the provincial teak business now involves recycled timber from old houses. Specially licensed cuts from fallen teak wood may also be used for decorative carving or furniture (but not house construction). The latest threat to the teak forests is a controversial dam project that developers claim is necessary to prevent food disasters in the Chao Phraya River basin; so far environmental groups have been able to keep the dam at bay.

The province of Phrae and its neighbouring province of Nan have been neglected by tourists and travellers alike because of their remoteness from Chiang Mai, but from Den Chai – on the northern train route – they're easily reached by bus along Route 101.

## PHRAE
อ.เมืองแพร่
• ☎ (54) • pop 21,000

This provincial capital is only 23 km from the Den Chai station on the Chiang Mai line. Like Chiang Mai and Lampang, Phrae has an old city partially surrounded by a moat alongside a river (here, the Yom River). Unlike Chiang Mai, Phrae's old city still has lots of quiet lanes and old teak houses – if you're a fan of traditional Thai teak architecture, you'll find more of it here than in any other city of similar size anywhere in Thailand. The local temple architecture has successfully resisted Central Thai influence over the centuries as well. It's a bit unusual since you'll find a mix of Burmese, Northern Thai (Nan and Lanna) and Lao styles.

South-east of the old city, the newer, more modern Phrae looks like any other medium-sized town in Thailand.

If you're in the market for baskets or woven mats, a shop called Kamrai Thong (no roman-script sign) near the Pratuchai gate carries a fine selection of handwoven basketry.

## Information

Phrae's GPO stands near the centre of the old city near the traffic circle. Long-distance calls can be made at the attached CAT office daily from 8 am to 8 pm.

Bangkok Bank and Krung Thai Bank, both on Charoen Meuang Rd, offer foreign exchange services during normal banking hours (8.30 am to 3.30 pm); both also have ATMs.

## Wat Luang
วัดหลวง

This is the oldest wat in the city, probably dating to the founding of the city in the 12th or 13th century. **Phra That Luang Chang Kham**, the large octagonal Lanna-style chedi, sits on a square base with elephants coming out of all four sides, surrounded by kutis and coconut palms. As is sometimes seen in Phrae and Nan, the chedi is usually swathed in Thai Lü silk.

The veranda of the main wihǎan is in the classic Luang Prabang-Lan Xang style but has unfortunately been bricked in with laterite. Opposite the front of the wihǎan is **Pratu Khong**, part of the city's original entrance gate. No longer used as a gate, it now contains a statue of Chao Pu, an early Lanna ruler. The image is sacred to local residents, who leave offerings of fruit, flowers, candles and incense.

Also on the wat grounds is a **museum** displaying temple antiques, ceramics and religious art from the Lanna, Nan, Pegu and Mon periods. A 16th century, Phrae-made sitting Buddha on the 2nd floor is particularly exquisite. There are also some 19th century photos with English labels on display, including some gruesome shots of a beheading. The museum is usually open weekends only, but the monks will sometimes open it mid-week upon request.

## Wat Phra Non
วัดพระนอน

South-west a few hundred metres from Wat Luang is a 300 year old wat named after its highly revered reclining Buddha image. The bòt was built around 200 years ago and has a very impressive three-tiered roof with a separate two-tiered portico and gilded carved wooden facade with *Ramayana* scenes. The wihǎan behind the bòt contains the Phra Non (a reclining Buddha), swathed in Thai Lü cloth with bead and foil decoration.

## Wat Jom Sawan
วัดจอมสวรรค์

Outside the old city on Ban Mai Rd, this temple was built by local Shan early this century, and shows Shan and Burmese influence throughout. The well preserved wooden wihǎans and bòt have high, tiered, tower-like roofs like those found in Mandalay. A large copper-crowned chedi has lost most of its stucco to reveal the artful brickwork beneath. A prized temple possession in the main wihǎan is a tripitaka (Buddhist scriptures) section consisting of 16 ivory pages engraved in Burmese. As in Lampang, temples like this were originally sponsored by Burmese teak merchants who immigrated to Northern Thailand at the turn of the century.

## Other Temples

Just outside the north-eastern corner of the moat, **Wat Sa Baw Kaew** is a Shan-Burmese-style temple similar to Wat Jom Sawan. **Wat Phra Ruang**, inside the old city, is typical of Phrae's many old city wats, with a Nan-style, cruciform-plan bòt, a Lao-style wihǎan and a Lanna chedi.

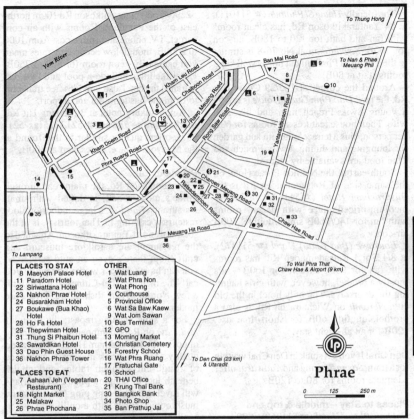

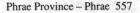

**Phrae**

0    125    250 m

To Thung Hong

Ban Mai Road

To Nan & Phae
Meuang Phii

Yom River

Kham Leu Road

Chaiboon Road

Rawp Meuang Road

Rong Saw Road

Yantarakikoson Road

Kham Doem Road

Phra Ruang Road

Charoen Meuang Road

Ratsadamdoen Road

Chaw Hae Road

Meuang Hit Road

To Wat Phra That
Chaw Hae & Airport (9 km)

To Lampang

To Den Chai (23 km)
& Utaradit

NORTHERN THAILAND

| PLACES TO STAY | OTHER |
| --- | --- |
| 8 Maeyom Palace Hotel | 1 Wat Luang |
| 11 Paradorn Hotel | 2 Wat Phra Non |
| 22 Siriwattana Hotel | 3 Wat Phong |
| 23 Nakhon Phrae Hotel | 4 Courthouse |
| 24 Busarakham Hotel | 5 Provincial Office |
| 27 Boukawe (Bua Khao) | 6 Wat Sa Baw Kaew |
| Hotel | 9 Wat Jom Sawan |
| 28 Ho Fa Hotel | 10 Bus Terminal |
| 29 Thepwiman Hotel | 12 GPO |
| 31 Thung Si Phaibun Hotel | 13 Morning Market |
| 32 Sawatdikan Hotel | 14 Christian Cemetery |
| 33 Dao Phin Guest House | 15 Forestry School |
| 36 Nakhon Phrae Tower | 16 Wat Phra Ruang |
| | 17 Pratuchai Gate |
| PLACES TO EAT | 19 School |
| 7 Aahaan Jeh (Vegetarian | 20 THAI Office |
| Restaurant) | 21 Krung Thai Bank |
| 18 Night Market | 30 Bangkok Bank |
| 25 Malakaw | 34 Photo Shop |
| 26 Phrae Phochana | 35 Ban Prathup Jai |

One day an art historian is going to have to sort out this temple mix – I suspect there's a uniform design of local (Nan-Phrae) provenance that hasn't yet been identified.

### Ban Prathup Jai (Prathapjai)
ข้านประทับใจ

You can see lots of good woodcarving in Phrae. On the western outskirts of town is Ban Prathup Jai (Impressive House), also called Ban Sao Roi Tan (Hundred Pillar-Filled House), a large Northern-style teak house which was built using more than 130 teak logs, each over 3000 years old. Opened in 1985, the house took four years to build, using timber taken from nine old rural houses. The interior pillars are ornately carved. It's open daily 8 am to 5 pm; admission is 20B.

### Places to Stay – bottom end

Several inexpensive hotels can be found along Charoen Meuang Rd, including *Ho Fa*, *Siriwattana* and *Thepwiman*, all of which have rooms for 80 to 120B; Thepwiman is the best of the bunch, followed closely by Ho Fa.

The friendly *Thung Si Phaibun* (☎ 511011), at 84 Yantarakitkoson Rd, has clean rooms with fan and bath for 120 to 180B, air-con for 300B. *Sawatdikan* at No 76-8 is similar to the Thung Si Phaibun but not as well kept; rooms start at 80B.

Around the corner at 105/29 Chaw Hae Rd, the new *Dao Phin Guest House* is run by a young Swiss-French man and his Thai wife. Their house features six rooms for 60B per person, plus a terrace/solarium and garden for lounging and dining. Swiss-French and Thai food are available by request.

South-east of the Nakhon Phrae Hotel on the same side of Ratsadamnoen Rd is the *Busarakham Hotel* (☎ 511437), a low to medium-priced place with decent rooms with fan for 140/160B single/double, 300B air-con.

*Boukawe (Bua Khao) Hotel* (☎ 511372), at 8/1 Soi 1 Ratsadamnoen Rd, has rooms with fan for 90B, air-con for 160B – it's mostly a brothel, however, with girls haunting the doorways. The only hotel in the old city, *Neramit* on Wichairacha Rd, is also a brothel, quoting 60B for short-time use, 120B for an all-night stay.

**Den Chai** If you get stuck in Den Chai waiting for a train, *Saeng Sawang* and *Yaowarat* offer adequate rooms for 80 to 120B.

### Places to Stay – middle & top end

*Nakhon Phrae Hotel* (☎ 511969) at 29 Ratsadamnoen Rd is a short walk from the old city. Large singles/doubles with fan and hot water cost 350B in the old wing; across the street in the new wing standard air-con rooms are 500 or 700B with TV and fridge. Local tourist information is available in the lobbies of both wings.

*Paradorn (Pharadon)* (☎ 511177), at 177 Yantarakitkoson Rd, has moderately priced singles/doubles with fan and bath for 180/220B, air-con rooms for 270 to 500B. Information on local attractions is available in the lobby, but the hotel is looking a bit run-down these days.

Towards the top of the scale in Phrae is the *Maeyom Palace Hotel* (☎ 522906; fax 522904) on Yantarakitkoson Rd 100m north-east of the Paradorn. Rooms with air-con, carpet, TV, phone and fridge cost from 1000 to 2000B, though low occupancy rates mean you can easily get a room for 600 to 750B. Hotel facilities include a pool and two restaurants; the hotel also provides free transport to/from the bus terminal and airport.

A new luxury hotel at 3 Meuang Hit Rd, *Nakhon Phrae Tower* (☎ 521321; fax 521-937), offers quality similar to that found at the Maeyom Palace. Rates start at 800B.

### Places to Eat

Yantarakitkoson Rd, the main road through Phrae's modern half, is dotted with small restaurants. *Ban Fai*, a large indoor/outdoor restaurant catering to Thai tourists, is at the southern end of Yantarakitkoson. Attached to the restaurant are a folklore museum and craft shop; there's even an auto service so you can have your car worked on while you eat! The menu is Thai-Chinese-farang, with a few Northern-Thai dishes, too. Prices are moderately high.

For a slow evening repast, the open-air *Malakaw* on Ratsadamnoen Rd (diagonally opposite the Busarakham Hotel) offers good quality food and drink in a rustic ambience of rough-cut wooden tables and chairs beneath lots of hanging plants. Vegetarians will revel in the hèt fang pîng (roasted straw mushrooms served with a chilli dip), when available, and the assortment of yam salads, including a delicious yam hèt hūu nūu or 'mouse-ear mushroom' salad. Malakaw is open daily from 3.30 pm to midnight.

Also on Ratsadamnoen Rd near the Nakhon Phrae Hotel and Busarakham Hotel are several other eating spots, including the inexpensive *Phrae Phochana*, which specialises in standard Thai fare. Two Chinese coffee shops right next to the Nakhon Phrae Hotel take turns holding court throughout the day – *Sing Ocha* in the morning, *Ah Hui Ocha* in the evening.

Not far from Wat Sa Baw Kaew and the Maeyom Palace Hotel off Ban Mai Rd is *Aahaan Jeh* (no roman or English sign), a Thai vegetarian place open 7 am to 7 pm.

A good night market convenes just outside the Pratuchai intersection every evening. Several food vendors also set up nightly in the soi opposite the Sawatdikan Hotel. There's another night market a block or two behind the Paradorn Hotel on weekday evenings only.

## Getting There & Away

**Air** THAI flies to Phrae daily from Bangkok for 1325B; the flight takes an hour and 20 minutes. There are also daily THAI flights between Nan and Phrae (300B, 25 minutes). The THAI office (☎ 511123) is at 42-44 Ratsadamnoen Rd, near the Nakhon Phrae Hotel. The Phrae airport is nine km south-east of town via the same road that goes to Wat Phra That Chaw Hae; THAI operates a free shuttle service between the airport and the THAI office.

**Bus** Ordinary buses from Bangkok's Northern Bus Terminal depart at 11.30 am, 6.30 and 9 pm for 132B. Air-con buses cost 238B and leave at 8.30, 8.45 and 8.50 pm; VIP (sleeper) buses cost 370B and leave at 8.30 and 8.45 pm.

From Chiang Mai's Arcade bus station, ordinary buses leave several times daily between 8 am and 5 pm (55B, four hours). An air-con bus leaves from the same station at 10 am and 10 pm (76B, 98B 1st class). From Sukhothai, ordinary buses are 48B, air-con 63B.

**Train** Trains to Den Chai station from Bangkok are 90B for 3rd class, 188B for 2nd class and 389B for 1st class, plus supplementary charges as they apply. The only trains that arrive at a decent hour are the No 101 ordinary (3rd class only, departs Bangkok at 7.05 am and arrives in Den Chai at 5.50 pm) and the No 59 rapid (2nd class only, leaves at 10 pm and arrives at 7.10 am). On the No 59 you can get a 2nd class sleeper.

Blue songthaews and red buses (No 193) leave the Den Chai station frequently for Phrae and cost 20B. In the opposite direction you can catch them anywhere along the south end of Yantarakitkoson Rd.

## Getting Around

A samlor anywhere in the old town costs 10B. Motorcycle taxis are available at the bus terminal; a trip from here to, say, the Pratuchai gate should cost you around 15 to 20B.

## AROUND PHRAE PROVINCE
### Wat Phra That Chaw Hae
วัดพระธาตุช่อแฮ

On a hill about nine km south-east of town off Route 1022, this wat is famous for its 33m-high gilded chedi. Chaw Hae is the name of the cloth that worshippers wrap around the chedi – it's a type of satin said to have originated in Xishuangbanna (Sipsongpanna, literally '12,000 fields in Northern Thai'). Like Chiang Mai's Wat Doi Suthep, this is an important pilgrimage site for Thais living in the North. The **Phra Jao Than Jai** Buddha image here – similar in appearance to Phra Jinnarat in Phitsanulok – is reputed to impart fertility to women who make offerings to it.

The bòt has a gilded wooden ceiling, rococo pillars and walls with lotus-bud mosaics. Tiered naga stairs lead to the temple compound; the hill-top is surrounded by a protected forest of mature teak trees.

Songthaews between the city and Phra That Chaw Hae are frequent and cost 10B.

### Phae Meuang Phii
แพะเมืองผี

The name means 'Ghost-Land', a reference to this strange geological phenomenon about 18 km north-east of Phrae off Route 101. Erosion has created bizarre pillars of soil and rock that look like giant fungi. The area has recently been made a provincial park; there are shaded tables and food vendors near the entrance – you may need a drink after wandering around the baked surfaces between the eroded pillars.

Getting there by public transport entails a bus ride nine km towards Nan, getting off at the signposted turn-off for Phae Meuang Phii, and then catching a songthaew another six km to a second right-hand turn-off to the park. From this point you must walk or hitch about 2.5 km to reach the entrance.

## Mabri Hill Tribe
ชนเผ่ามาบรี

Along the border of Phrae and Nan provinces live the remaining members of the Mabri (sometimes spelt Mrabri or Mlabri) hill tribe, whom the Thais call *phīi thong leŭang* ('spirits of the yellow leaves'). The most nomadic of all the tribes in Thailand, the Mabri customarily move on when the leaves of their temporary huts turn yellow, hence their Thai name. Now, however, their numbers have been greatly reduced (possibly to as few as 150) and experts suspect that few of the Mabri still migrate in the traditional way.

Traditionally, the Mabri are strict hunter-gatherers but many now work as field labourers for Thais, or other hill-tribe groups such as the Hmong, in exchange for pigs and cloth. Little is known about the tribe's belief system, but it is said that the Mabri believe they are not entitled to cultivate the land for themselves. A Mabri woman typically changes partners every five or six years, taking any children from the previous union with her. The Mabris' knowledge of medicinal plants is said to be enormous, encompassing the effective use of herbs for fertility and contraception, and for the treatment of snake or centipede poisoning. When a member of the tribe dies, the body is put in a tree top to be eaten by birds.

In Phrae Province there is a small settlement of around 40 Mabri living in Rong Khwang district (north-east of the provincial capital, near Phae Meuang Phii) under the protection/control of American missionary Eugene Long. Long calls himself 'Boonyuen Suksaneh' and the Mabris' village 'Ban Boonyuen' – a classic scenario right out of Peter Mathiessen's *At Play in the Fields of the Lord*. Ban Boonyuen can only be reached on foot or by elephant; the nearest village linked by road is 12 km away.

Several Mabri families abandoned Ban Boonyuen in early 1992 and are now living in Hmong villages in Phrae and Nan. The remaining 100 or so Mabri live across the provincial border in Nan. The Thai government operates a 'Pre-Agricultural Development of Mabri Society Project' in both provinces to ease the Mabri into modern rural society without an accompanying loss of culture. According to project leaders, the effort is necessary to protect the Mabri from becoming a slave society within Northern Thailand's increasingly capitalist rural economy. Because of their anti-materialist beliefs, the Mabri perform menial labour for the Hmong and other hill tribes for little or no compensation.

# Nan Province

One of Thailand's 'remote provinces' (an official Thai government designation), Nan was once so choked with bandits and PLAT insurgents that travellers were discouraged from visiting. Before the early 1980s the Thai government couldn't get any roads built in the province because guerrillas would periodically destroy highway building equipment at night.

With the successes of the Thai army and a more stable political machine in Bangkok during the last two decades, Nan has opened up and more roads are being built. The roads that link the provincial capital with the nearby provinces of Chiang Rai, Phrae and Utaradit pass through exquisite scenery of rich river valleys and rice fields. Like Loei in the North-East, this is a province to be explored for its natural beauty and its likeable people, who live close to traditional rural rhythms.

Nan remains a largely rural province with not a factory or condo in sight. Most of the inhabitants are agriculturally employed, growing sticky rice, beans, corn, tobacco and vegetables in the fertile river plains. Nan is also famous for two fruits: *fai jiin* (a Chinese version of Thailand's indigenous *má-fai*) and *sôm sǐi thong*, golden-skinned oranges. The latter are Nan's most famous export, commanding high prices in Bangkok and Malaysia. Apparently the cooler winter weather in Nan turns the skin orange (lowland Thai oranges are mostly green) and imparts a unique sweet-tart flavour. Thung Chang

JOE CUMMINGS

JOE CUMMINGS

## Northern Thailand
Top: A sea of fog surrounds Doi Kong Mu at dawn, Mae Hong Son
Bottom: A misty morning in Mae Sariang, Yuam River valley near the Myanmar border

JOE CUMMINGS

JOE CUMMINGS

JOE CUMMINGS

### Northern Thailand

Top: Familiar teaming of farmer and ox, Northern rice fields
Middle: Aspiring beauty queen contestants, Chiang Mai
Bottom: After the rice harvest, Um Phang

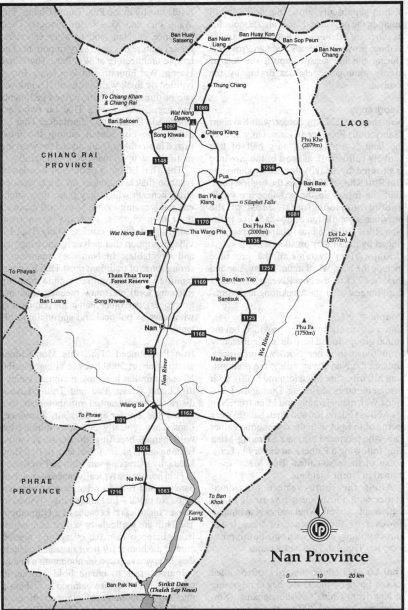

**Nan Province**

0     10     20 km

district supposedly grows the best sôm sĩi thong in the province. Nan is also famous for its *phrík yài hâeng*, long hot chillies similar to those grown in China's Sichuan Province. During the hot season, you'll see lots of highly photogenic chillies drying by the roadside.

### Geography

Nan shares a 227 km border with Sayaburi (Sainyabuli) Province in Laos. Only 25% of the land is arable (and only half of that actively cultivated), as most of the province is covered by heavily forested mountains; **Doi Phu Kha**, at 2000m, is the highest peak. Half the forests in the province are virgin upland monsoon forest. Most of the province's population of 364,000 live in the Nan River valley, a bowl-shaped depression ringed by mountains on all sides.

Major river systems in the province include the Nan, Wa, Samun, Haeng, Lae and Pua. At 627 km, the Nan River is Thailand's third longest after the Maekhong and Mun.

### People

Nan is a sparsely populated province, but the ethnic groups found here differ significantly from those in other Northern provinces. Outside the Nan River valley, the predominant hill tribes are Mien (around 8000), with smaller numbers of Hmong. During the Indochina War, many Hmong and Mien from Nan (as well as Chiang Rai and Phetchabun) were recruited to fight with the communist Pathet Lao, who promised to create a Hmong-Mien king following a Pathet Lao victory in Laos. Some of these so-called 'Red Meos' even trained in North Vietnam.

Along the south-western provincial border with Phrae are a few small Mabri settlements as well. What makes Nan unique, however, is the presence of three lesser known groups seldom seen outside this province: the Thai Lü, Htin and Khamu.

**Thai Lü** This ethnic minority, often called Lua or Lawa by the Thais, began migrating to Nan from China's Xishuangbanna (Sipsongpanna) around 200 years ago and now reside mostly in the Pua, Thung Chang, Tha Wang Pha and Mae Jarim districts. Their influence on Nan (and to a lesser extent, Phrae) culture has been very important. The temple architecture at Wat Phra That Chae Haeng, Wat Phumin and Wat Nong Bua – typified by thick walls with small windows, two or three-tiered roofs, curved pediments and naga lintels – is a Thai Lü (who are Theravada Buddhists) inheritance. Thai Lü fabrics are considered among the most prized in Northern Thailand and the weaving motifs show up in many Nan handicrafts.

The Thai Lü build traditional wooden or bamboo-thatched houses on thick wooden stilts, beneath which they place their kitchens and weaving looms. Many still make all their own clothes, typically sewn from indigo-dyed cotton fabrics. Many Thai Lü villages support themselves by growing rice and vegetables. In Nan they maintain a strong sense of tradition; most Thai Lü communities still recognise a chao meuang (meuang lord) and maw meuang (meuang astrologer), two older men in the community who serve as political and spiritual consultants.

**Htin** Pronounced 'Tin', this Mon-Khmer group of about 3000 lives in villages in the 50 or so families in remote mountain valleys of Chiang Klang, Pua and Thung Chang districts. A substantial number also live across the border in Sayaburi Province, Laos. They typically subsist by hunting for wild game, breeding domestic animals, farming small plots of land and, in Ban Baw Kleua, by extracting salt from salt wells.

Htin houses are typically made of thatched bamboo and raised on bamboo or wooden stilts. No metal – including nails – is used in house construction because of a Htin taboo. The Htin are particularly skilled at manipulating bamboo to make everything needed around the house; for floor mats and baskets they interweave pared bamboo with a black-coloured grass to create bold geometric patterns. They also use bamboo to fashion a musical instrument of stepped pipes – similar to the *angklung* of Central Thailand

and Indonesia – which is shaken to produce musical tones. The Htin don't weave their own fabrics, often buying clothes from neighbouring Miens.

**Khamu** Like the Thai Lü, the Khamu migrated to Nan around 150 years ago from Sipsongpanna. There are now around 5000 in Nan (more than anywhere else in Thailand), mostly in the Wiang Sa, Thung Chang, Chiang Klang and Pua districts. Their villages are established near streams; their houses have dirt floors like those of the Hmong but their roofs sport crossed beams similar to the Northern Thai kalae (locally called *kapkri-aak*). The Khamu are skilled at metalwork and perform regular rituals to placate Salok, the spirit of the forge. Khamu villages are usually very self-sufficient; villagers hold fast to tradition and are known to value thrift and hard work. Ban Huay Sataeng in Thung Chang district is one of the largest and easiest Khamu villages to visit in the province.

## NAN
อ.เมืองน่าน
• ☎ *(54)* • *pop 25,000*

Just over 668 km from Bangkok, little-known Nan is steeped in history. For centuries Meuang Nan was an isolated, independent kingdom with few ties to the outside world. Ample evidence of prehistoric habitation exists, but it wasn't until several small meuangs (ancient Thai river-valley states) consolidated to form Nanthaburi on the Nan River in the mid-1300s – concurrent with the founding of Luang Prabang and the Lan Xang (Million Elephants) kingdom in Laos – that the city became a power to contend with. Associated with the powerful Sukhothai kingdom, the city-state took the title Waranakhon (in Sanskrit its Varanagara, or Excellent City) and played a significant role in the development of early Thai nationalism.

Towards the end of the 14th century Nan became one of the nine Northern Thai-Lao principalities that comprised Lan Na Thai ('million Thai fields', now known as Lanna) and the city-state flourished throughout the 15th century under the name Chiang Klang or Middle City, a reference to its position roughly midway between Chiang Mai (New City) and Chiang Thong (Golden City, today's Luang Prabang). The Burmese, however, took control of the kingdom in 1558 and transferred many inhabitants to Myanmar as slaves; the city was all but abandoned until western Thailand was wrested from the Burmese in 1786. The local dynasty then regained local sovereignty and remained semi-autonomous until 1931 when Nan finally accepted full Bangkok sponsorship.

Parts of the old city wall and several early wats dating from the Lanna period can be seen in present-day Nan. Meuang Nan's wats are quite distinctive. Some temple structures show Lanna influence, while others belong to the Thai Lü legacy brought from Sipsongpanna, the Thai Lü's historical homeland.

### Orientation & Information
**Maps** Useful maps of the capital and province are available at Doi Phukha Guest House.

**Immigration** One of the closest immigration offices is in Thung Chang, about a hundred km north of Nan. You should be able to extend visas here.

**Money** Bangkok Bank and Thai Farmers Bank on Sumonthewarat Rd, near the Nan Fah and Dhevaraj hotels, operate foreign exchange services. Both also have ATMs.

**Post & Communications** The GPO on Mahawong Rd in the centre of the city is open from 8.30 am to noon and 1 to 3.30 pm, Monday to Friday, and from 8 am to noon on weekends and holidays. The attached CAT office offers international phone service daily from 7 am to 10 pm.

## Nan National Museum
พิพิธภัณฑ์แห่งชาติน่าน

Housed in the 1903 vintage palace of Nan's last two feudal lords (Phra Chao Suriyapongpalidet and Chao Mahaphrom Surathada), this museum first opened its doors in 1973. Recent renovations have made it one of the most up-to-date provincial museums in Thailand. Unlike most provincial museums in the country, this one also has English labels for many items on display.

The ground floor is divided into six exhibition rooms with ethnological exhibits covering the various ethnic groups found in the province, including the Northern Thais, Thai Lü, Htin, Khamu, Mabri, Hmong and Mien. Among the items on display are silverwork, textiles, folk utensils and tribal costumes. On the 2nd floor of the museum are exhibits on Nan history, archaeology, local architecture, royal regalia, weapons, ceramics and religious art.

The museum's collection of Buddha images includes rare Lanna styles as well as the floppy-eared local styles, usually wooden standing images in the 'calling for rain' pose (with hands at the sides, pointing down), which show a marked Luang Prabang influence. The astute museum curators posit a Nan style of art in Buddhist sculpture; some examples on display seem very imitative of other Thai styles, while others are quite distinctive – the ears curve outwards. Also on display on the 2nd floor is a rare 'black' (actually reddish-brown) elephant tusk said to have been presented to a Nan lord over 300 years ago. The tusk is held aloft by a wooden garuda sculpture.

The museum is open Wednesday to Sunday from 9 am to noon and 1 to 4 pm. Admission is 10B. A building adjacent to the museum has a few books on Thai art and archaeology for sale.

## Wat Phumin
วัดภูมินทร์

Nan's most famous temple is celebrated for its cruciform bòt which was constructed in 1596 and restored during the reign of Chao Anantavorapitthidet (1867-74). Murals on the walls depicting the Khatta Kumara and Nimi jatakas were executed during the restoration by Thai Lü artists; the bòt exterior exemplifies the work of Thai Lü architects as well. The murals are considered of historic as well as aesthetic importance since they incorporate scenes of local life from the era in which they were painted.

The ornate altar in the centre of the bòt has four sides with four Sukhothai-style sitting Buddhas in *marawichai* pose ('victory over Mara'; one hand touching the ground) facing in each direction.

## Wat Phra That Chae Haeng
วัดพระธาตุแช่แห้ง

Two km past the bridge which spans the Nan River, heading south-east out of town, this very old temple dating from 1355 is the most sacred wat in Nan Province. It is set in a square, walled enclosure on a hill with a view of Nan and the valley. The Thai Lü-influenced bòt features a triple-tiered roof with carved wooden eaves, and dragon reliefs over the doors. A gilded Lanna-style chedi sits on a large square base next to the bòt with sides measuring 22.5m long; the entire chedi is 55.5m high.

## Wat Phra That Chang Kham
วัดพระธาตุช้างค้ำ

This is the second most important temple in the city after Wat Phumin; the founding date is unknown. The main wihãan, reconstructed in 1458, has a huge seated Buddha image and faint murals in the process of being painstakingly uncovered. (Earlier this century an abbot reportedly ordered the murals to be whitewashed because he thought they were distracting worshippers from concentrating on his sermons.)

Also in the wihãan is a collection of Lanna-period scrolls inscribed (in Lanna script) not only with the usual Buddhist scriptures but with the history, law and astrology of the times. A Nan-style *thammat* (a throne once used by abbots during sermons) sits to one side.

NORTHERN THAILAND

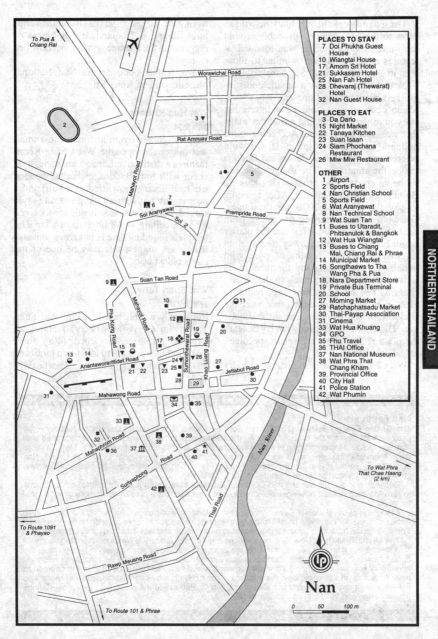

PLACES TO STAY
7 Doi Phukha Guest
  House
10 Wiangtai House
17 Amorn Sri Hotel
21 Sukkasem Hotel
25 Nan Fah Hotel
28 Dhevaraj (Thewarat)
   Hotel
32 Nan Guest House

PLACES TO EAT
3 Da Dario
15 Night Market
22 Tanaya Kitchen
23 Suan Isaan
24 Siam Phochana
   Restaurant
26 Miw Miw Restaurant

OTHER
1 Airport
2 Sports Field
4 Nan Christian School
5 Sports Field
6 Wat Aranyawat
8 Nan Technical School
9 Wat Suan Tan
11 Buses to Utaradit,
   Phitsanulok & Bangkok
12 Wat Hua Wiangtai
13 Buses to Chiang
   Mai, Chiang Rai & Phrae
14 Municipal Market
16 Songthaews to Tha
   Wang Pha & Pua
18 Nara Department Store
19 Private Bus Terminal
20 School
27 Morning Market
29 Ratchaphatsadu Market
30 Thai-Payap Association
31 Cinema
33 Wat Hua Khuang
34 GPO
35 Fhu Travel
36 THAI Office
37 Nan National Museum
38 Wat Phra That
   Chang Kham
39 Provincial Office
40 City Hall
41 Police Station
42 Wat Phumin

Worawichai Road

To Pua &
Chiang Rai

Rat Amnuay Road

Premprida Road

Soi Aranyawat

Suan Tan Road

Mahayot Road

Pha Kong Road

Anantaworarittidet Road

Mahawong Road

Sulnonthewarat Road

Khao Luang Road

Jettabut Road

Mahaphrom Road

Suriyaphong Road

Rawp Meuang Road

Thali Road

Nan River

To Wat Phra
That Chae Haeng
(2 km)

To Route 1091
& Phayao

To Route 101 & Phrae

Nan

0    50    100 m

NORTHERN THAILAND

The magnificent chedi behind the wihãan dates to the 14th century, probably around the same time the temple was founded. It features elephant supports similar to those seen in Sukhothai and Si Satchanalai.

Next to the chedi is a small, undistinguished bòt from the same era. Wat Chang Kham's current abbot told me an interesting story involving the bòt and a Buddha image that was once kept inside. According to his holiness, in 1955 art historian AB Griswold offered to purchase the 145-cm-tall Buddha inside the small bòt. The image appeared to be a crude Sukhothai-style walking Buddha moulded of plaster. After agreeing to pay the abbot 25,000B for the image, Griswold began removing the image from the bòt – but as he did it fell and the plaster around the statue broke away to reveal an original Sukhothai Buddha of pure gold underneath. Needless to say, the abbot made Griswold give it back, much to the latter's chagrin. The image is now kept behind a glass partition, along with other valuable Buddhist images from the area, in the abbot's kuti. Did Griswold suspect what lay beneath the plaster? The abbot refuses to speculate, at least on record.

Wat Chang Kham is also distinguished by having the largest tripitaka (Buddhist scripture) library in Thailand. It's as big as or bigger than the average wihãan, but now lies empty.

The wat is opposite the Nan National Museum on Pha Kong Rd.

## Wat Hua Khuang
วัดหัวข่วง

Largely ignored by art historians, this small wat diagonally opposite Wat Chang Kham features a distinctive Lanna/Lan Xang-style chedi with four Buddha niches, a wooden tripitaka library (now used as a kuti) and a noteworthy bòt with a Luang Prabang-style carved wooden veranda. Inside are a carved wooden ceiling and a huge naga altar. The temple's founding date is unknown, but stylistic cues suggest this may be one of the city's oldest wats.

## Wat Suan Tan
วัดสวนตาล

Reportedly established in 1456, Wat Suan Tan (Palm Grove Monastery) features an interesting 15th century chedi (40m high) that combines prang and lotus-bud motifs of obvious Sukhothai influence. The heavily

NORTHERN THAILAND

### Nan Festivals
The Golden Orange Festival (Thetsakaan Som Sii Thong) is held during December-January – the peak harvest time for the oranges. Among the festival events are a parade of floats decorated with Nan oranges and the coronation of an Orange Queen. During the hot season (March to May), in years when there's a bumper crop of phrík yài and the chilli-growers have extra income to spend, Nan occasionally celebrates a Chilli Festival (Ngaan Phrík) with pepper-festooned floats, chilli-eating contests and the coronation of – what else – a Chilli Queen.

Between mid-September and mid-October, Nan celebrates Thaan Kuay Salaak, a holiday unique to Nan in which special offerings dedicated to one's ancestors are presented to monks in the local temples.

At the end of the Buddhist Rains Retreat (mid-October to mid-November), during the *thâwt kathin* (robes-offering) for Wat Phra That Chang Kham, impressive long-boat races are held on the Nan River. The all-wooden 30m-long boats display sculpted naga heads and tails and hold up to 50 rowers.

The Mien usually hold New Year celebrations around mid-January in Nan's northern highlands.

Although not a festival per se, one local rite unique to Nan that's worth observing (if you have the opportunity) is the Seup Chataa (Extend Life) ceremony. Although at one time the ritual was performed annually, it is now most often held when someone is seriously ill or other bad fortune is deemed to have occurred. In the ceremony, the supplicant sits beneath a pyramid-like structure of reeds and flowers while monks and a shaman skilled at Seup Chataa execute a prescribed series of offerings (usually eggs and fruit) and sacred chants. ■

restored wihãan contains an early Sukhothai-style bronze sitting Buddha.

Wat Suan Tan is on Suan Tan Rd, near the north-eastern end of Pha Kong Rd.

## Trekking

Nan has nothing like the organised trekking industry found in Chiang Rai and Chiang Mai, but one company leads two or three day excursions into the mountains.

Fhu Travel Service (☎ 710636) at 453/4 Sumonthewarat Rd offers treks to Mabri, Hmong, Mien, Thai Lü and Htin villages combined with raft trips on the Nan River. A one day 'soft' trek costs 500B per person (minimum of five to six people, otherwise 600 to 700B); a two day/one night trek is 1000 to 1140B, depending on the number of participants; two nights/three days is 1500B per person (four person minimum); and three nights/four days is 2800 to 3000B. Fhu tends to concentrate on the northern areas of the province.

Doi Phukha Guest House offers one day tours along the Nong Bua-Doi Phu Kha loop for 500B each with four to six people.

Fees should include guide services, transport and all meals and accommodation.

## Places to Stay

**Guesthouses** *Doi Phukha Guest House* (☎ 771422), 94/5 Soi 1, Sumonthewarat Rd (Soi Aranyawat), offers tidy rooms in a large wooden house for 70/90B a single/double. Breakfast is available, along with information on exploring Nan.

The *Nan Guest House* (☎ 771849) is in another large house at 57/16 Mahaphrom Rd (actually at the end of a soi off Mahaphrom Rd) near the THAI office. Singles/doubles/triples with shared bath cost 60/80/100B; for rooms with private bath, add 20B per person.

*Wiangtai House* (☎ 710247), at 21/1 Soi Wat Hua Wiang Tai (off Sumonthewarat Rd near the Nara Department Store), has upstairs rooms in a large modern house for 120B (one large bed) and 150/180B (double/triple). Bathrooms are shared but very clean.

**Hotels** *Amorn Si* (☎ 710510) at 62/1 Anantaworarittidet Rd has very basic single/double rooms for 150/200B; it's at a very busy intersection so may not be the quietest choice. *Sukkasem* (☎ 710141) at 29/31 Anantaworarittidet Rd has better rooms costing 150 to 170B with fan and bath, 300B with air-con.

The renovated, all-wood *Nan Fah* (☎ 710-284) at 438-440 Sumonthewarat (next to the Dhevaraj Hotel) has a bit of atmosphere; one of the teak pillars supporting the hotel extends for three storeys, and there's an antique shop on the ground floor. All rooms come with air-con and cost from 350B with one bed, 600B for two beds. On the downside, the thin wooden walls are easily penetrated by street noise and by music from the ground floor's Phin Pub (open till 1 am).

The all air-con *Dhevaraj (Thewarat) Hotel* (☎ 710094) at 466 Sumonthewarat Rd is a four-storey place built around a tiled courtyard with a fountain. It's not really fancy but it's a pleasant place and is the best hotel Nan has to offer. Large, clean rooms on the 2nd floor, with fan and private bath, are 300/400B single/double – a bit steep due to the lack of competition, but the rooms are a cut above the usual fan room. Rooms towards the back of the hotel are quieter than those towards the front. Rooms on the 3rd floor are all air-con and cost 500/600B single/double. On the top floor are 'VIP' rooms with double-paned windows; these cost 700/900B single/double.

**Out of Town** About six km from town on Route 1168, the road to Mae Jarim, *Sawika Resort* (☎ 772598) has well appointed bungalows for 500B and up.

## Places to Eat

A night market assembles on the corner of Pha Kong and Anantaworarittidet Rds every night; it's not that spectacular, but the vendors along the sidewalks nearby have fairly good food. Another group of food vendors sets up along the soi opposite the Dhevaraj Hotel.

The most dependable restaurant in the

vicinity of the Nan Fah and Dhevaraj hotels is the old brick and wood *Siam Phochana*. It's a very popular morning spot for jók with a choice of fish, shrimp, chicken or pork; the menu has all the other Thai and Chinese standards as well, and is open 7 am to 9 pm. *Miw Miw*, opposite the Nan Fah Hotel, is a bit cleaner than Siam Phochana and has good jók, noodles and coffee.

If you turn left at the soi next to Siam Phochana and follow it a couple of hundred metres you'll come to the semi-outdoor *Suan Isaan*, the best choice in town for Isaan food – it's clean and the service is good.

The popular *Phin Pub*, behind the craft and antique shop on the ground floor of the Nan Fah Hotel, is decorated with Northern Thai antiques; when the weather is dry a few tables are put outdoors. Local Thai ensembles perform folk music on *phin* (Thai lute) and *saw* (Thai violin) in the early evenings, followed by modern Thai folk and pop later. Prices are very reasonable considering the quality of the food and entertainment.

A couple of Chinese-Thai restaurants next to the Sukkasem Hotel prepare the usual aahãan taam sàng at medium prices.

At 75/23-24 Anantaworarittidet Rd, the clean *Tanaya Kitchen* serves reasonably priced vegetarian dishes (along with meat dishes as well).

The relatively new *Da Dario* (☎ 750258) at 37/4 Rat Amnuay Rd in the northern part of town is an Italian/Thai restaurant run by a Swiss man who previously ran the Tip Top Restaurant. Among the specialities are Caesar salad and pizza; prices are reasonable and service is good.

## Things to Buy

Good buys include local textiles, especially the Thai Lü weaving styles from Sipsong-panna. Typical Thai Lü fabrics feature red and black designs on white cotton in floral, geometric and animal designs; indigo and red on white is also common. A favourite is the 'flowing-water design' *(lai náam lãi)* showing stepped patterns representing streams, rivers and waterfalls.

Local Mien embroidery and Hmong appliqué are of excellent quality – not as mass-produced as that typically found in Chiang Mai. Htin grass-and-bamboo baskets and mats are worth a look, too.

The nonprofit Thai-Payap Association, one of Thailand's most successful village self-help projects, has a shop at 24 Jettabut Rd near the morning market and bus terminal. Supported by Britain's Ockenden Venture from 1979 to 1990, the association now involves over 20 villages and has become totally self-sufficient. The handiwork offered through Thai-Payap is among the highest quality available, often including more intricate, time-consuming designs. All proceeds go directly to the participating villages – even the administrative staff are trained village representatives.

The arts and antique shop on the ground floor of the Nan Fah Hotel has a wide selection of local crafts, including silverwork and jewellery. There are also several small artisan-operated shops in the same vicinity along Sumonthewarat Rd and along Mahawong and Anantaworarittidet Rds.

## Getting There & Away

**Air** You can fly to Nan on THAI from Chiang Mai (thrice weekly, 510B), Phitsanulok (thrice weekly, 575B), Phrae (300B) or Bangkok (daily, 1530B). The THAI office is on Mahaphrom Rd.

**Bus** Baw Khaw Saw (government) buses run from Chiang Mai, Chiang Rai and Phrae to Nan. The fare from Chiang Mai's Arcade bus station is 83B (115B air-con, 148B 1st class air-con) and the trip takes from six to seven hours. The air-con buses leave in the morning before 11 am from both ends. From Chiang Rai there's one daily bus at 9.30 am (No 611, 74B) which takes six to seven gruelling hours via treacherous mountain roads – get a window seat as there's usually lots of motion sickness. Buses from Phrae to Nan leave frequently, cost 33B and take from two to 2½ hours.

From Nan, buses to Chiang Mai, Chiang Rai and Phrae leave from a terminal west of the large market on Anantaworarittidet Rd.

Ordinary buses to Utaradit, Phitsanulok, Sukhothai and other points south as far as Bangkok leave from the Baw Khaw Saw terminal off Khao Luang Rd. Regular government-run air-con buses to Bangkok cost 225B (one at 6 pm), 1st class air-con is 319B (one in the morning, three in the evening) and super-VIP buses are 445B (two nightly). The trip takes 18 to 19 hours.

Private VIP Bangkok buses leave from offices located along the eastern end of Anantaworarittidet Rd, not far from the Baw Khaw Saw terminal. Sombat Tour runs VIP buses to Bangkok for as low as 320B – check the number of seats before booking, though.

As provincial roads improve, eventually you should be able to bus from Nan to Nakhon Thai and connect with the highway to Loei from Phitsanulok.

**Bus & Train** The northern train line makes a stop in Den Chai, which is a 38B, three hour bus ride from Nan.

A Bangkok-bound rapid train leaves Den Chai at 7 pm (arriving at Bangkok's Hualamphong station at 5.25 am); to be sure of meeting this train, take a 1.15 or 2.30 pm Den Chai-bound bus from Nan's government bus station. To Chiang Mai there's a train that departs Den Chai at midnight, arriving at Chiang Mai at 5 am.

See Getting There & Away in the Phrae section for more Den Chai train information.

**Songthaews** Pickups to districts in the northern part of the province (Tha Wang Pha, Pua, Phaa Tuup) leave from the petrol station opposite Sukkasem Hotel on Anantaworarittidet Rd. Southbound songthaews (for Mae Jarim, Wiang Sa, Na Noi) depart from the parking lot opposite the new Ratchaphatsadu Market on Jettabut Rd.

**Getting Around**
Doi Phukha Guest House rents Honda Dreams for 200B per day, bicycles for 30B. Oversea Shop (☎ 710258) at 488 Sumonthewarat Rd (a few doors down from the Dhevaraj Hotel) rents bicycles and motor-

bikes at similar rates and can also handle repairs.

Samlors around town cost 10 to 15B.

## AROUND NAN PROVINCE
### Doi Phu Kha National Park
อุทยานแห่งชาติดอยภูคา

This recently established national park is centred around 2000m Doi Phu Kha in the Pua and Baw Kleua districts of north-eastern Nan (about 75 km from Nan). There are several Htin, Mien, Hmong and Thai Lü villages in the park and vicinity, as well as a couple of caves and waterfalls and endless opportunities for forest walks. As yet there is no established visitor accommodation in the park; in the meantime rangers will allow visitors to stay in park buildings at no charge. Tents are available for rent. This area gets quite cool in the winter months – evening temperatures of 5 to 10°C are not uncommon – so dress accordingly.

This area was once a hotbed of Thai communist activity; rumour says there are mines on Doi Phu Kha left over from the PLAT days, so stick to obvious footpaths or ask for a ranger guide (the going rate is 150B a day).

To reach the park by public transport you must first take a bus or songthaew north of Nan to Pua (13B), and then pick up one of the infrequent songthaews to the park headquarters (15B). A songthaew to the summit of Doi Phu Kha costs 35 to 40B. If you come by motorcycle, be forewarned that Route 1256 from Pua deteriorates as you get closer to the summit. Beyond the summit the stretch to Ban Baw Kleua is very rough in spots.

**Ban Baw Kleua** is a Htin village southeast of the park where the main occupation is the extraction of salt from local salt wells (Baw Kleua means 'salt well'). Route 1256 meets Route 1081 near Baw Kleua; Route 1081 can be followed south back to Nan (107 km) via a network of paved and unpaved roads.

### Nong Bua
วัดหนองบัว
This neat and tidy Thai Lü village near the

NORTHERN THAILAND

town of Tha Wang Pha, approximately 30 km north of Nan, is famous for Lü-style **Wat Nong Bua**. Featuring a typical two-tiered roof and carved wooden portico, the bòt design is simple yet striking – note the carved naga heads at the roof corners. Inside the bòt are some noteworthy but faded jataka murals; the building is often locked when religious services aren't in progress, but there's usually someone around to unlock the door. Leave a donation for temple upkeep and restoration at the altar.

You can also see Thai Lü weaving in action in the village. The home of Khun Janthasom Phrompanya, near the wat, serves as a local weaving centre – check there for the locations of looms, or to look at fabrics for purchase. Large yâams are available for just 45B, while nicely woven neck scarves cost more. There are also several weaving houses just behind the wat.

Originally from Sipsongpanna (Xishuangbanna) in China's Yunnan Province, the Thai Lü migrated to Nan in 1836 in the wake of a conflict with a local *chao meuang* (lord of a Thai river-valley state). Phra Chao Atityawong, ruler of the Nan kingdom at the time, allowed the Thai Lü to stay and grow vegetables in what is now Tha Wang Pha district. Nong Bua today is surrounded by picturesque vegetable farms.

**Getting There & Away** Songthaews to Tha Wang Pha (12B) leave from opposite Nan's Sukkasem Hotel. Get off at Samyaek Long-

bom, a three-way intersection before Tha Wang Pha, and walk west to a bridge over the Nan River, then left at the dead end on the other side of the bridge to Wat Nong Bua. It's 3.1 km from the highway to the wat.

If you're coming from Nan via your own transport on Route 1080, you'll cross a stream called Lam Nam Yang just past the village of Ban Fai Mun but before Tha Wang Pha. Take the first left off Route 1080 and follow it to a dead end; turn right and then left over a bridge across the Nan River and walk until you reach another dead end, then left two km until you can see Wat Nong Bua on the right.

### Tham Phaa Tuup Forest Reserve
ถ้ำผาตูบ

This limestone cave complex is about 10 km north of Nan and is part of a new wildlife reserve. Some 17 caves have been counted, of which nine are easily located by means of established (but unmarked) trails.

From Nan, you can catch a songthaew bound for Pua or Thung Chang; it will stop at the turn-off to the caves for 6B. The vehicles leave from the petrol station opposite the Sukkasem Hotel.

### Sao Din
เสาดิน

Literally 'Earth Pillars', Sao Din is an erosional phenomenon similar to that found at Phae Meuang Phii in Phrae Province – tall columns of earth protruding from a barren

NORTHERN THAILAND

**Nong Bua Festival**
Every three years in early December the Thai Lü at Nong Bua pay homage to their ancestral spirits. On the first day participants don traditional indigo outfits, build a village gate to fend off bad spirits and place offerings at 20 selected spirit houses around the village. The day ends with a feast.
On the second day the villagers form a procession in which they carry trays piled high with fruit, incense sticks, betel nut, candles, farm implements and weaponry. The chao meuang, or one of his assistants, carries a basket containing 20 live chickens. When the procession passes one of the 20 selected spirit houses, a feather plucked from one of the chickens is placed in the diminutive house, and then the chicken is tossed into the air. Everyone in the crowd scrambles to catch the chicken for good luck. When the group arrives at the spirit house of Nong Bua's first chao meuang, the participants sacrifice a water buffalo, an ox and two pigs (one white, one black). The meat is cooked and eaten in a feast following the sacrifice. Nowadays Thais from as far away as Bangkok attend the celebration. ■

depression. The area covers nearly 20 rai (3.2 hectares) off Route 1026 in Na Noi district about 30 km south of Nan.

Sao Din is best visited by bicycle or motorcycle since it's time-consuming to reach by public transport. If you don't have your own wheels, take a songthaew to Na Noi from the southbound songthaew terminal opposite the Ratchaphatsadu Market in Nan. From Na Noi you must get yet another songthaew bound for Fak Tha or Ban Khok, getting off at the entrance to Sao Din after five km or so. From here you'll have to walk or hitch four km to Sao Din itself. There are also occasional direct songthaews from Na Noi.

North-west of Sao Din, off Route 1216 West, is a smaller set of earth pillars called **Hom Chom**.

### Other Attractions

There are a couple of interesting destinations in and around the Thai Lü village of **Pua**, roughly 50 km north of Nan. In Pua itself you can check out another famous Thai Lü temple, **Wat Ton Laeng**, which is admired for its classic three-tiered roof. **Silaphet Falls** is south-east of Pua just off the road between Pua and Ban Nam Yao. The water falls in a wide swath over a cliff and is best seen at the end of the monsoon season in November. On the way to the falls and west of the road is the Mien village of **Ban Pa Klang**, worth a visit to see silversmiths at work. This village supplies many silver shops in Chiang Mai and Bangkok.

Other Mien villages that specialise in silverwork can be found along Route 101 between Nan and Phrae in the vicinity of **Song Khwae** (not to be confused with the village of the same name on Route 1097 farther north).

Off Route 1148, north of the village of Ban Sakoen, is a huge, 200m-wide cave called **Tham Luang**. The path to the cave is not signposted, but if you ask at the police checkpoint in Ban Sakoen you should be able to get directions or you might even find a guide.

The **Thaleh Sap Neua** (Northern Lake) formed by the Sirikit Dam is an important freshwater fishery for Nan, as well as a recreational attraction for Nan residents. **Ban Pak**

**Nai** on its north-western shore is the main fishing village. Just before the Nan River feeds into the lake at its extreme northern end, there is a set of river rapids called **Kaeng Luang**.

One area in Nan Province you're not encouraged to visit is the mountainous ridge along the Thai-Lao border. This is a 'restricted area' patrolled by the Thai military, who claim communist insurgents are still holed up here. More likely the real dangers of the area involve undetonated mines left by both insurgency and counter-insurgency forces during the 1960s and 1970s, as well as an ongoing opium trade. The province's two highest peaks, **Phu Khe** (2079m) and **Doi Lo** (2077m), are found in the restricted area.

### Border Crossing into Laos

Ban Huay Kon (140 km from Nan) in Thung Chang District is now a legal border crossing for Lao and Thais, and it may be promoted to an international crossing in the foreseeable future. From this crossing it's just 152 km to Luang Prabang or about 300 km to the Chinese border at Boten, Laos. From the Lao side of the border crossing, a dirt road leads north-north-east about 45 km to the banks of the Maekhong River in Laos' Udomxai Province. From here you can either take a boat downriver to Luang Prabang or cross the river and pick up Route 2 to Muang Xai, the provincial capital. From Muang Xai it's only a couple of hours to the international border with China's Yunnan Province.

Historically minded Nan residents are excited by the prospect of linking together again the five chiangs (cities) of the Lanna-Lan Xang-Sipsongpanna diaspora: Chiang Mai, Chiang Rai, Chiang Thong (the original name for Luang Phabang), Chiang Rung (Yunnan's Jinghong) and Chiang Klang (Nan).

There is an immigration office in the district capital of Thung Chang, 100 km north of Nan; if you find out that the border crossing is open to foreigners, you should stop in here first to get a Thai exit stamp in your passport.

# North-Eastern Thailand

In many ways, the north-eastern region of Thailand is the kingdom's heartland. Partly due to the area's general nondevelopment, the older Thai customs remain more intact here than elsewhere in the country. The region also hosts fewer tourists – in a typical year only 2% of the country's annual international arrivals venture into North-Eastern Thailand.

Compared to the rest of Thailand, the pace is slower, the people friendlier and inflation is less effective in the Isaan provinces, and although fewer people speak or understand English, travel in the North-East is easy.

Sites of historical and archaeological significance abound in the North-East; many of them have been restored or excavated. Scattered around the region are 202 known *prasats, prangs* and *kus*, 182 of which are of Khmer origins. Most of them are found in four provinces: Buriram (61 sites), Nakhon Ratchasima (26), Surin (33) and Si Saket (12). Generally speaking, prasat (from the Sanskrit architectural term *prasada)* refers to large temple sanctuaries with a cruciform floor plan, while ku and prang ku are smaller Khmer-style *chedis* (or stupas). However, many Thais use these terms interchangeably. Prasat is sometimes translated in Thai tourist literature as 'castle' or 'palace', but these Khmer monuments were never used as royal residences.

The Khorat Plateau extends across most of North-Eastern Thailand and is divided by the Phu Phan mountain range into two wide drainage basins, the Sakon Nakhon Basin in the upper North-East (fed by the Maekhong River and its tributaries) and the Khorat Basin in the lower North-East (fed by the Chi and Mun rivers).

Isaan (the collective term for the region) officially consists of 18 provinces: Buriram, Chaiyaphum, Kalasin, Khon Kaen, Loei, Mahasarakham, Mukdahan, Nakhon Phanom, Nakhon Ratchasima, Nong Bualamphu, Nong Khai, Roi Et, Sakon Nakhon, Si Saket, Surin, Ubon Ratchathani, Udon Thani and Yasothon.

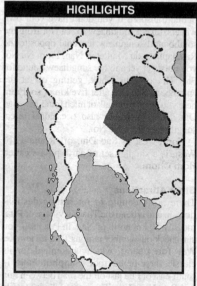

## HIGHLIGHTS

- Impressive Angkor ruins of Phanom Rung and Prasat Hin Phimai, as well as smaller, unexcavated ruins along the Maekhong River from Loei
- Nakhon Phanom – for its fine views of the Isaan countryside and important religious site of the Lao-style Wat Phra That Phanom
- Traditional cotton and silk-weaving towns dotted around Nakhon Ratchasima (Khorat), Khon Kaen, Roi Et and Udon Thani
- Khao Yai National Park with its pristine monsoon forests – an ASEAN National Heritage Site
- Important Bronze Age archaeological sites of Ban Chiang and Ban Prasat
- Cool and quiet North-Eastern forest monasteries
- Khao Phra Wihaan – another major Angkor site just across the Cambodian border

## History

The region has a long history, beginning with the 2000 year old bronze culture of Ban Chiang, which predates both Mesopotamia and China as a metallurgical and agricultural site.

Thais use the term *isāan* to classify the region, the people *(khon isāan)* and the food *(aahāan isāan)* of North-Eastern Thailand. The name comes from Isana, the Sanskrit name for the Mon-Khmer kingdom which flourished in what is now North-Eastern Thailand and pre-Angkor Cambodia; Isana was a precursor to the Funan empire (1st to 6th centuries AD). Funan was in turn absorbed by the Chenla empire during the late 6th to 8th centuries and divided into Upper (Water) and Lower (Land) Chenla, which corresponded with parts of modern-day Isaan, southern Laos and north-western Cambodia. After the 9th century Chenla was superseded by the Angkor empire, which extended well into Isaan and beyond.

Isaan remained more or less autonomous from early Thai kingdoms until the coming of the French in the 1800s created the Indochinese state of Laos, thus forcing Thailand to define its north-eastern boundaries. Rama V divided the region into four *monthon* (from the Pali-Sanskrit 'mandala') or semi-autonomous satellite states, including Lao Phuan (north-eastern Isaan), Roi Et (central Isaan), Lao Klang (south-western Isaan) and Ubon (south-eastern Isaan). The monthon system was abolished in favour of the Bangkok-ruled *jangwàat* (province) system in 1933.

Traditionally Thailand's poorest region due to the infertility of the soil and lack of rain in comparison with the rest of the country, the North-East was fertile ground for the communist movement. Ho Chi Minh spent 1928-29 proselytising in Udon Thani, Sakon Nakhon and Khorat (Nakhon Ratchasima's more common name); in the 1940s a number of Indochinese Communist Party leaders fled to Isaan from Laos and helped strengthen the Communist Party of Thailand. From the 1960s until 1982 or so, Isaan was a hotbed of guerrilla activity, especially in the provinces of Buriram, Loei, Ubon Ratchathani, Nakhon Phanom and Sakon Nakhon. Almost immediately following the amnesty of 1982, the Communist Party's North-Eastern strongholds began a rapid dissolution. The process was hastened by a decade of economic growth which drew large numbers of Isaan peasants from the forests and rice fields to various provincial capitals and to Bangkok.

Opinions today differ on just how far Isaan has been able to ride along on the coat-tails of Thailand's strong economy. The area still has the lowest per capita income of the country's four major regions, but it is definitely more prosperous overall than it was 20 years ago.

## Culture

Isaan culture and language are marked by a mixture of Lao and Khmer influence. The Khmers have left behind Angkor Wat-like monuments near Surin, Khorat, Buriram and other North-Eastern towns. Near the Maekhong River/Lao border in Nakhon Phanom Province are several Lao-style temples, including Wat Phra That Phanom. Many of the people living in this area speak Lao or Thai dialects which are very close to Lao dialects spoken in Laos – in fact there are more people of Lao heritage in North-Eastern Thailand than in all

NORTH-EASTERN THAILAND

### Bai Sii Ceremony

North-Eastern Thais commonly participate in *bai sīi* (sacred thread) ceremonies on auspicious occasions, such as birthdays, farewells, times of serious illness, and during certain festivals such as Khon Kaen's annual phùuk siaw, or 'tying friends' festival. In the bai sīi ceremony, the 32 guardian spirits known as *khwǎn* are bound to the guest of honour by white strings tied around the wrists. Each of the 32 khwǎn are thought to be guardians over different organs in a person's body. (See the Khon Kaen section later in this chapter.)

Khwǎn occasionally wander away from their owner, which isn't considered much of a problem except when that person is about to embark on a new project or on a journey away from home, or when they're very ill. At these times it's best to perform the bai sīi to ensure that all the khwǎn are present and attached to the person's body. A *maw phawn*, or wish priest – usually an elder who has spent some time as a monk – presides over the ritual. Those participating in the ritual sit on mats around a tiered vase-like centrepiece, or *phakhuan*, which is decorated with flowers, folded banana leaves and branches with white cotton strings hanging down; pastries, eggs, bananas, liquor and money are placed around the base as offerings to the spirits in attendance.

After a few words of greeting, the maw phawn chants in a mixture of Isaan and Pali to convey blessings on the honoured guest, while all in attendance place their hands in a prayer-like, palms-together pose. For part of the chanting segment, everyone leans forward to touch the base of the phakhuan; if there are too many participants for everyone to reach the base, it's permissible to touch the elbow of someone who can reach it, thus forming a human chain.

Once the maw phawn has finished chanting, each person attending takes two of the white strings from the phakhuan and ties one around each wrist of the honoured guest(s) while whispering a short, well-wishing recitation. When all have performed this action, the guest is left with a stack of strings looped around each wrist and small cups of rice liquor are passed around, sometimes followed by an impromptu *ram wong* (circle dance). For the intended effect, the strings must be kept around the wrists for a minimum of three full days. Some Isaan people believe the strings should be allowed to fall off naturally rather than cut off – this can take weeks. ■

of Laos. In certain areas of the lower North-East, Khmer is the most common language.

Isaan food is famous for its pungency and choice of ingredients. Well known dishes include *kài yâang* (grilled spiced chicken) and *sôm-tam* (spicy salad made with grated papaya, lime juice, garlic, fish sauce and fresh chillies). North-Easterners eat glutinous rice with their meals, rolling the almost translucent grains into balls with their hands.

The music of the North-East is also highly distinctive in its folk tradition, using instruments such as the *khaen*, a reed instrument with two long rows of bamboo pipes strung together; the *ponglang*, a xylophone-like instrument made of short wooden logs; and the *phin*, a type of small three stringed lute played with a large plectrum. The most popular song forms are of the *lûuk thûng* (literally, 'children of the fields') type, a very rhythmic style in comparison to the classical music of Central Thailand.

The best silk in Thailand is said to come from the North-East, around Khorat, Khon Kaen and Roi Et. A visit to North-Eastern silk-weaving towns can uncover bargains, as well as provide an education in Thai weaving techniques. Cotton fabrics from Loei, Nong Khai and Nakhon Phanom are highly regarded, especially those woven using the *mát-mii* (tie-dye) or ikat method.

For real antiquity, Udon Thani Province offers prehistoric cave drawings at Ban Pheu, north of Udon Thani, and a look at the ancient ceramic and bronze culture at Ban Chiang to the east. This latter site, excavated by the late Chester Gorman and his team of anthropologists from the University of Pennsylvania, may prove to be the remains of the world's oldest agricultural society and first bronze metallurgy.

Travellers who want to know more about North-Eastern Thailand should read the works of Pira Sudham, a Thai author born in Buriram. His autobiographical *People of Esarn (Isaan)* is especially recommended.

### Getting There & Away
The main train and bus lines in the North-East are between Bangkok and Nong Khai,

and between Bangkok and Ubon Ratchathani. The North-East can also be reached from Northern Thailand by bus or from Phitsanulok, with Khon Kaen as the 'gateway'.

# Nakhon Ratchasima Province

Thailand's largest province (20,500 sq km) is most well known for silk weaving. Some of the country's best silk is made in the village of Pak Thong Chai, 30 km south-west of Khorat on Route 304. Many of the Bangkok silk houses have their cloth made there, so don't expect to get any special bargains just because you went all that way. There are also a couple of silk shops in Khorat which are just as good – sometimes better – for their selection and price. Still, Pak Thong Chai is worth a trip if you're interested in observing Thai silk-weaving methods.

Khorat's other big attraction is the Angkor-period Khmer ruins scattered about the province. Most are little more than a jumble of stones or a single prang, but the restorations at Prasat Hin Phimai and Prasat Phanomwan are very impressive. In addition to Khmer religious shrines, there are some 192 ancient city sites – Mon, Lao and Khmer – scattered around the province. Most are visible only to archaeologists trained to look for the odd earthen rampart, boundary stone or laterite foundation. Little is known about the early history of the province except that, according to a 937 AD inscription, it was part of a kingdom known as Sri Janas (Si Janat), which apparently extended over the entire Khorat Plateau. The inhabitants of Sri Janas – or at least its royal inhabitants – practised a mixture of Mahayana Buddhism and Shiva worship, hence it was probably an Angkor satellite.

### NAKHON RATCHASIMA (KHORAT)
นครราชสีมา
• ☎ *(44)* • *pop 202,403*
Exactly 250 km from Bangkok, *amphoe meuang* (provincial capital) Nakhon Ratchasima

was once the capital of Lao Klang, a Thai *monthon* that covered present-day Khorat, Chaiyaphum and Buriram provinces. Up until the mid-Ayuthaya period it was actually two towns, Sema and Khorakpura, which merged under the reign of King Narai. To this day, Khorat has a split personality of sorts, with the older, less commercial half to the west, and the newer central half inside the city moats to the east, although neither Sema nor Khorakpura were originally here but in present-day Sung Noen (35 km south-east).

No longer the quaint Isaan town it once was, busy Khorat has become an important transportation hub and burgeoning industrial centre, and is Thailand's second largest city. Since 1988 new factory registrations have averaged 1300 per year. Yet only in 1992 did the city get its first international-class hotel. Often cited only as a train or bus stop from which one reaches the nearby Phimai ruins, Khorat is a fairly interesting place if you don't mind putting up with the generally grubby air, which can be almost as bad as Bangkok's. Those who prefer a quieter setting might want to spend the night in Phimai instead, making day trips to Khorat; those who like city life might consider the opposite tactic.

One of seven air bases in Thailand used by the US armed forces to launch air strikes on Laos and Vietnam in the 1960s and 1970s was just outside Khorat. A few retired GIs still live in the area with their Thai families, and the Veterans of Foreign Wars Cafeteria is still open on Phoklang Rd. But the heavy US influence that was obvious in the late 1970s after the base was closed has all but faded away. Yes, the big massage parlours are still there, but the clientele is almost exclusively Thai.

Khorat's most popular annual event is the Thao Suranari Festival, a celebration of Thao Suranari's victory over the Lao. It's held from late March to early April and features parades, *lí-khe* (Thai folk dance-drama), *phleng khorâat* (Khorat folk song) and a beauty contest. Thousands of participants from around Nakhon Ratchasima Province and beyond attend the festivities.

## Information

**Tourist Offices** The TAT office (☎ 213666; fax 213667) on Mittaphap Rd (western edge of town) is worth a visit, since it has plenty of information on the North-East and a good map of Khorat. To get there, walk straight across from the entrance of the Khorat train station to Mukkhamontri Rd, turn left and walk (or catch a No 2 bus) west until you reach the highway to Bangkok – this is Mittaphap Rd. TAT is just across the road, on the south-west corner. The office is open daily from 8.30 am to 4.30 pm.

A tourist police contingent (☎ 213333) is attached to the TAT office.

**Money** The best area for banks is Chomphon Rd, where you'll find Bangkok Bank, Thai Farmers Bank and Siam Commercial Bank, all of which offer foreign-exchange services from 8.30 am until 3.30 pm Monday to Friday. Bangkok Bank of Commerce, opposite the Fah Thai Hotel on Phoklang Rd, has an exchange window open daily from 8.30 am to 8 pm.

**Post & Communications** A conveniently located post office on Mittaphap Rd is open Monday to Friday from 8.30 am to 4.30 pm, Saturday from 9 am to 1 pm. There is another branch on Jomsurangyat Rd between Klang Plaza 2 shopping centre and the Anachak Hotel, and another on Atsadang Rd. International telephone calls are best made from the CAT office attached to the Atsadang post office; its open daily between 7 am and 11 pm.

## Mahawirawong National Museum
พิพิธภัณฑ์แห่งชาติมหาวีรวงศ์

In the grounds of Wat Sutchinda, directly across from the government buildings off Ratchadamnoen Rd and just outside the city moat, this museum has a good collection of Khmer art objects, especially door lintels, as well as objects from other periods. It's open from 9 am to noon and 1 to 4 pm Wednesday to Sunday. Admission is 10B.

## Thao Suranari Memorial
อนุสาวรีย์ท้าวสุรนารี

At the Chumphon Gate to central Khorat, on the west side, is this much-worshipped memorial shrine to Thao Suranari (also known as Khun Ying Mo), a courageous Thai woman who led the local citizens in a battle against Lao invaders from Vientiane during the rule of Rama III. Hundreds of unique offerings, such as a miniature model of a bus donated by local bus drivers, find their way to the shrine in the hope that Khun Ying Mo's spirit will protect the offerers from danger or ill will.

**Khorat Song** In the evenings you can see performances of phleng khorâat, the traditional Khorat folk song, in an area opposite the shrine near some shops selling preserved pork. It's usually performed by groups of four singers hired by people whose supplications to Thao Suranari have been honoured. To show gratitude to the spirit, they pay for the performance. Over 100 groups are for hire, usually for 300 to 600B per performance.

## Wat Phra Narai Maharat
วัดพระนารายณ์

This monastery of indeterminate age is important for two reasons: it contains a Khmer sandstone sculpture of Phra Narai (Vishnu) and, more significantly, Khorat's *làk meuang*, or city phallus-pillar. It's on Prajak Rd between Atsadang and Chomphon Rds.

## Wat Sala Loi
วัดศาลาลอย

This distinctive modern 'Temple of the Floating Pavilion' is 400m east of the north-eastern corner of the city moat and has a *bòt* (central sanctuary or chapel in a Thai temple) shaped like a Chinese junk.

## Wat Pa Salawan
วัดป่าสาละวัน

A Thammayut 'forest monastery' once surrounded by jungle, Salawan has been engulfed by the city, but it's still a fairly quiet escape. The abbot, Luang Phaw Phut, is quite well known as a meditation teacher and has developed a strong lay following in the area. A few relics belonging to the legendary Ajaan Man are on display in the main *wihāan* (counterpart to a *bòt*), a large but simple wooden affair. A cemetery on the grounds has a couple of markers with photos of US veterans who lived their later years in Khorat. Wat Pa Salawan is in the south-east sector of the city behind Khorat's train station.

## Swimming

Landlocked Khorat is quite warm most of the year – a swim at one of the several local public pools will revive all but the most wilted. Each of the following charges 20B per day per person: Chanya Swimming Pool (☎ 252305) on Seup Siri Rd; Rama Swimming Pool (☎ 242019) on Mittaphap Rd; Puttachart Swimming Pool (☎ 251815) at 29/1 Phetmatukang Rd; and Sripattana Hotel (☎ 242944) on Suranari Rd (this pool has a good snack bar). Thep Nakhon (off Mittaphap Rd in the north-western section of town) charges 60B a day but is worth it for the newer, more high-tech facilities.

## Places to Stay – bottom end

**Guesthouses** Khorat's first and longest-running guesthouse, *Doctor's House* (☎ 255846), is at 78 Soi 4, Seup Siri Rd, in the western area of the city. The house is quiet and comfortable, and has four large singles/doubles for 80/160B or 230B with air-con. The friendly proprietors speak English. A No 1 yellow songthaew will take you past here, or if you phone from the bus or train station, the guesthouse staff will give you a ride.

The new *Ratana Guest House* (☎ (01) 927-0354), a bit farther south along Seup Siri on Soi Suksan 39, is another friendly place in a quiet neighbourhood. Clean rooms in a modern, two-storey house cost 80 to 150B. Take the same No 1 yellow songthaew that continues past the Doctor's House and get off opposite the army camp, then look for a sign reading 'Guest House'.

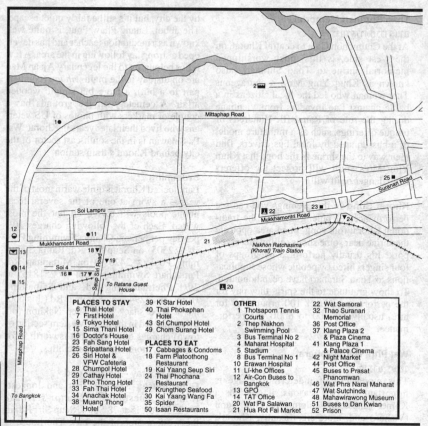

PLACES TO STAY
6 Thai Hotel
7 First Hotel
9 Tokyo Hotel
15 Sima Thani Hotel
16 Doctor's House
23 Fah Sang Hotel
25 Sripattana Hotel
26 Siri Hotel &
VFW Cafeteria
28 Chumpol Hotel
29 Cathay Hotel
31 Pho Thong Hotel
33 Fah Thai Hotel
34 Anachak Hotel
38 Muang Thong
Hotel

39 K Star Hotel
40 Thai Phokaphan
Hotel
43 Sri Chumpol Hotel
49 Chom Surang Hotel

PLACES TO EAT
17 Cabbages & Condoms
18 Farm Platoothong
Restaurant
19 Kai Yaang Seup Siri
24 Thai Phochana
Restaurant
27 Krungthep Seafood
30 Kai Yaang Wang Fa
35 Spider
50 Isaan Restaurants

OTHER
1 Thotsaporn Tennis
Courts
2 Thep Nakhon
Swimming Pool
3 Bus Terminal No 2
4 Maharat Hospital
5 Stadium
8 Bus Terminal No 1
10 Erawan Hospital
11 Li-khe Offices
12 Air-Con Buses to
Bangkok
13 GPO
14 TAT Office
20 Wat Pa Salawan
21 Hua Rot Fai Market

22 Wat Samorai
32 Thao Suranari
Memorial
36 Post Office
37 Klang Plaza 2
& Plaza Cinema
41 Klang Plaza 1
& Palace Cinema
42 Night Market
44 Post Office
45 Buses to Prasat
Phanomwan
46 Wat Phra Narai Maharat
47 Wat Sutchinda
48 Mahawirawong Museum
51 Buses to Dan Kwian
52 Prison

**Hotels** Visit the TAT office for a map and complete list of Khorat's hotels. *Fah Sang* (☎ 242143), at 112-114 Mukkhamontri Rd not far from Khorat train station, has OK rooms and a friendly staff, though the location is noisy. Rooms with fan and bath are 130B for singles, and 200 to 230B for doubles. Air-con singles/doubles with hot water cost 330/350B.

*Pho Thong* (☎ 242084), 658 Phoklang Rd, has rooms from 150 to 200B with fan and bath, 300 to 400B with air-con. It's on the corner of Ratchadamnoen Rd at the west city gate, right in the centre of things,

and is overall better value than the Fah Sang. In the same vicinity is the quiet and friendly – and even better value – *Siri Hotel* (☎ 242-831) at 167-8 Phoklang Rd, well located a couple of blocks west of the city moats. Rooms cost 120 to 160B with a fan or 240 to 280B with air-con. The VFW Cafeteria is next door.

The cheapest place on Phoklang Rd, *Chumpol Hotel* (☎ 242453) at No 701-2, costs just 100B for a basic but clean room in a classic Thai-Chinese hotel.

*Muang Thong Hotel* (☎ 242090) at 46 Chumphon Rd is a classic old wooden hotel

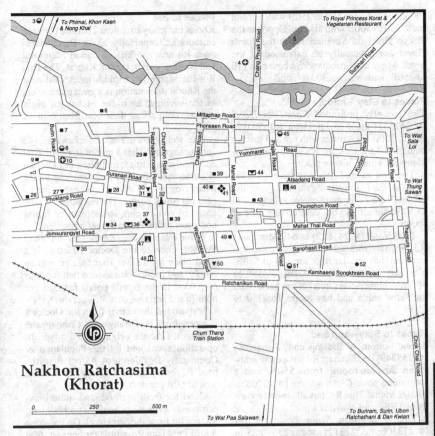

**Nakhon Ratchasima (Khorat)**

To Phimai, Khon Kaen & Nong Khai

To Royal Princess Korat & Vegetarian Restaurant

Chang Phuak Road

Suranari Road

Mittaphap Road

Phonsaen Road

Burin Road

Ratchadamnoen Road

Chumphon Road

Chakkri Road

Yommarat Road

Prajak Road

Manat Road

Kudan Road

Pholan Road

Suranari Road

Atsadang Road

To Wat Sala Loi

To Wat Thung Sawan

Phoklang Road

Chumphon Road

Mahat Thai Road

Kudan Road

Thaosura Road

Jomsurangyat Road

Wachasaam Road

Chainarong Road

Sanphasit Road

Ratchanikun Road

Kamhaeng Songkhram Road

Chum Thang Train Station

Chok Chai Road

0    250    500 m

To Wat Paa Salawan

To Buriram, Surin, Ubon Ratchathani & Dan Kwian

NORTH-EASTERN THAILAND

that's seen better days – look for the green-painted building inside the moat near the Thao Suranari Shrine. Rooms are a rock-bottom 80B a night – be sure to get a room off the street; and stay away if you're bothered by its reputation as the town brothel.

The *Thai Phokaphan* (☎ 242454), 104-6 Atsadang Rd, is inside the city moats, across the street from the more expensive *K Star Hotel* and the KR massage parlour. Good one bed/two bed rooms cost 150/300B, 350/500B with air-con. It's near the night market but well off the street and not too noisy.

The *Cathay* (☎ 242889) at 3692/5-6 Rat-

chadamnoen Rd has reasonable rates (150 to 200B), and is not far from the bus terminal for Buriram, Surin, Ubon Ratchathani and Chiang Mai. Closer still is the *First Hotel* (☎ 255203) at 132-36 Burin Rd, where ordinary rooms with fan cost 190 to 250B.

The *Sri Chumpol Hotel* (☎ 242460) at 122 Chumphon Rd is a bit quieter than the other Thai-Chinese places on Phoklang and Ratchadamnoen Rds, and it's cleaner than most. Fan-and-bath rooms with one bed cost 150B, two beds costs 220B.

The *Tokyo Hotel* on Suranari Rd has OK rooms – quieter than most of those on

Phoklang Rd – for 180 to 250B with fan and bath, 350 to 500B with air-con. Opposite the Tokyo Hotel on Suranari Rd is the *Tokyo Guest Land*, actually an extension of the hotel, where large rooms with a bath cost 140 to 250B, with air-con 300 to 500B.

### Places to Stay – middle

The recently upgraded *Fah Thai Hotel* (☎ 242533) at 3535 Phoklang Rd charges 280 to 350B for a room with fan and private bath, 480B for air-con. It's good for a Phoklang Rd Thai-Chinese place.

The well located *Anachak Hotel* (☎ 243-925) at 62/1 Jomsurangyat Rd, near the Klang Plaza 2 shopping centre, charges 400 to 500B for simple but comfortable air-con rooms.

*Thai Hotel* (☎ 241613) at 640 Mittaphap Rd, not far from the main city centre bus terminal, has similar digs for 480 to 580B, plus less expensive fan rooms for 350 to 400B. A higher-class hotel at the back bears the same name and has rooms for 750 to 850B.

### Places to Stay – top end

At the bottom of the top end, *Sripattana* (☎ 255349) on Suranari Rd has newly renovated air-con rooms from 550B, and a swimming pool. *Chom Surang* (☎ 257088), 2701/2 Mahat Thai Rd, has all air-con rooms from 750B, and also has a pool.

The 130-room *Sima Thani Hotel* (☎ 213100; fax 213121; ☎ (2) 253-4885 in Bangkok) originally opened in 1992 as a Sheraton but is now owned by a Thai hotel group. Superior singles/doubles start at 1800/2000B, and deluxe rooms cost 2000/2300B. On the premises are a lobby bar, restaurant, pub and swimming pool.

Not to be outdone, Thailand's Dusit Group has opened its own 188-room *Royal Princess Korat* (☎ 256629) at 1137 Suranari Rd on the north-eastern outskirts of the city. Rates are in the same league as Sima Thani's.

Accor Asia Pacific will soon be opening a new 160-room *Hotel Ibis*, with room rates in the 800 to 1200B range; this new hotel 'brand' promises good value in this category.

### Places to Eat

Khorat has many excellent Thai and Chinese restaurants, especially along Ratchadamnoen Rd near the Thao Suranari Memorial and western gate to central Khorat. The Hua Rot Fai Market on Mukkhamontri Rd near the Khorat train station is a great place to eat in the evening, as is the Manat Rd night market; both are at their best from 6 to 10 pm.

The well known *Thai Phochana* at 142 Jomsurangyat Rd has a mix of standard Thai and local specialities, including mìi khorâat (Khorat-style noodles) and yam kòp yâang (roast frog salad). Also good here is kaeng phèt pèt (duck curry). The restaurant is now enclosed and air-con, so automotive fumes and street noise are no longer a problem.

*Farm Platoothong Restaurant* on Seup Siri Rd, close to the Doctor's House, is a good place for a slow Thai splurge – great service and food. You can also fish for your own food in the farm's ponds for 20B per hour (a rod and reel cost 30B per day).

Just around the corner from the Doctor's is a new branch of Bangkok's *Cabbages & Condoms*. Like the original it's a nonprofit operation sponsored by the Population & Community Development Association; the food is good but a bit pricey for Khorat, around 60B per dish.

Good for fresh seafood, and quite inexpensive, is *Krungthep Seafood* on Phoklang Rd, not far from the Siri Hotel. On the same side of Phoklang Rd, a little farther east, *Bibi Muslim* does tasty Muslim curries and khâo mòk kài.

The *Vegetarian Restaurant (Sala Mangsawirat)* has moved once again, this time to an out-of-the-way location on Suranari Rd towards Khorat Teacher's College. If you manage to get out there, you'll find great Thai vegetarian dishes for 8 to 10B. It's open from around 10 am to 3 pm.

**Isaan**  Two very unassuming Isaan places along the east side of Wacharasarit Rd between Sanphasit and Kamhaeng Songkhram Rds, *Suan Sin* and *Samran Laap*, serve locally popular Isaan fare such as plaa chonábòt (freshwater fish steamed with vegetables and served with a tart-spicy sauce), súp haang wua (oxtail soup) and lin yâang (barbecued tongue). It also serves lâap and other Isaan standards.

For the best kài yâang and sôm-tam in town, check out *Kai Yaang Seup Siri*, near Doctor's House on Seup Siri Rd. There are two Isaan places next door to each other here – look for the one with chickens on the grill out the front. They start serving around 10.30 am and are usually sold out by 4 pm.

Also good, and open longer hours, is *Kai Yaang Wang Fa*, on Ratchadamnoen Rd opposite the shrine.

**Western** *VFW Cafeteria* next to the Siri Hotel on Phoklang Rd has cheap American-style breakfasts, as well as steaks, ice cream, pizza and salads. It gets mixed reviews, however, so let's just say it's a good imitation of an American 'greasy spoon', for all that term implies, both positive and negative. The central tables are often taken by a tight-knit group of US Vietnam War veterans talking in their standard military-issue mid-western accents.

Cleaner and more reliable – if more expensive – are the various US-style restaurants in Klang Plaza 2 shopping centre, including *KFC, Dunkin Donuts, Black Canyon Coffeeshop* and *Royal Home Bakery*. Klang Plaza also has a large supermarket, should you want to shop for groceries.

Many expats swear by *The Spider* on a *soi* (lane) parallel to Jomsurangyat Rd. It's an air-con restaurant/pub with the best farang food in town, plus a list of Thai dishes.

### Entertainment
Khorat is a regional headquarters for lí-khe troupes, who maintain several offices along Mukkhamontri Rd near the Seup Siri Rd intersection. Hired performances start at 1000B for a small ensemble – you provide the venue and the troupe will bring their costumes, stage sets and so on – much like a travelling carnival.

The *Phlap-Phla Dawan Restaurant* in the Sima Thani Hotel hosts a well executed cultural performance of Thai, Lao and Khmer dancing several evenings per week – check with the hotel for the latest schedule.

Several cinemas in town show motion pictures daily. The better movies, including occasional foreign flicks, seem to turn up at the Plaza, which is behind the Klang Plaza 2 shopping centre off Ratchadamnoen and Jomsurangyat Rds.

The city boasts seven massage parlours, three Thai-style nightclubs and a couple of hotel discos. For a complete list, see the TAT office.

### Things to Buy
A night market along Manat Rd features cheap clothes, fruit, flowers, sunglasses, watches and food vendors – nothing spectacular, but it's a fine place to while away an hour or so.

Klang Plaza 2 shopping centre on Jomsurangyat Rd offers five floors of shops purveying everything from videos to houseware. There's another Klang Plaza on Atsadang Rd near the Thai Phokaphan Hotel.

Khorat has many shops that specialise in Khorat silk. Several are found along Ratchadamnoen Rd near the Thao Suranari Memorial, including Ratri, Thusnee (Thatsani) and Today. Over on Chomphon Rd are a couple of others – Chompol and Jin Chiang.

### Getting There & Away
**Air** THAI flies to Khorat from Bangkok daily; the fare is 555B one way. The THAI office (☎ 257211/5) is at 14 Manat Rd, off Mahat Thai Rd inside the city moat.

**Bus** Ordinary buses leave the Northern Bus Terminal in Bangkok every 15 or 20 minutes from 5 am to 10.15 pm. The fare is 64B and the trip takes four hours. Air-con buses cost 115B. In Khorat, air-con buses to Bangkok arrive and depart from the air-con bus terminal on Mittaphap Rd.

For buses to other places in Thailand, there are two main bus terminals. Bus terminal 1, off Burin Rd in the city centre near the intersection of the Mittaphap Rd loop and the highway north to Nong Khai, has buses to

Khon Kaen, Phitsanulok, Chiang Mai and Chiang Rai, plus a few buses to Bangkok. This bus terminal can be extremely congested. Buses between Khorat and Khon Kaen cost 48B and leave regularly throughout the day.

Buses to other points in the North-East (eg Loei, Roi Et, Nakhon Phanom, Ubon Ratchathani, Udon Thani etc) or in eastern Central Thailand (eg Rayong, Pattaya, Chanthaburi) leave from bus terminal 2, off the highway to Nong Khai north of the city centre. Direct buses between Khorat and Chanthaburi on the south-east coast run hourly between 4.30 am and 4 pm. The fare is 86B (155B air-con) and the journey takes about eight hours.

The following table lists air-con buses (unless otherwise noted) to/from Khorat.

| City | Fare | Duration |
| --- | --- | --- |
| Chiang Mai* | 325B | 8 hours |
| (ordinary) | 180B | 9 hours |
| Chiang Rai* | 356B | 9 hours |
| (ordinary) | 198B | 10 hours |
| Loei | 174B | 3 hours |
| Nakhon Phanom | 159B | 4½ hours |
| Nong Khai | 157B | 3½ hours |
| (ordinary) | 87B | 4 hours |
| Pattaya | 125B | 3 hours |
| Phitsanulok* | 184B | 4 hours |
| (ordinary) | 102B | 5 hours |
| Rayong | 167B | 4 hours |
| Roi Et | 120B | 2½ hours |
| Sakon Nakhon | 128B | 4 hours |
| (ordinary) | 91B | 4½ hours |
| Ubon | 181B | 4½ hours |
| (ordinary) | 100B | 5½ hours |
| Udon | 135B | 3 hours |
| (ordinary) | 75B | 4 hours |
| Yasothon | 120B | 3 hours |

* Leaves from Bus Terminal No 1; all others in list leave from Bus Terminal No 2

**Train** An express train bound for Ubon Ratchathani departs Bangkok's Hualamphong station at 9 pm, arriving in Khorat at 1.53 am – hardly the best time to look for a hotel.

Rapid trains on the Ubon train line depart at 6.50 am and 6.45 pm, arriving in Khorat at 11.31 am and 11.51 pm respectively. These are much more convenient arrival

times, especially the morning arrival which leaves plenty of daylight time to explore the city.

There are also ordinary diesel trains on this line at 9.10 am (3rd class only), 11.05 am (2nd and 3rd class), 11.45 am (3rd class only), 3.25 pm (3rd class only), 6.45 pm (2nd and 3rd class), 9.50 pm (2nd and 3rd class), 10.45 pm (3rd class only) and 11.25 pm (3rd class only), which all arrive in Khorat about 5½ to six hours after departure. The 1st class fare (express train only) is 230B, 2nd class is 117B and 3rd class 51B. Add 20B for the rapid trains and 30B for the express. The train passes through some great scenery on the Khorat Plateau, including a view of the enormous white Buddha figure at Wat Theppitak on a thickly forested hillside.

### Getting Around

Samlors around the city cost 15 to 20B; tuk-tuks cost 20 to 30B for a short hop, 40 to 50B for longer trips.

The city also has a fairly extensive bus system. From the Khorat train station, bus No 1 heads east along Phoklang Rd; No 2 heads east along Mukkhamontri Rd and No 3 goes east along Jomsurangyat Rd. In the opposite direction, bus Nos 1, 2 and 3 all end up heading west on Mukkhamontri Rd towards the TAT office. The fare on each line is 3B. Comfortable air-con versions of bus No 2 are also available for 5B.

### AROUND NAKHON RATCHASIMA
### Pak Thong Chai
ปักธงชัย

Thirty-two km south of Khorat, on Route 304, is Pak Thong Chai, one of Thailand's most famous silk-weaving villages. Several varieties and prices of silk are available, and most weavers sell directly to the public. However, prices are not necessarily lower than in Khorat or Bangkok. Around 70 silk factories are located in the district. Pak Thong Chai Silk and Cultural Centre offers demonstrations of the silk-weaving process as well as the opportunity to purchase silks at reasonable prices.

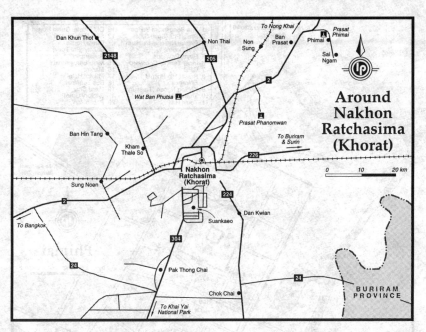

**Around Nakhon Ratchasima (Khorat)**

NORTH-EASTERN THAILAND

*Achaan Pan* and *Pak Thong Chai* hotels are both on the main road through town and have rooms from 70B.

Bus No 1303 to Pak Thong Chai leaves bus terminal No 1 in Khorat every 30 minutes, the last leaves at 4 pm. The fare is 11B.

### Dan Kwian
ต่านแกวียน

Travellers interested in Thai ceramics might pay a visit to Dan Kwian, 15 km south-east of Khorat. This village has been producing pottery for hundreds of years; originally it was a bullock-cart stop for traders on their way to markets in old Khorat (Dan Kwian means 'bullock cart checkpoint'). Dan Kwian pottery is famous for its rough texture and rust-like hue – only kaolin from this district produces such results.

Several more or less permanent shops line the highway. Prices are very good – many exporters shop for Thai pottery here. It's not all pottery either – clay is shaped and fired into all kinds of art objects, including jewellery. A TAT office in the village is open daily from 8.30 am to 4.30 pm.

To get here from Khorat, hop on a songthaew from the south or east city gates; the fare to Dan Kwian is 6B.

### Phimai
พิมาย

The small town of Phimai is nothing much, but staying a night or two is pleasant enough if you're here to visit Prasat Hin Phimai. If you want to visit the ruins as a day trip from Khorat, an 8 am bus would give you plenty of wandering time at the ruins with time to spare for the return bus trip in the late afternoon. If Khorat's not your cup of tea, do it the other way around; stay in Phimai and day trip to Khorat.

Outside the town entrance, a couple of km down Route 206, is Thailand's largest

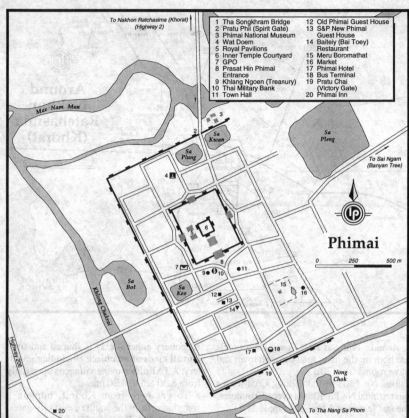

| | | | |
|---|---|---|---|
| 1 | Tha Songkhram Bridge | 12 | Old Phimai Guest House |
| 2 | Pratu Phii (Spirit Gate) | 13 | S&P New Phimai |
| 3 | Phimai National Museum | | Guest House |
| 4 | Wat Doem | 14 | Baiteiy (Bai Toey) |
| 5 | Royal Pavilions | | Restaurant |
| 6 | Inner Temple Courtyard | 15 | Meru Boromathat |
| 7 | GPO | 16 | Market |
| 8 | Prasat Hin Phimai | 17 | Phimai Hotel |
| | Entrance | 18 | Bus Terminal |
| 9 | Khlang Ngoen (Treasury) | 19 | Pratu Chai |
| 10 | Thai Military Bank | | (Victory Gate) |
| 11 | Town Hall | 20 | Phimai Inn |

**Phimai**

NORTH-EASTERN THAILAND

banyan tree, a mega-florum spread over an island in a large pond (actually a state irrigation reservoir). The locals call it **Sai Ngam**, meaning 'Beautiful Banyan'; you can walk through the banyan branches via wooden walkways built over the pond. Food vendors and astrologers offer their services to picnickers in the vicinity.

Around town you'll see one of North-Eastern Thailand's trademarks, the *rót kasèt*, or farm truck. These low-tech vehicles, fancifully painted with technicolour sunsets, swaying palms and bright geometric patterns, feature inexpensive Kubota engines mounted in an open engine housing. The engines are easily detached to run a plough, water pump or long-tail boat. A garage in town, U Prasan, around the corner from the Phimai Hotel, specialises in the painting and repair of these oddities.

Since 1991 the town has hosted a festival during the first week of November to celebrate Prasat Hin Phimai history. Events vary from year to year but typically include a sound & light show at the ruins, classical dance-drama performances, historical and cultural exhibits and a lamp-lit procession between temples.

**Information** The Baiteiy (Bai Toey) restaurant distributes a town map; the owner, Khun Siriluk, speaks English. A branch of the Thai Military Bank near the historical park entrance has an exchange window open until 5 pm.

**Prasat Hin Phimai National Historical Park** The Angkor-period Khmer shrine monument located in the park, 60 km north-east of Khorat, makes Phimai worth a visit. Originally started by Khmer King Jayavarman V in the late 10th century and finished by King Suriyavarman I (1002-49) in the early 11th century, this Hindu-Mahayana Buddhist temple projects a majesty that transcends its size. The 28m tall main shrine, of cruciform design, is made of white sandstone, while the adjunct shrines are of pink sandstone and laterite. The lintel sculpture over the doorways to the main shrine are particularly impressive. The Phimai temple, like many other Khmer monuments in this part of Thailand, predates the famous Angkor Wat complex in Cambodia. When the Angkor empire was at its peak, and encompassed parts of Thailand, Phimai was directly connected to the Angkor capital by road.

Reconstruction work by the Fine Arts Department has been completed, and although the pieces do not quite fit together as they must have originally, this only seems to add to the monument's somewhat eerie quality. Between the main entrance and the main street of the small town is a ruined palace and, farther on, an open-air museum features Khmer sculpture.

Admission to the complex is 20B; it is open daily from 7.30 am to 6 pm.

**Phimai National Museum** The exhibits at this nicely designed new museum are mostly dedicated to Isaan sculpture, with many of the best lintels and statues from Phimai, Phanom Rung, Phanomwan and other Khmer sites in Thailand as well as ceramics from nearby Ban Prasat. The museum's most prized possession, a stone sculpture of Angkor King Jayavarman VII, comes from Prasat Hin Phimai – it looks very much like

a sitting Buddha. An open-air sculpture garden next to the main hall displays ornate boundary stones and other Khmer figures from Phimai. A small bookshop is attached to the museum.

Opening hours are Wednesday to Sunday from 9 am to 4 pm; admission is 20B.

**Places to Stay** Two spartan but comfortable guesthouses in Phimai are on opposite sides of an alley off the main street leading to the ruins. *Old Phimai Guest House* (☎ (44) 471725) has dorm beds for 80B, plus singles/doubles/triples/quadruples for 120/150/200/350B with shared bath in a large house. Opposite is the similar *S&P New Phimai Guest House*, with slightly more basic rooms and a smaller communal space. Rates here are 50B for dorm beds, and 80/100/150B for singles/doubles/triples with shared facilities. Both guesthouses rent bicycles.

*Phimai Hotel*, around the corner from the bus terminal, is a bit dingy these days. Adequate rooms, but not as good value as the guesthouses, cost 120B for a single/double fan room with shared bath, 180 to 230B with attached bath or 330 to 400B for air-con.

The newer and better *Phimai Inn* (☎ (44) 471175) is about two km south-west of the old town (20B by samlor) on Highway 206. Clean and comfortable rooms cost 250B with fan and private bath, 350B with air-con. The hotel rents bicycles.

**Places to Eat** Good Thai and Chinese food is available at the *Baiteiy (Bai Toey)* restaurant near the hotel and guesthouses. Daily lunch specials are just 30B; there are also more expensive à-la-carte items, several vegetarian dishes, western breakfasts and ice cream.

Around the corner from the Baiteiy, on a smaller east-west street, are two modest restaurants specialising in lâap and kâwy (spicy Isaan-style salads made with meat, poultry or fish) and sticky rice. There is also a decent collection of food vendors at a night market just north of the regular day market; it gets

NORTH-EASTERN THAILAND

going around 6 pm and ends around midnight.

On a tributary of the Mun River about two km north-west of town, the *Rim Moon* is a typical upcountry garden restaurant.

**Getting There & Away** Bus No 1305 leaves for Phimai every half hour during the day from Khorat's bus terminal 1 behind the Erawan Hospital on Suranari Rd. Take the No 2 city bus (3B) east on Mukkhamontri Rd (from the train station) and get off at the hospital, then walk through a side street to the bus terminal.

The trip to Phimai (16B) takes from one to 1½ hours, depending on the number of passengers that are picked up along the way. The bus terminal in Phimai is around the corner from the Phimai Hotel and down the street from Prasat Hin Phimai. The last Phimai bus leaves Khorat bus terminal at 7.45 pm; from Phimai the last bus is at 6 pm.

**Getting Around** Phimai is small enough to walk easily between the bus terminal, Phimai Hotel, guesthouses and the ruins. Samlor trips in town cost 10 to 20B one way. If you would like to see more of the town and environs (eg Sai Ngam), you can rent bicycles from Old Phimai Guest House and S&P New Phimai Guest House for 8B per hour or 25B per day.

These guesthouses can also arrange day trips to the ruins of Phanom Rung and Meuang Tam (see the Buriram Province section) for 300B per person, minimum of four people.

### Prasat Phanomwan

ปราสาทพนมวัน

Although not as large as Prasat Hin Phimai, the 11th century ruins at Prasat Phanomwan are nonetheless impressive. Though basically unrestored, the sanctuary is on the grounds of a temple (Wat Phanomwan) that is still used for worship and has resident monks. Inside the sanctuary, surrounded by a moat that fills only in the rainy season, are a number of Buddha images plus a couple of

Shivalingams (phallus images) and a Nandi (Shiva's bull mount), which indicate that the Khmers must have originally built Phanomwan as a Hindu temple. Fifty metres south-west of the main sanctuary is a building that houses other sculpture and artefacts.

A French team is working on a restoration of Phanomwan.

**Getting There & Away** Prasat Phanomwan is off Highway 2 about 15 km north-east of Khorat on the way to Phimai – ask to be let off at Ban Saen Meuang (5B), then hop on a local songthaew, hitchhike or walk the six km through Ban Saen Meuang, Ban Nong Bua and Ban Makham to get to Prasat Phanomwan.

There are also three direct buses a day to Phanomwan from Khorat's Phosaen Gate, at 7 and 10 am and noon. The fare is 7B.

### Ban Prasat

บ้านปราสาท

Forty-five km north-east of amphoe meuang Nakhon Ratchasima near the banks of Lam Than Prasat (off Highway 2 between Non Sung and Phimai), Ban Prasat is the oldest archaeological site in the Khorat Basin. Excavations completed in 1991 show that the site, which is also known as the Ku Tan Prasat Mound, was inhabited by an agricultural-ceramic culture at least 3000 years ago. This culture lasted around 500 years and predated Udon Thani Province's Ban Chiang by 1000 years.

Archaeological evidence suggests the Ban Prasat culture spun thread for weaving cloth, made sophisticated coloured pottery, planted rice, raised domestic animals and – towards the end of the culture's 500 year zenith – developed bronze metallurgy. Other layers uncovered indicate the site was later taken over by a pre-Dvaravati Mon city, followed by a 10th century settlement whose main legacy is a small brick sanctuary known locally as **Ku Than Prasat**. This structure shows both Dvaravati and Khmer characteristics, and may have been a cultural transition point between Mon kingdoms to the west and the Khmer principalities to the east.

Several preserved excavation pits are on display; the visitors' centre houses pottery and skeletons found in the pits and is open Wednesday to Sunday from 8.30 am to 4 pm.

## KHAO YAI NATIONAL PARK
อุทยานแห่งชาติเขาใหญ่
• ☎ (44)

Established in 1961, this is Thailand's oldest national park; it covers 2172 sq km and includes one of the largest intact monsoon forests in mainland Asia. Considered by many park experts to be among the world's best national parks, Khao Yai was recently designated an ASEAN National Heritage Site and has been nominated for similar international status by the UN. The terrain covers five vegetation zones: evergreen rainforest (100 to 400m); semi-evergreen rainforest (400 to 900m); mixed deciduous forest (northern slopes at 400 to 600m); and hill evergreen forest (over 1000m), plus savannah and secondary-growth forest in areas where agriculture and logging occurred before the area was protected.

Some 200 to 300 wild elephants reside within the park boundaries; other recorded mammals include sambar deer, barking deer, gaur, wild pig, Malayan sun bear, Asiatic black bear, tiger, leopard, serow and various gibbons and macaques. In general these animals are most easily spotted during the rainy season from June to October. Khao Yai also has Thailand's largest population of hornbills, including the great hornbill (nók kòk or nók kaahang in Thai), king of the bird kingdom, as well as wreathed hornbill (nók ngaa cháang, literally, 'elephant-tusk bird'), Indian pied hornbill (nók khàek) and rhinoceros hornbill (nók râet). Hornbills breed from January to May, the best time to see them. They also feed on figs, so ficus trees are good places to find them. Caves in the park are home to rare wrinkle-lipped bats and Himalayan ribbed bats.

The park has over 50 km of hiking trails, many of them formed through the movement

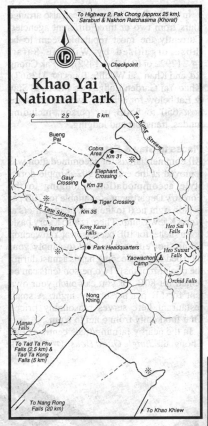

of wildlife. Elevations range from 100 to 1400m where the western edge of Cambodia's Dongrek mountain range meets the southern edge of the Khorat Plateau. You can get a rather inaccurate trail map from the park headquarters. It's easy to get lost on the longer trails so it's advisable to hire a guide. Rangers may be able to act as guides for 100B per day. If you do plan to go walking, it is a good idea to take boots as leeches can be a problem – although mosquito repellent does help to keep leeches away. There are also three wildlife-watching towers in the park.

In nearby Pak Chong, you can also arrange tours from two or three different agencies. Currently the most reputable seem to be those organised by Wildlife Safari (☎ 312922 or (01) 212-1492), 39 Pak Chong Rd, and Khao Yai Wildlife Tours (☎ 313567), Khao Yai Garden Lodge (see Places to Stay & Eat below for details). Two day packages cost 650 to 850B per person, including guides, transport and lodging.

### Places to Stay & Eat

All commercial visitor accommodation was removed at the end of 1992. Simple dorm-style accommodation belonging to the Forestry Department is available for 20B per person right next to the park headquarters at Kong Kaew Camp. There is also a very basic dorm shelter for 10B per person at Yaowachon Camp. For either you need to supply your own bedding (a sleeping bag is a must during the cooler months). Two person tents can be rented for 80B. Or you can pitch your own tent for 5B per person per night. A small restaurant here serves reasonably priced Thai food daily from 6 am to 6 pm.

In the nearby farming/trade centre of Pak Chong, the *Jungle Guest House* (☎ 313836),

off Soi 3 at 752/11 Kongwaksin Rd, offers basic dorm accommodation for 70B per night, simple rooms for 80B per person or newer rooms in a Thai-style wooden house for 150/200B. Rates include breakfast. The guesthouse is a 10 minute walk from the bus terminals on Friendship Highway; turn right from the Khorat bus terminal (or left from the Bangkok bus terminal), then left at the traffic lights, left again at Soi 1 and then follow the signs about 50m to the guesthouse. Although the guesthouse is basically OK, we've received a flood of complaints about the money-oriented tours led by this guesthouse under the name of 'Jungle Adventure Tours'.

*Phubade (Phubet) Hotel* (☎ 314964), 781/1 Thetsaban Rd 15, is also just off Friendship Highway – walk past the night market toward the road to Khao Yai and take a left at Thetsaban Rd 15, then a left at the sign that reads 'Hotel'. Clean, well maintained rooms catering to businesspeople and Thai government officials cost 200 to 240B with fan and private bath, 330 to 360B with air-con.

*Khao Yai Garden Lodge* (☎ 313567) is seven km out of town on the way to Khao

The North-East, with its many cotton and silk-weaving towns, produces some of the country's finest textiles.

Yai. Take a blue songthaew from the market for 6B or a regular Khao Yai bus for 8B. Or call the lodge and someone will pick you up in town for free. The Thai-German couple who run the lodge claim there are over 200 species of botanical and hybrid orchids in their garden. Basic singles cost 100B, while better rooms with fan and shared bath are 100B per person. There are also more expensive rooms with garden views and tasteful decor for 300 to 1200B. The affiliated Khao Yai Wildlife Tours offers well run, two day Khao Yai trips for 850B, including room, breakfast and guide service.

Also on the road to Khao Yai, the *Wan-Ree Resort, Golden Valley Resort* and *Juldis Khao Yai Resort* offer up-market bungalows in the 1000 to 2500B range.

Near the main highway intersection in Pak Chong is an excellent night market purveying a wide range of Thai and Chinese food from around 5 to 11 pm. There are also a few decent Thai restaurants on the highway through town.

### Getting There & Away
From Bangkok take a bus (every 15 minutes from 5 am to 10 pm; 35B ordinary, 65B air-con) from the Northern Bus Terminal to Pak Chong. From Pak Chong you can catch a songthaew to the park gates for 10B from in front of the 7-Eleven. You may also be able to take a direct bus from Bangkok at certain times of year – enquire at the Northern Bus Terminal. Minivans to the terminal are available from next to Pak Chong's air-con bus terminal for 100B.

From Khorat take a Bangkok-bound bus and simply get off in Pak Chong (23B ordinary, 47B air-con).

You can also easily get to Pak Chong from Ayuthaya by ordinary train for 23B in 3rd class, 47B in 2nd class; the trip takes around three hours. From Bangkok the train costs 36B in 3rd class, 82B in 2nd class, not including the surcharge (30B) for rapid trains. The ordinary train takes around four hours from Bangkok; the rapid is half an hour shorter.

Hitchhiking in the park is usually easy.

# Buriram Province

Buriram is a large province (18th largest out of 76) with a small capital and a long history. During the Angkor period this area was an important part of the Khmer empire. The restored ruins at Phanom Rung (formally known as Prasat Hin Khao Phanom Rung) are the most impressive of all Angkor monuments in Thailand; other lesser known ruins in the province include Prasat Meuang Tam, Ku Rasi, Prasat Ban Khok Ngiu, Prasat Nong Hong, Prasat Ban Thai Charoen, Prasat Nong Kong, Prang Ku Samathom, Prang Ku Khao Plaibat, Prang Ku Suwan Taeng, Prang Ku Khao Kadong and many others. If one includes all ancient city sites (including Dvaravati and pre-Dvaravati), the province contains 143, second in number only to Nakhon Ratchasima Province.

Most of the ruins in Buriram are little more than piles of bricks by the side of a road or out in a field. As the Fine Arts Department and/or the local community continue restoration in the province, more of the Khmer monuments mentioned here may become worth seeing.

Contemporary Buriram Province is famous among Thais for the 320 hectare **Dong Yai Forest** protected by monk Prajak Kuttajitto, who 'ordained' trees with monastic robes and sacred thread so people wouldn't cut them down. In 1991 he and his followers were finally run out of the forest by the Thai military, but not without the sustained protests of thousands of sympathetic Thai citizens.

### BURIRAM
อ.เมืองบุรีรัมย์
• ☎ (44) • pop 29,500
Buriram is a small provincial capital where there is not a great deal to do. Nevertheless, the town is a good base for visiting Khmer temple ruins around the province, such as Phanom Rung. See the following special Phanom Rung Historical Park section for details about these fine Khmer ruins.

# Phanom Rung Historical Park

ประสาทหินเขาพนมรุ้ง

**P**hanom Rung is on an extinct volcanic cone (383m above sea level) that dominates the flat countryside for some distance in all directions. To the south-east you can clearly see Cambodia's Dongrek Mountains, and it's in this direction that the capital of the Angkor empire once lay. The prasat's temple complex is the largest and best restored of all the Khmer monuments in Thailand (it took 17 years to complete the restoration) and, although it's not the easiest place to reach, it's well worth the effort.

During the week of the nationwide Songkhran Festival in April, the local people have their own special celebration, Phanom Rung Festival, which commemorates the restoration of Phanom Rung. During the day there is a procession up Phanom Rung Hill and at night sound & light shows and dance-dramas are performed in the temple complex.

Phanom Rung is Khmer for 'big hill', but the Thais have added their own word for hill *(khāo)* to the name as well as the word for stone *(hīn)* to describe the prasat. Its full name is Prasat Hin Khao Phanom Rung.

## Phanom Rung

พนมรุ้ง

The temple was constructed between the 10th and 13th centuries with the bulk of the work being done during the reign of King Suriyavarman II (1113-50), which by all accounts was the apex of Angkor architecture.

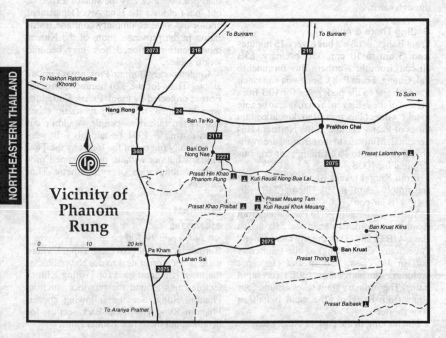

The complex faces east, towards the original Angkor capital. Of the three other great Khmer monuments of South-East Asia, Cambodia's Angkor Wat faces west, its Prasat Khao Wihaan faces north and Thailand's Prasat Hin Phimai faces south-east. Nobody knows for sure whether these orientations have any special significance, especially as most smaller Khmer monuments in Thailand face east (towards the dawn – typical of Hindu temple orientation).

A small museum on the grounds contains some sculpture from the complex and photographs of the 17 year restoration process.

There is a 20B admission fee (between 8 am and 5.30 pm) to the Phanom Rung Historical Park. *The Sanctuary Phanomrung*, by Dr Sorajet Woragamvijya, is an informative booklet put out by the Lower North-East Study Association (LNESA). Sometimes it is available for sale near the entrance to the complex for 20B (vendors may ask 50B, but the LNESA says visitors shouldn't pay more than 20B). Several English-speaking guides also offer their services at the complex – fees are negotiable.

Downhill a bit from the main sanctuary, a number of new structures have been built to house collections of art and artefacts found on the site. When finished, the buildings will become part of a museum complex that may have a separate admission fee – for now they're free.

The best time to visit Phanom Rung is before 10 am in the morning – this beats most bus tours, and it's cooler and the light is better for photography.

**Design** One of the most remarkable design aspects of Phanom Rung is the promenade leading to the main gate. This is the best surviving example in Thailand. It begins on a slope 400m east of the main tower, with three earthen terraces. Next comes a cruciform base for what may have been a wooden pavilion. To the right of this is a stone hall known locally as the White Elephant Hall. On the north side of this hall are two pools that were probably once used for ritual ablutions before entering the temple complex. Flower garlands to be used as offerings in the temple may also have been handed out here. After you step down from the pavilion area, you'll come to a 160m avenue paved with laterite and sandstone blocks, and flanked by sandstone pillars with lotus-bud tops, said to be early Angkor style (1100-80). The avenue ends at the first and largest of three *naga* (cobra deities) bridges.

These naga bridges are the only three which have survived in Thailand. The first is flanked by 16 five-headed nagas in the classic Angkor style – in fact these figures are identical to those found at Angkor Wat. After passing this bridge and climbing the stairway you come to the magnificent east gallery leading into the main sanctuary. The central prasat has a gallery on each of its four sides and the entrance to each gallery is itself a smaller version of the main tower. The galleries have

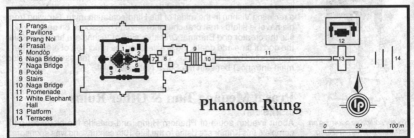

1 Prangs
2 Pavilions
3 Prang Noi
4 Prasat
5 Mondòp
6 Naga Bridge
7 Naga Bridge
8 Pools
9 Stairs
10 Naga Bridge
11 Promenade
12 White Elephant Hall
13 Platform
14 Terraces

**Phanom Rung**

0    50    100 m

NORTH-EASTERN THAILAND

NORTH-EASTERN THAILAND

## Phra Narai Lintel

An interesting story goes with the Phra Narai (Lord Narayana) lintel. In the 1960s local residents noticed the lintel was missing from the sanctuary and an investigation determined that it must have disappeared between 1961 and 1965. A mysterious helicopter was reportedly seen in the vicinity during this period. The Thais later discovered the lintel on display at the Art Institute of Chicago; the lintel had been donated by a James Alsdorf.

The Thai government as well as several private foundations tried unsuccessfully for many years to get the artwork returned to its rightful place. As the complex was reaching the final stages of restoration in preparation for the official opening in May 1988, a public outcry in Thailand demanded the return of the missing lintel. In the USA, Thai residents and US sympathisers demonstrated in front of the Chicago museum. The socially conscious Thai pop group Carabao recorded an album entitled *Thap Lang* (Lintel) that featured a picture of the Statue of Liberty cradling the Phra Narai lintel in her left arm on its cover! The chorus of the title song went: 'Take back Michael Jackson – Give us back Phra Narai'.

In December 1988 the Alsdorf Foundation returned the Phra Narai lintel to Thailand in exchange for US$250,000 (paid by private sources in the USA) and an arrangement whereby Thailand's Fine Arts Department would make temporary loans of various Thai art objects to the Art Institute of Chicago on a continual basis. Rumour in Thailand has it that of the seven Thais involved in the original theft and sale of the lintel, only one is still alive. The other six are supposed to have met unnatural deaths. ∎

curvilinear roofs and false balustraded windows. Once inside the temple walls, have a look at each of the galleries and the *gopura* (entrance pavilions), paying particular attention to the lintels over the porticoes. The craftwork at Phanom Rung represents the pinnacle of Khmer artistic achievement, on a par with the reliefs at Angkor Wat in Cambodia.

**Sculpture** The Phanom Rung complex was originally built as a Hindu monument and exhibits iconography related to the worship of Vishnu and Shiva. Excellent sculptures of both Vaishnava and Shaiva deities can be seen in the lintels or pediments over the doorways to the central monuments and in various other key points on the sanctuary exterior.

On the east portico of the *mondòp* (antechamber to the prasat or main sanctuary) is a Nataraja (Dancing Shiva), in the late Baphuan or early Angkor style, while on the south entrance are the remains of Shiva and Uma riding their bull mount, Nandi. The central cell of the prasat contains a Shivalingam.

Several sculpted images of Vishnu and his incarnations, Rama and Krishna, can be found on various other lintels and cornices. Probably the most beautiful is the **Phra Narai lintel**, a relief depicting Lord Narayana, a reclining Vishnu in the midst of the Hindu creation myth. Growing from his navel is a lotus that branches into several blossoms, on one of which sits the creator god Brahma. On either side of Vishnu are heads of Kala, the god of time and death. He is asleep on the milky sea of eternity, here represented by a naga snake. This lintel sits above the eastern gate (the main entrance) beneath the Shiva Nataraja relief.

# Prasat Meuang Tam & Other Ruins
ปราสาทเมืองต่ำ

About five km south of Phanom Rung, and outside the historical park complex, this Khmer site dates to the late 10th century and was sponsored

*Khmer sculpture adorning an entrance to Phanom Rung.*

Influences from classical Indian religious architecture characterise Phanom Rung's boldly carved stone temple buildings.

BERNARD NAPTHINE

Perched atop an extinct volcano in the middle of the Khorat Plateau, Phanom Rung is the best preserved and most dramatic of Thailand's Angkor-period monuments.

JOE CUMMINGS

Despite its origins as a Khmer-built Shaivite temple, Phanom Rung counts as one of the most important Buddhist pilgrimage points in Thailand today.

JOE CUMMINGS

Sandstone lintels over the porticoes, such as this one depicting the Indian deity Shiva, demonstrate that Phanom Rung was originally built as a place of Hindu worship. By the end of the Angkor empire – which extended from Cambodia west all the way to Kanchanaburi – Thailand's Khmer rulers had converted to Buddhism.

JOE CUMMINGS

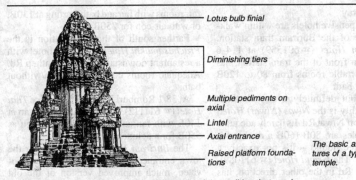

Lotus bulb finial

Diminishing tiers

Multiple pediments on axial

Lintel

Axial entrance

Raised platform foundations

*The basic architectural features of a typical Khmer-era temple.*

by King Jayavarman V. The laterite wall is still in fair condition, but much of the prasat has tumbled down. Restoration is moving steadily along, but unless you're attempting an exhaustive tour of Khmer ruins in Thailand you could skip this one. On the other hand, if you have the time, it gives you a good idea of what Prasat Phanom Rung looked like before it was restored. Admission is 20B.

West of Meuang Tam and south of Phanom Rung are the harder-to-find Khmer ruins of **Kuti Reusii Nong Bua Lai, Kuti Reusii Khok Meuang** and **Prasat Khao Praibat**. East of these are **Prasat Lalomthom, Prasat Thong** and **Prasat Baibaek**. We haven't explored any of these but they're spotted on the Vicinity of Phanom Rung map in case anyone is interested in taking a look. To find these it would be best to hire a local guide from the Phanom Rung complex or in the village of Prasat Meuang Tam.

From Prasat Meuang Tam you could continue south-east via Ban Kruat and Ban Ta Miang (along routes 2075 and 2121) to **Prasat Ta Meuan**, a secluded Khmer ruins complex on the Thai-Cambodian border (see the Surin section later in this chapter for details). From Ta Miang you could then proceed north to amphoe meuang Surin or continue east along the border to Si Saket and Ubon provinces.

## Getting to the Ruins

Phanom Rung can be approached from Nakhon Ratchasima (Khorat), Buriram or Surin. From Khorat, take a Surin-bound bus and get out at Ban Ta-Ko, which is a few km past Nang Rong (the turn-off north to Buriram). The fare should be about 20B; Ban Ta-Ko is well marked as the turn-off for Phanom Rung. Once in Ta-Ko you have several options. At the Ta-Ko intersection you can wait for a songthaew that's going as far as the foot of Phanom Rung (12 km, 15B) or one that's on the way south to Lahan Sai. If you take a Lahan Sai truck, get off at the Ban Don Nong Nae intersection (you'll see signs pointing the way to Phanom Rung to the east). From Ta-Ko to Don Nong Nae will cost 4B. From Don Nong Nae, get another songthaew to the foot of the hill for 10B or charter a pickup for 40B one way.

If you don't have the patience to wait for a songthaew, take a motorcycle taxi from Ta-Ko to Don Nong Nae (30B) or all the way to Phanom Rung for between 60 and 70B each way. A return trip will cost 120 to 150B; for an extra 50B the drivers will add Meuang Tam. These rates include waiting for you while you tour the ruins.

There are also a couple of morning songthaews from Buriram Market that go directly to Don Nong Nae; these are met by songthaews that go straight to the ruins.

From Surin, take a Khorat-bound bus and get off at Ban Ta-Ko on Highway 24, then follow the directions as from Khorat.

NORTH-EASTERN THAILAND

## Places to Stay

Several inexpensive hotels are within walking distance of the Buriram train station. *Chai Jaroen Hotel* (☎ 601559) at 114-6 Niwat Rd, in front of the train station, has fairly comfortable rooms from 80 to 120B with fan and bath.

Cheaper but definitely a step or three down in quality is the *Nivas (Niwat) Hotel*, on a soi just off Niwat Rd. Its barely adequate singles/doubles are 80B (60B a double for less than three hours) – it's not exactly a family place. The *Grand Hotel* (☎ 611089), along Niwat Rd in the other direction, has fair rooms with fan and bath starting at 130B, or with air-con for 250B.

Farther south of the train station is the *Prachasamakhi Hotel*, a Chinese hotel with a restaurant downstairs on Sunthonthep Rd. Adequate rooms cost 60/80B with/without bath.

At 38/1 Romburi Rd is the fairly nice *Thai Hotel* (☎ 611112), where clean rooms start at 140B with fan and bath, and go as high as 550B for a deluxe room.

The *Buriram Hotel* (☎ 611740) near the town entrance from Route 218 is a renovated, much improved version of the old

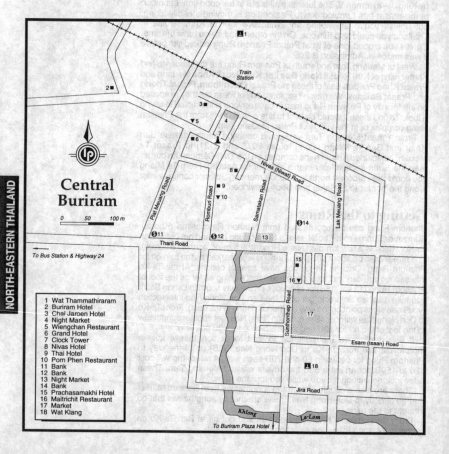

**Central Buriram**

0    50    100 m

→ To Bus Station & Highway 24

1  Wat Thammathiraram
2  Buriram Hotel
3  Chai Jaroen Hotel
4  Night Market
5  Wiengchan Restaurant
6  Grand Hotel
7  Clock Tower
8  Nivas Hotel
9  Thai Hotel
10 Porn Phen Restaurant
11 Bank
12 Bank
13 Night Market
14 Bank
15 Prachasamakhi Hotel
16 Maitrichit Restaurant
17 Market
18 Wat Klang

Train Station

Plat Meuang Road

Romburi Road

Nivas (Niwat) Road

Samatakan Road

Lak Meuang Road

Thani Road

Sunthonthep Road

Esarn (Isaan) Road

Jira Road

Khlong   La-Lom

To Buriram Plaza Hotel

NORTH-EASTERN THAILAND

Krung Rome. Plain, clean air-con rooms are from 400B.

Buriram's first tourist-class hotel, the 229-room *Buriram Plaza*, is on the southern outskirts of town on the way to Surin. Rooms with all the amenities start at 875B.

**Nang Rong** You can also stay closer to Phanom Rung by spending the night at this tiny town off the highway. *Honey Inn* (☎ 671131) at 8/1 Soi Ri Kun is run by a local schoolteacher who speaks English. Large, clean rooms cost 100/150B a single/double. To find it, walk 100m from the bus stop to the main road, turn east and go 100m past a petrol station on the left, then turn left just before the hospital, and it's about 150m farther on the right (past a reservoir). Or take a samlor for 20B. Good food is available here also.

The run-down *Nang Rong Hotel* has rooms for 100B a single/double, plus an attached restaurant.

**Places to Eat**
In front of the train station is a small night market with good, inexpensive food. This area also has a few restaurants that are open during the day for breakfast and lunch. The restaurant on the corner of the clock tower opens early in the morning and sells coffee, tea and paa-thông-kōh (light Chinese pastries).

At the Samatakan and Thani Rds intersection there is a larger night market that has mostly Chinese as well as a few Isaan vendors. More Isaan food can be found at the *Wiengchan Restaurant* on Nivas Rd near the Grand Hotel.

The *Maitrichit Restaurant* on Sunthonthep Rd near the Prachasamakhi Hotel has a large selection of Thai and Chinese standards which are served from morning until night. Also good is the *Porn Phen (Phawn Phen)* near the Thai Hotel on Romburi Rd.

Just after you turn left (east) from Ban Don Nong Nae on the way to Phanom Rung via Route 2221 there is a nice little family-owned place called *Baan Nit (Nit's House)*

where you can get good home-cooked local food. Nit only has a few tables, but out in this area there's not a lot of choice.

**Getting There & Away**
**Air** Bangkok Airways has tentative plans to build an airport near Buriram in 1997, but for now the nearest airport is in Khorat.

**Bus** Ordinary buses from Khorat to Buriram leave about every 20 minutes between 4.30 am and 7.30 pm. The trip takes about 2½ hours and costs 40B. From Surin ordinary buses head for Buriram at a similar frequency for 30B; this trip takes about an hour.

From Bangkok there are four air-con departures from the Northern Bus Terminal for 179B, plus seven ordinary buses for 79B.

**Train** Buriram is on the Bangkok-Ubon Ratchathani train line. Fares are 67B in 3rd class, 155B in 2nd class and 316B in 1st class, not including supplementary charges for rapid (30B) or express (50B) service. The fastest 3rd class trains to Buriram from Bangkok are the 11.05 am (No 931) and 9.50 pm (No 933) diesel railcars, which each take around five hours to reach Buriram. Rapid and express trains arrive only a half-hour faster than these – see the Nakhon Ratchasima Getting There & Away section earlier in this chapter for departure times from Bangkok.

From Khorat there are six trains to Buriram between 11.30 am and 9.51 pm; the 3rd class fare is 17B, 2nd class is 40B for a journey of around 1¾ hours. Trains from Surin take only 50 minutes and cost just 6B in 3rd class.

# Chaiyaphum Province

Bounded by Phetchabun, Lopburi, Nakhon Ratchasima and Khon Kaen provinces, right in the centre of Thailand, Chaiyaphum might as well be in the middle of nowhere considering its low tourist profile. The least visited of any province in the country, it's so remote

NORTH-EASTERN THAILAND

from national attention that even many Thai citizens can't tell you exactly where it is – or even whether it's in the North or the North-East.

The several Khmer shrine ruins in the province – none of them major sites – indicate that the territory was an Angkor and later Lopburi satellite during the 10th and 11th centuries.

## CHAIYAPHUM
• ☎ (44) • pop 25,600

During the late 1700s a Lao court official brought 200 Lao from Vientiane to settle this area, which had been abandoned by the Khmers 500 years earlier. The community paid tribute to Vientiane but was also careful to cultivate relations with Bangkok and Champasak. When Vientiane's Prince Anou declared war on Siam in the early 1800s, the Lao ruler of Chaiyaphum, Jao Phraya Lae, wisely switched allegiance to Bangkok, knowing full well that Anou's armies didn't stand a chance against the more powerful Siamese. Although Jao Phraya Lae lost his life in battle in 1806, the Siamese sacked Vientiane in 1828 and ruled most of western Laos until the coming of the French near the turn of the century. Today a statue of Jao Phraya Lae (renamed Phraya Phakdi Chumphon by the Thais) stands in a prominent spot in central Chaiyaphum.

Chaiyaphum residents celebrate a week-long festival in Jao Phraya Lae's honour each year in mid-January. Activities focus on his statue and on a shrine erected on the spot where he was killed by Vientiane troops in 1806 – at the base of a tamarind tree about three km west of town off the road to Ban Khwao (Route 225).

The town itself is a typical, medium-grade Thai trade centre with little to hold most visitors for more than a day or so. The districts around Chaiyaphum (especially Kut Lalom to the south) are known for trained elephants and elephant trainers, and it's not uncommon to see an elephant or two walking down the capital streets. Since work demand for elephants in Thailand is steadily declining due to the timber ban, many Chaiyaphum

elephants are being sold to 'elephant camps' for tourists in the North or to circuses in Europe. The city started an annual elephant roundup a few years ago that gained in popularity until the provincial governor had a nightmare in which elephants were injuring people. The roundup has since been cancelled.

The main reason people visit Chaiyaphum nowadays is to tour **Ban Khwao** (15 km west) and other nearby silk villages. Silk can also be purchased at Chaiyaphum shops or in the municipal market in the centre of town. Yin's Guest House (see Places to Stay below) can arrange inexpensive silk village tours. You can also catch a bus to Ban Khwao from the south side of Tantawan Rd just west of Non Meuang Rd. If you've never observed the silk process – from the cultivation of mulberry trees and propagation of silkworms to the dyeing and weaving of silk thread – you're in for an interesting day.

## Prang Ku
ปรางค์กู่

This hollow Khmer prang was constructed during the reign of the final Angkor king, Jayavarman VII (1121-1220) as a 'healing station' on the Angkor temple route between the Angkor capital in Cambodia and Prasat Singh in Kanchanaburi Province. Chaiyaphum residents consider this a very holy spot; many make daily offerings of flowers, candles and incense. The Buddha figure inside the ku purportedly hails from the Dvaravati period (6th to 10th centuries). Also on the small grounds are a Shivalingam pedestal and a venerable old tamarind tree.

Prang Ku is about a km east of the Jao Phraya Lae monument.

## Taat Tohn National Park
อุทยานแห่งชาติตาดโตน

Eighteen km north-west of Chaiyaphum via Route 2051, this seldom visited, 218 sq km park at the edge of the Laen Da mountain range is centred around the scenic waterfalls of **Taat Tohn**, **Taat Klang** and **Phaa Phiang**. Taat Tohn Falls are the largest, reaching 50m

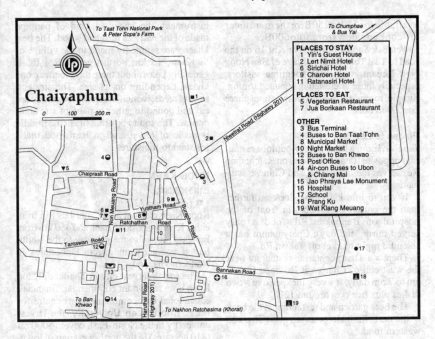

**Chaiyaphum**

0   100   200 m

To Taat Tohn National Park & Peter Sopa's Farm

To Chumphae & Bua Yai

Niwetrat Road (Highway 201)

Chaiprasit Road

Non Meuang Road

Yutitham Road

Ratchathan Road

Burapha Road

Tantawan Road

Bannakan Road

Haruthai Road (Highway 201)

To Ban Khwao

To Nakhon Ratchasima (Khorat)

**PLACES TO STAY**
1 Yin's Guest House
2 Lert Nimit Hotel
6 Sirichai Hotel
9 Charoen Hotel
11 Ratanasiri Hotel

**PLACES TO EAT**
5 Vegetarian Restaurant
7 Jua Borikaan Restaurant

**OTHER**
3 Bus Terminal
4 Buses to Ban Taat Tohn
8 Municipal Market
10 Night Market
12 Buses to Ban Khwao
13 Post Office
14 Air-con Buses to Ubon & Chiang Mai
15 Jao Phraya Lae Monument
16 Hospital
17 School
18 Prang Ku
19 Wat Klang Meuang

wide during the May to October monsoon. Most of the vegetation in the park is associated with dry dipterocarp forest. Little wildlife research has been carried out in the park, but since it lies halfway between Nam Nao National Park on the Chaiyaphum-Phetchabun border and Khao Yai National Park on the Nakhon Nayok-Nakhon Ratchasima-Prachinburi border, it's bound to harbour an interesting variety of resident and migrating species.

Park bungalows are available at the usual 400 to 800B rates. It's best to have your own wheels to find the park since there's no regular public transport from Chaiyaphum. Alternatively, you can get a songthaew from Chaiyaphum as far as Ban Taat Tohn (around 7B), then hire a pickup truck on to the park for 50 to 80B.

**Places to Stay**

*Yin's Guest House* (also known as Joshua's), about 300m north of the main bus terminal,

is a complex of wooden houses run by a Thai-Norwegian couple who charge 60/80B a single/double. Tours of nearby silk villages can be arranged for 50B per person.

The *Ratanasiri Hotel* (☎ 821258), on the corner of Non Meuang and Ratchathan Rds, is an efficiently run place with one floor of rooms with fan for 180 to 240B and two floors with air-con and hot water for 300 to 350B. All rooms come with TV.

The *Sirichai Hotel* (☎ 811461), on the opposite side of Non Meuang Rd farther north, has slightly more up-market rooms with air-con for 360B, plus a few rooms with fan in the 190 to 250B range. Farther east off Yutitham Rd at No 196/7 Soi 1, the run-down *Charoen Hotel* (☎ 812760) has fan rooms for 120 to 280B, air-con for 260 to 280B.

Top-end for Chaiyaphum is the popular *Lert Nimit Hotel* (☎ 811522; fax 822335) on Niwetrat Rd east of the bus terminal on the road to Chumphae (Route 201). Well kept rooms with fan and attached bath are

NORTH-EASTERN THAILAND

available for 200 to 250B, or there are nicer air-con bungalows for 550 to 600B.

*Peter & Sopa's Farm*, near Km 16 on the road to Taat Tohn, in the village of Ban Nong Ngu Leuam, welcomes longtime visitors, especially those interested in organic farming. Simple rooms in a quiet, rural atmosphere cost 60 to 80B.

### Places to Eat

*Jua Borikaan*, a large indoor-outdoor restaurant opposite Ratanasiri Hotel on Ratchathan Rd, serves the usual Thai and Chinese standards.

If you're into kài yâang, look no farther than the cluster of vendors in front of the hospital on Bannakan Rd (food is only served during the day). Chaiyaphum has a splendid night market off Taksin Rd.

There's a Thai vegetarian restaurant near the west end of Chaiprasit Rd open from 7 am to 7 pm daily. It's very inexpensive – two dishes plus rice cost around 12B.

The beer garden and restaurant at the back of the Lert Nimit Hotel serves good Thai and western food.

### Getting There & Away

Chaiyaphum can be reached by bus from Khon Kaen, Khorat and Lom Sak, each of which is about two hours away and costs about 35B.

Buses from Bangkok's Northern Bus Terminal cost 147B air-con (seven hours, nine departures daily) or 65B ordinary (eight hours, every half hour from 6.15 am to 11 pm).

# Khon Kaen & Roi Et Provinces

Khon Kaen and Roi Et are mostly rural provinces where farming and textiles are the main occupations. At the heart of the Isaan region, these provinces are good places to explore Isaan culture – its language, food and music.

Roi Et Province is also known for the crafting of the quintessential Isaan musical

instrument, the khaen, a kind of panpipe made of the *mái kuu* reed and wood. The best khaens are reputedly made in the village of Si Kaew, 15 km north-west of Roi Et. It generally takes about three days to make one khaen, depending on its size. The straight, sturdy reeds, which resemble bamboo, are cut and bound together in pairs of six, eight or nine. The sound box that fits in the middle is made of *tôn pràtuu*, a hardwood that's resistant to moisture.

## KHON KAEN
อ.เมืองขอนแก่น
• ☎ *(43)* • *pop 130,300*

Khon Kaen is about a 2½ hour bus trip from either Khorat or Udon Thani, and 450 km from Bangkok. It is also the gateway to the North-East if you are coming from Phitsanulok in Northern Thailand.

The fourth largest city in Thailand, Khon Kaen is an important commercial, financial, educational and communications centre for Isaan. **Khon Kaen University**, the largest university in the North-East, covers 5000 rai (810 hectares) in the north-west part of town. The city has grown fantastically over the last five years, with lots of added neon and the heaviest automotive traffic in the North-East after Khorat; unlike Khorat the air is fairly clean. A 3.5-km long airstrip built for American B-52s in nearby Nam Pheung may soon be converted into a maintenance centre for Boeing, McDonnell Douglas and/or Airbus craft – if this comes to pass the centre will be another major boost for the local economy.

With its western restaurants, air-con hotels and modern banking facilities, Khon Kaen makes a good spot to take a rest from small-town and village travel in the North-East. It can also be used as a base for day trips to **Chonabot** (57 km south-west), a centre for good quality mát-mii silk, and the Khmer ruins of **Prasat Peuay Noi** (66 km south-east).

### History

The city is named after **Phra That Kham Kaen**, a revered chedi at Wat Chetiyaphum in the village of Ban Kham in Nam Phawng district, 32 km north-east of the amphoe meuang. Legend says that early in this millennium a *thâat* (reliquary stupa) was built over a tamarind tree stump that miraculously came to life after a contingent of monks carrying Buddha relics to Phra That Phanom (in today's Nakhon Phanom Province) camped here overnight. There was no room at That Phanom for more relics, so the monks returned to this spot and enshrined the relics in the new That Kham Kaen (Tamarind Heartwood Reliquary). A town developed nearby but was abandoned several times until 1789, when a Suwannaphum ruler founded a city at the current site, which he named Kham Kaen after the chedi. Over the years the name changed to Khon Kaen (Heartwood Log).

## Information

**Tourist Office** The TAT (☎ 244498; fax 244497) has a branch office in Khon Kaen at 15/5 Prachasamoson Rd, open daily from 8.30 am to 4 pm. The English-speaking staff distribute good maps of the city and can answer queries on Khon Kaen and surrounding provinces.

**Foreign Consulates** At the time of writing, the Lao People's Democratic Republic had opened a Khon Kaen consulate (☎ 223698, 221961) at 123 Photisan Rd. Foreigners have successfully obtained 15 day tourist visas here in three days for 750 to 1000B, depending on nationality. Apparently this is an experimental programme, since the Lao embassy in Bangkok does not issue such visas directly.

There is also a Vietnamese consulate (☎ 241586; fax 241154) in Khon Kaen at 65/6 Chatapadung Rd.

**Money** Every major Thai bank has at least one branch in Khon Kaen, most of them clustered along the south side of Si Chan Rd west of Na Meuang Rd, and along Na Meuang Rd between Si Chan and Reun Rom Rds. Bangkok Bank on Si Chan Rd has an ATM and foreign-exchange window.

**Post & Communications** The main post office on the corner of Si Chan and Klang Meuang Rds is open weekdays from 8.30 am to 4.30 pm, and on Saturday from 9 am to noon. There is a CAT international phone office attached; you can also make international phone calls at the CAT office on Sun Ratchakan Rd in the northern part of town.

**Language Course** AUA (American University Alumni) (☎ 241072) has a branch at Khon Kaen University where Thai instruction may be available.

## Things to See

For visitors, about the only tourist attraction is the very well curated **Khon Kaen National Museum**, which features Dvaravati objects,

### Khon Kaen's Festivals

Khon Kaen's biggest annual event is the Silk and Phuuk Siaw Festival, held for 10 days and nights from late November through early December. Centred at Ratchadanuson Park and in the field in front of the Sala Klang (Provincial Hall), the festival celebrates the planting of the mulberry tree, a necessary step in the production of silk. Another aspect of the festival is *phùuk siaw*, or tying friends, a reference to the *bai sĭi* ceremony in which sacred threads are tied around one's wrists for spiritual protection. The ritual also implies a renewal of the bonds of friendship and reaffirmation of local tradition. Other activities include parades, Isaan music, folk dancing, and the preparation and sharing of Isaan food.

The Flowers and Khaen Music Festival takes place during Songkhran, the Thai lunar new year in mid-April. Along with the customary ritual bathing of important Buddha images at local temples, activities in Khon Kaen include parades of floats bedecked with flowers and plenty of khaen-centred Isaan music. ■

PLACES TO STAY
8  Suksawat Hotel
10  Rot Sukhon Hotel
14  Khon Kaen Hotel
15  Saen Samran Hotel
16  Si Mongkon Hotel
17  Roma Hotel
19  Villa Hotel
22  New Vanasiri Hotel
25  Muang Inn
26  Kaen Inn
32  Kosa Hotel
33  Charoen Thani Princess
34  Hotel Sofitel Raja Orchid
36  Deema Hotel
37  Kaen Nakom Hotel
38  Amarin Plaza Hotel
41  Thani Bungalow
42  Khon Kaen Reunrom Hotel

PLACES TO EAT
1  Kai Yaang Rabiap
6  Khaen Luang
7  First Choice
9  Pizza & Bake
12  Khrua Weh
13  Raan Paa Phawng
18  Thawng 24 Naw
20  Vegetarian Restaurant
23  Harry's Wine Bar
24  The Parrot

OTHER
2  Provincial Hall
3  National Museum
4  THAI Office
5  Bus Terminal
11  TAT Office
21  Funan
27  School
28  Night Market
29  Air-Con Bus Terminal
30  Wat Si Chan
31  Hospital
35  Post Office
39  School
40  Market
43  Wat That

Khon Kaen

To Udon Thani

To Airport & Phitsanulok

To Chonabot (57 km)

To Kalasin

To Prasat Peuay Noi (66 km)

Beung Thung Sang

Beung Kaen Nakhon

Khon Kaen University

Ratchadanuson Park

Train Station

NORTH-EASTERN THAILAND

sēma (ordination marker) stones from Kalasin and Meuang Fa Daet, and bronze and ceramic artefacts from Ban Chiang. It's open Wednesday to Sunday from 9 am to noon and 1 to 5 pm. Admission is 10B.

On the banks of Khon Kaen's 603 rai (in the rainy season) **Beung Kaen Nakhon** (Kaen Nakhon Pond) is the Isaan-style **Wat That**, with elongated spires on the prasat – typical of this area. At the south end of Beung Kaen Nakhon, **Wat Nong Wang Muang** features a new nine tier chedi. This lake and **Beung Thung Sang** in the north-eastern section of town are favourite venues for evening strolls.

**Places to Stay – bottom end**
As Khon Kaen is a large city and an important transit point, there are many hotels to choose from. The part-wooden, part-cement *Saen Samran* (a roman-script sign reads 'Sansumran') at 55/9 Klang Meuang Rd has reasonable rooms for 160 to 200B with fan or 250B with air-con. Just a bit farther down the street is the lower-priced *Si Mongkon* at No 61-67; grungy rooms here cost 90B with fan, 400B with air-con.

*Suksawat* (☎ 239611), off Klang Meuang Rd, is quieter since it's a bit off the main streets; rooms are 70B with shared facilities,

90 to 140B with fan and bath. The *Sawatdee* (☎ 221600), 177-9 Na Meuang Rd, starts at 150B for rooms with fan, up to 600B for air-con.

The newish *Coco Guest House*, in a bar area behind the First Choice restaurant between Na Meuang and Klang Meuang Rds, has simple, modern singles/doubles for 100/200B, air-con 300B. The nearby *New Vanasiri Hotel* (☎ 235816), off Si Chan Rd near Soi Yimsiri, has OK rooms with fan and bath for 120 to 180B.

*Thani Bungalow* (☎ 221470), on Reun Rom Rd, has clean bungalows with fan and bath for 200B, and rooms with air-con and hot water for 400B. It's near the train station and Hua Rot Fai Market.

### Places to Stay – middle

Khon Kaen excels in this category, with a fine selection of places in the 400 to 600B range.

The friendly, long-running *Roma Hotel* (☎ 236276) at 50/2 Klang Meuang Rd has large rooms with fan for 230 to 280B, plus refurbished air-con rooms for 500 to 800B. *Deema Hotel* (☎ 321562; fax 321561) at 133 Chetachon Rd, near the bus terminal and market, has clean rooms with private hot water bath and fan for 250B, air-con for 350 to 450B.

The newish, four-storey *Muang Inn* (☎ 238667; fax 243176), at a convenient location on Na Meuang Rd, offers tidy air-con rooms with telephone in the 500 to 1000B range. The new *Amarin Plaza Hotel* off Lang Muang Rd has nice air-con rooms with hot water for 480B.

*Phu Inn* (☎ 243174), a similar mid-range spot near the market at 26 Satityutitham Rd, has 98 air-con rooms for 400 to 600B. The relatively new *Khon Kaen Reunrom Hotel* (☎ 223522; fax 220567) at 335 Ruen Rom Rd, near the train station, has 72 air-con rooms for 450 to 500B; all rooms come with TV, fridge and hot water – good value in this range.

Toward the eastern end of Si Chan Rd, near Wat Si Chan, the *Kaen Nakorn Hotel* (☎ 224268; fax 224272) has 150 clean and comfortable air-con rooms for 300 to 600B.

The *Villa* (☎ 236640), on the corner of Klang Meuang and Ammat Rds, is mostly a short-time place attached to a massage parlour/'entertainment complex', but it has air-con rooms for 300 to 500B.

### Places to Stay – top end

More expensive places include the *Khon Kaen Hotel* (☎ 237711) on Phimphaseut Rd, which has air-con singles/doubles for 600/700B, and the similar *Rosesukon (Rot Sukhon) Hotel* (☎ 238576), near the Khon Kaen Hotel on Klang Meuang Rd, where singles/doubles cost 700/800B. Both hotels also have more expensive suites in the 1200 to 2000B range.

The popular *Kosa Hotel* (☎ 225014) on Si Chan Rd has rooms with all the amenities for 990 to 1800B. The attached up-market coffee shop/massage parlour attracts a steady flow of Thai businessmen. Next door the new 280-room *Hotel Sofitel Raja Orchid* (☎ 322-155; fax 322150) is under construction.

Until recently the top hotel in the city was the friendly 200-room *Kaen Inn* (☎ 237744; fax 239457) at 56 Klang Meuang Rd; doubles cost 800 to 1200B with air-con, TV, telephone and fridge. On the premises are Chinese and Japanese restaurants, a karaoke lounge, coffee shop, barber room and snooker club. This hotel is often full.

The new 320-room *Charoen Thani Princess* (☎ 220400; fax 220438; ☎ (2) 281-3088 in Bangkok) towers over the city at 260 Si Chan Rd. Well appointed singles/doubles with all mod-cons, including cable TV, cost 1484 to 1648B. Facilities include conference rooms, a banquet-style Chinese restaurant, coffee shop and pool. An attached entertainment complex is under construction.

### Places to Eat

**Thai & Isaan** Khon Kaen has a lively night market with plenty of good food stalls next to the air-con bus terminal; look for the busy *Khun Aem* jók stall, which serves exemplary broken-rice congee. Opposite the Villa Hotel, the 24 hour *Thawng 24 Naw* is a khâo tôm place with all the usual Thai and Chinese standards.

NORTH-EASTERN THAILAND

*Raan Paa Phawng* (no English sign), on Klang Meuang Rd south of Khrua Weh (see below), has the best kài yâang in town, plus several varieties of sôm-tam. It's only open from around 9 am to 4 pm. Another good spot for local Isaan food is *Kai Yaang Rabiap*, on Theparak Rd near the corner of Lang Sunratchakan Rd.

*Khrua Weh* (Tiam An Hue in Vietnamese) is an excellent Vietnamese restaurant in an old house on Klang Meuang Rd near Prachasamoson Rd. Prices are moderate and the bilingual menu features many Thai and Isaan dishes as well. Yam kài weh, a spicy chicken and mint salad, is a house speciality, as are kà-yaw sòt, fresh spring rolls.

The mid-price, air-con *First Choice* opposite Khon Kaen Hotel offers an extensive selection of Thai and vegetarian dishes. It opens at 7 am for breakfast.

A good night market convenes along Ruen Rom Rd between Klang Meuang and Na Meuang Rds each evening from around sunset to 11 pm.

**Western** *The Parrot*, on Si Chan Rd near Kosa Hotel, offers good western breakfasts (with wholemeal toast and Dutch coffee) for 40 to 55B. The lengthy menu includes grilled salmon, submarine sandwiches, pizza and good Thai food. Friendly service is a plus, and bread is available for purchase by the loaf.

Around the corner on Soi Yimsiri, *Harry's Wine Bar* (☎ 239755) features imported wines by the glass or bottle, and a range of fixed-price meals in English and US styles, as well as sandwiches, burgers, ice cream and Thai food; prices are moderate. Both of these restaurants are popular with the local expat crowd as well as well-to-do Thais; Harry's is open from 10.30 am to midnight, the Parrot from 8 am to 10 pm.

The family-oriented *Pizza & Bake* has two locations, one near the THAI office on Maliwan Rd west of the train line and another on the corner of Phimphaseut and Klang Meuang Rds. Pizza is the main focus, but the restaurant also prepares a variety of other European and Thai dishes.

**Vegetarian** *Ob-Un Vegetarian Restaurant* (English sign reads 'Vegetarian Food') off the north side of Si Chan Rd serves Thai vegetarian dishes for 15 to 25B and is open daily from 8 am to 9 pm. The *Vegetarian Restaurant* on Lang Muang Rd is similar.

### Entertainment

*Khaen Luang* (☎ 241922) on Phimphaseut Rd is a large nightclub that features Isaan music – predominantly maw lam and lûuk thûng – and folk dancing nightly. You can sit at tables at the front or on cushions and mats at the back; Thai and Isaan food is served.

*Funan*, on Si Chan Rd near the train line, is a wooden shophouse where local college and university students hang out and listen to live *phleng phêua chii-wít* (modern Thai folk songs) and occasional jazz. *Top West*, down a soi on the opposite side of the street, has duplicated the 'old west' theme found all over the country.

*Music World* opposite the Prachasamran Rd T-junction features live Thai pop bands in a heavy-metal decor.

*Thai Classical Massage* at the Khon Kaen Hotel offers traditional massage. The Kosa Hotel also has a massage annexe but it's definitely not the traditional kind.

### Things to Buy

Khon Kaen is a good place to buy handcrafted Isaan goods such as silk and cotton fabrics (you can get mát-mii cotton as well as silk), silver and basketry. A speciality of the North-East is the *māwn khwāan* (axe pillow), a stiff triangle-shaped pillow used as a support while sitting on the floor. These come in many sizes, from small enough to carry in a handbag to large enough to fill your entire backpack. Perhaps the most practical way to acquire axe pillows while on the road is to buy them unstuffed *(mâi sài nûn,* 'no kapok inserted') – the covers are easily carried and you can stuff them when you get home.

If textiles are your main interest, try Prathamakhan at 79/2-3 Reun Rom Rd just west of Na Meuang Rd, Rin Mai Thai at 412 Na Meuang Rd, and the Handicraft Centre for Development of Isaan Women, 90/85 Chetakhon Rd.

Several shops selling local preserved foods and other Isaan products can be found along Klang Meuang Rd between Prachasamoson and Si Chan Rds, including Jerat, Naem Laplae and Heng Nguan Hiang. The emphasis in these shops is *nãem* and other types of sausage or processed meats such as *sâi kràwk, mũu yãw, kun siang mũu* and *kuu siang kài*. Still, behind the stacks of sausage you can often ferret out some good handicraft purchases.

### Getting There & Away

**Air** THAI flies four times daily between Bangkok and Khon Kaen (1080B one way, 55 minutes). There is no longer a THAI flight between Phitsanulok and Khon Kaen, although you should check to see if this has changed.

The Khon Kaen THAI office (☎ 236523, 239011) is at 183/6 Maliwan Rd. The airport is a few km west of the city centre off Highway 12; minivan shuttles between the airport and the city are available through THAI.

Orient Express Air (☎ 344631) flies daily from Chiang Mai for 1115B one way, from Udon Thani twice a week for 800B and from Ubon Ratchathani on Saturday for 1100B. It has an office at the airport.

**Bus** Ordinary buses arrive at and depart from a terminal on Prachasamoson Rd, while air-con buses use a depot near the market off Klang Meuang Rd.

An air-con bus from Bangkok's Northern Bus Terminal costs 193B. Departures are every half hour between 8.30 am and 11.30 pm. There are also a couple of VIP bus departures daily that cost 295B. This is a seven to eight hour bus trip.

The Phitsanulok to Khon Kaen road runs through spectacular scenery, including a couple of national parks. Ordinary buses to Khon Kaen leave Phitsanulok hourly between 10 am and 4.30 pm, then again every hour from 6.30 pm to 1 am. The trip takes about five hours and costs 92B. Air-con

buses leave Phitsanulok less frequently for 129 to 156B depending on the company.

Air-con night buses between Khon Kaen and Chiang Mai (11 to 12 hours) are available for 268B (8 pm; old route via Tak) or 307B (8 and 9 pm; new route via Utaradit). An 8 pm VIP bus is also available for 345B. An ordinary bus takes 12 hours and costs 192B.

Other air-con bus destinations include Chiang Rai (339B, 13 hours), Nakhon Phanom (264B, four hours), Ubon (125B, five hours), Nong Khai (79B, five hours) and Loei (95B, four hours).

Ordinary buses leave Khorat for Khon Kaen roughly every half hour from 5.30 am until 5.30 pm, arriving 2½ to three hours later. The cost is 48B. Other destinations include Udon Thani (32B, two hours), Chaiyaphum (34B, two hours) and Surin (69B, 5½ hours).

**Train** Rapid No 33 and express No 945 depart from Bangkok's Hualamphong station at 6.15 and 8.20 am, arriving in Khon Kaen at 2.08 and 3.25 pm respectively. The only overnight sleeper train that arrives at a semi-decent hour is express No 3, which leaves Bangkok at 8.30 pm and arrives in Khon Kaen at 4.43 am. A non-sleeper express railcar, No 947, leaves at 8.40 pm and arrives at 4.20 am. Direct 3rd class trains are only available from Saraburi and farther north-east (eg Khorat).

Trains from Khorat leave four times daily between 6 am and 10.30 pm, arriving in Khon Kaen 4½ to five hours later. The 3rd class fare is 27B.

### Getting Around

A regular songthaew system plies the central city for 3B per person. There aren't many tuk-tuks or samlors in town so if you want to charter a vehicle you usually have to pay a songthaew driver 30 to 50B.

### AROUND KHON KAEN
#### Chonabot

This small town south-east of amphoe meuang Khon Kaen is famous throughout Thailand for mát-mii cotton and silk. Mát-mii is a method of tie-dyeing the threads

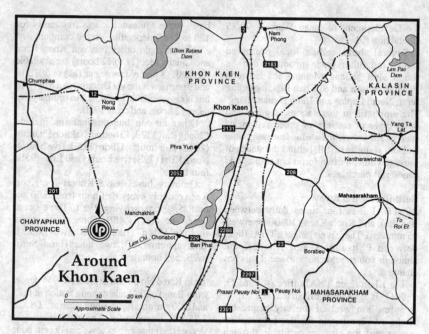

**Around Khon Kaen**

0        10        20 km

Approximate Scale

NORTH-EASTERN THAILAND

before weaving and is similar to Indonesian ikat. The easiest place to see the fabrics is at the **Suun Silapahattakam Pheun Baan** (Local Handicraft Centre) on Pho Sii Sa-aat Rd opposite Wat Pho Sii Sa-aat, about 10 km from the Highway 2/Ban Phai junction off Route 229 in the northern part of town. The centre is really more of a village. It displays and sells silk, cotton, ceramics, fishtraps and other assorted handicrafts (including some weavings from Laos), and is open from 9 am to 6 pm daily.

Better-quality cloth can be found at silk-weaving houses along nearby streets – look for looms beneath the wooden homes. Even if you're not interested in buying it's worth wandering around to see the amazing variety of simple wooden contraptions devised to spin, tie, weave and dry silk.

Some of the more reputable weaving households include those belonging to Khun Songkhram, Khun Suwan, Khun Thongsuk and Khun Chin. Very little English is spoken

in Chonabot so it helps considerably if you bring someone along who can speak Thai.

**Getting There & Away**  Songthaews to Chonabot leave the ordinary bus terminal in Khon Kaen hourly between 5.30 am and 5.30 pm for 12B; the last one back from Chonabot leaves the market around 3.30 or 4 pm. The trip lasts around 45 minutes to an hour.

There is a train station in Ban Phai, about 11 km west of Chonabot. From Khon Kaen to Ban Phai there are nine trains daily between 5 am and 10.16 pm (in the reverse direction six trains depart from Ban Phai between 8.47 am and 6.15 pm). The 3rd class fare is 6B for a journey of around 40 minutes. Songthaews (5B) between the Ban Phai train station and Chonabot leave frequently from around 6 am to 6 pm.

Chonabot can also be reached from the south (eg Khorat) via bus or train to Ban Phai. Ban Phai is 167 km north-east of Khorat.

## Prasat Peuay Noi

Also known as Ku Peuay Noi, and locally known as That Ku Thong, this 12th century Khmer temple ruin is now undergoing restoration at Khon Kaen government expense. About the size of Buriram's Prasat Meuang Tam, the monument consists of a large central sandstone sanctuary surmounted by a Lopburi-style prang and surrounded by stone slab walls with two major gates. The site is very rich in sculpted lintels; during restoration many of them have been gathered together to one side of the monument in a sort of impromptu sculpture garden.

**Getting There & Away** Although Prasat Peuay Noi can be time-consuming to approach if you don't have your own transport, it's a rewarding visit for the quiet scenery along the way, even if you're not a Khmer temple buff. On your own from Khon Kaen, proceed 44 km south on Highway 2 to Ban Phai, then east on Highway 23 (signposted to Borabeu), 11 km to Route 2297. Follow Route 2297 for 24 km south-east through a scenic tableau of rice fields and grazing cattle to the town of Peuay Noi. The ruins are at the western end of town on the south side of the road; you can't miss their grey eminence on your right as you enter the town.

By public transport from Khon Kaen, take a bus or train to Ban Phai, then a songthaew to Peuay Noi. Start early in the morning if you plan to do this in one day; the last songthaew back to Ban Phai from Peuay Noi leaves around 3 pm. Hitching may be possible. See the Chonabot Getting There & Away section earlier for details on transport to Ban Phai.

## ROI ET
อ.เมืองร้อยเอ็ด
• ☎ (43) • pop 34,000

Roi Et is the fairly small but growing capital of a province which, three centuries ago, probably served as a buffer between Thai and Lao political conflict. Old Roi Et had 11 city gates and was surrounded by its 11 vassal colonies. The name Roi Et means 'one hundred and one'; this could be an exaggeration of the number 11.

The capital is now on an entirely new site,

with the large **Beung Phlan Chai** artificial lake in the centre. Paddleboats are available for hire on the lake. An island in the middle, reached by north, west and south causeways, features a fitness park surrounding a tall walking Buddha – demonstrating perhaps that even the Buddha walked for health?

Silk and cotton fabrics from Roi Et are high in quality and generally cheaper than in Khorat and Khon Kaen.

A branch of Bangkok Bank near the Ban Chong Hotel offers foreign-exchange services.

## Wat Neua
วัดเหนือ

This wat, in the northern quarter of town, is worth seeing for its 1200 year old chedi from the Dvaravati period called Phra Satuup Jedi. This chedi exhibits an unusual four cornered bell-shaped form that is rare in Thailand. Around the bòt are a few old Dvaravati *sema* (ordination stones) and to one side of the wat is an inscribed pillar, erected by the Khmers when they controlled this area during the 11th and 12th centuries.

## Wat Burapha
วัดบุรพา

The tall, standing Buddha that towers above Roi Et's minimal skyline is the Phra Phuttha-ratana-mongkon-mahamuni (Phra Sung Yai for short) at Wat Burapha. Despite being of little artistic significance, it's hard to ignore. From the ground to the tip of the *ùtsànìt* (flame-top head ornament), it's 67.8m high, including the base. You can climb a staircase through a building which supports the figure to about as high as the Buddha's knees and get a view of the town.

## Places to Stay

Accommodation in Roi Et costs less than in many provincial capitals. The friendly *Ban Chong (Banjong)* (☎ 511235) at 99-101 Suriyadet Bamrung Rd has adequate rooms with fan and bath from 80 to 140B. On the same street at No 133 is the *Saithip*, where fan-cooled rooms cost 200 to 220B, air-con 280 to 300B; this one's often full.

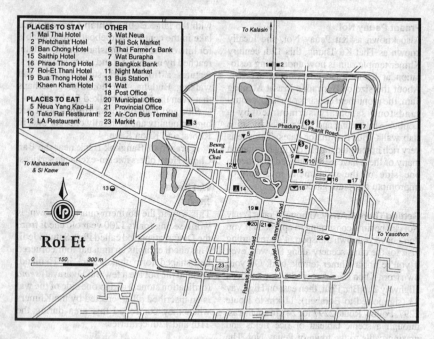

PLACES TO STAY
1  Mai Thai Hotel
2  Phetcharat Hotel
9  Ban Chong Hotel
15 Saithip Hotel
16 Phrae Thong Hotel
17 Roi-Et Thani Hotel
19 Bua Thong Hotel &
   Khaen Kham Hotel

PLACES TO EAT
5  Neua Yang Kao-Lii
10 Tako Rai Restaurant
12 LA Restaurant

OTHER
3  Wat Neua
4  Hai Sok Market
6  Thai Farmer's Bank
7  Wat Burapha
8  Bangkok Bank
11 Night Market
13 Bus Station
14 Wat
18 Post Office
20 Municipal Office
21 Provincial Office
22 Air-Con Bus Terminal
23 Market

To Kalasin

Phadung Phanit Road

Beung
Phlan
Chai

To Mahasarakham
& Si Kaew

Roi Et

0    150    300 m

Rattakit Khlaikhla Road

Sunyadet

Bamrung Road

To Yasothon

**NORTH-EASTERN THAILAND**

The *Khaen Kham* (☎ 511508) at 52-62 Rattakit Khlaikhla Rd has clean rooms with fan and bath for 140 to 180B, air-con for 260 to 300B. A coffee shop is attached. Also on Rattakit Khlaikhla Rd is the cheaper *Bua Thong* (☎ 511142) at No 46, with basic rooms with fan and bath for 90B, air-con for 200B.

The noisy *Phrae Thong Hotel* (☎ 511127) at 45-47 Ploenchit Rd, next to a Chinese temple, has comfortable rooms for 110 to 160B with fan, 200 to 250B with air-con.

*Mai Thai* (☎ 511136) at 99 Haisok Rd has all air-con rooms for 475 to 611B. The *Petcharat Hotel* (☎ 511741, 514058; fax 511837) opposite the Mai Thai has clean mid-range air-con rooms with hot water for 280 to 480B, or 25% more if you pay by credit card. Ask for a room off the road.

The relatively new *Roi-Et Thani Hotel* (☎ 520387; fax 520401), near the Phrae Thong Hotel, has 150 rooms for 800/900B a single/double, all with air-con, bath, phone

(with jacks for modem/fax), TV, minibar and carpet, plus nicer VIP rooms for 1750B. There are two restaurants on the premises.

**Places to Eat**

Around the edge of Beung Phlan Chai are several medium-price garden restaurants. The *Neua Yaang Kao-Lii* is on the north-western side and has a pleasant atmosphere, a menu in English and good food; the name-sake house speciality is cook-it-yourself Korean beef. Another good lakeside place is the indoors *LA*.

You'll find a string of cheaper restaurants along Ratsadan Uthit Rd, which runs east off the lake from the north-eastern corner.

*Tako Rai*, on Sukkasem Rd around the corner from the Ban Chong Hotel, serves some of the best Isaan food in town. The night market area is a couple of streets east of the Ban Chong and Saithip hotels. A decent night market assembles each evening along a street a block south of the post office.

## Things to Buy

If you want to buy local handicrafts, the best place to go is the shopping area along Phadung Phanit Rd, where you'll find māwn khwaan, phâa mát-mii (tie-dyed silk and cotton fabric), sticky-rice baskets, khaens and Buddhist paraphernalia. Phaw Kaan Khaa, at 377-9 Phadung Phanit Rd, has a particularly good selection of fabrics, but as always you must bargain well to get good prices. Charin (Jarin) at 383-385 Phadung Phanit Rd is also good; the owner speaks some English and he also sells gourmet Thai groceries.

Roi Et's street fabric vendors have better prices but less of a selection (and are lower quality) than the shops. On the street, four metres of yeoman-quality cotton mát-mii costs as low as 150B. Weavers themselves buy from a weaving supply shop at 371 Phadung Phanit Rd; here you may see local betel-munchers squatting on the floor checking out dyes, pattern books and pre-knotted skeins.

## Getting There & Away

Buses from Udon Thani to Roi Et are 34B (air-con 68B), and from Khon Kaen 30B (air-con 55B). If you're coming straight from Bangkok's Northern Bus Terminal, you can catch an air-con bus for 220B at 8.30 or 10 am, or every half hour from 8.30 to 11 pm. The trip takes about eight hours. VIP buses cost 420B and leave at 7.30 and 8.10 pm nightly (in the reverse direction at 7.30 pm only).

Ordinary bus destinations include Surin (38B), Yasothon (20B), Ubon Ratchathani (44B) and Khon Kaen (30B).

## Getting Around

Samlors around town are 10 to 15B; motorised samlors cost 15 to 30B.

## AROUND ROI ET
### Ku Phra Khona

Around 60 km south-east of amphoe meuang Roi Et, in Suwannaphum district, are the ruins of an 11th century Khmer shrine. The monument comprises three brick prangs

facing east from a sandstone pediment, surrounded by a sandstone slab wall with four gates. The middle prang was replastered in 1928 and Buddha niches were added. A Buddha footprint shrine, added to the front of this prang, is adorned with the Khmer monument's original Bayon-style naga (dragon-headed serpent) sculptures.

The two remaining prangs have been restored but retain their original forms, which also show Bayon (1017-87) influence. The northern prang features a Narai (Vishnu) lintel over one door and a Ramayana relief on the inside gable.

**Getting There & Away** Suwannaphum can be reached by frequent buses (20B) and songthaews (12B) from the capital via Route 215. From Suwannaphum it's another 17 km south via Route 214 to Ku Phra Khona; any Surin-bound bus can stop on the highway at the town of Ku, which is at the T-intersection with Route 2086 east to Phon Sai. The ruins are in a wat compound known locally as Wat Ku. The ruins could also be approached from Surin, 78 km south.

# Udon Thani Province

## UDON THANI
### อ.เมืองอุดรธานี
• ☎ (42) • pop 95,000

Just over 560 km from Bangkok, Udon (often spelt Udorn) is one of several North-Eastern cities that boomed virtually overnight when US air bases were established nearby during the Vietnam War (there were seven bases in Thailand until the USA pulled out in 1976).

Although the bases are long gone, the US presence lives on, albeit to a much more limited degree. A small number of retired US military personnel and missionaries have settled in the area and a US consulate is still active. Outside the town near the village of Ban Dung a huge Voice of America (VOA) transmitter was recently constructed at a cost of US$200 million. To reach points throughout

South-East Asia, China and Korea, the Ban Dung VOA station runs up an estimated US$3.5 million power bill every year.

In addition to being a US playground, Udon functions as a transport hub and an agricultural market centre for surrounding provinces. Except as a base for touring nearby Ban Chiang, Ban Pheu or *khít*-weaving villages, the city has little to offer, unless you've spent a long time already in the North-East and are seeking western amenities like air-con coffee houses, flashy ice-cream or farang food (though for all of these, Khon Kaen is better).

### Information

**Tourist Office** The TAT (☎ 325406) has recently built an office at 16/5 Mukkhamontri Rd near Nong Prajak. This office has printed material on Udon, Loei and Nong Khai provinces, and is open from 8.30 am to 4.30 pm daily.

**Foreign Consulates** There's a small US consulate (☎ 244270) in the north-western section of the city at 35/6 Suphakit Janya Rd, near Nong Prajak. The staff can assist US citizens with the extension or replacement of their passports and other emergency situations. The consulate also distributes a useful packet of information on Udon for prospective US expat residents. Opening hours are from 7.30 am to 4.30 pm Monday to Friday.

**Indochina Visas** Kannika Tour (☎ 241378), at 36/9 Si Sattha Rd, and Aranya Tour (☎ 247320), 105 Mak Khaeng Rd, can arrange visas and/or tours for Laos, Cambodia and Vietnam. Most of their clientele are Thai but they're happy to work with foreigners as well.

**Money** Several banks along the main avenues provide foreign-exchange services. Only the Bangkok Bank on Prajak Silpakorn Rd has an after-hours exchange window, usually open until 8 pm.

**Post & Communications** The GPO on Wattana Rd is open Monday to Friday from 8.30 am to 4.30 pm and on weekends and holidays from 9 am to noon. The upstairs telephone office is open from 7 am to 10 pm daily.

**Medical Services** Wattana Hospital, on Suphakit Janya Rd near Nong Prajak and the US consulate, is the best medical facility in the upper North-East.

### Things to See & Do

In the north-east corner of the Thung Si Meuang (City Field) is the **Lak Meuang**, or city phallus-pillar, where the city's guardian deity is thought to reside. Encrusted with gold leaf and surrounded by offerings of flowers, candles and incense, the pillar shrine sits next to a smaller shrine containing Phra Phuttha Pho Thong, a Buddha stele of undetermined age. Next to this is a sacred banyan tree used as a repository for broken or abandoned spirit houses and Chinese house shrines.

To get away from the busy central area, go for a walk around **Nong Prajak**, a reservoir/park in the north-western part of town.

### Places to Stay – bottom end

Udon has a plethora of hotels in all price ranges. The central *Krung Thong Hotel* (☎ 295299) at 195-9 Pho Si Rd offers fair rooms for 90B with shared bath, 140/190B with fan and bath, or 200/300B with air-con. *Queen Hotel* at 6-8 Udon-dutsadi Rd has simple rooms with fan and bath from 100 to 150B, air-con for 200B. *Sriswast (Si Sawat) Hotel* at 123 Prajak Silpakorn Rd costs 100B for a room with fan and shared bath in the old building, or 140 to 280B for rooms with fan and private bath in the new building. It's a bit noisy, according to one report, charming according to others. It definitely has more character than most hotels in this range.

Nicer than any of the above yet no more expensive, the *Tang Porn Dhiraksa Hotel* (☎ 221032) on Mak Khaeng Rd has large, fairly quiet fan rooms for 120B with shared bath, 180B with attached bath.

Another decent place in this range is *Prachapakdee (Prachaphakdi) Hotel* (☎ 221804) at 156/8 Prajak Silpakorn Rd.

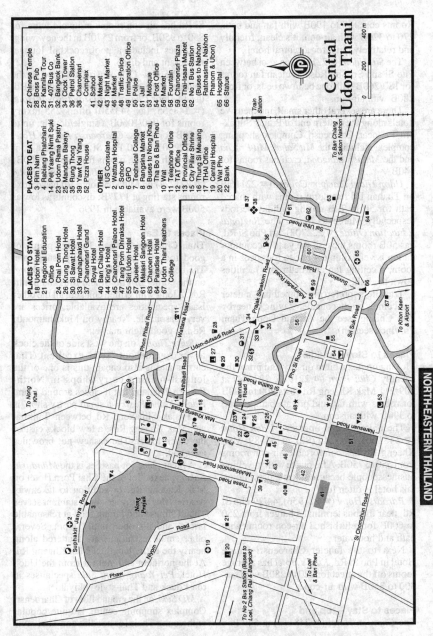

# Central Udon Thani

0   200   400 m

**PLACES TO STAY**

18  Udon Hotel
21  Regional Education
    Office
24  Chai Pom Hotel
26  Krung Thong Hotel
30  Si Sawat Hotel
33  Prachaphakdi Hotel
37  Charoensri Grand
    Royal Hotel
40  Ban Chiang Hotel
44  King's Hotel
45  Charoensri Palace Hotel
47  Tang Porn Dhiraksa Hotel
55  Siri Udon Hotel
57  Queen Hotel
61  Malasin Sangoen Hotel
63  Charoen Hotel
64  Paradise Hotel
67  Udon Thani Teachers
    College

**PLACES TO EAT**

3   Rim Nam
4   Rabiang Phatchani
14  Pet Yaang Nimit Suki
23  Udom Rama Pastry
25  Mandarin Bakery
35  Rung Thong
39  Yawt Kai Yang
52  Pizza House

**OTHER**

1   US Consulate
2   Wattana Hospital
5   School
6   GPO
7   Technical College
8   Rangsina Market
9   Buses to Nong Khai,
    Tha Bo & Ban Pheu
10  Wat
11  Telephone Office
12  TAT Office
13  Provincial Office
15  City Pillar Shrine
16  Thung Si Meuang
17  THAI Office
19  Central Hospital
20  Wat Pho
22  Bank
27  Chinese Temple
28  Boss Pub
29  Karnika Tour
31  407 Bus Co
32  Bangkok Bank
34  Clock Tower
36  Petrol Station
38  Charoensri
    Complex
41  School
42  Market
43  Night Market
46  Market
48  Traffic Police
49  Immigration Office
50  Police
51  Jail
53  Mosque
54  Post Office
56  Market
58  Fountain
59  Charoensri Plaza
60  Thai-Isaan Market
62  No 1 Bus Station
    (Buses to Nakhon
    Ratchasima, Nakhon
    Phanom & Ubon)
65  Hospital
66  Statue

NORTH-EASTERN THAILAND

Rooms cost 150 to 190B with fan and bath, 270 to 320B with air-con; it's clean, friendly and relatively quiet for a central hotel.

The *Siri Udon* (☎ 221658) on a soi between Pho Si and Sri Suk Rds has clean fan rooms for 180/260B with one bed/two beds, or from 280B with air-con.

There are several other small, inexpensive hotels along the eastern end of Prajak Silpakorn Rd near Charoensri Complex shopping complex, including the *Mit Sahai, Mit Pracha* and the *Malasri Sangoen*; each has rooms for 140B.

*Udon Thani Teachers College* (☎ 221169) on Thahan Rd lets dorm rooms with shared bath for 30 to 70B during holiday periods (especially March to May). The *Regional Education Office* (☎ 222702), off Pho Si Rd, has 50B rooms most of the year. Accommodation is very simple – one to four beds in a room, a ceiling fan and bathroom facilities down the hall.

Travellers preferring something quieter and calmer might consider staying in nearby Ban Chiang (see the Around Udon Thani Province section).

### Places to Stay – middle

Moving up just a bit in quality and price, the friendly *Chai Porn* (☎ 221913, 222144) at 209-211 Mak Khaeng Rd costs 200 to 290B for rooms with fan and private bath, or 300 to 390B with air-con.

The enlarged and upgraded *Udon Hotel* (☎ 248160; fax 242782) at 81-89 Mak Khaeng Rd has comfortable air-con rooms from 550 to 750B. A favourite with travelling businesspeople because it has a parking lot, this hotel is often full.

*Paradise Hotel* (☎ 221956), 44/29 Pho Si Rd, near the bus terminal, charges from 250 to 600B for refurbished air-con rooms with bath and hot water.

Next to the fancier Charoensri Palace Hotel in Pho Si Rd, *King's Hotel* has average rooms off the street for 220 to 280B with fan, 300 to 360B with air-con.

### Places to Stay – top end

The *Charoen Hotel* (☎ 248115) at 549 Pho Si Rd has air-con rooms in its old wing for 850 to 950B, or from 2570B in the new wing. Facilities include a pool, cocktail lounge, restaurant and disco.

At the new Charoensri Complex, at the south-eastern end of Prajak Silpakorn Rd, the 14-floor *Charoensri Grand Royal Hotel* (☎ 343555; fax 343550) offers 255 luxury rooms for 960/1060B a single/double, up to 2120B for suites. *Charoensri Palace Hotel* (☎ 222601) at 60 Pho Si Rd comes a poor third with air-con rooms from 450 to 900B.

The new 130-room *Ban Chiang Hotel* (☎ 221227) on Mukkhamontri Rd has deluxe rooms starting at 1777B; discounts as low as 500B were available in 1996.

### Places to Eat

**Thai, Chinese & Isaan** There is plenty of good food in Udon, especially Isaan fare. The best kài yâang place is *Yawt Kai Yang*, on the corner of Pho Si and Mukkhamontri Rds. Along with grilled chicken, all the other Isaan specialities are available; prices are very reasonable. Nearby on Mukkhamontri Rd is a good night market.

*Rung Thong*, on the west side of the clock tower roundabout, sells excellent Thai curries and is also cheap; this is one of the longest-running curry shops in North-Eastern Thailand but it closes around 5 pm. *Udorn Rama Pastry*, a small pastry shop, is on Prajak Silpakorn Rd between Tamruat and Mak Khaeng Rds, a few blocks east of the clock tower. The cashew-nut brownies are good.

A nicer place for pastries is the *Mandarin Bakery*, next door to the Chai Porn Hotel on Mak Khaeng Rd. In addition to takeaway pastries, this roomy air-con restaurant serves Thai, Chinese and farang food at reasonable prices, and it's open until 11 pm. Several other small restaurants are scattered along nearly the entire length of Mak Khaeng Rd. At the northern end, not far from the Udon Hotel, *Pet Yaang Nimit Suki* specialises in roast duck and Thai-style sukiyaki.

*MD Suki*, on the ground floor of Charoensri Complex shopping centre, is quite popular with young Thais for noodles and Thai-style sukiyaki. There's also a good food centre on the 3rd floor of this shopping centre, and a *KFC* downstairs.

On the banks of the Nong Prajak reservoir off Suphakit Janya Rd are two decent open-air Thai restaurants, *Rim Nam* and *Rabiang Phatchani*.

**Western** The 3rd floor of the Charoensri Complex at the south-eastern end of Prajak Silpakorn Rd contains *KFC, Sunmerry Bakery* and a huge supermarket. You'll find coffee shops on both the ground and 2nd floors, including the popular *Black Canyon*, with more than 20 kinds of coffee. The *Steak & Pizza House* on the 2nd floor is only passable.

Although it's inconveniently located, the *International Bar Steak House* (☎ 245341), also known as John's International Bar, has the best western food in town. Outdoor dining is at shaded tables around a pond; there's also an indoor dining area in a small tin-roofed brick hut. The menu is very reasonably priced and the clientele is an equal mix of Thais and expats. The disadvantage is that it's a bit out of town and hard to find – you have to really want farang food to come this far. It's off the highway north of the city at 325 Muu 4, Ban Leuam Rawp Meuang. To get there, take a tuk-tuk north to the highway, enter the Thai Samet School grounds and follow the signs for about a km to the restaurant. It's near the No 2 bus terminal, which is about a 150m walk from the school.

Two other places with farang food are the *Pizza House*, 63/1 Naresuan Rd, and *TJ's Restaurant*, 337 Nong Sam Rong Rd.

## Entertainment

The *Chao Phraya Theatre* at 150 Ratchaphatsadu Rd has a sound room that plays the original soundtracks of English-language films – probably the only such theatre in North-Eastern Thailand. For somewhere to go at night, the *Charoen Hotel* has a comfortable bar and also a disco. *La Reine* at the Udon Hotel is a popular cabaret-style club.

*Boss Pub* on Udon-dutsadi Rd, 200m from the clock tower, offers live jazz, reggae and Thai pop nightly.

Mak Khaeng Rd, in the vicinity of the Udon Hotel, has a few modern massage parlours left over from the US GI era; nowadays the clientele is mostly Thai.

## Things to Buy

Udon's main shopping district is centred around Pho Si Rd between the fountain circle and Mak Khaeng Rd.

Mae Lamun is a good local craft shop on Prajak Silpakorn Rd just east of Mak Khaeng Rd; it's on the 2nd floor of a shop selling Buddhist paraphernalia. Mae Lamun has a selection of quality silks and cottons, silver, jewellery, Buddha images and ready-made clothes tailored from local fabrics. Prices start high but are negotiable. Another good craft shop – especially for pillows – is Thi Non Michai at 208 Pho Si Rd.

The new Charoensri Complex, off Prajak Silpakorn Rd, promises to become the largest shopping centre in Isaan, possibly in all of Thailand. If completed as planned it will feature 22,000 sq m of retail space, a 3000 sq m supermarket, swimming pools and an amusement park. At the time of writing, it was filling up with standard Thai department stores, a flock of designer clothing boutiques, several restaurants and coffee shops (see Places to Eat above), and the attached Charoensri Grand Royal Hotel (see Places to Stay).

## Getting There & Away

**Air** THAI flies to Udon from Bangkok daily. The flight takes an hour and costs 1310B. The Udon office (☎ 246697, 243222) is at 60 Mak Khaeng Rd.

Orient Express Air (☎ 343818, 346994) flies from Chiang Mai daily for 1300B each way, and from Khon Kaen twice a week for 800B.

**Bus** Buses for Udon leave Bangkok's Northern Bus Terminal throughout the day from 5 am to 11 pm. The trip takes 10 to 11 hours, and the fare is 134B (241B air-con).

Buses leave the main bus terminal in Khorat every half hour during the day and arrive in Udon five hours later. The cost is 82B (135B air-con).

Getting out of Udon by bus, you must first sort out the tangle of departure points scattered around the city. Ordinary buses to Nong Khai (15 buses a day, 5.30 am to 3.30 pm; 15B) leave from Rangsina Market on the northern outskirts of town; take city bus No 6 or a songthaew north along Udon-dutsadi Rd to get to Talaat Rangsina. You can also get buses to Tha Bo, Si Chiangmai and Ban Pheu from here. The No 2 bus terminal is on the north-western outskirts of the city next to the highway, and has buses to Loei, Nakhon Phanom, Chiang Rai, Si Chiangmai, Nong Khai and Bangkok.

The No 1 bus terminal is off Sai Uthit Rd near the Charoen Hotel in the south-eastern end of town. Buses from here go mostly to points south and east of Udon, including Khorat, Sakon Nakhon, Nakhon Phanom, Ubon Ratchathani, Khon Kaen, Roi Et and Bangkok, and also to Beung Kan.

There are also private air-con buses to Bangkok. The company with the best local reputation is 407 Co (☎ 221121) at 125/3 Prajak Silpakorn Rd.

**Train** The 8.30 pm *Nong Khai Express* from Bangkok arrives in Udon at 6.25 am the next day. Rapid trains leave Bangkok on the Nong Khai line at 6.15 am and 7 pm, arriving in Udon at 3.57 pm and 5.15 am. The 1st class fare is 457B, 2nd class is 219B, plus applicable charges for sleeper and express service.

A special, all-inclusive 3rd class fare (120B) applies to faster diesel railcar trains to Udon, which leave Bangkok at 8.20 and 8.40 am, arriving at 5.05 and 6.05 pm respectively. Although both the English and Thai train schedules list a 95B 3rd class fare for ordinary *(thammadaa)* trains, there are actually no ordinary trains on the Bangkok to Udon run – only diesel railcar, rapid and express.

**Getting Around**
**Samlor** Drivers in Udon practically doubled their rates overnight when 50 Yanks were brought in to work on the VOA station outside the town in 1990-91; apparently the engineers were throwing their dollars around with abandon. With a permanent contingent of VOA employees in the area, just about any farang who happens through Udon will have to deal with this two tier price system (which exists to some extent everywhere in Thailand – it's just grossly exaggerated in Udon). Reasonable fares are 10 to 15B on short sprints (eg the No 1 bus terminal to the Paradise Hotel), 15 to 20B for a medium-length trip (eg No 1 bus terminal to the Prachaphakdee Hotel) and up to 25B for a longer jaunt (eg Charoensri Plaza to Nong Prajak park).

**Bus** A more hassle-free way to get around is by city bus. The most useful city bus for visitors is the yellow bus No 2, which plies a route from the No 2 bus terminal, south along Suphakit Janya Rd, and then along Pho Si Rd past the Charoen Hotel. The No 6 bus runs between the No 2 bus terminal and Rangsina Market, while bus No 23 runs between bus terminals Nos 1 and 2. The fare for all city buses is 3B.

**Car** Three car-rental places opposite the Udon Hotel offer sedans, jeeps and vans for hire starting at around 1400B. Should you want to hire a car with driver, a cheaper alternative is to negotiate for one of the old four door Nissan and Toyota taxis waiting along Phanphrao Rd at the southern end of Thung Si Meung. Figure on no more than 800B per day for one of these, including the services of a driver. These drivers are happy to go anywhere in the province, or as far out of the province as Nong Khai.

## AROUND UDON THANI PROVINCE
### Ban Chiang
บ้านเชียง

Ban Chiang, 50 km east of Udon Thani, now plays host to a steady trickle of tourists from all over Thailand and a few from beyond. As well as the original excavation at **Wat Pho Si Nai** at the village edge (open to the public), there is a new **national museum** with extensive Ban Chiang exhibits. This is worth a trip if you're at all interested in the historic Ban

Chiang culture, which goes back at least 2000 years. The museum is open daily from 9 am to 4 pm; entry is 10B. A map of the area is available at the museum.

The Ban Chiang culture, an agricultural society which once thrived in North-Eastern Thailand, is known for its early bronze metallurgy and clay pottery, especially pots and vases with distinctive burnt-ochre swirl designs, most of which were associated with burial sites. The area has been declared a UNESCO World Heritage site.

The locals attempt to sell Ban Chiang artefacts, real and fake, but neither type will be allowed out of the country, so don't buy them. Some of the local handicrafts, such as thick handwoven cotton fabric, are good buys; over 50 local families are involved in hand-crafted textile production.

**Places to Stay** Five minutes walk from the museum is the recently opened *Lakeside Sunrise Guest House* (☎ (42) 208167), with rooms in a new house for 80 to 150B.

**Getting There & Away** Songthaews run regularly between Udon and Ban Chiang from late morning until around 3.45 pm for 18B.

In the reverse direction the songthaews operate from around 5.30 am until noon. Alternatively, take a bus bound for Sakon Nakhon or Nakhon Pathom and get off at the Ban Pulu turn-off, a 10 minute samlor ride from Ban Chiang. Buses leave in either direction several times a day, but the last leaves Ban Chiang in the late afternoon.

**Ban Pheu**
บ้านผือ

Ban Pheu district, 42 km north-west of Udon Thani, has a peculiar mix of prehistoric cave paintings, bizarre geological formations and Buddhist shrines, the bulk of which are at Phra Phutthabat Bua Bok, 12 km outside Ban Pheu on Phra Bat hill. The area has recently been declared **Phu Phra Bat Historical Park**.

The formations are an interesting mix of balanced rocks, spires and whale-sized boulders, with several shrines and three wats built in and around the formations. A trail meandering through the park takes around two hours to negotiate at a normal walking pace.

At the entrance to the area is the largest temple in the historical park, **Wat Phra That**

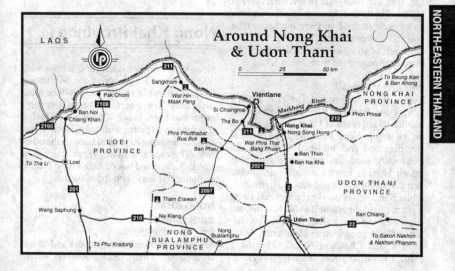

**Phra Phutthabat Bua Bok**. Prehistoric paintings are in several caves and feature wild animals, humans and cryptic symbols. To the south-east of the main wat are the caves of **Tham Lai Meu** and **Tham Non Sao Eh**, and to the west are **Tham Khon** and **Tham Wua Daeng**. For Isaan residents, this is an important place of pilgrimage. For visitors, the side-by-side progression from rock art to Buddhist temples represents a localised evolution of thought and aesthetics.

Entry to the park costs 20B. A crude trail map is available at the park entrance, although it doesn't include all the caves nor all the trail branches.

Also in the Ban Pheu district – but outside the park – is **Wat Pa Baan Kaw**, a respected meditation temple under the tutelage of Ajaan Tun (Phikkhu Kippapanyo).

**Getting There & Away** Ban Pheu has one hotel (90B with shared bath) if you want to spend some time here. Otherwise, Phra Phutthabat can be visited as a long day trip from either Udon or Nong Khai. From Udon it's a 13B songthaew ride to Ban Pheu; it's 24B from Nong Khai. From Ban Pheu, take a songthaew for 5B to the village nearest the site, Ban Tiu, then walk or hitch the two km to Phra Phutthabat. You could also charter a motorcycle in the Ban Pheu market to take you all the way to Phra Phutthabat.

Easiest of all would be to visit the park by bicycle or motorbike from Nong Khai.

### Weaving Villages

Two villages renowned for khít pattern fabrics are **Ban Na Kha** and **Ban Thon**, around 16 km north of Udon via Highway 2 on the way to Nong Khai. Khít is a geometric, diamond-grid minimal weft brocade commonly used for the centre square of māwn khwaan fabrics or other decorative items. Ban Na Kha is just east of Highway 2, while Ban Thon is two km farther east along a laterite road. Shops in Ban Na Kha that are somewhat used to dealing with foreign visitors include Songsi Isaan Handicraft, 184/1 Muu 1, and Chanruan Nakha, 92 Muu 1 (Muu 1 is within 100m of the highway).

**Ban Nong Aw Tai**, in the district of Nong Wua Saw, about 40 km south-west of Udon via Route 210, produces high-quality silk. In this same district is **Wat Tham Kok Duu**, a famous meditation wat presided over by abbot Phra Ajaan Kham Fong, whose simple, direct style of teaching has garnered a large number of lay students. Nong Wua Saw is actually now part of a new province, Nong Bualamphu, that recently split off from Udon Thani Province.

### Tham Erawan

If you happen to be travelling along Route 210 between Loei Province and Udon, you can stop off and visit Tham Erawan, a large cave shrine high up on the side of a limestone mountain. A huge seated Buddha in the cave can be seen gazing out over the plains from several km away.

The cave is at the back of **Wat Tham Erawan**, which is two km north of a turn-off between Km 31 and 32 markers on Route 210 – near the village of Ban Hong Phu Thawng, west of the town of Na Klang. There is a smaller cave wat near this turn-off – keep going north until you can see the larger, higher cave in the distance.

# Nong Khai Province

Nong Khai Province is long and narrow, with 300 km of its length along the Maekhong River. At its widest point, the province measures only 50 km across. Even if you can't cross into Laos, Nong Khai is a fascinating province to explore, with long, open views of the Maekhong River and Laos on the other side. The capital exhibits vague touches of Lao influence, and one of Asia's most bizarre sculpture gardens is on the outskirts.

### NONG KHAI
อ.เมืองหนองคาย
• ☎ (42) • pop 25,000

More than 620 km from Bangkok and 55 km from Udon Thani, Nong Khai is where

Highway 2 (also known as Mittaphap Highway, Friendship Highway and Asia 12) ends, at the Thai-Lao Friendship Bridge over the Maekhong River. Across the river is the Lao People's Democratic Republic.

Nong Khai was once part of the Vientiane (Wiang Chan) kingdom, which for much of its history vacillated between independence and tribute to either Lan Xang (1353 to 1694) or Siam (late 1700s to 1893). In 1827 Rama III gave a Thai lord, Thao Suwothamma, the rights to establish Meuang Nong Khai at the present city site. In 1891, under Rama V, Nong Khai became the capital of Monthon Lao Phuan, an early Isaan satellite state which included present-day Udon, Loei, Khon Kaen, Sakon Nakhon, Nakhon Phanom and Nong Khai provinces, as well as Vientiane. The area came under several attacks by Jiin Haw (Yunnanese) marauders in the late 1800s. The 1886 vintage **Prap Haw Monument** (*pràp haw* means 'putting down the Haw') in front of Nong Khai's city hall commemorates Thai-Lao victories over Haw invasions in 1877 and 1885. When western Laos was partitioned off from Thailand by the French in 1893, the monthon capital was moved to Udon, leaving Nong Khai to fade into a provincial backwater.

Today's Nong Khai has a row of old buildings of French-Chinese architecture along Meechai Rd, east of Soi Si Khun Meuang and parallel to the river. Unfortunately, local developers have razed some of the most historic buildings in Nong Khai and have replaced them with the ugly egg-carton architecture common all over urban Asia. Let's hope Nong Khai residents make a plea for historical preservation, or there'll soon be no historic buildings left. The arrival of the Thai-Lao Friendship Bridge largely shifts the focus of international trade from Nong Khai's historic central area to the bridge area west of the city, so perhaps this will alleviate the pressure to replace older architecture.

The opening of the bridge on 8 April 1994 marked the beginning of a new era of development for Nong Khai as a regional trade and transport centre. New multistorey hotels and office buildings are rising up along the out-

---

**Maekhong**

The Thai name for the river is Mae Nam Khong. Mae Nam means river (literally, 'mother water') and Khong is its name, hence the term 'Maekhong River' is a bit redundant. Westerners have called it the 'Mekong River' for decades and the Thais themselves sometimes call it 'Maekhong' for short (on the Laos side they prefer 'Nam Khong'); in this book I'm compromising and calling it Maekhong River. By agreement between the Thai and Lao governments, all islands in the Maekhong River – including sandbars that appear only in the dry season – belong to Laos. ■

---

skirts of town in the vicinity of the new Highway 2 (Mittaphap Highway) bypass which leads to the Thai-Lao Bridge.

The restaurant next to the immigration office and pier is a good place to sit and watch the ferry boats cross back and forth between Thailand and Laos. Since pedestrians aren't permitted on the new bridge, this ferry will probably continue to operate until regular bus service is established between Nong Khai and Vientiane.

Sunset boat rides are available daily at around 5 pm aboard a floating restaurant behind Wat Hai Sok. The city is constructing a new riverfront promenade for strolling along the Maekhong. At present the promenade begins at the far eastern end of town and ends two blocks west of Phochai Rd. Shops along Meechai Rd near the pier are jammed with Lao, Vietnamese and Chinese goods.

Like many other cities in the North-East, Nong Khai has a large Rocket Festival (Ngaan Bun Bang Fai) during the full moon of May, and a Candle Festival (Ngaan Hae Thian) at the beginning of *phansǎa*, or the Buddhist Rains Retreat, in late July. The city also holds its own Nong Khai Festival in March.

### Information

**Lao Visas** Nong Khai is one of six crossings open to non-Thai foreigners along the Thai-Lao border (the other five are Chiang Khong, Nakhon Phanom, That Phanom, Mukdahan

NORTH-EASTERN THAILAND

and Chong Mek) and citizens of the two countries are allowed to cross at will for day trips. Thais can get visas fairly easily for longer trips.

For foreign visitors, visas to Laos are now readily available through travel agencies in Bangkok or at the Lao consulate (☎ (43) 223698, 221961) in Khon Kaen. Several visa brokers in Nong Khai can also arrange the necessary paperwork for visits of up to two weeks. Current prices vary from 1900 to 2600B; waiting periods of four to 10 days are typical, depending on the broker. You'll need four passport photos for the visa. Among the more reliable brokers are The Meeting Place, Chez Pierrot and Fah Sai Travel Agency (☎ /fax 411094) at 1000/3 Kaew Worawut Rd west of Mutmee Guest House. (For details on The Meeting Place and Chez Pierrot see Places to Stay later in this section.) Fah Sai can arrange a 15 day visa in four days for 1900B or in one day for 2700B; the latter price includes transfer to Vientiane and one night at a Vientiane guesthouse.

See Getting There & Away later in this section for information on transport to/from Laos. Lonely Planet's *Laos* guidebook contains extensive visa and travel information.

**Money** Several banks along Meechai Rd offer ATMs and foreign-exchange services.

**Post & Communications** The GPO on Meechai Rd is open from 8.30 am to 4.30 pm Monday to Friday, and 9 am to noon on weekends and holidays. The upstairs telephone office is open from 7 am to 10 pm daily.

**Bookshops** Wasambe Bookshop (☎/fax 460272; e-mail wasambe@loxinfo.co.th), on the soi leading to Mutmee Guest House, sells new and used English-language novels, books on spirituality, guidebooks (especially for Thailand and Laos), maps and a small but growing collection of German, French and Dutch titles. Fax and e-mail services are also available here. The owner is an ex-Peace Corps volunteer who has also lived in Morocco and Nepal.

**Thai-Lao Friendship Bridge**

The US$30 million, Australian-financed Saphaan Mittaphap Thai-Lao spans the Maekhong River from Ban Jommani (three km west of Nong Khai) to Tha Na Laeng (19 km south-east of Vientiane) on the Lao side. The 1174m bridge opened to vehicular traffic in April 1994 amidst much hoopla about how it would improve transport and communications between the two countries. Historically it is only the second bridge to have been erected anywhere along the Maekhong's entire length (the first is in China).

In spite of its two 3.5m wide traffic lanes, two 1.5m footpaths and space for a train line down the centre, the bridge has done little to fulfil its design potential. City planners say that eventually a rail link will be extended from the Nong Khai railhead across the 12.7m wide bridge. On the Lao side a new train line (the country's first!) will skirt Vientiane to the south-east and terminate in the vicinity of That Luang. The bottom of the bridge features 13.4m minimum clearance for boats at the river's highest projected water level. An 8.2 km highway bypass was added to link the bridge with Highway 2/Asia 12 just south of the city.

For bridge transport information, see Getting There & Away later in this section.

**Wat Pho Chai (Phra Sai)**

วัดโพธิ์ชัย

This temple off Prajak Rd in the southeastern part of town is renowned for its large Lan Xang-era sitting Buddha. The head of the image is pure gold, the body is bronze and the utsanit is set with rubies. The altar on which the image sits features elaborately executed gilded wooden carvings and mosaics, while the ceiling bears wooden rosettes in the late Ayuthaya style. During the annual Songkhran Festival in April, the Phra Sai image is taken out in procession around town.

Murals in the bòt depict the image's travels from the interior of Laos to the banks of the Maekhong, where it was put on a raft. A storm capsized the raft and the image sat at the bottom of the river from 1550 to 1575, when it was salvaged and placed in Wat Haw Kawng (now called Wat Pradit Thammakhun) on the Thai side of the river. The highly revered image was moved to Wat Pho Sai during the reign of King Mongkut (1852-68).

The main wihãan is open daily from 7 am to 5 pm.

## Phra That Nong Khai

Also known as **Phra That Klang Nam** (Holy Reliquary in the Middle of the River) this Lao chedi is submerged in the Maekhong River and can only be seen in the dry season when the Maekhong lowers about 30m. The chedi slipped into the river in 1847 and continues to slide – it's near the middle now. For the best view of the chedi, walk east along Meechai Rd past the Marine Police post, then past three wats on the right, then turn left on Soi Paphraw (Paa Phrao) 3. Follow this soi until it ends at the new riverside promenade and look for the chedi in the river off to your right. Once the top of the chedi has cleared the river surface during the dry season, coloured flags are fastened to the top to make it easier to spot.

You can get a closer look at the chedi by taking the nightly floating restaurant cruise from the Wat Hai Sok pier – see Places to Eat for details.

## Sala Kaew Ku

ศาลาแก้วกู่

Also called **Wat Khaek** (Indian Temple) by locals, this strange Hindu-Buddhist shrine, established in 1978, is a tribute to the wild imagination of Luang Puu Bunleua Surirat. Luang Puu (Venerable Grandfather) is a Brahmanic yogi-priest-shaman who merges Hindu and Buddhist philosophy, mythology and iconography into a cryptic whole. He has developed a large following in North-Eastern Thailand and Laos, where he lived for many years before moving to Nong Khai (he still maintains a temple across the river in Laos). He is supposed to have studied under a Hindu *rishi* in Vietnam; according to legend Luang Puu was walking in the mountains when he fell through a sinkhole and

landed in the rishi's lap! He remained in the cave, called Kaew Ku (Jewel Grotto), for several years.

The focus of the temple is the many bizarre cement statues of Shiva, Vishnu, Buddha and every other Hindu or Buddhist deity imaginable, as well as numerous secular figures, all supposedly cast by unskilled artists under Luang Puu's direction. The style of the figures is remarkably uniform, with faces which look like benign Polynesian masks. The tallest, a Buddha seated on a coiled naga with a spectacular multiheaded hood, reaches 25m. A sound system wired into the park sometimes plays a bizarre mixture of avant-garde electronic and pop musical selections – Luang Puu's favourite artist is Donna Summer!

The main shrine building was recently demolished and a new one was under construction when we visited. If the old floor plan is reincorporated, there should be two large rooms, upstairs and down, full of framed pictures of Hindu or Buddhist deities, temple donors, Luang Puu at various ages, plus smaller bronze and wooden figures of every description and provenance, guaranteed to throw an art historian into a state of disorientation.

If the building is locked, you can ask one of the attendants to open it for you; there are two stairways to the 2nd level, one for males and one for females.

In Nong Khai, it is said that any person who drinks water offered by Luang Puu will turn all his possessions over to the temple. Luang Puu is rather ill these days and spends most of his time lying down beneath a small pavilion at the edge of the sculpture garden.

The grounds are open daily from 7.30 am to 5.30 pm; entry is 5B.

**Getting There & Away** To get to Sala Kaew Ku, board a songthaew heading south-east towards Beung Kan and ask to get off at Wat Khaek, which is four or five km outside of town, near St Paul Nong Khai School. The fare should be about 7B. A chartered tuk-tuk costs 20 to 25B.

If you have your own wheels, look for a

NORTH-EASTERN THAILAND

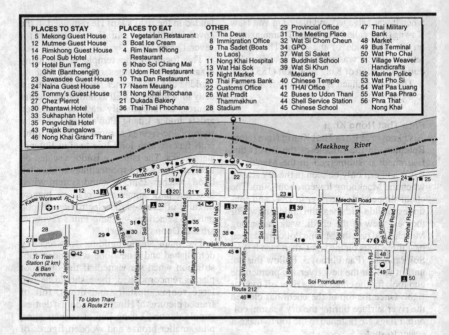

NORTH-EASTERN THAILAND

sign on the right about two turn-offs past St Paul's that reads 'Salakeokoo', referring to the official name, Sala Kaew Ku. It's an easy three km bike ride from town.

## Hat Jommani

This sand 'beach' along the Maekhong River only appears during the dry season. Next to the Thai-Lao Friendship Bridge in Ban Jommani, three km west of Nong Khai, the beach is a favourite picnic spot for local Thais. During the season a rustic thatched shelter with straw mats becomes a restaurant serving delicious kài yâang (grilled chicken), plaa yâang (grilled fish), sôm-tam and cold beer.

## Places to Stay – bottom end

**Guesthouses** Just west of Wat Hai Sok, *Mutmee (Mat-mii) Guest House* has 25 rooms in a couple of old houses and in rustic bungalows. Rates vary from 70B for a single in a simple, unscreened room to 160B for a hut with one large bed, screened windows

and private bath; most rooms fall in the 110 to 120B range. There's also one three bed room with shared bath for 60B per bed and a couple of larger, more private rooms with attached bath for 200 to 250B. The guesthouse has a pleasant garden restaurant next to the river. A corner of Wat Hai Sok leased by the guesthouse contains a pair of spirit houses built to honour two Lao princesses who drowned in the river nearby.

The soi leading to Mutmee Guest House has become a miniature travellers' centre, with a well stocked bookshop, small bakery and simple studios offering t'ai chi and yoga instruction.

In town, the *Mekong Guest House* (☎ 412119) has 16 basic but clean singles/doubles overlooking the river for 50B per person, plus a couple of larger rooms for 130B. Between the Mekong and Mutmee guesthouses, on a quiet spot near the river, the *Rimkhong Guest House* has 12 decent rooms with shared bath for 80/150B.

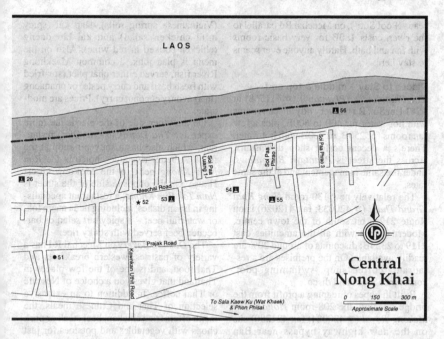

LAOS

Soi Paa Luang 1

Soi Paa Phrao

Soi Paa Phrao 3

Meechai Road

★ 52    53

54

55

Prajak Road

Kaewkan Uthit Road

● 51

To Sala Kaew Ku (Wat Khaek)
& Phon Phisai

**Central Nong Khai**

0    150    300 m
Approximate Scale

26    56

*Sawasdee Guest House* (☎ 412502) is in one of Nong Khai's old shophouses, restored and refurbished to provide small but very clean rooms for 80 to 120B with fan, 280B with air-con (add 40B for hot water). A small inner courtyard is pleasant for sitting. The house is at 402 Meechai Rd, opposite Wat Si Khun Meuang. It would be great if more historic Nong Khai shophouses could be preserved like this one.

Australian-managed *The Meeting Place* (☎ 421223) at 1117 Soi Chuenjit has a few rooms for 100B each with shared facilities, plus an expat-oriented bar. Tourist visas for Laos are available here for 2600B. French-managed *Chez Pierrot* (☎ /fax 460968) runs a similar guesthouse-bar-visa service at 1160 Soi Samoson; Lao visas cost 2500B here.

Towards the eastern end of town, at the end of the river extension of Phochai Rd, are two guesthouses that catch overflow from the more popular central places. *Tommy's*, run by a local Thai musician, is a cluster of basic rooms in an old wooden house; rates are just 50/70B for singles/doubles. On the other side of the soi to the west, *Naina* offers small, side-by-side rooms in a wooden building for 80/100B per night; a drawback is the collection of noisy fighting cocks on the grounds.

**Hotels** Two cheapies on Banthoengjit Rd are the *Banthoengjit* and the *Kheng Houng (Huang)*, with somewhat dismal rooms for 100 to 150B.

*Pongvichita (Phongwichit)* (☎ 411583) at 1244/1-2 Banthoengjit Rd, across the street from the Sukhaphan, is fairly clean and businesslike, with one/two bed rooms for 200/350B with fan and bath, 450/500B with air-con.

*Prajak Bungalows* (☎ 412644) at 1178 Prajak Rd has quiet off-street singles/doubles with fan for 220/300B, or 400/450B with air-con and hot water. The poorly managed *Phunsap Hotel* (the English sign

NORTH-EASTERN THAILAND

reads 'Pool Sub'), on Meechai Rd parallel to the river, costs 180B for very basic rooms with fan and bath. Hardly anyone ever seems to stay here.

## Places to Stay – middle & top end

The *Phanthavee (Phantawi)* (☎ 411568) at 1241 Hai Sok Rd has very tidy air-con rooms with hot water for 400 to 600B, plus a few fan rooms for 250B, or 300B with hot water. There's a decent coffee shop downstairs. Across the street is *Phantawi Bungalows*, under the same management and at the same rates.

The relatively new 130-room *Nong Khai Grand Thani* (☎ 420033; fax 412026) is on Route 212 a bit south of the town centre. Modern rooms with all the amenities cost 2119 to 2354B; discounts of around 20% are readily available. On the premises are a restaurant, coffee shop, swimming pool, conference room and disco.

Built in hopes of reaping a profit from the bridge opening, the 208-room *Holiday Inn Mekong Royal* (☎ 420024; fax 421280) sits on the new highway bypass near Ban Jommani, east of the town centre. Plush rooms start at 2119B; hotel facilities include a restaurant, coffee shop, cocktail lounge, pool and conference rooms. Just past the Holiday Inn, the new *Jommanee Royal Hotel* (☎ 420042; fax 420660) charges 840 to 960B for comfortable rooms overlooking the Maekhong River.

About 200m west of the bridge, the new *Phantavy II* (☎ 411008) offers decent rooms for 400 to 500B, VIP rooms for 1500B. The similarly priced *North-East Resort* (also known as Jommanee Villa; ☎ 412100) sits on the edge of the river between the train station and bridge – look for a sign reading 'NE'. The noisy jet skis one sees on the river come from this place.

## Places to Eat

*Udom Rot*, which overlooks the Maekhong and Tha Sadet (the ferry pier for boats to and from Laos), has good food and atmosphere, and Isaan-Lao crafts for sale at the front. Recommended dishes include pàw pía yuan

(Vietnamese spring rolls), lâap kài (spicy mint chicken salad) and kài lâo daeng (chicken cooked in red wine). Also on the menu is plaa jòhk, a common Maekhong River fish, served either phàt phèt (stir-fried with fresh basil and curry paste) or phanaeng (in a savoury coconut curry). Prices are moderate.

On the other side of the pier is the more expensive *Tha Dan* (Customs Pier) restaurant, which also has a souvenir shop at the front. A better riverside choice is the *Rim Nam Khong* next to the Mekong Guest House. On the opposite side of the street is *Nam Tok Rim Khong*, a restaurant specialising in Isaan dishes, including neúa náam tòk, or waterfall beef – a spicy/tart salad of barbecued beef served with sticky rice.

The *Dukada Bakery* on Meechai Rd has a variety of pastries, western breakfasts and Thai food, and is one of the few places in Thailand that gives you a choice of Nescafé or Thai coffee. In addition to an extensive selection of Thai and Chinese meals, the menu offers fried chicken, beef steak or pork chops with vegetables and potatoes for just 35B.

For Chinese food, *Nong Khai Phochana* on the corner of Banthoengjit and Rimkhong Rds is good – selections include Chinese roast duck, red pork, kũaytĩaw and bà-mìi. Very good Vietnamese food is available from *Naem Meuang* on the corner opposite Nong Khai Phochana; the house speciality is the namesake nãem meuang, spicy Isaan-style pork sausage.

*Khao Soi Chiang Mai* on Rimkhong Rd, not far from Nong Khai Phochana and Naem Meuang, serves authentic khâo sòi (Shan-style curry noodles) as well as delicious khanõm jiin náam ngíaw (spicy Yunnanese-style noodles).

*Boat*, farther west on Rimkhong Rd, serves ice cream, sundaes, milk shakes and good Thai food; you can choose to sit in the indoor air-con section or in the outdoor riverfront section.

Two doors south of Pongvichita Hotel, the ráan-khâo-tôm-style *Thai Thai Phochana* has all the usual Thai and Chinese dishes. It's open all night. Diagonally opposite the Pong-vichita is a major jók shop, with a choice of chicken or pork jók.

Along a soi inside Wat Hai Sok several coffee and noodle vendors set up each morning. Good kaa-fae thũng (filtered coffee) costs just a few baht. At a pier behind the wat, a floating restaurant leaves around 5 pm nightly to view the sunset and Phra That Nong Khai (the latter is visible in the dry season only) a little way down the Maekhong River. The menu includes a few regional dishes as well as Thai standards; prices are reasonable and cold beer is available.

Out of all the guesthouses in town, the Mutmee has the best food, including many vegetarian dishes, home-baked bread and wine.

*Espresso Corner*, in the same building as Fah Sai Travel Agency on Kaew Worawut Rd west of Mutmee Guest House, serves real coffee, pasta, pizza, desserts, banana pancakes and sandwiches at reasonable prices. On the premises is a small paperback library.

## Things to Buy

A shop called Village Weaver Handicrafts at 786/1 Prajak Rd sells high-quality, moderately priced woven fabrics and ready-made clothes. The staff can also tailor clothing in a day or two from fabric purchased. The shop was established by the Good Shepherd Sisters as part of a project to encourage local girls to stay in the villages and earn money by weaving rather than leaving home to seek work in urban centres. The hand-dyed mát-mii cotton is particularly good here, and visitors are welcome to observe the methods in the weaving workshop behind the shop. It's past the bus terminal – 10B by samlor from the centre of town. The Thai name for the project is Hattakam Sing Thaw.

## Getting There & Away

**Air** The nearest airport is approximately 55 km south at Udon Thani. THAI and Orient Express Air both fly to Udon; see the Udon Thani Getting There & Away section for flight details. THAI operates an express van direct from Udon airport to Nong Khai for 100B per person; the trip takes around 35 minutes.

**Bus** Nong Khai's main bus terminal off Prajak Rd has buses to Si Chiangmai, Beung Kan, Loei, Udon Thani, Ubon Ratchathani, Tha Bo, Bangkok and Rayong.

Buses to Nong Khai (No 221) leave Udon Thani approximately every half hour throughout the day from Udon's Rangsina Market bus terminal. The trip takes about 1¼ hours and costs 15B.

Buses between Loei and Nong Khai (No 506) leave every half hour in either direction and cost 61B; Nakhon Phanom buses (No 224) run at a similar frequency and cost 98B.

If you're coming from Loei Province, you can get buses from Chiang Khan or Pak Chom without having to double back to Udon Thani. From Nakhon Phanom you can travel via Beung Kan along the Maekhong River or you can cut through Sakon Nakhon and Udon Thani.

**Bangkok** Ordinary buses to Nong Khai from Bangkok's Northern Bus Terminal leave 12 times daily between 4.10 am and 10 am. The trip is a long 11 to 12 hours and costs 146B (177B in the reverse direction for some reason). Second class air-con buses cost 263B, and leave three times a day at 8.40 am, 9.15 and 9 pm. First class air-con and VIP buses leave nightly between 7 and 9.30 pm; 1st class costs 319 to 328B, VIP 405B. Most people prefer to take the Bangkok-Nong Khai train – you can wander around a bit rather than sit on a narrow bus seat for 10 or more hours.

**Laos** Shuttle buses ferry passengers back and forth across the bridge from a designated terminal near the Thai-Lao Friendship Bridge for 10B per person; there are departures every 20 minutes from 8 am to 5.30 pm. You must arrange your own transport to the bridge bus terminal from Nong Khai; figure around 25B by tuk-tuk. The bus stops at Thai immigration control on the bridge, where you pay 10B to have your passport stamped with an exit visa. You then reboard the bus and pay a fee of 20B to have your passport stamped (40B between 12 and 2 pm and on weekends) after crossing the bridge stop at Lao immigration and customs.

The bridge is open daily from 8 am to 6 pm. If you're driving, a toll of 20B is collected for cars, 30B for trucks under one tonne, 50B for mini or medium buses, 100B for bus coaches and 100 to 300B for larger trucks depending on the number of wheels.

**Train** From Bangkok, the Nong Khai express leaves Hualamphong station daily at 8.30 pm, arriving in Nong Khai at 7.20 am – about the same speed as the bus but considerably more comfortable. Two rapid trains leave daily at 6.15 am and 7 pm, arriving at 4.50 pm and 6.15 am. Basic one way fares are 497B in 1st class and 238B in 2nd class, not including surcharges for express or rapid service (50B and 30B) or sleeping berths.

There are no longer any 3rd class trains to Nong Khai, but you can take a 3rd class diesel railcar as far as Udon Thani (95B) and hop on a bus from there for another 15B – see the Udon Thani Getting There & Away section for schedule information.

### Getting Around
Samlors around the town centre cost 10B; tuk-tuks are 10 to 20B.

Nana Motor (☎ 411998) at 1160 Meechai Rd rents motorcycles at reasonable rates. Suzuki 4WD Caribians can be rented from Village Weaver Handicrafts at 786/1 Prajak Rd.

### AROUND NONG KHAI PROVINCE
### Wat Phra That Bang Phuan
วัดพระธาตุบังพวน

Twelve km south of Nong Khai on Highway 2 and then 11 km west on Highway 211, Wat Bang Phuan is one of the most sacred sites in the North-East because of the old Indian-style stupa here. It's similar to the original chedi beneath the Phra Pathom Chedi in Nakhon Pathom, but no-one knows when either chedi was built. Speculation claims that it must have been in the early centuries AD or possibly even earlier – supposedly the chedi enshrines some chest bones of the Buddha himself.

In 1559 King Jayachettha of Chanthaburi

(not the present Chanthaburi in Thailand, but Wiang Chan – known as Vientiane – in Laos) extended his capital across the Maekhong and built a newer, taller, Lao-style chedi over the original as a demonstration of faith (just as King Mongkut did in Nakhon Pathom). Rain caused the chedi to lean precariously and in 1970 it fell over. The Fine Arts Department restored it in 1976-77 with the Sangharaja, Thailand's Supreme Buddhist Patriarch, presiding over the re-dedication in 1978. The current chedi stands 34.25m high on a 17.2 sq m base.

Actually, it is the remaining 16th century Lao chedis in the compound (two contain semi-intact Buddha images in their niches) that give the wat its charm. There is also a roofless wihăan with a large Buddha image, and a massive round brick base that must have supported another large chedi at one time. A small museum displays site relics and a collection of old wooden spirit houses; admission is free, although donations are appreciated.

**Getting There & Away** To get to Wat Phra That Bang Phuan, get a Si Chiangmai or Sangkhom-bound songthaew or bus in Nong Khai and ask for Ban Bang Phuan (12B). Most Sangkhom-bound buses automatically stop at Phra That Bang Phuan. Otherwise get any bus south on Highway 2 and get off in Ban Nong Song Hong, the junction for Route 211. From there take the next bus (from either Udon or Nong Khai) that's going to Si Chiangmai and get off near the wat. The fare should be about 10B to the road leading off Route 211; it's an easy walk to the wat from that point.

### Tha Bo
ท่าบ่อ

Along the Maekhong River and Route 211 between amphoe meuang Nong Khai and the Loei Province border are several smaller towns and villages where life revolves around farming and minimal trade between Laos and Thailand.

Surrounded by banana plantations and

vegetable fields flourishing in the fertile Maekhong floodplains, Tha Bo (population 16,000) is the most important market centre between Nong Khai and Loei. An open-air market along the main street probably offers more wild plants and herbs than any market along the Maekhong, along with Tha Bo's most famous local product – tomatoes. Tomato exports from Tha Bo often exceed 80,000 tonnes. Tobacco is also grown in impressive quantities.

The **Huay Mong Dam**, which crosses the Maekhong at the western edge of town, irrigates 10,800 hectares of land around Tha Bo. This relatively small-scale pumping project is one of the most successful hydrology efforts in Thailand, running at a higher efficiency than any of the country's larger dam facilities and with less extreme environmental impact. There is a pleasant public park next to the dam.

Aside from the market and dam, the town's only other claim to fame is **Wat Ong Teu** (also known as Wat Nam Mong), an old Lao-style temple sheltering a 'crying Buddha'. According to local legend, the left hand of the 300 year old bronze image was once cut off by art thieves; tears streamed from the Buddha's eyes until the hand was returned. The wat is three km west of town off Route 211.

**Places to Stay & Eat** *Suksan Hotel*, on the main street through town, has basic rooms for 70B. Out on the road from Nong Khai at the town's eastern entrance is *SP Guest House*, a former flophouse hotel with rooms for 80 to 100B. *Tha Bo Bungalow*, on a back street not far from the town centre, has passable rooms with fan and bath for 100B.

Quieter accommodation is available at *Isan Orchid Guest Lodge* (☎ (42) 431665) at 87/9 Kaew Worawut Rd, a large modern house in the middle of village-like surroundings near the river. Owned by a retired American but managed by Thais, the house has large, comfortable air-con rooms from 500 to 750B, including a European breakfast. A smaller bungalow next to the main house is available for 700 to 850B. The

manager can arrange pick up from Udon airport as well as trips to Phra Phutthabat Bua Bok; bicycles can be borrowed at no charge.

There are several modest noodle and rice shops on the main street plus a couple of kài yâang places. Near the river at the northeastern end of town is *Suan Aahaan Taling Naam*, a garden restaurant specialising in 'mountain chicken', which denotes a method of grilling whole chickens standing on end rather than horizontally.

**Getting There & Away** All songthaews and buses from Nong Khai (25 km to the east) bound for Si Chiangmai will drop passengers in Tha Bo for 10B. If you're cycling from Nong Khai, you have a choice of the scenic but unpaved river road or the paved and fast – but less scenic – Route 211. Eventually the river road will be paved, in which case it will become the fastest and most direct route to Tha Bo and farther west.

## Si Chiangmai
ศรีเชียงใหม่

Just across the river from Vientiane, Si Chiangmai has a large number of Lao and Vietnamese who make their living from the manufacture of rice-paper spring-roll wrappers. You can see the translucent disks drying in the sun on bamboo racks all over town. Si Chiangmai is one of the leading exporters of spring-roll wrappers in the world! Many of the Vietnamese and Lao residents are Roman Catholic and there is a small cathedral in town. A local bakery bakes fresh French rolls every morning in an outdoor brick oven.

Wat Hin Maak Peng, Ban Pheu and various local villages can be visited from Si Chiangmai – enquire at Tim Guest House for the latest information.

Ferries now cross regularly to Vientiane; there are immigration and customs offices in town. However, foreigners are usually referred to Nong Khai for river crossings.

**Places to Stay & Eat** *Tim Guest House* (☎ (42) 451072), the only guesthouse in town, is run by a friendly young Swiss-French man

NORTH-EASTERN THAILAND

who speaks English, French, German and Thai. Rooms start at 50B for a small single to 100B for a large double with a river view (but over the street). Simple Thai and farang food is served in a dining area downstairs, and the owner is building a floating restaurant in front on the river. Maps of the vicinity, massage and herbal sauna, laundry service, and bicycle and motorcycle rental are available. Boat trips along the Maekhong River to Nong Khai, Wat Hin Maak Peng and Sangkhom can also be arranged. The guesthouse is on Rim Khong Rd near the river in the centre of town – walk west from the bus terminal and turn right at Soi 17, then turn left at the end of the road and you'll find it on the left.

Adjacent to Tim is the basic *Hotel Suthisuwan*, with rooms for 60 to 100B.

**Getting There & Away** Probably because of its importance as a spring-roll wrapper capital, Si Chiangmai has an abundance of public transport. Bus fares to/from Si Chiangmai are:

| To/From | Fare |
| --- | --- |
| Bangkok | |
| (air-con) | 175 to 205B |
| Khon Kaen | 55B |
| (air-con) | 90B |
| Khorat | 87B |
| (air-con) | 140B |
| Nong Khai | 15B |
| Pak Chom | 35B |
| Sangkhom | 12B |
| Udon Thani | 25B |

## Wat Hin Maak Peng
วัดหินหมากเป้ง

Sixty-four km north-west of Nong Khai between Si Chiangmai and Sangkhom, Wat Hin is worth a trip just for the scenery along Route 211 from Nong Khai. This monastery is locally known for its *thutong* (Pali: *dhutanga*) monks – men who have taken ascetic vows in addition to the standard 227 precepts. These vows include eating only once a day, wearing only forest robes made from discarded cloth, and a strong emphasis on meditation. There are also several mâe chiis living here.

The place is very quiet and peaceful, set in a cool forest with lots of bamboo groves overlooking the Maekhong. The monastic kutis are built among giant boulders that form a cliff high above the river; casual visitors aren't allowed into this area, though. Below the cliff is a sandy beach and more rock formations. Directly across the river a Lao forest temple can be seen. Fisherfolk occasionally drift by on house rafts.

The abbot at Wat Hin Maak Peng requests that visitors to the wat dress politely – no shorts or sleeveless tops. Those that don't observe the code will be denied entrance.

**Getting There & Away** To get there, take a songthaew from Nong Khai to Si Chiangmai (15B) and ask for a songthaew directly to Wat Hin (there are a few) or to Sangkhom, which is just past the entrance to Wat Hin – the other passengers will let you know when the truck passes it (the bus usually makes a stop here anyway). The second songthaew is 10B. On the way to Wat Hin you might notice a large topiary at Ban Phran Phrao on the right side of the highway.

## Sangkhom
สังคม

The tiny town of Sangkhom could be used as a rest stop on a slow journey along the Mae-khong River from Loei to Nong Khai. Wat Hin Maak Peng is nearby and there are some good hikes to caves and waterfalls in the area. The guesthouses hand out maps of the area.

Opposite the River Huts guesthouse, in the middle of the Maekhong River, the Lao island of **Don Klang Khong** appears during the dry season. Beginning around December a couple of rustic outdoor eating areas with thatched-roof shelters and tables and chairs are set up in the river shallows. On the Thai side you can get local boys to paddle you across to the island in canoes – no visa necessary.

One of the largest local waterfalls is **Than Thip Falls**, three km from Route 211 between Km 97 and 98, and a few km west of Sangkhom. The waterfall has two major levels; the upper level is cleaner and has a deep pool (during or just after the rainy season) which is good for a dip. The falls are a long walk from the road – this is a trip best accomplished by motorcycle. **Than Thong Falls**, 11.5 km east of Sangkhom at Km 73 off the north (river) side of Route 211, is more accessible but can be rather crowded on weekends and holidays.

**Places to Stay & Eat** The town's two guesthouses are off the main road through town and near the river.

A flood in 1993 forced two of the guesthouses to shift to less flood-prone locations. The friendly and efficient *River Huts* has moved to a more secluded location well off the main road, where thatched huts overlooking the river are 60/70B for singles/doubles. The food is good and there are bicycles for rent.

Out on the main road is the original *Bouy Guest House*, a very pleasant place with huts on the river. Singles/doubles next to the river are 70/90B, or 60/80B nearer the road. Its better than average restaurant is worth a stop for lunch even if you're not staying overnight. Sandwiches as well as Thai food are available.

Two or three other guesthouses seem to come and go with the seasons, including *Mama's* and *Suphamit*.

There are a couple of riverside restaurants. Ask around and you may be able to find a taste of náam yân, the sweetest moonshine from Laos.

**Getting There & Away** Buses from Nong Khai are 30B, and the trip takes about two hours. From Loei it's 50B and three or four hours. Pak Chom is 1½ hours away and costs 20B. From nearby Si Chiangmai, the fare is 12B. West of Pak Chom, songthaews are less frequent because the road worsens; the fare to Chiang Khan is 15B.

## BEUNG KAN
บึงกาฬ

This is a small dusty town on the Maekhong River, 185 km east of Nong Khai by Route

212. You may want to break your journey here if you are working your way around the north-eastern border from Nong Khai to Nakhon Phanom (as opposed to the easier but less interesting Udon Thani-Sakon Nakhon-Nakhon Phanom route). Between Nong Khai and Nakhon Phanom you'll pass many towns with 'Beung' or 'Nong' (Nawng) in their names; both terms refer to shallow bodies of fresh water fed by seasonal streams (a *beung* is usually larger than a *nãwng*).

The closer you get to Nakhon Phanom Province, the more Vietnamese you will see working in the rice fields or herding cows along the road. Nearly all the farmers in this area, whether ethnic Vietnamese or Thai, wear a simple Vietnamese-style straw hat to fend off the sun and rain.

The town of Beung Kan itself isn't much but there are some mildly interesting spots nearby. During the dry season the Maekhong River recedes away from Beung Kan and reaches its narrowest point along the Thai-Lao border. East of town is **Nam Song Sii** (Two Colour River), where the broad, muddy Huay Songkhram replenishes the Maekhong.

In the hope that it will soon be granted provincial status, amphoe Beung Kan has constructed a Sala Jangwat Beung Kan (Beung Kan Provincial Office) next to the highway; so far Beung Kan is still part of Nong Khai Province.

## Wat Phu Thawk
## (Wat Chedi Khiri Wihaan)
วัดภูทอก ( วัดเจดีย์คีรีวิหาร )

Travellers interested in North-Eastern forest wats can visit this nearby wat, a massive sandstone outcropping in the middle of a rather arid plain and a real hermit's delight. The entire outcropping, with its amazing network of caves and breathtaking views, belongs to the wat. The wat mountain is climbed by a seven level series of stairs representing the seven levels of enlightenment in Buddhist psychology. Monastic kutis are scattered around the mountain, in caves and on cliffs. As you make the strenuous

**NORTH-EASTERN THAILAND**

climb, each level is cooler than the one before. It is the cool and quiet isolation of this wat that entices monks and mâe chiis from all over the North-East to come and meditate here.

This wat used to be the domain of the famous meditation master Ajaan Juan, a disciple of the fierce Ajaan Man who disappeared many years ago. Ajaan Juan died in a plane crash a few years ago, along with several other monks who were flying to Bangkok for Queen Sirikit's birthday celebration. The plane went down just outside Don Muang airport. Many North-Easterners have taken this incident as proof that the present queen is a source of misfortune.

To get to Wat Phu Thawk, you'll have to take an early morning songthaew south on Route 222 to Ban Siwilai (25 km, 7B), then another songthaew east (left) on a dirt road, 20 km to the wat (10B). This songthaew carries merit-makers. Hitching might be possible if you miss the truck. A reader reported getting a type of local tuk-tuk to the wat in the afternoon from Siwilai for 10B. If solitude is your main objective, it's best to tour Phu Thawk early in the morning before the parade of Thai pilgrims begins.

## Ban Ahong
บ้านอาฮง

This village at Km 115 on Route 212 between Beung Kan and Nong Khai (23 km west of Beung Kan) makes an interesting alternative to staying overnight in Beung Kan. The friendly Hideaway Guest House (see Places to Stay & Eat) next to the Maekhong River is just a 200m walk from one of Isaan's smallest and most intriguing wats. Set amongst giant boulders along the river, **Wat Pa Ahong** has only one permanent monastic resident, the highly respected Luang Phaw Praeng. Due to Luang Phaw's skills as a gardener, the wat grounds boast lovely flowers year-round. Luang Phaw also fashions charming sculpture and furniture from bamboo roots, and is locally renowned for the traditional medicines he creates from local herbs. An occasional thutong monk or

young novice stops by for a few weeks at a time.

The narrow stretch of Maekhong River opposite the wat has some refreshing pools for swimming during the dry season when the river is fairly clear. This area is also considered a highly auspicious spot to spend the evening of *wan àwk phansãa*, the end of the Buddhist Rains Retreat. According to the local legend, supernatural lights, *bawng fai phayaa nàak* (dragon rockets), emerge from beneath the Maekhong River on this evening each year and arc across the sky three times. Several hundred Thai and Lao residents gather along the river for the yearly event. At other times of year there's frequent talk of UFO appearances. Similar stories circulate at Phon Phisai farther south-west towards Nong Khai.

Hideaway Guest House can arrange boat trips to nearby river islands for 10B.

### Places to Stay & Eat
**Beung Kan** Hotels in Beung Kan are all in the 80 to 200B price range. The small and funky *Samanmit, Neramit* and *Santisuk* are all on Prasatchai Rd not far from the town clock tower; the Samanmit has the best overall appearance, while the Santisuk has a nice eating area downstairs.

In addition to a few nondescript foodstalls in town, the *Mae Nam Restaurant* overlooking the river offers decent Thai and Isaan meals, although it's a bit pricey for the overall quality.

**Ban Ahong** *Hideaway Guest House*, behind the village school next to the river (turn off at Km 115), has a circle of simple, quiet huts on stilts for 50B a single, 80B a double. Meals are available; there is a pleasant riverside sitting area nearby, and you can go for walks in the village.

### Getting There & Away
The bus from Nong Khai to Beung Kan is 35B. Buses from Nakhon Phanom to Beung Kan are 45B.

NORTH-EASTERN THAILAND

# Loei Province

Loei is one of Thailand's most beautiful and unspoiled provinces. The geography is mountainous and the temperature goes from one extreme to the other, the weather being hotter here than elsewhere in Thailand during the hot season and colder during the cold season. This is the only province in Thailand where temperatures occasionally drop to 0°C.

The culture is an unusual mix of Northern and North-Eastern influences, which has produced many local dialects. The rural life of Loei outside the provincial capital has retained more of a traditional village flavour than many other places in Thailand, with the possible exceptions of Nan and Phetchabun, also once classified as remote or closed provinces.

Within the province, Phu Kradung, Phu Luang and Phu Reua national parks, as well as the districts of Tha Li and Chiang Khan, are good places to explore for natural attractions.

## LOEI

อ.เมืองเลย

• ☎ (42) • pop 22,000

Nearly 520 km from Bangkok, 140 km from Udon Thani, 269 km from Phitsanulok via Lom Sak and 200 km via Nakhon Thai, the provincial capital of Loei holds little of interest to the ordinary traveller. Cotton is one of Loei's big crops, so it's a pretty good place to buy cotton goods, especially the heavy cotton quilts (quite necessary in the cool months) made in Chiang Khan district – they're priced by the kg.

About five km north of Loei is a water recreation park with a large swimming pool called **Loei Land**. The admission is a reasonable 30B per day.

During the first week of February, Loei holds a Cotton Blossom Festival which culminates in a parade of cotton-decorated floats and, naturally, a Cotton Blossom Queen beauty contest. Loei also celebrates the annual Rocket Festival in May with fervour. The city has even imported the colourful Phi Ta Khon procession from nearby Dan Sai district (see the Dan Sai entry later in this section for details).

### Places to Stay – bottom end

At the time of writing, there were two guesthouses in Loei. *Muangloei Guest House* is within walking distance of the bus terminal at 103/72 Soi Aw Daw Ruamjai. Basic singles/doubles cost 60/90B; manager Somdy Mingolo speaks some English and French, and distributes travel information on Loei Province. Luggage may be stored here while you go hiking at Phu Kradung or other national parks.

*Friendship Guest House* (☎ 832408) is south of the post office and Cotton Inn at 257/41 Soi Buncharoen. This soi is just north of Wat Si Bun Reuang; coming from the town centre along Charoenrat Rd, take a left at this soi and walk 250m, then another left about 30m and you'll see it on your right. Large rooms in a modern house with toaster and coffee-maker cost 200B for up to five people. Out the back along the river is a wooden building with two rooms for 80B a single/double. Toilet and shower facilities are shared. The owner Khun Dum speaks some English.

*Sarai Thong Hotel*, off Ruamjit Rd, has 56 none-too-clean rooms in three buildings, costing from 90 to 160B. All rooms have a fan and bath. Service isn't great, but it's off the street so it's usually quiet. *Srisawat (Si Sawat)* on Ruamjit Rd near the Sarai Thong has grubby singles/doubles for 60/100B and similar facilities to Sarai Thong.

The *Di Phakdi* (☎ 811294) on Ua Ari Rd, around the corner from the Thai Udom Hotel and opposite the cinema, has minimalist rooms from 120B with fan and bath.

### Places to Stay – middle & top end

*Phu Luang Hotel* (☎ 811532/570) at 55 Charoenrat Rd, near the market, costs 420 to 700B for air-con singles/doubles. On the premises are a so-so restaurant and nightclub.

NORTH-EASTERN THAILAND

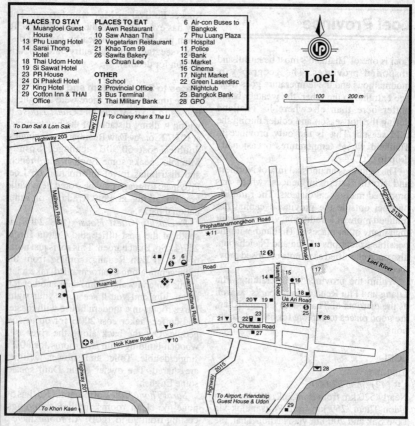

NORTH-EASTERN THAILAND

**PLACES TO STAY**
4   Muangloei Guest
    House
13  Phu Luang Hotel
14  Sarai Thong
    Hotel
18  Thai Udom Hotel
19  Si Sawat Hotel
23  PR House
24  Di Phakdi Hotel
27  King Hotel
29  Cotton Inn & THAI
    Office

**PLACES TO EAT**
9   Awn Restaurant
10  Saw Ahaan Thai
20  Vegetarian Restaurant
21  Khao Tom 99
26  Sawita Bakery
    & Chuan Lee

**OTHER**
1   School
2   Provincial Office
3   Bus Terminal
5   Thai Military Bank

6   Air-con Buses to
    Bangkok
7   Phu Luang Plaza
8   Hospital
11  Police
12  Bank
15  Market
16  Cinema
17  Night Market
22  Green Laserdisc
    Nightclub
25  Bangkok Bank
28  GPO

**Loei**

0     100     200 m

At 122/1 Charoenrat Rd, across from the
Bangkok Bank, is the friendly *Thai Udom
Hotel* (☎ 811763), where rooms with fan
cost 200/280B with one/two beds, and air-
con rooms cost 300/400B. Overall it's a
better choice than the Phu Luang, especially
if you take a room away from the street.

Over on Chumsai Rd near the Green
Laserdisc nightclub is the well run *King
Hotel* (☎ 811701), where rooms cost 280/
350B with fan and bath, or 420/500B with
air-con and hot water. Also in this vicinity,
just off Chumsai Rd, is the *PR House*
(☎ 811416), with modest apartments for rent

with fan and solar-heated shower for 180 to
240B per night or air-con for 350B, less for
long-term stays.

The four-storey, all air-con *Cotton Inn*
(*Meuang Fai*; ☎ 811302; fax 812353), near
the THAI office and GPO on Charoenrat Rd,
has very pleasant rooms with all the amenities for 400 to 700B. It's a well run place with
a decent coffee shop and inexpensive
laundry service.

**Places to Eat**
The night market near the intersection of
Ruamjai and Charoenrat Rds has cheap eats

and other items of local provenance. Look for the local speciality, khài pîng (eggs-in-the-shell toasted on skewers).

*Chuan Lee* and *Sawita Bakery* are two pastry/coffee shops on the same side of Charoenrat Rd, not far from the Thai Udom Hotel and Bangkok Bank. Chuan Lee is the older of the two and is more of a traditional Chinese coffee shop; it's very good and also serves a few curries at lunch and dinner. Sawita is newer, has air-con and offers a long menu of Thai and farang dishes, including fruit salads, spaghetti, ice cream and cookies. Prices are very reasonable.

Along Nok Kaew Rd near the roundabout are two moderately priced Thai restaurants: the *Duang Isaan* specialises in North-Eastern food; and *Saw Aahaan Thai* serves all kinds of Thai dishes in an indoor-outdoor setting. *Awn Restaurant* (no English sign), a simpler place on Nok Kaew Rd near Soi Saeng Sawang, serves kài yâang and sôm-tam.

Just off the roundabout on Ruamphattana Rd, the *Khao Tom 99* serves aahãan taam sãng (food according to order) until past midnight. There's a good Thai vegetarian restaurant near PR House.

### Entertainment

Most of the town seems to be asleep by 10 pm. Farther east on Chumsai Rd from the Isaan restaurant and opposite the King Hotel, the *Green Laserdisc* features live music and karaoke. Younger Thais go dancing at the *Galaxy* near the Phu Luang Hotel and the night market. Live Thai pop bands play at the side-by-side *Pegases* and *Robot* on Ruamphattana Rd.

### Getting There & Away

**Air** The Loei airport, six km south of town on the road to Udon Thani, has closed for repairs. In the past THAI has operated flights between Loei and Phitsanulok. If/when the airport reopens there may be flights from Bangkok as well.

**Bus** Buses to Loei leave Udon regularly until late afternoon for 38B. The 150 km trip takes about four hours. From Nong Khai the fare is 60B and the trip takes five or six hours.

Loei can also be approached from Phitsanulok by bus via Lom Sak or Nakhon Thai. A direct bus between Phitsanulok and Loei is 58B, and takes four to five hours; as far as Lom Sak it's 34B from either end. Buses between Loei and Dan Sai cost about 25B.

To Chiang Mai ordinary buses cost 136B, air-con 300B; the trip takes about eight hours via Utaradit.

Air-con buses from Bangkok's Northern Bus Terminal leave at 9 am and 12.30, 8.30, 9 and 9.30 pm, arriving in Loei about 10 hours later for a fare of 188B. A VIP bus leaves nightly at 9 pm and costs 340B. Ordinary buses cost 136B and leave at 4.35, 6.30, 7.50 and 10.30 am, and 2, 8.30 and 9.30 pm. In Loei you can get air-con buses to Bangkok from an agency on Ruamjai Rd (188B in 2nd class air-con, 375B VIP) or from the King Hotel.

## AROUND LOEI PROVINCE
### Phu Kradung National Park
อุทยานแห่งชาติภูกระดึง

At 1360m, Phu Kradung is the highest point in Loei. On top of this bell-shaped mountain is a large plateau with 50 km of marked trails to cliffs, meadows, waterfalls and montane forests of pine, beech and oak. The weather is always cool on top (average year-round temperature 20°C), hence the flora is more like that in a temperate zone. Lower down are mixed deciduous and evergreen monsoon forests as well as sections of cloud forest. The 359 sq km park is a habitat for various forest animals, including elephants, Asian jackals, Asiatic black bears, barking deer, sambars, serows, white-handed gibbons and the occasional tiger. A Buddhist shrine near the park headquarters is a favourite local pilgrimage site.

The main trail scaling Phu Kradung is six km long and takes about three hours to climb (or rather walk – it's not that challenging since the most difficult parts have bamboo ladders and stairs for support). The climb is quite scenic and there are rest stops with food

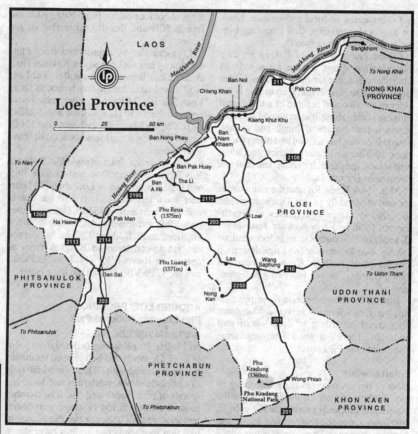

Loei Province

LAOS

Mekhong River

To Nong Khai

Sangkhom

Ban Noi

Chiang Khan

211

Pak Chom

NONG KHAI
PROVINCE

Kaeng Khut Khu

Ban Nong Pheu

Ban
Nam
Khaem

2108

To Nan

Ban Pak Huay

Tha Li

Heuang River

Ban
A Hii

2195

2115

LOEI
PROVINCE

1268

Na Haew

Pak Man

Phu Reua
(1375m)

203

Loei

2113

2114

Dan Sai

Phu Luang
(1571m)

Lao

Wang
Saphung

210

To Udon Thani

2250

Nong
Kan

UDON THANI
PROVINCE

To Phitsanulok

PHITSANULOK
PROVINCE

PHETCHABUN
PROVINCE

203

Phu
Kradung
(1360m)

Wong Phlan

201

Phu Kradang
National Park

KHON KAEN
PROVINCE

To Phetchabun

201

NORTH-EASTERN THAILAND

vendors along the way. It's another three km to the park headquarters. You can hire porters to carry your gear balanced on bamboo poles for 10B per kg.

During the hottest months, from March to June, it's best to start the climb about dawn to avoid the heat. Temperatures in December and January can drop as low as 3 to 4°C; blankets are available for hire. Bring sweaters and thick socks this time of year.

Phu Kradung is closed to visitors during the rainy season from mid-July to early October because it is considered too hazardous, being very slippery and subject to mud

slides. The park can get crowded during school holidays (especially March to May when Thai schools are closed).

A visitors' centre at the base of the mountain distributes detailed maps and collects a 25B admission fee; this entrance is only open from 7 am to 3 pm.

**Places to Stay & Eat** Lots of young Thais, mainly friendly college students, camp in the park. Tents already set up cost 40B a night, and boards for the bottom of the tents are available. Check the tents before paying – some are in quite ragged condition. You can set up your own tent for 5B per person. Blankets and pillows can be rented for 10B each. Cabins with water and electricity cost from 500 to 1200B depending on size, but even a 600B bungalow will sleep up to 10 people. There are several small restaurants on the plateau.

About two km from the summit, *Phu Kradung Guest House* has small A-frame doubles for 200B and large multi-bed bungalows with rustic kitchens for 600B.

If you get stuck in Phu Kradung town, *Phu Kradung House* has rooms with fan for 100 to 150B.

**Getting There & Away** Buses to Phu Kradung town leave the Loei bus terminal every half hour from 6 am until 5.30 pm (but don't forget the park entrance closes at 3 pm) for the 77 km, 20B trip. From amphoe Phu Kradung, hop on a songthaew (7B) to the park visitors' centre at the base of the mountain, seven km away.

The last bus back to Loei from amphoe Phu Kradung leaves around 6 pm.

## Phu Reua National Park
อุทยานแห่งชาติภูเรือ

This relatively small park of 121 sq km surrounds Phu Reua (Boat Mountain), so named because a cliff jutting from the peak is shaped like a Chinese junk. The easy 2½ hour hike to the summit (1375m) passes from tropical to broad-leaf evergreen forest to pine forest. In December, temperatures near the summit approach freezing at night.

The park entrance is about 50 km west of the provincial capital on Route 203. Although there is public transport from Loei to the town of Phu Reua, it is difficult to find songthaews all the way to the park except on weekends and holidays. A well marked 16 km trail from the park visitors' centre covers a good sample of what the park has to offer, including fine views of a mountain range in Sayabuli Province, Laos.

**Places to Stay & Eat** Tents can be pitched for 5B. Forestry Department bungalows cost

from 250 to 500B a night for up to five people. On weekends and holidays, food is sometimes available from vendors in the park; at other times you may be able to arrange food through the park rangers.

In the nearby town of Phu Reua, you could stay at the *Phu Reua* (250 to 500B), *Rai Waranya* (400 to 2000B) or the *Nam Taka* (400B).

**Getting There & Away** Nine buses a day run between Loei and Dan Sai between 5 am and 5 pm, passing through Phu Reua town on the way. The fare should be around 15B.

## Phu Luang National Park
อุทยานแห่งชาติภูหลวง

Yet another mountain retreat, Phu Luang (1571m) is less visited than either Phu Kradung or Phu Reua. Wildlife is reportedly abundant in the park's higher elevations.

**Restrictions** Thailand's Forestry Department keeps a tight rein on this national park in order to preserve its wilderness (in contrast to Phu Kradung National Park, which becomes quite trashy on weekends and holidays).

No group larger than 10 people is admitted to the park, and visits are restricted to three days and two nights. The park service's control is further enhanced by relatively steep fees totalling 696B for adults, 589B for children aged 12 and under. These fees include permits, two nights lodging, seven meals, transport from amphoe meuang Loei to the lodging site, guide service and government tax. Guide service usually includes nature walks near the mountain summit and trips to scenic cliffs, springs and waterfalls. Lectures are given in Thai only. The programme ends around 3 pm on the third day.

Permits must be arranged in advance with a 50% deposit – to be sure of obtaining permission apply 15 days ahead (you can just show up but there's no guarantee of space). Khun Somdy at Muangloei 2 Guest House in Loei can help with the arrangements, or you can write to the District Officer, Amphoe

NORTH-EASTERN THAILAND

Wang Saphung, Loei 42130, or telephone the park headquarters (☎ (42) 841141, 879032).

To get to the park you'll need your own wheels (hitchhiking is also a possibility); take Route 201 south from Loei for around 20 km to just north of Wang Saphung, then take Route 2250 south-west another 26 km. From there a nine km road leads south to the park entrance.

### Dan Sai
ด่านซ้าย

About 80 km west of Loei is the small town of Dan Sai, which is famous for its unique Bun Prawet Festival. The three day festival is part of the larger Rocket Festival that takes place throughout the North-East in May. Nobody seems to know how or when Dan Sai's distinctive festival first began.

The first day is celebrated with the procession of Phi Ta Khon, a type of masked parade. Participants wear huge masks made from carved coconut-tree trunks, topped with a wicker sticky-rice steamer! The procession is marked by a lot of music and dancing. On the second day Dan Sai residents fire off the usual bamboo rockets, and on the third day they retire to **Wat Pon Chai** to listen to Buddhist sermons.

### Pak Chom
ปากชม

Pak Chom is the first town of any size you come to in Loei Province if travelling west along the Maekhong River from Nong Khai. It owes much of its erstwhile development to nearby **Ban Winai Refugee Camp**, which was essentially a transplant of Hmong soldiers and families from the secret CIA/USAF base at Long Tieng (Long Chen), Laos, evacuated just before the 1975 Pathet Lao takeover. Ban Winai is officially closed and many of the 30,000 Hmong tribespeople at the camp have begun voluntary repatriation to Laos.

There is nothing much to do in Pak Chom except take walks along the river or to nearby villages. The town name means 'Mouth of the Chom', a reference to the confluence of

the Chom and Maekhong rivers here. During the dry season, locals pan for gold on Don Chom, a large island at the river junction.

**Places to Stay & Eat** *Pak Chom Guest House*, on the western edge of town next to the river, has a commanding view of the river and of limestone formations on the opposite banks. The couple who own it have added a few more huts and it's a suitable spot for long-term stays if you're seeking peace and quiet – no dogs or roosters in sight! Huts cost 60/80B a single/double; food and boat rentals are available.

To find the guesthouse coming from Chiang Khan on Route 211, get off the bus at the Km 147 marker and walk along a dirt road to the left. Coming from Loei along Route 2108, get off at the T-intersection in town, turn left and look for the Km 147 marker or follow the guesthouse signs. Coming from Nong Khai, walk straight across the intersection where the road makes a 90° turn left towards Chiang Khan, and walk about 500m until you see the sign pointing right to the Pak Chom Guest House. The huts are another 300m towards the river.

**Getting There & Away** From Chiang Khan, buses to Pak Chom are 15B. Buses from Sangkhom or Loei cost 25B.

### CHIANG KHAN
เชียงคาน
• ☎ *(42)*

Chiang Khan is about 50 km north of Loei, on the Maekhong River in a large valley surrounded by mountains. The wooden shophouses along the back streets give the place a bit of a frontier atmosphere and there are some nice views of the river.

Boat trips upriver as far as the Mae Nam Heuang river junction or downriver to Kaeng Khut Khu can be arranged at the Nong Sam and Zen guesthouses for 100 to 250B per person, depending on the size of the group and length of the trip (see Places to Stay).

Visas can be extended at the immigration office, next to the GPO, in Chiang Khan.

Recent reports say the officials here tend to be obnoxious – some solicit bribes above and beyond the usual 500B extension fee.

Chiang Khan comes alive during wan àwk phansãa, the end of the Buddhist Rains Retreat in October. At that time there's a week-long festival which features displays of large carved wax prasats at each of the temples in town as well as boat races on the river. At night there are performances of *mãw lam* (Isaan-style musical comedy) in the field facing the GPO.

## Wats

The town's wats feature a style of architecture rarely seen in Thailand – wihãans with colonnaded fronts and painted shutters that seem to indicate a French (via Laos) influence. A good example in the centre of town is **Wat Pa Klang** (Wat Machatimaram), which is about 100 years old and features a new glittery superstructure; in the grounds of this wat is a small Chinese garden with pond, waterfall and Chinese-style sculptures of Buddha and Kuan Yin.

**Wat Mahathat** in the centre of town is Chiang Khan's oldest temple; the bòt, constructed in 1654, has a new roof over old walls, with faded murals on the front.

Temple structures at **Wat Santi** and **Wat Thakhok** are similar to those at Wat Pa Klang (minus the Chinese garden). The walls of the temple buildings are stained red from all the red dust and mud that builds up in the dry and rainy seasons.

**Wat Tha Khaek** is a 600 to 700 year old temple, two km outside Chiang Khan, on the way to Ban Noi and Kaeng Khut Khu. The seated Buddha image in the bòt is very sacred and it is said that holy water prepared in front of the image has the power to cure any ailing person who drinks it or bathes in it.

Other well known monastic centres in the area include **Phu Pha Baen**, 10 km east of Chiang Khan, where monks meditate in caves and on tree platforms, and **Wat Si Song Nong**, west of Kaeng Khut Khu (within easy walking distance) on the river. This is a small forest wat where the highly respected Ajaan Maha Bun Nak resides.

## Kaeng Khut Khu
แก่งคุดคู้

About four km downstream from Chiang Khan is the Kaeng Khut Khu, a stretch of rapids (best in the dry, hot season) with a park on the Thai side and a village on the Laos side. You can hire a boat to reach the rapids. The park has thatched-roofed picnic areas with reed mats on raised wooden platforms. Vendors sell delicious Isaan food – kài yâang, sôm-tam and khâo niãw – as well as kûng tên (literally 'dancing shrimp', fresh river prawns served live in a light sauce of lime juice and chillies), kûng thâwt (the same fried whole in batter) and drinks. One large restaurant called Khrua Nucha serves sit-down meals. This is a nice place to spend a few hours.

Nearby **Wat Noi** houses three very old stone Buddha images; they're placed on a ledge high above a larger, modern Buddha in the wat's new bòt.

## Places to Stay
**Chiang Khan** The *Chiang Khan Guest House* (☎ 821029) has fair rooms for 60B, or 80B with two beds and a shared bath. The dining area overlooks the river and inexpensive food is served. At night it's a bit of a Thai hang-out. It's between sois 19 and 20 on Chai Khong Rd, which runs along the Maekhong.

Also on Chai Khong Rd, in an older building between sois 9 and 10, is the *Ton Khong Guest House* (☎ 821097), an OK place with rooms for 80/150B a single/double with shared facilities.

Turn away from the river altogether on Soi 12 and you'll find the simple *Zen Guest House* (☎ 821119), which offers mattress-on-the-floor rooms for 60/100B a single/double. Massage, herbal saunas and bike rentals are available. Staff also organise boat trips.

For hotels, there's the atmospheric *Suksombun Hotel* (☎ 821064) on Chai Khong Rd just past Soi 9. Rooms are 100B with fan and shared bath, or 150B with private bath. Around the corner on Soi 9 is the *Phoonsawad (Phunsawat)*, which charges just 60 to 80B for rooms with shared bath; add 10B for hot water.

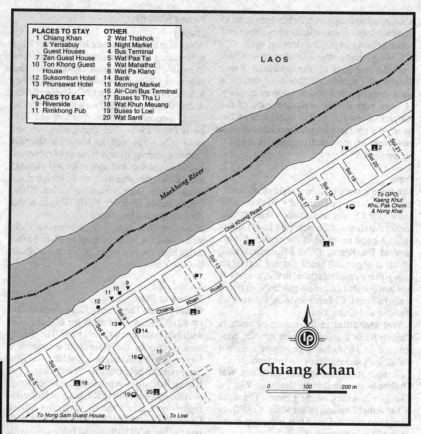

PLACES TO STAY
1  Chiang Khan
   & Yensabuy
   Guest Houses
7  Zen Guest House
10 Ton Khong Guest
   House
12 Suksombun Hotel
13 Phunsawat Hotel

PLACES TO EAT
9  Riverside
11 Rimkhong Pub

OTHER
2  Wat Thakhok
3  Night Market
4  Bus Terminal
5  Wat Paa Tai
6  Wat Mahathat
8  Wat Pa Klang
14 Bank
15 Morning Market
16 Air-Con Bus Terminal
17 Buses to Tha Li
18 Wat Khun Meuang
19 Buses to Loei
20 Wat Santi

Chiang Khan

South-west of town on the river is the easy-going *Nong Sam Guest House* (☎ 821457), run by an Englishman and his Thai wife. Large, comfortable, screened singles/doubles with ceiling fans in brick and wood bunga-lows cost 120/150B. Nong Sam organises boat trips and has motorcycle rentals.

**Kaeng Khut Khu** For most people a day trip to Kaeng Khut Khu from Chiang Khan is sufficient, but accommodation is available near the rapids for those inclined to spend the night. *Chiang Khan Hill Resort* (☎ 821285) offers solid brick bungalows near the rapids

starting at 300B and going up to 1600B depending on the size and amenities. Huts at *Seeview Huts*, near Ban Noi on the road between the rapids and the highway, cost 200B. The quiet huts are well off the road and next to the river, with a pleasant dining area. The nearby *Cootcoo Resort* (☎ 821248) has similar accommodation for 120B.

**Places to Eat**
*Riverside* and *Rimkhong Pub* are modest res-taurants in old shophouses on the river; they're open evenings and weekends only, and serve decent Thai and Isaan meals.

Most of the more modest eating places in town are clustered on Soi 9 and around the intersection of Soi 9 and Chiang Khan Rd. The most popular dish in town seems to be the local version of phàt thai, which here contains thin rice noodles fried with bean sprouts, eggs and pork (rather than egg, tofu, sprouts, peanuts and dried shrimp). Practically every restaurant in town lists this dish first on its menu! A few places serve khànom jiin (thin white wheat noodles with chilli sauce), a dish which the locals call by its Lao name, khào pûn.

For cheap breakfasts, head for the morning market off Soi 9 near Wat Santi. Between 5 and 7.30 am there are a couple of stalls selling kafae thûng (Thai coffee), curries and paathông-kǒh (Chinese pastries). The simple riverside restaurant at the Suksombun Hotel serves good Thai and Chinese standards.

### Getting There & Away

Songthaews to Chiang Khan leave almost hourly from the Loei bus terminal for 14B (one hour). From Chiang Khan the bus to Loei departs from near the Shell petrol station.

For transport between Chiang Khan and Nong Khai, see the Pak Chom, Sangkhom and Si Chiangmai sections earlier in this chapter.

### THA LI DISTRICT
อ.ท่าลี่

Perhaps the most beautiful part of Loei is the area which borders Laos from Dan Sai district in the west to Pak Chom in the east, including the district of Tha Li. Much of the district is the Thai half of a valley surrounded by the Khao Noi, Khao Laem and Khao Ngu mountains on the Thai side, and Phu Lane, Phu Hat Son and Phu Nam Kieng on the Lao side. The small town of Tha Li itself is 50 km from Loei on Route 2115, only about eight km from the Lao border. The border is formed by the Heuang River, a tributary of the Maekhong (which joins the border east of here towards Chiang Khan).

Now that relations between Laos and Thailand have normalised, local commerce back and forth across the Heuang River seems to be growing daily. Ban Nong Pheu, perched on the border, is bustling with a mixture of legal and black-market trade. Handmade products such as cotton fabrics and straw mats, and contraband goods such as ganja and lâo khǎo (white liquor), come across from Laos in exchange for finished goods like medicine and machine parts. These are 'wild west' villages where travellers go at their own risk – mostly they're easy-going and safe but a lot goes on beneath the apparently calm surface. Sayabuli, the Lao province on the other side of the border, is considered one of the most insecure and lawless in Laos; smuggling is the main source of local income and an armed Hmong guerrilla movement is believed to exist in Sayabuli's mountain ranges.

On the Thai side the village men are prodigious drinkers but rarely touch beer or Mekong whisky. Instead they drink lâo khǎo, a clear, colourless, fiery liquid with a very high alcohol content, distilled from glutinous rice. In a pun referring to Thailand's famous Mekong whisky, they call it 'Mae Heuang' after the local tributary. Inside nearly every bottle is inserted a thick black medicinal root called yaa dong, which is said to dissolve away the aches and pains of the day's work and prevent hangovers. It does seem to mellow the flavour of the lâo khǎo, which has a taste somewhere between high-proof rum and tequila.

Near Ban Pak Huay is one of the best places for swimming in the Heuang River, between January and May when the water is clear.

There is now one guesthouse in Ban Pak Huay, or you can usually spend the night at a village temple for a small donation. The wat with the Lao-style chedi off Route 2115 between Tha Li and Pak Huay has hosted several overnight farang visitors.

### Ban Nong Pheu & Beyond
บ้านหนองผือ

Fifty km west of Chiang Khan along rugged Route 2195, Ban Nong Pheu is a market village for local Thai-Lao trade across the Heuang River, where dozens of ferries flit back and forth all day long. Sit by the border post for an hour or two and you'll be amazed at all the merchandise that comes on and off the narrow boats – cases of Fab detergent, bags of cement, chickens and pigs, lumber, roots, rice. At a wat compound a short walk from the river is an outdoor market where a lot of the goods change hands; there are also a few noodle stalls and cold drink vendors to re-energise visitors who have made it to this little corner of the world. This market doesn't meet every day of the week – enquire in Loei or Chiang Khan for the current schedule. The river traffic is busiest on market days.

About 10 km farther west along Route 2195 is **Ban A Hii**, another market village on the river that's similar to Ban Nong Pheu but usually less lively. The recently paved road continues past Ban A Hii to nondescript **Pak Man** and ends after about 45 km at **Na Haew**. This road is not paved to a very high standard; within a year of sealing it was already buckling.

From Na Haew, Route 1268 now continues west and north along the Lao border as far as **Rom Klao** in Phitsanulok Province. A 33 km stretch of Route 1268 north of Rom Klao to **Huay Mun** in Utaradit Province is unsealed but will probably be reconstructed soon; at the moment there's no public transport along this route but it would make an interesting if somewhat rugged bike trip. From Huay Mun you can continue farther north into **Nan Province** (the provincial border is around 100 km away) along mostly unsealed roads, or head west via routes 1239 and 1045 to the amphoe meuang **Utaradit**.

### Places to Stay

Near the junction of routes 2195 and 2115, the low-profile *OTS Guest House* in Ban Pak Huay offers a few simple rooms in a private home for 50B.

### Getting There & Away

Songthaews from Loei leave almost hourly for Tha Li. The trip takes an hour and costs 15B. Songthaews between Tha Li and Ban A Hi, or Ban Pak Huay, cost 7B.

## NAM NAO NATIONAL PARK

One of Thailand's most beautiful and valuable parks, Nam Nao (Cold Water) covers nearly 1000 sq km, at an average elevation of 800m, at the intersection of Chaiyaphum, Phetchabun and Loei provinces. Although the park was first opened in 1972 it remained a People's Liberation Army of Thailand (PLAT) stronghold until the early 1980s. Marked by the sandstone hills of the Phetchabun Mountains, the park features dense mixed evergreen deciduous forest on mountains and hills, open dipterocarp-pine-oak forest on plateaux and hills, dense bamboo mountain forest with wild banana stands in river valleys, and savannah on the plains. A fair system of trails branches out from the park headquarters; the scenic and fairly level Phu Khu Khao trail cuts through pine forests and grass meadow for 24 km. The park also features several waterfalls and caves. The park's highest peak, **Phu Phaa Jit**, reaches 1271m.

Although it's adjacent to 390,000 acre **Phu Khiaw Wildlife Sanctuary**, a highway bisecting the park has unfortunately made wildlife somewhat more accessible to poachers, so many native species are in decline. There are no villages within the park boundaries, however, so incidences of poaching and illegal logging remain fairly minor. Elephants and banteng are occasionally spotted, as well as Malayan sun bears, tigers, leopards, Asian jackals, barking deer, gibbons, langurs and flying squirrels. Rumours of rhinoceros persist (last seen in 1971, but tracks were observed in 1979) and the bizarre fur-coated Sumatran rhino may survive here. Phu Khiaw itself is a sandstone mountain covered with thick forests in Khon San district that harbours crocodiles, banteng, gaur, tigers, elephants, serow, leopards and barking deer. Three rivers are sourced here, the Chi, Saphung and Phrom.

The park headquarters is 55 km east of Lom Sak. A small museum in the visitors' centre contains a collection of confiscated guns and traps used by poachers, an ecological map and bird list. Temperatures are fairly cool year-round, especially nights and mornings;

the best time to go is from November to February, when morning frost occasionally occurs.

The Forestry Department operates 10 bungalows (400 to 1200B) and camping areas; tents are available for rent. Vendors next to the visitors' centre offer noodles, Thai and Isaan food.

Daily buses run through the park from Lom Sak, Chumphae or Khon Kaen (103 km). Look for the park office sign on Highway 12 at Km 50; the office is two km from here.

## LOM SAK
หล่มสัก

It's a scenic trip to/from Phitsanulok via this small town in Phetchabun Province off Highway 12 on the way to/from Loei and Khon Kaen. The ongoing construction of the nearby **Huay Khon Kaen Dam** has brought a small measure of development to Lom Sak.

### Places to Stay & Eat
Most convenient to the bus stop is *Sawang Hotel* with rooms for 80 to 110B, but traffic noise can be intense. Near the centre of town, the motel-like *Baan Kaew Guest House* offers better, and quieter, rooms for 140B. On the southern outskirts of town towards the highway, opposite Nakhon Lom Hospital, *Nakhon Inn* has quiet rooms around a courtyard for 120B a single/double with fan, 180B with air-con. A new seven-storey wing is under construction next door; when completed it will probably have rooms in the 400 to 800B range.

*Chawn Ngoen* serves very good Thai food in a large *sãalaa* (*sala*; an open-sided covered resting place) off the main north-south street. Lom Sak's most famous restaurant is the Chinese *Drai-woh*, named for a once-popular detergent called 'Drive-O'! It's the kind of place that inspires Thais to say, 'If you haven't eaten at Drive-O you haven't really been to Lom Sak'. Specialities here include pèt phalóh tâo-hûu náam daeng (five spice duck stew), pîng kài (grilled chicken) and khanõm jìip (Chinese dumplings).

Alongside Talaat Mai, a large outdoor market in the centre of town, are two decent and inexpensive Chinese vegetarian restaurants. One is open from 6 am to 8 pm, while the other closes late afternoon.

# Nakhon Phanom Province

Nakhon Phanom Province has a large Lao and Vietnamese presence, although the capital is largely ethnic Chinese. If you've come to this province to visit That Phanom, you'll probably have to stop here first to change buses, unless you go directly to That Phanom from Sakon Nakhon via Route 223. The province is dotted with temples with Lao-style *thâat* (four sided, curvilinear chedis).

## NAKHON PHANOM
อ.เมืองนครพนม

• ☎ *(42)* • *pop 33,400*

Nakhon Phanom is 242 km from Udon Thani and 296 km from Nong Khai. It's a rather ordinary town which just happens to have a panoramic view of the Maekhong River and the craggy mountains of Laos beyond – in fact the Sanskrit-Khmer name means 'City of Hills'. A landscaped promenade was recently added along the river at either end of town to take advantage of the views.

Just south of the Grand View Hotel is a river 'beach', where locals and visitors gather to watch the sun set and buy snacks from the evening and weekend vendors. On hot, still days an upside-down mirror image of the river island **Don Don** appears to hang in the air above the real thing.

The interior murals of the bòt at **Wat Si Thep**, in town on the street of the same name, show *jatakas* (life stories of the Buddha) along the upper part, and kings of the Chakri dynasty along the lower part. On the back of the bòt is a colourful triptych done in modern style.

The Lao town on the other side of the Maekhong River is **Tha Khaek**. Foreigners

## Nakhon Phanom Festival

On the full moon of the 11th lunar month (usually late October) at the end of the Buddhist Rains Retreat, Nakhon Phanom residents celebrate Wan Phra Jao Prot Lok – a holiday in honour of Buddha's ascent to the Devaloka (Deity World) to offer the residing devas a Dhamma sermon. Besides the usual wat offering, festival activities include the launching of *reua fai*, or fire boats, on the Maekhong. Originally these eight to 10m boats were made of banana logs or bamboo but modern versions can be fashioned of wood or synthetic materials. The boats carry offerings of cakes, rice and flowers; at night the boats are launched on the river and illuminated in a spectacular display.

During this same festival in the daytime, the city hosts longboat races similar to those seen in many towns along the Maekhong. ∎

are now permitted to cross by ferry provided they hold valid Lao visas. Thai and Lao government officials are currently mulling over the possibility of adding a third bridge over the Maekhong River here (the first, between Thailand's Nong Khai Province and Laos' Vientiane Province, is already open, while the second, at Chiang Khong, is under construction). This would link Nakhon Phanom with the Vietnamese seaport of Vinh on the Gulf of Tonkin via the 240 km Route 12 across Laos and Vietnam.

### Information

**Tourist Office** The TAT (☎ 513490/1) has a new office in a beautiful colonial-style building on the corner of Sala Klang and Sunthon Wijit Rds. The staff distribute information on Nakhon Phanom, Mukdahan and Sakon Nakhon provinces.

**Post & Communications** The GPO, on the corner of Ratchathan and Sunthon Wijit Rds, is open from 8.30 am to 4.30 pm Monday to Friday, and from 9 am to noon on weekends and holidays. The separate CAT telephone office on Sala Klang Rd is open daily from 7 am to 10 pm.

### Places to Stay – bottom end

Conveniently located on the Maekhong River, the *River Inn* (☎ 511305) offers OK rooms with fan and bath from 180B, with some air-con rooms available for 350B.

The cheapest place in town is the *First Hotel* (☎ 511253) at 370 Si Thep Rd, which

has somewhat run-down rooms with fan and bath for 140 to 160B, or with air-con for 250B. The similar *Charoensuk Hotel* on Bamrung Meuang Rd costs 150/180B with fan and bath. A bit better is the *Grand Hotel* (☎ 511-526) on the corner of Si Thep and Ruamjit Rds, which has simple but well kept rooms for 160B, or 390B with air-con.

### Places to Stay – middle & top end

The *Windsor Hotel* (☎ 511946) at 692/19 Bamrung Meuang Rd is a former budget place which is currently under renovation and will cost in the 300 to 550B range.

The *Si Thep Hotel* (☎ 511036) at 708/11 Si Thep Rd costs 200B for rooms with fan and bath in the old wing, 400B for air-con rooms with hot water in the new wing. VIP rooms with fridge and TV are 650B.

The *Nakhon Phanom Hotel* (☎ 511455) at 403 Aphiban Bancha Rd has comfortable air-con rooms with carpet, TV and hot water for 400B, and VIP rooms with fridge and nicer furnishings for 560B.

The newer, all air-con *Mae Nam Khong Grand View Hotel* (☎ 513564; fax 511037), overlooking the river at the southern end of town, offers spacious rooms with all the amenities for 1050B a night, including breakfast. Farther south along the same road, the even newer, 130-room *Nakhon Phanom River View* is due to open soon.

### Places to Eat

Most of the town's better Thai and Chinese restaurants are along the river on Sunthon

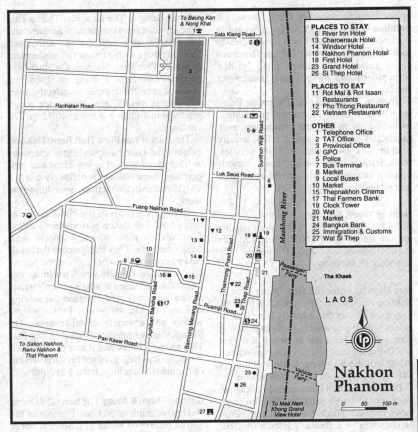

PLACES TO STAY
6 River Inn Hotel
13 Charoensuk Hotel
14 Windsor Hotel
16 Nakhon Phanom Hotel
18 First Hotel
23 Grand Hotel
26 Si Thep Hotel

PLACES TO EAT
11 Rot Mai & Rot Isaan Restaurants
12 Pho Thong Restaurant
22 Vietnam Restaurant

OTHER
1 Telephone Office
2 TAT Office
3 Provincial Office
4 GPO
5 Police
7 Bus Terminal
8 Market
9 Local Buses
10 Market
15 Thepnakhon Cinema
17 Thai Farmers Bank
19 Clock Tower
20 Wat
21 Market
24 Bangkok Bank
25 Immigration & Customs
27 Wat Si Thep

Nakhon Phanom

0    50    100 m

Wijit Rd; they include *Plaa Beuk Thong (Golden Giant Catfish)*, *New Rapmit*, *Ban Suan*, *Rim Nam* and *New Suan Mai*. New Suan Mai, Plaa Beuk Thong and Rim Nam are the best of the bunch; Rim Nam has an open-air, floating platform at the back that gets a breeze. At these restaurants, giant Maekhong catfish is occasionally available and served phàt phèt (stir-fried with basil and curry paste), tôm yam (in a spicy lemongrass broth), phàt kratiam (garlic-fried) or òp mâw din (baked in a clay pot).

There are several good, inexpensive restaurants serving dishes like noodles and

curry and rice along Bamrung Meuang Rd north of the Windsor and Charoensuk hotels. Two small rice shops between the Charoensuk Hotel and Honey Massage, *Rot Mai* and *Rot Isaan*, serve local specialities, including jàew háwn, a sukiyaki-style soup with noodles, beef and vegetables. Other popular dishes at these restaurants are lâap pèt (spicy duck salad), ling wua (beef tongue) and yâang sěua ráwng hâi (literally 'grilled crying tiger' – beef grilled with chillies).

*Pho Thong* on the opposite side of Bamrung Meuang Rd is a larger place serving Isaan food. Other well known local Isaan spots include *Somtom Khun Taew*, on Sunthon Wijit Rd, and *Nawt Laap Pet* at 494 Aphiban Bancha Rd. Local specialities to look for include súp naw mái (spicy bamboo-shoot salad), plaa châwn phão (grilled serpentfish) and hãwy khom (freshwater snails).

*Vietnam Restaurant* on Thamrong Prasit Rd naturally serves Vietnamese specialities, including nãem meuang (barbecued pork meatballs) and yáw (spring rolls), usually sold in 'sets' (sùt), with cold rice noodles, fresh lettuce leaves, mint, basil, various dipping sauces, sliced starfruit and sliced green plantain.

### Getting There & Away

**Air** THAI (☎ 512494) fields daily flights to/from Bangkok for 1605B each way. The flight takes an hour and 10 minutes. The airport is 16 km away.

**Bus** Regular buses run from Nong Khai to Nakhon Phanom via Sakon Nakhon for 50B. There are air-con buses hourly from 6 to 11 am for 80B. If you want to go through Beung Kan, you can get a bus to Beung Kan first (40B), then change to a Nakhon Phanom bus (45B). All the way from Udon Thani costs 64B by ordinary bus, 114B with air-con.

Between Nakhon Phanom and Mukdahan there are 13 buses daily for 29B; ordinary buses between Nakhon Phanom and Sakon Nakhon run on a similar schedule for 27B. Buses south to That Phanom run frequently throughout the day and cost 15B.

Air-con buses run between Khorat and Nakhon Phanom thrice daily for 180B.

From Bangkok there are several air-con buses to Nakhon Phanom each evening between 7 and 8 pm for 241B in 2nd class or 310 to 375B in 1st class, plus 7 and 7.40 pm VIP departures for 480B.

## AROUND NAKHON PHANOM

### Renu Nakhon
เรณูนคร

The village of Renu Nakhon is known for the weaving of cotton and silk fabrics, especially mát-mii designs. The local Phu Thai, a Thai tribe separate from mainstream Siamese and Lao, also market their designs here. Each Saturday there's a big handicraft market near Wat Phra That Renu Nakhon. On other days you can buy from a string of shops and vendors near the temple or directly from weavers in the village. Prices for rough grades of mát-mii are as low as 40B for a 170 cm length.

The thâat at **Wat Phra That Renu Nakhon** exhibits the same basic-style characteristics as That Phanom's but in less elongated proportions. Renu Nakhon is definitely worth a visit if you're in the vicinity, even during the week.

During local festivals the Phu Thai sometimes hold folk-dance performances called *fáwn lákhon thai*, which celebrate their unique heritage. They also practise the bai sĭi custom common in other parts of the North-East as well as Laos, in which a shaman ties loops of sacred string around a person's wrists during a complicated ceremony involving offerings of blessed water, fruit, flowers, whisky and a variety of other items. On Saturday at the handicraft market, the Phu Thai put on a music and dance performance for tourists, as well as an abbreviated version of the bai sĭi ceremony, from 1 to 3 pm.

### Getting There & Away

The turn-off to Renu Nakhon is south of Nakhon Phanom at the Km 44 marker on Route 212. Since it's only 10 km farther to That Phanom, you could visit Renu on the way, or if you are staying in That Phanom, visit Renu as a day trip. From Route 212, it's seven km west on Route 2031 (5B by songthaew from the junction).

### Tha Khaek
ท่าแขก

This Lao town across the river from Nakhon Phanom traces its roots to French colonial construction in 1911-12. Before the war (and during the war until the NVA and Pathet Lao cut the road north to Vientiane), Tha Khaek was a thriving provincial capital and a gambling centre for day-tripping Thais. Today it's a quiet transport and trade outpost with surviving French colonial architecture similar to that found in Vientiane and Savannakhet.

The *Khammouan Hotel*, a large four-storey, white, curved-front building facing the Maekhong, has clean rooms with TV, fridge, air-con, hot water and good mattresses from 180B. The *Thakhek May Hotel*, a few blocks away from the river on Thanon Vientiane, offers simple rooms in a two-storey square building for 100 to 175B.

If you hold a valid Lao visa, you can catch a 25B ferry ride across the river; the border is open Monday to Friday from 8.30 am to 5 pm, until 12.20 pm Saturday. Buses from Tha Khaek to Vientiane cost 3500 kip (around 125B) and take 10 hours. For more information see Lonely Planet's *Laos* guidebook.

## THAT PHANOM

ธาตุพนม

Fifty-three km south of Nakhon Phanom and 70 km south-east of Sakon Nakhon, the centre of activity in this small town is Wat Phra That Phanom.

The short road between Wat Phra That Phanom and the old town on the Maekhong River passes under a large Lao arch of victory, which is a miniature version of the arch on Lan Xang Rd in Vientiane (which leads to Vientiane's own Wat That Luang). This section of That Phanom is interesting, with a smattering of French-Chinese architecture reminiscent of old Vientiane or Saigon.

Hundreds of Lao merchants cross the river for the market on Monday and Thursday from around 8.30 am to noon. There are two market locations in town, one on the highway near the wat and one on the river north of the pier. The latter is where the Lao congregate on their twice weekly visits. Exotic offerings include Lao herbal medicines, forest roots, Vietnamese pigs and animal skins; the maddest haggling occurs just before the market closes, when Thai buyers

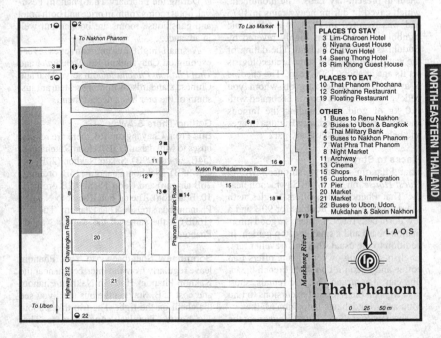

PLACES TO STAY
3 Lim-Charoen Hotel
6 Niyana Guest House
9 Chai Von Hotel
14 Saeng Thong Hotel
18 Rim Khong Guest House

PLACES TO EAT
10 That Phanom Phochana
12 Somkhane Restaurant
19 Floating Restaurant

OTHER
1 Buses to Renu Nakhon
2 Buses to Ubon & Bangkok
4 Thai Military Bank
5 Buses to Nakhon Phanom
7 Wat Phra That Phanom
8 Night Market
11 Archway
13 Cinema
15 Shops
16 Customs & Immigration
17 Pier
20 Market
21 Market
22 Buses to Ubon, Udon, Mukdahan & Sakon Nakhon

To Lao Market
To Nakhon Phanom
Kuson Ratchadamnoen Road
Chayangkun Road
Phanom Phanirak Road
Highway 212
Maekhong River
To Ubon
LAOS
That Phanom
0   25   50 m

NORTH-EASTERN THAILAND

try to take advantage of the Lao reluctance to carry unsold merchandise back to Laos.

About 20 km south of town (turn-off for Wan Yai, between Km 187 and 188) is a wooded park next to **Kaeng Kabao**, a set of rapids in the Maekhong River. Nearby hills afford views over the river and Laos on the other side. The usual food vendors make this a good spot for an impromptu picnic – it's an easy bicycle ride from That Phanom.

During the That Phanom Festival in mid-February, hordes of visitors descend from all over Isaan. Lao cross over to visit the wat, Thais cross over to Laos, and the town hardly sleeps for seven days.

## Information

The Thai Military Bank on Chayangkun Rd offers foreign-exchange services.

## Wat Phra That Phanom

The centrepiece of this wat is a huge thâat, or Lao-style chedi, more impressive than any chedi in present-day Laos. The monument, which caved in during heavy rains in 1975 and was restored in 1978, is a talismanic symbol of Isaan and is highly revered by Buddhists all over Thailand. The dating of the wat is disputed, but some archaeologists set its age at about 1500 years. The chedi is 57m (or 52m, depending on whom you believe) high and the spire is decorated with 110 kg of gold. Surrounding the famous chedi is a cloister filled with Buddha images and behind the wat is a shady park.

## Places to Stay & Eat

That Phanom's first guesthouse, *Niyana Guest House*, on Soi Withi Sawrachon near the That Phanom pier, offers singles with shared bath for 70B, doubles for 90B and a few dorm beds for 50B. There's a good information board and a small rooftop garden. In addition to the usual Thai and traveller fare, English-speaking owner Niyana offers Lao coffee and khâo jii, Lao-style French bread. She can also arrange bicycle rentals, short boat trips on the river and excursions to Phu Muu and Mukdahan's Indochina Market.

The new *Rim Khong Guest House* near the

boat landing features nine clean rooms in a modern L-shaped building with hard mattresses, ceiling fan and cold water shower for 400/600B a single/double. It seems pretty overpriced for this town, so rates will probably drop.

The old town also has three hotels. To reach *Saeng Thong Hotel*, turn right onto Phanom Phanarak Rd as you pass under the arch coming from the wat; it's on the left side of the street 30m down. An adequate room with a fan and shared bath costs 80B. It's a funky place (established 1958) with an inner courtyard and lots of character, but pretty basic. *Chai Von (Wan) Hotel*, on the opposite side of Phanom Phanarak Rd to the north of the arch (turn left as you pass under the arch), is similar in character but much better kept than the Saeng Thong. Rooms cost 60B with shared bath, 80B with private Thai-style bath.

*Lim-Charoen Hotel,* on Chayangkun Rd near the bus terminal, has rooms for 100B, but you're better off at the cheaper hotels.

During the February That Phanom Festival, hotel rooms zoom in price and both hotel and guesthouse rooms are booked out well in advance.

A small night market convenes every evening on Chayangkun Rd. *Somkhane* and *That Phanom Phochana* both serve Thai and Chinese standards. A floating restaurant just south of the pier has a decent menu.

## Getting There & Away

**Bus** From Chayangkun Rd, there are regular buses to Mukdahan (15B), Ubon Ratchathani (54B, air-con 99B), Sakon Nakhon (20B, air-con 35B), Nakhon Phanom (15B ordinary, 26B air-con) and Udon Thani (62B ordinary, 105B air-con). The air-con Khorat to Nakhon Phanom bus stops at That Phanom. The fare (160B) is the same all the way to Nakhon Phanom.

**Songthaew** Songthaews to That Phanom leave regularly from the intersection near the Nakhon Phanom Hotel in Nakhon Phanom and cost 15B. Stay on the bus until you see the chedi on the right. The trip takes about 1½ hours. The last songthaew to That

Phanom leaves around 6 pm; in the reverse direction the last vehicle leaves That Phanom for Nakhon Phanom at 8 pm.

**Ferry** A ferry ride across to Laos costs 10B per person. At the moment only Thai and Lao citizens are permitted to cross the border here.

# Sakon Nakhon Province

Sakon Nakhon Province is well known among Thais as the one-time home of two of the most famous Buddhist monks in Thai history, Ajaan Man and Ajaan Fan Ajaro. Both were ascetic thutong monks who were thought to have attained high levels of proficiency in *vipassana* meditation. Though born in Ubon Ratchathani, Ajaan Man spent most of his later years at Wat Pa Sutthawat in Sakon Nakhon. Some say he died there, while others say he wandered off into the jungle in 1949 and disappeared. Whatever the story, the wat now has an Ajaan Man museum with a display of some of his monastic possessions.

Ajaan Fan Ajaro, a student of Ajaan Man, established a cave hermitage for the study of meditation at Tham Kham on the mountain of Khao Phu Phaan. He was also affiliated with Wat Pa Udom Somphon in his home district of Phanna Nikhom, 37 km from Sakon Nakhon towards Udon Thani on Route 22. A museum commemorating the life of Ajaan Fan is there. Ajaan Fan died in 1963.

The end of the Buddhist Rains Retreat in November is fervently celebrated in Sakon with the carving and display of wax prasats, as well as parades.

## SAKON NAKHON
สกลนคร
• ☎ (42) • *pop 24,800*
As a secondary agricultural market centre (after Udon Thani) for the upper Isaan, the provincial capital is mostly a conglomeration of shops selling farm equipment. For most visitors, the only reason to stay in the city is to visit Wat Choeng Chum and Wat Narai Jeng Weng.

Along the eastern edge of town is **Nong Han**, Thailand's largest natural lake. Don't swim in the lake – it's infested with liver flukes, which can cause a nasty liver infection known as opisthorchiasis. The villages around the lake have recorded among the highest incidences of opisthorchiasis in the world, since many of the villagers eat snails gathered from water plants in the lake. These snails play host to the flukes, which bore through human or animal skin and breed in the internal organs. (See Health in the Facts for the Visitor chapter for more information.)

One of Sakon's claims to fame is the relative popularity of dogmeat dishes. Contrary to common Thai stereotype, not all natives of Sakon are fond of eating dog – in fact, it's a custom mostly relegated to the Soh ethnic minority of Tha Lae district, around 42 km north-west of amphoe meuang Sakon Nakhon. A dog market in Tha Lae slaughters up to 100 animals a day and purveys the meat for 25 to 35B per kilo – at least 60% cheaper than beef. The market also sells cooked dog in curries, satay, meatball soups and so on for onsite dining and takeaway. By national law, however, it's illegal to buy and sell live dogs for dining purposes.

## Ajaan Man Museum
In the grounds of Wat Pa Sutthawat, on the south-west outskirts of town (off the road to Kalasin), this recently completed museum contains an exhibition of the personal effects of Thailand's famous forest monk. The very modern building looks a bit like a modern Christian church, with arches and stained glass windows. A bronze image of Ajaan Man surrounded by flowers sits on a pedestal at one end. Articles and photos associated with the monk's history are on display behind glass. The museum building is usually open from 8 am to 6 pm daily.

## Wat Phra That Choeng Chum
วัดพระธาตุเชิงชุม
Next to the Nong Han Lake in town, this wat features a 25m-high, Lao-style chedi which

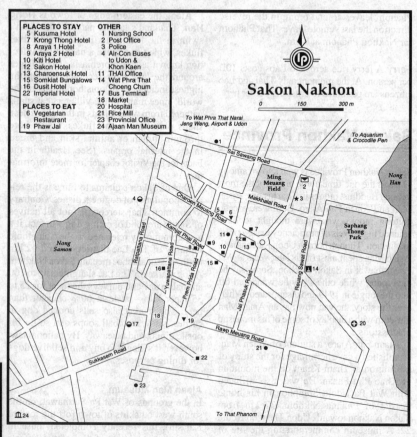

**Sakon Nakhon**

| PLACES TO STAY | OTHER |
|---|---|
| 5  Kusuma Hotel | 1  Nursing School |
| 7  Krong Thong Hotel | 2  Post Office |
| 8  Araya 1 Hotel | 3  Police |
| 9  Araya 2 Hotel | 4  Air-Con Buses |
| 10  Kiti Hotel | to Udon & |
| 12  Sakon Hotel | Khon Kaen |
| 13  Charoensuk Hotel | 11  THAI Office |
| 15  Somkiat Bungalows | 14  Wat Phra That |
| 16  Dusit Hotel | Choeng Chum |
| 22  Imperial Hotel | 17  Bus Terminal |
| | 18  Market |
| PLACES TO EAT | 20  Hospital |
| 6  Vegetarian | 21  Rice Mill |
| Restaurant | 23  Provincial Office |
| 19  Phaw Jai | 24  Ajaan Man Museum |

0    150    300 m

To Wat Phra That Narai
Jeng Weng, Airport & Udon

To Aquarium
& Crocodile Pen

Nong Han

was erected during the Ayuthaya period over a smaller 11th century Khmer prang. To view the prang you must enter through the adjacent wihăan. If the door to the chedi is locked, ask one of the monks to open it – they're used to having visitors. Around the base of the prang is a collection of Lao and Khmer Buddha images.

Also on the grounds is a small Lan Xangera bòt and a wihăan built in the cruciform shape reminiscent of Lanna styles found in Northern Thailand. Lûuk nímít, spherical ordination markers that look like cannonballs, are arranged on the grass near the

wihăan; next to the monastery's east gate is the base for an original Khmer Shivalingam.

A drum tower donated by the local Vietnamese population bears the inscription 'Viêt Kieu Luu Liem' – so this wat features Thai, Lao, Vietnamese and Khmer elements. A new wihăan under construction promises to dwarf all the other temple buildings.

### Wat Phra That Narai Jeng Weng
วัดพระธาตุนารายณ์เจงเวง

About five km west of town at Ban That (three km past the airport), this wat has a

10th to 11th century Khmer prang in the early Bapuan style. Originally part of a Khmer Hindu complex, the five level sandstone prang features a reclining Vishnu lintel over its eastern portico and a dancing Shiva over its northern one.

To get to the temple by public transport, catch a songthaew west towards the airport on Sai Sawang Rd and get off at Talaat Ban That Naweng (5B). From here it's a pleasant one km walk to the wat through a village. The wat is called Phra That Naweng (contraction of Narai Jeng Weng) for short.

### Aquarium & Crocodile Pen
North-east of the post office is a small park containing a fish hatchery, crocodile pen and aquarium. The latter features a couple of dozen large tanks with freshwater fish from Thailand and various parts of the world. It's not a world-class attraction but it's free.

### Places to Stay
The *Araya 1* on Prem Prida Rd has one/two bed rooms with fan for 150/250B and air-con rooms for 250/300B; diagonally opposite is the wooden *Araya 2*, with rooms with fan for only 70/90B or with attached bath for 120 to 200B. There is a Thai-Chinese restaurant below. On the same block as the Araya 2 are *Somkiat Bungalows* at 150/200B (a truck-driver favourite because of its inside parking lot) and *Kiti Hotel*, with basic but OK rooms for 200B.

The *Krong Thong Hotel* (☎ 711097) at 645/2 Charoen Meuang Rd has decent rooms with fan for 100 to 180B, air-con 250B. Also along Charoen Meuang Rd are several similar hotels in the 100 to 200B price range, including the *Kusuma, Charoensuk* and *Sakon* – all fair choices.

Sakon's top-end places consist of two hotels. The *Imperial* (☎ 711119) at 1892 Sukkasem Rd has rooms in its old wing for 290B with fan and bath, 390 to 490B with air-con; in the new wing VIP rooms with TV and carpet are 590 to 790B. The *Dusit Hotel* is not associated with any of the up-market Dusit Group hotels around the country. This one has OK air-con rooms with TV for 400B, or VIP for 650B.

On the south-western outskirts of town the new 70-room, up-market *Versailles Hotel* is under construction.

### Places to Eat
*Best House Suki* on Prem Prida Rd has a nice outdoor eating area, and serves seafood and jàew (Isaan-style sukiyaki – a noodle hot-pot). Night markets are open each evening near the roundabout at Charoen Meuang and Jai Phasuk Rds, and also at the intersection of Charoen Meuang and Sukkasem Rds. Both are very popular nightspots, open until late.

Along Prem Prida Rd are three inexpensive Thai-Chinese restaurants that seem to do half the restaurant business in the city. They're apparent clones of one another; the offerings at all three are similar (buffet-style curries and stir-fries) and all sport names that end in rák (love): *Mitrak* (Friend Love), *Yawt Rak* (Peak of Love) and *Na Rak* (Loveable). All serve passable food at cheap prices.

*Phaw Jai* at the three way intersection of Sukkasem, Prem Prida and Rawp Meuang Rds also serves a good variety of Thai and Chinese dishes.

The small *Vegetarian Restaurant* at 400/1 Charoen Meuang Rd, between Sukkasem and Prem Prida Rds, features decent Thai veggie dishes for 8 and 12B, but it's only open from 6 am to 1 pm, Monday to Saturday. Another vegetarian restaurant known simply as *Aahaan Jeh* (Vegetarian Food) is on Prem Prida Rd.

Five km out of town on the way to Kalasin is *Phen Laap Pet*, a Sakon institution that recently moved from its original Prem Prida Rd location. The menu offers a choice of lâap pèt khão or lâap pèt daeng (white duck salad and red duck salad – 'red' means with duck blood). Other house specialities are yam (another kind of Isaan salad, usually with vegetables or seafood), khài yát sâi (ground pork and vegetable omelette) and plaa sãam rót, or three-flavour fish (a whole fish fried with onions, chillies and garlic).

### Getting There & Away
**Air** Should you wish to fly in or out of Sakon Nakhon, THAI operates three flights a week

from Bangkok (1530B one way). The office in Sakon (☎ 712259/60) is on Sukkasem Rd.

**Bus** Direct buses to Sakon are available from Ubon Ratchathani (69B, six hours), Nakhon Phanom (26B, 1½ hours), Kalasin (35B, 2½ hours), That Phanom (20B, 1½ hours), Khon Kaen (50B, 4 hours) and Udon Thani (42B, 3½ hours). Buses from Sakon to Bangkok are 150B (10 departures a day) or 271B air-con (one evening departure a day). Buses between Khorat and Sakon (air-con only) are 138B and leave six times daily.

Private air-con buses to Udon and Khon Kaen leave three times daily from the Udon Thani-Sakon Doen Rot bus terminal, next to the Esso petrol station on Ratpattana Rd.

## AROUND SAKON NAKHON
### Phu Phaan National Park
อุทยานแห่งชาติภูพาน

This 645 sq km nature preserve is in the Phu Phaan Mountains near the Sakon Nakhon-Kalasin border. Deer, monkeys and other smaller forest animals are common to the park, and wild elephants and tigers are occasionally seen as well.

The mountain forests are thick and the area is fairly undeveloped. It has been used as a hiding spot by two guerrilla forces – the Thai resistance against the Japanese in WWII and later the PLAT guerrillas in the 1970s.

The park has only a few hiking trails but there are good views along Route 213 between Sakon Nakhon and Kalasin. Three waterfalls – **Tat Ton**, **Hew Sin Chai** and **Kham Hom** – can be visited fairly easily.

The **Tham Seri Thai** cave was used by the Thai Seri during WWII as an arsenal and mess hall.

# Yasothon & Mukdahan Provinces

Once encompassed by Ubon Ratchathani and Nakhon Phanom provinces, these adjacent provinces in the lower North-East are two of Thailand's newest and Isaan's smallest. Both are mostly rural in character, with small capital cities serving as market centres for surrounding farms.

## YASOTHON
อ.เมืองยโสธร
• ☎ (45) • pop 29,800

Yasothon is a bit out of the way, but if you happen to be in the area (say, in Ubon Ratchathani, which is about 100 km away) during May, it might be worth the two hour bus trip (from Ubon) to catch the annual Rocket Festival which takes place from 8 to 10 May. The festival (Bun Bang Fai in Thai) is prevalent throughout the North-East as a rain and fertility rite, and is celebrated most fervently in Yasothon, where it involves parades and a fantastic fireworks display. The name of the town, which has the largest Muslim population in the North-East, comes from the Sanskrit 'Yasodhara', which means preserver or maintainer of glory, and is also the name of one of Krishna's sons by Rukmini in the *Mahabharata*.

In town, **Phra That Phra Anon** (also known as Phra That Yasothon) at Wat Mahathat is a highly venerated Lao-style chedi. It's said to be 1200 years old and to enshrine holy relics of Phra Anon (Ananda), Buddha's first disciple.

The village of **Ban Si Than** in Pha Tiu district, about 20 km east of Yasothon off Route 202, is renowned for the crafting of firm, triangle-shaped mãwn khwaan, which are said to rival those of Roi Et.

**Phra That Kong Khao Noi**, in Ban Taat Thong off Highway 23 (between Km 194 and 195) heading toward Ubon Ratchathani, is an unusual brick-and-stucco chedi dating from the late Ayuthaya period.

### Places to Stay
*Udomphon*, at 80/1-2 Uthairamrit Rd, and *Surawet Wattana*, at 128/1 Changsanit Rd, each cost 150 to 200B for rooms with fan and bath. If you can't get into either of these, try the *Yot Nakhon* (☎ 711122), 141-143/1-3 Uthairamrit Rd, where rooms are from 180/300B with/without air-con.

NORTH-EASTERN THAILAND

## Getting There & Away

A bus to Yasothon from Ubon costs 27B; from Khorat it's 65B ordinary or 134B aircon.

## MUKDAHAN

อ.เมืองมุกดาหาร

• ☎ (42) • pop 25,000

Fifty-five km south of That Phanom, 170 km north of Ubon Ratchathani and directly opposite the city of Savannakhet in Laos, Mukdahan is known for its beautiful Maekhong scenery and as a Thai-Lao trade centre. Among Thais it's most known for the **Talaat Indojiin**, or Indochina Market, a Thai-Lao-Vietnamese affair that gathers around Wat Si Mongkon Tai near the Mukdahan pier. On weekends the market spills over onto nearby streets; you'll see khaens (the Isaan panpipe) and bolts of cloth from around Isaan in addition to the usual Lao, Vietnamese and Chinese imports. The more formal **Danang**

**Market** in the town centre contains shopfronts selling many of the same goods.

According to agreements between the Thai and Lao governments, a bridge between Mukdahan and Savannakhet on the opposite bank of the Maekhong River will be built within six years. Vietnam, Laos and Thailand have likewise agreed to accelerate development of Laos' Route 9 to link Mukdahan, Savannakhet and Danang along an east-west trade corridor. Japan may offer financial assistance, and the Asian Development Bank is also interested. Such discussions have prompted lots of construction around town as speculators position themselves for an anticipated economic boom. South of Hotel Muk, the ambitious **Haw Kaew Mukdahan** (Mukdahan Jewel Hall), is a huge space-needle-style shopping and business centre.

In spite of all the construction, Mukdahan might make a nice stopover between Nakhon Phanom or That Phanom and Ubon. For a view of the town, climb the 500m **Phu Narom**

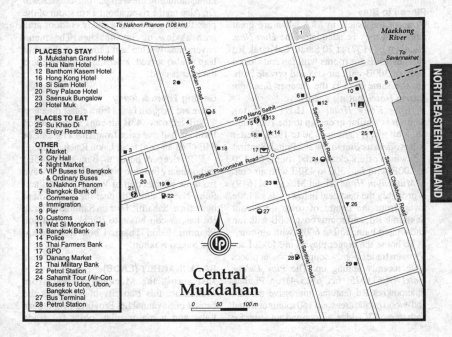

PLACES TO STAY
3 Mukdahan Grand Hotel
6 Hua Nam Hotel
12 Banthom Kasem Hotel
16 Hong Kong Hotel
18 Si Siam Hotel
20 Ploy Palace Hotel
23 Saensuk Bungalow
29 Hotel Muk

PLACES TO EAT
25 Su Khao Di
26 Enjoy Restaurant

OTHER
1 Market
2 City Hall
4 Night Market
5 VIP Buses to Bangkok & Ordinary Buses to Nakhon Phanom
7 Bangkok Bank of Commerce
8 Immigration
9 Pier
10 Customs
11 Wat Si Mongkon Tai
13 Bangkok Bank
14 Police
15 Thai Farmers Bank
17 GPO
19 Danang Market
21 Thai Military Bank
22 Petrol Station
24 Sahamit Tour (Air-Con Buses to Udon, Ubon, Bangkok etc)
27 Bus Terminal
28 Petrol Station

To Nakhon Phanom (106 km)

Maekhong River

To Savannakhet

Wiwit Surakan Road

Song Nang Sathit

Samut Sakdarak Road

Phithak Phanomkhet Road

Phithak Sathiri Road

Samran Chaikhong Road

**Central Mukdahan**

0    50    100 m

NORTH-EASTERN THAILAND

hill, three km south of town. **Phu Muu**, a favourite local picnic spot with scenic views, is 34 km south of amphoe meuang Mukdahan off Route 212 – just south of Ban Taw Khet and the Mukdahan Province line between Km 29 and 30.

The Bangkok Bank of Commerce on Samut Sakdarak Rd in town has a currency-exchange service.

### Phu Pha Thoep National Park
อุทยานแห่งชาติภูผาเทิบ

Sixteen km south of Mukdahan, off Route 2034, is a hilly area of caves and unusual mushroom-shaped rock formations. Besides the rock formations, the park is a habitat for barking deer, wild boar, monkeys and civets. The main entrance to the park is actually 25 km from town, just south of the Ubon Ratchathani provincial line. About two km south-west into the park, next to a waterfall, is a collection of dozens of small Buddha images.

### Places to Stay

None of the hotels in Mukdahan are great deals, but they're adequate. The *Hua Nam Hotel* (☎ 611137) at 20 Samut Sakdarak Rd charges 150B for rooms with fan and shared bath, or 300B with air-con and private bath. On the same road is the cheaper *Banthom Kasem Hotel*, but it's a real dive.

*Hong Kong Hotel* at 161/1-2 Phitak Santirat is similar in design to the Hua Nam but a bit nicer; rates are 150 to 190B. Better still is *Saensuk Bungalow* at 2 Phitak Santirat Rd, which offers clean, quiet rooms for 120 to 200B with fan, 300 to 450B with air-con.

*Mukdahan Hotel* (Hotel Muk; ☎ 611619) is probably the best deal in town – it's a little away from the centre of town on Samut Sakdarak Rd, and rooms cost 160B with fan and shared bath, 250 to 600B with air-con.

To house the bigger players in Muk's Lao-Vietnam trade boom, a couple of posher places have recently sprung up. The *Ploy Palace Hotel* (☎ 611075; fax 612574) on Phithak Phanomkhet Rd features impressive marble-and-wood public areas and 150 rooms outfitted with stereo TV, fridge, air-con and hot water for

1500 to 2000B. The nearby *Mukdahan Grand* (☎ 612020) has 200 similar but larger rooms in the same price range.

On Highway 212 the up-market 150-room *Mukthara* is under construction.

### Places to Eat

The night market along Song Nang Sathit Rd has kài yâang, sôm-tam, khâo jii (Lao baguette sandwiches) and páw-pía – Vietnamese spring rolls, either fresh (sòt) or fried (thâwt). *Khao Tom Suanrak*, next to Hua Nam Hotel, is a Chinese rice-soup place that's open all night. Another place that's open in the wee hours is the *Suwa Blend Restaurant/Pub* next to the Hotel Muk. House specialities are American-style breakfasts and khâo tôm.

*Enjoy Restaurant* (no English sign), on the left side of Phitak Santirat Rd on the way to Hotel Muk from the town centre, serves good Vietnamese food.

South of the pier along the river is a string of moderately priced indoor-outdoor restaurants, including the well patronised *Su Khao Di*. Also on the river, about a km south of the pier, the *Riverside* has a shady outdoor area with a view of Savannakhet. The menu covers mostly Thai and Chinese dishes, but lâap is also served. Prices are moderate and the beer is cold.

### Getting There & Away

There are frequent buses from either direction – 29B ordinary (48B air-con) from Nakhon Phanom, half that price from That Phanom, or 34B (77B air-con) from Ubon Ratchathani.

VIP (sleeper) buses to Bangkok (445B) and ordinary buses to Nakhon Phanom leave from the intersection of Wiwit Surakan and Song Nang Sathit Rds near the government bus office. Sahamit Tour on Samut Sakdarak Rd has air-con buses to Bangkok, Nakhon Phanom, Udon Thani, Ubon Ratchathani and Sakon Nakhon.

### SAVANNAKHET (LAOS)

Just across the Maekhong River from Mukdahan, this Lao city of 45,000 is the capital of Savannakhet Province in southern Laos and a major relay point for trade between Thailand and Vietnam. The 570 km Route 9 extends east all the way to the Vietnamese border at Lao Bao, where it continues eastward to the port of Dong Ha on the lower Gulf of Tonkin. There is talk of building a bridge here over the Maekhong River, but at the moment a competing proposal for a bridge farther north (between Nakhon Phanom Province and Laos' Khammuan Province) has a slight edge because the relative distance between the Lao-Thai border and the Gulf of Tonkin is much shorter.

Like Vientiane and Luang Prabang, Savan has a number of French colonial and Franco-Chinese buildings, but with less of a western presence and almost no tourists.

### Places to Stay
For 3000 to 5000 kip (107 to 178B) you can get basic rooms at the *Hotel Santyphab* on Thanon Tha Dan, two blocks east of the main ferry pier. On the river in an old French colonial villa is the Vietnamese-owned *Mekong Hotel*, with large, high-ceiling rooms, ceiling fans, air-con, tile floors and lots of wood panelling. Rates are 5000 kip (178B) for singles/doubles if you don't turn on the air-con, 7500 kip (267B) with air-con.

### Getting There & Away
Ferries cross the Maekhong River between Savan and Mukdahan frequently between 8.30 am and 5 pm weekdays, and until 12.30 pm Saturday for 30B from Thailand, 850 kip from Laos. Buses to Vientiane cost 7000 kip (250B) and take 12 hours; to Pakse 2500 kip (89B) and six hours.

It's now legal for foreigners to enter and exit the country via Savannakhet; other than a visa, no special permission is needed.

# Ubon Ratchathani Province

Ubon is the North-East's largest province and the provincial capital is one of the larger towns in Thailand. About 300 km of the province borders on Laos and around 60 km borders Cambodia. The local TAT office is trying to promote the area where the three countries meet as the 'Emerald Triangle' in counterpart to Northern Thailand's Golden Triangle. The 'emerald' in the title ostensibly refers to the many hectares of intact monsoon forest in this part of the province – largely due to the fact that it has been sparsely populated because of war tensions. Now that the Khmer Rouge has stopped military activities in the area, travel in the tri-border zone is considered safe.

Ubon's Mun and Chi river basins were centres for Dvaravati and Khmer cultures many centuries ago. Following the decline of the Khmer empires, the area was settled by groups of Lao in 1773 and 1792. By the early Ratanakosin era it had become part of Monthon Ubon, a south-eastern Isaan satellite state extending across present-day Surin, Si Saket and Ubon provinces – as well as parts of southern Laos – with Champasak, Laos, as monthon capital. Today the Lao influence in the province predominates over the Khmer.

## UBON RATCHATHANI
อ.เมืองอุบลราชธานี
• ☎ (45) • pop 90,000
Ubon (sometimes spelt Ubol, though the 'l' is pronounced like an 'n') is 557 km from Bangkok, 271 km from Nakhon Phanom and 311 km from Khorat. Situated on the banks of the Mun (pronounced Moon) River – Thailand's second longest waterway after the Maekhong – Ubon is a financial, educational, communications and agricultural market centre for eastern Isaan. Like Udon Thani and Khorat, it served as a US air base in the Vietnam War days. The city's main attractions are the October candle festival, a few wats and a national museum.

### Information
**Tourist Office** The TAT (☎ 243770/1) has a very helpful branch office at 264/1 Kheuan Thani Rd, opposite the Sri Kamol Hotel. The office distributes free maps of Ubon (on the

reverse is a list of city bus routes) and other information handouts; it's open daily from 8.30 am to 4.30 pm.

**Post & Communications** Ubon's GPO is near the intersection of Luang and Si Narong Rds. It's open from 8.30 am to 4.30 pm Monday to Friday, 9 am to noon on weekends. The telephone office is next door and is open daily from 7 am to 11 pm.

**Medical Services** The Rom Kao Hospital on Uparat Rd near the bridge is the best medical facility in the lower North-East.

## Ubon National Museum
พิพิธภัณฑ์แห่งชาติอุบล

Housed in a former palace of the Rama VI era, west of the TAT office on Kheuan Thani Rd, the National Museum is a good place to learn about Ubon's history and culture before exploring the city or province. Most of the exhibits have bilingual labels.

Flanking the main entrance are a large Dvaravati-period sema stone and some Pallava-inscribed pillars from the Khmer era. The room to the left of the entrance has general information on Ubon history and geography. This is followed by a prehistory room with displays of stone and bronze implements, burial urns and pottery resembling that found in Ban Chiang, plus reproductions of the Phaa Taem rock paintings. The rooms next to it cover the historical era and contain many real treasures of mainland South-East Asian art, including Hindu-Khmer sculpture from the Chenla, Bapuan and Angkor eras, Lao Buddhas, Ubon textiles, local musical instruments and folk utensils (rice containers, fish traps, betel-nut holders).

Among the museum's most prized possessions are a rare standing Dvaravati Buddha image and a Dong Son bronze drum.

The museum is open daily from 9 am to noon and 1 to 4 pm. Admission is 10B.

## Wat Thung Si Meuang
วัดทุ่งศรีเมือง

Off Luang Rd, near the centre of town, this wat was originally built during the reign of Rama III (1824-51) and has a *hǎw trai* (tripitaka library) in good shape. It rests on high-angled stilts in the middle of a small pond. Nearby is an old *mondòp* (small square building) with a Buddha footprint symbol. The bòt's interior is painted with 150 year old jataka murals.

## Wat Phra That Nong Bua
วัดพระธาตุหนองบัว

This wat on the road to Nakhon Phanom on the outskirts of town (catch a white city bus for 2B) is based almost exactly on the Mahabodhi stupa in Bodhgaya, India. It's a much better replica than Wat Jet Yot in Chiang Mai, which is also purported to be a Mahabodhi reproduction, but was designed by people who never saw the real thing. The jataka reliefs on the outside of the chedi are very good. Two groups of four niches on each side of the four sided chedi contain Buddhas standing in stylised Gupta or Dvaravati closed-robe poses.

## Wat Supatanaram
วัดสุปัฏนาราม

Called Wat Supat for short, the unique bòt at this temple features a mix of Khmer, European and Thai styles. In contrast to the usual Thai or Lao-style temple structures of the region, the bòt is made entirely of stone, like the early Khmer stone prasats; the roof corners display dragons instead of the usual *jâo fáa*, or sky spirits.

In front of the bòt is the largest wooden bell in Thailand.

## Wat Jaeng
วัดแจ้ง

This wat on Sanphasit Rd has a typical Lao-style bòt (known locally by the Lao term, *sim*). The carved wooden veranda depicts a *kotchasi*, a mythical cross between an elephant and a horse; above that is Erawan, Indra's three-headed elephant mount.

## Warin Chamrap District Temples
Ubon city district is separated from Warin Chamrap to the south by the Mun River. Two

NORTH-EASTERN THAILAND

well known wats in this district are forest monasteries *(wát pàa)* founded by the famous monk and meditation master Ajaan Chaa. The venerable ajaan died in January 1992, aged 75, after a productive and inspirational life, but his teachings live on at these two hermitages.

**Wat Nong Pa Phong** About 10 km past the train station, in Warin Chamrap district, is Wat Nong Pa Phong. This very famous forest wat was founded by Ajaan Chaa, who also founded many other branch temples in Ubon Ratchathani Province and one in Sussex, England; monks under his lineage have also founded monasteries in other parts of the world. All of these temples are known for their quiet discipline and daily routine of work and meditation.

Dozens of westerners have studied here during the past 20 years and many live here or at branch temples as ordained monks.

Ajaan Chaa, a former disciple of the most famous North-Eastern teacher of them all, Ajaan Man, was known for his simple and direct teaching method which seemed to cross all international barriers. His funeral, which was held here in 1993, drew thousands of followers from around the world.

The wat features a small museum and a chedi where Ajaan Chaa's ashes are interred. To get to the wat from Ubon, take a pink city bus No 3 to the Baw Khaw Saw terminal, then catch a songthaew going to the wat.

**Wat Pa Nanachat Bung Wai** The abbot here is English and most of the monks are European, American or Japanese. As English is the main language spoken here, Wat Pa Nanachat is a better place to visit than Wat Nong Pa Phong if you are interested in more than sightseeing. The wat is very clean, cool and quiet.

Generally only those with a serious interest in Buddhism – preferably with previous practice experience – are permitted to stay overnight. Both men and women are welcome, but men are required to shave their heads if they want to stay beyond three days. Write in advance to avoid disappointment (Wat Pa Nanachat, Ban Bung Wai, Amphoe Warin, Ubon Ratchathani 34310); during the March to May hot season monks go on retreat and overnight guests aren't usually accepted.

From Ubon, take a white city bus No 1 south down Uparat Rd, cross the bridge over the Mun River and get off as the bus turns right in Warin Chamrap for the train station. From there, catch any songthaew heading south (though heading west eventually, on Route 2193 towards Si Saket) and ask to be let off at Wat Nanachat – everybody knows it. You can also get there by catching a Si Saket bus from Ubon for 4B to Bung Wai, the village across the road from Wat Nanachat. There is a sign in English at the edge of the road – the wat is in the forest behind the rice fields. You can also hire a tuk-tuk direct to the wat from town for about 70B.

### Ko Hat Wat Tai
เกาะหาดวัดใต้
This is a small island in the Mun River on the southern edge of town. During the hot and dry months, from March to May, it is a favourite picnic spot and there are 'beaches' where you can swim. You can get there by boat from the northern shore of the river.

**Ubon Ratchathani's Candle Festival**
The Candle Festival (Ngaan Hae Thian) is most grandly celebrated in Ubon Ratchathani, with music, parades, floats, beauty contests and enormous carved candles of all shapes – human, animal, divine and abstract. The evening processions are impressive. The festival begins around Khao Phansaa, the first day of the Buddhist Rains Retreat in late July, and lasts five days. Spirits are high and hotels are full. It's worth a trip this time of year just to see the festival. ■

NORTH-EASTERN THAILAND

Ubon Ratchathani

0    100    200 m

*Approximate Scale*

To Yasothon

1

To Royal Park Hotel, Wat Phra
That Nong Bua & Mukdahan

3 ★        ★ 4

● 2

Ratchathani Road

▼ 5        7 ●        ● 8

■ 6

10

✛ 11

9 ●

12 ●

■ 13

Upalisan Road

16 ■        18

▼ 17

Suriyat Road

● 15

14 ●

19 ▼   20        21 ▼        ★ 22        23 ⊕

Sanphasit Road

30 ■        ■ 29        26

28 ▼   27 ▼   ● 25        24 ▼

Phichit Rangsan Road

34 ■        37        ● 38

31 ■        ▼ 35

⊕ 32   ■ 33        36 ● Phalorangrit Road

Phalo Chai Road

39 ●

40

41 ■

Si Narong Road

46

42        ● 45        47

43 🏛   44 ⓘ        Kheuan Thani Road

48 ■   ▼ 49        50 ■        ● 51        52 ■   ■ 53

Phrom Bat Road

54 ▼        60

55        ⊕ 56        57 ■   ■ 58        59

Hat Khu Deua

To Warin Chamrap District
(Wat Paa Nanachat
& Train Station)

Mun River

Ko Hat
Wat Tai

Jaeng Sanit Road

Chayangkun Road

Lang Meuang Road

Chawala Nok Road

Uparat Road

Pha Daeng Road

Nakhon Baan Road

Ratchabut Road

Luang Road

Theyathi Road

Phon Phaen Road

Burapha Nai Road

NORTH-EASTERN THAILAND

**PLACES TO STAY**
6  Ruanrangsi Mansion
   Park
7  Pathumrat Hotel
12  Regent Palace Hotel
13  Racha Hotel
16  Suriyat Hotel
27  Lai Thong Hotel
30  Tokyo Hotel
31  Tohsang Hotel
33  Bodin Hotel
41  Krung Thong Hotel
48  Ubon Hotel
50  Ratchathani Hotel
52  Sri Kamol Hotel
53  New Nakornluang
   Hotel
58  Si Isaan Hotel

**PLACES TO EAT**
5  Fern Hut
17  Kai Yaang Wat
   Jaeng
19  Indochine
   Restaurant
21  Sincere
   Restaurant
24  Vegetarian
   Restaurant
28  Italian Pizza
35  Sakhon Restaurant

49  Jiaw Kii (Chiokee)
   Restaurant
54  Arawy

**OTHER**
1  Buses for Mukdahan,
   Udon & Sakon
   Nakhon
2  Ubon Teachers'
   College
3  Border Police
4  Highway Police
8  THAI Office
9  Buses to Roi Et,
   Khon Kaen, Udon &
   Yasothon
10  Ordinary Bus
   Terminal
11  Airfield
14  Highway Department
   Office
15  Chaw Wattana
   Motorcycles
18  Market
20  Wat Jaeng
22  Police
23  Sanphasit Prasong
   Hospital
25  Buses to Phibun
   Mangsahan &
   Khong Jiam

26  Market No 5
29  Wat Paa Yai
32  Central Memorial
   Hospital
34  Wat Sutha-
   tsanaram
36  Air-Con Buses to
   Chiang Mai &
   Phitsanulok
37  Wat Paa Noi
38  Cinema
39  Province &
   District Offices
40  Wat Thung Si
   Meuang
42  City Shrine
43  Ubon National
   Museum
44  TAT Office
45  Municipal
   Office
46  GPO
47  Wat Liap
51  Saiyan Tour
55  Wat Supa-
   tanaram
56  Rom Kao
   Hospital
57  Night Market
59  Wat Luang
60  Wat Klang

## Hat Khu Deua
หาดคูเดื่อ

Hat Khu Deua is a 'beach' area on the northern bank of the river west of town, off Lang Meuang Rd. Several thatched sala offer shade for picnicking or napping by the river; you can even stay overnight in simple raft houses at no charge.

## Places to Stay – bottom end

*Suriyat Hotel* at 47/1-4 Suriyat Rd has divey rooms with fan for 130 to 180B, or 300B with air-con. A better choice in this range is the *Si Isaan (Far East*; ☎ 254204) at 220/6 Ratchabut Rd, where singles/doubles are 150/180B with fan and private bath, or in a separate building there are air-con rooms for 300B. In the old wing the mosaic railing on the staircase is worth a look.

The *New Nakornluang Hotel* (☎ 254768) at 84-88 Yutthaphan Rd has decent fan rooms with private bath for 150 to 250B, air-con for 250B.

The well kept *Tokyo Hotel* (☎ 241739; fax 263140) is at 178 Uparat Rd where it meets Chayangkun Rd, near the town centre, and is preferable to all of the foregoing if you can afford another 20B or so. Comfortable singles/doubles with fan and bath cost 150/200B or 230/280B with air-con. It's currently undergoing a major renovation so rates may rise.

## Places to Stay – middle

The friendly *Racha Hotel* (☎ 254155) at 149/21 Chayangkun Rd, north of the town centre, charges 200/240B for clean rooms with fan and bath, or 350/400B with air-con.

At 24 Si Narong Rd is the *Krung Thong* (☎ 241609), with air-con rooms for 450B, fan-cooled rooms for 280 to 400B.

The *Bodin (Badin)* on Phalo Chai Rd has singles/doubles with fan for 380B and air-con rooms for 450B. It's a bit overpriced for the hotel's shabby condition, though it's a favourite with the 'salespeople' crowd.

*Ubon Hotel (Kao Chan*; ☎ 241045) at 333 Kheuan Thani Rd used to be the city's No 1 lodgings but has gone steadily downhill over the years. Singles/doubles with fan and bath – some quite OK, others rather dank – cost 250/400B or 350/450B with air-con. Similar in price but in better condition is the *Ratchathani Hotel* (☎ 244388) at 229 Kheuan Thani Rd, where decent rooms are 280/400B with fan or 450/600B with air-con.

## Places to Stay – top end

The flashy 168-room *Pathumrat Hotel* (☎ 241501; fax 242313) at 173 Chayangkun Rd, once the top hotel in Ubon, has standard air-con rooms for 550B, 'deluxe' rooms for 700B and rooms with video for 1000B. Facilities include a coffee shop, restaurant, travel agency and massage parlour.

The 116-room *Regent Palace Hotel* (☎ 245-454; fax 241804) at 265-271 Chayangkun Rd has clean, quiet, carpeted rooms with TV and phone for 660B a single or double, including tax and service charge. Facilities include a lobby coffee shop, cocktail lounge and snooker club.

Another very good top-end place is the efficient *Sri Kamol (Si Kamon) Hotel* (☎ 241136; fax 243792) at 22/2 Ubonsak Rd near the Ratchathani Hotel. Large, comfortable rooms with all the amenities are 1050 to 1150B, or 1800B superior (with fridge and video); discounts of up to 40% are available and all rates include a Thai or western complimentary breakfast.

The 76-room *Tohsang Hotel* (☎ 241925; fax 244814) at 251 Phalo Chai Rd offers large, pleasant rooms with air-con, TV and minibar for 950 to 1230B. Facilities include a coffee shop and Chinese restaurant.

The relatively new *Lai Thong Hotel* (☎ 264271; fax 264270) at 50 Phichit Rangsan Rd has 124 comfortable rooms with all the amenities for 1070 to 1160B, including an American-style breakfast. There's a swimming pool on the premises.

*Ruanrangsi Mansion Park* (☎ 244744), in the Ruanrangsi Complex off Ratchathani Rd, offers up-market apartments for rent by the week or month (4000 to 12,500B). The landscaped grounds are conveniently adjacent to the Fern Hut Restaurant, various shops and a branch post office.

## Places to Eat

**Noodles & Rice** On Si Narong Rd, the *Choeng Ubon* (next to the Krung Thong Hotel) and *Song Rot* (opposite the GPO) make good kŭaytĭaw. *Mae Mun 2* and *Thiang Rak* on Kheuan Thani Rd (not far from the Ratchathani Hotel and on the same side of the street) are late-night khâo tôm places that can prepare just about any Thai or Chinese dish you can name.

*Maw Khao Maw Kaeng* ('Rice Pot – Curry Pot') next to the Sahamit bus office on Kheuan Thani Rd serves good Central Thai curries and hàw mòk (thick, fish-coconut curry steamed in banana leaves).

The *Arawy* (no romanised sign) toward the south end of Ratchabut Rd has a good Thai-Chinese buffet.

If you're looking for somewhere a little nicer, try the popular *Never Say Never* at 458/7-8 Suriyat Rd. It's a clean, air-con place with an extensive Thai menu but prices are moderate.

The cheapest string of rice and noodle places in town runs along Sanphasit Rd just opposite Sanphasit Prasong Hospital.

**Regional** Ubon is famous for its Isaan food – many Thai gourmets claim it has the best in all of Isaan. Lâap pèt (spicy duck salad) is the local speciality, often eaten with tôm fák (squash soup) and Chinese mushrooms. Good places for lâap pèt include *Jaak Kaan Laap Pet* on Suriyat Rd, *Piak Laap Pet* on Jaeng Sanit Rd (next to a radio relay station) and *Suan Maphrao*, near Km 288 on the road to Yasothon.

Ubon is also big on kài yâang (grilled Lao-style chicken) and everyone in town agrees that the best is at *Kai Yaang Wat Jaeng*, which has moved from its original location west of Wat Jaeng to a block north of Suriyat Rd. The chicken is sold from 9 am to 2 pm only, after which the vendor switches to curries. At this rustic, outdoor spot, a half chicken costs 35B, sticky rice is 5B and sôm-tam 5 to 10B. Other specialities include hàw mòk – choice of fish (plaa), or chicken (kài).

A favourite with local families, the simple *Sakhon*, on Pha Daeng Rd near the provincial courthouse, is a long-running Ubon institution with a full array of Isaan dishes. An English menu is available.

*Indochine (Indojiin)* on Sanphasit Rd near Wat Jaeng specialises in tasty Vietnamese food, including good-value set meals. It's only open from 10 am to 6 pm. A little farther east along the same side of the road, the air-con *Sincere Restaurant* serves an interesting Thai-French cuisine. It's open from 9 am to 11 pm; closed Sunday.

**Italian** Good pizza and pasta is available at the Italian-managed *Italian Pizza* on the corner of Phon Phaen and Phichit Rangsan Rds near the Lai Thong Hotel.

**Vegetarian** Ubon has just one vegetarian restaurant at the moment. It's in Warin, near the train station, and is called *Bua Buchaa*. Another possible source of vegetarian food is the *Hong Fa Restaurant* opposite the Pathumrat Hotel on Chayangkun Rd. The cooks at Hong Fa will prepare vegetarian Chinese dishes on request; this is where Chinese Buddhists eat when taking vegetarian vows.

**Breakfasts & Bakeries** The French-Lao influence in Ubon means people are somewhat more accustomed to pastries and western breakfasts than in many parts of Thailand. *Chiokee (Jiaw Kii)* on Kheuan Thani Rd is very popular among local office workers for both Chinese and western breakfasts. Prices are good and it serves everything from khâo tôm to ham and eggs. One of its specialities is jók (broken-rice soup or congee).

*Fern Hut*, down a soi opposite the teachers' college (*wítháyalai khruu* in Thai), sells good cakes and other baked items.

In Warin, on Pathumthepphakdi Rd near a Bangkok Bank branch, *Warin Bakery* offers decent baked goods, coffee and breakfasts.

**Night Markets** Ubon has two night markets which are open from dusk to dawn, one by the river near the bridge *(talàat yài* or big market), and the other near the bus terminal on Chayangkun Rd – convenient to hotels on Chayangkun and Suriyat Rds.

### Entertainment

**Nightclubs** The *High Class Executive Club* at 2/1 Uparat Rd (near the river and bridge), offers live music, karaoke and disco. The Pathumrat Hotel (see Places to Stay) boasts the disco-style *Champ* and the cabaret-style *Pathumma*. *Rot Isaan*, on Si Narong Rd next to the Krung Thong Hotel, is a smoky Thai-style nightclub. There are also several nightclubs along Theyati Rd.

**Massage** *Thai Massage Clinic* (☎ 254746) at 369-371 Sanphasit Rd offers traditional massage from 9 am to 9 pm daily. Rates are 100B per hour.

Ubon also has several àap òp nûat (bathe-steam-massage) places that probably got their start during the days when a US air base was located outside town. The least seedy is the Pathumrat Hotel's *Long Beach*.

### Things to Buy

One of the major local specialities is silver betel-nut containers moulded using the lost-wax process. The Ubon National Museum on Kheuan Thani Rd has a good exhibit of locally produced betel boxes; to see them being made visit Ban Pa-Ao, a silversmithing village between Ubon and Yasothon off Highway 23.

Phanchat (☎ 243433) at 158 Ratchabut Rd carries a range of Ubon handicrafts, including fabrics and silverwork, as do several other shops – Ket Kaew, Mit Ying, Dampun – along Ratchabut Rd. Kofak (☎ 254698) at 39 Phalochai Rd also sells Isaan products. For locally woven fabrics, have a look in Yai Bua (☎ 243287), 182 Sanphasit Rd, and Maybe (☎ 254932), 124 Si Narong Rd.

### Getting There & Away

**Air** THAI has two daily flights from Bangkok to Ubon. The fare is 1405B and the flight takes an hour.

NORTH-EASTERN THAILAND

Orient Express Air (☎ 264832) flies from Chiang Mai to Ubon via Khon Kaen four times a week for 1950B, and from Udon Thani on Saturday for 1180B. In the reverse direction Khon Kaen flights stop over in Udon.

**Bus** Two air-con buses a day go to Ubon from Nakhon Phanom, at 7 am and 2 pm, leaving from the intersection of Bamrung Meuang and Ratsadon Uthit Rds near the Windsor Hotel. The fare is 98B. Ordinary buses from the Baw Khaw Saw station leave regularly from morning until late afternoon for 67B. The trip takes 5½ hours on the tour bus and six to seven hours on the rot thammadaa (ordinary bus).

If you're coming from Northern Thailand, you'll find air-con buses to Ubon from both Phitsanulok (305B) and Chiang Mai (445B).

Ordinary buses to Ubon from Bangkok cost 161B for the 10½ hour route, 159B for the 9½ hour route. Both types leave the Northern Bus Terminal in Bangkok hourly from around 4.30 am to nearly midnight. First class air-con buses cost 287 to 290B depending on the bus, and leave once in the morning around 9 am and six times in the evening between 8 and 10.30 pm. There is one 400B VIP departure nightly at 8 pm.

Other fares to/from Ubon are listed below. Some fares differ according to alternative routes taken between the same terminals – longer routes are usually cheaper – or class of air-con service.

| Destination | Fare |
| --- | --- |
| Buriram | 55B |
| (air-con) | 120B |
| Kantharalak | |
| (for Khao Phra Wihaan) | 28B |
| Khong Jiam | 32B |
| Khon Kaen | 70B |
| (air-con) | 125B |
| Khorat | 87 to 102B |
| (air-con) | 146 to 184B |
| Mahasarakham | 53B |
| (air-con) | 96B |
| Mukdahan | 43B |
| (air-con) | 77B |
| Phibun Mangsahan | 12B |
| Phimai | 74B |
| (air-con) | 133B |
| Prakhon Chai (for Phanom Rung) | 70B |
| Roi Et | 44B |
| (air-con) | 62 to 79B |
| Sakon Nakhon | 69B |
| (air-con) | 125B |
| Si Saket | 20B |
| (air-con) | 32 to 40B |
| Surin | 43B |
| (air-con) | 80B |
| That Phanom | 54B |
| (air-con) | 99B |
| Udon Thani | 97B |
| (air-con) | 125 to 175B |
| Yasothon | 28B |
| (air-con) | 38 to 50B |

**Train** The Ubon Ratchathani express leaves Bangkok nightly at 9 pm, arriving in Ubon at 6.50 am the next morning. The basic 1st class fare is 460B, 2nd class 221B, not including surcharges for express service or a sleeping berth. Rapid trains leave at 6.50 am, 6.45 and 10.45 pm, arriving in Ubon about 11 hours later. There is no 1st class on the rapid trains. Ordinary trains take only about an hour longer to reach Ubon; there are three departures daily in either direction; the fare is 95B.

Rapid trains from Khorat leave at 11.48 am and 11.54 pm, arriving in Ubon at 4.45 pm and 5.05 am. The basic fares are 106B in 2nd class and 45B in 3rd class.

The all-air-con *Sprinter* leaves Bangkok at 6.05 am and arrives in Ubon at 2.30 pm; the fare is 411B, including a couple of aeroplane-style meals.

Ubon's train station is in Warin Chamrap; take a white No 2 city bus to reach Chayangkun Rd in the city centre.

**Getting Around**

A city bus system runs large buses along the main avenues (3B), very convenient for getting from one end of town to the other cheaply. Samlors around town are 10 to 20B depending on distance.

Motorcycles, vans and cars can be rented at Chaw Wattana (☎ 241906), 39/8 Suriyat Rd. Other rental places, on Chayangkun Rd, include Chi Chi Tour (☎ 241464), Ubonsak Travel (☎ 311038) and Ubon Tour (☎ 243570).

## AROUND UBON PROVINCE
### Phibun Mangsahan to Khong Jiam
โขงเจียม

The small riverside district of Khong Jiam is 75 km east of Ubon via Route 217 to Phibun Mangsahan and then over the Mun River by bridge at the western end of Route 2222. Visitors often stop in Phibun to see a set of rapids called **Kaeng Sapheu** next to the river crossing. Phibun Mangsahan is also the location for the Ubon immigration office; visa extensions as well as exit visas (for crossings into Laos) are available here. The office is about a km from town on the way south to Chong Mek – look for a large communications antenna nearby.

**Ban Khawn Sai**, half a km west of Phibun on Route 217 between Km 23 and 24, is a small village whose main livelihood is the forging of bronze gongs for temples and classical Thai music ensembles. You can watch the gong-makers hammering the flat metal discs into beautiful instruments and tempering them in rustic fires – often in temporary shelters just off the road. Should you care to make a purchase or two, small gongs cost 400 to 500B each, larger ones 4000 to 5000B; the huge two metre gongs run as high as 50,000B.

Farther east along Route 2222 you can stop at **Sae Hua Maew Falls** and **Wat Tham Hehw Sin Chai**. The latter is a cave temple with a waterfall cascading over the front of the cave; it's just a two km walk south-west of Khong Jiam. Also in the vicinity are two other waterfalls, **Pak Taew Falls** in Nam Yuen district – a tall vertical drop – and the low but wide **Taton Falls**.

**Khong Jiam** itself sits on a picturesque peninsula formed by the confluence of the Mun and Maekhong rivers. Huge conical fish traps are made here for local use – they look very much like the fish traps that appear in the 3000-year-old prehistoric murals at Pha Taem (see later in this section). Thais visit Khong Jiam to see the so-called **Mae Nam Song Sii** (Two Colour River), the contrasting coloured currents formed at the junction of the Mun and Maekhong rivers. Along the Maekhong side is a simple but pleasant park with benches and food vendors.

For 150B per hour you can charter long-tail boats with 15 person capacities from a rustic landing next to the Pak Mun Restaurant to see Two Colour River and various small river islands; Thais can cross the Maekhong to Laos. Provincial officials on both sides of the border are trying to arrange permanent permission for day crossings by foreigners. (Foreigners are permitted to cross into Laos 32 km farther south at Chong Mek, however.)

**Places to Stay & Eat – Khong Jiam** *Apple Guest House* (☎ (45) 351160) on Kaewpradit Rd has rooms in a couple of two-storey buildings off the main road through town. There are two large, clean rooms upstairs and six smaller rooms downstairs, all with shared bath. Rates are a very reasonable 90B per fan room or 250B air-con; windows are screened and soap and towels provided. Good meals can be purchased in a separate dining area; bicycles and motorcycles are available for rent.

Near the river, the friendly, motel-like *Khong Jiam Guest House* (☎ (45) 351160; fax 351074) has rooms with fan and bath for 100/150B, 300B for a one bed room with air-con. Also on the river, *Ban Rim Khong* offers six timber bungalows overlooking the river for 1000B with TV, fridge, bath and carpet. Two km outside of town toward Phibun, *Khong Chiam Marina Resort* (☎ (45) 361011) has bungalows for 380 to 780B with fan, depending on size, or air-con for 450 to 600B.

On the Mun River side of town are two restaurants, the floating *Songsat* and the *Hat Mae Mun* on a hillside overlooking the river. The latter has the better food – try the delicious yam mét mámûang sãam sũan, a warm cashew-nut salad made with tomatoes, chillies and fresh green peppercorn.

Along the Maekhong side, *Araya* is very popular on weekends and serves a variety of freshwater fish, Thai-Lao standards, river turtle (ta-phâap náam) and wild pig. Two other restaurants in this vicinity are *Nam Poon* and *Mae Nam Song Sii*. *Pak Mun* is a nice wooden restaurant overlooking the junction of the two rivers at the eastern end of town.

**Places to Stay & Eat – Phibun Mangsahan**
*Phiboonkit Hotel* (☎ (45) 441201), near the bus stop in the centre of Phibun, has fan rooms for 100B with shared bath, 150/200B with attached bath or air-con for 300/400B.

Three km north of town, *Sanamchai Guest House* (☎ (45) 441289) has modern bungalows for 150 to 250B with fan, 260B with air-con. There are a pub and garden restaurant opposite the guesthouse.

Near the bridge to Route 2222 is a simple *restaurant* famous for salabao (Chinese buns) and nǎng kòp (frog skin, usually fried). Thais visiting Pha Taem always stop here on the way to stock up on salabao and nǎng kòp.

**Getting There & Away** From Ubon, direct buses to Khong Jiam (74 km) cost 30B and leave from Market No 5 between 9 am and 1 pm. When direct buses aren't running to Khong Jiam, catch a Phibun bus (12B) from Warin train station between 5 am and 3.30 pm, and change to a Khong Jiam bus (12B) in Phibun.

If you're driving or cycling to Khong Jiam from the Sirinthon Reservoir area via Routes 217 and 2296, you'll have to cross the Mun River by vehicle ferry (30B per vehicle).

**Pha Taem**
ผาแต้ม

In Khong Jiam district, 94 km north-east of Ubon, near the confluence of the Mun and Maekhong rivers, is a tall stone cliff called Pha Taem. The cliff is about 200m long and features prehistoric colour paintings that are at least 3000 years old. Mural subjects include fish traps, *plaa bèuk* (giant Maekhong catfish), turtles, elephants, human hands and a few geometric designs – all very reminiscent of prehistoric rock art found at widely separated sites around the world.

A 500m trail descends from the cliff edge to the base past two platforms where visitors can view the rock paintings; from the top of the cliff you get a bird's eye view of Laos. Vendors sell snacks and beverages near the top of the cliff. A cliff-top visitors' centre is planned for future construction and will contain exhibits pertaining to the paintings and local geology.

On the road to Pha Taem is **Sao Chaliang**, an area of unusual stone formations similar to Phu Pha Thoep in Mukdahan.

**Getting There & Away** Pha Taem is 20 km beyond Khong Jiam via Route 2112, but there's no direct public transport there. The bus from Ubon to Khong Jiam will pass the final turn-off to Pha Taem on request; then you can walk or hitch five km to the cliff.

By car, bike or motorcycle, go east on Route 217 to Phibun Mangsahan, then turn left (north) across the Mun River on Route 2222 and follow this road to Khong Jiam. From Khong Jiam, take Route 2134 northwest to Ban Huay Phai and then go north-east at the first turn-off to Pha Taem.

**Chong Mek & the Emerald Triangle**
ช่องเม็ก

South of Khong Jiam via Route 217 is the small trading town of Chong Mek on the Thai-Lao border. Chong Mek has the distinction of being the only town in Thailand where you can cross into Laos by land if you possess a valid Lao visa. Some people report that you have to obtain a Thai exit stamp at the Thai immigration office in Phibun Mangsahan before you'll be allowed to leave Thailand at Chong Mek. I've never had a problem crossing here in either direction, but to be safe you might consider stopping in Phibun first. The southern Lao capital of Pakse is about an hour by road and ferry from Ban Mai Sing Amphon, the village on the Lao side of the border.

Thai visitors come to Chong Mek to drink *oh-líang* (Chinese-style iced coffee) and to shop for Lao and Vietnamese souvenirs.

About five km west of Chong Mek is the north-eastern shore of the huge **Sirinthon Reservoir**, an impoundment of a Mun River tributary. On forested hills near the dam at the northern end of the reservoir is a recreation area frequented by local picnickers.

A North-Eastern forest monastery in the Ajaan Man-Ajaan Chaa tradition, **Wat Pa**

**Wanaphothiyaan** sits on a peninsula jutting from the reservoir's northern shore. Also known locally as Wat Ko (Island Monastery) or Wat Kheuan (Dam Monastery), it's similar in concept to Wat Pa Nanachat Bung Wai in Warin, although there are only about 10 monks, most of them Thai. Until recently the abbot was an Australian monk. Serious, experienced meditators may apply to practice here; as at Wat Pa Nanachat, men must shave their heads after three days. To reach here by public transport, take a songthaew bound for Nikhom Neung from Phibun and get off at the wat pier (thâa wát kàw), where you can get a boat out to the wat for 20B.

Farther south, near the intersection of the Lao, Thai and Cambodian borders (an area sometimes referred to as the 'Emerald Triangle' for its relatively healthy forest cover), is the little known **Phu Chong Nayoi National Park**. Established in 1987, the 687 sq km park's predominant attractions include the **Bak Taew Yai Waterfall** (3.5 km from the park headquarters), which plunges 40m over a cliff in two separate but parallel streams, a number of interesting rock formations, a couple of fresh springs and some nice views of the surrounding countryside from a cliff called **Phaa Pheung**. The park's highest point reaches 555m. Fauna includes the endangered white-winged wood duck.

**Getting There & Away** Songthaews run between Phibun and Chong Mek for 12B.

# Surin & Si Saket Provinces

These adjacent provinces between Buriram and Ubon border Cambodia and are dotted with ancient Khmer ruins built during the 11th and 12th century Angkor empire. The only other major attraction in the area is the Surin Annual Elephant Roundup. Few elephants are still used as work animals in Surin; instead they are brought out for ceremonial occasions such as parades and monastic ordinations.

## SURIN
สุรินทร์
• ☎ (44) • pop 40,000

Surin, 452 km from Bangkok, is a quiet provincial capital except during the Elephant Roundup in late November. At that time a carnival atmosphere reigns, with elephants providing the entertainment. If you ever wanted to see a lot of elephants in one place (there are more elephants now in Thailand than in India), this is your chance.

Culturally, Surin represents an intersection of Lao, Central Thai, Khmer and Suay peoples, resulting in an interesting mix of dialects and customs. A fifth group contributing to the blend was the many volunteers and UN employees working with local refugee camps here during the 1970s and 1980s; with the huge refugee industry winding down, their influence is beginning to wane.

To see Surin's elephants during the off season, visit **Ban Tha Klang** in Tha Tum district, about 40 km north of Surin. Many of the performers at the annual festival are trained here, but their presence is seasonable – enquire in Surin before making a trip.

Silk weaving can be observed at several local villages, including **Khwaosinarin** and **Ban Janrom**.

### Prasat Ta Meuan
The most atmospheric – and most difficult to reach – of Surin's temple ruins is a series of three sites known collectively as Prasat Ta Meuan in Ban Ta Miang district on the Cambodian border. Ban Ta Miang is 25 km east of Ban Kruat or 49 km west of Kap Choeng via Route 2121. This trip is best done by hired bicycle, motorcycle or car – Pirom's House (see Places to Stay) can also arrange day trips by van if you can get a small group together.

The first site, **Prasat Ta Meuan** proper, was built in the Jayavarman VII period (1121-1220 AD) as a rest stop for pilgrims. It's a fairly small monument with a two door, eight window sanctuary constructed of laterite blocks; only one sculpted sandstone lintel over the rear door remains.

To the south, about 500m along a winding

NORTH-EASTERN THAILAND

NORTH-EASTERN THAILAND

Around Si Saket &
Ubon Ratchathani

road, is the more impressive **Prasat Ta Meuan Tot**, which is said to have been a 'healing station' or 'hospital' like Prang Ku outside Chaiyaphum. Large fig trees, cut back to stumps, have attached themselves to the ruins, which consist of a *gopura* (entrance pavilion), mondòp and main sanctuary surrounded by a laterite wall.

Farther south, right next to the Cambodian border, is the largest site, **Prasat Ta Meuan Thom**. Built mostly of sandstone blocks on a laterite base on a slope that drops off at the southern end to face the Cambodian border, the walled complex has been rather badly

reassembled into a jumble of sculpted blocks. Unfortunately, some of the sculpted blocks from the highly ornate southern gate have ended up haphazardly inserted into other structures in the compound. Just beyond the southern gate the forest is cordoned off by barbed wire and red skull-and-crossbone signs – in Khmer and English – warning of undetonated mines.

Mines and undetonated hand grenades in the vicinity of the Prasat Ta Meuan sites are a real danger; don't veer from the cleared paths around and between the monuments. During the dry season firefights between the

Khmer Rouge and Phnom Penh government troops can be heard almost daily nearby. A Thai military checkpoint along Route 2121 screens all visitors; sometimes the area is temporarily closed to nonresidents. You can enquire in amphoe meuang Surin as to the current situation, although this is no guarantee. When we last visited, Surin residents told us the area was closed, yet the checkpoint sentries allowed us to pass without any attempt to turn us back. Automatic rifle and mortar fire could be heard in the distance as we toured the ruins.

If you happen to be in this area on a weekend, check out the Khmer-Thai **Chong Jom (Chawng Jawm) Market** near Ban Dan. The latter is eight km north of the border via Route 214, 57 km south of amphoe meuang Surin.

**Other Khmer Temple Ruins**

The southern reach of Surin Province along the Cambodian border harbours several minor Angkor-period ruins, including **Prasat Hin Ban Phluang** (30 km south of Surin). The solitary sandstone sanctuary, mounted on a laterite platform, exhibits well sculpted stone lintels.

A larger Khmer site can be seen 30 km north-east of town at **Prasat Sikhoraphum**. Sikhoraphum (or Si Khonphum) features five Khmer prangs, the tallest of which reaches 32m. The doorways to the central prang are decorated with stone carvings of Hindu deities in the Angkor Wat style. Sikhoraphum can be reached by bus or train from amphoe meuang Surin.

The ruined **Prasat Phumphon** in Sangkha district (59 km south-east of amphoe meuang Surin via Route 2077) is the oldest Khmer prasat in Thailand, dating to the 7th or 8th century AD. Unless you're adamant about ticking off every Khmer site in Thailand, you'll most likely be disappointed by this jumble of bricks.

Surin can also be used as a base for visiting the Khmer ruins at **Phanom Rung** and **Prasat Meuang Tam**, about 75 km south-west of Surin in Buriram Province (see the Buriram Province section earlier in this chapter for details).

**Places to Stay**

*Pirom's House* (☎ 515140) at 242 Krung Si Nai Rd has dorm beds for 50B per person and singles/doubles for 70/120B in a traditional wooden house. Try to get a room with a mosquito net – the house sits next to a lotus pond. Pirom knows the area well and can suggest ideas for day trips around Surin, including excursions to lesser known Khmer temple sites. He can also lead van tours himself for 340 to 450B per person.

*Country Roads Cafe & Guesthouse* (☎/fax 515721), a bit out of the town centre at 165/1 Sirirat Rd, behind the bus terminal, has rooms for 100B. Run by a Texan and his Thai wife, the guesthouse has just six rooms and is primarily a restaurant/bar. General information on the area is readily dispensed in English.

Hotel rates may increase during the Elephant Roundup and hotels may fill up, but otherwise, *Krung Si* (☎ 511037), 15/11-4 Krung Si Nai Rd, charges from 120 to 200B, and *New Hotel* (☎ 511341/322), next to the train station at 22 Thanasan Rd, charges from 150 to 270B and has some air-con rooms from 280B. *Thanachai Hotel*, just off the roundabout on Thetsaban 1 Rd near the post office, has somewhat dark and dingy rooms for 60/80B.

Moving up-market just a bit, the very clean and well run *Nid Diew* (☎ 511274; fax 514041) at 155-61 Thanasan Rd offers rooms with fan for 380 to 800B with air-con and hot water. *Memorial Hotel* (☎ 511637) on Lak Meuang Rd, just west of Thanasan Rd, has good rooms for 240/260B with fan, 400/500B with air-con.

The business-like *Phetkasem Hotel* (☎ 511274/576), is at 104 Jit Bamrung Rd. All rooms are air-con, and rates are from 760 to 1300B. Surin's top-end place to stay, the *Tarin Hotel* at 60 Sirirat Rd, has 205 rooms and rates up to 1400B with all the amenities, including breakfast.

**Places to Eat**

Along the northern end of Thanasan Rd between the Saeng Thong Hotel and the train station are a number of good, inexpensive

NORTH-EASTERN THAILAND

Thai and Chinese restaurants. Along this stretch the long-running *Surin Phochana* serves dependable curries and noodles.

A small night market assembles in front of the train station each evening. There is also a larger night market next to the main municipal market along Krung Si Nai Rd, close to Pirom's House and the Krung Si Hotel.

The popular *Phaw Kin*, near the intersection of Lak Meuang and Krung Si Nai Rds, serves excellent Isaan food at very reasonable prices.

*Country Roads Cafe* specialises in imported liquors, videos, steaks, barbecues, burgers and Thai food. The owner has all the cafe's beef custom-cut and packaged from French cattle in nearby Sakon Nakhon Province.

### Getting There & Away

**Bus** Ordinary buses to Surin leave 17 times a day from Bangkok's Northern Bus Terminal between 6 am and 10.50 pm for 108B. Second class air-con buses cost 152B and leave nightly at 9 and 11 pm, while 1st class air-con buses depart at 11 am, 9.30, 10 and 10.10 pm for 195B. During the Elephant Roundup, there are many special air-con buses to Surin organised by major hotels and tour companies.

Surin lies about halfway between Ubon Ratchathani and Khorat; buses from either direction take around four hours and cost 43B ordinary, 80B air-con.

**Train** Most people travel to Surin by rapid train No 31, which leaves Bangkok at 6.50 am, arriving in Surin at 2.21 pm. The 2nd class fare is 199B, including the rapid surcharge. Book your seats at least two weeks in advance for travel during November. A faster train is the air-con diesel No 931 to Surin at 11.05 am, arriving at 5.35 pm for 20B less (no surcharges for 3rd class; 50B surcharge in air-con 2nd class). If you prefer night train travel, the rapid No 51 leaves Bangkok at 10.45 pm and arrives in Surin at 6.40 am.

Ordinary 3rd class trains take around nine hours from Bangkok, cost 73B, and leave daily at 3.25 and 11.25 pm. Surin can also be

reached by train from any other station along the Ubon line, including Buriram, Si Saket and Ubon Ratchathani.

### Getting Around

Samlors around central Surin cost 10 to 20B per trip.

## SI SAKET
ศรีสะเกษ
• ☎ (45) • *pop 34,700*

Si Saket's provincial capital has gained on Surin's; however, with nothing like Surin's Elephant Roundup to provide support, the town has less of a tourist infrastructure – a boon for visitors in search of laid-back, authentic Isaan ways. Also, Si Saket Province has more Khmer ruins of significance within its borders than Surin.

When Khao Phra Wihaan, a major Angkor site just over the provincial border in Cambodia, first opened the town's fortunes began to change as it became the gateway for visitors to the ruins. The capture of the site by the Khmer Rouge has slowed things down considerably.

### Khao Phra Wihaan
เขาพระวิหาร

Lying just across the Cambodian border opposite Si Saket Province's Kantharalak, the Khmer ruins of Khao Phra Wihaan (other common spellings include Kao Prea Vihar and Khao Phra Viharn) are virtually inaccessible from the Cambodian side and until a Khmer Rouge ceasefire was reached in Cambodia they were also off-limits from the Thai side. After a year of negotiations between the Cambodian and Thai governments, the ruins finally opened to the public in 1991, then closed down again during the Phnom Penh offensive against the Khmer Rouge in 1993-94. As of mid-1996 the ruins remained under the control of the Khmer Rouge. Enquire with the TAT in Bangkok or Ubon Ratchathani to find out the latest situation.

Khao Phra Wihaan was built over two centuries under a succession of Khmer kings, beginning with Rajendravarman II in the mid-10th century and ending with Suryavarman II in the early 12th century – it was the latter who also commanded the construction of Angkor Wat. The hill itself was sacred to Khmer Hindus for at least 500 years before the completion of the temple complex, however, and there were smaller brick monuments on the site prior to the reign of Rajendravarman II.

Phra Wihaan sits atop a 600m hill at the edge of the Dangrek (Dong Rek) mountain range, commanding a view of the Thai plains to the west. Built originally as a Hindu temple in the classic Bapuan and early Angkor styles, the complex extends a linear 850m, encompassing four gopuras, and a large prasat or sanctuary surrounded by a courtyard and galleries. A stepped naga approach ascends approximately 120m from the foot of the hill to the sanctuary.

The temple complex is semi-restored – the general condition is somewhere between that of Prasat Phanomwan in Khorat and Phanom Rung in Buriram. One naga balustrade of around 30m is still intact; the first two gopuras have all but fallen down and many of the temple buildings are roofless, but abundant examples of stone carving are intact and visible. The doorways to the third gopura have been nicely preserved and one (the inner door facing south) is surmounted by a well executed carved stone lintel depicting Shiva and his consort Uma sitting on Nandi (Shiva's bull), under the shade of a symmetrised tree. A Vishnu creation lintel is also visible on the second gopura; in contrast to the famous Phanom Rung lintel depicting the same subject, this one shows Vishnu climbing the churning stick rather than reclining on the ocean below.

The main prasat tower in the final court at the summit is in need of major restoration before the viewer can get a true idea of its former magnificence. Many of the stone carvings from the prasat are either missing or lie buried in nearby rubble. The galleries leading to the prasat have fared better and have even kept their arched roofs. Eventually the complex may undergo a total restoration but at the moment the money from entrance

fees is supposedly going towards the improvement of the road to Phra Wihaan from the Cambodian side (currently Cambodian officials must walk six to eight hours to reach the Thai border).

**Getting There & Away** Highway 221 leads 95 km south from Si Saket to Phum Saron – 11 km short of the temple – via Kantharalak. Catch a songthaew from near the bus terminal adjacent to the main day market in Si Saket for 20B. If you miss the infrequent direct songthaew service, you may have to take a bus first to Kantharalak (20B) and pick up another songthaew to Phum Saron (7B). Buses to Kantharalak leave every half hour from around 6 am to 5 pm. From either Kantharalak or Phum Saron, you'll have to hire a motorcycle taxi to the border entrance to Khao Phra Wihaan – figure 200B return from Kantharalak or Phum Saron with a couple of hours waiting time (50 to 100B one way). On weekends, when the temple complex is open, there are also direct songthaews from Si Saket all the way to the border entrance for 18B.

If the site is open, you must complete an entry form at the Thai army checkpoint and present a passport or other picture ID (so far these entry forms are available in Thai only – you'll have to appeal for assistance if you don't read Thai). Back when Khao Phra Wihaan was open the admission fees for Thais were 5B for students, 60B for adults; for foreign visitors they were 100B for children, 200B for adults. When the site first opened in January 1992, half the foreign visitors' fee was collected on either side of the border to ensure that the Thais and Cambodians each got their share of the loot.

At the Cambodian checkpoint you had to leave your ID as a security deposit. Even when Khao Phra Wihaan was open, visitors could only tour the immediate surroundings to the complex. Whether or not Khmer Rouge-Phnom Penh firefights in the area have ceased by the time you arrive, there will still be plenty of land mines and live ordnance in the fields and forests nearby; stick to the designated safety lanes leading to the

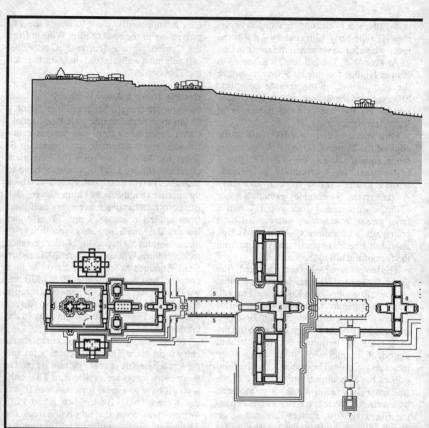

ruins. Avoid visiting on weekends, when the site is packed with hundreds of local Thai visitors.

**Phaa Maw i Daeng**

If border entry to Khao Phra Wihaan is closed, you can still walk to the edge of this cliff around 400m from the temple site on the Thai side. In addition to good views of the plains below and the Dangrek mountain range in the distance, you can also make out the Khao Phra Wihaan ruins over a chasm on a hill opposite the cliff – binoculars would certainly enhance the view. In early 1994 we

watched from the relative safety of this cliff as Phnom Penh troops bombarded a Khmer Rouge position on the plains below.

A railed stairway cut into the edge of the cliff leads down to a well sculpted relief executed directly onto the upper cliff face. The relief depicts three figures whose identities are an enigma to archaeologists and art historians. Although they give the general impression of representing deities, angels or kings, the iconography corresponds to no known figures in Thai, Mon or Khmer mythology. Stylistically the relief appears to date back to the Koh Ker (921-45 AD) period of

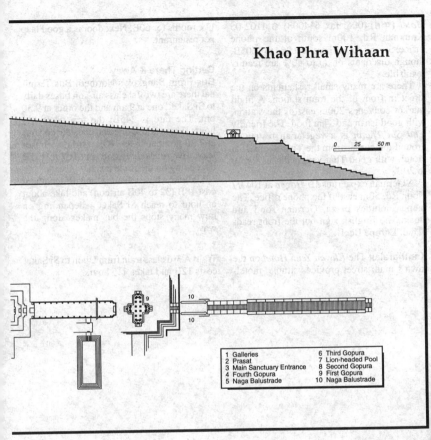

# Khao Phra Wihaan

0    25    50 m

1 Galleries
2 Prasat
3 Main Sanctuary Entrance
4 Fourth Gopura
5 Naga Balustrade
6 Third Gopura
7 Lion-headed Pool
8 Second Gopura
9 First Gopura
10 Naga Balustrade

Khmer art, when King Jayavarman IV ruled from his capital at Koh Ker, Cambodia.

## Other Khmer Ruins

Forty km west of Si Saket in Uthumphon Phisai district, **Prasat Hin Wat Sa Kamphaeng Yai** features a striking 10th century sandstone prang with carved doorways. The ruined sanctuary is on the grounds of Wat Sa Kamphaeng Yai's modern successor. About eight km west of town via Route 2084 is the similar but smaller **Prasat Hin Wat Sa Kamphaeng Noi**.

Other minor Khmer sites in the province include **Prasat Prang Ku**, **Prasat Ban Prasat** and **Prasat Phu Fai**.

## Places to Stay & Eat

**Si Saket** *Phrom Phiman* (☎ 612677) at 849/1 Lak Meuang Rd has good rooms with fan for 280 to 330B, air-con rooms from 380 to 420B. Everything else in town is in the 100 to 160B range for simple rooms with fan: *Santisuk* (☎ 611496), 573 Soi Wat Phra To; *Si Saket* (☎ 611846), 384-5 Si Saket Rd; and *Thai Soem Thai* (☎ 611458), also on Si Saket Rd.

A nicer place to stay is the new *Kessiri*

*Hotel* (☎ 614006; fax 614008) at 1102-05 Khukhan Rd, 100m south of the phone office. Swank rooms here cost 964 to 1605B, though discounts of up to 40% are readily available.

There are many small restaurants on the street in front of the train station. A night market convenes 200m east of the station, with good Isaan and Thai food. The friendly *Chu Sin Thaan* is a vegetarian restaurant around the corner from the Thai Soem Thai Hotel, with good Thai veggie dishes for 10 to 20B.

A German expat runs *Mr Hagen* at 1043/7 Ubon Rd, 50m east of the phone office. The menu includes pizza, German food and steak. The English sign out the front reads 'Thai: Europe Beef'.

**Kantharalak** The *Khwan Yeun Hotel* on the town's main street provides simple, motel-like rooms for 60B. Next door is a good lâap pèt restaurant.

### Getting There & Away

**Bus** From Bangkok's Northern Bus Terminal there are two 1st class air-con buses daily to Si Saket, one at 9 am and the other at 9.30 pm. The fare is 245B; the trip takes 8½ hours. There is also one 2nd class air-con bus at 7.30 pm that costs 180B. Ordinary buses leave five times daily and cost 107 to 131B depending on the route taken.

Ordinary buses from Ubon Ratchathani cost 18B (32 to 40B air-con) and take about an hour to reach Si Saket – depending on how many stops the bus makes along the way.

**Train** A 3rd class train from Ubon to Si Saket costs 12B and takes 1½ hours.

# Southern Thailand

Bounded by water on two sides, the people of Southern Thailand – the *Thai pàk tâi* – are by and large a seafaring lot. One consequence of this natural affinity with the ocean is the abundance of delectable seafood, prepared Southern style. Brightly painted fishing boats, hanging nets and neat thatched huts add to the pàk tâi setting; travellers who do a stint in Southern Thailand are likely to come face to face with more than a few visions of 'tropical paradise', whatever their expectations might be.

Officially as well as ethnolinguistically, Southern Thailand is made up of 14 provinces: Chumphon, Krabi, Nakhon Si Thammarat, Narathiwat, Pattani, Phang-Nga, Phattalung, Phuket, Ranong, Satun, Songkhla, Surat Thani, Trang and Yala. See the Culture of the South section later in this chapter for more details on the unique culture of Southern Thailand.

Three of Thailand's most important exports – rubber, tin and coconut – are produced in the South, so the standard of living is a bit higher than in other provincial regions. However, Southern Thais claim that most of the wealth is in the hands of ethnic Chinese. In any of the Southern Thai provinces, it is obvious that the Chinese are concentrated in the urban provincial capitals while the poorer Muslims live in the rural areas. The urban concentration of Chinese is a fact of life throughout South-East Asia which becomes more noticeable in Southern Thailand and the Islamic state of Malaysia because of religious and cultural differences.

## HIGHLIGHTS

- National marine parks of Ko Surin and Ko Similan – for Thailand's best coral colonies
- Craggy limestone cliffs and dense jungles of Khao Sok National Park – home to the *Rafflesia*, the largest flower in the world
- Try the watersports and cuisine of Phuket and Ko Samui, or escape to quieter hideaways on Ko Pha-Ngan, Ko Tao, Ko Tarutao or Ko Lanta
- Nakhon Si Thammarat – one of the only places where life-size shadow puppets are still made
- Experience the character of the deep south towns of Trang, Satun, Ko Yo, Pattani and Narathiwat, or explore their little-known beaches
- Visit Krabi Province for some of Asia's hottest rock-climbing spots – over 150 routes on high-quality limestone surfaces
- Kayaking tours through Ang Thong National Marine Park – an archipelago dotted with small islands, sandy beaches and hidden lagoons

## Chumphon Province

### CHUMPHON
อ.เมืองชุมพร
• ☎ (77) • *pop 15,000*
About 500 km south of Bangkok and 184 km from Prachuap Khiri Khan, Chumphon is the junction town where you turn west to Ranong and Phuket or continue south on the newer road to Surat Thani, Nakhon Si Thammarat and Songkhla. In reference to its function as

667

MYANMAR (BURMA)

Isthmus of Kra

Chumphon

Kraburi

Ranong

Lang Suan

Phato

Kapoe

Khuraburi

Chiaw Lan Dam

Khao Sok National Park

Takua Pa

Phanom

Kapong

Thai Muang

Phang-Nga

Takua Thung

Krabi

Ko Yao Yai

Phuket

Ko Phi Phi

Ko Lanta

Pak Meng

Ko Libong

Sikao

Trang

Kantang

Palian

Thung Wa

Pak Bara

Ko Tarutao National Marine Park

Ko Tarutao

Ko Adang

La-Ngu

Ko Rawi

Satun

Thaleh Ban National Park

ANDAMAN SEA

INDIAN OCEAN

GULF OF THAILAND

Ko Tao

Ang Tong National Marine Park

Ko Pha-Ngan

Ko Phalual

Chaiya

Phun Phin

Surat Thani

Don Sak

Khanom

Ko Samui

Sichon

Khao Luang (1835m)

Ron Phibun

Nakhon Si Thammarat

Thung Song

Khlong Thorn

Hua Sai

Thaleh Luang

Phattalung

Khukhut Waterbird Sanctuary

Rattaphum

Thaleh Sap

Songkhla

Chana

Hat Yai

Kuan Khalong

Padang Besar

Saba Yoi

Sadao

Changlun

Alor Setar

Pattani

Yaring

Saiburi

Yala

Ruso

Narathiwat

Yaha

Bannang Sata

Tak Bai

Ban Taba

Sungai Kolok

Kota Baru

Bang Lang Dam

Betong

MALAYSIA

Southern Thailand

0    50    100 km

SOUTHERN THAILAND

a crossroads, the name derives from the Thai *chumnumphon*, which means 'meeting place'. The provincial capital is a busy place, but of no particular interest except that this is where Southern Thailand really begins in terms of ethnic markers like dialect and religion.

Pak Nam, Chumphon's port, is 10 km from Chumphon, and in this area there are a few beaches and a handful of islands with good reefs for diving. The best local beach is four-km-long Hat Thung Wua Laen (12 km north of town), also known locally as 'Hat Cabana' because the long-running Chumphon Cabana Resort is located here. You can catch a bus there from Pracha Lothit Rd.

Sometime in March or April the city hosts the Chumphon Marine Festival, which features cultural and folk art exhibits, a windsurfing competition at Hat Thung Wua Laen and a marathon. In October, the five day Lang Suan Buddha Image Parade & Boat Race Festival includes a procession of temple boats and a boat race on the Lang Suan River, about 60 km south of the capital.

Pak Nam is a major departure point for boats to Ko Tao, a popular island north of Ko Samui and Ko Pha-Ngan. Hence many travellers bound for Ko Tao stop for a night or two in Chumphon.

### Information
**Money** Several banks in town offer foreign exchange services and ATMs; most are located along Sala Daeng Rd.

**Post & Communications** The GPO on Poramin Mankha Rd is open Monday to Friday from 8.30 am to 4.30 pm, weekends 9 am to noon. The CAT office on the 2nd floor of the same building is open for international telephone service daily from 8.30 am to 9 pm.

**Books & Maps** A new DK Book Store has been established opposite the Jansom Chumphon Hotel, but so far it's predominantly Thai-oriented and carries only a few English-language titles. Maps of Chumphon may be purchased here, however.

### Organised Tours
Several travel agents and guesthouses organise outdoor tours to the surrounding areas. Infinity, one of the best, can arrange diving trips from 2000B per day. Tri Star Adventure Tours offers a series of interesting jungle treks, local cave trips and island tours lasting from two to five days and starting at 1250B per person. A one day cave exploration costs 400B and up depending on the number of people. Tri Star can be contacted through any travel service or guesthouse.

### Places to Stay – bottom end
Places continue to spring up as more people use Chumphon as a gateway to Ko Tao. North of the bus terminal, on the opposite side of the street, *Infinity Travel Service* (☎ 501937) at 68/2 Tha Taphao Rd has three basic but clean rooms with shared bath in an attached guesthouse for 60B per person. They provide plenty of information on boats to Ko Tao and things to do in the area, and also allow travellers to shower while waiting for boat or bus transfers.

The *Sooksamer Guest House* (☎ 502430) at 118/4 Suksamoe Rd, also known as Pat's Place, is a cosy place with clean, bright rooms in a home-like atmosphere for 120B. Pat, the English-speaking owner, can cook both Thai and European food, and is happy for you to use the shower if you drop by to eat a meal on your way to Pak Nam for a Ko Tao boat. Information on Chumphon Province and Ko Tao is plentiful.

*Chumphon Guest House* (☎ 501242), also known as Miow House, is around the corner from Sooksamer on Krom Luang Chumphon Rd and features basic, clean rooms in an old house for 80 to 120B with shared facilities. The proprietors can arrange car and motorcycle rental as well as local tours.

*Mayaze's Resthouse* (☎ 504452), down a *soi* (lane) east of Infinity Travel, offers five immaculate rooms for 150/200B single/double with fan, 250B single/double with air-con, and 300B triple/quad with air-con. Shared bathroom facilities are equally immaculate.

Other cheaper hotels can be found along

PLACES TO STAY
2 Chumphon Guest House
3 Thai Prasert Hotel
6 Jansom Chumphon Hotel
7 Sooksamer Guest House
9 TC Super Mansion
10 Si Chumphon Hotel
12 Chumphon Suriwong Hotel
13 Paradorn Inn
15 Morakhot Hotel
17 Suriya Hotel
23 Infinity Guest House & Travel Service
24 Mayaze's Resthouse
25 Tha Taphao Hotel
29 Si Taifa Hotel

PLACES TO EAT
1 Night Market
4 Curry Shops
11 Esan
14 Tiw Restaurant
26 Day & Night Market
28 Night Market
31 Tang Soon Kee

OTHER
5 Shopping Centre
8 Provincial Hospital
16 Cinema
18 Bank
19 Buses to Ao Thung Wua Laen
20 Chok Anan Tour
21 Songthaews to Ko Tao Boat Pier
22 Minivans to Ranong
27 Bus Terminal
30 Cinema
32 Hospital
33 Market
34 GPO & Telephone Office
35 Wat Suphannimit

Krom Luang Chumphon Road

Train Station

Tawee Sinka Road

Sala Daeng Road

Tha Taphao Road

Pracha Uthit Road

Phint Khadi Road

Phisit Phayadan Road

Suksamoe Road

Phisit Phayap Road

Poramin Mankha Road

Tha Chang Road

Khlong  Tha  Taphao

To Pak Nam (14 km), Hat Thung Wau Laen & Hat Sairi (21 km)

To Highway 4

**Chumphon**

0    100    200 m

Sala Daeng Rd in the centre of town. The *Si Taifa Hotel* is a clean old Chinese hotel built over a restaurant with large rooms for 140B with shared bath, 200B with shower and Thai-style toilet, or 350B air-con. Each floor has a terrace where you can watch the sun set over the city. There's also the *Thai Prasert* at 202-204 Sala Daeng Rd, with rooms from 70 to 90B; and the rather drab *Suriya*, 125/24-26 Sala Daeng Rd, which costs a bit more – neither of them are particularly good.

Farther north on Sala Daeng Rd, *Si Chumphon Hotel* (☎ (77) 511280) is a clean and efficient Chinese hotel with rooms for

200 to 350B with fan and bath, 350 to 500B for air-con. The nearly identical *Chumphon Suriwong Hotel* charges 210B for single/double fan rooms with bath, 280B for three or four people, and just 280/380B single/double for air-con.

The quiet, apartment-style *TC Super Mansion* on the east side of town near the provincial hospital offers decent rooms for 280B with fan, 330B air-con.

**Tha Yang & Pak Nam** Near the piers for boats to/from Ko Tao the *Tha Yang Hotel* (☎ (77) 521953) has clean air-con rooms for

315 to 490B; the indoor/outdoor Reun Thai Restaurant next door has good seafood.

At Pak Nam the *Siriphet Hotel* (☎ 521304) has basic rooms from 80B.

### Places to Stay – middle & top end

At the *Tha Taphao Hotel* (☎ 511479), on Tha Taphao Rd near the bus terminal, comfortable rooms cost 290B for singles/doubles with fan and bath, 550B standard air-con, or 800B for a decked-out superior room. More expensive is the large *Paradorn Inn* (☎ 511-598), at 180/12 Paradorn Rd, where standard rooms with air-con and TV cost 500B or 640B with TV and fridge.

Top of the heap is the newer *Jansom Chumphon Hotel* (☎ 502502; fax 502503) with all air-con rooms starting at 824B. The disco here is locally known as the 'Khao Tom-teque' because of the khâo tôm meals served after midnight.

### Places to Eat

Food vendors line the south side of Krom Luang Chumphon Rd between Sala Daeng Rd and Suksamoe Rd nightly from around 6 pm to 10 or 11 pm.

The curry shops along Sala Daeng Rd are proof that you are now in Southern Thailand. Over on Tha Taphao Rd is a smaller night market and a very popular Chinese place called *Tang Soon Kee*. Up on Tawee Sinka Rd near the Chumphon Suriwong Hotel is the *Esan*, with good North-Eastern Thai food in the evenings. Several more Isaan-style places can be found along Krom Luang Chumphon Rd.

*Sarakrom Wine House*, opposite the Tha Taphao Hotel on Sala Daeng Rd, is a clean, slightly upscale Thai restaurant. The menu is printed in Thai, English and German. The wine list is dominated by wines from South Africa, along with wines from Chile, France and Australia.

Chumphon Province is famous for klûay lép meu naang, or 'princess fingernail bananas'. They're very tasty and cheap – 25B wild buy around a hundred of these small, slender bananas.

### Getting There & Away

**Bus** From Bangkok's Southern Bus Terminal ordinary buses cost 112B and depart at 3.30, 4, 6.05 and 6.50 am only. First class air-con buses are 202B and leave at 2, 9.40 and 10 pm; 2nd class costs 157B and leaves nightly at 9 pm. There is also a 9.40 pm VIP departure for 280B. In the reverse direction the air-con buses leave from Chok Anan Tour, off Pracha Uthit Rd.

Buses run regularly between Surat Thani and Chumphon for 60B (80B air-con, 3½ hours), and to/from Ranong for 35B, Bang Saphan 30B, Prachuap Khiri Khan 45B and Phuket 102B. In Chumphon the main terminal for these buses is found on the west side of Tha Taphao Rd.

Air-con minivans run to/from Ranong daily every two hours between 8 am and 5.30 pm for 70B from Infinity Travel; other places do the same trip for 90B. There is also a minivan to Bangkok which meets the Ko Tao boat at the Pak Nam pier, and leaves from Chumphon Travel Service at noon and 5 pm, costing 300B. Others go to Surat Thani (90B, 2½ hours, several departures per day), Hat Yai and Phattalung (150B, four to five hours); these leave from the north side of Krom Luang Chumphon Rd.

**Train** Rapid and express trains from Bangkok take about 7½ hours to reach Chumphon and cost 172B in 2nd class or 356B in 1st class, not including rapid or express surcharges. There are only two ordinary trains to Chumphon, both of which originate at the Thonburi (Bangkok Noi) station rather than Hualamphong; these cost 82B (3rd class only). See the Phetburi Getting There & Away section in the Central Thailand chapter for departure times.

There are several ordinary 3rd class trains daily to Prachuap Khiri Khan (34B), Surat Thani (34B) and Hat Yai (99B). Southbound rapid and express trains – the only trains with 1st and 2nd class service – are much less frequent and can be difficult to book out of Chumphon.

**Boat to Ko Tao** This small island north of Ko Samui and Ko Pha-Ngan (all covered in the Surat Thani Province section later in this chapter) can be reached by boat from Tha Reua Ko Tao (Ko Tao boat pier), 10 km south-east of town. The regular daily boat leaves at midnight, costs 200B and takes about six hours to reach Ko Tao. From Ko Tao the boat usually leaves at 10 am and arrives at Tha Reua Ko Tao around 3.30 pm.

Songthaews run to both piers frequently between 6 am and 6 pm for 10B. After 6 pm, Infinity and most other travel services and guesthouses can send a van to the pier around 9.30 pm for 50B per person. Going by van means you won't have to wait at the pier for six hours before the boat departs. The only other alternative is a 60B motorcycle taxi ride to the pier.

A more expensive but faster boat is the speed boat from the Tha Yang pier, which takes only 2½ hours and costs 400B. Depending on the weather, it usually departs at 9.30 am daily (8 am in the reverse direction). Regular air-con minibuses to/from Bangkok's Khao San Rd guesthouses and travel agencies also connect with the slow boat for 300B.

You can also charter a boat to Ko Tao from Pak Nam for around 2500B.

### Getting Around
Motorcycle taxis around town cost a flat 10B per trip. Songthaews to the port of Chumphon (Pak Nam Chumphon) are 13B per person. To Hat Sairi they cost 15B and to Thung Wua Laen 13B. Buses to Tako Estuary (for Hat Arunothai) are 15B. A motorcycle taxi out to Thung Wua Laen should be no more than 50B. The Chumphon Travel Service can arrange motorcycle and car rental.

### AROUND CHUMPHON
#### Islands
Islands close to Chumphon include Ko Samet, Ko Mattara, Ko Maphrao, Ko Rang Kachiu, Ko Ngam Yai and Ko Raet. Landing on Ko Rang Kachiu is restricted as this is where the precious swiftlets' nests are collected for the gourmet market. If you want to visit, you can request permission from the Laem Thong Bird Nest Company in Chumphon. For several years now, rumour has said

the birds' nest island may open to tourism, but so far this hasn't happened. The other islands in the vicinity are uninhabited; the reefs around Ko Raet and Ko Mattara are the most colourful.

There are many other islands a bit farther out that are also suitable for diving – get information from the diving centre at Chumphon Cabana Resort on Thung Wua Laen beach or from Chumphon Travel Service on Tha Taphao Rd in town. You can also hire boats and diving equipment here during the diving season, June to October. Fishing is also popular around the islands.

### Meditation Temple
Around 48 km south of town in Sawi district, Wat Tham Phan Meuang is a Thammayut monastery offering instruction in *vipassana*. There is one Thai monk who can speak English and translate.

### AROUND CHUMPHON PROVINCE
The best beaches in Chumphon Province are north of Chumphon at **Ao Phanang Tak**, **Ao Thung Wua Laen** and **Ao Baw Mao**. Nearer to town, in the vicinity of Pak Nam Chumphon, are the lesser beaches of **Hat Pharadon Phap** and **Hat Sairi**. About 40 km south of Chumphon, past the town of Sawi, is the Tako Estuary and the fair beach of **Hat Arunothai**. Most of these beaches have at least one set of resort bungalows.

### Places to Stay & Eat
**Hat Pharadon Phap & Hat Sairi** The air-con *Porn Sawan Home Beach Resort* (☎ (77) 521521) is at Pak Nam Chumphon and has rooms starting at 840B. *Sai Ree Lodge* (☎ (77) 521212) at nearby Hat Sairi has concrete bungalows with corrugated roofs for 950B with fan, 1150B with air-con. Farther north along Hat Sairi, *Sweet Guest House* (☎ (77) 521324) offers fan rooms for 300B, air-con for 400 to 500B.

**Hat Thung Wua Laen** Twelve km north of Chumphon on Hat Thung Wua Laen – also known as Hat Cabana – the well established *Chumphon Cabana Resort* (☎ (77) 501990;

SOUTHERN THAILAND

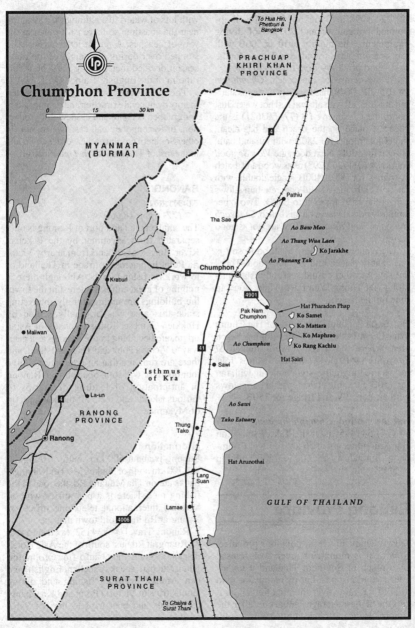

# Chumphon Province

**MYANMAR (BURMA)**

**PRACHUAP KHIRI KHAN PROVINCE**

To Hua Hin, Phetburi & Bangkok

0    15    30 km

Pathiu

Tha Sae

*Ao Baw Mao*

*Ao Thung Wua Laen*

Ko Jarakhe

*Ao Phanang Tak*

4

Chumphon

4901

Pak Nam Chumphon

Hat Pharadon Phap

Ko Samet

Ko Mattara

Ko Maphrao

Ko Rang Kachiu

Hat Sairi

*Ao Chumphon*

Kraburi

41

Sawi

*Isthmus of Kra*

Maliwan

La-un

4

**RANONG PROVINCE**

Ranong

Thung Tako

*Ao Sawi*

*Tako Estuary*

Hat Arunothai

Lang Suan

*GULF OF THAILAND*

4006

Lamae

**SURAT THANI PROVINCE**

To Chaiya & Surat Thani

(2) 224-1994 in Bangkok) has 26 well-appointed bungalows and 20 sets of diving equipment. The nightly tariff is 500B with fan, or from 900B for air-con. They offer the best – and priciest – dive trips in the area.

At the centre of the beach, *Chuanphun* (☎ (01) 726-0049) has a variety of rooms starting at 578B, all with air-con and hot water. Just north, the *Cleanwave* (☎ (77) 503621) is the cheapest place on the beach and has clean, motel-like rooms for 250B with fan and bath, air-con for 550B. Next door, the *View Seafood Resort* (☎ (01) 726-0293) rents wood and thatch A-frames for 300B/400B single/double with fan and bath, more solid concrete bungalows across the road for 600 to 800B. Two other similarly priced places on this beach, *Seabeach Bungalow* and *Khun Rim Lay*, are not as good value.

The restaurant at View Seafood Resort is reasonably priced and is quite good. There are several other casual seafood restaurants along Hat Thung Wua Laen where you can dine on the beach.

**Hat Sapli** A couple km north of Hat Thung Wua Laem is this newly developing beach area, where the friendly, well situated *Si Sanyalak* (☎ (01) 477-6602) features four rooms in a longhouse-style building with fan for 350B each, plus two separate bungalows with air-con, TV and fridge for 750B.

**Hat Arunothai** *Chumphon Sunny Beach* (☎ (77) 541895) is at the Tako Estuary on Hat Arunothai, about 50 km south of Chumphon. Bungalows are 400 to 450B with fan or 550B with air-con.

# Ranong Province

This is Thailand's least populous province; 67% of it is mountains, over 80% forests. Like much of Southern Thailand it undergoes two monsoons, but its mountains tend to hold the rains over the area longer, so it gets the highest average annual rainfall in the country. Hence, it's incredibly green overall,

with lots of waterfalls, although it's swampy near the coastline so there isn't much in the way of beaches. A recent letter writer who stopped over during the height of the rainy season decided that Ranong must be a corruption of the English 'Rained On'!

The provincial economy is supported mainly by mineral extraction and fishing, along with rubber, coconut and cashew-nut production. In Ranong they call cashews *ka-yuu* (in other Southern provinces the word is *ka-yii* and in the rest of Thailand it's *mét má-mûang*).

## RANONG
อ.เมืองระนอง
• ☎ *(77)* • *pop 18,000*
The small capital and port of Ranong is only separated from Myanmar by the Pakchan River. Burmese residents from nearby Victoria Point hop across to trade in Thailand or to work on fishing boats. Although there is nothing of great cultural interest in the town, the buildings are architecturally interesting since this area was originally settled by Hokkien Chinese. Tourists, mostly of Asian origin, are beginning to use Ranong as a gateway to Victoria Point and Thahtay Island, and there are rumours that an international dive tour operator will soon open shop in Ranong in anticipation of leading dive trips to various islands and reefs off the southern tip of Myanmar.

### Information
Ranong is about 600 km south of Bangkok and 300 km north of Phuket. Most of Ranong's banks are on Tha Meuang Rd, the road to the fishing pier. There is a post office with an attached international telephone office on Ruangrat Rd in the old town district.

Ranong Travel (☎ 834153; fax 811154) at 37 Ruangrat Rd, just south of the Asia Hotel, dispenses good travel info (the proprietor, Khun Nuansri, speaks excellent English) and can arrange deep-sea fishing and diving jaunts, trips to Victoria Point and Ko Chang, car rentals and boat trips to the Ko Surin islands.

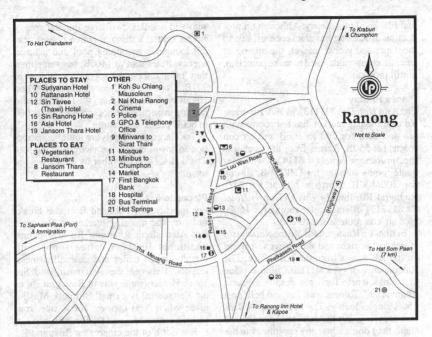

**PLACES TO STAY**
- 7 Suriyanan Hotel
- 10 Rattanasin Hotel
- 12 Sin Tavee (Thawi) Hotel
- 15 Sin Ranong Hotel
- 16 Asia Hotel
- 19 Jansom Thara Hotel

**PLACES TO EAT**
- 3 Vegetarian Restaurant
- 8 Jansom Thara Restaurant

**OTHER**
- 1 Koh Su Chiang Mausoleum
- 2 Nai Khai Ranong
- 4 Cinema
- 5 Police
- 6 GPO & Telephone Office
- 9 Minivans to Surat Thani
- 11 Mosque
- 13 Minibus to Chumphon
- 14 Market
- 17 First Bangkok Bank
- 18 Hospital
- 20 Bus Terminal
- 21 Hot Springs

## Nai Khai Ranong
ในค่ายระนอง

During the reign of Rama V, a Hokkien named Koh Su Chiang became governor of Ranong (thus gaining the new name Phraya Damrong Na Ranong) and his former residence, Nai Khai Ranong, has become a combination clan house and shrine. It's on the northern edge of town and is worth a visit while you're in Ranong.

Of the three original buildings, one still stands and is filled with mementoes of the Koh family glory days. The main gate and part of the original wall also remain. Koh Su Chiang's great-grandson Koh Sim Kong is the caretaker and he speaks some English. Several shophouses on Ruangrat Rd preserve the old Hokkien style, too. Koh Su Chiang's mausoleum is set into the side of a hill a bit farther north on the road to Hat Chandamri.

## Hot Springs & Wat Hat Som Paen
บ่อน้ำร้อน/วัดหาดส้มแป้น

About one km east of the Jansom Thara Hotel is the Ranong Mineral Hot Springs at Wat Tapotaram. Water temperature hovers around 65°C, hot enough to boil eggs. You can bathe in rustic rooms (10B per person) where you scoop water from separate hot and cool water tanks and sluice the mixed water over your body Thai style. Don't get inside the tanks and spoil the water. The Jansom Thara Hotel also pipes water from the springs into the hotel, where you can take a 42°C mineral bath in their large public spa for 100B.

If you continue on the same road past the hot springs for about seven km, you'll come to the village of Hat Som Paen, a former tin-mining community. At Wat Hat Som Paen, visitors feed fruit to the huge black carp (plaa phluang) in the temple stream. The faithful believe these carp are actually thewada, a type of angel, and it's forbidden to catch and eat them. Legend has it that those who do will contract leprosy.

Another three km down a bumpy dirt road is **Marakot Thara**, an emerald-green reservoir

SOUTHERN THAILAND

that fills an old tin quarry. Although tin production in Ranong has slackened off due to the depressed global market, the mining of calcium compounds, used to make porcelain, is still profitable.

## Places to Stay

The *Asia Hotel* (☎ 811113), at 39/9 Ruangrat Rd near the day market, has fair rooms with fan and bath for 200 to 260B and air-con rooms for 550B. Across from the market is the *Sin Ranong Hotel* (☎ 811454) with adequate rooms with fan for 150/170B, air-con for 300/400B. North a bit, at No 81/1 Ruangrat Rd, the *Sin Tavee (Thawi) Hotel* (☎ 811213) offers similar rooms for 160B, plus air-con rooms for 240/280B.

Farther up Ruangrat Rd are the *Rattanasin Hotel* on the right and the *Suriyanan Hotel* on the left across from the post office. The Rattanasin is a typical Thai-Chinese place that looks worse for wear despite a recent 'renovation'. Rooms with fan and bath cost 150B single/double. The Suriyanan is dark and decaying, but the staff are friendly and claim they don't allow any prostitutes in the hotel. A basic room is 80B with a fan, and 100B with fan and bath.

*Ranong Inn Hotel* (☎ 822777; fax 821527), at 29/9 Phetkasem Rd, a few km south of the town centre on the highway to Kapoe, is a clean, new place with nice rooms for 240B with fan and private bath, 430B with air-con and TV. In the same direction, the two-year-old *Eiffel Inn* (☎ 823271) – you can't miss it, there's a 15m Eiffel Tower model in the parking lot – offers fancy bungalows with TV, fridge, phone and hot water showers for 1500B (discounted rates of 600B are readily dispensed).

Across the highway on the road to the hot springs is *Jansom Thara Hotel* (☎ 811510; fax 821821; ☎ (2) 448-6096 in Bangkok), which has just about everything you could possibly want in a hotel. Standard rooms come with air-con and colour TV and there's in-house video, hot water bath with spa (piped in from the hot springs), and a refrigerator stocked with booze. There are also two restaurants, one of which specialises in Chinese dim

sum and noodles, two large mineral spas, a fitness centre, a disco, a coffee house/cocktail lounge, a swimming pool and a travel agency. Rates start at 1400B, but sometimes they offer discounted rooms for as low as 771B. Opposite the Jansom Thara Hotel on Highway 4, the *Spa Inn* (☎ 811715) is also cashing in on piped-in hot springwater for 600 to 800B per air-con room.

Two large new hotels are under construction in town, one in the vicinity of Jansom Thara Hotel and the other by a lake west of town.

## Places to Eat

For inexpensive Thai and Burmese breakfasts, try the morning market on Ruangrat Rd. Also along Ruangrat Rd are several traditional Hokkien coffee shops with marble-topped tables and enamelled metal teapots. Between the Rattanasin and Sin Tavee Hotels (same side of Ruangrat Rd as the Rattanasin) is a small Burmese Muslim place where you can get curry, rice, roti, pickled cucumbers and tea for 20B.

Just north of the cinema on Ruangrat Rd is a tiny vegetarian restaurant serving very inexpensive Thai veggie dishes; it's open Monday to Saturday from around 7 am to 6 pm. In the same vicinity, the moderately priced *Sri Prae* at 313/2 Ruangrat Rd is very popular with locals for stuffed crab and other seafood.

*Chaou Thong* at 8-10 Ruangrat Rd is a clean, air-con place with Thai food and western breakfasts. It's open from 6 am to 9.30 pm. A couple of km north of town on the highway, between Caltex and PT petrol stations, the *Mandalay* specialises in Burmese and Thai-style seafood. *Pak Nam Seafood*, out past Jansom Thara Resort on the road to Hat Chandamri, serves delicious and relatively inexpensive Thai seafood in a terraced dining area overlooking the seaside.

## Getting There & Away

**Air** Ranong airport, 20 km south of town off Highway 4, opened in November 1995. Bangkok Airways is the main carrier, with daily two hour flights from Bangkok for

1980B one way. This flight continues on to Phuket from Ranong three days a week for 800B. Bangkok Airways' Ranong office (☎ 835096) is at 50/18 Muu 1 Phetkasem Rd, a couple of km south of town on Highway 4.

THAI flies between Ranong and Surat Thani four times a week for 485B each way.

**Bus** You can get to Ranong via Chumphon (35B), Surat Thani (60B, 80B air-con), Takua Pa (45B) and Phuket (80B, 100B air-con). The bus terminal in Ranong is out of town near the Jansom Thara Hotel, but buses stop in town on Ruangrat Rd before proceeding on to the terminal.

To/from Bangkok, ordinary buses cost 140B, air-con 250B, VIP 350 to 390B.

Air-con minivans run between Surat Thani and Ranong for 110B. Departure from Ranong's Luv Wan Rd (near the Rattanasin Hotel) is at around 8 am, arriving in Surat Thani at around noon. From Surat Thani the van leaves at around 1 pm and returns to Ranong at 4 pm.

Daily air-con minibuses to Chumphon cost 70B and depart between 7 am and 5.30 pm from opposite Sin Tavee Hotel, where you can book a seat in advance. Buses to Khuraburi cost 35B and take an hour and 20 minutes.

### Getting Around

Songthaews ply the roads around Ranong and out to the hot springs and Hat Som Paen (No 2), Hat Chandamri (No 3) and Saphaan Plaa (No 2). The fare is 5B to any of these places. See the Around Ranong section for details. Motorcycle taxis (look for the orange vests) will take you anywhere in town for 15B, or to the area around the Jansom Thara for 20B.

Mayline, a minimart next to the Jansom Thara Hotel, rents Honda Dreams for 200B per day. Ranong Travel can assist with motorcycle and car rentals.

### AROUND RANONG
### Hat Chandamri
หาดชาญดำริ

Touted as the nearest beach to Ranong, Hat Chandamri is really more of a mud flat. A sister hotel to the Jansom Thara in Ranong, the *Jansom Thara Resort* (☎ (77) 821611; fax 821821) has similarly equipped bungalows (but no spas) for 1400B (discounts to 900B frequently available). From the dining terrace overlooking the bay you can eat seafood and watch the sun set over Myanmar's Victoria Point.

Hat Chandamri is 10 km north-west of Ranong, about 50B by motorcycle taxi or 5B by songthaew.

### Fishermen's Pier
สะพานปลา

The provincial fishing port, Tha Thiap Reua Pramong, is eight km south-west of Ranong. It's called **Saphaan Plaa** (Fish Bridge) for short and is always bustling with activity as fishing boats are loaded and unloaded with great cargoes of flapping fish. About half the boats are Burmese, as the fish traders buy from anyone who lands fish here. Boats can be chartered here for day trips to nearby islands. Unless you want to see heaps of fish or charter a fishing boat, there's really no reason to go out to the port.

### Victoria Point, Myanmar

This small port at the southernmost tip of mainland Myanmar is only separated from Thailand by the broad estuary of the Pakchan River. To the British it was Victoria Point and to the Thais it's Ko Sawng, which means Second Island. The Burmese name, Kaw Thaung, is probably a corruption of the latter.

The main business here is trade with Thailand, followed by fishing. Among the Burmese, Victoria Point is perhaps best known for producing some of the country's best kickboxers. Most residents are bilingual, speaking Thai and Burmese. Many people born and raised around Victoria Point, especially Muslims, also speak Pashu, a dialect that mixes Thai, Malay and Burmese. Nearby islands are inhabited by bands of nomadic Moken or sea gypsies.

At the moment Victoria Point is only accessible to foreigners by boat from Ranong, Thailand. It's probably not worth making a

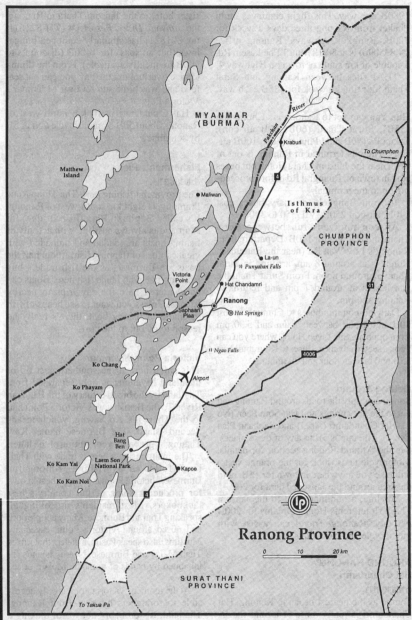

# Ranong Province

SOUTHERN THAILAND

special trip to Ranong just to visit Victoria Point, but if you're in the area and decide to cross over, you'll find it's similar to Southern Thailand except that many more men wear the *longyi* (the Burmese sarong).

Boats to Victoria Point leave the pier in Ranong regularly from around 7 am till 3 pm for 30B per person. Immediately as you exit the Victoria Point jetty there's a small immigration office on the right, where you must pay US$5 for a day permit. For the same rate you can stay up to three nights but then you're required to buy US$50 worth of foreign exchange certificates (FECs). If you want to stay longer, you can extend your permit up to 29 days upon payment of US$36 and the exchange of US$200 into FECs, a currency exchange that allows the Myanmar government to collect a 9.45% tax on every FEC exchanged for kyat (the Burmese currency). Whether this will allow you to travel further north is another matter – road travel is impossible and boat travel beyond the immediate Victoria Point area is so far forbidden.

Our experience indicates it's better to deal with the small immigration office at the pier rather than with the larger one on the road leading to the motel. The staff at the larger office may claim only day visits are allowed.

**Organised Tours** Jansom Thara Hotel in Ranong offers Victoria Point and island tours aboard four boats with capacities ranging from 15 to 200 people. A half-day tour costing 600B per person sails from Ranong, visits a couple of pagodas in Victoria Point and returns to Ranong around 11 am. The full day tour costing 850B goes to Pulau Besin for beach swimming and lunch and returns at 2 pm. Rates include immigration procedures on both sides, guide and boat transport; lunch costs an extra 120B per person.

Ranong Travel can arrange similar tours starting at 400B.

**Places to Stay** So far there's only one place in Victoria Point itself which is approved for foreigners, the simple *Victoria Point Motel* not far from the waterfront. For simple double rooms with private cold water bath, Thais pay 350B, foreigners US$25, Burmese around 80B.

On nearby Thahtay Island, well-heeled Thai and Singaporean gamblers shack up at the *Andaman Club* (☎ (01) 956-4354), a huge five star hotel complex sporting a casino and a Jack Nicklaus-designed 18 hole golf-course. All 191 rooms come with sea views and start at 3000B. Guests with reservations are able to take a 125B boat direct from Jansom Thara Resort on Hat Chandamri, about 10 km north-west of Ranong.

### Isthmus of Kra
คอคอดกระ

About 60 km north of Ranong, in Kraburi district, is the Isthmus of Kra, the narrowest point between water in Thailand. Barely 50 km separates the Gulf of Thailand from the Indian Ocean at this point. Just off Highway 4 is a monument commemorating this geographical wonder. At one time the Thai government had plans to construct the so-called Kra Canal here, but the latest word is that the canal – if it's built – will run east from Satun Province through Songkhla, about 500 km farther south.

### Waterfalls
น้ำตก

Of the several well known waterfalls in Ranong Province, **Ngao Falls** and **Punyaban Falls** are within walking distance of Highway 4. Ngao is 13 km south of Ranong while Punyaban is 15 km north. Just ride a songthaew in either direction and ask to be let off at the *náam tòk* (waterfall).

### Ko Chang
Don't confuse this island off the coast of Ranong with the much larger Ko Chang in Trat Province. As with many of the islands in this area, estuarial effluent from the Pakchan River inhibits clarity in the Andaman waters surrounding Ko Chang, but natural mangroves on the east coast and a hilly, forested interior are attractions enough for

some. Birdlife includes hornbills, sea eagles and Andaman kites.

A couple of trails meander around the island and so far there are no motor vehicles. Nor is there electricity – the few resorts on the island either do without or generate their own. Beaches are found along the western shore; though they're not classic white-sand strands, regular visitors enjoy the laid-back atmosphere.

Bungalow operations on the island can arrange boat trips to Ko Phayam and other nearby islands for around 150B per person (including lunch) in a group of six or more.

**Places to Stay** Several beach places have opened up over the last couple of years, though for the most part they're only open from November to April. Starting at the northern end of the island, *Rasta Baby* (☎ (77) 833077 in Ranong) is a seven-bungalow spot run by a dreadlocked Thai and his American wife. You can choose from two price schemes: 200B for room, breakfast and dinner, or 100B for room only. Meals are often prepared communally. Sharing the same small beach with Rasta Baby, *Ko Chang Contex* (☎ (77) 812730 in Ranong) is run by a Thai family with similar arrangements, along with an à la carte restaurant menu.

South and west, the *Eden Bistro Café* offers two small bungalows with shared bath for 100B each, and one large bungalow with attached shower for 150B. Just down the beach from Eden, *Sunset* offers nicely built bungalows in a shady, breezy spot for 100B each.

*Cashew Resort*, the oldest and largest place on the island, charges 100B for simple huts with shared facilities. Service has slipped over the years, perhaps because the proprietors were the only game on the island for so long.

A few hundred metres past the pier for boats from the mainland are the friendly *Chang Thong* and *Pheung Thong*, side-by-side operations run by brother and sister. Bamboo or plasterboard huts cost 80B here; Chang Thong's restaurant serves decent Thai

food. Nearby *Sabai Jai*, a well run Swedish-Thai joint effort, has a six-bed dorm for 30B per bed as well as several thatched huts for 80 to 100B. Facilities are simple but clean and well maintained; the proprietors bake their own bread and the restaurant focuses on western food.

The rather unfriendly *Ko Chang Resort* sits on a section of rocky headlands and offers huts with shared bath for 100B, with attached bath for 150B. Monkeys are chained to table legs in the restaurant, not a good sign.

At the southern end of the island at Ao Lek (Small Bay), *N & X Bungalows* offers more of the same thatched huts for 100B each. At least three other bungalow operations are under construction at this end of the island.

**Getting There & Away** From Ranong take a songthaew (red No 2, 5B) to Saphaan Plaa, getting off by the petrol station toward the main pier. Look for signs advertising Ko Chang bungalows and follow them down a zigzag soi a couple of hundred metres, where you'll find long-tail boats that run to Ko Chang. If you have a heavy bag a motorcycle taxi can bring you to this landing for 20B. Depending on the tides, two or three boats leave every morning from November to April; turn up around 8 am to see when they're going, as they don't usually leave before this hour. They return to the mainland in the early afternoon.

The cost is negotiable depending on how many passengers board; if you book a bungalow through Ranong Travel in town, you may get a free boat ride along with a ride down to Saphaan Plaa. Otherwise count on paying anywhere from 30 to 100B per person.

## LAEM SON NATIONAL PARK
อุทยานแห่งชาติแหลมสน

The Laem Son (Pine Cape) Wildlife & Forest Preserve stretches 315 sq km over the Kapoe district of Ranong and Khuraburi district in Phang-Nga. This area includes about 100 km of Andaman Sea coastline – the longest protected shore in the country – as well as over

20 islands. Much of the coast here is covered with mangrove swamps, home to various species of birds, fish, deer and monkeys, including the crab-eating macaques which are easily seen while driving along the road to the park headquarters.

The best known and most accessible beach is **Hat Bang Ben**, where the main park offices, restaurant and bungalows are. This is a long, sandy beach backed by shady casuarina trees and it is said to be safe for swimming year-round. From Hat Bang Ben you can see several islands, including the nearby Ko Kam Yai, Ko Kam Noi, Ko Yipun, Ko Kang Kao and, to the north, Ko Phayam. The park staff can arrange boat trips out to any of these islands for 800B per boat per day. During low tide you can walk to a nearby island just a couple of hundred metres away from Hat Bang Ben.

**Ko Phayam** is inhabited by around 100 Thais, who mostly make their living by fishing or growing cashews. There are good swimming beaches on Phayam and on the western side of some of the Kam islands, as well as some live coral. Although underwater visibility isn't great, it's a little better here than on Ko Chang since it's farther from the mouth of the Pakchan River. The beach on **Ko Kam Noi** has relatively clear water for swimming and snorkelling (April is the best month) plus the added bonus of fresh water year-round and plenty of grassy areas for camping. One island on the other side of Ko Kam Yai which can't be seen from the beach is **Ko Kam Tok** (also called Ko Ao Khao Khwai). It's only about 200m from Ko Kam Yai and, like Ko Kam Noi, has a good beach, coral, fresh water and a camping area. **Ko Kam Yai** is 14 km south-west of Hat Bang Ben.

About three km north of Hat Bang Ben, across the canal, is another beach, **Hat Laem Son**, which is almost always deserted and is 'undeveloped' according to park authorities (which means they won't guarantee your safety). The only way to get there is to hike from Bang Ben. In the opposite direction, about 50 km south of Hat Bang Ben, is **Hat Praphat**, very similar to Bang Ben with casuarina trees and a long beach. A second

park office is located here and this one can be reached by road via the Phetkasem Highway (Highway 4).

In the canals you ford coming into the park, you may notice large wooden racks which are used for raising oysters.

### Places to Stay & Eat

Camping is allowed anywhere amongst the casuarina trees for 5B per person. National park bungalows have dorm-like 10 person and 16 person wooden houses – 700B and 900B respectively – but will allow individuals to stay for 100B per night. Similar park accommodation is also available on Ko Kam Yai but should be arranged in advance: call ☎ (77) 823255 in Ranong or ☎ (2) 579-0529 in Bangkok for information.

A few hundred metres before the park entrance (9.5 km from the Highway 4 junction) is the private *Wasana Resort*, a new place run by a Thai-Dutch couple. Clean bamboo bungalows with mosquito nets, fan and private bath cost 250B, larger concrete bungalows with verandahs are 500B; discounts for long-term stays are available. Nearby *Andaman Peace Resort* (☎ (77) 821796) offers five different models of concrete bungalow for 600 to 1500B. Just outside the park entrance, the lacklustre *Komain Villa* offers small bungalows for 200B per night.

The food at the park canteen isn't bad, although Wasana Resort is a better choice.

**Ko Phayam** There are only a few places to stay on Ko Phayam. On the west side of the island is one small beach with a couple of bungalows in the 100 to 150B range, plus a nicer, larger beach with five bungalows for 150B each. On the east side is the more expensive *Payam Island Resort* (☎ (77) 812297; (2) 390-2681 in Bangkok) with bungalows from 400 to 2500B. There is also the *Thawon Resort* (☎ (77) 811186) with bungalows for 100B and 150B.

### Getting There & Away

The turn-off for Laem Son is about 58 km down the Phetkasem Highway (Highway 4) from Ranong, between Km 657 and 658. Any bus heading south from Ranong can drop you off here or you could hitch fairly easily – there is plenty of traffic along Highway 4. Once you're off the highway, however, you'll have to wait a bit to flag down pickup trucks going to the village near Laem Son. If you can't get a ride all the way, it's a two km walk from the village to the park. At the new police box at the junction you may be able to hire a motorcycle taxi for 30B. The road is now paved all the way to the park, so if you have your own vehicle it's a breeze.

Boats to Ko Phayam are irregular, unless you are willing to charter one for 2000B. Sometimes the Ko Chang boats continue to Ko Phayam – enquire at Ranong's Jansom Thara Hotel, Ranong Travel or at Saphaan Plaa.

Boats out to the various islands can be chartered from the park's visitors' centre; the general cost is 800B per day. You can arrange to go as far as the Similan or Surin islands (see in the Phang-Nga Province section below for descriptions) for 900 and 1200B per person respectively.

# Phang-Nga Province

## KHURABURI, TAKUA PA & THAI MUANG
ศุระบุรี,ตะกั่วป่าและ,ท้ายเมือง
These districts of Phang-Nga Province are of minor interest in themselves but are departure points for other destinations. From Khuraburi you can reach the remote Surin and Similan islands, or from Takua Pa you can head east to Khao Sok National Park and Surat Thani.

Takua Pa is also about halfway between Ranong and Phuket so buses often make rest stops here. Just off the highway is the *Extra Hotel* with rooms from 140B if you want to stop for the night.

In the district of Thai Muang is **Thai Muang Beach National Park**, where sea turtles come to lay eggs between November

and February. **Thap Lamu**, about 23 km north of Thai Muang, has a pier with boats to the Similan Islands.

## HAT BANG SAK & HAT KHAO LAK
หาดบางสัก/หาดเขาหลัก
Twenty-five km south of Takua Pa, the beach at Khao Lak is a pretty stretch of sand studded with granite boulders. An offshore coral reef suitable for snorkelling is 45 minutes away by long-tail boat, and some of the bungalow resorts here offer dive excursions to this reef as well as to the Similan and Surin island groups. Another 12 km south on Highway 4 is Hat Bang Sak, a long sandy beach backed by casuarina trees.

The area to the immediate south of Hat Khao Lak is encompassed by the 125 sq km **Khao Lak - Lamru National Park**, a beautiful collection of sea cliffs, 1000m hills, beaches, estuaries, forested valleys and mangroves. Wildlife seen in the area includes hornbills, drongos, tapirs, gibbons, monkeys and Asiatic black bear. The visitors' centre, just off Highway 4 between Km 56 and 57, has little in the way of maps or printed info, but there's a very nice open-air restaurant perched on a shady slope overlooking the sea.

### Activities
Poseidon Bungalows (☎ /fax (01) 229-6767) can arrange guided treks along the coast or in the inland forests of Khao Lak - Lamru National Park, as well as long-tail boat trips up the scenic Khlong Thap Liang estuary. The latter passes through mangrove communities of crab-eating macaques.

Live coral formations can be found just off Hat Khao Lak and along the western tip of the bay near Poseidon. Sea Dragon Dive Center, on Highway 4 opposite the main entrance to Hat Khao Lak, is the main diving operation in the area. In addition to selling and renting diving/snorkelling equipment, it offers PADI-certified scuba instruction and dive trips to the Similan Islands. Sea Dragon's three day, two night Similan excursion costs 7600B for divers, including food,

SOUTHERN THAILAND

transport, accommodation and all equipment, or 5500B for non-divers. These are among the lowest rates available for dive excursions to the Similans since most companies work out of Phuket. Local dive trips to nearby coral reefs cost 1000B per day including equipment and two tanks.

Poseidon Bungalows offers three day, two night snorkelling-only trips to the Similan Islands for 3300B per person. These trips depart twice a week during the November to April dive season. For both Poseidon and Sea Dragon, count on five hours each way to reach the islands; such trips operate only between October and April due to climatic conditions. For further information on getting to the Similans, see the Similan Islands National Marine Park section further on in this chapter.

## Places to Stay & Eat

**Hat Khao Lak** The south end of Hat Khao Lak has the least expensive lodgings, beginning with the original *Khao Lak Resort*, where bungalows cost 100 to 150B with shared bath, 200 to 350B with private bath; the lease on this lot expires soon, so the place may change proprietors and rates. *Khao Lak View Bungalow*, all the way at the south end of the main beach, has a collection of new thatched huts for 100B per night, plus more expensive ones under construction.

Moving toward the centre of Hat Khao Lak the rates and accommodation quality begin to rise. The slightly up-market *Nang Thong Bay Resort* (☎ (01) 723-1181) has a variety of bungalows, all with private bath, starting at 350B. This is the only place in Khao Lak where you can change money (cash or travellers' cheques). Motorbikes are available for 200B per day, Suzuki jeeps 800B. A *Nong Thong Bay II* is under construction and will cost more. The nearby *Garden Beach Resort* (☎ (01) 723-1179) has similar rates and also offers motorcycle and jeep hire.

At the northern end of Hat Khao Lak, *Khao Lak Bungalows* (☎ (01) 723-1197) offers small rooms with shared bath for 150B or larger Thai-style bungalows with private

bath for 800B. This entire beach is moving up-market, so expect the low end to rise steadily from the 150B range within the next few years till rates become comparable with Phuket. The deluxe *Khao Lak Laguna Resort* will open toward the south end of the beach in early 1997.

A cluster of simple thatched-roof beach restaurants toward the centre of the beach (follow the sign for Talking Stone Bar) offer reasonably priced Thai dishes and seafood.

**National Park Environs** There is no official accommodation in Khao Lak - Lamru National Park as yet, but a long-running place at the southern edge of the park deserves kudos for its commitment to nature conservation. *Poseidon Bungalows* (☎ /fax (01) 229-6767), in a sheltered bay south of Hat Khao Lak, rents basic thatched huts for 100B single/ double with shared bath, larger huts with private bath for 280B or 350B for three people. The huts are non-intrusively dispersed among huge boulders and beach forest, affording quiet and privacy. The proprietors dispense information on the area and organise boat excursions and dive trips to the local reef and to the Similan Islands. A pleasant restaurant built on stilts over the sea serves Thai and European food.

## Getting There & Away

Any bus coming down Highway 4 between Thai Muang and Takua Pa will stop at Khao Lak if asked (look for the Sea Dragon Dive Center on the east side of the highway). If you miss Khao Lak heading south, get off at the Thap Lamu highway junction and catch a motorcycle taxi for 30B; this is the best way to reach Poseidon.

## SURIN ISLANDS NATIONAL MARINE PARK

อุทยานแห่งชาติหมู่เกาะสุรินทร์

A national park since 1981, the Surin Islands are famous for excellent diving and sportfishing. The two main islands (there are five in all) of Ko Surin Neua and Ko Surin Tai (North Surin Island and South Surin Island) are about 70 km from Khuraburi and less than five km from Thailand's marine border with Myanmar. The park office and visitors' centre are on the south-west side of the north island at Ao Mae Yai, where boats anchor. Admission to the park is 20B.

On the southern island is a village of sea gypsies (*chao leh* or *chao náam*) and this is also where the official camping ground is located. The best diving is said to be in the channel between these two islands. The chao náam hold a large ceremony, involving ancestral worship, on Ko Surin Tai during the full moon in March. The island may be off limits during that time, so ask at the park office.

Most visitors to the islands are Thai tourists, who tend to arrive on national holidays; the remainder of the time Surin is little visited.

Surrounding the Surin Islands are the most well-developed coral colonies in Thai seas, according to Piprell & Boyd's *Diving in Thailand*, though the Similans boast a richer variety of fish species. There are seven major dive sites in the immediate vicinity, of which the best are found at the south-eastern point of Surin Neua; at Ko Chi, a small island off the north-eastern shore of Surin Neua; and Richelieu Rook, a seamount about 14 km south-east of Surin Tai. Whale sharks – the largest fish in the world – are reportedly spotted near Richelieu on 50% of all dive trips, most commonly during the months of March and April. Snorkelling is excellent in many areas due to relatively shallow reef depths of five to six metres.

The little-explored Burma Banks, a system of submerged seamounts around 60 km north-west of Ko Surin, are so prized by Thai dive operations that the GPS (Global Positioning System) coordinates are kept virtually secret. Actually the only way to visit the Burma Banks – unless you have your own boat – is by seven to 10 day live-aboard dive trips out of Phuket. The three major banks, Roe, Silvertip and Rainbow, provide four to five star diving experiences, with fields of psychedelic coral laid over flat, underwater plateaux and loads of large

oceanic as well as smaller reef marine species. Sharks – silvertip, reef, nurse, leopard and at least a half-dozen other species – abound.

### Places to Stay & Eat

Accommodation at the park longhouses is 100B per person or you can rent an entire six-person bungalow for 600B, an eight-person one for 800B. At the campground, two-person tents cost 40B a night or you can use your own (or camp without a tent) for 10B per night per person. The park also offers a daily package of three good meals (mostly seafood) for 250B, or you can order meals separately. Electric power is generated from 6 to 11 pm.

Should you get stuck in Khuraburi, the *Rungtawan* next to the bus stop has adequate rooms for 150B. If the attached sing-song cafe is too noisy, the only other possibility is *Tararain Resort*, two km outside town, with three-person bungalows for 300B.

### Getting There & Away

The mainland office of Surin Islands National Marine Park is in Ban Hin Lat, from where boats to the islands depart. The road to Ban Hin Lat turns off Highway 4 at Km 110, seven km north of the Khuraburi turn-off, about 70 km south of Ranong. Buses between Khuraburi and Ranong cost 35B and take about an hour and 20 minutes; ask to be let off at the turn-off for Ban Hin Lat. To/from Phuket, buses cost 50B and take about three hours. From Khuraburi to the Ban Hin Lat pier costs 30B by motorcycle taxi.

You can charter a boat out to the Surin Islands from Ban Hin Lat either through the park officers (who will merely serve as brokers/interpreters) or from the Phae Plaa Chumphon pier at Ban Hin Lat. A boat that takes up to 30 people can be chartered for 6000B return – it takes four to five hours each way. Group tours sometimes go from Ban Hin Lat for 800B return per person. Ordinarily boat travel is only considered safe between December and early May, between the two monsoons. Enquire at the park office (☎ (76) 491378) to see when the latest departures are.

SOUTHERN THAILAND

You can also get boats to the Surin Islands from Hat Patong in Phuket. A regular charter boat from Phuket takes 10 hours, or you can get a Songserm express boat during the diving season (December to April) that takes only three hours 15 minutes. However, the fare for the express boat is 1700B per person – if you have more than a couple of people it's cheaper to go from Khuraburi.

## SIMILAN ISLANDS NATIONAL MARINE PARK

อุทยานแห่งชาติหมู่เกาะสิมิลัน

The Similan Islands are world-renowned among diving enthusiasts for incredible underwater sightseeing at depths ranging from two to 30m. Beside attractive sand beaches, huge, smooth granite rock formations plunge into the sea and form seamounts, rock reefs and dive-throughs. As elsewhere in the Andaman Sea, the best diving months are December to May when the weather is good and the sea is at its clearest (and boat trips are much safer).

The Similans are also sometimes called Ko Kao, or Nine Islands, because there are nine of them – each has a number as well as a name. The word 'Similan' in fact comes from the Malay word *sembilan* for nine. Counting in order from the north, they are Ko Bon, Ko Ba-Ngu, Ko Similan, Ko Payu, Ko Miang (which is actually two islands close together), Ko Payan, Ko Payang and Ko Hu Yong. They're relatively small islands and uninhabited except for park officials and occasional tourist groups from Phuket.

Princess Chulabhorn, the present Thai monarch's youngest daughter, has a cottage on Ko Miang, a royal association that adds an extra layer of protection to the islands' national park status. The Thai navy operates a sea turtle preserve on Ko Ba-Ngu, another bonus for enforcement of park preservation.

The park office and visitors' centre is on Ko Miang. Admission to the islands is 20B.

## Organised Tours

**From Phuket** Overnight diving excursions from Phuket are fairly reasonable in cost – about 3500B a day including food, accommodation, diving equipment and underwater guides. Non-divers may be able to join these trips for around half the cost – snorkellers are welcome.

Package deals out of Phuket typically start at 9000B for a three day/two night dive trip, and go up to 37,000B for a seven day, seven night Similan and Burma Banks trip on Siam Diving Center's (☎ (76) 330936; fax 330608) live-aboard MV *Sai Mai*. The latter also offers longer, more exotic dive excursions such as a 10 day/10 night whale shark expedition costing over 50,000B per person.

Songserm Travel (☎ (76) 222570) in Phuket operates a one day excursion trip to the Similans every Tuesday, Thursday and Saturday at 8 am for 1600B per person including lunch. Considering it takes 3½ hours each way, this doesn't leave a lot of time for island exploration.

**From Hat Khao Lak** Sea Dragon at Hat Khao Lak does three day/two night dive trips to the Similans for 7600B, while Poseidon Bungalows has a snorkelling trip for 3300B; see the Hat Khao Lak section for more detail.

## Places to Stay

Bungalows cost the same in the Similans as in the Surin Islands, while tents are 100B for two persons, 150B for three. All facilities are located on Ko Miang. Reservations can be made through the park headquarters on ☎ (77) 411914.

## Getting There & Away

The Similans can be reached from Thap Lamu (about 40 km south of Takua Pa off Highway 4, or 20 km north of Thai Muang), Hat Khao Lak or Phuket.

Boats run to the Similans November to May only; during the remainder of the year the seas are too heavy. From Thap Lamu and Khao Lak the islands are only 60 km away, about three hours by boat. Figure on roughly 3000B return to charter a boat for eight people from Thap Lamu; you can sometimes hitch a ride with Thai tour boats from Thap Lamu for about 800B per person. From

SOUTHERN THAILAND

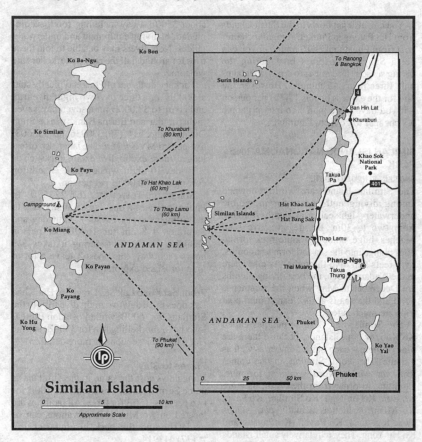

Similan Islands

November to March the Parks Division in Thap Lamu runs boats daily that cost 700B each way; they stop only at Island No 4 (Ko Miang), however.

## AO PHANG-NGA & PHANG-NGA
อ่าวพังงา/อ.เมืองพังงา
☎ (76) pop 9000

Over 95 km from Phuket, the area around Ao Phang-Nga is quite scenic – lots of limestone cliffs, odd rock formations, islands that rise out of the sea like inverted mountains, not to mention caves and quaint fishing villages.

Phang-Nga would make a good motorcycle trip from Phuket, or, if you have time, you could spend a few days there.

On the way to Phang-Nga turn left off Highway 4 at Km 31, just five km past the small town of Takua Thung, to get to **Wat Tham Suwankhuha** (Heaven Grotto Temple), a cave shrine full of Buddha images. The shrine consists of two main caverns, a larger one containing a 15m reclining Buddha and tiled with *laikhram* and *benjarong*, two coloured patterns more common in pottery, and a smaller cavern displaying spirit flags and a rishi statue. Royal seals of several kings, including Rama V, Rama VII and Rama IX – as well as those of lesser royalty – are inscribed on one wall of the latter cave.

Other nearby caves in the province include **Tham Reusisawan** (Hermit Heaven; three km south of Phang-Nga) and **Tham Phung Chang** (Elephant Belly Cave; also three km south). **Manohra Falls** is nine km north of Phang-Nga.

Phang-Nga's best beach areas are on the west coast facing the Andaman Sea. Between Thai Muang in the south and Takua Pa in the north are the beaches of Hat Thai Muang and Hat Bang Sak – see the earlier Khuraburi, Takua Pa & Thai Muang section for more details.

In Phang-Nga itself, a small town wedged between verdant limestone cliffs, there's little to see or do unless you happen to be there during the annual Vegetarian Festival in October (see the Phuket section for information on this unusual festival).

In the centre of town along Highway 4 are several banks open during regular banking hours. The post and telephone office is about two km from the bus station.

### Organised Tours
**Boat Trips** Between Takua Thung and Phang-Nga is the road to **Tha Dan**, where you can find the Phang-Nga customs pier. At an adjacent pier boats can be hired to tour Ao Phang-Nga, visiting a Muslim fishing village on stilts, half-submerged caves, strangely shaped islands (yes, including those filmed in the 007 flick, *The Man with the Golden Gun*) and other local oddities.

Tours from the pier cost between 150 and 400B; from Phuket they cost at least 300 to 600B per person. A former postman from Ko Panyi (one of Ao Phang-Nga's islands) named Sayan Tamtopol has been doing overnight tours of Ao Phang-Nga for several years now, and these continue to receive good reviews from travellers. The tour costs 300B per person and includes a boat tour of **Tham Lawt** (a large water cave), **Ko Phing Kan** (Leaning Island), **Ko Khao Tapu** (Nail Mountain Island), **Ko Maju**, **Tham Naga**, **Khao Khian** (Drawing Cave; containing

cave murals), a former mangrove charcoal factory and **Ko Panyi**, a mangrove swamp, plus dinner, breakfast and accommodation in a Muslim fishing village on Ko Panyi. Sayan also leads morning (rainy season) and afternoon (dry season) trips for 150B. Both include a seafood lunch and return in the afternoon. The overnight trip is recommended over the day trip; the latter tends to be a bit rushed. Sayan Tour (☎ 430348) now has an office next to the bus terminal in Phang-Nga or he can be contacted at the Thawisuk Hotel in the same town. Beware of touts posing as Sayan at Tha Dan.

You can also take a ferry to Ko Panyi on your own for 25B.

Whatever you do, try to avoid touring the bay in the middle of the day (10 am to 4 pm) when hundreds of package tourists crowd the islands. The Ko Panyi Muslim village is very commercialised during the day when hordes of tourist boats invade to eat lunch at the village's many overpriced seafood restaurants and buy tacky souvenirs at the many stalls. The village returns to its normal self after the boats depart. On Ko Panyi, always ask the price before eating as the restaurants often overcharge.

**Canoe Tours** Sea Canoe (☎ 212172; fax 212-252; e-mail @seacanoe.com), a company based in Phuket at 367/4 Yaowarat Rd, offers inflatable-kayak excursions on the bay. The kayaks – a type of their own design, called Sea Explorers – are able to enter semi-submerged caves inaccessible by the long-tail boats. A day paddle costs 2675B per person and includes meals, beverages and equipment, while an all-inclusive, three day camping trip is 7500B per person. Many other companies in the area offer similar inflatable canoe trips for about half these prices, but Sea Canoe was the first and is still the most ecologically conscious in terms of the way in which they organise and operate their tours. Any travel agency can book their trips.

### Places to Stay
**Phang-Nga** Phang-Nga has several small hotels. The *Thawisuk* is right in the middle

of town, a bright blue building with the English sign 'Hotel'. Fairly clean, quiet rooms upstairs go for 100B a single/double with fan and bath, plus towel and soap on request. You can sit and have a beer on the roof of Thawisuk while watching the sun set over Phang-Nga's rooftops and the limestone cliffs surrounding the town.

The *Lak Meuang* (☎ 411125/288), on Phetkasem Rd, just outside town towards Krabi, has rooms for 200B with fan and bath, 480B air-con, plus an OK restaurant downstairs. The *Rak Phang-Nga*, across the street from Thawisuk towards Phuket, is 80 to 100B but somewhat dirty and noisy. Opposite the Rak Phang-Nga is the *Ratanapong Hotel*, which has cleaned up its act and now offers OK singles for 120 to 150B, doubles for 200 to 230B, triples for 280B and quadruples for 350B; air-con rooms are also available for 300/430B single/double.

Farther down the road towards Phuket is the *Muang Thong*, with clean, quiet singles/doubles for 120/180B with fan, 250 to 320B with air-con. Outside town, even farther towards Phuket, is *New Lak Meuang II*, with all air-con rooms from 350B.

**Tha Dan** About 100m before the tour pier are the *National Park Bungalows*, which cost 350 to 750B a night. Farther on towards town, before the customs pier, the *Phang-Nga Bay Resort Hotel* (☎ 411067/70) costs 90B up. Facilities include a swimming pool and a decent restaurant. All rooms come with TV, telephone and fridge.

### Places to Eat
*Duang Restaurant*, next to Bangkok Bank on the main road, has a bilingual menu and a good selection of Thai and Chinese dishes, including Southern Thai specialities. Prices have crept up a little higher than the standard of the food would indicate.

South-west of the market, not far from the bus terminal, the new and clean *Nawng James* (Little Brother James) serves very good and inexpensive khâo man kài, won-ton and noodles. Diagonally opposite Nawng

James is the *Bismilla*, a tidy restaurant serving Muslim food.

Several foodstalls on the main street of Phang-Nga sell cheap and delicious khanǒm jiin with chicken curry, náam yaa (spicy ground-fish curry) or náam phrík (sweet and spicy peanut sauce). One vendor in front of the market (opposite Bangkok Bank) serves khanǒm jiin with an amazing 12 varieties of free vegetable accompaniments – but only from 1 to 8 pm daily; an adjacent vendor does khâo mòk kài from 6 am to noon. Roti kaeng (flatbread and curry) is available in the morning market from around 5 to 10 am. There are also the usual Chinese khâo man kài places around town.

### Getting There & Away
Buses for Phang-Nga leave from the Phuket bus terminal on Phang-Nga Rd, near the Thepkasatri Rd intersection, hourly between 6 am and 6 pm. The trip to Phang-Nga takes two hours and the one way fare is 26B. Air-con buses leave about every two hours from 10 am to 4.30 pm and cost 50B. Alternatively you can rent a motorcycle in Phuket.

Buses to/from Krabi cost 28B and take 1½ hours; to/from Surat Thani they cost 50B and take 3½ hours.

Ordinary buses to/from Bangkok cost 192B and take 14 hours, while air-con is 346B and VIP is 515B, both taking 13 hours.

### Getting Around
Most of the town is easily accessible on foot. Sayan Tour at the bus terminal can assist with motorcycle rental. Songthaews between Phang-Nga and Tha Dan (the Phang-Nga customs pier) cost 10B.

### AROUND PHANG-NGA
#### Ko Yao
Ko Yao Yai and Ko Yao Noi (Big Long Island and Little Long Island) are directly south of the provincial capital, in the middle of the bay almost equidistant between the provinces of Phuket and Krabi. Together they encompass 137 sq km of forest, beaches and rocky headlands with views of the surrounding karst formations characteristic of Ao

Phang-Nga. Contrary to first assumptions, Ko Yao Noi is the main population centre of the two, although even there fishing, coconuts and a little tourism sustains a relatively small group of year-rounders. **Hat Paa Sai** and **Hat Tha Khao**, both on Yao Noi, are the best beaches. Bring along a mountain bike if you want to explore the island's numerous dirt trails.

**Ta Khai**, the largest settlement on the island, is a subdistrict seat and a source of minimal supplies. Boat trips to neighbouring islands, bird-nest caves and sea gypsy funeral caves are possible. **Ko Bele**, a small island east of the twin Ko Yai, features a large tidal lagoon, three white-sand beaches, and easily accessible caves and coral reefs around the entire island. Long-tail boats from Ko Yao Noi or from Ao Nang in Krabi can be chartered for around 500 to 1000B per day depending on the size of the boat.

**Places to Stay** On Ko Yao Noi, the only island with regular visitor lodgings, *Sabai Corner* is an environmentally sensitive resort associated with Sea Canoe (☎ (76) 212172; 367/4 Yaowarat Rd, Phuket), which arranges kayak trips here – both self-paddles or guided trips – from November to August. Thatch and wood bungalows cost 300 to 700B a night.

The only other place to stay on Yao Noi is *Long Beach Village* (☎ /fax 381623; ☎ (2) 272-0650 in Bangkok), which has large wood and thatch bungalows for 500 to 1000B a night.

**Getting There & Away** Although both islands fall within the Phang-Nga Province boundaries, the easiest places to find boat transport to Ko Yao Noi are Phuket, Ao Leuk (Krabi Province) or Ao Nang (Krabi Province).

In Phuket city, catch a songthaew from in front of the Ranong Rd to Bang Rong on Ao Paw for 20B. From the public pier at Ao Paw there are usually two mail boats a day to Ko Yao Noi, one between 8 and 9 am and another around noon. The fare is 30B per passenger and the trip takes 45 minutes to an hour. Between departures or after hours you can charter a long-tail boat out to the island

for 400B one way. Coming back to Phuket from Yao Noi, the mail boats leave between 6 and 7 am and around 11 am. There is also one daily boat to Ko Yao Noi from the Tha Laem Hin pier, just north-east of Phuket city, at 3 pm; this one costs 25B one way and takes 1½ hours; it returns to Phuket at 10 am in the morning.

You can also get boats from Ko Yao Noi north-east across Ao Phang-Nga to Tha Laem Sak at Ao Leuk, Krabi. These cost around 40B on regular ferries, or 500B to charter. From Krabi's Ao Nang you can charter a boat for about 500B each way.

If you want to take a look around Ko Yao Yai, directly south of Yao Noi, catch a shuttle boat from Ko Yao Noi's Tha Manaw pier (10B each way), or charter a long-tail boat or kayak from Sabai Corner.

# Phuket Province

Dubbed 'Pearl of the South', by the tourist industry, Phuket (pronounced 'Poo-get') is Thailand's largest island (810 sq km) and a province in itself. It is Thailand's wealthiest province, and although tourism is its biggest source of income (along with tin, rubber and cashews), the island is still big enough to accommodate escapists of nearly all budget levels. Formerly called Ko Thalang and before that Junk Ceylon, Phuket has a culture all of its own, combining Chinese and Portuguese influences (like neighbouring western Malaysia) with that of the chao náam, an indigenous ocean-going people, and the Southern Thais. About 35% of the island's population are Thai Muslims and mosques outnumber Buddhist wats 38 to 37.

Lying in the Andaman Sea off Southern Thailand's west coast, the island's terrain is incredibly varied, with rocky beaches, long, broad, sandy beaches, limestone cliffs, forested hills and tropical vegetation of all kinds. Great seafood is available all over the island and several offshore islands are known for good snorkelling and scuba diving.

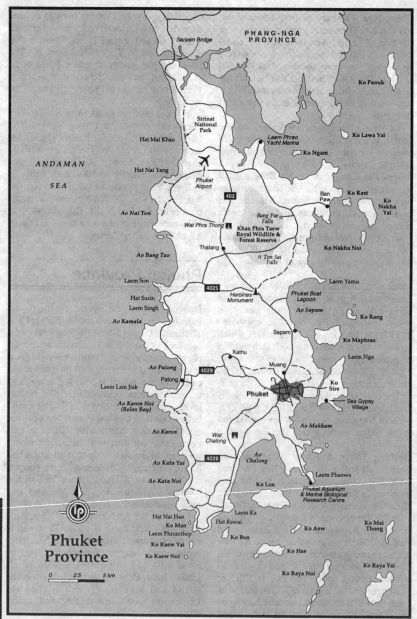

PHANG-NGA
PROVINCE

Sarasin Bridge

Ko Panuk

Sirinat
National
Park

Hat Mai Khao

Laem Phrao
Yacht Marina

Ko Lawa Yai

Ko Ngam

ANDAMAN

Hat Nai Yang

Phuket
Airport

Ban
Paw

Ko Raet

SEA

402

Ko
Nakha
Yai

Ao Nai Ton

Bang Pae
Falls

Wat Phra Thong

Khao Phra Taew
Royal Wildlife &
Forest Reserve

Ko Nakha Noi

Ao Bang Tao

Thalang

Ton Sai
Falls

Laem Son

4025

Laem Yamu

Hat Surin
Laem Singh

Heroines
Monument

Phuket Boat
Lagoon

Ao Kamala

Ao Sapam

Ko Rang

Sapam

Ko Maphrao

Kathu

Laem Nga

Ao Patong

4029

Muang

Patong

Laem Lam Jiak

Phuket

Ko
Sire

Ao Karon Noi
(Relax Bay)

Sea Gypsy
Village

Ao Makham

Ao Karon

Wat
Chalong

Ao Kata Yai

4028

Ao
Chalong

Ao Kata Noi

Laem Phanwa

Phuket Aquarium
& Marine Biological
Research Centre

Ko Lon

Phuket
Province

Hat Nai Han
Ko Man
Laem Phromthep
Ko Kaew Yai

Laem Ka

Hat Rawai

Ko Aew

Ko Mai
Thong

Ko Bon

Ko Kaew Noi

Ko Hae

0    2.5    5 km

Ko Raya Noi

Ko Raya Yai

Comparisons with Ko Samui, off the east coast, as well as with other Thai islands, are inevitable, of course. All in all, there is more to do in Phuket, but that means more to spend your money on, too. There are more tourists in Phuket than on any other island but they are concentrated at certain beaches – Patong, Karon and Kata. Beaches like Nai Han and Kamala are relatively quiet, in spite of major tourist developments at both, while Nai Yang, Nai Thon and Mai Khao to the north are still pristine. The beaches of Ko Samui, by contrast, are development-saturated around the entire perimeter of the island.

Development on Phuket has been influenced by the fact that it is connected to the mainland by a bridge, and hence it receives much more vehicular traffic than any other island in the country. And Phuket's high per-capita wealth means there's plenty of money available for investment. A turning point was probably reached when a Club Méditerranée was established at Hat Kata, followed by the construction of the more lavish Phuket Yacht Club on Hat Nai Han and Le Meridien on Karon Noi (Relax Bay). This marked an end to the decade-long cheap bungalow era, which started in the early 1970s when a 10B guesthouse was attached to a laundry on Patong Beach. The cheapies have long since been bought out and replaced by all manner of hotel and bungalow developments, some ill-conceived, others quite appealing.

The era of going for quick money regardless of the cost to the environment has passed. Most beachside resorts are nowadays looking toward long-term, sustainable practices – not all of them, but a far greater percentage than on Ko Samui, Ko Pha-Ngan, Ko Tao, and even Ko Chang (though the total number of beach places on the latter is still small enough that the total impact of negative environmental practices is so far minimal). For this long-term outlook, the Phuket visitor pays a premium in terms of somewhat higher prices overall.

On the other hand the general growth of commercialism seen along the island's main roads detracts from the island's appeal –

there seems to be a snake farm, bungee-jumping operation, gaudy billboard, half-built condo project, travel agency or tacky craft shop every half km in the southern half of the island. The island's beaches and relatively unspoiled northern interior remain its main attractions, and the provincial authorities as well as the business sector seem to recognise this.

The geography of Phuket is more varied than any other island in Thailand, and its large size has allowed microclimates to develop in different areas of the island. Check out the whole island if you have time. Don't ignore the interior of the island, which offers rice paddies, plantations of rubber, cashew nut, cacao, pineapple and coconut, as well as Phuket's last bit of island rainforest.

### Diving & Snorkelling

Although there are many, many places to dive around Thailand, Phuket is indisputably the primary centre for the Thai scuba-diving industry and one of the world's top 10 dive destinations. The island itself is ringed by good to excellent dive sites, including several small islands to the south and east – Ko Hae, Ko Raya (Noi & Yai), Ko Yao (Noi & Yai), Hin Daeng and Shark Point (a habitat for harmless leopard sharks) at the southern tip of the island. Excursions further afield to Ao Phang-Nga islands to the east, and to the world-famous Surin and Similan islands to the north-west, are also for the most part operated from Phuket.

Most Phuket diving operations are centred at Patong Beach, with a sprinkling of branch offices in town or on other beaches. Many companies stagger regularly scheduled dives throughout the week so that different dive groups don't bump into one another; for example, Santana might go to Ko Raya Yai on Monday and Shark Point Tuesday while Calypso might do Shark Point Monday and Raya Yai Tuesday, and so on. Typical one day dive trips to nearby sites such as these cost 1250B, including two dives, tanks and weights, transport, divemaster service, breakfast and lunch. Non-divers – including snorkellers – are often permitted to join such dive trips for 500 to 600B. PADI open-water certification courses cost 7200 to 7800B for four days of instruction and all equipment.

A few companies – generally the larger, more well established ones – offer extended three to seven-day trips on live-aboard dive boats, ranging from 10,000 to 20,000B, to Ko Phi Phi, Ko Similan, Ko Surin and the Burma Banks.

Most dive shops also rent the following equipment: regulator (150B a day), BCD (150B), mask, fins & snorkel (100B), wet-suit (100 to 150B).

Among the more reputable dive companies on the island are:

Andaman Divers – Patong Beach (☎ /fax 341126)
Calypso Divers – Kata-Karon Beach (☎ /fax 330869)
Dive Inn – Patong Beach (☎ 341927; fax 342453)
Fantasea Divers – Patong Beach (☎ 340088; fax 340309)
Marina Divers – Karon Beach (☎ 330272/516)
PIDC Divers – Ao Chalong (☎ 280644; fax 381219)
Santana – Patong Beach, also Kata & Karon (☎ 294220; fax 340360)
Sea Bees Submarine Diving – Ao Chalong (☎ /fax 381765)
Sea Hawk Divers – Patong Beach (☎ /fax 341179)
Siam Diving Center – Karon Beach (☎ 330936; fax 330608)
South East Asia Divers – Patong Beach (☎ 340406; fax 340608)

## Yachting

Phuket is one of South-East Asia's main yacht destinations and you'll find all manner of craft anchored along its shores, from 80-year-old wooden sloops that look like they can barely stay afloat to the latest in high-tech world motor cruisers. Marina-style facilities with year-round anchorage are available at two bays on the protected east side of the island: Laem Phrao Yacht Marina (☎ /fax 327109) at Laem Phrao at the north-east tip; and Phuket Boat Lagoon (☎ 239055; fax 239056) at Ao Sapam, about 20 km north of Phuket town on the east shore.

Phuket Boat Lagoon offers an enclosed marina with tidal channel access, serviced pontoon berths, 60 and 120 ton travel lifts, hard-stand area, laundry, coffee shop, fuel,

water, repairs and maintenance services. Laem Phrao has moorings and a jetty, workshop, sundries shop, ice, restaurant, fuel, water, showers and toilets. Construction of another marina, the Yacht Haven, has just begun next to the Laem Phra Yacht Marina and will boast 130 pontoon berths by early 1997. In season (December to April) Ao Nai Han is a popular anchorage at the southern end of the island, while Ao Chalong, on the island's south-eastern edge, offers year-round anchorage with limited facilities.

You can often travel by yacht between Phuket and Penang (Malaysia) as a paying passenger or as crew. Ask around at these marinas or at Patong Beach to see what's available. You may also find yachts going further afield, particularly to Sri Lanka. December and early January are the best months to look for them. The crossing takes about 10 to 15 days.

For information on yacht charters – both bareboat and crewed – yacht sales and yacht deliveries, contact the following:

Big A Yachting – Ao Chalong (☎ 381934; fax 381934)
Phuket Boating Association – Phuket Boat Lagoon (☎ /fax 381322)
Phuket Yacht Services – Laem Phrao Marina (☎ 224999)
South East Asia Yacht Charters – Patong Beach (☎ 340406)
Sunsail Yacht Charters – Phuket Boat Lagoon (☎ 239057; fax 238940)
Thai Marine Leisure – Patong Beach (☎ 344261; fax 344262)
Thai Yachting – Patong Beach (☎ 341153; fax 341154)

Charters aboard 32 to 44 foot yachts start at 8750B a day, while larger ones (39 to 85 foot yachts) start at 12,000B a day. Day trips usually include crew, lunch and soft drinks, plus snorkelling and fishing gear.

## Sea Canoeing

Several companies based in Phuket offer inflatable canoe tours of scenic Ao Phang-Nga; see the Ao Phang-Nga & Phang-Nga section for details.

## Cycling

Tropical Trails (☎ 282914, 248239) offers fully supported half-day and full-day 'cycle safaris' around Phuket as well as on neighbouring Ko Yao. Half-day fun rides cost 975B for adults, 575B for children, while a full-day tour is 1550/875B. The Ko Yao full-day trip costs 1950/1140B. Rates include hotel pickup (plus boat transport for Ko Yao), van support, mountain bike and equipment, a guided hike, snorkelling, 'cultural break stops', lunch, insurance and a Thai massage.

## PHUKET
อ.เมืองภูเก็ต
• ☎ (76) • pop 50,000

Centuries before Phuket began attracting sand-and-sea hedonists it was an important trade centre for Arab, Indian, Malay, Chinese and Portuguese traders who exchanged goods from the world at large for tin and rubber. Francis Light, the British colonialist who made Penang the first of the British Straits Settlements, married a native of Phuket and tried unsuccessfully to pull this island into the colonial fold as well. Although this polyglot, multi-cultural heritage has all but disappeared from most of the island, a few vestiges can be seen and experienced in the province's *amphoe meuang* (provincial capital), Phuket.

In the older town centre you'll see plenty of Sino-Portuguese architecture, characterised by ornate two-storey Chinese *haang tháew* or 'row companies', fronted by Romanesque arched porticoes with 'five-foot ways' that were a 19th century tradition in Malaysia, Singapore, Macau and Hainan Island. For a time it seemed this wonderful old architecture was all being torn down and replaced with modern structures but in recent years a preservation ethic has taken hold.

## Information

**Tourist Office** The TAT office (☎ 212213, 211036) on Phuket Rd has maps, information brochures, a list of the standard songthaew fares out to the various beaches and also the recommended charter costs for a vehicle. It is open daily from 8.30 am to 4.30 pm.

The tourist police can be reached at ☎ 212046/213.

**Foreign Consulates** Phuket has a French consulate (☎ 321199) at 89 Muu 3, Patong Beach, Kathu, and an Italian consulate (☎ 391151) at 89/2 Sakdidet Rd, Muu 7.

**Money** Several banks along Takua Pa, Phang-Nga and Phuket Rds offer exchange services and ATMs. Bank of Asia, opposite the TAT office on Phuket Rd, has an exchange window open from 8.30 am until 8 pm daily.

**Post & Communications** The GPO, housed in an architectural gem on Montri Rd, is open Monday to Friday from 8.30 am to 4.30 pm, Saturday and Sunday 9 am to noon. During much of 1995 and 1996 the GPO was closed for renovations and temporarily moved around the corner to a large modern shophouse on Phang-Nga Rd, but by the time you read this it should be back on Montri Rd.

Mail Boxes Etc (☎ 256409; fax 256411) has a branch at 168/2 Phuket Rd, almost opposite The Books. MBE rents private mail boxes, sells packaging and mailing materials and offers laminating, binding, passport photo and business card services.

The Phuket Telecommunications Centre, nearby on Phang-Nga Rd, offers Home Direct service and is open daily 8 am to midnight.

**Bookshops** Phuket has one very good bookshop, The Books, at 53-55 Phuket Rd near the TAT office. The selection of English-language reading material includes magazines, guidebooks and novels. There's a smaller branch at Robinson Ocean Plaza, off Ong Sim Phai Rd near the municipal market.

**Periodicals & Online Services** The monthly English-language *Phuket Gazette* publishes lots of info on activities, events, dining and entertainment in town as well as around the island. The same publisher issues the *Gazette*

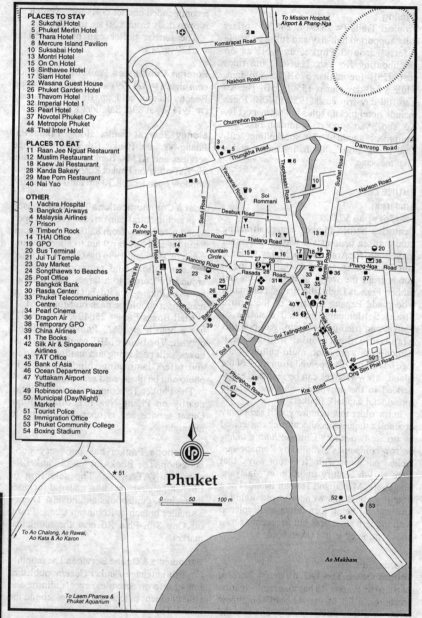

**PLACES TO STAY**
2  Sukchai Hotel
5  Phuket Merlin Hotel
6  Thara Hotel
8  Mercure Island Pavilion
10  Suksabai Hotel
13  Montri Hotel
15  On On Hotel
16  Sinthavee Hotel
17  Siam Hotel
22  Wasana Guest House
26  Phuket Garden Hotel
31  Thavorn Hotel
32  Imperial Hotel 1
35  Pearl Hotel
37  Novotel Phuket City
44  Metropole Phuket
48  Thai Inter Hotel

**PLACES TO EAT**
11  Raan Jee Nguat Restaurant
12  Muslim Restaurant
18  Kaew Jai Restaurant
28  Kanda Bakery
29  Mae Porn Restaurant
40  Nai Yao

**OTHER**
1  Vachira Hospital
3  Bangkok Airways
4  Malaysia Airlines
7  Prison
9  Timber'n Rock
14  THAI Office
19  GPO
20  Bus Terminal
21  Jui Tui Temple
23  Day Market
24  Songthaews to Beaches
25  Post Office
27  Bangkok Bank
30  Rasda Center
33  Phuket Telecommunications
     Centre
34  Pearl Cinema
36  Dragon Air
38  Temporary GPO
39  China Airlines
41  The Books
42  Silk Air & Singaporean
     Airlines
43  TAT Office
45  Bank of Asia
46  Ocean Department Store
47  Yuttakarn Airport
     Shuttle
49  Robinson Ocean Plaza
50  Municipal (Day/Night)
     Market
51  Tourist Police
52  Immigration Office
53  Phuket Community College
54  Boxing Stadium

To Mission Hospital,
Airport & Phang-Nga

Komarapat Road

Nakhon Road

Chumphon Road

Damrong  Road

Thungkha Road

Narison Road

Thepkasatri Road

Yaowarat Road

Soi
Rommani

Deebuk  Road

Satul  Road

Suthat  Road

To Ao
Patong

Krabi      Road

Thalang Road

Phang-Nga      Road

Pattana Rd

Petkasiri Rd

Fountain
Circle

Ranong Road

Rasada          Road

Takua Pa Road

Monti Road

Soi 9

Soi "Phuthon"

Bangkok Road

Phuket Road

Phunphon Road

Sol Talingchan

Ong Sim Phai Road

Kra  Road

To Ao Chalong, Ao Rawai,
Ao Kata & Ao Karon

# Phuket

0    50    100 m

Ao Makham

To Laem Phanwa &
Phuket Aquarium

SOUTHERN THAILAND

*Guide*, a 128-page listing of services and businesses on the island. Phuket Net is an Internet service (e-mail info@phuket.net or Web address http://www. phuket.net) that provides tourism and business-oriented information on the islands.

**Medical Services** Phuket's better hospitals are:

Bangkok Phuket Hospital – Yongyok Uthit Rd (☎ 254421)
Mission Hospital – Thepkasatri Rd (☎ 212386)
Phuket International Hospital – Airport Bypass Rd (☎ 249400)

Feedback we've received about these hospitals indicates that, although they're well equipped, better treatment is available in Bangkok.

### Things to See & Do
For historic **Sino-Portuguese architecture** your best bets are Thalang, Deebuk, Yaowarat, Ranong, Phang-Nga, Rasada and Krabi Rds; the most magnificent individual examples in town are the Standard Chartered Bank – Thailand's oldest foreign bank – on Phang-Nga Rd and the Thai Airways office on Ranong Rd, but there are lots of more modest buildings of interest along these streets.

Phuket's main **market** on Ranong Rd is fun to wander through and is a good place to buy Thai and Malay sarongs as well as baggy fisherman pants. A few old **Chinese temples** can be found in this area.

Walk up **Khao Rang**, sometimes called Phuket Hill, north-west of town, for a nice view of the city, jungle and sea. If, as many people say, Phuket is a corruption of the Malay word *bukit* (hill), then this is probably the hill it was named after.

### Thai Language Study
A branch of AUA (☎ 217756) at Phuket Community College, Phuket Rd, Saphan Hin, offers Thai-language instruction.

### Places to Stay – bottom end
Near the centre of town, and close to the songthaew terminal for most outlying beaches, is the *On On Hotel* (☎ 211154) at 19 Phang-Nga Rd. This hotel's old Sino-Portuguese architecture (established 1929) gives it real character, though the rooms are basically just four walls and a bed. Rates are 100B for a single with ceiling fan and shared facilities, 150/220B single/double with fan and attached bath, 250/360B with air-con. The simple *Pengman* (☎ 211486, ext 169) nearby at 69 Phang-Nga Rd, above a Chinese restaurant, costs 100B single/double for basic but quite clean rooms with ceiling fan and shared bath.

The *Thara Hotel* (☎ 216208) on Thepkasatri Rd costs 120B with fan and bath; the nearby *Suksabai Hotel* (☎ 212287) is a bit better at 120B for similar but cleaner rooms, plus air-con for 280B. The dark *Siam Hotel*, 13-15 Phuket Rd, is basically a brothel with adequate rooms with fan and bath for 150B. In the same category are the *Sukchai* (☎ 223313), 17/1 Komarapat Rd, at 120B with fan and bath, 200 to 280B with air-con, and *Taweekit* at 7/3 Chao Fa Rd which costs about the same.

*Wasana Guest House* (☎ 211754, 213385) at 159 Ranong Rd (next to the fresh food market) has clean rooms for 161B with fan and bath or 268B with air-con.

*Thai Inter Hotel* (☎ 220275) at 22 Phunphon Rd is convenient to the airport shuttle drop-off in town if you've just flown into Phuket or are trying to catch an early morning flight. Fan rooms cost 240B, air-con 300B, both with attached bath.

### Places to Stay – middle
The *Thavorn (Thawon) Hotel* (☎ 211333) at 74 Rasada Rd is a huge place consisting of an original, less expensive wing out the back and a flashier place up front. In the back wing, large rooms with ceiling fan and private bath cost 200/250B single/double, while in the front building all rooms come with TV, air-con, hot water and carpet and cost 500 to 600B. The cheaper rooms are better value. There's also a swimming pool.

## Vegetarian Festival

Phuket's most important festival is the Vegetarian Festival, which takes place during the first nine days of the ninth lunar month of the Chinese calendar. This is usually late September or October.

Basically, the festival celebrates the beginning of the month of 'Taoist Lent', when devout Chinese abstain from eating all meat and meat products. In Phuket, the festival activities are centred around five Chinese temples, with the Jui Tui temple on Ranong Rd the most important, followed by Bang Niaw and Sui Boon Tong temples. Events are also celebrated at temples in the nearby towns of Kathu (where the festival originated) and Ban Tha Reua.

The TAT office in Phuket prints a helpful schedule of events for the Vegetarian Festival each year. If you plan to attend the street processions, consider bringing earplugs to make the noise of the firecrackers more tolerable. The festival also takes place in Trang, Krabi and other Southern Thai towns.

Besides abstention from meat, the Vegetarian Festival involves various processions, temple offerings and cultural performances and culminates with incredible acts of self-mortification – walking on hot coals, climbing knife-blade ladders, piercing the skin with sharp objects and so on. Shopowners along Phuket's central streets set up altars in front of their shopfronts offering nine tiny cups of tea, incense, fruit, candles and flowers to the nine emperor gods invoked by the festival. Those participating as mediums bring the nine deities to earth for the festival by entering into a trance state and piercing their cheeks with all manner of objects – sharpened tree branches (with leaves still attached!), spears, trombones, daggers; some even hack their tongues continuously with saw or axe blades. During the street processions these mediums stop at the shopfront altars, where they pick up the offered fruit and either add it to the objects piercing their cheeks or pass it on to bystanders as a blessing. They also drink one of the nine cups of tea and grab some flowers to stick in their waistbands. The shopowners and their families stand by with their hands together in a wai gesture, out of respect for the mediums and the deities by whom they are temporarily possessed.

The entire atmosphere is one of religious frenzy, with deafening firecrackers, ritual dancing, bloody shirt fronts and so on. Oddly enough, there is no record of this kind of activity associated with Taoist Lent in China. Some historians assume that the Chinese here were somehow influenced by the Hindu festival of Thaipusam in nearby Malaysia, which features similar acts of self-mortification. The local Chinese claim, however, that the festival was started by a theatre troupe from China who stopped off in nearby Kathu around 150 years ago. The story goes that the troupe was struck seriously ill and that they decided the illness had befallen them because they had failed to propitiate the nine emperor gods of Taoism. The nine day penance they performed included self-piercing, meditation and a strict vegetarian diet. ■

The *Montri Hotel* (☎ 212936), 12/6 Montri Rd, is similar but without a swimming pool; rather unkempt rooms cost 180B with fan, 320 to 480B with air-con.

The clean and friendly *Imperial Hotel 1* (☎ 212311) at 51 Phuket Rd has good rooms for 250/300B with fan, 400/450B with air-con.

In the centre of town, at 81 Phang-Nga Rd, the renovated *Sinthavee Hotel* (☎ 212153) offers comfortable air-con rooms for 471/589B a single/double or 850/950B for deluxe rooms. All rooms come with carpet, hot water bath and refrigerators (add TV/video for deluxe); other facilities include a 24 hour coffee shop, business centre, spa and disco.

### Places to Stay – top end

The *Pearl Hotel* (☎ 211044) at 42 Montri Rd has 212 rooms from 1354B, a rooftop restaurant, fitness centre, swimming pool and so on. The *Phuket Merlin Hotel* (☎ 211866) at 158/1 Yaowarat Rd has 180 rooms for 1236B up and again there's a swimming pool and fitness centre.

The *Phuket Garden Hotel* (☎ 216900/8) on Bangkok Rd costs 1200 to 2400B with a pool and all the usual facilities.

One of the best located top-enders is the plush 248-room *Metropole Phuket* (☎ 215-050; fax 215990), right in the centre of things on Montri Rd. 'Superior' singles/ doubles cost 2400/2600B; 2800/3000B for deluxe. Facilities include two Chinese restaurants, a coffee shop, three bars, swimming pool, fitness centre, business centre and airport shuttle service. Another well located spot is the new *Mercure Island Pavilion* (☎ 210444; fax 210458) at 133 Satun Rd, where spacious, well appointed rooms go for 1413 to 2237B.

A short walk east of the Phuket Telecommunications Centre on Phang-Nga Rd is the towering 251-room *Novotel Phuket City* (☎ 233402; fax 233335), where state-of-the-art rooms start at 2900B.

## Places to Eat

**Town Centre** If there's one thing the town of Phuket is known for, it's good food – even if you're staying at the beach it's worth a trip into the city to sample authentic, Phuket-style cooking (a blend of Thai, Malay and Straits Chinese influences). Meals in the city tend to cost at least 50% less (often many times less) than meals at the beach.

One long-running local institution is *Raan Jee Nguat*, a Phuket-style restaurant run by Hokkien Chinese, across the street from the now defunct Siam Cinema on the corner of historic Yaowarat and Deebuk Rds. Jee Nguat serves Phuket's most famous dish – delicious khanŏm jiin náam yaa phukèt – Chinese noodles in a pureed fish and curry sauce, Phuket style, with fresh cucumbers, long green beans and other fresh vegetables on the side – for under 15B. Also good are khài plaa mòk, a Phuket version of hàw mòk (eggs, fish and curry paste steamed in banana leaves), and the kari mai fan, similar to Malaysian laksa, but using rice noodles. The curries are highly esteemed as well. Don't leave it too late, though; they open early in the morning but close around 2 pm.

Very popular with Thais and farangs alike, and deservedly so, is the *Mae Porn*, a restaurant on the corner of Phang-Nga Rd and Soi Pradit, close to the On On and Sinthavee hotels. There's an air-con room as well as outdoor tables. They sell curries, seafood, fruit shakes – you name it and Mae Porn has it – all at very reasonable prices. Another popular spot in town is *Kanda Bakery* on Rasada Rd just south of the Bangkok Bank. It's open early in the morning with fresh-baked whole-wheat bread, baguettes, croissants, cakes and real brewed coffee; they also serve a variety of khâo tôm specialities any time of day.

Another good local discovery is the simple Muslim restaurant on the corner of Thepkasatri and Thalang Rds – look for the star and crescent. This friendly family-run place serves delicious and inexpensive mátsaman kài (chicken-potato curry), roti kaeng (flatbread and curry – in the morning only) and khâo mòk kài (chicken biryani – usually gone by 1 pm).

Fried rice and Thai pastry fans shouldn't miss *Kaew Jai* (no English sign), at 151 Phang-Nga Rd between Phuket and Montri Rds. More basic than Kanda Bakery, this is the Thai idea of pastry heaven – especially the custard cake and cashew cake – even if the service is a bit surly. Among the highly varied fried rice dishes on hand are khâo phàt náam phrík phão (fried rice with roasted chilli paste), khâo phàt khreûang kaeng (rice fried in curry paste) and khâo phàt bai kà-phrao (with holy basil), each with a choice of chicken, pork, crab, shrimp or squid. In the same vicinity on Phang-Nga Rd are two or three other inexpensive Phuket-style ráan khâo kaeng (rice-and-curry shops), including the *Aik Ocha*; try the tasty cashew-nut curry.

Venerable *Nai Yao* is still hanging on in an old wooden building with a tin roof near the Honda dealer on Phuket Rd. It features an excellent, inexpensive seafood menu (bilingual), cold beer and, at night, tables on the sidewalk. The house speciality is the unique and highly recommended tôm yam hâeng (dry tôm yam), which can be ordered with chicken, shrimp or squid.

Another Phuket institution, perfect for an intimate night out, is *Krajok Sii* (☎ 217903), in an old shophouse on Takua Pa Rd just south of Phang-Nga Rd on the west side of street. It's hard to spot as there's no romanised sign; look for the coloured glass transom (the restaurant's name means 'coloured glass') over the door. There aren't more than a dozen tables in the tastefully decorated dining room, but it's worth waiting for a table as the kitchen specialises in home-made Phuket cuisine, including delicious hàw mòk thaleh (steamed seafood curry), green mango salad, shrimp toast and other delights. Prices are reasonable, but portions are small as befits traditional Thai cooking.

The 24 hour coffee shop at the *Sinthavee Hotel* has cheap lunch specials and late-night khâo tôm service. For a splurge, the dim sum service (11 am to 2 pm) at the Hotel Metropole's *Fortuna Pavilion* is an excellent choice. Their popular Thai buffet lunch is good for 130B, but come early.

*Kaw Yam (Khao Yam)*, on Thungkha Rd in front of the Phuket Merlin, has a clean, middle-class, indoor-outdoor atmosphere enjoyed by local office workers for breakfast and lunch. The kitchen serves very well prepared khâo yam, the Southern Thai rice salad, as well as khanŏm jiin and many other Phuket specialities. Prices are inexpensive to moderate. Just as good for khanŏm jiin but cheaper is *Khwan Khanom Jiin* (no English sign) next door.

The tourist-oriented Rasda Center, a shopping complex off Rasada Rd, has several small, up-market eating places like *Krua Thai* (fancy Thai cuisine) and *Le Café* (good coffees). There's also a 24 hour supermarket in the complex, part of Phuket Shopping Centre.

There's a *KFC* in the Robinson Ocean Plaza off Ong Sim Phai Rd towards the south end of town. Next door to the shopping complex is Phuket's municipal market. Around three sides of this market you'll find an inexpensive night market. The popular smaller night market that used to be on Phuket Rd near Nai Yao and the TAT office is now defunct.

**Khao Rang (Phuket Hotel)** *Thungkha Kafae* is an outdoor restaurant at the top of the hill with a very pleasant atmosphere and good food. Try the tôm khàa kài (chicken coconut soup) or khài jiaw hãwy naang rom (oyster omelette).

**Ao Chalong** Just past Wat Chalong (on the left past the five-road intersection) is *Kan Aeng* (☎ 381323), a good fresh seafood place

that used to sit on a pier over the bay itself. Now housed in an enclosed air-con restaurant (open-air dining is still available as well), it still sets a standard for Phuket seafood though prices have risen considerably. You order by weight, choosing from squid, oysters, cockles, crab, mussels and several kinds of fish, and then specify the method of cooking, whether grilled (phão), steamed (nêung), fried (thâwt), parboiled (lûak – for squid), or in soup (tôm yam).

### Entertainment
The *Pearl Cinema*, on the corner of Phang-Nga and Montri Rds near the Pearl Hotel, occasionally shows English-language films. The *Alliance Française* (☎ 222988), at 3 Soi 1, Pattana Rd, shows French films (subtitled in English) weekly. They also have a TV with up-to-date news broadcasts and a library.

The major hotels have discos and/or karaoke clubs. The *Timber 'n Rock*, on the eastern side of Yaowarat Rd just south of Thungkha Rd, is a well run pub with an attractive woodsy decor, lots of Phuket and Thai food and live music after 9 pm. This is perhaps the only non-hotel bar in town with cocktails.

Traditional Thai massage is available at *Green Leaf Thai Style Massage* (☎ 211083), 206/1-2 Phuket Rd. Municipal law allows only one modern massage parlour to operate – you'll find it in the Pearl Hotel.

### Things to Buy
Although there are loads of souvenir shops and clothing boutiques surrounding the beach resorts of Patong, Kata and Karon, the best shopping bargains on the island are found in the provincial capital. There are two main markets, one off the south side of Ranong Rd near the centre of town, and a second off the north side of Ong Sim Phai Rd a bit south-east of town centre. The Ranong Rd market traces its history back to the days when pirates, Indians, Chinese, Malays and Europeans traded in Phuket and offers a wide variety of sarongs and fabrics from Thailand, Malaysia, Indonesia and India.

You'll also find inexpensive clothing and crafts here.

At the newer Ong Sim Phai Rd Market the focus is more on fresh produce. Adjacent to the market is the large Robinson Ocean Plaza, which contains Robinson Department Store as well as smaller shops with moderately priced clothing and housewares. Along Yaowarat Rd between Phang-Nga and Thaland Rds are a number of Indian-run tailor and fabric shops, while Chinese gold shops are lined up along Ranong Rd opposite the Ranong Rd Market. Other shopping venues include the small Rasda Center/Phuket Shopping Centre on Rasada Rd.

### Getting There & Away
**Air** THAI operates nearly a dozen daily flights from Bangkok for 2000B one way. The flight takes just over an hour, except for departures which have a half-hour stop-over in Surat Thani, Hat Yai or Nakhon Si Thammarat. There are also regular flights to and from Hat Yai (780B), Narathiwat (990B), Nakhon Si Thammarat (640B) and Surat Thani (475B).

THAI flies between Phuket and several international destinations, including Penang, Langkawi, Kuala Lumpur, Singapore, Hong Kong, Taipei and Sydney. Other international airlines with offices in Phuket are: Malaysia Airlines (☎ 216675), 1/8-9 Thungkha Rd; Silk Air (☎ 213891), 95/20 Montri Rd; Singapore Airlines (same offices as Silk Air); Dragonair (☎ 217300), 37/52 Montri Rd; and China Airlines (☎ 223939), Bangkok Rd.

THAI has two Phuket offices: one at 78 Ranong Rd (☎ 211195) and the other at 41/33 Montri Rd (☎ 212880).

Bangkok Airways (☎ 225033) flies between Ko Samui and Phuket daily for 1330B each way. Their office is 158/2-3 Yaowarat Rd.

Southern Helicopter Service (☎ 327111; fax 327113) at the airport charters a Kawasaki BK117 helicopter, which carries up to seven passengers, for 48,000B per hour. The service covers all of Phuket and Ao Phang-Nga, including Ko Phi Phi. Southern Flying Group (☎ 247237) does small aeroplane charters.

**Bus** From Bangkok, one 1st class air-con and one VIP bus leave the Southern Bus Terminal at 6.50 pm for 368 and 570B respectively. The trip takes 13 to 14 hours. Ordinary buses leave 10 times a day from 7.30 am until 10.30 pm for 210B; these buses take around 15 hours.

Several private tour buses run from Bangkok to Phuket regularly with fares of 378B one way or 700B return. Most have one bus a day which leaves at 6 or 7 pm. The ride along the west coast between Ranong and Phuket can be hair-raising if you are awake, so it is fortunate that this part of the trip takes place during the wee hours of the morning.

From Phuket, most tour buses to Bangkok leave at 3 pm. Several agencies have their offices on Rasada and Phang-Nga Rds in the city's centre. The main bus terminal for government buses is off the north side of Phang-Nga Rd between the Phuket Telecommunications Centre and the Novotel Phuket City.

Fares and trip durations for bus trips to and from Phuket's government terminal include:

| Destination | Fare | Hours |
| --- | --- | --- |
| Hat Yai | 112B | 8 |
| (air-con) | 192 to 202B | 7 |
| Krabi | 47B | 4½ |
| (air-con) | 85B | 4 |
| Nakhon Si Thammarat | 80 to 93B | 8 |
| (air-con) | 129B | |
| Phang-Nga | 26B | 2½ |
| (air-con) | 50B | 1½ |
| Surat Thani | 77B | 6 |
| (air-con) | 139B | |
| Takua Pa | 38B | 3 |
| Trang | 78B | 6 |
| (air-con) | 140B | 5 |

**Taxi & Minivan** There are share taxis between Phuket and other provincial capitals in the south; taxi fares are generally double the fare of an ordinary bus (Krabi 80B, Surat Thani 150B, Trang 120B). The taxi stand for Nakhon Si Thammarat, Surat Thani, Krabi, Trang and Hat Yai is on Phang-Nga Rd, near the Pearl Cinema.

Some companies run air-con minivans (rot tûu) with through tickets to Ko Samui from Phuket – part of a minivan circuit that covers Phuket, Surat, Krabi and Ranong. As in share taxis, fares are about double the public bus fares. You can also get vans to Hat Yai (220B), Krabi (150B), Penang (550B), Kuala Lumpur (650B) and Singapore (700B). Vans can be booked at the same intersection as the share taxis.

**Boat**  A ferry service between Phuket and Malaysia's Langkawi Island has come and gone several times. When running it usually costs around 800B; enquire at Songserm Travel (☎ 216820), 64/2 Rasda Center, Rasada Rd.

## Getting Around
**The Airport**  A company called Yuttakarn runs an airport shuttle bus service between the town and airport (29 km) for 70B per person. The drop-off point in town is a bit out of the way on a soi off Phunphon Rd. There's a similar service to Patong, Kata or Karon beaches for 100B.

Taxis ask 300B for the trip from the airport to the city, 400B to the beaches; in the reverse direction you should be able to negotiate a fare of 150 to 200B.

**Songthaew**  Large bus-size songthaews run regularly from Ranong Rd near the market to the various Phuket beaches for 10 to 30B per person – see the following Phuket Beaches section for details. Beware of tales about the tourist office being five km away, or that the only way to reach the beaches is by taxi, or even that you'll need a taxi to get from the bus station to the town centre (the bus station is more or less *in* the town centre). Officially beach songthaews run from 7 am to 5 pm; after that time you must charter your own mini-songthaew to the beaches.

Smaller songthaews or tuk-tuks around town cost a standard 7B, but some travellers have reported that at times drivers have insisted on 10B.

**Car**  Several agencies in town rent Suzuki jeeps for 900B per day, including insurance. If you rent for a week or more you can get the price down to 800B per day. In the centre

of town your best choice is Pure Car Rent (☎ 211002) at 75 Rasada Rd. Avis charges a bit more (around 1100B a day) but has outlets around the island at Le Meridien, Phuket Arcadia, Dusit Laguna, Phuket Cabana, Club Med, Phuket Island Resort and the airport. Hertz is similar and has branches at the airport, Banyan Tree Resort and Holiday Inn.

**Motorcycle**  Motorcycle taxis around town are 10B. You can hire motorcycles (usually 100cc Japanese bikes) in Phuket along Rasada Rd between Phuket and Yaowarat Rds or from various places at the beaches. Costs are in the 150 to 200B per day range. Take care when riding a bike – if you have an accident you're unlikely to find that medical attention is up to international standards. People who ride around in shorts and T-shirt and a pair of thongs are asking for trouble. A minor spill whilst wearing reasonable clothes would leave you bruised and shaken, but for somebody clad in shorts it could result in enough skin loss to end your travels right there.

Bigger bikes (over 125cc) can be rented at a couple of shops at Patong and Karon.

## AROUND THE ISLAND
### Ko Sire
This island, four km east of the capital and separated from the main island by a canal, is known for its chao náam (sea gypsy) village and a hill-top reclining Buddha.

There are a couple of places to stay on Ko Sire, including *Madam Puye Bungalow* for 200B and *Siray Resort* for 300 to 500B.

### Laem Phanwa
A classic Sino-Portuguese mansion called **Phanwa House**, on the grounds of the Cape Panwa Sheraton Resort on Laem Phanwa, is open to the public. The mansion has a library and a collection of antique furniture and art; high tea is served daily on the veranda.

At the tip of the cape, **Phuket Aquarium & Marine Biological Research Center** displays a varied collection of tropical fish. Admission is 20B.

On **Laem Phanwa** by itself is the very plush *Cape Panwa Hotel* (☎ (76) 391123; fax 391177; ☎ (2) 233-3433 in Bangkok), where luxury digs start at 3237B, about half that from April to November.

## Khao Phra Taew Royal Wildlife & Forest Reserve

This mountain range in the northern interior of the island protects 2333 hectares of virgin island rainforest. There are some nice jungle hikes in this reserve, along with a couple of waterfalls, Ton Sai and Bang Pae. The falls are best seen in the rainy season between June and November. Because of its royal status, the reserve is better protected than the average Thai national park.

Near Bang Pae Falls, the Phuket Gibbon Rehabilitation Centre (☎ (76) 381065 or (01) 212-7824) is open to the public daily 10 am to 4 pm. Financed by donations, the centre adopts gibbons which have been kept in captivity and re-introduces them to the wild.

To get to Khao Phra Taew from the provincial capital, take Thepkasatri Rd north about 20 km to the district of Thalang, and turn right at the intersection for Ton Sai Waterfall three km down the road.

Also in Thalang district, just north of the crossroads near Thalang village, is **Wat Phra Thong**, Phuket's 'Temple of the Gold Buddha'. The image is half buried – those who have tried to excavate it have met with unfortunate consequences. Parts of the movie *Good Morning Vietnam* were filmed in Thalang.

## PHUKET BEACHES & NEARBY ISLANDS
• ☎ (76)

Phuket beach accommodation has come a long way since 1977 when I first stayed at Kata and Nai Han in simple thatched-roof huts for 10B a night. Nowadays 80 or 100B is rock-bottom. Any remaining accommodation costing under 300B will probably be upgraded within the next couple of years to a minimum of 500B as Phuket completes the final stages of moving from rustic beach hideaway to full-fledged international resort.

**Warning**
All of the western Phuket beaches, including Surin, Laem Singh and Kamala, have strong riptides during the monsoons. Take care when swimming, or don't go in the water at all if you're not a strong swimmer.

## Patong
ป่าตอง
Directly west of Phuket, Patong is a large curved beach around Ao Patong. Over the last 10 years, Hat Patong has been rapidly turning into another Pattaya in all respects. It is now a strip of hotels, up-market bungalows, German restaurants, expensive seafood places, beer bars, nightclubs and coffee houses. Ironically, though this began as Phuket's most expensive beach, the prices are stabilising as the local accommodation market has become saturated with over 80 places to stay. As it becomes funkier and rowdier, Patong is rapidly becoming the cheapest beach on the island for accommodation.

**Information** Patong has many foreign-exchange booths, plus its own post and telephone office off Soi Perm Pong and Thawiwong Rd.

**Dive Shops** Patong is the diving centre of the island. See Diving & Snorkelling at the beginning of the Phuket Province section for a list of established dive shops.

**Boat Trips** Several different companies on Patong do one day cruises to nearby islands. For excursions to the Similan and Surin islands off the Andaman coast of Phang-Nga Province, see the sections on those islands under the Ranong Province section earlier in this chapter.

**Boat Charter** Motor yachts, sailboats and catamarans can sometimes be chartered with or without crew. Read the earlier Yachting section or check with dive shops around Patong to find out who has what.

SOUTHERN THAILAND

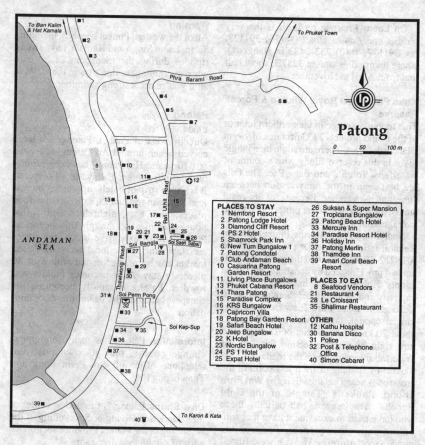

Patong

0    50    100 m

**PLACES TO STAY**
1 Nemtong Resort
2 Patong Lodge Hotel
3 Diamond Cliff Resort
4 PS 2 Hotel
5 Shamrock Park Inn
6 New Tum Bungalow 1
7 Patong Condotel
9 Club Andaman Beach
10 Casuarina Patong
   Garden Resort
11 Living Place Bungalows
13 Phuket Cabana Resort
14 Thara Patong
15 Paradise Complex
16 KRS Bungalow
17 Capricorn Villa
18 Patong Bay Garden Resort
19 Safari Beach Hotel
20 Jeep Bungalow
22 K Hotel
23 Nordic Bungalow
24 PS 1 Hotel
25 Expat Hotel

26 Suksan & Super Mansion
27 Tropicana Bungalow
29 Patong Beach Hotel
33 Mercure Inn
34 Paradise Resort Hotel
36 Holiday Inn
37 Patong Merlin
38 Thamdee Inn
39 Amari Coral Beach
   Resort

**PLACES TO EAT**
8 Seafood Vendors
21 Restaurant 4
28 Le Croissant
35 Shalimar Restaurant

**OTHER**
12 Kathu Hospital
30 Banana Disco
31 Police
32 Post & Telephone
   Office
40 Simon Cabaret

**Hash House Harriers** Phuket's chapter of the running-and-drinking HHH meets regularly at the Expat Bar on Bangla Rd. Hashes (foot races) are held on Saturday afternoons; all interested people are welcome to participate.

**Places to Stay – bottom end** Rates on Patong vary according to season. In the high season (December to March, and August) you'll be doing very well to find something under 300B a night. On the beach there is nothing under 500B, but on and off Rat Uthit Rd, especially in the Paradise Complex and

along Soi Saen Sabai, there are several non-descript guesthouses with rooms for around 250B. During off months some of the 400B places will drop as low as 200B or even 100B, but that's about it. Most of the bungalows of yore have been replaced by tacky modern apartment buildings, often with faulty plumbing. Bottom-end places usually come with fan and shared bath; more expensive rooms in this category will have a private bath and perhaps air-con. During the rainy season, May to November, you may be able to knock about 100B off rates for the following hotels.

*Asia Guest House* – Paradise Complex (☎ 340962); 350 to 600B

*Best Guest House* – Paradise Complex (☎ 340958); 250B

*Boomerang Cafe & Inn* – Rat Uthit Rd; 250 to 600B

*Capricorn Villa* – Rat Uthit Rd (☎ 340390); 200 to 700B

*Charlis Guesthouse* – Soi Saen Sabai (☎ 341216); 350B

*Club Oasis* – Thawiwong Rd (☎ 293076); 250 to 500B

*Duangjit Villas* – Thawiwong Rd (☎ 340778); 300 to 700B

*888 Inn* – Paradise Complex (☎ 341306); 400 to 700B

*Jeep Bungalow* – Rat Uthit Rd (☎ 340100); 300B

*K Hotel* – Rat Uthit Rd (☎ 340833; fax 340124); 400 to 800B

*PS II* – Rat Uthit Rd (☎ 342207/8); 250 to 650B

*Shamrock Park Inn* – Rat Uthit Rd (☎ 340991); 450B

*Suksan Mansion* – Soi Saen Sabai; 350B

*Super Mansion* – Soi Saen Sabai; 300B with fan and 400B with air-con

**Places to Stay – middle** The middle range at Patong Beach is roughly 500 to 1000B, which always includes air-con and private bath; the more expensive ones will have hot water showers, lower priced ones cold water only. Prices in this category can usually be negotiated downwards 100 to 200B during the rainy season.

*Andaman Resortel* – Soi Saen Sabai (☎ 341516; fax 340847); 800 to 1000B

*Casa Summer Breeze* – Soi Saen Sabai (☎ 340464; fax 340493); 600 to 800B

*Coconut Village Resort* – Thawiwong Rd (☎ 340161; fax 340144); from 1000B

*Cosmos Inn* – Soi Kep-Sup (☎ /fax 292069); 500 to 800B

*Expat Hotel* – (☎ /fax 340300); 490 to 690B

*KRS Bungalow* – Thawiwong Rd (☎ 340938; fax 340322); 350 to 600B

*The Living Place* – Sawatdirak Rd (☎ /fax 340121); 400 to 800B

*Neptuna Hotel* – Thawiwong Rd (☎ 340824; fax 340627); 750 to 1400B

*Nerntong Resort* – Hat Kalim (☎ 340572; fax 340571); from 620B

*New Tum Bungalow 1* – Rat Uthit Rd (☎ 340159); 300 to 750B

*Nordic Bungalow* – Soi Bangla (☎ 340284); 350 to 750B

*PS I* – Rat Uthit Rd (☎ 340184); 500 to 700B

*Paradise Resort Hotel* – Thawiwong Rd (☎ 340172); 550B

*Patong Bed & Breakfast* – Bangla Rd (☎ 340819; fax 340818); 500 to 1500B

*Safari Beach Hotel* – Thawiwong Rd (☎ 341170); from 800B

*Swiss Garden Bungalow* – 750B

*Thamdee Inn* – (☎ 340452); 650 to 950B

*Tropicana Bungalow* – (☎ 340204; fax 340206); 500 to 1000B

The *Sky Inn* (☎ 342486) on the 9th floor of the Patong Condotel, caters to a primarily gay clientele and costs 900 to 1000B in high season, as low as 500B during the rainy season.

**Places to Stay – top end** At the lower end of the top price range, roughly around 2000 to 3000B, you'll find a number of all air-con places with swimming pools, modest room service, phones and most of the other amenities desired by the average mainstream visitor and package tourist.

*Beach Resortel* – (☎ 340544; fax 340848); 1200 to 2500B

*Casuarina Patong Garden Resort* – towards the north end of Thawiwong Rd (☎ /fax 340123); 1800 to 3000B

*Mercure Inn Patong Beach* – 89/71 Thawiwong Rd (☎ 340328; fax 340330); 1766 to 2590B

*Patong Beach Hotel* – (☎ 340301; fax 340541); from 2119B

*Thara Patong* – (☎ 340135; fax 340446); 1035 to 2000B

*Patong Bay Garden Resort* – (☎ 340297/8; fax 340560); from 1710B

*Patong Beach Bungalow* – (☎ 340117; fax 340213); bungalows for 1500 to 3500B

*Patong Merlin Hotel* – south end of Thawiwong Rd (☎ 340037; fax 340394); 1500 to 3500B

*Patong Villa* – (☎ 340132; fax 340133); 1000 to 2000B*Patong Resort* – (☎ 340551; fax 340189); from 1391B

Moving up a couple of notches to places with true world-class standards, rates start at 3000B and reach epic proportions for large suites with the best bay views. Many top-end places add a 500 to 700B peak season surcharge between late December and mid-January.

*Amari Coral Beach Resort* – (☎ 340106; fax 340115); 3000B from 1 November to 31 March, 1815/1935B single/double the remainder of the year – add 500B for superior rooms, 2500B for suitesClub Andaman Beach – 77/1 Thawiwong Rd (☎ 340530; fax 340527); bungalows from 3708B

*Diamond Cliff Resort* – Kalim Beach (☎ 340501; fax 340507); from 3766B

*Holiday Inn Resort Phuket* – (☎ 340608/9; fax 340435); from 3200B

*Kalim Guest House* – Kalim Beach (☎ 340353; fax 340701); 1800 to 2200B

*Patong Lodge Hotel* – Kalim Beach (☎ 340286; fax 340287); 1600 to 1800B

*Phuket Cabana Resort* – (☎ 340138; fax 340178); 2340 to 13,000B

*Thavorn Palm Beach Hotel* – northern Patong (☎ 340034); 2400 to 4500B

**Places to Eat** Patong has stacks of restaurants, some of them quite good. The seafood restaurants are concentrated along Bangla Rd; *Restaurant 4* is the best priced and is popular with Thais. Opposite Casuarina Patong Garden Resort on the beach is a string of inexpensive seafood vendors who provide umbrellas and sling chairs for beach dining. For inexpensive noodle and rice vendors, check the soi near The Living Place.

Around the intersection of Rat Uthit Rd and Bangla Rd are a few inexpensive Thai and farang cafes worth trying. *Le Croissant*, on Bangla Rd, carries French pastries, French wines, sandwiches, salads, baguettes and imported cheeses. A couple of sois south, *Viva Mexico* does Mexican food.

Two OK Indian restaurants, the *Tandoor* and *Shalimar*, can be found on Soi Kep-Sup near the Cosmos Inn.

Every Wednesday and Friday evening from 7 to 10 pm the *Merlin Hotel* serves a buffet of French, Italian, German, Thai and Chinese food – accompanied by a traditional Thai dance performance – for less than 400B per person.

**Entertainment** There are many bars around town, as well as a few cabarets and discos. *Banana Discotheque* at 96 Thawiwong Rd is still one of the more popular dance clubs, while *Rock Hard* on the corner of Bangla and Rat Uthit Rds is one of the larger and more

popular nightclub/bars. If you like transvestite shows, check out the *Simon Cabaret* at 100/6-8 Muu 4.

**Things to Buy** A string of shops and stalls along the central part of Thawiwong Rd sell clothing, silk, jewellery and souvenirs from all over Thailand. Prices are higher than average.

**Getting There & Around** Songthaews to Patong from Phuket leave from Ranong Rd, near the day market and fountain circle; the fare is 15B. The after-hours charter fare is 130B.

Tuk-tuks circulate Patong for 5 to 7B per ride. Patong Big Bike on Rat Uthit Rd rents 250cc to 750cc bikes.

### Karon
กะรน

Karon is a long, gently curving beach with small sand dunes and a few palms and casuarina trees. Some insist on calling it two beaches: Karon Yai and Karon Noi. Karon Noi, also known as Relax Bay, can only be reached from Hat Patong and is completely monopolised by Le Meridien Hotel. The main section of Karon now features a paved promenade with streetlights, and the entire area has blended with Hat Kata to the south to produce a self-contained village inhabited by a mixture of tourists, seasonal residents and year-rounders. It is still a fairly peaceful beach where a few fisherfolk cast nets, and where you can buy fresh seafood from their boats, though the rice fields between the beach and the surrounding hills have been abandoned or filled with high-rise hotels.

**Places to Stay** Karon is lined with multistorey inns and deluxe bungalows, along with a dwindling number of places with rooms or huts for under 400B. During the low season – May to November – you can often get a 400B room for as low as 150B, a 1000B room for 500B, and a 2000B room for 800 to 1000B. See the Kata Getting There & Away section for details on transport to Karon.

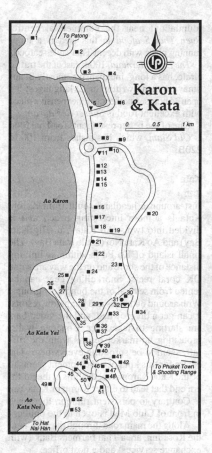

**Karon & Kata**

*To Patong*

0    0.5    1 km

Ao Karon

Ao Kata Yai

*To Phuket Town & Shooting Range*

Ao Kata Noi

*To Hat Nai Han*

**PLACES TO STAY**

1  Le Meridien
2  Thepsomboon Inn
3  Felix Karon Swissotel
4  Lume & Yai Bungalows
6  Phuket Ocean Resort
7  Phuket Golden Sand Inn
8  The Islandia Travelodge
9  Karon Guest House
10  Crystal Beach Hotel
12  My Friend & Karon Beach
     Front Pension
13  South Sea Resort
14  Karon Villa
15  Karon Royal Wing
16  Karon Seaview
     Bungalow
17  Phuket Arcadia
18  Thavorn Palm Beach
19  Karon Inn
20  Karon Village
22  Phuket Island View
23  Happy Hut
24  Kata Tropicana
25  Ruam Thep Inn
26  Laem Sai Village
27  Marina Cottages
28  Fantasy Hill
30  Lucky Guest House &
     Charlie's Guest House
33  Rose Inn
34  Bougainville Terrace
     House
35  Peach Hill Hotel
36  Smile Inn
37  Dome Bungalow
38  Club Med
40  Kata Sanuk Village
41  Sea Bees Bungalow
42  Bell Guest House
43  Kata Beach Resort
44  The Boathouse
45  Kata Delight
46  Friendship Bungalow
47  Sea Wind Hotel
48  Cool Breeze
49  Kata Thani Amari
     Resort
51  Pop Cottage
52  Kata Noi Riviera
53  Mountain Beach
     Resort

**PLACES TO EAT**

5  Seafood Restaurants
11  Ruen Thai Seafood
29  Kampong-Kata Hill
39  Coconut Garden
50  Islander's

**OTHER**

21  Maxim Supermarket
31  Good Earth
32  Post Office

Most of the places under 700B are located well off the beach, often on small hillocks to the east of the main road. On the north of the headland straddling Karon and Kata is the *Kata Tropicana* (☎ /fax 330408), with well maintained bungalows for 350 (150B in the low season) to 800B. *Happy Hut* (☎ 330230) next door has clean 150 to 250B bungalows; both of these are well off the beach, though. At the northern end of the beach, bungalows at *Lume & Yai* (☎ /fax 396096) cost 300 to 500B.

In the commercial centre of Karon, near the roundabout, quiet *Karon Seaview Bungalow*

(☎ 396912) offers OK concrete duplexes and row houses for 200 to 400B. On the main road away from the beach is the *Crystal Beach Hotel* (☎ 396580/5); it's good value at 300 to 400B for air-con rooms. Farther south and nearer the beach is the popular and friendly *My Friend Bungalow* (☎ 396344), with 45 rooms for 150 to 400B; the cafe out front is a plus. *Fantasy Hill Bungalow* (☎ 330106), farther south still on a small hill off the main road, has good budget bungalows for 150 to 300B.

In the mid-range (averaging 500B and up) are the *Karon Village* (☎ 381431), 600 to 800B; *Karon Guest House* (☎ 396860; fax 396117), 300 to 700B; *Phuket Ocean Resort* (☎ 396599; fax 396470), 1150 to 1250B; *Karon Beach Front Pension* (☎ 396569), 500 to 700B; and *Ruam Thep Inn* (☎ (01) 723-0231), 350 to 800B.

The remaining places on Karon are new resort-type hotels – which have nearly tripled in number over the last two years – with rooms starting at 1000B or above, with air-con, swimming pools etc. Prices at most places have come down a bit over the last two years due to competition.

Among the top end are:

*Felix Karon Swissotel* – (☎ 396666; fax 396853); 81 rooms, from 2072B
*The Islandia Travelodge Resort* – (☎ 396200; fax 396491); 128 rooms, 2000 to 4500B
*Karon Beach Resort* – (☎ 330006; fax 330529); 81 rooms, 2010 to 3510B
*Karon Inn* – (☎ 396519; fax 330529); 100 rooms, 1150 to 2150B
*Karon Villa & Karon Royal Wing* – (☎ 396139; fax 396122); 324 rooms, from 2707B
*Le Meridien Hotel* – (☎ 340480; fax 340479); 470 rooms, from 3767B
*Phuket Arcadia Hotel* – (☎ 396038; fax 396136); 225 rooms, from 3531B
*Phuket Golden Sand Inn* – (☎ 396493; fax 396117); 95 rooms, 500 to 1200B
*Phuket Island View* – (☎ 396452; fax 396632); 81 rooms, 1500B
*South Sea Resort* – (☎ 396611; fax 396618); 100 rooms, from 3472B
*Thavorn Palm Beach Hotel* – (☎ 396090; fax 396555); 210 rooms, 1700 to 4473B

**Places to Eat** As usual, almost every place to stay provides some food. The cheapest Thai and seafood places to eat are off the roundabout near the commercial centre. *Ruen Thai Seafood* in this area is a long-running place with decent Thai-style seafood.

*The Little Mermaid*, 100m east of the traffic circle, has a long, inexpensive, mostly Scandinavian menu written in 12 languages; it's open 24 hours. Another cosy inexpensive place with excellent food is *Sunset Restaurant*.

One of the better restaurants for Thai food is *Old Siam*, which has dishes from 100 to 220B.

## Kata

กะตะ

Just around a headland south from Karon, Kata is a more interesting beach and is divided into two – Ao Kata Yai (Big Kata Bay) and Ao Kata Noi (Little Kata Bay). The small island of Ko Pu is within swimming distance of the shore and on the way are some OK coral reefs. Snorkelling gear can be rented from several of the bungalow groups. With around 30 hotels and bungalow resorts, it can get a bit crowded, and the video bars are starting to take over. Concrete walls, protecting up-market resorts from the riff-raff, seem to be sprouting everywhere. The centre for this kind of development seems to be the Kata-Karon area, the hills at the northern end that lead to either Karon or Kata Yai.

Contrary to persistent rumour, the beach in front of Club Med is open to the public.

Along the main road through the area, near the Rose Inn, are a Thai Farmers Bank (with exchange services) and a post office.

**Places to Stay** Bungalow rates have really gone up in Kata in recent years and are now a bit more expensive than at Karon. The crowd of 34 places to stay ranges from 100 to 200B at *Bell Guest House*, quite a distance back from the beach toward the south end of Kata Yai, to around 4000B at the classy *Boathouse Inn*, just a step above the Club Méditerranée on Kata Yai. In general the less expensive places tend to be off the beach between Kata Yai (north) and Kata Noi (south) or well off the beach on the road to the island interior.

*Friendship Bungalow* (☎ 330499), a popular place off the beach at the headland between Kata Yai and Kata Noi, is 350 to 700B. Rooms at the *Cool Breeze* (☎ 330484) in Kata Noi start at 150B (certain huts only; others with toilet and shower are more expensive). *Coastline Bungalow* (☎ 330498), just down from the Cool Breeze, has large, two-storey brick cottages for a mere 350B, all with private bath. Two new budget apartment-style places worth checking out – both basic but clean and friendly – are *Lucky Guest House* at 250 to 350B and *Charlie's Guest House* (☎ 330855) at 200 to 280B; both are found toward the back road that parallels the beach, north-east of Rose Inn and Good Earth.

A sprinkling of other spots starting at under 500B include *Kata Noi Riviera* (☎ 330726), 300 to 600B; *Kata Sanuk Village* (☎ 330476), 200 to 450B; *Dome Bungalow* (☎ 330620), 200 to 500B; *P & T Kata House* (☎ 33151), 200 to 300B; *Sea Bees* (☎ (01) 723-1070), 250 to 350B; and *Rose Inn* (☎ 330135; fax 3830591), 250 to 500B. All of the bungalows will give discounts during the low season from May to October.

Recommended medium-range places (all air-con) in Kata are *Peach Hill Hotel* (☎ 330-603; fax 330895), in a nice setting with a pool from 350 to 800B; and *Smile Inn* (☎ 330926; fax 330925), a clean, friendly place with a nice open-air cafe and air-con rooms with hot water showers for 700B (800B including breakfast). Other mid-priced lodgings are available at *Pop Cottage* (☎ 330794), from 300 to 800B; *Flamingo* (☎ 330776), 350 to 700B; *Chao Kheun Inn* (☎ 330403), 750 to 1500B; and *Kata Garden Resort* (☎ 330627; fax 330446), 500 to 1300B.

Moving up in price a bit, one of the more exemplary places at the lower end of the top end is the long-running *Marina Cottage* (☎ 330517; fax 330516), a medium-scale, low-rise, low-density place on shady, palm-studded grounds near the beach. Marina Cottage doesn't accept tour groups and takes reservations only through selected travel agents, yet manages to keep rates for its comfortable, well designed Thai-style bungalows in the 1000 to 3000B range.

The palatial, 202-room *Kata Thani Amari Resort* (☎ 330417; fax 330426) on the beach at Kata Noi has up-market rooms and bungalows on nicely landscaped grounds for 2000 to 4200B.

*The Boathouse* (☎ 330557; fax 330561; ☎ (2) 438-1123 in Bangkok), the brainchild of architect and Phuket resident ML Tri Devakul, is a 36-room boutique resort that manages to stay full year-round without resorting to off-season rates. In spite of rather ordinary-looking if capacious rooms, the hotel hosts a steady influx of Thai politicos, pop stars, artists, celebrity authors (the hotel hosts periodic poetry/fiction readings) and the ordinary rich on the strength of its stellar service and acclaimed restaurant, and because it commands a choice spot right on the south end of Kata Yai. Rooms start at 3700B.

Other top-end places on Kata are:

*Bougainville Terrace House* – (☎ 330087; fax 330463); 21 rooms, 1404 to 2808B
*Club Méditerranée* – (☎ 381455; fax 330461); 300 rooms, 2600 to 4600B
*Kata Beach Resort* – (☎ 330530; fax 330128); 280 rooms, from 2010B
*Kata Delight* – (☎ 330481); 19 rooms, 900 to 3200B
*Laem Sai Village* – (☎ 212901); 17 rooms, 1800 to 2500B
*Mountain Beach Resort* – (☎ 330565; fax 330567); 33 rooms, 100 to 1600B
*Sea Wind Hotel* – (☎ /fax 330564); 22 rooms, 1936 to 2178B

**Places to Eat** Most of the restaurants in Kata offer standard tourist food and service. The best restaurant in the entire area, including Karon and Patong to the north, is the open-air *Boathouse Wine & Grill*, which started out as a restaurant only but now has 36 rooms attached to its original location at the south end of Kata Yai. The wine collection here is so far the only one in Thailand to have been cited for excellence by *Wine Spectator* magazine, and the nightly seafood buffet is excellent. It's a pricey place but the atmosphere is casual and service is tops. On weekends one of the chefs conducts cooking classes, open to the public.

Another standout, though considerably less expensive, is the *Kampong-Kata Hill*

*Restaurant*, a Thai-style place decorated with antiques and situated on a hill a bit inland from the beach. It's open only for dinner, from 5 pm till midnight.

The *Dive Café* serves a multi-course Thai dinner for two for 100B per person. *Good Earth* is a casual spot that sells used books and serves fresh pastries, four kinds of coffee and nine teas. The very large and medium-priced *Islander's* (☎ 330740) strives to provide something for everyone, including seafood, Italian, barbecue and fresh baked goods; if you call they'll provide free transport to/from your hotel. Swiss-managed *Coconut Garden* also does Thai, Italian and seafood.

**Getting There & Away** Songthaews to both Kata and Karon leave frequently from the Ranong Rd Market in Phuket from 7 am to 5 pm for 15B per person. After-hours charters cost 130B. The main songthaew stop is in front of Kata Beach Resort.

### Nai Han
ในหาน

A few km south of Kata, this beach around a picturesque bay is similar to Kata and Karon but, in spite of the 1986 construction of the Phuket Yacht Club, not as developed. This is mainly thanks to the presence of Samnak Song Nai Han, a monastic centre in the middle of the beach that claims most of the beachfront land. To make up for the loss of saleable beachfront, developers started cutting away the forests on the hillsides overlooking the beach. Recently, however, the development seems to have reached a halt. This means that Nai Han is usually one of the least crowded beaches on the southern part of the island.

The TAT says Nai Han beach is a dangerous place to swim during the monsoon season (May to October), but it really varies according to daily or weekly weather changes – look for the red flag, which means dangerous swimming conditions.

**Places to Stay** Except for the Yacht Club, there's really not much accommodation available on or even near the beach. If you follow the road through the Yacht Club and beyond to the next cape, you'll come to the simple *Ao Sane Bungalows* (☎ 288306), which cost 100 to 300B depending on the season and condition of the huts. Farther on at the end of this road is the secluded *Jungle Beach Resort* (☎ /fax 381108). The nicely made cottages are well spaced along a naturally wooded slope with a small beach below. Low-season rates start at 300B for a sturdy hut without bath; high-season rates peak at 4000B for a large terraced cottage with private bath.

Well back from the beach, near the road into Nai Han and behind a small lagoon, is the motel-like *Nai Han Resort* (☎ 381810), with decent rooms for 500 to 600B with fan, 800B for air-con. Near the other side of the lagoon, *Romsai Bungalows* (☎ 381338) has simple huts for 300B in the December to April high season, as low as 100 or 150B the remainder of the year.

The *Phuket Yacht Club* (☎ 381156; fax 381164) sits on the northern end of Nai Han. Originally built at the astronomical cost of 145 million baht, the hotel has given up on the idea of becoming a true yacht club (apparently the bay currents aren't right for such an endeavour) with a mobile pier. The pier has been removed but luxurious 'state rooms' are still available for 7768B a night and up. On the other end of the bay from the Yacht Club, up on the hillside overlooking the bay, there used to be a set of bungalows known as *Sunset*, which were torn down around four years ago. Rumour has it this operation will be re-born sometime in the near future, so check this area out – it would be a prime location.

**Getting There & Away** Nai Han is 18 km from Phuket and a songthaew (leaving from the intersection of Bangkok Rd and the fountain circle) costs 20B per person. Tuk-tuk charters are 130B one way.

### Rawai
ราไวย์

Rawai was one of the first coastal areas on Phuket to be developed, simply because it was near Phuket and there was already a

PLACES TO STAY
2  Jungle Beach Resort
3  Ao Sane Bungalows
4  Phuket Yacht Club
5  Nai Han Resort
6  Romsai Bungalows
8  Rawai Garden Resort
9  Rawai Plaza & Bungalow
10  Siam Phuket Resort
11  Salaloy Resort
13  Laem Kha Beach Inn
14  Phuket Island Resort

OTHER
1  Phuket Shell Museum
7  Samnak Song Nai Han
12  Pier
15  Phra Phrom Shrine
16  Pier

ANDAMAN SEA

Nai Han
& Rawai

0        1        2 km

rather large fishing community there. Once other nicer beach areas like Patong and Karon were 'discovered', Rawai gradually began to lose popularity and today it is a rather spiritless place – but at least it's not crowded.

The beach is not so great, but there is a lot happening in or near Rawai: there is a local sea-gypsy village; Hat Laem Kha (better than Rawai) is to the north; boats go to the nearby islands of Ko Lon, Ko Hae, Ko Aew, Ko Phi and others; and there's good snorkelling off **Laem Phromthep** at the southern tip of Phuket island, easy to approach from Rawai. In fact, most of the visitors who stay at Rawai these days are divers who want to be near Phromthep or boat facilities for offshore diving trips.

Laem Phromthep is also a popular viewing point at sunset, when lots of shutterbugs gather to take the famous Phromthep shot. On a hill next to the viewpoint is a shrine to Phra Phrom (Brahma).

The diving around the offshore islands is not so bad, especially at Kaew Yai and Kaew Noi, off Phromthep and at Ko Hae. It's a good idea to shop around for boat trips to these islands to find the least expensive passage – the larger the group, the cheaper the cost per person.

**Places to Stay** The long-running *Salaloy Resort*, at 52/2 Wiset Rd, has bungalows for 300B with fan, up to 800B with air-con. Their well patronised seafood restaurant is one of the better – and more moderately priced – ones in the area.

The *Rawai Garden Resort* (☎ 381292) has eight rooms for 250B, while *Rawai Plaza & Bungalow* (☎ 381346; fax 381647) has 50 rooms and bungalows ranging from 450 to 900B. The relatively new *Siam Phuket Resort* (☎ 381346; fax 3812347) offers sturdy-looking bungalows in the 750 to 1300B range.

Round at Laem Kha, the well managed

SOUTHERN THAILAND

*Phuket Island Resort* (☎ 381010/7; fax 381018) has 290 air-con rooms from 2000B, a swimming pool and other mod-cons. The *Laem Kha Beach Inn* (☎ 381305) has 20 rooms starting at 450B, up to 1200B for larger ones.

**Places to Eat** Aside from the restaurants attached to the resorts in Rawai (Salaloy is the best), the only places to eat are the seafood and noodle vendors set up along the roadside near the beach.

**Getting There & Away** Rawai is about 16 km from Phuket and getting there costs 15B by songthaew from the circle at Bangkok Rd. Tuk-tuk charters cost 90B from Phuket.

## Laem Singh & Kamala
แหลมสิงห์/หาดกมลา

North of Ao Patong, 24 km from Phuket, Laem Singh (Cape Singh) is a beautiful little rock-dominated beach. You could camp here and eat at the rustic roadside seafood places at the north end of Singh or in Ban Kamala, a village farther south. If you're renting a motorbike, this is a nice little trip down Route 402 and then over dirt roads from Surin to Kamala. Just before Surin, in Ban Thao Village No 2, is one of Southern Thailand's most beautiful mosques, a large, whitewashed, immaculate structure with lacquered wooden doors.

Hat Kamala is a lovely stretch of sand and sea south of Surin and Laem Singh. The north end, the nicest area, is shaded by casuarina trees and features a small thatch-roofed snack bar with free sling chairs and umbrellas available. The middle of the beach is now dominated by resorts and seafood restaurants. Bangkok's Safari World has leased a 160 acre plot near the beach for the construction of a US$60 million entertainment park called Phuket Fantasea; so far little protest has been launched but it remains to be seen whether this potentially destructive project will go through.

**Places to Stay** The up-market *Phuket Kamala Resort* (☎ 324396; fax 324399) dominates

the centre of the beach and costs 1250 to 1900B.

On the other side of the road from the beach are a couple of less expensive options. The quiet *Bird Beach Bungalows* and *Kamala Beach House* offer small but solid cottages for 350 to 500B. In this same area are several laundry services and minimarts, evidence that Kamala is attracting long-termers.

In the village there are several small houses for rent starting at around 500B a night. At the southern end of the bay, overlooking but not on the beach, is *Kamala Beach Estate* (☎ 314111; fax 324115), where fully equipped, high-security, modern time-share apartments go for 1900 to 6400B a night. Around the headland further south, the similar *Kamala Bay Terrace* (☎ 270801; fax 270818) has more luxurious apartments and time-shares for 2700 to 13,000B per night.

**Places to Eat** The best value for eating is the friendly thatched-roof place at the north end of the beach. Near Bird Beach Bungalow are the decent *Kamala Seafood* and *Jaroen Seafood*, both family-run Thai seafood places that cater to farangs. *Paul's Place Pub & Kitchen*, next to Kamala Beach Estate at the south end of the bay, is the most up-market place to eat; it offers good views of the bay and reliable Thai and western food.

## Surin
สุรินทร์

A little north of Laem Singh, Surin has a long beach and sometimes fairly heavy surf. When the water is calm, there's fair snorkelling here. It's long been a popular place for local Thais to come and nibble at seafood snacks sold by vendors along the beach.

**Places to Stay** Surin's northern end has been dubbed 'Pansea Beach' by developers and is claimed by the exclusive Amanpuri and Pansea resorts. *Amanpuri Resort* (☎ 324-333; fax 324100) plays host to Thailand's celebrity traffic, each of whom gets a 133 sq m pavilion and a personal attendant; the staff to guest ratio is 3½ to one. It's owned by Indonesian Adrian Zecha and designed by the architect who designed the former Shah of Iran's Winter Palace. You can expect to pay 6900B and up per day for a room here. The Amanpuri was once censured by the local community for the improper display of Buddha images.

The former Pansea has been re-christened *The Chedi* (☎ 32417; fax 324252) and now offers 110 rooms starting at 3000B. The Chedi has its own golf-course.

Toward the southern end of Surin, *Surin Sweet Apartment* (☎ (01) 721-1153) and *Taengthai Guesthouse* offer simple but modern rooms in the 300 to 600B range.

## Ao Bang Tao
บางเทา

North of Surin around a cape is Ao Bang Tao, an eight km sandy beach with an 18 hole golf-course that has attracted much upscale development. A steady breeze makes it a haven for sailboarders; since 1992 the annual Siam World Cup windsurfing championships have been held here (formerly at Pattaya's Jomtien Beach). A system of lagoons inland from the beach has been incorporated into the resorts and golf-course, hence this is sometimes referred to as 'Laguna Beach'.

**Places to Stay** With one exception, Bang Tao is strictly for the well-to-do nowadays. Least expensive is the quiet and secluded *Bangtao Lagoon Bungalow* (☎ 324260; fax 324168) at the south end of the bay, with small cottages for 250B, medium-sized ones for 600B, or 1000 to 1600B for the largest.

Rooms at the plush *Dusit Laguna Resort* (☎ 324320; fax 324174) start at 3884B, with suites costing considerably more, not including tax. From 20 December to 20 February there is a 400B peak-season surcharge. Another top-end place at the northern end of the bay is the *Royal Park Travelodge Resort* (☎ 324021; fax 324243), where rooms start at 2543B in the low season, up to 3178 in the high.

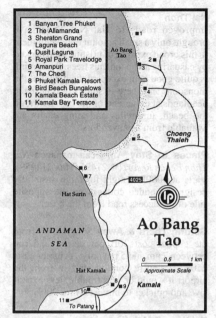

1 Banyan Tree Phuket
2 The Allamanda
3 Sheraton Grand Laguna Beach
4 Dusit Laguna
5 Royal Park Travelodge
6 Amanpuri
7 The Chedi
8 Phuket Kamala Resort
9 Bird Beach Bungalows
10 Kamala Beach Estate
11 Kamala Bay Terrace

Ao Bang Tao

Bringing yet more beachside luxury to the bay are the *Sheraton Grand Laguna Beach Resort* (☎ 324101; fax 324108) and the *Banyan Tree Phuket* (☎ 324374; fax 324375). The Sheraton features a sprawling 370 rooms starting at 4000B, while the more exclusive Banyan Tree has 86 villas (all with open-air sunken bathtubs, 34 with private pools) from 6350B. The Sheraton is the only place on this beach with a fitness centre.

Finally, *The Allamanda Phuket* (☎ 324359; fax 324360) offers 94 rooms for 2800 to 5600B, while the equally new *Laguna Beach Club* (☎ 324352; fax 324353) rivals the Sheraton and Dusit in providing 252 rooms for 4000 to 5000B.

**Getting There & Away** A songthaew from Phuket's Ranong Rd to Surin, Kamala or Bang Tao costs 15B. Tuk-tuk charters are 200B to Surin and Kamala, 170B to Bang Tao.

SOUTHERN THAILAND

## Nai Thon

Improved roads to Hat Nai Thon have brought only a small amount of development to this broad expanse of pristine sand backed by casuarina and pandanus trees. Swimming is quite good here except at the height of the monsoon, and there is some coral near the headlands at either end of the bay. Down on the beach, umbrellas and sling chairs are available from Thai vendors.

**Places to Stay** American-managed *Nai Thon Beach Resort* (☎ 214954; fax 214959), starts at 4000B a night for large, tastefully designed wooden cottages on the opposite side of the access road from the beach.

**Getting There & Away** Songthaews from the capital cost 30B per person and run between 7 am and 5 pm only. A charter costs 250B; if you're coming straight from the airport it would be less trouble, less expensive and quicker to hire a taxi for 200B.

## Nai Yang & Mai Khao
ในยาพ/ไม้ขาว

Both of these beaches are near Phuket airport, about 30 km from Phuket. Nai Yang, a fairly secluded beach favoured by Thais, is actually part of Sirinat National Park, a newly decreed protected area that combines former Nai Yang National Park with a wildlife reserve at Mai Khao. The park encompasses 22 sq km of coastline, plus 68 sq km of sea, from the western Phang-Nga provincial border south to the headland that separates Nai Yang from Nai Thon.

About five km north of Nai Yang is Hat Mai Khao, Phuket's longest beach. Sea turtles lay their eggs on the beach here between November and February each year. A new visitors' centre with toilets, showers and picnic tables has recently been constructed at Mai Khao (replacing the old headquarters at the north end of Nai Yang), from which there are some short trails through the casuarinas to a steep beach. Take care when swimming at Mai Khao, as there's a strong year-round undertow. Except on

weekends and holidays you'll have this place almost entirely to yourself; even during peak periods, peace and solitude are usually only a few steps away, as there's so much space here.

About a km off Nai Yang is a large reef at a depth of 10 to 20m. Judging from the lie of the reef, there could be surfable reef break here during the south-west monsoon.

**Places to Stay & Eat** Camping is allowed on both Nai Yang and Mai Khao beaches. The park accommodation on Nai Yang costs 200B in a dorm-like longhouse, 300B in a four-bed bungalow, 600B in a 12-bed one. Two-person tents can be rented for 60B a night.

Commercial development has been permitted toward the southern end of Hat Nai Yang, well back from the beach itself. *Garden Cottage* (☎ /fax 327293), back from the beach quite a bit but still within five minutes walk, features tidy cottages with air-con, fridge and private bath for 750 to 1200B.

The fancy *Pearl Village Beach Hotel* (☎ 327006; fax 327338) commands 8.1 hectares at the southern end of the beach. Air-con rooms and cottages start at 3500B. Also at this end is the *Crown Nai Yang Suite Hotel* (☎ 317420), an ugly, multistorey place that rents modern boxes for 1250B and up.

A group of vendors just past the Crown sell inexpensive seafood. The Garden Cottage has a reasonably priced, indoor/outdoor restaurant.

**Getting There & Away** A songthaew from Phuket to Nai Yang costs 20B, while a tuk-tuk charter is 250B.

## Other Beaches & Nearby Islands

At **Ko Hae**, a few km south-west of Ao Chalong, the *Coral Island Resort* (☎ 281060; fax 381957) has up-market bungalows from 2300B with air-con. Sometimes the island itself is called Coral Island. It's a good spot for diving and snorkelling if you don't plan on going further out to sea.

Two islands about 1½ hours by boat south

of Phuket, **Ko Raya Yai** and **Ko Raya Noi** (also known as Ko Racha Yai/Noi), are highly favoured by divers and snorkellers for their hard coral reefs. Because the coral is found in both shallow and deep waters, it's a good area for novice scuba divers and snorkellers as well as accomplished divers. Visibility can reach 15 to 30m. On Ko Raya Yai, accommodations are available at *Jungle Bungalow* (☎ 228550) at *Raya Resort* (☎ 327-803, (01) 723-1195) starting at 300B for simple palm-thatch bungalows, and at *Raya Andaman Resort* (☎ 381710; fax 381713) for 750 to 950B for air-con digs.

For information on attractions and accommodations on the island of Ko Yao Noi, off Phuket's north-western shore, see the Phang-Nga Province section earlier.

**Getting There & Away** Passenger boats to Ko Raya Yai leave from the pier at Hat Rawai daily around 8.30 am, returning at 11 am, for 100 to 150B per person (the boats carrying cargo are cheaper). You can also charter a long-tail boat from Rawai or from Ao Chalong for 1000 to 1200B.

# Surat Thani Province

## CHAIYA
ไชยา

About 640 km from Bangkok, Chaiya is just north of Surat Thani and best visited as a day trip from there. Chaiya is one of the oldest cities in Thailand, dating back to the Srivijaya empire. In fact, the name may be a contraction of Siwichaiya, the Thai pronunciation of the city that was a regional capital between the 8th and 10th centuries. Previous to this time the area was on the Indian trade route in South-East Asia. Many Srivijaya artefacts in the National Museum in Bangkok were found in Chaiya, including a famous Avalokitesvara Bodhisattva bronze that's considered to be a masterpiece of Buddhist art.

### Wat Phra Boromathat, Wat Kaew & Chaiya National Museum

The restored **Borom That Chaiya** stupa at Wat Phra Boromathat, just outside of town, is a fine example of Srivijaya architecture and strongly resembles the *candis* of central Java – a stack of ornate boxes bearing images of Kala, a peacock (a symbol for the sun), Erawan, Indra and the Buddha (facing east as usual). In the courtyard surrounding the revered *chedi* (stupa) are several pieces of sculpture from the region, including an unusual two-sided *yoni* (the uterus-shaped pedestal that holds the Shivalingam), rishis performing yoga and several Buddha images.

A ruined stupa at nearby **Wat Kaew** (also known as Wat Long), also from the Srivijaya period, again shows central Javanese influence (or perhaps vice versa) as well as Cham (9th century southern Vietnam) characteristics.

The **national museum** near the entrance to Wat Phra Boromathat displays prehistoric and historic artefacts of local provenance, as well as local handicrafts and a shadow puppet exhibit. Admission to the museum is 10B; it's open Wednesday to Sunday from 9 am to 4 pm.

You can catch any songthaew heading west from the main intersection south of the train station to Wat Boromathat for 3B. This same songthaew route passes the turn-off for Wat Kaew, which is about a half km before the turn-off for Boromathat. Wat Kaew is less than a half km from this junction on the left, almost directly opposite Chaiya Witthaya School.

### Wat Suan Mokkhaphalaram
วัดสวนโมกขพลาราม

Wat Suanmok (short for Wat Suan Mokkhaphalaram – literally, Garden of Liberation), west of Wat Kaew, is a modern forest wat founded by Ajaan Buddhadasa Bhikkhu (Thai: Phutthathat), Thailand's most famous monk. Born in Chaiya in 1906, Buddhadasa ordained as a monk when he was 21 years old, spent many years studying the Pali scriptures and then retired to the forest for

SOUTHERN THAILAND

six years of solitary meditation. Returning to ecclesiastical society, he was made abbot of Wat Phra Boromathat, a high distinction, but conceived of Suanmok as an alternative to orthodox Thai temples. During Thailand's turbulent 1970s, he was branded a communist because of his critiques of capitalism, which he saw as a catalyst for greed. Buddhadasa died in July 1993 after a long illness.

Buddhadasa's philosophy was ecumenical in nature, comprising Zen, Taoist and Christian elements as well as the traditional Theravada schemata. Today the hermitage is spread over 120 hectares of wooded hillside and features huts for up to 70 monks, a museum/library, and a 'spiritual theatre'. This latter building has bas-reliefs on the outer walls which are facsimiles of sculptures at Sanchi, Bharhut and Amaravati in India. The interior walls feature modern Buddhist painting – eclectic to say the least – executed by the resident monks.

At the affiliated International Dhamma Hermitage, across the highway 1.5 km from Wat Suanmok, resident monks hold meditation retreats during the first 10 days of every month. Anyone is welcome to participate; a 50B donation per day is requested to cover food costs.

### Places to Stay

Travellers could stay in Surat Thani for visits to Chaiya or request permission from the monks to stay in the guest quarters at Wat Suanmok. *Udomlap Hotel*, an old Chinese-Thai hotel in Chaiya, has rooms for 80 to 100B.

### Getting There & Away

If you're going to Surat Thani by train from Bangkok, you can get off at the small Chaiya train station, then later catch another train to Phun Phin, Surat's train station.

From Surat you can either take a songthaew from Talaat Kaset II in Ban Don (18B to Wat Suanmok or 20B to Chaiya) or get a train going north from Phun Phin. The trains between Phun Phin and Chaiya may be full but you can always stand or squat in a 3rd class car for the short trip. The ordinary train

costs 8B in 3rd class to Chaiya and takes about an hour to get there. The songthaew takes around 45 minutes. Or you can take a share taxi to Chaiya from Surat for 30B per person; in Chaiya, Surat-bound taxis leave from opposite the Chaiya train station.

Suanmok is about seven km outside town on the highway to Surat and Chumphon. Until late afternoon there are songthaews from the Chaiya train station to Wat Suanmok for 8B per passenger. From Chaiya you can also catch a Surat-bound bus from the front of the movie theatre on Chaiya's main street and ask to be let off at Wat Suanmok. (Turn right on the road in front of the train station.) The fare to Wat Suanmok is 5B. If buses aren't running you can hire a motorcycle taxi for 20B anywhere along Chaiya's main street.

## SURAT THANI/BAN DON
อ.เมืองสุราษฎร์ธานี
• ☎ *(77)* • *pop 41,800*

There is little of particular historical interest in Surat Thani, a busy commercial centre and port dealing in rubber and coconut, but the town's waterfront lends character nonetheless. It's 651 km from Bangkok and the first point in a southbound journey towards Malaysia that really feels and looks like Southern Thailand. For most people Surat Thani (often known as Surat) is only a stop on the way to Ko Samui or Ko Pha-Ngan, luscious islands 32 km off the coast – so the Talaat Kaset bus station in Ban Don and the ferry piers to the east become the centres of attention.

### Information

**Tourist Office** The friendly TAT office (☎ 288818/9), at 5 Talaat Mai Rd near the south-western end of town, distributes plenty of useful brochures and maps. It's open daily from 8.30 am to 4.30 pm.

**Money** There's a string of banks – one on every block for five blocks – along Na Meuang Rd south-west of Chonkasem Rd; all have ATMs and most offer foreign

**Surat Thani Festivals**
In mid-October Chak Phra and Thawt Phaa Paa celebrations occur on the same day (first day of the waning moon in the 11th lunar month) at the end of the Buddhist rains retreat and are major events for Surat Thani. Thawt Phaa Paa, or 'Laying-Out of Forest Robes', begins at dawn with the offering of new monastic robes to the monks, while Chak Phra or 'Pulling of the Buddha Image' takes place during the day and evening. In the latter local, lay devotees place sacred Buddha images on boats for a colourful procession along the Tapi River. A similar landborne procession uses trucks and hand-pulled carts. Lots of foodstalls and musical performances, including *li-khe*, are set up for the occasion. ■

exchange. Bangkok Bank at 193 Na Meuang Rd has an exchange booth open daily from 8.30 am to 5 pm.

**Post & Communications** The GPO is on Na Meuang Rd. A new telecommunications centre on Don Nok Rd, open daily 7 am to 11 pm, is the place to make international calls.

**Travel Agencies** Several travel agents in town handle travel to the islands or elsewhere in Southern Thailand, including Phantip Travel (☎ 272230) at 442/24-5 Talaat Mai Rd and Songserm Travel (☎ 285-124; fax 285127) at 30/2 Mu 3 Bangkoong Rd, with another office opposite the pier. Phantip is the most reliable travel agent in town overall for the average transport transaction; Songserm is notorious for its couldn't-care-less attitude because its parent company monopolises nearly all boat transport to the islands.

**Places to Stay – bottom end**
For many of Surat Thani's cheaper hotels, business consists largely of 'short-time' trade. This doesn't make them any less suitable as regular hotels – it's just that there's likely to be rather more noise as guests arrive and depart with some frequency. In fact, in many ways it's better to zip straight through Surat Thani since there's nothing of interest to hold you. You're quite likely to sleep better on the night boat than in a noisy hotel. Another alternative is to stay near the train station in Phun Phin (see under Places to Stay & Eat – Phun Phin later in this section).

All of the following are within walking (or samlor) distance of the Ban Don boat pier.

The *Surat Hotel* (☎ 272243) on Na Meuang Rd, between the Grand City Hotel and bus station, costs 150 to 300B for rooms with fan and bath. At the rear are some quiet, renovated rooms. Across the street from the Surat, the *Phanfa Hotel* has similar rooms for 120B.

The *Grand City Hotel* (☎ 272960) at 428 Na Meuang Rd has been renovated and has plain but clean rooms with fan and bath for 160/190B singles/doubles, and air-con rooms for 330/500B.

Off Ban Don Rd, near the municipal pier on a fairly quiet street off Si Chaiya Rd, is the *Seree (Seri) Hotel* (☎ 272279). You get adequate but somewhat airless rooms with fan and bath for 290B, air-con rooms for 330B.

One block from the night boat pier on Si Chaiya Rd is the *Thai Hotel* (☎ 272932), which is 140/180B for dingy but fairly quiet singles/doubles with fan and bath.

The best budget value in Surat is the *Ban Don Hotel* (☎ 272167) on Na Meuang Rd towards the morning market, with clean singles/doubles with fan and bath for 160/220B. Enter the hotel through a Chinese restaurant. The *Thai Rung Ruang Hotel* (☎ 273249), 191/199 Mitkasem Rd, is also good with rooms from 260/320B (fan) for singles/doubles, and 430/450B (air-con).

On the corner of Na Meuang Rd and the road between the river and bus station is the scruffy, not-too-clean *Ratchathani Hotel* (☎ 272972/143), which starts at 230B for rooms with fan and bath and from 300B for air-con.

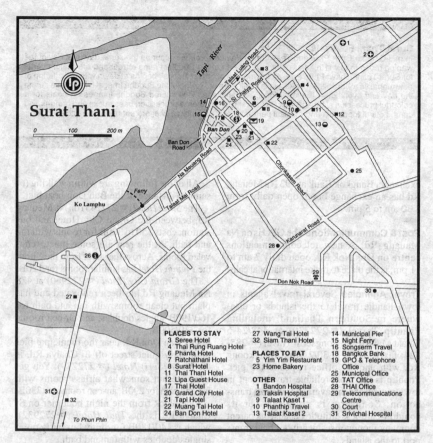

# Surat Thani

0    100    200 m

PLACES TO STAY
3  Seree Hotel
4  Thai Rung Ruang Hotel
6  Phanfa Hotel
7  Ratchathani Hotel
8  Surat Hotel
11 Thai Thani Hotel
12 Lipa Guest House
17 Thai Hotel
20 Grand City Hotel
21 Tapi Hotel
22 Muang Tai Hotel
24 Ban Don Hotel

27 Wang Tai Hotel
32 Siam Thani Hotel

PLACES TO EAT
5  Yim Yim Restaurant
23 Home Bakery

OTHER
1  Bandon Hospital
2  Taksin Hospital
9  Talaat Kaset 1
10 Phanthip Travel
13 Talaat Kaset 2

14 Municipal Pier
15 Night Ferry
16 Songserm Travel
18 Bangkok Bank
19 GPO & Telephone
   Office
25 Municipal Office
26 TAT Office
28 THAI Office
29 Telecommunications
   Centre
30 Court
31 Srivichai Hospital

## Places to Stay – middle

Although these two don't cost much more than the foregoing budget places, the facilities are considerably better. Popular with travelling businesspeople, the *Tapi Hotel* (☎ 272575) at 100 Chonkasem Rd has fan-cooled rooms for 250 to 370B, air-con for 500 to 670B. The similar but older *Muang Tai* (☎ 272367) at 390-392 Talaat Mai Rd has fan-cooled rooms from 200B and air-con rooms from 300B.

## Places to Stay – top end

Surat Thani also has a number of more expensive hotels, including the *Wang Tai* (☎ 283020/39; fax 281007) at 1 Talaat Mai Rd. It's a big hotel with nearly 300 rooms, a swimming pool and prices from 680B. The *Siam Thani* (☎ 273081), at 180 Surat Thani-Phun Phin Rd, starts at 840B (as low as 580B in low season) and has a swimming pool. There's a good restaurant on the premises. The *Siam Thara*, on Don Nok Rd near the Talaat Mai Rd intersection, has air-con rooms for 560 to 640B.

## Places to Eat

The Talaat Kaset market area, next to the bus

terminal, and the morning market, between Na Meuang and Si Chaiya Rds, are good food-hunting places. Many stalls near the bus station specialise in khâo kài òp, a marinated baked chicken on rice which is very tasty. During mango season, a lot of street vendors in Surat sell incredible khâo niāw má-mûang, coconut-sweetened sticky rice with sliced ripe mango.

*Yim Yim Restaurant* on Talaat Luang Rd serves reasonably priced seafood, including Surat's celebrated large white oysters, served raw in a lime-garlic-chilli marinade. *Athit Restaurant*, opposite Sun Hiam Chinese Restaurant on the same street as the Thai Hotel, is an air-con beer house with snacks and ice cream. Just around the corner from Bangkok Bank, off Na Meuang Rd in an old wooden building, is an exemplary Southern-style khanŏm jiin place.

*J Home Bakery*, around the corner from the Grand City Hotel, is a dark, poorly ventilated air-con place, but it has inexpensive western breakfasts, a few baked goods, plus Thai and Chinese dishes from a bilingual menu. Another bakery choice is the *Valaisak Bakery* next to the Tapi Hotel. *Homeburger Restaurant*, next to the Phanfa Hotel, does hamburgers, pizza, steak and some Thai dishes.

Next door to J Home is the inexpensive and popular *Yong Hua Long*, a decent Chinese restaurant with roast duck and a large buffet table.

## Places to Stay & Eat – Phun Phin

You may find yourself needing accommodation in Phun Phin, either because you've become stranded there due to booked-out trains or because you've come in from Samui in the evening and plan to get an early morning train out of Surat before the Surat to Phun Phin bus service starts. If so, there are a couple of cheap, dilapidated hotels just across from the train station. The *Tai Fah* has rooms for 100B with shared bath, 120B with attached bath. Slightly better at the same location is the *Sri Thani*, also with rooms at 100B. If you can afford a few baht more, around the corner on the road to Surat, but

still quite close to the train station, is the better *Queen* (☎ 311003), where rooms cost 150 to 200B with fan and 250 to 300B with air-con.

Across from the Queen is a good night market with cheap eats. The Tai Fah and Sri Thani do Thai, Chinese and farang food at reasonable prices.

## Getting There & Away

**Air** THAI flies to Surat Thani from Bangkok (daily, 1785B), Chiang Mai (twice a week, 3060B), Hat Yai (1450B). There are also quite frequent services to Nakhon Si Thammarat, Phuket and Ranong. The THAI office (☎ 272610) in Surat is at 3/27-28 Karunarat Rd.

Orient Express Air (☎ 210071), a relatively new service, offers five weekly flights between Surat and Chiang Mai for 2450B each way; this flight continues on to Hat Yai for 1150B.

A THAI shuttle van between Surat Thani and the airport costs 40B per person. THAI also runs a more expensive limo service for 150B.

**Bus, Share Taxi & Minivan** First class air-con buses leave Bangkok's Southern Bus Terminal in Thonburi daily at 8, 8.20 and 8.30 pm, arriving in Surat 11 hours later; the fare is 285B. There is also one 2nd class air-con departure at 10 pm that costs 222B and one VIP departure at 8 pm for 350B. Private companies also run 'Super VIP' buses with only 30 seats for 450B.

Ordinary buses leave the ordinary Southern Bus Terminal at 9.20 and 11 pm for 158B.

Take care when booking private air-con and VIP buses out of Surat. A company called Harmony Tours has been known to sell tickets for VIP buses to Bangkok, then pile hapless travellers onto an ordinary air-con bus and then refuse to refund the fare difference. If possible get a recommendation from another traveller or enquire at the TAT office.

Public buses and share taxis run from the Talaat Kaset 1 or 2 markets. Muang Tai bus company books air-con bus tickets to several destinations in Southern Thailand from its desk in the lobby of the Surat Hotel, including VIP buses to Bangkok. Phantip Travel handles minivan bookings.

Other fares to/from Surat are:

| Destination | Fare | Hours |
|---|---|---|
| Hat Yai | 85B | 5 |
| (air-con) | 120B | 4 |
| (share taxi or van) | 150B | 3½ |
| Krabi | 51B | 4 |
| (air-con) | 91B | 3 |
| (share taxi or van) | 150B | 2 |
| Nakhon Si Thammarat | 36B | 2½ |
| (air-con) | 55B | 2 |
| (share taxi) | 60B | 2 |
| Narathiwat | 127B | 6 |
| Phang-Nga | 50B | 4 |
| (air-con) | 100B | 3 |
| (share taxi) | 80B | 2½ |
| Phuket | 77B | 6 |
| (air-con) | 112B | 5 |
| (share taxi or van) | 150B | 4 |
| Ranong | 70B | 5 |
| (air-con) | 80B | 4 |
| (share taxi or van) | 150B | 3½ |
| Satun | 76B | 4 |
| Trang | 50B | 3 |
| (share taxi) | 100B | 3 |
| Yala | 100B | 6 |

**Train** Trains for Surat, which don't really stop in Surat but in Phun Phin, 14 km west of town, leave Bangkok's Hualamphong terminal at 1.30 pm (rapid), 2.35 pm (special express), 3.15 pm (special express), 3.50 pm (rapid), 5.05 pm (rapid), 6.30 pm (rapid), 7.20 pm (express) and 7.45 pm (rapid), arriving 10½ to 11 hours later. The 6.30 pm train (rapid No 41) is the most convenient, arriving at 5.44 am and giving you plenty of time to catch a boat to Samui, if that's your destination. Fares are 470B in 1st class (available only on the 2.35 and 3.15 pm special express) and 224B in 2nd class, not including rapid/express/special express surcharges or berths.

There are no direct 3rd class trains to Surat from Bangkok, but you can travel from Chumphon to Surat on the ordinary Nos 119 or 149 for 25B.

The all 1st class special express No 981 (formerly called the Sprinter) leaves Bangkok

daily at 10.35 pm and arrives in Phun Phin at 7.20 am for 370B. No sleeping berths are available on this train.

The Phun Phin train station has a 24 hour left-luggage room that costs 5B for the first five days, 10B thereafter. The advance ticket office is open daily from 6 to 11 am and noon to 6 pm.

It can be difficult to book long-distance trains out of Phun Phin – for long-distance travel, it may be easier to take a bus, especially if heading south. The trains are very often full and it's a drag to take the bus 14 km from town to the Phun Phin train station and be turned away. You could buy a 'standing room only' 3rd class ticket and stand for an hour or two until someone vacates a seat down the line. Advance train reservations can be made without going all the way out to Phun Phin station at Phantip travel agency on Talaat Mai Rd in Ban Don, near the market/bus station. You might try making an onward reservation *before* boarding a boat for Samui. The Songserm Travel Service on Samui can also assist travellers with reservations.

Here is a list of other train fares out of Surat (not including surcharges on rapid, express or air-con coaches):

| Destination | Fare | | |
|---|---|---|---|
| | 1st class | 2nd class | 3rd class |
| Bangkok | 470B | 224B | – |
| Chaiya | – | | 8B |
| Chumphon | 71B | 34B | 25B |
| Hat Yai | 228B | 114B | 55B |
| Nakhon Si Thammarat | | | |
| (Thung Song) | 103B | 54B | 26B |
| Prachuap Khiri Khan | 255B | 127B | – |

**Train/Bus/Boat Combinations** These days many travellers are buying tickets from the State Railway of Thailand that allow them to go straight through to Ko Samui or Ko Pha-Ngan from Bangkok on a train, bus and boat combination. For example, a 2nd class air-con sleeper that includes bus to boat transfers through to Samui costs 679B. See the Getting There & Away sections under each island for more details.

## Getting Around

Buses to Ban Don from Phun Phin train station leave every 10 minutes or so from 6 am to 8 pm for 6B per person. Some of the buses drive straight to the pier (if they have enough tourists on the bus), while others will terminate at the Ban Don bus station, from where you must get another bus to Tha Thong (or to Ban Don if you're taking the night ferry).

If you arrive in Phun Phin on one of the night trains, you can get a free bus from the train station to the pier, courtesy of the boat service, for the morning boat departures. If your train arrives in Phun Phin when the buses aren't running (which includes all trains except No 41), then you're out of luck and will have to hire a taxi to Ban Don for about 60 to 70B, or hang out in one of the Phun Phin street cafes until buses start running around 5.15 am.

Orange buses run from Ban Don bus station to Phun Phin train station every five minutes from 5 am to 7.30 pm for 6B per person. Empty buses also wait at the Tha Thong pier for passengers arriving from Ko Samui on the express boat, ready to drive them directly to the train station or destinations further afield.

Around town, share tuk-tuks cost 5B and samlors are 10B.

## KHAO SOK NATIONAL PARK
อุทยานแห่งชาติเขาสก

This 646 sq km park is in the western part of Surat Thani Province, off Route 401 about a third of the way from Takua Pa to Surat Thani. The park features 65,000 hectares of thick native rainforest with waterfalls, limestone cliffs, numerous streams, an island-studded lake formed by the Chiaw Lan Dam, and many trails, mostly along rivers. Connected to the **Khlong Saen Wildlife Sanctuary** and three smaller preserves (thus forming the largest contiguous nature preserve on the Thai peninsula), Khao Sok shelters a plethora of wildlife, including wild elephant, leopard, serow, banteng, gaur, dusky langur, tiger and Malayan sun bear as well as over 175 bird species. In 1986 Slorm's stork – a new species for Thailand – was confirmed.

One floral rarity found in the park is *Rafflesia kerri meyer*, know to the Thais as *bua phut* or wild lotus, the largest flower in the world. Found only in Khao Sok and an adjacent wildlife sanctuary (different varieties of the same species are found in Malaysia and Indonesia), mature specimens reach 80 cm in diameter. The flower has no roots or leaves of its own; instead it lives parasitically inside the roots of the liana, a jungle vine. Once a year buds burst forth from the liana root and swell to football size. When the bud blooms it emits a potent stench (said to resemble that of a rotting corpse) that attracts insects responsible for pollination.

A map of hiking trails within the park is available from the park headquarters near the park entrance. Three trails lead to the waterfalls of Than Sawan (seven km), Sip-Et Chan (four km) and Than Kloy (eight km). Guesthouses near the park entrance can arrange guided hikes that include waterfalls, caves and river-running. Leeches are quite common in certain areas of the park, so take the usual precautions – wear closed shoes when hiking and apply plenty of repellent.

The park is 1.5 km off Route 401 between Takua Pa and Surat Thani at Km 109. Besides the camping area at the park headquarters, there are several private bungalow operations featuring 'tree house' style accommodation.

Entrance to the park is 3B; rangers can lead jungle tours or rafting trips for 150B per day. Rainforest Safari (☎/fax (76) 330852) in Phuket arranges treks and elephant rides in Khao Sok for 2200 to 4000B.

### Places to Stay & Eat

Khao Sok has a camping area and several places to stay. The national park has a house, with rooms for 350B. Tents can be rented for 50B per person. A small restaurant near the entrance serves inexpensive meals.

Accommodation is also available at several places just outside the park between the highway and the visitors' centre. *Khao*

SOUTHERN THAILAND

*Sok River Huts* (radio ☎ 421155/613, both ext 107), offers six rooms with bath for 200/300B a single/double, or a tree house with bath for 400B, and meals for 40 to 70B. *Bamboo House*, off the main road to the park, has seven rooms for 100/150B with shared bath, 170/250B with private bath, plus 120B extra for three meals a day.

*Art's Riverview Jungle Lodge*, off the same road beyond the Bamboo House about a km from the park, has seven rooms for 200 to 300B, plus tree houses for 400B and two large houses with rooms with private bath and deck for 600B; meals cost 250B a day or you can order à la carte at breakfast and lunch, 80B for a set Thai dinner. All places have guides for jungle trips. Meals are available for 40 to 60B.

Past Art's and the Bamboo House is *Our Jungle House*, a friendly, family-run place which has nicely designed tree houses with private bath for 400B, plus smaller, less expensive rooms in the main house, where the dining rooms are.

Under the same management as Dawn of Happiness in Krabi, *Khao Sok Rainforest Resort* (☎ (01) 464-4362; fax (75) 612914) offers sturdy cottages raised on stilts with large verandahs overlooking the forest, with attached showers and toilets, for 300 to 600B. A longhouse-style dorm is planned along with air-con luxury bungalows – which seem rather out of place in what purports to be an eco-sensitive resort

*Tree Tops Jungle Safaris* started the Khao Sok experience several years ago, but these days they accept only package tours booked through Green Wood Travel in Bangkok (☎ /fax (2) 252-5316) or Phuket (☎ (76) 270662; fax 272406). A typical package for four nights (two nights at Tree Tops, two nights at their raft house) with meals is 4600 to 4900B. Accommodation consists of raft houses as well as tree houses.

## Getting There & Away

From Phun Phin or Surat Thani catch a bus bound for Takua Pa and get off at Km 109 (the park's entrance) on Highway 401. The bus will cost you 75B air-con, 28B ordinary.

You can also come from the Phuket side of the peninsula by bus, but you'll have to go to Takua Pa first; Surat-bound buses from Phuket don't use Highway 401 anymore.

## KO SAMUI
เกาะสมุย
• ☎ (77) • pop 35,000

Ko Samui is part of an island group that used to be called Muu Ko Samui, though you rarely hear that term these days. Thailand's third-largest island at 247 sq km, it's surrounded by 80 smaller islands. Six of these, Pha-Ngan, Ta Loy, Tao, Taen, Ma Ko and Ta Pao, are inhabited as well.

Samui's first settlers were islanders from Hainan Island (now part of the People's Republic of China) who took up coconut farming here around 150 years ago. You can still see a map of Hainan on the *săan jâo* or Chinese spirit shrine near Siam City Bank in Na Thon, the oldest town on the island. The island has had a somewhat legendary status among Asian travellers for the last 20 years or so, but it wasn't until the late 1980s that it escalated to the touristic proportions of other similar getaways found between Goa and Bali. Since the advent of the Don Sak auto/bus ferry and the opening of the airport, things have been changing fast. During the high seasons, late December to February and July to August, it can be difficult to find a place to stay, even though most beaches are crowded with bungalows and resorts. The port town of Na Thon teems with foreign travellers getting on and off the ferry boats, booking tickets onward, and collecting mail at the post office. With nearly a dozen daily flights to Samui from Bangkok, the island is rushing headlong into top-end development.

Airport or no airport, Samui is still an enjoyable place to spend some time, and more than a few people have been making regular visits for nearly 20 years. It still has some of the best accommodation values in Thailand and a casual, do-as-you-please atmosphere that makes it quite attractive. Even with an airport, it still has the advan-

SARA JANE CLELAND

RICHARD NEBESKY

RICHARD NEBESKY

## Southern Thailand

Top: Striking limestone cliffs and outcrops dot the Andaman coastline, Krabi
Bottom Left: Simple thatched bungalows at Hat Lamai, Ko Samui
Bottom Right: Last run for the day, Ban Mae Hat, Ko Tao

JOE CUMMINGS

PAUL BEINSSEN

### Southern Thailand

Top: The painted wooden upper decks of a sea-bound vessel
Bottom: The three islands of Ko Tao's Ko Nang Yuan linked by a narrow sandbar

tage of being off the mainland and far away from Bangkok. Coconuts are still an important part of the local economy – up to two million are shipped to Bangkok each month.

But there's no going back to 1971, when the first two tourists arrived on a coconut boat from Bangkok, much to the surprise of a friend who had been living on the island for four years as a Peace Corps volunteer. The main difference is that there are now many more places to stay, most of them in the mid to high range by Thai standards. And of course, with this 'something for everyone' climate have come more people, more traffic, more noise and more rubbish, but so far not in intolerable proportions. Samui residents are beginning to formulate policies to deal with these social and environmental challenges and the prognosis is, tentatively, optimistic – only time will tell.

Perhaps due to the Hainanese influence, Samui culture differs from that of other islands in Southern Thailand and its inhabitants refer to themselves as *chao samūi* (Samui folk) rather than Thais. They can be even friendlier than the average upcountry Thai, in my opinion, and have a great sense of humour, although those who are in constant contact with tourists can be a bit jaded. Nowadays many of the resorts, restaurants, bars and other tourist enterprises are owned or operated by Bangkok Thais or Europeans, so you have to get into the villages to meet true chao samūi.

The island has a distinctive cuisine, influenced by the omnipresent coconut, still the main source of income for chao samūi, who have disproportionately less ownership in beach property than outsiders. Coconut palms blanket the island, from the hillocks right up to the beaches. The durian, rambutan and langsat fruits are also cultivated.

The population of Ko Samui is for the most part concentrated in the port town of Na Thon, on the western side of the island facing the mainland, and in 10 or 11 small villages scattered around the island. One road encircles the island with several side roads poking into the interior; this main road is now paved all the way around.

## Ecology & Environment

Samui's visitors and inhabitants produce over 50 tonnes of garbage a day, much of it plastic. Not all of is properly disposed of, and quite a few plastic bottles end up in the sea, where they wreak havoc on marinelife. Remember to request glass water bottles instead of plastic, or to try to fill your own water bottle from the guesthouse or hotel restaurant's large, reusable canisters. On Ko Tao the TAT arranges monthly volunteer rubbish collections with half a dozen dive agencies who offer discounts to customers who participate; ask your Samui dive shop if a beach cleanup is planned.

## Information

**When to Go** The best time to visit the Samui group of islands is during the hot and dry season, February to late June. From July to October it can be raining on and off, and from October to January there are sometimes heavy winds. However, many travellers have reported fine weather (and fewer crowds) in September and October. November tends to get some of the rain which also affects the east coast of Malaysia at this time. Prices tend to soar from December to July, whatever the weather.

**Tourist Offices** A TAT office at the northern end of Na Thon, past the post office on the west side of the road, dispenses the usual handy brochures and maps. TAT says this is a temporary office and that it is looking for a new location elsewhere in town. The office is open daily 8.30 am to 4.30 pm.

**Maps** In Surat or on Ko Samui, you can pick up TAT's helpful Surat Thani map, which has maps of Surat Thani, the province, Ang Thong National Marine Park and Ko Samui, along with travel info. A couple of private companies now do good maps of Ko Samui, Pha-Ngan and Tao, which are available in tourist areas of Surat and on the islands for 35 to 40B. The most accurate and up-to-date is V Hongsombud's *Guide Map of Koh Samui, Koh Pha-Ngan & Koh Tao*.

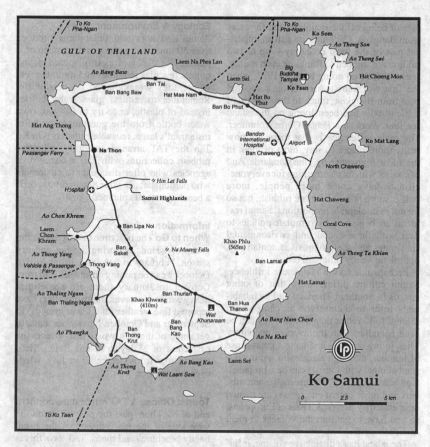

**Ko Samui**

*Map labels:*

To Ko Pha-Ngan

GULF OF THAILAND

Ao Bang Baw

Laem Na Phra Lan

To Ko Pha-Ngan

Ko Som

Ao Thong Son

Ao Thong Sai

Hat Choeng Mon

Ban Tai

Ban Bang Baw

Hat Mae Nam

Laem Sai

Hat Bo Phut

Big Buddha Temple

Ko Faan

Ko Mat Lang

Hat Ang Thong

Ban Bo Phut

Passenger Ferry

Na Thon

Bandon International Hospital

Ban Chaweng

Airport

North Chaweng

Hospital

Hin Lat Falls

Samui Highlands

Hat Chaweng

Ao Chon Khram

Ban Lipa Noi

Coral Cove

Laem Chon Khram

Ban Saket

Na Muang Falls

Khao Phlu (565m)

Ao Thong Ta Khian

Ao Thong Yang

Vehicle & Passenger Ferry

Thong Yang

Ban Lamai

Hat Lamai

Ao Thaling Ngam

Ban Thaling Ngam

Khao Khwang (410m)

Ban Thurian

Wat Khunaraam

Ban Hua Thanon

Ao Bang Nam Cheut

Ao Phangka

Ban Thong Krut

Ban Bang Kao

Ao Na Khai

Ao Thong Krut

Wat Laem Saw

Ao Bang Kao

Laem Set

To Ko Taen

0  2.5  5 km

**Immigration** Travellers have been able to extend their Tourist Visas at the Ko Samui immigration office in Na Thon, 6/9 Thawiraphakdi Rd, for 500B. Hours are Monday to Friday 8.30 am to 3.30 pm.

**Money** Changing money isn't a problem in Na Thon, Chaweng or Lamai, where several banks or exchange booths offer daily exchange services.

**Post & Communications** The island's main post office is in Na Thon, but in other parts of the island there are privately run branches. Many bungalow operations also sell stamps and mail letters, but most charge a commission.

International telephone service is available on the 2nd floor of the CAT office, attached to the Na Thon GPO, daily 7 am to 10 pm. Many private phone offices around the island will make a connection for a surcharge over the usual TOT rates.

**Travel Agencies** Surat Thani travel agents Phantip (☎ 421221/2) and Songserm (☎ 421-288) have offices in Na Thon.

**Medical Services** A new medical facility, Bandon International Hospital (☎ 425382/3; fax 425342) has recently opened in Bo Phut. Although we haven't yet received any feedback on the quality of the hospital's staff or facilities, emergency ambulance service is available 24 hours and credit cards are accepted for treatment fees.

**Dangers & Annoyances** Several travellers have written to say take care with local agents for train and bus bookings. Bookings sometimes don't get made at all, the bus turns out to be far inferior to what was expected or other hassles develop.

Take care with local boat trips to nearby islands. Visitors have reported swamped boats on windy days, sometimes being forced to spend the night stranded on an uninhabited island.

**Waterfalls**
Besides the beaches and rustic, thatched-roof bungalows, Samui has a couple of waterfalls. **Hin Lat Falls** is worth a visit if you're waiting in town for a boat back to the mainland. You can get there on foot – walk three km or so south of town on the main road, turning left at the road by the hospital. Go straight along this road about two km to arrive at the entrance to the waterfall. From here, it's about a half-hour walk along a trail to the top of the waterfall.

**Na Muang Falls**, in the centre of the island (the turn-off is 10 km south of Na Thon), is more scenic and somewhat less frequented. A songthaew from Na Thon should be about 20B. Songthaews can also be hired at Chaweng and Lamai beaches.

**Temples**
For temple enthusiasts **Wat Laem Saw**, at the southern end of the island near the village of Bang Kao, features an interesting and highly venerated old Srivijaya-style chedi. At the northern end, on a small rocky island joined to Samui by a causeway, is the so-called **Temple of the Big Buddha**, or Phra Yai. Erected in 1972, the modern image stands about 12m in height, and makes a nice sil-

houette against the tropical sky and sea behind it. The image is surrounded by *kutis* (meditation huts), mostly unoccupied. The monks prefer to receive visitors there. A sign in English requests that proper attire (no shorts) be worn on the temple premises. There is also an old semi-abandoned temple, **Wat Pang Ba**, near the northern end of Hat Chaweng, where 10 day vipassana courses are occasionally held for farangs; the courses are led by farang monks from Wat Suanmok in Chaiya.

Near the car park at the entrance to Hin Lat Falls is another trail left to **Suan Dharmapala**, a meditation temple. Another wat attraction is the ghostly **Mummified Monk** at Wat Khunaraam, which is off Route 4169 between Ban Thurian and Ban Hua Thanon.

## Ang Thong National Marine Park
อุทยานแห่งชาติหมู่เกาะทะเลอ่างทอง
This archipelago of around 40 small islands combines dense vegetation, sheer limestone cliffs, hidden lagoons and white sand beaches to provide a nearly postcard-perfect opportunity to enjoy Gulf islands at their best. The park itself encompasses 18 sq km of islands, plus 84 sq km of marine environments. From Ko Samui, a couple of tour operators run day trips out to the Ang Thong archipelago, 31 km north-west. A typical tour costs 350B per person, leaves Na Thon at 8.30 am and returns at 5.30 pm. Lunch is included, along with snorkelling in a sort of lagoon formed by one of the islands, from which Ang Thong gets its name (Golden Jar), and a climb to the top of a 240m hill to view the whole island group. Some tours also visit Tham Bua Bok, a cavern containing lotus-shaped cave formations. Tours depart daily in the high season, less frequently in the rainy season. The tours are still getting rave reviews. Bring hiking shoes, snorkelling gear and plenty of sunscreen and drinking water.

At least once a month there's also an overnight tour, as there are bungalows on Ko Wua Ta Lap, site of the park headquarters. These cost 500B per person and include three meals and accommodation at the bungalows. You

**SOUTHERN THAILAND**

may be able to book a passage alone to the Ang Thong islands; enquire at Songserm Travel Service or Ko Samui Travel Centre in Na Thon.

You can also arrange to join a more active but more expensive Ang Thong kayak trip through Sea Canoe at the Blue Lagoon Hotel on Hat Chaweng. Yet another alternative would be to get a group together, charter your own boat and design your own Ang Thong itinerary. At the park headquarters on Ko Wat Ta Lap you can rent bungalows for 400B a night or tents for 50B. For reservations, call Ang Thong National Marine Park at ☎ (77) 283025.

### Muay Thai
At the northern end of Na Thon there's a Thai boxing ring with regularly scheduled matches. Admission is around 100B to most fights. The quality of the mostly local contestants isn't exactly top-drawer.

### Diving
Many dive operations have opened around the island. Gear hired for beach dives costs around 500B per day. Dives from boats start from 1000B, and a four day certification course is about 5500B. An overnight dive trip to Ko Tao, including food and accommodation, costs around 3500B, or you can do a longer four day, three night trip for around 5000B.

The highest concentration of dive shops is found on Hat Chaweng. Among the more established are:

Aqua Divers – Hat Chaweng (☎ 442172)
Chang Divers – Hat Chaweng, Hat Lamai (☎ 424121)
The Dive Shop – Hat Chaweng (☎ /fax 230232)
Matlang Divers – Na Thon & Hat Chaweng (☎ 442172)
Samui International Diving School – Na Thon & Hat Chaweng (☎ 421056; fax 421465)

### Sea Kayaking
Sea Canoe (☎ 422037; fax 422401) at Blue Lagoon Hotel on Hat Chaweng offers guided kayak trips to nearby islands – Ko Mat Lang off the coast of Hat Chaweng is a three hour paddle, while the trip to Ko Ang Thong lasts

all day. From Christmas to August Sea Canoe also offers a three day Ang Thong kayaking/camping trip.

### Na Thon
หน้าทอน
Na Thon (pronounced *nâa thâwn*), on the north-west side of the island, is where express and night passenger ferries from the piers in Surat disembark. Car ferries from Don Sak and Khanom land at Ao Thong Yang, about 10 km south of Na Thon (see the Samui Beaches section later). If you're not travelling on a combination ticket you'll probably end up spending some time in Na Thon on your way in or out, waiting for the next ferry. Or if you're a long-term beachcomber, it makes a nice change to come into Na Thon once in a while for a little town life.

Although it's basically a tourist town now, Na Thon still sports a few old teak Chinese shophouses and cafes along Ang Thong Rd.

**Places to Stay** If you want or need to stay in Ko Samui's largest settlement (population 4000), there are seven places to choose from at the time of writing.

If you're looking for something inexpensive, take a look at the *Seaview Guest House* (☎ 420052) on Thawi Ratchaphakdi Rd, which has Khao San-style rooms with fan and shared bath for 150B, fan and private bath for 180 to 200B, and air-con for 300B – none of the rooms actually have sea views.

The *Palace Hotel* (Thai name *Chai Thaleh*) has clean, spacious rooms starting at 250 to 280B with fan or 350 to 400B with air-con. The *Win Hotel* farther down the road has all air-con rooms with TV and telephone for 420B, plus a nice coffee shop downstairs. Around the corner from the Win Hotel is the similar four-storey *Seaview Hotel* (☎ 421481) with rooms for 350/380B single/double with air-con, TV, phone and fridge.

On the main road north out of town is the *Dum Rong Town Hotel*, which charges from 500B for rooms with fan and bath. *Chao Koh Bungalow*, just north of town nearer to the sea, is 300 to 800B. On the southern edge of

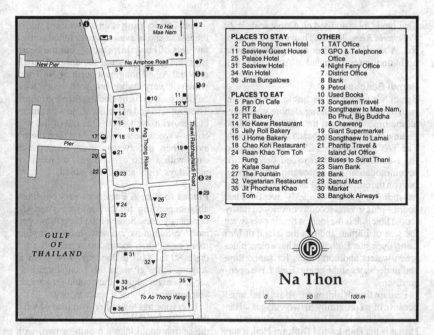

| PLACES TO STAY | OTHER |
|---|---|
| 2 Dum Rong Town Hotel | 1 TAT Office |
| 11 Seaview Guest House | 3 GPO & Telephone |
| 25 Palace Hotel | Office |
| 31 Seaview Hotel | 4 Night Ferry Office |
| 34 Win Hotel | 7 District Office |
| 36 Jinta Bungalows | 8 Bank |
|  | 9 Petrol |
| PLACES TO EAT | 10 Used Books |
| 5 Pan On Cafe | 13 Songserm Travel |
| 6 RT 2 | 17 Songthaew to Mae Nam, |
| 12 RT Bakery | Bo Phut, Big Buddha |
| 14 Ko Kaew Restaurant | & Chaweng |
| 15 Jelly Roll Bakery | 19 Giant Supermarket |
| 16 J Home Bakery | 20 Songthaew to Lamai |
| 18 Chao Koh Restaurant | 21 Phantip Travel & |
| 24 Raan Khao Tom Toh | Island Jet Office |
| Rung | 22 Buses to Surat Thani |
| 26 Kafae Samui | 23 Siam Bank |
| 27 The Fountain | 28 Bank |
| 32 Vegetarian Restaurant | 29 Samui Mart |
| 35 Jit Phochana Khao | 30 Market |
| Tom | 33 Bangkok Airways |

**Na Thon**

0        50        100 m

town, the *Jinta Bungalows* has pretty basic rooms for 150 to 250B.

**Places to Eat** There are several good restaurants and watering holes in Na Thon. On the road facing the harbour, the *Chao Koh Restaurant* is still serving good seafood and Thai standards at reasonable prices. *Ko Kaew* is a similar standby. A good place for breakfast is the *Jelly Roll*, a bakery with home-made pastries and coffee. Other meals include burgers, sandwiches and pizza.

Farther down the road towards Thong Yang are the *Pha-Ngan* and *Sri Samui* restaurants, both quite good Thai seafood places. Towards the Palace Hotel is a Thai rice and noodle place that's open all night, *Raan Khao Tom Toh Rung* (no English sign) – the cheapest place to eat on this strip. During the high season, many of these restaurants fill up at night with travellers waiting for the night ferry.

On the next street back from the harbour

is another branch of the Jelly Roll bakery, *Jelly Roll II*, then the *J Home Bakery* and a few old Chinese coffee shops like *Kafae Samui*. Farther south on this street is the *Fountain*, an Italian place specialising in pasta and pizza. At the intersection of Na Amphoe and Ang Thong Rds, you can't miss the popular bakery/cafe *RT 2*, which has an extensive Thai menu (dishes 35B and up) as well as fresh baked goods. After midnight the only places open are the Raan Khao Tom Toh Rung and the flashy Thai nightclub *Pan On Cafe*, which is rather expensive, dark and well chilled.

The third street back from the harbour is mostly travel agencies, photo shops and other small businesses. Two small supermarkets, Samui Mart and Giant Supermarket are also back here. The Charoen Laap day market is still thriving on this street as well. The *RT Bakery* on the same street is similar to the previously described RT 2.

One of the few places in town still serving

Thai (and Chinese) food on a large scale is *Jit Phochana Khao Tom* on Thawi Ratchaphakdi Rd. A small vegetarian restaurant opens at night on the southern end of Ang Thong Rd.

## Samui Beaches

Samui has plenty of beaches to choose from, with bungalows appearing at more small bays all the time. Transport has also improved, so getting from beach to beach is no problem. The TAT has registered 250 places to stay on the island. The most crowded beaches for accommodation are **Chaweng** and **Lamai**, both on the eastern side of the island. Chaweng has more bungalow 'villages' – over 80 at last count – plus several recently developed flashy tourist hotels. It is the longest beach, over twice the size of Lamai, and has the island of **Mat Lang** opposite. Both beaches have clear blue-green waters and coral reefs for snorkelling and underwater sightseeing. Both have open-air discos.

Perhaps there's a bit more to do in Hat Lamai because of its proximity to two villages – Ban Lamai and Ban Hua Thanon. At the wat in Ban Lamai is the **Ban Lamai Cultural Hall**, a sort of folk museum displaying local ceramics, household utensils, hunting weapons and musical instruments. The drawback to Lamai is the rather sleazy atmosphere of the strip of beer bars behind the beach; Chaweng's bar-and-disco strip is decidedly more sophisticated and more congenial for couples or single women.

Chaweng is definitely the target of current up-market development because of its long beach. Another factor is that only Chaweng (and the northern part of Lamai) has water deep enough for swimming from October to April; most other beaches on the island become very shallow during these months.

For more peace and quiet, try the beaches along the north, south and west coasts. **Mae Nam, Bo Phut and Big Buddha** are along the northern end; Bo Phut and Big Buddha are part of a bay that holds **Ko Faan** (the island with the 'big Buddha'), separated by a small headland. The water here is not quite as clear as at Chaweng or Lamai, but the feeling of seclusion is greater, and accommodation is cheaper.

**Hat Thong Yang** is on the western side of the island and is even more secluded (only a few sets of bungalows there), but the beach isn't that great by Samui standards. There is also Hat Ang Thong, just north of Na Thon, which is very rocky but with more local colour (such as fishing boats) than the others. The southern end of the island now has many bungalows as well, set in little out-of-the-way coves – worth seeking out. And then there's everywhere in between – every bay, cove or cape with a strip of sand gets a bungalow nowadays, right around the island.

**Places to Stay & Eat** Prices vary considerably according to the time of year and occupancy rates. Some of the bungalow operators on Samui have a nasty habit of tripling room rates when rooms are scarce, so a hut that's 80 to 100B in June could be 200B in August. Rates given in this section can only serve as a guideline – they could go lower if you bargain or higher if space is tight.

Everyone has his or her own idea of what the perfect beach bungalow is. At Ko Samui, the search could take a month or two, with so many operations to choose from. Most offer roughly the same services and accommodation for 100 to 400B, though some cost quite a bit more. The best thing to do is to go to the beach you think you want to stay at and pick one you like – look inside the huts, check out the restaurant, the menu, the guests. You can always move if you're not satisfied.

Beach accommodation around Samui now falls into four basic categories, chronicling the evolution of places to stay on the island. The first phase included simple bungalows with thatched roofs and walls of local, easily replaceable materials; the next phase brought concrete bathrooms attached to the old-style huts, a transition to the third phase of cement walls and tile roofs – the predominant style now, with more advanced facilities like fans and sometimes air-con. The latest wave is luxury rooms and bungalows indistinguishable from mainland inns and hotels.

Generally anything that costs less than

100B a night will mean a shared bath, which may be preferable when you remember that mosquitoes breed in standing water. For a pretty basic bungalow with private bath, 100 to 150B is the minimum on Ko Samui.

Theft isn't unknown on the island. If you're staying in a beach bungalow, consider depositing your valuables with the management while off on excursions around the island or while you're swimming at the beach. Most of the theft reports have come from Lamai and Mae Nam beaches.

Food is touch and go at all the beaches – one meal can be great, the next at the very same place not so great. Fresh seafood is usually what they do best and the cheapest way to eat it is to catch it yourself and have the bungalow cooks prepare it for you, or buy it in one of the many fishing villages around the island, direct from the fisherfolk themselves, or in the village markets. Good places to buy are in the relatively large Muslim fishing villages of Mae Nam, Bo Phut and Hua Thanon.

The island has changed so much in the years between editions of this book that I hesitate to name favourites. Cooks come and go, bungalows flourish and go bankrupt, owners are assassinated by competitors – you never can tell from season to season. Prices have remained fairly stable here in recent years, but they are creeping up. It's easy to get from one beach to another, so you can always change bungalows. With the establishment of several places charging well over 3000B per night, the jet-set seems to be discovering Samui. Finally, if Samui isn't to your liking, move islands! Think about Ko Pha-Ngan or Ko Tao.

What follows are some general comments on staying at Samui's various beaches, moving clockwise around the island from Na Thon.

## Ban Tai (Ao Bang Baw)
บ้านใต้ (อ่าวบางบ่อ)

Ban Tai is the first beach area north of Na Thon; so far there are just a handful of places to stay here. The beach has fair snorkelling and swimming. The *Axolotl Village* (☎ 420-017), run by an Italian-German partnership, caters to Europeans (the staff speak English, Italian, German and French) with tastefully designed, mid-range rooms for 300B or bungalows for 400 to 600B. Meditation and massage rooms are available – a massage costs 150B per hour. A very pleasant restaurant area overlooking the beach has an inventive international menu.

Next door to the Axolotl is the similar-looking and similarly priced *Blue River*, under Thai management. Also at Ban Tai is *Sunbeam*, a set of bungalows in a very nice setting. Huts are 250 to 300B, all with private bath.

## Hat Mae Nam
หาดแม่น้ำ

Hat Mae Nam is 14 km from Na Thon and expanding rapidly in terms of budget bungalow development – definitely still the cheapest area on the island.

At the headland (Laem Na Phra Lan) where Ao Bang Baw ends and Mae Nam begins is the *Home Bay Bungalows*, with basic huts for 80B and bungalows with bath for 200 to 400B. Next is *Coco Palm Village* (150 to 300B), followed by *Plant Inn*, also spelt *Phalarn*, with bungalows from 80 to 150B. Also in this area are *Naplarn Villa*, *Harry's* and *OK Village* – all in the 100 to 400B range. The beach in front of Wat Na Phalaan is undeveloped and the locals hope it will stay that way – topless bathing is strongly discouraged here.

The next group of places east includes *Anong Villa*, *Shangrilah Bungalows* (many bad reports on this one), *Maenam Resort*, *Palm Point Village* (nice ambience) and *Shady Shack Bungalows*, where prices start at 100 to 150B. *Maenam Resort* (☎ 425116) is a good mid-range place with spacious bungalows for 250 to 700B, while *Seafan Resort* offers spacious air-con bungalows and a pool for 1200 to 3500B.

Ban Mae Nam's huge *Santiburi Dusit Resort* (☎ 425038; (2) 238-4790 in Bangkok) – complete with tennis courts, waterways, ponds, bakery and sports facilities – costs from 6000B.

SOUTHERN THAILAND

Right in Ban Mae Nam, without beach views, are *Lolita Bungalows* and *Suksom Villa*, both in the 200 to 500B range.

Down on Hat Mae Nam proper is *Friendly*, which has clean, well kept huts for 80B, or 100 to 200B with private bath. Also good are *New La Paz Villa* (150 to 200B, or up to 550 with air-con) and *Silent* (80 to 150B).

Moving towards Bo Phut you'll find *Moon Hut Bungalows*, *Rose Bungalows*, *Laem Sai Bungalows*, *Maenam Villa* and *Rainbow Bungalows*, all with old-style Samui huts for 80 to 150B a night.

There are at least 10 or 15 other bungalow operations between Laem Na Phra Lan and Laem Sai, where Ao Mae Nam ends. The *Ubon Villa* (100 to 150B) is one of the better ones.

## Hat Bo Phut
หาดบ่อผุด

This beach has a reputation for peace and quiet, and those who come here regularly hope it will stay that way; this is not the place to show up looking for a party. The beach tends to be a little on the muddy side and the water can be too shallow for swimming during the dry season – a blessing wrapped in a curse which keeps development rather low-key and has preserved Bo Phut's village atmosphere.

Near Bo Phut village there's a string of bungalows in all price ranges, including the farthest north budget-friendly *Sunny* and *Chalee Villa*, both 100 to 300B, followed by the *Bophut Guest House* (80 to 200B), *Sandy Resort* (400 to 800B), *World Resort* (150 to 1000B), *New Sala Thai* (100 to 200B), *Calm Beach Resort* (100B fan up to 500B air-con) and the long-running, well run *Peace Bungalow* (150 to 350B).

More money to spend? Go for the semi-luxurious *Samui Palm Beach* (☎ 425494) at 1200 to 2200B or *Samui Euphoria* (☎ 425098; fax 425107), a posh spot with rooms and bungalows for 2800B and up.

Proceeding east, a road off the main round-island road runs to the left and along the bay towards the village. One of the golden oldies here is *Ziggy Stardust* (☎ 425410), a clean, well landscaped and popular place with huts for 200 to 300B and a couple of nicer family bungalows for 500 to 1200B. Next to Ziggy's is the *Siam Sea Lodge*, a small hotel with rooms for 250B with fan, hot water and fridge, or 400B with ocean view. You'll find several more cheapies along this strip, including *Miami*, in the 120 to 200B range, and *Oasis*, with huts in the 80 to 150B range. In the same vicinity on the inland side (no sea view), *Smile House* starts at 250B and offers the bonus of a swimming pool.

Up the street from Smile House and facing the ocean is a newer place, *The Lodge* (☎ 425337; fax 425336), which features a two-storey design reminiscent of old Samui architecture. Rooms with air-con and TV cost 800 to 1000B (200B less in low season). Next door you'll find the original *Boon Bungalows*, still holding on with cheap, closely spaced huts for 50 to 100B a night.

If you continue through the village along the water, you'll find the isolated *Sand Blue* with huts for 150 to 400B, and *Sky Blue* in the 80 to 150B range. This area is sometimes called Hat Bang Rak.

The village has a couple of cheap local-style restaurants as well as French, German, Spanish and Italian restaurants. The Austra-lian-managed *Boathouse* has good western and Thai food in a nice setting, and great cocktails. They are also an agent for a PADI diving school. *Bird in the Hand* next door to The Lodge serves good, reasonably priced Thai and western food in a rustic setting overlooking the water. A little farther east on Bo Phut's main street, *Ubon Waan Som Tam* serves cheap and tasty Isaan food.

## Big Buddha Beach (Hat Phra Yai)
หาดพระใหญ่

This now has nearly 20 bungalow opera-tions, including the moderately expensive air-con *Comfort Resort Nara Garden* (☎ 425364), with rooms for 600 to 1500B and a swimming pool. *Family Village* gets good reviews and costs 200 to 700B. *Big*

*Buddha Bungalows* (200 to 350B) is still OK. *Sun Set* is about the cheapest place here, with simple huts at 80 to 300B. *Como's*, *Champ Resort*, *Beach House*, *Kinnaree* and *Number One* are in the 150 to 300B range. The Beach House also has huts for 200 to 400B. *Niphon* has bungalows costing from 200 to 650B.

## Ao Thong Son & Ao Thong Sai
อ่าวท้องสน/อ่าวท้องใทร

The big cape between Big Buddha and Chaweng is actually a series of four capes and coves, the first of which is Ao Thong Son. The road to Thong Son is a bit on the hellish side, but that keeps this area quiet and secluded. *Samui Thongson Resort* has its own cove and bungalows for 200B with fan, 850 to 1200B with air-con; knock off about 25% May to November. *Thongson Bay Bungalows* next door has old-style bungalows for 100 to 150B; farther on is the similar *Golden Pine* with 100 to 200B bungalows.

The next cove over is as yet undeveloped and there isn't even a dirt road there yet. The third, Ao Thong Sai, has *Imperial Tongsai Bay* (☎ 425015), a heavily guarded resort with a private beach, swimming pool and tennis courts. Rates start at 4700B.

## Hat Choeng Mon
หาดเชิงมน

The largest cove following Ao Thong Sai has been called by several names, but the beach is generally known as Hat Choeng Mon. It's clean, quiet and recommended for families or people who don't need nightlife and a variety of restaurants. If you want to stay here, you can find restaurants and nightlife at nearby Chaweng.

In Hat Choeng Mon you'll find the well run, popular *PS Villa* (200 to 400B), along with *Choeng Mon Bungalow Village* (150 to 650B), *Chat Kaew Resort* (200 to 1000B), *Island View* (100 to 300B) and the well laid-out *Sun Sand Resort* (starting at 950B), which has sturdy thatched-roof bungalows connected by wooden walkways on a breezy hillside. Across from the beach is **Ko Faan**

**Yai**, an island that can be reached on foot at low tide.

Between Choeng Mon Bungalow Village and PS Villa are two top-end places. The *Imperial Boat House Hotel* (☎ 425041; fax (2) 261-9533 in Bangkok) has a three-storey hotel plus separate two-storey bungalows built to resemble rice barges; rates are 2200 to 6000B. Just north is *The White House* (☎ 245315), a collection of deluxe bungalows for 1200 to 2900B.

Next is a smaller bay called Ao Yai Noi, just before North Chaweng. This little bay is quite picturesque, with large boulders framing the beach. The secluded *IKK* bungalows are 200 to 500B and the *Coral Bay Resort* has larger, well spaced bungalows with air-con on grassy grounds for 1500 to 2200B.

## Hat Chaweng
หาดแฉวง

Hat Chaweng, Samui's longest beach, also has the island's highest concentration of bungalows and tourist hotels. Prices are moving up-market fast; accommodation is now perhaps 60 to 80B at the lowest in the off season, and up to 8000B at the Central Samui. There is a commercial 'strip' behind the central beach jam-packed with restaurants, souvenir shops and discos. The beach is beautiful here, and local developers are finally cleaning up some of the trashy areas behind the bungalows that were becoming a problem in the 1980s.

One minus here are the obnoxious trucks mounted with loudspeakers that drive up and down the strip announcing bullfight (bull against bull, Thai style) matches at a nearby stadium; the noise of the loudspeakers drowns out all conversation and any music being played or performed in local bars and restaurants. Another blight on the scene is the ongoing construction of a multistorey hotel in the centre of the beach that obviously flaunts the island's 12m height restriction for all beach structures. One hopes a group of honest Samui residents will take on the task of reversing whatever decision allowed this monstrosity to begin.

SOUTHERN THAILAND

Chaweng has km after km of bungalows – perhaps 70 or more in all – so have a look around before deciding on a place. There are basically three sections: North Chaweng, Hat Chaweng proper and Chaweng Noi.

**North Chaweng** Places here are mostly in the 100 to 800B range, with simple bungalows with private bath at the northernmost end. Besides being less expensive than lodgings farther south, the North Chaweng places are out of earshot of central Chaweng's throbbing discos. *Papillon Resort* and *Samui Island Resort*, the northernmost, offer concrete bungalows starting at 300B, though rates can be half this in low season. The friendly *Matlang Resort* (☎ 230468) has better-than-average bungalows for 150 to 400B, and the same can be said for *Marine Bungalows* and *Venus Resort* next door. In this same area, the most inexpensive place, *Blue Lagoon Bungalow*, charges 100 to 400B. After that you have the OK *Family* (150 to 300B), *K John Resort* (100 to 400B) and the rather aggressively commercial *Moon* (200 to 300B).

At the end nearest to central Chaweng are a small group of up-market places starting at 2000B or more: *Samui Villa Flora* (☎ 422272), *Chaweng Blue Lagoon Hotel* (☎ 422037; fax 422401) and *Amari Palm Reef Resort*. The Amari is the nicest of the three, with individual two-storey, Thai-style cottages and two swimming pools; it's also the most environmentally conscious luxury resort on the island, using filtered sea water for most first uses and recycling grey water for landscaping. Rooms and bungalows start at 2990/3220B for singles/doubles, 3680B for a mezzanine (two-storey) cottage and up to 4485B for a terrace room or suite. The Blue Lagoon is Sea Canoe's Samui home, and charges 2200B per room but sometimes runs special rates of 1500B. There are also two mid-range places in the area, the *JR Palace* (400B to 1200B) and *The Island* (400 to 1500B); that latter has a very popular open-air restaurant.

Off the road that leads away from the beach toward the interior is the new *Novotel*

*Ko Samui Resort* (☎ 422472; fax 422473; ☎ (2) 267-0810 in Bangkok). Novotel's 74 rooms and suites are built in stepped, two-storey hotel wings built on a slight slope with sea as well as lagoon views. Rates start at 2200B for deluxe doubles and continue up to 4200B for suites.

**Hat Chaweng Central** The central area, Hat Chaweng proper, is the longest and has the most bungalows and hotels. This is also where the strip behind the hotels and huts is centred, with restaurants (most with videos), bars (yes, the girlie bar scene is sneaking in), discos, video parlours, pool halls, tourist police, TAT mini-office, post office, minimarts, one hour photo-developing labs, tailors, souvenir shops and currency exchange booths.

Water sports are big here, too, so you can rent sailboards, go diving, sail a catamaran, charter a junk and so on. Parasailing costs around 400B and water-skiing is 250 to 300B per hour. This area also has the highest average prices on the island, not only because accommodation is more up-market but simply because this is the prettiest beach on the island. In general, the places get more expensive as you move from north to south; many places are owned by the same families who owned them under different names 10 or 15 years ago, and some have just added the word 'Resort' to the name.

The *Reggae Pub* has built a huge new zoo-like complex off the beach with many bars, an artificial waterfall, a huge open-air dance floor with high-tech equipment and trendy DJs who play music customers can bop to most of the night. Another popular dance place is the *Green Mango*, which stays open later – this is where people usually end the night (it was the reverse two years ago!). New clubs include *The Doors Pub*, a rock'n'roll place whose decor pays tribute to Jim Morrison et al, the *Santa Fe*, a huge place with an American South-West theme, beach entrance and state-of-the-art sound and lighting and *Phra Chan Samui Club*, an enclosed air-con place that's open all night.

Rather than list all the places on Chaweng

Central, I'll just give examples across the spectrum, starting at the north:

*Charlie's Hut* – 100 to 350B
*Chaweng Garden Beach* – (☎ /fax 422265); 450 to 900B
*Chaweng Villa* – (☎ /fax 422130); 600 to 1000B (air-con)
*Coconut Grove* – (☎ 422268); 100 to 300B
*Joy Resort* – 200 to 1000B
*Long Beach Lodge* – (☎ 422372); 200 to 750B
*Lucky Mother* – 100 to 300B
*Malibu Resort* – (☎ 422386); 300 (fan) to 1500B (air-con)
*Munchies Resort* – 300 to 1500B
*Montien House* – (☎ 422169; fax 422145); 500B (fan) to 1000B (air-con)
*Poppies Samui* – (☎ 422389; fax 422420); 2000 to 3000B
*The Princess Village* – (☎ 422216; fax 422382); 1200 to 3400B

The queen of the central Chaweng properties is *Central Samui Beach Resort* (☎ 230500; fax 422385), a huge neo-colonial-style place with rooms starting at 4200B. If you're getting the idea that this isn't the beach for bottom-budget backpackers, you're right, but surprisingly a few popular cheapies have survived between the Beachcomber and Central Bay Resort. From the northern end is *Silver Sand* (300 to 400B), followed by the least expensive, *Charlie's Hut I*, with rustic huts in the 80 to 100B range. I've heard several complaints of rude staff and theft here, along with pot 'busts' that result in on-the-spot fines and no confiscation of the dope.

Better but more expensive huts can be found at *Charlie's Hut II* for 150 to 250B, while next door *Viking* starts at 100B, followed by the similarly priced *Thai House* and *Charlie's Hut*. In peak season these places fill early, so to save money it may be easier to go to another beach entirely – or try North Chaweng.

**Chaweng Noi** This area is off by itself around a headland at the southern end of central Hat Chaweng. One place that straddles the headland on both bays is the aptly named *First Bungalows* (they were the first to build on this beach 16 years ago), with

wooden bungalows for 600B and concrete-and-tile types for 700B up. The *New Star* starts at 350B. Nearby *Fair House* has fan-cooled rooms for 400B, air-con up to 1200B.

The plush, multistorey *Imperial Samui* is built on a slope in the middle of Chaweng Noi proper and costs 3000 to 5000B for air-con accommodation with telephone and colour TV – up to 40% less in the off season. The Imperial's 56 cottages and 24-room hotel are built in a pseudo-Mediterranean style with a 700 sq m salt-water swimming pool and a terrace restaurant with a view. The *Chaweng Noi*, at the southern end of the beach, is the only cheap place left – huts cost 100 to 150B. Finally there's the *Tropicana Beach Resort* with all air-con rooms at 650 to 1200B.

### Coral Cove (Ao Thong Yang)
อ่าวท้องยาง
Another series of capes and coves starts at the end of Chaweng Noi, beginning with scenic Coral Cove. Somehow the Thais have managed to squeeze three places around the cove, plus one across the road. The only one with immediate beach access is *Coral Cove Resort*, where basic huts start at 150B and go up to 300B for a decent bungalow with fan, 500 to 850B with air-con. At the southern end of the cove is the new *Samui Yacht Club* (☎ /fax 422400), with luxurious Thai-style bungalows for 3300 to 4300B (1000B less in the low season).

The *Hi Coral Cove* on a lovely, remote spot above the bay is 80 to 400B – good value if you don't mind walking to the beach. The *Coral Mountain Chalets*, on the hill opposite the road, costs 350 to 500B.

### Ao Thong Ta Khian
อ่าวท้องตะเคียน
This is another small, steep-sided cove, similar to Coral Cove and backed by huge boulders. The *Samui Silver Beach Resort* has bungalows overlooking the bay for 400B with fan or 850B with air-con, and a pleasant restaurant with a beach view. On the other side of the road is the *Little Mermaid*, with

bungalows for 200 and 350B. This is a good spot for fishing, and there are a couple of good seafood restaurants down on the bay.

## Hat Lamai
หาดละไม

After Chaweng, this is Samui's most popular beach for travellers. Hat Lamai rates are just a bit lower than at Chaweng overall, are without the larger places like the Central Samui or the Imperial (yet) and have fewer of the 500B-plus places. As at Chaweng, the bay has developed in sections. There is a long central beach flanked by hilly areas. There continue to be reports of burglaries and muggings at Lamai. Take care with valuables – have them locked away in a guesthouse or hotel office if possible. Muggings mostly occur in dark lanes and along unlit parts of the beach at night.

**Northern Hat Lamai** Accommodation at the north-eastern end of the beach is quieter and more moderately priced, though the beach is a bit thin on sand. At the top of the beach is the inexpensive *New Hut*, with 80B huts which can accommodate two people; the proprietor here has been known to eject guests who don't eat in the restaurant. Farther south and almost as inexpensive is an oldie, *Thong Gaid Garden*, with huts for 150 to 250B. *Comfort Bungalow* has undergone a facelift and new ownership, now costing 500 to 1000B for all air-con rooms plus there's a pool. The semi-secluded *Royal Blue Lagoon Beach Resort* (☎ 424086; fax 424195) sounds fancier than its 350 to 1000B tariffs indicate; it also has a pool and a good restaurant in a nice setting. Less expensive are the *Island Resort* (200 to 250B), *Rose Garden* (150 to 450B) and *Suksamer* (150 to 300B). There are a sprinkling of others here that seem to come and go with the seasons.

One relatively new northern Lamai place that looks like it's here to stay is the American-run *Spa Resort* (☎ 230855; fax 424126), a new-agey place that offers herbal sauna, massage, natural foods, meditation and yes, even colon cleansing. Bob Weir of Grateful

Dead fame reportedly checked in for a few days in 1996. At the moment simple bungalows here cost 250 to 500B near the beach, 100 to 200B for smaller ones near the road. The restaurant serves vegetarian and seafood. As accommodation alone, these huts are overpriced relative to the neighbourhood; fees for health services are extra. Other activities include t'ai chi, chi kung, yoga and mountain biking.

**Hat Lamai Central** Down into the main section of Lamai is a string of places for 100 to 600B including *Mui, Utopia, Magic, Coconut Villa* and the *Weekender*. The Weekender has a wide variety of bungalows and activities to choose from, including a bit of nightlife. Moving into the centre of Ao Lamai, you'll come across *Coconut Beach* (80 to 200B), *Animal House* (skip this one, it's received several complaints) and *Lamai Inn* (300 to 800B).

This is the part of the bay closest to Ban Lamai village and the beginning of the Lamai 'scene'. Just about every kind of service is available here, including exchange offices, medical service units, supermarkets, one hour photo labs, clothing shops, bike and jeep rental places, travel agencies with postal and international telephone services, restaurants (many with videos), discos, bars, bungee-jumping and foodstalls. The girlie bar scene has invaded this part of the island, with several lanes lined with Pattaya-style outdoor bars. By and large it's a farang male-dominated scene, but unlike in Pattaya and other similar mainland places, where western males tend to take on Thai females as temporary appendages, you may see more than a few western women spending their holiday with Thai boys on Lamai.

Next comes a string of slightly up-market 100 to 600B places: *Thai House Inn, Marina Villa, Sawatdi, Mira Mare, Sea Breeze* and *Varinda Resort*. The *Aloha* (☎ 424014) is a two-storey up-market resort where bungalows start at 1050B, rooms from 2200B. All of these have fairly elaborate dining areas; the Aloha has a good restaurant with seafood, Thai and European food. Also in this area are the *Galaxy Resort*, with fully equipped bungalows for 1400 to 1600B and more basic air-con ones for 400 to 450B, which is reasonable value. *Golden Sand* is still looking good at 450 to 800B for air-con bungalows.

Finishing up central Hat Lamai is a mixture of places costing anywhere from 80 to 600B. *Paradise* has been here 20 years and is the second longest-running place on the beach, with thatched huts from 100 to 150B and concrete bungalows for 400 to 600B. Standing apart in terms of providing high-quality, friendly service is *Bill's Resort* (☎ 233054; fax 424286), where bungalows are close together but spacious inside and cost 200 to 400B. The *White Sand* is another Lamai original and huts are now 80B and up. A farang flea market is held here on Sundays – many travellers sell handmade jewellery. The long-standing *Palm* with bungalows in the 150 to 250B price range. The *Nice Resort* has huts for 150B up but they're really too close together. Finally, there's the *Sun Rise*, where acceptable huts go for 100 and 200B, new bungalows for 400B with fan or 700B with air-con.

A place with good French bread, croissants and cakes is *Will Wait* in the centre of the village. They open very early for breakfast, close after 10 pm and are popular for inexpensive travellers' food. Also popular on the 'strip' is *Shi Bar-Restaurant*, which serves Middle Eastern fare such as hummus, pita and falafel along with a few Thai dishes starting at 30B. Lamai has two large dance clubs, the older *Bauhaus Pub* and the newer *Mix Pub*, the most local dance venue on the island. Interspersed with DJ-ed music are short drag shows and Thai boxing demos.

**Ao Bang Nam Cheut** At this point a headland interrupts Ao Lamai and the bay beyond is known as Ao Bang Nam Cheut, named after the freshwater stream that runs into the bay here. During the dry months the sea is too shallow for swimming here, but in the late rainy season when the surf is too high elsewhere on the island's beaches, south Lamai is one of the best for swimming. Look for the well known, phallus-like 'Grandmother' and 'Grandfather' rock formations.

Closer to the road than the coast is the *Samui Park*, a concrete block with rooms and a few bungalows from 650 to 1250B. Down further, *Noi* offers huts starting at 80B and bungalows from 150B. Next is *Chinda House*, with air-con bungalows for 800 to 2000B. The *Swiss Chalet* has large bungalows overlooking the sea for 200B and the restaurant does Swiss as well as Thai food. Then comes the old-timer *Rocky*, with a few thatched huts for 150 to 250B, and renovated and newer ones for 400 to 800B.

## Ao Na Khai & Laem Set
อ่าวหน้าคาย/แหลมเส็ต

Just beyond the village of Ban Hua Thanon at the southern end of Ao Na Khai is an area sometimes called Hat Na Thian. As at Lanai, the places along the southern end of the island are pretty rocky, which means good snorkelling (there's a long reef here), but perhaps not such good swimming. Prices in this area seem fairly reasonable – 100B here gets you what 200B might in Chaweng. The hard part is finding these places, since they're off the round-island road, down dirt tracks, and most don't have phones. You might try exploring this area on a motorcycle first. The *Cosy Resort* has 11 well spaced, simple huts for 100 to 200B. Next is the *Royal Resort*, with bungalows for 350B with fan and up to 1200B with air-con. The cheaper *Wanna Samui Resort* has bungalows with fan for 250 and air-con for 950B.

Down a different road in the same area is the drab concrete *Samui Orchid Resort* (☎ 424017) which, with huts for 650 to 1200B and a swimming pool, makes an unsuccessful attempt to be up-market.

Turn right here, follow the coast and you'll come to the basic *Sonny View* (80B) and the nicely designed *Na Thian* (100 to 150B). At the end of the road, at the foot of Khao Thaleh, the secluded *Laem Set Inn* (☎ 424393; fax 424394) commands a pretty corner of sand-and-boulder beach. Some of the buildings here are old Samui-style homes that have been salvaged by the English owner from other parts of the island. Rustic but charming bungalows start at 1150B with veranda, hot water shower and sea view. More contemporary air-con rooms facing the sea cost from 2500B. On the premises are a minor art gallery and a good Thai restaurant (pricey, small portions according to one reader). At Laem Set you pay for atmosphere and ecological sensitivity more than for amenities; some people will find this just what they're looking for, while others may feel they can find better value on the more popular beaches.

## Ao Bang Kao
อ่าวบางเก่า

This bay is at the very south end of the island between Laem Set and Laem So (Saw). Again, you have to go off the round-island road a couple of km to find these places: *River Garden* (60 to 150B), *Diamond Villa* (100 to 300B), *Samui Coral Beach* (150 to 400B) and *Waikiki* (300 to 400B).

## Ao Thong Krut & Ko Taen
อ่าวต้องกรุตและเกาะแตน

Next to the village of Ban Thong Krut on Ao Thong Krut is, what else, *Thong Krut*, where huts with private bath are 150 to 250B (100B in low season).

Ban Thong Krut is also the jumping-off point for boat trips to four offshore islands: **Ko Taen**, **Ko Raap**, **Ko Mat Daeng** (which has the best coral) and **Ko Mat Sum**. Ko Taen has three bungalow villages along the east coast beach at Ao Awk: *Tan Village*, *Ko Tan Resort* and *Coral Beach*, all in the range of 80 to 250B a night. Ko Mat Sum has good beaches – some travellers have camped here. Lately rubbish has been a problem though, perhaps because there are fewer bungalow proprietors to organise cleanups.

Boats to Ko Taen cost 50B each way. If you want to have a good look at the islands, you can charter a boat at the *Sunset Restaurant* in Thong Krut from 9 am to 4 pm for 900 to 1100B; the boats carry up to 10 people. The Sunset Restaurant has good seafood (best to arrange in advance) and delicious coconut shakes.

## West Coast

Several bays along Samui's western side have places to stay, including Thong Yang, where the Don Sak ferry docks. The beaches here turn to mud flats during low tide, however, so they're more or less for people seeking to get away from the east coast scene, not for beach fanatics.

**Ao Phangka** Around Laem Hin Khom on the bottom of Samui's western side is this little bay, sometimes called Emerald Cove. The secluded *Emerald Cove* and *Sea Gull* have huts with rates from 80 to 300B – it's a nice setting and perfectly quiet. Between them are the newer and slightly cheaper *Gem House* and *Pearl Bay*. During the low season there are so few guests on this cove that the bungalow proprietors tend to let the rubbish pile up.

**Ao Taling Ngam** Dominating the northern end of this shallow curving bay from its perch atop a steep hill, *Baan Taling Ngam* (☎ 423019; fax 423220; ☎ (2) 236-0400 in Bangkok) is Samui's most ultra-exclusive resort at the moment. Managed by the Mandarin Oriental hotel group, Baan Taling Ngam boasts tennis courts, two swimming pools, a fitness centre and a full complement of equipment and instructors for kayaking, windsurfing and diving. As it's not right on the beach, a shuttle service transports guests back and forth. Luxuriously appointed guest accommodation containing custom-made Thai-style furnishings start at 4000B for a deluxe room in the low season (April to December 14) up to 10,000B for a cliff villa or deluxe suite in the high season, not including 17% tax and service.

Sharing the same bay just below Baan Taling Ngam, *Wiesenthal* (☎ /fax 233165) offers nine bungalows well spaced amidst a coconut grove for 300B single/double, 800B for a family-size bungalow. The Swiss-managed restaurant serves good Thai and European food.

Ao Taling Ngam is a 15 to 20B songthaew ride from Na Thon or the vehicle ferry pier. Baan Taling Ngam of course provides airport/ferry transfers for all guests.

SOUTHERN THAILAND

**Ao Thong Yang** The vehicle ferry jetty is here in Ao Thong Yang. Near the pier are *In Foo Palace* (100 to 400B), *Coco Cabana Beach Club* (350B and up) and the motel-like *Samui Ferry Inn* (400 to 900B). The Coco Cabana is the best of the lot.

The vehicle ferry jetty may be moved to another location in the near future; or this one may remain in operation and a second built elsewhere along the coast. Either way the local accommodation will be affected by the change, possibly winding down and eventually closing.

**Ao Chon Khram** On the way to Na Thon is sweeping Ao Chon Khram, with the *Lipa Lodge* and *International*. The Lipa Lodge is especially nice, with a good site on the bay. Most huts are 100 to 150B, with a few as high as 650B. There is a good restaurant and bar here, not bad for the money. On the other hand, the International is nothing special at 200 to 500B. Between them is the up-market *Rajapruek Samui Resort* (1150 to 3500B), and farther north the isolated and slightly more expensive *The Siam Residence Resort*.

### Getting There & Away

**Air** Bangkok Airways flies nearly a dozen times daily to Ko Samui from Bangkok. There is an office in Na Thon near the Win Hotel and another at the airport (☎ 425012). The fare is 2540B one way – no discount for a return ticket. The flight duration is one hour and 20 minutes.

Bangkok Airways also offers daily flights to Samui from Phuket (1120B, 50 minutes), Hua Hin (1640B, one hour) and U-Tapao (1660B, one hour).

During high season flights may be completely booked out as much as six weeks in advance, so be sure to plan accordingly. If Samui flights are full, you might try flying to Surat Thani from Bangkok and other places aboard THAI (see the Surat Thani Getting There & Away section for details). From Surat Thani airport you can catch a THAI bus directly to Ko Samui (via the Don Sak vehicle ferry) for 200B.

There is talk that the Samui airport may be expanded to accommodate international flights sometime within the next five years.

**Bus** The government bus/ferry combo fare from Bangkok's Northern Bus Terminal is 327B. Most private buses from Bangkok charge around 350B for the same journey. From Khao San Rd in Bangkok it's possible to get bus/ferry combination tickets for as low as 220B, but service is substandard and theft is more frequent than on the more expensive buses.

**Train** The State Railway of Thailand also does train/bus/ferry tickets straight through to Samui from Bangkok. These save you only 10 or 20B on 2nd class seat tickets; for everything else a combo ticket costs around 50B more than separate train, bus (from the train station to piers) and boat tickets – which may be worth it to avoid the hassles of separate bookings/connections. See the Surat Thani Getting There & Away section for details on train travel.

**Boat** To sort out the ferry situation you have to understand that there are two ferry companies and three ferry piers on the Surat Thani coast (actually four but only three are in use at one time) and two on Ko Samui. Neither ferry company is going to tell you about the other. Songserm Travel runs express ferry boats from the Tha Thong pier, six km north-east of central Surat, and slow night boats from the Ban Don pier in town. These take passengers only. The express boats used to leave from the same pier in Ban Don as the night ferry – when the river is unusually high they may use this pier again.

Samui Ferry Co runs vehicle ferries from Don Sak (or Khanom when the sea is high). This is the company that gets most of the bus/boat and some of the train/bus/boat combination business.

Which boat you take will depend on what's next available when you arrive at the bus terminal in Surat or train station in Phun Phin – touts working for the two ferry companies will lead you to one or the other.

During the low season (any time except

December to February or August), young Thais may throng the piers around departure time for the Ko Samui boats, inviting farangs to stay at this or that bungalow. This same tactic is employed at the Na Thon and Thong Yang piers upon arrival at Ko Samui. During the high tourist season, however, this isn't necessary as every place is just about booked out. Some of the more out-of-the-way places to stay put touts on the boats to pass around photo albums advertising their establishments.

**Tha Thong – Express Boat** From November to May three express boats go to Samui (Na Thon) daily from Tha Thong and each takes two to 2½ hours to reach the island. From November to May the departure times are usually 7.30 am, noon and 2.30 pm, though these change from time to time. From June to October there are only two express boats a day, at 7.30 am and 1.30 pm – the seas are usually too high in the late afternoon for a third sailing in this direction during the rainy season. The express ferry boats have two decks, one with seats below and an upper deck that is really just a big luggage rack – good for sunbathing. Passage is 105B one way, 170B return, but this fare seesaws from season to season; if any rivals to Songserm appear on the scene (as has happened twice in the last four years), Songserm tends to drop its fares immediately to as low as 50B one way to drive the competition out of business.

From Na Thon back to Surat, there are departures at 7.15 am, noon and 2.45 pm from November to May, or 7.30 am and 2.45 pm from June to October. The 7.15 am boat includes a bus ride to the train station in Phun Phin; the afternoon boats include a bus to the train station and to the Talaat Kaset bus station in Ban Don.

**Ban Don – Night Ferry** There is also a slow boat for Samui that leaves the Ban Don pier each night at 11 pm, reaching Na Thon around 5 am. This one costs 70B for the upper deck (including pillows and mattresses), or 50B down below (straw mats only).

The locals use this boat extensively and the craft itself is in better shape than some of the express boats. It's particularly recommended if you arrive in Surat Thani too late for the fast boat and don't want to stay in Ban Don. And it does give you more sun time on Samui, after all.

The night ferry back to Samui leaves Na Thon at 9 pm, arriving at 3 am; you can stay on the boat, catching some more sleep, until 8 am. Ignore the touts trying to herd passengers onto buses to Bangkok, as these won't leave till 8 am or later anyway.

Don't leave your bags unattended on the night ferry, as thefts can be a problem. The thefts usually occur after you drop your bags on the ferry well before departure and then go for a walk around the pier area. Most victims don't notice anything's missing until they unpack after arrival on Samui.

**Don Sak – Vehicle Ferry** Tour buses run directly from Bangkok to Ko Samui, via the vehicle ferry from Don Sak in Surat Thani Province, for around 327B. Check with the big tour bus companies or any travel agency.

From Talaat Mai Rd in Surat Thani you can also get bus/ferry combination tickets straight through to Na Thon. These cost 70B for an ordinary bus, 90B for an air-con bus. Pedestrians or people in private vehicles can also take the ferry directly from Don Sak, which leaves at 8, 10 am, 2 and 5 pm, and takes one hour to reach the Thong Yang pier on Samui. In the opposite direction, ferries leave Thong Yang at 7.30 and 10 am, noon, 2 and 4 pm; in this direction the trip takes around an hour and 45 minutes.

Without bus fare included, the straight fare for pedestrians is 50B, for a motorcycle and driver 75B, and for a car and driver 190B. Passengers in private vehicles pay the pedestrian fare. The ferry trip takes about 1½ hours to reach Don Sak, which is 60 km from Surat Thani.

Buses between the Surat Thani bus station and Don Sak cost 14B and take 45 minutes to an hour to arrive at the ferry terminal. If you're coming north from Nakhon Si Thammarat, this might be the ferry to take, though from Surat Thani the Tha Thong ferry is definitely more convenient.

From Ko Samui, air-con buses to Bangkok leave from near the old pier in Na Thon at 1.30 and 3.30 pm daily, both arriving in Bangkok around 5 am due to a stopover in Surat. Other through bus services from Na Thon include Hat Yai (200B), Krabi (191B) and Phuket (193B); all of these buses leave Na Thon around 7 am, arriving at their respective destinations around six hours later. Check with the several travel agencies in Na Thon for the latest routes.

### Getting Around

It is quite possible to hitch around the island, despite the fact that anyone on the island with a car is likely to want to boost their income by charging for rides.

**The Airport**  The Samui airport departure tax is 100B. Bangkok Airways has an air-con van service for 60B per person to/from its Na Thon office and the north/north-west beaches, 80B to/from Lamai. For other beaches you'll have to rely on songthaews or taxis. Chartered taxis from the airport cost 250B to anywhere on the island.

**Car & Motorcycle**  You can rent motorcycles from several places in Na Thon as well as at various bungalows around the island. The going rate is 150B per day for a 100cc bike, but for longer periods you can get the price down (say 280B for two days, 400B for three days etc). Rates are generally lower in Na Thon and it makes more sense to rent them there if you're going back that way. Take it easy on the bikes; several farangs die or are seriously injured in motorcycle accidents every year on Samui, and, besides, the locals really don't like seeing their roads become race tracks.

Suzuki Caribian jeeps can be hired for around 700 to 800B per day from various Na Thon agencies as well as at Chaweng and Lamai. Aside from all the small independents doing rentals, Hertz has branches at Samui airport (☎ 425011) and at the Baan Taling Ngam and Chaweng Blue Lagoon resorts.

**Local Transport**  Songthaew fares are 15B

from Na Thon to Lamai, 10B to Mae Nam or Bo Phut, 15B to Big Buddha, 20B to Chaweng or Choeng Mon. From the car-ferry landing in Thong Yang, rates are 20B for Lamai, Mae Nam and Bo Phut/Big Buddha, 25B for Chaweng, 30B for Choeng Mon. A few years ago official fares were posted for these routes, but nowadays songthaew drivers like to over-charge newcomers, so take care. Songthaews run regularly during daylight hours only. A regular bus between Thong Yang and Na Thon costs 10B. Note that if you're arriving in Thong Yang on a bus (via the vehicle ferry), your bus/boat fare includes a ride into Na Thon, but not elsewhere.

## KO PHA-NGAN
เกาะพะงัน
• ☎ (77) • *pop 10,000*

Ko Pha-Ngan, about a half-hour boat ride north of Ko Samui, has become the island of choice for those who find Samui too crowded or too expensive. It started out as sort of 'back-door escape' from Samui but is well established now, with a regular boat service and over 156 places to stay around the 190 sq km island. It's definitely worth a visit for its remaining deserted beaches (they haven't all been built upon) and, if you like snorkelling, for its live-coral formations.

In the interior of this somewhat smaller island are four year-round waterfalls and a number of more seasonal ones. Boulders carved with the royal insignia of Rama V, Rama VII and Rama IX, all of whom have visited the falls, can be found at **Than Sadet Falls**, which cascades along Khlong Than Sadet in the north-eastern part of the island. **Phaeng Falls** is off the main road between Thong Sala and Chalok Lam, almost in the centre of the island. A third falls, **Than Prapat Falls**, is situated near the eastern shore in an area that can be reached by road or boat, while **Than Prawet Falls** is in the north-east near Ao Thong Nai Pan.

Although hordes of backpackers have discovered Ko Pha-Ngan, the lack of an airport and relative lack of paved roads have so far spared it from tourist-hotel and package-tour

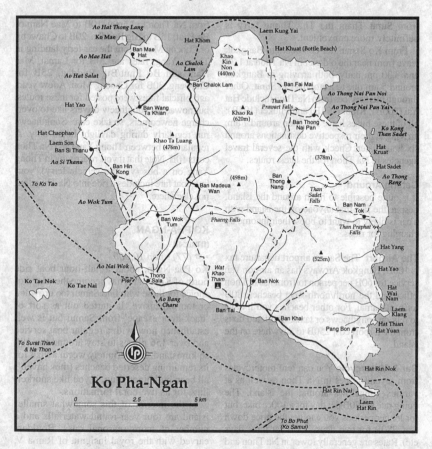

## Ko Pha-Ngan

0        2.5        5 km

development. Compared to Samui, Ko Pha-Ngan has a lower concentration of bungalows, less crowded beaches and coves, and an overall less 'modern' atmosphere. Pha-Ngan aficionados say the seafood is fresher and cheaper than on Samui's beaches, but it really varies from place to place. As Samui becomes more expensive for both travellers and investors, more and more people will be drawn to Pha-Ngan. But for the time being, overall living costs remain about half what you'd pay on Samui.

Except at the island's party capital, Hat Rin, the island hasn't yet been cursed with video and blaring stereos; unlike on Samui, travellers actually interact instead of staring over one another's shoulders at a video screen.

## Wat Khao Tham
### วัดเขาถ้ำ

This cave temple is beautifully situated on top of a hill near the little village of Ban Tai. An American monk lived here for over a decade and his ashes are interred on a cliff overlooking a field of palms below the wat. It's not a true wat since there are only a couple of monks and a nun in residence (among other requirements, a quorum of five monks is necessary for wat status).

Ten day meditation retreats taught by an American-Australian couple are held here during the latter half of most months. The cost is 1800B; write in advance to Khao Tham, Ko Pha-Ngan, Surat Thani, for information or pre-register in person. A bulletin board at the temple also has information.

## Thong Sala
ท้องศาลา

About half of Ko Pha-Ngan's total population of 10,000 live in and around the small port town of Thong Sala. This is where the ferry boats from Surat and Samui (Na Thon) dock, although there are also smaller boats from Mae Nam and Bo Phut on Samui that moor at Hat Rin.

The town sports several restaurants, travel agents, clothing shops and general stores. You can also rent motorcycles here for 150 to 250B per day.

**Information** Bovy Supermarket on the main street leading from the pier sells just about anything you might need – sunglasses, sunscreen, liquor, snorkelling gear, cereal, cosmetics, even Frisbees – for short or long-term stays on the island.

**Money** If you're continuing on to other areas of the island and need to do some banking, this is the place to do it. Krung Thai Bank, Siam City Bank and Siam Commercial Bank buy and sell travellers' cheques and can arrange money transfers and credit card cash advances; Siam Commercial generally has the best service.

Hat Rin also has some foreign exchange services, as complete as those available in Thong Sala.

**Post & Communications** The post office is at the southern end of town, in the direction of Hat Rin; it's open Monday through Friday 8.30 am to noon and 1 to 4.30 pm, Saturday 9 am to noon. Café de la Poste, opposite the post office, sells stamps and offers a parcel/packaging service as well as phone service.

**Medical Services** The new Ko Pha-Ngan Hospital, about 2.5 km north of Thong Sala off the road to Chalok Lam, offers 24 hour emergency services. Anything that can wait till Bangkok should wait till Bangkok, where medical facilities are of higher quality.

**Places to Stay & Eat** Aside from a couple of local brothels, the only place to get a room in town is the *Pha-Ngan Central Hotel* (☎ 377068; fax 377032), on the bay about 150m south of the pier. All rooms come with air-con and TV and cost 600B or 700B facing the sea.

Several cafes near the pier cater to farang tastes and also sell boat tickets. *Café de la Poste*, opposite the post office, offers imported cheeses, coffee, sandwiches, pizza, pasta and vegetarian dishes. There are a couple of karaoke bars in Thong Sala.

## Ao Nai Wok
There are a few beach bungalows within a couple of km north of the pier. Although the beach here isn't spectacular, it's a fairly nice area to while away a few days – especially if you need to be near Thong Sala for some reason. People waiting for an early boat back to Surat or on to Ko Tao may choose to stay here (or south of Thong Sala at Ao Bang Charu) since transport times from other parts of the island can be unpredictable.

Turn left at the first main crossing from the pier, then walk straight till the road crosses a concrete bridge, and then turn left again when the road dead-ends at a T-junction. Soon you'll come to *Phangan* (60B with shared bath, up to 300B with bath), *Charn* (80 to 120B, all with bath), *Siriphun* (100 to 400B, all with bath) and *Tranquil Resort* (60B with shared bath, up to 200B with bath). All are within about two km. Siriphun seems particularly good value and it still has the best kitchen locally; Siriphun also has some larger houses for long-term rentals and has become a headquarters for Thong Sala Scuba Diving.

SOUTHERN THAILAND

## Laem Hat Rin

This long cape juts south-east and has beaches along both its westward and eastward sides. The eastward side has the best beach, Hat Rin Nok, a long sandy strip lined with coconut palms. The snorkelling here is pretty good, but between October and March the surf can be a little hairy. The western side more or less acts as an overflow for people who can't find a place to stay on the eastern side, as the beach is often too shallow for swimming. Together these beaches have become the most popular on the island.

The eastern beach, or Hat Rin Nok (Outer Rin Beach), has gradually become a more or less self-contained town, complete with travel agencies, moneychangers, mini-marts, restaurants, bars, tattoo shops and two large generators which supply electric power to the area (at 8B per unit, twice the national average – one reason accommodation prices are higher here). Hat Rin Nok is famous for its monthly 'full moon parties', featuring all-night beach dancing and the ingestion of various illicit substances – forget about sleeping on these nights. Suan Saranrom (Garden of Joys) psychiatric hospital in Surat Thani has to take on extra staff during full moon periods to handle the number of farangs who freak out on magic mushrooms, acid or other abundantly available hallucinogens. There are plenty of other drugs available from the local drug mafia and drug-dependent visitors, and the police occasionally conduct raids. Travellers should be watchful of their personal safety at these parties, especially female travellers; assaults have occasionally been reported.

Lately the district authorities and TAT have stepped in and tried to establish a more wholesome full moon event featuring water sports and cultural events during the daytime, and keeping close watch at night so that things don't get out of hand. As a result the infamous Hat Rin full moon party will probably fold up and go away any day now, or else become a mainstream tourist event. Still, even when the moon isn't full, several establishments blast dance music all night long – head for the western side if you prefer a quieter atmosphere.

**Places to Stay** The bungalows here are stacked rather closely together and are among the most expensive on the island. Starting from the south, *Paradise Bungalows* is one of the oldest establishments and offers a variety of cottages from near the beach to inland on the rocks, plus rooms in a motel-like structure perpendicular to the beach, starting at 150B. The newer *Beach Blue* continues the trend of renting motel-like rows of rooms extending away from the beach for 120B a night. Next are the slightly more up-market *Anant Bungalows* and *Haadrin Resort* with rooms in the 150 to 500B range. Nicely kept *Phangan Orchid Resort* is similar, while *Sea Garden Bungalows* is on the cheaper side with huts for 80 to 150B. *Sunrise Bungalows*, more or less in the middle of the beach, is another long-runner; huts made of local materials are priced 60 to 300B depending on position relative to the beach and the current occupancy rate.

*Pha-Ngan Bayshore Resort* (☎ (01) 725-0430), Hat Rin's first semi-upscale establishment, occupies the middle section of the beach and charges around 400 to 500B a night. Next is *Tommy Resort*, another old-timer and home to Samui International Diving School; bungalows here cost from 100 to 300B. *Palita Lodge*, a large group of wooden bungalows next door, costs 80 to 200B and boasts one of the better beach restaurants. Toward the north end of the beach is the badly maintained *Seaview Haadrin Resort* amidst trashy grounds; the usual bungalows cost 100 to 300B but consider this place only as a last resort.

Built into the rocky headland at the north end of Hat Rin, *Mountain Sea Bungalows* shares a set of cement stairs (inundated by the surf at high tide) with *Serenity*. Each has huts with and without bath for 80 to 200B; an advantage to staying here is that it's relatively quieter here at night than at places right on the beach.

Behind the main row of beach lodgings a second row of bungalows is beginning to open, including *Bumblebee Huts* and *Haad Rin Hill* in the 80 to 150B range. Perched on the slopes of the hill in the centre of Hat Rin's southernmost point are the similarly priced *Leela Bungalows* and *Lighthouse*, plus one or two others that come and go with each high season.

Across the ridge on the west side is Hat Rin Nai (Inner Rin Beach), which overall is much quieter than Hat Rin Nok. Here you'll find long-runners *Palm Beach* (50 to 150B) and *Sunset Bay Resort* (80 to 200B), plus a string of places in the 70 to 250B range: *Dolphin*, *Charung*, *Haad Rin Village*, *Friendly* and *Family House*. The *Rin Beach Resort* has a few larger huts with private bath and fan from 300B as well as concrete air-con bungalows for 800B.

At the northern end of Hat Rin Nai, around a small headland, are the newer *Bang Son Villa*, *Blue Hill*, *Star*, *Bird*, *Sun Beach*, *Sandy*, *Sea Side*, *Rainbow*, *Coral*, *Sooksom* and *Laidback Shack*, all in the 50 to 100B range. For 80B, the nicest thatched bungalows are those at Blue Hill, situated on a hill above the beach.

Along the road that joins Hat Rin Nok and Hat Rin Nai, in the centre of the cape, you'll find the *Pooltrub (Phuntrap) Resort*, which has upgraded to the 100 to 300B range with solidly built bungalows on landscaped grounds. It's a short walk to Hat Rin Nai.

On both sides of Hat Rin, hammers and saws are busy putting together new huts, so there may be quite a few more places by now. Not only are the cliffs on each side of the bay filling up, but a few one-storey hotels are now under construction back from the beach due to the popularity of the area.

Restaurants here are getting almost as expensive as on Samui, but the seafood is good and fresh, particularly at *Sand* and *Crab*. The *Haadrin Bakery & Restaurant* offers a wide variety of cakes, rolls and other baked goods. On the road between the two beaches, *Namaste Chai Shop* serves good Indian food.

Songthaew taxis go back and forth between Hat Rin and Thong Sala for 40B. This road was paved with concrete in 1996. The steeper, windier passages are more dangerous now than before the paving, since everyone drives faster and the smooth surface doesn't afford much braking traction. Motorcycles can be rented in Hat Rin Nok; take extra care when riding motorbikes on this road as lots of people wipe out on the steep downhill slopes; there is no shoulder on the road either, so watch out for passing vehicles.

### Other Beaches

Beach bungalow operations are still mostly concentrated north and south of Thong Sala and especially on the southern end of the island at Hat Rin, but now there are many other places to stay around the island as well. Because there are few paved roads on Pha-Ngan, transport can be a bit of a problem, though the situation is constantly improving as enterprising Thais set up taxi and boat services between the various beaches.

Many of the huts on Pha-Ngan have been established by entrepreneurs from Ko Samui with several years' experience in the bungalow business. Huts with shared bathing facilities go for 60 to 100B a night on average, as low as 40B between May and October; many of these do not have electricity or running water. Some have generators which are only on for limited hours in the evening – the lights dim when they make a fruit shake. For many people, of course, this adds to Pha-Ngan's appeal.

Other places are moving into the 100 to 300B range, which almost always includes a private bath, and there a few scattered spots on the west and south-east coasts with resort-like amenities for 500B and up. As travel to Pha-Ngan seems particularly seasonal, you should be able to talk bungalow rates down 30% to 40% when occupancy is low. During the peak months (December to February and July and August), there can be an acute shortage of rooms at the most popular beaches and even the boats coming to the island can be dangerously overcrowded.

Since many of the cheaper bungalows make the bulk of their profits from their restaurants rather than from renting huts, bungalow owners have been known to eject guests who don't take meals where they're

SOUTHERN THAILAND

staying after a few days. The only way to avoid this, besides foregoing your own choice of restaurants, is to get a clear agreement beforehand on how many days you can stay. This seems to be a problem only at the cheaper (40 to 60B) places.

There are a number of beaches with accommodation on Pha-Ngan; the following are listed moving in an anti-clockwise direction away from Thong Sala.

**Ao Bang Charu** South of Thong Sala, the shallow beach here is not one of the island's best, but it's close to town and so is popular with people waiting for boats or bank business.

*Petchr Cottage*, *Sundance*, *Pha-Ngan Villa* and *Moonlight* have similar basic thatched huts in the 60 to 120B range, with a few wood or concrete huts costing a bit more. Following a coconut grove to the south are the distinctive high-pitched roofs of *Charm Beach Resort*, a nicely landscaped place starting in the same range and going up to 400B. *Chokkhana Resort* has big, solidly built hexagonal cottages in addition to more traditional huts, up to 500B. Charm Beach and Chokkhana Resort have decent restaurants.

Farther south-east towards Ban Tai, past a school, *First Villa* offers cement-block, tiled roof cottages but lacks atmosphere. A bit farther on, *First Bay Resort* has even more characterless small concrete huts.

**Ban Tai & Ban Khai** Between the villages of Ban Tai and Ban Khai is a series of sandy beaches with well-spaced bungalow operations, mostly in the 50 to 100B range (a few also have 200B bungalows). Not all bungalows here are signed from the paved road; to really survey the area you must walk along the beach. *Dewshore* and *P Park* can be reached from a road in the centre of Ban Tai; Dewshore offers well constructed huts for 50 to 200B, while the P Park couldn't be more dilapidated.

Starting at the southern outskirts of Ban Tai you'll find *Birdville*, *Pink*, *Mac Bay Resort*, *Liberty*, *Jup*, *Sabai*, *Bay Hut*, *Lee's Garden*,

*Baan Khai Bay*, *Pha-Ngan Rainbow*, *Green Peace*, *Pha-Ngan Island Resort* (300 to 450B) and *Golden Beach*.

In Ban Khai the locals also rent rooms to travellers, especially from December to February when just about everything is filled up. You can get a hut for a month at very low rates here. 'Dark moon parties' are held on the beach at Ban Khai on the day of the month when there's no moon as an alternative to Hat Rin's infamous full moon raves.

Long-tail boats to other parts of the island can be chartered from Ban Khai. At one time there was a regular boat service to/from Hat Rin, but with the paving of the road all the way to Hat Rin it has been discontinued.

Songthaew taxis from Thong Sala to Ban Tai or Ban Khai cost 15B per person; a motorbike taxi is 20B.

**East Coast Beaches** Between Hat Rin and the village of Ban Nam Tok are several little coves. There you'll find the white-sand beaches of **Hat Yuan** (2.5 km north of Hat Rin) and **Hat Wai Nam** (3.5 km). The beach at Hat Yuan has no places to stay but would be perfect for camping if you bring your own food; it's connected by an inland trail with Hat Rin. Around a smaller headland at the north-eastern end of Hat Yuan, there is accommodation at Hat Thian's *The Sanctuary*, a new age-oriented spot built into boulders overlooking the beach. Bungalows with shared facilities cost 60 to 100B, with attached bathroom 100 to 300B; instruction in yoga, tai chi, meditation and massage is available. The Sanctuary can be reached on foot or boat (February to November only) from Hat Rin. Over the next headland at Hat Wai Nam is a no-name place that's only open December to April. At the time of writing there is nothing else until **Hat Sadet**. A dirt track (traversable on foot but only partially by motorcycle) runs along the coast from Hat Rin before heading inland to Ban Nam Tok and Than Sadet Falls.

**Hat Yao** (five km from Hat Rin) and **Hat Yang** (six km) are virtually deserted. After that, 2.5 km north of Ban Nam Tok by dirt track, is the pretty double bay of **Ao Thong**

**Reng,** where *No Name* bungalows are 50B. Above the beach on the headland, *Than Wung Thong Resort* offers huts for 60 to 150B. North of the headland, a pretty cove ringed by Hat Sadet features a string of places whose names change regularly, all in the 50 to 80B range. The rough dirt track from Thong Sala is usable, subject to weather; a boat to/from Hat Rin (50B) and Thong Sala (70B) makes the trip by water every morning between September and April.

**Ao Thong Nai Pan** This bay is really made up of two bays, **Ao Thong Nai Pan Yai** and **Ao Thong Nai Pan Noi.** The latter is the best all-round swimming beach. On the beach at Thong Nai Pan Yai, south-east of Ban Thong Nai Pan village, are the *White Sand, AD View* and *Nice Beach,* all with huts from 60B with shared bath up to 300B for nicer ones with attached bath. The other end of the beach features the similarly priced *Pen's* and *Pingjun Resort,* along with the more basic *Chanchit Dreamland* at 70B per hut.

Up on Thong Nai Pan Noi are the very nicely situated *Panviman Resort* (☎/fax 377048; ☎ (2) 587-8491, fax 587-8593 in Bangkok) and *Thong Ta Pan Resort.* Panviman sits on a cliff between two beaches and offers 40 rooms in wooden bungalows or a two-storey building for 300B with fan up to 1500B with air-con, all with private bath. The more basic but clean Thong Ta Pan Resort, at the north end of the smaller bay, costs 80 to 150B. Between them is the similarly priced *Rocky Blue* and *Big Yogurst. Star Huts* (☎ 84280) at Thong Nai Pan Noi receives high marks for well maintained huts with fans for 100/150B single/double in high season, nicer huts for up to 300B.

Songthaew taxis from Thong Sala to Thong Nai Pan cost 60B. Panviman runs its own taxi service from the Thong Sala pier.

**Hat Khuat & Chalok Lam** These are two pretty bays with beaches on the northern end of Pha-Ngan, still largely undeveloped because of the distances involved from major transport points to Samui and the mainland. Some of the island's least expen-

sive accommodation is found here – hence it's popular with long-termers – but that means more likelihood of being evicted from your hut if you don't buy meals from the bungalow kitchens. Be sure to establish whether you'll be required to buy meals before taking a hut.

Hat Khuat (Bottle Beach) is the smaller of the two and currently has four sets of bungalows, all in the 60 to 250B range – *Bottle Beach, Bottle Beach II, OD Bungalows* and *Sea Love.* West of Hat Khuat, 2.5 km across Laem Kung Yai, is **Hat Khom,** where the *Coral Bay* rents standard huts for 40 and 50B. You can walk to Hat Khuat from Ban Chalok Lam, but until they build a better bridge over Khlong Ok, no jeeps or motorcycles can get to it – all the better for quiet days and nights.

The fishing village of Ban Chalok Lam at the centre of Ao Chalok Lam features several small mom-and-pop grocery stores, laundry services and lots of fish drying at the side of the main street. You can also rent bikes and diving equipment. The food situation has improved; of the several restaurants, the best are *Seaside* and *Porn.* There are also a few inexpensive noodle stands around.

The Dive Inn here offers scuba courses in English or German. Starting from the north-eastern corner of the village, *Mr Phol's* offers very basic huts, with no beach to speak of, for 50B a night. Further on in this direction, *Fanta* is larger and a bit better, with several rows of huts starting at 40B per person and a fair chunk of beach frontage.

Across Khlong Ok via a rickety footbridge, *Try Tong Resort* offers largish wooden cabins facing the bay and canal for 50 to 200B. There's no beach at Try Thong save for a small chunk with boulders at the surf line. Further on toward Hat Khom is *Thai Life,* with simple huts for 40B, and better bungalows with facilities for up to 200B.

At the other end of long Hat Chalok Lam, west of the village, is the slightly nicer *Wattana* with huts for 60 to 80B and bungalows with fan for 150 to 250B. The beach is better here, too.

SOUTHERN THAILAND

The road between Thong Sala and Ban Chalok Lam is paved all the way now, and songthaews do the route regularly for 25B per person, or you can do the same trip by motorcycle for 30B. These fares are really keyed to the old days when the road wasn't so good, so expect the fare to drop as the number of songthaews plying this route increases.

Ao Chalok Lam is a good place to hire boats for explorations of the northern coast as many fishermen dock here (particularly from February to September). During this season boats run regularly from here to Hat Khuat twice a day for 20B per person. On some days the service may be cancelled due to high surf, so anyone electing to stay at Bottle Beach should leave a couple of extra days for planned departure from the island just in case. A new concrete pier was recently completed in Ban Chalok Lam, so boat services may increase.

**Ao Hat Thong Lang & Ao Mae Hat** As you move west on Pha-Ngan, as on Samui, the sand gets browner and coarser. The secluded beach and cove at Ao Hat Thong Lang has no accommodation at the moment.

An all-weather road leads west from Chalok Lam to Ban Mae Hat, a small fishing village with a few bungalow resorts. The beach at Ao Mae Hat isn't fantastic, but there is a bit of coral offshore. Close by, a little inland via a well-marked dirt track (200m off the road from Chalok Lam near Km 9), is Wang Sai Falls, also know as Paradise Falls. Toward the north-east end of the bay, *Maehaad Bungalows* has good, simple thatched huts for 50B plus wood and thatch huts with private bath for up to 150B, while the *Mae Hat Bay Resort* and *Crystal Island Garden* have small wooden huts in the same price range. Moving south-westward, the *Island View Cabana* offers good clapboard huts from 50B to as high as 250B for nicer ones. The Island View also has a good restaurant.

*Bang Sai Resort*, at the south-western end of Mae Hat, offers nice-sized bungalows built among boulders on a hillside; all have views of beach and bay. Rates run from 60 to 200B, depending on position on the slope. A open-air restaurant is situated well away from the huts, down on the beach.

Opposite the beach on the islet of Ko Mae are five huts that go for just 40B.

The paved section of the road from Chalok Lam gives out at Km 10 (counting from Thong Sala), but a new road under construction will eventually link with Hat Yao to the south-west. Songthaew/motorcycle taxis from Thong Sala cost 25/30B.

**Hat Salat & Hat Yao** These coral-fringed beaches are fairly difficult to reach – the road from Ban Si Thanu to the south is very bad in spots, even for experienced dirt-bikers – come by boat if possible. Hat Yao is a very long, pretty beach with a reasonable drop-off that makes it one of the island's best swimming beaches.

Hat Salat has *My Way* with huts for 60B. Down at Hat Yao are the basic *Benjawan*, *Dream Hill*, *Blue Coral Beach*, *Sandy Bay*, *Ibiza*, *Bayview* and *Hat Thian*; the latter two are isolated on a beach north of Hat Yao around the headland, and the road is very steep and rocky. All of these places offer basic 40 to 120B huts. Along the best section of beach is *Haad Yao Bungalows*, which sensibly charges extra for basic accommodation if you don't eat there and has 200 to 500B bungalows; its tall security fence, however, lends a definite air of paranoia and posted signs say it's for sale.

Around a small headland to the south of Hat Yao is *Rock Garden*, which lives up to its name with all manner of creative rock placements, including a steep rock path leading down to the bungalows from the road; tread carefully. Its isolation may appeal to those looking for a long-term hideaway.

**Hat Chaophao & Ao Si Thanu** Hat Chaophao is a rounded beach two headlands south of Hat Yao; then around a larger headland at the south end of Ao Chaophao is Ao Si Thanu. In these areas you begin to see the occasional mangrove along the coast; inland there's a pretty lagoon at the south end of Hat Chaophao near Laem Son.

There are four places to stay along the beach at Hat Chaophao. The popular *Sea Flower, Sri Thanu* and *Great Bay* all have bungalows with private bath for 80 to 180B, and some without for 50 to 80B; we've heard complaints about sexual harassment of female travellers and general cheating (promising one room rate, than upping it when you checkout) at Great Bay. *Hat Chaophao*, sandwiched between the others, has only 300B bungalows. At the south end of the bay, past curving Laem Niat, *Bovy Resort* has standard huts with attached bath for only 50 to 70B; it's owned by the same family who own Bovy Supermarket in Thong Sala, so is usually kept well stocked with food.

On the rounded, pine-studded cape of Laem Son, at the north end of Ao Si Thanu proper, lies *Laem Son Bungalows*, with simple, quiet, shaded huts for 40 to 70B. South over a creek comes *Seaview Rainbow* with similar rates. Down towards the south end of the bay, *Lada* offers 200B bungalows with fan and bath. *Loy Fah* and *Chai*, both sitting high on a point at the southern end of the bay on the cape of Laem Si Thanu, offer good views and sturdy huts. Nicely landscaped Loy Fah, the better run of the two, offers good-sized wooden cottages for 150B, cement for 200B, all with fan, mosquito net, toilet and shower. Loy Fah also has two large, 400B cottages at the bottom of the cliff on a private cove. In the low season you can knock 40% off these rates. Down at the southern base of the cliff is the similarly priced *Nantakarn*, but it's not as good value.

**Ao Hin Kong/Ao Wok Tum** This long bay – sometimes divided in two by a stream which feeds into the sea – is just a few km north of Thong Sala but so far has hardly any development. At the centre of Hin Kong, not far from the village of Ban Hin Kong, is the basic *Lipstick Cabana* for 40 to 150B. On the southern end of the village is the similarly priced *Hin Kong*. Down at the southern end of Ao Wok Tum on the cape between this bay and Ao Nai Wok are *Tuk* and *Kiat*, both in the 40 to 60B range. A little farther down

around the cape that separates Ao Wok Tum from Ao Nai Wok are *OK, Darin, Sea Scene, Porn Sawan, Cookies* and *Beach*, most with simple 30 to 80B huts – Darin, Sea Scene and Porn Sawan also have bungalows with private bath in the 120 to 300B range. Songthaews to this area cost 30B per person but you won't see them outside ferry departure/arrival times.

See the earlier Thong Sala section for accommodation just north of Thong Sala at Ao Nai Wok.

### Getting There & Away
**Ko Samui – Express Boats** Songserm Co express boats to Ko Pha-Ngan leave from the Na Thon pier on Ko Samui every day November to May at 10 am and 3 pm, the remainder of the year 10 am and 4 pm. The trip takes 50 minutes and costs 50B one way. Boats back to Samui leave Pha-Ngan's Thong Sala pier at 6.15 and 1 pm daily; in this direction the fare is 60B.

**Ko Samui – Other Boats** A small boat goes direct from Samui's Bang Rak (near Bo Phut village) to Hat Rin on Ko Pha-Ngan for 50 to 60B (depending on who's got the concession, the boat sometimes leaves from Bo Phut instead). This boat departs Bang Rak/Bo Phut just about every day at 10.30 am and 3.30 pm, depending on the weather and number of prospective passengers, and takes 40 to 45 minutes to reach the bay at Hat Rin. In the reverse direction it usually leaves at 9.30 am and 2.30 pm and takes 30 to 40 minutes.

From January to September there is also one boat a day from Hat Mae Nam on Samui to Ao Thong Nai Pan on Pha-Ngan, with a stop at Hat Rin. The fares are 120B and 60B respectively and the boat usually leaves Mae Nam around 1 pm. In the reverse direction the boat starts from Ao Thong Nai Pan around 8 am.

A new company called Rossarin Tour has 35-passenger speed boats that go between Samui's Hat Mae Nam and Thong Sala for 150B; this boat only takes about half an hour to reach Thong Sala.

SOUTHERN THAILAND

**Surat Thani – Night Ferry** You can also take a slow night ferry direct to Pha-Ngan from the Ban Don pier in Surat. It leaves nightly at 11 pm, takes 6½ hours to arrive at Thong Sala, and costs 100B on the upper deck, 60B on the lower.

As with the night ferry to Samui, don't leave your bags unattended on the boat – there have been several reports of theft.

**Surat Thani – Other Boats** A couple of years ago a fast jetboat and another express boat competed with Songserm for about a year, but Songserm immediately dropped its fares to a loss level and ran them out of business. With increasing tourism in the islands, it's only a matter of time before someone else steps in and gives Songserm a run for its money.

**Ko Tao** Subject to weather conditions, there are daily express boats between Thong Sala and Ko Tao, 47 km north, at 2.30 pm. The trip takes 2½ hours and costs 150B one way.

Rossarin Tour operates speed boats between Thong Sala and Ko Tao a couple of times a day for 350B per person; the crossing only takes about an hour.

**Train/Bus/Boat Combinations** At Bangkok's Hualamphong station you can purchase train tickets that include a bus from the Surat Thani train station (Phun Phin) to the Ban Don pier and then a ferry to Ko Pha-Ngan. These generally cost around 30 to 50B more than buying each ticket separately yourself.

### Getting Around

A couple of roads branch out from Thong Sala, primarily to the north and the south. One road goes north-west from Thong Sala a few km along the shoreline to the villages of Ban Hin Kong and Ban Si Thanu. From Ban Si Thanu the road travels north-east across the island to Ban Chalok Lam. Another road goes straight north from Thong Sala to Chalok Lam. There is also a very poor dirt road along the west coast from Ban Si Thanu to Ao Hat Yao and Ao Hat Salat.

Hat Khuat (Bottle Beach) can be reached on foot from Ban Fai Mai (two km) or Ban Chalok Lam (four km) or there are boats.

The road south from Thong Sala to Ban Khai passes an intersection where another road goes north to Ban Thong Nang and Ban Thong Nai Pan. The paved road to Hat Rin is now passable year-round, so there's regular transport between Thong Sala and Hat Rin. Even with the paving, only experienced motorbike riders should attempt the section between Ban Khai and Hat Rin. Steep grades, blind turns and a slippery road surface (which will only become more slippery with use) make it the most dangerous piece of road on the island, perhaps anywhere in Southern Thailand.

Songthaews and motorcycle taxis handle all the public transport along island roads. Some places can only be reached by motorcycle; some places only by boat or foot.

You can rent motorcycles in Thong Sala for 150 to 250B a day.

**Songthaew & Motorcycle Taxi** From Thong Sala, songthaews to Hat Chaophao and Hat Yao are 30B and 40B per person respectively, while motorcycle taxis cost 40B and 50B. To Ban Khai, it's 15B by songthaew, or 20B by motorcycle; if you're only going as far as Wat Khao Tham or Ban Tai the fare remains the same for motorcycles but drops to 10B for a songthaew.

A songthaew from Thong Sala to Ban Chalok Lam is 25B, a motorcycle taxi 30B. To get to Hat Rin from Thong Sala, a songthaew costs 50B one way while a motorbike is 70B. You can also get there by boat, see the following Boat section.

Thong Nai Pan can be reached from Thong Sala by songthaew (60B) or motorcycle (90B). See the following Boat section for water transport to Thong Nai Pan.

**Boat** There are daily boats from Ao Chalok Lam to Hat Khuat at noon and 4 pm (returning at 9 am and 3.30 pm) for 20 to 30B per person depending on the number of passengers. The service operates from January to September, depending on the weather.

Thong Nai Pan can be reached by boat

from Hat Rin in southern Pha-Ngan at noon for 60B, but these boats generally run only between January and September, depending on the weather. When the ferry arrives at the Thong Sala pier from Surat or Samui, there may be boats waiting to take passengers on to Hat Rin for 50B – it takes about 45 minutes, but with the road paved all the way to Hat Rin these boat services are fading.

Regular boat service between Ban Khai and Hat Rin has all but halted, though boat pilots will still take one to three persons for 50B each, four or more for 20B each. Although the boat is slower, it's a lot easier on the nerves than the Hat Rin's 'death highway'.

## KO TAO
เกาะเต่า

Ko Tao translates as 'Turtle Island', named for its shape. It's only about 21 sq km and the population of 750 are mostly involved in fishing, growing coconuts and catering to tourism. Snorkelling and diving are particularly good here due to the relative abundance of coral, though most of the beaches are too shallow for swimming.

Since it takes three to five hours to get there from the mainland (from either Chumphon or Surat Thani via Ko Pha-Ngan), Ko Tao doesn't get people coming over for day trips or for quick overnighters. Still, the island can become quite crowded during high season, when Mae Hat, Hat Sai Ri and Ao Chalok Ban Kao have people sleeping on the beach waiting for huts to vacate.

**Ban Mae Hat**, on the western side of the island, is where inter-island boats land. The only other villages on the island are **Ban Hat Sai Ri** in the centre of the northern part and **Ban Chalok Ban Kao** to the south. Just a km off the north-west shore of the island is **Ko Nang Yuan**, which is really three islands joined by a sand bar.

The granite promontory of **Laem Tato** at the southern tip of Ko Tao makes a nice hike from Ban Chalok Ban Kao.

## Information
Ban Mae Hat, a one-street town with a busy

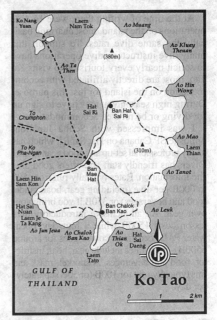

pier, is the only commercial centre on the island. Here you'll find a police station, post and telephone office (open daily from 8.30 am to 4 pm), travel agents, dive shops, restaurants and general stores. There is no bank on the island, but several moneychangers offer exchange services below the usual bank rates.

Boat tickets can be purchased at a booking office by the harbour as well as from travel agents.

## Diving & Snorkelling
Relative to its size, Ko Tao has a large number of diving shops, with some of Thailand's lowest prices for training and/or excursions. Underwater visibility is high and the water is cleaner than around most other inhabited islands in the Gulf. Because of the farang presence, the best diving spots have English names, such as White Rock, Shark Island, Chumphon Pinnacle, Green Rock and South-West Pinnacles. Newer spots are being discovered all the time.

At the time of writing there were 16 dive operations on the island, most charging basically the same dive rates. To support this many dive instructors, dive operations have to solicit nearly every tourist who visits Ko Tao; most are directly affiliated with accommodation on the island for just this purpose. During high season you may have to sign up for diving or be refused accommodation.

I was impressed with Scuba Junction, opposite SP Cabana on Hat Sai Ri, which has a very professional set-up and good gear. Master Divers has friendly staff and offers good dive site information. Rates typically run from 500 to 600B per dive (including gear, boat, guide, food and beverages) or 350B if you bring your own gear. An all-inclusive introductory dive lesson costs 1500B while a four day, open-water PADI certificate course goes for around 6500B – these rates include gear, boat, instructor, food and beverages. A snorkel, mask and fins typically rent for 100B (or 50B separately) per day.

## Places to Stay

With the steady transformation of Ko Tao into a diving resort, huts have moved up-market relative to Ko Pha-Ngan, standing sort of in between Samui and Pha-Ngan in terms of costs and amenities. Few bungalows are made with local materials any more, perhaps a boon to the environment. At last count there were about 650 huts in 48 locations around the island. At most places electricity is provided by generators from 6 pm to midnight. Simple thatched or wooden huts typically cost 80 to 150B per night, while larger wood, brick or concrete bungalows with private bath range from 200 to 600B.

During the peak season – December to March – it can be difficult to find accommodation anywhere on the island – no matter what the time of the day – and people end up sleeping on the beach or in restaurants for one or two nights until a hut became available. What is more common is that all the cheaper huts are occupied and the only the places costing 250B or more are available.

On arrival at Ban Mae Hat it may be best to follow a tout who can find vacant huts, otherwise your chances of finding a place on your own might be very slim.

Some bungalows with associated diving operations will refuse accommodation to visitors who don't sign up for a dive trip or instruction. Some of the cheaper operations – especially those at the north end of Hat Sai Ri and at Ao Tha Then – will give you the boot if you don't buy food at their restaurant; we still receive reports of visitors being locked out of their bungalows or being violently ejected. In the off season it can be a problem finding a bungalow operation that hasn't closed down till next high season.

**Ao Mae** At Hat Ao Mae, just north of Ban Mae Hat, the shallow bay has plenty of coral. *Crystal* offers basic plywood huts for 150B and concrete and wood bungalows with bath for 500 to 650B – the most expensive on the island and rather overpriced considering the lackadaisical staff. Friendly, quiet *Dam* has nice thatched huts with shared facilities and small verandas with hammocks for 100B to 150B; it's often full because it's one of the best value places on the west side of the island.

On the headland overlooking the bay are *Queen Resort* (100 to 200B for standard bungalows) and *Tommy Resort* (80B for a room over the restaurant/office, and from 250 to 500B for a nicer bungalow). Just beyond Tommy, the *View Cliff Restaurant & Bungalows* offers basic huts with shared bath for 100B, larger huts with shower and toilet for 250 to 350B.

**Hat Sai Ri** Around the headland to the north is the longest beach on the island, with a string of bungalow and dive operations starting with *AC Resort I & II*, which has sturdy bungalows with attached bath and nice landscaping in the 200 to 350B range. *Haad Sai Ree Resort* and *Ko Tao Cabana* have similar accommodations at the same rates. Up next, *SB Cabana* has clean wooden bungalows with attached toilet and shower for 200 to 250B. *Bing Bungalow*, on the other side of the road, has cheaper huts for 100B with shared bath, 200B with attached bath. *Big Fish Dive Resort* and *Ban's Diving Resort* each offer sturdy bungalows starting at 150B.

The air-con stucco cottages at *Sunset Bari Resort* go for a Mediterranean look, start at 500B and are the poshest digs on the island; there's a swimming pool on the premises. Farther north along Hat Sai Ri are four places in the 80 to 250B range: *Sai Ri Cottage*, *New Way*, *Haad Sai Ree Villa* and *O-Chai*. New Way is one of the places that locks guests out of their rooms if they don't purchase a sufficient amount of food.

North of the beach in an area sometimes called Ao Ta Then are several inexpensive bungalow operations with very basic huts – most off the beach and built high on the rocks – including *Golden Cape*, *Silver Cliff*, *Sun Sea*, *Sun Lord*, *Eden Resort* and *Mahana Bay* in the 50 to 150B range. Farther north, the lone *CFT* has basic huts for 70B and bungalows with attached bath for up to 300B.

**Ao Muang & Ao Kluay Theuan** On the northern and north-eastern tip of the island, accessible only by boat, are two coral-fringed coves without bungalow accommodation. As the pressure for places to stay increases, new operations should start appearing at both.

**Ao Hin Wong** South of Ao Kluay Theuan by sea, or two km north-east of Ban Hat Sai Ri by trail, tranquil Ao Hin Wong has a handful of huts called *Hin Wong Bungalows* for 80 to 100B. In spite of the lack of competition the restaurant serves good food.

**Ao Mao, Laem Thian & Ao Tanot** Continuing clockwise around the island, Ao Mao, connected by a two km dirt trail with Ban Hat Sai Ri, is another cove with no beach accommodation so far. On the cape which juts out

over the north end of Ao Tanot, *Laem Thian* has huts built among the rocks from 60B.

Ao Tanot proper, to the south, is one of the island's best spots for snorkelling and features a good set of bungalow operations, the proprietors of which so far cooperate to keep the beach clean. The well landscaped *Tanote Bay Resort* charges 50 to 100B for simple but well maintained huts, while *Poseidon* has rather shabby huts for 50 to 80B. The friendly *Diamond Beach* offer huts from 50 to 100B. *Bamboo Hut*, a new place, has decked bungalows for 100B; the kitchen specialises in spicy Southern Thai-style food.

**Khao Mae Hat** On the way to Ao Tanot from Mae Hat, a path forks off the main track and leads up the slopes of 310m Khao Mae Hat in the centre of the island to *Two View Resort*, so named because it affords sunrise and sunset views of both sides of the island. It's a 15 minute walk up the path. There are only five bungalows, starting at 50B. Two View advertises three day meditation retreats and five day Thai massage courses.

**Ao Leuk & Hat Sai Daeng** Ao Leuk, connected by a 2.2 km dirt road with Ban Mae Hat, has the lone *Ao Leuk Resort*, with huts from 60B. Another km or so south is Hat Sai Daeng, where *Kiet* offers simple huts from 60B or nicer ones with private bath for up to 300B.

**Ao Thian Ok & Laem Tato** Farther west on the side of the impressive Laem Tato is pretty Ao Thian Ok with *Rocky* at 80 to 300B. We continue to receive complaints from people who have been ejected from the place for not buying enough meals there.

**Ao Chalok Ban Kao** This nicely situated coral beach, about 1.7 km south of Ban Mae Hat by road, has become quite crowded. In peak season it can be very difficult to find a free hut here and travellers end up sleeping on the floor of a restaurant for a night or two until something becomes available.

On the hill overlooking the western part of the bay you'll find *Laem Khlong* (100 to 500B, no beach) and *Viewpoint*, with lots of bungalows for 80 to 350B and grumpy staff. Next is *Sunshine*, with basic but clean bungalows for 150 to 400B, all with fan and attached bath. *Buddha View Dive Resort* next door has similar bungalows as well as rooms in a multistorey building for 200B; the restaurant is one of the better ones outside of Hat Sai Ri. Next are two cheaper places, the well run *Carabao* (50 to 80B) and the rather dilapidated *K See* (100 to 150B with bath). Towards the eastern end of the bay, the friendly *Ko Tao Cottages* has the some of the island's most luxurious bungalows for 550 to 650B.

Around a couple of small points to the south along Laem Tato is a beach which can only be reached on foot and at low tide. Here *Tatoo Lagoon* offers basic huts for 60B, plus more elaborate ones with attached bath for up to 300B. Connected by a network of bridges and walkways, bungalows at the newish *Pond Resort* perch on rocks overlooking the bay and start at 200B. Also on the hillside are the more basic *Banana Rock* and *Aud Bungalow* for 100 to 200B.

**South-West of Mae Hat** As might be expected, beaches just south of town get better the farther south you go. A few hundred metres south-west of Mae Hat, across a stream and down a footpath, *Paew* has sturdy bungalows for 100 to 350B, while *Coral Beach* offers standard but clean huts with shared facilities for 80 to 100B, 150B with attached bath. Between the two is the new, up-market *Sensi Paradise Resort* (☎ /fax (77) 377196), with solid cottages made from local materials for 350 to 700B depending on size, as well as a few larger places with sleeping lofts suitable for families for 1500B; all accommodation comes without air-con.

A couple of km farther south of Ban Mae Hat is a series of small beaches collectively known as **Hat Sai Nuan**, where you'll find

*Siam Cookie* (80 to 250B) and *Cha* (60 to 80B).

Around at **Laem Je Ta Kang** (about 1.2 km west of Ao Chalok Ban Kao) is another tiny beach with *Tao Thong Villa* (50 to 80B). South of Laem Je Ta Kang, by itself on **Ao Jun Jeua**, is *Sunset* (70 to 150B). The latter commands a beautiful point that juts out into the sea. The only way to get to these is to walk along the dirt track from Mae Hat or take a long-tail boat.

**Ko Nang Yuan** This pretty little tripartite island is occupied by *Ko Nangyuan Dive Resort* (☎ (01) 726-0085) where, as the name suggests, the emphasis is on diving. Accommodation starts at 150B (100B long-term) for standard bungalows and go up to 1500B for air-con villas. Regular daily boats to Nang Yuan leave from the Ban Mae Hat pier daily at 10 am and return at 4 pm, for 40B round trip. You can easily charter a ride there for 50B. Note that the management does not allow any plastic bottles on the island – these will be confiscated on arrival.

**Places to Eat**
In Ban Mae Hat there's a string of simple seafood restaurants south of pier – *Mae Haad, Lucky, Neptune, Baan Yaay* – all with dining platforms built over the water's edge. The *Swiss Bakery* on the road that leads to the pier sells very good breads and pastries.

There are also several restaurants on Hat Sai Ri, most associated with bungalows. Back from the beach on a slight slope, *Chaba Restaurant* is an atmospheric place with a choice of outdoor or loft dining areas; the Thai seafood is very good here although the spices are toned down for western tastes.

**Getting There & Away**
**Bangkok** Bus/boat combination tickets from Bangkok cost 450 to 650B and are available from travel agents on Khao San Rd.

Beware of travel agents on Ko Tao selling boat/train combos. Usually this involves receiving a 'voucher' that you're supposed to be able to exchange for a train ticket in Surat Thani or Chumphon; more than a few travellers have found the vouchers to be worthless. If you book train reservations a few days (or more) in advance, any legitimate agency on Ko Tao should be able to deliver the train tickets themselves. It's same-day or day-before reservations that usually involve voucher problems.

**Chumphon** Two boats from the mainland – a slow boat and a 'speed boat' – leave daily from Chumphon to Ko Tao. Departures may be fewer if the swells are high. The slow boat leaves Chumphon at midnight, takes five or six hours or so to reach Ko Tao and costs 200B one way. In the opposite direction it departs from Ko Tao at 10 am. See the Chumphon section for more details.

The speed boat departs Chumphon at 9.30 am (from Ban Mae Hat at 8 am) and takes about 2½ hours. The speed boat fare is 400B. See the Chumphon section for more details.

**Surat Thani** Every third day, depending on the weather, a boat runs between Surat Thani (Tha Thong) and Ko Tao, a seven to eight hour trip for 220B one way. From Surat, boats depart at 11 pm and return from Ban Mae Hat at 9 am.

**Ko Pha-Ngan** Depending on weather conditions, boats run daily between the Thong Sala pier on Ko Pha-Ngan and Ban Mae Hat on Ko Tao. The trip takes anywhere from 2½ to three hours and costs 150B per person. Boats leave Thong Sala at 2.30 pm and return from Ko Tao at 9 am the next day. Twice a day – again depending on marine conditions – Rossarin Tour runs an 800 hp, 35-passenger speed boat that costs 350B and does the trip in an hour.

**Getting Around**
The various pickups cost 20B per person to anywhere on the island during the day, but to charter one after hours costs whatever it takes to motivate someone – usually 100B. Long-tail boats can also be chartered for 500 to 800B a day depending on the number of passengers carried.

Walking is an easy way to get around the

island, but some trails aren't clearly marked and can be difficult to follow. You can walk around the whole island in a day, though the up-and-down, rocky paths make it a challenging proposition. The *Guide Map of Koh Samui, Koh Pha-Ngan & Koh Tao* by V Hongsombud offers a rough outline of the trails.

# Nakhon Si Thammarat Province

Much of this large Southern province is covered with rugged mountains and forests, which were, until recently, the last refuge of Thailand's communist insurgents. The province's eastern border is formed by the Gulf of Thailand and much of the provincial economy is dependent on fishing and shrimp farming. Along the north coast are several nice beaches: **Khanom, Nai Phlao, Tong Yi, Sichon** and **Hin Ngam**.

In the interior are several caves and waterfalls, including **Phrom Lok Falls, Thong Phannara Cave** and **Yong Falls**. Besides fishing, Nakhon residents earn a living by growing coffee, rice, rubber and fruit (especially *mongkhút*, or mangosteen).

## KHAO LUANG NATIONAL PARK
อุทยานแห่งชาติเขาหลวง
This 570 sq km park in the centre of the province surrounds **Khao Luang**, at 1835m the highest peak in peninsular Thailand. The park is known for beautiful mountain and forest walks, cool streams, waterfalls (Karom and Krung Ching are the largest) and fruit orchards. Wildlife includes clouded leopard, tiger, elephant, banteng, gaur and Javan mongoose, plus over 200 bird species.

To get to the park, take a songthaew (15B) from Nakhon Si Thammarat to the village of Khiriwong at the base of Khao Luang. Twice a year the villagers lead groups on a special climb up the mountain – ask at the TAT office in Nakhon Si Thammarat for details.

# Culture of the South

A lthough under Thai political domination for several centuries, the South has always remained culturally apart from the other regions of Thailand. Historically, the peninsula has been linked to cultures in ancient Indonesia, particularly the Srivijaya empire, which ruled a string of principalities in what is today Southern Thailand, Malaysia and Indonesia. The Srivijaya dynasty was based in Sumatra and lasted nearly 500 years (8th to 13th centuries). The influence of Malay-Indonesian culture is still apparent in the ethnicity, religion, art and language of the *Thai pàk tâi*, the Southern Thais.

The Thai pàk tai dress differently, build their houses differently and eat differently from Thais in the North. Many are followers of Islam, so there are quite a few mosques in Southern cities; men often cover their heads and the long sarong is favoured over the shorter *phâakhamãa* worn in the Northern, Central and North-Eastern regions. There are also a good many Chinese living in the South – their influence can be seen in the old architecture and in the baggy Chinese pants worn by rural non-Muslims.

Southern Thais speak a dialect that confounds even visitors from other Thai regions. Diction is short and fast: *pai nãi* (Where are you going?) becomes *p'nái*, and *tham arai* (What are you doing?) becomes *'rái*. The clipped tones fly into the outer regions of intelligibility, giving the aural impression of a tape played at the wrong speed. In the provinces nearest Malaysia – Yala, Pattani, Narathiwat and Satun – many Thai Muslims speak Yawi, an old Malay dialect with similarities to modern Bahasa Malaysia and Bahasa Indonesia.

Architecture is also different in the South and follows three basic threads. In rural areas, simple bungalows constructed from thatched palm leaves and bamboo strips affixed to wood or bamboo frames are common. A Malay style of construction emphasises sturdy houses of wood with square tile roofs. In the older cities you'll come across splendid examples of Sino-Portuguese architecture, featuring arched windows and porticoes and curved tiled roofs.

Southern Thai cuisine combines Chinese, Malay and Thai elements to create brightly coloured, heavily spiced dishes. Look for *khanõm jiin nàam yaa*, thin noodles doused in a fish curry sauce, and *roti kaeng*, Malay-style flatbread served with a curry dip. Seafood is an everyday staple.

## People

Southern Thais are stereotypically regarded as rebellious folk, considering themselves reluctant subjects of Bangkok rule and Thai (Central Thai) custom. Indeed, Thai Muslims (ethnic Malays) living in the provinces bordering on Malaysia complain of persecution by Thai government troops who police the area for insurgent activity. There has even been some talk of these provinces seceding from Thailand.

The majority of the people in the upper Southern provinces are Thai Buddhists, while the lower are dominated by Muslims of Thai and Malay descent. In the cities throughout the South live a large minority of Chinese. In addition to these groups, there are small numbers of Sakai in the interior, and Moken or sea gypsies along the coast and on nearby islands.

Ban Sakai is the centre of Thailand's last remaining Sakai tribes, called 'Ngaw' by Thais apparently because their frizzy hair and dark-skinned complexions remind Thais of the outer skin of the rambutan fruit (*ngáw* in Thai). Anthropologists speculate that the Sakai are the direct descendants of a Proto-Malay race that once inhabited the entire Thai-Malay peninsula and beyond. It is believed that the Sakai's numbers decreased as they were pushed farther back into the jungle by the Austro-Thai cultures from the North. At any rate, the Sakai continue to

JOE CUMMINGS

Much of Southern Thailand once belonged to the powerful Srivijaya kingdom based in Palembang, Sumatra, during the 8th to 13th centuries. This mondòp at Wat Phra Mahathat in Nakon Si Thammarat, one of the most important wats in the South, shows possible Sumatran influence in its roofline.

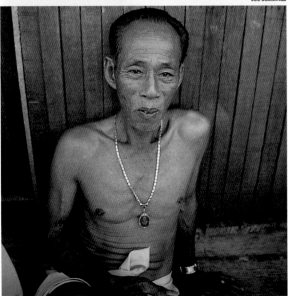
SARA JANE CLELAND

A Southern Thai fisherman, sporting a hefty amulet for good luck, takes a break after a morning of fishing – one of the main industries of the South.

Inspired by the resources common to the region, Southern Thai dishes feature a tantalising array of fresh seafood as well as the milk, oil and grated flesh of coconuts, used heavily to flavour soups, curries and condiments.

TAT

A Southern Thai fishing boat, adorned by coloured strips of cloth to appease the sea spirits, moored at Ao Hat Rin Nai, Ko Pha-Ngan.

RICHARD NEBESKY

lead a traditional village life of hunting and gathering, practising very little agriculture and expressing themselves through their own unique language, music and dance. Recently a development project has got the Sakai involved in tending rubber plantations.

The Moken, known to the Thais as *chao náam* or 'water people', are a somewhat nomadic people who sail from island to island, stopping off to repair their boats or fishing nets. With stones tied to their waists as ballast, chao náam divers can reportedly descend up to 60m while breathing through an air hose held above the water surface. Ko Sire, four km east of Phuket and separated from the main island by a canal, is known for its chao náam village. How much longer the chao náam can hold out here in the face of Thai land encroachment is uncertain. Thai fishing trawlers continue to infringe on the chao náam's traditional fishing grounds – even though these are supposedly protected by a three km limit. On top of this, local housing developers are wreaking havoc on local mangroves, an important source of food and wood for the chao náam.

## Religion
Many Southern Thais are Muslims, particularly in the four Southern provinces bordering Malaysia. In Satun Province, for example, 80% of the people profess Islam. In fact, throughout the entire province there are only 11 or 12 Buddhist temples, versus 117 mosques. Urban Chinese worship at Buddhist, Taoist and Confucianist shrines and temples, while the Thais usually make twice-monthly visits to their local wats. Many of the chao náam practice animism, which revolves around the placation of spirits who inhabit the sea, island forests and even their boats. This often takes the form of leaving offerings of food, liquor and coloured strips of cloth at local shrines. The Moken gather at yearly festivals to assure continuing fish harvests, with more involved ceremonies and much merry-making.

## Handicrafts
Nakhon Si Thammarat and Phattalung are home to the uniquely Thai life-size shadow puppets, *năng yài*, carved from buffalo hide. Nakhon Si Thammarat is also known for its dance masks and for nielloware *(khrêuang thõm)*, a silver and black alloy/enamel jewellery technique borrowed from China many centuries ago. Another indigenous handicraft is *yaan lipao*, basketry woven from a hardy local grass into intricate contrasting designs.

Ko Yo, in Songkhla Province, is famous for its cotton weaving – every other house on this little island has a loom or two. The provinces of Pattani and Narathiwat are renowned for colourful batik textiles, which share many design characteristics with the batiks of Malaysia and Indonesia.

## Music & Dance
Two features of Southern Thai culture are *mánohra*, the classical Southern Thai dance-drama, and *năng thálung*, or shadow play. (See Thai Arts & Architecture in the Facts about the Country chapter for more details.)

Trang has a unique Indian-influenced music and dance tradition. *Lí-khe paà* (also called *lí-khe bòk* and *lí-khe ram ma-naa)* is a local folk opera with a story line that depicts Indian merchants taking their Thai wives back to India for a visit. It's part farce, part drama, with Thais costumed as Indians with long beards and turbans. Also in Trang, traditional funerals and Buddhist ordinations often feature a musical ensemble called *kaa-law*, which consists of four or five players sitting on a small stage under a temporary coconut-leaf roof or awning. The instruments include two long Indian drums, a *pìi haw* (a large oboe) and two gongs.

SOUTHERN THAILAND

## NAKHON SI THAMMARAT
อ.เมืองนครศรีธรรมราช
• ☎ (75) • pop 71,500

Nakhon Si Thammarat is 780 km from Bangkok. Centuries before the 8th century Srivijaya empire subjugated the peninsula, there was a city-state here called Ligor or Lagor, capital of the Tambralinga kingdom, which was well known throughout Oceania. Later, when Sri Lankan-ordained Buddhist monks established a cloister at the city, the name was changed to the Pali-Sanskrit Nagara Sri Dhammaraja (City of the Sacred Dharma-King), rendered in Thai phonetics as Nakhon Si Thammarat. An overland route between the western port of Trang and eastern port of Nakhon Si Thammarat functioned as a major trade link between Thailand and the rest of the world, as well as and between the western and eastern hemispheres.

During the early development of the various Thai kingdoms, Nakhon Si Thammarat also became a very important centre of religion and culture. Thai shadow play (năng thălung) and classical dance-drama (lákhon – the Thai pronunciation of Lagor) were developed in Nakhon Si Thammarat; buffalo-hide shadow puppets and dance masks are still made here.

In the past Nakhon Si Thammarat natives were stereotyped as somewhat rough and prone to criminal activity, but a new civic pride has developed in recent years and the natives are now quite fond of being called khon khawn (Nakhon people). Bovorn (Bowon) Bazaar, a cluster of restaurants and handicraft shops off Ratchadamnoen Rd, serves as a commercial centre for the city's revitalisation process.

### Orientation & Information
Nakhon Si Thammarat can be divided into two sections, the historic half south of the clock tower and the new city centre north of the clock tower and Khlong Na Meuang. The new city has all the hotels and most of the restaurants, as well as more movie theatres per sq km than any other city in Thailand.

The TAT office (☎ 346515/6) is housed in a 70 year old building in the north-west corner of the Sanaam Naa Meuang (City Park) off Ratchadamnoen Rd, near the police station. They distribute the usual helpful information printed in English, and can also assist with any tourism-related problems.

The GPO is also on Ratchadamnoen Rd, along with an upstairs telephone office with international service (open from 8 am to 11 pm).

### Suan Nang Seu Nakhon Bowonrat
The Suan Nang Seu or Book Garden, at 116 Ratchadamnoen Rd next to Bovorn Bazaar and Siam Commercial Bank, is Nakhon's intellectual centre (look for the traditional water jar on a platform in front). Housed in an 80 year old building that once served variously as a sinsae (Chinese doctor) clinic, opium den and hotel, this nonprofit bookshop specialises in books (mostly in Thai) on local history as well as national politics and religion. It also co-ordinates Dhamma lectures and sponsors local arts and craft exhibits.

### Nakhon Si Thammarat National Museum
พิพิธภัณฑ์แห่งชาตินครศรีธรรมราช

This is past the principal wats on Ratchadamnoen Rd heading south, across from Wat Thao Khot and Wat Phet Jarik, on the left – 2B by city bus or 3B by songthaew. Since the Tampaling (or Tambralinga) kingdom traded with Indian, Arabic, Dvaravati and Champa states, much art from these places found its way to the Nakhon Si Thammarat area, and some is now on display in the national museum here. Notable are Dong-Son bronze drums, Dvaravati Buddha images and Pallava (south Indian) Hindu sculpture. Locally produced art is also on display.

If you've already had your fill of the usual Thai art history surveys from Ban Chiang to Ayuthaya, go straight to the Art of Southern Thailand exhibit in a room on the left of the foyer. Here you'll find many fine images of Nakhon Si Thammarat provenance, including Phutthasihing, U Thong and late Ayuthaya styles. The Nakhon Si Thammarat-produced

Ayuthaya style seems to be the most common, with distinctive, almost comical, crowned faces. The so-called Phutthasihing-style Buddha looks a little like the Palla-influenced Chiang Saen Buddha, but is shorter and more 'pneumatic'.

Admission to the museum is 10B and hours are Wednesday to Sunday from 9 am to 4 pm.

## Wat Phra Mahathat
วัดพระมหาธาตุ

This is the city's most historic site, reputed to have been founded by Queen Hem Chala over a thousand years ago. Bronze statues representing the queen and her brother stand in front of the east wall facing Ratchadamnoen Rd, and her spirit is said to be associated with the large standing Buddha in the southeastern cloister. Locals make daily offerings of flower garlands to both this Buddha image and the statue of the queen, believing her spirit watches over the city and all its residents.

This is the biggest wat in the South, comparable to Wat Pho and other large Bangkok wats. If you like wats, this one is well worth a trip. Reconstructed in the mid-13th century, the huge complex features a 78m chedi, crowned by a solid gold spire weighing several hundred kg. Numerous smaller grey-black chedis surround the main chedi. The temple's bòt (central sanctuary) contains one of Thailand's three identical Phra Singh Buddhas, one of which is supposed to have been originally cast in Sri Lanka before being brought to Sukhothai (through Nakhon Si Thammarat), Chiang Mai and later, Ayuthaya. The other images are at Wat Phra Singh in Chiang Mai and the National Museum in Bangkok – each is claimed to be the original.

Besides the distinctive bòt and chedi there are many intricately designed wihǎans (Buddhist image sanctuaries) surrounding the chedi, several of which contain crowned Nakhon Si Thammarat/Ayuthaya-style Buddhas in glass cabinets. One wihǎan houses a funky museum with carved wooden kruts (garudas, Vishnu's mythical bird-mount),

old votive tablets, Buddha figures of every description including a standing Dvaravati figure, a Buddha styled after the Siwichai naga (dragon-headed serpent), pearl-inlaid alms bowls and other oddities. A 12m whale skeleton lies in the back of the complex under the north cloister.

A mondòp, the fortress-looking structure toward the north end of the temple grounds, holds a Buddha footprint – one of the better designs in Thailand.

Wat Phra Mahathat's full name, Wat Phra Mahathat Woramahawihaan, is sometimes abbreviated as Wat Phra Boromathat. It's about two km from the new town centre – hop on any bus or songthaew going down Ratchadamnoen Rd.

## Wat Na Phra Boromathat
วัดหน้าพระบรมธาตุ

Across the road from Wat Phra Mahathat, this is the residence for monks serving at Mahathat. There is a nice Gandhara-style fasting Buddha in front of the bòt here.

## Other Temples, Shrines, Churches & Mosques

In addition to the original Sri Lankan monks who arrived in 13th century Nakhon to teach Theravada Buddhism, many other missionaries – Catholics from Portugal, Hindus from India, Muslims from the Middle East and Mahayana Buddhists from Japan – also stationed themselves in the city. A legacy of these visitors is the variety and number of non-Theravadin places of worship surviving today.

Three Hindu temples can be found along the west side of Ratchadamnoen Rd inside the city walls. Brahman priests from these temples take part each year in the Royal Ploughing Ceremony in Bangkok. One temple houses a locally famous Shivalingam (phallic shrine) which is worshipped by women hoping to bear children. Farther north on the east side of Ratchadamnoen Rd toward the town centre stands the green-hued Matsayit Yamia (Friday Mosque), and there are at least two other mosques in the

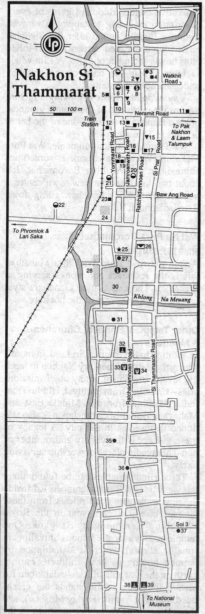

**PLACES TO STAY**
4   Taksin Hotel
5   Phetpailin Hotel
7   Thai Fa Hotel
10  Si Thong Hotel
11  Nakhon Garden Inn
12  Montien Hotel
13  Siam Hotel
14  Thai Hotel
16  Muang Thong Hotel
17  Thai Lee Hotel
18  Nakhon Hotel
19  Bue Loung (Bua Luang) Hotel
23  Laem Thong Hotel

**PLACES TO EAT**
2   Dam Kan Aeng
9   Yong Seng Restaurant
15  Bovorn Bazaar

**OTHER**
1   Taxis to Surat, Chumphon & Ranong
3   THAI Office
6   Minivans to Sichon & Khanom
8   Bangkok Bank
20  Songthaews to Khao Luang
21  Shared Taxi Stand
22  Bus Station
24  Market
25  Police Station
26  Main Post Office & Telephone Office
27  Lak Meuang (City Pillar)
28  Handicraft Shops
29  TAT Office
30  Sanaam Naa Meuang (City Park)
31  Prison
32  Wat Sema Muang
33  Shiva Shrine
34  Brahma Shrine
35  Provincial Offices
36  Clock Tower
37  Suchart's Workshop
38  Wat Phra Mahathat
39  Wat Na Phra Boromathat

area. On the same side of the road opposite Christian Hospital is quaint Bethlehem Church.

Nakhon's most important non-Buddhist shrine, the Lak Meuang or City Pillar, stands at the north end of Sanaam Naa Meuang. In typical Thai design, it's a small, open-sided pavilion containing a phallic-shaped pillar festooned with the daily offerings of hundreds of local residents.

**Nakhon Si Thammarat Festivals**
Every year in mid-October there is a Southern Thai festival called Chak Phra Pak Tai held in Songkhla, Surat Thani and Nakhon Si Thammarat. In Nakhon Si Thammarat the festival is centred around Wat Mahathat and includes performances of năng thálung and lákhon as well as the parading of Buddha images around the city to collection donations for local temples.

In the third lunar month (February to March) the city holds the colourful Hae Phaa Khun That, in which a lengthy cloth jataka painting is wrapped around the main chedi at Wat Phra Mahathat. ■

## Shadow Puppet Workshop

Traditionally, there are two styles of shadow puppets, *năng thálung* and *năng yài*; the former are similar in size to the typical Malay-Indonesian style puppets while the latter are nearly life-size and unique to Thailand. Both are intricately carved from buffalo-hide. Performances of Thai shadow theatre are rare nowadays (usually only during festivals), but there are two places in town where you can see the puppets being made.

The acknowledged master of shadow puppet craft – both manufacture and performance – is Suchart Subsin (Suchaat Sapsin), a Nakhon resident with a workshop at 110/18 Si Thammasok Soi 3, not far from Wat Phra Mahathat. Khun Suchart has received several awards for his mastery and preservation of the craft and has performed for the king. His workshop is open to the public; if enough people are assembled he may even be talked into providing a performance at his small outdoor studio. Puppets can be purchased here at reasonable prices – and here only, as he refuses to sell them through distributors. On some puppets the fur is left on the hide for additional effect – these cost a bit more as special care must be taken in tanning them.

Another craftsperson, Mesa Chotiphan, welcomes visitors to her workshop in the northern part of town. Mesa sells to distributors but will also sell direct at lower prices. Her house is at 558/4 Soi Rong Jeh, Ratchadamnoen Rd (☎ 343979). If you call she will pick you up from anywhere in the city. To get there on your own, go north from the city centre on Ratchadamnoen Rd and after about half a km north of the sports field, take the soi opposite the Chinese cemetery (before reaching the golf-course and military base).

## Places to Stay – bottom end

Most of Nakhon Si Thammarat's hotels are near the train and bus stations. The best budget value in town is the friendly *Thai Lee Hotel* (☎ 356948) at 1130 Ratchadamnoen Rd, where clean rooms with ceiling fan, shower and toilet cost 120/200B single/double.

On Yommarat (spelt 'Yammaraj' on some signs) Rd, almost across from the train station, is the *Si Thong Hotel* (☎ 356357), with adequate rooms for 120 to 180B with fan and bath. Also on Yommarat Rd is the *Nakhon Hotel* (☎ 356318), with similar rates and facilities as the Si Thong. Avoid the nearby *Yaowarat*, which is almost exclusively used as a brothel.

On Jamroenwithi Rd (walk straight down Neramit Rd opposite the train station two blocks and turn right into Jamroenwithi Rd) is the large *Siam Hotel* (☎ 356090); rooms with fan and bath cost from 130B. Farther south on this street is the *Muang Thong Hotel*, where 100B will get you a clean room with fan and bath. A block north of the Siam, on the same side of the street, is the *Thai Fa Hotel* (☎ 356727), a small, two-storey place with adequate rooms for 100 to 150B.

The *Laem Thong Hotel* (☎ 356478) at 1213/5-6 Yommarat Rd was recently closed for renovations; when opened again it will probably cost around 200B a night.

SOUTHERN THAILAND

## Places to Stay – middle & top end

Once Nakhon Si Thammarat's flashiest hotel, the *Thai Hotel* (☎ 341509) on Ratchadamnoen Rd, two blocks from the train station, now seems rather ordinary with fan-cooled singles/doubles for 270/300B, and air-con rooms from 440 to 600B. The six-storey *Taksin Hotel* (☎ 342790) stands off Si Prat Rd amidst a string of massage places and costs 590B for all air-con rooms with hot water showers.

The *Bue Loung (Bua Luang) Hotel* (☎ 341-518), on Soi Luang Meuang off Jamroenwithi Rd, has large, clean singles/doubles with fan and bath for 170B, air-con for 270B, or add TV and fridge for 340B.

On Yommarat Rd next to the train station, the fading, eight-storey *Montien Hotel* (☎ /fax 341908) has large rooms with fan and attached bath from 220B and air-con for 420B – a bit overpriced considering the low upkeep. The nearby *Phetphailin* (☎ 341896; fax 343283), a block north, is similar but costs 180B with fan, 380B air-con,

The quiet *Nakhon Garden Inn* (☎ 344831; fax 342926) at 1/4 Pak Nakhon Rd, east of the centre, has 50 rooms with air-con and TV costing 500 to 600B.

Nakhon's new top spot, the *Southern BM Hotel* (no telephone yet), is under construction on Pattanakan Kukwang Rd in the extreme south-eastern corner of town. It will have all the amenities expected by Bangkok business travellers and is projected to cost 1600B for a standard single/double room, 1800B for a deluxe room.

## Places to Eat

There are lots of funky old Chinese restaurants along Yommarat and Jamroenwithi Rds. The latter street is the city's main culinary centre. At night the entire block running south from the Siam Hotel is lined with cheap food vendors – Muslim stands opposite the hotel sell delicious roti klûay (banana pancake), khâo mók (chicken biryani) and mátàbà (pancakes stuffed with chicken or vegetables) in the evening and by day there are plenty of rice and noodle shops. *Yong Seng* (no English sign) is a good, inexpensive Chinese restaurant on Jamroenwithi Rd.

To try some of Nakhon's excellent Thai coffee, stop by *Hao Coffee* at Bovorn Bazaar. Basically an update of an original Hokkien-style coffee shop once run by the owner's family in Nakhon, Hao Coffee serves international coffees as well as Southern Thai Hokkien-style coffee (listed as 'Hao coffee' on the menu) served with a tea chaser. Ask for fresh milk (nom sòt) if you abhor powdered non-dairy creamer.

Bovorn Bazaar offers several other culinary delights. Adjacent to Hao Coffee is *Khrua Nakhon*, a large open-air restaurant serving real Nakhon cuisine, including khâo yam (Southern-style rice salad), kaeng tai plaa (spicy fish curry), khanõm jiin (curry noodles served with a huge tray of veggies) and seafood. The restaurant also has egg-and-toast breakfasts; you can order Hao coffee from next door if you'd like. With a banyan tree in front and a modest display of Southern Thai folk art, the atmosphere is hard to beat. Get there early as it's only open from 7 am to 3 pm. Behind Khrua Nakhon is *Ban Lakhon*, in an old house, which is also very good for Thai food and is open for dinner.

On the corner of the alley leading into Bovorn Bazaar, *Ligor Home Bakery* bakes fresh European-style pastries daily. At night the bakery closes and Nakhon's most famous roti vendors set up along the alley. In Nakhon, roti klûay is a tradition – the vendors here use only fresh mashed bananas, no banana preserves or the like. Other offerings here include roti with curry (roti kaeng), with egg (roti khài) or as mátàbà. They also do great khanõm jìip, dumplings stuffed with a chicken-shrimp mixture, along with Nakhon coffee and better than average milk tea. On the north-western corner of Ratchadamnoen and Watkhit Rds, the popular Thai-Chinese *Dam Kan Aeng* is packed with hungry customers every night.

## Entertainment

Beyond the cinemas in town, there's not a lot of nightlife. *Rock 99% Bar & Grill*, an American roadhouse-style pub inside Bovorn Bazaar, offers draught beer, cocktails and western pop music, as well as pizza, baked potatoes and sandwiches; this is where the few expats that live in Nakhon Si Thammarat hang out. It's open from 6 pm to 2 am.

### Getting There & Away
**Air** THAI has four flights a week to/from Bangkok (1770B), three flights a week to/from Phuket (690B) via Hat Yai, three flights a week to/from Narathiwat (835B) and three flights weekly to/from Surat Thani (340B). The THAI office (☎ 342491) in Nakhon is at 1612 Ratchadamnoen Rd.

**Bus & Minivan** Air-con buses bound for Nakhon Si Thammarat leave Bangkok's Southern Bus Terminal daily every 30 minutes or so from 5 to 8 pm, arriving 12 hours later, for 342B. Air-con buses in the reverse direction leave at about the same times. There are also two 2nd class air-con departures (266B) and one VIP departure (420B) nightly. Ordinary buses leave Bangkok at 6.40, 7 and 8.30 am, 4.30, 5.30 and 6.30 pm for 190B.

Ordinary buses from Surat Thani cost 37B and leaves four times a day, while air-con departures are slightly less frequent and cost around 60B. Direct buses run from Songkhla via a bridge over the entrance to Thaleh Noi (the inland sea). Check with one of the tour-bus companies on Niphat Uthit 2 Rd in Hat Yai. Muang Tai Tours, on Jamroenwithi Rd in Nakhon Si Thammarat, does a 70B trip to Surat that includes a good meal and a video movie. There are a couple of other private bus companies on Jamroenwithi Rd in the vicinity of the Siam Hotel.

Hourly buses between Nakhon Si Thammarat and Krabi cost 50B per person (70B air-con) and take about three hours. Other routes include Trang (37B ordinary, 60B air-con), Phattalung (30B ordinary, 50B air-con), Phuket (92B ordinary, 130B air-con) and Hat Yai (53B ordinary, 60B air-con, 80B minivan).

Minivans to Krabi leave from in front of the municipality office every half hour from 7 am to 3 pm for 71B; the trip takes 2½ hours. You can also catch minivans to Phuket (130B, five hours). To Ko Samui there is one

air-con bus a day from the main terminal at 11.20 am (100B, three hours).

**Share Taxis** This seems to be the most popular form of inter-city travel out of Nakhon. The huge share-taxi terminal on Yommarat Rd has taxis to Thung Song (25B), Khanom (40B), Sichon (30B), Krabi (80B), Hat Yai (80B), Trang (60B), Phuket (140B) and Phattalung (70B). A second smaller stand on Thewarat Rd has taxis to Surat (60B), Chumphon (130B) and Ranong (180B).

**Train** Most southbound trains stop at the junction of Thung Song, about 40 km west of Nakhon Si Thammarat, from where you must take a bus or taxi to the coast. However, two trains actually go all the way to Nakhon Si Thammarat (there is a branch line from Khao Chum Thong to Nakhon Si Thammarat): the rapid No 47, which leaves Bangkok's Hualamphong station at 7.45 pm, arriving in Nakhon Si Thammarat at 10.50 am, and the express No 15, which leaves Bangkok at 7.20 pm and arrives in Nakhon Si Thammarat at 10 am. Most travellers will not be booking a train directly to Nakhon Si Thammarat, but if you want to, 1st class costs 652B, 2nd class 308B, not including surcharges for rapid/express service or sleeping berths. There are no direct 3rd class trains to Nakhon Si Thammarat.

### Getting Around
City buses run north-south along Ratchadamnoen and Si Thammasok Rds for 3B. Blue songthaews do similar routes for 4B during the day, 5B at night. Motorbike taxis cost 10B.

### AROUND NAKHON SI THAMMARAT PROVINCE
#### Laem Talumpuk
แหลมตะลุมพุก
This is a small scenic cape not far from Nakhon Si Thammarat. Take a bus from Neramit Rd going east to Pak Nakhon for 10B, then cross the inlet by ferry to Laem Talumpuk.

## Hat Sa Bua
หาดสระบัว

Sixteen km north of Nakhon Si Thammarat in the Tha Sala district, off Route 401 to Surat and about 11B by songthaew, are some semi-deserted white-sand beaches with few tourists. As yet accommodation isn't available, but there are some very reasonably priced restaurants here.

## Hat Sichon & Hat Hin Ngam
หาดสิชล/หาดหินงาม

Hat Sichon and Hat Hin Ngam are stunning beaches 37 km north of Nakhon Si Thammarat in Sichon district. Another good beach, **Hat Tong Yi**, is accessible only by boat and is hence almost always deserted – it's between Sichon and Hin Ngam (a chartered boat to Tong Yi from either beach costs 200 to 250B).

Get the bus for Hat Hin Ngam or Sichon from the Nakhon Si Thammarat bus station for 18B or take a share taxi for 30B. Hat Sichon comes first; Hin Ngam is another 1.5 km. Beach accommodation at Sichon is available at: *Prasansuk Villa* (☎ (75) 536299), 30 rooms, 280 to 420B; *Sailom Bungalow* (☎ (75) 536299), 22 rooms, 120 to 500B; or on Hat Hin Ngam at *Hin Ngam Bungalow* (☎ (75) 536204), six bungalows, 120B. The clientele at these places is almost entirely Thai.

## Ao Khanom
อ่าวขนอม

About 25 km from Sichon, 70 km from Surat and 80 km from Nakhon Si Thammarat is the bay of Ao Khanom. Not far from the vehicle-ferry landing for Ko Samui in Khanom is a string of four white-sand beaches – Hat Nai Praet, Hat Nai Phlao, Hat Na Dan and Hat Pak Nam. Most of the places to stay here offer five to 10 solid, plain bungalows with private bath for 500 to 800B a night; the lower end of this range may have fan only, while the upper end offers air-con.

At Nai Phlao these include *Khanom Hill Resort* (☎ (75) 529403), *GB Resort*, *Nai Phlao Bay Resort* (☎ (75) 529039) and *Supa Villa* (☎ (75) 529237). The eight-bungalow

*Fern Bay Resort* (☎ (75) 528226) at Nai Phlao is a bit cheaper at 300 to 450B, while the *Khanab Nam Diamond Cliff Resort* (☎ (75) 529144; fax 529111) handles the top end with 22 rooms for 500 to 3500B. The latter is the only place with a swimming pool, though the Nai Phlao Bay Resort is promising one by the end of 1997.

At Hat Na Dan the *Watanyoo Villa* (☎ (75) 529224) has fan-cooled bungalows for 120 to 300B.

# Phattalung Province

Over 840 km from Bangkok and 95 km from Hat Yai, Phattalung is one of the South's only rice-growing provinces and has prospered as a result. The eastern portion of the province is washed by the Thaleh Noi or Little Sea, a northern extension of the brackish Thaleh Sap.

## PHATTALUNG
อ.เมืองพัทลุง

• ☎ (74) • pop 34,000

The provincial capital is fairly small (you can walk around the perimeter of central Phattalung in an hour, even stopping for rice). Judging from the number of *hang thong* (gold dealers) on Poh Saat Rd, there's a large Chinese population.

Phattalung is famous for the original nǎng thálung (shadow play) which was probably named after Phattalung – *nǎng* means hide (untanned leather), and *thálung* is taken from Phattalung. The Thai shadow-play tradition remains only in Nakhon Si Thammarat and Phattalung, though the best performances are seen in the former. A typical performance begins at midnight and lasts four to five hours. Usually they take place during *ngaan wat* (temple fairs).

The town is situated between two picturesque, foliage-trimmed limestone peaks, Khao Ok Thalu (literally, 'Punctured-Chest Mountain') and Khao Hua Taek (or 'Broken-Head Mountain'). Local myth has it that these two mountains were the wife and mistress of a third mountain to the north, Khao Meuang, who fought a fierce battle over the adulterous husband, leaving them with their 'wounds'. The names refer to their geographic peculiarities – Ok Thalu has a tunnel through its upper peak, while Hua Taek is sort of split at the top.

Like most Thai towns, Phattalung's street plan is laid out in a grid pattern. Most of the local sights are nearby.

## Information

The tourist centre (☎ 611201), on the corner of Ramesuan and Kanasan Rds near the town hall, is actually a trade handicraft information/retail office also acting as tourist office for the area. It's open weekdays 8 am to 4 pm.

To change money your best option is to go to the Thai Farmers Bank on Ramet Rd, near the intersection of Nivas (Niwat) Rd. The post office on Rot Fai Rd offers international telephone service upstairs daily from 8 am to 8 pm.

## Wat Khuhasawan
## วัดคูหาสวรรค์

On the western side of town, the Ayuthaya-

### PLACES TO STAY
6 Hoa Far (Haw Fa) Hotel
12 Phattalung Hotel
14 Thai Hotel

### PLACES TO EAT
7 Night Market
16 Khrua Cook

### OTHER
1 Municipal Office
2 Provincial Office
3 Tourist Centre
4 Wat Kuhasawan
5 Market
8 Buses to Thaleh Noi,
 Nakhon Si Thammarat
 & Hat Yai
9 Post Office
10 Share Taxis to Lam Pam
11 Minivans to Hat Yai
 & Songkhla
13 Bangkok Bank
15 Cinema
17 Buses to Bangkok, Hat
 Yai, Surat Thani &
 Songkhla

**Phattalung**

0    100    200 m

To Tham Malai & Nakhon Si Thammarat

Khao Hua Taek

Khuhasawan Road

Nivas Road

Poh Saat Road

Train Station

Yutham Road

Ramet (Ramesuan) Road

Pracha

Datra-Nakarin Road

Bamrung Road

To Highway 4 & Trang

To Wat Wang (4 km) & Lam Pam

To Hat Yai

SOUTHERN THAILAND

period Wat Khuhasawan has one large cave with rather ugly statues, but the cave is high and cool. A tall passageway leads deeper into the cave – lights can be switched on by the monks. Steps lead around the cave to the top of the mountain for a nice view of rice fields and mountains farther west.

To the right of the main cave is an old hermit's cave – the monk who lived here died in 1973 and is commemorated by a statue at the second level of stairs. Good views of Khao Ok Thalu and most of Phattalung city can be had from certain points around this cave.

### Places to Stay

Ramet Rd is the main drag; here you will find two of Phattalung's three principal hotels.

At 43 Ramet Rd, the *Phattalung Hotel* is the cheapest place at 100B with fan and bath but the rooms are dark and dirty. The larger and friendlier *Thai Hotel*, on Disara-Nakarin Rd, off Ramet Rd near Bangkok Bank, has spacious rooms for 150/180B single/double with fan and bath, up to 350B with air-con. The *Hoa Far (Haw Fa) Hotel*, on the corner of Poh Saat and Khuhasawan Rds, has large, clean rooms with fan and bath for 140 to 170B, air-con rooms for 250B.

### Places to Eat

One of the best restaurants in Phattalung is *Khrua Cook* on Pracha Bamrung Rd – turn left off Disara-Nakarin Rd just past the Thai Hotel. One of the house specialities is deep-fried fish with mango salad for 40B. Also on Pracha Bamrung Rd look for *Khrua Muang Lung*, a place with Muslim curries.

Most cheap restaurants in Phattalung are on the grubby side; there are several standard Thai-Chinese places on Pracha Bamrung Rd near the Disara-Nakarin Rd intersection. The market off Poh Saat Rd is a good place for cheap takeaways. For breakfast, try the local speciality khâo yam (dry rice mixed with coconut, peanuts, lime leaves and shrimp); it's delicious. About three km west of town where Highway 4 meets Highway 41 is a Muslim Market. Several foodstalls here sell Muslim food like khâo mòk kài (chicken biryani) and the Southern Thai version of kài yâang.

### Getting There & Away

**Bus & Share Taxi** Buses from the Baw Khaw Saw (government bus) station in Nakhon Si Thammarat take two hours and cost 30B; share taxis are 50B. Air-con buses and minivans to/from Hat Yai are 27B and 30B respectively and take about the same time. There is only one minivan a day to/from Songkhla, for 35B.

Buses to/from Trang cost 15B and take 1½ hours. Other routes include Phuket (90B ordinary, 165B air-con; seven hours), Surat Thani (60B ordinary, 90B air-con; 4½ hours) and Bangkok (209B ordinary, 376B air-con; 12 hours). Most buses heading out of town stop along Ramet Rd near the Phattalung Hotel; you can also catch out of town buses at the Muslim Market, three km west of town.

**Train** Special express trains from Bangkok leave Hualamphong station at 2.35 and 3.15 pm, arriving in Phattalung at 5.04 and 5.30 am. The cheaper rapid No 43 leaves Bangkok at 3.50 pm and arrives in Phattalung at 6.56 am. Basic fares are 611B 1st class (express only) and 288B 2nd class, plus appropriate surcharges. There are also 3rd class trains to Phattalung from Surat Thani (42B) and Nakhon Si Thammarat (22B).

**Boat** It's possible to travel across the inland sea by regularly scheduled ferry boat from Phattalung to Sathing Phra in Songkhla Province – see under Khukhut Waterbird Sanctuary in the Songkhla Province section following for details.

### AROUND PHATTALUNG
### Wat Wang
วัดวัง

Over 100 years old, this is the oldest wat in Phattalung. The palace of a Thai prince was originally located just east of the wat *(wang* means palace), but only the wall remains. The original chedi is in front of the wat. A closed bòt has a decaying set of murals with Buddhist and *Ramayana* themes. You have to open the doors and windows to see them.

Wat Wang is about four km east of Phattalung on the road to Lam Pam. Take a songthaew from next to the post office (4B).

## Lam Pam
ลำปำ

If you follow Phattalung's main street, Ramet Rd, east over the train tracks past Wat Wang, you'll come to Lam Pam on the banks of the Thaleh Luang, the upper part of the South's inland sea (Thaleh Noi). For 5B you can ride a songthaew from next to the post office out to Lam Pam in 15 minutes, or hire a motorcycle for 10B.

Under shady trees next to the freshwater 'sea' are beach chairs and tables where you can relax, enjoy the breeze and order food – crab, mussels, other shellfish, squid, plus beer, soda etc. Although the inland sea itself is not at all spectacular, this is a nice spot to while away a few hours drinking beer and eating the fabulous speciality *plaa mèuk klûay yâang* (literally banana squid – an egg-carrying squid roasted over charcoal), along with *miang kham*, the unique do-it-yourself concoction of dried shrimp, peanuts, lime, garlic, ginger, chilli, toasted coconut and salty-sweet sauce wrapped in wild tea leaves.

The *Lampam Resort* (☎ (74) 611486) has bungalows for 250B (fan) and 500B (air-con).

## Tham Malai
ถ้ำมาลัย

Three km north of Phattalung, near the train line, is a hill with a large cave, Tham Malai, at its base. On top of the hill are some Chinese shrines, though a Thai *mâe chii* (Buddhist nun) resides there. There are excellent views of Phattalung and surrounding mountains from the top.

The cave itself is only slightly more interesting than the shrines. Bring a torch (flashlight) and you can explore the various rooms within the cavern. The cave is more or less in its natural state, with its stalagmites and stalactites still intact. Even without a light, it's worth exploring a bit – when the cave reaches its darkest point, you'll come upon an opening leading back around to daylight.

If the canal running parallel to the train line has enough water, you can get a boat for 5B as far as Tham Malai – easiest in December and January. If the water is too low, walk along the tracks until you come to a footbridge which will take you over the canal onto a path leading to the cave.

## Bullfighting

A rustic stadium four to five km south of town on Highway 4 (4B by songthaew) holds Southern Thai-style bullfights – in which two Brahmin bulls butt each other till one retreats – on occasional Sundays. Matches start around 10 am and last at least six hours. Entry is 20B; most of the spectators are men, who bet furiously before and during the matches.

## Thaleh Noi Wildlife Preserve
อุทยานนกน้ำทะเลน้อย

Thaleh Noi, a small inland sea or lake 32 km north-east of Phattalung, is protected by the Forestry Department – no fishing or hunting is permitted anywhere on or along its shores, islands or waters. Among the 182 species of resident and migratory waterfowl found here, the most prominent is the *nók i kong*, with its long, funny feet which quiver like malfunctioning landing gear as the bird takes flight, and the *nók pèt daeng*, a small, red-headed 'duck bird', related to the whistling teal, that skitters along the water. This is also the last natural habitat in Asia for the beautiful painted stork or *nók kàap bua*, and an important sanctuary as well for the great egret, purple heron, spot-billed pelican and bronze-winged jacana. The best time for bird sightings is November and December; the least number of birds is seen from May to August.

The sea itself is sort of a large swamp similar to the Everglades in the southern USA. The major forms of vegetation are water vines and *dôn kòk*, a reed which the nók i kong uses to build large 'platforms' over the water for nesting purposes. The local Thais also use these same reeds, after drying them in the sun, to make woven floor mats which are sold throughout Phattalung.

The village near the park entrance to Thaleh Noi is a good place to observe the reed-weaving methods.

The Forestry Department has a few bungalows for rent for 100 to 300B.

**Getting There & Away** To get there, take a Thaleh Noi bus from the local bus stop on Poh Saat Rd in Phattalung. The bus stops at the sanctuary after about an hour's journey and costs 10B. Long-tail boats can be hired at the pier to take passengers out and around Thaleh Noi for 150 to 400B, depending on how long and how far you go. The last bus back to Phattalung leaves around 5 pm.

# Songkhla Province

## SONGKHLA
อ.เมืองสงขลา
• ☎ (74) • pop 85,000

Songkhla, 950 km from Bangkok, is another former Srivijaya satellite on the east coast. Not much is known about the pre-8th century history of Songkhla, a name derived from the Yawi 'Singora' – a mutilated Sanskrit reference to a lion-shaped mountain (today called Khao Daeng) opposite the harbour. Originally the settlement lay at the foot of Khao Daeng, where two cemeteries and the ruins of a fort are among the oldest structural remains.

About three km north of Khao Daeng village off the road to Nakhon Si Thammarat is the tomb of Suleiman (1592-1668), a Muslim trader who was largely responsible for Songkhla's commercial eminence during the 17th century. Just south of Suleiman's tomb, a Dutch graveyard testifies to a 17th century Dutch presence as well (look for large granite slabs in an overgrown area next to a Total warehouse). Suleiman's son Mustapha subsequently fell out of grace with Ayuthaya's King Narai, who burned the settlement to the ground in the next century. Songkhla later moved across the harbour to its present site on a peninsula between the Thaleh Sap Songkhla (an inland sea) and

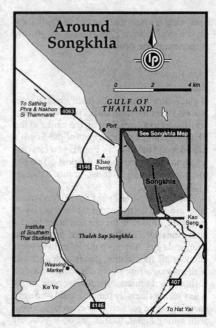

the South China Sea (or Gulf of Thailand, depending on how you look at it). Today's inhabitants are a colourful mixture of Thais, Chinese and Muslims (ethnic Malays), and the local architecture and cuisine reflect this combination. Older Southern Thais still refer to the city as Singora or Singkhon.

The seafood served along the white Hat Samila is excellent, though the beach itself is not that great for swimming, especially if you've just come from the Ko Samui archipelago. In fact, beaches are not Songkhla's main attraction, even if the TAT promotes them as such – although the evergreen trees along Hat Samila give it a rather nice visual effect. However, the town has plenty of other curiosities to offer.

In recent years Songkhla has become increasingly westernised due to the influx of multinational oil company employees – particularly British and Americans. Several farang bars have opened up around town to serve oil workers.

## Orientation

The town has a split personality, with the charming older town west of Ramwithi Rd towards the waterfront, and the new town east of Ramwithi Rd – a modern mix of business and suburbia.

## Information

**Foreign Consulates** The Malaysian consulate (☎ 311062/104) is next to Khao Noi at 4 Sukhum Rd, near Hat Samila. There is also a Chinese consulate (☎ 311494) on Sadao Rd, not far from the Royal Crown Hotel.

**Post & Communications** The post office is opposite the department store/market on Vichianchom Rd; international calls can be made upstairs daily from 8 am to 8 pm.

## Thaleh Sap Songkhla

ทะเลสาบสงขลา

Stretching north-west of the city is the huge brackish lake or 'inland sea' of Thaleh Sap Songkhla. Parts of the Thaleh Sap are heavily fished, the most sought-after catch being the famous black tiger prawn. Illegal gill-net trawling for the prawn is now threatening the overall fish population; legal fishermen have begun organising against gill-net use.

The city's waterfront on the inland sea buzzes with activity: ice is loaded onto fishing boats on their way out to sea, baskets and baskets of fish are unloaded onto the pier from boats just arrived, fish markets are set up and disassembled, long-tail boats doing taxi business between islands and mainland tool about. The fish smell along the piers is pretty powerful though, so be warned.

## National Museum

พิพิธภัณฑ์แห่งชาติ

This is in a 100 year old building of southern Sino-Portuguese architecture, between Rong Meuang and Jana Rds (off Vichianchom Rd). It's a quiet, breezy building with a tranquil garden in front. The museum contains exhibits from all national art-style periods, particularly the Srivijaya, including a 7th to 9th century Shivalingam found in Pattani. Also on display are Thai and Chinese ceramics and sumptuous Chinese furniture owned by the local Chinese aristocracy. The museum is open Wednesday to Sunday, 9 am to noon and 1 to 4 pm; admission is 10B.

## Temples & Chedis

On Saiburi Rd towards Hat Yai, **Wat Matchimawat** typifies the Sino-Thai temple architecture of 17th century Songkhla. One of the wihãan contains an old marble Buddha image and a small museum. Another temple with similar characteristics, **Wat Jaeng** on Ramwithi Rd, is currently under renovation.

There is a Sinhalese-style chedi and royal pavilion atop **Khao Tang Kuan**, a hill rising up at the northern end of the peninsula; to reach the top you'll have to climb 305 steps.

## Beaches

Besides the strip of white sand along **Hat Samila**, there's the less frequented **Hat Son Awn** on a slender cape jutting out between the Gulf of Thailand and Thaleh Sap, north of Samila.

## Other Attractions

Songkhla is Southern Thailand's educational centre: there is a university, several colleges, technical schools and research institutes, a nursing college and a military training camp, all situated in or near the town.

Suan Tun, a topiary park across from the Samila Hotel, has yew hedges trimmed into animal shapes.

If you are interested in seeing some traditional Songkhla architecture, walk along the back streets parallel to the inland sea waterfront – Nang Ngam, Nakhon Nai and Nakhon Nawk Rds all have some older Songkhla architecture showing Chinese, Portuguese and Malay influence, but it's disappearing fast.

A few km south of Hat Samila is **Kao Seng**, a quaint Muslim fishing village – this is where the tourist photos of gaily painted fishing vessels are taken. Songthaews run regularly between Songkhla and Kao Seng for 7B per person.

SOUTHERN THAILAND

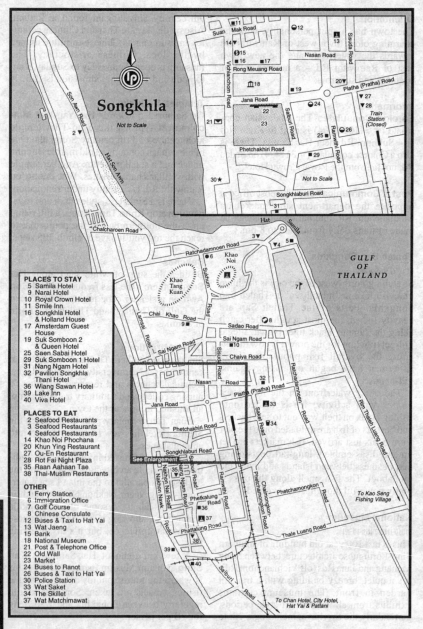

**Songkhla**

*Not to Scale*

**GULF OF THAILAND**

**PLACES TO STAY**
5  Samila Hotel
9  Narai Hotel
10 Royal Crown Hotel
11 Smile Inn
16 Songkhla Hotel & Holland House
17 Amsterdam Guest House
19 Suk Somboon 2 & Queen Hotel
25 Saen Sabai Hotel
29 Suk Somboon 1 Hotel
31 Nang Ngam Hotel
32 Pavilion Songkhla Thani Hotel
36 Wiang Sawan Hotel
39 Lake Inn
40 Viva Hotel

**PLACES TO EAT**
2  Seafood Restaurants
3  Seafood Restaurants
4  Seafood Restaurants
14 Khao Noi Phochana
20 Khun Ying Restaurant
27 Ou-En Restaurant
28 Rot Fai Night Plaza
35 Raan Aahaan Tae
38 Thai-Muslim Restaurants

**OTHER**
1  Ferry Station
6  Immigration Office
7  Golf Course
8  Chinese Consulate
12 Buses & Taxi to Hat Yai
13 Wat Jaeng
15 Bank
18 National Museum
21 Post & Telephone Office
22 Old Wall
23 Market
24 Buses to Ranot
26 Buses & Taxi to Hat Yai
30 Police Station
33 Wat Saket
34 The Skillet
37 Wat Matchimawat

Suan Mak Road
Nasan Road
Sisuda Road
Rong Meuang Road
Vichianchom Road
Jana Road
Saiburi Road
Platha (Pratha) Road
Ramwithi Road
Phetchakhiri Road
Songkhlaburi Road
Train Station (Closed)
Not to Scale

Chalcharoen Road
Son Awn Road
Hat Son Awn

Hat Samila

Ratchadamnoen Road
Khao Noi
Khao Tang Kuan
Sukhum Road
Lamsai Road
Chai Khao Road
Sadao Road
Sai Ngam Road
Chaiya Road
Nasan Road
Jana Road
Phetchakhiri Road
Songkhlaburi Road
See Enlargement
Platha (Pratha) Road
Saket Road
Ratchadamnoen Road
Rim Thanon Luang Road
Phetchamongkon
Chamongkon-Phetchamongkon Road
Thale Luang Road
Nakhon Nai Road
Nakhon Nawk Road
Nang Ngam Road
Saiburi Road
Phetkalung Road
Ramwithi Road
Phattalung Road

To Kao Seng Fishing Village
To Chan Hotel, City Hotel, Hat Yai & Pattani

## Hash House Harriers

With all the expats living in Songkhla, there would have to be an HHH chapter. Songkhla's HHH, founded in 1981, usually holds hashes on Saturday at 4.30 pm at different locations around the city. Information is available in the lobbies of the Pavilion and Royal Crown hotels.

## Thai Language Study

The new AUA branch (☎ 311258), a block east of the Pavilion Songkhla Thani Hotel on Platha Rd, offers small-group classes in Thai language.

## Places to Stay – bottom end

The popular and clean *Amsterdam Guest House* at 15/3 Rong Meuang Rd has nice rooms with shared bath for 150 and 180B. It is run by a friendly Dutch woman. On the same street, near the corner of Vichianchom Rd, *Holland House* has clean rooms with shared facilities for 200B and an apartment for 350B; Dutch breakfasts are available.

One of the best deals in Songkhla is the friendly *Narai Hotel* (☎ 311078) at 14 Chai Khao Rd, near the foot of Khao Tang Kuan. It's an older wooden hotel with clean, quiet singles/doubles with fan and shared bath (though each room comes with a washbasin) for 110B. A huge double room with bath is 200B.

Another place with character is the *Nang Ngam Hotel*, a small Chinese hotel on Nang Ngam Rd near Yaring Rd. Rather basic rooms are 80B, but for anyone who wants to be in the heart of the old Chinese district this is the place.

The refurbished *Songkhla Hotel*, on Vichianchom Rd across from the Fishing Station, has good 140B rooms with shared bath, 180B with private bath. Just up the street from the Songkhla Hotel, the former Choke Dee has been reincarnated as the *Smile Inn* (☎ 311258), a clean place with medium-size rooms with ceiling fan and private cold water shower for 280B, or identical rooms with air-con for 380B.

The *Suk Somboon 1* on Phetchakhiri Rd is not bad for 160/240B a single/double,

although they're just wooden rooms off a large central area, and you have to ask for that price – posted rates start at 180B. Rooms in the air-con wing next door are 380B.

The *Wiang Sawan* on Saiburi Rd, not far from Wat Matchimawat, has rooms from 200B, a bit overpriced for what you get.

## Places to Stay – middle

The *Saen Sabai* (☎ 311090) at 1 Phetchakhiri Rd is well located and has clean, if small, rooms in an early Bangkok-style building for 150B with fan and shared bath, 270B with private bath, or 300B with air-con. Nearby is the *Suk Somboon 2* on Saiburi Rd, with fan-cooled singles/doubles for 160/300B. Next door is a new all air-con wing with rooms for 350B with TV, bathtub and fridge.

The *Queen* (☎ 311138) at 20 Saiburi Rd, next door to the Suk Somboon 2, has decent air-con rooms from 280/350B. The similarly priced *Charn (Chan)* (☎ 311903) is on the same road but on the outskirts of the central area on the way to Hat Yai.

The newish *Viva Hotel* (☎ 321033/7; fax 312608), at 547/2 Nakhon Nawk Rd, has modern air-con rooms from 500B.

## Places to Stay – top end

Catering mostly to visiting oil company employees and their families, the five-storey *Royal Crown Hotel* (☎ 312174; fax 321027) on Sai Ngam Rd costs 1020 to 1288B for rooms with air-con, TV with in-house video, fridge and carpet; the tariff includes continental breakfast.

The newest and poshest place to stay is the nine-storey, 180-room *Pavilion Songkhla Thani Hotel* (☎ 311355; fax 323716) at 17 Platha Rd, east of Ramwithi Rd. Large, luxurious rooms with wood panelling, air-con, IDD phones, satellite TV, carpeting and so on cost a bargain 900B at the time of the hotel's opening in 1996 but will most likely rise to around 1800B in the future. The lobby is very swanky compared to the Royal Crown's.

The *Samila Hotel* on the beachfront will reportedly be demolished and rebuilt as a new super-luxury hotel to open in 1997. The popular *Lake Inn* (☎ 314240) is a rambling multistorey place with great views right on the Thaleh Sap. Rooms are 450B with air-con, carpet, hot water, TV, minibar, 525B with the same plus a bathtub, or 600B with a balcony and lake view.

The *Haad Kaew Princess Resort* (☎ 331-059) on the other side of the Thaleh Sap on the road to Ranot has its own beachfront and a swimming pool (available to non-guests for 30B a day). The landscaped grounds are a plus. Nice air-con rooms with all the amenities cost from 1117B.

### Places to Eat
There are lots of good restaurants in Songkhla but a few tend to overcharge foreign tourists. The best seafood place according to locals is the *Raan Aahaan Tae* on Nang Ngam Rd (off Songkhlaburi Rd and parallel to Saiburi Rd). Look for a brightly lit place just south of the cinema. The seafood on the beach is pretty good too – try the curried crab claws or spicy fried squid.

Competing with Tae for the best seafood title is *Buakaew* on Hat Samila – there are several other seafood places in this vicinity. Fancier seafood places are found along Son Awn Rd near the beach – *Seven Sisters, Mark, Suda, Ying Muk, Smile Beach, Son Awn* – but these also tend to have hordes of young Thai hostesses kept on to satisfy the Thai male penchant for chatting up *áw-áw* (young girls).

Along Nang Ngam Rd in the Chinese section are several cheap Chinese noodle and congee shops. At the end of Nang Ngam Rd along Phattalung Rd (near the mosque) are several modest Thai-Muslim restaurants, including *Sharif*, *Suda* and *Dawan*. *Khao Noi Phochana*, on Vichianchom Rd near the Songkhla Hotel, has a very good lunchtime selection of Thai and Chinese rice dishes.

*Auntie Bar & Restaurant* and *Ty Brezh French Restaurant* on Sisuda Rd cater to expat tastes. There are several fast-food spots at the intersection of Sisuda and Platha Rds, including *Jam's Quik* and *Fresh Baker*, both with burgers, ice cream and western breakfasts; there are also a few popular Thai

and Chinese restaurants. The kíaw náam (wonton soup) place next to Fresh Baker is cheap and quite good.

Farther south along Sisuda Rd near the Chalerm Thong cinema and the old train station is a hawkers' centre and night market called Rot Fai Night Plaza. In this section *Ou-en* is a very popular Chinese restaurant with outdoor tables; the house speciality is Peking duck. The very clean *Khun Ying*, next door to the Jazz Pub on Sisuda Rd near the Platha Rd intersection, has inexpensive curries and khanŏm jiin during the daytime only.

Of the several expat pubs around town, *The Skillet* on Saket Rd has the cleanest kitchen and best food, including sandwiches, pizza, chilli, breakfast and steaks.

### Entertainment
The *Easy Pub, Lipstick, Cheeky* and *The Skillet* on Saket Rd next to Wat Saket cater to oil company employees and other expats in town with imported liquors, air-con and cable TV offering a mix of music videos and sports. The *Offshore, Anytime* and *King on Sadao* are similar.

Thais tend to congregate at bars with live music in the vicinity of the Sisuda and Platha Rds intersection.

### Getting There & Away
**Air** THAI operates several daily flights to/from nearby Hat Yai; see the Hat Yai section for details. A taxi from Hat Yai airport to Songkhla costs 340B. In the reverse direction you should be able to find a car or songthaew to the airport for 150 to 200B.

**Bus, Minivan & Share Taxi** Air-con public buses leave Bangkok's Southern Bus Terminal daily at 5, 6.45 and 7.30 pm, arriving in Songkhla 13 hours later, for 425B. Ordinary buses are 236B from Bangkok, but there are only a couple of departures a day and the trip lasts at least 16 hours. The privately owned tour buses out of Bangkok (there are several available) are quicker but cost around 350B. VIP buses are available for 500 to 630B depending on the number of seats.

Air-con buses from Surat Thani to Songkhla and Hat Yai cost 120B one way. From Songkhla to Hat Yai, big green buses leave every 15 minutes (9B) from Saiburi Rd, around the corner from the Songkhla Hotel, or they can be flagged down anywhere along Vichianchom or Saiburi Rds towards Hat Yai.

Air-con minivans to Hat Yai are 15B: these arrive and depart from a parking area in front of Wat Jaeng. Share taxis are 15B to Hat Yai if there are five other passengers, 90B if chartered; after 8 pm the rates go up to 20B and 120B respectively. Share taxis cost 50B to Pattani and 50B to Yala.

See the Hat Yai Getting There & Away section for more options, as Hat Yai is the main transport hub for Songkhla Province.

**Train** The old railway spur to Songkhla no longer has a passenger service. See Hat Yai's Getting There & Away section for trains to/from nearby Hat Yai.

### Getting Around
For getting around in town, red mini-songthaews circulate Songkhla and take passengers, for 5B, to any point on their route. Motorcycle taxis anywhere in town cost 10B.

## KO YO
เกาะยอ
An island on the inland sea, Ko Yo (pronounced Kaw Yaw) is worth visiting just to see the cotton-weaving cottage industry there. The good-quality, distinctive *phâa kàw yaw* is hand-woven on rustic looms and available on the spot at 'wholesale' prices – meaning you still have to bargain but have a chance of undercutting the usual city price.

Many different households around this thickly forested, sultry island are engaged in cotton-weaving, and there is a central market off the highway so you don't have to go from place to place comparing prices and fabric quality. At the market, prices for cloth and ready-made clothes are excellent if you bargain, and especially if you speak Thai. If you're more interested in observing the weaving process, take a walk down the road behind the market where virtually every other house has a loom or two – listen for the clacking sound made by the hand-operated wooden looms. As the island gradually gets taken over by condo and vacation home developments, it's bound to have an impact on the weaving villages.

There are also a couple of semi-interesting wats, Khao Bo and Thai Yaw, to visit. Along the main road through Ko Yo are several large seafood restaurants overlooking Thaleh Sap. *Pornthip* (about half a km before the market) is reportedly the best.

### Folklore Museum
At the northern end of the island at Ban Ao Sai, about two km past the Ko Yo cloth market, is a large folklore museum run by the Institute of Southern Thai Studies, a division of Si Nakharinwirot University. Opened in 1991, the complex of Thai-style pavilions overlooking the Thaleh Sap Songkhla contains well curated collections (but unfortunately with no English labels) of folk art as well as a library and souvenir shop. Displays include pottery, beads, shadow puppets, basketry, textiles, musical instruments, boats, religious art, weapons and various household, agricultural and fishing implements. Among these is a superb collection of coconut-grater seats carved into various animal and human shapes.

On the institute grounds are a series of small gardens, including one occasionally used for traditional shadow theatre performances, a medicinal herb garden and a bamboo culture garden.

Admission to the museum is 50B for farangs, 30B for Thais.

### Getting There & Away
From Hat Yai, direct Ko Yo buses – actually large wooden songthaews – leave from near the clock tower on Phetkasem Rd frequently throughout the day. The fare to Ko Yo is 8B; although the bus terminates on Ko Yai further on, it will stop in front of the cloth market on Ko Yo (ask for *nâa talàat*, 'in front

of the market'). To get off at the museum, about two km past the market, ask for *phíphítaphan*. From Songkhla, buses to Ranot pass through Ko Yo for the same fare.

Nakhon Si Thammarat or Ranot-bound buses from Hat Yai also pass through Ko Yo via the new bridge system (part of Route 4146) and will stop at the market or museum. Another way to get there is to take a Hat Yai-Songkhla bus to the junction for Ko Yo (5B), then catch the Songkhla-Ranot bus for 3B to the market or museum.

## KHUKHUT WATERBIRD SANCTUARY
อุทยานนกน้ำคูขุด

On the eastern shore of the Songkhla inland sea, about 30 km north of Songkhla near Sathing Phra, is a 520 sq km sanctuary for waterbirds. Together with the similar Thaleh Noi Wildlife Preserve in Phattalung, the wetlands are habitat for over 200 resident and migrant bird species from the entire Thaleh Sap, including bitterns, egrets and herons (these three are called *nók yang* in Thai), rare Javanese pond herons, fishing eagles (*nók yiaw*), cormorants (*nók kaa*), storks, kites, hawks, falcons, plovers, sandpipers, terns (*nók nang*) and kingfishers.

A book available at the park office has very detailed information on the waterbirds and maps showing habitat. The best birdwatching months are November and December, the worst are May to August.

You can arrange boat trips through the park service – it's 150B for a one hour birdwatching excursion, or 400B for a three hour trip to see birds and stop at two islands.

### Places to Stay & Eat
At the time of writing there were no guest-houses or hotels in Sathing Phra (the former *Khukhon Guest House* is now a restaurant only), but it's easy to find rooms in the village for 100B a night.

About five km from the turn-off to the park towards Songkhla (opposite the Km 129 marker), the friendly *Sathing Phra Resort* rents bungalows near the Gulf side of the peninsula for 150 to 300B; you can also

pitch a tent here for 50B. A motorcycle taxi from Sathing Phra to the resort costs 10B.

A rustic eating area over the lake near the park office serves good Thai food. The Sathing Phra Resort offers reasonably priced seafood.

### Getting There & Away
Buses to Sathing Phra are 13B from Songkhla – take a red Ranot-bound bus. From the bus stop in front of the Sathing Phra district office you can walk the three km to the park or get a motorcycle taxi for 7 to 10B.

You can also get boats to Khukhut from Phattalung. A long-tail boat (40B) usually leaves Lam Pam daily around 12.30 pm and takes about two hours.

## HAT YAI
หาดใหญ่
• ☎ *(74)* • *pop 139,400*

Hat Yai, 933 km from Bangkok, is Southern Thailand's commercial centre and one of the kingdom's largest cities, though it is only a district of Songkhla Province. A steady stream of customers from Malaysia keeps Hat Yai's central business district booming. Everything from dried fruit to stereos is sold in the shops along Niphat Uthit Rds Nos 1, 2 and 3, not far from the train station. Many travellers stay in Hat Yai on their way to and from Malaysia.

Culturally, Hat Yai is very much a Chinese town at its centre, with loads of gold shops and Chinese restaurants. A substantial Muslim minority is concentrated in certain sections of the city, for example near the mosque off Niphat Songkhrao Rd.

### Information
**Tourist Office** The TAT office (☎ 243747) is at 1/1 Soi 2 Niphat Uthit 3 Rd and is open daily from 8.30 am to 4.30 pm. The tourist police (☎ 1699 or 246733) can be found opposite the Florida Hotel.

**Immigration** The Hat Yai immigration office (☎ 243019, 233760) is on Phetkasem Rd near the railway bridge, in the same complex as a police station. The nearest Malaysian consulate is in Songkhla.

**Money** Hat Yai is loaded with banks. Several after-hours exchange windows are along Niphat Uthit 2 and 3 Rds near the Thamnoonvithi Rd (pronounced Thammanun Withi) intersection.

**Post & Communications** Hat Yai's GPO is on Niphat Songkhrao 1 Rd just south of the stadium and is open from 8.30 am to 4.30 pm weekdays, 9 am to noon weekends. The adjacent telephone office is open from 7 am to 11 pm daily. There is also a more convenient branch post office on Rattakan Rd, just north of the train station. A private packing service is available next door to the Rattakan post office.

**Film & Photography** The Chia Colour Lab at 58-60 Suphasan Rangsan Rd, next to the Singapore Hotel, offers a good selection of films and quality processing. There are many other photo shops in the city's centre.

### Wat Hat Yai Nai
วัดหาดใหญ่ใน
A few km west of town, off Phetkasem Rd towards the airport, is Wat Hat Yai Nai. A very large (35m) reclining Buddha is on the premises (Phra Phut Mahatamongkon). Inside the image's gigantic base is a curious little museum/souvenir shop/mausoleum. To get there, hop on a songthaew near the intersection of Niphat Uthit 1 and Phetkasem Rds and get off after crossing the U Taphao Bridge.

### Bullfighting
Bullfighting, involving two bulls in opposition rather than a person and a bull, takes place as a spectator sport twice monthly in Hat Yai. Fights take place on the first Saturday of each month, or on the second Saturday if the first Saturday is a *wan phrá* or Buddhist worship day (full or new moon). The venue changes from time to time, but lately they've been held at an arena at the Khlong Wat

intersection about five km out of town (50B by tuk-tuk). Matches take place continuously from 10 am until 3 pm and admission is 600 to 700B all day or 100 to 200B per round – although many hundred times that amount changes hands during the non-stop betting by Thai spectators.

Because the times and venues for these bullfights tend to change every other year or so, check with the TAT office for the latest.

### Places to Stay – bottom end
Hat Yai has dozens of hotels within walking distance of the train station. During Chinese New Year, prices double for most lower-end rooms.

Cheaper places near the station include the *Cathay Guest House* (☎ 243815), on the corner of Thamnoonvithi and Niphat Uthit 2 Rds three blocks from the station, with rooms ranging from 120 to 180B; there is also a 60B dorm. The Cathay has become a travellers' centre in Hat Yai because of its good location, helpful staff and plentiful travel info for trips onward, including tips on travel in Malaysia. It has a laundry service and serves inexpensive breakfasts as well as other meals (and also the staff don't mind if you bring in takeaways and eat in the lounge). There is a reliable bus ticket agency downstairs with irregular hours.

Cheaper still are some of the older Chinese hotels in the central area. Rooms are very basic but they're usually secure and service is quite OK – you can get towels and soap on request. The *Tong Nam Hotel* at 118-120 Niphat Uthit 3 Rd is a basic Chinese hotel that has recently upgraded its rooms a bit; rooms now start at 150B with fan, up to 300B with air-con and private bath. *Kim Hua*, opposite and farther south on the same road, is 200 to 270B for fan and attached bath.

On Niphat Uthit 1 Rd is the *Mandarin Hotel*, with standard rooms for 170B a double with fan and bath, 270B with air-con, 250B triple. The *Grand Hotel*, at 257-9 Thamnoonvithi Rd, is better, with fairly clean if overpriced rooms with fan and bath for 300B. At 138/2-3 Thamnoonvithi Rd the *Prince Hotel* (☎ 243160) offers small, musty

SOUTHERN THAILAND

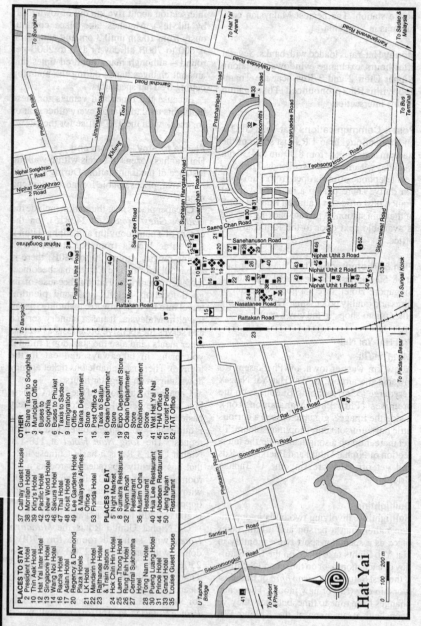

SOUTHERN THAILAND

**PLACES TO STAY**
2  President Hotel
37  Cathay Guest House
38  Mortlen Hotel
39  King's Hotel
10  Thin Aek Hotel
12  Hat Yai Inter Hotel
42  Pacific Hotel
13  Singapore Hotel
43  New World Hotel
14  Wang Noi Hotel
46  Sakura Hotel
16  Racha Hotel
47  Thai Hotel
17  Asian Hotel
48  Kosit Hotel
20  Regency & Diamond
49  Lee Gardens Hotel
Plaza Hotels
& Malaysia Airlines
21  LK Hotel
Office
22  Mandarin Hotel
53  Florida Hotel
23  Rajthanee Hotel
& Train Station

**PLACES TO EAT**
24  Hok Chin Hin Hotel
5  Night Market
25  Laem Thong Hotel
8  Sumatra Restaurant
26  Rung Fah Hotel
32  Niyom Rosh
27  Central Sukhontha
Restaurant
Hotel
36  Muslim Ocha
28  Tong Nam Hotel
Restaurant
30  Pueng Luang Hotel
40  Hua Lee Restaurant
31  Prince Hotel
44  Abedeen Restaurant
33  Grand Hotel
50  Jeng Nguan
35  Louise Guest House
Restaurant

**OTHER**
1  Share Taxis to Songkhla
3  Municipal Office
4  Buses to
Songkhla
6  Buses to Phuket
7  Taxis to Sadao
9  Immigration
Office
11  Diana Department
Store
15  Post Office &
Taxis to Satun
18  Soean Department
19  Expo Department Store
29  Odean Department
Store
34  Robinson Department
Store
41  Wat Hat Yai Nai
45  THAI Office
51  Tourist Police
52  TAT Office

rooms for 140 to 280B; a large room with two beds is 240B.

The *Weng Aun* is an old Chinese hotel across from King's Hotel on Niphat Uthit 1 Rd, four doors down from the Muslim Ocha restaurant. Very basic singles start at 110B. The friendly *Thin Aek Hotel* at 16 Duangchan Rd (behind Diana Department Store on Niphat Uthit 3 Rd) is another old Chinese relic; it's mostly a holding place for Bangladeshis trying to immigrate to Malaysia, but the owner caters to farang travellers as well. Rooms are 80B with shared bath, 100B with shower, 120B with shower and two large beds (four can sleep for 150B). The toilet is outside for all rooms.

Another good deal is the *Hok Chin Hin Hotel* (☎ 243258) on Niphat Uthit 1 Rd, a couple of blocks from the train station. Very clean rooms with bath and fan cost 150B single, 240B double; there's a good coffee shop downstairs. Hat Yai used to have more hotels like this, but they're closing down one by one.

There's a rash of places in town calling themselves 'guesthouses' that are really small budget hotels. *Louise Guest House* (☎ 220966) at 21-23 Thamnoonvithi Rd is an apartment-style place with rooms for 200B with air-con, or 290B with air-con and hot water – not a bad bargain compared to some of the previously described places. *Lada Guest House* (☎ 220233), next to the Robinson Dept Store complex near the train station, is similar with rooms with fan from 160B and air-con from 250B. Near the Songkhla bus stand off Phetkasem Rd is *Sorasilp Guest House* (☎ 232635), where clean rooms with fan and bath are 150 to 300B.

## Places to Stay – middle

For some reason hotels in Hat Yai take a disproportionate leap upward in quality once you go from 100 to 150B a night to 200B and above.

Very popular with Malaysian visitors as well as travellers is the *King's Hotel* (☎ 234140) on Niphat Uthit 1 Rd. Rooms start at 350B with fan and bath, 410B with air-con and hot water. Not far from the train

station on Thamnoonvithi Rd is the *Laem Thong Hotel* (☎ 352301), with fairly comfortable singles/doubles for 260B with fan and bath, or 350 to 600B with air-con. The *OH Hotel (Oriental)* (☎ 230142), at 137-9 Niphat Uthit 3 Rd, has very good fan-cooled singles/doubles in the old wing for 250B. In the new wing rooms with air-con, TV, phone and hot water cost 400/450B single/double. Beside the OH, the *Tawan Ok Hotel* (☎ 243-071) is a clean, friendly place with fan rooms for 200B, air-con for 300B.

*Rung Fah* (☎ 244808), at 117/5-6 Niphat Uthit 3 Rd, is a slightly upgraded old Chinese place. Clean rooms cost 170 to 200B with fan and bath or 300B with air-con – a bargain. The *Thai Hotel* (☎ 244437) on Rat Uthit Rd south-west of the train station has fan-cooled rooms from 130B and air-con rooms up to 300B. There are also cheaper rooms on the top floor for 100B.

The friendly *Pueng Luang (Pheung Luang) Hotel* (☎ 244548), at 241-5 Saeng Chan Rd, has huge fan rooms with bath for 250B plus a few smaller ones for 200B. Air-con rooms go for just 350B. The *Wang Noi* (☎ 231024), 114/1 Saeng Chan Rd, has clean rooms for 200 to 220B with fan or 300 to 370B with air-con; it seems to be a relatively quiet location. Also good is the *Pacific Hotel* (☎ 244062), at 149/1 Niphat Uthit 2 Rd, with clean air-con rooms for 400B.

The clean and friendly *Singapore Hotel* (☎ 237478), at 62-66 Suphasan Rangsan Rd, has clean rooms with fan and bath for 200B, air-con 350B, and air-con rooms with two beds, TV and hot water for 400B.

The *Tawan Ork Hotel* (☎ 243071) at 131/1-3 Niphat Uthit Rd offers 32 clean rooms for a straightforward 300B with fan, 400B with air-con. The *Montien Hotel* (☎ 234386; fax 230043) on Niphat Uthit 1 Rd is a large 180-room place that once occupied the city's top end; decent air-con doubles cost 330B, 370B with TV.

## Places to Stay – top end

The top end in Hat Yai is mainly geared towards Malaysian weekenders, which keeps rates considerably lower than in Bangkok or

Chiang Mai. The *Rajthanee* (☎ 232288; fax 232188), at the Hat Yai train station, couldn't be more convenient if you have an early morning train to catch or just like to be near the rails; good standard rooms with air-con, hot water, TV and phone cost 540B.

The nicest hotel in town is the 238-room *Central Sukhontha Hotel* (☎ 352222; fax 352223) at 3 Sanehanuson Rd, where spacious rooms with all the amenities – including IDD phone – cost 1800 to 2800B; facilities include a swimming pool, 24 hour cafe, fitness centre, business centre and shopping mall (with a branch of Central Department Store).

All of the following are fully air-con:

*Asian Hotel* – 55 Niphat Uthit 3 Rd (☎ 353400; fax 234890); 104 rooms, from 800B

*Diamond Plaza* – 62 Niphat Uthit 3 Rd (☎ 353147; fax 239824); 280 rooms, from 920B

*JB Hotel* – 99 Chuti Anuson Rd (☎ 234300/8; fax 243499); 209 rooms, from 1400B

*Emperor* – 1 Ranrattankhon Rd (☎ 235457; fax 234165); 108 rooms, 420 to 756B

*The Florida* – 8 Siphunawat Rd (☎ 234555/9; fax 234553); 119 rooms, from 715B

*Grand Plaza Hotel* – 24/1 Sanehanuson Rd (☎ 234340; fax 230050); 145 rooms, from 689B

*Hat Yai Central Hotel* – 180 Niphat Uthit 3 Rd (☎ 230000/11; fax 230990); 250 rooms, 707B

*Hat Yai Inter Hotel* – 42-44 Niphat Uthit 3 Rd (☎ 231022; fax 232539); 210 rooms, doubles from 420B

*Lee Gardens Hotel* – 1 Lee Pattana Rd (☎ 234422; fax 231888); doubles from 690B

*LK Hotel* – 150 Saeng Chan Rd (☎ 235681; fax 238112); 196 rooms, doubles 850B including breakfast

*New World* – 144-158 Niphat Uthit 2 Rd (☎ 23100; fax 231105); 133 rooms, from 535B

*President* – 420 Phetkasem Rd (☎ 244477; fax 235355); 110 rooms, doubles from 620B

*Racha Hotel* – 40-42 Niphat Uthit 1 Rd (☎ 230951/5; fax 234668); 65 rooms, from 453B

*The Regency* – 23 Prachathipat Rd (☎ 353333; 234102); 189 rooms, doubles from 798B

*The Royal Hotel* – 106 Prachathipat Rd (☎ 232162); 139 rooms, 470 to 1000B

*Sakura Hotel* – 185/1 Niphat Uthit 3 Rd (☎ 246688; fax 235936); 453B

*Scala Hotel* – 43/42-43 Tanrattanakhon Rd (☎ 246983); 84 rooms, 400 to 710B

*Siam City Hotel* – 25-35 Niphat Uthit 2 Rd (☎ 353111; fax 231060)

**Places to Eat**

Hat Yai is Southern Thailand's gourmet mecca, offering fresh seafood from both the Gulf of Thailand and the Andaman Sea, bird's nests, shark fins, Muslim roti and curries, Chinese noodles and dim sum. Lots of good, cheap restaurants can be found along the three Niphat Uthit Rds, in the markets off side streets between them, and also near the train station.

**Chinese** Start the day with inexpensive dim sum at *Shangrila* on Thamnoonvithi Rd near the Cathay Guest House. Specialities include khanŏm jìip (dumplings), salabao (Chinese buns) and khâo nâa pèt (roast duck on rice). In the evenings the Chinese-food action moves to *Hua Lee* on the corner of Niphat Uthit 3 and Thamnoonvithi Rds; it's open till the wee hours.

*Jeng Nguan* is an old feasting stand-by near the end of Niphat Uthit 1 Rd (turn right from the station; it's on a corner on the left-hand side). Try the tâo hûu thâwt kràwp (fried bean curd), hûu chalãam (shark-fin soup), bàmìi plaa phàt (fried noodles with fish), or kíaw plaa (fish wonton). It's open from 9 am until late at night.

Several hotels in town also have good splurge-style Chinese restaurants, including *China Town* (Scala Hotel), *Hong Kong* (Lee Gardens Hotel) and *Dynasty* (Dusit JB Hotel).

**Malay & Indian** The *Muslim-O-Cha* (Muslim Ocha), across from the King's Hotel, is still going strong, with roti kaeng (roti chanai in Malay) in the mornings and curries all day. This is one of the few Muslim cafes in town where women – even non-Muslim – seem welcome. There are a couple of other Muslim restaurants near this one. *Makanan Muslim* at the corner of Saeng Chang and Prachathipat Rds is a clean open-air place with roti and mátàbà.

On Niyomrat Rd between Niphat Uthit 1 and 2 are *Abedeen*, *Sulaiman* and *Mustafa*, all specialising in Muslim food. Sulaiman has the best selection of dishes, including Indian paratha, dal, chapati, biryani, and various mutton, chicken, fish and veggie dishes. Abedeen is good for tôm yam kûng (spicy shrimp lemon-grass soup).

*Sumatra Restaurant*, next to the Pakistan Mosque near the Holiday Plaza Hotel, does Malay dishes like rojak (peanut-sauce salad) and nasi biryani (spiced rice plate).

**Thai** Although Chinese and Malay food rules in Hat Yai, there are a few Thai places as well. An old, established Thai restaurant is *Niyom Rot* (the English sign says 'Niyom Rosh') at 219-21 Thamnoonvithi Rd. The plaa krabàwk thâwt, whole sea mullet fried with eggs intact, is particularly prized here.

Although the name is Lao, the *Viang Chan* (no English sign) at 12 Niphat Uthit 2 Rd serves Thai and North-Eastern Thai dishes along with Chinese. The food centre below the Tong Nam Hotel has both Thai and Chinese dishes.

*A & A Food Centre* on Niphat Uthit 2 Rd serves inexpensive Thai and Chinese food on a coupon system.

**Night Markets** The extensive night market along Montri 1 Rd specialises in fresh seafood; you can dine on three seafood dishes and one vegetable dish for less than 200B here if you speak Thai. There are smaller night markets along Suphasan Rangsan Rd and Siphuwanat Rd.

**Other** *Royal Bakery*, at 41 Thamnoonvithi Rd (between Niphat Uthit 1 & 2 Rds), has assorted Chinese and western pastries, while the *Boat Bakery* opposite Lee Gardens Hotel and the *Cake House* next door are similar. Another good one is *Little Home Bakery* at 8 Niphat Uthit 2 Rd. Adjacent to Robinson Dept Store on Thamnoonvithi Rd are *KFC*, *Mister Donut* and *Burger King*.

For something very different, cruise down Thanon Nguu (Snake Street – Soi 2, Channiwet Rd), Hat Yai's most popular spot for snake fetishists. After a live snake is slit lengthwise with a scalpel, the blood is drained and drunk with honey, Chinese rice wine or herbal liquor. Besides the blood, the heart, gall bladder and penis are also highly regarded. Skins are sold to manufacturers of wallets, belts and other accessories, while the meat is given away to customers for soup. Rates range from 100B for the evisceration of a small-to-medium cobra to 2000B for a king cobra three or four metres in length.

### Entertainment

Most of the many clubs and coffee shops in town cater to Malaysian clientele. The bigger hotels have discos: among the most popular are the *Disco Palace* (Emperor Hotel), the *Metro* (JB Hotel), the *Diana Club* (Lee Gardens Hotel) and the *Inter* (Hat Yai Inter Hotel). Cover charges are only 100 to 150B.

The *Post Laserdisc* on Thamnoonvithi Rd, a block east of the Cathay Guest House, is a music video/laserdisc restaurant/bar with an excellent sound system and well placed monitors. It has mostly western movies, and programmes change nightly – the fairly up-to-date music videos are a filler between the films. The daily schedule starts at 10 am and goes until 1 am – mostly Thais and farangs come here. There's no admission charge and drink prices are only a little higher than at the average bar. Meals are served as well, including breakfast.

Opposite the Post Laserdisc, *Sugar Rock* is one of the more durable Hat Yai pubs, with good food, good prices and a low-key atmosphere.

### Things to Buy

Shopping is Hat Yai's No 1 draw, with most of the market action taking place along Niphat Uthit 2 and 3 Rds. Here you'll find Thai and Malaysian batik, cheap electronics and inexpensive clothing.

SMS Muslim Panich, 17 Niphat Uthit 1, has an excellent selection of south Indian sarongs, plus Thai, Malay and Indonesian batiks; although the markets are cheaper they can't compare with SMS in terms of quality and selection.

DK Book House, about 50m from the train station on Thamnoonvithi Rd, carries English-language books and maps.

Hat Yai has three major department stores on Niphat Uthit 3 Rd (Diana, Ocean and

Expo) and two on Thamnoonvithi Rd (World and Robinson), plus the newer Central Dept Store next to the Central Sukhontha Hotel.

### Getting There & Away – Within Thailand

**Air** THAI operates flights between Hat Yai and Bangkok every day. Flights take one hour and 20 minutes; the fare is 2280B one way. There are also THAI flights to Hat Yai from Phuket daily for 780B. THAI's office is at 166/4 Niphat Uthit 2 Rd.

Orient Express Air (☎ 335771) flies to Hat Yai from Chiang Mai, with a stopover in Surat Thani, five times a week for 2900B one way. Surat to Hat Yai costs 1150B one way. The OEA office is in the New World Hotel.

**Bus** To Songkhla the green buses leave from outside the small clock tower on Phetkasem Rd. Share taxis leave from around the corner near the President Hotel.

Air-con buses from Bangkok are 428B (VIP 500 to 625B) and leave the Southern Bus Terminal at 7 am and 4, 5.30, 6, 6.15, 6.30, 7, 8 and 8.20 pm. The trip takes 14 hours. Private companies sometimes have fares as low as 300B. Ordinary government buses cost 227B and leave Bangkok at 9.45 and 10.50 pm.

There are lots of buses running between Phuket and Hat Yai; ordinary buses are 122B (eight hours) and air-con 197B (six hours). Air-con minivans to Nakhon Si Thammarat are available for 100B from the Rado Hotel on Sanehanuson Rd. Three daily buses go to Pak Bara (for Ko Tarutao) for 35B (three hours).

Magic Tour (☎ 234535), a travel agency downstairs from the Cathay Guest House, does express air-con buses and minivans to Phuket (200B), Krabi (130B), Ko Samui (250B) and Surat Thani (130B). Other buses from Hat Yai include:

| Destination | Fare | Hours |
|---|---|---|
| Bangkok | 238B | 16 |
| (air-con) | 425B | 14 |
| (VIP) | 625B | 14 |
| Ko Samui | 200B | 7 |
| Krabi | – | – |
| (air-con only) | 125B | 4 |

| | | |
|---|---|---|
| Narathiwat | 50B | 3 |
| (air-con) | 65B | 3 |
| Padang esar | 18B | 1½ |
| Pattani | 35B | 2 |
| (air-con) | 43B | 1½ |
| Phattalung | 27B | 2 |
| Satun | 27B | 2 |
| (air-con) | 40B | 1 |
| Sungai Kolok | – | |
| (air-con only) | 96B | 4 |
| Surat Thani | 86B | 6½ |
| (air-con) | 120B | 5½ |
| Trang | 40B | 2 |
| Yala | 35B | 2½ |

Agencies which arrange private buses include:

Golden Way Travel – 132 Niphat Uthit 3 Rd (☎ 233917; fax 235083)
Hat Yai Swanthai Tours – 108 Thamnoonvithi Rd (☎ 246706)
Magic Tour – ground floor, Cathay Guest House (☎ 234535)
Pan Siam – 99 Niphat Uthit 2 Rd (☎ 237440)
Sunny Tour – Niphat Uthit 2 Rd (☎ 244156)
Universal On-Time Co – 147 Niphat Uthit 1 Rd (☎ 231609)

**Share Taxi** Share taxis are a good way of getting from one province to another quickly in the South. There are seven share-taxi stands in Hat Yai, each specialising in certain destinations (see the following page).

In general, share-taxi fares cost about the same as an air-con bus, but the taxis are about 30% faster. Share taxis also offer door-to-door drop-offs at the destination. The downside is that the drivers wait around for enough passengers (usually five minimum) for a departure. If you hit it right the taxi may leave immediately; otherwise you may have to wait for half an hour or more. The drivers also drive at hair-raising speeds – not a pleasant experience for highly-strung passengers.

According to the TAT, the city may soon be establishing a single share-taxi stand on Siphuwanat Rd. Whether or not it will work (each of the current share-taxi stands takes advantage of the quickest route out of the city towards its respective destination) remains to be seen; they've been promising this for at least two years.

## Share Taxi Fares

| Destination | Fare | Hours | Taxi Stand |
|---|---|---|---|
| Songkhla | 15B | ½ | near the President Hotel, off Phetkasem Rd |
| Phattalung | 50B | 1¼ | Suphasan Rangsan Rd, near Wat Cheu Chang |
| Trang | 60B | 2½ | Suphasan Rangsan Rd, near Wat Cheu Chang |
| Sungai Kolok | 120B | 3½ | Suphasan Rangsan Rd, near Wat Cheu Chang |
| Betong | 100B | 3½ | Suphasan Rangsan Rd, near Wat Cheu Chang |
| Nakhon Si Thammarat | 70B | 2½ | Suphasan Rangsan Rd, near Wat Cheu Chang |
| Phuket | 220B | 6 | Duangchan Rd |
| Surat Thani | 150B | 5 | Duangchan Rd |
| Krabi | 150B | 5 | Duangchan Rd |
| Narathiwat | 80B | 3 | Niphat Uthit 1 Rd |
| Sadao | 25B | 1 | Siam Nakarin Department Store, Phetkasem Rd |
| Khukhut | 25B | 1 | Siam Nakarin Department Store, Phetkasem Rd |
| Ranot | 30B | 2 | Siam Nakarin Department Store, Phetkasem Rd |
| Yala | 60B | 2 | Niphat Uthit 2 Rd, near Cathay Guest House |
| Satun | 35B | 1½ | Rattakan Rd, near the post office |
| La-Ngu | 50B | 1½ | Rattakan Rd, near the post office |

**Train** Trains from Bangkok to Hat Yai leave Hualamphong station daily at 2.35 pm (special express No 19), 3.15 pm (special express No 11) and 4.02 pm (rapid No 43), arriving in Hat Yai at 6.34 am, 6.53 am and 8.29 am. The basic fare is 664B 1st class (express only), 313B 2nd class. In the reverse direction to Bangkok you can take the 3.32 pm (rapid No 46), 4.50 pm (rapid No 44), 5.52 pm (special express No 12) and 6.24 pm (special express No 20), arriving in Bangkok at 8.35 am, 9.30 am, 10 am and 10.35 am. Third class trains to Hat Yai start only as far north as Chumphon (99B) and Surat Thani (55B).

The advance booking office at Hat Yai station is open from 7 am to 5 pm daily. The station's Rajthanee Restaurant in the Rajthanee Hotel is good and not that expensive; there's a cheaper eating area on the platform. A left-luggage office (the sign reads 'Cloak Room') is open daily from 5.30 to 11 am and 1 to 7 pm. The cost is 5B per piece for the first five days, 10B thereafter.

### Getting There & Away – International

Hat Yai is a very important travel junction – almost any Thailand-Malaysia overland trip involves a stop here.

**Air** Both THAI and Malaysia Airlines fly from Penang; there are also Silk Air flights from Singapore.

THAI (☎ 243711) has offices in the centre of town at 166/4 Niphat Uthit 2 Rd (☎ 245851) and 190/6 Niphat Uthit 2 Rd (☎ 231272). Malaysia Airlines (☎ 245443) has its office in the Lee Gardens Hotel, with a separate entrance on Niphat Uthit 1 Rd.

Hat Yai international airport has a post office with an IDD telephone in the arrival area; it's open from 8.30 am to 4.30 pm weekdays, 9 am to noon Saturday, closed Sunday. Other airport facilities include the Sky Lounge Cafe & Restaurant on the ground floor near the domestic check-in, a less expensive coffee shop on the 2nd floor departure level and foreign-exchange kiosks.

**Bus** From Padang Besar at the Malaysian border, buses are 18B and take an hour and a half to reach Hat Yai. Bus services operate every 10 minutes between 6 am and 7.20 pm.

Magic Tour (☎ 234535), a travel agency downstairs from the Cathay Guest House, does express air-con buses and minivans to Penang (200B and five hours by bus), Kuala Lumpur, Singapore, and destinations within Thailand. Golden Way Travel (☎ 233917; fax 235083), 132 Niphat Uthit 3 Rd, runs VIP buses (30 reclining seats) to Singapore for 400B including all meals; super VIP (24 seats) costs 550B. See the list on the following page for other buses out of Hat Yai.

| Destination | Fare | Hours |
|---|---|---|
| Butterworth | | |
| (for Penang) | 200B | 6 |
| Kuala Lumpur* | 250 to 350B | 12 |
| Singapore* | 300 to 550B | 15 |

*\* Denotes private tour-bus companies; see the list on page 776 for contact details*

**Warning** Care should be taken in selecting travel agencies for bus trips into Malaysia. There are still reports of bus companies demanding 'visa fees' before crossing the border – since visas aren't required for most nationalities, this is a blatant rip-off. The offending company collects your passport on the bus and then asks for the fee – holding your passport hostage. Refuse all requests for visa or border-crossing fees – all services are supposed to be included in the ticket price. Chaw Weng Tours is allegedly one agency to be careful of.

**Share Taxis** Share taxis are a popular way of travelling between Hat Yai and Penang in Malaysia. They're faster than the tour buses, although less comfortable and more expensive. Big old Thai-registered Chevys or Mercedes depart from Hat Yai around 9 am every morning. You'll find them at the train station or along Niphat Uthit 2 near the King's Hotel. In Penang you can find them around the cheap travellers' hotels in Georgetown. The cost is about 200B/M$20 – this is probably the fastest way of travelling between the two countries, and you cross the border with a minimum of fuss.

From Hat Yai the fare to Padang Besar is 25B for the one hour trip; taxis are on Duangchan Rd. For Penang the stand is on Niphat Uthit 1 Rd and the three hour trip costs 200B.

**Getting Around**
**The Airport** The THAI van costs 40B per person for transport to the city; there's also a private 150B THAI limo service. A regular taxi costs 150B from the airport to the city, about half that in the reverse direction.

**Car** Hertz (☎ 751007) has an office at Hat Yai international airport. You may also be able to arrange car rental through travel agencies in town.

**Local Transport** The innumerable songthaews around Hat Yai cost 5B per person. Watch out when you cross the street or they'll mow you down.

## AROUND HAT YAI
### Ton Nga Chang Falls
น้ำตกโตนงาช้าง
Elephant Tusk Falls, 24 km west of Hat Yai via Highway 4 in Rattaphum district, is a 1200m seven-tier cascade that falls in two streams (thus resembling two tusks). If you're staying over in Hat Yai, the falls make a nice break from the hustle and bustle of the city. The waterfall looks its best at the end of the rainy season, October to December.

To get to the falls take a Rattaphum-bound songthaew (10B) and ask to get off at the *náam tòk* (waterfall).

# Krabi Province

Krabi Province has scenic karst formations (similar to those in Phang-Nga Province) near the coast and even in the middle of the Krabi River. Over 150 islands offer excellent recreational opportunities; many of the islands belong to the **Hat Noppharat Thara - Ko Phi Phi National Marine Park**. Hundreds of years ago, Krabi's waters were a favourite hide-out for Asian pirates because of all the islands and water caves. Latter-day pirates now steal islands or parts of islands for development – land encroachment is reportedly taking place on Phi Phi Don, Poda, Bubu, Jam (Pu), Po, Bilek (Hong), Kamyai and Kluang.

The interior of the province, noted for its tropical forests and the Phanom Bencha mountain range, has barely been explored. Birdwatchers come from far and wide to view Gurney's pitta (formerly thought to be extinct) and Nordmann's greenshank.

SOUTHERN THAILAND

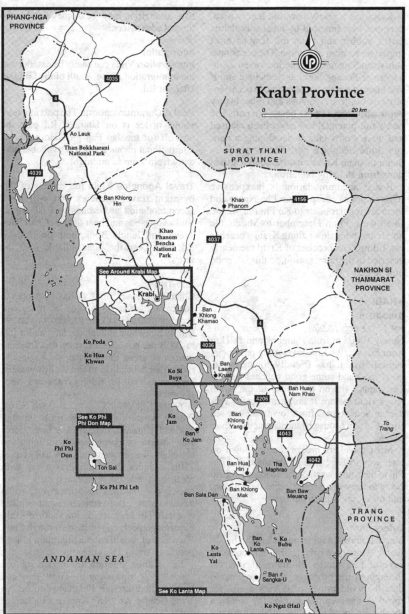

Krabi has a nearly new, but hardly used, deep-sea port financed by local speculators in tin, rubber and palm oil, Krabi's most important sources of income. The occasional ship from Singapore (sometimes even a Singapore or Penang junk) anchors here and if you know the right people you can occasionally buy tax-free cigarettes and other luxury items while one of these boats is in port. The port's full potential has never been realised and there's now talk of developing a new, substitute deep-sea port farther south in Satun to spare Krabi's natural tourist attractions from shipping pollution.

Beach accommodation is inexpensive (though not as cheap as Ko Pha-Ngan) and there are regular boats to Ko Phi Phi, 42 km south-west. From December to March, the hotels and bungalows along Krabi's beaches can fill up. The beaches of Krabi are nearly deserted in the rainy season, so this is a good time to go.

## KRABI
อ.เมืองกระบี่
• ☎ (75) • *pop 18,000*

Nearly 1000 km from Bangkok and 180 km from Phuket, the fast-developing provincial capital, Krabi, has friendly townspeople, good food and some good beaches nearby. The capital sits on the banks of the Krabi River right before it empties into the Andaman Sea. Across from town you can see Bird, Cat and Mouse Islands, named for their shapes.

Most travellers breeze through town on their way to Ko Lanta to the south, Ko Phi Phi to the south-west, or the beaches near Ao Nang to the west. Some elect to stay in town and make day trips to the latter.

## Orientation
**Maps** Bangkok Guide publishes the handy *Guide Map of Krabi* (50B) that contains several mini-maps of areas of interest throughout the province. If it's kept up to date it should prove to be very useful for travel in the area. *Krabi Holiday Guide*, a locally produced pamphlet, is also informa-

tive, though it may be somewhat biased toward advertisers.

## Information
**Immigration** Visas can easily be extended at the immigration office, south of the GPO on Utarakit Rd.

**Post & Communications** The post and telephone office is on Utarakit Rd past the turn-off for the Jao Fah pier. Home direct international phone service is available here daily from 7 am to midnight.

**Travel Agencies** Krabi has dozens of fly-by-night travel agencies that will book accommodation at beaches and islands as well as tour-bus and boat tickets. Chan Phen Travel and Jungle Book, both on Utarakit Rd, have been the most reliable over the years.

## Eco-Trips
Chan Phen Travel runs half-day boat tours to nearby estuaries for a look at mangrove ecology (200 to 350B per person), or you can simply hire a boat at Saphaan Jao Fah for 100 to 200B per hour. Bird species that frequent mangrove areas include the sea eagle and ruddy kingfisher. In mud and shallow waters, keep an eye out for fiddler crabs and mudskippers.

At the Khao Nor Chuchi Lowland Forest Project, visitors can follow trails through lowland rainforest, swim in clear forest pools and observe or participate in local village activities like rubber-tapping. A daily fee of 250B includes these activities along with meals and lodging in thatched huts – proceeds go towards reforestation, rural development, nature education and wildlife research. The project is 56 km south of Krabi but arrangements can be made through Chan Phen Travel; you'll need a minimum of four people to arrange this trip.

Sea Canoe operate their famous sea canoe/kayak trips along the coast; they can be contacted through Phranang Inn on Ao Nang (see the Ao Nang Area section further on).

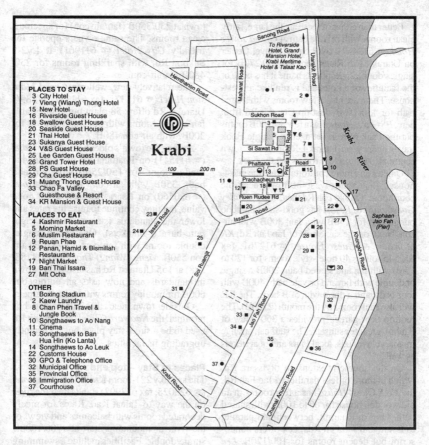

**PLACES TO STAY**
3  City Hotel
7  Vieng (Wiang) Thong Hotel
15  New Hotel
16  Riverside Guest House
18  Swallow Guest House
20  Seaside Guest House
21  Thai Hotel
23  Sukanya Guest House
24  V&S Guest House
25  Lee Garden Guest House
26  Grand Tower Hotel
28  PS Guest House
29  Cha Guest House
31  Muang Thong Guest House
33  Chao Fa Valley
     Guesthouse & Resort
34  KR Mansion & Guest House

**PLACES TO EAT**
4  Kashmir Restaurant
5  Morning Market
6  Muslim Restaurant
9  Reuan Phae
12  Panan, Hamid & Bismillah
     Restaurants
17  Night Market
19  Ban Thai Issara
27  Mit Ocha

**OTHER**
1  Boxing Stadium
2  Kaew Laundry
8  Chan Phen Travel &
     Jungle Book
10  Songthaews to Ao Nang
11  Cinema
13  Songthaews to Ban
     Hua Hin (Ko Lanta)
14  Songthaews to Ao Leuk
22  Customs House
30  GPO & Telephone Office
32  Municipal Office
35  Provincial Office
36  Immigration Office
37  Courthouse

Krabi

**Places to Stay – bottom end & middle Guesthouses** The cheapest places in Krabi are the many guesthouses. Some only stay around a season or two, others seem fairly stable. The ones in the business district feature closet-like rooms above modern shop buildings, often with faulty plumbing – OK for one night before heading to a nearby beach or island but not very suitable for long-term stays.

The small *Riverside Guest House*, on Kongkha Rd near the Jao Fah Pier and Customs House, has decent 90B rooms with shared facilities and a restaurant with good

vegetarian food. The local Rotary Club meets here Thursday afternoons. Next door to the Riverside, *S&R Guest House* has similar rooms for 100B.

On Prachacheun Rd, *Swallow Guest House* (☎ 611645) is a popular place with shipshape rooms for 80/100B a single/double with private bath. On Ruen Rudee Rd are several other places with the usual upstairs rooms and slow plumbing, including the *KL* with rooms for 80/100B a single/double with shared bath. Around the corner on Maharat Rd is the *Seaside*, of the same ilk.

SOUTHERN THAILAND

Better than either of these are the large, fairly clean rooms with private bath at *Grand Tower Hotel* (☎ 612457), over Grand Travel Center on Utarakit Rd. Rates here are 230/270B for singles/doubles; despite its name it has none of the facilities of a hotel and is run like a guesthouse. There are also a few rooms with shared bath for 130/150B. Just up Utarakit Rd from here, *PS Guest House* has a few 80/100B rooms out the back of a travel agency. Jungle Book travel agency on Utarakit Rd near the town centre also rents a few rooms out the back.

Quieter and more comfortable are the guesthouses just south-west of town near the courthouse. On Jao Fah Rd the *Chao Fa Valley Guesthouse & Resort* has good-sized bamboo bungalows for 150B with fan, 300B with aircon. Next, on the same side of Jao Fah Rd, *KR Mansion & Guest House* (☎ 612761; fax 612545) offers 40 hotel-style rooms for 120 to 150B with fan and shared bath; 200B a single or double with fan and private bath; 400B with four beds; and a dorm with 50B beds. The KR will also rent rooms by the month (2700B). The rooftop beer garden provides a 360° view of Krabi – great for sunsets. The staff can arrange motorcycle rentals, local tours and boat tickets as well.

On the southern extension of Issara Rd, which is more or less parallel to Jao Fah Rd, the *V&S Guest House* has a few rooms in an old wooden house for 60 to 100B with shared bath. On Soi Ruamjit, between and parallel to Issara and Jao Fah Rds, *Lek* offers nondescript but decent rooms for 100/120B. *Lee Garden*, opposite Lek, is rather grim but costs about the same – if you can find anyone to rent a room from. Farther down the soi on the right is the even more dingy *Muang Thong* with 120B rooms. Both Lee Garden and Muang Thong should be considered only if everywhere else is full.

Along Utarakit Rd, in the vicinity of the post office, *Cha Guest House* is a plain building with cement rooms with shared facilities for 60/80B, but it is the cheapest place in town.

**Hotels** The *Riverside Hotel* (☎ 612128) at 287/11 Utarakit Rd is the best hotel deal in town at 230/350B (fan/air-con) for spacious, clean rooms. The same owners operate the friendly *City Hotel* (☎ 611961) at 15/2-3 Sukhon Rd, with sparkling rooms for 250/480B fan/air-con.

The relatively new, well run *Grand Mansion Hotel* (☎ 611371; fax 611372) at 289/1 Utarakit Rd offers 58 plain but comfortable fan-cooled rooms with hot water shower for 300B, with air-con 480B.

Among the town's older hotels, *New Hotel* (☎ 611541) on Phattana Rd has somewhat seedy rooms for 150/250B with fan and bath, 350B with air-con. The *Thai Hotel* (☎ 620560) on Issara Rd used to be good value, but they continue to raise the rates and lower the standards (stained carpets, cigarette-burned blankets). Overpriced single/double rooms with fan cost 300/330B, air-con 550B. *Vieng (Wiang) Thong* (☎ 611188/288) at 155 Utarakit Rd has also fallen down in standards and now asks an outrageous 600B for mouldy rooms with stained carpets.

Outside town near the Talaat Kao bus terminal, the *Naowarat Hotel* on Utarakit Rd used to be a short-stay place but is currently upgrading its facilities.

### Places to Stay – top end

The swanky 221-room *Krabi Meritime Hotel* (☎ 620028; fax 612992) stands near the river on the way to Talaat Kao. Rates for nicely decorated rooms with balconies and views of the river or mountains start at 1700/1900B single/double. Facilities include a swimming pool, nightclub, fitness centre and convention facilities.

### Places to Eat

What Krabi lacks in hotels it more than makes up for in good eating places. The *Reuan Phae*, an old floating restaurant on the river in front of town, is fine for a beer or rice whisky while watching the river rise and fall with the tide. Although the food at Reuan Phae is not that great overall, certain dishes, including the fried shrimp cakes (thâwt man kûng) and spicy hàw mók tháleh (steamed curried fish), are well worth trying. Farther south down Utarakit Rd is a night market near the big pier (called Saphaan Jao Fah), with great seafood at low prices and a host of Thai dessert vendors.

One of the better and most reasonably priced restaurants in town for standard Thai dishes and local cuisine is the *Kotung* near Saphaan Jao Fah pier. The tôm yam kûng is especially good, as is anything else made with fresh seafood.

*Pe-pe*, on the corner of Maharat and Prachacheun Rds, is a clean place that serves good, inexpensive noodles and khâo man kài; it's very popular at lunchtime.

For cheap Thai breakfasts, the morning market off Si Sawat Rd in the middle of town is good. Another cheap and tasty breakfast spot is *Mit Ocha*, a funky coffee shop on the corner of Khongkha and Jao Fah Rds, opposite the customs house. Besides Thai-style coffee and tea, the old Chinese couple here serve khanŏm jiin (served with chunks of pineapple as well as the usual assorted veggies), and custard and sticky rice wrapped in banana leaves (khâo nĭaw săngkha-yaa) – help yourself from the plates on the tables. It's a good place to hang out if you're waiting for the morning boat to Phi Phi.

The nicely decorated *Ban Thai Issara* on Ruen Rudee Rd, run by a New Zealand woman and her Thai husband, specialises in western breakfasts and a mixed menu of decent Thai and farang food; the selection of home-baked breads and imported cheeses is particularly good. It's only open 8 am to 5 pm. *Pizzeria Firenze*, at 10 Khongkha Rd, does good pizza, pasta, wine, gelato and Italian breads. *Coffee Corner* opposite the Grand Tower Hotel has a good selection of coffee, including espresso; it's open during the daytime only.

*Thammachart*, below the Riverside Guest House, serves good vegetarian food oriented toward farang palates. *Ice Ink Restaurant*, opposite Ban Thai Issara, is a Thai curry place with lots of vegetarian dishes, especially tofu.

*Reuan Mai* is a very good sŭan aahăan near Krabi Hospital on the way to Talaat Kao; it's mostly a locals' place but well worth seeking out for the high-quality Thai food.

**Southern Thai & Muslim** Places for fine spicy Thai-Malay Muslim cuisine continue to multiply as the earnings of the local populace rise with tourism development. *Panan* (no English sign), on the corner of Ruen Rudee and Maharat Rds, has khâo mòk kài (chicken biryani) in the mornings, inexpensive curries and kŭaytĭaw the rest of day. The roman-script sign reads 'Makanan Islam' (Malay for Muslim food). Next door are two other decent Muslim places, *Bismillah* and *Hamid*, with signs in Thai/Yawi only.

Not far from the morning market, on Preusa Uthit Rd, the *Muslim Restaurant* serves roti chanai, the Malaysian-style breakfast of flat bread and curry. Look for a sign that says 'Hot Roti Curry Service'. They have other Thai-Malay dishes as well. *Kashmir Restaurant*, nearby at the office of Waterfall Resort, serves good Muslim food and caters to tourists as well as locals; in the morning the restaurant serves western breakfasts as well as roti kaeng.

### Getting There & Away

**Air** When the renovation of the airport is complete (estimated late 1997 or early 1998 opening), Bangkok Airways will operate regular flights to Krabi from Bangkok.

**Bus, Share Taxi & Minivan** Government buses to/from Bangkok cost 193B ordinary, 368 to 377B air-con or 440B VIP (540B for super VIP – 24 seats). Air-con buses leave Bangkok's Southern Bus Terminal between 6.30 and 8 pm; in the reverse direction they leave Krabi between 2 and 5 pm.

Buses to/from Phuket leave hourly during daylight hours, cost 46B (85B with air-con) and take three to four hours. Share taxis to/from Phuket cost 70B; air-con minivans cost 170B.

Buses for Krabi leave Phang-Nga several times a day for 25B ordinary, 43B air-con.

Ordinary buses between Surat Thani and Krabi make the four hour trip 13 times daily between 5 am and 2.30 pm for 60B. Air-con buses depart three times a day between 5.30 am and 2 pm for 150B and take around 3½ hours. Through various agencies in town you can pay 140 to 150B for a private air-con bus to Surat or 150B for air-con minivan. These agencies also arrange minivans to Hat Yai (150B) and Phuket (170B).

Government buses to/from Hat Yai cost 78B (127B air-con) and take five hours; from Trang it's 36B (66B air-con) and 2½ hours. There are also share taxis to/from Trang, Hat Yai and Satun; fares are roughly twice the ordinary bus fare.

Out-of-province buses to/from Krabi arrive at and depart from Talaat Kao, a junction about four km north of Krabi on the highway between Phang-Nga and Trang. To get to the centre of Krabi, catch a songthaew for 5B or motorcycle taxi for 10B. Private air-con buses leaves from Songserm Travel Centre on Utarakit Rd.

Songthaews to Ban Hua Hin (for Ko Lanta) leave from Phattana Rd in town, with a second stop in Talaat Kao, for 30B. They leave about every half hour from 10 am to 2 pm and take 40 minutes to reach Ban Hua Hin. There are also more expensive air-con minivans available from Krabi travel agencies.

**Boat**  Krabi can be reached by sea from Ko Phi Phi and Ko Lanta. See the respective Phi Phi and Lanta sections for details.

### Getting Around

Any place in town can easily be reached on foot, but if you plan to do a lot of exploring out of town, renting a motorcycle might be a good idea. Several travel agencies and guesthouses can arrange motorcycle rentals for 200B a day, 150B for multi-day rentals.

Songthaews to Ao Leuk (for Than Bokkharani National Park) leave from the intersection of Phattana and Preusa Uthit Rds for 20B. To Ao Nang (15B) they leave from Phattana Rd near the New Hotel – departures are about every 15 minutes from 7 am to 6 pm during the high season (December to March), till 4 or 4.30 pm the remainder of the year. Boats to the islands and beaches mostly leave from Jao Fah pier. See the Ao Nang Area Getting There & Away section for boat details.

## AROUND KRABI
### Su-Saan Hawy (Shell Cemetery)
สุสานหอย

Nineteen km west of Krabi, on Laem Pho, is the so-called Shell Fossil Cemetery, a shell 'graveyard' where 75-million-year-old shell fossils have formed giant slabs jutting into the sea.

To get there, take a songthaew from the Krabi waterfront for 20B – ask for 'Su-Saan Hawy'.

### Wat Tham Seua
วัดถ้ำเสือ

In the other direction, about five km north and then two km east of town, is Wat Tham Seua (Tiger Cave Temple), one of Southern Thailand's most famous forest wats. The main wihāan is built into a long, shallow limestone cave, on either side of which dozens of kutis (monastic cells) are built into various cliffs and caves.

The abbot is Ajaan Jamnien, a Thai monk in his 40s who has allowed a rather obvious personality cult to develop around him. The usual pictures of split cadavers and decaying corpses on the walls (useful meditation objects for countering lust) are interspersed with large portraits of Ajaan Jamnien, who is well known as a teacher of vipassana and *metta* (loving-kindness). It is said that he was apprenticed at an early age to a blind lay priest and astrologer who practised folk medicine and that he has been celibate his entire life. Many young women come here to practise as eight-precept nuns.

The best part of the temple grounds can be found in a little valley behind the ridge where the bòt is located. Follow the path past the main wat buildings, through a little village with nuns' quarters, until you come to some steep stairways on the left. The first leads to an arduous climb to the top of a karst hill with a good view of the area.

The second stairway, next to a large statue of Kuan Yin, leads over a gap in the ridge and into a valley of tall trees and limestone caves. Enter the caves on your left and look for light switches on the walls – the network

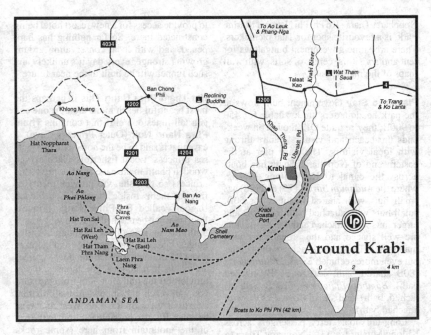

Around Krabi

of caves is wired so that you can light your way chamber by chamber through the labyrinth until you rejoin the path on the other side. There are several kutis in and around the caves, and it's interesting to see the differences in interior decorating – some are very spartan and others are outfitted like oriental bachelor pads.

A path winds through a grove of trees surrounded by tall limestone cliffs covered with a patchwork of foliage. If you continue to follow the path you'll eventually end up where you started, at the bottom of the staircase.

**Getting There & Away** To get to Wat Tham Seua, take a songthaew from Utarakit Rd to the Talaat Kao junction for 5B, then change to any bus or songthaew east on Highway 4 towards Trang and Hat Yai and get off at the road on the left just after Km 108 – if you tell the bus operators 'Wat Tham Seua' they'll let you off in the right place. It's a two km walk straight up this road to the wat.

In the mornings there are a few songthaews from Phattana Rd in town that pass the turn-off for Wat Tham Seua (10B) on their way to Ban Hua Hin. Also in the morning there is usually a songthaew or two going direct to Wat Tham Seua from Talaat Kao for around 6B.

### Hat Noppharat Thara
หาดนพรัตน์ธารา

Eighteen km north-west of Krabi, this beach used to be called Hat Khlong Haeng (Dry Canal Beach) because the canal that flows into the Andaman Sea here is dry except during, and just after, the monsoon season. Field Marshal Sarit gave the beach its current Pali-Sanskrit name, which means Beach of the Nine-Gemmed Stream, as a tribute to its beauty. Recently the Thai navy has cleared the forest backing the beach to make way for a new royal residence.

The two-km-long beach, part of Hat

SOUTHERN THAILAND

Noppharat Thara - Ko Phi Phi National Marine Park, is a favourite spot for Thai picnickers. There are some government bungalows for rent and a visitors' centre of sorts, with wall maps of the marine park.

**Places to Stay** Government bungalows at the park headquarters are available for 450 to 900B; they're quite OK, though on weekends the beach and visitors' centre throng with local visitors. The park pier at the eastern end of Noppharat Thara has boats across the canal to Hat Khlong Muang, where the *Andaman Inn* (☎ (75) 612728) has small huts with shared facilities for 50B, small huts with attached bath for 150B and larger huts with attached bath for 250B. Huts are well spaced and the grounds are well maintained. Down the beach are the similar but even more secluded *Emerald Bungalows* (80B shared bath; 150 to 350B attached bath), *Bamboo Bungalows* (100B with attached bath) and *Sara Cove* (300B with attached bath).

Long-tail boats ferry passengers across Khlong Muang from Hat Nopparat Thara to the Andaman Inn for free.

### Ao Nang Area
อ่าวนาง

South of Noppharat Thara is a series of bays where limestone cliffs and caves drop right into the sea. The water is quite clear and there are some coral reefs in the shallows. The longest beach is along Ao Nang, a lovely spot easily reached by road from Krabi.

Over the headlands to the south are the beaches of **Phai Phlong, Ton Sai, Rai Leh**, and then the cape of Laem Phra Nang, which encompasses **Hat Tham Phra Nang** (Princess Cave Beach) on the western side, a beach facing east usually called **East Rai Leh**, and another beach called **Hat Nam Mao**.

All these beaches are accessible either by hiking over the headland cliffs or by taking a boat from Ao Nang or Krabi – although for several years now rumours have said that a tunnel road will be built to Hat Phai Phlong

to provide access for a new resort hotel being constructed there. So far nothing has happened, and with local conservation groups growing stronger every day it's unlikely any such tunnel will be built in the near future.

**Hat Tham Phra Nang** This is perhaps the most beautiful beach in the area. At one end is a tall limestone cliff that contains **Tham Phra Nang Nok** (Outer Princess Cave), a cave that is said to be the home of a mythical sea princess. Local fisherfolk place carved wooden phalli in the cave as offerings to the princess so that she will provide plenty of fish for them. Inside the cliff is a hidden 'lagoon' called **Sa Phra Nang** (Princess Pool) that can be reached by following a cave trail into the side of the mountain. A rope guides hikers along the way and it takes about 45 minutes to reach the pool – guides are available from local guesthouses. If you turn left off the trail after 50m from the start, you can reach a 'window' in the cliff that affords a view of Rai Leh West and East beaches. It's also possible to climb to the top of the mountain from here (some rock-climbing is involved) and get an aerial view of the entire cape and the islands of **Ko Poda** and **Ko Hua Khwan** (also known as Chicken Island) in the distance.

A second, larger cave on Laem Phra Nang was discovered only a few years ago. The entrance is in the middle of the peninsula near a batch of beach huts on East Rai Leh. This one is called **Tham Phra Nang Nai** (Inner Princess Cave) and consists of three caverns. All three contain some of the most beautiful limestone formations in the country, including a golden 'stone waterfall' of sparkling quartz. Local mythology says that this cave is the grand palace of the sea princess while Tham Phra Nang on the beach is her summer palace. The cliffs around Ao Phra Nang have become a worldwide mecca for rock-climbers and it's easy to arrange equipment, maps and instruction from beach bungalows on Hat Rai Leh.

The islands off Laem Phra Nang are good areas for snorkelling. Besides Ko Poda and Ko Hua Khwan there is the nearer island of

**Ko Rang Nok** (Bird Nest Island) and, next to that, a larger, unnamed island (possibly part of the same island at low tide) with an undersea cave. Some of the bungalows do reasonably priced day trips to these as well as other islands in the area.

**Ao Phai Phlong** This peaceful, palm-studded cove is worth boating to for the day. At the moment there is no accommodation here. A few years back a hotel conglomerate was rumoured to have purchased the land but so far there are no signs of construction.

**Rock-Climbing** Limestone cliffs on the huge headland between Hat Tham Phra Nang and Hat Rai Leh East, and on nearby islands, offer practically endless rock-climbing opportunities. Most surfaces provide high-quality limestone with steep, pocketed walls, overhangs, and the occasional hanging stalactite. Over 150 routes have been identified by zealous climbers, most in the mid to high difficulty level (grades 16 to 25). They bear names like Lord of the Thais, The King and I, Andaman Wall, One-Two-Three, Sleeping Indian Cliffs and Thaiwan Wall. Novices often begin with Muay Thai, a 50m wall with around 20 climbs in the 17 to 21 grade range at the south end of East Rai Leh. Certain areas are off limits because they're part of Hat Noppharat Thara - Ko Phi Phi National Marine Park, including the cliff next to the Dusit resort.

Virtually any of the lodgings in this area can arrange guided climbs or rock-climbing instruction. A half-day climb with instruction and guidance costs around 400B, while an all-day is 700B, three days 2000B; all equipment is included. Tex Rock Climbing at Railay Bay Bungalows is the best equipped of the local outfits.

**Diving** Baby Shark Divers at Railay Village, Phra Nang Diving School at Viewpoint Resort, and Seafan's Divers next to Phranang Inn on Ao Nang beach do dive trips. Going rates are 1200 to 1600B for a day trip to nearby islands, while three to four day certification courses cost 7500B. The most convenient local dive spots are Ko Poda Nai and Ko Poda Nawk. At nearby Ko Mae Urai, a km west of Poda Nawk, two submarine tunnels lined with soft and hard corals offer lots of tropical fish and are suitable for all levels of divers. Another fairly interesting dive site is the sunken boat just south of Ko Rang Nok, a favoured fish habitat. Fun three day snorkelling/camping trips – sometimes led by chao náam (sea gypsies) – can be arranged for 1000 to 1500B per person.

**Paddling** Tours of the coast, islands and semi-submerged caves by inflatable canoe or kayak can be arranged through Sea Canoe at Phranang Inn at Ao Nang or Krabi Canoe, also at Ao Nang. One of the best local paddles is the canyon river cruise, an estuary trip that cuts through 200m foliaged limestone cliffs, mangrove channels and tidal lagoon tunnels (euphemistically called 'hongs', from the Thai word for 'room'). There are also shorter, more expensive sunset paddles from Ao Nang to Rai Leh, Phra Nang and back.

**Places to Stay & Eat** A large and growing number of bungalows and inns can be found along Ao Nang and nearby beaches.

**Ao Nang** Because it's easily accessible by road, this beach has become fairly developed of late. The more expensive places usually have booking offices in amphoe meuang Krabi. The oldest resort in the area, *Krabi Resort* (☎ (75) 612160; (2) 208-9165 in Bangkok), at the northern end of Ao Nang, has luxury bungalows that cost 2367 to 5476B on the beach, 1415B away from the beach, and 2047B in the new hotel wing. Most of the guests are with package tours or conferences. There are the usual resort amenities, including a swimming pool, bar and restaurant. Bookings can be made at the Krabi Resort office on Phattana Rd in Krabi and guests receive free transport out to the resort.

Off Route 4203, the road leading to the beach's north end, *Beach Terrace* (☎ (01) 722-0060; fax 722-0061) has modern bunga-

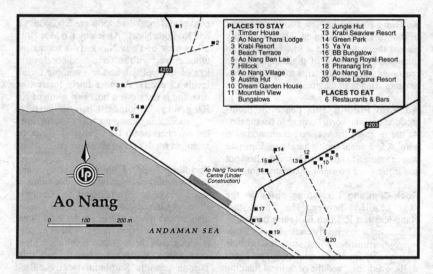

PLACES TO STAY
1 Timber House
2 Ao Nang Thara Lodge
3 Krabi Resort
4 Beach Terrace
5 Ao Nang Ban Lae
7 Hillock
8 Ao Nang Village
9 Austria Hut
10 Dream Garden House
11 Mountain View
   Bungalows
12 Jungle Hut
13 Krabi Seaview Resort
14 Green Park
15 Ya Ya
16 BB Bungalow
17 Ao Nang Royal Resort
18 Phranang Inn
19 Ao Nang Villa
20 Peace Laguna Resort

PLACES TO EAT
6 Restaurants & Bars

Ao Nang

Ao Nang Tourist Centre (Under Construction)

0   100   200 m

ANDAMAN SEA

lows for 1340B with air-con, hot water, TV and fridge. The *Ao Nang Ban Lae* (☎ (01) 228-4326) next door has six simple but well maintained bungalows for 150 to 250B. On the opposite side of the road, *Ban Ao Nang* (☎ (01) 722-0258) is a modern hotel with rooms for 850 to 1980B. About half a km from the beach are *Timber House* and *Ao Nang Thara Lodge*, with mid-range cottages for 400B and 900B respectively.

Down on the beach heading south you'll come to *Ao Nang Beach, Wanna's Place* and *Sea Breeze*, all 100 to 150B for fairly simple huts, and *Gift's* (☎ /fax (01) 723-1128), a nicer spot with larger huts with bath for 250 to 350B. Next along the beach a huge shopping centre called *Ao Nang Tourist Centre* is currently under construction.

The beach road intersects Route 4203 to Krabi just before you arrive at *Phra-Nang Inn* (☎ (75) 612173/4), a tastefully designed 'tropical hotel' with sweeping views of the bay and a small pool. Large air-con rooms start at 1776B a night in the high season (usually December to February), 1300B the remainder of the year. They have a good restaurant. A second, similarly designed branch recently opened across the road. Sea

Canoe, which operates see canoe/kayak tours in the area, has its local headquarters here.

Next door is the *Ao Nang Villa* (☎ (75) 620576), with 90 upgraded cottages with all the amenities for 750 to 4500B. Right around the corner on Route 423, the newer *Ao Nang Royal Resort* (☎ (75) 611606) has decent bungalows for 700B with fan and private bath, up to 1200B with air-con.

Up Route 4203, 100 or so metres from the beach, is the small *BB Bungalow* with relatively modern but simple accommodation for 150 to 350B. *Ya Ya* next door (not to be confused with Ya Ya on East Hat Rai Leh) is similar. Farther up the road, about 200m from the beach, the *Green Park* is one of the better cheapies with well maintained huts for 80B with shared bath, 100/150B with attached bath – as low as 50B in the low season. Moving further away from the beach along Route 4203 is *Krabi Seaview Resort* (☎ (75) 611648), with modern A-frames for 500/980B fan/air-con, followed by *Jungle Hut* with adequate bungalows for 70B with shared bath, 120 to 200B with private bath – down to 50B in the low season. On the opposite side of Route 4203, well back from

SOUTHERN THAILAND

the road, the *Peace Laguna Resort* (☎ (75) 611972) has gone more up-market with new bungalows for 450B with fan and private bath, 600 to 1000B with air-con.

Farther east along Route 4203 is the newer *Mountain View Bungalows*, with small fan-cooled bungalows for 150 to 250B and larger ones for 350B, followed by the simple *Ao Nang Village*, with plain but serviceable huts for 100 to 200B. The adjacent *Dream Garden House*, *Penny's Bed & Breakfast* and *Austria Hut* offer more up-market rooms for 600 to 1000B. Farther on yet, *Hillock* offers motel-like rooms for around 100B.

At the north end of the beach, past where Highway 4203 turns inland, is a short string of thatched-roof bars and restaurants. *Sala Thai*, the last in the series, has the best Thai-style seafood, while *Khon Thai* is the best bar.

**Hat Ton Sai** This beach can only be reached by boat from Ao Nang, Ao Nam Mao or Krabi. New management has taken over *Ton Sai Huts* here, providing accommodation for 80 to 350B per night.

**Hat Rai Leh (West)** At the centre of this pretty bay, *Railay Bay Bungalows* (☎ (01) 722-0236) packs in nearly a hundred huts right across the peninsula to East Hat Rai Leh. Rates range from 200 to 400B depending on the size of the hut and number of guests, possibly lower in the off season. The *Sand Sea* next door features two rows of cottages facing each other, some thatched, some with hard walls, for 300 to 400B, lower in the off season. The similar *Railay Village* has small cottages with glass fronts in two facing rows for about the same rates. All three have pleasant dining areas. At the northern end of the beach is a private home development where it's possible to rent vacant beach homes from the caretakers for 400 to 4500B a night. Contact the caretakers at the site or phone/fax directly to ☎ (01) 464-4338; or write to Dick Balsamo, PO Box 8, Krabi 81000.

West Rai Leh can be reached by boat from Ao Nang, Ao Nam Mao or Krabi, or on foot from Hat Tham Phra Nang and Hat Rai Leh (east) (but these must be approached by boat as well).

**Hat Tham Phra Nang** The only place to stay at this beautiful beach is the *Dusit Rayavadee* (☎ (2) 238-0032 in Bangkok), a tastefully designed and fairly unobtrusive resort with 179 luxurious rooms in cement-and-stucco or wooden cottages starting at 8000B.

The beach is not Dusit's exclusive domain – a wooden walkway has been left around the perimeter of the limestone bluff so that you can walk to Hat Tham Phra Nang from East Rai Leh. From West Rai Leh a footpath leads through the forest around to the beach.

Phra Nang is accessible by boat or foot only.

**Hat Rai Leh (East)** The beach along here tends towards mud flats during low tide, while the north-east end of the bay is vegetated with mangrove; most people who stay here walk over to Hat Tham Phra Nang for beach activities.

Railay Bay Bungalows has another entrance on this side (see Hat Rai Leh West). *Ya-Ya* has some interesting bungalow designs, including some treehouse-style huts, but some of the rooms were in very poor repair on my last visit; guests complained of grouchy staff, faulty plumbing and doors that wouldn't close. There's a rock-climbing club of sorts here, but the main activity now centres around the separate Tex Rock Climbing in front of Railay Bay Bungalows. Rates run 100 to 200B in December and January, half that the rest of the year.

*Coco Bungalows*, farther north-east toward the mangrove area, is set back from the shoreline and offers simple, quiet bungalows for 100 to 150B and one of the better restaurants in the area.

Set on a hill overlooking Rai Leh East and the mangrove, *Viewpoint Resort* (☎ (01) 476-0270) offers clean, well maintained two-storey cottages for 400 to 500B, negotiable in the off season. Phra Nang Diving School, with headquarters at Viewpoint, offers reasonable dive courses and excursions.

A bit farther, near the Phra Nang Nai caves, the *Diamond Cave Bungalows* rents poorly maintained huts in a rubber grove for 80B up. An outdoor bar set against a rock cliff next to the cave and bungalows is atmospheric, but the night-time din carries for some distance – light sleepers beware.

**Ao Nam Mao** This large bay, around a headland to the north-east of East Rai Leh, about 1½ km from the Shell Cemetery, has a coastal environment similar to that of East Rai Leh – mangroves and shallow, muddy beaches.

Here you'll find the environmentally friendly *Dawn of Happiness Beach Resort* (☎ (75) 612730; fax 612251), where natural, locally available building materials are used wherever possible and no sewage or rubbish ends up in the bay. Thatched bungalows with private baths and mosquito nets cost 200 to 400B per night depending on the season. The staff can arrange trips to nearby natural attractions.

Ao Nam Mao is accessible by road via Route 4204. If you phone from Krabi, the Dawn of Happiness will arrange free transport.

**Getting There & Away** Hat Noppharat Thara and Ao Nang can be reached by songthaews that leave about every 15 minutes from 7 am to 6 pm (high season) or 4 pm (low season) from Utarakit Rd in Krabi, near the New Hotel. The fare is 15B and the trip takes 30 to 40 minutes.

You can get boats to Ton Sai, West Rai Leh and Laem Phra Nang at several places. For Ton Sai, the best thing to do is get a songthaew out to Ao Nang, then a boat from Ao Nang to Ton Sai. It's 15B per person for two people or more, 30B if you don't want to wait for a second passenger to show up. You may have to bargain to get this fare. Boats also go between Ao Nang and Ko Phi Phi for 150B, October to April only.

For West Rai Leh or anywhere on Laem Phra Nang, you can get a boat direct from Krabi's Jao Fah pier for 40B. It takes about 45 minutes to reach Phra Nang. However, boats will only go all the way round the cape

to West Rai Leh and Hat Phra Nang from October to April when the sea is tame enough. During the other half of the year they only go as far as East Rai Leh, but you can easily walk from there to West Rai Leh or Hat Phra Nang. You can also get boats from Ao Nang for 20B all year-round, but in this case they only go as far as West Rai Leh and Hat Phra Nang (again, you can walk to East Rai Leh from there). From Ao Nang you'll have to pay 20B per person for two or more passengers, 40B for just one.

Another alternative is to take a songthaew as far as Ao Nam Mao, to the small fishing bay near the Shell Cemetery, for 15B and then a boat to Laem Phra Nang for 20B (three or more people required).

Some of the beach bungalows have agents in Krabi who can help arrange boats – but there's still a charge.

## THAN BOKKHARANI NATIONAL PARK
อุทยานแห่งชาติธารโบกขรณี

Than Bokkharani National Park was established in 1991 and encompasses nine caves throughout the Ao Leuk area in northern Krabi Province as well as the former botanical gardens for which the park was named.

The park is best visited just after the monsoons – when it has been dry a long time the water levels go down and in the midst of the rains it can be a bit murky. In December Than Bokkharani looks like something cooked up by Disney, but it's real and entirely natural. Emerald-green waters flow out of a narrow cave in a tall cliff and into a large lotus pool, which overflows steadily into a wide stream, itself dividing into many smaller streams in several stages. At each stage there's a pool and a little waterfall. Tall trees spread over 40 rai (6.4 sq km) provide plenty of cool shade. Thais from Ao Leuk come to bathe here on weekends and then it's full of laughing people playing in the streams and pools. During the week there are only a few people about, mostly kids doing a little fishing. Vendors sell noodles, roast chicken, delicious batter-fried squid and sôm-tam under a roofed area to one side.

SOUTHERN THAILAND

## Caves

Among the protected caves scattered around the Ao Leuk district, one of the most interesting is **Tham Hua Kalok**, set in a limestone hill in a seldom-visited bend of mangrove-lined Khlong Baw Thaw. Besides impressive stalactite formations, the high-ceilinged cave features 2000 to 3000 year old cave paintings of human and animal figures and geometric designs.

Nearby **Tham Lawt** (literally, 'Tube Cave') is distinguished by a navigable stream flowing through it – it's longer than Phang-Nga's Tham Lawt but shorter than Mae Hong Son's.

## Places to Stay

*Ao Leuk Bungalow*, on the highway half a km before Than Bok, offers decent if over-priced cottages for 200B with private bath; you may be able to bargain for a lower rate if there are empty rooms.

In nearby Ao Leuk Tai, the wooden *Thai Wiwat Hotel* next to the district office has plain rooms for 80B.

## Getting There & Away

Than Bok, as the locals call it, is off Highway 4 between Krabi and Phang-Nga, near the town of Ao Leuk, one km south-west towards Laem Sak. To get there, take a songthaew from the intersection of Phattana and Preusa Uthit Rds in Krabi to Ao Leuk for 17B; get off just before town and it's an easy walk to the park entrance on the left.

To visit Tham Lawt and Tham Hua Kalok you must charter a boat from Tha Baw Thaw, around 6.5 km south-west of Than Bok. The tours are run exclusively by Ao Leuk native Uma Kumat and his son Bunma. They'll take one or two people for 100B; up to 10 can charter a boat for 250B. The boats run along secluded Khlong Baw Thaw and through Tham Lawt before stopping at Tham Hua Kalok. The pier at Tha Baw Thaw is 4.3 km from Than Bok via Route 4039, then two km by dirt road through an oil palm plantation. You must provide your own transport to Tha Baw Thaw.

## KHAO PHANOM BENCHA NATIONAL PARK

อุทยานแห่งชาติเขาพนมเบญจา

This 50 sq km park is in the middle of virgin rainforest along the Phanom Bencha mountain range. The main scenic attractions are the three-level **Huay To Falls, Khao Pheung Cave** and **Huay Sadeh Falls**, all within three km of the park office. Other less well known streams and waterfalls can be discovered as well. Clouded leopards, black panthers, Asiatic black bears, deer, leaf monkeys, gibbons and various tropical birds make their home here. The park has a camping ground where you are welcome to pitch your own tent for 5B per person per night.

## Getting There & Away

Public transport direct to Khao Phanom Bencha National Park from Krabi or Talaat Kao is rare. Two roads run to the park off Highway 4. One is only about half a km from Talaat Kao – you could walk to this junction and hitch, or hire a truck in Talaat Kao all the way for 100B or so. The other road is about 10 km north of Krabi off Highway 4. You could get to this junction via a songthaew or a bus heading north to Ao Leuk.

It would be cheaper to rent a motorcycle in Krabi for a day trip to Phanom Bencha than to charter a pickup. Try to have someone at the park watch your bike while hiking to nearby falls – motorcycle theft at Phanom Bencha has been a real problem lately.

## KO PHI PHI

เกาะพีพี

Ko Phi Phi actually consists of two islands about 40 km from Krabi, Phi Phi Leh and Phi Phi Don. Both are part of Hat Noppharat Thara - Ko Phi Phi National Marine Park, though this means little in the face of the blatant land encroachment now taking place on Phi Phi Don.

Only parts of Phi Phi Don are actually under the administration of the Park Division of the Forestry Department. Phi Phi Leh and the western cliffs of Phi Phi Don are left to

SOUTHERN THAILAND

the nest collectors, and the part of Phi Phi Don where the chao náam (sea gypsies) live is also not included in the park.

**Money** Near Ton Sai pier on Phi Phi Don, Krung Thai Bank has an exchange booth open daily 8.30 am to 3.30 pm.

## Ko Phi Phi Don
พีพีดอน

Phi Phi Don is the larger of the two islands, a sort of dumbbell-shaped island with scenic hills, awesome cliffs, long beaches, emerald waters and remarkable bird and sea life. The

'handle' in the middle has long, white-sand beaches on either side, only a few hundred metres apart. The beach on the southern side curves around **Ao Ton Sai**, where boats from Phuket and Krabi dock. There is also a Thai-Muslim village here. On the northern side of the handle is **Ao Lo Dalam**.

The uninhabited (except for beach huts) western section of the island is called Ko Nawk (Outer Island), and the eastern section, which is much larger, is Ko Nai (Inner Island). At the north of the eastern end is Laem Tong, where the island's chao náam population lives. The number of chao náam

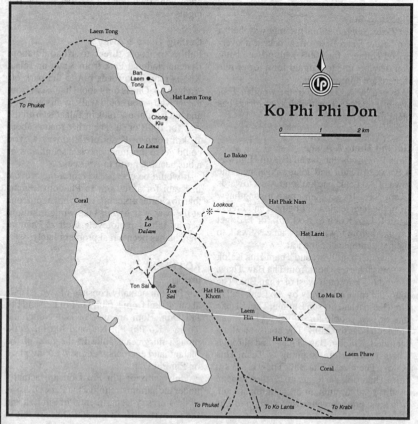

here varies from time to time, but there are generally about 100.

**Hat Yao** (Long Beach) faces south and has some of Phi Phi Don's best coral reefs. Ton Sai, Lo Dalam and Hat Yao all have beach bungalows. Over a ridge north-west from Hat Yao is another very beautiful beach, **Hat Lanti**, with good surf. For several years the locals wouldn't allow any bungalows here out of respect for the large village mosque, situated in a coconut grove above the beach – but money talked, and the chao náam walked. Farther north is the sizeable bay of **Lo Bakao**, where there is a small resort, and near the tip of Laem Tong are three luxury resorts.

Unfortunately, the park administrators have allowed development on Phi Phi Don to continue unchecked. Rumour has it that park officials won't dare even set foot on Ko Phi Phi for fear of being attacked by village chiefs and bungalow developers profiting from tourism. Beautiful Ao Ton Sai is becoming very littered, and more and more bungalows have been crowded onto this section of the island. The noise of the generators is only drowned out by the sounds of Arnold firing large weapons at his enemies during the latest Schwarzenegger epic showing at every other bungalow restaurant.

A friend who visited Ton Sai had this report:

Bay packed with boats, small and large, grimy and grand luxe. New hotels building by the pier; scaffolding, dust and din, tin shacks for construction workers all about. Plenty of illegally obtained shell art, hamburgers, pizza, beer bars – Pattaya without the prostitutes. Huge piles of garbage and endless rows of dreary, crowded bungalow developments. Where's the nature? Everywhere the horrid smell of rotting cashew fruit. No-one harvests the nuts any more and no-one fishes. Why bother when you can ferry farangs around the coral reefs?

Other parts of Phi Phi Don aren't this bad, though the once-brilliant coral reefs around the island are suffering from anchor drag and runoff from large beach developments. The least disturbed parts of the island so far are those still belonging to those chao náam who haven't cashed in.

However, development on Ko Phi Phi has stabilised to a significant degree over the last couple of years and it seems a near-truce between park authorities and greedy developers has come about. Still, there's much room for improvement in terms of rubbish collection and waste disposal.

If you go to the island and want to air your opinion on the what's going on there with regard to the environment, please contact one of the organisations listed under Ecology & Environment in the Facts about the Country chapter with your assessments, whether good or bad.

## Phi Phi Leh

Phi Phi Leh is almost all sheer cliffs, with a few caves and a sea lake formed by a cleft between two cliffs that allows water to enter into a bowl-shaped canyon. The so-called **Viking Cave** contains prehistoric paintings of stylised human and animal figures alongside later paintings of ships (Asian junks) no more than 100 years old.

The cave is also a collection point for swiftlet nests. The swiftlets like to build their nests high up in the caves in rocky hollows which can be very difficult to reach. Agile collectors build vine-and-bamboo scaffolding to get at the nests but are occasionally injured or killed in falls. Before ascending the scaffolds, the collectors pray and make offerings of tobacco, incense and liquor to the cavern spirits.

Those who want to collect swiftlet nests must bid for a licence which gives them a franchise to harvest the nests for four years. In one year there are only three harvests, as the birds build seasonally, and the first harvest fetches the highest prices. The collectors sell the nests to intermediaries who then sell them to Chinese restaurants in Thailand and abroad. Known as 'white gold', premium teacup-sized nests sell for US$2000 per kilo – Hong Kong alone imports US$25 million worth every year. The nests are made of saliva which the birds secrete – the saliva hardens when exposed to the air. When cooked in chicken broth, the nests soften and separate and look like bean thread noodles. The Chinese value the expensive bird secretions highly, believing them to be a medicinal food that imparts vigour.

No-one is allowed to stay on Phi Phi Leh because of the bird-nest business, but boats can be hired from Phi Phi Don for the short jaunt over to see the caves and to do a little snorkelling at the coral reefs in Ao Ma-Ya.

### Diving

Several places in Ton Sai village – nine at last count – can arrange diving and snorkelling trips around the island or to nearby islands. The typical all day snorkelling trip includes lunch, water, fruit and equipment for 300B. Guided dive trips start at 500B for two dives. An open-water certification course costs 6700 to 7000B, a bit more expensive than elsewhere in Thailand.

Mask, fins and snorkel can be rented for 50B a day.

### Organised Tours & Boat Charters

From Ko Phi Phi Don, boats to Ko Phi Phi Leh can be chartered for 200B per trip. A half-day trip to Phi Phi Leh or Bamboo Island costs 500B, a full day 800B. Fishing trips average 1600B a day.

### Places to Stay

During the high tourist months of December to February, July and August, nearly all the accommodation on Phi Phi Don gets booked out. As elsewhere during these months, it's best to arrive early in the morning to stake out a room or bungalow. During the off season, rates are negotiable.

**Ao Ton Sai** *Ton Sai Village* (☎ (01) 612-1434) offers 30 very comfortable bungalows with air-con, hot water, TV and minibar for 1883B including breakfast; it's also a little removed from others on this beach so is a bit quieter. *Phi Phi Island Cabana Hotel*, the oldest resort on the island, is joined to the *PP Marina* with access to both Ton Sao and Lo Dalam. A bungalow with fan costs 1200B while a standard room in a three-storey hotel

building are 2300B and up to 9300B for the Andaman Suite.

*Phi Phi Hotel* (☎ (01) 712-0138; fax (74) 245721) features 64 rooms in a multistorey building off the beach near the pier. Rooms are 1800B with all the amenities but its proximity to the sometimes noisy pier is a minus. *Chao Koh Phi Phi Lodge* consists of fairly basic but clean concrete bungalows with bath and fan for 300 to 500B, a bit off the beach.

**Lo Dalam** *Chong Khao* is set inland with a path leading to both Lo Dalam and Ton Sai beaches. Fairly quiet rooms in a row house or bungalow range from 100 to 200B with shared facilities, 250B with attached bath.

*PP Princess Resort* (☎ (75) 612188; fax 620615) has large, well-spaced upscale wooden bungalows with glass doors and windows for 1390 to 2990B. The bungalows feature nice deck areas and are connected by wooden walkways.

*Charlie Beach Resort* (☎ (01) 723-0495) features thatched-roof bungalows and a beach bar in a atmospheric setting; there's live folk music at night. Rooms cost 300 to 750B, all with bath and fan, depending on size and position on the beach. *Phi Phi Pavilion Resort* (☎ (75) 620633) is another thatched-roof place but in this case with air-con for 700B. Most bungalows have sea views.

Friendly *PP Viewpoint Resort I & II* (☎ (01) 722-0111) are situated on a hillside; No I overlooks Lo Dalam while No II doesn't have a bay view. Rates range from 450B for a room to 500 to 750B for a bungalow, depending on size and location. Monthly rentals for 4500B are also available.

Beside the Viewpoint, *Home Parklong Seasight* consists of five rooms in the home of a local entrepreneur for 550 to 750B a night, probably less in low season. Facilities are shared, so this is a bit pricey.

**Hat Hin Khom** This beach a little south-east of Ton Sai has become the preferred budget beach of late, replacing Hat Yao, because it's not as crowded and the source of freshwater for showers is more constant. *Phi Phi Don Resort* (☎ (01) 722-0083) charges 500 to 800B for cement and stucco bungalows with tin roofs, all with fan and bath and 24 hour power. Many are right on the beachfront. *PP Andaman* has thatched huts – many in need of repair – for 150 to 200B, plus sturdier cement and stucco ones for 350B.

*Bayview Resort* (☎ (01) 723-1134) is an up-market place with modern-looking cottages geared to the Thai market, though plenty of farangs stay here as well. A cottage with fan and cold water shower costs 1300B, while one with air-con and hot water costs 1600 to 1900B.

Off by itself on a little cove at the southeast end of Hat Hin Khao, *Maphrao Resort* offers thatched A-frame huts in a natural setting for 100 to 320B. Showers are shared for the 100B bungalows, while 200B and 300B huts have attached showers. The restaurant is good and tables are arranged overlooking the beach rather than in the more typical large mess hall style.

**Hat Yao** Bungalows on this beach are practically piled onto one another, with very little space in between. A shortage of freshwater means most showers employ salt water. *Pee Pee Paradise Pear Resort* (☎ (01) 228-4370) has bungalows in all shapes and sizes, ranging from 200 to 800B. All come with toilet, shower and fan. This one's a little tidier and more well spaced than others on Hat Yao.

*PP Long Beach* has huts starting at 100B on the hillside, 120B for better locations, 150B for newer huts, all with shared shower. For 200 to 300B you can get a hut with private bath and fan. The *Coral Bay Resort* still appears to be looking for a new owner or is closed down for repairs.

**Lo Bakao** *Pee Pee Island Village* is the only resort on this beautiful, secluded stretch of sand. From November to April rooms start at 1400B and reach as high as 2100B. The remainder of the year they cost 800 to 1000B; air-con is available at the upper end of the price bracket.

**Laem Tong** This is another nice beach, with pricey resorts and its own pier. *Phi Phi Palm Beach* (☎ (01) 723-0052) is only accessible by boat for a minimum transport charge of 200B or 100B per person. High-tone cottages with everything start at 4173B; the premises are well landscaped and there's a good swimming pool. *PP Coral Resort* (☎ (75) 212901, (01) 211-1575) offers wooden cottages on the beach for 1600 to 1800B high season, 1400 to 1600B low season. The 70 well appointed bungalows at *PP International Resort* (☎ /fax (01) 723-1250) cost 2200/3200B single/double (add 350B peak season charge late December to late February). This one has the advantage of being at the end of the beach with a view of the next rocky cape.

**Interior** A little village of sorts has developed in the interior of the island near Ao Ton Sai and Hat Hin Khom. Amidst the gift shops, scuba shops and cafes there are several budget-oriented places to stay. *Tara Inn* has minimal rooms for 350/400B single/double with attached bath. *PP Twin Palm* (no sign) is simply a few rooms in a house for 100/200/300B single/double/triple; *Jong Guest House* is similar. *Orchid House* continues the same theme for 150B; the proprietor seems friendly and helpful.

*Gypsy I* offers solid concrete bungalows with tin roofs and attached toilet and shower for 300B, while *Gypsy II* has rather ill-repaired thatched bungalows for 150B with attached bath.

*P P Valentine* is one of the more promising budget places in this area, with sturdy thatched-roof huts with flowers growing around them for 250 to 350B. Friendly *Rim Na Villa* costs 350/550B for singles/doubles, fan and attached bath. *Rim Kao* and *Chan House* round out the offerings with motel-like rooms for 250 to 300B.

Rates for all of the above may drop to as low as 50 to 100B a night between May and November, except in August.

**Places to Eat**
Most of the resorts, hotels and bungalows around the island have their own restaurants.

SOUTHERN THAILAND

Cheaper and sometimes better food is available at the restaurants and cafes in Ton Sai village, although virtually all of it is prepared for farang, not Thai, palates so the Thai dishes aren't usually very authentic. *PP Pizza* and *Mama's Restaurant*, predictably, offer Italian food. The very popular *Garlic Restaurant* in the island centre has good and reasonably priced seafood and some of the better Thai dishes on the island.

*PP Bakery* prepares decent breakfasts, baked goods and sandwiches; prices are very moderate.

### Getting There & Away

Ko Phi Phi is equidistant from Phuket and Krabi, but Krabi is your most economical point of departure. Until recently, boats travelled only during the dry season, from late October to May, as the seas are often too rough during the monsoons for safe navigation.

Nowadays the boat operators risk sending boats out all year-round – we've received several reports of boats losing power and drifting in heavy swells during the monsoons. It all depends on the weather – some rainy season departures are quite safe, others are risky. If the weather looks chancy, keep in mind that there usually aren't enough life jackets to go around on these boats.

Another cautionary note regards the purchase of return-trip boat tickets. From Krabi there are currently two boat services and if you buy a return ticket from one company you must use that service in both directions. Neither service will recognise tickets from its competitor; not only that, they will refuse to sell you a new ticket back to Krabi if you hold a return ticket from the competitor. The advisable thing, then, is to buy one way tickets only.

Most boats from Phuket and all boats from Krabi moor at the original pier at Ao Ton Sai. A few boats from Phuket, notably the Fast Ferry Siam's *Jet Cruise*, use the new pier at Laem Tong.

**Krabi** From Krabi's Jao Fah pier, there are usually four boats a day. Three regular boats depart at 9 am, 1 and 3 pm for 125B per person and take about two hours. A faster air-con boat leaves at 9 am, costs 150B and takes an hour and 20 minutes. These fares are sometimes discounted by agents in town to as low as 100B. Departures are sometimes delayed because boats often wait for buses from Bangkok to arrive at the Krabi pier. From Ko Phi Phi back to Krabi the boats leave at the same times.

**Ao Nang** You can also get boats from Ao Nang on the Krabi Province coast for 150B per person from October to April; there's usually only one departure a day at around 8 am. The trip lasts an hour and 20 minutes.

**Phuket** A dozen different companies operate boats from various piers on Phuket, ranging in price from 250B to 450B for the boats which take an hour and 40 minutes to two hours. Any guesthouse or hotel on Phuket can arrange tickets; the more expensive fares include bus or van pickup from your hotel. Boats leave frequently between 8 am and 3.30 pm from May to September.

Fast Ferry Siam (☎ (76) 245194) runs the fast *Jet Cruise*, which leaves Phuket at 8.30 pm (from Laem Thong at 2.30 pm) and takes 50 minutes.

Various tour companies in Phuket offer day trips to Phi Phi for 500 to 950B per person, including return transport, lunch and a tour. If you want to stay overnight and catch another tour boat back, you have to pay another 100B. Of course it's cheaper to book one way passage on the regular ferry service.

**Other Islands** As Ko Lanta is becoming more touristed, there are now fairly regular boats between that island and Ko Phi Phi from October to April. Boats generally leave from the pier on Lanta Yai around 8 am, arriving at Phi Phi Don around 9.30 am. In the reverse direction the departure is usually at 1 pm. Passage is 150B per person. It's also possible to get boats to/from Ko Jam; the same approximate departure time, fare and trip duration applies.

## Getting Around

Transport on the island is mostly on foot, although fishing boats can be chartered at Ao Ton Sai for short hops around Phi Phi Don and Phi Phi Leh. Touts meet boats from the mainland to load people onto to long-tail boats going to Hat Yao (Long Beach) for 20B per person. Other boat charters around the island from the pier at Ton Sai include Laem Thong (300B), Lo Bakao (200B) and Viking Cave (200B).

## KO JAM (KO PU) & KO SI BOYA
เกาะจำ(ปู)/เกาะสีบอยา

These large islands are inhabited by a small number of fishing families and are perfect for those seeking complete removal from the videos, farang restaurants, beach bars and so on. About the only entertainment is watching the local fishermen load or unload their boats, swimming or taking long walks on the beach. *Joy Resort* on the south-western coast of Ko Jam offers spacious bungalows for 200 to 450B. Ko Jam's southern tip is occupied by a private residential development.

There is one set of bungalows on the western side of Ko Si Boya called *Jung Hut* for 100 to 200B per night.

## Getting There & Away

Boats to both islands leave once or twice a day from Ban Laem Kruat, a village about 30 km from Krabi, at the end of Route 4036, off Highway 4. Passage is 15B to Si Boya, 20B to Ban Ko Jam.

You can also take boats bound for Ko Lanta from Krabi's Jao Fah pier and ask to be let off at Ko Jam. There are generally two boats daily which leave at 10.30 am and 1.30 pm; the fare is 130B as far as Ko Jam.

## KO LANTA
เกาะลันตา

Ko Lanta (population 18,000) is a district of Krabi Province that consists of 52 islands. The geography here is typified by stretches of mangrove interrupted by coral-rimmed beaches, rugged hills and huge umbrella trees. Twelve of the islands are inhabited

and, of these, three are easily accessible: **Ko Klang, Ko Lanta Noi** and **Ko Lanta Yai**. You can reach the latter by ferry from either Ban Hua Hin, on the mainland across from Ko Lanta Noi, or from Baw Meuang, farther south.

Ko Lanta Yai is the largest of the three islands – piers are found in **Ban Sala Dan**, at the northern tip of the island, and at the district capital **Ban Ko Lanta**, on the lower east coast. The western sides of all the islands have beaches. The best are along the south-west end of Lanta Yai, but practically the whole west coast of Lanta Yai is one long beach interrupted by the occasional stream or shell bed. There are coral reefs along parts of the western side of Lanta Yai and along the Khaw Kwang (Deer Neck) cape at its north-western tip. A hill on the cape gives a good aerial view of the island.

The people in this district are a mixture of Muslim Thais and chao náam who settled here long ago. Their main livelihood is the cultivation of rubber, cashew and bananas, along with a little fishing on the side. There is now a long string of inexpensive and moderately priced bungalow operations on Lanta Yai and you can camp on any of the islands – all have sources of fresh water. The village of **Ban Sangka-U** on Lanta Yai's southern tip is a traditional Muslim fishing village and the people are friendly. Ban Sala Dan at the northern end is the largest village on the island and is connected to the mainland by power lines. Ban Ko Lanta town has a post office and long pier; there's not much to the town but the buildings are more solid-looking than those in Sala Dan and the ferry service accommodates larger vehicles.

An unpaved road nearly encircles the island; only the south-eastern tip around Ban Sangkha-U is devoid of vehicles. In the centre of the island is **Tham Mai Kaew**, a five or six cavern limestone cave complex. A narrow, 1.5 km dirt track through a rubber plantation leads to the cave from the lower of the two cross-island roads. This track ends at the home of a Muslim family who guide visitors through five caverns for 50B per person.

Ko Si Boya

Ko Jam

KRABI PROVINCE

Ban Huay Nam Khao

4206

4043

4

Ban Ko Jam

To Ko Phi Phi

Ban Hua Hin

Ban Tha Maphrao

4042

Ban Sala Dan

Ban Khlong Mak

Ko Lanta Noi

Ban Baw Meuang

TRANG PROVINCE

ANDAMAN SEA

Ban Phra-at

Ko Klang

Ban Thung Yii Pheng

Ban Je Lil

Ban Naa

Ban Ko Lanta

Ko Bubu

Ko Po

1 Deer Neck Cabanas & Khaw Kwang Beach Bungalows
2 Golden Bay Cottages
3 Lanta Villa & Lanta Island Resort
4 Lanta Sea House & Lanta Garden Home
5 Memory & Lanta Palm Beach
6 Rapala Long Beach Resort
7 Relax Bay Tropicana
8 Blue Lanta
9 Lanta Coral Beach
10 Paradise
11 Miami
12 Dream Team
13 Sea Sun
14 Waterfall Bay Resort

Ko Lanta Yai

Ban Ko Lanta

Ban Hua Laem Klang

Ban Hua Laem

Ban Sangka-U

Ko Lanta

0      5      10 km

SOUTHERN THAILAND

The little island between Ko Lanta Noi and Ko Klang has a nice beach called **Hat Thung Thaleh** – hire a boat from Ko Klang. Also worth exploring is Ko Ngai (Hai) – see the Trang Province section for more details, as Ko Ngai is more accessible from that province.

### Ko Lanta National Marine Park
อุทยานแห่งชาติหมู่เกาะลันตา

In 1990, 15 islands in the Lanta group (covering an area of 134 sq km) were declared part of the new Ko Lanta National Marine

Park in an effort to protect the fragile coastal environment. **Ko Rok Nok** is especially beautiful, with a crescent-shaped bay featuring cliffs and a white-sand beach and a stand of banyan trees in the interior. The intact coral at **Ko Rok Nai** and limestone caves of **Ko Talang** are also worth seeing. Dive shops in Ban Sala Dan can arrange dives to these islands as well as **Ko Ha, Ko Bida, Hin Bida** and **Hin Daeng**.

Ko Lanta Yai itself is only partially protected since most of the island belongs to chao náam. As on Ko Phi Phi, many bungalows have been built on shorelands under the nominal protection of the Forestry Department. The interior of the island consists of rubber, cashew and fruit plantations, with a few stands of original forest here and there, mostly in the hilly southern section of the island. The park headquarters is situated at the southern tip of Ko Lanta Yai.

## Places to Stay

**Ko Lanta Yai** Outside of Ban Sala Dan, Ko Lanta doesn't have a regular electrical service yet but power lines may be extended southward in the near future. Quiet nights are still the rule at the less expensive places, while generators are buzzing at new up-market bungalows. Two Krabi hotels have bought tracts of land here in anticipation of the arrival of a power grid – rumours say ex-Prime Minister Chuan Leekpai also has land on the island.

Ko Lanta has the opportunity of becoming a model for environmentally conscious island tourism if the beach developers here will cooperate to keep the island clean and noise-free. Deforestation is becoming a problem as unscrupulous developers cut down trees to build up-market bungalows with hectares of decks. The simple places catering to backpackers still use renewable bamboo. As seems obvious elsewhere in Thailand, the national park system cannot be relied upon to protect the lands, although in the last two years no new beach places have been added to the island, so perhaps a limit is being enforced.

The best beach areas are found along the north-west side of the island just south of Ban Sala Dan, and this is where all the development is concentrated. Because it's long, wide and flat, this is a perfect beach for walking and jogging. Few places on this end costs less than 400B a night during high season (November to May). During low season prices plummet to 80B a night but the road along the west coast of the island becomes nearly impassable during the south-west monsoon; only the four northernmost beach bungalow operations actually stay open during low season. At this time proprietors make little effort to clean the beach of accumulating refuse and hence it's rather unappealing that half of the year.

At the northernmost section of the beach near Ban Sala Dan is the locally owned *Khaw Kwang Beach Bungalows* (☎ (01) 722-0106), the oldest of the beach places and still commanding the best stretch of beach. It's actually on the south-east side of the small peninsula of the same name that juts west from the island. Nicely separated thatched huts with private bath cost 180 to 300B depending on proximity to the beach; there are also some large VIP bungalows for 600B. The proprietors offer fishing and snorkelling trips to nearby islands. The adjacent *Deer Neck Cabanas* faces the western side of this tiny cape and is similar.

Starting about 2½ km south of Ban Sala Dan along the western side of the island are a cluster of places in varying price ranges. *Lanta Villa* and *Golden Bay Cottages* are in the 200 to 400B range, followed by the newly renovated *Lanta Island Resort* (formerly the Lanta Royal Beach), where plain bungalows with fan are 300B, air-con ones up to 800B. The latter is popular with tour groups. This is followed by the similar *Lanta Sea House* with bungalows for 400 to 600B. *Lanta Garden Home* next door has more basic huts with shared bath for 100B, up to 400B with private bath.

Just around a headland famous for a triple-trunked coconut palm are *Memory* (closed when I visited last) and the friendly *Lanta Palm Beach*, where good huts rent for 100 to 150B.

A couple of km farther south along the beach is the new, up-market, poorly designed *Rapala Long Beach Resort* in the 200 to 400B range. The nearby *Relax Bay Tropicana* features spacious bungalows with large decks for 200 to 600B; huts are perched around a rocky hillside overlooking the sea. The beach along this stretch – and for the next two km – is nothing special.

Another km south are the *Blue Lanta* and *Lanta Coral Beach*. Blue Lanta has spacious grounds with simple thatched huts amidst coconut palms for 100B with attached bath. Older huts without bath – which typically cost 50B – are currently being renovated. Lanta Coral Beach has bungalows for 50 to 80B with shared bath, 100 to 250B with private bath. Farther south another km or so the beach begins improving again and the accommodation becomes cheaper. The *Paradise* offers OK bungalows with good beach frontage for 100 to 250B, while the *Miami* immediately south is a bit simpler and costs 80 to 200B.

Sitting by itself on a rather rocky stretch of beach is the beautifully landscaped *Dream Team* with well kept, large, screened bungalows for 200 to 300B. A better sand beach is only about 10 minutes away on foot. Just before the road ends is the secluded *Sea Sun* with 80/100B cement bungalows.

Right at the end of the road, the well designed, eco-oriented *Waterfall Bay Resort* (☎ (01) 722-0014; (75) 612084 in Krabi) offers 18 well-spaced wooden bungalows with thatched roofs overlooking a secluded bay. The bungalows cost 300 to 600B depending on their position relative to the beach. All have two rooms, one below and one above as a loft, making it very suitable for family stays. The namesake waterfall is a 30 to 40 minute walk, and boat trips to Ko Rok Nai and Ko Rok Nok can be arranged. The restaurant serves Indian, Thai and farang food. As Waterfall is often booked out when open (October to mid-June only), it's best to book in advance through its office in Krabi. A 4WD vehicle picks guests up from the pier in Sala Dan. From the resort a dirt track continues to the park headquarters and Ban Sangka-U. This is a good spot to stay if you're interested in hiking into the park interior.

In Ban Ko Lanta, on the island's lower east coast near the pier for boats to/from Baw Meuang on the mainland, *No Name* provides very basic accommodation for 50B a night.

**Ko Bubu** This tiny island has one bungalow village with 13 huts. Rates are 100B per person in a dormitory, 200B in a bungalow with shared bath or 500B in a two-bed bungalow with private bath.

To get to Bubu from Lanta you can charter a boat from Samsan pier (Ban Ko Lanta) for 150 to 200B. From Krabi the boat to Ban Sala Dan on Ko Lanta Yai continues on to Baw Meuang with a stop at Bubu. You can also get boats from Baw Meuang. More information is available at the Samsan pier on Ko Lanta or from Thammachart (☎ (75) 612536), on Kongkha Rd near the Jao Fah pier in Krabi.

**Places to Eat**
If you get tired of bungalow food there are a couple of basic places to eat in Ban Sala Dan at the northern end of Lanta Yai. *Seaview* and *Seaside* are two small moderately priced restaurants over the water with Thai food and seafood. The *Swiss Bakery* next to the pier has good coffee and pastries. Restaurants on the beach near Lanta Garden Home come and go with the seasons, usually offering Swiss, French or Italian food.

**Getting There & Away**
**Krabi** The slow way to get to Ko Lanta is to take a songthaew (30B) from Phattana Rd in Krabi all the way to Ban Hua Hin, and then a vehicle ferry across the narrow channel to Ban Khlong Mak on Ko Lanta Noi. From there, get a motorcycle taxi (20B) across to another pier on the other side, then another vehicle ferry to Ban Sala Dan on Ko Lanta Yai. Both ferries cost 3B for pedestrians, 5B for a bicycle and one rider, 10B per motorcycle and 50B in a car or truck. Both ferries run frequently 6 am to 6 pm except on Fridays when they close at noon so that the Muslim pilots can visit local mosques.

Ban Hua Hin is 26 km down Route 4206 from Ban Huay Nam Khao, which is about 44 km from Krabi along Highway 4. Songthaews from Krabi (Talaat Kao junction) to Ban Hua Hin run regularly until about 3 pm. Count on two hours to complete the trip, including ferry crossing. If you're travelling by private car or motorcycle, the turn-off for Route 4206 is near the village of Ban Huay Nam Khao (Km 64) on Highway 4.

If you're coming from Trang, there's no direct public transport to Ban Hua Hin, but you can take a bus from Trang to Ban Huay Nam Khao (25B), then transfer to a songthaew going south-west to the Ban Hua Hin pier.

The quickest way to reach Ko Lanta from Krabi is to take a boat from Krabi's Jao Fah pier, only available October to April. Boats usually depart at 10.30 am and 1.30 pm and take one to 1½ hours to reach Ban Sala Dan; the fare is 150B. In the reverse direction boats leave at 8 am and 1 pm.

**Ban Baw Meuang** You can also take a boat from Ban Baw Meuang, which is about 35 km from Ban Huay Nam Khao at the end of Route 4042 (about 80 km in total from Krabi). The turn-off for Route 4042 is at Km 46 near the village of Sai Khao. It's 13 km from Ban Sai Khao to Ban Baw Meuang on this dirt road. The boats from Ban Baw Meuang are fairly large, holding up to 80 people, and they take an hour to reach Samsan pier on Lanta Yai's eastern shore. This ferry departs daily at 12.30 and 2 pm; the fare is 40B per person.

**Ko Phi Phi** During the dry season, October to April, there is one boat a day from Ko Phi Phi at 1 pm for 150B per person. They take about an hour and 20 minutes to reach Ban Sala Dan; in the opposite direction boats leave Ko Lanta around 8 am. There are also occasional boats to Lanta from Ko Jam.

### Getting Around
Most of the bungalows on Ko Lanta will provide free transport to and from Ban Sala Dan. Motorcycle taxis are available from Ban Sala Dan to almost anywhere along the beaches for 10 to 40B depending on the distance. From Ban Ko Lanta, motorcycle taxi fares fall in the same range.

Motorcycles can be rented in Ban Sala Dan for a steep 250B a day.

# Trang Province

The province of Trang has a geography similar to that of Krabi and Phang-Nga, with islands and beaches along the coast and lime-stone-buttressed mountains inland, but is much less frequented by tourists. Caves and waterfalls are the major attractions in the interior of the province – Trang seems to have more than its share.

Twenty km north of the capital is a 3500 rai (5.6 sq km) provincial park, which preserves a tropical forest in its original state. In the park there are three waterfalls and government rest houses. To the north is Thaleh Song Hong (Sea of Two Rooms), a large lake surrounded by limestone hills. Hills in the middle of the lake nearly divide it in half, hence the name.

## TRANG
อ.เมืองตรัง
• ☎ (75) • pop 49,400
Historically, Trang has played an important role as a centre of trade since at least the 1st century AD. It was especially important between the 7th and 12th centuries, when it was a sea port for ocean-going sampans sailing between Trang and the Straits of Malacca. Nakhon Si Thammarat and Surat Thani were major commercial and cultural centres for the Srivijaya empire at this time, and Trang served as a relay point for communications and shipping between the east coast of the Thai peninsula and Palembang, Sumatra. Trang was then known as Krung Thani and later as Trangkhapura (City of Waves), until the name was shortened during the early years of the Ratanakosin period.

During the Ayuthaya period, Trang was a common port of entry for seafaring western visitors, who continued by land to Nakhon Si Thammarat or Ayuthaya. The town was then located at the mouth of the Trang River, but King Mongkut later gave orders to move the city to its present location inland because of frequent flooding. Today Trang is still an important point of exit for rubber from the province's many plantations.

### Post & Communications
The GPO and the telephone office are on the corner of Phra Ram VI and Kantang Rds.

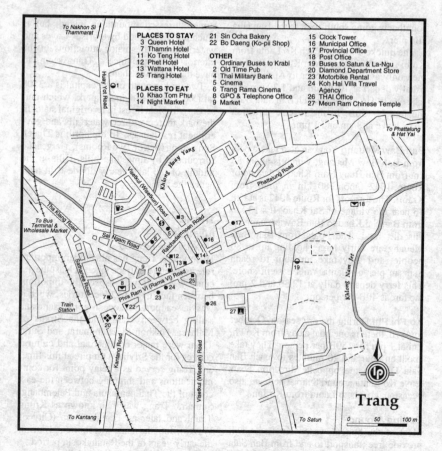

**PLACES TO STAY**
3  Queen Hotel
7  Thamrin Hotel
11  Ko Teng Hotel
12  Phet Hotel
13  Wattana Hotel
25  Trang Hotel

**PLACES TO EAT**
10  Khao Tom Phui
14  Night Market

21  Sin Ocha Bakery
22  Bo Daeng (Ko-pii Shop)

**OTHER**
1  Ordinary Buses to Krabi
2  Old Time Pub
4  Thai Military Bank
5  Cinema
6  Trang Rama Cinema
8  GPO & Telephone Office
9  Market

15  Clock Tower
16  Municipal Office
17  Provincial Office
18  Post Office
19  Buses to Satun & La-Ngu
20  Diamond Department Store
23  Motorbike Rental
24  Koh Hai Villa Travel
    Agency
26  THAI Office
27  Meun Ram Chinese Temple

**Trang**

0    50    100 m

## Things to See

Trang's main attractions are the nearby beaches and islands, plus the fact that it can be reached by train. Among Thais, one of Trang's claims to fame is that it often wins awards for 'Cleanest City in Thailand' – its main rival in this regard is Yala. One odd aspect of the city is the seeming lack of Thai Buddhist temples. Most of those living in the central business district are Chinese, so you do see a few joss houses but that's about it. Meun Ram, a Chinese temple between sois 1 and 2, Visetkul Rd, sometimes sponsors performances of Southern Thai shadow theatre.

## Places to Stay

A number of hotels are found along the city's two main thoroughfares, Phra Ram VI Rd and Visetkul (Wisetkun) Rd, which run from the clock tower. The long-running *Ko Teng* on Phra Ram VI Rd recently closed due to an illness in the family and it's not certain whether it will reopen. If it does, count on large singles/doubles for a reasonable 140/200B, and a good restaurant downstairs. This was one of the main sources of information on what to see and do around Trang, so it will be a shame if it doesn't reopen.

The *Wattana Hotel* (☎ 218184), on the

**Trang Festivals**

At nearby Hat Jao Mai, a unique sailboat regatta is held on the first weekend of May. This one differs from the usual Phuket affair in that only wooden sailboats of the traditional Andaman Sea type may enter. These boats feature square or triangular sails dyed with natural pigments from the *samèt* or cajeput tree. In addition to the races, events include live musical and theatrical performances, including lí-khe pàa and nǎng thálung.

The Vegetarian Festival is also celebrated fervently in Trang in September or October (see the Phuket section for details on this festival). ∎

same street, offers upgraded rooms for 230 to 280B with fan and bath or 430/480B for air-con.

Over on Ratchadamnoen Rd is the inexpensive *Phet Hotel* (☎ 218002), with fair rooms with fan and shared bath for 80B, or with attached bath for 100 to 150B. They also have a restaurant downstairs.

On Visetkul Rd are the *Queen Hotel* (☎ 218522), with large clean rooms with fan for 230B, or 350B with air-con, and the business-like *Trang Hotel* (☎ 218944), near the clock tower, with upgraded fan-cooled rooms for 450B or air-con from 500B.

The 10-storey *Thamrin* (☎ 211011; fax 218057) is an up-market place on Kantang Rd near the train and bus stations. Modern air-con rooms cost 600B standard, 900B deluxe, not including tax and service.

**Kantang** If you happen to become stranded in nearby Kantang waiting for a boat to Hat Jao Mao or the islands, there are three inexpensive places to stay. *Siri Chai Hotel* (☎ 251172), on the main road leading to the port from the train station, has small but fairly clean singles for 140B, doubles for 240B – or you can have a room for two hours for 100B!

Near the main market near the waterfront, *JT Hotel* (☎ 251755) has fan rooms for 200B, air-con for 300B. *Chula Pah Guest House* (☎ 251318), about a half km north of the main intersection, near the harbourmaster station, costs 250B for a very clean fan room, 350B with air-con.

**Places to Eat**

Plenty of good restaurants can be found in the vicinity of the hotels. Next door to the Queen Hotel is the *Image Restaurant*, which has a very broad selection of rice and noodle dishes. *Nam Muy* is a large Chinese restaurant opposite the old Ko Teng; although it looks fancy, the menu is medium-priced.

Two khâo tôm places on Phra Ram VI Rd, *Khao Tom Phui* and *Khao Tom Jai Awn*, serve all manner of Thai and Chinese standards in the evenings till 2 am. Phui has been honoured with the Shell Chuan Chim designation for its tôm yam (available with shrimp, fish or squid), sea bass in red sauce (plaa kraphõng náam daeng) and stir-fried greens in bean sauce (pûm pûy kha-náa fai daeng).

The *Muslim Restaurant* opposite the Thamrin Hotel on Phra Ram VI serves inexpensive roti kaeng, curries and rice. Diamond Department Store on the nearby corner has a supermarket on the 1st floor, and a small hawkers' centre on the third.

**Khanõm Jiin** Trang is famous for khanõm jiin (Chinese noodles with curry). One of the best places to try it is at the tables set up on the corner of Visetkul and Phra Ram VI Rds. You have a choice of dousing your noodles in náam yaa (a spicy ground fish curry), náam phrík (a sweet and slightly spicy peanut sauce), or kaeng tai plaa (a very spicy mixture of green beans, fish, bamboo shoots and potato). To this you can add your choice of fresh grated papaya, pickled veggies,

SOUTHERN THAILAND

cucumber and bean sprouts – all for just 8B per bowl.

Across the street from this vendor, in front of the municipal offices, is a small night market that usually includes a couple of khanõm jiin vendors.

**Ko-píi Shops** Trang is even more famous for its coffee and ráan kafae or ráan ko-píi (coffee shops), which are easily identified by the charcoal-fired aluminium boilers with stubby smokestacks seen somewhere in the middle or back of the open-sided shops. Usually run by Hokkien Chinese, these shops serve real filtered coffee (called kafae thũng in the rest of the country) along with a variety of snacks, typically paa-thông-kõ, salabao (Chinese buns), khanõm jìip (dumplings), Trang-style sweets, mũu yâang (barbecued pork) and sometimes noodles and jók (thick rice soup).

When you order coffee in these places, be sure to use the Hokkien word ko-píi rather than the Thai kafae, otherwise you may end up with Nescafé or instant Khao Chong coffee – the proprietors often think this is what farangs want. Coffee is usually served with milk and sugar – ask for ko-píi dam for sweetened black coffee or ko-píi dam, mâi sài náam-taan for black coffee without sugar.

The best ráan ko-píi in town are the Bo Daeng (open from 6 am till midnight), next to a Chinese clan house and Bangkok Bank on Phra Ram VI Rd near Kantang Rd, and Khao Ocha (open from 6 am to 8 pm) on Visetkul Rd Soi 5. Sin Ocha Bakery, on Kantang Rd near Phra Ram VI Rd and the train station, was once the queen of Trang coffee shops (under it's old name, Sin Jiaw), but was recently completely renovated and made into a modern cafe. Ko-píi is still available here, along with international pastries and egg and toast breakfasts.

**Entertainment**
Old Time Pub, off Huay Yot Rd a bit north of the town centre, is a cosy, air-con place with good service and no hassling from jii-khõh (Thailand's 'hoodlums'). The Relax Pub at 25/50 Huay Yot Rd is a dark, expensive place with the usual parade of Thai female singers.

**Things to Buy**
Trang is known for its wickerwork and, especially, mats woven of bai toei (pandanus leaves), which are called sèua paa-nan, or Panan mats. Panan mats are important bridal gifts in rural Trang, and are a common feature of rural households. The process of softening and drying the pandanus leaves before weaving takes many days. They can be purchased in Trang for about 100 to 200B.

The province also has its own distinctive cotton-weaving styles. The villages of Na Paw and Na Meun Si are the most highly regarded sources for these fabrics, especially the intricate diamond-shaped lai lûuk kâew pattern, once reserved for nobility.

The best place in town for good buys is the Tha Klang wholesale market along Tha Klang Rd.

**Getting There & Away**
**Air** THAI operates three flights weekly from Bangkok (2005B) and six from Phuket (435B). The Trang THAI office (☎ 218066) is at 199/2 Visetkul Rd. The airport is four km south of Trang; THAI runs shuttle vans back and forth for 50B per person.

**Bus & Share Taxi** A bus from Satun or Krabi to Trang is 37B; from Hat Yai it's 40B. A share taxi from the same cities is around 70B. Air-con buses from Krabi cost 70B and take three to four hours. From Phattalung it's 15B by bus, 30B by share taxi.

From Ban Huay Nam Khao, the junction for Highway 4 and the road to Ko Lanta, a bus to Trang is 25B.

Air-con buses to/from Bangkok are 375B (203B for an ordinary bus) or 565B for a VIP bus. The air-con buses take about 12 hours.

**Train** Only two trains go all the way from Bangkok to Trang, the rapid No 41, which leaves Hualamphong station at 6.30 pm, arriving in Trang at 9.55 am the next day, and the express No 13, which leaves Bangkok at

5.05 pm and arrives in Trang at 7.35 am. The fare is 597B 1st class, 282B 2nd class, not including rapid or express surcharges. There are no direct 3rd class trains to Trang; you must change in Thung Song, a rail junction town in Nakhon Si Thammarat Province. From Thung Song there are two trains daily to Trang, leaving at 9.30 am and 3.20 pm, arriving an hour and 45 minutes later.

If you want to continue on to Kantang on the coast, there is one daily ordinary train out of Trang at 5.02 pm which arrives in Kantang at 5.20 pm; the rapid No 41 also terminates in Kantang, arriving at 10.25 am. The fare from Trang to Kantang is 5B in 3rd class (5.02 pm train only) or 28B in 2nd class on the rapid No 41.

**Boat** At the harbour at nearby Kantang, Thai-Langkawi Ferry Line (☎ 251917) used to operate ferries back and forth to Pulau Langkawi, just across the border in Malaysia; at times the service has gone as far afield as Medan (Indonesia) and Singapore, but for the moment the only boat option is the ferry across the Trang River estuary to Tha Som. See the Beaches section next for details.

**Getting Around**
Samlors around town cost 10B per trip, tuk-tuks 20B.

Honda 100cc motorbikes can be rented from a shophouse (☎ 218473) at 44A Phra Ram VI Rd for 200B per day.

Big orange buses to the harbour at Kantang leave frequently from Kantang Rd in the vicinity of the station for 10B. There are also air-con minivans which do the same trip every hour or so for 20B each; a motorcycle taxi will cost 60 to 70B, but this is really too long a jaunt for a comfortable pillion ride.

**TRANG BEACHES**
Trang Province has several sandy beaches and coves along the coast, especially in the Sikao and Kantang districts. On Route 403 between Trang and Kantang is a turn-off west onto an unpaved road that leads down to the coast through some interesting Thai-

Muslim villages. At the end, it splits north and south. The road south leads to Hat Yao, Hat Yong Ling and Hat Jao Mai. The road north leads to Hat Chang Lang and Hat Pak Meng.

**Hat Jao Mai & Ko Libong**
หาดเจ้าไหมและเกาะลิบง
Hat Jao Mai and Ko Libong are in Kantang district, about 35 km from Trang. The wide white-sand beach of Hat Jao Mai is five km long and gets some of Thailand's biggest surf (probably the source of the Trang's original unshortened name, City of Waves). Hat Jao Mai is backed by casuarina trees and limestone hills with caves, some of which contain prehistoric human skeletal remains. **Tham Jao Mai** is the most interesting of the caves, a large cavern with lots of stalactites and stalagmites. In their only known appearance on the Thai-Malay peninsula, rare black-necked storks frequent Jao Mai to feed on molluscs and crustaceans.

This beach is part of the 231 sq km **Hat Jao Mai National Park**, which includes Hat Chang Lang farther north and the islands of Ko Muk, Ko Kradan, Ko Jao Mai, Ko Waen, Ko Cheuak, Ko Pling and Ko Meng. In this area the endangered dugong (also called manatees or sea cows) can sometimes be spotted.

**Places to Stay** Camping is permitted on Jao Mai and there are a few bungalows for rent as well. *Sinchai's Chao Mao Resort* (☎ (01) 464-4140) offers a couple of two room wooden cottages with shared facilities for 200B. Cheaper but no bargain are three 100B dilapidated huts. Bathing is done at a well. *Ban Chaom Talay* (☎ (01) 979-1540) near the pier for Ko Libong is being constructed by two Mahidol University professors who speak perfect English. They haven't set room rates yet but this will probably become a very good source of information on the area.

Off the coast here is **Ko Libong**, Trang's largest island. There are three fishing villages on the island, so boats from Kantang port are easy to get for the one hour trip. The Botanical Department maintains free shel-

**SOUTHERN THAILAND**

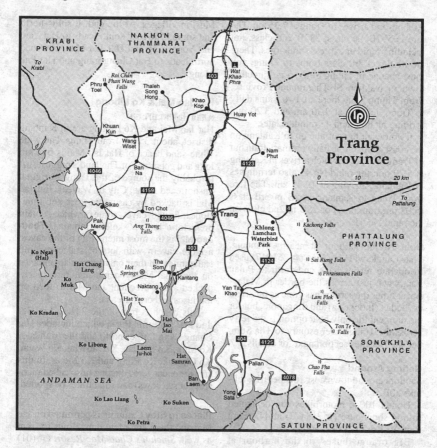

ters on Laem Ju-Hoi, a cape on the western tip of Ko Libong. On the south-western side of the island is a beach where camping is permitted. The *Libong Beach Resort* (☎ (75) 214676 in Trang) has A-frame thatched bungalows for 350 to 500B. About one km from the pier on Libong is the *Tongkran Bungalow* with basic huts for 50B.

**Getting There & Away** The best way to reach Hat Jao Mai by public transport is to catch a bus, train or taxi from Trang to Kantang harbour, then hop on one of the frequent ferries across to Tha Som on the opposite shore of the Trang River estuary. Tickets cost 1B for pedestrians, 5B for motorcycles, 12B car and 15B pickup; the ferry operates daily 6 am to 8 pm. From Som Tha there are frequent songthaews to Hat Jao Mai. A long-tail boat from the pier at Hat Jao Mai to Ko Libong costs just 20B.

### Hat Yong Ling & Hat Yao
หาดหยงหลิง/หาดยาว
A few km north of Hat Jao Mai are these two white-sand beaches separated by limestone cliffs. There is no accommodation here as yet.

SOUTHERN THAILAND

## Hat Chang Lang
หาดฉางหลาง

Hat Chang Lang is part of the Hat Jao Mai National Park, and this is where the park office is located. The beach is about two km long and very flat and shallow. At the northern end is Khlong Chang Lang, a stream that empties into the sea.

## Ko Muk & Ko Kradan
เกาะมุก/เกาะกระดาน

Ko Muk is nearly opposite Hat Chang Lang and can be reached by boat from Kantang or Pak Meng. The coral around Ko Muk is lively, and there are several small beaches on the island suitable for camping and swimming. The best beach, Hat Sai Yao, is on the opposite side of the island from the mainland and is nicknamed Hat Farang because it's 'owned' by a farang from Phuket.

Near the northern end is **Tham Morakot** (Emerald Cave), a beautiful limestone tunnel that can be entered by boat during low tide. At the southern end of the island is pretty Phangka Cove and the fishing village of Hua Laem.

Ko Kradan is the most beautiful of the islands that belong to Hat Jao Mai National Park. Actually, only five of six precincts on the island belong to the park: one is devoted to coconut and rubber plantation. There are fewer white-sand beaches on Ko Kradan than on Ko Muk, but the coral reef on the side facing Ko Muk is quite good for diving.

**Places to Stay & Eat** *Ko Muk Resort* (Trang office: 25/36 Sathanee Rd, next to the train station; ☎ (75) 212613), on Muk facing the mainland next to the Muslim fishing village of Hua Laem, has simple but nicely designed bungalows for 200B with shared bath, 250 to 300B with bath. The beach in front tends toward mud flats during low tide; the beach in front of the nearby village is slightly better but modest dress is called for. The resort organises boats to nearby islands like Ko Ngai, Waen, Kradan and Lanta. The newer *Morning Calm Resort* (☎ (01) 979-1543) on the opposite side of the island offers 50 bun-

galows, all with fan and attached bath, for 200 to 800B depending on size.

*Ko Kradan Resort* (☎ (75) 211391 in Trang; (2) 392-0635 in Bangkok) has OK bungalows and ugly cement shophouse-style rooms with fans and private bath for 700 to 900B a night and up. The beach isn't bad, but this resort still gets low marks for serving lousy, expensive food and for littering the area – a perfect example of the worst kind of beach resort development.

**Getting There & Away** The easiest place to get a boat to either Ko Muk or Ko Kradan is Kantang. Songthaews or vans from Trang to Kantang leave regularly and cost 10B. Once in Kantang you must charter another songthaew to the ferry pier for 20B, where you can get a regular long-tail boat to Ko Muk for 50B (or charter for 300B), to Ko Kradan for 100B or to Ko Libong for 25B (noon daily).

You can also get to the islands from Hat Pak Meng. There are two piers, one at the northern end of the beach and one at the southern end. Boats are more frequent from the southern pier, especially during the rainy season. Boats costs 30 to 60B per person to Ko Muk (depending on the number of passengers), 120B to Ko Kradan.

## Hat Pak Meng
หาดปากเมง

Thirty-nine km from Trang in Sikao district, north of Hat Jao Mai, Yao and Chang Lang, is another long, broad, sandy beach near the village of Ban Pak Meng. The waters are usually shallow and calm, even in the rainy season. A couple of hundred metres offshore are several limestone rock formations, including a very large one with caves. Several vendors and a couple of restaurants offer fresh seafood. There are unnamed brick bungalows for rent at 200 to 300B a night, plus the *Relax Parkmeng Resort* (☎ (75) 218940) with thatched bungalows in the 150 to 300B range and *Pakmeng Resort* (☎ (75) 210321) with sturdier bungalows with fan and bath for 300 to 500B.

Around the beginning of November, locals flock to Hat Pak Meng to collect *hãwy taphao*, a delicious type of clam. The tide reaches its lowest this time of year, so it's relatively easy to pick up the shells.

About halfway between Pak Meng and Trang, off Route 4046, is the 20m-high **Ang Thong Falls**.

**Getting There & Away** Take a van (20B) or songthaew (15B) to Sikao from Trang, and then a songthaew (10B) to Hat Pak Meng. There are also one or two direct vans daily to Pak Meng from Trang for 30B. A paved road now connects Pak Meng with the other beaches south, so if you have your own wheels there's no need to backtrack through Sikao.

**Hat Samran & Ko Sukon**
หาดสำราญและเกาะสุกร

Hat Samran is a beautiful and shady white-sand beach in Palian district, about 40 km south-west of Trang city. From the customs pier at nearby Yong Sata you should be able to get a boat to **Ko Sukon** (also called Ko Muu), an island populated by Thai Muslims, where there are more beaches.

*Sukon Island Resort* (☎ (75) 219679 in Trang; 211460 on the island) has bungalow accommodation for 200 to 500B a night.

**Ko Ngai (Hai)**
เกาะไหง(ไห)

This island is actually part of Krabi Province to the north, but is most accessible from Trang. It's a fairly small island, covering about 3000 rai (4.8 sq km), but the beaches are fine white sand and the water is clear. The resorts on the island operate half-day boat tours of nearby islands, including Morakot Cave on Ko Muk, for around 200B per person.

**Places to Stay** Along the east shore of Ko Ngai are two 'resorts'. Towards the middle of the island is *Koh Hai Villa* (☎ (75) 218029 in Trang; (2) 318-3107 in Bangkok), with fan-cooled bungalows for 300B a day and tents

for 150B. The vapid food here is overpriced, and the staff are surly.

At the southern end is *Ko Ngai Resort* (☎ (75) 210496 in Trang; (2) 246-4399 in Bangkok), where one-bed seaside huts cost 300B, double rooms in large bungalows are 600 to 900B and a six-bed bungalow is 1200B. Tents are also available for 150B.

You can book any of these through the Koh Hai Villa Travel Agency in Trang (☎ (75) 210496; (2) 246-4399 in Bangkok) at 112 Phra Ram VI Rd. Each resort has its own office in the city, but this one is the most conveniently located if you're staying in the central business district.

**Getting There & Away** Four boats a day leave from the southern pier at Pak Meng for 50B per person or charter for 300 to 500B.

**Ban Tung Laem Sai**

Ban Tung Laem Sai in Sikao district has an alternative homestay for visitors interested in ecotourism. The homestay is operated by Yat Fon, a local nonprofit organisation that promotes community development and environmental conservation. The staff can educate visitors about local mangroves, coral reefs, coastal resources and the Thai-Muslim way of life. No sunbathing or drinking is allowed in the vicinity. Contact Khun Suwit at Yat Fon, 105-107 Ban Pho Rd in Trang, for reservations and transport.

**WATERFALLS**

A lightly trafficked, paved road runs south from Highway 4 near the Trang-Phattalung border past a number of scenic waterfalls where the Trang and Palian rivers (or their tributaries) meet the Khao Banthat Mountains. **Ton Te Falls**, 46 km from Trang, is the loftiest. It's best seen during or just after the rainy season, say from September to November, when the 320m vertical waterfall reaches its fullest.

**Chao Pha Falls** in the Palian district near Laem Som has about 25 stepped falls of five to 10m each, with pools at every level. The semi-nomadic Sakai tribe are sometimes seen in this area.

Perhaps the most unusual waterfall in the province is **Roi Chan Phan Wang** (literally, 'Hundred Levels – Thousand Palaces'), about 70 km north-west of Trang in Wang Wiset district, a little-explored corner of the province. Surrounded by rubber groves, dozens of thin cascades of water tumble down limestone rock formations into pools below. The entire area is well shaded and a good spot for picnics. There is no public transport to the falls, however, and the road is none too good – motorcycle or jeep would be the best choice of transport.

### CAVES

A limestone cave in the north-eastern district of Huay Yot, **Tham Phra Phut**, contains a large Ayuthaya-period reclining Buddha. When the cave was rediscovered earlier this century, a cache of royal-class silverwork, nielloware, pottery and lacquerware was found hidden behind the image – probably stashed there during the mid-18th century Burmese invasion.

Also in this district, near the village of Ban Huay Nang, is **Tham Tra** (Seal Cave), with mysterious red seals carved into the cave walls which have yet to be explained by archaeologists. Similar symbols have been found in the nearby cave temple of **Wat Khao Phra**.

More easily visited is **Tham Khao Pina**, off Highway 4 between Krabi and Trang at Km 43, which contains a large, multilevel Buddhist shrine popular with Thai tourists. Another famous cave, **Tham Khao Chang Hai** near Na Meun Si village, Nayong district, contains large caverns with impressive interior formations.

### KHLONG LAMCHAN WATERBIRD PARK
อุทยานนกน้ำลำชาน

This large swampy area in the Nayong district, east of Trang, is an important habitat for several waterbird species – similar to Thaleh Noi or Khukhut in Songkhla Province. Accommodation is available.

# Satun Province

Bordering Malaysia, Satun (or Satul) is the west coast's southernmost province. Besides crossing the Malaysian border by land or sea, the principal visitor attractions are Ko Tarutao National Marine Park and Thaleh Ban National Park.

Before 1813 Satun was a district of the Malay state of Kedah: the name 'Satun' comes from the Malay *setul*, a type of tree common in this area. At the time Kedah, along with Kelantan, Trengganu and Perlis, paid tribute to Siam. The Anglo-Siamese Treaty of 1909 released parts of these states to Britain and they later became part of independent Malaysia.

### SATUN
อ.เมืองสตูล

• ☎ (74) • *pop 22,000*

Satun itself is not that interesting, but you may enter or leave Thailand here by boat via Kuala Perlis in Malaysia. Sixty km north-west of Satun is the small port of Pak Bara, the departure point for boats to Ko Tarutao.

As in Thailand's other three predominantly Muslim provinces (Yala, Pattani and Narathiwat), the Thai government has installed a loudspeaker system in the streets which broadcasts government programmes at 6 am and 6 pm (beginning with a wake-up call to work and ending with the Thai national anthem, for which everyone must stop and stand in the streets), either to instil a sense of nationalism in the typically rebellious Southern Thais, or perhaps to try and drown out the prayer calls and amplified sermons from local mosques. As in Pattani and Narathiwat, one hears a lot of Yawi spoken in the streets.

### Information

**Immigration** The relatively new Wang Prachan Customs complex at the Tammalang pier south of town contains an immigration office where anyone arriving or departing Satun to/from Malaysia by boat will have their

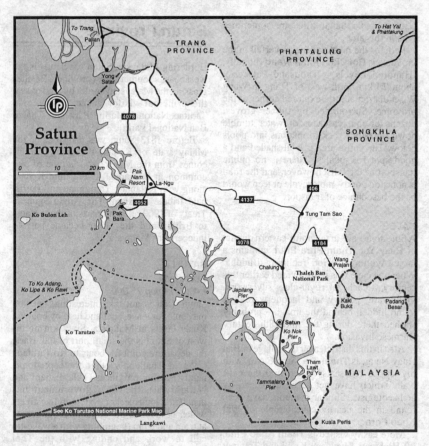

Satun Province

To Trang
Palian
TRANG PROVICE
Yong Satar
To Hat Yai & Phattalung
PHATTALUNG PROVINCE
4078
Satun Province
0   10   20 km
Pak Nam Resort
La-Ngu
SONGKHLA PROVINCE
406
4137
Tung Tam Sao
Ko Bulon Leh
4052
Pak Bara
4078
Chalung
4184
Wang Prajan
Thaleh Ban National Park
To Ko Adang, Ko Lipe & Ko Rawi
Jepilang Pier
4051
Kaki Bukit
Padang Besar
Ko Tarutao
Satun
Ko Nok Pier
Tham Lawt Pu Yu
MALAYSIA
Tammalang Pier
See Ko Tarutao National Marine Park Map
Langkawi
Kuala Perlis

papers processed. You can also use this office for visa extensions.

**Money** If you are going to Kuala Perlis in Malaysia, remember that banks on the east coast of Malaysia are not open on Thursday afternoon or Friday, due to the observance of Islam. If you're heading south at either of these times, be sure to buy Malaysian ringgit on the Thai side first so you won't be caught short on the Muslim sabbath.

**Post & Communications** The main post and telephone office is on the corner of Samanta Prasit and Satun Thani Rds.

### Khao Phaya Wang
เขาพญาวัง

If you find yourself with time to kill in Satun, you might consider a visit to the park along the western side of Khao Phaya Wang, a limestone outcropping next to Khlong Bambang. Steps lead up the vine-choked cliff on the khlong side of the Phaya Wang and at the top there are views of the winding green khlong, rice fields and coconut plantations. Pandan mats are available at the cool, bamboo-shaded picnic area next to the canal below. Vendors sell sôm-tam, khâo niãw, kài thâwt, kûng thâwt and miang kham.

### Places to Stay & Eat

The *Rain Tong Hotel (Rian Thong)* is at the end of Samanta Prasit Rd, next to the Rian Thong pier, where boats go to and from Malaysia. Large, clean rooms with ceiling fan and attached shower and toilet cost 100 to 150B. Near the municipal offices on Hatthakam Seuksa Rd is the two-storey *Udomsuk Hotel* (☎ 711006), with reason-

ably clean rooms with ceiling fan and attached bath for 120B single, 130B double. The *Satun Thani Hotel* near the centre of town is OK but noisy, with single fan rooms for 190B, double fan rooms for 250B, air-con for 290/390B.

At the up-market *Wang Mai Hotel* (☎ 711-607/8), near the northern end of town off Satun Thani Rd, all rooms come with air-con, carpeting, hot water and TV for 550/590B single/double, 650B for deluxe, or 1300B VIP.

The new *Sinkiat Thani Hotel* (☎ 721055; fax 721059) in the centre of town on Buriwanit

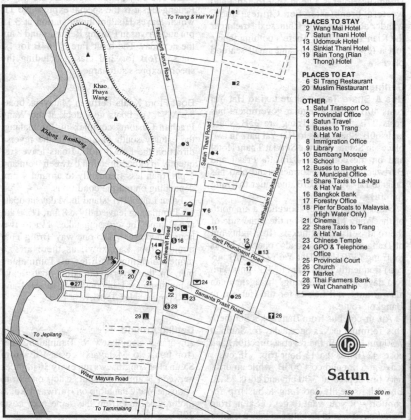

Rd has comfortable rooms similar to those at the Wang Mai but in better condition for 630B single/double.

Near the gold-domed Bambang Mosque in the centre of town are several cheap Muslim food shops, including the reliable *Suhana Restaurant*, almost opposite the mosque on Buriwanit Rd. Up on Satun Thani Rd across from the Satun Thani Hotel, *Si Trang* specialises in Southern Thai curries but it isn't Muslim. Roti kaeng and Malay-style curries are also available at a clean Muslim shop a few doors east of the Rian Thong Hotel.

A no-name coffee shop next to the Udomsuk Hotel is a good spot for Thai and western breakfasts. For Chinese food, wander about the little Chinese district near the Rian Tong Hotel. There's nothing fancy, just a few noodle shops and small seafood places.

### Getting There & Away
**Bus & Share Taxi** A share taxi to Hat Yai costs 40B, while a regular government bus costs 27B. Buses to Trang are 35B, share taxis 60B. Share taxis to Hat Yai park in two places in Satun, near the Sinkiat Thani Hotel and on the corner of Samanta Prasit and Buriwanit Rds. The former stand also has taxis to La-Ngu for 25B, the latter to Trang for 40B.

Satul Transport Co, about half a km north of the Wang Mai Hotel on the same side of the road, sells THAI tickets (for flights out of Trang or Hat Yai), and also operates buses to Trang (37B) and Hat Yai (27B, 30B air-con) frequently from 6 am to 4.30 pm. With two days advance booking, the agency can also arrange rail tickets for the Hat Yai to Bangkok route.

An air-con bus from Bangkok's Southern Bus Terminal leaves once a day for Satun at 7.30 pm (4 pm in the reverse direction) and costs 427B for the 15 hour trip. VIP buses leave at 6 pm and cost 500B, while an ordinary bus departs at 7.30 pm and costs 234B. But this is really too long a bus trip for comfort – if you want to get to Satun from Bangkok, it would be better to take a train to

Padang Besar on the Malaysian border and then a bus or taxi to Satun. Padang Besar is 60 km from Satun. See the following Train section.

A new highway between Satun and Perlis in Malaysia is still in the planning stages. If the proposal is approved by the Thai and Malaysian governments, the highway would cut travel time between the two towns but it would also unfortunately mean cutting through some of Southern Thailand's dwindling rainforest – many Thais have organised to protest the proposal.

**Train** The only train that goes all the way to Padang Besar is the special express No 11, which leaves Hualamphong station at 3.15 pm and arrives in Padang Besar around 8 am the next day. The basic fare is 744B for 1st class, 376B for 2nd class, including the special express surcharge.

**Boat** From Kuala Perlis in Malaysia, boats are M$4. All boats now dock at the Wang Prachan Customs complex in Tammalang, the estuary south of Satun. In the reverse direction the fare is 40B. Boats leave frequently in either direction between 9 am and 1 pm, than less frequently to around 4 pm, depending on marine conditions.

From Langkawi Island in Malaysia boats for Tammalang leave daily at 8 am, 11.30 am and 2 pm. The crossing takes 1½ to two hours and costs M$15 one way. Bring Thai money from Langkawi, as there are no moneychanging facilities at Tammalang pier. In the reverse direction boats leave Tammalang for Langkawi at 9.30 am, 1 and 3.30 pm and cost 150B.

### Getting Around
An orange songthaew to Tammalang pier (for boats to Malaysia) costs 10B from Satun. The songthaews run every 20 minutes between 8 am and 5 pm; catch one from opposite Wat Chanathip on Buriwanit Rd. A motorcycle taxi from the same area costs 20B.

## KO TARUTAO NATIONAL MARINE PARK

อุทยานแห่งชาติทางทะเลหมู่เกาะตะรุเตา

This park is actually a large archipelago of 51 islands, approximately 30 km from Pak Bara in La-Ngu district, which is 60 km north-west of Satun. Ko Tarutao, the biggest of the group, is only five km from Langkawi Island in Malaysia. Only five of the islands (Tarutao, Adang, Lipe, Rawi and Klang) have any kind of regular boat service to them, and of these, only the first three are generally visited by tourists.

The Forestry Department has been considering requests from private firms to build hotels and bungalows in Tarutao National Park. This would be a very unfortunate event if it means Ko Tarutao is going to become like Ko Phi Phi or Ko Samet, both of which are national parks that have permitted private development with disastrous results. So far nothing has transpired.

### Ko Tarutao

เกาะตะรุเตา

The park's namesake is about 151 sq km and features waterfalls, inland streams, beaches, caves and protected wildlife that includes dolphins, dugongs, sea turtles and lobster. Nobody lives on this island except for employees of the Forestry Department. The island was a place of exile for political prisoners between 1939 and 1947, and remains of the prisons can be seen near Ao Talo Udang on the southern tip of the island, and at Ao Talo Wao on the middle of the east coast. There is also a graveyard, charcoal furnaces and fermentation tanks for making fish sauce. Wildlife on the island includes dusky langur, mousedeer, wild pig, fishing cat and crab-eating macaque; dolphins and whales may be sighted offshore. Four types of sea turtle swim the surrounding waters – Pacific ridley, hawksbill, leatherback and green. All four lay eggs on the beaches here between September and April.

Tarutao's largest stream, Khlong Phante Malaka, enters the sea at the north-west tip of the island at Ao Phante; the brackish waters flow out of **Tham Jara-Khe** (Crocodile Cave – the stream was once inhabited by ferocious crocodiles, which seem to have disappeared). The cave extends for at least a km under a limestone mountain – no-one has yet followed the stream to the cave's end. The mangrove-lined watercourse should not be navigated at high tide, when the mouth of the cave fills.

The park pier, headquarters and bungalows are also here at Ao Phante Malaka. A 50B park fee is payable on arrival. The best camping is at the beaches of **Ao Jak** and **Ao San**, two bays south of park headquarters. For a view of the bays, climb Topu Hill, 500m north of the park office. There is also camping at Ao Makham (Tamarind Bay), at the south-west end of the island, about 2.5 km from another park office at Ao Talo Udang.

There is a road between Ao Phante Malaka, in the north, and Ao Talo Udang, in the south, of which 11 km was constructed by political prisoners in the 1940s, and 12 km was more recently constructed by the park division. The road is, for the most part, overgrown, but park personnel have kept a path open to make it easier to get from north to south without having to climb over rocky headlands along the shore.

**Ko Rang Nok** (Bird Nest Island), in Ao Talo Udang, is another trove of the expensive swiftlet nests craved by Chinese throughout the world. Good coral reefs are at the north-west part of Ko Tarutao at **Pha Papinyong** (Papillon Cliffs), at Ao San and in the channel between Ko Tarutao and Ko Takiang (Ko Lela) off the north-east shore.

### Ko Adang

เกาะอาดัง

Ko Adang is 43 km west of Tarutao, and about 80 km from Pak Bara. Ko Adang's 30 sq km are covered with forests and freshwater streams, which supply water year-round. Green sea turtles lay their eggs here between September and December. At **Laem Son** (Pine Cape), on the southern tip of the island where the pier and park office are located, visitors can stay in a thatched longhouse. Camping is also allowed. The restaurant is a

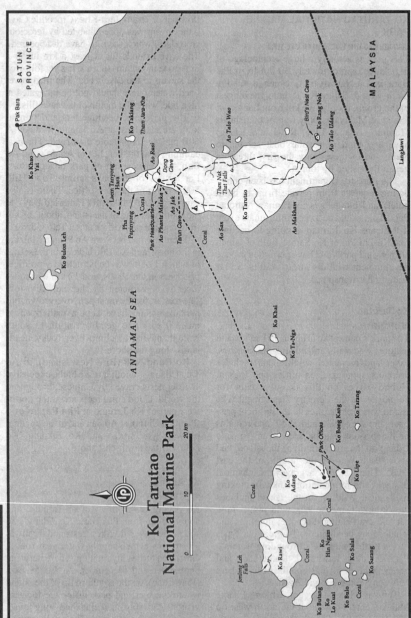

little expensive considering the low quality of the food served – but then considering the transport problems, perhaps not. As on Tarutao, it's a good idea to bring some food of your own from the mainland.

An interesting hike can be undertaken along the island's west coast to a pretty beach two km from the park station. Inland a little way from the beach is a waterfall once – perhaps still – used by passing pirate ships as a freshwater source. Around on the east coast, three km from Laem Son, is another waterfall and the chao náam village of **Talo Puya**.

## Ko Rawi & Ko Lipe
เกาะราวี/เกาะลิเป

Ko Rawi is just east of Ko Adang, and a bit smaller. Off the west coast of Ko Adang, and the south-east coast of Ko Rawi, are coral reefs with many live species of coral and tropical fish.

Ko Lipe is immediately south of Ko Adang and is inhabited by about 500 chao náam (*orang rawot* or *orang laut* in Malay) who are said to have originated on the Lanta islands in Krabi Province. They subsist on fishing and some cultivation of vegetables and rice on the flatter parts of the island. One can camp here, or rent a hut from the chao náam for 100 to 200B a night at any of several bungalow operations in or near the main village along the east coast. There is a coral reef along the southern side of the small island and several small beachy coves. The chao náam can provide boat hire to nearby islets ringed by coral reefs. For some reason the chao náam on this island prefer to be called 'chao leh' – a term despised by other Moken on islands to the north, who prefer the term chao náam. They also go by the term Thai Mai (New Thai).

Between Ko Tarutao and Ko Adang-Rawi is a small cluster of three islands called **Mu Ko Klang** (Middle Island Group), where there is good snorkelling. One of the islands, Ko Khai, also has a good white-sand beach. Boats from Ko Tarutao take about 40 minutes to reach Ko Khai.

## Other Islands

**Ko Kabeng**, a 10 minute boat ride from Pak Bara, is of mild interest. The beaches here are often littered and murky, so it's basically just a convenient place to stay in Pak Bara, but if you have time to kill visit the charcoal factory at Khlong La-Ngu or check out the cashew orchards. Pak Nam Resort can also arrange boat trips to other, more pristine islands in the area, or if you speak enough Thai you could hire a fishing boat directly from Ko Kabeng's little harbour at the fishing village of Ban Jet Luk.

Twenty-two islands stretching between Ko Kabeng and the boundaries of Ko Tarutao belong to the little-visited, 495-sq-km **Ko Phetra National Marine Park**. Uninhabited **Ko Khao Yai**, the largest in the group, boasts several pristine beaches suitable for swimming and snorkelling. Crab-eating macaques are plentiful here (local Muslims don't hunt them). There's a castle-shaped rock formation on one shore; during low tide boats can pass beneath a natural arch in the formation. The park headquarters is on nearby **Ko Lidi**, which features a number of picturesque and unspoiled caves, coves, cliffs and beaches. Camping facilities are available here. Between Ko Lidi and Ko Khao Yai is a channel bay known as Ao Kam Pu, a tranquil passage with cascading waters during certain tidal changes and some coral at shallow depths.

## Places to Stay & Eat

Officially the park is only open from November to May. Visitors who show up on the islands during the monsoon season can stay in park accommodation, but they must transport their own food from the mainland unless staying with the chao náam on Ko Lipe.

Bungalows may be booked in advance at the park office in Pak Bara (☎ (74) 711383; no English spoken) or through the Forestry Department (☎ (2) 579-0529) in Bangkok. For Ko Tarutao and/or Ko Adang, bring as much of your own food as you can from Satun or Pak Bara – the park restaurants are expensive and not very good.

SOUTHERN THAILAND

**Ko Tarutao** Park accommodation on Ko Tarutao costs 400B for a large 'deluxe' two room bungalow sleeping four, or 600B for cottages that sleep up to six people. A four-bed room in a longhouse goes for 280B. Full rates for all rooms and bungalows must be paid even if only one person takes a bed. Tent camping (bring your own) is permitted at Ao San and Ao Jak for 10B per person.

**Ko Adang** At Laem Son a bed in a privately owned longhouse costs 40B per person, while two-person bungalows are 200B. A small restaurant provides basic meals and sundries; it's closed in the rainy season. You can pitch your own tent for 10B.

**Ko Lipe** On Ko Lipe you have a choice of places to stay and eat among the chao náam, although it's starting to become more difficult as the chao náam are being pushed from the beaches into the jungle by Chinese businesspeople who are developing the beaches for tourism.

There are several places to stay, including the *Pattaya Beach Bungalow* where a room in a bamboo longhouse costs 100B with shared facilities, 200 to 270B with attached toilet. *Shaolea* has a longhouse with rooms for 50/80B single/double as well as 150B huts with shared bath, 200B with attached bath.

Another choice is the larger *Lipe Island Resort* with bungalows for 70B shared bath, 220 to 400B with private bath. Under construction is the new *Seaview Bungalows* near Pattaya Beach Bungalows, which will have small bamboo bungalows for 100B, larger ones for 150B.

**Pak Bara & La-Ngu** There is some accommodation in these jumping-off points for the park. In Pak Bara, *Andrew's Guest House* has simple rooms with shared bath for 50B. Just over a km before the pier in Pak Bara, along the shore among the casuarina trees, are the *Marina Bungalows, Suan Som Bungalows, Saengthien Bungalows, Krachomsai Bungalows* and *Ban Sontong Bungalows*, all with huts for around 120 to 200B a night.

A 10 minute, 10B boat ride north of Pak Bara, on rocky, palm-fringed Ko Kabeng, the quiet *Pak Nam Resort* (☎ (74) 781129) offers beds (mattresses on the floor) in a longhouse for 100B per person and thatched A-frame bungalows for 180 to 260B.

Pak Nam Resort and Marina Bungalows have the best food of all the Pak Bara lodgings. There are several foodstalls near the Pak Bara pier that do fruit shakes and seafood.

La-Ngu has a couple of cheap hotels on its main street, but Pak Bara has a much better atmosphere.

### Getting There & Away – Ko Tarutao

**Pak Bara** Boats to Tarutao leave regularly between November and April from the pier in Pak Bara, 60 km north-west of Satun and 22 km from Ko Tarutao. During the rest of the year boat service is irregular, since the park is supposedly closed. Satun Province officials have discussed constructing a new pier in Tan Yong Po district, nearer Satun, that will serve tourist boats to Tarutao and other islands, possibly on a year-round basis.

For now, boats leave Pak Bara for Tarutao in season daily at 10.30 am and 3 pm. The return fare is 200B, one way 100B, and it takes one to two hours, depending on the boat. Food and beverages are available on the boat. Departures back to Pak Bara are at 9 am and 2 pm.

I recommend buying one way tickets for each segment of your journey because there is more than one boat company handling these routes and they don't always recognise one another's tickets (they claim they do, but that's another story). Also if the boat you have a ticket for doesn't make it to the islands due to bad weather or an engine mishap, you won't have to worry about getting a refund for both tickets. Some companies will refuse to refund an unused return ticket; Charan Tours has a particularly bad reputation in this regard. If you have a choice, go with Andrew Tour.

There are also occasional tour boats out to Tarutao, but these are usually several hundred baht per person, as they include a guided tour, meals etc. Your final alternative is to charter a boat with a group of people. The cheapest are the hang yao (long-tail boats), which can take eight to 10 people out from Pak Bara's commercial pier for 800B. On holidays, boats may travel back and forth to Tarutao every hour or so to accommodate the increased traffic.

**Other Piers** It is also possible to hire boats to Ko Tarutao from three different piers on the coast near Satun. The nearest is the Ko Nok pier, four km south of Satun (40 km from Tarutao). Then there is the Tammalang pier, nine km from Satun, on the opposite side of the estuary from Ko Nok pier. Tammalang is 35 km from Tarutao. Finally there's the Jepilang pier, 13 km east of Satun (30 km from Tarutao); this one seems most geared to boat charters.

### Getting There & Away – Ko Adang & Ko Lipe

On Tuesday, Thursday and Saturday (November to May), a boat leaves Pak Bara at 10.30 am for Ko Adang and Ko Lipe, with a stop at Ko Tarutao along the way, for 280B each way. The boat continues on from Ko Tarutao to Adang and Lipe at 12.30 pm, arriving at the Ko Adang pier around 3 pm, for 180B each way. The following day (Wednesday, Friday and Sunday) the boat starts out from Ko Lipe at 9 am. A one way ticket costs 360B, return 560B. Since there is no pier at Ko Lipe, you must take a one minute long-tail boat ride from the larger boat; sometimes there's an extra 20B charge for this.

### Getting There & Away – Pak Bara

To get to Pak Bara from Satun, you must take a share taxi or bus to La-Ngu, then a songthaew on to Pak Bara. Taxis to La-Ngu leave from in front of the defunct Thai Niyom Hotel when there are enough people to fill a taxi for 25B per person. Buses leave frequently from in front of the public library along the same road and they cost 15B. From La-Ngu, songthaew rides to Pak Bara are 8B and terminate right at the harbour; you can

take a motorcycle taxi this same distance for 20B.

From Hat Yai, there are three daily buses to La-Ngu and Pak Bara which cost 34B and take 2½ hours. If you miss one of the direct La-Ngu buses, you can also hop on any Satun-bound bus to the junction town of Chalung (20B, 1½ hours), which is about 15 km short of Satun, then get a songthaew north on Route 4078 for the 10B, 45 minute trip to La-Ngu. Or take a share taxi from Hat Yao to La-Ngu for 50B; there is also a mini-van service from Hat Yai for 50B, a better deal since it goes all the way to Pak Bara.

You can also travel to La-Ngu from Trang by songthaew for 30B, or by share taxi for 50B.

## KO BULON LEH
เกาะบุโหลนแล

Approximately 20 km west of Pak Bara is the small island group of Ko Bulon, of which the largest island is Ko Bulon Leh. Though considerably smaller than the major islands of Ko Tarutao, Bulon Leh shares many of the geographical characteristics, including sandy beaches and coral reefs. Aside from the beach in front of Pansand Resort on the east shore, one of the best coral sites can be found along the north-east side of the island. There are some small villages in the northern part of the island near Ao Pangka. Nearby Ko Bulon Don sports a chao leh village and some nice beaches, but no accommodation so far. Ko Bulon Mai Phai further out is uninhabited and pristine.

*Pansand Resort* (☎ (01) 722-0279) has A-frame bungalows on Bulon Leh's best beach costing 80/100B in a simple hut with shared bath, 200/250B for a larger hut with fan, 650 to 800B for better bungalows with deck and private bath. There's also a dorm for 70B per bed. Two-person tents can be hired for 60B or you can pitch your own for 10B. Facilities include badminton, volleyball, table tennis and boats for hire. Pansand can also arrange boat trips to nearby uninhabited islands in both Ko Tarutao National Marine Park and Ko Phetra National Marine

Park. More information is available from First Andaman Travel (☎ (75) 218035; fax 211010), 82-84 Visetkul Rd in Trang (opposite the Queen Hotel).

*Bulon Leh Bungalows*, on the north-east shore close to Pansand, and *Pangka Bay Resort* on the north shore offer similar bungalows for 100 to 200B. *Moronay* reputedly has the best food on the island, including good seafood. *Jeb's*, behind Moronay, runs a small shop with basic necessities and a small cafe with Thai and western food.

### Getting There & Away

Boats to Ko Bulon Leh depart from the Pak Bara pier at 2 pm and cost 100B per person round trip. The trip takes an hour and a half each way. On the return, boats usually leave Bulon Leh at 9 am.

## THALEH BAN NATIONAL PARK
อุทยานแห่งชาติทะเลบัน

This 196 sq km park on the Thailand-Malaysia border encompasses the best preserved section of white meranti rainforest (named for the dominant species of dipterocarp trees) on either side of the border. Although the forest straddles the border, the Malaysian side is becoming steadily deforested by agricultural development. The terrain is hilly, with a maximum elevation of 740m at Khao Chin. The area east of Highway 4184 is primary forest on granitic rock reaching up to 700m high; there are many small streams in this section.

The park headquarters, situated on a 100 rai lake in a valley formed by limestone outcroppings, is only two km from the border. Five km north of the office and only 500m off Highway 4184 is **Yaroi Falls**, a 700m, nine-tiered waterfall with pools suitable for swimming. Climb the limestone cliffs next to the park buildings for a view of the lake and surrounding area. A network of trails leads to a number of other waterfalls and caves in the park, including **Rani Falls, Ton Pliw Falls, Chingrit Falls, Ton Din Cave** and **Pu Yu Tunnel Cave (Tham Lawt Pu Yu)**. Rangers will guide you along the trails

for a small fee but little English is spoken. To the west the park extends all the way to the Andaman Sea to a beach and mangrove area just two km south of the Wang Prachan Customs complex.

Wildlife found within park boundaries tends to be of the Sundaic variety, which includes species generally found in Peninsular Malaysia, Sumatra, Borneo and Java. Common mammals include mouse deer, serow, tapir, various gibbons and macaques. Some of the rare bird species found here are the great argus hornbill, rhinoceros hornbill, helmeted hornbill, banded and bluewing pitta, masked finfoot, dusky crag martin and black Baza hawk. Honey bears and wild pigs are commonly seen near the park headquarters and up in the limestone are 150 cm monitor lizards and 40 cm tree geckos. More elusive residents include clouded leopard and dusky leaf langur.

On Sunday morning a border market selling produce, clothing and housewares convenes along both sides of the border; you're permitted to cross free of visa formalities for this occasion.

The park entrance is about 37 km east of Satun's provincial capital or 90 km south of Hat Yai via Route 406 and Route 4184; coming from Malaysia it's about 75 km from Alor Setar. The best time to visit is from December to March, between seasonal monsoons. It can rain any time of year here but the heaviest and longest rains generally fall in July, August, October and November. In January and February nights can be quite cool.

### Places to Stay & Eat

Near the park office (☎ (74) 797073; (2) 579-0529 in Bangkok) beside the lake are longhouses sleeping six to 20 people for 500 to 800B per night. If you're in a group of less than six people and accommodation isn't already booked you can stay in these bungalows for 100B per person. It costs 5B per person to set up your own tent.

The park restaurant provides a nice view of the lake and simple Thai food for 30 to 50B per meal. It's open 8 am to 8 pm daily.

Next to the restaurant is a small shop with a few toiletries and snacks.

### Getting There & Away
The park is about 40 km from Satun in *tambon* Khuan Sataw. Take a songthaew or share taxi from near the Rian Tong Hotel in Satun to Wang Prajan on Route 4184 for 20B. Wang Prajan is just a few km from the park entrance. Sometimes these vehicles might take you to the park gate, otherwise you can hitch or hop on one of the infrequent songthaews from Wang Prajan into the park. If you're coming from Hat Yai you can also pick these songthaews up in Chalung; some are marked 'Thale Ban-Wangprachan' in English.

A songthaew leaves from the entrance nearly every hour from 8 am until 1 pm to Chalung and Hat Yai.

# Yala Province

Yala is the most prosperous of the four predominantly Muslim provinces in Southern Thailand, mainly due to income from rubber production. It is also the number one business and education centre for the region.

## YALA
อ.เมืองยะลา
• ☎ (73) • *pop 68,500*
The fast-developing capital is sometimes known as 'the cleanest city in Thailand' and has won awards to that effect several times in the last 25 years (its main competitor is Trang). It's a city of parks, wide boulevards and orderly traffic.

One of the biggest regional **festivals** in Thailand is held in Yala during the last six days of June to pay respect to the city guardian spirit, Jao Phaw Lak Meuang. Chinese New Year is also celebrated here with some zest, as there are many Chinese living in the capital. The Muslim population is settled in the rural areas of the province, for the most part, though there is a sizeable Muslim quarter near the train station in town – you'll know it by the sheep and goats wandering in the streets and by the modern mosque – one of Yala's tallest buildings and the largest mosque in Thailand.

### Information
The post & telephone office on Sirirot Rd offers international telephone service daily from 8 am to 10 pm.

### Things to See & Do
During the dry season there are nightly musical performances in Chang Pheuak Park, in the south-east part of the city just before the big Lak Meuang (City Pillar) roundabout, off Pipitpakdee Rd. **Phrupakoi Park**, just west of the roundabout, has a big artificial lake where people can fish, go boating and eat in floating restaurants. Yala residents seem obsessed with water recreation, possibly as a consequence of living in the only land-locked province in the entire South. There is a public swimming pool in town at the Grand Palace restaurant and disco.

### Places to Stay – bottom end & middle
Yala has quite a few hotels at low to moderate price levels. In the town centre are lots of old Chinese hotels – like Hat Yai in the old days. Starting from the bottom, the *Shanghai Hotel* at 36-34 Ratakit Rd and *Saen Suk* are nearly identical Chinese hotels with Chinese restaurants on the ground floor. Both are on the same block on Ratakit Rd, in the business district not far from the train station. They have somewhat dreary rooms from 80B and 70B respectively; the Saen Suk is a bit cleaner, and its restaurant is also better, specialising in generous plates of chicken rice (khâo man kài) for 15B. Next door to the Shanghai, the *Muang Thong Hotel* is similar. Nearby, on the other side of Ratakit Rd, the *Metro Hotel* at No 7/1-2 has better rooms for 80 to 150B and a better restaurant downstairs.

The *Hawaii* and *Aun Aun* hotels, on Pipitpakdee Rd, are the first hotels you see as you walk into town from the train station.

SOUTHERN THAILAND

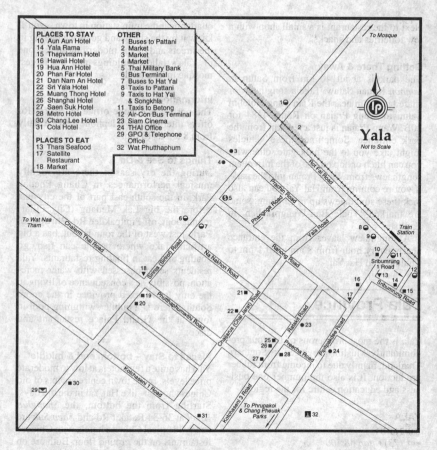

**PLACES TO STAY**
10  Aun Aun Hotel
14  Yala Rama
15  Thepvimarn Hotel
16  Hawaii Hotel
19  Hua Ann Hotel
20  Phan Far Hotel
21  Dan Nam An Hotel
22  Sri Yala Hotel
25  Muang Thong Hotel
26  Shanghai Hotel
27  Saen Suk Hotel
28  Metro Hotel
30  Chang Lee Hotel
31  Cola Hotel

**PLACES TO EAT**
13  Thara Seafood
17  Satellite
     Restaurant
18  Market

**OTHER**
1  Buses to Pattani
2  Market
3  Market
4  Market
5  Thai Military Bank
6  Bus Terminal
7  Buses to Hat Yai
8  Taxis to Pattani
9  Taxis to Hat Yai
    & Songkhla
11  Taxis to Betong
12  Air-Con Bus Terminal
23  Siam Cinema
24  THAI Office
29  GPO & Telephone
     Office
32  Wat Phutthaphum

Yala
Not to Scale

The Hawaii is OK at 150B, but the Aun Aun is more economical at 90B without bath, 120B with. The manager at Aun Aun also speaks good English. Another central cheapie, the *Dan Nam An* (no English sign) on Na Nakhon Rd, costs 80B single/double but it's not very well kept.

Over on Sirirot Rd are two newer side-by-side Chinese hotels, the *Hua Ann Hotel* and the *Phan Far Hotel*, both with clean, sizeable rooms with fan and private bath in the 130 to 170B range; the Hua Ann also has air-con rooms for 260B. Both hotels have coffee shops downstairs in the typical layout.

The *Thepvimarn Hotel* (☎ 212400), a left turn from the station on Sribumrung (Si Bamrung) Rd, across from the Yala Rama, is the best value in this range. It's a friendly place, with clean, large rooms with fan and bath for 180B, or 370B with air-con. On Kotchaseni 1 Rd, the *Cola Hotel* has 170/200B rooms (250B air-con) similar to those at the Thepvimarn.

The *Sri Yala Hotel* (☎ 212815) at 18-22 Chai Jarat Rd (the street sign says 'Chaijarus') offers clean rooms for 180B single/double with fan, 240/340B air-con, plus a restaurant and a popular coffee shop.

SOUTHERN THAILAND

## Places to Stay – top end

The *Yala Rama* (☎ 212563; fax 214532) stands at 21 Sribumrung Rd near the air-con bus terminal. A room with fan and bath goes for 300B, while air-con rooms are 500B. All rooms have two beds. The coffee shop and nightclub here are quite popular.

The plush *Chang Lee Hotel* (☎ 211223; fax 211773) on Sirirot Rd just north of the post office, was only partially completed when I visited but was already renting rooms at a soft opening rate of 900B. When finished rooms will cost 1300B standard, 1600B superior; all rooms come with air-con, carpeting, hot water, TV and phone. Facilities include a swimming pool (not finished yet), business centre, karaoke, nightclub and coffee shop.

## Places to Eat

There are plenty of inexpensive places to eat in central Yala near all the hotels, especially Chinese restaurants along Ratakit and Ranong Rds.

The popular *Thara Restaurant* (no English sign) at the corner of Pipitpakdee and Sribamrung Rds serves excellent seafood at moderate prices. House specialities include kûng phǎo (grilled prawns) and plaa òp bai toei (fish baked in pandanus leaves). The *Suay Suay* indoor/outdoor restaurant, on Sribumrung Rd near the Yala Rama Hotel, and the big *Satellite* restaurant, on the corner of Pipitpakdee and Ranong Rds, specialise in steamed cockles. In the morning Satellite also does good jók and Chinese dumplings.

The day market on Sirirot Rd has a good selection of fresh fruit. The Muslim foodstalls nearby serve roti kaeng in the early morning – a cheap and filling breakfast.

## Getting There & Away

**Air** The nearest commercial airport is in Narathiwat, on the coast south-east of Yala. Although THAI doesn't serve Yala, they maintain a ticket office almost opposite Bangkok Bank at 91 Pipitpakdee Rd.

**Bus & Share Taxi** Air-con buses between Bangkok and Yala are 460B, VIPs are 530 to 715B and ordinary buses cost 255B for the 16 hour haul. In Yala long-distance buses leave from a small terminal near the Thepvimarn and Yala Rama hotels.

Buses to/from Pattani cost 12B for the one hour trip. Buses south to Sungai Kolok or Pattani leave from Sirorot Rd, north of the train tracks. An ordinary bus to Kolok is only 14B but takes three to 3½ hours.

Short to medium-distance buses north (to Hat Yai etc) leave from Sirirot Rd, south of the train tracks. Buses to/from Hat Yai cost 41B and take 2½ hours; by share taxi or air-con minivan the trip is 60B and takes two hours.

There are several share-taxi stands in the vicinity of Yala's train station; some of them offer services to the same places, some differ. Just wander around this area and the drivers and their touts will find you. Other share-taxi possibilities include Sungai Kolok (70B), Betong (70B), Pattani (25B) and Narathiwat (45B).

**Train** The rapid No 45 leaves Bangkok daily at 1.30 pm and arrives in Yala at 8.14 am the next day. The special express No 19 leaves at 2.35 pm and arrives at 8.35 am. Fares are 346B 2nd class, 738B 1st class, not including air-con (mandatory on the special express) and rapid or special express surcharges.

From Hat Yai, ordinary trains are 23B for 3rd class and take 2½ hours. From Sungai Kolok, at the Malaysian border, trains are 22B for a 2½ hour trip. To/from Surat Thani the 3rd class fare is 91B.

## AROUND YALA
## Wat Naa Tham
วัดหน้าถ้ำ

Outside town, about eight km west off the Yala-Hat Yai highway, is Wat Khuhaphimuk (also called Wat Naa Tham – the Cave-Front Temple), a Srivijaya-period cave temple established around 750 AD. Inside the cave is Phra Phutthasaiyat, a long, reclining Buddha image sculpted in the Srivijaya style. For Thais, this is one of the three most venerated Buddhist pilgrimage points in Southern Thailand (the other two are Wat Boromathat in Nakhon Si Thammarat and Wat Phra Boromathat Chaiya in Surat Thani). There is a small museum in front of the cave, with artefacts of local provenance.

To get there, take a songthaew going west towards the town of Yaha via Route 4065, and ask to get off at the road to Wat Naa Tham – the fare is 3B. It's about a one km walk to the wat from the highway.

Two km past Wat Naa Tham is **Tham Silpa**, a well known cave with Buddhist polychrome murals from the Srivijaya era as well as prehistoric monochromatic paintings of primitive hunters. A monk from Wat Naa Tham may be able to guide you there. There are several other caves in the vicinity worth exploring for their impressive stalactite and stalagmite formations.

## BAN SAKAI
บ.ซาไก

The well known village of Ban Sakai is in Tharato district, about 80 km south of Yala on the way to Betong.

At Ban Sakai, 3.5 km off Highway 410, there's a small **museum**, souvenir shop, herb garden and a trail that leads through a small valley to a cascade. The road between the highway and village is quite bad but is currently under reconstruction.

Highway 410 through this area passes some beautiful limestone scenery and many coconut, banana, and rubber plantations; the latter are sometimes terraced, a rarity in South-East Asia. Banglang Dam stands off Highway 410 near Km 45 and in this same area is **Tharato Falls**, part of **Banglang National Park**; the entrance for the latter is off the highway between Kms 55 and 56.

## BETONG
เบตง

Betong is 140 km south-west of Yala on the Malaysian border and is Thailand's southernmost point. The area surrounding Betong is mountainous and jungle-foliated; morning fog is not uncommon in the district. Three km north of town is a pleasant hot springs.

Until 1990 the Communist Party of Malaysia had its hidden headquarters in Betong District at a camp called Wan Chai, home to 180 guerrillas of the 12th Regiment. Most were ethnic Chinese, and more than half were women. All uniforms and weapons were made at the camp; they even operated their own radio station which broadcast the 'Voice of Malayan Democracy'. In December 1989 the CPM finally laid down arms; many guerrillas were given minor land grants in the area by the Thai government in return for their capitulation. Others – mainly Chinese – have blended into the Betong woodwork and now make their way as peddlers, Chinese-language tutors, odd-job labourers, rubber tappers and tailors. A number of former CPM members live in nearby 'Peace Village' and regale visiting journalists with tales of jungle life and how they once lived on elephant, tiger and bear meat. The Pattani United Liberation Organisation (PULO), Thai-Muslim separatists who want Yala and other Muslim provinces to secede from Thailand, still have minor forces in this area but the word is that they, too, will soon give up the fight.

A **gateway** over town entrance combines an onion-shaped mosque turret, curved Chinese temple roof and spire-like Buddhist stupa to symbolise the town's unique synthesis of Malay, Chinese and Thai cultures. The Chinese influence predominates and you'll hear Hokkien, Tae Jiu and Cantonese spoken more than any other language; many people also speak English. It's a very wealthy district compared to Sungai Kolok or Padang Besar, the two other major border crossings between Thailand and Malaysia. Lots of new shophouses are going up, and all the new hotels have karaoke lounges.

There's little of general interest for the visitor; a strange park, sports and culture complex is under construction on a hill overlooking the city. A large **Chinese temple** stands on a lower slope of the hill. Near the traffic circle in the centre of town is a three metre, cylindrical red **mailbox**, touted as the world's tallest mail receptacle.

Betong is a legal crossing for all nationalities.

The little town is often crowded on weekends as Malaysians come across to shop for cheaper Thai merchandise including, for Malaysian men, Thai women.

### Places to Stay & Eat

Most hotels in Betong are in the 250 to 500B range – Malaysian price levels – for basic fan or air-con rooms. Hotels include the *Cathay*, *Fortuna*, *My House* and *Khong Kha*. Payment in Malaysian ringgit is as acceptable as baht at most hotels. One of the hassles for single male visitors is constantly being approached by pimps at many of the hotels.

The *Betong Hotel*, 13/6 Sarit Det Rd, is OK for 120 to 250B. *Sri Betong* at 2-4 Thamwithi Rd has decent fan rooms for 200B, air-con for 400B, plus more expensive VIP rooms up to 700B. Cheaper is the spartan *Metro* at 7/1-3 Rattakit Rd, where fan rooms are 60B single with shared bath, 120B for a double with bath.

The best budget bet is *Fa Un Rong Hotel* on Jantharothai Rd for 120B with fan, 220B with air-con. Another decent place to stay is the *Sri Charoen (Sea World Long) Hotel* at 17 Soi Praphan Phesat, where good rooms with a bit of a view cost 150B with fan and bath, 220 to 280B with air-con. The hotel's business card is written in Chinese and prices are quoted in Malaysian currency.

The *Betong Merlin* (☎ (73) 230222; fax 231357) stands on a hill overlooking Betong and is still top of the heap in this town. Rooms with all the amenities start at 875B. In addition to the places in the town centre, there are several expensive resorts outside town serving as getaways for Yala's nouveau riche.

Betong has more Muslim and Chinese restaurants than Thai. The town is famous for kài betong, the tasty local chicken, and also roasted or fried mountain frogs, which are said to be even more delicious than the mountain frogs of Mae Hong Son. *Arabia Ocha* on Sukhayang Rd does good Malay Muslim food. Best places for kài betong are *New City* and *Ta Yern*, both on Sukhayang Rd below the Merlin. The latter is good for all kinds of Chinese food as well.

### Getting There & Away

A shared Mercedes taxi to Betong from Yala is 70B; bus is 38B. The Malaysian border crossing is about five km from the centre of Betong. A taxi ride to the border is M$6 (drivers prefer Malaysian ringgit but will accept 60B).

### RAMAN
รามัน

Twenty-five km south-east of Yala by road or train, Raman is well known as a centre for the Malay-Indonesian martial art of *silat*. Two very famous teachers of silat reside here, Hajisa Haji Sama-ae and Je Wae. If you're interested in pure Thai-Muslim culture, this is the place.

# Pattani Province

### PATTANI
อ.เมืองปัตตานี
• ☎ *(73)* • *pop 41,000*

The provincial capital of Pattani provides a heavy contrast with Yala. In spite of its basic function as a trading post operated by the Chinese for the benefit (or exploitation, depending on your perspective) of the surrounding Muslim villages, the town has a more Muslim character than Yala. In the streets, you are more likely to hear Yawi, the traditional language of Java, Sumatra and the Malay peninsula (which when written uses the classic Arabic script plus five more letters), than any Thai dialect. The markets are visually quite similar to markets in Kota Baru in Malaysia. The town as a whole is a bit dirtier than Yala, but the riverfront area is interesting.

Pattani was until rather recently the centre of an independent principality that included Yala and Narathiwat. It was also one of the earliest kingdoms in Thailand to host international trade; the Portuguese established a trading post here in 1516, the Japanese in 1605, the Dutch in 1609 and the British in 1612. During WWII, Japanese troops landed in Pattani to launch attacks on Malaya and Singapore.

## Orientation & Information

The centre of this mostly concrete town is at the intersection of Naklua and Yarang Rds, the north-south road between Yala and Pattani harbour, and Ramkomud Rd, which runs east-west between Songkhla and Narathiwat. Inter-city buses and taxis stop at this intersection. Ramkomud Rd becomes Rudee Rd after crossing Yarang Rd, and it is along Rudee Rd that you can see what is left of old Pattani architecture – the Sino-Portuguese style that was once so prevalent in Southern Thailand.

Pattani's main post office is on Pipit Rd, near the bridge. The attached CAT office provides overseas telephone service daily between 7 am and 10 pm.

As in Yala, Narathiwat, Satun and Trang, all street signs are in tortured English transliterations of Thai (better than no transliterations at all, for those who can't read Thai).

## Mosques

Thailand's second-largest mosque is the **Matsayit Klang**, a traditional structure of green hue, probably still the South's most important mosque. It was built in the early 1960s.

The oldest mosque in Pattani is the **Matsayit Kreu-Se**, built in 1578 by an immigrant Chinese named Lim To Khieng who had married a Pattani woman and converted to Islam. Actually, neither To Khieng, nor anyone else, ever completed the construction of the mosque (see the boxed aside on this legend).

The brick, Arab-style building has been left in its original semi-completed, semi-ruined form, but the faithful keep up the surrounding grounds. The mosque is in the village of Ban Kreu-Se, about seven km east of Pattani next to Highway 42 at Km 10; a gaudy Tiger Balm Gardens-style Chinese temple has been built next to it.

The tree that Ko Niaw hanged herself from has been enshrined at the **San Jao Leng Ju Kieng** (or San Jao Lim Ko Niaw), the site of an important Chinese-Muslim festival in late February or early March. During the festival a wooden image of Lim Ko Niaw is carried through the streets; additional rites include fire-walking and seven days of vegetarianism. The shrine is in the northern end of town towards the harbour.

Another festival fervently celebrated in Pattani is Hari Rayo, the Muslim month of fasting during the 10th lunar month.

## Beaches

The only beach near town is at **Laem Tachi**, a cape that juts out over the northern end of Ao Pattani. You must take a boat taxi to get there, either from the Pattani pier or from Yaring district at the mouth of the Pattani River. This white-sand beach is about 11 km long, but is sometimes marred by refuse from Ao Pattani, depending on the time of year and the tides.

## Places to Stay & Eat

The *Palace Hotel* (☎ 349171) at 38 Soi Talaat Tetiwat, off Prida Rd, is a decent place

---

**SOUTHERN THAILAND**

### The Uncompleted Mosque

The story goes that To Khieng's sister, Lim Ko Niaw, sailed from China on a sampan to try and persuade her brother to abandon Islam and return to his homeland. To demonstrate the strength of his faith, he began building the Matsayit Kreu-Se. His sister then put a Chinese curse on the mosque, saying it would never be completed. Then, in a final attempt to dissuade To Khieng, she hanged herself from a nearby cashew-nut tree. In his grief, Khieng was unable to complete the mosque, and to this day it remains unfinished – supposedly every time someone tries to work on it, lightning strikes. ■

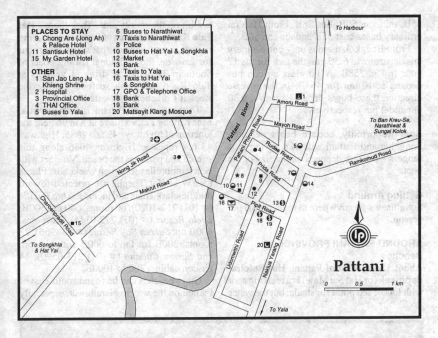

**PLACES TO STAY**
9 Chong Are (Jong Ah)
& Palace Hotel
11 Santisuk Hotel
15 My Garden Hotel

**OTHER**
1 San Jao Leng Ju
Khieng Shrine
2 Hospital
3 Provincial Office
4 THAI Office
5 Buses to Yala

6 Buses to Narathiwat
7 Taxis to Narathiwat
8 Police
10 Buses to Hat Yai & Songkhla
12 Market
13 Bank
14 Taxis to Yala
16 Taxis to Hat Yai
& Songkhla
17 GPO & Telephone Office
18 Bank
19 Bank
20 Matsayit Klang Mosque

with rooms for 140B with fan and bath, 200B double or air-con, plus another 50B if you want TV. The *Santisuk* (☎ 349122), at 29 Pipit Rd, has OK rooms for 80B without a bath, 130 with private bath and 200 to 350B with air-con.

*My Garden* (☎ 331055; fax 348200) at 8/28 Chareonpradit Rd, about a km outside town, is a good value middle-range hotel – 275B for a large double with fan and bath, 440 to 495B for air-con, 660B with TV. The disco is very popular on weekends. Samlor or songthaew drivers may know it by its former name, the Dina.

The *Chong Are (Jong Ah)* restaurant, next to the Palace Hotel on Prida Rd, serves decent Thai and Chinese food.

**Things to Buy**
Thai Muslims in Southern Thailand have their own traditional batik methods that are similar but not identical to the batik of north-east Malaysia. The best place to shop for local batik is at the Palat Market *(talàat nát paalát)*, which is off Highway 42 between Pattani and Saiburi in Ban Palat. The market is held all day Wednesday and Sunday only. If you can't make it to this market, the shops of Muslim Phanit and Nadi Brothers on Rudee Rd in Pattani sell local and Malaysian batik at perhaps slightly higher prices.

**Getting There & Away**
**Air** Pattani has an airport and until mid-1994 THAI operated twice-weekly flights to/from Narathiwat and Hat Yai. These flights still haven't been resumed – check at Pattani's THAI office (☎ 349149) on 9 Prida Rd to see if these or other flights out of Pattani have been reinstated.

**Bus & Share Taxi** Pattani is only 40 km from Yala. Share taxis are 25B and take about half an hour; buses cost only 12B but take around an hour. From Narathiwat, a share taxi is

45B, minivan 50B, bus 28B. From Hat Yai ordinary buses cost 35B and air-con 50B.

From Bangkok there is only one ordinary bus departure at 6.30 pm; the fare for the 17 hour trip is 258B. A 1st class air-con bus departs at 10 am for 464B. In the reverse direction these buses depart Pattani at 6.30 pm and 2 pm respectively.

**Boat**  Reportedly, certain boats between Songkhla and Pattani will take paying passengers – the fare depends on the size of the boat.

### Getting Around
Songthaews go anywhere in town for 5B per person.

### AROUND PATTANI PROVINCE
### Beaches
About 15 km west of Pattani, **Hat Ratchadaphisek** (or Hat Sai Maw) is a relaxing spot with lots of sea pines for shade, but the water

is a bit on the murky side. Then there's **Hat Talo Kapo**, 14 km east of Pattani near Yaring district, a pretty beach that's also a harbour for *kaw-lae*, the traditional fishing boats of Southern Thailand. A string of vendors at Talo Kapo sell fresh seafood; during the week it's practically deserted.

To the north of Pattani is **Hat Thepha**, near Khlong Pratu village at Km 96 near the junction of highways 43 and 4085. Highway 43 has replaced Highway 4086 along this stretch and parallels the beach. Vendors with beach umbrellas set up on weekends. Places to stay at Hat Thepha are oriented toward middle-class Thais and include: *Club Pacific* (☎ (01) 712-1020), 60 rooms, 600 to 1500B; *Leela Resort* (☎ (01) 712-0144), 38 rooms, 400B up; *Sakom Bay Resort* (☎ 238966), 23 rooms, 200B for fan to 600B with air-con; and *Sakom Cabana* (☎ (01) 213-0590), 14 air-con cabins; 700 to 1000B.

Other beaches can be found south-east of Pattani on the way to Narathiwat, especially

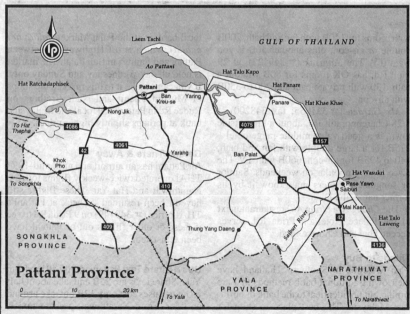

SOUTHERN THAILAND

**Pattani Province**

GULF OF THAILAND

Laem Tachi

Ao Pattani

Hat Talo Kapo

Hat Ratchadaphisek

Pattani

Ban Kreu-se

Yaring

Hat Panare

Panare

Hat Khae Khae

Nong Jik

4075

To Hat Thepha

4086

42

4061

Yarang

Ban Palat

4157

Khok Pho

To Songkhla

410

42

Hat Wasukri

Pase Yawo

Saiburi

Mai Kaen

Hat Talo Laweng

409

Thung Yang Daeng

Saiburi River

42

4136

SONGKHLA PROVINCE

NARATHIWAT PROVINCE

YALA PROVINCE

0    10    20 km

To Yala

To Narathiwat

in the Panare and Saiburi districts where there are km of virtually deserted beach. **Hat Chala Lai** is a broad white-sand beach 43 km south-east of Pattani, near Panare. Eight km farther on towards Narathiwat is **Hat Khae Khae**, a pretty beach studded with boulders. Three km north of Panare is **Hat Panare**, which is another colourful kaw-lae harbour.

If you have your own wheels, follow Highway 4136 along the coast south of where the broad Saiburi River empties into the Gulf. Near Saiburi is **Hat Wasukri**, also called Chaihat Ban Patatimaw, a beautiful white-sand beach with shade. It's 53 km from Pattani. You'll find miles of deserted beach starting at around Km 22, a few km before you reach the Narathiwat provincial border. The cleanest and prettiest stretch, **Hat Talo Laweng**, is found near a Muslim cemetery just south of the tidy Muslim village of Laweng, where you could probably rent rooms from local villagers. The people here make their living from fishing and coconuts. Highway 4136 veers off to Mai Kaen just before Laweng if you're heading north to Pattani. None of these beaches is signposted but you can't miss them if you're on Highway 4136.

A good place to watch the building of kaw-lae is in the village of Pase Yawo (Ya-Waw), near the mouth of the Saiburi River. It's a tradition that is slowly dying out as the kaw-lae is replaced by flat-sterned boats painted in the same style.

# Narathiwat Province

## NARATHIWAT
อ.เมืองนราธิวาส
• ☎ (73) • pop 40,500

Narathiwat is a pleasant, even-tempered little town, one of Thailand's smallest provincial capitals, with a character all of its own. Many of the buildings are old wooden structures, a hundred or more years old. The local businesses seem to be owned by both Muslims and Chinese, and nights are partic-

ularly peaceful because of the relative absence of male drinking sessions typical of most upcountry towns in Thailand. The town is right on the sea, and some of the prettiest beaches on Southern Thailand's east coast are just outside town. A new promenade has been installed along the waterfront at the south end of town.

Local radio stations broadcast in a mix of Yawi, Thai and Malay, with musical selections to match – everything from North-Eastern Thailand's *lûuk thûng* to Arabic-melodied *dangdut*. Many signs around town appear in Yawi as well as Thai, Chinese and English.

Every year during the third week of September, the Narathiwat Fair features kaw-lae boat racing, a singing dove contest judged by the queen, handicraft displays and silat martial arts exhibitions. Other highlights include performances of the local dance forms, *ram sam pen* and *ram ngeng*.

### Information
The post office is at the southern end of Pichitbamrung Rd. An attached international phone office is open daily from 7 am to 10 pm.

### Hat Narathat
หาดนราทัศน์
Just north of town is a small Thai-Muslim fishing village at the mouth of the Bang Nara River, lined with the large painted fishing boats called reua kaw-lae which are peculiar to Narathiwat and Pattani. Near the fishing village is Hat Narathat, a sandy beach four to five km long, which serves as a kind of public park for locals, with outdoor seafood restaurants, tables and umbrellas. The constant breeze here is excellent for windsurfing, though only the occasional visiting Malaysian seems to take advantage of this. Shade is provided by a mixture of casuarinas and coco palms.

The beach is only two km north of the town centre – you can easily walk there or take a samlor. This beach extends all the way north to Pattani, interrupted only by the

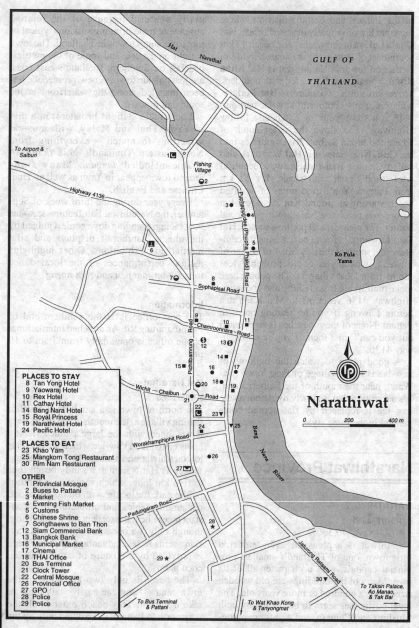

**GULF OF THAILAND**

Hat Narathat

To Airport & Saiburi

Highway 4136

Fishing Village

Phupha Phakdi (Phuphadee) Road

Ko Pula Yama

Sophapisai Road

Chamroonnara – Road

Pichitbamrung Road

Wichit – Chaibun Road

Bang Nara River

**Narathiwat**

0    200    400 m

Worakhamphiphit Road

Padungaram Road

Jaturong Ratsami Road

To Bus Terminal & Pattani

To Wat Khao Kong & Tanyongmat

To Taksin Palace, Ao Manao, & Tak Bai

**PLACES TO STAY**
8   Tan Yong Hotel
9   Yaowaraj Hotel
10  Rex Hotel
11  Cathay Hotel
14  Bang Nara Hotel
15  Royal Princess
19  Narathiwat Hotel
24  Pacific Hotel

**PLACES TO EAT**
23  Khao Yam
25  Mangkorn Tong Restaurant
30  Rim Nam Restaurant

**OTHER**
1   Provincial Mosque
2   Buses to Pattani
3   Market
4   Evening Fish Market
5   Customs
6   Chinese Shrine
7   Songthaews to Ban Thon
12  Siam Commercial Bank
13  Bangkok Bank
16  Municipal Market
17  Cinema
18  THAI Office
20  Bus Terminal
21  Clock Tower
22  Central Mosque
26  Provincial Office
27  GPO
28  Police
29  Police

SOUTHERN THAILAND

occasional stream or river mouth; the farther north you go the cleaner and prettier the beach becomes. Almost the entire coast between Narathiwat and Malaysia, 40 km south, is sandy beach as well.

### Matsayit Klang (Central Mosque)
มัสยิดกลาง

Toward the south end of Pichitbamrung Rd stands an old wooden mosque built in the Sumatran style. It was reportedly built by a prince of the former kingdom of Pattani over a hundred years ago. Today it's of secondary importance to the newer Arabian modernist-style provincial mosque at the north end of town, but is architecturally more interesting.

### Taksin Palace
พระตำหนักทักษิณ

About seven km south of town is Tan-yongmat Hill, where Taksin Palace (Phra Taksin Ratchaniwet) is located. The royal couple stay here for about two months between August and October every year. When they're not in residence, the palace is open to the public daily from 8.30 am to noon and 1 to 4.30 pm. The buildings themselves are not that special, but there are gardens with the Bangsuriya palm, a rare fan-like palm named after the embroidered sun-shades used by monks and royalty as a sign of rank. A small zoo and a ceramics work-shop are also on the grounds, and in front is Ao Manao, a pretty, curved bay lined with sea pines. Vendors on the beach offer food and drinks, along with umbrellas and sling chairs. The locals believe Ao Manao to be the province's prettiest, but it's not as nice as some stretches further north or south.

A songthaew from the town to the palace area is 5B. Songthaew services stop around sunset.

### Wat Khao Kong
วัดเขากง

The tallest seated-Buddha image in Thailand is at Wat Khao Kong, six km south-west on the way to the train station in Tanyongmat. Called Phra Phuttha Taksin Mingmongkon,

the image is 25m high and made of bronze. The wat itself isn't much to see. A songthaew to Wat Khao Kong is 5B from the Narathiwat Hotel.

### Places to Stay

The cheapest places to stay are all on Puphapugdee (Phupha Phakdi) Rd along the Bang Nara River. The best deal is the *Narathiwat Hotel* (☎ 511063), a funky wooden building that's quiet, breezy, clean and comfortable. Rooms on the waterfront cost 110B with shared bath. The downstairs rooms can sometimes get a bit noisy from the night trade – try to get an upstairs room. Mosquitoes could be a problem, so don't forget your repellent or mozzie coils.

Another OK place, a bit farther north on the same side of the street, is the quiet *Cathay Hotel* (☎ 511014) – signed in Yawi, English, Thai and Chinese – where spacious, clean if somewhat cheerless rooms with attached bath and ceiling fan cost 120B. The elderly Chinese owner speaks good English. There's a view of the river from the roof.

Across the street and next to the Si Ayuthaya Bank, is the *Bang Nara Hotel*, which is a barely disguised brothel with large rooms for 100B with shared bathroom.

The *Rex Hotel* (☎ 511134), at 6/1-3 Chamroonnara Rd, is a fair place at 170B for rooms with fan, 320B for air-con. Similar rooms with fan for 120 to 160B, 280 to 300B air-con, are available at the *Yaowaraj Hotel* on the corner of Chamroonnara and Pichitbamrung Rds. Because of its busy location, it's not as quiet as the previously mentioned places.

The recently renovated *Pacific Hotel* (☎ 511076) costs 300B for large, clean rooms with fan and bath, plus air-con for 330 to 410B.

The top end for the moment is the *Tan Yong Hotel* (☎ 511477), on Sophapisai Rd, with air-con rooms from 500B. Most of the guests are Malaysians and Thai government officials. A new upscale place is under construction off the west side of Pichitbamrung Rd, the *Royal Princess Narathiwat* (☎ 511-027). When completed it will offer 126 rooms in an eight-storey building in the 1500 to 2000B range.

Seven km south of town at Ao Manao, *Ao Manao Resort* features large but closely spaced cement cottages with fan and bath for 400 to 600B a night. It's back from the beach about 400m.

### Places to Eat

For eating, the night market off Chamroonnara Rd behind the Bang Nara Hotel is good. There are also several inexpensive places along Chamroonnara Rd, especially the khâo kaeng place next to the Yaowaraj Hotel, for curries. A cluster of foodstalls on Sophaphisai Rd at Puphapugdee Rd serves inexpensive noodle dishes.

On Puphapugdee Rd at the north-west corner of a soi leading to the back of the Central Mosque, an elderly couple operate a small shop (in a wooden building with a tile roof) selling delicious and inexpensive khâo yam. Malay-style fried rice noodles are served on the side with each order. Curries and rice are also available at this shop. Other places in town have khâo yam in the morning, but this one's best so go early before they run out. Farther south on the same side of the street is a Muslim shop with khâo mók and duck over rice. Along Wichit Chaibun Rd west of Puphapugdee Rd are several inexpensive Muslim food shops.

*Mangkorn Tong Restaurant* is a small seafood place on Puphapugdee Rd that has a floating dining section out back. The food's quite good and prices are reasonable.

The outdoor *Rim Nam* restaurant, on Jaturong Ratsami Rd a couple of km south of town, has good medium-priced seafood and curries. South of Rim Nam is the similar but larger *Bang Nara*; both restaurants are popular with Malaysian tour groups these days.

### Things to Buy

Two batik factories near town, M Famabatik (☎ 512452) and Saenghirun Batik (☎ 513151) will sell batik direct to visitors at decent prices.

### Getting There & Away

**Air** THAI has four flights weekly between Narathiwat and Phuket, connecting with flights to Bangkok. The fare to Phuket is 990B; through to Bangkok it's 2575B. There are also three flights a week to/from Nakhon Si Thammarat for 835B. The THAI office (☎ 511161, 513090/2) is at 322-324 Puphapugdee Rd; a THAI van between Nara airport (12 km north via Highway 4136) and the THAI office costs 30B per person.

**Bus & Taxi** Share taxis between Yala and Narathiwat are 45B, buses 35B (with a change in Pattani). Buses cost 28B from Pattani. From Sungai Kolok, buses are 18B, share taxis and minivans 40B. To Hat Yai it's 120B by share taxi or 100B by air-con minivan; the latter leave several times a day from opposite the Rex Hotel for 100B per person.

To/from Tak Bai, the other border crossing, it is 10B by songthaew (catch one in front of the Narathiwat Hotel), 20B by taxi.

**Train** The train costs 13B for 3rd class seats to Tanyongmat, 20 km west of Narathiwat, then it's either a 15B taxi to Narathiwat, or 10B by songthaew.

### Getting Around

Motorcycle taxis around town cost 10B. Wicker-chair samlors from Malaysia are mainly used for carrying goods back and forth to market; these cost from 10 to 25B depending on distance and amount of cargo.

## AROUND NARATHIWAT
### Wadin Husen Mosque
มัสยิดวาดินฮูเซ็น

One of the most interesting mosques in Thailand, the Wadin Husen was built in 1769 and mixes Thai, Chinese and Malay architectural styles to good effect. It's in the village of Lubosawo in Bajo (Ba-Jaw) district, about 15 km north-west of Narathiwat off Highway 42, about 8B by songthaew.

### Wat Chonthara Sing-He
วัดชลธาราสิงเห

During the British colonisation of Malaysia (then called Malaya), the Brits tried to claim Narathiwat as part of their Malayan empire.

SOUTHERN THAILAND

The Thais constructed Wat Chonthara Sing-He (also known as Wat Phitak Phaendin Thai) in Tak Bai district near the Malayan border to prove that Narathiwat was indeed part of Siam, and as a result the British relinquished their claim.

Today it's most notable because of the genuine Southern Thai architecture, rarely seen in a Buddhist temple – the Thai-Buddhist equivalent of the Wadin Husen Mosque. A wooden wihăan here very much resembles a Sumatran-style mosque. An 1873 wihăan on the grounds contains a reclining Buddha decorated with Chinese ceramics from the Song dynasty. Another wihăan on the spacious grounds contains murals painted by a famous Songkhla monk during King Mongkut's time. The murals are religious in message but also depict traditional Southern Thai life. There is also a larger, typical Thai wihăan.

Wat Chon is 34 km south-east of Narathiwat in Tak Bai. It's probably not worth a trip from Narathiwat just to see this 100 year old temple unless you're a real temple freak, but if you're killing time in Tak Bai or Sungai Kolok this is one of the prime local sights. It's next to the river and the quiet, expansive grounds provide a retreat from the busy border atmosphere.

To get there from Narathiwat, take a bus or songthaew bound for Ban Taba and get off in Tak Bai. The wat is on the river about 500m from the main Tak Bai intersection.

## SUNGAI KOLOK & BAN TABA
• ☎ (73)

These small towns in the south-east of Narathiwat Province are departure points for the east coast of Malaysia. There is a fair batik (Thai: *paa-té*) cottage industry in this district.

Be prepared for culture shock coming from Malaysia, warned one traveller. Not only are most signs in Thai script, but fewer people speak English in Thailand than in Malaysia.

### Sungai Kolok
สุไหงโก-ลก

The Thai government once planned to move the border crossing from Sungai Kolok to Ban Taba in Tak Bai district, which is on the coast 32 km east. The Taba crossing is now open and is a shorter and quicker route to Kota Baru, the first Malaysian town of any size, but it looks like Sungai Kolok will remain open as well for a long time. They're even building new hotels in Sungai Kolok and have established a TAT office next to the immigration post.

Still, as a town it's a bit of a mess, with an estimated 3000 prostitutes who produce the town's second most important source of revenue. The rest of the economy is given over to Thai-Malaysia shipping; there's an entire district in the north-east part of town dedicated to warehouses which store goods moving back and forth between countries.

The border is open from 5 am to 5 pm (6 am to 6 pm Malaysian time). On slow days they may close the border as early as 4.30 pm.

**Information** The TAT office (☎ 612126), next to the immigration post, is open daily from 8.30 am to 5 pm. The post and telephone office is on Thetpathom Rd, while immigration is near the Merlin Hotel on Charoenkhet Rd.

### Ban Taba
บ้านตาบา

Ban Taba, five km south of bustling Tak Bai, is a blip of a town with a large market and a few hotels. Takbai Border House, a large customs complex built in the hope of diverting traffic from Kolok, is under-used and neglected. From the customs and market area you can see Malaysia right across the Kolok River. A few hundred metres north of the complex, Hat Taba is a beach park of sorts planted with casuarinas and featuring a few open-air shelters. You can change money at street vendors by the ferry on the Thai side.

A ferry across the river into Malaysia is 5B. The border crossing here is open the same hours as in Sungai Kolok. From the Malaysian side you can get buses direct to Kota Baru for M$1.50.

### Places to Stay & Eat – Sungai Kolok
According to the TAT there are 46 hotels in

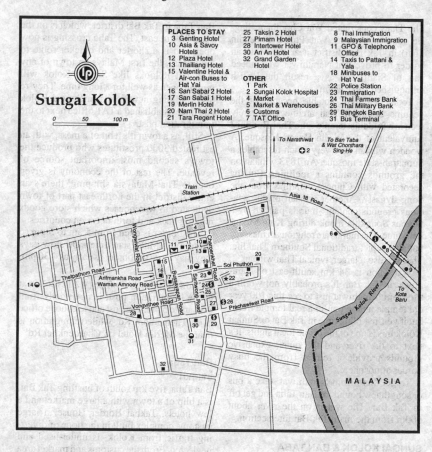

**PLACES TO STAY**
3 Genting Hotel
10 Asia & Savoy Hotels
12 Plaza Hotel
13 Thailiang Hotel
15 Valentine Hotel & Air-con Buses to Hat Yai
16 San Sabai 2 Hotel
17 San Sabai 1 Hotel
19 Merlin Hotel
20 Nam Thai 2 Hotel
21 Tara Regent Hotel

25 Taksin 2 Hotel
27 Pimarn Hotel
28 Intertower Hotel
30 An An Hotel
32 Grand Garden Hotel

**OTHER**
1 Park
2 Sungai Kolok Hospital
4 Market
5 Market & Warehouses
6 Customs
7 TAT Office

8 Thai Immigration
9 Malaysian Immigration
11 GPO & Telephone Office
14 Taxis to Pattani & Yala
18 Minibuses to Hat Yai
22 Police Station
23 Immigration
24 Thai Farmers Bank
26 Thai Military Bank
29 Bangkok Bank
31 Bus Terminal

**Sungai Kolok**

0    50    100 m

Train Station

To Narathiwat

To Ban Taba & Wat Chonthara Sing-He

Asia 18 Road

Wongwiwat Road

Charoenkhet Road

Thetpathom Road

Arifmankha Road

Waman Amnoey Road

Bussayawan Road

Satnoeng Road

Soi Phuthon

Vongvithee Road

Prachawiwat Road

Sungai Kolok River

To Kota Baru

MALAYSIA

---

Sungai Kolok, most in operation to accommodate the weekend trips of Malaysian males and bearing names like *Marry, Come In, Honey, My Love* and *Hawaii*. Of the cheaper hotels, only a handful are under 150B and they're mainly for those only crossing for a couple of hours. So if you have to spend the night here it's best to pay a little more and get away from the short-time trade. Most places in Sungai Kolok will take Malaysian ringgit as well as Thai baht for food or accommodation.

The most inexpensive places are along Charoenkhet Rd. Here you can find the fairly clean *Thailiang Hotel* (☎ 611132) at No 12 for

150B, the *Savoy Hotel* (☎ 611093) at No 8/2 for 120 to 150B, and the *Asia Hotel* (☎ 611101) at No 4-4/1 for 160B (fan and bath), or 200 to 250B with air-con. The *Pimarn Hotel* (☎ 611464) at No 76-4 is also good at 150B with fan and bath.

On the corner of Thetpathom and Waman Amnoey Rds is the pleasant *Valentine Hotel* (☎ 611229), with rooms for 180B with fan, 260 to 330B with air-con. There's a coffee shop downstairs.

Other reasonably decent hotels in the 100 to 200B range include the *An An Hotel* (☎ 611058) at 183/1-2 Prachawiwat Rd, the *Taksin 2* (☎ 611088) at 4 Prachasamran Rd, the *San*

SOUTHERN THAILAND

*Sabai 2* (☎ 611313) at 38 Waman Amnoey Rd, the cheaper *San Sabai 1* (☎ 612157) at 32/34 Bussayapan Rd, and the *Nam Thai 2* (☎ 611163) at Soi Phuthon, Charoenkhet Rd. Some of these hotels also offer air-con rooms for 200 to 360B.

Top-end hotels in Sungai Kolok include:

*Genting Hotel* – Asia 18 Rd (☎ 613231; fax 611259); from 600B
*Grand Garden* – 104 Arifmankha Rd (☎ 611219; fax 613501); from 550B
*Intertower Hotel* – Prachawiwat Rd (☎ 611192; fax 613400); from 399B
*Marina Hotel* – 173 Soi 3, Charoenkhet Rd (☎ 613881; fax 613385); from 638B
*Merlin Hotel* – 40 Charoenkhet Rd (☎ 611003; fax 611431); from 410B
*Plaza Hotel* – off Bussayapan Rd (☎ 611875; fax 613402); from 374B
*Tara Regent Hotel* – Soi Phuthon, Charoenkhet Rd (☎ 611401; fax 611801); from 390B

The town has plenty of foodstalls selling Thai, Chinese and Malaysian food. There's a good Chinese vegetarian restaurant between the Asia and Savoy hotels that's open daily 7 am to 6 pm. A cluster of reliable Malay food vendors can be found at the market and in front of the train station.

### Places to Stay – Ban Taba
*Masaya Resort* (☎ 581125) has good rooms for 170 to 250B with fan and bath, 300B with air-con or 370B with air-con and TV. It's set back off the road leading from the Malaysian border and a bit difficult to find; take a motorcycle taxi there for 5B. The *Pornphet* (☎ 581331), a motel-like place near the beach north of Taba, isn't bad for 250 to 370B, all air-con.

### Getting There & Around
**Bus & Share Taxi** Air-con buses to/from Bangkok cost 533B, take 18 hours and depart from Bangkok at 6.30 pm (from Sungai Kolok at 12.30 pm). Standard bus fares are 296B, departing from Bangkok at 9 pm or from Sungai Kolok at 9 am – but you would have to be a dyed-in-the-wool masochist to ride this entire 20 hour trip by ordinary bus. To Surat Thani, standard buses are 143B (taking 10 hours), air-con 256B (nine hours).

Share taxis from Yala to Sungai Kolok costs 65B, from Narathiwat 40B; in Sungai Kolok the taxi stand is at the west end of Thetpathom Rd. There are also buses from Narathiwat for 18B (25B air-con). From Sungai Kolok taxis to Narathiwat leave from in front of the An An Hotel.

Air-con buses to Hat Yai cost 98B and leave from the Valentine Hotel at 7 am, 9 am, 1 and 3 pm. From Hat Yai, departure times are the same. The trip takes about four hours. Share taxis to Hat Yai cost 120B and leave from next to the Thailiang Hotel.

The border is about a km from the centre of Sungai Kolok or the train station. Transport around town is by motorcycle taxi – it's 10B for a ride to the border. Coming from Malaysia, just follow the old train tracks to your right, or, for the town, turn left at the first junction and head for the high-rises.

From Rantau Panjang (Malaysian side), a share taxi to Kota Baru costs M$4 per person (M$15 to charter the whole car) and takes about an hour. The regular yellow-and-orange bus to KB costs M$2.50.

**Train** The daily special express No 19 to Sungai Kolok departs Bangkok at 2.35 pm and arrives at 10.20 am the next day. This train has 1st (808B) and 2nd class fares (378B), not including the special-express surcharge of 50B (and 1st or 2nd class sleeping berths if you so choose).

You can also get trains to Sungai Kolok from Yala and Tanyongmat (for Narathiwat), but buses are really faster and more convenient along these routes.

From Sungai Kolok to points farther north (via Yala), however, the train is a reasonable alternative. A train to Hat Yai takes about 4½ hours and costs 31B for a 3rd class seat, 65B for 2nd class. Train Nos 124 and 132 leave Sungai Kolok at 6.30 and 9 am, arriving in Hat Yai at 11.37 am and 1.49 pm.

From Sungai Kolok special express No 20 leaves at 3 pm and arrives in Bangkok at 10.35 am the next day, with stops in Hat Yai (6.40 pm), Surat Thani (11.48 pm) and Hua Hin (6.42 am) among other towns along the way.

# Glossary

**aahăan** – food

**aahăan pàa** – jungle food

**ajaan** – respectful title for teacher, from the Sanskrit term *acharya*

**amphoe** – district; next subdivision down from province; sometimes spelt *amphur*

**amphoe meuang** – provincial capital

**ao** – bay or gulf

**bâan** – house or village; often spelt *ban*

**bai toey** – pandanus leaf

**bàw náam ráwn** – hot springs

**bhikku** – Buddhist monk in Pali; Thai pronunciation *phík-khù*

**bòt** – central sanctuary or chapel in a Thai temple; from the Pali *uposatha*

**chaa** – tea

**chaihàat** – beach; also spelt *hat*

**chao le (chao náam)** – sea gypsies

**chedi** – stupa; monument erected to house a Buddha relic; called *pagoda* in Myanmar, *dagoba* in Sri Lanka, *cetiya* in India

**dhammachakka** – Buddhist wheel of law

**doi** – mountain peak

**farang** – foreigner of European descent

**hàat** – beach; short for *chaihaat*; also *hat*

**hang yao** – long-tailed boat

**hăw trai** – a tripitaka (Buddhist scripture) library

**hĭn** – stone

**isăan** – general term for North-Eastern Thailand, from the Sanskrit name for the medieval kingdom Isana, which encompassed parts of Cambodia and North-Eastern Thailand

**jangwàat** – province

**jataka** – life-stories of the Buddha

**jii-khŏh** – Thai hoodlum

**jiin** – Chinese

**kâew** – crystal, jewel, glass, or gem; also spelt *keo*

**kafae thũng** – filtered coffee; sometimes called *ko-píi* in Southern Thailand

**kàp klâem** – drinking food

**ka-toey** – Thai transvestite

**kaw-lae** – traditional fishing boats of Southern Thailand

**khaen** – reed instrument common in North-Eastern Thailand

**khăo** – hill or mountain

**khlong** – canal

**khŏn** – masked dance-drama based on stories from the *Ramakian*

**khon isăan** – the people of North-Eastern Thailand

**klawng** – Thai drums

**ko** – island; also spelt *koh*; pronounced *kàw*

**kúay hâeng** – Chinese-style work shirt

**kuti** – meditation hut

**lâap** – spicy mint salad with mint leaves

**lăem** – cape (in the geographical sense)

**lákhon** – classical Thai dance-drama

**làk meuang** – city pillar/phallus

**lâo khăo** – white liquor

**lâo thèuan** – jungle liquor

**lí-khe** – Thai folk dance-drama

**longyi** – Burmese sarong

**mâe chii** – Thai Buddhist nun

**mâe náam** – river; literally 'mother water'

**maha that** – literally 'great element', from the Sanskrit-Pali *mahadhatu*; common name for temples which contain Buddha relics

**mát-mìi** – tie-dye silk method

**mâw hâwm** – Thai work shirt

**mãwn khwaan** – triangular pillow popular in Northern and North-Eastern Thailand

**metta** – Buddhist practice of loving kindness

**meuang** – city; pronounced *meu-ang*

**mondòp** – small square building in a *wat* complex generally used by laypeople, as opposed to monks; from the Sanskrit *mandapa*

**muay thai** – Thai boxing

**náam** – water
**náam phrík** – chilli sauce
**náam plaa** – fish sauce
**náam tòk** – waterfall
**naga** – dragon-headed serpent
**nakhon** – city; from the Sanskrit-Pali *nagara*; also spelt *nakhorn*
**năng** – Thai shadow play
**ngaan wát** – temple fair
**ngôp** – traditional Khmer rice farmer's hat
**noeng khăo** – hill

**pàak náam** – estuary
**paa-té** – batik
**paa-thông-kō** – Chinese 'doughnut', a common breakfast food
**pàk tâi** – Southern Thai
**phâakhamăa** – piece of cotton cloth worn as a wraparound by men
**phâasîn** – same as above for women
**phrá** – monk or Buddha image; an honorific term from the Pali *vara*, 'excellent'
**phrá phum** – earth spirits
**phuu khăo** – 'mountain' in Central Thai
**pìi-phâat** – classical Thai orchestra
**ponglang** – North-Eastern Thai marimba made of short logs
**prang** – Khmer-style tower on temples
**prasat** – small ornate building with a cruciform ground plan and needle-like spire, used for religious purposes, located on wat grounds; from the Sanskrit term *prasada*

**rai** – one *rai* is equal to 1600 sq metres
**reua hang yao** – long-tail taxi boat
**reuan tháew** – longhouse
**reu-sĭi** – a Hindu *rishi* or 'sage'
**rót thamádaa** – ordinary bus (non air-con) or ordinary train (not rapid or express)
**roti** – round flatbread, common street food; also found in Muslim restaurants

**săalaa (sala)** – an open-sided, covered meeting hall or resting place; from the Portuguese *sala* or 'room'
**sala klang** – provincial office
**samlor** – three-wheeled pedicab

**sēma** – boundary stones used to consecrate ground used for monastic ordinations; from the Sanskrit-Pali *sima*
**serow** – Asian mountain goat
**sêua mâw hâwm** – blue cotton farmer's shirt
**soi** – lane or small street
**sôm-tam** – green papaya salad
**sŏngkhran** – Thai New Year, held in mid-April
**songthaew** – literally 'two rows'; common name for small pickup trucks with two benches in the back, used as buses/taxis
**susăan** – cemetery

**talàat nàam** – floating market
**tambon** – 'precinct', next subdivision below *amphoe*; also spelled *tambol*
**thâat** – four-sided, curvilinear Buddhist reliquary, common in North-Eastern Thailand; also spelt *that*
**thale sàap** – inland sea or large lake
**thêp** – angel or divine being; from the Sanskrit *deva*
**thewada** – a kind of angel
**thutong** – monks who have taken extra vows, a series of 13 ascetic practices which usually involve wandering on foot from place to place with no set abode
**tripitaka** – Theravada Buddhist scriptures
**tuk-tuk** – motorised *samlor*

**vipassana** – Buddhist insight meditation

**wâi** – palms-together Thai greeting
**wang** – palace
**wát** – temple-monastery; from the Pali *avasa*, monk's dwelling
**wihăan** – counterpart to *bòt* in Thai temple, containing Buddha images but not circumscribed by *sema* stones. Also spelt *wihan* or *viharn*; from the Sanskrit *vihara*

**yàa dong** – herbal liquor; also the herbs inserted in *lâo khăo*
**yam** – Thai-style salad; usually made with meat or seafood

# Index

## TEXT

Map references are in **bold** type.

Abhisek Dusit Throne Hall 232
accommodation 151-4
    camping 153
    guesthouses & hostels 151-2
    hotels & resorts 152-3
    temple lodgings 153
    university campuses 153
administrative divisions 30, **32**
AIDS, *see* health
air travel 179-86, 190-6, **191**
    airline offices 190, 291-2
    airport facilities 192-3
    departure tax 196
    domestic 190-2
    glossary 180-1
    international 179
    to/from the airport 193-6
Allied War Cemeteries 330-1
amulets 223
Ancient City 350
Andaman Sea 22
Ang Thong 317
Ang Thong NMP 723-4
Ang Thong Province 317-8
Ao Bang Charu 742
Ao Bang Kao 734
Ao Bang Tao 711, **711**
Ao Chalok Ban Kao 749-50
Ao Cho 372
Ao Chon Khram 735
Ao Hat Thong Lang 744
Ao Hin Khok 371-2
Ao Hin Kong 745
Ao Khanom 760
Ao Mae 744, 748
Ao Manao 415
Ao Mao 749
Ao Na Khai 733-4
Ao Nai Wok 739
Ao Nang 786-90, **788**
Ao Noi 415
Ao Nuan 372
Ao Phai 372
Ao Phai Phlong 787

Ao Phang-Nga 686-8
Ao Phangka 734
Ao Phrao 373
Ao Phutsa 372
Ao Si Thanu 744-5
Ao Takiap 404
Ao Taling Ngam 734
Ao Thian 372
Ao Thong Krut 734
Ao Thong Nai Pan 743
Ao Thong Son 729
Ao Thong Ta Khian 731-2
Ao Thong Yang 735
Ao Ton Sai 794
Ao Wong Deuan 372
Aranya Prathet 394-5
architecture 51-7, 131, 186, 325,
    479, 492, 517, 611, 693
area codes, *see* telephone
    services
art styles 58-9
arts 49-72, *see also* individual
    entries
Ayuthaya 13, 300-11, **302**
Ayuthaya HP 304-7
Ayuthaya Historical Study
    Centre 308

Ban Ahong 626
Ban Chiang 612-3
Ban Hat Siaw 504
Ban Khai 742
Ban Khawn Sai 657
Ban Ko Lanta 797
Ban Mae Tao 512
Ban Na Kha 614
Ban Nong Pheu 635-6
Ban Phe 367
Ban Pheu 613-4
Ban Prasat 586-7
Ban Sakai 822
Ban Sala Dan 797
Ban Taba 831-3
Ban Tai 727, 742
Ban Thon 614
Bang Pan-In 311

Bang Saphan 417-9
Bangkok 208-99, **210-1, 214-5,**
    **225, 229, 237, 239, 246, 249,**
    **253, 256, 258**
    entertainment 278-86
    getting around 293-9
    getting there & away 291-3
    information 212-9
    places to eat 266-78
    places to stay 245-66
    shopping 286-91
    things to see & do 234-45
Bangkok international airport,
    *see* air travel
Banglamphu 246-51, **246**
Banharn Silapa-Archa 19
banks 143, see also money
bars 156
Baw Sang 462-3
beer, *see* drinks
Betong 822-3
Beung Kan 625-6
Big Buddha Beach 728-9
boat travel 206, *see also* rafting
    international 186, 188
    river & canal trips 147, 238-42,
    297-8, 472, 552
books 98-102
    arts & architecture 56
    bookshops 102, 213-6
    culture & society 99-100
    food 102
    hill tribes 100
    history & politics 101
    travel 98-9
border crossings
    Cambodia 141, 187, 383, 395
    China 187-8
    Laos 185-6, 423, 555, 571-2,
    615, 637
    Laos/China 422
    Malaysia 184-5, 833
    Myanmar 36, 142, 186-7, 349,
    505, 507, 512, 542, 547-8
boxing, *see* muay thai
Buddhaisawan Chapel 228

## Thanks

Thanks to the many travellers who wrote in with helpful hints, useful advice and funny and interesting stories.

Marie-Claire Aarts, Donna Accord, Peter Adams, AN Addison, A Addison, J Ainsworth, Kathleen Akin, JA Aluey, Heather Andres, Mark Andrews, NI Andrews, Mick Anstis, K Arniger, M Asher, Kris Attard, Todd Austin, Malcolm Ayres, Lara Azria, Michael Babcock, Anne Badger, A Balderson, Jennifer Ballagh, Dick & Beth Balsamo, Chris Bannister, Matthew Barclay, Audre Barnaid, Marg Barr-Brown, JC Barrett, George Bauguess, Jason Baxter, Gill Beddows, Lucie Benton, Ron Bernardi, David Bernardini, Brad Bernthal, Laurent Biais, Joe Bigalow, Charlotte Bishop, A Blackburn, Barbara Blackford, U Blaser, William Bloomhuff, S Boerke, Jon Bonnin, M Boonslva, Cheryl Borgmann, Martin Bottenberg, Anne Boulton, John & Jean Bowler, David Boxall, Rebecca Boyce, Peter Brennan, Henriette Breum, Sjoulije Broer, Kelly Ann Brogan, Michael Brorsen, Marvin Brown, Roxanna Brown, Benjamin Buikema, Carol Bullen, Lenny & Wendy Burnett, Anny Bussieres, Laurence Buytaert, Dan Byrne, Stuart Cadden, Gwen Cahill, Michael Cannon, N Carper, David Carson, R Carter, Sarah Chambers, D & S Chanel, Toby Charnaud, Denise Chavez, Pauline Chia, Woodrow Chow, Jacky Chrisp, Anne Christianes, Mike Clarke, Richard Clarke, S Coe, Jennifer Coffin, Simon Cole, Peter Coleman, Alec Connah, Andrew Coop, Richard Coughlin, Roland Couzens, S Creaser, Adam Cresswell, Kerstin Cronquist, Emily Culbert, Patrick Cullen, Connie Dahlin, Jurgen Dahm, Phillip Dale, Jeff Dane, Greg Darch, Cynthia Dargan, FJ Davey, John Davis, Jason Day, Norman & Kelcy Dean, N de Jong, Rik de Buyserie, Jeanette de Raaf, Peter Dekkers, Evert Delanghe, Jeff Delkin, Jessica Dempsey, Franz Dennenmoser, Diana Dennison, Julian Derry, Joseph Distlan, Paul & Sheila Doherty, Mike Doria, Joseph Doucet, Kerry Doyle, Vincent Duggan, Hans Durrer, Donna Eade, Richard Eden, Gabrielle Ellis, Joanne Ellis, Bethany Ellis, Jim Enright, Doreen Entwistle, Lukas Ernst, Elaine Evans, Salvati Fabio, Robert Falk, L Farr, Andreas Faul, Edwina Fenwick, B Fewtrell, Bill Flagg, Kimberlee Forbes, David Francis, Ray Frank, Michael Gardner, Christopher Garrenger, Jennie Germann, Richard Gillman, Stephen Ginn, Gary Giombi, Brian & Cindy Goke, Maurice Goldberg, Jesus Gonzalez, Olga Gonzalez, Josh Gonze, Alvin Goodwin, Lisa & Steven Gosling, Jasper Goss, Eli Graham, Rob Graham, Rick Graves, Guido Groenen, Mr & Mrs De Groot, Catherine Gunning, A Haddon, Claire Haddon, Amanda Haley, Judy Hall, Jeannie Hall, Ian Hammond, AA Hampton, Steven Hankey, Timmo Hannay, R Harrop, Dick Haugland, Sarah Haynes, Ashley Heath, Jennifer Hegle, S Hendrix, S & M Elliott-Herault, Chris Hetcalf, Christopher Hilborn, Lucy Hilts, Birgit Himmelsbach, Gunter Hoffman, John Hofmann, Colin Holst, Simon Honeybone, Vicki Howarth, Suzanne Huggins, Sue Hughes, Jeff Hurwitz, Dominick Isaac, Stuart Jarvis, Stewart & Sally Jeffrey, Katherine Johnson, Stein Jonasson, Kashi Jones & friends, Daniel Jordan, Tony Jurica, Dennis Keating, A Keister, J Keller, Vincent Kelly, Maria Kendro, A Kent, IHF Kerr, Julian King, M King, Matt King, Peter Kirsch, Nicholas Klar, Martin & Henny Knight, Rosalind Knowlson, Jacques Kooh, GF Kortschak, David Kulka, Alistair Lamb, Jean-Marc Lange, David Latchford, Kay Lawson, Clotilde Le Grand, Martin Leduc, Fiona & Sascha Leese, Philip Leese, Dave & Carol Leligdon, CM Lennie, Andrea Lindel, Bruce Linker, Annie Liu, Sharon London, David Loris, Caroline Lurie, Anthony Lynch, Vincent Lynch, Laurie MacKay, BE Mackin, Sheldon Madson, John Maidment, Ian Mann, Lyndal Mannix, Dave Marini, R Marom, John Martin, Nalli Massimo, Steven Mathers, Bettina Matthes, Curt Matthew, M Matthews, Alberto & Sara Mazzocchi, M McBride, Lisa & Pat McCarthy, D McFadden, Carolyn McLeod, Stephen McMillan, Rob Mellett, Angelo Mercure, S Meredith, Mark Micallef, Phil Miller, K Mills, Bruce Moore, Rebecca Moore, A Moores, Stephen Morey, Andrew Morolla, Michael Mortensen, Shelley Muzzy, Thomas Neihsen, Anne Newey, Roaxanna Ngerntongdee, N Nguyen, Mari Nicholson, MP Nunan, John O'Donnell, Carol O'Hare, Kevin & Harriett O'Mahoney, Jan O'Neill, Vicki Olsen, K Onsanit, Mark Ord, Jackie Origne, Marc Orts, Dan Orzech, Orly & Oren Oz, Tina Pacheco, Rolf Palmberg, Steve Palmier, James Parsons, James Pate, Rachel Paterson, John Paulsen, Steve Peache, Donald Peck, Warner Pel, Colin Pendry, Mark Peters, N Pik, Michelle Pirkl, Kyle Portman, Denise Powell, Eveline Powell, Owen Powell, Charlotte Prehnum, Ged Prescott, Neil & Suzy Purues, Lesley Quinn, David Ramm, Philippe Raoul, J Rasmussen, Fabrizio Rasore, Nicholas Redfearn, Janine Redfern, Leni Reeves, Valerie Rice, Peter Ridgway, Paul Robinson, Richard Robinson, Carol Rogers, Ann Rooney, Isabel Rothery, Naomi Rubine, Petra Russi, Kevin Ryan, Peng Sarnkam, H Saunders, Carmel Savege, Ed & Marie Scarpari, Janis Schaus, Bernd & Elke Scheffer, Margo Schlanger, Norbert Schmiedeberg, Bernd Schmirler, Kristian Scholte, Marcel Schrijvers, William Scorpion, Sophia Scott, Kaine Seeoophachar, Wiyada Sereewichyaswat, PA & G Sharp, Marion and Mark Sheffield, Glen Shen, P Shenton, Bill Shipp, Gudrun Siegel, Bevan Silvester, Lionie Sliz, Brad & Vicki Skinner, A & S Smith, Gill Smith, Rodney Smith, L Snideman, Marianne Soldavini, Rachel Speth, Shelley Stansfield, P Stewart, Ted Stirzaker, Carol Stock, Martianne Sullivan, Poonsak Suvannuparat, John Sweetman, Ryuhei Takahashi, Scott Takushi, Mizuno Tetsuyuki, Hilary Third, Sally Thomas, James Thompson, John Tigue, Chris Toland, M Toms, Carol Topalian, Peter Tse, David Unkovich, L Urwin, Sheryn Valter, Marie-Claire van de Wiel, Robert van Weperen, F van den Bouwhuijsen, Johanna van Hal, Ilona Veen, MC Verinue, Laurent Vermeulen, Caroline Ward, David Wayte, Peter Webster, Jonas Westberg, Lloyd Westby, M Willemse, John Williams, Karen Williams, Reg Williams, Jenny Williamson, Don Wills, R Wilson, Rupert Wilson, Sue Wilson, Zae Wilson, Stephen Winterstein, Wolfgang Wizsner, Michael Wolff, Douglas Wood, Martin Worswick, Phil & Linda Wotherspoon, Brande Wulff, Michael & Jackie Yates, B Young, Kathy Yu, Karen Yung, Carola Zentner, Myriem Zouaq

# LONELY PLANET JOURNEYS

JOURNEYS is a unique collection of travel writing – published by the company that understands travel better than anyone else. It is a series for anyone who has ever experienced – or dreamed of – the magical moment when they encountered a strange culture or saw a place for the first time. They are tales to read while you're planning a trip, while you're on the road or while you're in an armchair, in front of a fire.

JOURNEYS books catch the spirit of a place, illuminate a culture, recount a crazy adventure, or introduce a fascinating way of life. They always entertain, and always enrich the experience of travel.

---

## ISLANDS IN THE CLOUDS
### Travels in the Highlands of New Guinea
### *Isabella Tree*

Isabella Tree's remarkable journey takes us to the heart of the remote and beautiful Highlands of Papua New Guinea and Irian Jaya – one of the most extraordinary and dangerous regions on earth. Funny and tragic by turns, *Islands in the Clouds* is her moving story of the Highland people and the changes transforming their world.

*Isabella Tree*, who lives in England, has worked as a freelance journalist on a variety of newspapers and magazines, including a stint as senior travel correspondent for the *Evening Standard.* A fellow of the Royal Geographical Society, she has also written a biography of the Victorian ornithologist John Gould.

*'One of the most accomplished travel writers to appear on the horizon for many years . . . the dialogue is brilliant'* – Eric Newby

---

## SEAN & DAVID'S LONG DRIVE
### *Sean Condon*

Sean Condon is young, urban and a connoisseur of hair wax. He can't drive, and he doesn't really travel well. So when Sean and his friend David set out to explore Australia in a 1966 Ford Falcon, the result is a decidedly offbeat look at life on the road. Over 14,000 death-defying kilometres, our heroes check out the re-runs on tv, get fabulously drunk, listen to Neil Young cassettes and wonder why they ever left home.

*Sean Condon* lives in Melbourne. He played drums in several mediocre bands until he found his way into advertising and an above-average band called Boilersuit. *Sean & David's Long Drive* is his first book.

*'Funny, pithy, kitsch and surreal . . . This book will do for Australia what Chernobyl did for Kiev, but hey you'll laugh as the stereotypes go boom'*
*– Time Out*

# LONELY PLANET PHRASEBOOKS

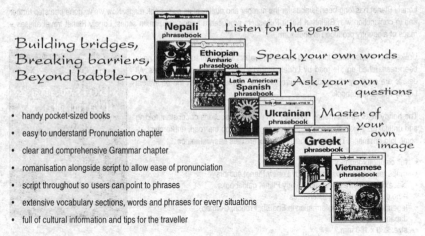

Building bridges,
Breaking barriers,
Beyond babble-on

*Listen for the gems*

*Speak your own words*

*Ask your own questions*

*Master of your own image*

- handy pocket-sized books
- easy to understand Pronunciation chapter
- clear and comprehensive Grammar chapter
- romanisation alongside script to allow ease of pronunciation
- script throughout so users can point to phrases
- extensive vocabulary sections, words and phrases for every situations
- full of cultural information and tips for the traveller

'...vital for a real DIY spirit and attitude in language learning' – Backpacker

'the phrasebooks have good cultural backgrounders and offer solid advice for challenging situations in remote locations' – San Francisco Examiner

'...they are unbeatable for their coverage of the world's more obscure languages' – The Geographical Magazine

---

Arabic (Egyptian)
Arabic (Moroccan)
Australia
 Australian English, Aboriginal and
 Torres Strait languages
Baltic States
 Estonian, Latvian, Lithuanian
Bengali
Burmese
Brazilian
Cantonese
Central Europe
 Czech, French, German, Hungarian,
 Italian and Slovak
Eastern Europe
 Bulgarian, Czech, Hungarian, Polish,
 Romanian and Slovak
Egyptian Arabic
Ethiopian (Amharic)
Fijian
Greek
Hindi/Urdu

Indonesian
Japanese
Korean
Lao
Latin American Spanish
Malay
Mandarin
Mediterranean Europe
 Albanian, Croatian, Greek, Italian,
 Macedonian, Maltese, Serbian,
 Slovene
Mongolian
Moroccan Arabic
Nepali
Papua New Guinea
Pilipino (Tagalog)
Quechua
Russian
Scandinavian Europe
 Danish, Finnish, Icelandic, Norwegian
 and Swedish

South-East Asia
 Burmese, Indonersian, Khmer, Lao,
 Malay, Tagalog (Pilipino), Thai and
 Vietnamese
Sri Lanka
Swahili
Thai
Thai Hill Tribes
Tibetan
Turkish
Ukrainian
USA
 US English, Vernacular Talk,
 Native American languages and
 Hawaiian
Vietnamese
Western Europe
 Basque, Catalan, Dutch, French,
 German, Irish, Italian, Portuguese,
 Scottish Gaelic, Spanish (Castilian)
 and Welsh

---

# LONELY PLANET TRAVEL ATLASES

Lonely Planet has long been famous for the number and quality of its guidebook maps. Now we've gone one step further and in conjunction with Steinhart Katzir Publishers produced a handy companion series: Lonely Planet travel atlases – maps of a country produced in book form.

Unlike other maps, which look good but lead travellers astray, our travel atlases have been researched on the road by Lonely Planet's experienced team of writers. All details are carefully checked to ensure the atlas corresponds with the equivalent Lonely Planet guidebook.

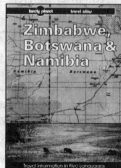

The handy atlas format means no holes, wrinkles, torn sections or constant folding and unfolding. These atlases can survive long periods on the road, unlike cumbersome fold-out maps. The comprehensive index ensures easy reference.

- full-colour throughout
- maps researched and checked by Lonely Planet authors
- place names correspond with Lonely Planet guidebooks
  – no confusing spelling differences
- legend and travelling information in English, French, German, Japanese and Spanish
- size: 230 x 160 mm

*Available now:*
Chile & Easter Island • Egypt • India & Bangladesh • Israel & the Palestinian Territories •Jordan, Syria & Lebanon • Kenya • Laos • Portugal • South Africa, Lesotho & Swaziland • Thailand • Vietnam • Zimbabwe, Botswana & Namibia

# LONELY PLANET TV SERIES & VIDEOS

Lonely Planet travel guides have been brought to life on television screens around the world. Like our guides, the programmes are based on the joy of independent travel, and look honestly at some of the most exciting, picturesque and frustrating places in the world. Each show is presented by one of three travellers from Australia, England or the USA and combines an innovative mixture of video, Super-8 film, atmospheric soundscapes and original music.

Videos of each episode – containing additional footage not shown on television – are available from good book and video shops, but the availability of individual videos varies with regional screening schedules.

*Video destinations include:* Alaska • American Rockies • Australia – The South-East • Baja California & the Copper Canyon • Brazil • Central Asia • Chile & Easter Island • Corsica, Sicily & Sardinia – The Mediterranean Islands • East Africa (Tanzania & Zanzibar) • Ecuador & the Galapagos Islands • Greenland & Iceland • Indonesia • Israel & the Sinai Desert • Jamaica • Japan • La Ruta Maya • Morocco • New York • North India • Pacific Islands (Fiji, Solomon Islands & Vanuatu) • South India • South West China • Turkey • Vietnam • West Africa • Zimbabwe, Botswana & Namibia

*The Lonely Planet TV series is produced by:*
**Pilot Productions**
Duke of Sussex Studios
44 Uxbridge St
London W8 7TG  UK

*Lonely Planet videos are distributed by:*
**IVN Communications Inc**
2246 Camino Ramon
California 94583, USA

107 Power Road, Chiswick
London W4 5PL  UK

*Music from the TV series is available on CD & cassette.*
*For video availability and ordering information contact your nearest Lonely Planet office.*

# PLANET TALK

## Lonely Planet's FREE quarterly newsletter

We love hearing from you and think you'd like to hear from us.

*When...*is the right time to see reindeer in Finland?
*Where...*can you hear the best palm-wine music in Ghana?
*How...*do you get from Asunción to Areguá by steam train?
*What...*is the best way to see India?

*For the answer to these and many other questions read PLANET TALK.*

Every issue is packed with up-to-date travel news and advice including:

- a letter from Lonely Planet co-founders Tony and Maureen Wheeler
- go behind the scenes on the road with a Lonely Planet author
- feature article on an important and topical travel issue
- a selection of recent letters from travellers
- details on forthcoming Lonely Planet promotions
- complete list of Lonely Planet products

*To join our mailing list contact any Lonely Planet office.*

*Also available: Lonely Planet T-shirts. 100% heavyweight cotton.*

---

# LONELY PLANET ONLINE

## Get the latest travel information before you leave or while you're on the road

Whether you've just begun planning your next trip, or you're chasing down specific info on currency regulations or visa requirements, check out Lonely Planet Online for up-to-the-minute travel information.

As well as travel profiles of your favourite destinations (including maps and photos), you'll find current reports from our researchers and other travellers, updates on health and visas, travel advisories, and discussion of the ecological and political issues you need to be aware of as you travel.

There's also an online travellers' forum where you can share your experience of life on the road, meet travel companions and ask other travellers for their recommendations and advice. We also have plenty of links to other online sites useful to independent travellers.

And of course we have a complete and up-to-date list of all Lonely Planet travel products including guides, phrasebooks, atlases, Journeys and videos and a simple online ordering facility if you can't find the book you want elsewhere.

*www.lonelyplanet.com*
*or*
*AOL keyword: lp*

# LONELY PLANET PRODUCTS

Lonely Planet is known worldwide for publishing practical, reliable and no-nonsense travel information in our guides and on our web site. The Lonely Planet list covers just about every accessible part of the world. Currently there are eight series: *travel guides*, *shoestring guides*, *walking guides*, *city guides*, *phrasebooks*, *audio packs*, *travel atlases* and *Journeys* – a unique collection of travel writing.

## EUROPE

Amsterdam • Austria • Baltic States phrasebook • Britain • Central Europe on a shoestring • Central Europe phrasebook • Czech & Slovak Republics • Denmark • Dublin • Eastern Europe on a shoestring • Eastern Europe phrasebook • Estonia, Latvia & Lithuania • Finland • France • Greece • Greek phrasebook • Hungary • Iceland, Greenland & the Faroe Islands • Ireland • Italy • Mediterranean Europe on a shoestring • Mediterranean Europe phrasebook • Paris • Poland • Portugal • Portugal travel atlas • Prague • Russia, Ukraine & Belarus • Russian phrasebook • Scandinavian & Baltic Europe on a shoestring • Scandinavian Europe phrasebook • Slovenia • Spain • Spanish phrasebook • St Petersburg • Switzerland • Trekking in Greece • Trekking in Spain • Ukrainian phrasebook • Vienna • Walking in Britain • Walking in Switzerland • Western Europe on a shoestring • Western Europe phrasebook

## NORTH AMERICA

Alaska • Backpacking in Alaska • Baja California • California & Nevada • Canada • Florida • Hawaii • Honolulu • Los Angeles • Mexico • Miami • New England • New Orleans • New York, New Jersey & Pennsylvania • Pacific Northwest USA • Rocky Mountain States • San Francisco • Southwest USA • USA phrasebook • Washington, DC & the Capital Region

## CENTRAL AMERICA & THE CARIBBEAN

Bermuda • Central America on a shoestring • Costa Rica • Cuba • Eastern Caribbean • Guatemala, Belize & Yucatán: La Ruta Maya • Jamaica

## SOUTH AMERICA

Argentina, Uruguay & Paraguay • Bolivia • Brazil • Brazilian phrasebook • Buenos Aires • Chile & Easter Island • Chile & Easter Island travel atlas • Colombia • Ecuador & the Galápagos Islands • Latin American Spanish phrasebook • Peru • Quechua phrasebook • Rio de Janeiro • South America on a shoestring • Trekking in the Patagonian Andes • Venezuela

*Travel Literature:* Full Circle: A South American Journey

## ANTARCTICA

Antarctica

## ISLANDS OF THE INDIAN OCEAN

Madagascar & Comoros • Maldives• Mauritius, Réunion & Seychelles

## AFRICA

Africa on a shoestring • Arabic (Moroccan) phrasebook • • Cape Town • Central Africa • East Africa • Egypt • Egypt travel atlas• Ethiopian (Amharic) phrasebook • Kenya • Kenya travel atlas • Malawi, Mozambique & Zambia • Morocco • North Africa • South Africa, Lesotho & Swaziland • South Africa, Lesotho & Swaziland travel atlas • Swahili phrasebook • Trekking in East Africa • West Africa • Zimbabwe, Botswana & Namibia • Zimbabwe, Botswana & Namibia travel atlas

*Travel Literature:* The Rainbird: A Central African Journey • Songs to an African Sunset: A Zimbabwean Story

# MAIL ORDER

onely Planet products are distributed worldwide.They are also available by mail order from Lonely Planet, so if you have difficulty finding a title please write to us. North American and South American residents should write to Embarcadero West, 155 Filbert St, Suite 251, Oakland CA 94607, USA; European and African residents should write to 10 Barley Mow Passage, Chiswick, London W4 4PH; and residents of other countries to PO Box 617, Hawthorn, Victoria 3122, Australia.

## NORTH-EAST ASIA

Beijing • Cantonese phrasebook • China • Hong Kong • Hong Kong, Macau & Guangzhou • Japan • Japanese phrasebook • Japanese audio pack • Korea • Korean phrasebook • Mandarin phrasebook • Mongolia • Mongolian phrasebook • North-East Asia on a shoestring • Seoul • Taiwan • Tibet • Tibet phrasebook • Tokyo

*Travel Literature*: Lost Japan

## MIDDLE EAST & CENTRAL ASIA

Arab Gulf States • Arabic (Egyptian) phrasebook • Central Asia • Iran • Israel & the Palestinian Territories • Israel & the Palestinian Territories travel atlas • Istanbul • Jerusalem • Jordan & Syria • Jordan, Syria & Lebanon travel atlas • Middle East • Turkey • Turkish phrasebook • Turkey travel atlas • Yemen

*Travel Literature:* The Gates of Damascus • Kingdom of the Film Stars: Journey into Jordan

## ALSO AVAILABLE:

Travel with Children • Traveller's Tales

## INDIAN SUBCONTINENT

Bangladesh • Bengali phrasebook • Delhi • Hindi/Urdu phrasebook • India • India & Bangladesh travel atlas • Indian Himalaya • Karakoram Highway • Nepal • Nepali phrasebook • Pakistan • Rajasthan • Sri Lanka • Sri Lanka phrasebook • Trekking in the Indian Himalaya • Trekking in the Karakoram & Hindukush • Trekking in the Nepal Himalaya

*Travel Literature:* In Rajasthan • Shopping for Buddhas

## SOUTH-EAST ASIA

Bali & Lombok • Bangkok • Burmese phrasebook • Cambodia • Ho Chi Minh City • Indonesia • Indonesian phrasebook • Indonesian audio pack • Jakarta • Java • Laos • Lao phrasebook • Laos travel atlas • Malay phrasebook • Malaysia, Singapore & Brunei • Myanmar (Burma) • Philippines • Pilipino phrasebook • Singapore • South-East Asia on a shoestring • South-East Asia phrasebook • Thailand • Thailand travel atlas • Thai phrasebook • Thai audio pack • Thai Hill Tribes phrasebook • Vietnam • Vietnamese phrasebook • Vietnam travel atlas

## AUSTRALIA & THE PACIFIC

Australia • Australian phrasebook • Bushwalking in Australia • Bushwalking in Papua New Guinea • Fiji • Fijian phrasebook • Islands of Australia's Great Barrier Reef • Melbourne • Micronesia • New Caledonia • New South Wales & the ACT • New Zealand • Northern Territory • Outback Australia • Papua New Guinea • Papua New Guinea phrasebook • Queensland • Rarotonga & the Cook Islands • Samoa • Solomon Islands • South Australia • Sydney • Tahiti & French Polynesia • Tasmania • Tonga • Tramping in New Zealand • Vanuatu • Victoria • Western Australia

*Travel Literature:* Islands in the Clouds • Sean & David's Long Drive

# THE LONELY PLANET STORY

Lonely Planet published its first book in 1973 in response to the numerous 'How did you do it?' questions Maureen and Tony Wheeler were asked after driving, bussing, hitching, sailing and railing their way from England to Australia.

Written at a kitchen table and hand collated, trimmed and stapled, *Across Asia on the Cheap* became an instant local bestseller, inspiring thoughts of another book.

Eighteen months in South-East Asia resulted in their second guide, *South-East Asia on a shoestring*, which they put together in a backstreet Chinese hotel in Singapore in 1975. The 'yellow bible', as it quickly became known to backpackers around the world, soon became *the* guide to the region. It has sold well over half a million copies and is now in its 9th edition, still retaining its familiar yellow cover.

Today there are over 240 titles, including travel guides, walking guides, language kits & phrasebooks, travel atlases and travel literature. The company is the largest independent travel publisher in the world. Although Lonely Planet initially specialised in guides to Asia, today there are few corners of the globe that have not been covered.

The emphasis continues to be on travel for independent travellers. Tony and Maureen still travel for several months of each year and play an active part in the writing, updating and quality control of Lonely Planet's guides.

They have been joined by over 70 authors and 170 staff at our offices in Melbourne (Australia), Oakland (USA), London (UK) and Paris (France). Travellers themselves also make a valuable contribution to the guides through the feedback we receive in thousands of letters each year and on our web site.

The people at Lonely Planet strongly believe that travellers can make a positive contribution to the countries they visit, both through their appreciation of the countries' culture, wildlife and natural features, and through the money they spend. In addition, the company makes a direct contribution to the countries and regions it covers. Since 1986 a percentage of the income from each book has been donated to ventures such as famine relief in Africa; aid projects in India; agricultural projects in Central America; Greenpeace's efforts to halt French nuclear testing in the Pacific; and Amnesty International.

*'I hope we send people out with the right attitude about travel. You realise when you travel that there are so many different perspectives about the world, so we hope these books will make people more interested in what they see. Guidebooks can't really guide people. All you can do is point them in the right direction.'*

– Tony Wheeler

# LONELY PLANET PUBLICATIONS

**Australia**
PO Box 617, Hawthorn 3122, Victoria
tel: (03) 9819 1877  fax: (03) 9819 6459
e-mail: talk2us@lonelyplanet.com.au

**USA**
Embarcadero West, 155 Filbert St, Suite 251,
Oakland, CA 94607
tel: (510) 893 8555  TOLL FREE: 800 275-8555
fax: (510) 893 8563
e-mail: info@lonelyplanet.com

**UK**
10 Barley Mow Passage, Chiswick,
London W4 4PH
tel: (0181) 742 3161  fax: (0181) 742 2772
e-mail: 100413.3551@compuserve.com

**France:**
71 bis rue du Cardinal Lemoine, 75005 Paris
tel: 1 44 32 06 20  fax: 1 46 34 72 55
e-mail: 100560.415@compuserve.com

**World Wide Web: http://www.lonelyplanet.com**